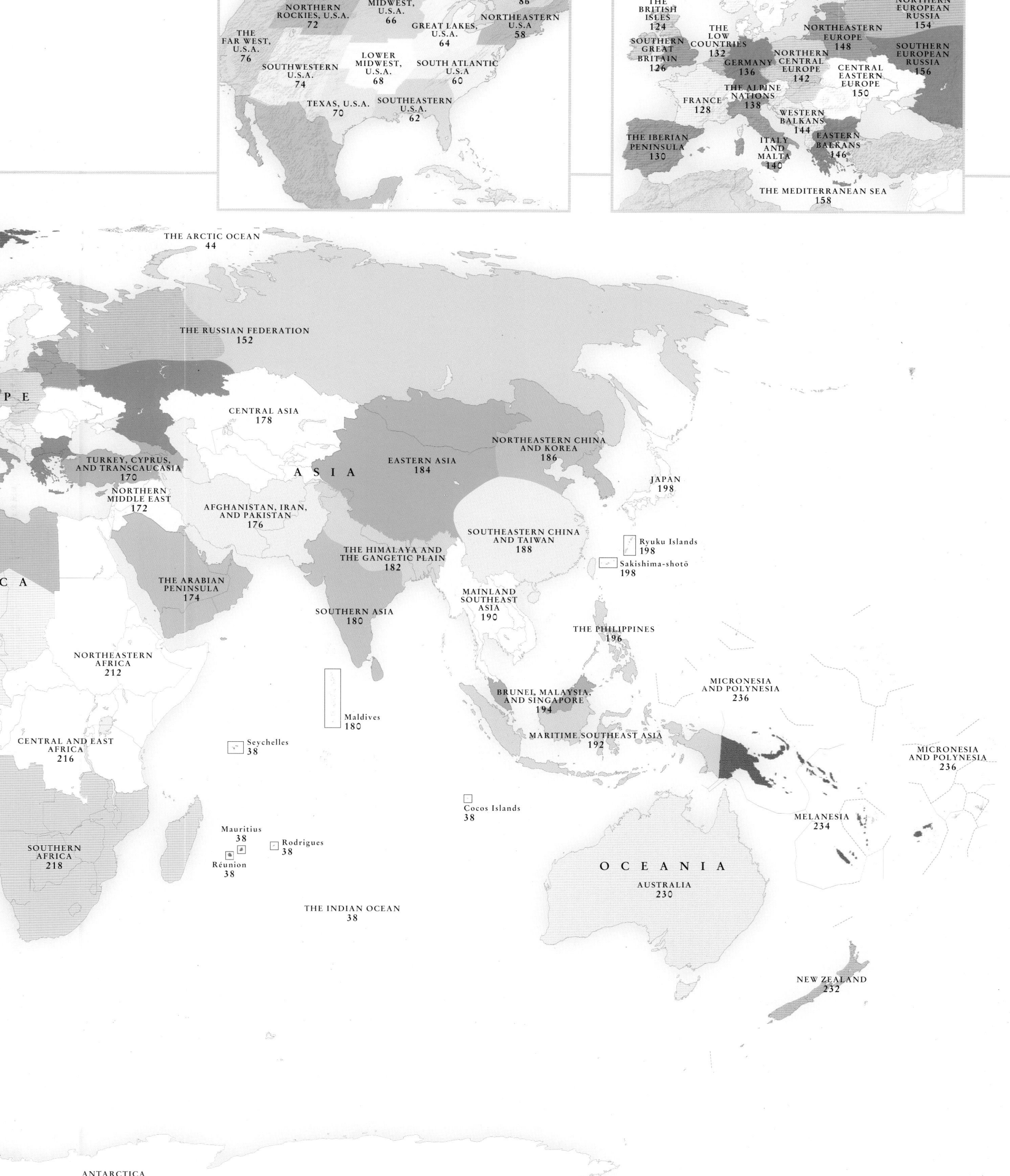

WESTERN CANADA
82

EASTERN CANADA
84

SOUTHEASTERN
CANADA
86

NORTHERN
ROCKIES, U.S.A.
72

UPPER
MIDWEST,
U.S.A.
66

GREAT LAKES,
U.S.A.
64

NORTHEASTERN
U.S.A
58

THE
FAR WEST,
U.S.A.
76

SOUTHWESTERN
U.S.A.
74

LOWER
MIDWEST,
U.S.A.
68

SOUTH ATLANTIC
U.S.A
60

TEXAS, U.S.A.
70

SOUTHEASTERN
U.S.A.
62

SCANDI
134

P9-BZQ-477

THE
BRITISH
ISLES
124

THE
LOW
COUNTRIES
132

NORTHEASTERN
EUROPE
148

NORTHERN
EUROPEAN
RUSSIA
154

SOUTHERN
GREAT
BRITAIN
126

GERMANY
136

NORTHERN
CENTRAL
EUROPE
142

CENTRAL
EASTERN
EUROPE
150

SOUTHERN
EUROPEAN
RUSSIA
156

FRANCE
128

THE ALPINE
NATIONS
138

THE IBERIAN
PENINSULA
130

ITALY
AND
MALTA
140

WESTERN
BALKANS
144

EASTERN
BALKANS
146

THE MEDITERRANEAN SEA
158

THE ARCTIC OCEAN
44

THE RUSSIAN FEDERATION
152

CENTRAL ASIA
178

TURKEY, CYPRUS,
AND TRANSCAUCASIA
170

EASTERN ASIA
184

NORTHEASTERN CHINA
AND KOREA
186

A S I A

JAPAN
198

NORTHERN
MIDDLE EAST
172

AFGHANISTAN, IRAN,
AND PAKISTAN
176

SOUTHEASTERN CHINA
AND TAIWAN
188

Ryuku Islands
198

THE HIMALAYA AND
THE GANGETIC PLAIN
182

Sakishima-shotō
198

THE ARABIAN
PENINSULA
174

MAINLAND
SOUTHEAST
ASIA
190

SOUTHERN ASIA
180

THE PHILIPPINES
196

NORTHEASTERN
AFRICA
212

MICRONESIA
AND POLYNESIA
236

Maldives
180

BRUNEI, MALAYSIA,
AND SINGAPORE
194

CENTRAL AND EAST
AFRICA
216

MICRONESIA
AND POLYNESIA
236

Seychelles
38

MARITIME SOUTHEAST ASIA
192

Cocos Islands
38

MELANESIA
234

Mauritius
38

Rodrigues
38

Réunion
38

SOUTHERN
AFRICA
218

O C E A N I A

AUSTRALIA
230

THE INDIAN OCEAN
38

NEW ZEALAND
232

ANTARCTICA
240

the **illustrated**

WORLD ATLAS

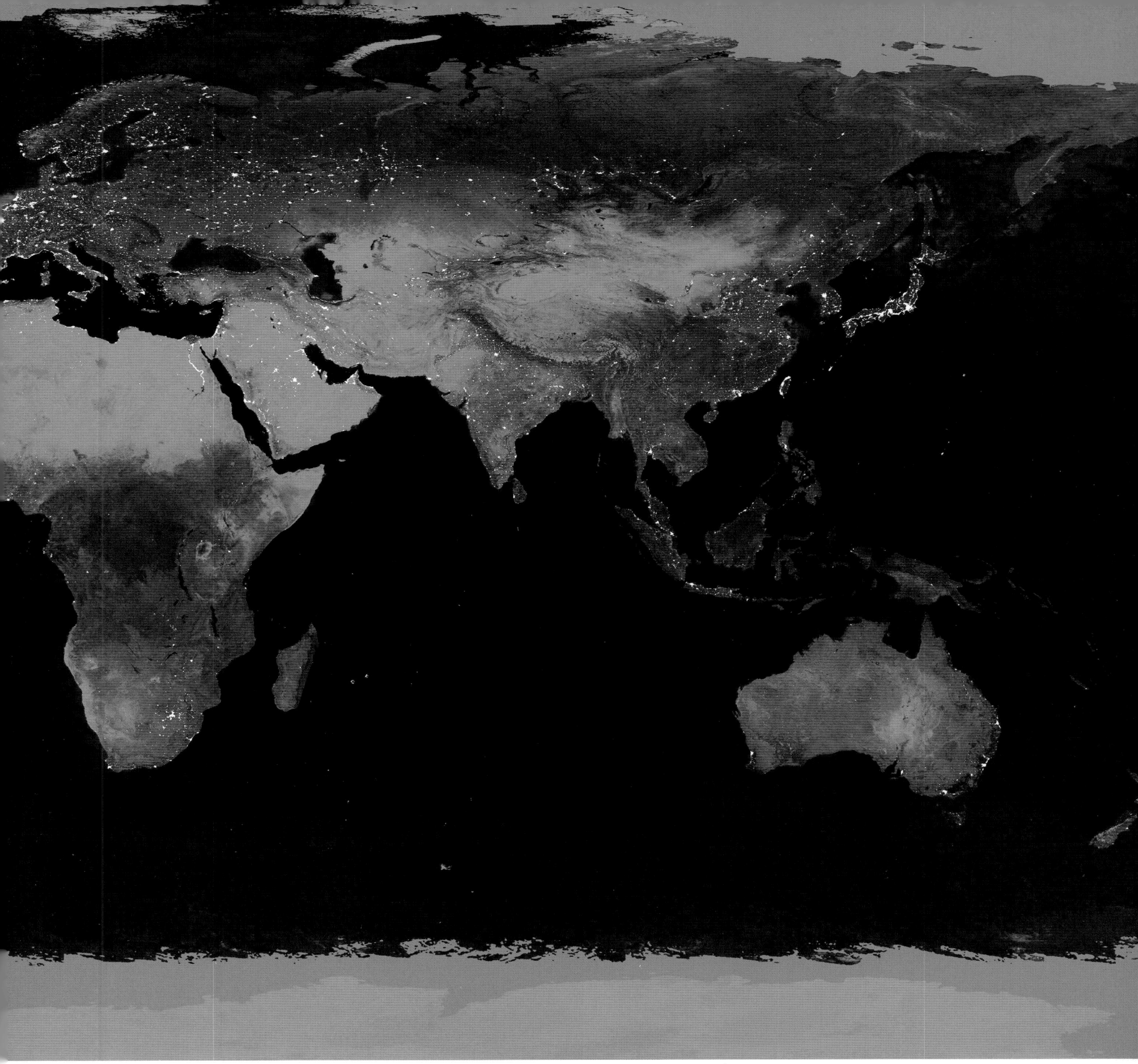

the **illustrated**

WORLD ATLAS

BARNES & NOBLE BOOKS
NEW YORK

This edition published by Barnes & Noble, Inc,
by arrangement with Weldon Owen Inc.

2004 Barnes & Noble Books

M 10 9 8 7 6 5 4 3 2 1

ISBN 0-7607-5359-8

Copyright © 2004 Weldon Owen Inc.

Library of Congress Cataloging-in-Publication Data available
upon request.

Printed and bound in Singapore

CARTOGRAPHIC CONSULTANTS

Dr William Cartwright
Associate Professor in Multimedia Cartography
School of Mathematical and Geospatial Sciences
RMIT University, Melbourne, Australia
Vice-President, International
Cartographic Association

Professor Michael P. Peterson
Department of Geography/Geology
University of Nebraska at Omaha, U.S.A.
Chair, International Cartographic Association
Commission on Maps and the Internet

REGIONAL MAPPING CONSULTANTS

Imran Ali
Cartographer, Pakistan

M. (John) Balodis
FMSIA Adjunct Professor
Curtin University, Perth, Australia

Professor Jean Carrière
Professeur titulaire
Directeur du Département de géographie
Université du Québec à Montréal, Canada

Dr Prem Chetri
School of Mathematical and Geospatial Sciences
RMIT University, Melbourne, Australia

Professor Benjamin Cohen
Department of Photogrammetry
and Cartography
University of Architecture, Civil Engineering
and Geodesy, Sofia, Bulgaria

Igor Drecki
Geographics Unit Manager
School of Geography and Environmental Science
University of Auckland, Auckland, New Zealand

Dr Francisco Escobar
Profesor Titular de Análisis Geográfico Regional
Departamento de Geografía
Universidad de Alcalá de Henares, Spain

Dr David Fairbairn
School of Civil Engineering and Geosciences
University of Newcastle, Newcastle, U.K.

Steve Foldi
Cartographer, Windsor, Australia

Scott Furey
School of Mathematical and Geospatial Sciences
RMIT University, Melbourne, Australia

Professor Dr Georg Gartner
Institut für Kartographie und Geo-Medientechnik
Technische Universitat Wien, Vienna, Austria

Ibrahim Hanna
Hydrogeologist, Syria

Hashim al Hashimi
Geo-Information Analyst
Environmental Research and Wildlife
Development Agency, United Arab Emirates

Dr Stephen Hutchinson
Southampton Oceanography Centre
University of Southampton, Southampton, U.K.

Dr Simon Jones
School of Mathematical and Geospatial Sciences
RMIT University, Melbourne, Australia

Professor Milan Konecny
Department of Geography, Faculty of Science
Masaryk University, Brno, Czech Republic

Professor Alexandra Koussoulakou
Department of Cadastre, Photogrammetry
and Cartography
The Aristotle University, Thessaloniki, Greece

Colin Kropman
Geographic Consultant, Sydney, Australia

Hyun Jong (David) Lee
Sung Kyun Kwan University, Seoul, South Korea

Antonio Hernández Navarro
Geodetic Coordinator
National Institute of Statistics,
Geography and Informatics (INEGI)
National Mapping Agency of Mexico,
Aguascaliente, Mexico

Professor Ferjan Ormeling,
University of Utrecht, Netherlands
Secretary-General, International
Cartographic Association

Will Pringle
Cartographic Director
Australian Geographic Pty Ltd,
Sydney, Australia

Professor Patrick Quilty
Honorary Research Professor
School of Earth Sciences
University of Tasmania, Hobart, Australia

Cristhiane da Silva Ramos
School of Mathematical and Geospatial Sciences
RMIT University, Melbourne, Australia

Rushan Gul Rozi
School of Mathematical and Geospatial Sciences
RMIT University, Melbourne, Australia

Afshin Alizadeh Shabini
University of Tehran, Tehran, Iran

Hussein Tawansi
Fellow Member, Institute of Quarrying
Sydney, Australia

Professor Dr Theodor Wintges
Munich University of Applied Sciences,
Munich, Germany

Assistant Professor Hiroyuki Yoshida
Faculty of Policy Management
SFC, Keio University, Endo, Japan

Jason Zhang
School of Mathematical and Geospatial Sciences
RMIT University, Melbourne, Australia

THEMATIC MAPPING CONSULTANTS

Dr Colin Arrowsmith
Senior Lecturer
School of Mathematical and Geospatial Sciences
RMIT University, Melbourne, Australia

Dr Paul Bahn
Archaeologist/author, Hull, U.K.

Robert Burnham
Senior Editor, *Astronomy* Magazine
Hales Corner, U.S.A

Dr Susan Canney
Department of Zoology
University of Oxford, Oxford, U.K.

Professor Bernard Comrie
Director, Department of Linguistics
Max Planck Institute for Evolutionary
Anthropology, Leipzig, Germany

Professor John Connell
School of Geosciences
University of Sydney, Sydney, Australia

Associate Professor Jim Forrest
Head, Department of Human Geography
Macquarie University, Sydney, Australia

Dr Stephen Gale
School of Geoscience
University of Sydney, Sydney, Australia

Dr Stephen Hutchinson
Southampton Oceanography Centre
University of Southampton, Southampton, U.K.

Dorothy F. Prescott
Senior Fellow
School of Anthropology, Geography
and Environmental Science
University of Melbourne, Melbourne, Australia

Professor John Robert Victor Prescott
Professor Emeritus and Professorial Fellow
School of Anthropology, Geography
and Environmental Studies
University of Melbourne, Melbourne, Australia

Professor Patrick Quilty
Honorary Research Professor
School of Earth Sciences
University of Tasmania, Hobart, Australia

Dr Anne I. Thackeray
Honorary Research Associate
Archaeology Division, School of Geography,
Archaeology and Environmental Studies
University of the Witwatersrand,
Johannesburg, South Africa

Richard Whitaker
Weathersmart Meteorological Services
Sydney, Australia

Associate Professor Charles Zika
Head, Department of History
University of Melbourne, Melbourne, Australia

Below: The dark-red Namib Desert is clearly visible at bottom center in this satellite photo of the southwestern coast of Africa.

Below left: These abstract patterns are sand beds in The Bahamas that have been carved by the tides and currents.

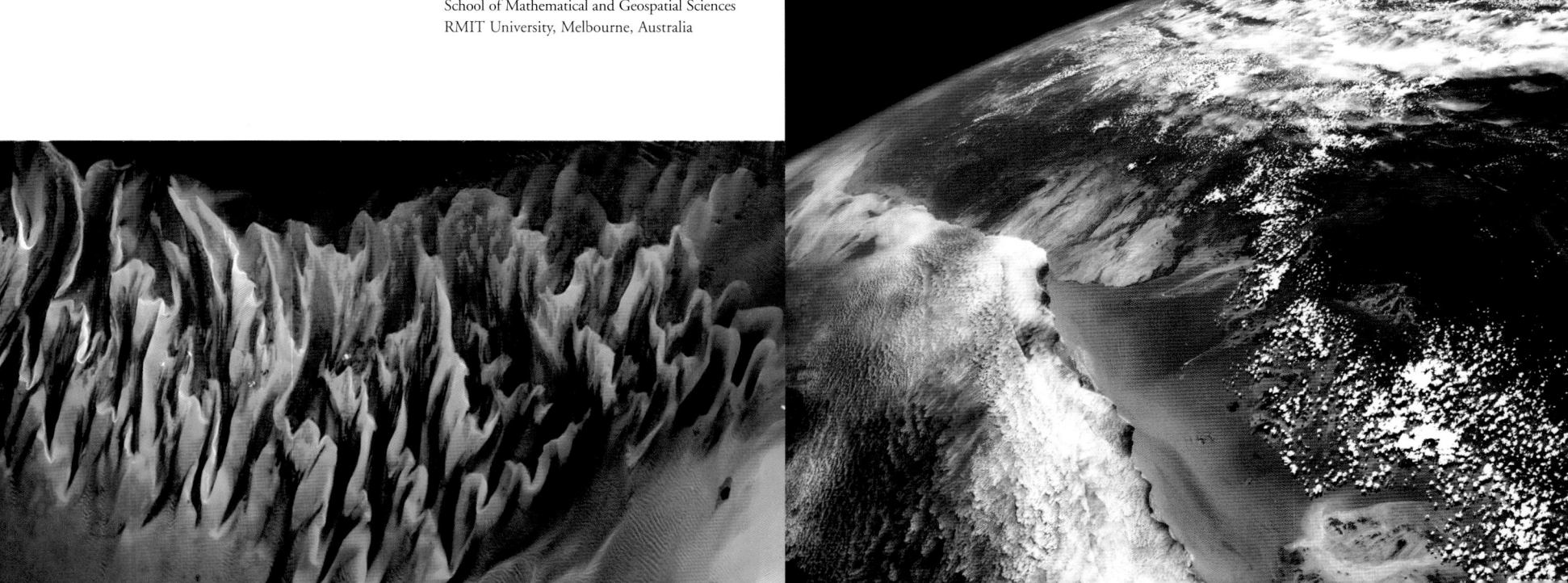

CONTENTS

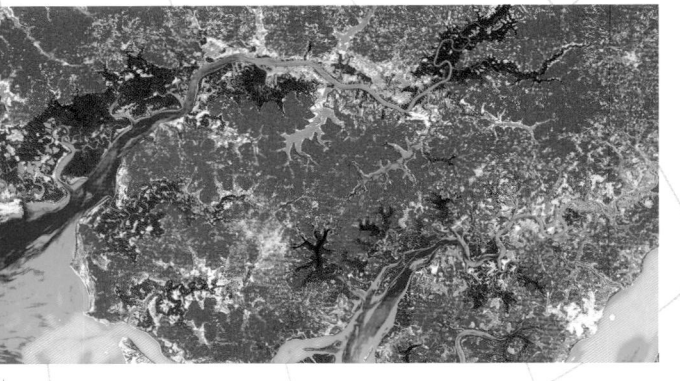
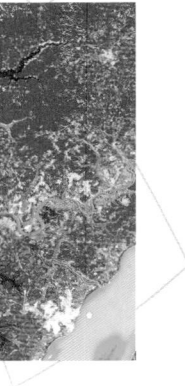
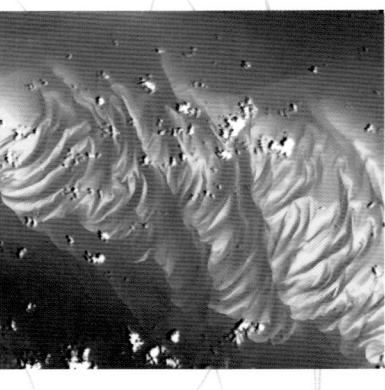
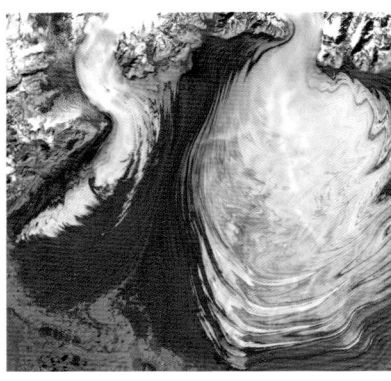
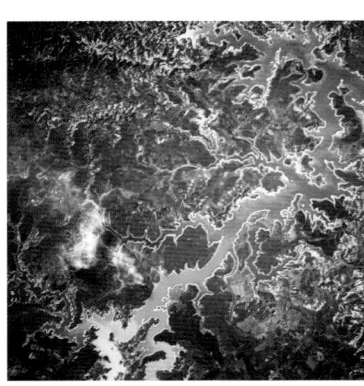

How to Use this Atlas

The atlas is organized into two major sections. The first, World View, provides an introductory survey of the physical, human, and economic geography of planet Earth. The second section, Mapping the World, contains detailed regional maps, arranged by continent, and includes physical, political, and human impact maps for the six largest continents. A reference section completes the atlas. It includes geographical comparisons, a fact file of the world's nations, a glossary, and a complete gazetteer.

Regional Maps

Each central map is accompanied by economic profile and population pattern maps. Included for selected regions are three-dimensional terrain maps and illustrations of significant cities. Annotated photographs of regional features support the central maps.

Grid reference
The location of each place, as listed in the gazetteer, is referenced against the grid frame.

Regional map
Each regional map includes detailed information on the physical landscape of a region, as well as its human geography.

Photographs
Photographs of natural features and human structures are included, with captions.

Locator map
This map indicates the location of the region within its continent.

Illustration
Illustrations highlight significant areas within a major city.

Population Patterns key

Population Patterns map
The population distribution of the area is plotted on this map.

Economic Profile key

Economic Profile map
The regional land use and economic activity are displayed on this map.

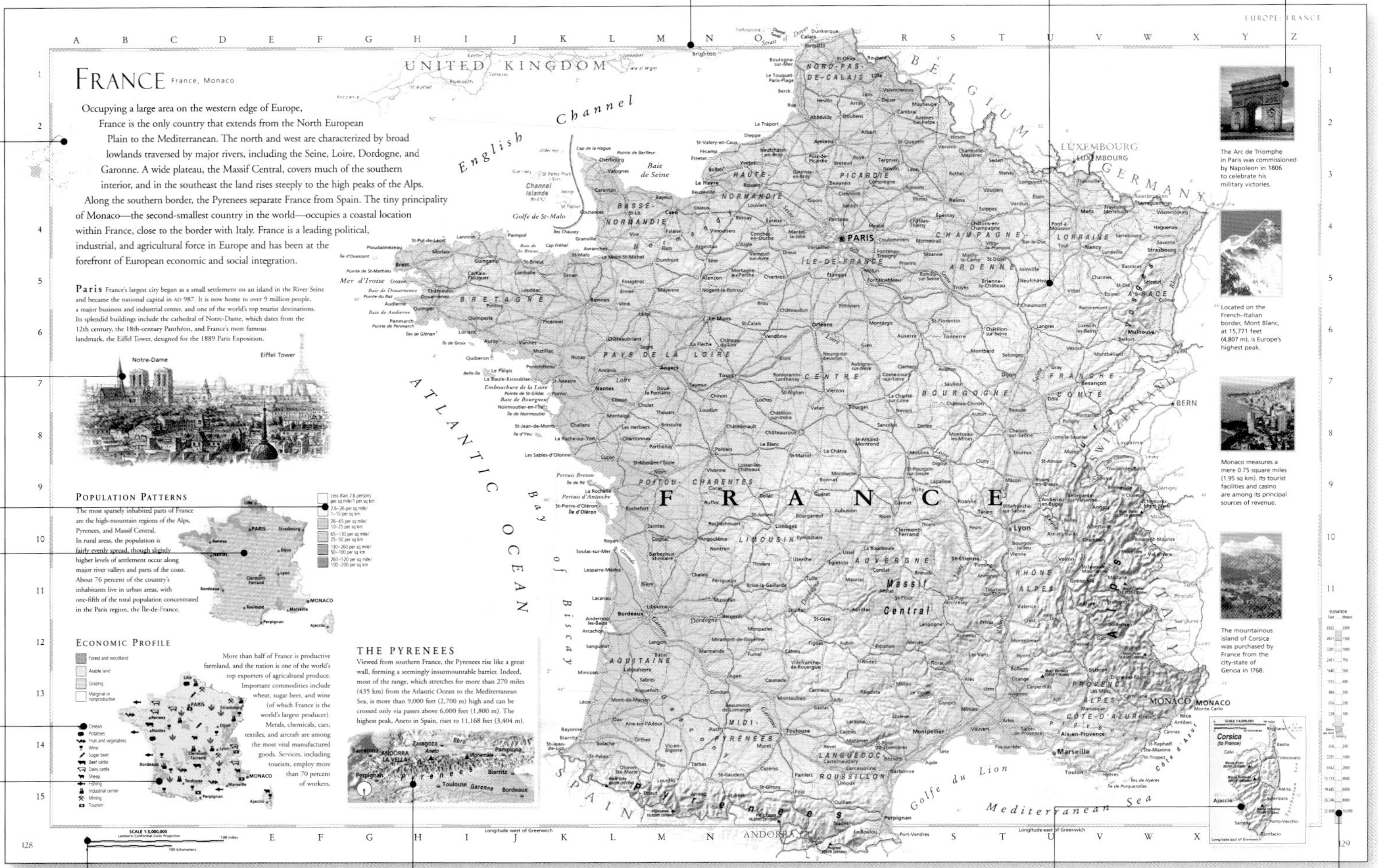

Scale
The scale of the main map, plus a scale bar and projection information, are included here.

Three-dimensional terrain map
This computer-generated map focuses on a specific physical feature.

Inset map
Associated regions that fall outside the area are included as detailed inset maps.

Elevation chart
This chart indicates elevation, the height above sea level, as well as ocean depths.

Thematic Maps

These pages include detailed world maps accompanied by illustrations, diagrams, charts, graphs, and photographs. They cover topics as diverse as our place in space, climate, wildlife, natural resources, exploration, population, religions, languages, indigenous peoples, transport and communications, economics, and governments.

Satellite Views

Included for the six largest continents are double-page spreads featuring images obtained from the satellites that orbit the globe. The photos reveal the diversity of population patterns, agricultural areas, and concentrations of industry across the continents. From space, the details of landscapes and the impact of human activity are often startlingly clear.

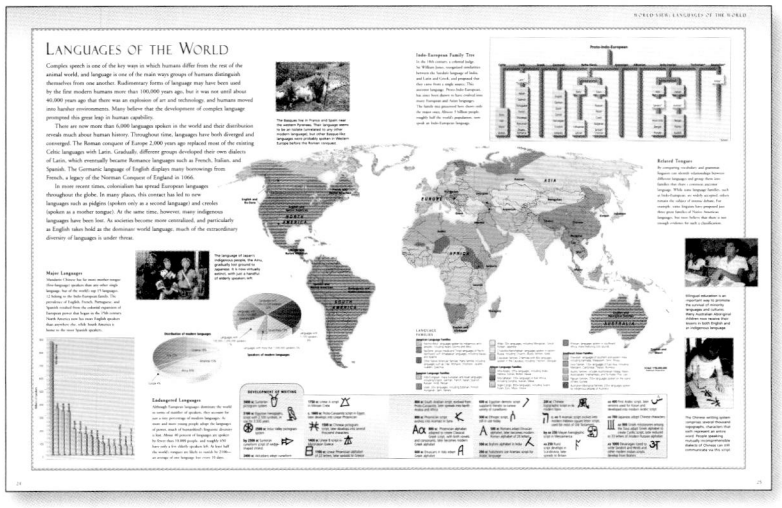

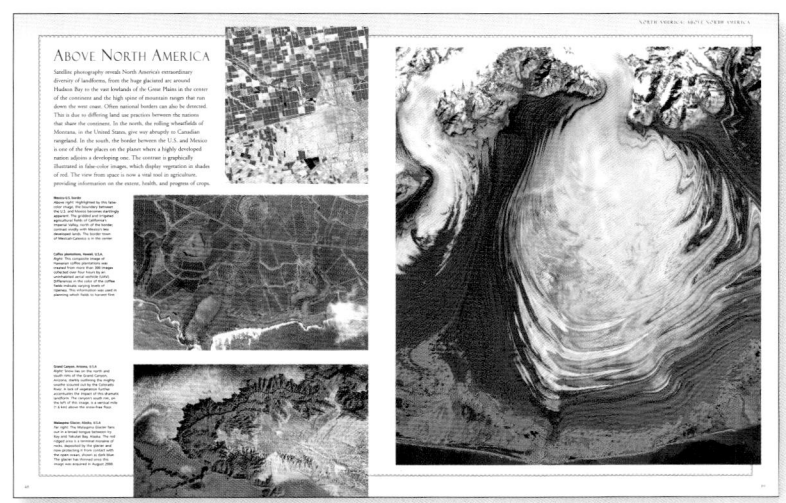

PHYSICAL CONTINENT MAPS

The central map displays the landform of each continent, including major waterways, mountain ranges, and geographical features. Smaller maps reveal the continental climate and vegetation zones. A side panel, containing a map, diagram, and photograph, reviews a significant natural hazard that occurs on the continent. Satellite photographs highlight major physical features of the continent.

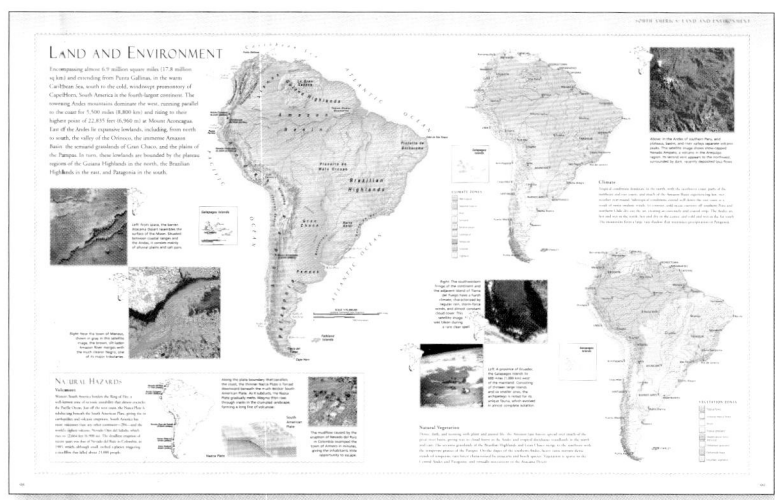

POLITICAL CONTINENT MAPS

The large political map displays the human geography of the continent. Supporting maps reveal the continental population distribution, and trade or political organizations. A series of historical maps highlight major political and social changes over time. A side panel includes flashpoint maps that focus on areas of current dispute and conflict. The maps are accompanied by a graph indicating the population of the largest cities.

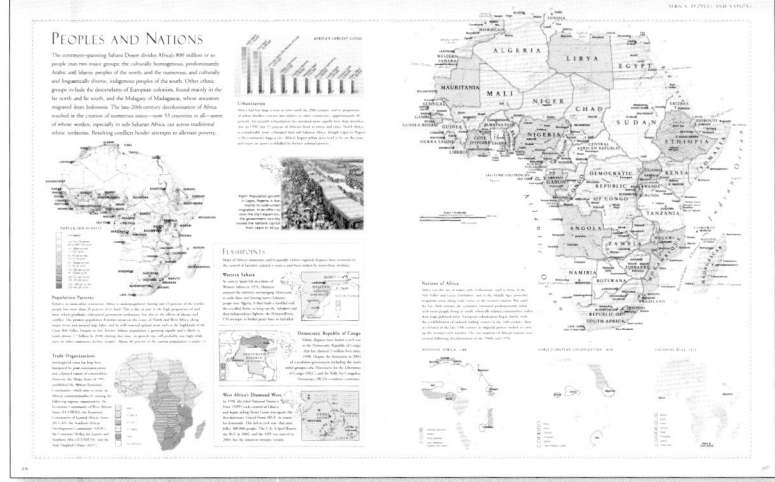

HUMAN IMPACT CONTINENT MAPS

The main map indicates land use and significant economic activities across the continent. A supporting map, accompanied by photographs, underlines the threats to the continent's environment. A side panel focuses on a dramatic environmental change as a result of human activity. A graph showing protected land illustrates the efforts of selected countries to reverse environmental damage.

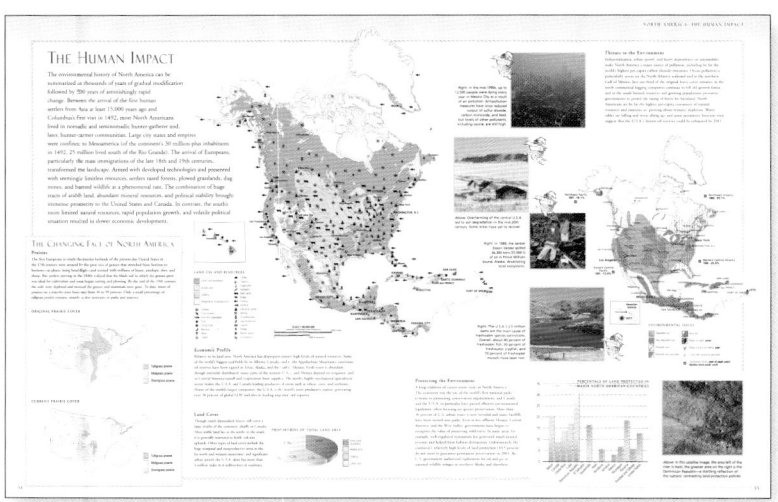

KEY TO REGIONAL MAPS

PHYSICAL FEATURES

ELEVATION

Feet	Meters
6562	2000
4921	1500
3281	1000
2461	750
1640	500
1312	400
984	300
656	200
328	100
0	0
Below sea level 0	0
656	200
3281	1000
6562	2000
13,123	4000
19,685	6000
26,246	8000
32,808	10,000

Ice cap
Ice shelf

▲ Mountain peak/volcano
Height, feet (meters)
+ **Pole**
△ Geomagnetic Pole
▲ Seamount
▼ Sea trench
Depth, feet (meters)

WATER FEATURES

Lake
Salt pan/Dry/Intermittent lake
Coastline
Major river
Minor river
✕ River source
▼ Waterfall

TRANSPORT

Major road
Main road
Minor road
Railway

GRATICULE FEATURE

125° Graticule number
Graticule line
Tropics/polar circle
Equator

BORDERS

International border
Defined maritime boundary
Equidistant lines
Disputed border
Demarcation/line of control/ceasefire line
State/territory border (Australia, Canada, U.S.A.)
International Date Line

NATIONAL/DEPENDENT TERRITORY CAPITAL CITIES

Over 5 million	■ **LONDON**
1–5 million	● **OTTAWA**
100,000–1 million	✳ **HELSINKI**
100,000–1 million	✳ **KINGSTON**
0–100,000	✳ **HONIARA**
0–100,000	✳ **BELMOPAN**

STATE/TERRITORY CAPITAL CITIES (Australia, Canada, U.S.A.)

Over 5 million	■ **Toronto**
1–5 million	● **Sydney**
100,000–1 million	✳ **Québec**
0–100,000	✳ Columbia

OTHER CITIES OR TOWNS

Over 5 million	■ **São Paulo**
1–5 million	● **Calicut**
100,000–1 million	○ **Luxor**
0–100,000	○ Lillehammer

□ Research base

Built-up area

TYPOGRAPHIC KEY

POLITICAL FEATURES

Country	**BELIZE**
Dependent territory with parent state	VIRGIN ISLANDS *(to U.S.A.)*
Internal administrative region	*UMBRIA*
State/Territory (Australia, Canada, U.S.A.)	VICTORIA

PHYSICAL FEATURES

Mountain range	*Allegheny Mountains*
Mountain peak	*Mt Davis*
Geographic feature	*Nullarbor Plain*
Peninsula	*Cape York Peninsula*
Headland/point/cape	*Cabo de São Vicente*
Island group	*Solomon Islands*
Island	*New Caledonia*
Pole	*North Pole*

WATER FEATURES

Ocean	*PACIFIC OCEAN*
Sea	*Irish Sea*
Bay/gulf	*Gulf of Mexico*
Channel/strait	*Bass Strait*
Undersea ridge	*Carlsberg Ridge*
Seamount/Sea trench	*Golden Dragon Seamount*
Lake/Salt pan/Dry/Intermittent lake	*Lake Titicaca*
Major river	*Nile*
Minor river	*Salween*
River source	*Source of the Amazon*
Waterfall	*Angel Falls*

GRATICULE FEATURES

Tropics/polar circle/equator	Tropic of Capricorn
Date line	International Date Line

INDEX TO MAP PAGES

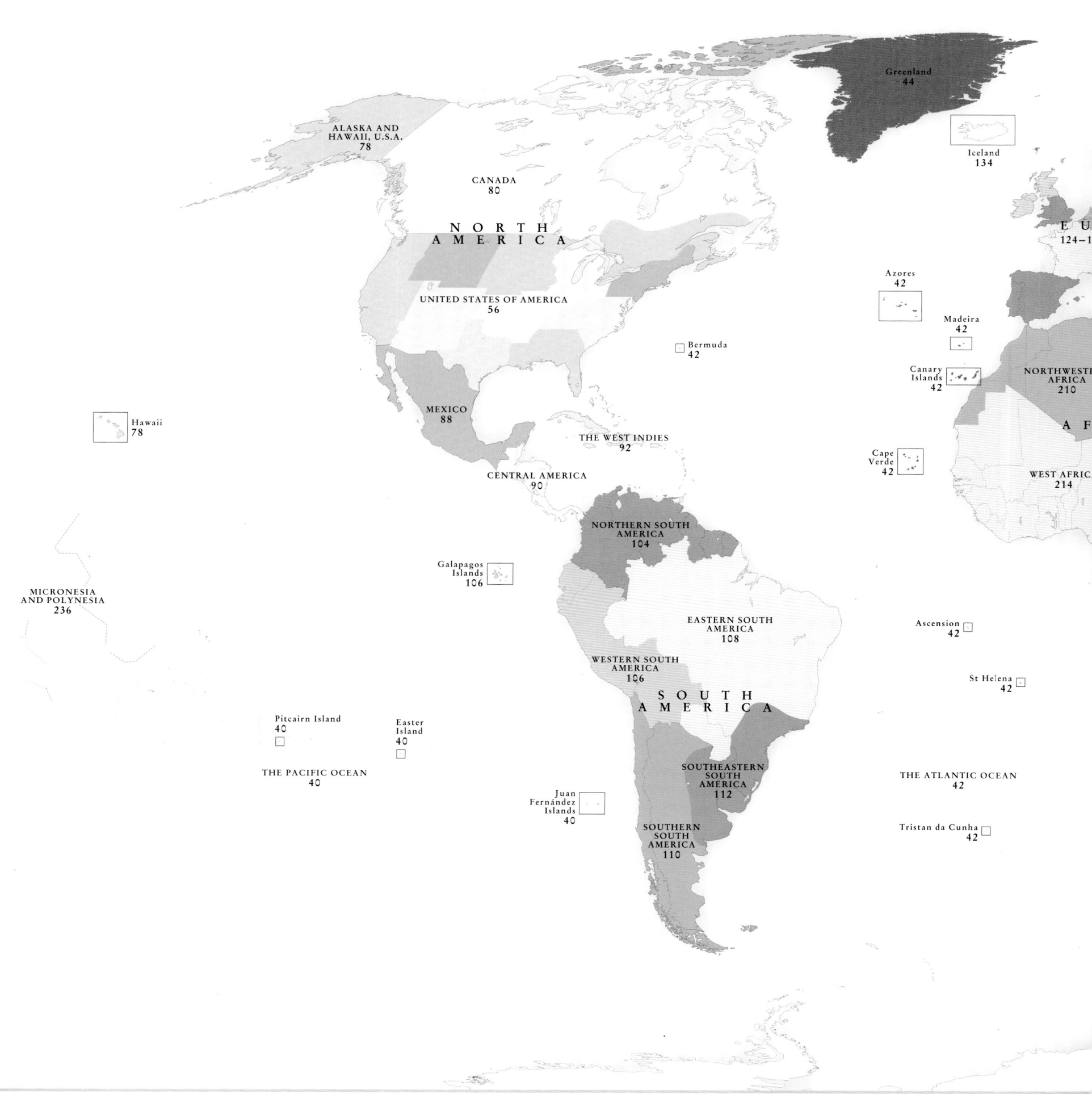

Greenland
44

ALASKA AND
HAWAII, U.S.A.
78

Iceland
134

CANADA
80

**NORTH
AMERICA**

E U
124–15

Azores
42

UNITED STATES OF AMERICA
56

Madeira
42

Bermuda
42

Canary
Islands
42

NORTHWESTE
AFRICA
210

Hawaii
78

MEXICO
88

A F

THE WEST INDIES
92

Cape
Verde
42

WEST AFRICA
214

CENTRAL AMERICA
90

NORTHERN SOUTH
AMERICA
104

Galapagos
Islands
106

EASTERN SOUTH
AMERICA
108

Ascension
42

MICRONESIA
AND POLYNESIA
236

WESTERN SOUTH
AMERICA
106

St Helena
42

**SOUTH
AMERICA**

Pitcairn Island
40

Easter
Island
40

THE PACIFIC OCEAN
40

SOUTHEASTERN
SOUTH
AMERICA
112

THE ATLANTIC OCEAN
42

Juan
Fernández
Islands
40

SOUTHERN
SOUTH
AMERICA
110

Tristan da Cunha
42

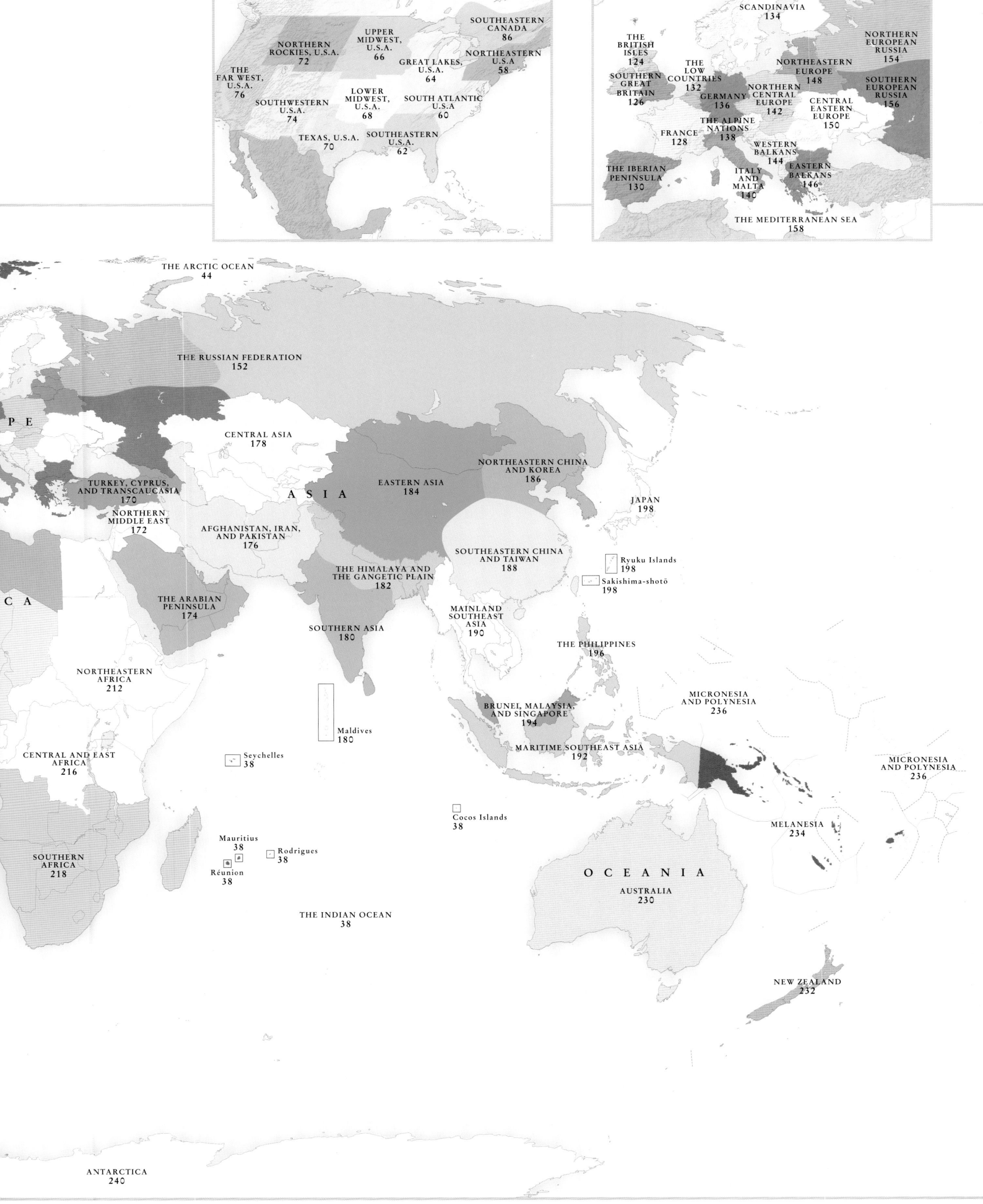

WESTERN CANADA
82

EASTERN CANADA
84

SOUTHEASTERN
CANADA
86

UPPER
MIDWEST,
U.S.A.
66

NORTHERN
ROCKIES, U.S.A.
72

GREAT LAKES,
U.S.A.
64

NORTHEASTERN
U.S.A
58

THE
FAR WEST,
U.S.A.
76

SOUTHWESTERN
U.S.A.
74

LOWER
MIDWEST,
U.S.A.
68

SOUTH ATLANTIC
U.S.A
60

TEXAS, U.S.A.
70

SOUTHEASTERN
U.S.A.
62

SCANDINAVIA
134

THE
BRITISH
ISLES
124

THE
LOW
COUNTRIES
132

NORTHEASTERN
EUROPE
148

NORTHERN
EUROPEAN
RUSSIA
154

SOUTHERN
GREAT
BRITAIN
126

GERMANY
136

NORTHERN
CENTRAL
EUROPE
142

CENTRAL
EASTERN
EUROPE
150

SOUTHERN
EUROPEAN
RUSSIA
156

FRANCE
128

THE ALPINE
NATIONS
138

WESTERN
BALKANS
144

THE IBERIAN
PENINSULA
130

ITALY
AND
MALTA
140

EASTERN
BALKANS
146

THE MEDITERRANEAN SEA
158

THE ARCTIC OCEAN
44

THE RUSSIAN FEDERATION
152

CENTRAL ASIA
178

NORTHEASTERN CHINA
AND KOREA
186

P E

TURKEY, CYPRUS,
AND TRANSCAUCASIA
170

EASTERN ASIA
184

A S I A

JAPAN
198

NORTHERN
MIDDLE EAST
172

AFGHANISTAN, IRAN,
AND PAKISTAN
176

Ryuku Islands
198

C A

SOUTHEASTERN CHINA
AND TAIWAN
188

Sakishima-shotō
198

THE HIMALAYA AND
THE GANGETIC PLAIN
182

THE ARABIAN
PENINSULA
174

MAINLAND
SOUTHEAST
ASIA
190

SOUTHERN ASIA
180

THE PHILIPPINES
196

NORTHEASTERN
AFRICA
212

MICRONESIA
AND POLYNESIA
236

Maldives
180

BRUNEI, MALAYSIA,
AND SINGAPORE
194

Seychelles
38

CENTRAL AND EAST
AFRICA
216

MARITIME SOUTHEAST ASIA
192

MICRONESIA
AND POLYNESIA
236

Cocos Islands
38

MELANESIA
234

Mauritius
38

Rodrigues
38

SOUTHERN
AFRICA
218

Réunion
38

O C E A N I A

THE INDIAN OCEAN
38

AUSTRALIA
230

NEW ZEALAND
232

ANTARCTICA
240

ll

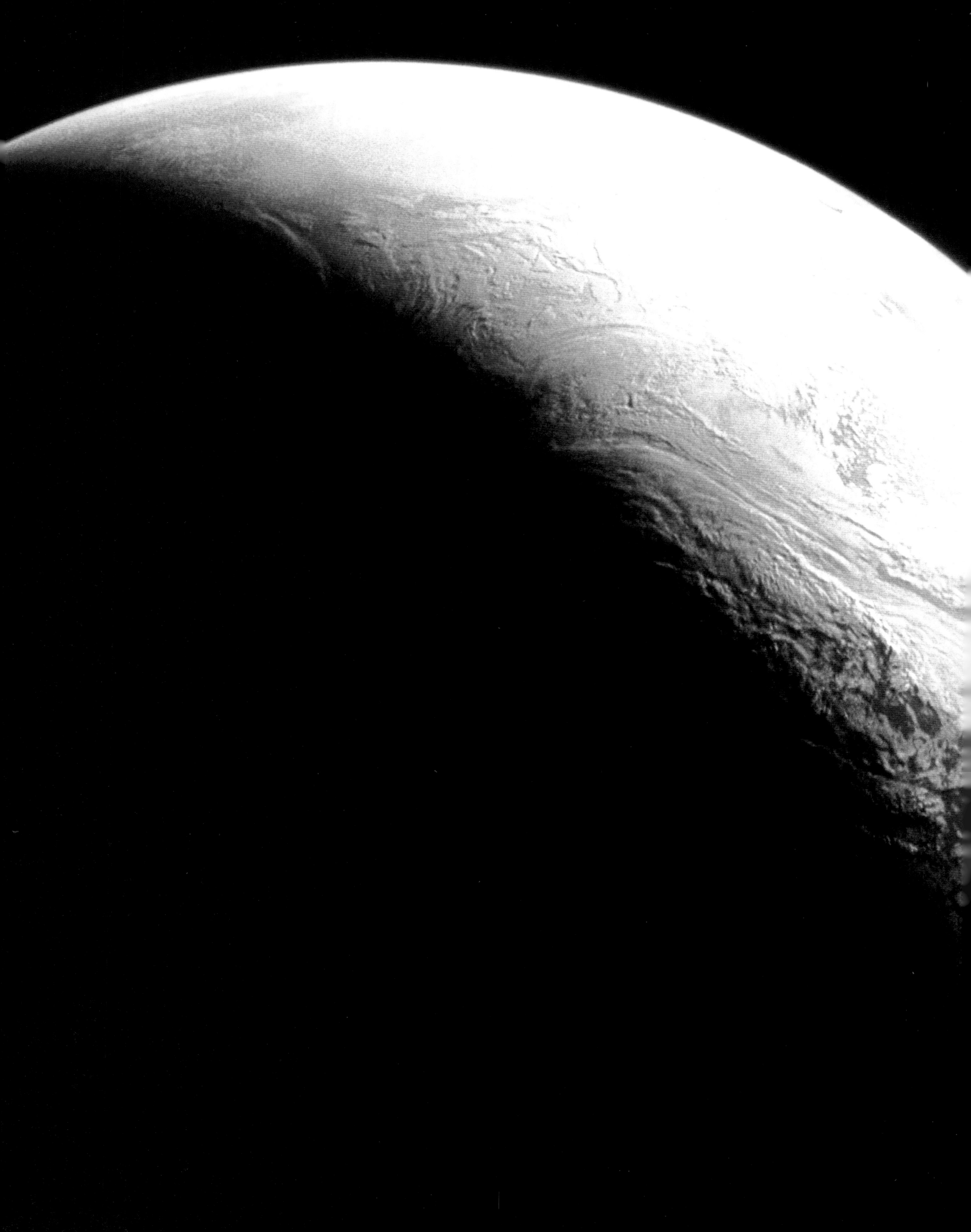

WORLD VIEW

This image of Earth was taken from the Apollo 4 spacecraft, which was launched on November 9, 1967. It is one of the earliest photographs of Earth taken from space. The dramatic distinction between day and night is clearly visible, and the side of the planet in daylight appears to form a crescent. It is difficult to distinguish any physical features on the sunlit side of Earth due to the significant amount of cloud cover.

OUR PLACE IN SPACE

As vast as our planet may seem when we map and describe its features, it is a mere speck compared to the immensity of the universe. Earth is the third of nine planets orbiting the Sun, which is just one of 200 billion stars in the Milky Way galaxy. The Milky Way, in turn, is simply one of perhaps 50 billion galaxies that populate space.

The solar system forms Earth's local neighborhood. At its center is the Sun, a giant ball of hydrogen and helium. Like other stars, the Sun shines because nuclear reactions in its core release tremendous amounts of energy. The planets fall into two main groups—the inner rocky planets of Mercury, Venus, Earth, and Mars, and the outer gas giants of Jupiter, Saturn, Uranus, and Neptune. The ninth planet, Pluto, fits into neither group and is probably an icy planetesimal. Other icy planetesimals orbit beyond Pluto, some traveling inward to become comets. Smaller, rocky bodies known as asteroids orbit in a loose band between Mars and Jupiter or occasionally pass near Earth. Meteoroids are pieces of rocky debris scattered through the solar system. We see them as meteors, or "shooting stars," when they burn up after entering Earth's atmosphere.

Beyond the solar system are other stars, some with their own planets. The Sun, other stars, and clouds of gas and dust make up the Milky Way galaxy, part of a cluster of galaxies known as the Local Group. This cluster belongs to the Local Supercluster, one of the many collections of galaxies thought to make up the honeycomb structure of the universe.

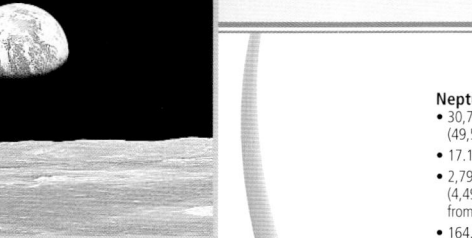

Earth rises over the Moon's dusty surface in this image captured by Apollo astronauts. Our planet's only natural satellite, the Moon is 2,160 miles (3,476 km) in diameter.

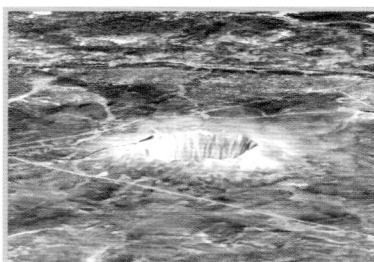

Erosion has erased most of Earth's impact scars, but a few can still be seen. A house-size meteorite that struck 50,000 years ago created Meteor Crater in Arizona, U.S.A.

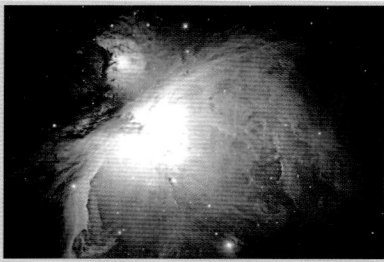
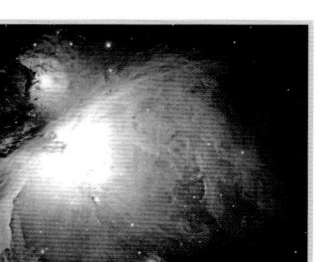

Throughout space, new stars are being born in clouds of gas and dust known as nebulas. The Orion nebula is one of many star-producing regions in the Milky Way galaxy.

Neptune
- 30,775 miles (49,528 km) wide
- 17.1 x Earth's mass
- 2,793 million miles (4,495 million km) from Sun
- 164.8 year orbit
- 16h 7m rotation
- 13 moons

Pluto
- 1,485 miles (2,390 km) wide
- 0.002 x Earth's mass
- 3,647 million miles (5,870 million km) from Sun
- 248 year orbit
- 6.4 day rotation
- 1 moon

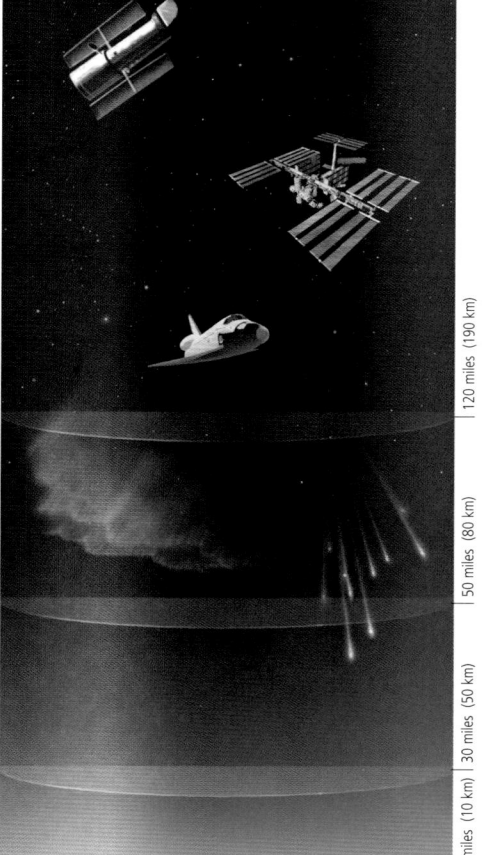

Where Space Begins
No sharp line separates space from Earth's atmosphere—the air just gradually becomes thinner with altitude. The atmosphere's last traces can be detected roughly 600 miles (1,000 km) above the ground.

Exosphere

Thermosphere

Mesosphere

Stratosphere

Troposphere

120 miles (190 km)

50 miles (80 km)

30 miles (50 km)

6 miles (10 km)

Sea level

To the Edge of the Universe

One light-year is the distance that light travels in a year, or 5.9 trillion miles (9.5 trillion km). On this scale, the Moon is just 1.3 light-seconds from Earth, while Pluto, the most distant planet, is 6 light-hours away. The Milky Way galaxy is 100,000 light-years across, and the nearest large galaxy, Andromeda, lies at a distance of 2.8 million light-years. The edge of the visible universe lies more than 13 billion light-years away.

The Local Group
With about 40 members, the Local Group is a cluster of galaxies held together by their mutual gravity. It features three large spiral galaxies—our own Milky Way, the Andromeda galaxy, and the Pinwheel.

The solar system
The Sun makes up 99.9 percent of the solar system's mass. Its powerful gravity keeps Earth and eight other planets in orbit, along with countless smaller bodies—more than 135 moons, millions of asteroids, and maybe trillions of comets.

The Milky Way
Our galaxy is made up of the Sun and about 200 billion other stars. The spiral is slowly turning, with the Sun taking 226 million years to complete one revolution.

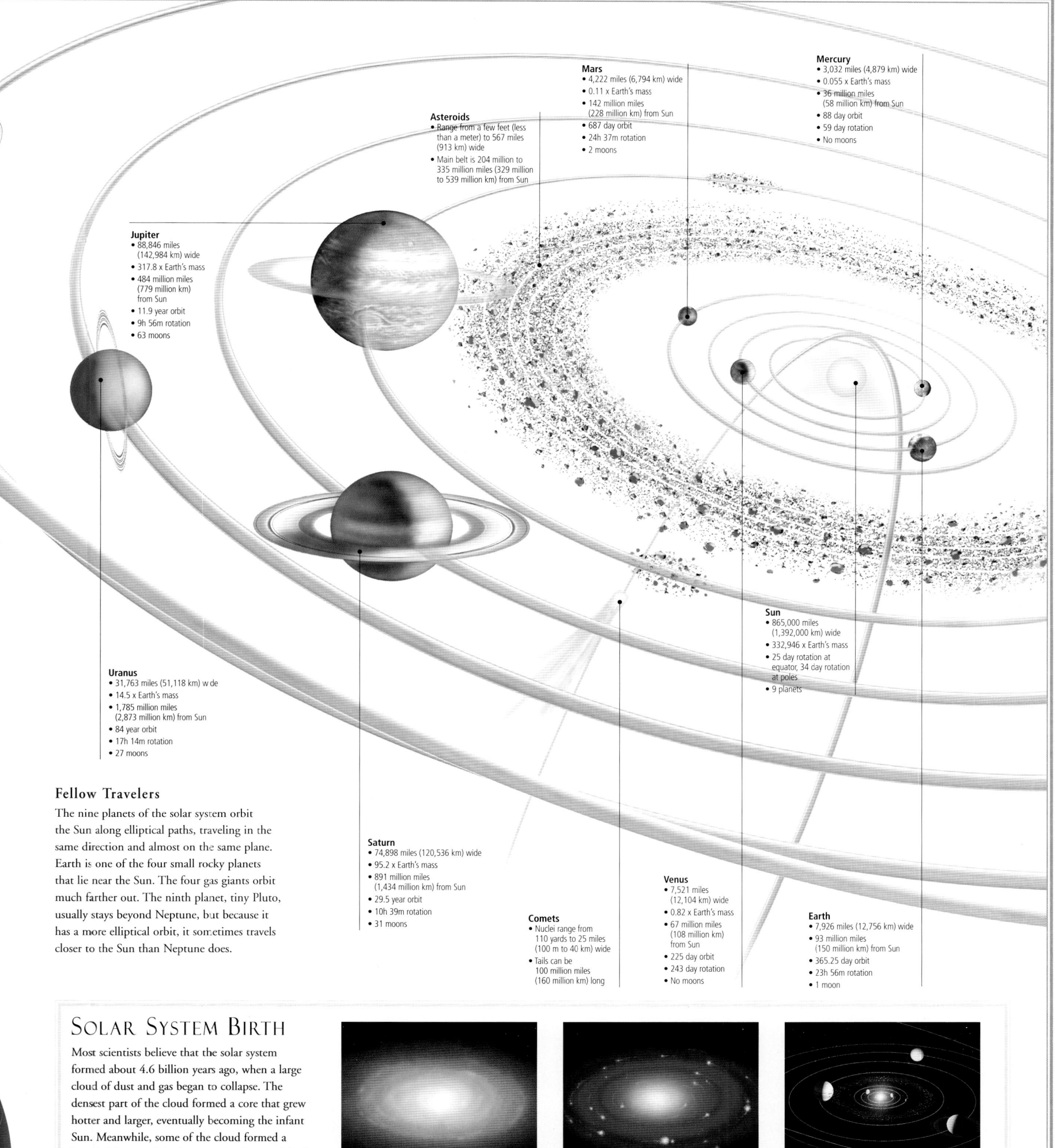

Mars
- 4,222 miles (6,794 km) wide
- 0.11 x Earth's mass
- 142 million miles (228 million km) from Sun
- 687 day orbit
- 24h 37m rotation
- 2 moons

Mercury
- 3,032 miles (4,879 km) wide
- 0.055 x Earth's mass
- 36 million miles (58 million km) from Sun
- 88 day orbit
- 59 day rotation
- No moons

Asteroids
- Range from a few feet (less than a meter) to 567 miles (913 km) wide
- Main belt is 204 million to 335 million miles (329 million to 539 million km) from Sun

Jupiter
- 88,846 miles (142,984 km) wide
- 317.8 x Earth's mass
- 484 million miles (779 million km) from Sun
- 11.9 year orbit
- 9h 56m rotation
- 63 moons

Sun
- 865,000 miles (1,392,000 km) wide
- 332,946 x Earth's mass
- 25 day rotation at equator, 34 day rotation at poles
- 9 planets

Uranus
- 31,763 miles (51,118 km) wide
- 14.5 x Earth's mass
- 1,785 million miles (2,873 million km) from Sun
- 84 year orbit
- 17h 14m rotation
- 27 moons

Fellow Travelers

The nine planets of the solar system orbit the Sun along elliptical paths, traveling in the same direction and almost on the same plane. Earth is one of the four small rocky planets that lie near the Sun. The four gas giants orbit much farther out. The ninth planet, tiny Pluto, usually stays beyond Neptune, but because it has a more elliptical orbit, it sometimes travels closer to the Sun than Neptune does.

Saturn
- 74,898 miles (120,536 km) wide
- 95.2 x Earth's mass
- 891 million miles (1,434 million km) from Sun
- 29.5 year orbit
- 10h 39m rotation
- 31 moons

Comets
- Nuclei range from 110 yards to 25 miles (100 m to 40 km) wide
- Tails can be 100 million miles (160 million km) long

Venus
- 7,521 miles (12,104 km) wide
- 0.82 x Earth's mass
- 67 million miles (108 million km) from Sun
- 225 day orbit
- 243 day rotation
- No moons

Earth
- 7,926 miles (12,756 km) wide
- 93 million miles (150 million km) from Sun
- 365.25 day orbit
- 23h 56m rotation
- 1 moon

SOLAR SYSTEM BIRTH

Most scientists believe that the solar system formed about 4.6 billion years ago, when a large cloud of dust and gas began to collapse. The densest part of the cloud formed a core that grew hotter and larger, eventually becoming the infant Sun. Meanwhile, some of the cloud formed a broad disk around the hot core. As dust particles in the disk collided, they formed solid bodies, which continued to grow through further collisions. Near the heat of the young Sun, the bodies were rocky and would become the small inner planets, while farther out they remained water- and gas-rich and ended up as the gas giant planets.

Spinning Disk
A cloud of dust and gas collapses and forms the solar nebula, a broad, thin disk rotating around a dense core.

Colliding Bodies
The core becomes the hot infant Sun, as lumps of dust in the disk collide and form solid bodies called planetesimals.

Sun and Planets
The Sun becomes a star and, through violent collisions, the planetesimals gradually grow and form the planets.

EARTH'S STRUCTURE

Beneath our feet, planet Earth is restless. The continents slowly drift, mountains are gradually built, earthquakes shake the ground, and volcanoes spectacularly erupt. Meanwhile, on the surface, wind and water sculpt intricate shapes from the land.

Deep inside Earth, the heat of its iron–nickel core stirs the rocks of the mantle above it. Like slowly boiling water, mantle rocks circulate in convection currents, rising as they heat up and forming a soft layer called the asthenosphere. As they move toward the thin rocky crust at the surface, the mantle rocks cool and become solid. Together, the crust and the solid upper mantle form Earth's outer layer, the lithosphere, which carries the continents and oceans.

The movements of the mantle cracked the lithosphere of the young Earth, splitting it into tectonic plates. Today, the convection currents continue to shift the plates, slowly but surely. Plates sliding past each other can rattle the ground in an earthquake. Plates moving apart can widen an ocean or create a new sea. And colliding plates may form mountains, volcanoes, or ocean trenches. Over millions of years, tectonic activity also alters the shape and position of the continents.

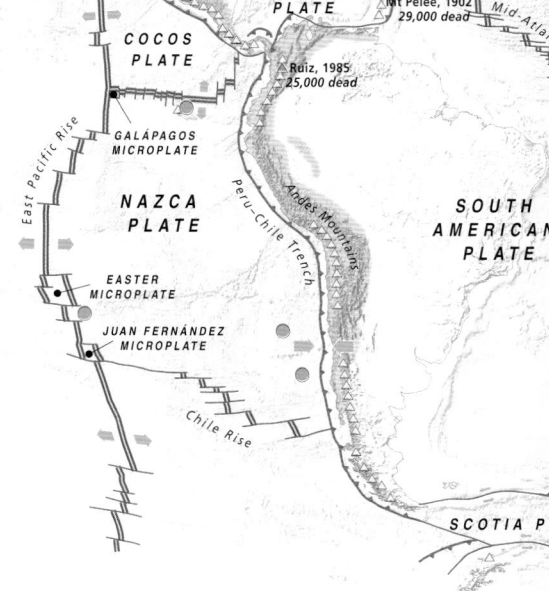

Tectonic Boundaries

The movements of the seven large and many small tectonic plates that make up Earth's surface have shaped much of the land and ocean floor. This map shows how the distribution of volcanoes and earthquakes relates closely to the plate boundaries.

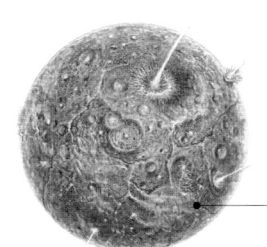

4.6–4.2 billion years ago
The infant Earth's surface is bombarded by meteorites and comets, as the interior starts to heat up and heavier elements sink to the core.

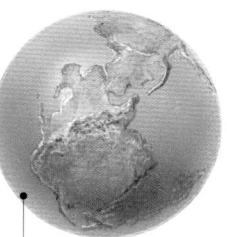

4.2–3.8 billion years ago
Bombardment slows. Lava flows released by the impacts cool and form the crust. Water from volcanoes and comets slowly forms the oceans.

90 million years ago
Pangaea has broken up and the South Atlantic Ocean has opened, but North America remains close to Europe, and Australia remains joined to Antarctica.

SCALE 1:109,600,000
Robinson Projection

Today
The continents had reached their present positions by roughly 12 million years ago. Continental collisions will eventually result in a new supercontinent.

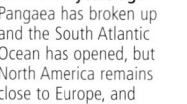

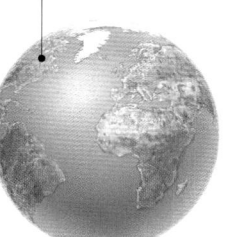

Inside Earth

Earth's core has two layers of iron and nickel—solid in the inner core, and liquid in the outer core. The mantle is made of layers of rock—solid in the lower mantle, soft in the asthenosphere, and solid in the upper mantle. The upper mantle and the rocky crust make up the lithosphere.

200 million years ago
The landmasses of the Northern and Southern hemispheres are joined in the single supercontinent of Pangaea, surrounded by one large ocean.

Crust
Lithosphere
Asthenosphere
Mantle
Outer core
Inner core

Moving Plates

Powered by convection currents in the mantle, Earth's tectonic plates are always on the move. Plate boundaries can be divergent (two plates pulling away from each other); convergent (two plates colliding); or transform (two plates sliding past each other).

Undersea collision
When two oceanic plates meet at a convergent boundary, one plate is subducted beneath the other, creating a trench such as the Mariana Trench. An arc of volcanic islands may appear parallel to the trench.

Mid-ocean ridge
Magma rising where two oceanic plates meet forces them apart, making a divergent boundary. It also creates new seafloor, forming an undersea mountain chain such as the Mid-Atlantic Ridge.

Hot-spot volcanoes
Volcanoes can appear when a powerful plume of magma pushes up from the mantle and bursts through the crust. The Hawaiian Islands formed at a volcanic hot spot.

Coastal collision
When oceanic and continental plates converge, the thinner oceanic plate is subducted, creating a deep trench in the ocean. Mountains such as the Andes may form on the land.

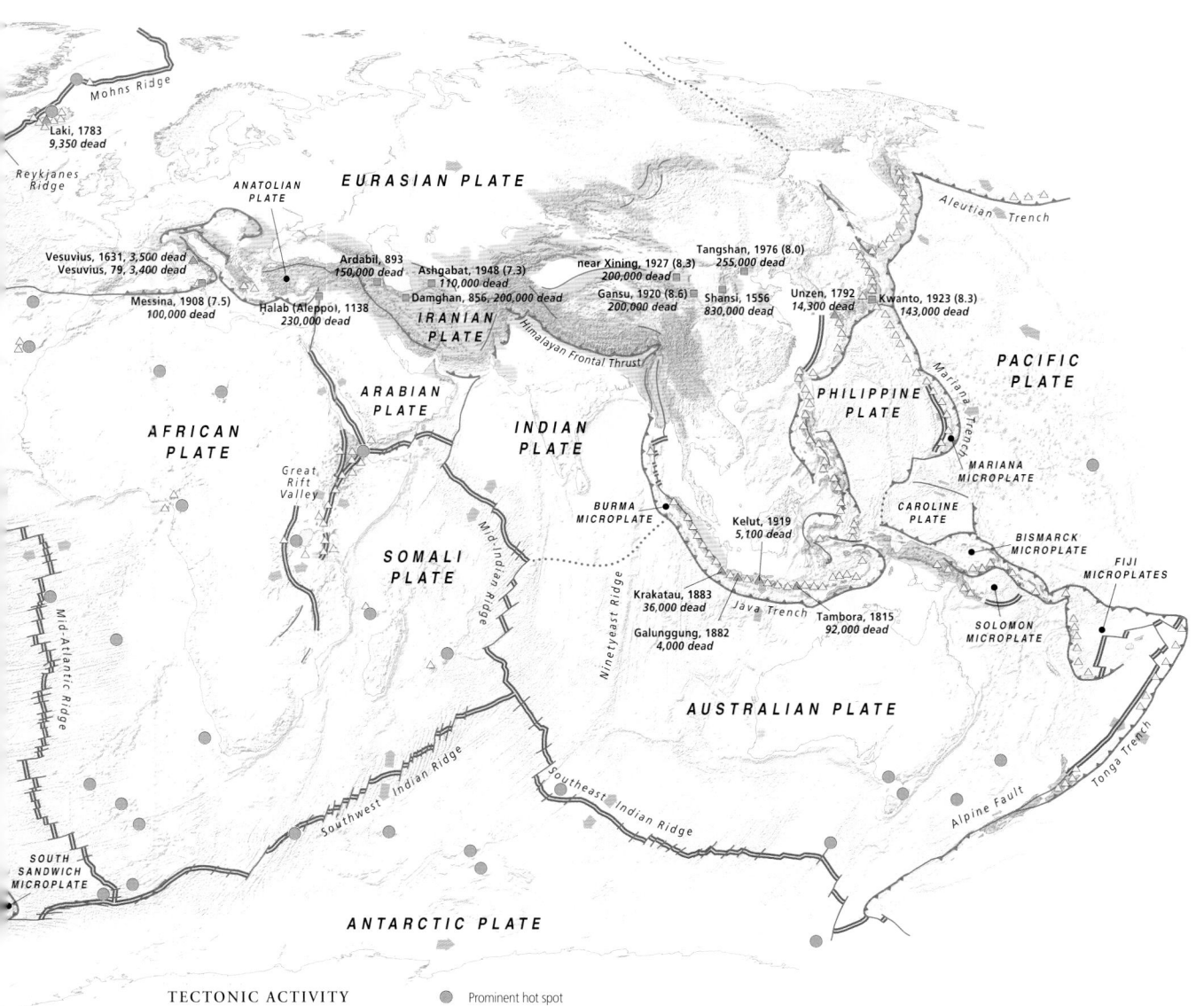

Laki, 1783
9,350 dead

Reykjanes
Ridge

Mohns Ridge

ANATOLIAN
PLATE

EURASIAN PLATE

Aleutian Trench

Vesuvius, 1631, 3,500 dead
Vesuvius, 79, 3,400 dead

Ardabil, 893
150,000 dead
Ashgabat, 1948 (7.3)
110,000 dead

Tangshan, 1976 (8.0)
255,000 dead

near Xining, 1927 (8.3)
200,000 dead

Messina, 1908 (7.5)
100,000 dead

Halab (Aleppo), 1138
230,000 dead

IRANIAN
PLATE

Damghan, 856, 200,000 dead

Gansu, 1920 (8.6)
200,000 dead

Shansi, 1556
830,000 dead

Unzen, 1792
14,300 dead

Kwanto, 1923 (8.3)
143,000 dead

Mariana Trench

ARABIAN
PLATE

INDIAN
PLATE

Himalayan Frontal Thrust

PHILIPPINE
PLATE

PACIFIC
PLATE

AFRICAN
PLATE

Great
Rift
Valley

MARIANA
MICROPLATE

CAROLINE
PLATE

SOMALI
PLATE

BURMA
MICROPLATE

Kelut, 1919
5,100 dead

BISMARCK
MICROPLATE

FIJI
MICROPLATES

Mid-Indian Ridge

Ninetyeast Ridge

Krakatau, 1883
36,000 dead

Java Trench

Tambora, 1815
92,000 dead

SOLOMON
MICROPLATE

Galunggung, 1882
4,000 dead

AUSTRALIAN PLATE

Mid-Atlantic Ridge

Southwest Indian Ridge

Southeast Indian Ridge

Alpine Fault

Tonga Trench

SOUTH
SANDWICH
MICROPLATE

ANTARCTIC PLATE

TECTONIC ACTIVITY

- ▨ Earthquake zone
- ■ Deadliest earthquakes: Location, year (magnitude, where known) *number dead*
- △ Volcanic zone
- ▲ Deadliest volcanoes: Location, year, *number dead*
- ● Prominent hot spot
- ▲▲ Convergent margin
- ═══ Divergent margin
- ─── Transform fault
- ········ Diffuse or uncertain
- ⇨ Direction of movement

50 million years from now
The Atlantic widens, the Mediterranean vanishes as Africa and Europe join up, Australia and Southeast Asia collide, and California slides up to Alaska.

The Story of Earth

About 4.6 billion years ago, Earth formed with the rest of the solar system from a swirling cloud of dust and gas. Since then, our planet has been in a state of flux. The theory of plate tectonics explains how the continents have drifted and altered over millions of years to reach their present state, and how they will continue to change in the future.

The Forces of Erosion

As wind and water move across the landscape, they wear down rocks and carry away the sediment, gradually reshaping Earth's surface. Water can flow through the terrain in rivers, seep underground through rocks, inch downhill in frozen form as glaciers, or crash along the coast as ocean waves. Winds can pick up loose rock particles, carry them long distances, and blast them at the surface. Temperature can also have a dramatic effect, with extremes of heat and cold both causing rocks to crack and split.

Ruth Glacier is one of many glaciers on North America's highest peak, Mount McKinley in Alaska. The ice has gouged out a U-shaped valley as gravity slowly drags it downhill.

The Goosenecks of the San Juan River in Utah, U.S.A., formed when the region was uplifted, boosting the meandering river's ability to carve its path into the rocks.

Off the coast of Victoria, Australia, ocean waves have carved the Twelve Apostles. These impressive rock stacks are islands of hard limestone that have resisted erosion.

The volcanic landscape of Cappadocia in Turkey has been shaped by the wind. The bizarre formations were created when the soft pumice layers eroded at a different rate to the harder tuff layers.

THE ROCK CYCLE

Earth's crust features three kinds of rock. Igneous rocks, such as granite and basalt, form when molten magma either cools below ground, or erupts as lava and cools at the surface. Sedimentary rocks, such as sandstone and limestone, are made from mud, silt, or sand broken down from other rocks, or from organic matter such as shells. Metamorphic rocks, such as marble and slate, are rocks that have been altered by heat or pressure. Earth's rocks constantly transform as they are processed through the rock cycle.

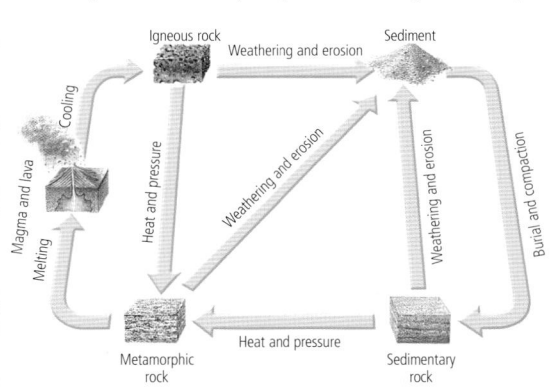

Igneous rock — Weathering and erosion — Sediment

Cooling

Magma and lava

Heat and pressure

Weathering and erosion

Weathering and erosion

Burial and compaction

Melting

Metamorphic rock — Heat and pressure — Sedimentary rock

Sliding plates
At transform boundaries, two plates slide horizontally past each other. California's San Andreas Fault is a transform boundary on land, but most such faults are in the ocean.

Continental rift
When two continental plates move apart at a divergent boundary, a wide valley, such as Africa's Great Rift Valley, is formed. Eventually, such a rift may be flooded by water from a nearby ocean and become a new sea.

Folding crust
When two continental plates collide, neither is subducted. Instead, the crusts buckle, forming high mountains such as the Himalayas.

CLIMATE AND WEATHER

The atmosphere that surrounds Earth is in a constant state of flux, subject to variations in temperature, wind, pressure, humidity, and precipitation that collectively create our weather. The long-term pattern of weather in a particular region is known as its climate and depends on three main factors: latitude, altitude, and proximity to the sea.

The world's weather is fueled by the Sun's uneven heating. Because Earth is a sphere, sunlight is more intense and the air is warmer at the Equator than at the poles. Warm air expands and rises, creating an area of low atmospheric pressure. As it rises, the air cools and its water vapor condenses into clouds, often bringing rain. Cold air is heavier and sinks, forming a high-pressure area with clear skies and settled weather. Wind is created when air flows from areas of high pressure to lower-pressure zones. Sometimes "wedges" of cold air, known as cold fronts, push under existing air, forcing it to rise rapidly and resulting in towering clouds and dramatic storms.

Constantly working toward equilibrium, the atmosphere carries warm air from the Equator toward the poles, and cold air toward the Equator. Earth's rotation deflects these air masses, creating complex patterns that are matched by the warm and cold currents in the ocean. The large-scale air and ocean currents determine the world's various climates, while smaller circulations and individual clouds within them bring our day-to-day weather.

Lightning is an electrical discharge created within a thunderstorm. The heat of the discharge makes the air expand explosively, causing a dramatic clap of thunder.

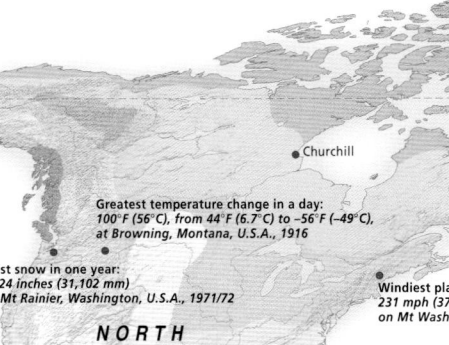

• Churchill

Greatest temperature change in a day:
100°F (56°C), from 44°F (6.7°C) to −56°F (−49°C), at Browning, Montana, U.S.A., 1916

Most snow in one year:
1,224 inches (31,102 mm) on Mt Rainier, Washington, U.S.A., 1971/72

Windiest place:
231 mph (372 km/h) on Mt Washington, U.S.A., 1934

NORTH AMERICA

SOUTH AMERICA

Driest place:
0.02 inches (0.5 mm) per year in Quillagua, Atacama Desert, Chile, 1964–2001

Global Circulation

The Sun strikes Earth more directly near the Equator than at the poles. The warm air of the tropics rises and moves toward the colder polar regions, then cools and sinks at about 30 degrees north and south latitude. Most of it travels back toward the Equator, but some continues to move poleward until it meets cold polar air at about 60 degrees north and south.

A tornado is a spinning column of air that extends from a thundercloud to the ground. Its powerful winds can exceed speeds of 300 mph (480 km/h).

The heat of the tropics can be dispersed to the middle latitudes by tropical storm systems known as cyclones, typhoons, or hurricanes. Hurricane Fran (pictured) hit North Carolina in 1996.

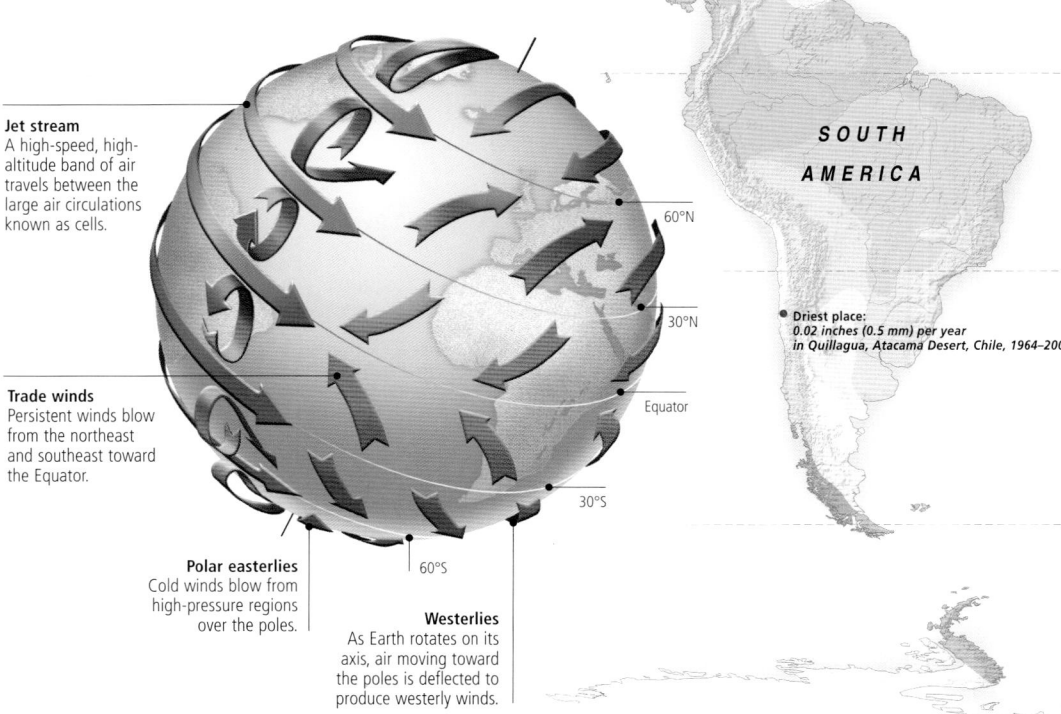

Jet stream
A high-speed, high-altitude band of air travels between the large air circulations known as cells.

Trade winds
Persistent winds blow from the northeast and southeast toward the Equator.

Polar easterlies
Cold winds blow from high-pressure regions over the poles.

Westerlies
As Earth rotates on its axis, air moving toward the poles is deflected to produce westerly winds.

60°N
30°N
Equator
30°S
60°S

The Water Cycle

Much of our weather is generated by the water cycle, the continuous interchange of moisture between oceans, land, plants, and clouds. Moisture enters the atmosphere when water in oceans, rivers, and lakes is heated by the Sun and evaporates, and when plants exude water as part of photosynthesis. It condenses as clouds and returns to Earth's surface when it falls as rain, hail, or snow.

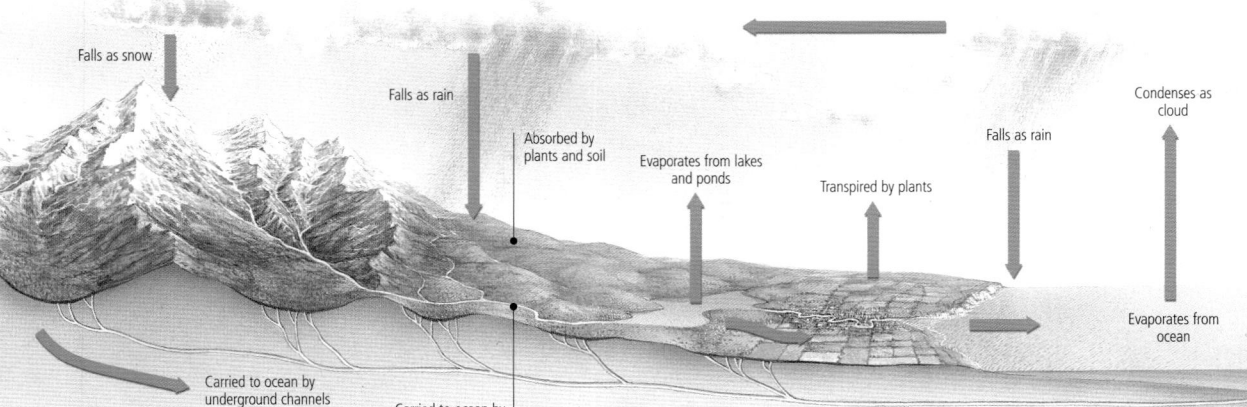

Falls as snow

Falls as rain

Absorbed by plants and soil

Evaporates from lakes and ponds

Transpired by plants

Falls as rain

Condenses as cloud

Evaporates from ocean

Carried to ocean by underground channels

Carried to ocean by rivers and streams

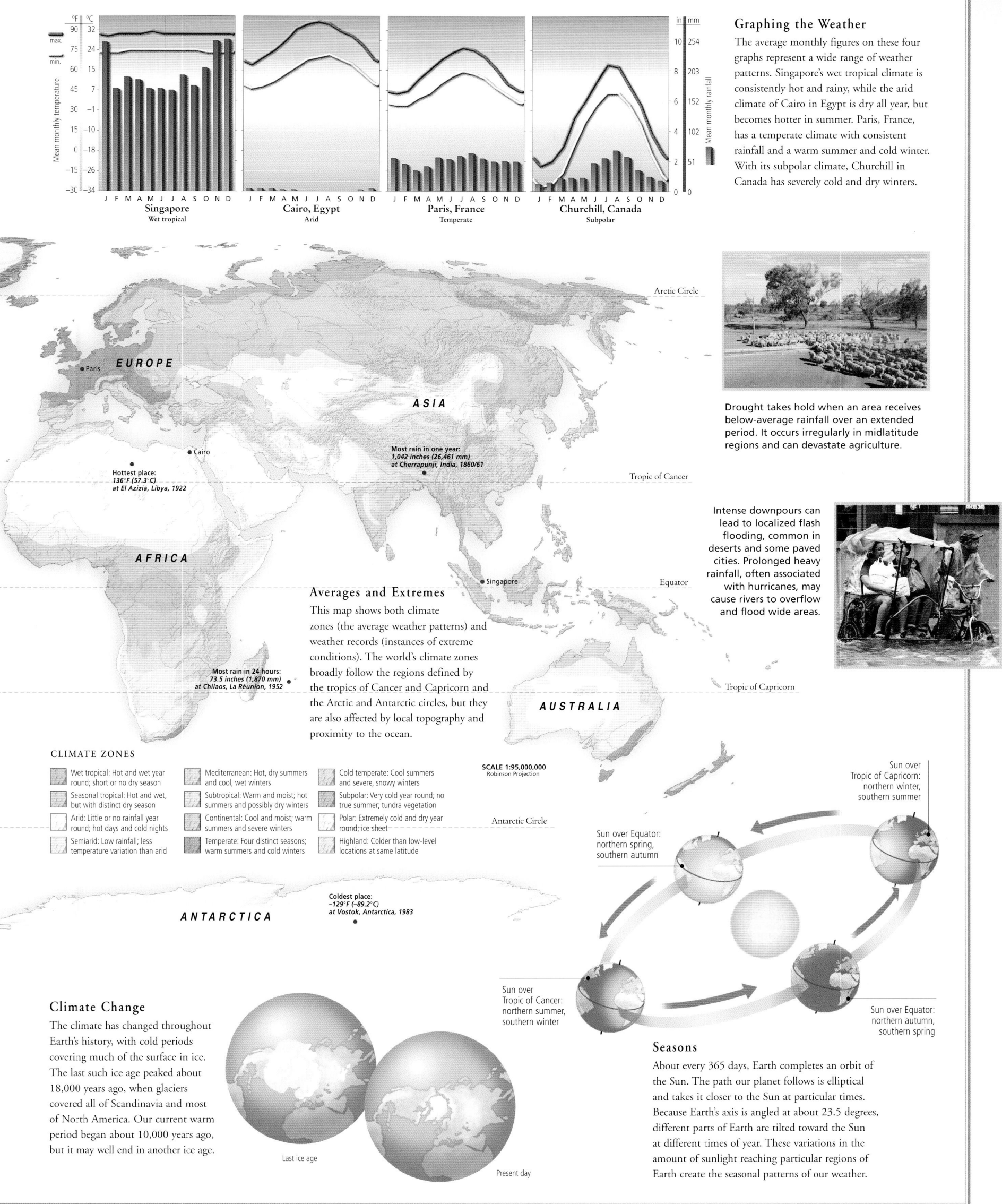

Graphing the Weather

The average monthly figures on these four graphs represent a wide range of weather patterns. Singapore's wet tropical climate is consistently hot and rainy, while the arid climate of Cairo in Egypt is dry all year, but becomes hotter in summer. Paris, France, has a temperate climate with consistent rainfall and a warm summer and cold winter. With its subpolar climate, Churchill in Canada has severely cold and dry winters.

Singapore Wet tropical

Cairo, Egypt Arid

Paris, France Temperate

Churchill, Canada Subpolar

Drought takes hold when an area receives below-average rainfall over an extended period. It occurs irregularly in midlatitude regions and can devastate agriculture.

Intense downpours can lead to localized flash flooding, common in deserts and some paved cities. Prolonged heavy rainfall, often associated with hurricanes, may cause rivers to overflow and flood wide areas.

Hottest place: 136°F (57.3°C) at El Azizia, Libya, 1922

Most rain in one year: 1,042 inches (26,461 mm) at Cherrapunji, India, 1860/61

Most rain in 24 hours: 73.5 inches (1,870 mm) at Chilaos, La Réunion, 1952

Coldest place: −129°F (−89.2°C) at Vostok, Antarctica, 1983

Averages and Extremes

This map shows both climate zones (the average weather patterns) and weather records (instances of extreme conditions). The world's climate zones broadly follow the regions defined by the tropics of Cancer and Capricorn and the Arctic and Antarctic circles, but they are also affected by local topography and proximity to the ocean.

SCALE 1:95,000,000
Robinson Projection

CLIMATE ZONES

- Wet tropical: Hot and wet year round; short or no dry season
- Seasonal tropical: Hot and wet, but with distinct dry season
- Arid: Little or no rainfall year round; hot days and cold nights
- Semiarid: Low rainfall; less temperature variation than arid
- Mediterranean: Hot, dry summers and cool, wet winters
- Subtropical: Warm and moist; hot summers and possibly dry winters
- Continental: Cool and moist; warm summers and severe winters
- Temperate: Four distinct seasons; warm summers and cold winters
- Cold temperate: Cool summers and severe, snowy winters
- Subpolar: Very cold year round; no true summer; tundra vegetation
- Polar: Extremely cold and dry year round; ice sheet
- Highland: Colder than low-level locations at same latitude

Climate Change

The climate has changed throughout Earth's history, with cold periods covering much of the surface in ice. The last such ice age peaked about 18,000 years ago, when glaciers covered all of Scandinavia and most of North America. Our current warm period began about 10,000 years ago, but it may well end in another ice age.

Last ice age

Present day

Seasons

About every 365 days, Earth completes an orbit of the Sun. The path our planet follows is elliptical and takes it closer to the Sun at particular times. Because Earth's axis is angled at about 23.5 degrees, different parts of Earth are tilted toward the Sun at different times of year. These variations in the amount of sunlight reaching particular regions of Earth create the seasonal patterns of our weather.

Sun over Tropic of Capricorn: northern winter, southern summer

Sun over Equator: northern spring, southern autumn

Sun over Equator: northern autumn, southern spring

Sun over Tropic of Cancer: northern summer, southern winter

THE IMPACT OF GEOGRAPHY

The history of humankind and the societies we live in today have been profoundly influenced by geography. The concentration of wealth and power in the hands of people of Eurasian origin is largely a legacy of the European empire-building that began in about AD 1500. When Europeans arrived to colonize the Americas, Africa, and Australasia, they brought with them military superiority provided by their steel weapons, guns, and cavalry horses; new, deadly diseases to which the local people had little resistance; better communication through writing; and centralized political organization. The fact that these critical advantages belonged to Europeans rather than to the colonized peoples can be largely explained by Earth's geography.

Until the end of the last ice age, about 13,000 years ago, all the world's peoples were hunter-gatherers. Following the change in climate, a transition to settled life and the adoption of agriculture occurred in many places, allowing populations to grow and, eventually, cities and states to form. In some regions of the world, such as Australia, farming was not developed because the land offered few plants and animals that could be domesticated. Eurasia, on the other hand, had more domesticable plant and animal species than any other continent. In the Americas and Africa, a north–south orientation gives the continents a highly varied climate and environment, which impeded the spread of agricultural and technological innovations. The east–west orientation of Eurasia produces a broadly similar climate throughout the extensive land mass. Innovations could spread relatively easily and quickly, yielding increased food production and allowing large, stratified societies to develop.

The crops of Southwest Asia took only a few hundred years to spread to Egypt (grain harvest depicted above), Europe, and India.

The Maya and Aztecs of Mesoamerica built great cities such as Tikal, but the region was isolated by desert to the north and the narrow Isthmus of Panama to the south.

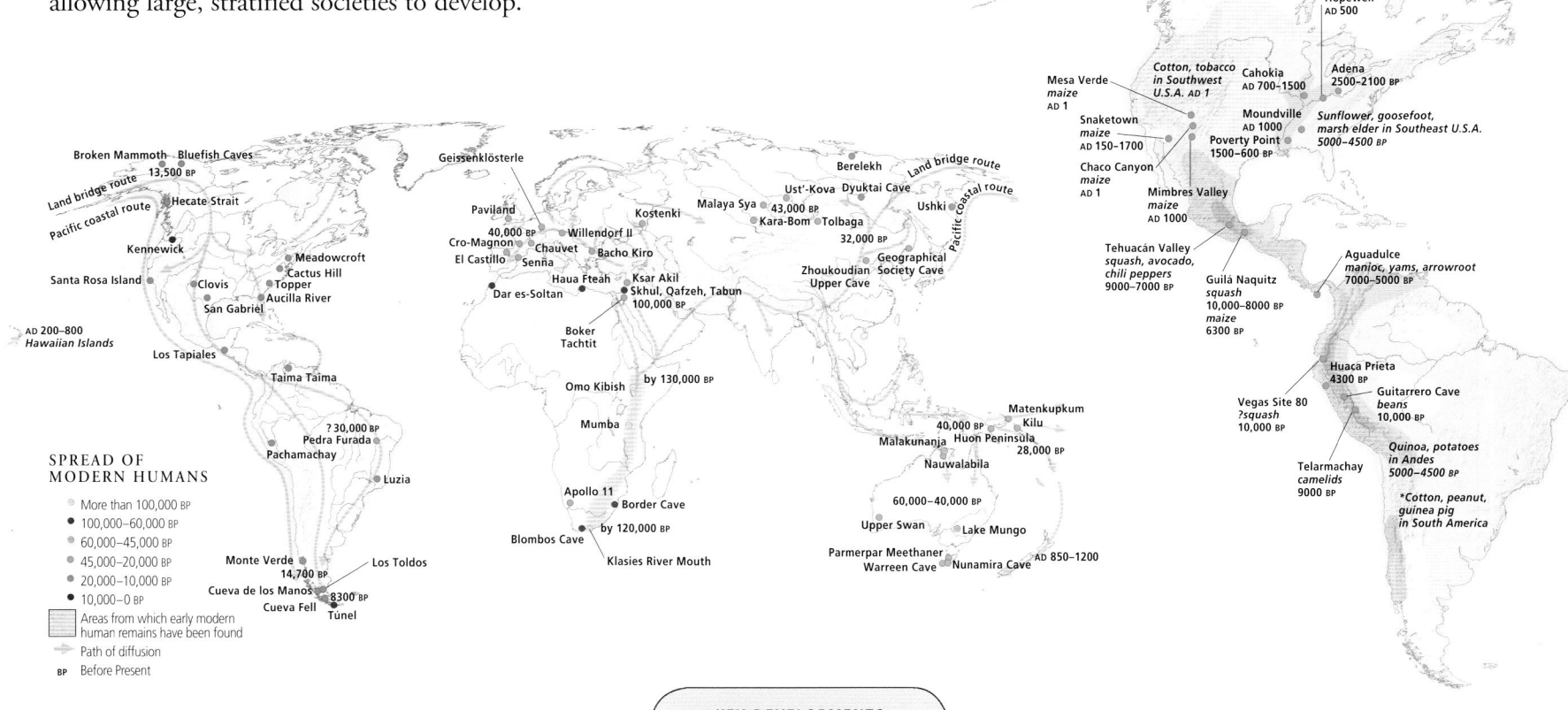

SPREAD OF
MODERN HUMANS

- More than 100,000 BP
- 100,000–60,000 BP
- 60,000–45,000 BP
- 45,000–20,000 BP
- 20,000–10,000 BP
- 10,000–0 BP

Areas from which early modern human remains have been found
→ Path of diffusion
BP Before Present

Colonizing the Globe

Advanced stone tools and social flexibility allowed anatomically modern humans to flourish in a wide range of habitats. By about 100,000 years ago, they had moved into Southwest Asia from Africa, and sometime between 60,000 and 40,000 years ago, they traveled to Australia by boat. Europe was colonized by 40,000 years ago, after which evidence of art, ritual, and symbolism begins to accumulate. By 15,000 years ago, humans had reached the Americas, either by crossing the Bering Land Bridge that existed during the ice age or by boat along a Pacific route. Far-flung islands such as New Zealand and Hawaii have been settled only in the last 2,000 years.

KEY DEVELOPMENTS

130,000 BP Modern humans (*Homo sapiens*) in Africa

100,000 BP Modern humans (*Homo sapiens*) in Southwest Asia; first evidence of deliberate burials (Israel)

77,000 BP Rare examples of art (Blombos Cave, South Africa)

70,000 BP Composite tools in Africa (Howieson's Poort industry)

60,000 BP Modern humans in East Asia and Australia—first sea voyages

40,000 BP Modern humans (Cro-Magnon) in Europe, associated with early evidence of burials, art, and music

37,000 BP Ivory carvings of animals in southwestern Germany

28,000 BP Female statuettes known as "Venus" figurines in Europe

"Venus of Willendorf"
26,000 BP–24,000 BP

26,000 BP First cremation (Australia)

16,000 BP First fired clay pottery (Japan)

15,000 BP Modern humans spread into America (possibly earlier)

13,000 BP Domesticated plants in Southwest Asia

12,500 BP Settled villages of hunter-gatherers in Southwest Asia

12,000 BP First animal domestication (dogs in the Levant)

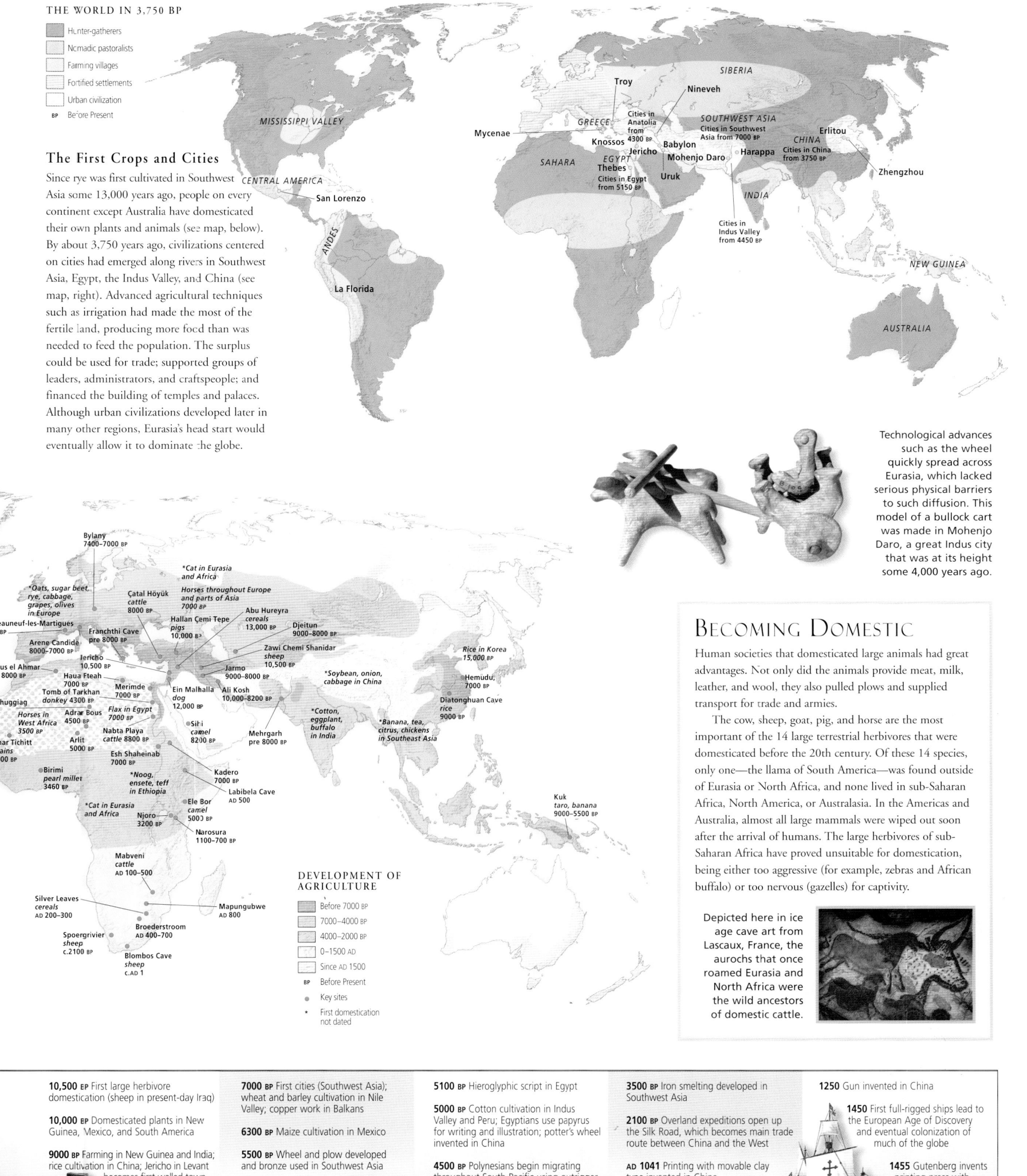

THE WORLD IN 3,750 BP

- Hunter-gatherers
- Nomadic pastoralists
- Farming villages
- Fortified settlements
- Urban civilization
- BP Before Present

MISSISSIPPI VALLEY

CENTRAL AMERICA
San Lorenzo

ANDES

La Florida

SIBERIA

GREECE
Troy
Mycenae
Knossos
Cities in Anatolia from 4300 BP
Jericho
Babylon
Mohenjo Daro

SOUTHWEST ASIA
Nineveh
Cities in Southwest Asia from 7000 BP
Uruk
Harappa

EGYPT
Thebes
Cities in Egypt from 5150 BP

SAHARA

CHINA
Erlitou
Cities in China from 3750 BP
Zhengzhou

INDIA
Cities in Indus Valley from 4450 BP

NEW GUINEA

AUSTRALIA

The First Crops and Cities

Since rye was first cultivated in Southwest Asia some 13,000 years ago, people on every continent except Australia have domesticated their own plants and animals (see map, below). By about 3,750 years ago, civilizations centered on cities had emerged along rivers in Southwest Asia, Egypt, the Indus Valley, and China (see map, right). Advanced agricultural techniques such as irrigation had made the most of the fertile land, producing more food than was needed to feed the population. The surplus could be used for trade; supported groups of leaders, administrators, and craftspeople; and financed the building of temples and palaces. Although urban civilizations developed later in many other regions, Eurasia's head start would eventually allow it to dominate the globe.

Technological advances such as the wheel quickly spread across Eurasia, which lacked serious physical barriers to such diffusion. This model of a bullock cart was made in Mohenjo Daro, a great Indus city that was at its height some 4,000 years ago.

Bylany 7400–7000 BP

*Cat in Eurasia and Africa

*Oats, sugar beet, rye, cabbage, grapes, olives in Europe 00 BP

Châteauneuf-les-Martigues

Çatal Höyük cattle 8000 BP

Horses throughout Europe and parts of Asia 7000 BP

Hallan Çemi Tepe pigs 10,000 BP

Abu Hureyra cereals 13,000 BP

Djeitun 9000–8000 BP

Franchthi Cave pre 8000 BP

Arene Candide 8000–7000 BP

mous el Ahmar ttle 8000 BP

Haua Fteah 7000 BP

Jericho 10,500 BP

Zawi Chemi Shanidar sheep 10,500 BP

Jarmo 9000–8000 BP

*Soybean, onion, cabbage in China

Rice in Korea 15,000 BP

Muhuggiag BP

Tomb of Tarkhan donkey 4300 BP

Merimde 7000 BP

Ein Malhalla 12,000 BP

Ali Kosh 10,000–8200 BP

Hemudu 7000 BP

Horses in West Africa 3500 BP

Flax in Egypt 7000 BP

Adrar Bous 4500 BP

Nabta Playa cattle 8800 BP

Siti camel 8200 BP

*Cotton, eggplant, buffalo in India

*Banana, tea, citrus, chickens in Southeast Asia

Diatonghuan Cave rice 9000 BP

Dhar Tichitt grains 4000 BP

Arlit 5000 BP

Mehrgarh pre 8000 BP

Birimi pearl millet 3460 BP

Esh Shaheinab 7000 BP

*Noog, ensete, teff in Ethiopia

Kadero 7000 BP

Labibela Cave AD 500

*Cat in Eurasia and Africa

Ele Bor camel 5000 BP

Njoro 3200 BP

Kuk taro, banana 9000–5500 BP

Narosura 1100–700 BP

Mabveni cattle AD 100–500

Silver Leaves cereals AD 200–300

Mapungubwe AD 800

Spoergrivier sheep c.2100

Broederstroom AD 400–700

Blombos Cave sheep c.AD 1

DEVELOPMENT OF AGRICULTURE

- Before 7000 BP
- 7000–4000 BP
- 4000–2000 BP
- 0–1500 AD
- Since AD 1500
- BP Before Present
- Key sites
- * First domestication not dated

BECOMING DOMESTIC

Human societies that domesticated large animals had great advantages. Not only did the animals provide meat, milk, leather, and wool, they also pulled plows and supplied transport for trade and armies.

The cow, sheep, goat, pig, and horse are the most important of the 14 large terrestrial herbivores that were domesticated before the 20th century. Of these 14 species, only one—the llama of South America—was found outside of Eurasia or North Africa, and none lived in sub-Saharan Africa, North America, or Australasia. In the Americas and Australia, almost all large mammals were wiped out soon after the arrival of humans. The large herbivores of sub-Saharan Africa have proved unsuitable for domestication, being either too aggressive (for example, zebras and African buffalo) or too nervous (gazelles) for captivity.

Depicted here in ice age cave art from Lascaux, France, the aurochs that once roamed Eurasia and North Africa were the wild ancestors of domestic cattle.

10,500 BP First large herbivore domestication (sheep in present-day Iraq)

10,000 BP Domesticated plants in New Guinea, Mexico, and South America

9000 BP Farming in New Guinea and India; rice cultivation in China; Jericho becomes first walled town

8500 BP Farming in Europe

Grain pots from Swiss Alps 6000 BP

7000 BP First cities (Southwest Asia); wheat and barley cultivation in Nile Valley; copper work in Balkans

6300 BP Maize cultivation in Mexico

5500 BP Wheel and plow developed and bronze used in Southwest Asia

5400 BP Sumerian cuneiform writing

Sumerian tablet c. 5000 BP

5100 BP Hieroglyphic script in Egypt

5000 BP Cotton cultivation in Indus Valley and Peru; Egyptians use papyrus for writing and illustration; potter's wheel invented in China

4500 BP Polynesians begin migrating throughout South Pacific using outrigger canoes; Minoans and Mycenaeans build first seagoing cargo ships

3700 BP The world's first codified laws are recorded in Babylon in Code of Hammurabi

3500 BP Iron smelting developed in Southwest Asia

2100 BP Overland expeditions open up the Silk Road, which becomes main trade route between China and the West

AD 1041 Printing with movable clay type invented in China

1050 Asian astrolabes arrive in Europe and revolutionize navigation

1183 Magnetic compass invented in China

1250 Gun invented in China

1450 First full-rigged ships lead to the European Age of Discovery and eventual colonization of much of the globe

1455 Gutenberg invents printing press with movable metal type in Germany

Columbus's ship *Santa Maria*

POPULATION

The number of people in the world has increased tenfold in the past 400 years, but such explosive growth is a very recent phenomenon. World population can expand only when there are more births than deaths, and for most of human history, birth and death rates both remained at high levels. The introduction of farming from around 8000 BC led to the first significant growth in human numbers, but the increase was gradual and it took until AD 1500 to move from 10 million to 500 million people.

In the developed regions, such as Europe and North America, death rates began to decline during the 18th century as revolutions in both agriculture and industry led to improved living conditions and health care. Birth rates stayed high, however, because people had not yet adjusted to the idea that all their children were likely to reach adulthood. Over the next 200 years, population figures exploded, but gradually birth rates started to drop and growth in these regions slowed. Today, some European populations are actually shrinking.

The developing parts of the world, however, are at an earlier stage in the process and are experiencing even more rapid growth. Although the birth rates in much of Asia, Africa, and South America are now falling, it will be many decades before their populations stabilize. Most experts believe that at this point there will be more than 10 billion people on Earth, but nobody knows whether our planet has the capacity to sustain such enormous numbers.

Where People Live

Earth's total population of 6 billion or so is distributed very unevenly. People have tended to live along river valleys or near the coast, with the largest concentrations being in China, India, and Europe. Rural-to-urban migration has led to about half the world's population now living in cities. Combined with explosive growth, it has also caused the proliferation of megacities in the developing world.

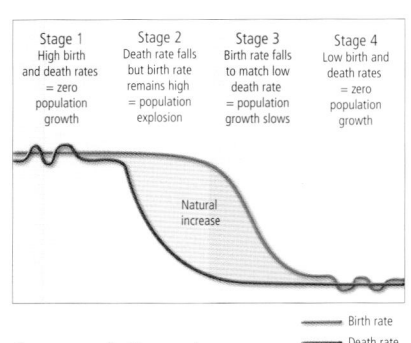

Stages of Growth

In Stage 1, birth and death rates are both high and there is little population growth. When health care and living conditions improve, death rates drop but birth rates initially remain high, leading to a natural increase in the population. During Stage 3, the birth rate gradually falls, eventually leading to the zero growth of Stage 4.

Stage 1	Stage 2	Stage 3	Stage 4
High birth and death rates = zero population growth	Death rate falls but birth rate remains high = population explosion	Birth rate falls to match low death rate = population growth slows	Low birth and death rates = zero population growth

Natural increase

— Birth rate
— Death rate

Urbanization

In the developed countries, the Industrial Revolution was followed by a massive shift of population from rural to urban areas. With later but more rapid industrialization, developing countries are experiencing a sudden increase in city dwellers. In the coming years, almost all the world's population growth will be in urban areas.

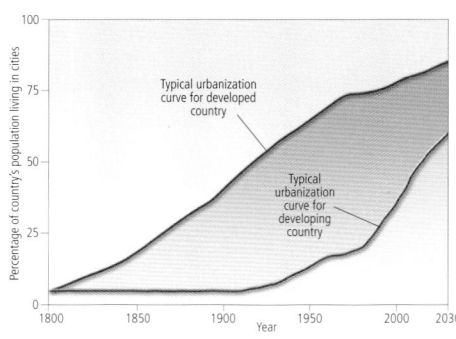

Typical urbanization curve for developed country

Typical urbanization curve for developing country

The walled towns of Europe, such as Albarracín, in Spain, reflect a time before technology allowed vast, sprawling cities to become a feature of the modern landscape.

In the Philippines and many other developing countries, extensive shantytowns have grown up, as millions have erected makeshift shelters on the outskirts of cities.

LARGEST POPULATIONS		MOST CROWDED COUNTRIES		FASTEST GROWING COUNTRIES*	
COUNTRY	POPULATION	COUNTRY	POPULATION DENSITY	COUNTRY	ANNUAL GROWTH
China	1,302,207,990	Monaco	26,784 per sq mile (16,620 per sq km)	Liberia	5.53%
India	1,080,264,390	Singapore	11,629 per sq mile (7,219 per sq km)	Sierra Leone	4.54%
United States	295,734,130	Vatican City	5,015 per sq mile (3,111 per sq km)	Eritrea	4.22%
Indonesia	241,973,880	Malta	2,073 per sq mile (1,286 per sq km)	Somalia	4.21%
Brazil	186,112,790	Maldives	1,877 per sq mile (1,164 per sq km)	Yemen	4.07%
Pakistan	156,689,150	Bangladesh	1,735 per sq mile (1,078 per sq km)	Afghanistan	3.68%
Bangladesh	144,319,630	Bahrain	1,667 per sq mile (1,035 per sq km)	Niger	3.63%
Russia	143,736,790	Taiwan	1,143 per sq mile (710 per sq km)	Democratic Republic of Congo	3.34%
Nigeria	140,601,620	Barbados	1,042 per sq mile (648 per sq km)	Oman	3.27%
Japan	127,417,240	Nauru	1,004 per sq mile (621 per sq km)	Uganda	3.11%

Countries with more than 1 million inhabitants

Top Ten Countries

The population of a country can be assessed in various ways, including the total number of inhabitants, the ratio of inhabitants to land, and the rate at which it is growing. Many of today's most populous countries are in Asia, but Africa and the Middle East are seeing the highest rates of growth. Apart from Bangladesh, the most densely populated countries listed here all have small land areas.

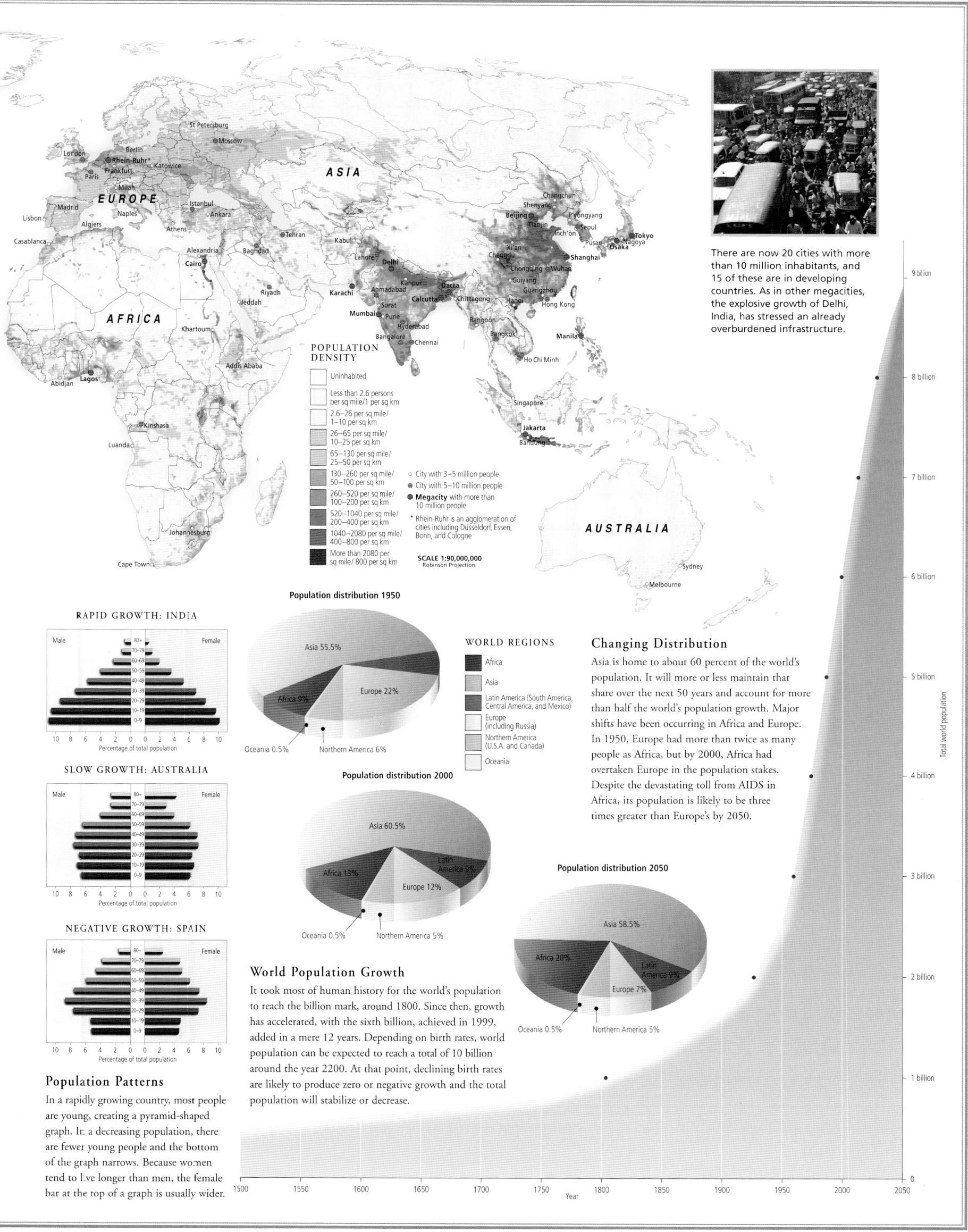

There are now 20 cities with more than 10 million inhabitants, and 15 of these are in developing countries. As in other megacities, the explosive growth of Delhi, India, has stressed an already overburdened infrastructure.

POPULATION DENSITY

- Uninhabited
- Less than 2.6 persons per sq mile/1 per sq km
- 2.6–26 per sq mile/1–10 per sq km
- 26–65 per sq mile/10–25 per sq km
- 65–130 per sq mile/25–50 per sq km
- 130–260 per sq mile/50–100 per sq km
- 260–520 per sq mile/100–200 per sq km
- 520–1040 per sq mile/200–400 per sq km
- 1040–2080 per sq mile/400–800 per sq km
- More than 2080 per sq mile/800 per sq km

○ City with 3–5 million people
● City with 5–10 million people
● **Megacity** with more than 10 million people

* Rhein-Ruhr is an agglomeration of cities including Düsseldorf, Essen, Bonn, and Cologne

SCALE 1:90,000,000
Robinson Projection

WORLD REGIONS
- Africa
- Asia
- Latin America (South America, Central America, and Mexico)
- Europe (including Russia)
- Northern America (U.S.A. and Canada)
- Oceania

Population distribution 1950
Asia 55.5%
Europe 22%
Africa 9%
Northern America 6%
Oceania 0.5%

Population distribution 2000
Asia 60.5%
Latin America 9%
Europe 12%
Africa 13%
Northern America 5%
Oceania 0.5%

Population distribution 2050
Asia 58.5%
Latin America 9%
Europe 7%
Africa 20%
Northern America 5%
Oceania 0.5%

RAPID GROWTH: INDIA
Male — Female
80+ 70–79 60–69 50–59 40–49 30–39 20–29 10–19 0–9
10 8 6 4 2 0 0 2 4 6 8 10
Percentage of total population

SLOW GROWTH: AUSTRALIA
Male — Female
80+ 70–79 60–69 50–59 40–49 30–39 20–29 10–19 0–9
10 8 6 4 2 0 0 2 4 6 8 10
Percentage of total population

NEGATIVE GROWTH: SPAIN
Male — Female
80+ 70–79 60–69 50–59 40–49 30–39 20–29 10–19 0–9
10 8 6 4 2 0 0 2 4 6 8 10
Percentage of total population

Population Patterns

In a rapidly growing country, most people are young, creating a pyramid-shaped graph. In a decreasing population, there are fewer young people and the bottom of the graph narrows. Because women tend to live longer than men, the female bar at the top of a graph is usually wider.

World Population Growth

It took most of human history for the world's population to reach the billion mark, around 1800. Since then, growth has accelerated, with the sixth billion, achieved in 1999, added in a mere 12 years. Depending on birth rates, world population can be expected to reach a total of 10 billion around the year 2200. At that point, declining birth rates are likely to produce zero or negative growth and the total population will stabilize or decrease.

Changing Distribution

Asia is home to about 60 percent of the world's population. It will more or less maintain that share over the next 50 years and account for more than half the world's population growth. Major shifts have been occurring in Africa and Europe. In 1950, Europe had more than twice as many people as Africa, but by 2000, Africa had overtaken Europe in the population stakes. Despite the devastating toll from AIDS in Africa, its population is likely to be three times greater than Europe's by 2050.

Total world population
9 billion
8 billion
7 billion
6 billion
5 billion
4 billion
3 billion
2 billion
1 billion
0
1500 1550 1600 1650 1700 1750 1800 1850 1900 1950 2000 2050
Year

LANGUAGES OF THE WORLD

Complex speech is one of the key ways in which humans differ from the rest of the animal world, and language is one of the main ways groups of humans distinguish themselves from one another. Rudimentary forms of language may have been used by the first modern humans more than 100,000 years ago, but it was not until about 40,000 years ago that there was an explosion of art and technology, and humans moved into harsher environments. Many believe that the development of complex language prompted this great leap in human capability.

There are now more than 6,000 languages spoken in the world and their distribution reveals much about human history. Throughout time, languages have both diverged and converged. The Roman conquest of Europe 2,000 years ago replaced most of the existing Celtic languages with Latin. Gradually, different groups developed their own dialects of Latin, which eventually became Romance languages such as French, Italian, and Spanish. The Germanic language of English displays many borrowings from French, a legacy of the Norman Conquest of England in 1066.

In more recent times, colonialism has spread European languages throughout the globe. In many places, this contact has led to new languages such as pidgins (spoken only as a second language) and creoles (spoken as a mother tongue). At the same time, however, many indigenous languages have been lost. As societies become more centralized, and particularly as English takes hold as the dominant world language, much of the extraordinary diversity of languages is under threat.

The Basques live in France and Spain near the western Pyrenees. Their language seems to be an isolate (unrelated to any other modern language), but other Basque-like languages were probably spoken in Western Europe before the Roman conquest.

Major Languages

Mandarin Chinese has far more mother-tongue (first-language) speakers than any other single language, but of the world's top 15 languages, 12 belong to the Indo-European family. The prevalence of English, French, Portuguese, and Spanish resulted from the colonial expansion of European power that began in the 15th century. North America now has more English speakers than anywhere else, while South America is home to the most Spanish speakers.

The language of Japan's indigenous people, the Ainu, gradually lost ground to Japanese. It is now virtually extinct, with just a handful of elderly speakers left.

Distribution of modern languages

- Oceania 19%
- Asia 32%
- Americas 15%
- Africa 30%
- Europe 4%

Speakers of modern languages

- Languages with 1,000–10,000 speakers 24%
- Languages with 10,000–100,000 speakers 23%
- Languages with 100–1,000 speakers 16%
- No estimate 13%
- Languages with 1–100 speakers 8%
- Languages with more than 1,000,000 speakers 5%
- Languages with 100,000–1,000,000 speakers 11%

Endangered Languages

Although European languages dominate the world in terms of number of speakers, they account for just a tiny percentage of modern languages. As more and more young people adopt the languages of power, much of humankind's linguistic diversity is lost. About 40 percent of languages are spoken by fewer than 10,000 people, and roughly 450 have only a few elderly speakers left. At least half the world's tongues are likely to vanish by 2100—an average of one language lost every 10 days.

[Bar chart — Millions of speakers, from 0 to 900: Mandarin Chinese, Hindi, English, Spanish, Bengali, Portuguese, Russian, Arabic, Japanese, German, Korean, French, Shanghainese (Wu), Javanese, Cantonese (Yue)]

DEVELOPMENT OF WRITING

3400 BC Sumerian pictogram system

3100 BC Egyptian hieroglyphs, script with 2,500 symbols, in use for 3,500 years

2500 BC Indus Valley pictogram system

by 2500 BC Sumerian cuneiform script of wedge-shaped strokes

2400 BC Akkadians adopt cuneiform

1750 BC Linear A script in Minoan Crete

c. 1600 BC Proto-Canaanite script in Egypt, later develops into Linear Phoenician

1500 BC Chinese pictogram script, later develops into several thousand characters

1400 BC Linear B script in Mycenaean Greece

1100 BC Linear Phoenician alphabet of 22 letters, later spreads to Greece

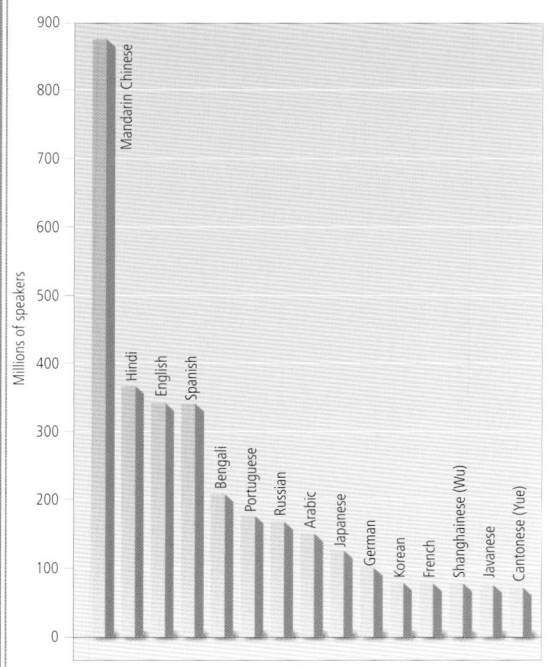

French and Native American

English and Na-Dene

English and Native American

NORTH AMERICA

Spanish and Native American

Spanish and Native American

SOUTH AMERICA

Portuguese and Native American

Indo-European Family Tree

In the 18th century, a colonial judge, Sir William Jones, recognized similarities between the Sanskrit language of India, and Latin and Greek, and proposed that they came from a single source. This ancestor language, Proto-Indo-European, has since been shown to have evolved into many European and Asian languages. The family tree presented here shows only the major ones. Almost 3 billion people, roughly half the world's population, now speak an Indo-European language.

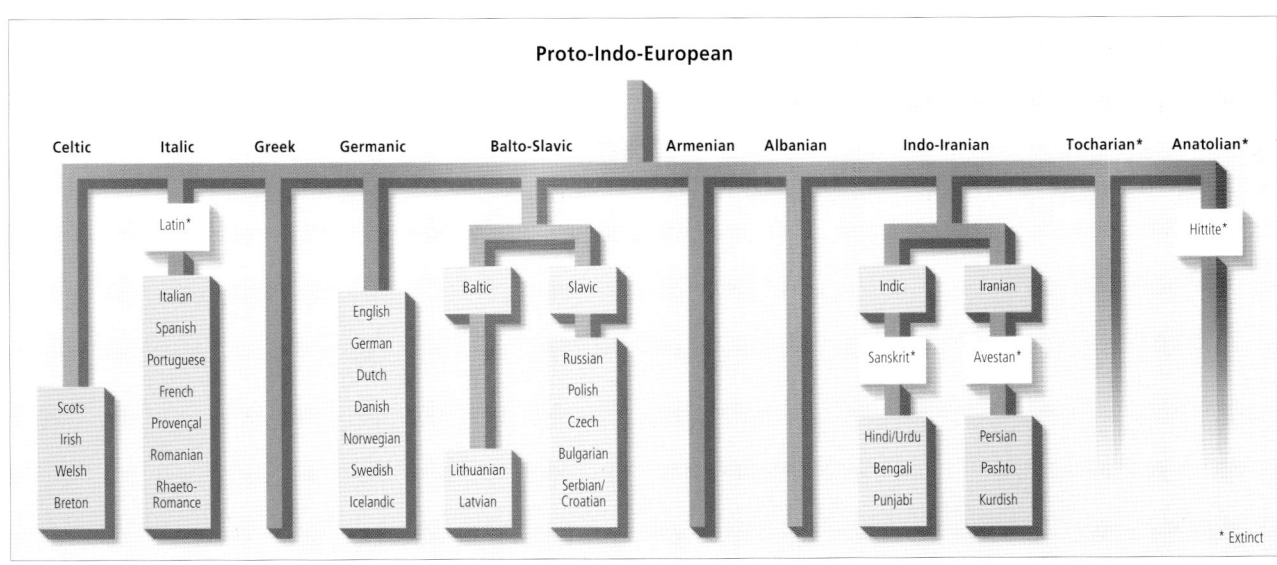

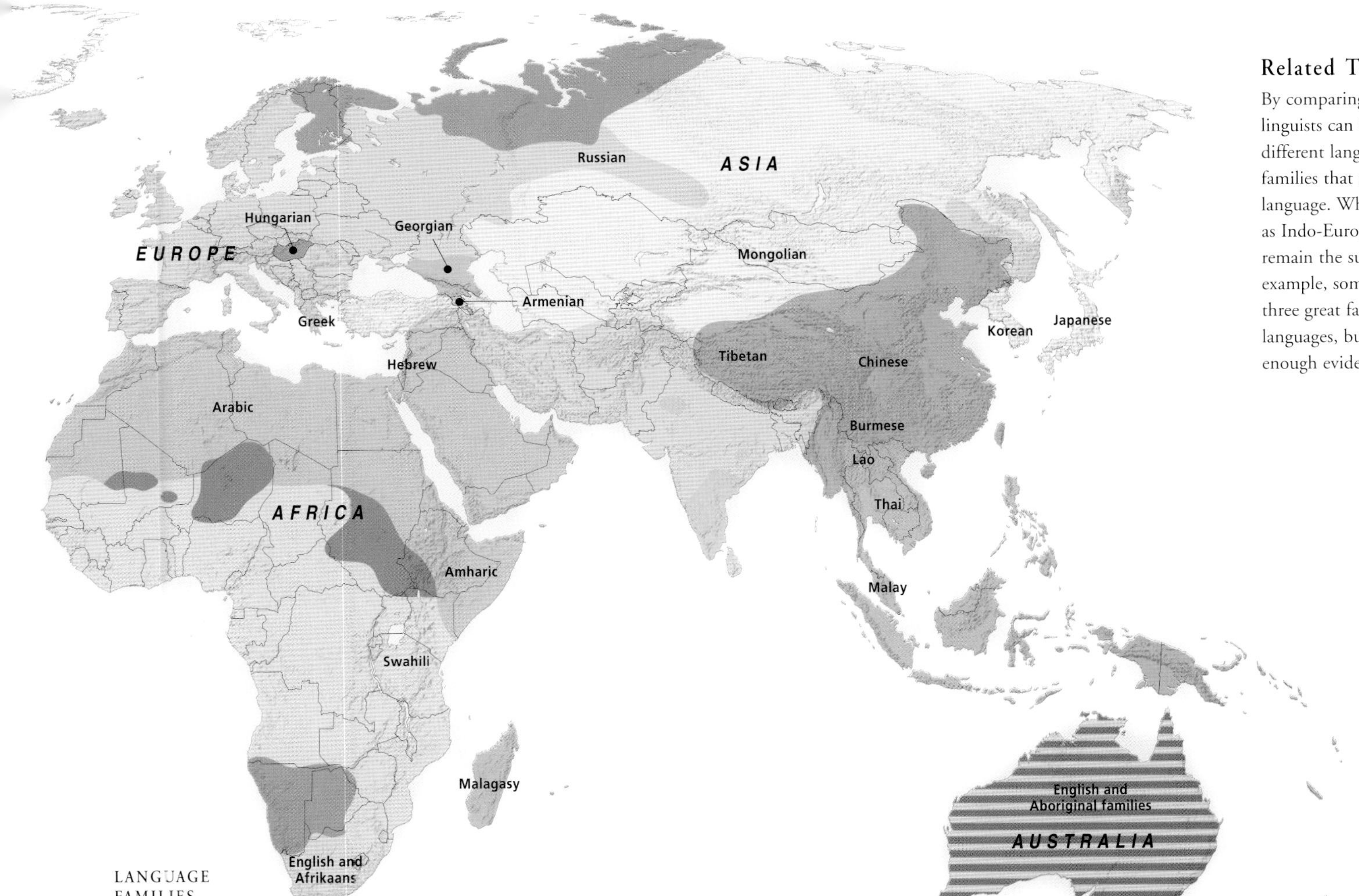

Proto-Indo-European

Celtic	Italic	Greek	Germanic	Balto-Slavic	Armenian	Albanian	Indo-Iranian	Tocharian*	Anatolian*

Latin*

Italian, Spanish, Portuguese, French, Provençal, Romanian, Rhaeto-Romance

Scots, Irish, Welsh, Breton

English, German, Dutch, Danish, Norwegian, Swedish, Icelandic

Baltic — Lithuanian, Latvian
Slavic — Russian, Polish, Czech, Bulgarian, Serbian/Croatian

Indic — Sanskrit* — Hindi/Urdu, Bengali, Punjabi
Iranian — Avestan* — Persian, Pashto, Kurdish

Hittite*

*Extinct

Related Tongues

By comparing vocabulary and grammar, linguists can identify relationships between different languages and group them into families that share a common ancestor language. While some language families, such as Indo-European, are widely accepted, others remain the subject of intense debate. For example, some linguists have proposed just three great families of Native American languages, but most believe that there is not enough evidence for such a classification.

(Map labels) Russian, Hungarian, Georgian, Armenian, Greek, Hebrew, Arabic, Mongolian, Tibetan, Chinese, Korean, Japanese, Burmese, Lao, Thai, Malay, Amharic, Swahili, Malagasy, English and Afrikaans, English and Aboriginal families, English and Maori

EUROPE, ASIA, AFRICA, AUSTRALIA

SCALE 1:90,000,000
Robinson Projection

Bilingual education is an important way to promote the survival of minority languages and cultures. Many Australian Aboriginal children now receive their lessons in both English and an indigenous language.

LANGUAGE FAMILIES

American Language Families
- Eskimo-Aleut: languages spoken by indigenous arctic peoples, including Asiatic Eskimo and Aleut
- Na-Dene: groups Haida and Tlingit languages of Pacific Northwest with Athabaskan languages, including Navajo and Apache
- Other Native American families: many families including languages such as Cree, Mohawk, Shoshone, Jacaltec, Guarani, Quechua

Eurasian Language Families
- Indo-European: many European and Asian languages, including English, German, French, Italian, Spanish, Russian, Hindi, Persian
- Uralic: 20+ languages, including Estonian, Finnish, Hungarian, Sami, Nenets

- Altaic: 50+ languages, including Mongolian, Turkish, Korean, Japanese
- Chukotko-Kamchatkan: languages spoken in eastern Russia, including Chukchi, Alutor, Itelmen, Kerek
- Caucasian families: 3 families with 40+ languages spoken in the Caucasus, including Chechen, Georgian

African Language Families
- Afro-Asiatic: 370+ languages, including Arabic, Hebrew, Somali, Berber, Hausa
- Nilo-Saharan: 100+ languages in East Africa, including Songhai, Nubian, Masai
- Niger-Congo: 900+ languages, including Swahili, Fulani, Zulu, Mossi, Shona

- Khoisan: languages spoken in southwest Africa, many featuring click sounds

Southeast Asian Families
- Dravidian: languages of southern and eastern India, including Kannada, Malayalam, Tamil, Telugu
- Sino-Tibetan: 130+ languages of East Asia, including Mandarin, Cantonese, Tibetan, Burmese
- Austric families: includes Austronesian (Malay, Maori), Austroasiatic (Vietnamese), and Tai-Kadai (Thai, Lao)
- Papuan families: 700+ languages spoken on the island of New Guinea
- Australian Aboriginal families: 250+ languages spoken by indigenous peoples of Australia

---

800 BC South Arabian script, evolved from Proto-Canaanite, later spreads into North Arabia and Africa

800 BC Phoenician script evolves into Aramaic in Syria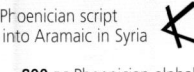

800 BC Phoenician alphabet adapted to create Classical Greek script, with both vowels and consonants; later becomes modern Greek alphabet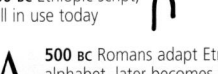

600 BC Etruscans in Italy adapt Greek alphabet

600 BC Egyptian demotic script supplants hieratic (a cursive variety of cuneiform)

500 BC Ethiopic script, still in use today

500 BC Romans adapt Etruscan alphabet, later becomes modern Roman alphabet of 26 letters

300 BC Brahmi alphabet in India

200 BC Nabateans use Aramaic script for Arabic language

200 BC Chinese logographic script in its modern form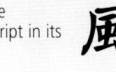

C. AD 1 Aramaic script evolves into modern Hebrew square letter script, used for most of Old Testament

by AD 250 Mayan hieroglyphic script in Mesoamerica

AD 250 Runic script develops in Scandinavia, later spreads to Britain

AD 400 First Arabic script, later versions used for Koran and developed into modern Arabic script

AD 700 Japanese adopt Chinese characters

AD 900 Greek missionaries among the Slavs adapt Greek alphabet to create Cyrillic script, later reduced to 33 letters of modern Russian alphabet

AD 1000 Devanagari (used to write Sanskrit and Hindi) and other modern Indian scripts develop from Brahmi

The Chinese writing system comprises several thousand logographs, characters that each represent an entire word. People speaking mutually incomprehensible dialects of Chinese can still communicate via this script.

THE GLOBAL ECONOMY

Global industrial output increased 50-fold during the 20th century. The wealth this generated, however, was shared by relatively few and led to an ever greater gap between rich and poor, both within countries and across the world. The richest 1 percent of the world's people receive as much income as the poorest 57 percent. More than 1.2 billion people live on less than US$1 a day, and 2.8 billion live on less than US$2 a day. Developing countries (ones yet to achieve effective industrial production levels) make up much of Asia, Africa, South America, and the Pacific; account for about 75 percent of world population; and share just 20 percent of world income.

During the 1990s, more than 50 developing countries became poorer and many others stagnated, victims of failed economic growth, declining aid from rich countries, rising debt repayments, and falling prices for the raw materials that make up the bulk of their export revenue. The HIV/AIDS epidemic has also been devastating, especially in sub-Saharan Africa, which has 70 percent of the world's 42 million cases.

Even within prosperous countries there can be great disparities in wealth, and in poor countries the brunt of the hardship is borne by disadvantaged groups. On average, men have a larger share of resources than women do, and urban dwellers are far better off than people in rural areas, with greater access to income, education, safe water and sanitation, and health services. On both a national and global level, future stability depends on a fairer distribution of the world's wealth.

Famine can be both a cause and an effect of armed conflict, which prevents farmers from producing and distributing food. While essential during a crisis, food aid does not provide a long-term solution.

Food Supply

More than 800 million people do not have enough to eat. The Dietary Energy Supply (DES) estimates the energy that is available for human consumption in the total food supply of each country. An adequate daily DES is 2,600 Calories (10,900 kilojoules) per person. A daily DES of fewer than 2,300 Calories (9,600 kilojoules) indicates widespread hunger and malnutrition.

DAILY DIETARY ENERGY SUPPLY (DES)

- More than 3,200 Calories (13,400 kilojoules) per person
- 2,900–3,200 Calories (12,000–13,400 kilojoules) per person
- 2,600–2,900 Calories (10,900–12,000 kilojoules) per person
- 2,300–2,600 Calories (9,600–10,900 kilojoules) per person
- 2,000–2,300 Calories (8,400–9,600 kilojoules) per person
- Fewer than 2,000 Calories (8,400 kilojoules) per person
- Insufficient data

HEALTH INDICATORS

The gulf between the haves and have-nots is reflected most keenly in a comparison of key health indicators. Most of the risk factors that contribute to the world's major health problems are related to patterns of consumption. Poor countries are home to 170 million underweight children, 3 million of whom die each year. At the same time, obesity contributes to about half a million deaths every year in North America and Western Europe. Unsafe water, sanitation, and hygiene lead to 1.7 million deaths every year. Other leading risk factors in Africa and Asia include unsafe sex, iron deficiency, and indoor smoke from solid fuels.

COUNTRY COMPARISON

- Norway (HDI 0.942)*
- Mexico (HDI 0.796)
- Indonesia (HDI 0.684)
- Pakistan (HDI 0.499)
- Sierra Leone (HDI 0.275)

* HDI Human Development Index

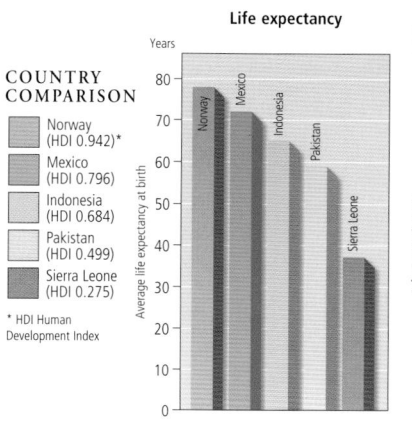
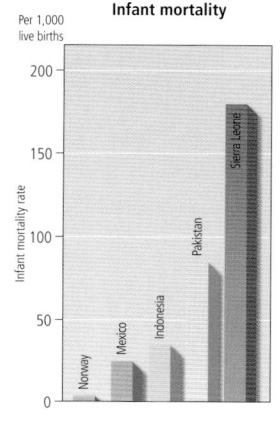
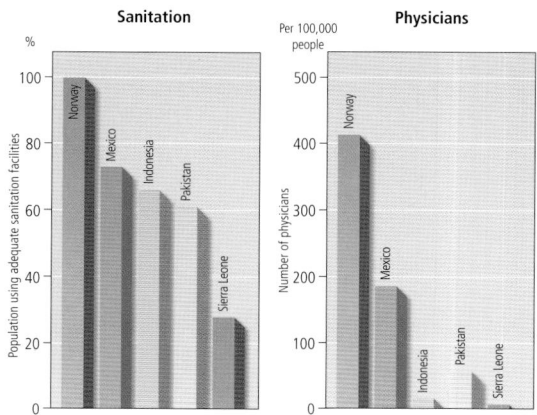

RICHEST COUNTRIES: GDP PER CAPITA*	
Luxembourg	US$44,000
United States	US$37,600
San Marino	US$34,600
Norway	US$31,800
Switzerland	US$31,700
Ireland	US$30,500
Canada	US$29,400
Belgium	US$29,000
Denmark	US$29,000
Japan	US$28,000

POOREST COUNTRIES: GDP PER CAPITA*	
East Timor	US$500
Somalia	US$550
Sierra Leone	US$580
Burundi	US$600
Democratic Republic of Congo	US$610
Tanzania	US$630
Malawi	US$670
Afghanistan	US$700
Comoros	US$720
Eritrea	US$740

** All GDP figures are in PPP (Purchasing Power Parity), which takes into account price differences between countries.*

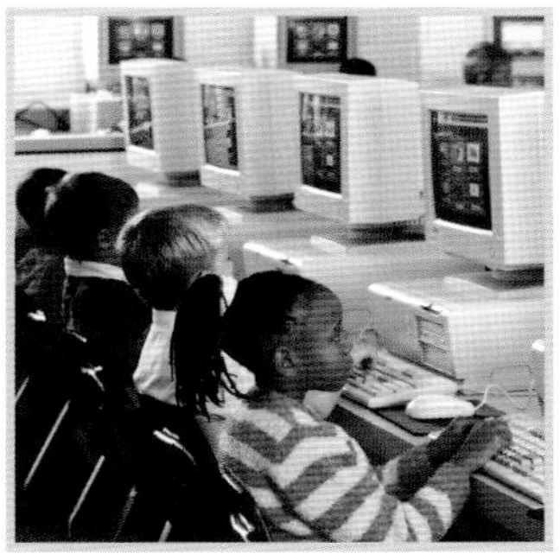

In developed countries, computers are now a feature of classrooms. With only 8 percent of the world connected to the Internet, the "digital divide" is likely to further disadvantage the poorest people.

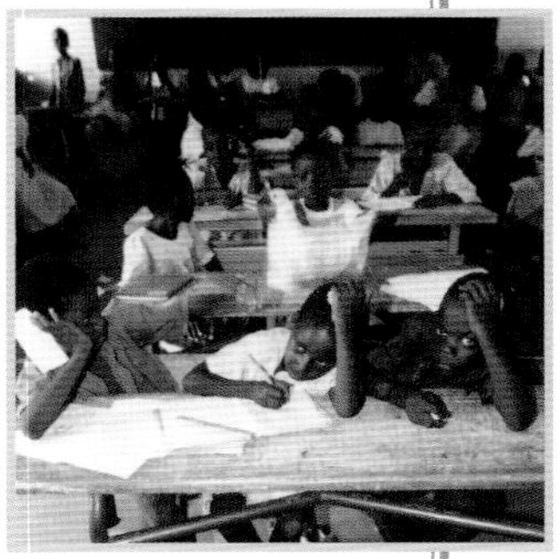

Although the 1990s saw primary school enrollments increase in every region, less than 60 percent of young children in sub-Saharan Africa attend school.

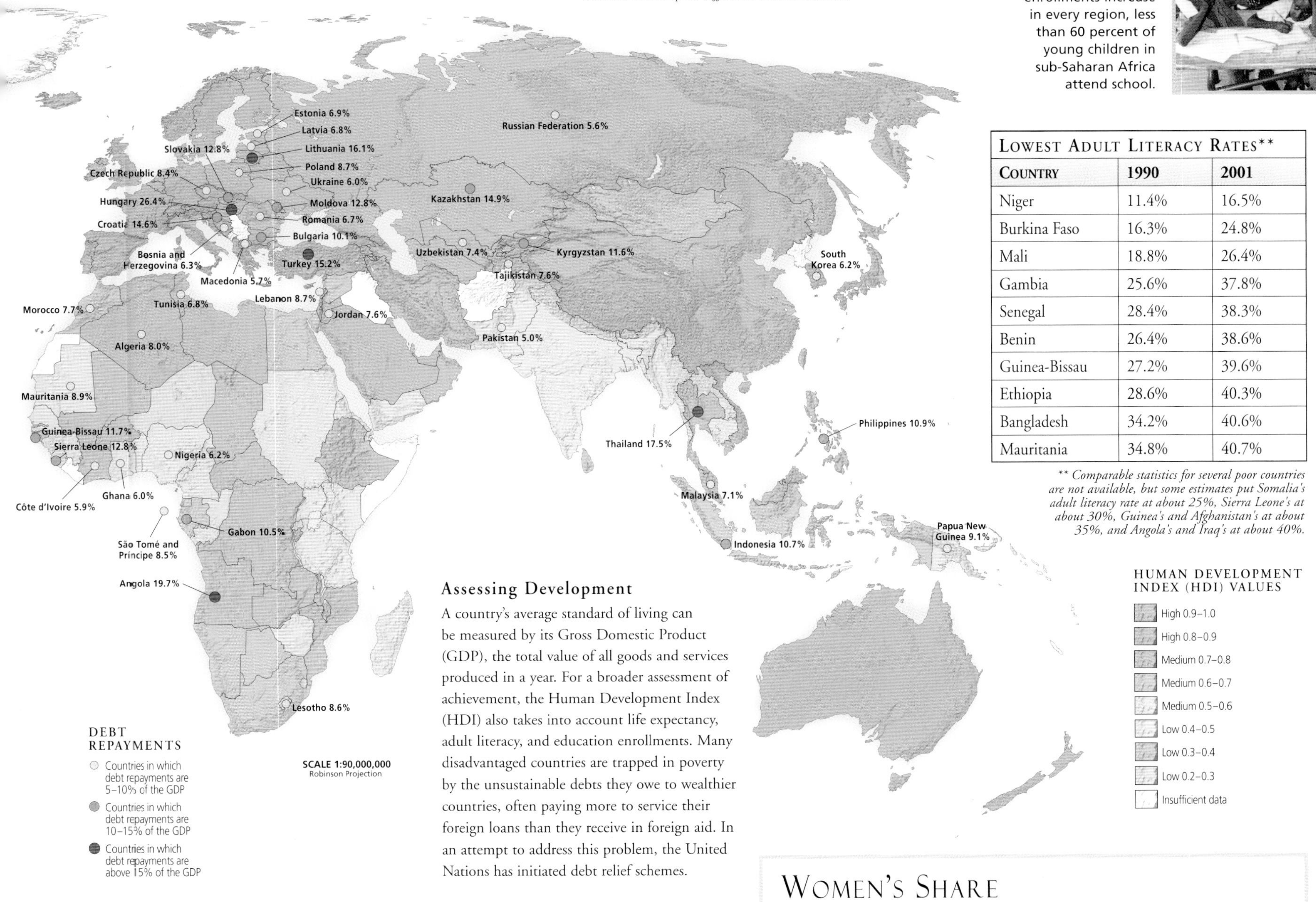
Estonia 6.9%
Latvia 6.8%
Lithuania 16.1%
Poland 8.7%
Ukraine 6.0%
Slovakia 12.8%
Czech Republic 8.4%
Hungary 26.4%
Moldova 12.8%
Romania 6.7%
Croatia 14.6%
Bulgaria 10.1%
Bosnia and Herzegovina 6.3%
Turkey 15.2%
Macedonia 5.7%
Lebanon 8.7%
Jordan 7.6%
Tunisia 6.8%
Morocco 7.7%
Algeria 8.0%
Mauritania 8.9%
Guinea-Bissau 11.7%
Sierra Leone 12.8%
Nigeria 6.2%
Ghana 6.0%
Côte d'Ivoire 5.9%
Gabon 10.5%
São Tomé and Príncipe 8.5%
Angola 19.7%
Lesotho 8.6%
Russian Federation 5.6%
Kazakhstan 14.9%
Uzbekistan 7.4%
Kyrgyzstan 11.6%
Tajikistan 7.6%
Pakistan 5.0%
South Korea 6.2%
Thailand 17.5%
Philippines 10.9%
Malaysia 7.1%
Indonesia 10.7%
Papua New Guinea 9.1%
DEBT REPAYMENTS
Countries in which debt repayments are 5–10% of the GDP
Countries in which debt repayments are 10–15% of the GDP
Countries in which debt repayments are above 15% of the GDP
SCALE 1:90,000,000
Robinson Projection
HUMAN DEVELOPMENT INDEX (HDI) VALUES
High 0.9–1.0
High 0.8–0.9
Medium 0.7–0.8
Medium 0.6–0.7
Medium 0.5–0.6
Low 0.4–0.5
Low 0.3–0.4
Low 0.2–0.3
Insufficient data

LOWEST ADULT LITERACY RATES**		
COUNTRY	1990	2001
Niger	11.4%	16.5%
Burkina Faso	16.3%	24.8%
Mali	18.8%	26.4%
Gambia	25.6%	37.8%
Senegal	28.4%	38.3%
Benin	26.4%	38.6%
Guinea-Bissau	27.2%	39.6%
Ethiopia	28.6%	40.3%
Bangladesh	34.2%	40.6%
Mauritania	34.8%	40.7%

*** Comparable statistics for several poor countries are not available, but some estimates put Somalia's adult literacy rate at about 25%, Sierra Leone's at about 30%, Guinea's and Afghanistan's at about 35%, and Angola's and Iraq's at about 40%.*

Assessing Development

A country's average standard of living can be measured by its Gross Domestic Product (GDP), the total value of all goods and services produced in a year. For a broader assessment of achievement, the Human Development Index (HDI) also takes into account life expectancy, adult literacy, and education enrollments. Many disadvantaged countries are trapped in poverty by the unsustainable debts they owe to wealthier countries, often paying more to service their foreign loans than they receive in foreign aid. In an attempt to address this problem, the United Nations has initiated debt relief schemes.

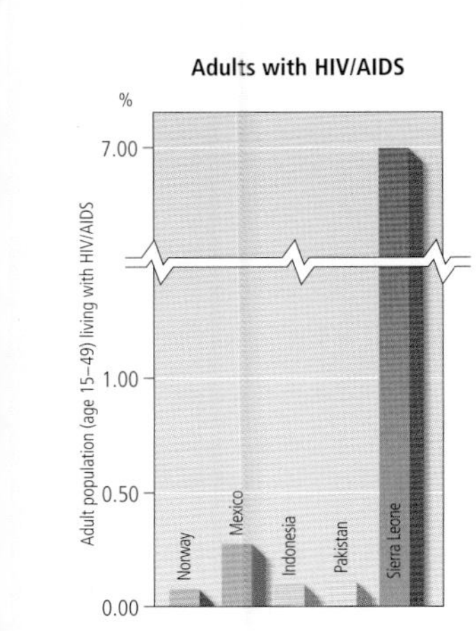
Adults with HIV/AIDS
%
7.00
1.00
0.50
0.00
Adult population (age 15–49) living with HIV/AIDS
Norway
Mexico
Indonesia
Pakistan
Sierra Leone

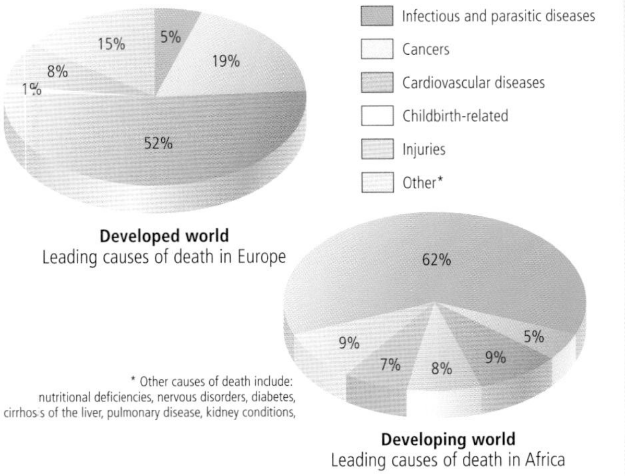
Infectious and parasitic diseases
Cancers
Cardiovascular diseases
Childbirth-related
Injuries
Other*
15%
5%
19%
8%
1%
52%
Developed world
Leading causes of death in Europe
62%
9%
7%
8%
9%
5%
Developing world
Leading causes of death in Africa

* Other causes of death include: nutritional deficiencies, nervous disorders, diabetes, cirrhosis of the liver, pulmonary disease, kidney conditions,

WOMEN'S SHARE

Throughout the world, women are poorer than their male compatriots, and three-fifths of the world's 1 billion poorest people are women. Ethiopian women, for example, earn an average of US$550 per year, compared to an average of US$1,074 for men. Education is an important factor—of the nearly 1 billion people who cannot read, two-thirds are women. Even in a country with well-educated women, such as Sweden, the average female income is less than 70 percent of the male income. Other causes of gender inequality include the poor pay that traditionally female work attracts and the lack of women in positions of power in politics and business.

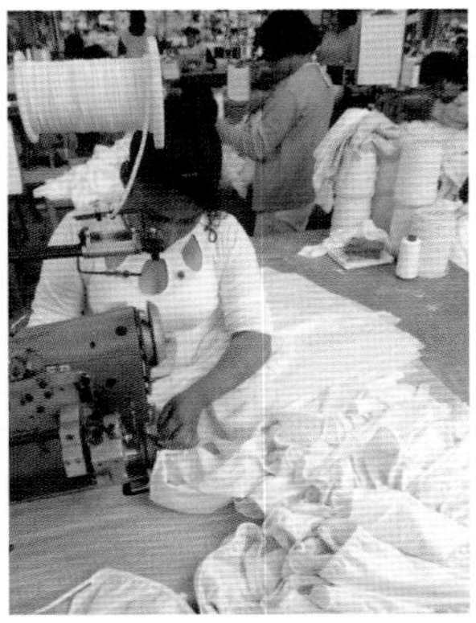

In developed and developing countries alike, women earn significantly less than men.

MAPPING THE WORLD

Part of the coastline of Guinea-Bissau in western Africa is visible in this color-enhanced satellite image. It was photographed from Landsat 7 using infrared, red and blue wavelengths. The blue ribbons are river systems; at center right is the River Geba. The light blue areas are silt that has been deposited as rivers flow into the Atlantic Ocean at the bottom of the image.

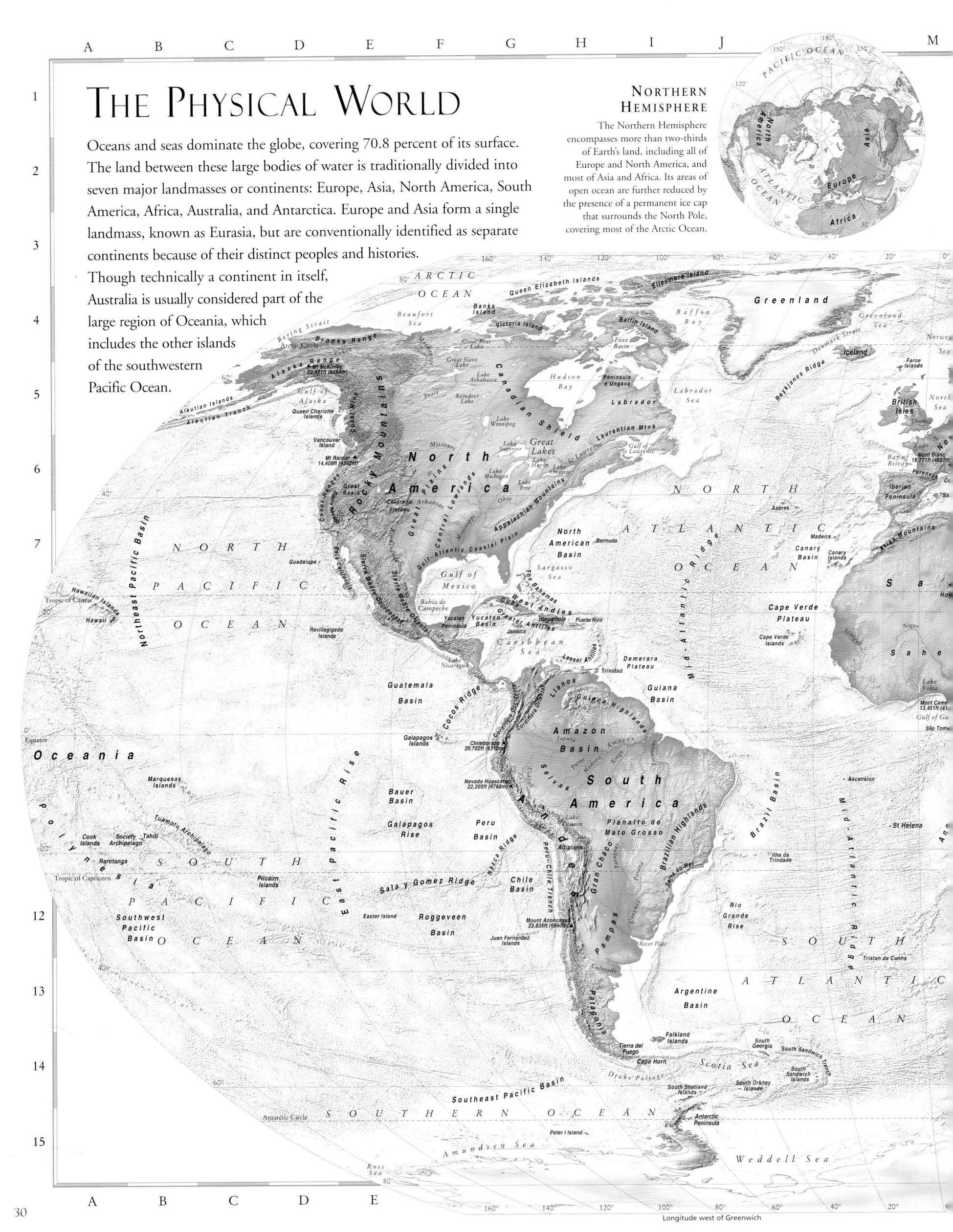

THE PHYSICAL WORLD

Oceans and seas dominate the globe, covering 70.8 percent of its surface. The land between these large bodies of water is traditionally divided into seven major landmasses or continents: Europe, Asia, North America, South America, Africa, Australia, and Antarctica. Europe and Asia form a single landmass, known as Eurasia, but are conventionally identified as separate continents because of their distinct peoples and histories. Though technically a continent in itself, Australia is usually considered part of the large region of Oceania, which includes the other islands of the southwestern Pacific Ocean.

NORTHERN HEMISPHERE

The Northern Hemisphere encompasses more than two-thirds of Earth's land, including all of Europe and North America, and most of Asia and Africa. Its areas of open ocean are further reduced by the presence of a permanent ice cap that surrounds the North Pole, covering most of the Arctic Ocean.

Longitude west of Greenwich

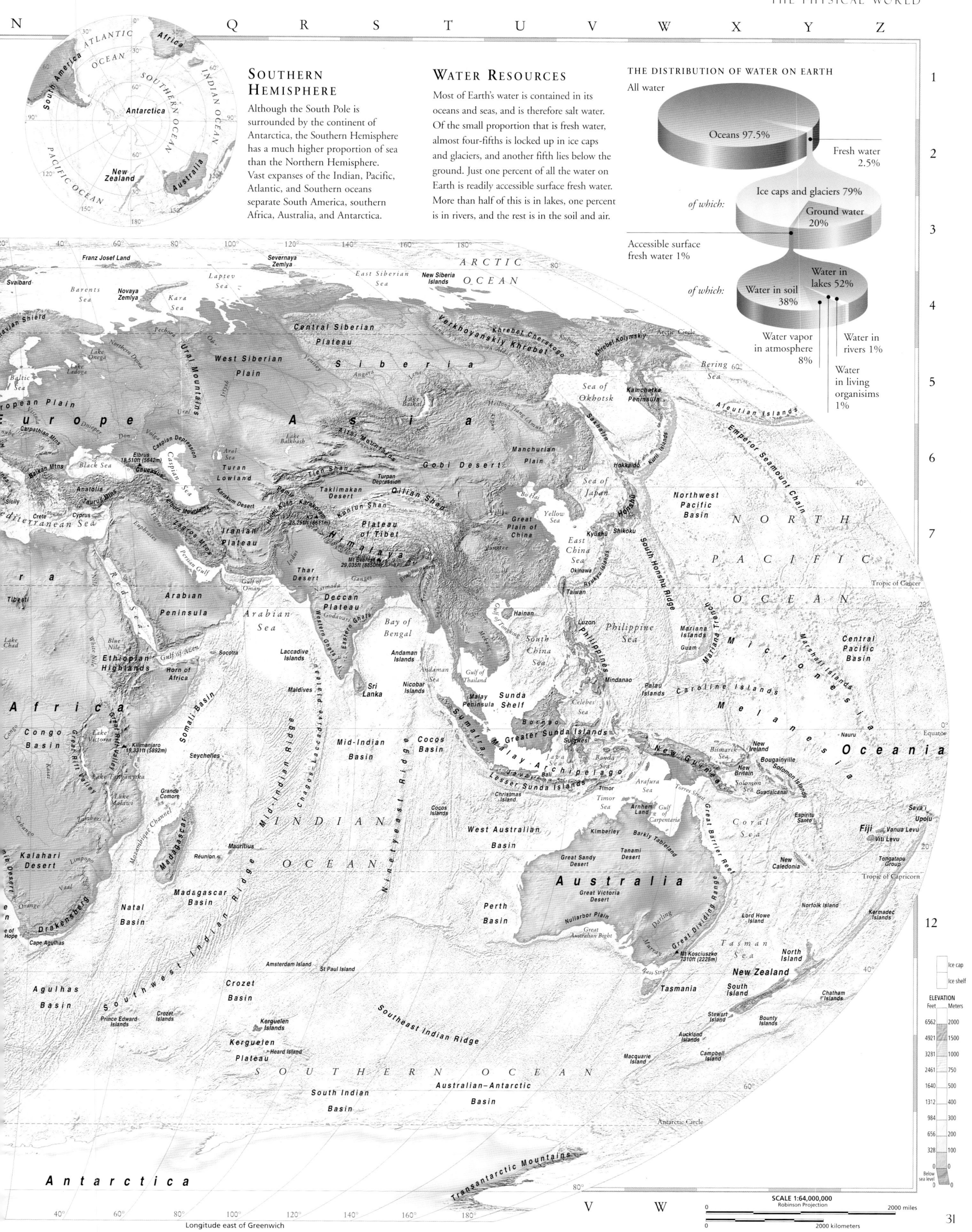

SOUTHERN HEMISPHERE

Although the South Pole is surrounded by the continent of Antarctica, the Southern Hemisphere has a much higher proportion of sea than the Northern Hemisphere. Vast expanses of the Indian, Pacific, Atlantic, and Southern oceans separate South America, southern Africa, Australia, and Antarctica.

WATER RESOURCES

Most of Earth's water is contained in its oceans and seas, and is therefore salt water. Of the small proportion that is fresh water, almost four-fifths is locked up in ice caps and glaciers, and another fifth lies below the ground. Just one percent of all the water on Earth is readily accessible surface fresh water. More than half of this is in lakes, one percent is in rivers, and the rest is in the soil and air.

THE DISTRIBUTION OF WATER ON EARTH

All water

Oceans 97.5%

Fresh water 2.5%

of which:

Ice caps and glaciers 79%

Ground water 20%

Accessible surface fresh water 1%

of which:

Water in soil 38%

Water in lakes 52%

Water vapor in atmosphere 8%

Water in rivers 1%

Water in living organisims 1%

ELEVATION

Feet	Meters
	Ice cap
	Ice shelf
6562	2000
4921	1500
3281	1000
2461	750
1640	500
1312	400
984	300
656	200
328	100
0	0
Below sea level	

SCALE 1:64,000,000
Robinson Projection

0 — 2000 miles

0 — 2000 kilometers

Longitude east of Greenwich

THE POLITICAL WORLD

With the exception of Antarctica, where territorial claims have been suspended, all the land on Earth is divided into 192 independent countries and about 60 dependent territories. The countries range in size from the largest, the vast Russian Federation, to the smallest, the Vatican City, which lies entirely within the city of Rome in Italy. Most dependent territories came about as the result of colonization and belong to a few, mainly European nations. Some areas of land, usually on the fringes of countries, are the focus of territorial disputes.

Dividing the World

About 150,000 miles (250,000 km) of land boundaries separate the world's countries and territories. These borders may follow landforms, waterways, the margins of traditional ethnic territories, lines of latitude or longitude, or arbitrary lines plotted by colonial administrators. Many seaboard nations have also established maritime boundaries. A nation's maritime territorial claim extends 12 nautical miles offshore, but exclusive fishing and economic zones are generally recognized up to 200 nautical miles offshore.

PACIFIC OCEAN
Yap   Caroline Islands   Pohnpei
Chuuk
Islands   Kosrae
FEDERATED STATES OF MICRONESIA

The Exclusive Economic Zone (EEZ) of the Federated States of Micronesia encompasses over 1.3 million square miles (3 million sq km) of ocean.

The Vatican City covers less than a fifth of a square mile (0.5 sq km) of the city of Rome.

Map labels

ARCTIC OCEAN
Beaufort Sea
Victoria Island
Ellesmere Island
Baffin Island
Baffin Bay
Greenland (to Denmark)
Jan Mayen (to Norway)
Arctic Circle
U.S.A. (Alaska)
ICELAND
REYKJAVÍK
Faroe Islands (to Denmark)
Hudson Bay
CANADA
Gulf of Alaska
Aleutian Islands (U.S.A.)
UNITED KINGDOM   DENM
DUBLIN
REPUBLIC OF IRELAND
LONDON   AMSTER
BRUSSELS   BELG
PARIS
OTTAWA
St Pierre and Miquelon (to France)
NORTH   FRANC
MONAC
ANDORRA   Co
UNITED STATES OF AMERICA
WASHINGTON, D.C.
Azores (to Portugal)
PORTUGAL   MADRID   SPAIN
LISBON
ALGIERS
NORTH   PACIFIC   OCEAN
Bermuda (to U.K.)
ATLANTIC
Madeira (to Portugal)
RABAT   MOROCCO
Tropic of Cancer
Guadalupe (to Mexico)
Canary Islands (to Spain)
LAÂYOUNE   ALGERI
THE BAHAMAS
NASSAU
WESTERN SAHARA (occupied by Morocco)
Hawaii (U.S.A.)
MEXICO
Gulf of Mexico
CUBA   OCEAN   MAURITANIA   MALI
HAVANA   NOUAKCHOTT
Revillagigedo Islands (to Mexico)
MEXICO CITY
DOMINICAN REPUBLIC
SANTO DOMINGO
HAITI   PORT-AU-PRINCE
Cayman Is (to U.K.)
CAPE VERDE
PRAIA
NIAME
Puerto Rico (to U.S.A.)
ST KITTS AND NEVIS
ANTIGUA AND BARBUDA
SENEGAL   BANJUL
DAKAR   BAMAKO   OUAGADOUG
GUATEMALA
BELIZE   KINGSTON   JAMAICA   DOMINICA
BELMOPAN
GAMBIA
BISSAU   BURKINA FASO   BENIN
GUATEMALA   HONDURAS
SAN SALVADOR   TEGUCIGALPA   ST LUCIA
EL SALVADOR   MANAGUA   ST VINCENT AND THE GRENADINES   BARBADOS
GUINEA-BISSAU   GUINEA   CÔTE D'IVOIRE   NIC
NICARAGUA   GRENADA
CONAKRY   YAMOUSSOUKRO   LOME   PORT
Clipperton Island (to France)
COSTA RICA   TRINIDAD AND TOBAGO   PORT OF SPAIN
FREETOWN   ACCRA   NOV
SAN JOSÉ   PANAMA CITY
SIERRA LEONE   MA
PANAMA   CARACAS   GEORGETOWN
MONROVIA   LIBERIA   EQUATO
GUINE
BOGOTÁ   VENEZUELA   PARAMARIBO
LIB
SÃO TOM
GUYANA   CAYENNE
SURINAME   FRENCH GUIANA (to France)
SÃO TOMÉ AND PRÍNCIPE
COLOMBIA
Galapagos Islands (to Ecuador)
QUITO
ECUADOR
Fernando de Noronha (to Brazil)
PERU
BRAZIL
KIRIBATI
International Date Line
SOUTH   PACIFIC   OCEAN
LIMA
Ascension (to U.K.)
BOLIVIA
LA PAZ   BRASÍLIA
American Samoa (to U.S.A.)
SUCRE
St Helena (to U.K.)
Cook Islands (to N.Z.)
PAPEETE   Tahiti
French Polynesia (to France)
AVARUA
PARAGUAY
Ilha da Trindade (to Brazil)
ASUNCIÓN   SOUTH
Tropic of Capricorn
ADAMSTOWN
Pitcairn Islands (to U.K.)
Sala y Gómez (to Chile)
Easter Island (to Chile)
CHILE   ARGENTINA   ATLANTIC
Juan Fernández Islands (to Chile)
SANTIAGO   URUGUAY
BUENOS AIRES   MONTEVIDEO
Tristan da Cunha (to U.K.)
OCEAN
Falkland Islands (to U.K.)
South Georgia (to U.K.)
Gough Island (to U.K.)
South Sandwich Islands (to U.K.)
South Shetland Islands (to U.K.)
South Orkney Islands (to U.K.)
Antarctic Circle
SOUTHERN OCEAN
Peter I Island (to Norway)
Antarctic Peninsula
AN
Weddell Sea

Longitude west of Greenwich

1

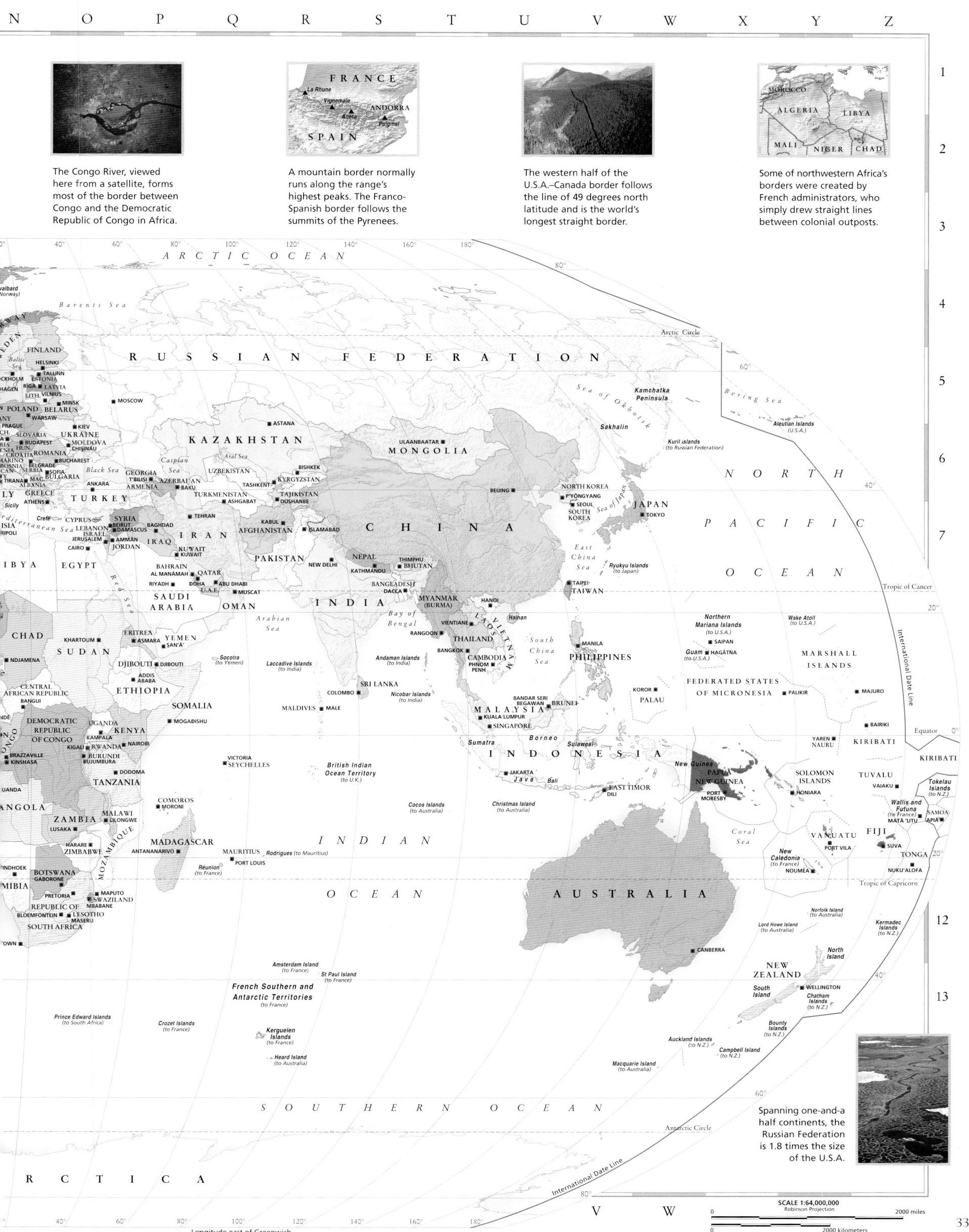

The Congo River, viewed here from a satellite, forms most of the border between Congo and the Democratic Republic of Congo in Africa.

A mountain border normally runs along the range's highest peaks. The Franco-Spanish border follows the summits of the Pyrenees.

The western half of the U.S.A.–Canada border follows the line of 49 degrees north latitude and is the world's longest straight border.

Some of northwestern Africa's borders were created by French administrators, who simply drew straight lines between colonial outposts.

2

3

Spanning one-and-a half continents, the Russian Federation is 1.8 times the size of the U.S.A.

Longitude east of Greenwich

SCALE 1:64,000,000
Robinson Projection

0   2000 miles

0   2000 kilometers

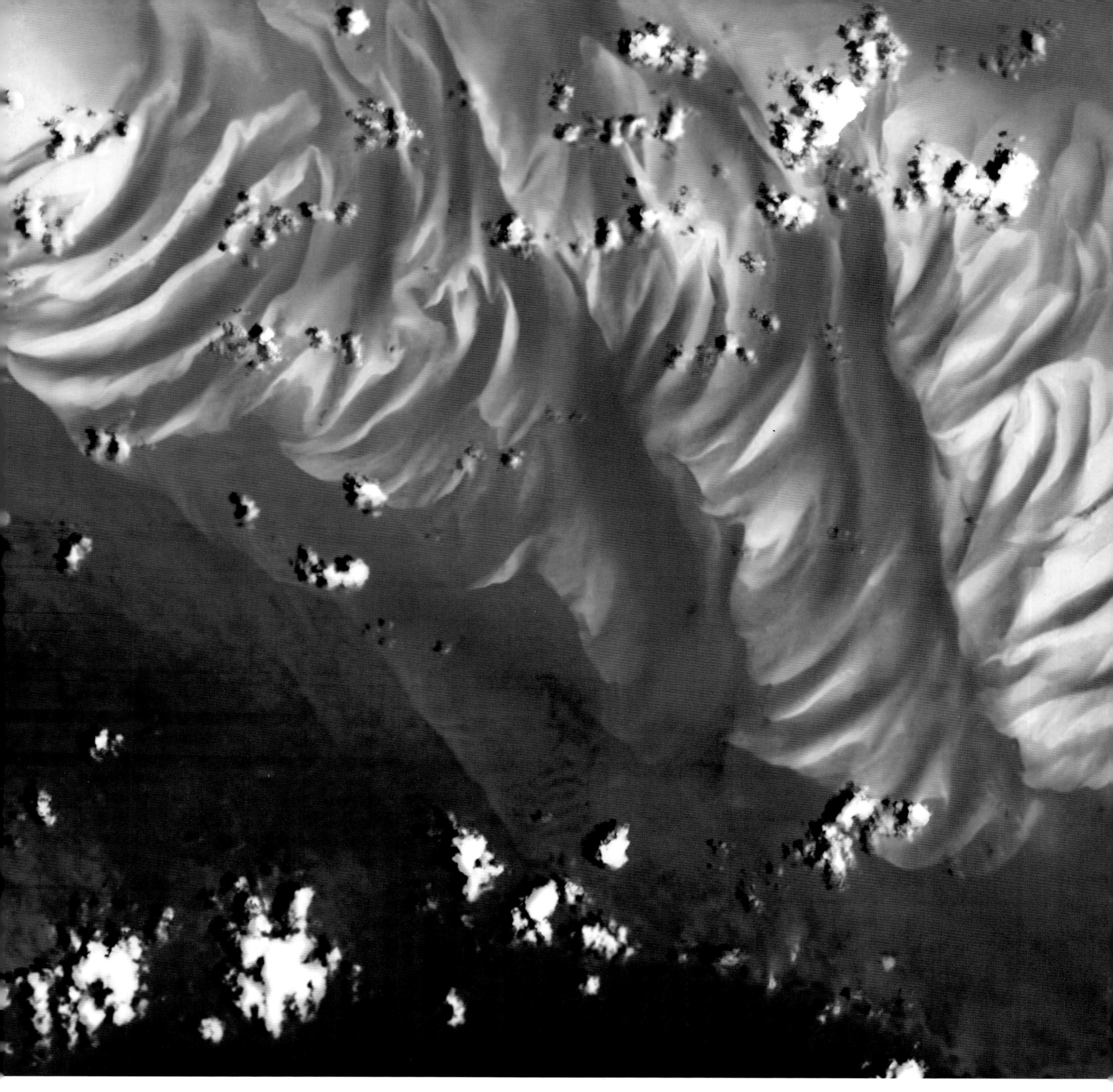

Taken from NASA's Terra satellite, this image shows underwater sand dunes in the waters of Tarpum Bay, southwest of Eleuthera Island in The Bahamas. These dunes, shaped by ocean currents, are made of sand eroded from limestone coral reefs.

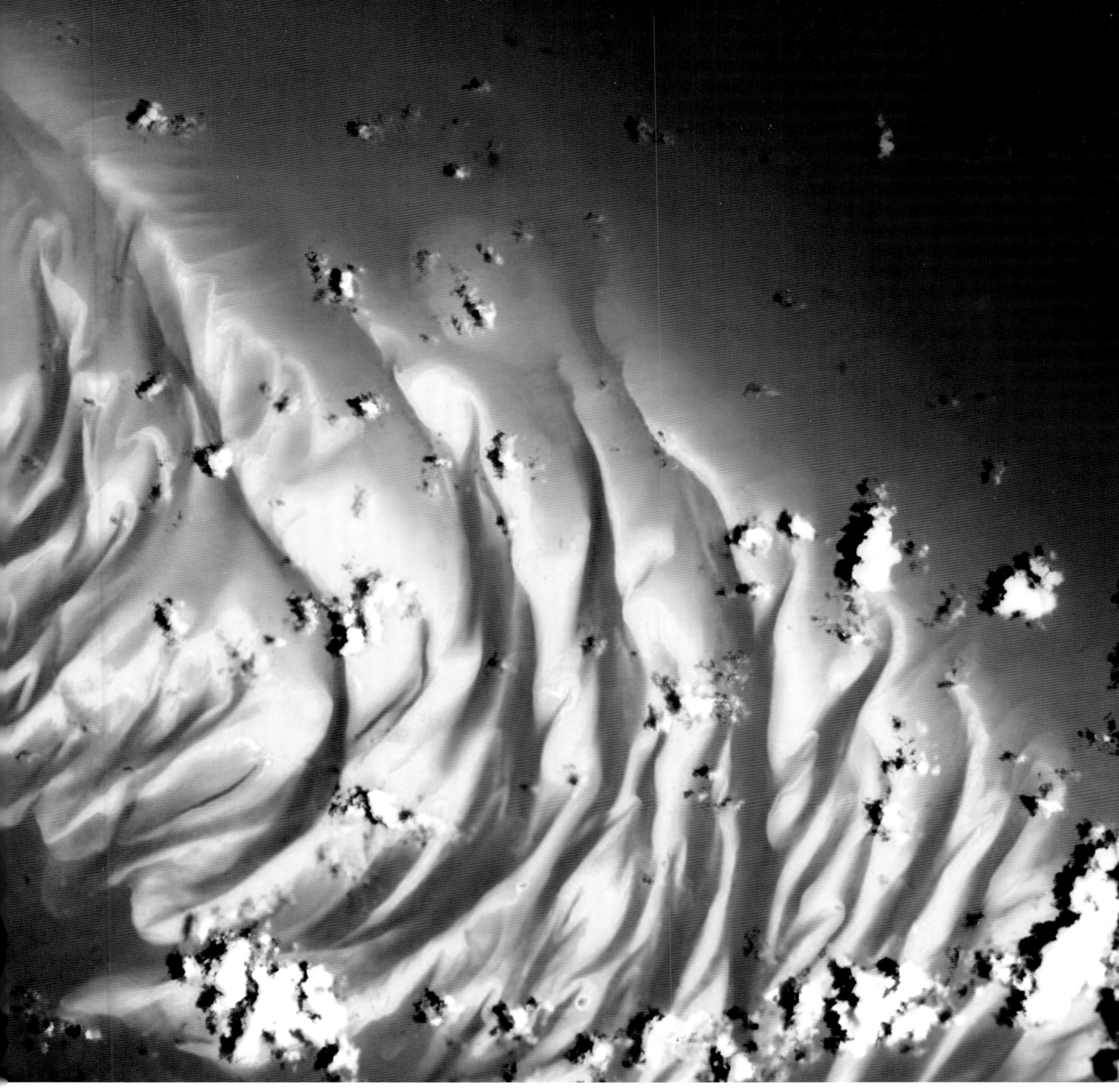

THE OCEANS

THE OCEANS

More than two-thirds of Earth's surface is covered by its five connected oceans. The Pacific, Atlantic, Indian, and Arctic have been recognized for centuries. The fifth ocean, the Southern, was demarcated by the International Hydrographic Organization only in the year 2000. It encompasses all the waters surrounding Antarctica up to 60 degrees south latitude, taking in areas formerly considered part of the Pacific, Atlantic, and Indian oceans. A region known as the Antarctic Polar Frontal Zone separates the icy waters of the Southern Ocean from the warmer waters to the north.

The oceans absorb more than 80 percent of the solar radiation that reaches Earth, and water has a remarkable capacity for storing heat. Consequently, the uppermost 10 percent of the oceans contains more heat than the entire atmosphere. As ocean currents carry immense quantities of heat around the globe, they modify the climate. The Gulf Stream, for example, carries warm water from the Caribbean past the eastern United States to northern Europe, making northern Europe significantly warmer than northern Canada at the same latitudes.

Recent technologies such as satellites, submersibles, and sounding equipment have dramatically enhanced our understanding of the sea. The underwater landscape contains Earth's greatest canyons and longest mountain chains. Bizarre lifeforms adapted to the cold, dark depths have been discovered. Even so, more than 90 percent of Earth's oceans are still to be explored.

SCALE 1:115,000,000
Robinson Projection

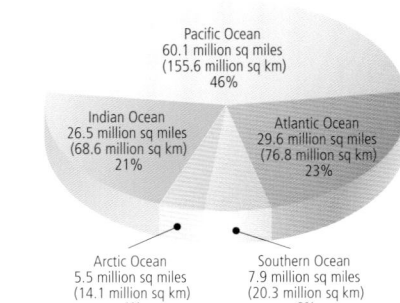

Pacific Ocean
60.1 million sq miles
(155.6 million sq km)
46%

Indian Ocean
26.5 million sq miles
(68.6 million sq km)
21%

Atlantic Ocean
29.6 million sq miles
(76.8 million sq km)
23%

Arctic Ocean
5.5 million sq miles
(14.1 million sq km)
4%

Southern Ocean
7.9 million sq miles
(20.3 million sq km)
6%

Ocean Size

Almost equal in size to the Indian, Atlantic, and Arctic combined, the Pacific is by far the largest ocean. Together, the five oceans cover about 130 million square miles (335 million sq km). They contain 335 million cubic miles (1,400 million cubic km) of water, which makes up 97 percent of all Earth's water and is 18 times greater than the volume of Earth's land.

Tidal Forces

Every day as Earth rotates, the Moon's gravity pulls on its oceans, creating high tide on the side facing the Moon. Centrifugal force produced by Earth's rotation creates high tide on the opposite side as well. When the Sun and Moon line up, their combined gravitational pull creates especially high tides, known as spring tides. When the Sun and Moon are at right angles to each other, the tidal range is small and neap tides occur.

In warm, shallow seas, vast reefs can be built by coral polyps, tiny animals that produce casings of limestone. Referred to as "the rain forests of the sea," coral reefs harbor a rich diversity of life.

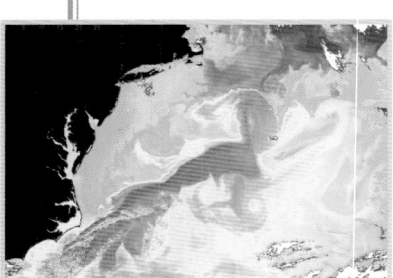

The Gulf Stream is a warm surface current in the Atlantic Ocean off the east coast of the United States. In this false-color satellite image, warmer waters are shown as red, and cooler waters are shown as blue.

Great Ocean Conveyor Belt

A "great ocean conveyor belt" transports heat around the globe. As surface currents carry warm water from the Pacific through the Indian and into the Atlantic, the water cools and evaporation increases its salinity. In the North Atlantic, this denser, colder water sinks, creating a deep current that carries it back to the Indian, Southern, and Pacific oceans. Changes in precipitation and ice melt may affect the belt's strength, which in turn may alter the global climate.

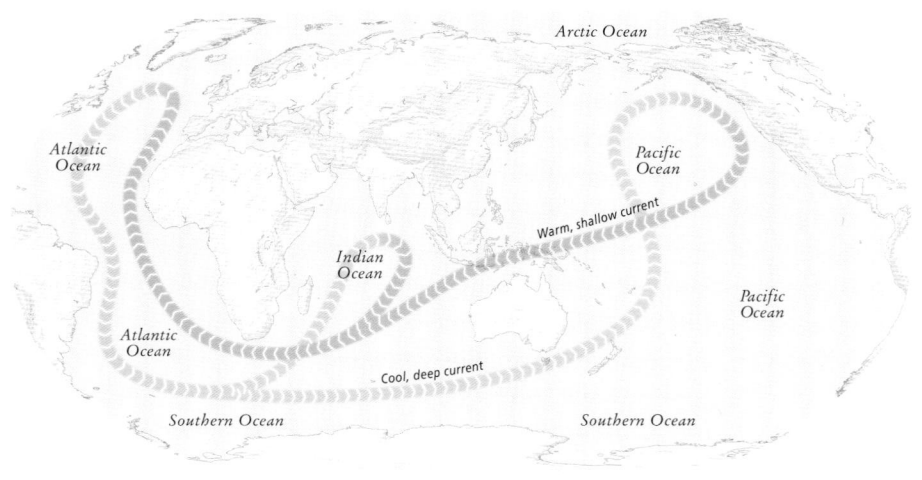

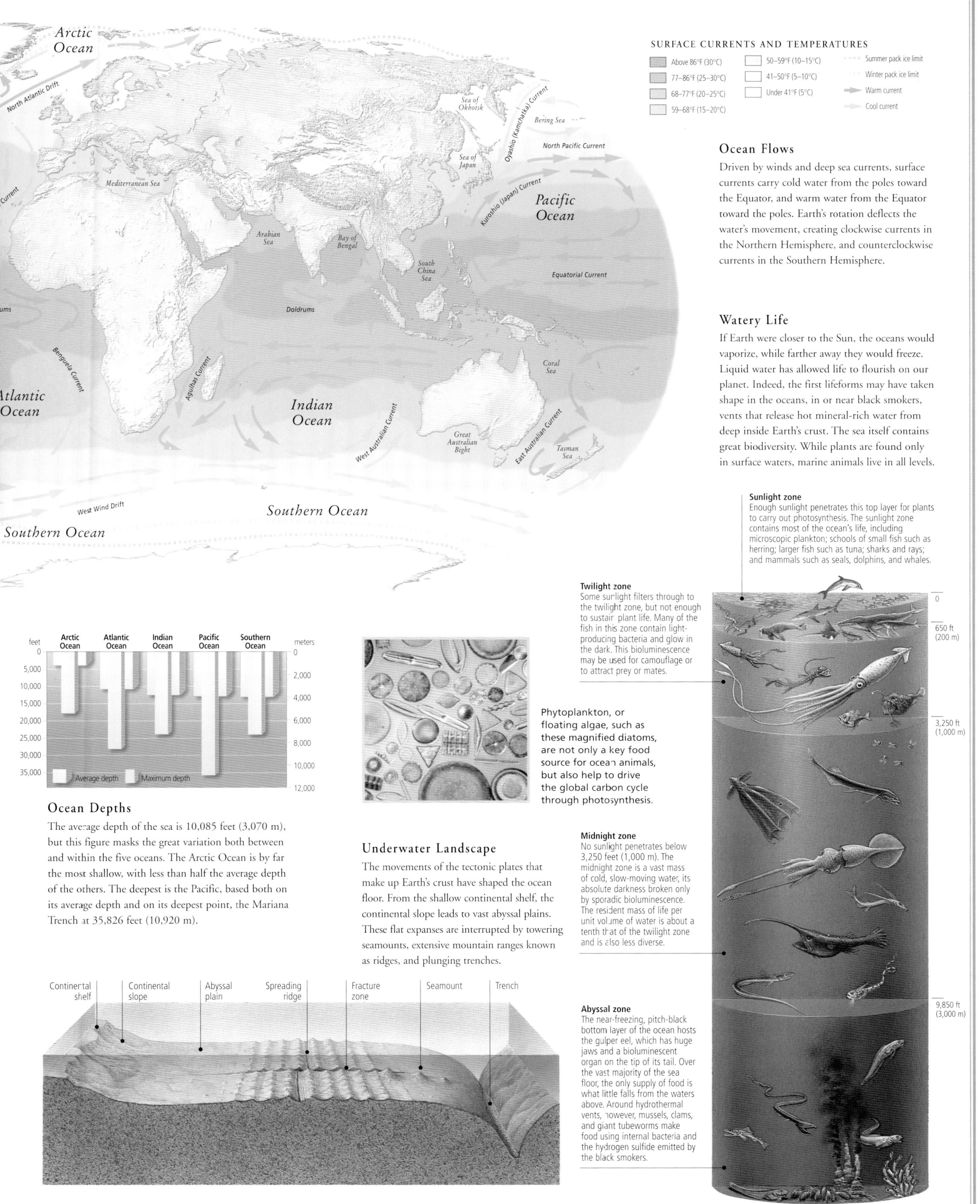

Map labels

Arctic Ocean

North Atlantic Drift

Mediterranean Sea

Atlantic Ocean

Southern Ocean

Benguela Current

Agulhas Current

West Wind Drift

Arabian Sea

Bay of Bengal

Indian Ocean

West Australian Current

Great Australian Bight

Doldrums

South China Sea

Sea of Japan

Sea of Okhotsk

Bering Sea

Oyashio (Kamchatka) Current

Kuroshio (Japan) Current

North Pacific Current

Pacific Ocean

Equatorial Current

Coral Sea

East Australian Current

Tasman Sea

Southern Ocean

SURFACE CURRENTS AND TEMPERATURES

- Above 86°F (30°C)
- 77–86°F (25–30°C)
- 68–77°F (20–25°C)
- 59–68°F (15–20°C)
- 50–59°F (10–15°C)
- 41–50°F (5–10°C)
- Under 41°F (5°C)
- Summer pack ice limit
- Winter pack ice limit
- Warm current
- Cool current

Ocean Flows

Driven by winds and deep sea currents, surface currents carry cold water from the poles toward the Equator, and warm water from the Equator toward the poles. Earth's rotation deflects the water's movement, creating clockwise currents in the Northern Hemisphere, and counterclockwise currents in the Southern Hemisphere.

Watery Life

If Earth were closer to the Sun, the oceans would vaporize, while farther away they would freeze. Liquid water has allowed life to flourish on our planet. Indeed, the first lifeforms may have taken shape in the oceans, in or near black smokers, vents that release hot mineral-rich water from deep inside Earth's crust. The sea itself contains great biodiversity. While plants are found only in surface waters, marine animals live in all levels.

Ocean depths chart

	Arctic Ocean	Atlantic Ocean	Indian Ocean	Pacific Ocean	Southern Ocean

feet: 0, 5,000, 10,000, 15,000, 20,000, 25,000, 30,000, 35,000

meters: 0, 2,000, 4,000, 6,000, 8,000, 10,000, 12,000

Average depth   Maximum depth

Ocean Depths

The average depth of the sea is 10,085 feet (3,070 m), but this figure masks the great variation both between and within the five oceans. The Arctic Ocean is by far the most shallow, with less than half the average depth of the others. The deepest is the Pacific, based both on its average depth and on its deepest point, the Mariana Trench at 35,826 feet (10,920 m).

Phytoplankton, or floating algae, such as these magnified diatoms, are not only a key food source for ocean animals, but also help to drive the global carbon cycle through photosynthesis.

Underwater Landscape

The movements of the tectonic plates that make up Earth's crust have shaped the ocean floor. From the shallow continental shelf, the continental slope leads to vast abyssal plains. These flat expanses are interrupted by towering seamounts, extensive mountain ranges known as ridges, and plunging trenches.

Continental shelf | Continental slope | Abyssal plain | Spreading ridge | Fracture zone | Seamount | Trench

Sunlight zone
Enough sunlight penetrates this top layer for plants to carry out photosynthesis. The sunlight zone contains most of the ocean's life, including microscopic plankton; schools of small fish such as herring; larger fish such as tuna; sharks and rays; and mammals such as seals, dolphins, and whales.

Twilight zone
Some sunlight filters through to the twilight zone, but not enough to sustain plant life. Many of the fish in this zone contain light-producing bacteria and glow in the dark. This bioluminescence may be used for camouflage or to attract prey or mates.

Midnight zone
No sunlight penetrates below 3,250 feet (1,000 m). The midnight zone is a vast mass of cold, slow-moving water, its absolute darkness broken only by sporadic bioluminescence. The resident mass of life per unit volume of water is about a tenth that of the twilight zone and is also less diverse.

Abyssal zone
The near-freezing, pitch-black bottom layer of the ocean hosts the gulper eel, which has huge jaws and a bioluminescent organ on the tip of its tail. Over the vast majority of the sea floor, the only supply of food is what little falls from the waters above. Around hydrothermal vents, however, mussels, clams, and giant tubeworms make food using internal bacteria and the hydrogen sulfide emitted by the black smokers.

0
650 ft (200 m)
3,250 ft (1,000 m)
9,850 ft (3,000 m)

THE INDIAN OCEAN

The third-largest ocean on Earth, the Indian Ocean covers 26.5 million square miles (68.6 million sq km), extending from the east coast of Africa to the west coast of Australia, and from the southern shore of Asia to the Southern Ocean. A series of major spreading ridges, including the Mid-Indian Ridge, runs southeast from the Arabian Sea to the center of the ocean, forking to form the Southwest Indian and Southeast Indian ridges. South of these two plate boundaries, broad basins are interrupted by the massive Kerguelen Plateau. To the north lie numerous plateaus and subsidiary, stable ridges, including the Ninetyeast Ridge, the longest straight ridge in the world, named for its location along the 90 degrees east meridian. The deepest part of the Indian Ocean is the Java Trench, south of the Indonesian island of Java, where the ocean floor drops to 23,376 feet (7,125 m) below sea level.

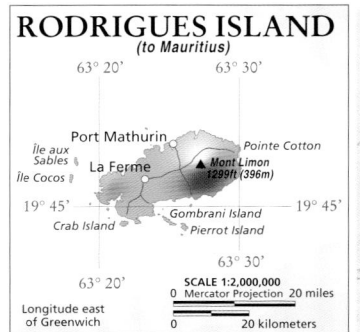

Residents watch a fiery lava flow from Piton de la Fournaise, an active volcano on the island of Réunion.

RODRIGUES ISLAND
(to Mauritius)

63° 20' 63° 30'

Port Mathurin
Île aux Sables
Île Cocos
La Ferme
▲ Mont Limon 1299ft (396m)
Pointe Cotton

19° 45' Gombrani Island 19° 45'
Pierrot Island
Crab Island

63° 30'
63° 20'

SCALE 1:2,000,000
Mercator Projection 20 miles
Longitude east of Greenwich
20 kilometers

SEYCHELLES

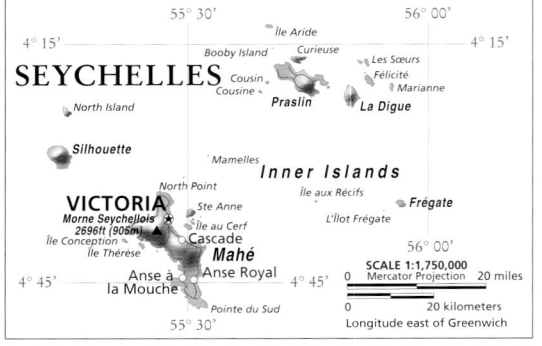

55° 30' 56° 00'
4° 15' 4° 15'
Île Aride
Booby Island Curieuse
Cousine Cousin Les Sœurs
Praslin Félicité
Marianne
North Island La Digue
Silhouette
Mamelles Inner Islands
North Point Île aux Récifs
VICTORIA Ste Anne Frégate
Morne Seychellois Île au Cerf L'Îlot Frégate
2696ft (905m) Cascade
Île Conception Mahé
Île Thérèse Anse Royal
Anse à 4° 45' 56° 00'
la Mouche
Pointe du Sud
4° 45' 55° 30'
SCALE 1:1,750,000
Mercator Projection 20 miles
0 20 kilometers
Longitude east of Greenwich

MAURITIUS

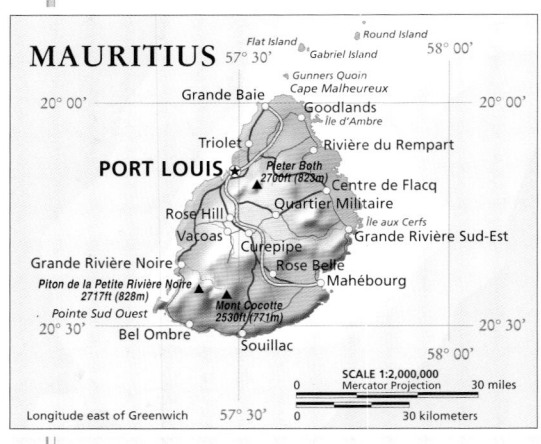

57° 30' Flat Island 58° 00'
Round Island
Gabriel Island
Gunners Quoin
Cape Malheureux
20° 00' Grande Baie Île d'Ambre 20° 00'
Goodlands
Triolet Rivière du Rempart
PORT LOUIS Pieter Both
2700ft (823m)
Rose Hill Centre de Flacq
Quartier Militaire
Vacoas Île aux Cerfs
Curepipe Grande Rivière Sud-Est
Grande Rivière Noire Rose Belle
Piton de la Petite Rivière Noire Mahébourg
2717ft (828m) Mont Cocotte
Pointe Sud Ouest 2530ft (771m)
20° 30' Bel Ombre 20° 30'
Souillac
58° 00'
SCALE 1:2,000,000
Mercator Projection 30 miles
Longitude east of Greenwich 57° 30' 30 kilometers

RÉUNION
(to France)

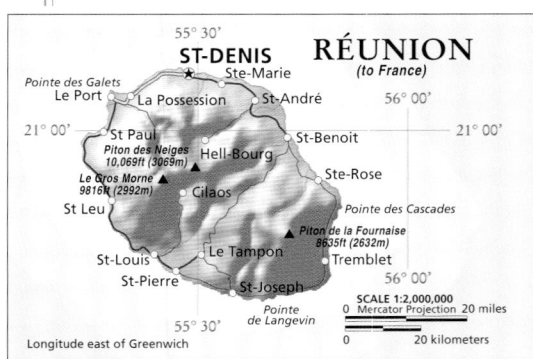

55° 30'
ST-DENIS
Ste-Marie
Pointe des Galets St-André
Le Port 56° 00'
La Possession
21° 00' 21° 00'
St-Paul St-Benoit
Piton des Neiges
10,069ft (3069m) Hell-Bourg Ste-Rose
Le Gros Morne Cilaos
9816ft (2992m)
St-Leu Piton de la Fournaise
8635ft (2632m)
St-Louis Le Tampon Tremblet
St-Pierre St-Joseph
Pointe
de Langevin
55° 30'
SCALE 1:2,000,000
Mercator Projection 20 miles
Longitude east of Greenwich 20 kilometers

NATURAL RESOURCES

Busy shipping routes crisscross the ocean, with much of the traffic originating in the Persian Gulf oil fields. Other major oil reserves lie off Saudi Arabia, Iran, India, and Australia; in total, the Indian Ocean generates 40 percent of world offshore production. Sands and placer deposits are mined along the shoreline, and potentially valuable manganese nodules litter the ocean floor, though these have not yet been successfully exploited. Fish stocks, especially shrimps along the coast and tuna in the open ocean, are vital to many seaboard nations. Commercial harvesting occurs on only a modest scale, though fleets come from as far afield as Russia and Japan.

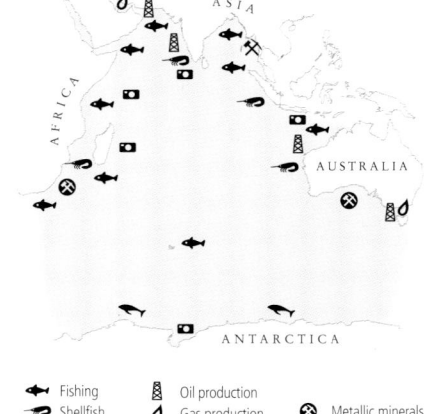

ASIA
AFRICA
AUSTRALIA
ANTARCTICA

Fishing
Shellfish
Whales
Oil production
Gas production
Mining
Metallic minerals
Tourism

Main map labels

30° 40° 50° 60°
Persian Gulf
Gulf of Oman
Tropic of Cancer
Murray Ridge
Arabian Peninsula
Red Sea
Arabian Sea
20°
Gulf of Aden East Sheba Ridge
West Sheba Ridge Socotra Arabian Basin
10° Horn of Africa Carlsberg Ridge
Ethiopian Highlands
Andrew Tablemount
Chain Ridge
Coco-de-Mer Seamounts
0° Equator
AFRICA Somali Basin Mid-Indian Ridge
Amirante Islands Seychelles
Zanzibar Island Mascarene Ridge
Amirante Trench
Aldabra Islands Farquhar Islands
10° Comoros Mascarene Basin
Mayotte
Île Tromelin Nazareth Bank Cargados Carajos Islands
Mascarene Plain Cargados Carajos Bank
Rodrigues Island
Bassas da India Mauritius
20° Réunion
Tropic of Capricorn
Mauritius Trench
Davie Ridge
Mozambique Channel
Madagascar Plateau Madagascar Basin
MADAGASCAR
30° Drakensberg Madagascar Ridge
Transkei Basin Mozambique Ridge
Mozambique Escarpment
Natal Basin
Cape Agulhas Walters Shoal
Agulhas Bank Natal Valley
Protea Seamount Crozet Basin
Africana Seamount
40° Agulhas Plateau Southwest Indian Ridge
Del Cano Rise Crozet Plateau Crozet Islands
Agulhas Basin
Prince Edward Fracture Zone Prince Edward Islands
50° Atlantic-Indian Ridge Conrad Rise
60° Enderby Abyssal Plain
Atlantic-Indian-Antarctic Basin
Antarctic Circle Cape Ann Cape Boothby
30° Lützow-Holm Bay
40° 50° 60°
Longitude east of Greenwich

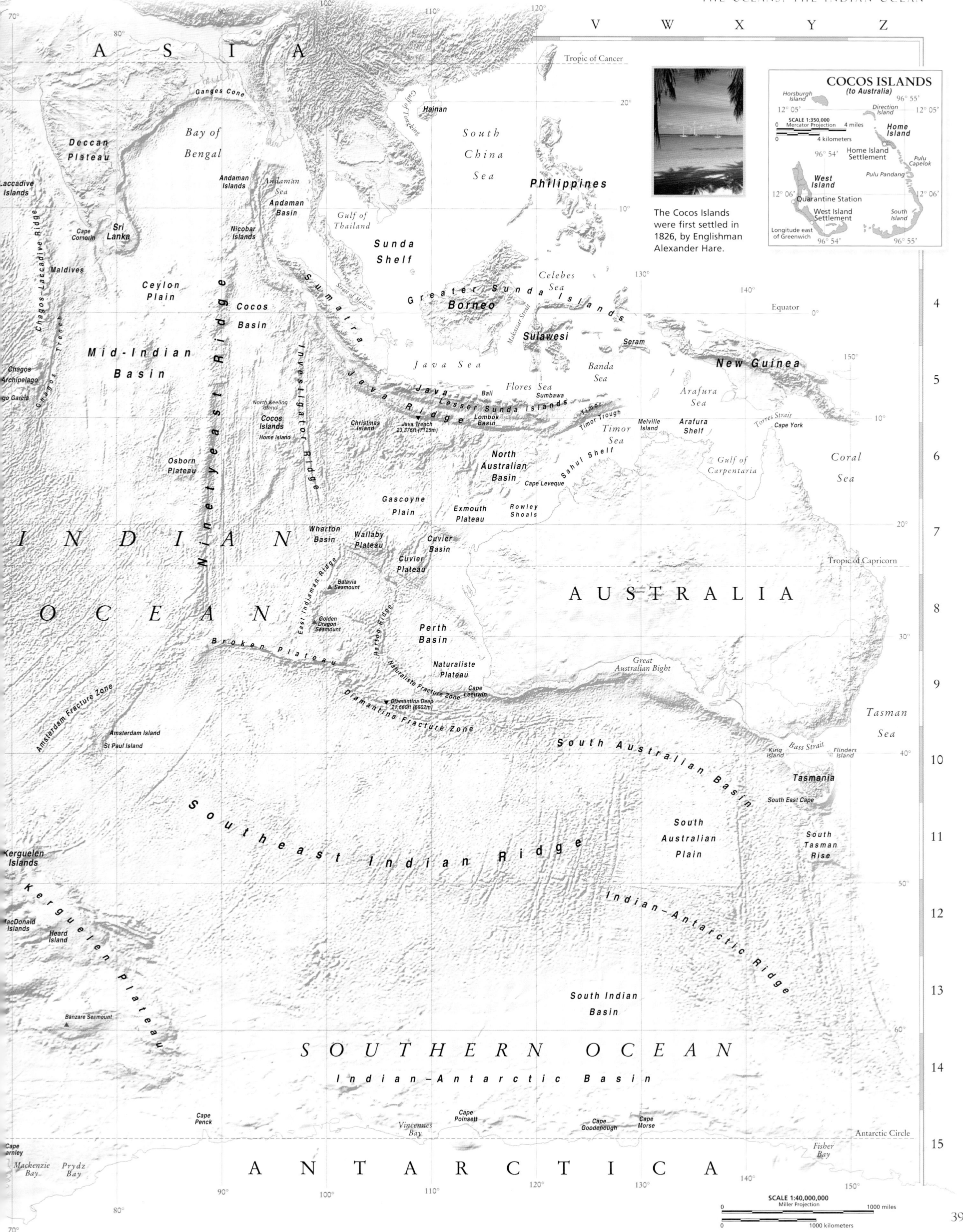

V   W   X   Y   Z

ASIA

Deccan
Plateau

Laccadive
Islands

Cape
Comorin

Sri
Lanka

Maldives

Chagos
Archipelago

go Garcia

Chagos-Laccadive Ridge

Chagos Trench

**Mid-Indian
Basin**

Bay of
Bengal

Ganges Cone

Andaman
Islands

Andaman
Sea

Andaman
Basin

Nicobar
Islands

Ceylon
Plain

Cocos
Basin

Ninetyeast Ridge

Sumatra

Strait of Malacca

Investigator Ridge

Java Ridge

Sunda
Shelf

Gulf of
Thailand

Hainan

Gulf of Tongking

South
China
Sea

Tropic of Cancer

Philippines

Greater Sunda

Borneo

Celebes
Sea

Sulawesi

Islands

Makassar Strait

Seram

Java Sea

Flores Sea

Bali

Sumbawa

Lesser Sunda Islands

Lombok
Basin

Banda
Sea

Timor

Timor Trough

Melville
Island

Arafura
Sea

New Guinea

Equator   0°

Arafura
Shelf

Torres Strait   Cape York

Coral
Sea

Gulf of
Carpentaria

North Keeling
Island

Christmas
Island

Java Trench
23,376ft (7125m)

Timor
Sea

Sahul Shelf

Cape Leveque

**North
Australian
Basin**

Cocos
Islands

Home Island

Osborn
Plateau

Gascoyne
Plain

Exmouth
Plateau

Rowley
Shoals

INDIAN

Wharton
Basin

Wallaby
Plateau

Cuvier
Basin

Cuvier
Plateau

East Indian Ridge

Batavia
Seamount

Hartog Ridge

AUSTRALIA

Tropic of Capricorn

OCEAN

Golden
Dragon
Seamount

Broken Plateau

Naturaliste Fracture Zone

Perth
Basin

Naturaliste
Plateau

Cape
Leeuwin

Great
Australian Bight

Diamantina Fracture Zone

Diamantina Deep
21,660ft (6602m)

Amsterdam Fracture Zone

Amsterdam Island

St Paul Island

Kerguelen
Islands

South Australian Basin

King
Island

Bass Strait

Flinders
Island

*Tasman
Sea*

**South
Australian
Plain**

South East Cape

Tasmania

South
Tasman
Rise

Southeast   Indian   Ridge

Kerguelen Plateau

MacDonald
Islands

Heard
Island

**South Indian
Basin**

Indian–Antarctic Ridge

Banzare Seamount

SOUTHERN   OCEAN

Indian–Antarctic   Basin

Cape
Barnley

Mackenzie
Bay

Prydz
Bay

Cape
Penck

Vincennes
Bay

Cape
Poinsett

Cape
Goodenough

Cape
Morse

Antarctic Circle

Fisher
Bay

ANTARCTICA

SCALE 1:40,000,000
Miller Projection
0 — 1000 miles
0 — 1000 kilometers

COCOS ISLANDS
(to Australia)

Horsburgh
Island

12° 05'

Direction
Island

12° 05'

Home
Island

SCALE 1:350,000
Mercator Projection
0 — 4 miles
0 — 4 kilometers

96° 55'

Home Island
Settlement

Pulu Pandang

Pulu
Capelok

**West
Island**

Quarantine Station

West Island
Settlement

96° 54'

12° 06'

South
Island

12° 06'

Longitude east
of Greenwich

96° 54'

96° 55'

The Cocos Islands
were first settled in
1826, by Englishman
Alexander Hare.

39

THE PACIFIC OCEAN

Not only is the Pacific the largest of the oceans, it is twice as large and holds twice as much water as the Atlantic Ocean, and exceeds the combined area of all of Earth's landmasses. Spanning 60.1 million square miles (155.6 million sq km), it separates the continents of Asia and Australia from the Americas. A divergent plate boundary running south from Mexico forms the East Pacific Rise, part of the great chain of mid-ocean ridges that winds round the globe. Trenches formed by subduction border the eastern continental shelves, and volcanic peaks line the shores above. In the west, a complex series of mainly convergent plate boundaries forms a number of deep trenches bordered by volcanic archipelagoes. These zones of volcanic and seismic activity that almost encircle the Pacific Ocean are known as the Ring of Fire. In contrast, the floor of the central Pacific is relatively stable, consisting mainly of wide basins scarred by long, west–east-trending fractures and studded with myriad seamounts, thousands of which breach the sea surface to form islands and atolls.

The Pacific Ocean yields approximately 50 percent of the world's tuna catch.

In the kelp forests off the west coast of North America, the diversity of species rivals that of tropical rain forests.

NATURAL RESOURCES

The Pacific yields 60 percent of the world's fish catch, with the Northwest Pacific alone providing one-quarter of the entire global catch in recent years. Offshore oil and gas reserves are especially important for China, the U.S.A., Australia, and New Zealand. Sand and gravel are mined in most seaboard nations, and phosphates are extracted off the coasts of Australia, California, and Peru. Metallic nodules are common on the ocean floor, but the high cost of retrieval means that they are not yet mined commercially. The Pacific has by far the most extensive coral reefs of any ocean, which in many regions generate significant revenue from tourism.

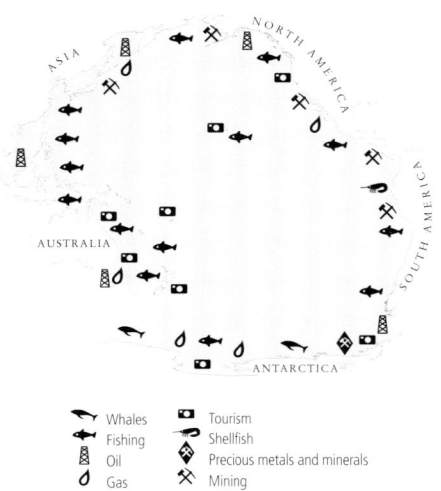

- ⚓ Whales
- 🐟 Fishing
- 🛢 Oil
- 💧 Gas
- 📷 Tourism
- 🦪 Shellfish
- 💎 Precious metals and minerals
- ⛏ Mining

THE MARIANA TRENCH

Arcing for 1,580 miles (2,550 km) around the Mariana Islands, the Mariana Trench is the deepest part of the Pacific Ocean and the world's deepest ocean trench. Formed as a result of the Pacific Plate being forced beneath the Philippine Plate—the Mariana Islands are the tips of volcanoes created by this subduction—it reaches 35,826 feet (10,920 m) below sea level at Challenger Deep. This site was named for the British survey ship *Challenger II*, the first vessel to survey the trench, in 1951. In 1960, Jacques Piccard and Donald Walsh descended here in the U.S. bathyscaph *Trieste* to a depth of 35,797 feet (10,911 m), a record that remains unsurpassed.

In May 2000, Kavachi, an undersea volcano in the Solomon Islands, erupted, giving birth to a new island.

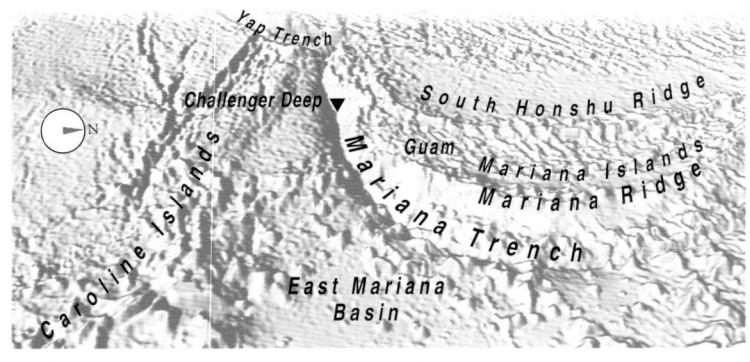

The humpback whales residing in Alaska in summer migrate to lower latitudes in winter.

The Pacific's coral reefs have six times as many fish species as those of the Caribbean Sea.

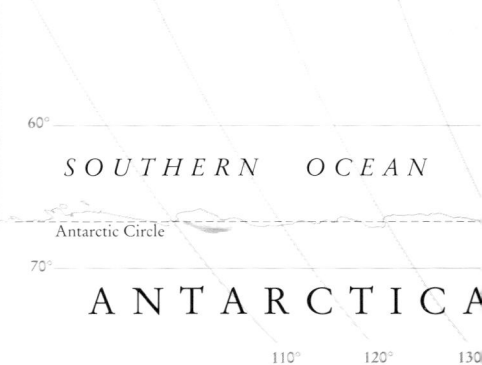

SCALE 1:50,000,000
Robinson Projection

0 ———— 1500 miles
0 ———— 1500 kilometers

Longitude east of Greenwich

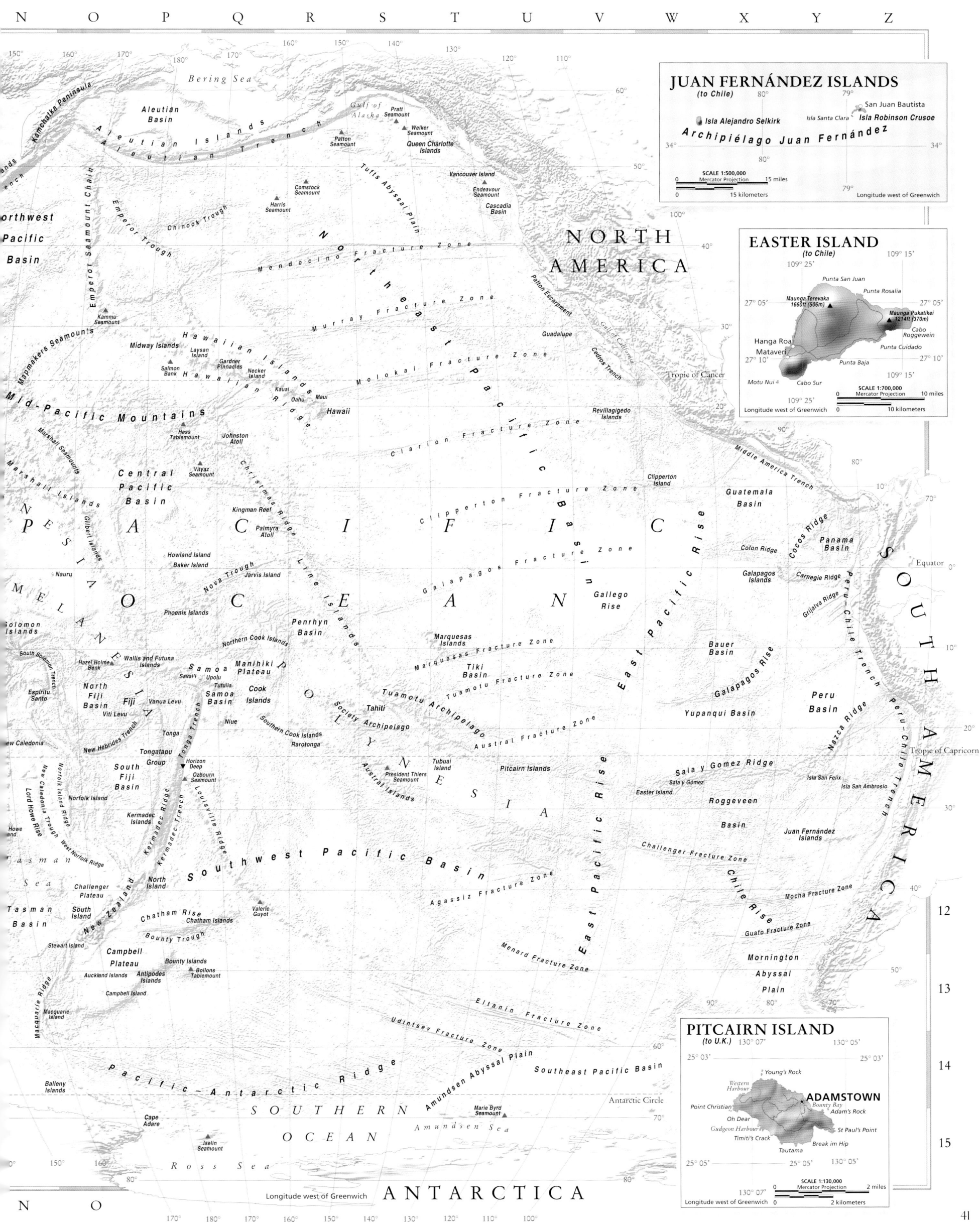

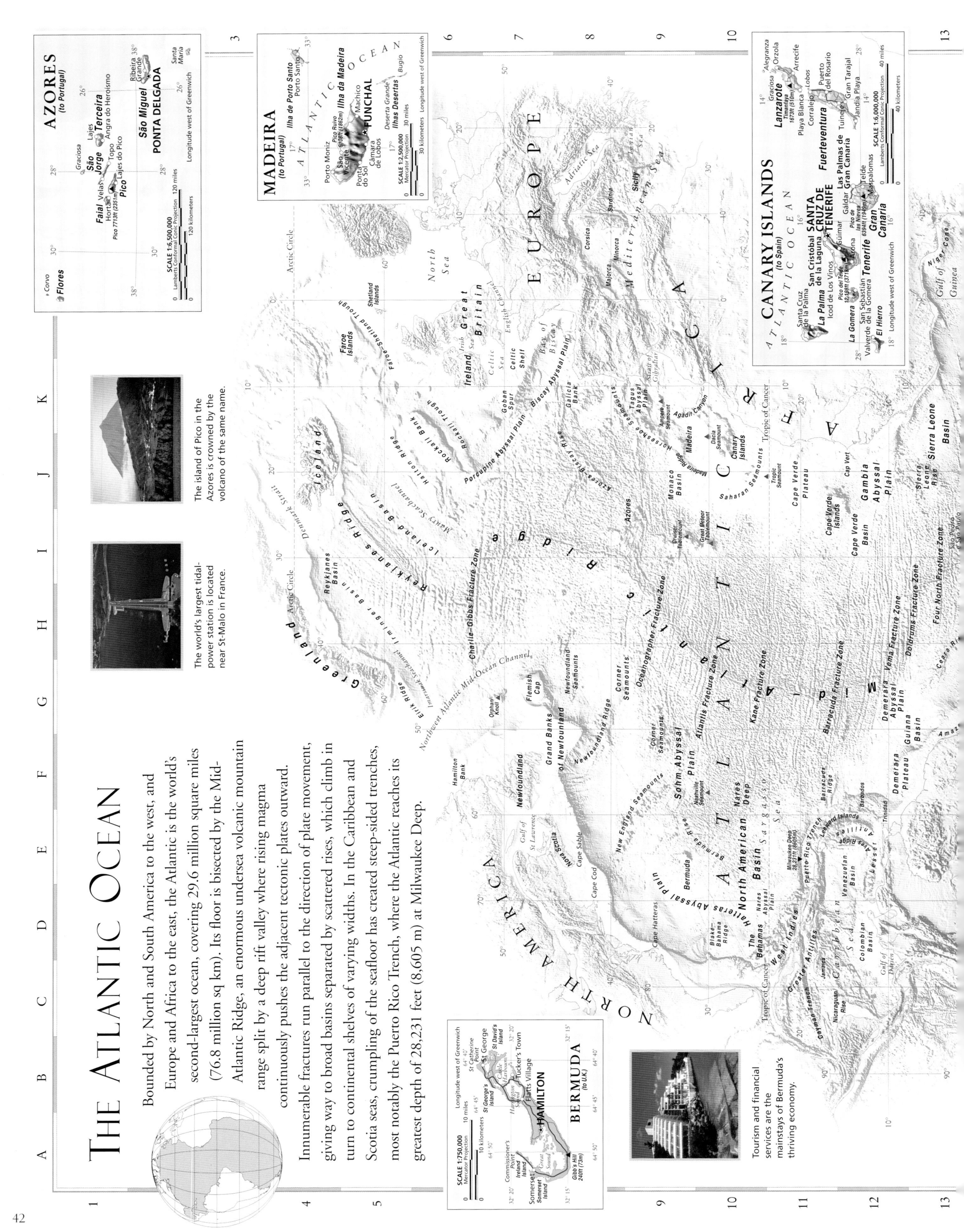

THE ATLANTIC OCEAN

Bounded by North and South America to the west, and Europe and Africa to the east, the Atlantic is the world's second-largest ocean, covering 29.6 million square miles (76.8 million sq km). Its floor is bisected by the Mid-Atlantic Ridge, an enormous undersea volcanic mountain range split by a deep rift valley where rising magma continuously pushes the adjacent tectonic plates outward. Innumerable fractures run parallel to the direction of plate movement, giving way to broad basins separated by scattered rises, which climb in turn to continental shelves of varying widths. In the Caribbean and Scotia seas, crumpling of the seafloor has created steep-sided trenches, most notably the Puerto Rico Trench, where the Atlantic reaches its greatest depth of 28,231 feet (8,605 m) at Milwaukee Deep.

The island of Pico in the Azores is crowned by the volcano of the same name.

The world's largest tidal-power station is located near St-Malo in France.

Tourism and financial services are the mainstays of Bermuda's thriving economy.

AZORES
(to Portugal)

Corvo
Flores
Graciosa
São Jorge
Terceira
Velas
Lajes
Topo Angra do Heroísmo
Lajes do Pico
Faial Velas
Horta
Pico 7713ft (2351m)
Pico
São Miguel
PONTA DELGADA
Ribeira 38°
Grande
Santa Maria

SCALE 1:6,500,000
Lamberts Conformal Conic Projection
0   120 kilometers
0   120 miles
Longitude west of Greenwich

MADEIRA
(to Portugal)

Porto Moniz
Porto Santo
Ilha de Porto Santo
Pico Ruivo
Ilha da Madeira Machico
Pico Ruivo 6106ft (1862m)
FUNCHAL
Câmara de Lobos
Ponta do Sol
Deserta Grande
Ilhas Desertas
Bugio
Ilha das Deserta
Cabo Girão

SCALE 1:2,500,000
Mercator Projection
0   30 kilometers
0   30 miles
Longitude west of Greenwich

CANARY ISLANDS
(to Spain)

Alegranza
Graciosa Orzola
Lanzarote Arrecife
Timanfaya
1673ft (510m) Corralejo Lobos
Playa Blanca
Puerto del Rosario
Fuerteventura
Gran Tarajal
Tuineje
La Palma
Santa Cruz
de la Palma
SANTA CRUZ DE TENERIFE
San Cristóbal
de la Laguna
Icod de los Vinos
Pico del Teide
12198ft (3718m)
Tenerife
La Gomera
San Sebastián
de la Gomera
El Hierro
Valverde
Las Nieves
Gáldar
Teror
Teide
6594ft (1949m)
Gran Canaria
Las Palmas de
Gran Canaria
Güímar Arona
Maspalomas

SCALE 1:6,000,000
Lamberts Conformal Conic Projection
0   40 kilometers
0   40 miles
Longitude west of Greenwich

BERMUDA
(to U.K.)

Commissioner's Point
Ireland Island
Somerset Island
St Catherine Point
St George
St David's Island
St George's Island
Castle Harbour
Tucker's Town
HAMILTON
Harrington Sound
Flatts Village
Gibb's Hill
260ft (73m)
Great Sound
Little Sound
Longitude west of Greenwich

SCALE 1:750,000
Mercator Projection
0   10 kilometers
0   10 miles

TRISTAN DA CUNHA
(to U.K.)

SETTLEMENT OF EDINBURGH

Queen Mary's Peak
2060m (6760ft)

Tristan da Cunha

SCALE 1:1,250,000
Mercator Projection

Stoltenhoff Island • Middle Island
Inaccessible Island • Nightingale Island

Longitude west of Greenwich

Rookery Point
Stonyhill Point
North Point
East Point

ST HELENA
(to U.K.)

JAMESTOWN

Diana's Peak
2700ft (823m)

Sugar Loaf Point
Bennett's Point
Barn Long Point
Prosperous Bay
Gill Point
Longwood
George Island
Egg Island
South West Point
Manati Bay
Sandy Bay
Speery Island • Castle Rock Point

Flagstaff

SCALE 1:750,000
Mercator Projection

Longitude west of Greenwich

ASCENSION
(to U.K.)

GEORGETOWN

The Peak
▲ 2818ft (859m)

North East Bay
English Bay
North Point
Porpoise Point
Two Boats Village
Unicorn Point
Clarence Bay
Main Base
Portland
South West Bay
Pillar Bay
Point
South Point

SCALE 1:750,000
Mercator Projection

Longitude west of Greenwich

SOUTH AMERICA

ATLANTIC OCEAN

SOUTHERN OCEAN

ANTARCTICA

Congo Cone
Angola Basin
Orange Cone
Cape Basin
Agulhas Basin
Cape Agulhas
Agulhas Bank
Cape of Good Hope
Namibia Abyssal Plain
Valdivia Seamount
Ewing Seamount
Erica Seamount
Schmidt-Ott Seamount
Vema Seamount
Meteor Rise
Discovery Seamount
Shona Ridge
Bouvetøya
Spiess Seamount
Maud Rise
Astrid Ridge
Lazarev Sea
Larsen Sea
Antarctic Circle
Raiser-
Pernambuco Abyssal Plain
Fernando de Noronha
Pernambuco Seamounts
Stocks Seamount
Grell Seamount
Hotspur Seamount
Abrolhos Bank
Vitória Seamount
Columbia Seamount
Ilhas Martin Vas
Ilha da Trindade
St Helena
Ascension
Bode Verde Fracture Zone
Saint Helena Fracture Zone
Tropic of Capricorn
Rio Grande Fracture Zone
Tristan da Cunha Fracture Zone
Gough Fracture Zone
Tristan da Cunha
Gough Island
Crawford Seamount
West Seamount
Zapiola Seamount
Santos Plateau
Rio Grande Gap
Rio Grande Rise
Argentine Basin
Argentine Abyssal Plain
Zapiola Ridge
Falkland Escarpment
Falkland Plateau
Falkland Islands
Burwood Bank
Shag Rocks
South Georgia
Scotia Ridge
Islas Orcadas Rise
East Scotia Basin
South Sandwich Islands
South Sandwich Trench
Scotia Sea
South Orkney Islands
Georg von Neumayer Ridge
Jane Basin
Powell Basin
South Shetland Islands
South Scotia Ridge
South Shetland Trough
Weddell Sea
Weddell Abyssal Plain
Berkner Island
Antarctic Peninsula
Alexander Island
Tierra del Fuego
Cape Horn
Yaghan Basin
Drake Passage
West Scotia Basin
Golfo San Matías
Golfo de San Jorge
Tropic of Capricorn
Antarctic Circle
Longitude west of Greenwich

The Atlantic's busiest shipping routes connect Western Europe with the U.S.A.

NATURAL RESOURCES

Upwellings of cold, nutrient-rich water on continental shelves give rise to huge plankton blooms that support large fish stocks, notably of cod and haddock in the north, and hake and tuna in the south. But the formerly productive Atlantic fisheries have been overexploited and many species are depleted. As much as one-third of the world's oil and gas may lie under the Atlantic coastal shelves; large deposits are being exploited in the North Sea and Gulf of Mexico, and off Newfoundland and West Africa. Sand and gravels are mined in U.S. and U.K. waters, and placer deposits of gemstones and other minerals are retrieved from many river mouths. Huge tides in Canada and France are harnessed to generate electricity.

Fishing
Whales
Shellfish
Precious metals and minerals
Mining
Oil production
Gas production
Tourism

EUROPE
AFRICA
NORTH AMERICA
SOUTH AMERICA
ANTARCTICA

SCALE 1:48,000,000
Miller Projection

Longitude west of Greenwich

CAPE VERDE

PRAIA

Santo Antão
São Vicente
Santa Luzia
São Nicolau
Sal
Santa Maria
Boa Vista
Maio
São Tiago
Fogo
Brava
Mt Fogo
2829m (9281ft)

Ponta do Sol
Porto Novo
Mindelo
Vila da Ribeira Brava
Tarrafal
Vila do Tarrafal
Pedra Badejo
Porto Rincão
São Filipe
Vila Nova Sintra
Curral Velho
Porto Inglês
Vila da Sal Rei

Branco
Raso

SCALE 1:7,000,000
Mercator Projection

Longitude west of Greenwich

ATLANTIC OCEAN

THE ARCTIC OCEAN

Covering 5.5 million square miles (14.1 million sq km), the Arctic Ocean is the world's smallest ocean. It is ringed by the continental fringes of North America, Europe, and Asia, as well as associated islands, including the largest island on Earth, Greenland. The ocean reaches depths of over 18,000 feet (5,500 m) and is divided into major basins by extensive undersea ranges, the largest of which, the Lomonosov Ridge, surpasses 10,000 feet (3,000 m) in height. Pack ice covers most of the sea surface year-round, expanding to reach most surrounding landmasses in winter. This shoreline has been inhabited by indigenous groups such as the North American Inuit, Asian Yakut, and European Saami for thousands of years. They have learned to cope with the Arctic's extreme climate, including months of darkness in winter, and exploit its restricted range of biological resources. Europeans first explored the Arctic Ocean in the 16th century, searching for a shortcut between Europe and Asia. More recently, outsiders have been lured here by the discovery of potentially vast undersea mineral reserves.

NATURAL RESOURCES

The Arctic Ocean's pack ice blocks sunlight, inhibiting photosynthetic processes and limiting marine life, but rich fisheries exist in areas of open ocean such as the Barents, Greenland, and Bering seas. Seals and whales were long a valuable resource for native peoples and, from the late 17th century, the basis of lucrative commercial trades operated by Europeans. Whaling is now banned, but sealing still takes place in Newfoundland and the White Sea. Sparse grazing lands fringe the ocean, providing food for wild caribou in North America and about 3 million domesticated reindeer in Scandinavia and Russia. Huge reserves of oil, coal, and gas have been tapped in northern Siberia and Alaska; even larger supplies are thought to lie offshore, but so far remain inaccessible.

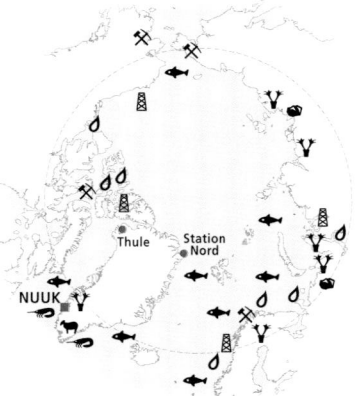

- Sheep
- Fishing
- Shellfish
- Mining
- Oil
- Gas
- Reindeer
- Coal

GREENLAND AND ICELAND

At the boundary between the Arctic and Atlantic oceans, the narrow Denmark Strait divides Greenland from the much smaller island of Iceland. About two-thirds of Greenland lies within the Arctic Circle, and the northern tip of the island lies just 500 miles (800 km) from the North Pole. More than 80 percent of the landmass is blanketed by the world's second-largest ice sheet. Cupped within a basin encircled by coastal peaks, it has an average thickness of about 5,000 feet (1,500 m). Iceland sits astride the Reykjanes Ridge, part of the Mid-Atlantic Ridge. Divergence of tectonic plates along this boundary steadily tears the island apart, giving rise to great faults as well as volcanoes and geysers.

ELEVATION

Feet	Meters
Ice cap	
Ice shelf	
6562	2000
4921	1500
3281	1000
2461	750
1640	500
1312	400
984	300
656	200
328	100
0	0
Below sea level	
0	0

The polar ice pack is 10 feet (3 m) thick on average, but ridges form that may be up to three times that depth.

Directly beneath the North Pole, the ocean is 13,410 feet (4,087 m) deep.

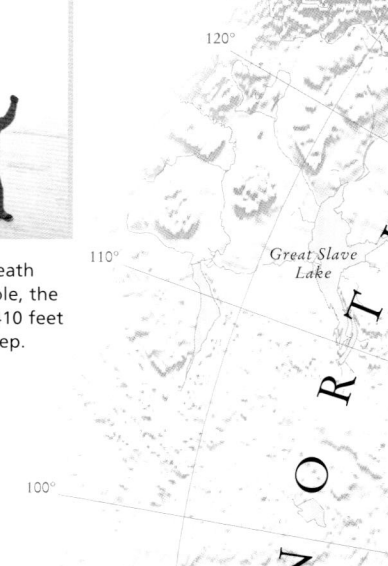

In winter, the Arctic fox grows a white coat to blend in with the snow.

About 3,000 people live on Svalbard, working mainly in coal extraction.

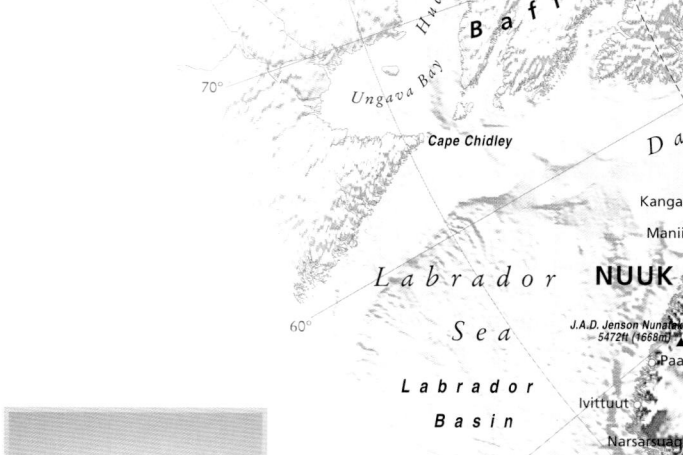

Yakut hunters in the Siberian Arctic employ modern means to catch traditional prey, including seals and walruses.

Thule

Station Nord

NUUK

NORTH AM

Macken

Great Bear Lake

Great Slave Lake

Coronation Gulf

Queen Maud Gulf

King William Island

Boot Penin

Hudson Bay

Southampton Island

Coats Island

Mansel Island

Foxe Basin

Foxe Peninsula

Melville Peninsula

Prince Charles Island

Hudson Strait

Baffin Isla

Ungava Bay

Cape Chidley

Dav

Kangaam

Maniitso

Labrador Sea

NUUK

J.A.D. Jenson Nunataker 5472ft (1668m)

Labrador Basin

Paami

Ivittuut

Narsarsuaq

Apostolens Tommelfinger 7510ft (2289m)

Nanortalik

Kap F

Baffin Island

Davis Strait

NUUK

Greenland

Ammassalik

Ittoqqortoormiit

Denmark Strait

Iceland

Reykjanes Ridge

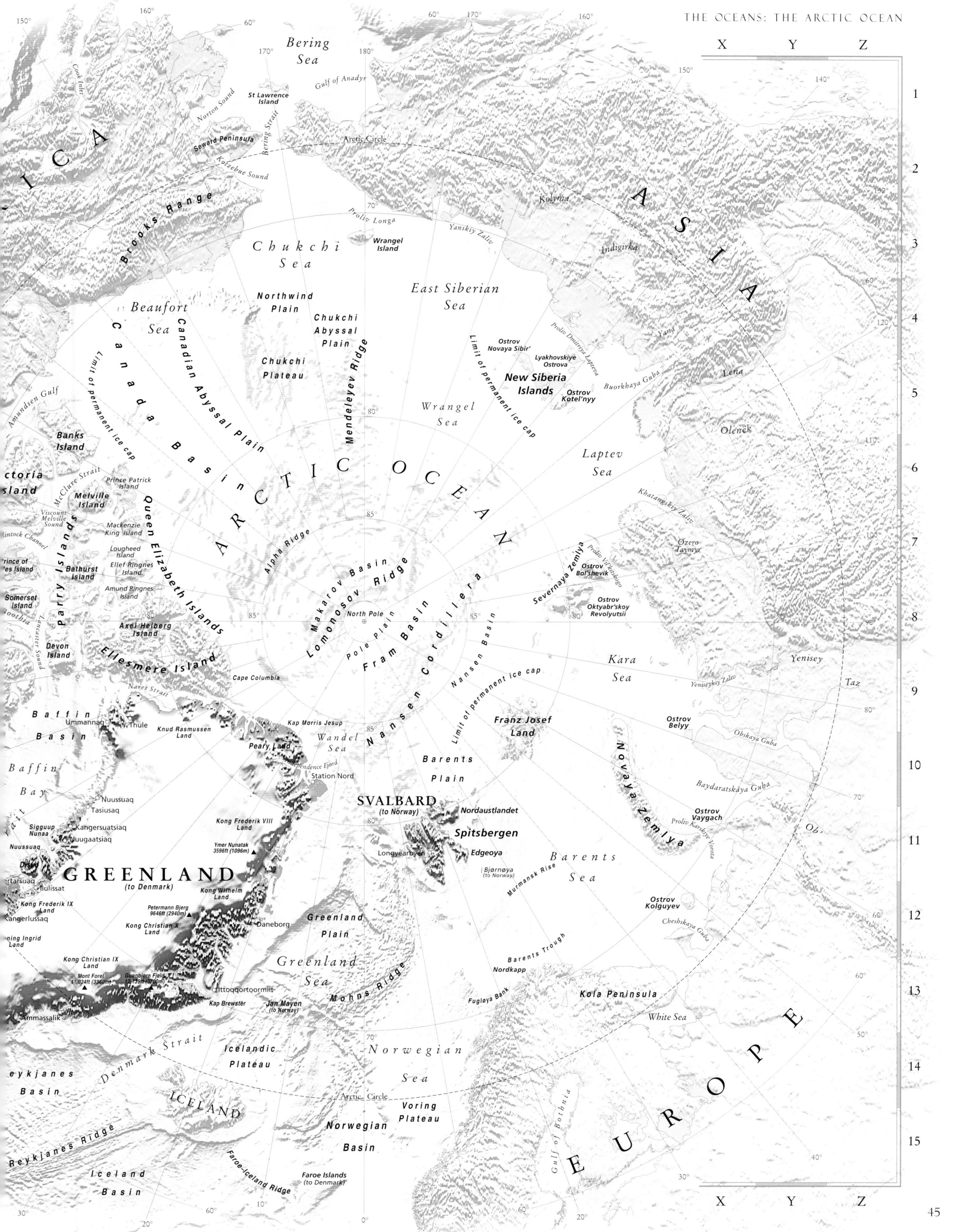

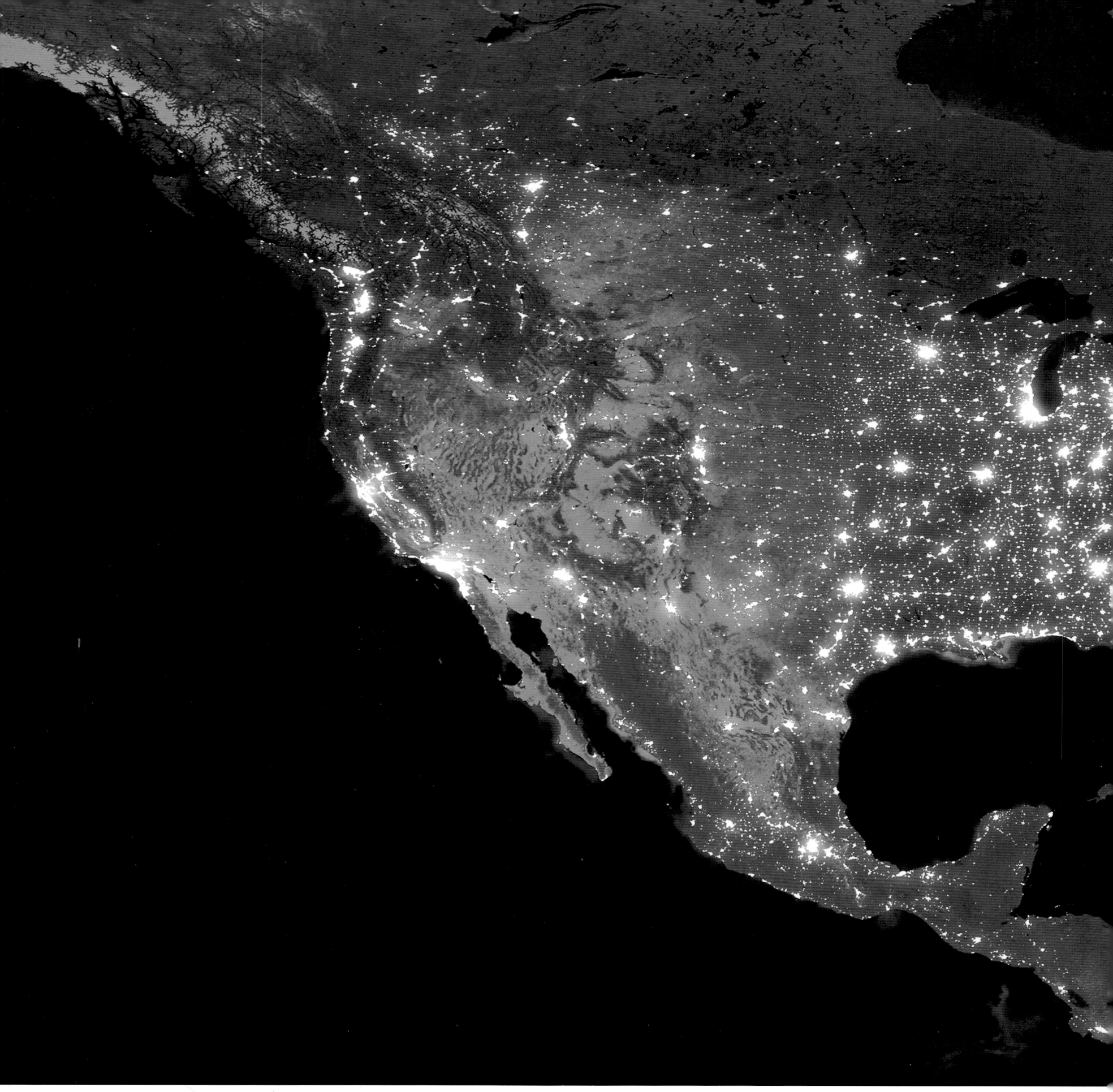

This image from space reveals the concentration of people and infrastructure in the eastern part of the North American continent. The interstate highways create a lattice pattern across the United States, connecting the bright areas of the city centers.

NORTH AMERICA

ABOVE NORTH AMERICA

Satellite photography reveals North America's extraordinary diversity of landforms, from the huge glaciated arc around Hudson Bay to the vast lowlands of the Great Plains in the center of the continent and the high spine of mountain ranges that run down the west coast. Often national borders can also be detected. This is due to differing land use practices between the nations that share the continent. In the north, the rolling wheatfields of Montana, in the United States, give way abruptly to Canadian rangeland. In the south, the border between the U.S. and Mexico is one of the few places on the planet where a highly developed nation adjoins a developing one. The contrast is graphically illustrated in false-color images, which display vegetation in shades of red. The view from space is now a vital tool in agriculture, providing information on the extent, health, and progress of crops.

Mexico-U.S. border
Above right: Highlighted by this false-color image, the boundary between the U.S. and Mexico becomes startlingly apparent. The gridded and irrigated agricultural fields of California's Imperial Valley, north of the border, contrast vividly with Mexico's less developed lands. The border town of Mexicali-Calexico is in the center.

Coffee plantations, Hawaii, U.S.A.
Right: This composite image of Hawaiian coffee plantations was created from more than 300 images collected over four hours by an uninhabited aerial vechicle (UAV). Differences in the color of the coffee fields indicate varying levels of ripeness. This information was used in planning which fields to harvest first.

Grand Canyon, Arizona, U.S.A
Right: Snow lies on the north and south rims of the Grand Canyon, Arizona, starkly outlining the mighty swathe scoured out by the Colorado River. A lack of vegetation further accentuates the impact of this dramatic landform. The canyon's south rim, on the left of this image, is a vertical mile (1.6 km) above the snow-free floor.

Malaspina Glacier, Alaska, U.S.A
Far right: The Malaspina Glacier fans out in a broad tongue between Icy Bay and Yakutat Bay, Alaska. The red ridged area is a terminal moraine of rocks, deposited by the glacier and now protecting it from contact with the open ocean, shown as dark blue. The glacier has thinned since this image was acquired in August 2000.

LAND AND ENVIRONMENT

Stretching from the Arctic Circle almost to the Equator, North America covers 9.5 million square miles (24.6 million sq km) and is the third-largest continent. It is bounded by ocean on all sides and linked to South America only by the slender Isthmus of Panama. As well as the mainland, it includes Greenland, the islands of the Caribbean (the West Indies), and the Hawaiian Islands, which lie 2,500 miles (4,000 km) away, in the middle of the Pacific Ocean. Mountains dominate the west and south of the mainland, coastal ranges running from Alaska to Panama and the Rocky Mountains arcing through Canada and the United States. East of the Rockies lie the plateau of the Great Plains and the lowlands of the Canadian Shield and U.S. Midwest. The lowlands extend to the Gulf of Mexico in the south; in the east and north, they are bounded by ancient mountains, including the Appalachian Mountains, the Laurentian Mountains, and the uplands of Labrador.

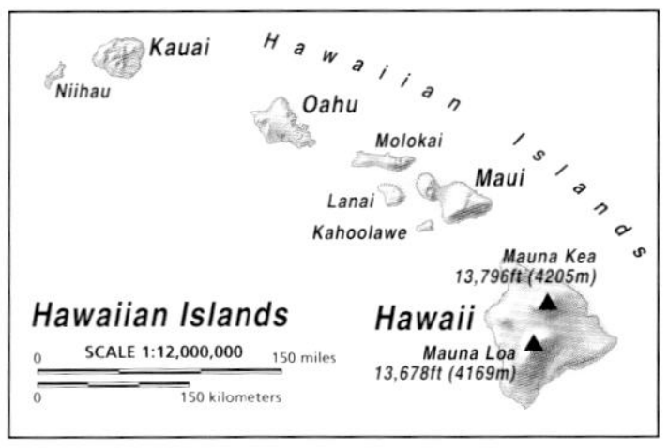

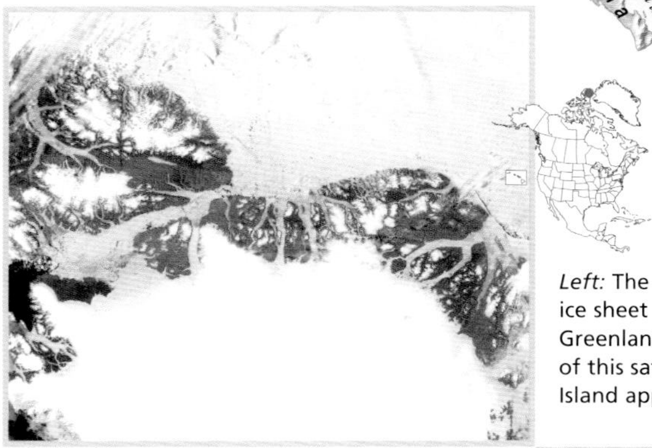

NATURAL HAZARDS

Tornadoes

Tornadoes occur in many parts of the world but are most strongly associated with and most common in the United States—about 1,000 are recorded there each year. At certain times of the year, cold air from the Arctic meets warm, moist air from the tropics over the central and eastern U.S.A., fueling atmospheric instability and thunderstorms. On occasions, wind patterns cause a storm to rotate, creating a spinning column of air, or tornado. Generating powerful updrafts and fearsome winds of up to 300 mph (480 km/h), a tornado can obliterate almost anything in its path.

AVERAGE NUMBER OF TORNADOES PER YEAR PER 10,000 SQUARE MILES (26,000 SQ KM)

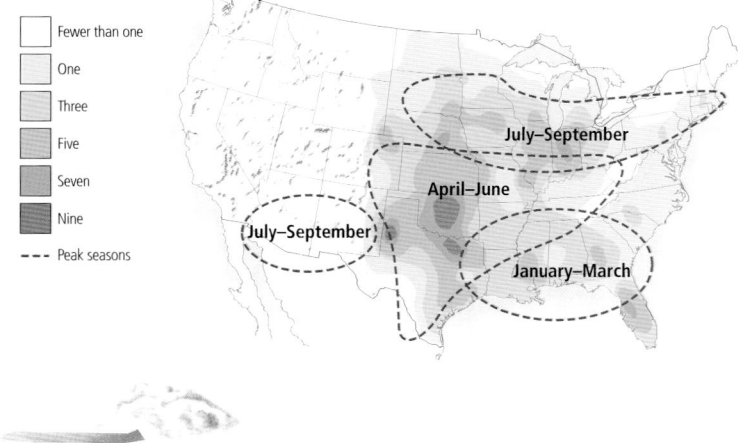

- Fewer than one
- One
- Three
- Five
- Seven
- Nine
- --- Peak seasons

July–September
April–June
July–September
January–March

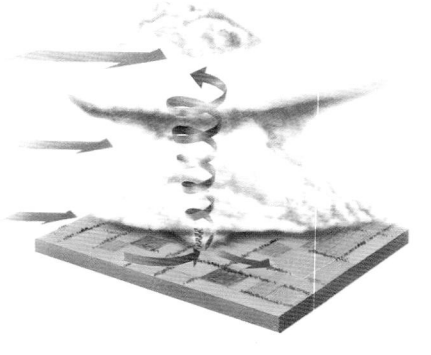

When a large storm turns, a spinning column of air may form at the heart of the cloud and move gradually downward. When it touches the ground, it becomes a tornado.

The outline of a tornado may be enhanced by condensation or the dust and debris it draws skyward.

Left: The world's second-largest ice sheet covers 80 percent of Greenland, shown at the bottom of this satellite image. Ellesmere Island appears at top left.

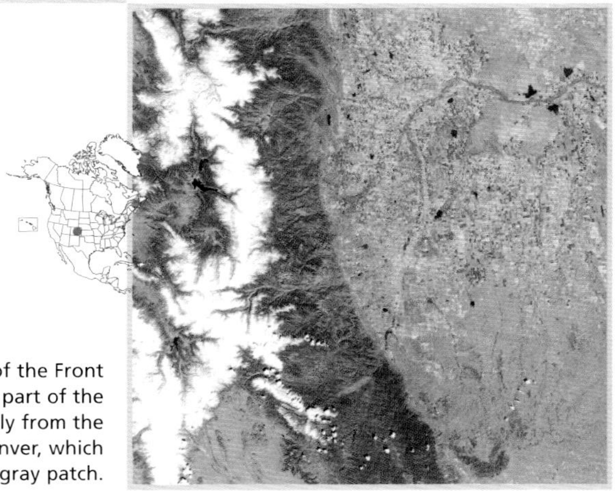

Right: The peaks of the Front Range, the tallest part of the Rockies, rise abruptly from the plains west of Denver, which appears here as a pale gray patch.

Hawaiian Islands
Kauai
Niihau
Oahu
Molokai
Lanai
Maui
Kahoolawe
Hawaiian Islands
SCALE 1:12,000,000
150 miles
150 kilometers
Hawaii
Mauna Kea 13,796ft (4205m)
Mauna Loa 13,678ft (4169m)

ASIA
Chukchi Sea
Bering Strait
Bering Sea
Aleutian Islands
Aleutian Range
PACIFIC OCEAN
Gulf of Alaska
Alaska Range
Mt McKinley 20,321ft (6194m)
Brooks Range
Yukon
Beaufort Sea
Banks Island
Victoria Island
Mackenzie Mountains
Coast Mountains
Great Bear Lake
Peace
Great Slave Lake
Athabasca
Lake Athabasca
Reindeer Lake
North
Saskatchewan
South
Queen Elizabeth Islands
Axel Heiberg Island
Ellef Ringnes Island
Ellesmere Island
Parry Islands
Melville Island
Bathurst Island
Devon Island
Somerset Island
Prince of Wales Island
Boothia Peninsula
Melville Peninsula
Foxe Basin
Baffin Bay
Baffin Island
Hudson
Pénin d'Ung
Hudson Bay
Canadian Shield
Lake Winnipeg
Lake Manitoba
Lake Nipigon
Lake Superior
Great Lakes
Lake Michigan
Great Plains
Central Lowlands
Missouri
Mississippi
Ohio
Arkansas
Gulf-Atlantic Coas
Mississippi Delta
Gulf of Mexico
Yucata Peninsu
Columbia
Cascade Range
Mt Rainier 14,409ft (4392m)
Snake
Great Salt Lake
Great Basin
Coast Ranges
Sierra Nevada
Mt Whitney 14,495ft (4418m)
Mojave Desert
Grand Canyon
Colorado Plateau
Mt Elbert 14,432ft (4399m)
Rocky Mountains
Colorado
Sonoran Desert
Baja California
Gulf of California
Sierra Madre Occidental
Rio Grande
Sierra Madre Oriental
Volcan Popocatepetl 17,887ft (5452m)
Pico de Orizaba 18,405ft (5610m)
Sierra Madre del Sur
Hawaiian Islands
G r
Gr
Ellesmere Island

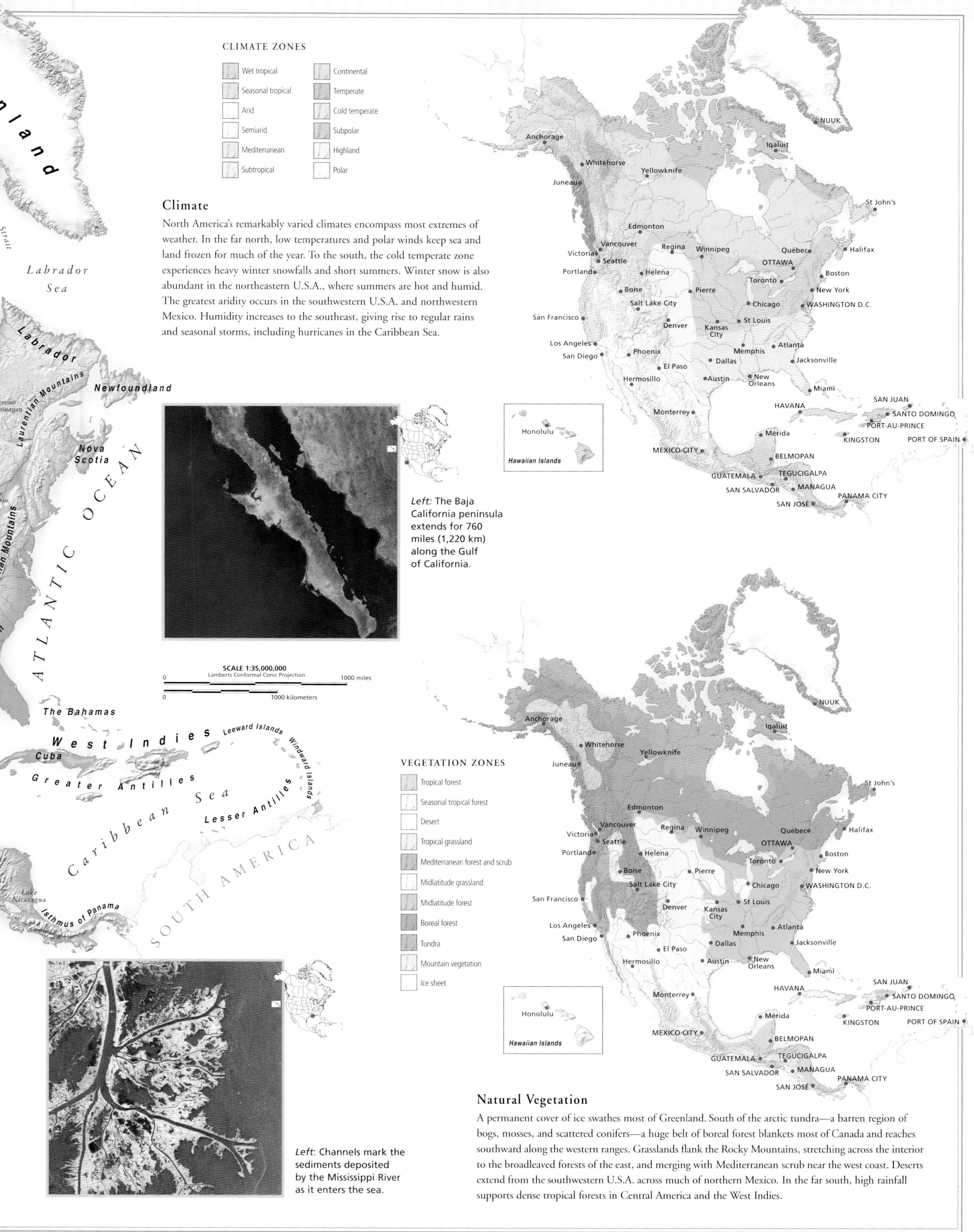

CLIMATE ZONES

- Wet tropical
- Seasonal tropical
- Arid
- Semiarid
- Mediterranean
- Subtropical
- Continental
- Temperate
- Cold temperate
- Subpolar
- Highland
- Polar

Climate

North America's remarkably varied climates encompass most extremes of weather. In the far north, low temperatures and polar winds keep sea and land frozen for much of the year. To the south, the cold temperate zone experiences heavy winter snowfalls and short summers. Winter snow is also abundant in the northeastern U.S.A., where summers are hot and humid. The greatest aridity occurs in the southwestern U.S.A. and northwestern Mexico. Humidity increases to the southeast, giving rise to regular rains and seasonal storms, including hurricanes in the Caribbean Sea.

Left: The Baja California peninsula extends for 760 miles (1,220 km) along the Gulf of California.

SCALE 1:35,000,000
Lamberts Conformal Conic Projection

0   1000 miles

0   1000 kilometers

VEGETATION ZONES

- Tropical forest
- Seasonal tropical forest
- Desert
- Tropical grassland
- Mediterranean forest and scrub
- Midlatitude grassland
- Midlatitude forest
- Boreal forest
- Tundra
- Mountain vegetation
- Ice sheet

Left: Channels mark the sediments deposited by the Mississippi River as it enters the sea.

Natural Vegetation

A permanent cover of ice swathes most of Greenland. South of the arctic tundra—a barren region of bogs, mosses, and scattered conifers—a huge belt of boreal forest blankets most of Canada and reaches southward along the western ranges. Grasslands flank the Rocky Mountains, stretching across the interior to the broadleaved forests of the east, and merging with Mediterranean scrub near the west coast. Deserts extend from the southwestern U.S.A. across much of northern Mexico. In the far south, high rainfall supports dense tropical forests in Central America and the West Indies.

PEOPLES AND NATIONS

North America has a population of about 500 million and includes 23 nations and 16 dependencies and territories. These can be divided broadly between the large, affluent, industrialized, predominantly English-speaking nations of Canada and the United States of America (U.S.A.), and the smaller, less affluent, mainly agricultural and Spanish-speaking countries and territories to the south. More than three-quarters of Americans and Canadians are descended from European immigrants, and one-eighth from African slaves; another eighth is of Hispanic origin. Native peoples now account for less than one percent of the population. In the south, Amerindian peoples are significantly outnumbered by mestizos—people of mixed Spanish and Amerindian descent—and also, in the West Indies, by people of African and mixed African–Spanish origin.

The population of Mexico City expanded dramatically in the second half of the 20th century, increasing sixfold between 1950 and 2000. In comparison, New York's population grew by just 25 percent in the same period. Mexico City overtook New York as North America's largest urban center in the mid-1990s and is now the world's third-biggest city.

FLASHPOINTS

Central America and the Caribbean have experienced frequent political instability, often as a result of uprisings or military coups. On several occasions, the United States has intervened, overtly and covertly, to protect its interests in the region.

Belize–Guatemala Border

Since 1821, when it became independent, Guatemala has laid claim to a large area of southern Belize and refused to recognize the latter's western boundary (though it finally recognized its independence in 1991). In recent years, incidents involving alleged illegal settlers and armed forces have led to a number of deaths and increased tension between the two countries.

South Cay

Honduras and Nicaragua have been in dispute over the tiny and uninhabited but potentially oil-rich island of South Cay (Cayo Sur) in the Caribbean Sea since 1999, when Honduras asserted its claim to the island by ratifying the 1986 Caribbean Sea Maritime Limits Treaty with Colombia. This has led to increased military activity on both sides of the common land border.

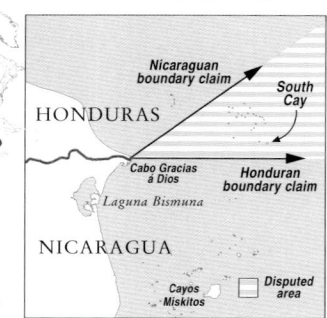

Guantanamo Bay, Cuba

Cuba achieved independence from Spain in 1898, following U.S. military intervention. Despite the 1959 communist revolution that brought Fidel Castro to power, the subsequent imposition by the U.S.A. of an embargo on trade with Cuba, and strong Cuban opposition to its presence, an American naval base still operates at Guantanamo Bay.

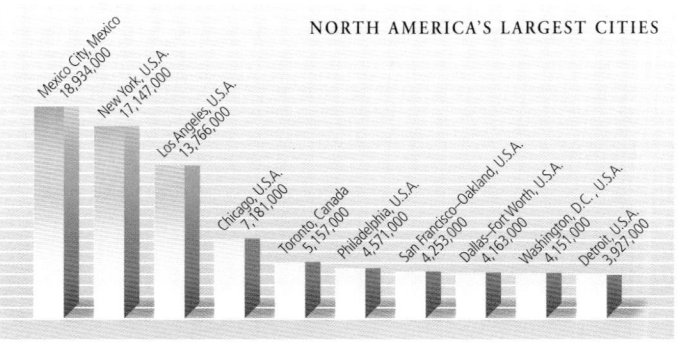

Mexico City, Mexico 18,934,000
New York, U.S.A. 17,147,000
Los Angeles, U.S.A. 13,766,000
Chicago, U.S.A. 7,181,000
Toronto, Canada 5,157,000
Philadelphia, U.S.A. 4,571,000
San Francisco–Oakland, U.S.A. 4,253,000
Dallas–Fort Worth, U.S.A. 4,163,000
Washington, D.C., U.S.A. 4,151,000
Detroit, U.S.A. 3,927,000

Urbanization

Most of North America's largest urban areas are located in the highly industrialized United States and Canada, where four-fifths of inhabitants live in towns and cities. Even in the traditionally agricultural regions of Mexico, Central America, and the West Indies, urbanization has increased dramatically, rising to approximately 65 percent. Many cities in these regions have struggled to cope with the enormous influx of new residents, resulting in widespread social deprivation, most prominent in the form of slums and shanty towns on city fringes.

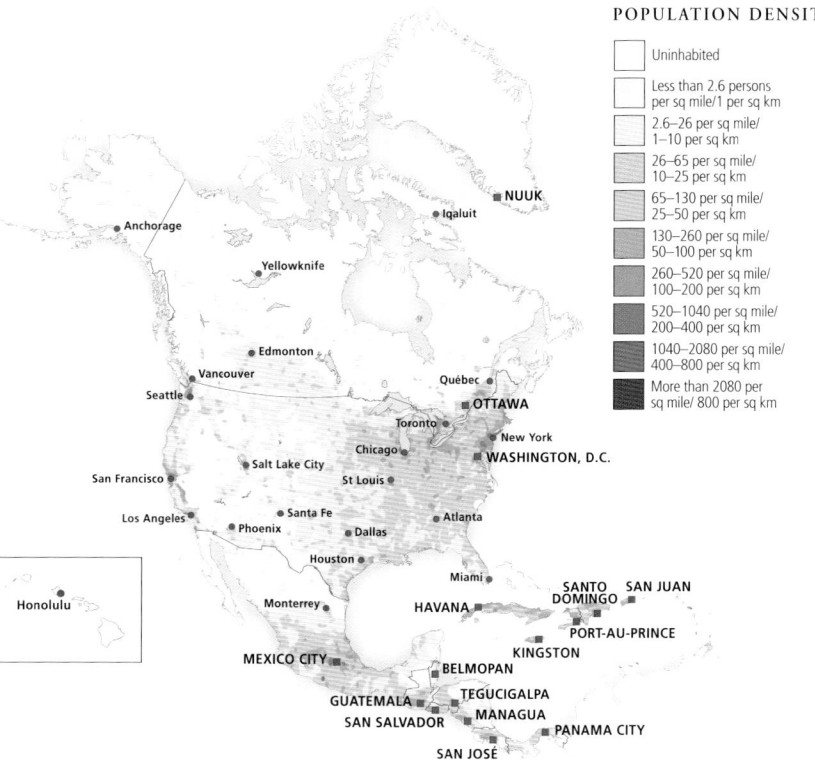

POPULATION DENSITY

- Uninhabited
- Less than 2.6 persons per sq mile/1 per sq km
- 2.6–26 per sq mile/ 1–10 per sq km
- 26–65 per sq mile/ 10–25 per sq km
- 65–130 per sq mile/ 25–50 per sq km
- 130–260 per sq mile/ 50–100 per sq km
- 260–520 per sq mile/ 100–200 per sq km
- 520–1040 per sq mile/ 200–400 per sq km
- 1040–2080 per sq mile/ 400–800 per sq km
- More than 2080 per sq mile/ 800 per sq km

Population Patterns

Rugged terrain, a harsh climate, and poor soil make the far north one of the world's most sparsely inhabited regions. Canada occupies two-fifths of the continent but, with 35 million inhabitants, has just 7 percent of its population. The U.S.A. has almost ten times as many people, who are heavily concentrated in the northeast and on the west coast. Both countries have low population growth by world standards. In contrast, growth is high in Mexico, Central America, and the West Indies, where the most densely settled areas are the uplands of the mainland and the Caribbean islands.

North American Trade Organizations

Signed by the U.S.A., Canada, and Mexico, the North American Free Trade Agreement (NAFTA) came into effect in 1994, creating the world's largest free-trade zone. The Central American Free Trade Zone (CAFTZ) includes El Salvador, Guatemala, Honduras, and Nicaragua. Mexico also belongs to the Latin American Integration Association (LAIA).

- North American Free Trade Agreement (NAFTA)
- Latin American Integration Association (LAIA)
- Central American Free Trade Zone (CAFTZ)

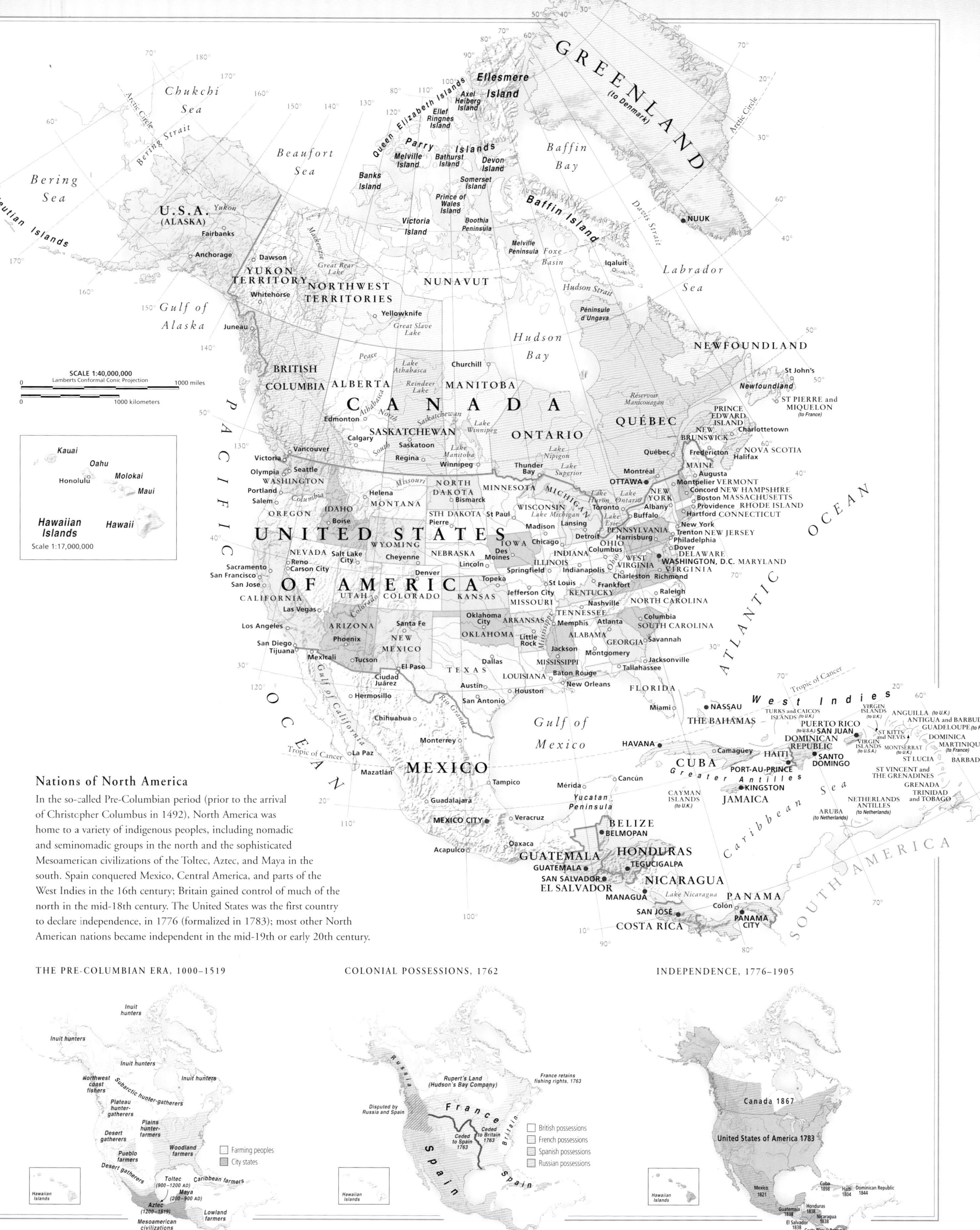

Nations of North America

In the so-called Pre-Columbian period (prior to the arrival of Christopher Columbus in 1492), North America was home to a variety of indigenous peoples, including nomadic and seminomadic groups in the north and the sophisticated Mesoamerican civilizations of the Toltec, Aztec, and Maya in the south. Spain conquered Mexico, Central America, and parts of the West Indies in the 16th century; Britain gained control of much of the north in the mid-18th century. The United States was the first country to declare independence, in 1776 (formalized in 1783); most other North American nations became independent in the mid-19th or early 20th century.

THE PRE-COLUMBIAN ERA, 1000–1519

COLONIAL POSSESSIONS, 1762

INDEPENDENCE, 1776–1905

THE HUMAN IMPACT

The environmental history of North America can be summarized as thousands of years of gradual modification followed by 500 years of astonishingly rapid change. Between the arrival of the first human settlers from Asia at least 15,000 years ago and Columbus's first visit in 1492, most North Americans lived in nomadic and seminomadic hunter-gatherer and, later, hunter-farmer communities. Large city states and empires were confined to Mesoamerica (of the continent's 30 million-plus inhabitants in 1492, 25 million lived south of the Rio Grande). The arrival of Europeans, particularly the mass immigrations of the late 18th and 19th centuries, transformed the landscape. Armed with developed technologies and presented with seemingly limitless resources, settlers razed forests, plowed grasslands, dug mines, and hunted wildlife at a phenomenal rate. The combination of huge tracts of arable land, abundant mineral resources, and political stability brought immense prosperity to the United States and Canada. In contrast, the south's more limited natural resources, rapid population growth, and volatile political situation resulted in slower economic development.

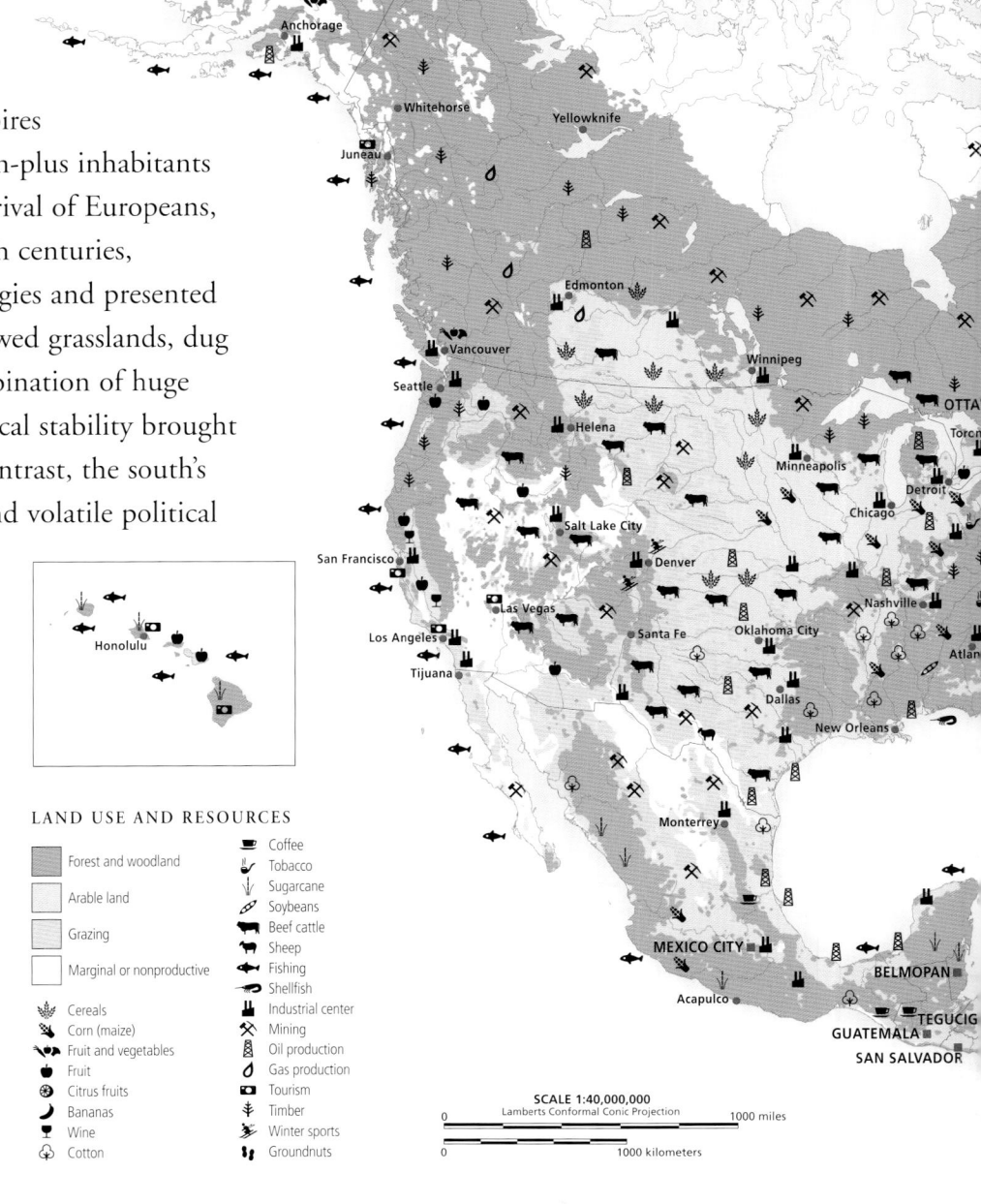

THE CHANGING FACE OF NORTH AMERICA

Prairies

The first Europeans to reach the interior lowlands of the present-day United States in the 17th century were amazed by the great seas of grasses that stretched from horizon to horizon—in places rising head-high—and teemed with millions of bison, antelope, deer, and sheep. But settlers arriving in the 1840s realized that the black soil in which the grasses grew was ideal for cultivation and soon began cutting and plowing. By the end of the 19th century, the soils were depleted and most of the grasses and mammals were gone. To date, losses of prairies on a state-by-state basis vary from 30 to 99 percent. Only a small percentage of tallgrass prairie remains, mainly as tiny remnants in parks and reserves.

ORIGINAL PRAIRIE COVER

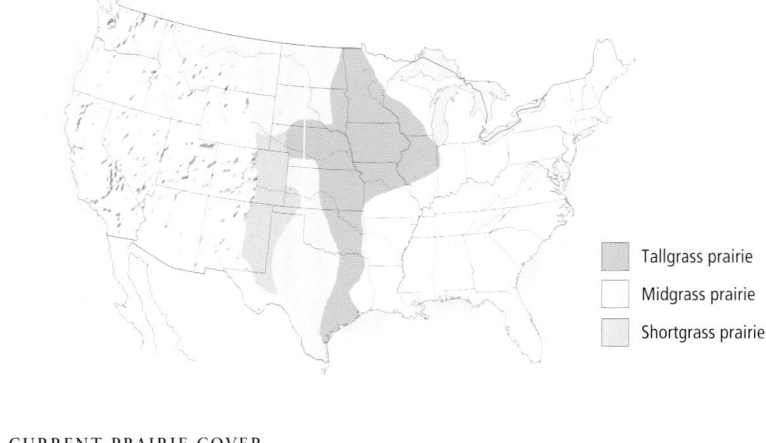

Tallgrass prairie
Midgrass prairie
Shortgrass prairie

CURRENT PRAIRIE COVER

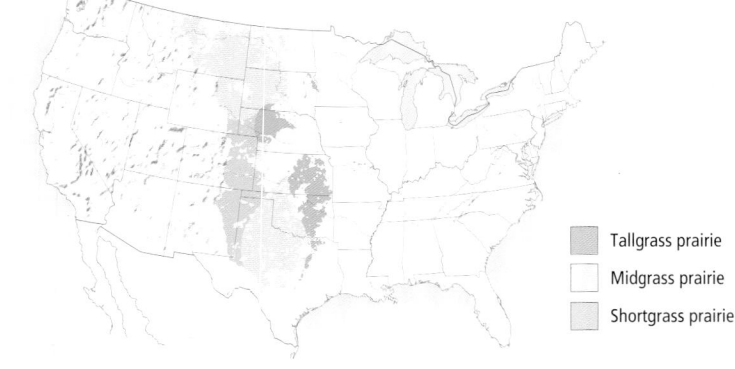

Tallgrass prairie
Midgrass prairie
Shortgrass prairie

LAND USE AND RESOURCES

Forest and woodland
Arable land
Grazing
Marginal or nonproductive

- Cereals
- Corn (maize)
- Fruit and vegetables
- Fruit
- Citrus fruits
- Bananas
- Wine
- Cotton

- Coffee
- Tobacco
- Sugarcane
- Soybeans
- Beef cattle
- Sheep
- Fishing
- Shellfish
- Industrial center
- Mining
- Oil production
- Gas production
- Tourism
- Timber
- Winter sports
- Groundnuts

SCALE 1:40,000,000
Lamberts Conformal Conic Projection
1000 miles
1000 kilometers

Economic Profile

Relative to its land area, North America has disproportionately high levels of natural resources. Some of the world's biggest coal fields lie in Alberta, Canada, and in the Appalachian Mountains; enormous oil reserves have been tapped in Texas, Alaska, and the Gulf of Mexico. Fresh water is abundant, though unevenly distributed: many parts of the western U.S.A. and Mexico depend on irrigation, and in Central America runoff and evaporation limit supplies. The north's highly mechanized agricultural sector makes the U.S.A. and Canada leading producers of crops such as wheat, corn, and soybeans. Home of the world's largest companies, the U.S.A. is the world's most productive nation, generating over 30 percent of global GDP, and also its leading importer and exporter.

Land Cover

Though much diminished, forests still cover a large swathe of the continent, chiefly in Canada. Most arable land lies in the north; in the south it is generally restricted to fertile volcanic uplands. Other types of land cover include the large marginal and nonproductive areas in the far north and western mountains, and significant urban sprawl: the U.S.A. alone has more than 4 million miles (6.4 million km) of roadways.

PROPORTIONS OF TOTAL LAND AREA

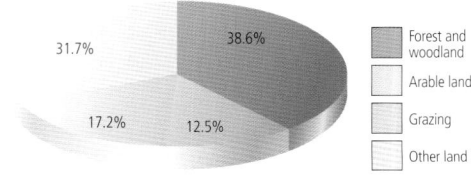

31.7%
38.6%
17.2%
12.5%

Forest and woodland
Arable land
Grazing
Other land

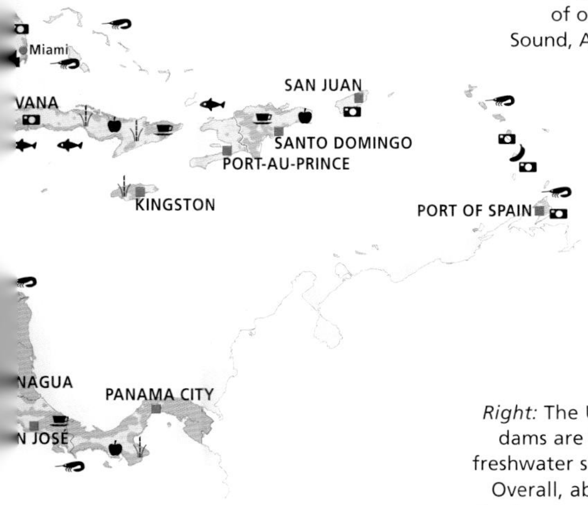

Right: In the mid-1990s, up to 12,500 people were dying every year in Mexico City as a result of air pollution. Antipollution measures have since reduced output of sulfur dioxide, carbon monoxide, and lead, but levels of other pollutants, including ozone, are still high.

Threats to the Environment

Industrialization, urban sprawl, and heavy dependence on automobiles make North America a major source of pollution, including by far the world's highest per-capita carbon dioxide emissions. Ocean pollution is particularly severe on the North Atlantic seaboard and in the northern Gulf of Mexico. Just one-third of the original forest cover remains; in the north commercial logging companies continue to fell old-growth forest, and in the south limited resources and growing populations pressurize governments to permit the razing of forest for farmland. North Americans are by far the highest per-capita consumers of natural resources and concerns are growing about resource depletion. Water tables are falling and rivers silting up, and some pessimistic forecasts even suggest that the U.S.A.'s known oil reserves could be exhausted by 2011.

Above: Overfarming of the central U.S.A. led to soil degradation in the mid-20th century. Some areas have yet to recover.

Right: In 1989, the tanker *Exxon Valdez* spilled 36,300 tons (37,000 t) of oil in Prince William Sound, Alaska, devastating local ecosystems.

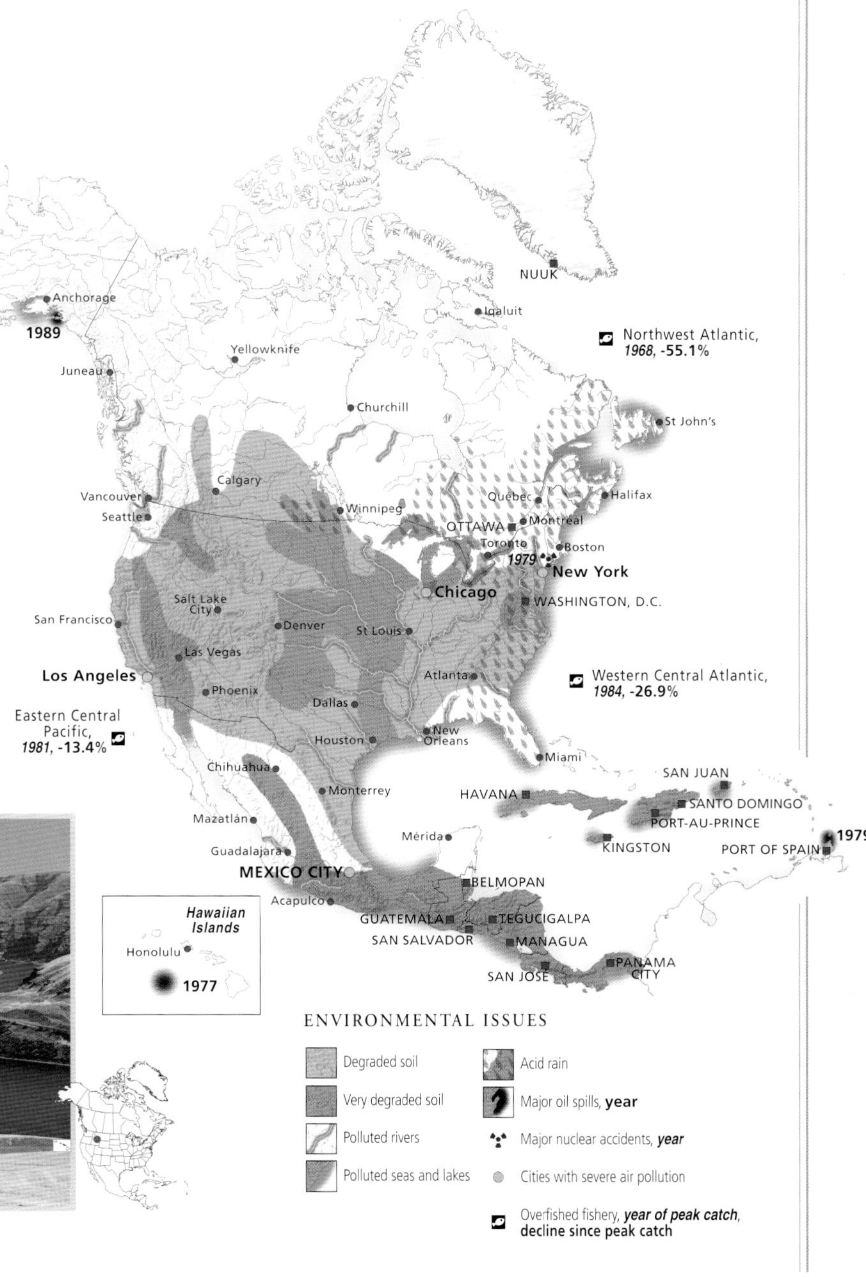

Right: The U.S.A.'s 2.5 million dams are the main cause of freshwater species extinctions. Overall, about 40 percent of freshwater fish, 50 percent of freshwater crayfish, and 70 percent of freshwater mussels have been lost.

Northeast Pacific, *1987, -18.1%*

1989

Northwest Atlantic, *1968, -55.1%*

1979

Western Central Atlantic, *1984, -26.9%*

Eastern Central Pacific, *1981, -13.4%*

Hawaiian Islands

Honolulu

1977

1979

ENVIRONMENTAL ISSUES

- Degraded soil
- Very degraded soil
- Polluted rivers
- Polluted seas and lakes
- Acid rain
- Major oil spills, **year**
- Major nuclear accidents, *year*
- Cities with severe air pollution
- Overfished fishery, *year of peak catch*, decline since peak catch

Protecting the Environment

A long tradition of conservation exists in North America. The continent was the site of the world's first national parks, is home to pioneering conservation organizations, and Canada and the U.S.A. in particular have passed effective environmental legislation, often focusing on species preservation. More than 30 percent of U.S. urban waste is now recycled and many landfills have been turned into parks. Even in less affluent Mexico, Central America, and the West Indies, governments have begun to recognize the value of preserving wilderness. In some areas, for example, well-regulated ecotourism has generated much-needed revenue and helped limit habitat destruction. Unfortunately, the continent's relatively high levels of land protection (10.5 percent) do not seem to guarantee permanent preservation: in 2001, the U.S. government authorized exploration for oil and gas in national wildlife refuges in northern Alaska and elsewhere.

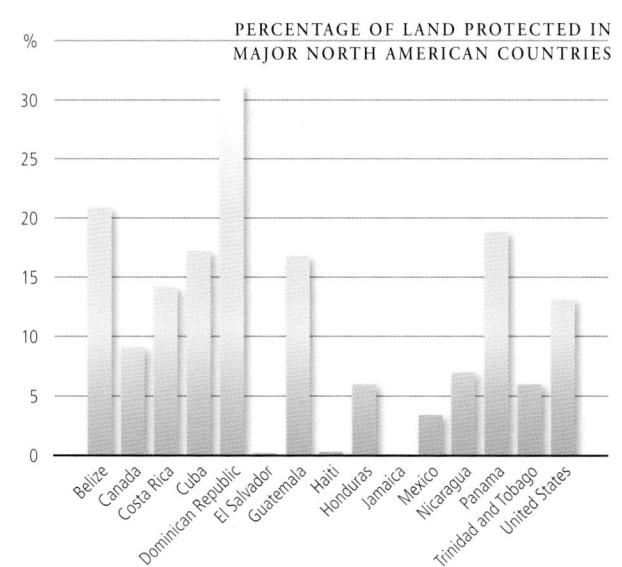

PERCENTAGE OF LAND PROTECTED IN MAJOR NORTH AMERICAN COUNTRIES

%

30

25

20

15

10

5

0

Belize · Canada · Costa Rica · Cuba · Dominican Republic · El Salvador · Guatemala · Haiti · Honduras · Jamaica · Mexico · Nicaragua · Panama · Trinidad and Tobago · United States

Above: In this satellite image, the area left of the river is Haiti; the greener area on the right is the Dominican Republic—a startling reflection of the nations' contrasting land-protection policies.

UNITED STATES OF AMERICA

A federal republic made up of 50 states, the United States of America (U.S.A.) is the world's third-largest country by size and population. Its contiguous 48 states span the center of North America, from the Pacific Ocean to the Atlantic shoreline. The other two states are Alaska, in the far northwest of the continent, and the island state of Hawaii, in the central Pacific Ocean. On the western side of the lower 48, coastal ranges and the central Rocky Mountains enclose a series of high, arid plateaus and peaks. Plains predominate in the center and east, the much-eroded Appalachian Mountains dividing the vast Mississippi River Basin from the Atlantic Coastal Plain. The U.S.A. declared independence from British rule in 1776 and, with help from France, defeated Britain in the Revolutionary War. It has since flourished to become the world's leading economic and political power.

The Rockies attain their highest elevations in Colorado, which has 53 peaks above 14,000 feet (4,270 m).

The Mississippi River nears the end of its 2,339-mile (3,765-km) journey at New Orleans in Louisiana.

POPULATION PATTERNS

The U.S.A. has a large population, but it is distributed over a wide area. Density is higher in the eastern half of the country, especially on the northeastern seaboard, but California is the most populous state. Although the western interior is the least densely inhabited area, it has the fastest-growing state populations. The majority of Americans, 69.1 percent, are non-Hispanic whites; Hispanics make up 12.5 percent of the population, blacks 12.3 percent, Asians 3.6 percent, and Native Americans 0.9 percent.

Less than 2.6 persons per sq mile/1 per sq km	130–260 per sq mile/ 50–100 per sq km
2.6–26 per sq mile/ 1–10 per sq km	260–520 per sq mile/ 100–200 per sq km
26–65 per sq mile/ 10–25 per sq km	520–1040 per sq mile/ 200–400 per sq km
65–130 per sq mile/ 25–50 per sq km	1040–2080 per sq mile/ 400–800 per sq km

ECONOMIC PROFILE

The U.S.A. is the most productive nation on Earth. It has the world's largest coal reserves and generates 40 percent of its oil. Intensive farming of rich agricultural lands yields half of the world's corn, one-fifth of its meat, and one-tenth of its wheat. The U.S.A. is also the top producer of soybeans and the biggest source of timber. Forestry, mining, and agriculture are far surpassed, however, in terms of contribution to GDP, by manufacturing—led by transport equipment, industrial machinery, electronic components, and computers—and services, which employ 73.5 percent of workers, primarily in the financial and health sectors.

Corn (maize)	Fishing
Cereals	Shellfish
Fruit	Industrial center
Citrus fruits	Mining
Cotton	Oil production
Tobacco	Tourism
Soybeans	Timber
Groundnuts	Winter sports
Beef cattle	Potatoes
Sheep	Wine

Forest and woodland	
Arable land	
Grazing	
Marginal or nonproductive	

Longitude west of Greenwich

Washington, D.C.
In 1790, 10 square miles (26 sq km) on the Potomac River were selected by Congress as the site of a new national capital and named the District of Columbia after Christopher Columbus. George Washington commissioned French engineer Pierre-Charles L'Enfant to plan a city, subsequently named after the president. Although L'Enfant was later dismissed, his plan for a rectangular grid and avenues radiating out from grand government buildings was broadly followed. The Capitol Building, home of the House of Representatives and the Senate, was commenced in 1793 and first hosted Congress in 1800.

Divided between the U.S.A. and Canada, Lake Superior is 383 miles (616 km) wide and fed by about 200 rivers.

The world's tallest trees, redwoods grow on California's rainy north coast.

ELEVATION

Feet	Meters
6562	2000
4921	1500
3281	1000
2461	750
1640	500
1312	400
984	300
656	200
328	100
0	0
Below sea level	
656	200
3281	1000
6562	2000
13,123	4000
19,685	6000
26,246	8000
32,808	10,000

SCALE 1:12,000,000
Lamberts Conformal Conic Projection
400 miles
400 kilometers

57

NORTHEASTERN U.S.A.

Connecticut, Maine, Massachusetts, New Hampshire, New Jersey, New York, Pennsylvania, Rhode Island, Vermont

The site of some of the continent's earliest European settlements and subsequently the entry point to North America for millions of immigrants, the northeastern seaboard is the most densely populated part of the U.S.A. On the southern half of the coastal plain lies a string of cities that have merged to form one massive, almost continuous urban area. Running from Boston south to Washington, D.C., it is sometimes referred to as the megalopolis or BosWash corridor. In the north, the shoreline is less developed and more rugged, deep bays and promontories lining southern Maine. To the west, the coastal plain is hemmed in by the ancient, forested peaks of the Appalachian Mountains. Studded with lakes and breached by rivers, including the Hudson, Delaware, and Connecticut, the Appalachians reach west to the shores of the Great Lakes, to the Adirondack Mountains, and north into Canada.

Measuring 3,500 miles (5,630 km) in length, the heavily indented Maine coast is fringed by rocky inlets and 1,200 islands.

The strongest winds ever measured were recorded on top of Mount Washington in New Hampshire's White Mountains.

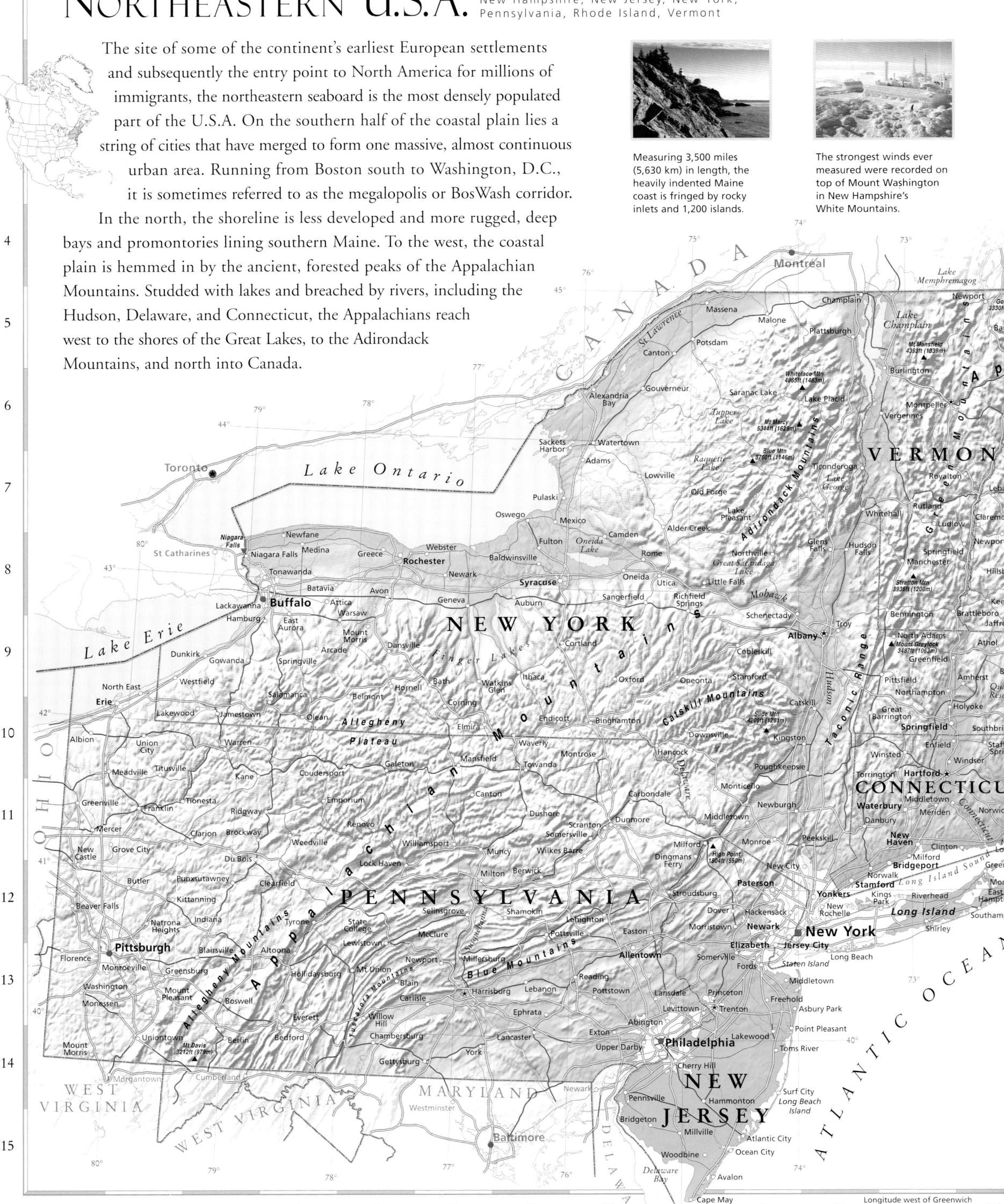

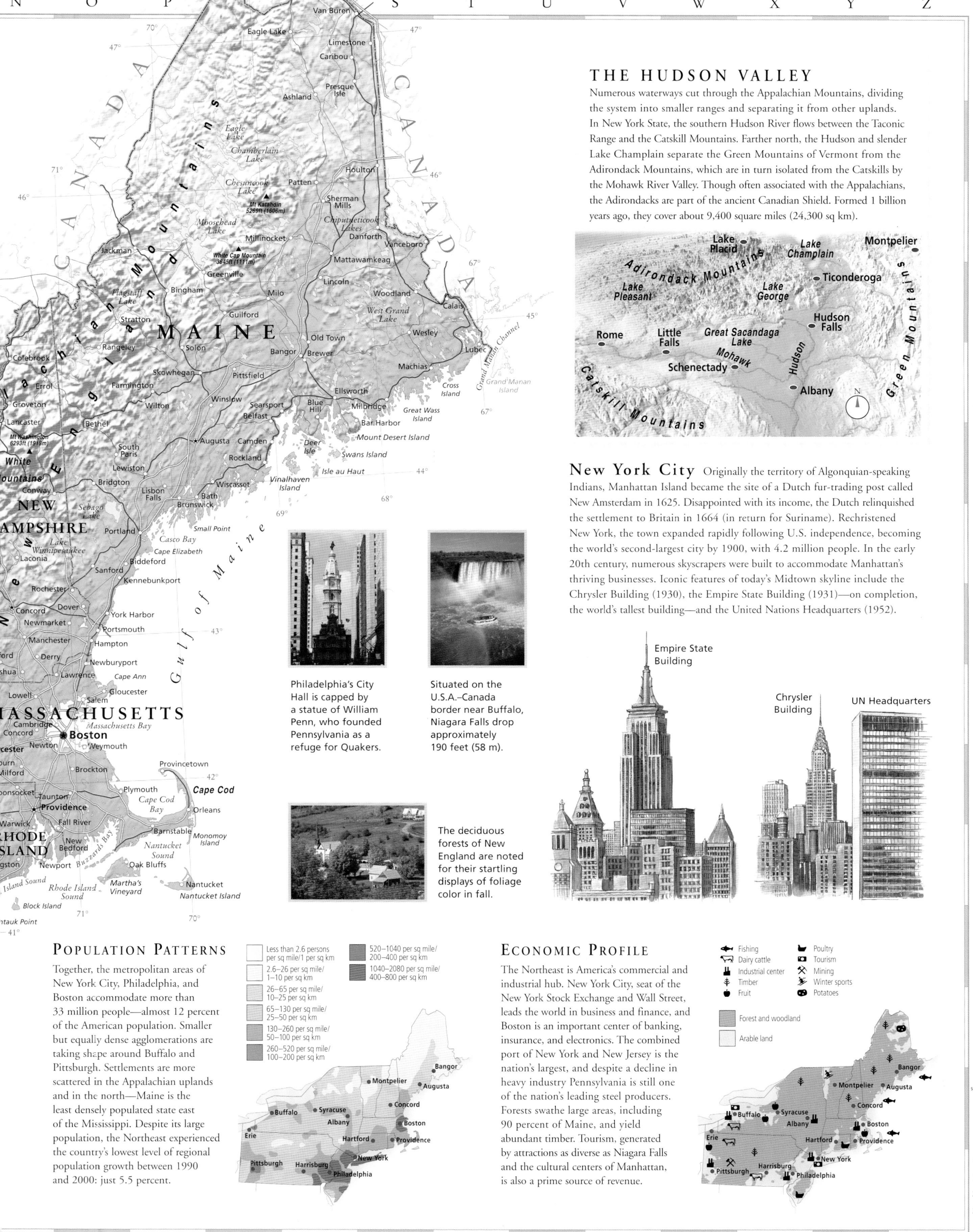

N O P Q R S T U V W X Y Z

Madawaska
Van Buren
Eagle Lake
Limestone
Caribou
Ashland
Presque Isle
Eagle Lake
Chamberlain Lake
Houlton
Chesuncook Lake
Patten
Mt Katahdin 5269ft (1606m)
Moosehead Lake
Sherman Mills
Chiputneticook Lakes
Danforth
Millinocket
Vanceboro
White Cap Mountain 3644ft (1111m)
Mattawamkeag
Jackman
Greenville
Bingham
Milo
Lincoln
Woodland
West Grand Lake
Calais
MAINE
Stratton
Guilford
Old Town
Wesley
Flagstaff Lake
Rangeley
Solon
Bangor
Brewer
Lubec
Skowhegan
Pittsfield
Machias
Grand Manan Channel
Grand Manan Island
Farmington
Winslow
Ellsworth
Cross Island
Colebrook
Wilton
Searsport
Milbridge
Great Wass Island
Errol
Bethel
Belfast
Blue Hill
Bar Harbor
Mt Washington 6293ft (1918m)
South Paris
Augusta
Camden
Mount Desert Island
White Mountains
Lewiston
Rockland
Swans Island
Conway
Bridgton
Wiscasset
Deer Isle
Isle au Haut
NEW HAMPSHIRE
Lisbon Falls
Bath
Vinalhaven Island
Sebago Lake
Brunswick
Portland
Small Point
Laconia
Casco Bay
Lake Winnipesaukee
Cape Elizabeth
Rochester
Sanford
Biddeford
Dover
Kennebunkport
Concord
Gulf of Maine
Newmarket
York Harbor
Portsmouth
Manchester
Hampton
Derry
Newburyport
Nashua
Cape Ann
Lawrence
Gloucester
Lowell
Salem
MASSACHUSETTS
Cambridge
Concord
Boston
Newton
Weymouth
Worcester
Auburn
Milford
Brockton
Provincetown
Woonsocket
Taunton
Plymouth
Cape Cod
Providence
Cape Cod Bay
Orleans
Warwick
Fall River
Barnstable
Monomoy Island
RHODE ISLAND
New Bedford
Nantucket Sound
Kingston
Newport
Buzzards Bay
Oak Bluffs
Nantucket
Block Island
Martha's Vineyard
Nantucket Island
Island Sound
Rhode Island Sound
Montauk Point

CANADA

THE HUDSON VALLEY

Numerous waterways cut through the Appalachian Mountains, dividing the system into smaller ranges and separating it from other uplands. In New York State, the southern Hudson River flows between the Taconic Range and the Catskill Mountains. Farther north, the Hudson and slender Lake Champlain separate the Green Mountains of Vermont from the Adirondack Mountains, which are in turn isolated from the Catskills by the Mohawk River Valley. Though often associated with the Appalachians, the Adirondacks are part of the ancient Canadian Shield. Formed 1 billion years ago, they cover about 9,400 square miles (24,300 sq km).

Lake Placid
Lake Champlain
Montpelier
Adirondack Mountains
Ticonderoga
Lake Pleasant
Lake George
Hudson Falls
Rome
Little Falls
Great Sacandaga Lake
Mohawk
Hudson
Schenectady
Albany
Green Mountains
Catskill Mountains

New York City

Originally the territory of Algonquian-speaking Indians, Manhattan Island became the site of a Dutch fur-trading post called New Amsterdam in 1625. Disappointed with its income, the Dutch relinquished the settlement to Britain in 1664 (in return for Suriname). Rechristened New York, the town expanded rapidly following U.S. independence, becoming the world's second-largest city by 1900, with 4.2 million people. In the early 20th century, numerous skyscrapers were built to accommodate Manhattan's thriving businesses. Iconic features of today's Midtown skyline include the Chrysler Building (1930), the Empire State Building (1931)—on completion, the world's tallest building—and the United Nations Headquarters (1952).

Philadelphia's City Hall is capped by a statue of William Penn, who founded Pennsylvania as a refuge for Quakers.

Situated on the U.S.A.–Canada border near Buffalo, Niagara Falls drop approximately 190 feet (58 m).

The deciduous forests of New England are noted for their startling displays of foliage color in fall.

Empire State Building
Chrysler Building
UN Headquarters

ELEVATION
Feet	Meters
6562	2000
4921	1500
3281	1000
2461	750
1640	500
1312	400
984	300
656	200
328	100
0	0
Below sea level	Below sea level
656	200
3281	1000
6562	2000
13,123	4000
19,685	6000
26,246	8000
32,808	10,000

POPULATION PATTERNS

Together, the metropolitan areas of New York City, Philadelphia, and Boston accommodate more than 33 million people—almost 12 percent of the American population. Smaller but equally dense agglomerations are taking shape around Buffalo and Pittsburgh. Settlements are more scattered in the Appalachian uplands and in the north—Maine is the least densely populated state east of the Mississippi. Despite its large population, the Northeast experienced the country's lowest level of regional population growth between 1990 and 2000: just 5.5 percent.

Less than 2.6 persons per sq mile/1 per sq km
2.6–26 per sq mile/1–10 per sq km
26–65 per sq mile/10–25 per sq km
65–130 per sq mile/25–50 per sq km
130–260 per sq mile/50–100 per sq km
260–520 per sq mile/100–200 per sq km
520–1040 per sq mile/200–400 per sq km
1040–2080 per sq mile/400–800 per sq km

Bangor
Montpelier
Augusta
Concord
Buffalo
Syracuse
Albany
Boston
Erie
Hartford
Providence
Pittsburgh
Harrisburg
New York
Philadelphia

ECONOMIC PROFILE

The Northeast is America's commercial and industrial hub. New York City, seat of the New York Stock Exchange and Wall Street, leads the world in business and finance, and Boston is an important center of banking, insurance, and electronics. The combined port of New York and New Jersey is the nation's largest, and despite a decline in heavy industry Pennsylvania is still one of the nation's leading steel producers. Forests swathe large areas, including 90 percent of Maine, and yield abundant timber. Tourism, generated by attractions as diverse as Niagara Falls and the cultural centers of Manhattan, is also a prime source of revenue.

Fishing
Dairy cattle
Industrial center
Timber
Fruit
Poultry
Tourism
Mining
Winter sports
Potatoes

Forest and woodland
Arable land

Bangor
Montpelier
Augusta
Concord
Buffalo
Syracuse
Albany
Boston
Erie
Hartford
Providence
Pittsburgh
Harrisburg
New York
Philadelphia

SCALE 1:3,000,000
Lamberts Conformal Conic Projection
0 100 miles
0 100 kilometers

SOUTH ATLANTIC U.S.A.

Delaware, District of Columbia, Kentucky, Maryland, North Carolina, South Carolina, Tennessee, Virginia, West Virginia

The northern perimeter of this region, formed by the Ohio River and the southern border of Pennsylvania—the so-called Mason and Dixon Line—is the traditional divide between North and South: prior to the Civil War it separated slave-owning states from abolitionists. History and terrain have created other regional distinctions. The thickly forested ridges of the Appalachian Mountains form a sparsely populated enclave of mining and timber towns. To the west lie the pastoral hills of central Tennessee and Kentucky's Bluegrass region, and the heavily cultivated lowlands of the Mississippi and Ohio rivers. In the east, the wooded Appalachian foothills, known as the Piedmont, descend to a broad coastal plain bordered by historic ports and barrier islands.

POPULATION PATTERNS

In the northeast, the population is heavily urbanized and concentrated in the Washington–Baltimore area, home to 7.6 million people. Elsewhere the proportion of rural dwellers is high, rising from 27 percent in Virginia to 51 percent in West Virginia. In Virginia and the Carolinas, people cluster in the Piedmont, but the cities here are relatively small; the largest urban centers outside the northeast are Nashville and Memphis in Tennessee. Population growth between 1990 and 2000 varied markedly, from –5.7 percent in the District of Columbia to 21.4 percent in North Carolina.

ECONOMIC PROFILE

Farming has declined in importance, though this is still the country's main source of tobacco and yields sizable crops of soybeans, corn, and vegetables. Kentucky is also renowned for horse-breeding. Manufacturing industries include whiskey in Kentucky and Tennessee; chemicals in Tennessee, Virginia, and Delaware; and textiles and high-tech goods in North Carolina. Service industries predominate in the northeast, with the government being a major employer. Appalachia has some of America's most productive coal fields. Fishing, mainly of shellfish, remains important around Chesapeake Bay.

Population density legend

- Less than 2.6 persons per sq mile/1 per sq km
- 2.6–26 per sq mile/1–10 per sq km
- 26–65 per sq mile/10–25 per sq km
- 65–130 per sq mile/25–50 per sq km
- 130–260 per sq mile/50–100 per sq km
- 260–520 per sq mile/100–200 per sq km
- 520–1040 per sq mile/200–400 per sq km
- 1040–2080 per sq mile/400–800 per sq km

Economic legend

- Corn (maize)
- Cotton
- Shellfish
- Tobacco
- Fishing
- Industrial center
- Timber
- Beef cattle
- Mining
- Fruit
- Poultry
- Soybeans
- Pigs
- Forest and woodland
- Arable land
- Grazing

Longitude west of Greenwich

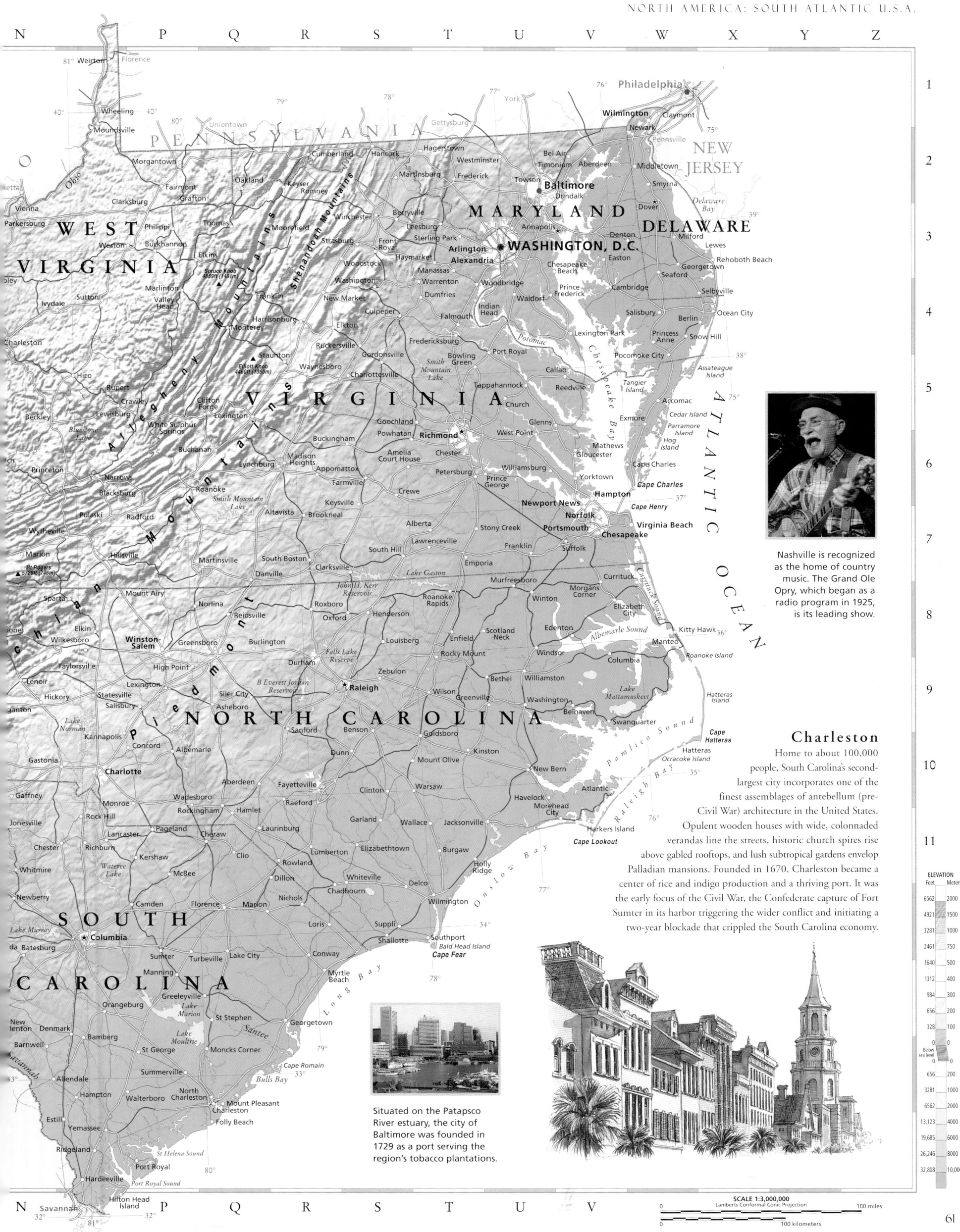

Nashville is recognized as the home of country music. The Grand Ole Opry, which began as a radio program in 1925, is its leading show.

Charleston

Home to about 100,000 people, South Carolina's second-largest city incorporates one of the finest assemblages of antebellum (pre-Civil War) architecture in the United States. Opulent wooden houses with wide, colonnaded verandas line the streets, historic church spires rise above gabled rooftops, and lush subtropical gardens envelop Palladian mansions. Founded in 1670, Charleston became a center of rice and indigo production and a thriving port. It was the early focus of the Civil War, the Confederate capture of Fort Sumter in its harbor triggering the wider conflict and initiating a two-year blockade that crippled the South Carolina economy.

Situated on the Patapsco River estuary, the city of Baltimore was founded in 1729 as a port serving the region's tobacco plantations.

ELEVATION

Feet	Meters
6562	2000
4921	1500
3281	1000
2461	750
1640	500
1312	400
984	300
656	200
328	100
0	0
Below sea level	
656	200
3281	1000
6562	2000
13,123	4000
19,685	6000
26,246	8000
32,808	10,000

SCALE 1:3,000,000
Lambert's Conformal Conic Projection

0   100 miles
0   100 kilometers

SOUTHEASTERN U.S.A.

Alabama, Florida, Georgia, Louisiana, Mississippi

In the southeastern corner of the United States, rolling hills and low plateaus cover much of the interior, rising in northern Alabama and Georgia to the southern edge of the Appalachian Mountains and descending along a broad sweep to the alluvial plain of the Mississippi River, the Gulf and Atlantic coastal plains, and the broad, flat Florida Peninsula. In the 16th century, Spanish explorers became the first Europeans to visit this predominantly swampy coastline, then home to various Indian groups. The Spanish founded the settlement of St Augustine, Florida, in 1565, now the oldest city in the country. In the late 17th century, French traders took control of the Mississippi Basin, establishing a port at New Orleans. Under the Treaty of Paris of 1763, New Orleans and the western Mississippi Valley passed to Spain, while the land to the east of the Mississippi, including Spanish Florida, came under British control. After the Civil War, continuing discrimination against the African-American population made the Southeast the focus of civil-rights protests, which reached a peak in the 1960s with mass demonstrations in Montgomery and Birmingham, Alabama, and the 1963 March on Washington for Jobs and Freedom.

Hurricanes regularly strike the Southeast. In August 1992, Hurricane Andrew caused US$25 billion worth of damage and 23 deaths.

The distinctive architecture of New Orleans reflects the origins of its early inhabitants. Founded by the French in 1718, it was ceded to Spain in 1763.

POPULATION PATTERNS

The Southeast's inhabitants are fairly evenly spread, though coastal wetlands limit settlement in parts of the Gulf Coast (notably the Mississippi Delta) and Florida. Population density and urbanization are lower in the three western states, particularly in Mississippi. In contrast, Georgia and Florida have large urban populations, with settlement focused on cities such as Atlanta (home to half of Georgia's people), Tampa, and Miami. The populations of these two states are growing rapidly, with Florida's projected to reach 20 million by 2010, due in part to its popularity as a retirement destination.

ECONOMIC PROFILE

Until the early 20th century, the Southeast was dependent on agriculture, especially the cultivation of cotton and tobacco. These crops remain significant, but farmers have diversified into soybeans, corn, peanuts, and, in Florida, citrus fruits. Extensive forests provide abundant timber, and the industrial sector has expanded to include textiles, transportation equipment, electronics, and the aerospace industry. Louisiana is one of the nation's leading producers of oil and gas, Georgia is home to major corporations—Atlanta is the headquarters of Coca-Cola and CNN (Cable News Network)—and Florida has a thriving tourist industry.

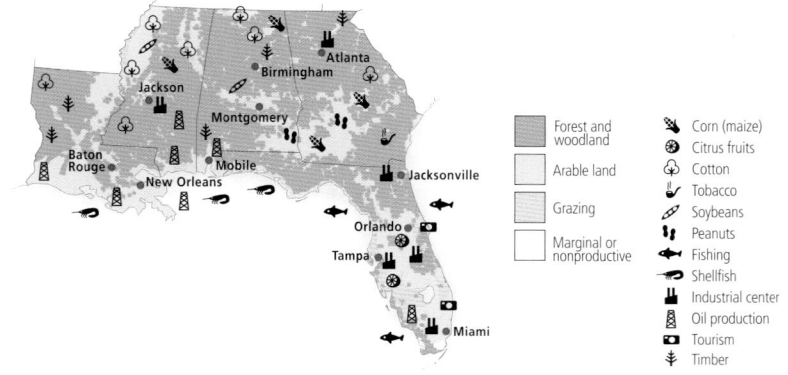

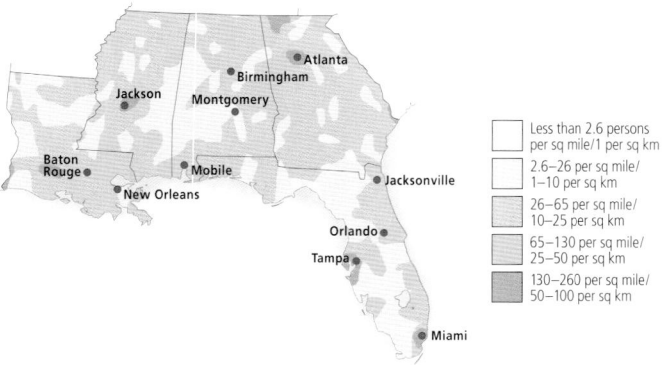

Population density legend:
- Less than 2.6 persons per sq mile/1 per sq km
- 2.6–26 per sq mile/1–10 per sq km
- 26–65 per sq mile/10–25 per sq km
- 65–130 per sq mile/25–50 per sq km
- 130–260 per sq mile/50–100 per sq km

Economic legend:
- Forest and woodland
- Arable land
- Grazing
- Marginal or nonproductive
- Corn (maize)
- Citrus fruits
- Cotton
- Tobacco
- Soybeans
- Peanuts
- Fishing
- Shellfish
- Industrial center
- Oil production
- Tourism
- Timber

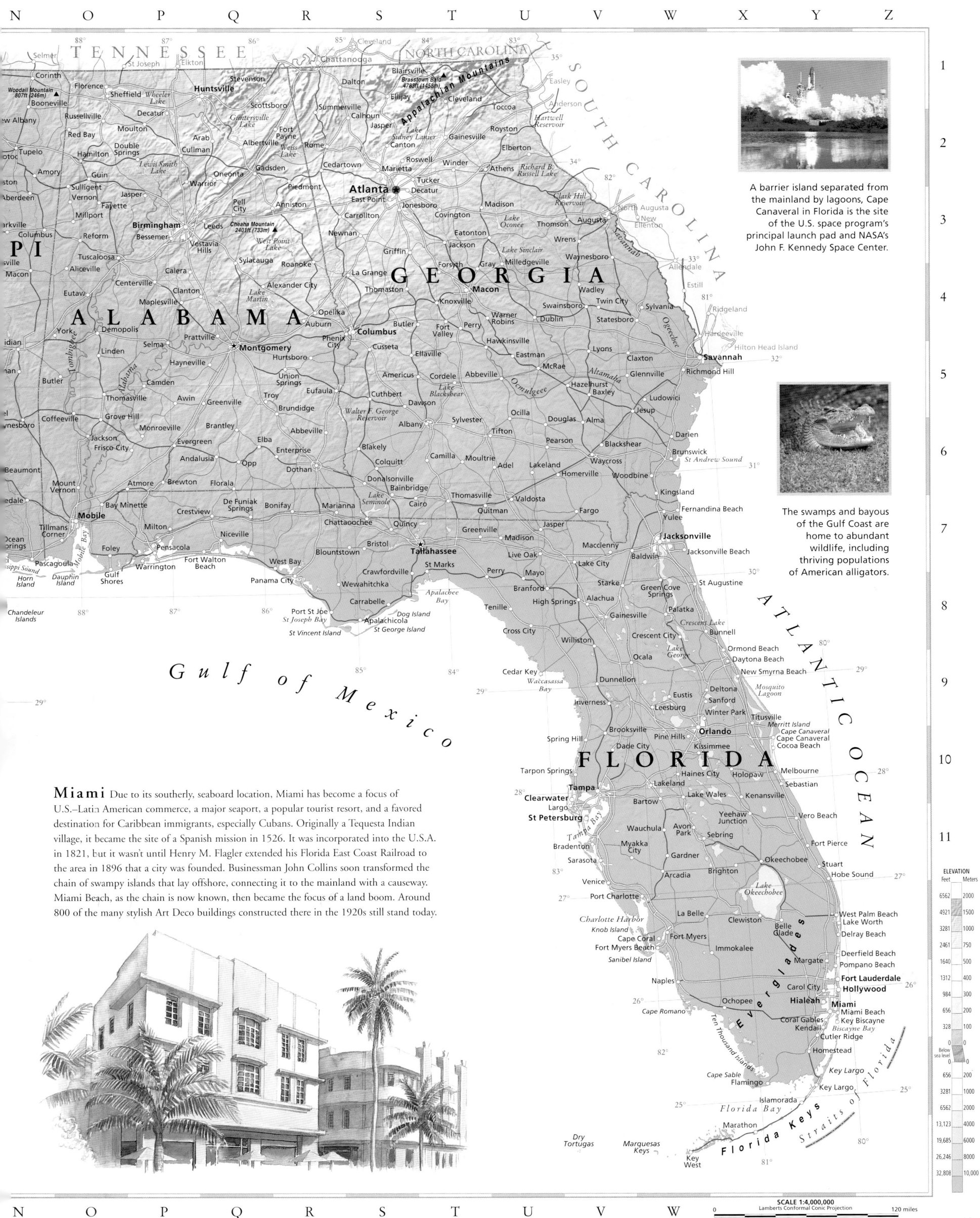

A barrier island separated from the mainland by lagoons, Cape Canaveral in Florida is the site of the U.S. space program's principal launch pad and NASA's John F. Kennedy Space Center.

The swamps and bayous of the Gulf Coast are home to abundant wildlife, including thriving populations of American alligators.

Miami Due to its southerly, seaboard location, Miami has become a focus of U.S.–Latin American commerce, a major seaport, a popular tourist resort, and a favored destination for Caribbean immigrants, especially Cubans. Originally a Tequesta Indian village, it became the site of a Spanish mission in 1526. It was incorporated into the U.S.A. in 1821, but it wasn't until Henry M. Flagler extended his Florida East Coast Railroad to the area in 1896 that a city was founded. Businessman John Collins soon transformed the chain of swampy islands that lay offshore, connecting it to the mainland with a causeway. Miami Beach, as the chain is now known, then became the focus of a land boom. Around 800 of the many stylish Art Deco buildings constructed there in the 1920s still stand today.

ELEVATION	
Feet	Meters
32,808	10,000
26,246	8000
19,685	6000
13,123	4000
6562	2000
4921	1500
3281	1000
2461	750
1640	500
1312	400
984	300
656	200
328	100
0	0
Below sea level	
0	0
656	200
3281	1000
6562	2000
13,123	4000
19,685	6000
26,246	8000
32,808	10,000

SCALE 1:4,000,000
Lambert's Conformal Conic Projection

0 120 miles

0 120 kilometers

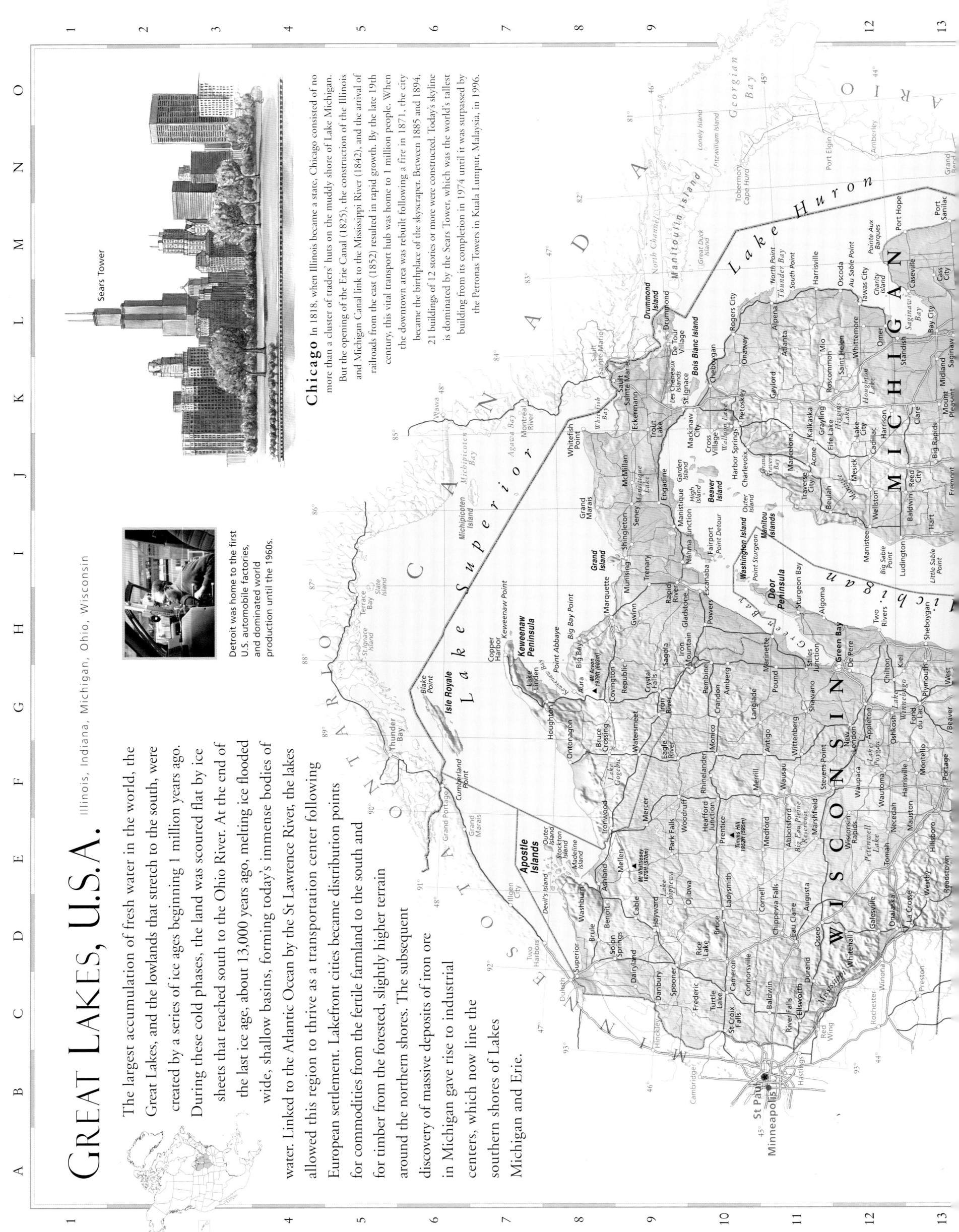

GREAT LAKES, U.S.A.

Illinois, Indiana, Michigan, Ohio, Wisconsin

The largest accumulation of fresh water in the world, the Great Lakes, and the lowlands that stretch to the south, were created by a series of ice ages beginning 1 million years ago. During these cold phases, the land was scoured flat by ice sheets that reached south to the Ohio River. At the end of the last ice age, about 13,000 years ago, melting ice flooded wide, shallow basins, forming today's immense bodies of water. Linked to the Atlantic Ocean by the St Lawrence River, the lakes allowed this region to thrive as a transportation center following European settlement. Lakefront cities became distribution points for commodities from the fertile farmland to the south and for timber from the forested, slightly higher terrain around the northern shores. The subsequent discovery of massive deposits of iron ore in Michigan gave rise to industrial centers, which now line the southern shores of Lakes Michigan and Erie.

Detroit was home to the first U.S. automobile factories, and dominated world production until the 1960s.

Sears Tower

Chicago In 1818, when Illinois became a state, Chicago consisted of no more than a cluster of traders' huts on the muddy shore of Lake Michigan. But the opening of the Erie Canal (1825), the construction of the Illinois and Michigan Canal link to the Mississippi River (1842), and the arrival of railroads from the east (1852) resulted in rapid growth. By the late 19th century, this vital transport hub was home to 1 million people. When the downtown area was rebuilt following a fire in 1871, the city became the birthplace of the skyscraper. Between 1885 and 1894, 21 buildings of 12 stories or more were constructed. Today's skyline is dominated by the Sears Tower, which was the world's tallest building from its completion in 1974 until it was surpassed by the Petronas Towers in Kuala Lumpur, Malaysia, in 1996.

64

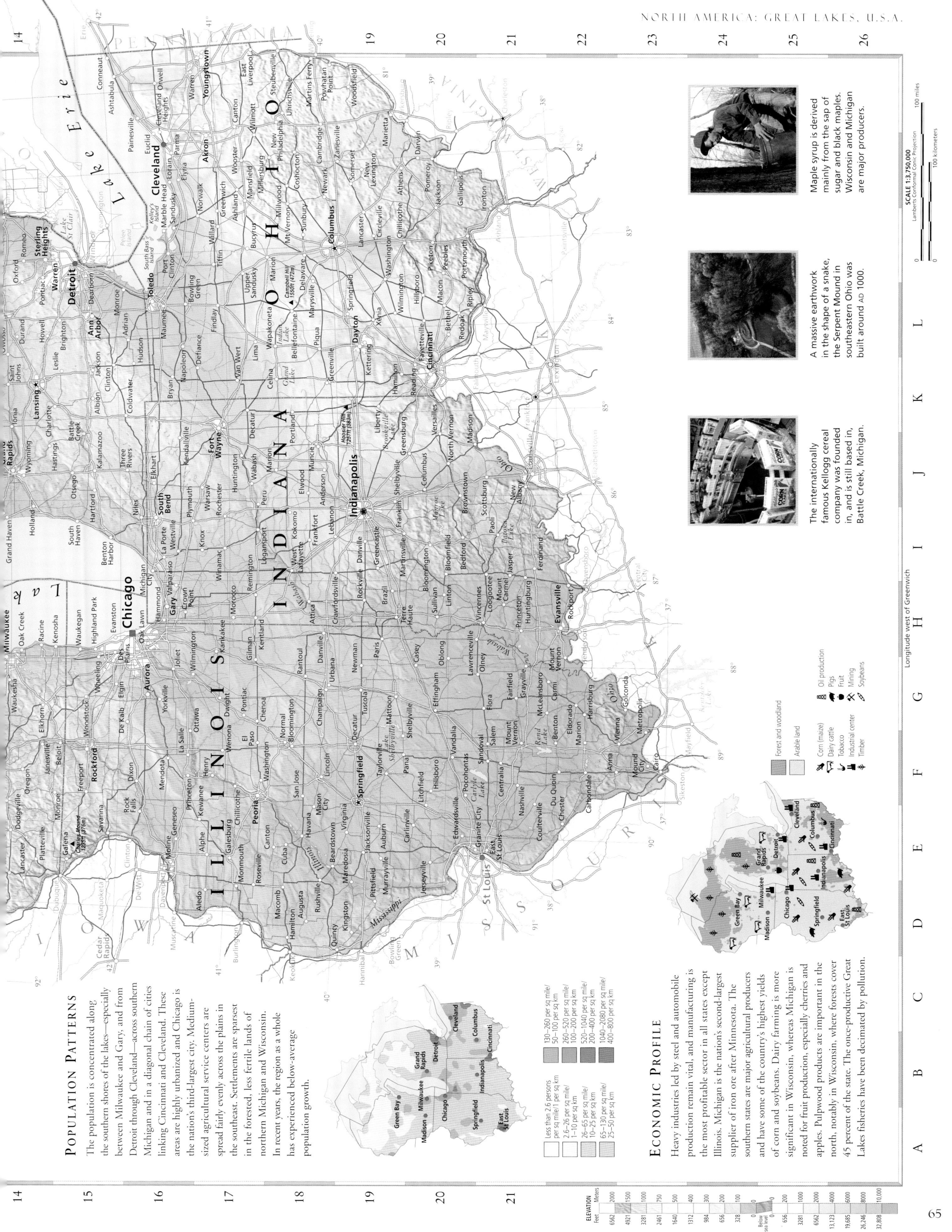

POPULATION PATTERNS

The population is concentrated along the southern shores of the lakes—especially between Milwaukee and Gary, and from Detroit through Cleveland—across southern Michigan and in a diagonal chain of cities linking Cincinnati and Cleveland. These areas are highly urbanized and Chicago is the nation's third-largest city. Medium-sized agricultural service centers are spread fairly evenly across the plains in the southeast. Settlements are sparsest in the forested, less fertile lands of northern Michigan and Wisconsin. In recent years, the region as a whole has experienced below-average population growth.

Less than 2.6 persons per sq mile/1 per sq km
2.6–26 per sq mile/1–10 per sq km
26–65 per sq mile/10–25 per sq km
65–130 per sq mile/25–50 per sq km
130–260 per sq mile/50–100 per sq km
260–520 per sq mile/100–200 per sq km
520–1040 per sq mile/200–400 per sq km
1040–2080 per sq mile/400–800 per sq km

ECONOMIC PROFILE

Heavy industries led by steel and automobile production remain vital, and manufacturing is the most profitable sector in all states except Illinois. Michigan is the nation's second-largest supplier of iron ore after Minnesota. The southern states are major agricultural producers and have some of the country's highest yields of corn and soybeans. Dairy farming is more significant in Wisconsin, whereas Michigan is noted for fruit production, especially cherries and apples. Pulpwood products are important in the north, notably in Wisconsin, where forests cover 45 percent of the state. The once-productive Great Lakes fisheries have been decimated by pollution.

Forest and woodland
Arable land

Corn (maize)
Dairy cattle
Tobacco
Timber
Oil production
Pigs
Fruit
Industrial center
Mining
Soybeans

The internationally famous Kellogg cereal company was founded in, and is still based in, Battle Creek, Michigan.

A massive earthwork in the shape of a snake, the Serpent Mound in southeastern Ohio was built around AD 1000.

Maple syrup is derived mainly from the sap of sugar and black maples. Wisconsin and Michigan are major producers.

SCALE 1:3,750,000
Lambert's Conformal Conic Projection

Longitude west of Greenwich

ELEVATION

65

Upper Midwest, U.S.A.

Iowa, Minnesota, Nebraska,
North Dakota, South Dakota

A seemingly boundless sea of crops is the image most strongly associated with the Upper Midwest, and indeed more than half of the land is used for cultivation and agriculture dominates the economy. Wheat fields swathe much of the Great Plains plateau on the western side of the region. Myriad streams and rivers follow the plateau's gentle eastward inclination, carving gullies and channels through hills and badlands, and feeding for the most part into the Missouri River. Undulating farmland—mainly fields of corn and soybeans—also covers most of Iowa and southern Minnesota. In the northeast, the plains are studded with lakes and marshes formed by the retreat of glaciers at the end of last ice age. The upper Mississippi and Missouri were vital transportation routes for Native Americans and early European explorers and trappers, but widespread intensive settlement did not take place until after the arrival of the railroads around 1870.

Population Patterns

The western part of this region is one of the most sparsely inhabited parts of the lower 48, and North and South Dakota are, respectively, the second and fourth least populous states. The east has larger settlements, especially along major rivers. The Upper Midwest generally experiences lower than average population growth: between 1990 and 2000, North Dakota had the country's lowest rate of growth, a mere 0.5 percent. The overall proportion of rural dwellers is significantly higher than average, reaching almost half in South Dakota.

Less than 2.6 persons per sq mile/1 per sq km
2.6–26 per sq mile/ 1–10 per sq km
26–65 per sq mile/ 10–25 per sq km
65–130 per sq mile/ 25–50 per sq km
130–260 per sq mile/ 50–100 per sq km

Economic Profile

These states are among the nation's largest agricultural producers. The west forms part of the Great Plains Wheat Belt; the so-called Corn Belt encompasses eastern Nebraska, Iowa, and southern Minnesota. Grazing of cattle and pigs occurs throughout the region. Minnesota is the nation's largest producer of iron ore, Nebraska and North Dakota have modest supplies of petroleum, and South Dakota's Black Hills are a prime source of gold. Farming is the basis of most manufacturing and services, though tourism and the insurance industry are also important.

Forest and woodland
Arable land
Grazing
Cereals
Corn (maize)
Beef cattle
Industrial center
Mining
Oil production
Soybeans
Pigs

CANADA

NORTH DAKOTA

SOUTH DAKOTA

NEBRASKA

MONTANA

WYOMING

COLORADO

Black Hills

Badlands

Sand Hills

Great Plains

Lake Sakakawea

Lake Oahe

Missouri

Cheyenne

Niobrara

North Platte

Lake McConaughy

Fortuna, Bowbells, Westhope, Rocklake, Langdon, Melita, Boissevain, Manitou, Kenmare, Dunseith, Tioga, Ray, Stanley, Minot, Towner, Rugby, Cando, Williston, New Town, Velva, Devil's Lake, Lakota, Watford City, Max, Harvey, New Rockford, Fessenden, Sheyenne, Grassy Butte, Killdeer, Halliday, Underwood, McClusky, Carrington, Pingree, Manning, Wilton, Tuttle, Beach, Hebron, Bismarck, Medina, Jamestown, Belfield, Dickinson, Mandan, Sterling, Dawson, Sentinel Butte 3428ft (1045m), White Butte 3530ft (1076m), Elgin, Breien, Napoleon, Edgeley, Baker, Mott, Linton, Wishek, Bowman, Reeder, Ashley, Ellenda, Hettinger, Selfridge, Lemmon, McIntosh, McLaughlin, Buffalo, Reva, Bison, Selby, Roscoe, Isabel, Mobridge, Grand, Moreau, La Plant, Gettysburg, Mell, Mud Butte, Faith, Dupree, Redfield, Belle Fourche, Howes, Blunt, Highmore, Wolsey, Spearfish, Billsburg, Hayes, Pierre, Sturgis, Rapid City, Wall, Mt Rushmore 5725ft (1745m), Custer, Kadoka, Murdo, Chamberlain, Plankiton, White, Hot Springs, Winner, Edgemont, Mission, Gregory, Pickstown, Oelrichs, Pine Ridge, Martin, Chadron, Merriman, Valentine, Bassett, Harrison, Ainsworth, O'Ne, Crawford, Hay Springs, Hemingford, Alliance, Hyannis, Thedford, Dunning, Taylor, Bartlett, Scottsbluff, Bridgeport, Arthur, Tryon, Stapleton, Ansley, St Pau, Hogback Mtn 5082ft (1549m), Oshkosh, Kimball, Sidney, Ogallala, North Platte, Gothenburg, Lexington, Kearney, Hasti, Holyoke, Grant, Maywood, Holdrege, Gr, Is, Imperial, McCook, Arapahoe, Alma, Red, KANSAS, Grand Forks, Duluth, Minneapolis, St Paul, Sioux Falls, Sioux City, Des Moines, Omaha, Lincoln

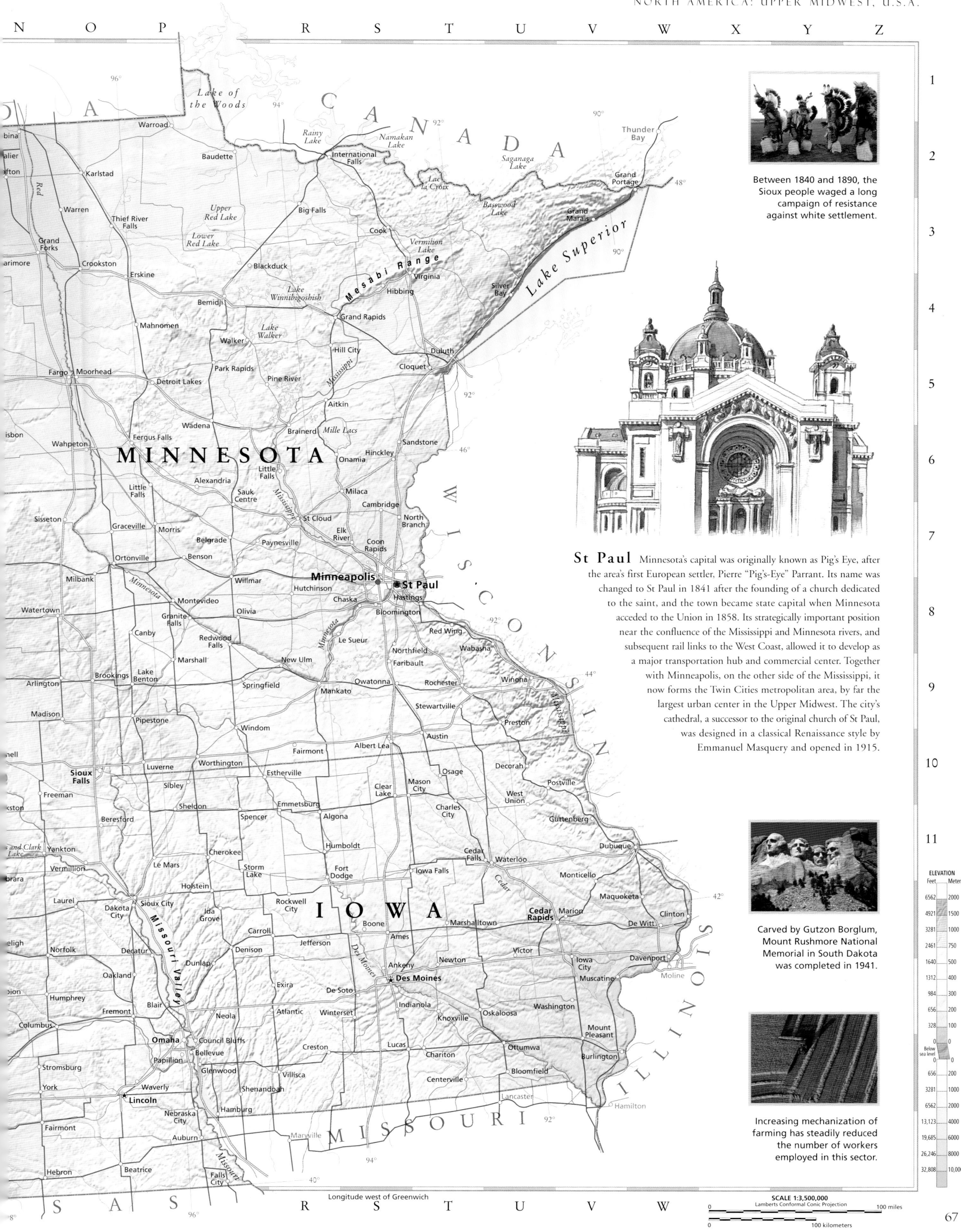

Between 1840 and 1890, the Sioux people waged a long campaign of resistance against white settlement.

St Paul Minnesota's capital was originally known as Pig's Eye, after the area's first European settler, Pierre "Pig's-Eye" Parrant. Its name was changed to St Paul in 1841 after the founding of a church dedicated to the saint, and the town became state capital when Minnesota acceded to the Union in 1858. Its strategically important position near the confluence of the Mississippi and Minnesota rivers, and subsequent rail links to the West Coast, allowed it to develop as a major transportation hub and commercial center. Together with Minneapolis, on the other side of the Mississippi, it now forms the Twin Cities metropolitan area, by far the largest urban center in the Upper Midwest. The city's cathedral, a successor to the original church of St Paul, was designed in a classical Renaissance style by Emmanuel Masquery and opened in 1915.

Carved by Gutzon Borglum, Mount Rushmore National Memorial in South Dakota was completed in 1941.

Increasing mechanization of farming has steadily reduced the number of workers employed in this sector.

ELEVATION

Feet	Meters
6562	2000
4921	1500
3281	1000
2461	750
1640	500
1312	400
984	300
656	200
328	100
Below sea level	0
656	200
3281	1000
6562	2000
13,123	4000
19,685	6000
26,246	8000
32,808	10,000

Longitude west of Greenwich

SCALE 1:3,500,000
Lamberts Conformal Conic Projection

0   100 miles
0   100 kilometers

LOWER MIDWEST, U.S.A.

Arkansas, Kansas, Missouri, Oklahoma

From the central Mississippi River, pioneers launched the great wave of westward expansion that began in the 1840s, turning this region into the "Gateway to the West." Most traveled along the Missouri River, over the hills of present-day Kansas and across the treeless plateau of the Great Plains. But the rugged, densely forested terrain of the Ozark Plateau and Ouachita Mountains in the east, the presence of large groups of displaced Native Americans in the so-called Indian Territory of the west, and early reports that the plains were a desert meant that the majority simply passed through. It wasn't until the end of the century that farmers turned the western plains into the major agricultural region that, despite occasional droughts such as those that created the Dust Bowl of the 1930s, it remains today.

Thermal springs are among the attractions that have made the Ozark Plateau a popular tourist center.

St Louis Sited at the heart of the mainland U.S.A., just south of the confluence of the Missouri and Mississippi rivers, St Louis was ideally placed to become a major transportation hub. It was founded by the French as a fur-trading post in 1764, came briefly under Spanish control, and was acquired by the U.S.A. as part of the Louisiana Purchase of 1803. Not only did St Louis cater to trappers and traders traveling north, northwest, and south along the rivers, it also became a major supply depot and departure point for exploratory parties venturing west and for thousands of pioneers setting off along the Santa Fe, Oregon, and California trails. The massive Gateway Arch commemorates the city's historic role in U.S. expansion. Standing almost 630 feet (192 m) high, it was designed by Eero Saarinen and erected in 1965.

POPULATION PATTERNS

The focus of early European settlement, the Mississippi and Missouri valleys are still the most densely populated areas, along with regional commercial and agricultural centers such as Oklahoma City and Wichita. Settlements are much more scattered on the western plains. More than a third of the region's inhabitants—including almost half of the population of Arkansas—live in rural areas. Limited economic diversity encourages migration to other areas, in turn keeping population growth well below the national average.

Population density	
2.6–26 per sq mile/1–10 per sq km	65–130 per sq mile/25–50 per sq km
26–65 per sq mile/10–25 per sq km	130–260 per sq mile/50–100 per sq km

ECONOMIC PROFILE

Wheat is the principal crop in the west—Kansas is the nation's leading producer—whereas corn, soybeans, and rice predominate in the better-watered east. Immense herds of cattle support meat-packing and beef-processing industries. Sizable oil and gas reserves helped Kansas and Oklahoma recover from the Dust Bowl droughts and remain an important source of revenue. Missouri is the leading producer of lead and has large iron ore reserves. St Louis and Kansas City are centers of automobile and aerospace equipment production, and Wichita is one of the world's leading aircraft manufacturers.

Forest and woodland
Arable land
Grazing

Cereals
Cotton
Beef cattle
Industrial center
Mining
Oil production
Rice
Soybeans
Pigs
Corn (maize)

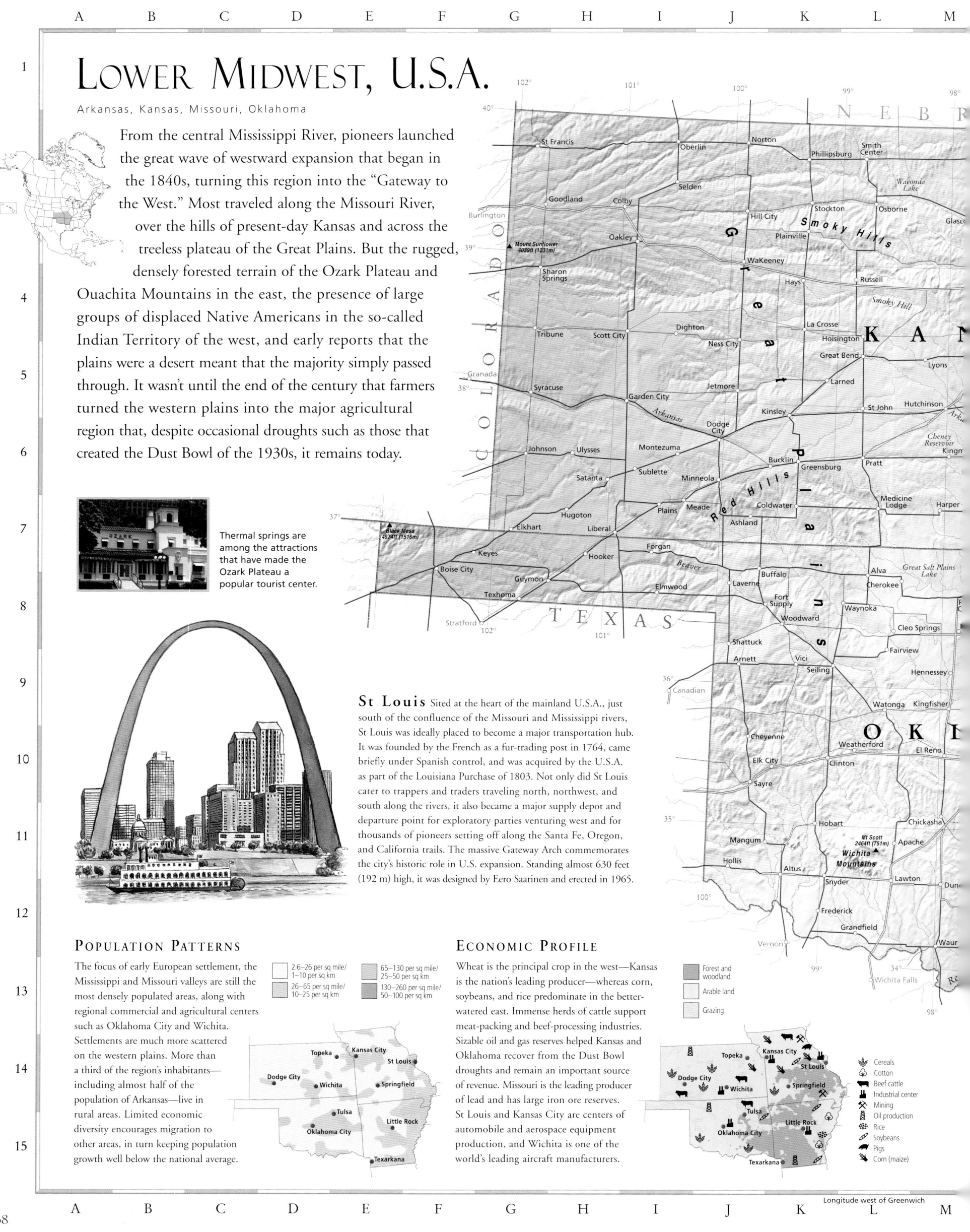

Aircraft production provides more than half of all the manufacturing employment in Wichita.

Central Oklahoma has the world's highest incidence of tornadoes. Most strike between April and June.

SCALE 1:3,000,000
Lamberts Conformal Conic Projection

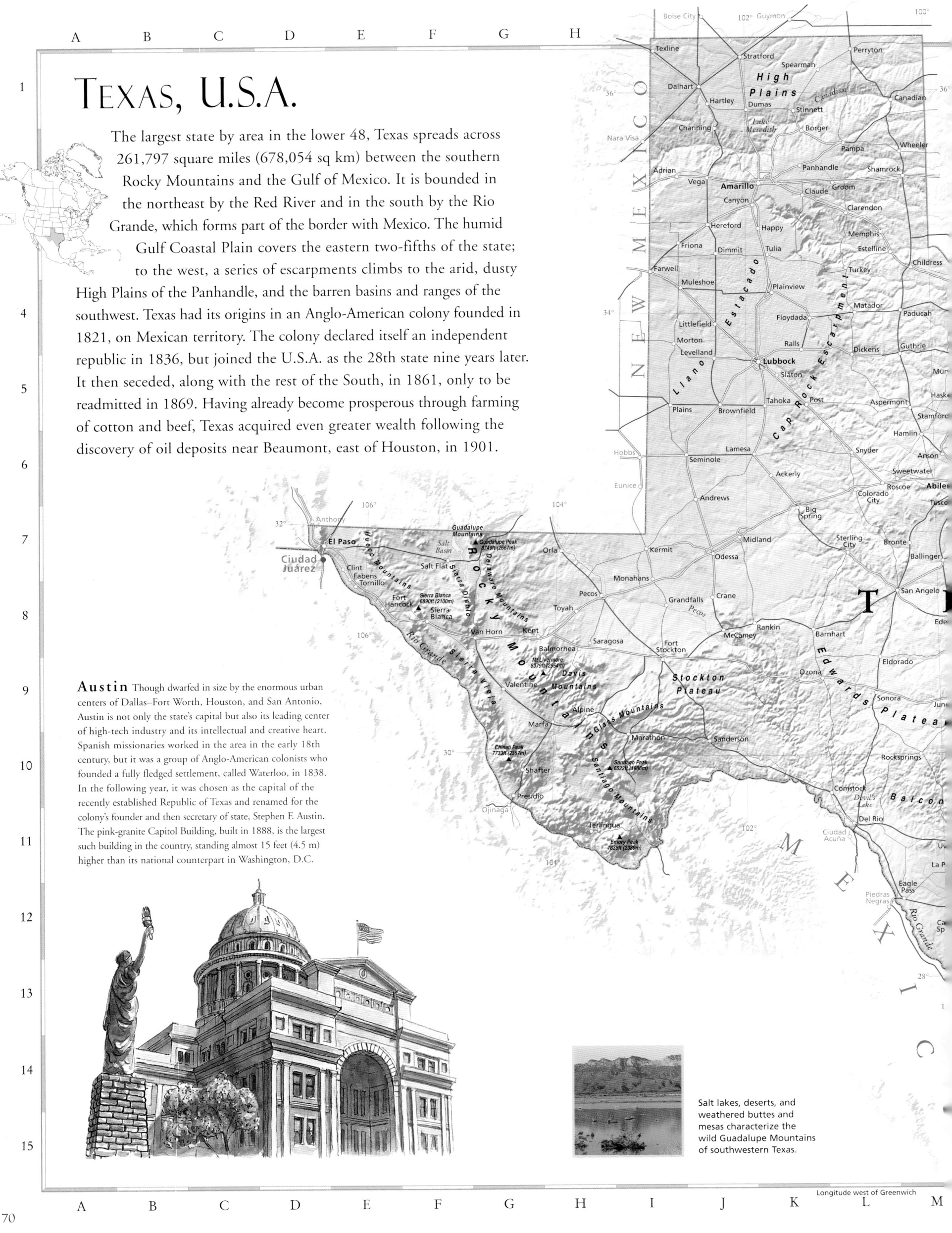

TEXAS, U.S.A.

The largest state by area in the lower 48, Texas spreads across 261,797 square miles (678,054 sq km) between the southern Rocky Mountains and the Gulf of Mexico. It is bounded in the northeast by the Red River and in the south by the Rio Grande, which forms part of the border with Mexico. The humid Gulf Coastal Plain covers the eastern two-fifths of the state; to the west, a series of escarpments climbs to the arid, dusty High Plains of the Panhandle, and the barren basins and ranges of the southwest. Texas had its origins in an Anglo-American colony founded in 1821, on Mexican territory. The colony declared itself an independent republic in 1836, but joined the U.S.A. as the 28th state nine years later. It then seceded, along with the rest of the South, in 1861, only to be readmitted in 1869. Having already become prosperous through farming of cotton and beef, Texas acquired even greater wealth following the discovery of oil deposits near Beaumont, east of Houston, in 1901.

Austin Though dwarfed in size by the enormous urban centers of Dallas–Fort Worth, Houston, and San Antonio, Austin is not only the state's capital but also its leading center of high-tech industry and its intellectual and creative heart. Spanish missionaries worked in the area in the early 18th century, but it was a group of Anglo-American colonists who founded a fully fledged settlement, called Waterloo, in 1838. In the following year, it was chosen as the capital of the recently established Republic of Texas and renamed for the colony's founder and then secretary of state, Stephen F. Austin. The pink-granite Capitol Building, built in 1888, is the largest such building in the country, standing almost 15 feet (4.5 m) higher than its national counterpart in Washington, D.C.

Salt lakes, deserts, and weathered buttes and mesas characterize the wild Guadalupe Mountains of southwestern Texas.

Longitude west of Greenwich

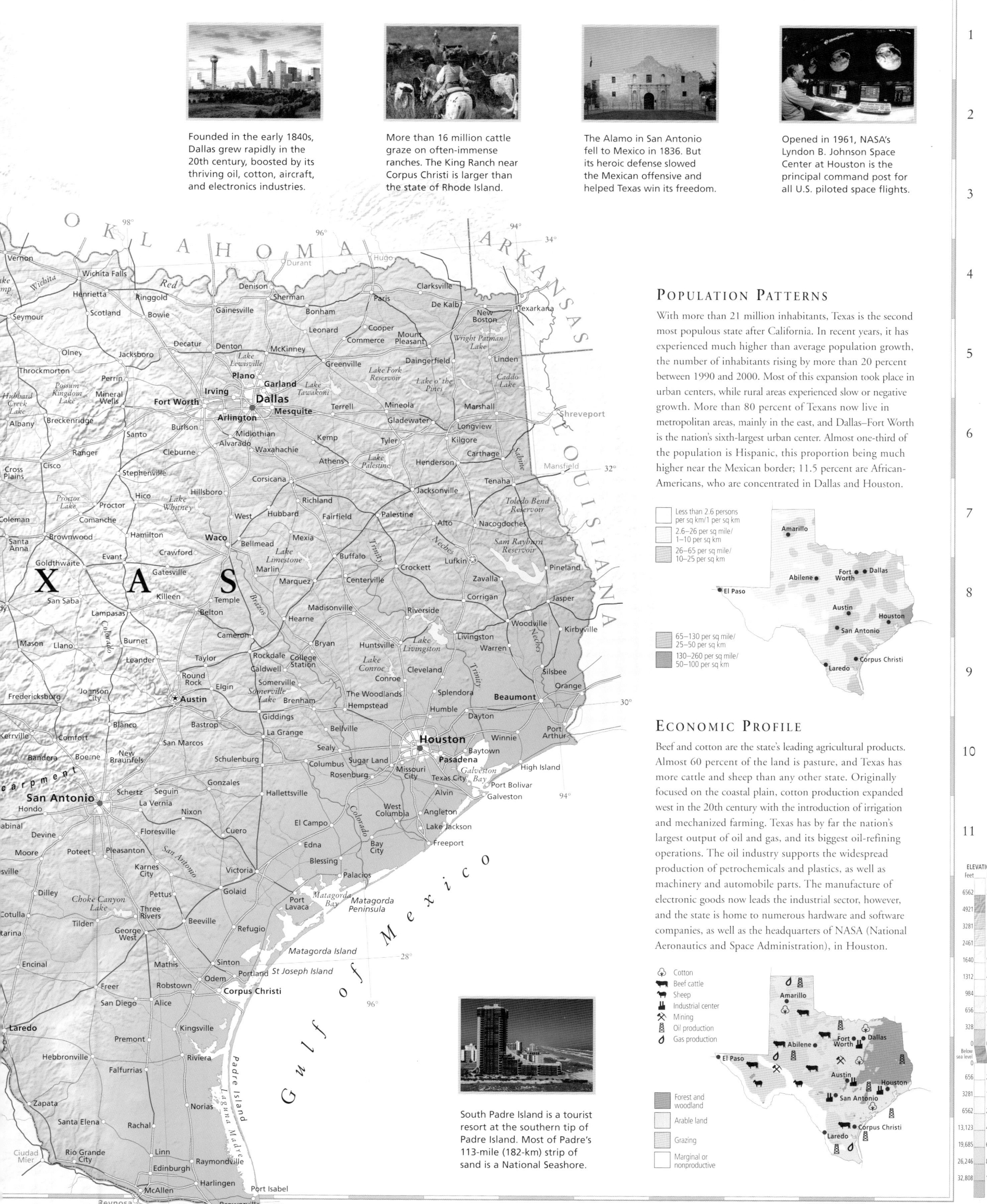

Founded in the early 1840s, Dallas grew rapidly in the 20th century, boosted by its thriving oil, cotton, aircraft, and electronics industries.

More than 16 million cattle graze on often-immense ranches. The King Ranch near Corpus Christi is larger than the state of Rhode Island.

The Alamo in San Antonio fell to Mexico in 1836. But its heroic defense slowed the Mexican offensive and helped Texas win its freedom.

Opened in 1961, NASA's Lyndon B. Johnson Space Center at Houston is the principal command post for all U.S. piloted space flights.

POPULATION PATTERNS

With more than 21 million inhabitants, Texas is the second most populous state after California. In recent years, it has experienced much higher than average population growth, the number of inhabitants rising by more than 20 percent between 1990 and 2000. Most of this expansion took place in urban centers, while rural areas experienced slow or negative growth. More than 80 percent of Texans now live in metropolitan areas, mainly in the east, and Dallas–Fort Worth is the nation's sixth-largest urban center. Almost one-third of the population is Hispanic, this proportion being much higher near the Mexican border; 11.5 percent are African-Americans, who are concentrated in Dallas and Houston.

Less than 2.6 persons per sq mile/1 per sq km
2.6–26 per sq mile/1–10 per sq km
26–65 per sq mile/10–25 per sq km
65–130 per sq mile/25–50 per sq km
130–260 per sq mile/50–100 per sq km

ECONOMIC PROFILE

Beef and cotton are the state's leading agricultural products. Almost 60 percent of the land is pasture, and Texas has more cattle and sheep than any other state. Originally focused on the coastal plain, cotton production expanded west in the 20th century with the introduction of irrigation and mechanized farming. Texas has by far the nation's largest output of oil and gas, and its biggest oil-refining operations. The oil industry supports the widespread production of petrochemicals and plastics, as well as machinery and automobile parts. The manufacture of electronic goods now leads the industrial sector, however, and the state is home to numerous hardware and software companies, as well as the headquarters of NASA (National Aeronautics and Space Administration), in Houston.

Cotton
Beef cattle
Sheep
Industrial center
Mining
Oil production
Gas production

Forest and woodland
Arable land
Grazing
Marginal or nonproductive

South Padre Island is a tourist resort at the southern tip of Padre Island. Most of Padre's 113-mile (182-km) strip of sand is a National Seashore.

ELEVATION
Feet	Meters
6562	2000
4921	1500
3281	1000
2461	750
1640	500
1312	400
984	300
656	200
328	100
Below sea level	0
656	200
3281	1000
6562	2000
13,123	4000
19,685	6000
26,246	8000
32,808	10,000

SCALE 1:3,750,000
Lamberts Conformal Conic Projection
100 miles
100 kilometers

NORTHERN ROCKIES, U.S.A.
Idaho, Montana, Wyoming

The Rocky Mountains form a broad diagonal band across northern Idaho and western Montana and Wyoming. In southern Idaho, the Columbia Plateau and Snake River Plain skirt the mountains. On their eastern flank, the Rockies level out on the Great Plains, an expanse of rolling pastures and wheat fields. Still little developed, the Northern Rockies are the traditional homeland of native peoples such as the Nez Perce, Shoshone, Cheyenne, and Sioux. The first Europeans to visit were Lewis and Clark, during their momentous expedition of 1804–06. Only a trickle of traders and trappers followed, until a gold rush in the early 1860s. Once the boom was over, prospectors turned their hands to mining other minerals, and to forestry and farming—still the foundations of the economy.

Old Faithful is one of 200 or so geysers in Yellowstone National Park, Wyoming. A major tourist destination, Yellowstone also encompasses 10,000 hot springs.

POPULATION PATTERNS

Population density is low—Wyoming is the nation's least populous state, despite being the ninth biggest by area—and there are few large cities, with only Boise's population surpassing 100,000. Towns line the major river valleys, and half of Wyoming's population is concentrated in the southeastern quarter of the state. Wide open spaces separate settlements elsewhere. The population is overwhelmingly white, but includes a much higher than average proportion of Native Americans. In 1990–2000, Idaho was the fifth fastest-growing state and Boise was the nation's seventh fastest-growing metropolitan area.

	Less than 2.6 persons per sq mile/1 per sq km
	2.6–26 per sq mile/ 1–10 per sq km
	26–65 per sq mile/ 10–25 per sq km
	65–130 per sq mile/ 25–50 per sq km

ECONOMIC PROFILE

Coal, oil, and gas are major sources of revenue in Montana and especially Wyoming (the nation's top coal producer), whereas mining in Idaho is focused on silver, lead, and molybdenum. Irrigation supports the cultivation of a range of crops, most notably potatoes in Idaho and wheat in the east. Huge numbers of cattle and sheep roam the plateaus and prairies. Forests are extensive, covering one-third of Idaho; timber is a vital resource there and in Montana. Most manufacturing involves the processing of raw materials. Tourism is a leading employer and revenue source.

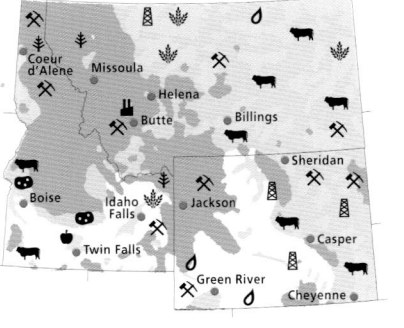

	Forest and woodland
	Arable land
	Grazing
	Marginal or nonproductive

- Cereals
- Potatoes
- Gas production
- Beef cattle
- Timber
- Industrial center
- Mining
- Oil production
- Fruit

THE TETON RANGE

Extending for 40 miles (64 km) across northwestern Wyoming, the Teton Range is one of the youngest and most imposing mountain ranges in the Rockies. Its jagged peaks began to form more than 1 million years ago when the land to the east dropped downward along a 50-mile (80-km) fault line. Today, 13,770-foot (4,197-m) Grand Teton, the highest peak in the range, rises 7,000 feet (2,135 m) above the valley of Jackson Hole.

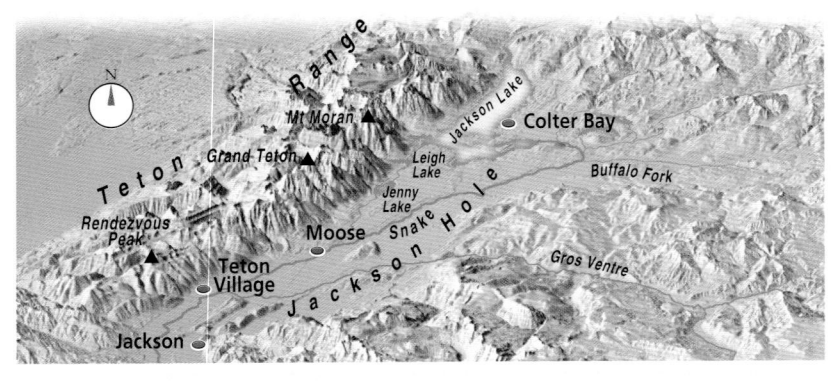

The Northern Rockies harbor the country's largest bison populations.

The Capitol Building in Boise was completed in 1920, 30 years after Idaho became a state.

ELEVATION
Feet / Meters

6562	2000
4921	1500
3281	1000
2461	750
1640	500
1312	400
984	300
656	200
328	100
0	0
Below sea level	
656	200
3281	1000
6562	2000
13,123	4000
19,685	6000
26,246	8000
32,808	10,000

Longitude west of Greenwich

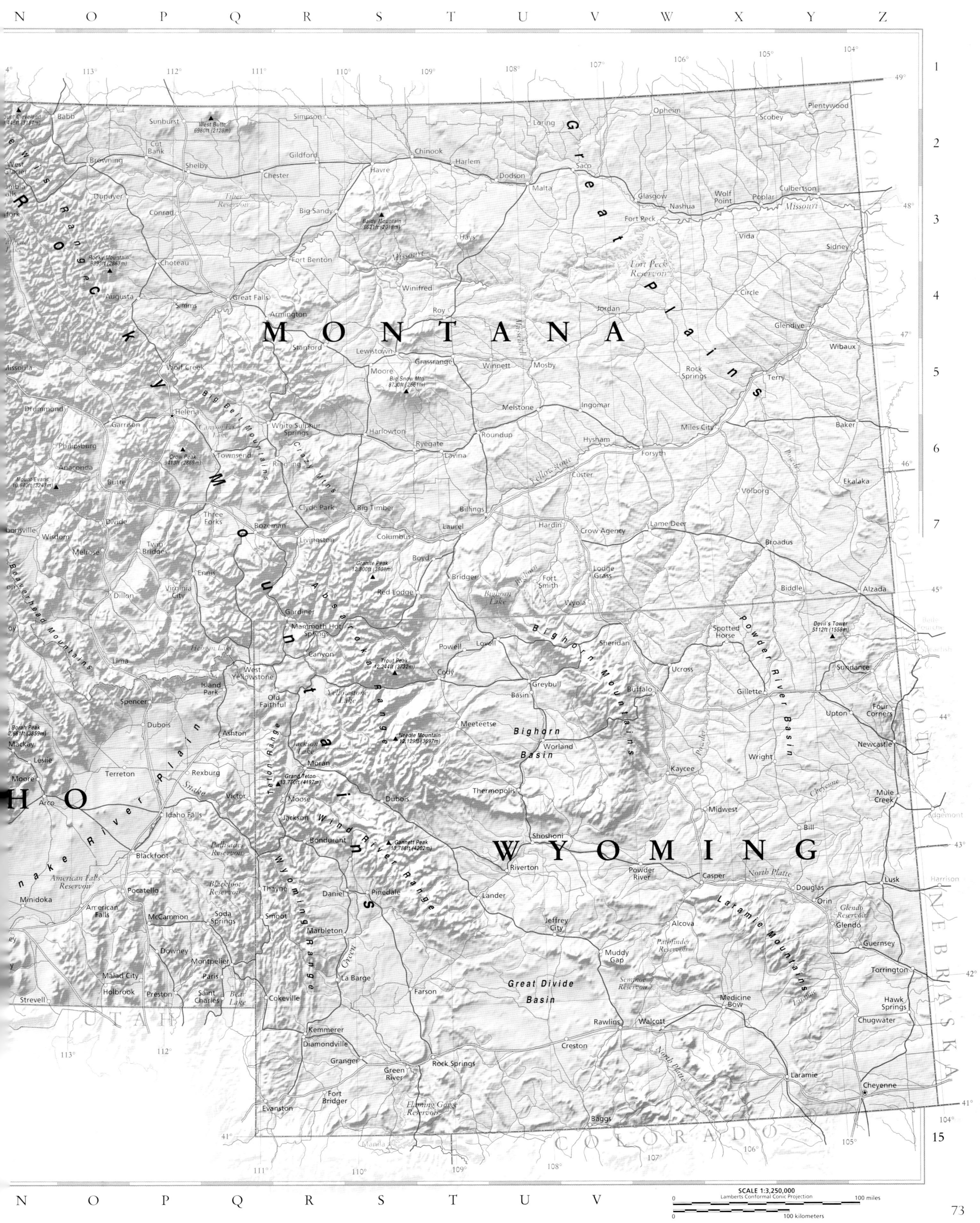

N O P Q R S T U V W X Y Z

113° 112° 111° 110° 109° 108° 107° 106° 105° 104°

Mt Cleveland
10,460ft (3184m)
Babb
Sunburst
Simpson
Loring
 Opheim
Scobey
Plentywood
49° 1

West
Glacier
Browning
Cut
Bank
Shelby
Gildford
Chinook
Harlem
Saco
Glasgow
Wolf
Point
Poplar
Culbertson
2

West Butte
6980ft (2128m)
Chester
Havre
Dodson
Malta
Fort Peck
Nashua
48°

Columbia
Falls
Dupuyer
Conrad
Tiber
Reservoir
Big Sandy
Baldy Mountain
6621ft (2018m)
Hays
Missouri
Fort Peck
Reservoir
Vida
Sidney
3

Rocky Mountain
9393ft (2863m)
Choteau
Fort Benton
Winifred
Circle

Augusta
Great Falls
Armington
Roy
Jordan
Glendive
Wibaux
47°

Missoula
Simms
MONTANA
Stanford
Lewistown
Grassrange
Winnett
Mosby
Rock
Springs
Terry
4

Wolf Creek
Moore
Big Snow Mtn
8730ft (2661m)
Melstone
Ingomar
Miles City
Baker
5

Drummond
Garrison
Helena
White Sulphur
Springs
Harlowton
Ryegate
Lavina
Roundup
Hysham
Forsyth
Custer
Volborg
Ekalaka
46°

Philipsburg
Crow Peak
9413ft (2869m)
Townsend
Ringling
Clyde Park
Big Timber
Billings
Lame Deer

Anaconda
Butte
Three
Forks
Bozeman
Livingston
Columbus
Laurel
Hardin
Crow Agency
Broadus
7

Mount Evans
10,641ft (3243m)
Divide
Granite Peak
12,800ft (3901m)
Boyd
Bighorn
Lake
Lodge
Grass
Biddle

Wisdom
Melrose
Twin
Bridges
Ennis
Red Lodge
Bridger
Fort
Smith
Wyola
Alzada
45°

Dillon
Virginia
City
Gardiner
Mammoth Hot
Springs
Spotted
Horse
Devil's Tower
5112ft (1558m)

Lima
Helton Lake
West
Yellowstone
Canyon
Trout Peak
12,244ft (3732m)
Powell
Lovell
Sheridan
Ucross
Sundance
Gillette

Island
Park
Old
Faithful
Yellowstone
Lake
Cody
Greybull
Buffalo
Powder River Basin
44°

Borah Peak
12,661ft (3859m)
Spencer
Dubois
Ashton
Needle Mountain
12,129ft (3697m)
Basin
Bighorn
Basin
Upton
Four
Corners

Mackay
Leslie
Terreton
Rexburg
Jackson
Lake
Moran
Meeteetse
Worland
Kaycee
Wright
Newcastle

Moore
Arco
Snake River Plain
Victor
Grand Teton
13,770ft (4197m)
Moose
Dubois
Thermopolis
Midwest
Bill
43°

Idaho Falls
Jackson
Bondurant
Gannett Peak
13,785ft (4202m)
WYOMING
Shoshoni
Mule
Creek

Blackfoot
Palisades
Reservoir
Riverton
Powder
River
Casper
North Platte
Lusk

American Falls
Reservoir
Pocatello
Blackfoot
Reservoir
Thayne
Daniel
Pinedale
Lander
Jeffrey
City
Alcova
Douglas
Orin
Glendo
Reservoir
42°

Minidoka
American
Falls
McCammon
Soda
Springs
Smoot
Marbleton
Muddy
Gap
Pathfinder
Reservoir
Medicine
Bow
Glendo
Guernsey

Downey
La Barge
Farson
Great Divide
Basin
Seminoe
Reservoir
Torrington

Malad City
Holbrook
Montpelier
Paris
Saint
Charles
Bear
Lake
Cokeville
Rawlins
Walcott
Medicine
Bow
Hawk
Springs
Chugwater

Strevell
Preston
Diamondville
Kemmerer
Granger
Green
River
Rock Springs
Creston
Laramie
41°

UTAH
Evanston
Fort
Bridger
Manila
Flaming Gorge
Reservoir
Baggs
COLORADO
Cheyenne
15

113° 112° 111° 110° 109° 108° 107° 106° 105° 104°

N O P Q R S T U V

SOUTHWESTERN U.S.A.

Arizona, Colorado, New Mexico, Utah

The immense Colorado Plateau constitutes the core of this arid region. Bounded to the west by basin and range country, to the north and east by the southern Rockies, and to the south by the Sonoran Desert, it is characterized by ancient, eroded landscapes where barren plateaus sit beneath forested, snow-capped peaks, and rivers have carved deep chasms between broad mesas and towering buttes. Scattered cliff-dwellings and pueblos testify to thousands of years of Native American habitation. Historic missions and adobe architecture recall Spanish occupation between the 16th and early 19th centuries, and subsequent Mexican rule over much of the Southwest until 1848. Today, the region's dry, sunny climate, thriving high-tech industries, and astounding scenery make it one of the most-visited and fastest-growing parts of the country.

THE GRAND CANYON

A deep gash in the southwestern corner of the Colorado Plateau, the Grand Canyon was carved over millennia by the Colorado River. Extending 277 miles (446 km) and measuring 15 miles (24 km) across at its widest point, it is up to 6,000 feet (1,800 m) deep. Erosion has exposed rocks at the bottom of the canyon that are about 2 billion years old. Now encompassed by the national park of the same name, the canyon attracts up to 5 million visitors annually.

Salt Lake City In 1846, fleeing persecution in Illinois, 148 Mormons migrated more than 1,000 miles (1,600 km) to present-day Utah. Settling in the Valley of the Great Salt Lake in 1847, they founded a new settlement, initially called Great Salt Lake City. By the late 19th century, it had become, and remains, one of the most important commercial centers in the western U.S.A. Its focal point, and the heart of the Mormon faith, is Temple Square, site of the six-towered Mormon Temple, begun in 1853 and completed 40 years later.

Longitude west of Greenwich

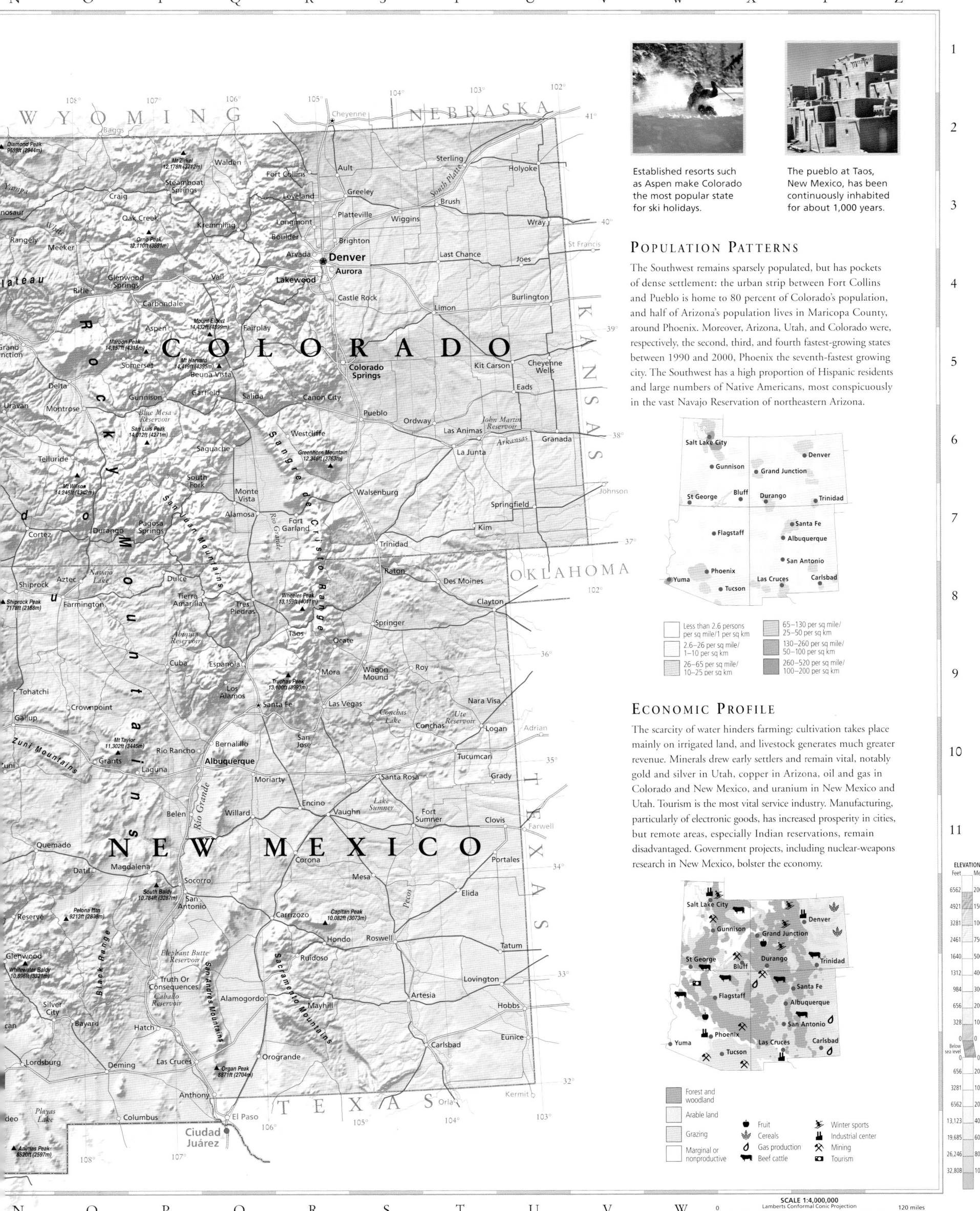

Established resorts such as Aspen make Colorado the most popular state for ski holidays.

The pueblo at Taos, New Mexico, has been continuously inhabited for about 1,000 years.

POPULATION PATTERNS

The Southwest remains sparsely populated, but has pockets of dense settlement: the urban strip between Fort Collins and Pueblo is home to 80 percent of Colorado's population, and half of Arizona's population lives in Maricopa County, around Phoenix. Moreover, Arizona, Utah, and Colorado were, respectively, the second, third, and fourth fastest-growing states between 1990 and 2000, Phoenix the seventh-fastest growing city. The Southwest has a high proportion of Hispanic residents and large numbers of Native Americans, most conspicuously in the vast Navajo Reservation of northeastern Arizona.

Less than 2.6 persons per sq mile/1 per sq km
2.6–26 per sq mile/ 1–10 per sq km
26–65 per sq mile/ 10–25 per sq km
65–130 per sq mile/ 25–50 per sq km
130–260 per sq mile/ 50–100 per sq km
260–520 per sq mile/ 100–200 per sq km

ECONOMIC PROFILE

The scarcity of water hinders farming: cultivation takes place mainly on irrigated land, and livestock generates much greater revenue. Minerals drew early settlers and remain vital, notably gold and silver in Utah, copper in Arizona, oil and gas in Colorado and New Mexico, and uranium in New Mexico and Utah. Tourism is the most vital service industry. Manufacturing, particularly of electronic goods, has increased prosperity in cities, but remote areas, especially Indian reservations, remain disadvantaged. Government projects, including nuclear-weapons research in New Mexico, bolster the economy.

Forest and woodland
Arable land
Grazing
Marginal or nonproductive

Fruit
Cereals
Gas production
Beef cattle

Winter sports
Industrial center
Mining
Tourism

ELEVATION

Feet	Meters
6562	2000
4921	1500
3281	1000
2461	750
1640	500
1312	400
984	300
656	200
328	100
Below sea level	
656	200
3281	1000
6562	2000
13,123	4000
19,685	6000
26,246	8000
32,808	10,000

SCALE 1:4,000,000
Lamberts Conformal Conic Projection
0 ___ 120 miles
0 ___ 120 kilometers

The Far West, U.S.A.

California, Nevada, Oregon, Washington

Geologically, the U.S. mainland's western fringe is its youngest and most active region. Plate movements here cause regular earthquakes in California and occasional volcanic eruptions in the Pacific Northwest. They have also given rise, over millions of years, to the two long mountain chains that parallel the shoreline. The Coast Ranges climb steeply from the sea, falling to sheltered lowlands, including the Central and Willamette valleys, which are enclosed in turn by the loftier peaks of the Cascade Range and Sierra Nevada. Farther east lies a jumble of arid landforms, including volcanic plateaus in the north, rows of north–south-trending basins and ranges in Nevada, and low-lying deserts in southeastern California. This intimidating terrain deterred early European immigrants, who clustered in coastal settlements and threaded their way along river valleys before being lured into the uplands by the discovery of gold and other minerals in the mid-19th century. In the 20th century, southern California's warm climate, available land, and thriving ports drew millions west, making it one of the nation's most populous regions.

Washington's Mount Rainier is crowned by the largest glacier system in the lower 48 states.

Crater Lake, Oregon, fills a caldera that was once part of an enormous volcano, Mount Mazama.

Population Patterns

California has the largest state population, of more than 34 million. More than 90 percent of these people live in urban areas, mainly around Los Angeles and San Diego, and San Francisco and Oakland. One-third of Californians are Hispanic or Latino. In the Pacific Northwest, densely populated areas include the shores of Puget Sound and Oregon's Willamette Valley. In the east, settlements are small and scattered; an exception is Las Vegas, a desert metropolis founded on gambling and tourism. Between 1990 and 2000, Nevada grew faster than any other state, increasing its population by 66 percent.

Less than 2.6 persons per sq mile/1 per sq km
2.6–26 per sq mile/1–10 per sq km
26–65 per sq mile/10–25 per sq km
65–130 per sq mile/25–50 per sq km
130–260 per sq mile/50–100 per sq km
260–570 per sq mile/100–200 per sq km
520–1040 per sq mile/200–400 per sq km

Economic Profile

The region has just a few pockets of arable land, most of which require irrigation, but they include California's productive Central Valley, and its Napa Valley vineyards, and the fertile Columbia Basin. The Pacific Northwest has enormous stands of timber and abundant hydroelectric power—Washington generates one-third of U.S. supplies. Nevada benefits from reserves of gold and mercury, and hosts major military test sites—85 percent of the land is government-owned. Seattle and San Francisco's famed Silicon Valley are world leaders in new technologies, and Seattle is also a major aircraft manufacturer. As well as the Hollywood film industry, Los Angeles is home to major TV and music corporations. Tourism is a vital industry throughout the region.

Forest and woodland
Arable land
Grazing
Marginal or nonproductive

Fruit and vegetables
Fruit
Wine
Beef cattle
Fishing
Industrial center
Mining
Tourism
Timber
Cereal
Citrus fruits
Dairy cattle

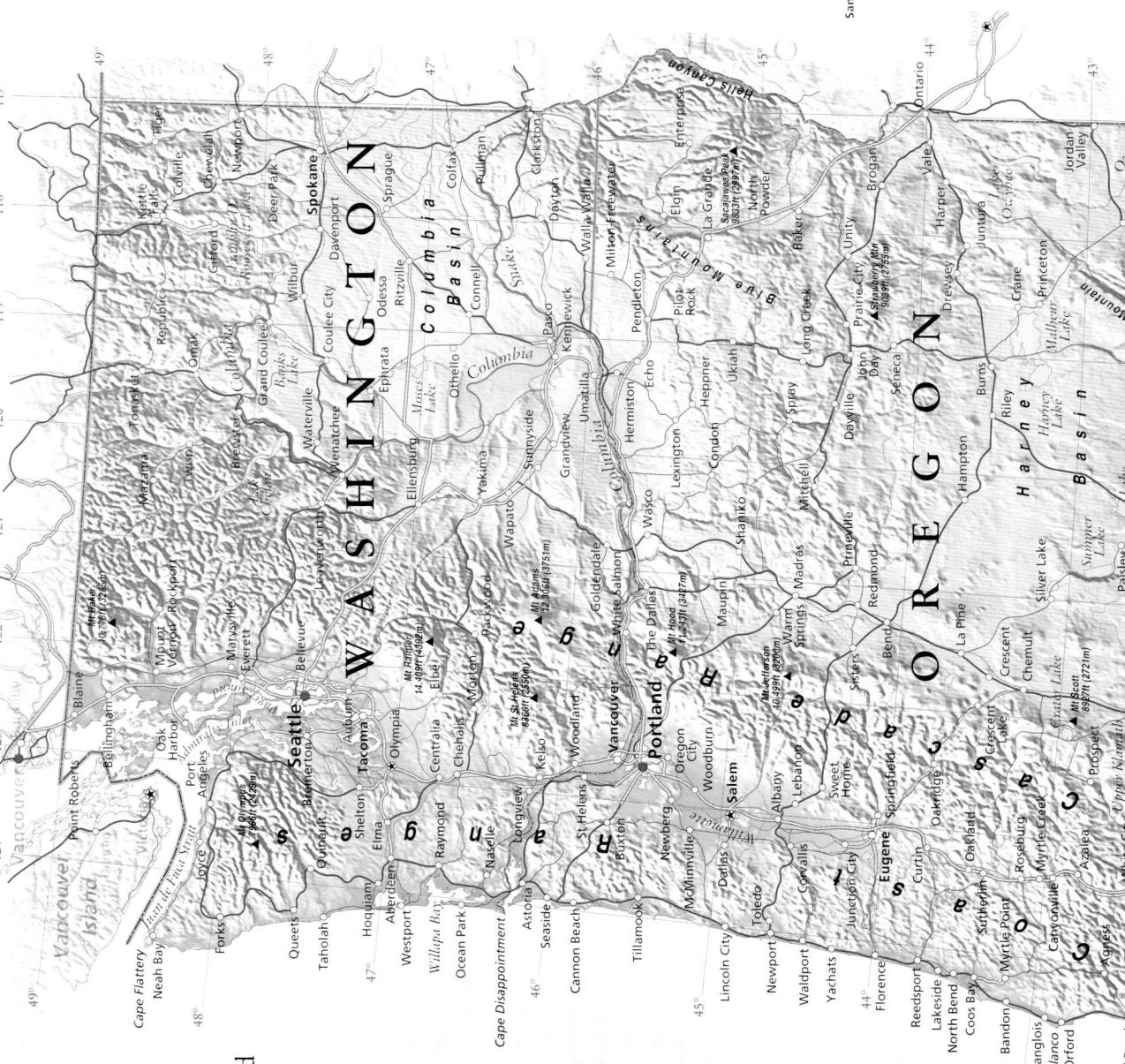

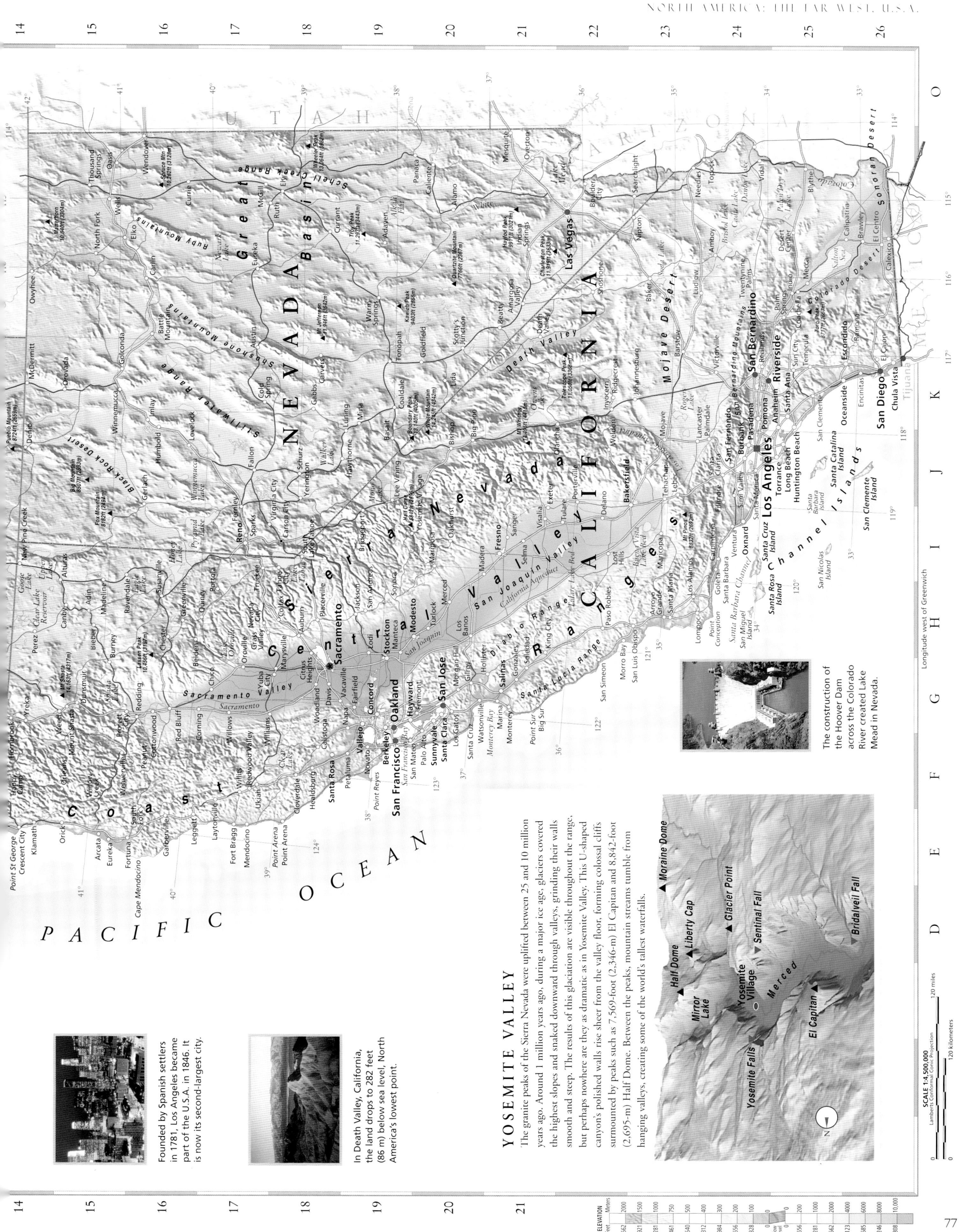

YOSEMITE VALLEY

The granite peaks of the Sierra Nevada were uplifted between 25 and 10 million years ago. Around 1 million years ago, during a major ice age, glaciers covered the highest slopes and snaked downward through valleys, grinding their walls smooth and steep. The results of this glaciation are visible throughout the range, but perhaps nowhere are they as dramatic as in Yosemite Valley. This U-shaped canyon's polished walls rise sheer from the valley floor, forming colossal cliffs surmounted by peaks such as 7,569-foot (2,346-m) El Capitan and 8,842-foot (2,695-m) Half Dome. Between the peaks, mountain streams tumble from hanging valleys, creating some of the world's tallest waterfalls.

Founded by Spanish settlers in 1781, Los Angeles became part of the U.S.A. in 1846. It is now its second-largest city.

In Death Valley, California, the land drops to 282 feet (86 m) below sea level, North America's lowest point.

The construction of the Hoover Dam across the Colorado River created Lake Mead in Nevada.

SCALE 1:4,500,000
Lambert's Conformal Conic Projection

0   120 miles
0   120 kilometers

ELEVATION
Feet   Meters
6562   2000
4921   1500
3281   1000
2461   750
1640   500
1312   400
984   300
656   200
328   100
0   Below sea level
656   200
3281   1000
6562   2000
13,123 4000
19,685 6000
26,246 8000
32,808 10,000

77

ALASKA AND HAWAII, U.S.A.

Alaska and Hawaii are the only two states that are not part of the lower 48, and both became states—the 49th and 50th, respectively—in the same year, 1959. Their territories, however, could hardly be more different. Separated from the rest of the country by western Canada, Alaska is by far the largest state and about 95 times the size of Hawaii—though it has only half as many inhabitants. Its huge, oblong landmass is mountainous, little developed, and mostly inhospitable: winters are severe across most of the state and one-third of the land is barren tundra. Hawaii is a chain of 137 volcanic islands, measuring 1,500 miles (2,400 km) in length and including eight major islands, located in the middle of the Pacific Ocean, about 2,400 miles (3,860 km) west of San Francisco. Cloaked with tracts of tropical forest and fringed by golden beaches, the Hawaiian Islands have fertile soils and are warm and, for the most part, well-watered year-round.

In summer, herds of caribou migrate to Alaska's Arctic tundra to breed.

The Trans-Alaska Oil Pipeline extends from Prudhoe Bay to the port of Valdez.

HAWAII

Hawaiian Islands

Kilauea
Kauai
Waimea   Lihue
Niihau
Kauai Channel

Waimea   Oahu
Wahiawa
Pearl City   Kaneohe
Ewa Beach   Honolulu
Pearl Harbor   Kaiwi Channel
Molokai
Kaunakakai   Maui
Lanai   Lahaina   Wailuku   Kailua
Lanai City   Kihei   Haleakala   Hana
Kahoolawe   10,023ft (3055m)
Alenuihaha Channel

Upolu Point
Waimea   Hawi
Honokaa
Keahole Point   Mauna Kea
Honokohau   13,796ft (4205m)   Honolulu
Hilo
Captain Cook   Mauna Loa   Keaau
13,678ft (4169m)
Kauna Point   Volcano
Kilauea
13,379ft (4078m)
Hawaii
Naalehu
Kauna Point
Ka Lae

PACIFIC OCEAN

SCALE 1:5,750,000
Lamberts Conformal Conic Projection   100 miles
0   100 kilometers

Longitude west of Greenwich

Named Denali by local Native American people, Mount McKinley is the tallest peak in North America, rising to 20,321 feet (6,194 m).

Kilauea, on the island of Hawaii, is the world's largest active volcanic crater. Its regular eruptions generate extensive lava flows.

Chukchi Sea
RUSSIAN FEDERATION
Wevok
Point Hope
Arctic Circle
Bering Strait
Kotze Sou
Shishmaref
Seward Peninsula
Brevig Mission   Teller
Sinuk
Nome
Cape Nome
Northwest Cape
Savoonga
St Lawrence Island
Northeast Cape
Nort Soun
Bering Sea
Emmonak   Stet
Scammon Bay
Hooper Bay   Chevak
St Matthew Island
Cape Mohican   Nunivak Island   Tanunak   Beth
Etolin Strait   Chefornak
Kipnuk
Kwigillingok
Quinhaga
Kuskokwim Bay   Goodnew
Platinum
Cape Newenham

St Paul Island
Pribilof Islands
St George Island

ELEVATION
Feet	Meters
6562	2000
4921	1500
3281	1000
2461	750
1640	500
1312	400
984	300
656	200
328	100
Below sea level	0
0	0
656	200
3281	1000
6562	2000
13,123	4000
19,685	6000
26,246	8000
32,808	10,000

Near Islands
Attu Island
Agattu Strait   Shemya Island
Agattu Island
Rat Islands
Buldir Island
Kiska Island
Segula Island
Rat Island   Little Sitkin Island
Semisopochnoi Island
Amchitka Island   Amchitka Pass
Gareloi Island
Tanaga Island
Amchitka Islands   Kanaga Island   Adak
Adak Island   Atka   Atka Island   Amlia Island
Andreanof Islands   Seguam Island
Seguam Pass
Amukta Pass
Yunaska Island
Islands of The Four Mountains
Umnak Island
Makushin Volcano   Akutan Island
6678ft (2036m)   Dutch Harbor
Unalaska Island
Fox Islands
Alaska
Shishaldin Volcano   Cold Bay
9371ft (2857m)   False Pass
Unimak Island   Sanak Islands
Unimak Pass

PACIFIC OCEAN

A swamp until the early 20th century, Waikiki Beach, Oahu, is Hawaii's, and one of the world's, best-known beaches.

Longitude west of Greenwich

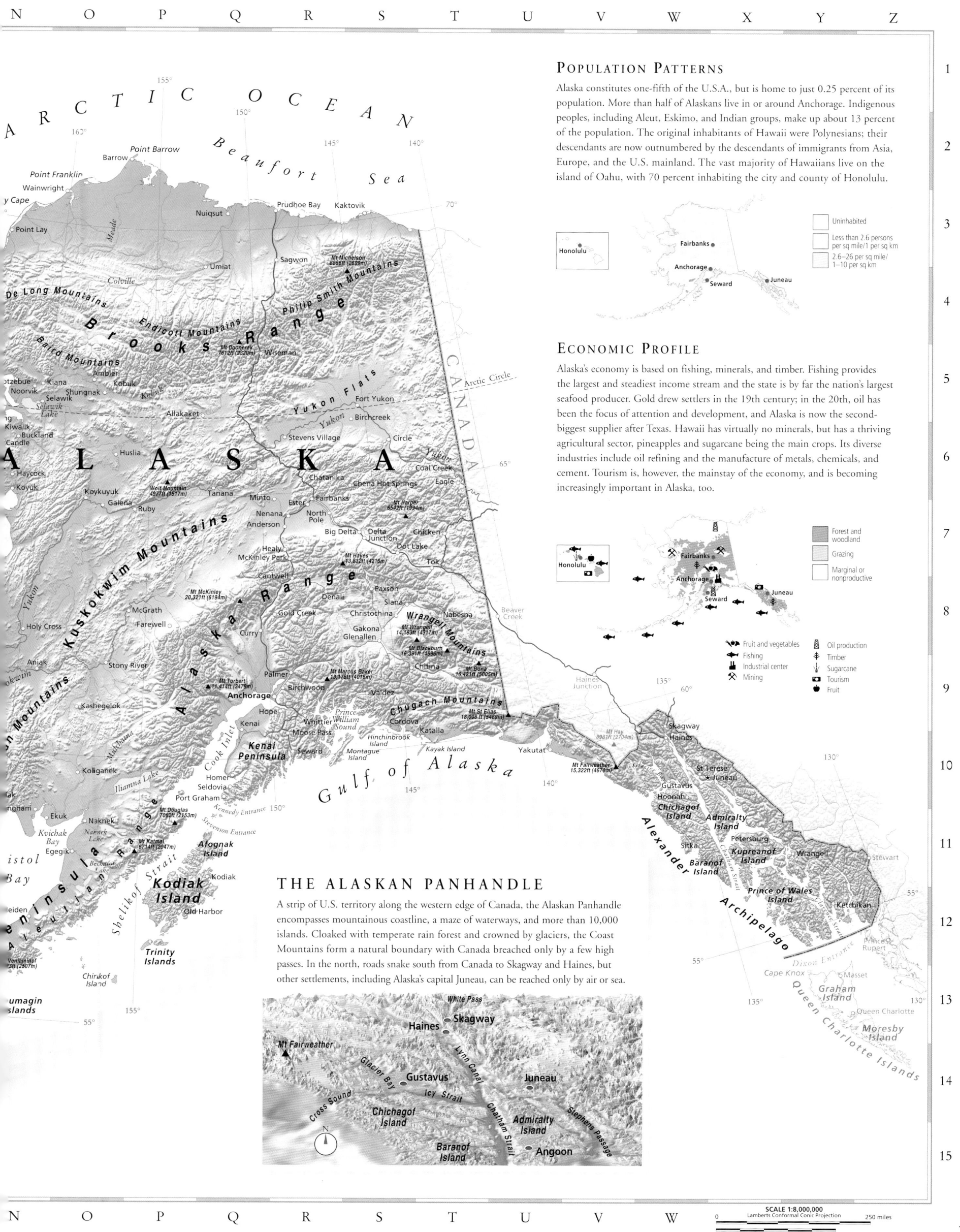

POPULATION PATTERNS

Alaska constitutes one-fifth of the U.S.A., but is home to just 0.25 percent of its population. More than half of Alaskans live in or around Anchorage. Indigenous peoples, including Aleut, Eskimo, and Indian groups, make up about 13 percent of the population. The original inhabitants of Hawaii were Polynesians; their descendants are now outnumbered by the descendants of immigrants from Asia, Europe, and the U.S. mainland. The vast majority of Hawaiians live on the island of Oahu, with 70 percent inhabiting the city and county of Honolulu.

Uninhabited

Less than 2.6 persons per sq mile/1 per sq km

2.6–26 per sq mile/ 1–10 per sq km

ECONOMIC PROFILE

Alaska's economy is based on fishing, minerals, and timber. Fishing provides the largest and steadiest income stream and the state is by far the nation's largest seafood producer. Gold drew settlers in the 19th century; in the 20th, oil has been the focus of attention and development, and Alaska is now the second-biggest supplier after Texas. Hawaii has virtually no minerals, but has a thriving agricultural sector, pineapples and sugarcane being the main crops. Its diverse industries include oil refining and the manufacture of metals, chemicals, and cement. Tourism is, however, the mainstay of the economy, and is becoming increasingly important in Alaska, too.

Forest and woodland

Grazing

Marginal or nonproductive

Fruit and vegetables

Fishing

Industrial center

Mining

Oil production

Timber

Sugarcane

Tourism

Fruit

THE ALASKAN PANHANDLE

A strip of U.S. territory along the western edge of Canada, the Alaskan Panhandle encompasses mountainous coastline, a maze of waterways, and more than 10,000 islands. Cloaked with temperate rain forest and crowned by glaciers, the Coast Mountains form a natural boundary with Canada breached only by a few high passes. In the north, roads snake south from Canada to Skagway and Haines, but other settlements, including Alaska's capital Juneau, can be reached only by air or sea.

SCALE 1:8,000,000
Lamberts Conformal Conic Projection

0   250 miles

0   250 kilometers

CANADA

Occupying most of the northern third of North America, Canada is the world's second-largest country by area, but also one of its most sparsely inhabited. A band of western ranges, including the Coast and Rocky mountains, and a number of lower, much older mountain chains in the east, enclose the vast Canadian Shield, an ancient, low, bowl-shaped plateau. Originally home to scattered Indian and Inuit peoples, Canada was visited in the 11th century by Viking explorers, who founded a short-lived settlement in Newfoundland. The French laid claim to the St Lawrence River Valley in the 16th century, but by 1763 most of North America was under British control. The self-governing British dominion of Canada was created in 1867. Initially, it included only Ontario, Québec, New Brunswick, and Nova Scotia, but other areas were gradually absorbed into the confederation, which now consists of ten provinces and three territories.

Mostly uninhabited, mountainous Baffin Island is Canada's largest island.

Waterlogged boreal forest, of spruce, fir, and birch, spans the entire country.

Toronto Canada's most populous city, with around 5 million inhabitants, and its leading commercial and financial center, Toronto originated in the 17th century as a trading post founded at the intersection of several Indian trails (Toronto is a Huron word meaning "meeting place"). Despite being chosen as the site for the capital of Ontario in 1793, the settlement remained undeveloped until the arrival of the Grand Trunk and Great Western railways in the 1850s, after which its population rose to more than half a million by 1921. The modern skyline is dominated by the CN Tower, which rises to 1,815 feet (553 m) and is the world's tallest self-supporting structure.

CN Tower

POPULATION PATTERNS

Vast areas of northern Canada are virtually uninhabited: Nunavut and the Yukon and Northwest territories encompass 41 percent of the land, but have just 0.3 percent of the population. Nunavut has no roads. About 80 percent of Canadians live in the temperate south, within 100 miles (160 km) of the U.S. border. The population is highly urbanized, with four-fifths living in towns and cities. It is also ethnically diverse, one-third of Canadians being of mixed descent. Most, however, are of European, especially British or French, origin. Indigenous peoples make up just 3 percent of the population. Both English and French are official languages and bilingualism is encouraged: 17 percent of Canadians can use both languages.

Uninhabited

Less than 2.6 persons per sq mile/1 per sq km

2.6–26 per sq mile/ 1–10 per sq km

26–65 per sq mile/ 10–25 per sq km

65–130 per sq mile/ 25–50 per sq km

130–260 per sq mile/ 50–100 per sq km

260–520 per sq mile/ 100–200 per sq km

520–1040 per sq mile/ 200–400 per sq km

1040–2080 per sq mile/ 400–800 per sq km

More than 2080 per sq mile/800 per sq km

ECONOMIC PROFILE

Almost half of the country is forested and Canada is the world's leading producer of pulp, paper, and wood. Ample fresh water is harnessed by hydroelectric plants to provide 60 percent of energy needs. Canada is among the world's top sources of zinc, uranium, nickel, bauxite, copper, and gold, and produces far more oil and gas than it uses. Arable land is limited in extent, covering just 7 percent of the country, but productive. Manufacturing is led by transportation equipment, food, machinery, and wood products. Services employ three-quarters of Canadians and generate two-thirds of GDP.

Cereals
Fruit and vegetables
Fruit
Beef cattle
Fishing
Industrial center
Mining
Oil production
Gas production
Timber

Forest and woodland
Arable land
Grazing
Marginal or nonproductive

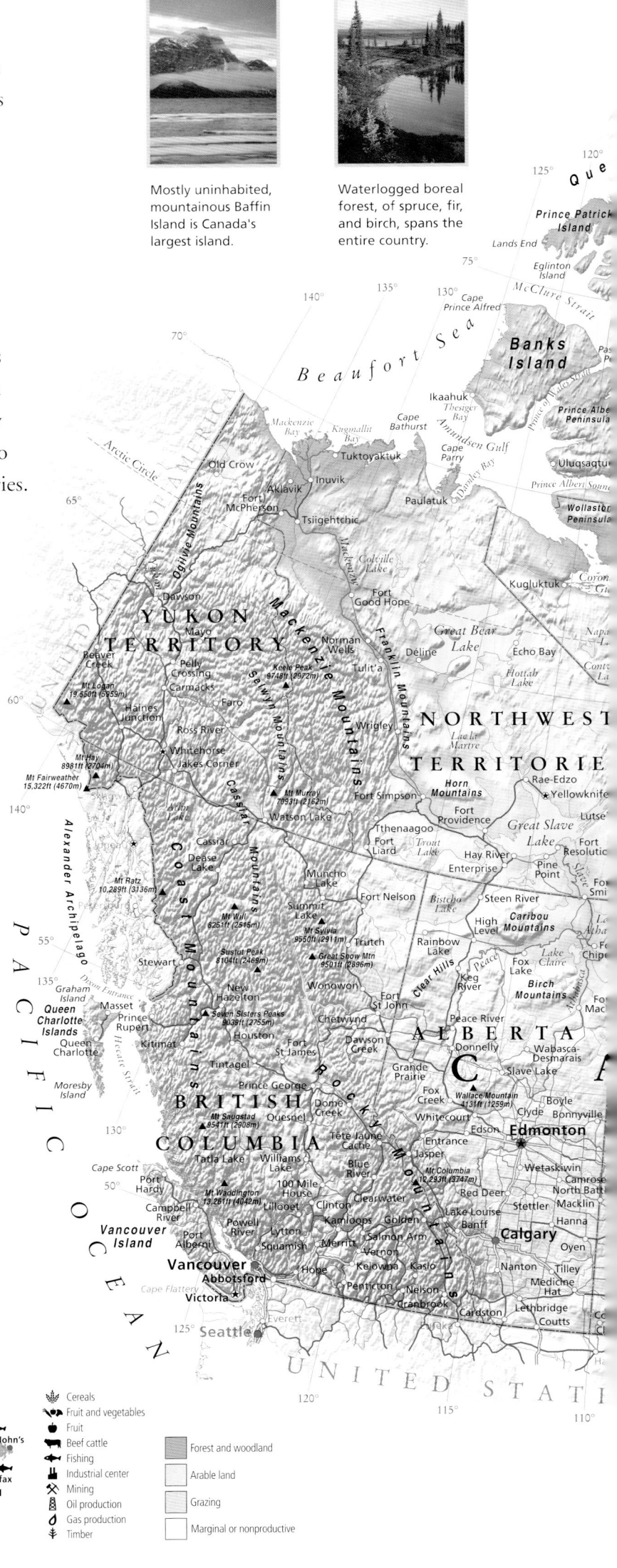

Longitude west of Greenwich

THE CANADIAN ROCKIES

Together with the adjacent Columbia Mountains, the Rockies formed a formidable barrier to Canadian expansion in the late 19th century. A number of passes became major communications routes, including Kicking Horse Pass near Lake Louise, which was threaded by the Canadian Pacific Railway, completed in 1885, and the Trans-Canada Highway, which opened in 1962. Yellowhead Pass, near Jasper, was the route chosen by the Canadian Northern Railway, in 1913.

In 1999, Canada created the territory of Nunavut as a homeland for the indigenous Inuit people.

The nation's famous Royal Canadian Mounted Police Force was first deployed in western Canada in 1873.

ELEVATION	
Feet	Meters
6562	2000
4921	1500
3281	1000
2461	750
1640	500
1312	400
984	300
656	200
328	100
Below sea level	0
656	200
3281	1000
6562	2000
13,123	4000
19,685	6000
26,246	8000
32,808	10,000

SCALE 1:15,000,000
Lamberts Conformal Conic Projection
0 — 400 miles
0 — 400 kilometers

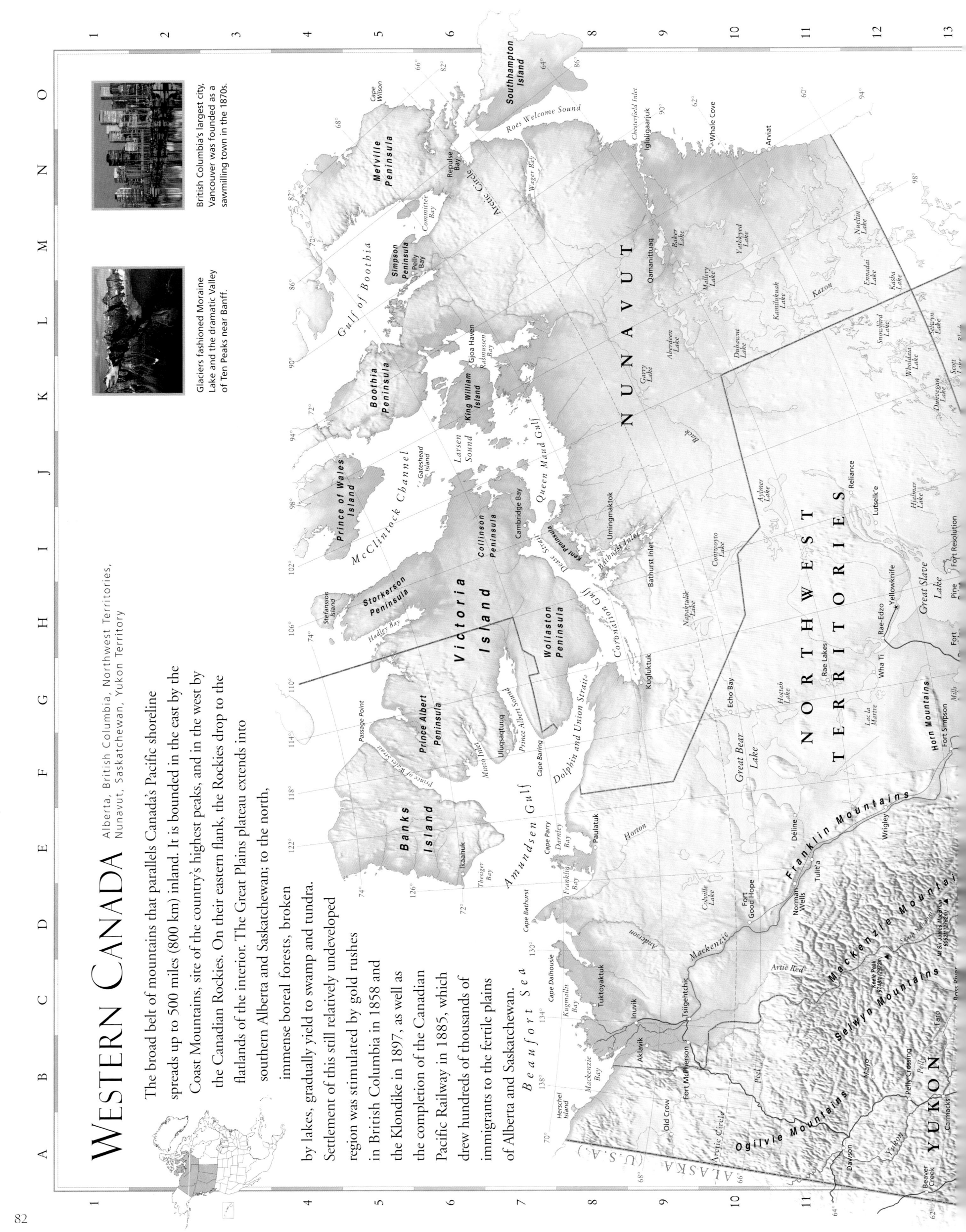

WESTERN CANADA

Alberta, British Columbia, Northwest Territories, Nunavut, Saskatchewan, Yukon Territory

The broad belt of mountains that parallels Canada's Pacific shoreline spreads up to 500 miles (800 km) inland. It is bounded in the east by the Coast Mountains, site of the country's highest peaks, and in the west by the Canadian Rockies. On their eastern flank, the Rockies drop to the flatlands of the interior. The Great Plains plateau extends into southern Alberta and Saskatchewan; to the north, immense boreal forests, broken by lakes, gradually yield to swamp and tundra. Settlement of this still relatively undeveloped region was stimulated by gold rushes in British Columbia in 1858 and the Klondike in 1897, as well as the completion of the Canadian Pacific Railway in 1885, which drew hundreds of thousands of immigrants to the fertile plains of Alberta and Saskatchewan.

British Columbia's largest city, Vancouver was founded as a sawmilling town in the 1870s.

Glaciers fashioned Moraine Lake and the dramatic Valley of Ten Peaks near Banff.

Southampton Island

Melville Peninsula

Simpson Peninsula

Gulf of Bootbia

Boothia Peninsula

Prince of Wales Island

McClintock Channel

Storkerson Peninsula

Victoria Island

Collinson Peninsula

Queen Maud Gulf

Wollaston Peninsula

Prince Albert Peninsula

Banks Island

Amundsen Gulf

Beaufort Sea

Dolphin and Union Strait

Coronation Gulf

NUNAVUT

NORTHWEST TERRITORIES

Great Bear Lake

Great Slave Lake

Franklin Mountains

Mackenzie Mountains

Selwyn Mountains

Ogilvie Mountains

Horn Mountains

YUKON

ALASKA (U.S.A.)

Arctic Circle

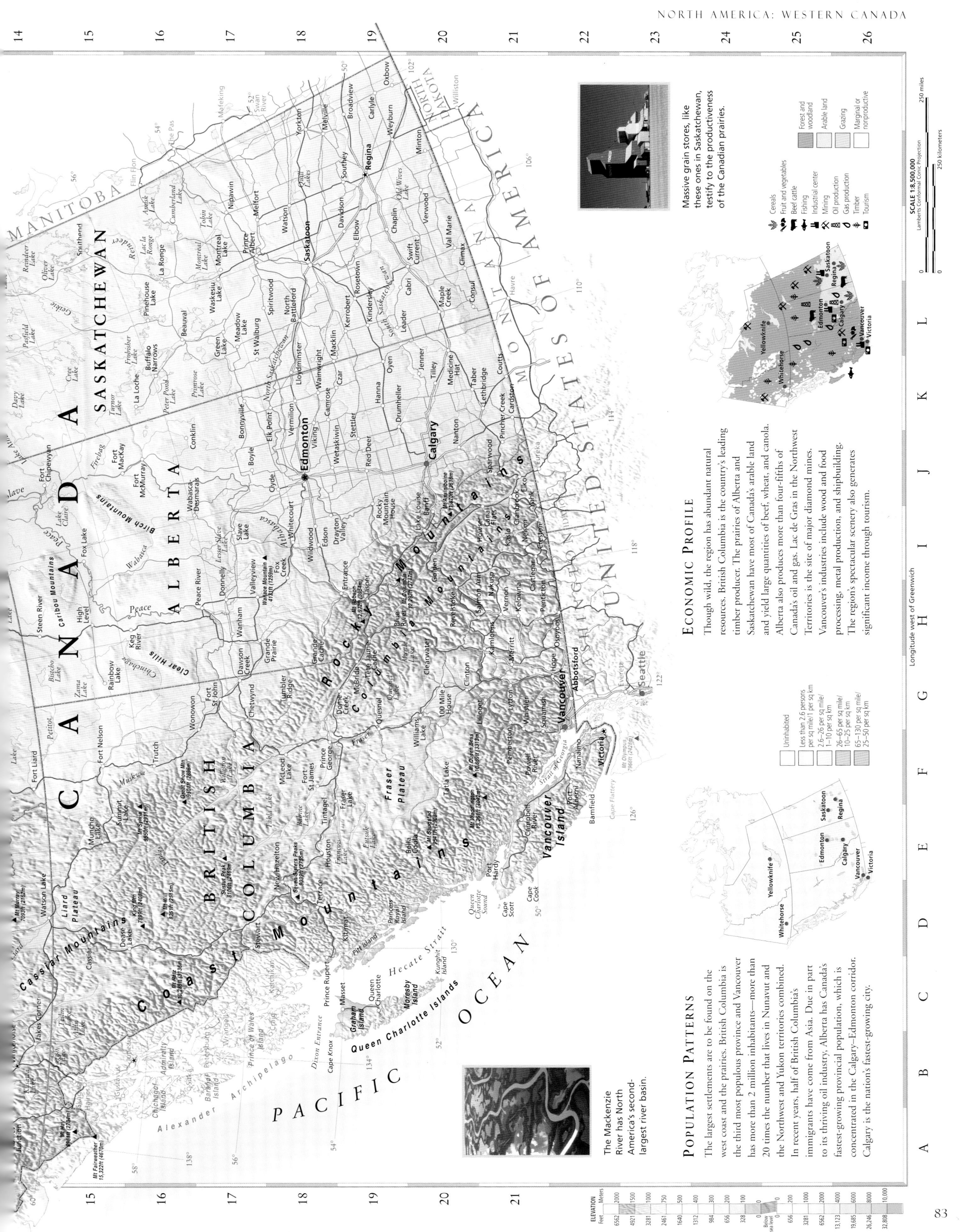

Massive grain stores, like these ones in Saskatchewan, testify to the productiveness of the Canadian prairies.

ECONOMIC PROFILE

Though wild, the region has abundant natural resources. British Columbia is the country's leading timber producer. The prairies of Alberta and Saskatchewan have most of Canada's arable land and yield large quantities of beef, wheat, and canola. Alberta also produces more than four-fifths of Canada's oil and gas. Lac de Gras in the Northwest Territories is the site of major diamond mines. Vancouver's industries include wood and food processing, metal production, and shipbuilding. The region's spectacular scenery also generates significant income through tourism.

Cereals
Fruit and vegetables
Beef cattle
Fishing
Industrial center
Mining
Oil production
Gas production
Timber
Tourism

Forest and woodland
Arable land
Grazing
Marginal or nonproductive

SCALE 1:8,500,000
Lambert's Conformal Conic Projection
250 miles
250 kilometers

Longitude west of Greenwich

The Mackenzie River has North America's second-largest river basin.

POPULATION PATTERNS

The largest settlements are to be found on the west coast and the prairies. British Columbia is the third most populous province and Vancouver has more than 2 million inhabitants—more than 20 times the number that lives in Nunavut and the Northwest and Yukon territories combined.

In recent years, half of British Columbia's immigrants have come from Asia. Due in part to its thriving oil industry, Alberta has Canada's fastest-growing provincial population, which is concentrated in the Calgary-Edmonton corridor. Calgary is the nation's fastest-growing city.

Uninhabited
Less than 2.6 persons per sq mile/1 per sq km
2.6–26 per sq mile/1–10 per sq km
26–65 per sq mile/10–25 per sq km
65–130 per sq mile/25–51 per sq km

ELEVATION
Feet   Meters
32,808 10,000
26,246 8000
19,685 6000
13,123 4000
6562   2000
3281   1000
1640   500
984   300
656   200
328   100
0   0
Below sea level

83

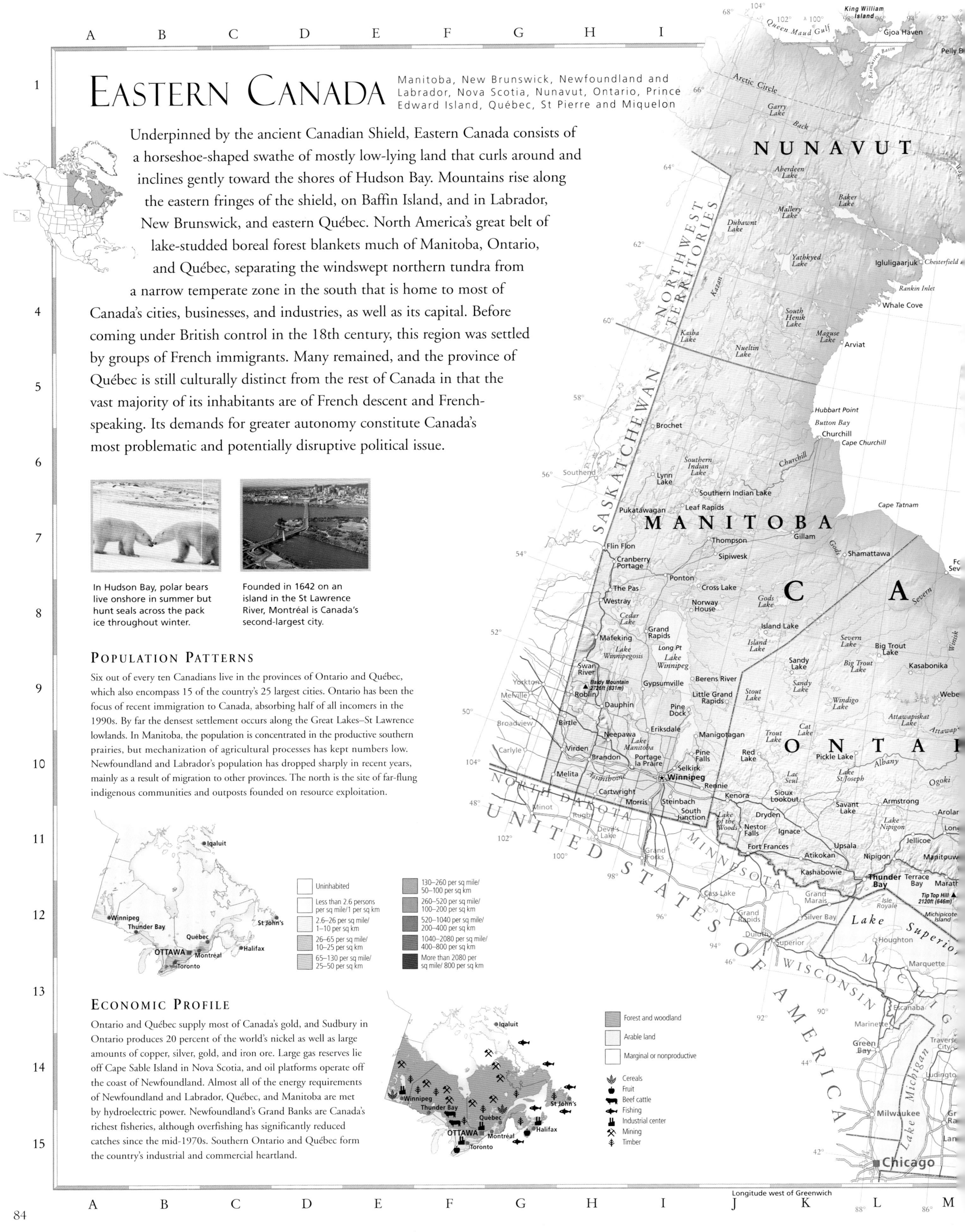

EASTERN CANADA

Manitoba, New Brunswick, Newfoundland and Labrador, Nova Scotia, Nunavut, Ontario, Prince Edward Island, Québec, St Pierre and Miquelon

Underpinned by the ancient Canadian Shield, Eastern Canada consists of a horseshoe-shaped swathe of mostly low-lying land that curls around and inclines gently toward the shores of Hudson Bay. Mountains rise along the eastern fringes of the shield, on Baffin Island, and in Labrador, New Brunswick, and eastern Québec. North America's great belt of lake-studded boreal forest blankets much of Manitoba, Ontario, and Québec, separating the windswept northern tundra from a narrow temperate zone in the south that is home to most of Canada's cities, businesses, and industries, as well as its capital. Before coming under British control in the 18th century, this region was settled by groups of French immigrants. Many remained, and the province of Québec is still culturally distinct from the rest of Canada in that the vast majority of its inhabitants are of French descent and French-speaking. Its demands for greater autonomy constitute Canada's most problematic and potentially disruptive political issue.

In Hudson Bay, polar bears live onshore in summer but hunt seals across the pack ice throughout winter.

Founded in 1642 on an island in the St Lawrence River, Montréal is Canada's second-largest city.

POPULATION PATTERNS

Six out of every ten Canadians live in the provinces of Ontario and Québec, which also encompass 15 of the country's 25 largest cities. Ontario has been the focus of recent immigration to Canada, absorbing half of all incomers in the 1990s. By far the densest settlement occurs along the Great Lakes–St Lawrence lowlands. In Manitoba, the population is concentrated in the productive southern prairies, but mechanization of agricultural processes has kept numbers low. Newfoundland and Labrador's population has dropped sharply in recent years, mainly as a result of migration to other provinces. The north is the site of far-flung indigenous communities and outposts founded on resource exploitation.

Uninhabited	130–260 per sq mile/50–100 per sq km
Less than 2.6 persons per sq mile/1 per sq km	260–520 per sq mile/100–200 per sq km
2.6–26 per sq mile/1–10 per sq km	520–1040 per sq mile/200–400 per sq km
26–65 per sq mile/10–25 per sq km	1040–2080 per sq mile/400–800 per sq km
65–130 per sq mile/25–50 per sq km	More than 2080 per sq mile/800 per sq km

ECONOMIC PROFILE

Ontario and Québec supply most of Canada's gold, and Sudbury in Ontario produces 20 percent of the world's nickel as well as large amounts of copper, silver, gold, and iron ore. Large gas reserves lie off Cape Sable Island in Nova Scotia, and oil platforms operate off the coast of Newfoundland. Almost all of the energy requirements of Newfoundland and Labrador, Québec, and Manitoba are met by hydroelectric power. Newfoundland's Grand Banks are Canada's richest fisheries, although overfishing has significantly reduced catches since the mid-1970s. Southern Ontario and Québec form the country's industrial and commercial heartland.

Forest and woodland	
Arable land	
Marginal or nonproductive	

- Cereals
- Fruit
- Beef cattle
- Fishing
- Industrial center
- Mining
- Timber

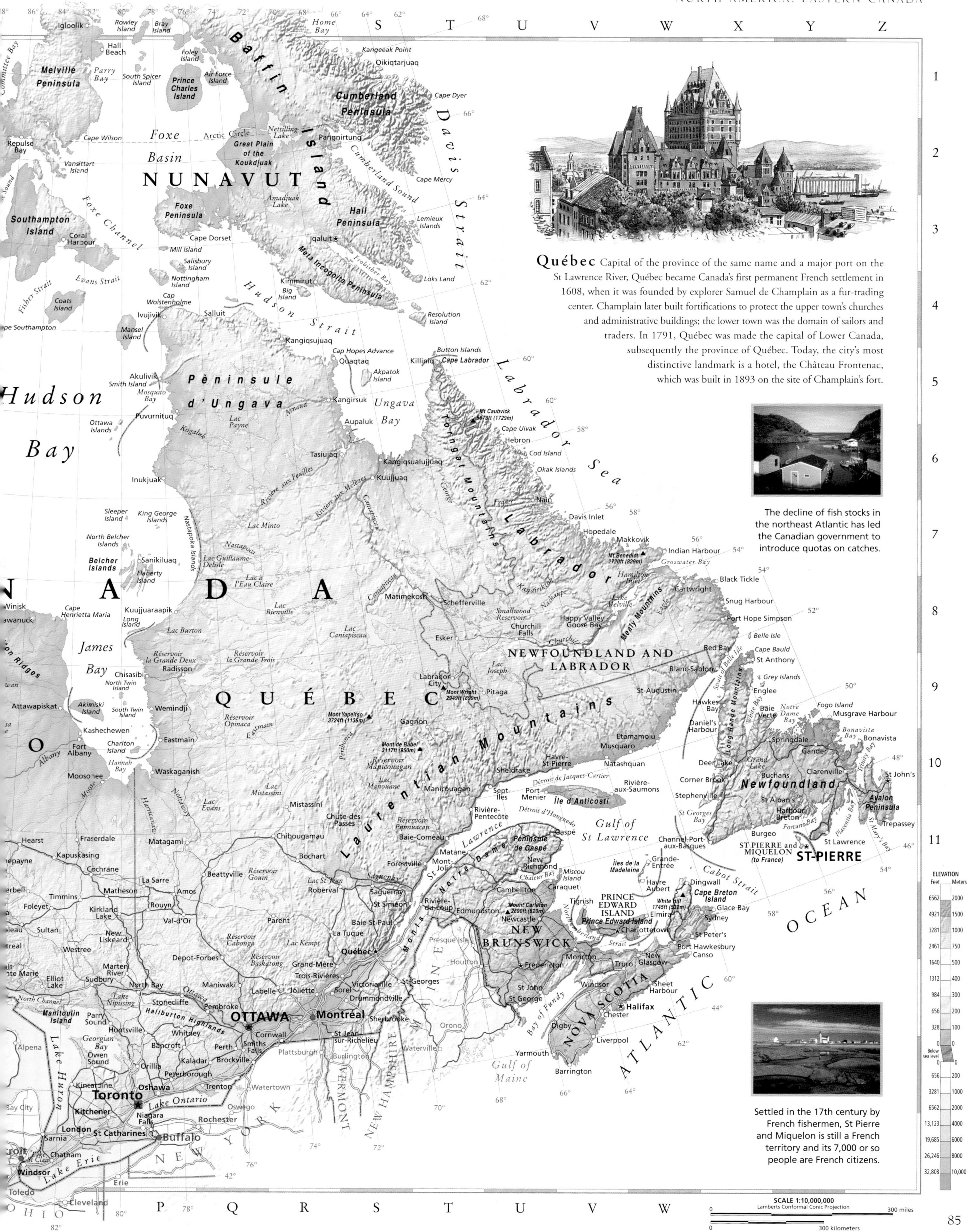

Québec Capital of the province of the same name and a major port on the St Lawrence River, Québec became Canada's first permanent French settlement in 1608, when it was founded by explorer Samuel de Champlain as a fur-trading center. Champlain later built fortifications to protect the upper town's churches and administrative buildings; the lower town was the domain of sailors and traders. In 1791, Québec was made the capital of Lower Canada, subsequently the province of Québec. Today, the city's most distinctive landmark is a hotel, the Château Frontenac, which was built in 1893 on the site of Champlain's fort.

The decline of fish stocks in the northeast Atlantic has led the Canadian government to introduce quotas on catches.

Settled in the 17th century by French fishermen, St Pierre and Miquelon is still a French territory and its 7,000 or so people are French citizens.

ELEVATION

Feet	Meters
6562	2000
4921	1500
3281	1000
2461	750
1640	500
1312	400
984	300
656	200
328	100
Below sea level	
656	200
3281	1000
6562	2000
13,123	4000
19,685	6000
26,246	8000
32,808	10,000

SCALE 1:10,000,000
Lamberts Conformal Conic Projection
0   300 miles
0   300 kilometers

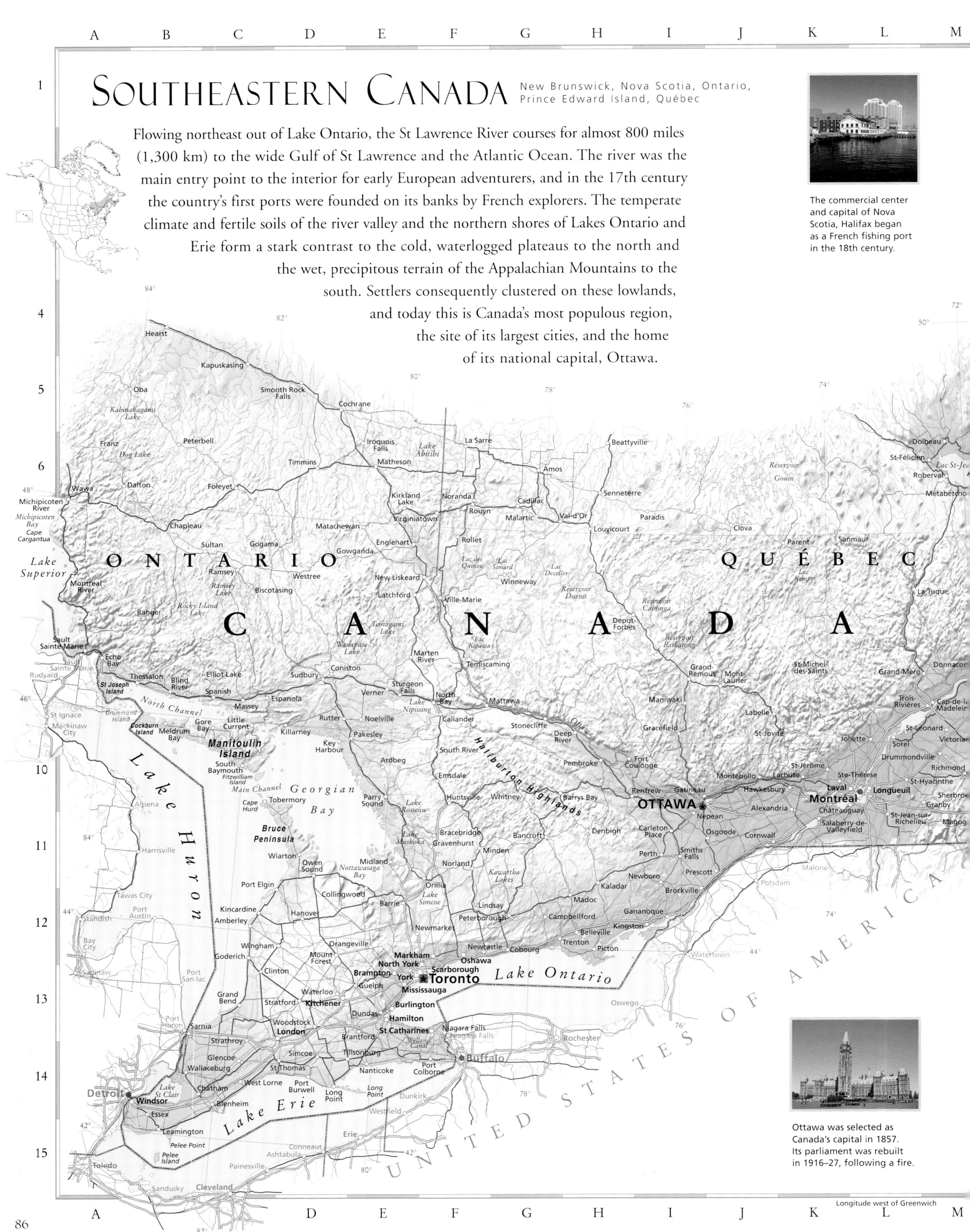

SOUTHEASTERN CANADA

New Brunswick, Nova Scotia, Ontario, Prince Edward Island, Québec

Flowing northeast out of Lake Ontario, the St Lawrence River courses for almost 800 miles (1,300 km) to the wide Gulf of St Lawrence and the Atlantic Ocean. The river was the main entry point to the interior for early European adventurers, and in the 17th century the country's first ports were founded on its banks by French explorers. The temperate climate and fertile soils of the river valley and the northern shores of Lakes Ontario and Erie form a stark contrast to the cold, waterlogged plateaus to the north and the wet, precipitous terrain of the Appalachian Mountains to the south. Settlers consequently clustered on these lowlands, and today this is Canada's most populous region, the site of its largest cities, and the home of its national capital, Ottawa.

The commercial center and capital of Nova Scotia, Halifax began as a French fishing port in the 18th century.

Ottawa was selected as Canada's capital in 1857. Its parliament was rebuilt in 1916–27, following a fire.

Longitude west of Greenwich

N O P Q R S T U V W X Y Z

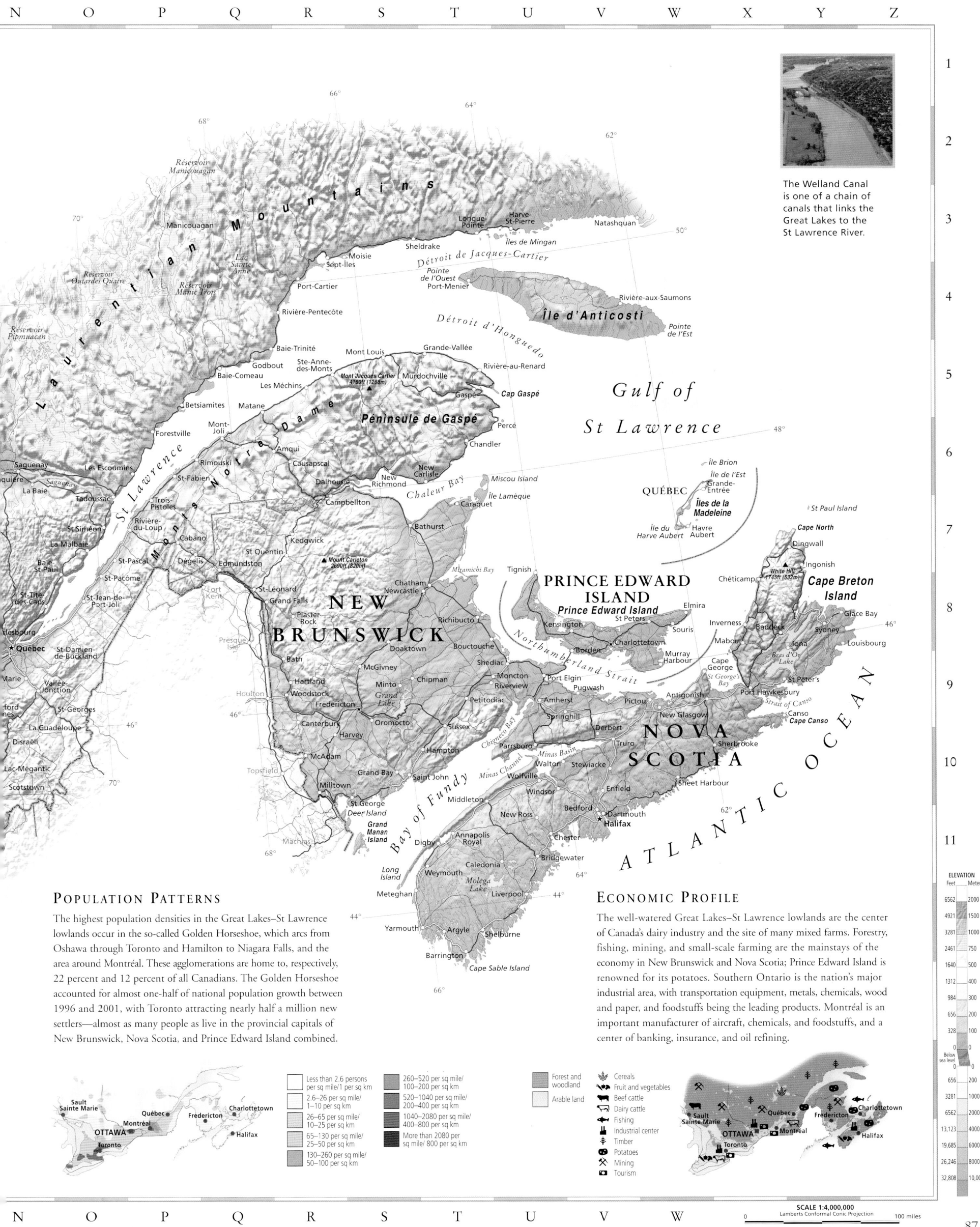

1

2

The Welland Canal
is one of a chain of
canals that links the
Great Lakes to the
St Lawrence River.

*Réservoir
Manicouagan*

Laurentian Mountains

70°

68°

66°

64°

62°

Manicouagan

*Lac
Sainte
Anne*

*Réservoir
Ontardes Quatre*

*Réservoir
Manic Trois*

Sheldrake

Moisie

Sept-Îles

50°

Longue-
Pointe

Harve-
St-Pierre

Natashquan

3

Îles de Mingan

Port-Cartier

Détroit de Jacques-Cartier

*Pointe
de l'Ouest*

Port-Menier

Rivière-aux-Saumons

4

*Réservoir
Pipmuacan*

Rivière-Pentecôte

Détroit d'Honguedo

Île d'Anticosti

*Pointe
de l'Est*

Baie-Trinité

Godbout

Mont Louis

Grande-Vallée

Ste-Anne-
des-Monts

Murdochville

Rivière-au-Renard

Baie-Comeau

*Mont Jacques Cartier
4160ft (1268m)* ▲

Cap Gaspé

*Gulf of
St Lawrence*

5

Betsiamites

Matane

Gaspé

Les Méchins

Péninsule de Gaspé

Percé

48°

Saguenay

Forestville

Mont-
Joli

Chandler

6

Île Brion

Île de l'Est

quière

Saguenay

Les Escoumins

St-Fabien

Amqui

Rimouski

Causapscal

New
Richmond

New Carlisle

Chaleur Bay

Miscou Island

Île Lamèque

Caraquet

QUÉBEC

**Îles de la
Madeleine**

Grande-
Entrée

La Baie

Tadoussac

Trois-
Pistoles

Dalhousie

*Île du
Harve Aubert*

Havre
Aubert

7

St Paul Island

St Siméon

Rivière-
du-Loup

Cabano

Campbellton

Bathurst

Tignish

Kedgwick

Miramichi Bay

Elmira

Cape North

Dingwall

La Malbaie

St-Pascal

Degelis

St Quentin

▲ *Mount Carleton
2690ft (820m)*

Chatham

Newcastle

**PRINCE EDWARD
ISLAND**

*White Hill
1745ft (532m)* ▲

Chéticamp

Ingonish

**Cape Breton
Island**

Baie
St-Paul

St-Pacôme

Fort
Kent

St-Léonard

Grand Falls

Prince Edward Island

St Peters

Inverness

Baddeck

Iona

Glace Bay

46°

lesbourg

St-Tite-
des-Caps

St-Jean-de-
Port-Joli

Edmundston

Plaster
Rock

Kensington

**NEW
BRUNSWICK**

Richibucto

Doaktown

Bouctouche

Northumberland Strait

St Peters

Charlottetown

Borden

Murray
Harbour

Mabou

Sydney

Louisbourg

St Peter's

★ Québec

St-Damien-
de-Buckland

*Presque
Isle*

Houlton

Bath

McGivney

Shediac

Port Elgin

Pugwash

Cape
George

Antigonish

*St George's
Bay*

Port Hawkesbury

Strait of Canso

Marie

*Vallée-
Jonction*

Hartland

Woodstock

Minto
*Grand
Lake*

Chipman

Moncton

Riverview

Petitcodiac

Amherst

Pictou

New Glasgow

**NOVA
SCOTIA**

Canso

Cape Canso

9

*tford
nes*

St-Georges

Canterbury

Fredericton

Oromocto

Sussex

Chignecto Bay

Springhill

Derbert

Sherbrooke

46°

La Guadeloupe

Disraëli

Harvey

Parrsboro

Walton

Minas Basin

Truro

Stewiacke

Lac-Mégantic

Scotstown

McAdam

Hampton

Grand Bay

Saint John

Minas Channel

Wolfville

Enfield

Sheet Harbour

10

70°

Topsfield

Milltown

Deer Island

St George

Middleton

New Ross

Windsor

Bedford

Dartmouth

★ Halifax

*Grand
Manan
Island*

Bay of Fundy

Digby

Annapolis
Royal

Chester

Bridgewater

11

Machias

*Long
Island*

Weymouth

Caledonia

*Molega
Lake*

Liverpool

64°

62°

A T L A N T I C   O C E A N

Meteghan

44°

Yarmouth

44°

Argyle

Shelburne

Barrington

Cape Sable Island

66°

POPULATION PATTERNS

The highest population densities in the Great Lakes–St Lawrence
lowlands occur in the so-called Golden Horseshoe, which arcs from
Oshawa through Toronto and Hamilton to Niagara Falls, and the
area around Montréal. These agglomerations are home to, respectively,
22 percent and 12 percent of all Canadians. The Golden Horseshoe
accounted for almost one-half of national population growth between
1996 and 2001, with Toronto attracting nearly half a million new
settlers—almost as many people as live in the provincial capitals of
New Brunswick, Nova Scotia, and Prince Edward Island combined.

ECONOMIC PROFILE

The well-watered Great Lakes–St Lawrence lowlands are the center
of Canada's dairy industry and the site of many mixed farms. Forestry,
fishing, mining, and small-scale farming are the mainstays of the
economy in New Brunswick and Nova Scotia; Prince Edward Island is
renowned for its potatoes. Southern Ontario is the nation's major
industrial area, with transportation equipment, metals, chemicals, wood
and paper, and foodstuffs being the leading products. Montréal is an
important manufacturer of aircraft, chemicals, and foodstuffs, and a
center of banking, insurance, and oil refining.

Sault
Sainte
Marie

Québec

Fredericton

Charlottetown

OTTAWA

Montréal

Halifax

Toronto

	Less than 2.6 persons per sq mile/1 per sq km	260–520 per sq mile/ 100–200 per sq km
	2.6–26 per sq mile/ 1–10 per sq km	520–1040 per sq mile/ 200–400 per sq km
	26–65 per sq mile/ 10–25 per sq km	1040–2080 per sq mile/ 400–800 per sq km
	65–130 per sq mile/ 25–50 per sq km	More than 2080 per sq mile/ 800 per sq km
	130–260 per sq mile/ 50–100 per sq km	

	Forest and woodland
	Arable land

🌾 Cereals
🍇 Fruit and vegetables
🐄 Beef cattle
🐄 Dairy cattle
🐟 Fishing
🏭 Industrial center
🌲 Timber
Potatoes
⚒ Mining
Tourism

Sault
Sainte
Marie

Québec

Fredericton

Charlottetown

OTTAWA

Montréal

Halifax

Toronto

ELEVATION

Feet	Meters
6562	2000
4921	1500
3281	1000
2461	750
1640	500
1312	400
984	300
656	200
328	100
0	0
	Below sea level
656	200
3281	1000
6562	2000
13,123	4000
19,685	6000
26,246	8000
32,808	10,000

SCALE 1:4,000,000
Lamberts Conformal Conic Projection

0 ———————— 100 miles

0 ———————— 100 kilometers

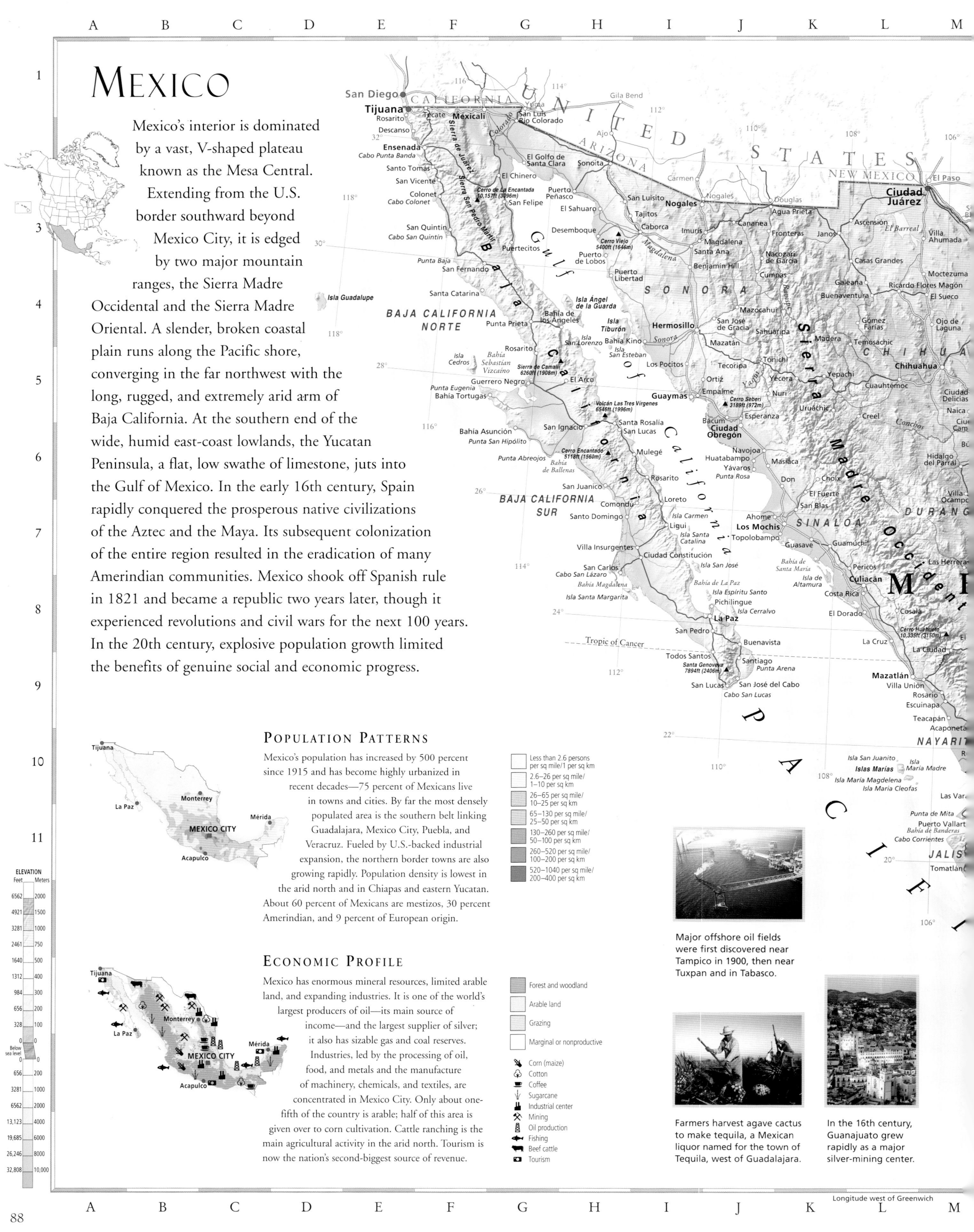

MEXICO

Mexico's interior is dominated by a vast, V-shaped plateau known as the Mesa Central. Extending from the U.S. border southward beyond Mexico City, it is edged by two major mountain ranges, the Sierra Madre Occidental and the Sierra Madre Oriental. A slender, broken coastal plain runs along the Pacific shore, converging in the far northwest with the long, rugged, and extremely arid arm of Baja California. At the southern end of the wide, humid east-coast lowlands, the Yucatan Peninsula, a flat, low swathe of limestone, juts into the Gulf of Mexico. In the early 16th century, Spain rapidly conquered the prosperous native civilizations of the Aztec and the Maya. Its subsequent colonization of the entire region resulted in the eradication of many Amerindian communities. Mexico shook off Spanish rule in 1821 and became a republic two years later, though it experienced revolutions and civil wars for the next 100 years. In the 20th century, explosive population growth limited the benefits of genuine social and economic progress.

POPULATION PATTERNS

Mexico's population has increased by 500 percent since 1915 and has become highly urbanized in recent decades—75 percent of Mexicans live in towns and cities. By far the most densely populated area is the southern belt linking Guadalajara, Mexico City, Puebla, and Veracruz. Fueled by U.S.-backed industrial expansion, the northern border towns are also growing rapidly. Population density is lowest in the arid north and in Chiapas and eastern Yucatan. About 60 percent of Mexicans are mestizos, 30 percent Amerindian, and 9 percent of European origin.

Less than 2.6 persons per sq mile/1 per sq km
2.6–26 per sq mile/ 1–10 per sq km
26–65 per sq mile/ 10–25 per sq km
65–130 per sq mile/ 25–50 per sq km
130–260 per sq mile/ 50–100 per sq km
260–520 per sq mile/ 100–200 per sq km
520–1040 per sq mile/ 200–400 per sq km

ECONOMIC PROFILE

Mexico has enormous mineral resources, limited arable land, and expanding industries. It is one of the world's largest producers of oil—its main source of income—and the largest supplier of silver; it also has sizable gas and coal reserves. Industries, led by the processing of oil, food, and metals and the manufacture of machinery, chemicals, and textiles, are concentrated in Mexico City. Only about one-fifth of the country is arable; half of this area is given over to corn cultivation. Cattle ranching is the main agricultural activity in the arid north. Tourism is now the nation's second-biggest source of revenue.

Forest and woodland
Arable land
Grazing
Marginal or nonproductive

Corn (maize)
Cotton
Coffee
Sugarcane
Industrial center
Mining
Oil production
Fishing
Beef cattle
Tourism

ELEVATION

Feet	Meters
6562	2000
4921	1500
3281	1000
2461	750
1640	500
1312	400
984	300
656	200
328	100
0 Below sea level	0
656	200
3281	1000
6562	2000
13,123	4000
19,685	6000
26,246	8000
32,808	10,000

Major offshore oil fields were first discovered near Tampico in 1900, then near Tuxpan and in Tabasco.

Farmers harvest agave cactus to make tequila, a Mexican liquor named for the town of Tequila, west of Guadalajara.

In the 16th century, Guanajuato grew rapidly as a major silver-mining center.

Longitude west of Greenwich

N O P Q R S T U V W X Y Z

Sited on a magnificent harbor, Acapulco is a vital Pacific port and popular tourist resort.

Around AD 1000, Chichén Itzá in Yucatán was the center of the Mayan civilization.

Mexico City

The small band of Spanish conquistadors that reached the Aztec capital of Tenochtitlán in 1519 discovered a magnificent city of 250,000 people, built on an island surrounded by lakes and dominated by grand ceremonial structures. The centuries that followed saw the destruction of Tenochtitlán's buildings by the Spanish, the draining of the lakes to prevent flooding, and the growth of a new capital. Today, Mexico City is the third-largest and fastest-growing urban area in the world, with more than 19 million inhabitants. The heart of the city is the Zócalo (Plaza de la Constitución), site of the Metropolitan Cathedral, built in the 1520s over a razed Aztec temple.

THE CORDILLERA NEO-VOLCÁNICA

The mountain range known as the Cordillera Neo-Volcánica stretches west to east across the southern end of the Mesa Central, passing south of Mexico City and dropping steeply to the eastern coastal plains just north of Veracruz. It incorporates several towering volcanic peaks, including Popocatépetl, Iztaccihuatl, and 18,405-foot (5,610-m) Pico de Orizaba, Mexico's highest mountain. Tectonic activity along the Pacific coast causes regular earthquakes here—a major tremor killed 9,500 people in Mexico City in 1985. In 1994 and 1996, it also gave rise to eruptions of Popocatépetl, which had previously been dormant for more than 50 years.

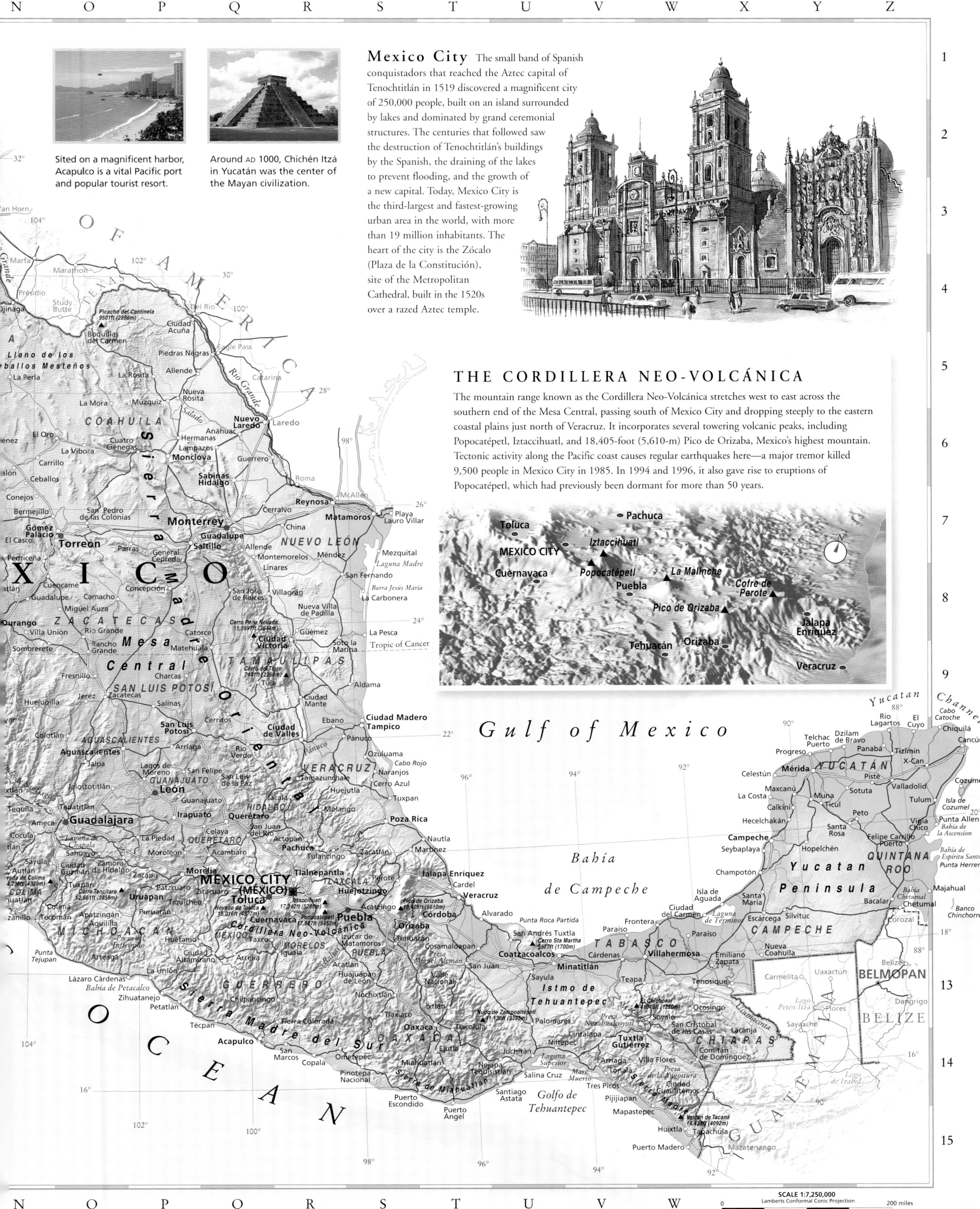

SCALE 1:7,250,000
Lamberts Conformal Conic Projection
200 miles
200 kilometers

CENTRAL AMERICA

Belize, Costa Rica, El Salvador, Guatemala, Honduras, Nicaragua, Panama

From the Mexican border, Central America dog-legs and tapers southeastward, connecting with Colombia in South America at the eastern end of the Isthmus of Panama. Forested mountain ranges parallel the Pacific coast, spreading east across Honduras and northern Nicaragua, and covering four-fifths of the entire landmass. Narrow coastal plains line the Pacific shore; wider, swampy lowlands border the Caribbean Sea. With the exception of the former British colony of Belize, the nations of Central America share a predominantly Hispanic culture stemming from a long period of Spanish domination and shaped to varying degrees by other imported and indigenous cultures. Central America's recent history has been clouded by coups, periods of repressive military rule, and guerilla warfare, especially in the north. The southern nations of Costa Rica and Panama have the highest standards of living and have been more stable, although the U.S.A. invaded Panama in 1989 to remove a corrupt military regime.

POPULATION PATTERNS

Most of the population is mestizo, though the ethnic makeup varies from country to country. Almost one-third of people in Belize are of African origin, and most Costa Ricans are of European descent. Indigenous peoples are in a small minority in most countries except Guatemala, where they form almost half of the population. Settlement has favored the west, especially the cool, fertile uplands, over the humid Caribbean plains, and the north is more populous—one-third of Central Americans live in Guatemala. Urbanization ranges from just over 40 percent in Guatemala to almost 66 percent in El Salvador.

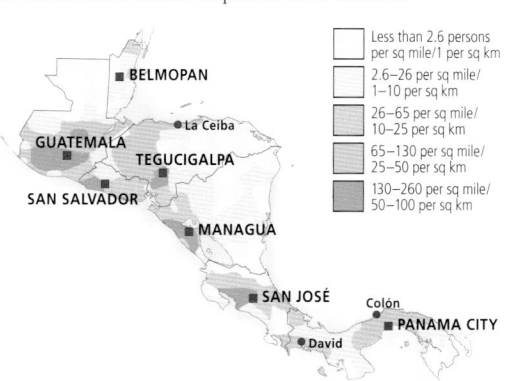

	Less than 2.6 persons per sq mile/1 per sq km
	2.6–26 per sq mile/1–10 per sq km
	26–65 per sq mile/10–25 per sq km
	65–130 per sq mile/25–50 per sq km
	130–260 per sq mile/50–100 per sq km

ECONOMIC PROFILE

Development is hampered by political unrest, poor infrastructure, and inequitable distribution of land. Many people grow corn, beans, squashes, and fruit for their own consumption, but much of the best farmland has been turned into large, often foreign-owned, cattle ranches and plantations producing sugar, bananas, and coffee. Mineral resources are, for the most part, scanty or undeveloped. Forests provide timber and chicle (used in chewing gum), but are not harvested sustainably. Industries are limited mainly to food processing and textiles. Services are most significant in Panama, where a free-trade zone is centered on Colón.

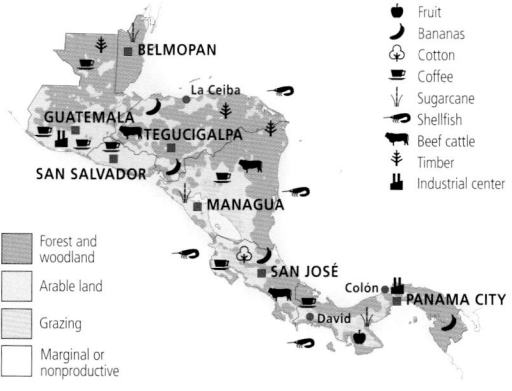

Fruit
Bananas
Cotton
Coffee
Sugarcane
Shellfish
Beef cattle
Timber
Industrial center

Forest and woodland
Arable land
Grazing
Marginal or nonproductive

Wildlife-rich rain forests are among the attractions that draw over 1 million overseas visitors a year to Costa Rica.

Lake Nicaragua is the world's only freshwater lake that is home to saltwater fish such as sharks and swordfish.

ELEVATION
Feet	Meters
6562	2000
4921	1500
3281	1000
2461	750
1640	500
1312	400
984	300
656	200
328	100
Below sea level	0
0	
656	200
3281	1000
6562	2000
13,123	4000
19,685	6000
26,246	8000
32,808	10,000

SCALE 1:4,000,000
Lamberts Conformal Conic Projection
0   100 miles
0   100 kilometers

Longitude west of Greenwich

Tegucigalpa Cathedral, a baroque, 18th-century construction, is the focal point of Honduras's capital.

The ruined city of Tikal, in northern Guatemala, was a ceremonial center of Mayan culture from 300 BC to AD 900.

Guatemala The National Palace stands on Plaza Mayor (also known as Parque Central), a popular gathering place at the heart of Guatemala, the capital of the country of the same name and the largest city in Central America, with close to 4 million inhabitants. Guatemala became the capital of Spanish-ruled Guatemala after the first capital, Antigua Guatemala, was flattened by an earthquake in 1773. Much of the modern capital, including the National Palace (completed in 1943), dates from a period of reconstruction following a series of violent tremors in 1917–18, which lasted for six weeks and razed large areas of the city center.

Honduras and Costa Rica are among the world's leading banana producers.

THE ISTHMUS OF PANAMA

The narrowest and one of the lowest points in Central America, the Isthmus of Panama was an obvious choice for the site of a canal linking the Pacific and Atlantic oceans. The idea was first proposed by the Spanish in the 16th century; work began in 1881 and was completed with U.S. assistance in 1914. Measuring 51 miles (82 km) in length, the canal can save ships traveling from the east to west coasts of the U.S.A. up to 8,000 miles (12,900 km) of sailing.

THE WEST INDIES

Antigua and Barbuda, The Bahamas, Barbados, Cuba, Dominica, Dominican Republic, Grenada, Haiti, Jamaica, St Kitts and Nevis, St Lucia, St Vincent and the Grenadines, Trinidad and Tobago

Forming the northern boundary of the Caribbean Sea, the islands of the West Indies arc east then south from Florida in the U.S.A. to the north coast of South America. They include two major island groups: the Greater Antilles, consisting of the large islands of Cuba, Hispaniola, Jamaica, and Puerto Rico, and the Lesser Antilles, a string of small, high, chiefly volcanic islands. Following the arrival of Christopher Columbus in 1492 at San Salvador in The Bahamas (his belief that he had reached Asia led to the region being called the "West" Indies), the islands were fought over by various imperial powers, who imported huge numbers of African slaves to work on plantations. Today, this history is reflected in the region's cultural diversity and large number of dependencies, including French Guadeloupe, British Montserrat, and the Netherlands Antilles.

The twin volcanic peaks of the Pitons rise almost sheer from the sea near Soufrière on the island of St Lucia.

Over 100 million tourists visit the West Indies each year. Tourism generates two-fifths of the region's GNP.

ELEVATION

Feet	Meters
6562	2000
4921	1500
3281	1000
2461	750
1640	500
1312	400
984	300
656	200
328	100
0	0
Below sea level	
656	200
3281	1000
6562	2000
13,123	4000
19,685	6000
26,246	8000
32,808	10,000

UNITED STATES OF AMERICA

THE BAHAMAS

Grand Bahama
Cooper's Town
Freeport
Pelican Point
Marsh Harbour
Great Abaco
Bimini Islands
Alice Town
Cornwall
Mastic Point
New Providence
NASSAU
Eleuthera
Tarpum Bay
Andros Town
Mangrove Cay
Cat Island
Andros Island
Kemp's Bay
Exuma Cays
Port Howe
Great Exuma Island
George Town
Long Isla
Deadman's

Straits of Florida
Great Bahama Bank
Santaren Channel
Cay Sal
Anguilla Cay

Tropic of Cancer

HAVANA (LA HABANA)
Guanabacoa
Marianao
Matanzas
Cárdenas
Mariel
Artemisa
Güines
Colón
Archipiélago de Sabana
Sagua la Grande
Archipiélago de Camagüey
Minas de Matahambre
Los Palacios
Surgidero de Batabanó
Santa Clara
Caibarién
Cayo Romano
Guane
Pinar del Río
Golfo de Batabanó
Jagüey Grande
Cienfuegos
Pico San Juan 3793ft (1156m)
Sancti Spiritus
Morón
Esmeralda
Cayo Sabinal
Cabo San Antonio
Lafé
Nueva Gerona
Archipiélago de los Canarreros
Santa Fé
Cayo del Rosario
Trinidad
Ciego de Ávila
Minas
Nuevitas
Cabo Corrientes
Isla de la Juventud
Cayo Largo
CUBA
Vertientes
Camagüey
Puerto Padre
Cabo Lucre
Las Tunas
Bar
Golfo de Guacanayabo
Santa Cruz del Sur
Holguín
Sagua de Tánamo
Cueto
Bayamo
Palma Soriano
Pilón
Sierra Maestra
Pico Turquino 6378ft (1944m)
Guantán
Guantánamo Naval Bas (to U.S.A.)
Cabo Cruz
Archipiélago de los Jardines de la Reina

Greater Antilles

Little Cayman
Cayman Brac
GEORGE TOWN
Grand Cayman
CAYMAN ISLANDS (to U.K.)
Cayman Trench

Rosario Bank
Misteriosa Bank

BELIZE
BELMOPAN
Dangriga

Swan Islands (to Honduras)

Montego Bay
Falmouth
Ocho Rios
South Negril Point
Savanna-la-Mar
Port Antonio
Mandeville
JAMAICA
KINGSTON

Pedro Bank

Gulf of Honduras
Islas de la Bahía
Isla de Utila
Isla de Guanaja
Isla de Roatán
Puerto Barrios
La Ceiba
Cabo Camarón
Punta Patuca
Banco Gorda
Rosalind Bank
Serranilla Bank
Alice Shoal

HONDURAS

South Cay
Cabo Gracias á Dios
Cayos Miskitos

NICARAGUA
Mosquito Coast

Isla de Providencia (to Colombia)

Punta de Perlas
Laguna de Perlas
Rama
Bluefields
Islas del Maíz (to Nicaragua)
Cayos de Albuquerque (to Colombia)
Isla de San Andrés (to Colombia)
Acoyapa

Punta del Mono

Bahía de San Juan del Norte
San Carlos
San Juan del Norte

Caribb

COSTA RICA
Limón
Cartagena
SAN JOSÉ

Golfo de los Mosquitos
Colón
Gulf of Darién
Almirante
Isthmus of Panama
PANAMA CITY (PANAMÁ)
PANAMA
Golfo de Uraba

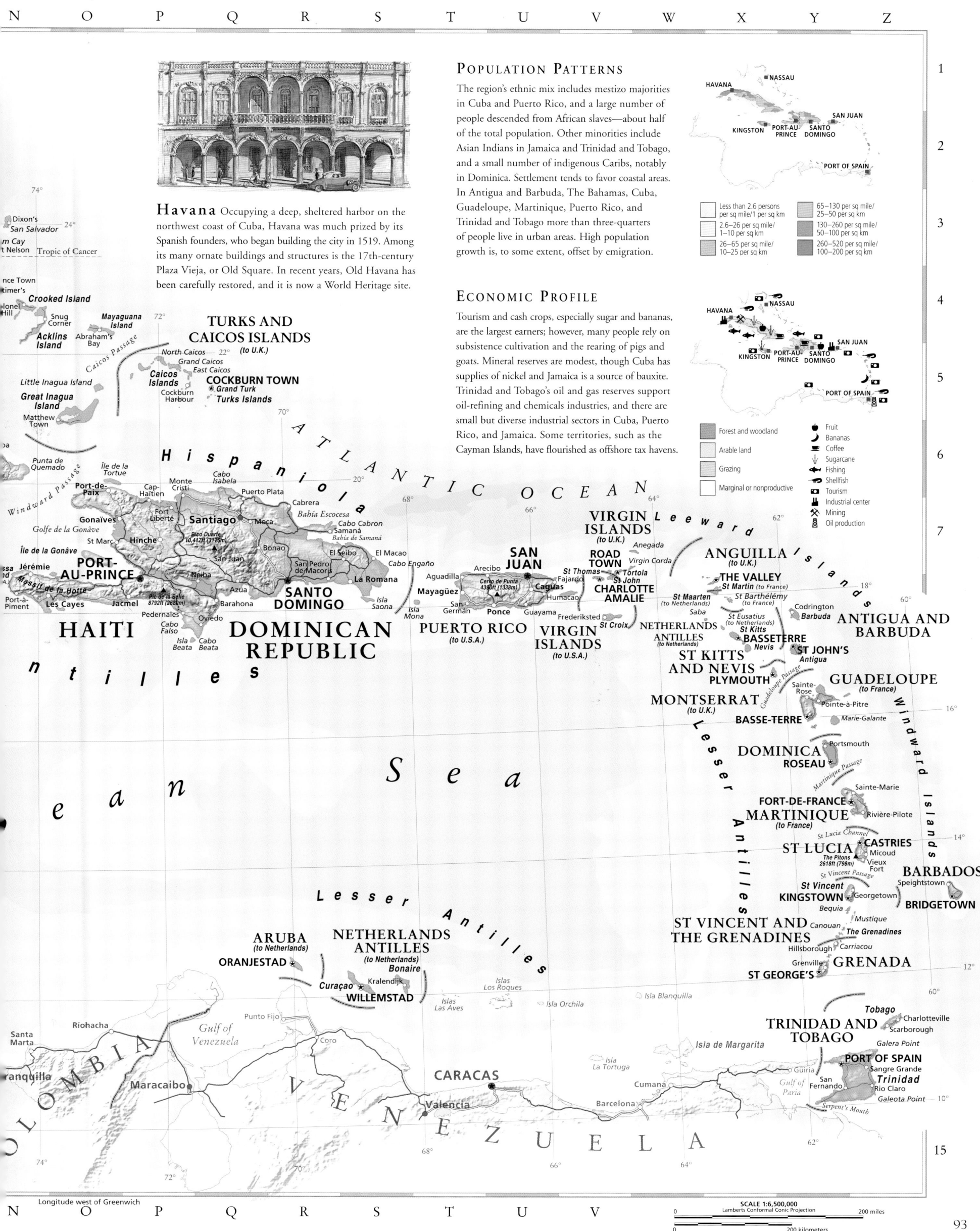

Population Patterns

The region's ethnic mix includes mestizo majorities in Cuba and Puerto Rico, and a large number of people descended from African slaves—about half of the total population. Other minorities include Asian Indians in Jamaica and Trinidad and Tobago, and a small number of indigenous Caribs, notably in Dominica. Settlement tends to favor coastal areas. In Antigua and Barbuda, The Bahamas, Cuba, Guadeloupe, Martinique, Puerto Rico, and Trinidad and Tobago more than three-quarters of people live in urban areas. High population growth is, to some extent, offset by emigration.

Less than 2.6 persons per sq mile/1 per sq km
2.6–26 persons per sq mile/1–10 per sq km
26–65 per sq mile/10–25 per sq km
65–130 per sq mile/25–50 per sq km
130–260 per sq mile/50–100 per sq km
260–520 per sq mile/100–200 per sq km

Economic Profile

Tourism and cash crops, especially sugar and bananas, are the largest earners; however, many people rely on subsistence cultivation and the rearing of pigs and goats. Mineral reserves are modest, though Cuba has supplies of nickel and Jamaica is a source of bauxite. Trinidad and Tobago's oil and gas reserves support oil-refining and chemicals industries, and there are small but diverse industrial sectors in Cuba, Puerto Rico, and Jamaica. Some territories, such as the Cayman Islands, have flourished as offshore tax havens.

Forest and woodland
Arable land
Grazing
Marginal or nonproductive

Fruit
Bananas
Coffee
Sugarcane
Fishing
Shellfish
Tourism
Industrial center
Mining
Oil production

Havana Occupying a deep, sheltered harbor on the northwest coast of Cuba, Havana was much prized by its Spanish founders, who began building the city in 1519. Among its many ornate buildings and structures is the 17th-century Plaza Vieja, or Old Square. In recent years, Old Havana has been carefully restored, and it is now a World Heritage site.

Longitude west of Greenwich

SCALE 1:6,500,000
Lamberts Conformal Conic Projection
0   200 miles
0   200 kilometers

The lights of South America reveal the focus of development around the continent's edges while the interior jungle remains mostly dark. The three brightest areas on the east coast are the sprawling cities of Rio de Janeiro, São Paulo, and Buenos Aires.

SOUTH AMERICA

ABOVE SOUTH AMERICA

From space, the details of South America's landscapes are revealed. The human impact is startling: many photographs record the scars of logging and burning in the vast tropical rain forests of Brazil; others are dominated by artificial features such as the enormous dams and reservoirs created for irrigation and hydroelectric power. Satellite photography can also help explain natural phenomena. The Andes Mountains run like a spine down the west coast of South America, creating what is known as a rain-shadow effect. Tradewinds from the east carry warm, moist tropical air over the forested interior. As the air climbs the high eastern slopes of the Andes, it cools, condenses, and falls as rain or snow, which runs into the Amazon River and Basin. The air warms again as it descends the western slopes and so holds its moisture as it crosses the Atacama Desert to the coast. This effect contributes to both the extreme dryness of the Atacama Desert, in the rain-shadow area, and the lushness of the Amazon Basin, which dominates the continent's interior and is one of the wettest places on the planet.

Atacama Desert, Chile
Below: Two banks of clouds flank Chile's Atacama Desert. Those on the left stop at the coast because the cold waters of the Humboldt (Peru) Current, just off shore, cause rain to fall over the ocean. On the right, the Andes stop a line of clouds, forcing rain to fall on the eastern slopes. Parts of the Atacama Desert have never recorded rain.

Rain forest, Brazil
Below right: The destruction of Brazil's forests is dramatically illustrated in this false-color image. The remaining tropical forest appears as bright red, while darker areas represent cleared land, and black and gray patches are recently burned areas. The vertical lines indicate land cleared along transportation routes.

Represa Três Marias, Brazil
Above: The serpentine Represa Três Marias winds across this true-color image of southeastern Brazil. This reservoir was built in 1960 to generate hydroelectric power for the state of Minas Gerais. It occupies some 60 miles (95 km) of the São Francisco River, which can be seen carrying sediment into the reservoir's southern end.

River Plate, Argentina
Right: In this satellite view of Argentina, the sediment-laden waters filling the bay of the River Plate reflect light and so appear bright. In contrast, the waters stretching north along the coast have absorbed light, perhaps because of a phytoplankton bloom, and so look very dark. Buenos Aires is the gray-green area at the bay's western end.

LAND AND ENVIRONMENT

Encompassing almost 6.9 million square miles (17.8 million sq km) and extending from Punta Gallinas, in the warm Caribbean Sea, south to the cold, windswept promontory of Cape Horn, South America is the fourth-largest continent. The towering Andes mountains dominate the west, running parallel to the coast for 5,500 miles (8,800 km) and rising to their highest point of 22,835 feet (6,960 m) at Mount Aconcagua. East of the Andes lie expansive lowlands, including, from north to south, the valley of the Orinoco, the immense Amazon Basin, the semiarid grasslands of Gran Chaco, and the plains of the Pampas. In turn, these lowlands are bounded by the plateau regions of the Guiana Highlands in the north, the Brazilian Highlands in the east, and Patagonia in the south.

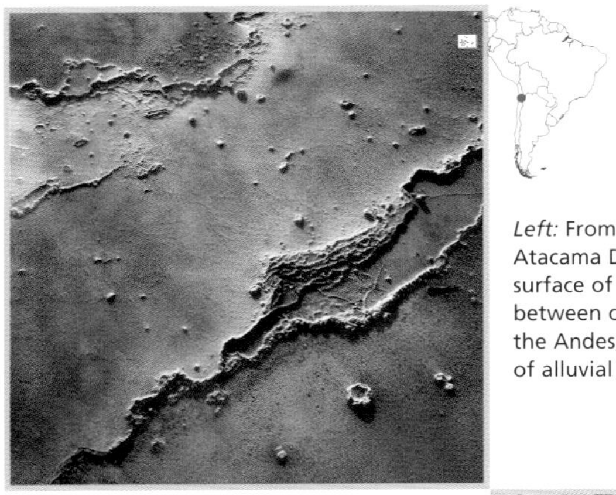

Left: From space, the barren Atacama Desert resembles the surface of the Moon. Situated between coastal ranges and the Andes, it consists mainly of alluvial plains and salt pans.

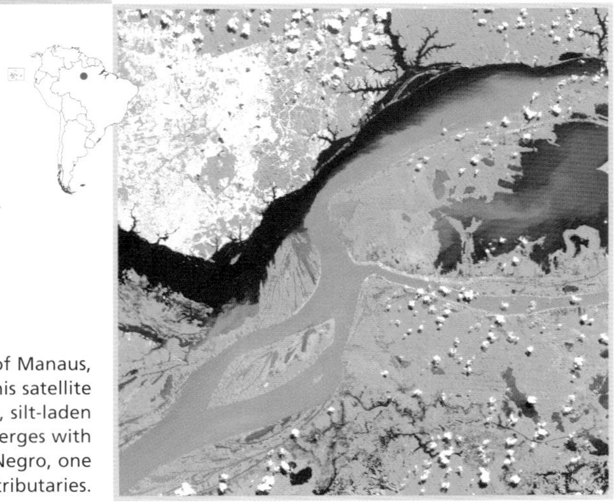

Galapagos Islands

Isla San Salvador
Fernandina
Isla Santa Cruz
Isla Isabela
Isla San Cristóbal

0   SCALE 1:12,500,000   100 miles
0   100 kilometres

Right: Near the town of Manaus, shown in gray in this satellite image, the brown, silt-laden Amazon River merges with the much clearer Negro, one of its major tributaries.

Caribbean Sea
Punta Gallinas
Gulf of Venezuela
Gulf of Darién
Lake Maracaibo
Gulf of Panama
Orinoco
ATLANTIC
Llanos
La Gran Sabana
Guiana Highlands
Cordillera Occidental
Cordillera Central
Cordillera Oriental
Cauca
Magdalena
Caquetá
Negro
Branco
Tumuc-Humac Mountains
Volcán Cotopaxi 19,344ft (5896m)
Chimborazo 20,702ft (6310m)
Putumayo
Amazon
A m a z o n
Gulf of Guayaquil
Punta Parinas
Marañón
Juruá
Purus
Madeira
B a s i n
Tapajós
Xingu
Araguaia
Tocantins
Nevado Huascarán 22,205ft (6768m)
Ucayali
A n d e s
Lake Titicaca
Altiplano
Planalto do Mato Grosso
Brazilian Highlands
PACIFIC
Atacama Desert
Pilcomayo
Gran Chaco
Paraguay
Paraná
Serra Geral
Serra do Mar
OCEAN
SCALE 1:35,000,000
Lamberts Conformal Conic Projection
0   1000
0   1000 kilometers
Mount Aconcagua 22,835ft (6960m)
Mesopotamia
Uruguay
Paraná
Lagoa dos Patos
River Plate
Pampas
Colorado
Negro
Lagoa Mirim
ATLANTIC OCEAN
Chico
Golfo de San Jorge
Falkland Islands
Golfo de Penas
Deseado
Bahía Grande
Tierra del Fuego
Patagonia
A n d e s
Cape Horn

NATURAL HAZARDS

Volcanoes

Western South America borders the Ring of Fire, a well-known zone of tectonic instability that almost encircles the Pacific Ocean. Just off the west coast, the Nazca Plate is subducting beneath the South American Plate, giving rise to earthquakes and volcanic eruptions. South America has more volcanoes than any other continent—204—and the world's highest volcano, Nevado Ojos del Salado, which rises to 22,664 feet (6,908 m). The deadliest eruption of recent years was that of Nevado del Ruiz in Colombia, in 1985, which, although small, melted a glacier, triggering a mudflow that killed about 23,000 people.

Nevado del Ruiz 17,716ft (5400m)
Volcán Cotopaxi 19,344ft (5896m)
Nevado Ojos del Salado 22,664ft (6908m)
Volcán Villarrica 9318ft (2840m)
Cerro Hudson 8530ft (2600m)

Along the plate boundary that parallels the coast, the thinner Nazca Plate is forced downward beneath the much thicker South American Plate. As it subducts, the Nazca Plate gradually melts. Magma then rises through cracks in the crumpled landscape, forming a long line of volcanoes.

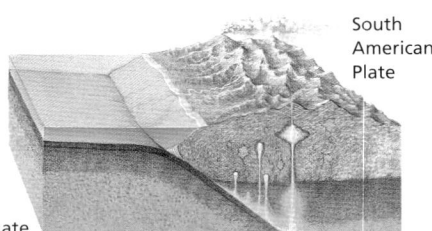

South American Plate

Nazca Plate

The mudflow caused by the eruption of Nevado del Ruiz in Colombia swamped the town of Armero in minutes, giving the inhabitants little opportunity to escape.

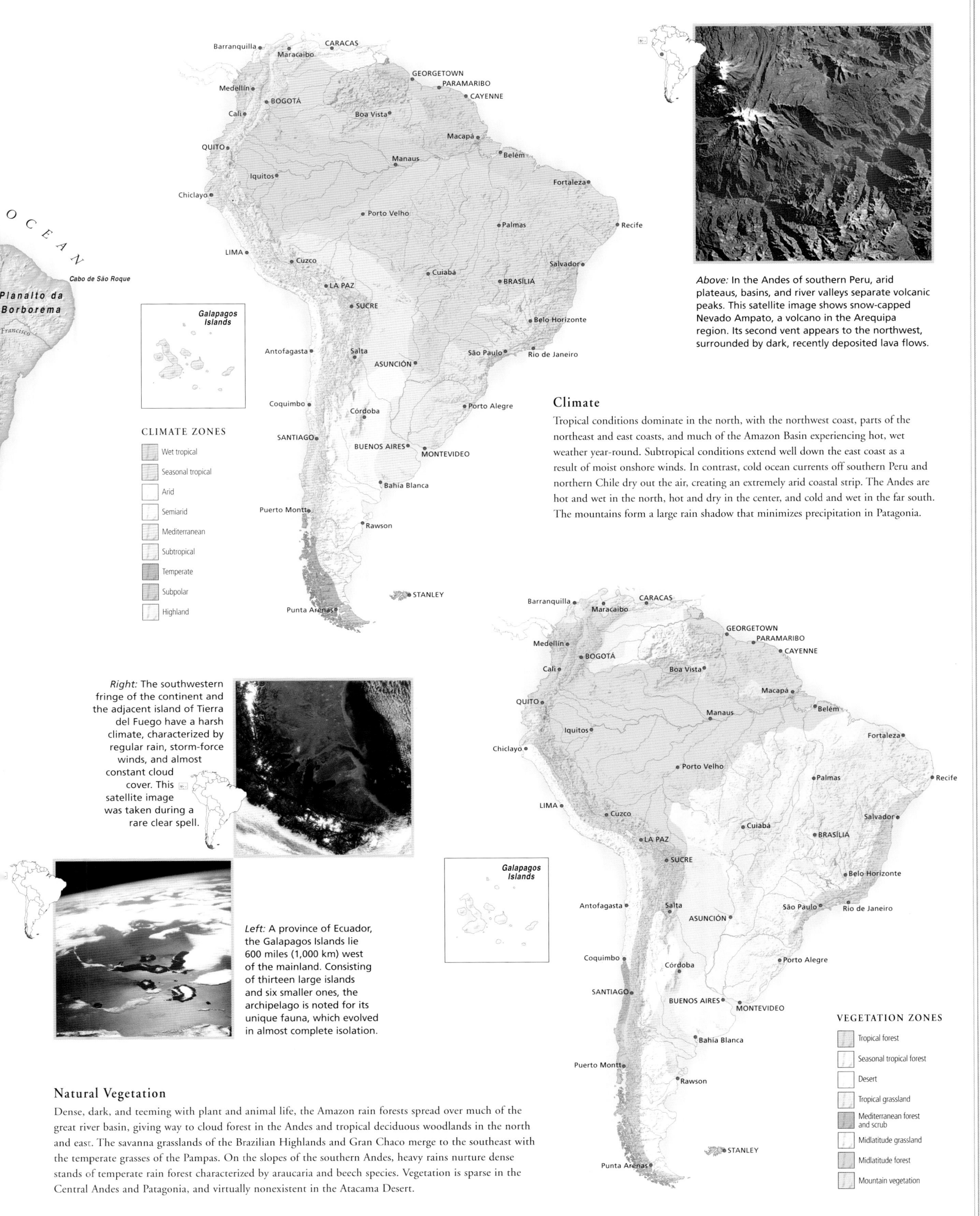

Above: In the Andes of southern Peru, arid plateaus, basins, and river valleys separate volcanic peaks. This satellite image shows snow-capped Nevado Ampato, a volcano in the Arequipa region. Its second vent appears to the northwest, surrounded by dark, recently deposited lava flows.

Climate

Tropical conditions dominate in the north, with the northwest coast, parts of the northeast and east coasts, and much of the Amazon Basin experiencing hot, wet weather year-round. Subtropical conditions extend well down the east coast as a result of moist onshore winds. In contrast, cold ocean currents off southern Peru and northern Chile dry out the air, creating an extremely arid coastal strip. The Andes are hot and wet in the north, hot and dry in the center, and cold and wet in the far south. The mountains form a large rain shadow that minimizes precipitation in Patagonia.

CLIMATE ZONES

- Wet tropical
- Seasonal tropical
- Arid
- Semiarid
- Mediterranean
- Subtropical
- Temperate
- Subpolar
- Highland

Right: The southwestern fringe of the continent and the adjacent island of Tierra del Fuego have a harsh climate, characterized by regular rain, storm-force winds, and almost constant cloud cover. This satellite image was taken during a rare clear spell.

Left: A province of Ecuador, the Galapagos Islands lie 600 miles (1,000 km) west of the mainland. Consisting of thirteen large islands and six smaller ones, the archipelago is noted for its unique fauna, which evolved in almost complete isolation.

VEGETATION ZONES

- Tropical forest
- Seasonal tropical forest
- Desert
- Tropical grassland
- Mediterranean forest and scrub
- Midlatitude grassland
- Midlatitude forest
- Mountain vegetation

Natural Vegetation

Dense, dark, and teeming with plant and animal life, the Amazon rain forests spread over much of the great river basin, giving way to cloud forest in the Andes and tropical deciduous woodlands in the north and east. The savanna grasslands of the Brazilian Highlands and Gran Chaco merge to the southeast with the temperate grasses of the Pampas. On the slopes of the southern Andes, heavy rains nurture dense stands of temperate rain forest characterized by araucaria and beech species. Vegetation is sparse in the Central Andes and Patagonia, and virtually nonexistent in the Atacama Desert.

99

PEOPLES AND NATIONS

Relative to its size, South America has a modest population of about 350 million. These people inhabit twelve nations and two overseas territories. Their dominant cultures and languages are those of the European colonial powers that, from the early 16th century onward, seized large parts of the continent. Portuguese is the official language in Brazil; Spanish predominates in most other areas. English, Dutch, and French are spoken in, respectively, the Falkland Islands and the former British colony of Guyana; the former Dutch colony of Suriname; and French Guiana, a French territory. Amerindian languages are restricted mainly to the Amazon Basin, the central Andes, and western Paraguay.

Left: São Paulo is the continent's largest city and the second-biggest urban agglomeration in the world after Tokyo in Japan. In 1947, São Paulo's city center had just three high-rise buildings; now it bristles with skyscrapers.

POPULATION DENSITY

	Uninhabited
	Less than 2.6 persons per sq mile/1 per sq km
	2.6–26 per sq mile/1–10 per sq km
	26–65 per sq mile/10–25 per sq km
	65–130 per sq mile/25–50 per sq km
	130–260 per sq mile/50–100 per sq km
	260–520 per sq mile/100–200 per sq km

FLASHPOINTS

Though it has been relatively stable since the mid-19th century, South America has recently experienced conflict between guerilla groups and governments, as well as several border disputes.

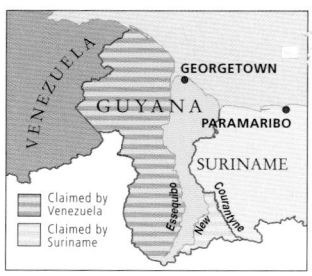

Guyana

Guyana has long faced significant territorial claims from its western and eastern neighbors, which, if realized, would see its territory drastically reduced. Venezuela disputes ownership of the entire area west of the Essequibo River, asserting that it inherited the land from Spain. Suriname claims the triangular region between the New (Upper Courantyne) and Courantyne rivers.

Northern Chile

In 1879–83, Chile defeated Bolivia and Peru in the War of the Pacific. As a result, it gained much of the Atacama region including southern Peru and coastal Bolivia. Peru regained some territory in 1929 as a result of negotiation, but Chile has refused to consider regular requests from Bolivia for sovereign access to the sea. This has led to repeated breakdowns in diplomatic relations.

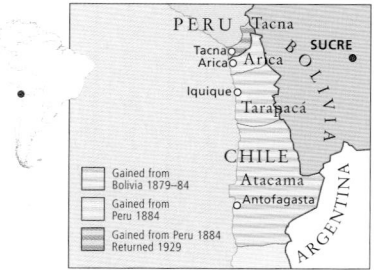

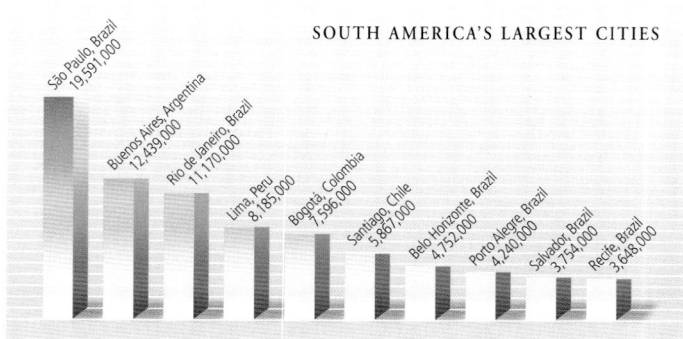

Colombia

Since the mid-1960s, guerillas belonging to the Revolutionary Armed Forces of Colombia (FARC) and the National Liberation Army (ELN) have been attempting to install a socialist government by force, a conflict that has cost 38,000 lives. Although the current government is supported by right-wing paramilitaries and the U.S.A., the guerilla groups control more than half of the country, and have formed alliances with drug traffickers.

Population Patterns

Sometimes referred to as "the hollow continent," South America has a sparsely populated interior ringed by areas of heavy coastal settlement. Among the most densely inhabited areas are the northeast and south coasts of Brazil, the Andean plateaus, and the River Plate region of Argentina and Uruguay. Most South Americans are descended from one or more of four main groups: native Amerindian peoples; early Spanish or Portuguese colonists; African slaves brought to the continent between the 16th and early 19th centuries; and more recent immigrants, especially from Italy, Spain, Portugal, Eastern Europe, and Japan.

SOUTH AMERICA'S LARGEST CITIES

- São Paulo, Brazil 19,591,000
- Buenos Aires, Argentina 12,439,000
- Rio de Janeiro, Brazil 11,170,000
- Lima, Peru 8,185,000
- Bogotá, Colombia 7,596,000
- Santiago, Chile 5,867,000
- Belo Horizonte, Brazil 4,752,000
- Porto Alegre, Brazil 4,240,000
- Salvador, Brazil 3,754,000
- Recife, Brazil 3,648,000

Urbanization

Prior to the early 16th century, major population centers lay on the Pacific Coast, in the Andes, and along the waterways of the Amazon Basin. The arrival by sea of Spanish and Portuguese colonists and traders caused a shift of settlement to seaboard towns. In the mid-20th century, rapid industrialization of these centers, combined with a lack of development, communications, and infrastructure in the interior, spurred large-scale migration to coastal cities. Continent-wide, urbanization has risen from less than 50 percent in 1950 to a current level of around 82 percent.

Nations of South America

Prior to the 16th century, South America was inhabited by about 20 million people living in diverse communities. Under the Treaty of Tordesillas of 1494, Spain and Portugal agreed to divide the world along a line of demarcation at roughly 46° west. Portugal colonized eastern South America and Spain laid claim to the west. Following the collapse of the Spanish and Portuguese empires in the early 19th century, their South American territories rapidly achieved independence. Guyana and Suriname attained political autonomy only in the late 20th century.

PRIOR TO IBERIAN CONQUEST, 1525

Coastal farmers
Forest hunter-gatherers
Forest hunter-gatherers
Forest farmers
Forest hunter-gatherers
Savanna hunter-gatherers
Grassland hunter-gatherers
Hunter-fishers
Inca Empire

Galapagos Islands

- Farming peoples
- Hunter-gatherers
- Inca Empire
- Chiefdoms

COLONIAL POSSESSIONS, 1750–63

Spain
Netherlands
France
Spain
Portugal

Galapagos Islands

INDEPENDENCE, 1810–33

Venezuela 1830
British Guiana (to Britain, 1831)
New Granada (Colombia) 1830
Suriname (to Netherlands, 1815)
Great Colombia 1819–30
French Guiana (to France, 1815)
Ecuador 1830
Brazil 1822
Peru 1821
Bolivia 1825
Paraguay 1811
Chile 1818
United Provinces of La Plata 1816
Uruguay 1828

Galapagos Islands (to Ecuador, 1832)

Falkland Islands (to Britain, 1833)

Map labels

Caribbean Sea
Barranquilla
Cartagena
Maracaibo
CARACAS
Cumaná
Gulf of Darién
Lake Maracaibo
Barquisimeto
Valencia
Ciudad Bolívar
GEORGETOWN
PARAMARIBO
CAYENNE
Cúcuta
San Cristóbal
VENEZUELA
GUYANA
SURINAME
FRENCH GUIANA (to France)
Gulf of Panama
Medellín
Bucaramanga
BOGOTÁ
Orinoco
Boa Vista
Esmeraldas
Pasto
COLOMBIA
Cali
Macapá
Equator
Negro
ATLANTIC OCEAN
Cauca
Magdalena
Equator
QUITO
ECUADOR
Guayaquil
Machala
Cuenca
Iquitos
Caquetá
Putumayo
Marañón
Amazon
Manaus
Santarém
Belém
São Luís
Fortaleza
Solimões
Juruá
PERU
Chiclayo
Trujillo
Rio Branco
Porto Velho
B R A Z I L
Madeira
Purus
Tapajós
Xingu
Tocantins
Teresina
Natal
Recife
Maceió
Callao
LIMA
Huancayo
Cuzco
BOLIVIA
La PAZ
Cochabamba
Santa Cruz
Cuiabá
BRASÍLIA
Goiânia
São Francisco
Aracaju
Salvador
PACIFIC OCEAN
Arequipa
Lake Titicaca
Tacna
Arica
SUCRE
Campo Grande
Belo Horizonte
Vitória
Iquique
PARAGUAY
Paraná
Antofagasta
Pilcomayo
ASUNCIÓN
Ciudad del Este
Foz do Iguaçu
São Paulo
Curitiba
Rio de Janeiro
Tropic of Capricorn
Salta
San Miguel de Tucumán
Corrientes
Posadas
Uruguay
Santa María
Florianópolis
Coquimbo
ARGENTINA
Córdoba
Santa Fé
Rosario
Melo
URUGUAY
Porto Alegre
Valparaíso
SANTIAGO
Mendoza
San Luis
Paraná
BUENOS AIRES
MONTEVIDEO
River Plate
Concepción
Colorado
Bahía Blanca
Mar del Plata
Salado
Neuquén
Negro
C H I L E
Valdivia
Puerto Montt
Chico
Rawson
Golfo de San Jorge
Golfo de Penas
Deseado
FALKLAND ISLANDS (to U.K.)
Bahía Grande
Río Gallegos
STANLEY
Punta Arenas
Ushuaia
Cape Horn

Galapagos Islands (to Ecuador)
Isla San Salvador
Isla Fernandina
Isla Santa Cruz
Isla San Cristóbal
Isla Isabela

SCALE 1:35,000,000
Lamberts Azimuthal Equal Area Projection
0   1000 miles
0   1000 kilometers

South American Trade Organizations

All South American nations except Guyana and Suriname are members of the Latin American Integration Association (LAIA), which also includes Mexico. Established by the Treaty of Montevideo in 1980, it aims to facilitate economic cooperation throughout Central and South America. Other important regional organizations include Mercosur (the Southern Common Market), a free trade zone formed by Argentina, Brazil, Paraguay, and Uruguay; and the Andean Group, which aims to establish a common market between Bolivia, Colombia, Ecuador, Peru, and Venezuela by 2005.

Galapagos Islands

- Mercosur (Southern Common Market)
- Andean Group
- Latin American Integration Association (LAIA)

THE HUMAN IMPACT

By the time of European colonization, human modification of the South American landscape was already widespread, though uneven. Hunter-gatherer lifestyles still predominated in some areas, but many of the continent's estimated 6 to 9 million inhabitants practiced agriculture, cultivating crops that would become staples worldwide, such as corn, potatoes, and beans. From 1800 BC, large settlements incorporating ceremonial buildings and irrigation systems took shape on the west coast. In the 15th century, the Inca expanded the practice of building terraces to increase agricultural output and constructed a road network covering 13,000 miles (21,000 km). After 1532, the pace of change accelerated. The Portuguese cleared huge swathes of tropical forest on the east coast to make way for sugar and, later, coffee plantations; less than 8 percent of that forest remains. The Andes, too, were stripped of timber, and the woodlands that covered the Pampas were cleared and planted with grasses to feed introduced livestock. Rapid population growth in the second half of the 20th century increased pressure on remaining wilderness areas, and has given rise to overcrowding and severe pollution and waste problems in cities.

Economic Profile

Though unevenly distributed, South America's abundant natural resources help make it a major exporter of primary produce. The continent provides one-quarter of the world's copper and one-fifth of its iron ore, as well as large supplies of tin and bauxite. Oil reserves have been located in areas such as Lake Maracaibo in Venezuela, the western Amazon Basin, and southern Patagonia. The immense pastures of the east and southeast support massive beef-cattle herds, and tropical plantations generate enormous cash crops of sugar, coffee, citrus fruits, and rubber. The southeastern Pacific Ocean is the world's second-most productive fishery. Plentiful metals and hydroelectric power have aided the development of industries, but most remain resource-based and South America is dependent on imports of many manufactured goods.

Land Cover

Forests still swathe more than half of the continent and account for 25 percent of global forest cover. South America has extensive reserves of cultivable land, though most is used as pasture. Other types of land cover include sprawling coastal settlements, wetlands, and the barren Andean uplands and western and southern deserts.

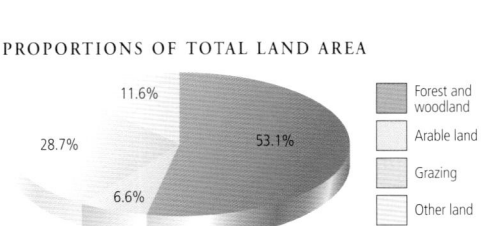

PROPORTIONS OF TOTAL LAND AREA

11.6%

28.7%

53.1%

6.6%

- Forest and woodland
- Arable land
- Grazing
- Other land

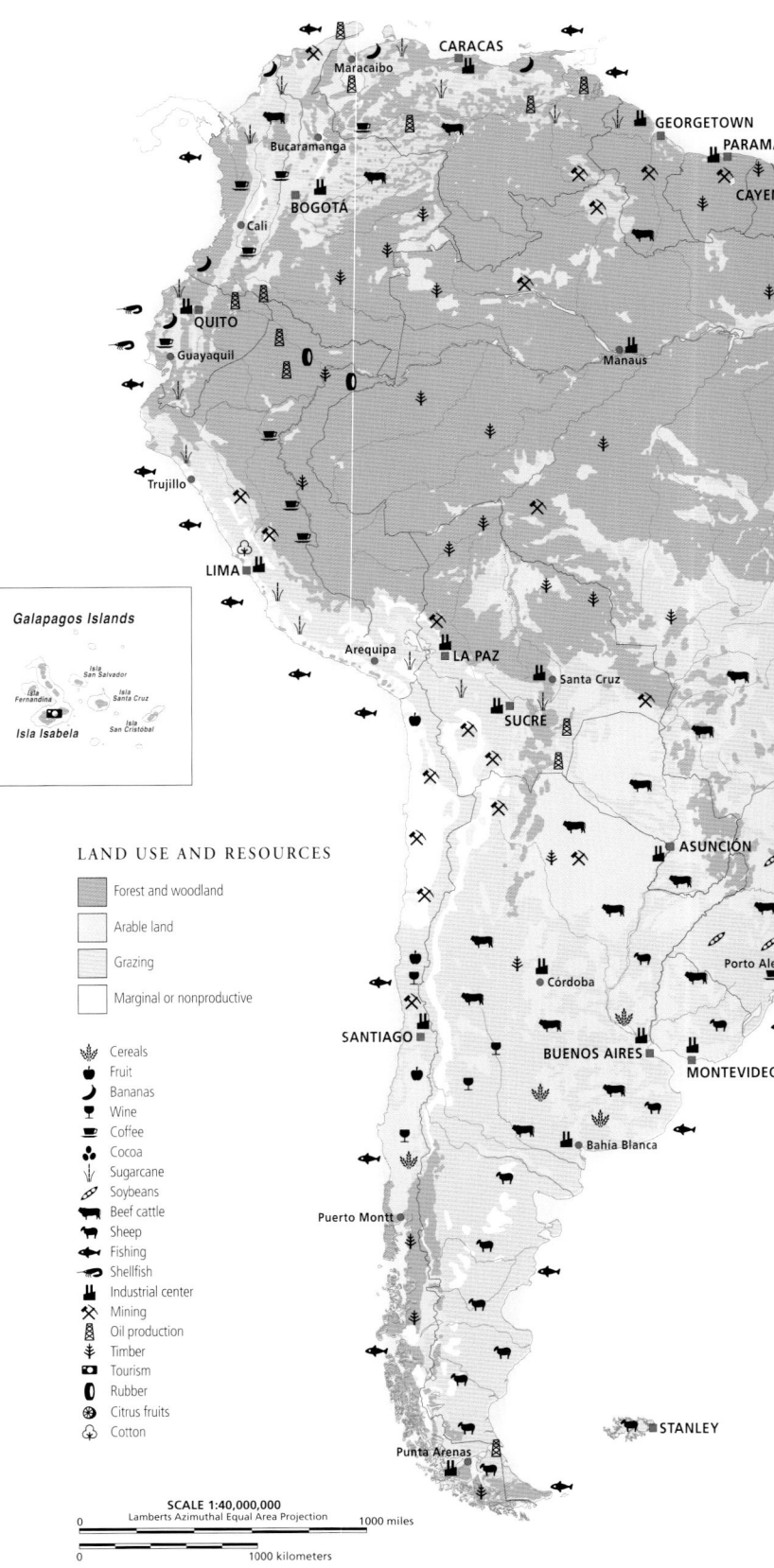

Galapagos Islands

Isla Fernandina
Isla San Salvador
Isla Santa Cruz
Isla Isabela
Isla San Cristóbal

LAND USE AND RESOURCES

- Forest and woodland
- Arable land
- Grazing
- Marginal or nonproductive

- Cereals
- Fruit
- Bananas
- Wine
- Coffee
- Cocoa
- Sugarcane
- Soybeans
- Beef cattle
- Sheep
- Fishing
- Shellfish
- Industrial center
- Mining
- Oil production
- Timber
- Tourism
- Rubber
- Citrus fruits
- Cotton

SCALE 1:40,000,000
Lamberts Azimuthal Equal Area Projection
0   1000 miles
0   1000 kilometers

THE CHANGING FACE OF SOUTH AMERICA

The Amazon Rain Forest

The Amazon rain forest covers an area as large as the United States and harbors at least 40 percent of the world's plant and animal species, as well as 180,000 indigenous people; it also recycles 10 percent of the world's airborne carbon. Since the mid-20th century, this ecologically vital and once-remote environment has come increasingly under threat. In 1960, faced with mounting pressure from a land-hungry citizenry, the Brazilian government adopted the vote-winning policy of populating the region. Ten percent of the rain forest was cleared within seven years. Currently, an area the size of New Jersey disappears every year and total losses now amount to an area as large as France. Despite this, Brazil recently announced another plan to cover the region with dams, settlements, and thousands of miles of roads. Conservation groups estimate this could result in the loss of between 33 and 42 percent of the remaining Amazon rain forest.

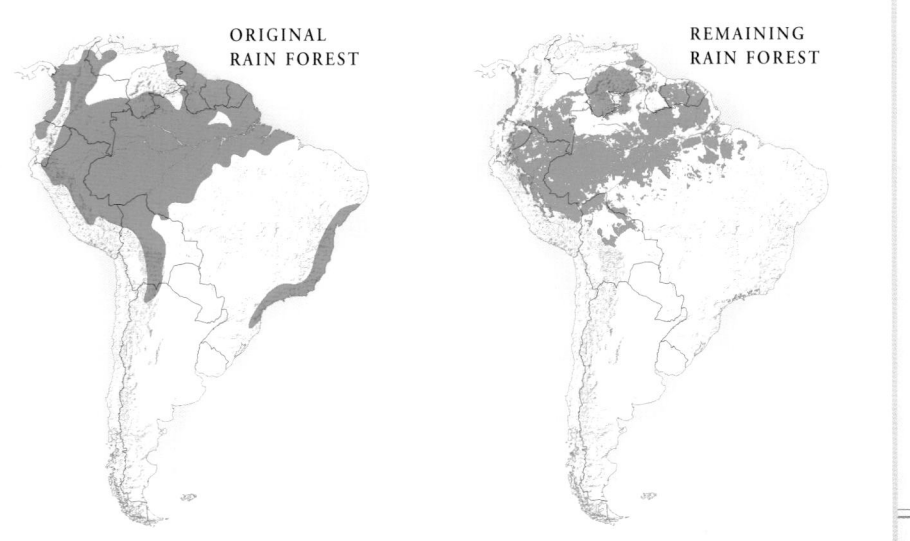

ORIGINAL RAIN FOREST

REMAINING RAIN FOREST

Protecting the Environment

Air pollution has been reduced in several cities, most notably Santiago, and Argentina has led the way in setting voluntary greenhouse-gas emission targets. South America's carbon dioxide emissions per capita are now below the world average. Modest reductions in deforestation rates have been recorded in some countries and government incentives for the creation of plantations have stimulated reforestation (although plantations do not fully compensate for the loss of natural forests, which support specialized ecosystems). Approximately 7.4 percent of the continent is now protected and Ecuador and Venezuela have, respectively, the highest and second-highest proportions of protected areas in the world. However, many South American preserves lack the funds and personnel to prevent degradation.

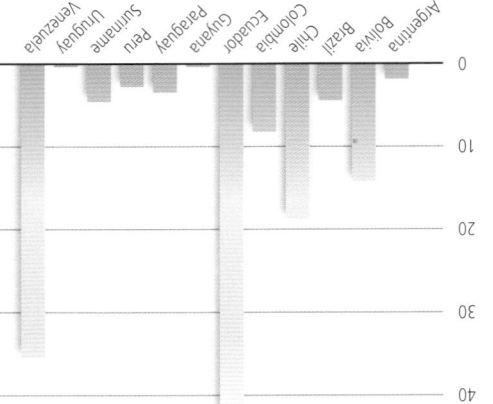

PERCENTAGE OF LAND PROTECTED IN MAJOR
SOUTH AMERICAN COUNTRIES

Skillful town planning has made Curitiba in Brazil a model of sustainability. It has dozens of parks, a traffic-free downtown zone, highly efficient public transport, and an effective recycling program.

Threats to the Environment

Over the past century, rapid population growth and widespread poverty, the concentration of land and power in the hands of wealthy individuals and corporations, corruption, and a lack of government control have contributed to widespread overexploitation of resources. Deforestation proceeds apace, from the rain forests of Guyana to the conifer forests of Chile, with logging, mining, and road-building being the main causes. Soil degradation resulting from deforestation, grazing, and overuse of chemicals affects about 15 percent of the continent. Massive hydroelectric projects threaten vital wetlands and continuing urbanization has exacerbated air and water pollution as well as waste-disposal problems.

ENVIRONMENTAL ISSUES

Degraded soil

Very degraded soil

Polluted rivers

Polluted seas and lakes

Acid rain

Major oil spills, year

Cities with severe air pollution

Overfished fishery, year of peak catch, decline since peak catch

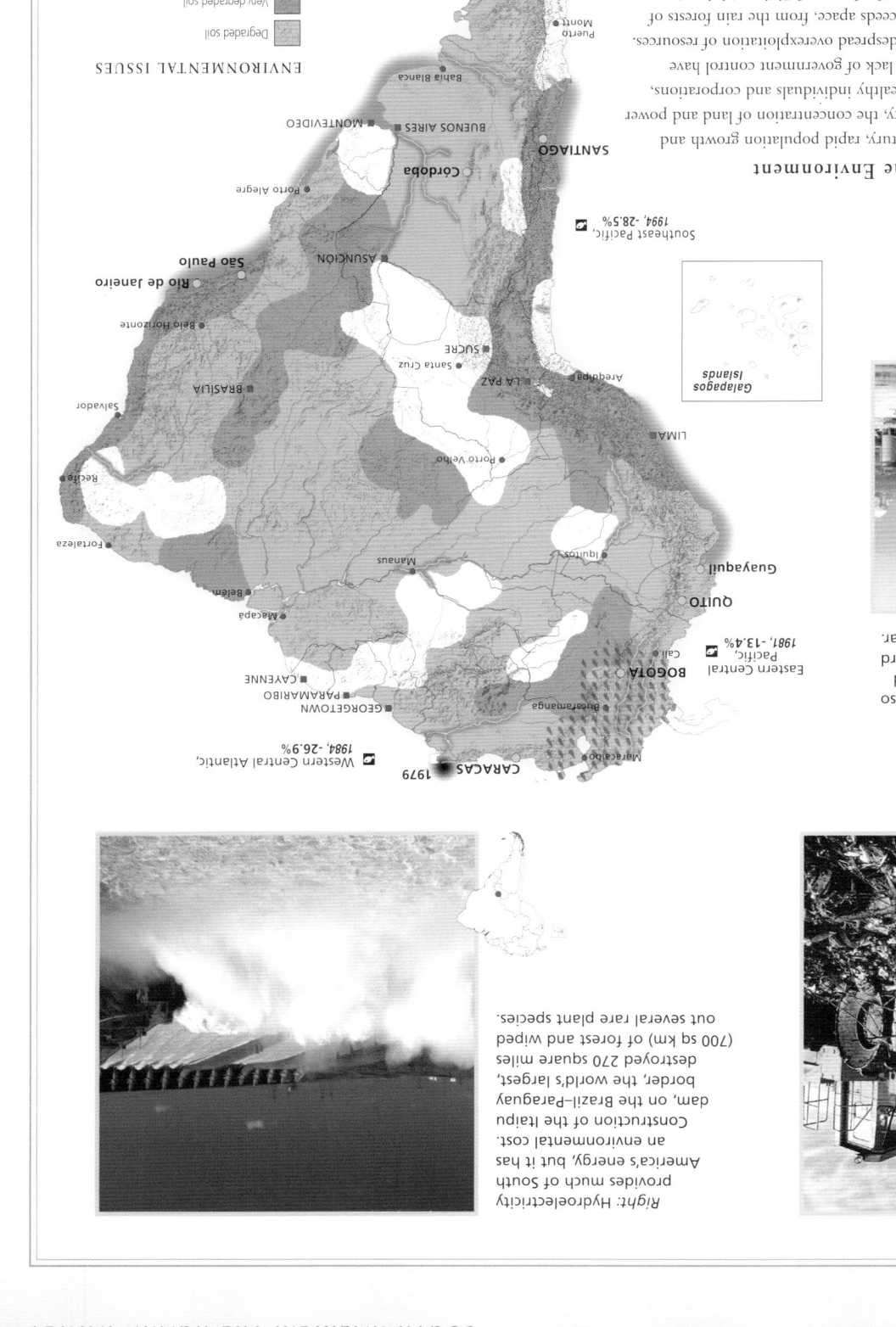

Western Central Atlantic, 1984, -26.9%

Eastern Central Pacific, 1981, -13.4%

Southeast Pacific, 1994, -28.5%

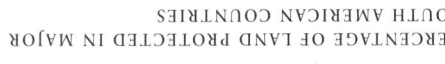
Galapagos Islands

Above: In 1972 in Peru, a combination of overfishing and an El Niño episode saw fish stocks plummet by two-thirds for the next 15 years. More than 80 percent of stocks in South American waters are now fully fished, overfished, or depleted.

Below: In 1980, the Brazilian industrial city of Cubatão was so polluted that it reportedly had no birds or insects and one-third of infants died in their first year.

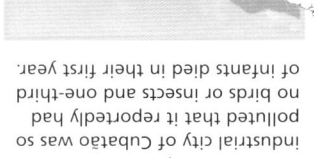

Right: Throughout South America, enormous amounts of domestic waste are deposited in open garbage dumps like this one in Buenos Aires. In Bolivia, Ecuador, and Peru, sanitary landfills can be found only in the capital cities.

Right: Hydroelectricity provides much of South America's energy, but it has an environmental cost. Construction of the Itaipu dam, on the Brazil–Paraguay border, the world's largest, destroyed 270 square miles (700 sq km) of forest and wiped out several rare plant species.

Longitude west of Greenwich

NORTHERN SOUTH AMERICA

Colombia, Guyana, Suriname, Venezuela

Nearing their northern limit in southern Colombia, the Andes Mountains divide into three separate chains, forming a rugged hinterland of valleys and ranges. This is paralleled to the east by a broad sweep of low land, including part of the heavily forested Amazon Basin in the south and, in the north, the Llanos, humid savanna grasslands drained by the Orinoco River. Beyond the Orinoco, the flat-topped Guiana Highlands sprawl across southern Venezuela, Guyana, Suriname, and French Guiana, descending in the north to densely forested lowlands and swampy coastal plains. Despite significant natural resources, and for a variety of reasons, the countries in this region have struggled to attain stability and prosperity. Colombia's government has fought a draining struggle against armed guerrillas and powerful drug-traffickers; oil-rich Venezuela's progress has been hindered by inefficient economic management and inequitable distribution of wealth; and the less-developed Guyana, Suriname, and French Guiana still lack infrastructure.

THE COLOMBIAN CORDILLERAS

The three northern branches of the Andes—the Cordillera Occidental, Cordillera Central, and Cordillera Oriental—are separated by the fertile valleys of the Cauca and Magdalena rivers. These valleys and adjacent slopes are the site of Colombia's largest cities (including the capital Bogotá) and most productive coffee and sugar plantations. They also contain vital natural resources, including oil, emeralds, and gold. In the north, the Cordillera Oriental splits again, its two arms enclosing the wide ocean inlet of Lake Maracaibo, site of Venezuela's second-largest city, Maracaibo, and the principal source of the country's enormous oil reserves.

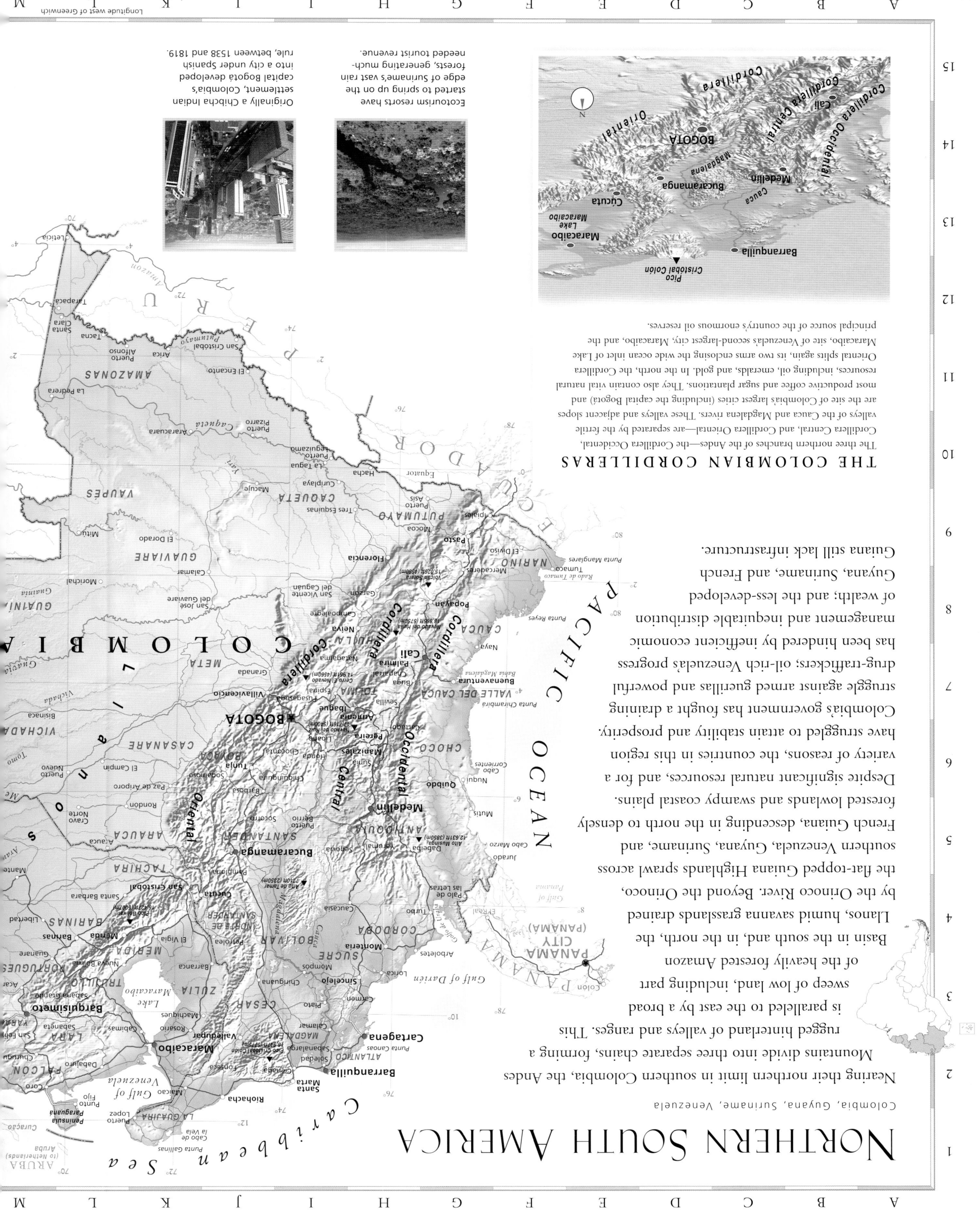

Ecotourism resorts have started to spring up on the edge of Suriname's vast rain forests, generating much-needed tourist revenue.

Originally a Chibcha Indian settlement, Colombia's capital Bogotá developed into a city under Spanish rule, between 1538 and 1819.

ECONOMIC PROFILE

The region has extensive mineral resources, limited arable land, and modest industries led by food and mineral processing and, in Colombia and Venezuela, textiles and consumer goods. Venezuela has benefited from and become highly dependent on its huge oil reserves, discovered in 1917 and found mainly around Lake Maracaibo. Colombia has more modest oil reserves, but large deposits of coal as well as gold and emeralds (of which it is the world's foremost supplier). Coffee is its leading official export, though illegally produced cocaine probably provides more revenue. Guyana and Suriname depend heavily on bauxite and sugar production.

POPULATION PATTERNS

The Andean valleys and the coast are by far the most densely populated regions, with more than 90 percent of Colombians inhabiting the eastern third of the country and 88 percent of Venezuelans living in coastal cities. Similar proportions of the populations of Guyana, Suriname, and French Guiana also live on the coastal plains. The interior is home only to scattered Amerindian peoples, cattle ranchers in the west, and remote communities originally founded by escaped slaves in the east. Most Colombians and Venezuelans are mestizo; in Guyana, Suriname, and French Guiana, the descendants of Asian—especially Indian—indentured workers marginally outnumber those of African slaves. Amerindian peoples now account for less than 3 percent of the regional population.

Dropping 3,212 feet (979 m), Angel Falls is the world's tallest waterfall. It was named for American pilot James Angel, who sighted the cascade in 1933.

The European Space Agency launches its "Ariane" satellite-carrying rockets from this facility outside Kourou in French Guiana.

Venezuela's Amerindian peoples live mainly in the Guiana Highlands. Culturally diverse, they speak more than 25 different languages.

Paramaribo

Originally an Amerindian village, Suriname's capital was settled by the French around 1640, then became a British colony in 1651. Sixteen years later Holland traded the colony, under the Treaty of Breda, for Nieuw Amsterdam, better known today as New York. Excluding short spells of British rule (1799–1802 and 1804–15), Paramaribo remained Dutch until Suriname attained independence in 1975. The city's heritage is apparent in its elegant Dutch colonial buildings, including these houses along Waterkant Straat, as well as the cathedral and the 17th-century fort. The city center has been declared a World Heritage site.

SCALE 1:7,700,000 Lamberts Conformal Conic Projection

200 miles
200 kilometers

ELEVATION

Feet	Meters
32,808	10,000
26,246	8000
19,685	6000
13,123	4000
6562	2000
3281	1000
656	200
0	sea level
Below	sea level

Feet	Meters
6562	2000
4921	1500
3281	1000
2461	750
1640	500
1312	400
984	300
656	200
328	100
0	sea level

Population density:

- Less than 2.6 persons per sq mile/ per sq km
- 2.6–26 per sq mile/ 1–10 per sq km
- 26–65 per sq mile/ 10–25 per sq km
- 65–130 per sq mile/ 25–50 per sq km
- 130–260 per sq mile/ 50–100 per sq km
- 260–520 per sq mile/ 100–200 per sq km
- 520–1040 per sq mile/ 200–400 per sq km

Economic profile symbols:

- Bananas
- Fishing
- Coffee
- Industrial center
- Sugarcane
- Mining
- Beef cattle
- Oil production
- Timber
- Forest and woodland
- Arable land
- Grazing
- Marginal or nonproductive

BOGOTÁ Bucaramanga CARACAS Maracaibo PARAMARIBO GEORGETOWN CAYENNE Pasto

ATLANTIC OCEAN

VENEZUELA GUYANA SURINAME FRENCH GUIANA (to France) BRAZIL

CARACAS PORT OF SPAIN TRINIDAD and TOBAGO GRENADA ST GEORGE'S NETHERLANDS ANTILLES (to Netherlands)

GEORGETOWN PARAMARIBO CAYENNE

Guiana Highlands Tumuc-Humac Mountains Acarai Mountains Sierra Pacaraima Sierra Parima

WESTERN SOUTH AMERICA

Bolivia, Ecuador, Peru

Separated from the Pacific Ocean by a slender coastal plain, the towering peaks of the Andes dominate the entire western side of this region, yielding in the east to well-watered, forest-cloaked lowlands, most of which drain into the vast Amazon Basin. Narrower in the north, the Andes broaden in southern Peru and Bolivia, splitting into two parallel chains, the Cordillera Occidental and the Cordillera Oriental. In the south, these ranges enclose an expansive, arid plateau known as the Altiplano. From around 1200 until shortly after the arrival of the Spanish conquistadors, Cuzco in the northern Altiplano was the capital of the Inca empire, which encompassed virtually the entire Andean sector of this region. Spanish rule left most of the region's wealth and resources in the hands of European-dominated elites. Dissatisfaction with this state of affairs has since fueled indigenous uprisings, labor unrest, Maoist guerrilla activity in Peru, and repeated changes of government. In turn, this has hampered economic development, especially in Bolivia, South America's poorest nation.

In the 16th century, the silver-mining center of Potosí in Bolivia was the New World's largest city, with 120,000 inhabitants.

The Galápagos Islands' wildlife includes a host of species unique to the archipelago, including the land iguana.

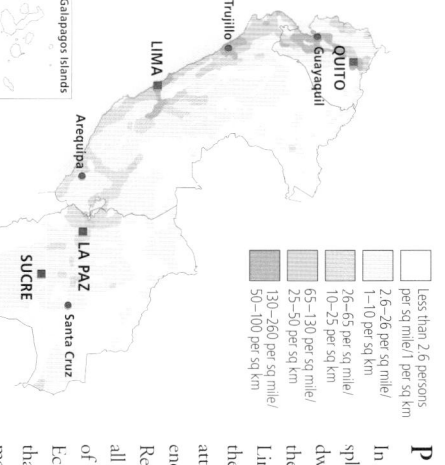

Quito

The world's second-highest capital city after La Paz in Bolivia, Ecuador's capital occupies a narrow valley on the slopes of spectacular Pichincha volcano in the Andes. Little trace remains of the Amerindian and Inca settlements that once stood here, but the city's rich array of buildings from the early period of Spanish settlement in the 16th and 17th centuries, including the elegant Monastery of San Francisco, Ecuador's oldest church, make it the best-preserved capital city in South America.

POPULATION PATTERNS

In Ecuador and Peru, the population is split evenly between coastal and mountain dwellers, with only a minority inhabiting the interior. One-third of Peruvians live in Lima. In Bolivia, the Altiplano is by far the most densely populated region, despite attempts in the late 20th century to encourage people to settle in the east. Relative to other South American nations, all three countries have high proportions of indigenous peoples—25 percent in Ecuador, 45 percent in Peru, and more than 50 percent in Bolivia. They live mainly in the Andean uplands.

| Less than 2.6 persons per sq mile/1 per sq km |
| 2.6–26 per sq mile/1–10 per sq km |
| 26–65 per sq mile/10–25 per sq km |
| 65–130 per sq mile/25–50 per sq km |
| 130–260 per sq mile/50–100 per sq km |

ECONOMIC PROFILE

Subsistence farming involving the cultivation of corn and potatoes and grazing of sheep and llamas takes place in the uplands. On the coast, Ecuador's fertile lowlands yield bananas (of which Ecuador is the world's largest exporter), coffee, and sugar. Peru's irrigated plains produce sugar, cotton, and rice. Peru and Bolivia are the leading producers of coca, the source of cocaine, an illegal but profitable crop. Metals, especially silver, copper, and tin, have long been mainstays of the economy; oil and gas have also become vital. Industries are mainly resource-based and include smelting, oil refining, food processing, and textiles.

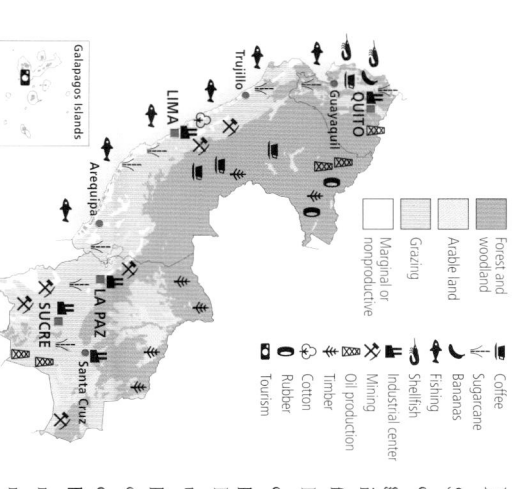

	Coffee
	Sugarcane
	Bananas
	Fishing
	Shellfish
	Mining
	Industrial center
	Oil production
	Timber
	Cotton
	Rubber
	Tourism

Forest and woodland
Grazing
Arable land
Marginal or nonproductive

The mountaintop citadel of Machu Picchu, near Cuzco in southern Peru, was built by the Inca in the mid-15th century.

The Aymara people are native to the Altiplano. Aymara women wear distinctive derby hats and woollen shawls.

La Paz (left) is Bolivia's administrative capital and seat of national government. Sucre is the constitutional capital and home of the supreme court.

THE ALTIPLANO

Consisting of a series of basins located at around 12,000 feet (3,650 m) between the Cordillera Occidental and the Cordillera Oriental, the Altiplano extends for 600 miles (965 km) from southeastern Peru to southwestern Bolivia. Its northernmost basin, situated on the border between Peru and Bolivia, is the site of Lake Titicaca, at an altitude of 12,500 feet (3,810 m) the highest navigable body of water on Earth, and La Paz, the world's highest capital city, which climbs from 10,650 feet (3,250 m) to 13,250 feet (4,050 m). Many of the surrounding mountains, including Nevado de Illimani near La Paz and Bolivia's highest peak Nevado Sajama, rise above 20,000 feet (6,100 m). Just to the northwest of the Altiplano, in the Peruvian Andes, the Amazon River begins its long, transcontinental journey of over 4,000 miles (6,400 km) to the Atlantic Ocean.

SCALE 1:8,500,000
Lambert's Conformal Conic Projection

0 250 miles
0 250 kilometers

Longitude west of Greenwich

Galapagos Islands
(to Ecuador)

SCALE 1:5,000,000

0 60 miles
0 60 kilometers

Longitude west of Greenwich

ELEVATION

Feet	Meters
6562	2000
4921	1500
3281	1000
2461	750
1640	500
1312	400
984	300
655	200
328	100
0	Below sea level
656	200
3281	1000
6562	2000
13,123	4000
19,685	6000
26,246	8000
32,808	10,000

EASTERN SOUTH AMERICA
Brazil, Paraguay

Encompassing more than 2.3 million square miles (6 million sq km) between the Andes and the eastern seaboard, the Amazon Basin is the world's largest drainage system. Cloaked with dense tropical rain forest embroidered by more than 1,000 tributaries, it dominates western and northern Brazil, its great river draining into the Atlantic Ocean near the town of Macapá. To the south rises the extensive plateau region of the Brazilian Highlands, which falls steeply to the coast in the east but descends more gently in the west to the swamps of the Pantanal, the low hills of eastern Paraguay, and the plains of Argentina. Here, the main drainage outlets are the Paraná River, which forms Paraguay's eastern boundary, and its major tributary, the Paraguay, which bisects the nation of the same name, dividing its eastern uplands from its semiarid western plains. Relatively small and landlocked, Paraguay has modest natural resources and a predominantly agricultural economy. In contrast, Brazil is South America's biggest and the world's fifth-largest country, with 5,400 miles (8,700 km) of coastline, the continent's largest population, and immense natural resources.

POPULATION PATTERNS

Brazil's population is concentrated on the coast, especially around São Paulo and Rio de Janeiro. About half of Brazilians are of European origin, 6 percent are of African descent, and 38 percent are of mixed African-European or African-Amerindian descent (so-called mulatos or pardos). Just 0.1 percent are Amerindian. These diverse groups are united by the Portuguese language. In Spanish-speaking Paraguay, 95 percent of the population is mestizo. Many Paraguayans also speak the indigenous Guaraní language. Paraguay is sparsely inhabited, and only 5 percent of the population lives west of the Paraguay River.

ECONOMIC PROFILE

Though hyperinflation, inequitable wealth distribution, and social problems have hampered development, Brazil has enormous economic potential. It is the world's second-largest iron-ore producer and third-biggest bauxite producer and it has the world's second-largest forests. Self-sufficient in food, it is the world's third-biggest meat producer and leading supplier of coffee, sugar, and oranges. Almost 90 percent of its energy comes from hydroelectric power. Industries include the manufacture of automobiles, petrochemicals, steel, shoes and textiles, and wood products. Paraguay generates all of its energy from hydroelectricity. It has a large "informal" or cash economy involving the resale of imported goods, often at street stalls.

Population density legend

- Less than 2.6 persons per sq mile/1 per sq km
- 2.6–26 per sq mile/1–10 per sq km
- 26–65 per sq mile/10–25 per sq km
- 65–130 per sq mile/25–50 per sq km
- 130–260 per sq mile/50–100 per sq km
- 260–520 per sq mile/100–200 per sq km

Economic activity legend

- Coffee
- Cocoa
- Sugarcane
- Soybeans
- Beef cattle
- Fishing
- Industrial center
- Mining
- Timber
- Citrus fruits

Land use legend

- Forest and woodland
- Arable land
- Grazing
- Marginal or nonproductive

THE PANTANAL

In western Brazil, the Planalto do Mato Grosso, an extension of the Brazilian Highlands, borders an immense plain known as the Pantanal. Tumbling down escarpments from the plateau, numerous rivers slow and meander across this plain. During the summer rainy season, the rivers overflow their banks, forming countless lakes and swamps and creating the world's largest freshwater wetland. Covering an area almost as big as Ohio, the Pantanal harbors an extraordinary diversity of wildlife. Though parts of the floodplain are protected by a national park, the ecosystem is threatened by poaching and pollution from mines and farms.

Fortaleza in Brazil derives its name from a 17th-century Dutch (then Portuguese) fort around which the city grew.

Western Paraguay is home to about 10,000 German-speaking Mennonites, whose forebears arrived in the 1920s from Eastern Europe.

Brasília A proposal for a new capital city was first presented to the Brazilian government in 1823 and subsequently incorporated in the constitution of 1891. The site was selected in 1956, partly to entice new settlers to the then-sparsely populated interior. Designed by Brazilian architects Lúcio Costa and Oscar Niemeyer in a monumental modernist style, Brasília became the national capital in 1960 and now has over 2 million inhabitants. Notable structures that helped it gain World Heritage status include its Cathedral and the National Congress—both designed by Niemeyer.

National Congress

Cathedral

Toucans abound in the rain forests of the Amazon Basin, 4 square miles (10 sq km) of which may harbor more than 400 bird species.

Brazil's Iguaçu Falls stand 269 feet (82 m) high and span 1.7 miles (2.7 km)—three times the width of the U.S.A.'s Niagara Falls.

Recife in northeastern Brazil was established in the 16th century by Portugal as a seaport serving the colonial sugar trade.

SCALE 1:14,000,000
Lamberts Conformal Conic Projection

400 miles

400 kilometers

Longitude west of Greenwich

ELEVATION

Feet	Meters
32,808	10,000
26,246	8000
19,685	6000
13,123	4000
6562	2000
4921	1500
3281	1000
2461	750
1640	500
1312	400
984	300
656	200
328	100
0	0
sea level	
Below	Below

SOUTHERN SOUTH AMERICA
Argentina, Chile, Uruguay

Below the Tropic of Capricorn, South America tapers and curls toward stormy Cape Horn, the continent's southern limit. In the west, the Andes form a great wall between Chile and Argentina, which is in turn separated from its eastern neighbor Uruguay by the Uruguay River and the estuary known as the River Plate. Twenty times as long as it is wide, Chile is divided into three climatically contrasting regions. The northern Atacama Desert is the driest place in the world. The center of the country, or Central Valley, roughly from Valparaíso to Temuco, experiences temperate weather and has rich, volcanic soils. In the south, thick, well-watered conifer forests climb steep Andean slopes. Arid plains spread eastward from the Andes across Argentina, merging with temperate grasslands that roll into low-lying Uruguay. In the 1970s, all three nations experienced military coups and periods of repressive government. A return to civilian rule in the late 1980s was followed by widespread economic reforms. Development was, however, hobbled by foreign debt and, especially in Argentina, crippling inflation.

Buenos Aires Argentina's capital was founded in 1580 by explorer Juan de Garay, on the site of an earlier abandoned Spanish settlement, and named for Santa Maria del Buen Aire (Saint Maria of the Good Air). Today a sprawling city of more than 12 million people and one of the world's most important ports, Buenos Aires has a strong European atmosphere. Undoubtedly its most colorful neighborhood is the portside district of La Boca. Traditionally the home of dancers and artists, and Italian immigrants, it is famed for its multicolored buildings, arts and crafts, and tango shows.

Founded in 1573, Córdoba became an important Spanish colonial center and is now Argentina's second city. Its cathedral dates from 1758.

Rainfall is almost nonexistent in the Atacama Desert of northern Chile, with localized showers occurring only a few times a century.

The Moreno Glacier forms a 200-foot (60-m) wall of ice across an arm of Lago Argentino in the foothills of the Argentine Andes.

SOUTHERN PATAGONIA

On the southern Chile–Argentina border, extensive icefields crown Andean peaks such as Cerro Murallón and Cerro Fitz Roy. Glaciers snake down from these summits, plowing through expansive conifer forests. In the west, they reach the ragged, island-studded coast. In the east, they fall to lakes such as Argentino—site of the huge Moreno Glacier—and Viedma, and fuel mountain streams that drain across the barren Patagonian plateau and feed in turn into major rivers such as the Chico and Gallegos.

FALKLAND ISLANDS
(to U.K.)

Argentina has long claimed ownership of the British-ruled Falkland Islands. An Argentine invasion in 1982 led to defeat in a brief war with the U.K.

SCALE 1:9,000,000
Lamberts Conformal Conic Projection

POPULATION PATTERNS

Almost 90 percent of the region's inhabitants live in cities, mainly in the central temperate belt, in and around the cities of Santiago in Chile, Buenos Aires and Córdoba in Argentina, and Montevideo in Uruguay. Settlements are sparse on Andean peaks, and in the cold, wet southwest. Chile's population is predominantly mestizo, with a small residual population of mainly Mapuche Indians. Argentina and Uruguay have more varied cultures, influenced by the large numbers of Spanish, Italian, and German immigrants who arrived after 1870. Indigenous groups still inhabit remote parts of Argentina but have almost vanished from Uruguay.

Uninhabited

Less than 2.6 persons per sq mile/1 per sq km
2.6–26 per sq mile/1–10 per sq km
26–65 per sq mile/10–25 per sq km
65–130 per sq mile/25–50 per sq km
130–260 per sq mile/50–100 per sq km
260–520 per sq mile/100–200 per sq km

ECONOMIC PROFILE

All three countries are strong exporters of primary goods. Chile is the world's leading supplier of copper and in the top five fish producers. Its forests provide abundant timber and the Central Valley yields large quantities of wheat, rice, fruit, and vegetables. Beef and wool from livestock grazed on the Pampas are the traditional mainstays of the Argentine and Uruguayan economies. Uruguay has few mineral resources, but Argentina has sizable oil reserves. Chile and Argentina have thriving wine industries, and Argentina is now the world's fifth-largest producer. All three capital cities are important commercial centers. Leading industries include food processing, chemicals, and textiles.

Cereals
Fruit
Wine
Beef cattle
Sheep
Fishing
Industrial center
Mining
Timber
Oil production

Forest and woodland
Arable land
Grazing
Marginal or nonproductive

ELEVATION
Feet	Meters
6562	2000
4921	1500
3281	1000
2461	750
1640	500
1312	400
984	300
656	200
328	100
0	Below sea level
656	200
3281	1000
6562	2000
13,123	4000
19,685	6000
26,246	8000
32,808	10,000

III

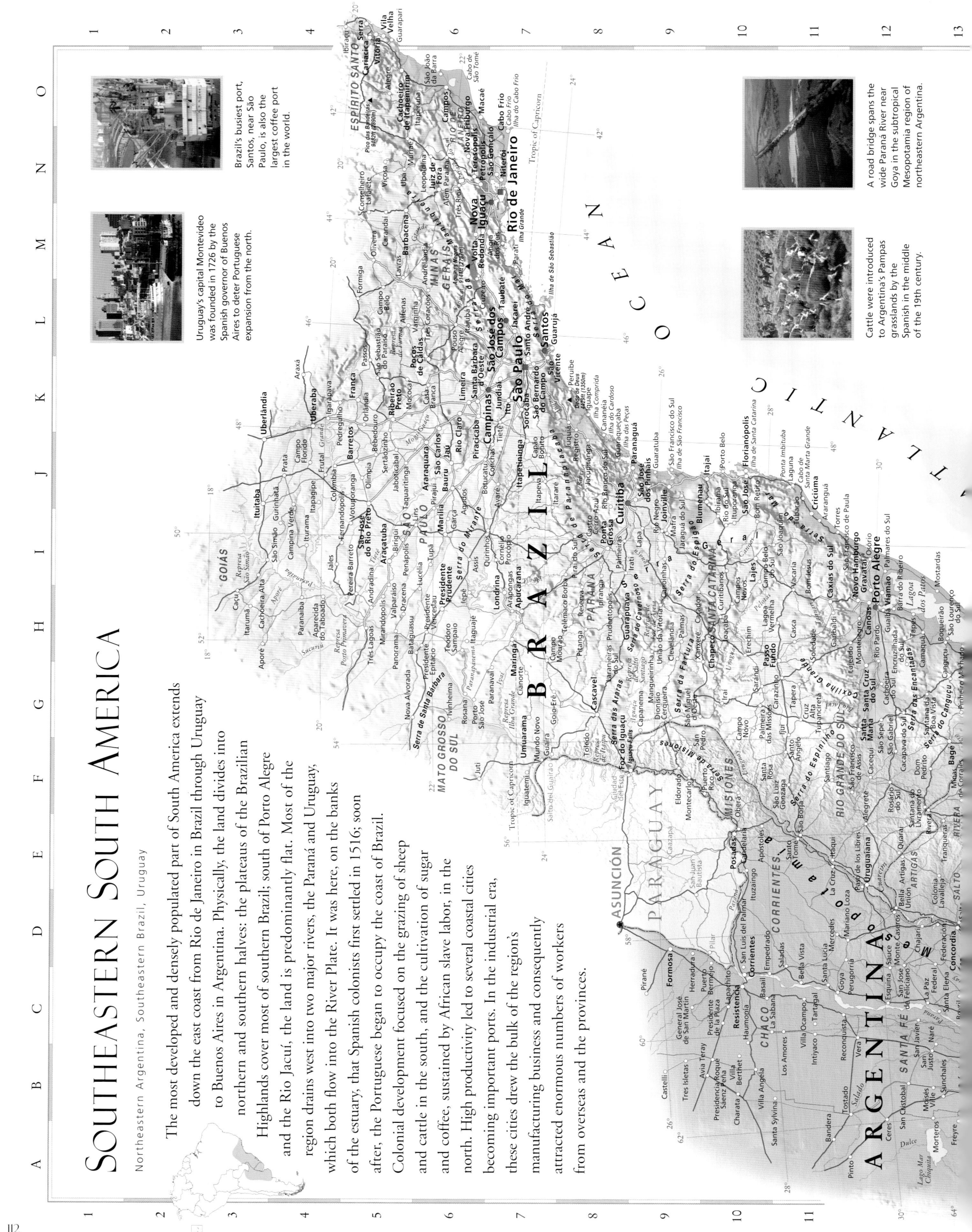

SOUTHEASTERN SOUTH AMERICA

Northeastern Argentina, Southeastern Brazil, Uruguay

The most developed and densely populated part of South America extends down the east coast from Rio de Janeiro in Brazil through Uruguay to Buenos Aires in Argentina. Physically, the land divides into northern and southern halves: the plateaus of the Brazilian Highlands cover most of southern Brazil; south of Porto Alegre and the Rio Jacuí, the land is predominantly flat. Most of the region drains west into two major rivers, the Paraná and Uruguay, which both flow into the River Plate. It was here, on the banks of the estuary, that Spanish colonists first settled in 1516; soon after, the Portuguese began to occupy the coast of Brazil. Colonial development focused on the grazing of sheep and cattle in the south, and the cultivation of sugar and coffee, sustained by African slave labor, in the north. High productivity led to several coastal cities becoming important ports. In the industrial era, these cities drew the bulk of the region's manufacturing business and consequently attracted enormous numbers of workers from overseas and the provinces.

Brazil's busiest port, Santos, near São Paulo, is also the largest coffee port in the world.

Uruguay's capital Montevideo was founded in 1726 by the Spanish governor of Buenos Aires to deter Portuguese expansion from the north.

A road bridge spans the wide Paraná River near Goya in the subtropical Mesopotamia region of northeastern Argentina.

Cattle were introduced to Argentina's Pampas grasslands by the Spanish in the middle of the 19th century.

POPULATION PATTERNS

The overwhelming majority of the region's inhabitants live in cities. Metropolitan Buenos Aires has more than 12 million people, almost one-third of the national population. Over 1.3 million Uruguayans, 40 percent of the country's inhabitants, live in Montevideo. Elsewhere, Uruguay is sparsely populated: the next largest city, Salto, is less than one-tenth the size of the capital. Southern Brazil includes the country's most populous urban centers, São Paulo and Rio de Janeiro (which accommodate about 17 percent of Brazil's huge population), as well as several other cities, including Curitiba and Porto Alegre. The state of São Paulo alone is home to 37 million people. Its capital's vast citizenry includes the biggest Japanese population outside Japan and South America's largest Jewish community.

ECONOMIC PROFILE

The southern lowlands are used chiefly for raising beef cattle and sheep, though wheat is also cultivated on the Pampas. Fruit, including oranges and bananas, and rice are grown along the Brazilian coast; sugarcane, soybeans, and coffee are planted across the uplands. Livestock exports and food processing underpin the industrial sector in Montevideo and Buenos Aires, though the latter is also a center of automobile production, oil refining, and printing. São Paulo is South America's industrial powerhouse. It generates 40 percent of Brazil's GDP and its factories employ 15 percent of the national population. Its major industries are the manufacture of automobiles, textiles, chemicals, and metals, and oil refining. Services are more significant in Rio de Janeiro, the headquarters of many large businesses.

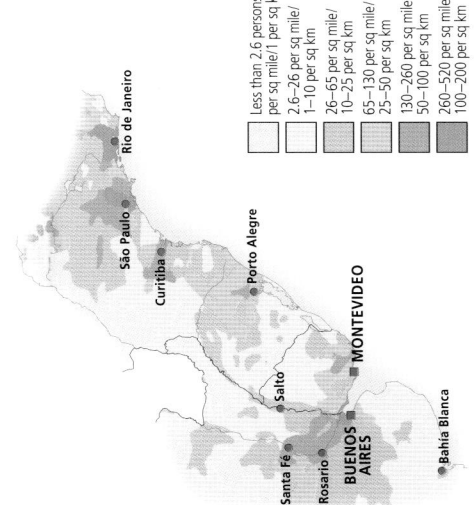

Uruguay has over 15 million sheep, and wool is one of the country's most valuable exports.

THE SERRA DO MAR

On their eastern flank, the Brazilian Highlands abut the coast along a 1,600-mile (2,600-km) escarpment, the southern part of which is known as the Serra do Mar (Sea Range). Averaging 3,000 feet (1,000 m) in height, this range rises almost sheer from the sea at several points. The precipitous slopes provide a mountainous backdrop to Rio de Janeiro and other coastal cities. Associated outcrops have created islands, such as Ilha de São Sebastião and Ilha Grande, and other coastal formations including Rio's famous Sugar Loaf Mountain.

Rio de Janeiro

One of the most distinctive landmarks in South America, the 100-foot (30-m) statue of Christ the Redeemer in Rio de Janeiro was built by engineer Heitor da Silva Costa and completed in 1931. From its site atop 2,428-foot (740-m) Mount Corcovado, it overlooks Guanabara Bay and the city of 11 million that spreads inland from the bay's northern and western shores. The name Rio de Janeiro, meaning "January River," was coined by the area's first Portuguese explorers: arriving in January, 1502, they assumed the bay was the mouth of a river. Portuguese settlers returned to occupy the bay in 1565, and a burgeoning sugar trade soon gave rise to a town. In 1763, Rio became the colonial capital, and in 1822, when Brazil achieved independence, it became the national capital, remaining so until 1960, when the country's seat of government was transferred to Brasília.

Sugar Loaf Mountain

Mount Corcovado

SCALE 1:7,500,000
Lamberts Conformal Conic Projection

Longitude east of Greenwich

Less than 2.6 persons per sq mile/1 per sq km
2.6–26 per sq mile/ 1–10 per sq km
26–65 per sq mile/ 10–25 per sq km
65–130 per sq mile/ 25–50 per sq km
130–260 per sq mile/ 50–100 per sq km
260–520 per sq mile/ 100–200 per sq km

Coffee
Sugarcane
Soybeans
Beef cattle
Fishing
Industrial center
Mining
Citrus fruits
Cereals
Sheep
Bananas
Tourism

Forest and woodland
Arable land
Grazing

Seen from a satellite, the bright lights of Europe reveal a highly urbanized continent. The pattern of human settlement along the coasts ensures that the outline of much of western Europe is clearly visible from space.

EUROPE

ABOVE EUROPE

Satellites and space shuttles have been collecting images of our planet from space for more than 40 years. These images are sometimes assigned "false colors" to emphasize particular elements. From above, the patterns of dense populations, concentrations of industry, and vast agricultural areas of Europe emerge in astonishing detail. Revealed also is a surprising amount of natural environment, including the high lands of the Alps and the icy plains that stretch east from the jagged Norwegian coast to the Ural Mountains. Satellites have tracked oil slicks off the Atlantic coasts, captured the eruptions of Mount Etna and Mount Vesuvius, and followed wildfires through the forests of France, Spain, and Portugal. Observations such as these can help civil defense authorities to plan disaster responses. Glaciers, sensitive indicators of global climate change, have also been monitored over decades.

Volga delta, The Russian Federation
Below: The Volga flows 2,291 miles (3,688 km) from near Moscow south to the landlocked Caspian Sea, where it empties its waters through a delta of about 500 outlets. In this false-color image the delta wetlands are shown as bright green. The long thin lines just offshore indicate artificially maintained shipping channels.

Aletsch Glacier, Switzerland
Right: Climate change can be measured by the varying rates of retreat of glaciers such as Switzerland's Aletsch Glacier, seen here curving across the center and upper right of the image. Glacial ice is shown as pale blue, and, from above, the moraine lines that mark its slow-moving path look almost like vehicle tracks.

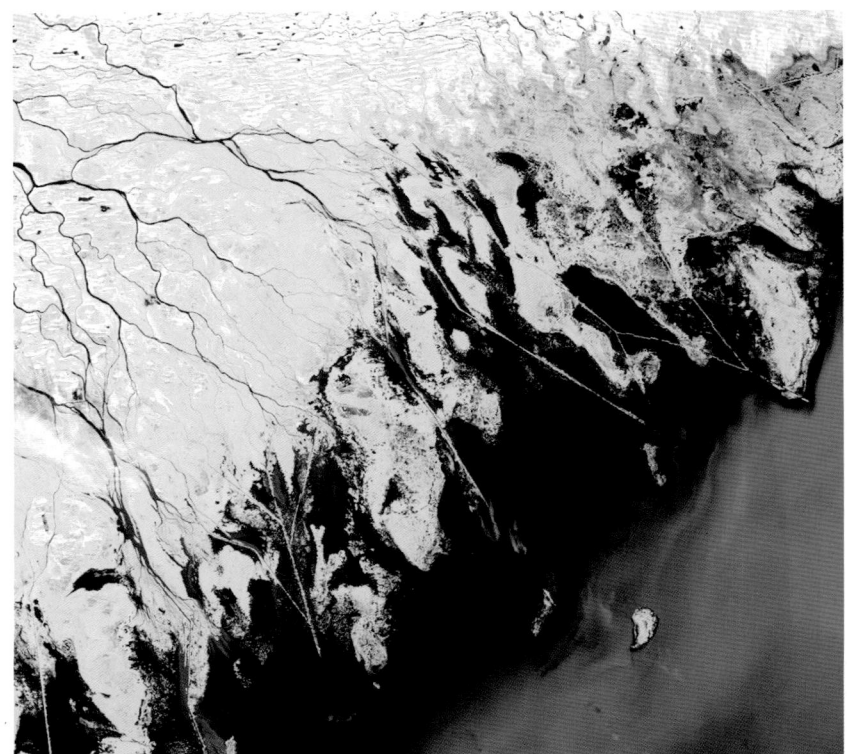

Nordrhein-Westfalen, Germany
Below: Coal mines fan into farmlands in this simulated natural color view of a 19 by 22 mile (30 by 36 km) region of Nordrhein-Westfalen, Germany. The white and dark blue patterns on the right are huge opencast coal mines. The myriad patches are agricultural fields; light green indicates crops, gray is bare soil. The thin dark lines are roads.

Mount Etna, Italy
Below right: Mount Etna, on the Italian island of Sicily, is Europe's largest and most active volcano. Here a dark, thick plume of smoke and ash from its November 2002 eruption is shown blowing southeast toward the city and airport of Catania. The white smoke is from forest fires sparked by ash fall on the slopes of the volcano.

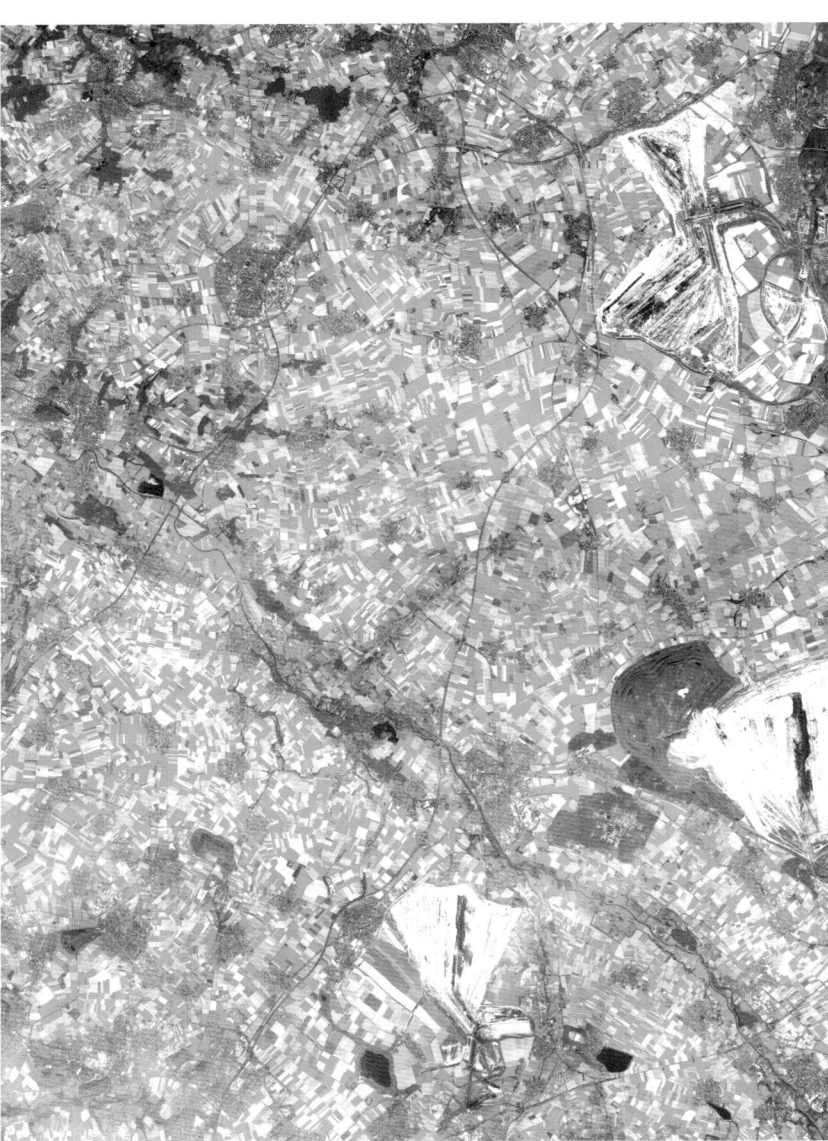

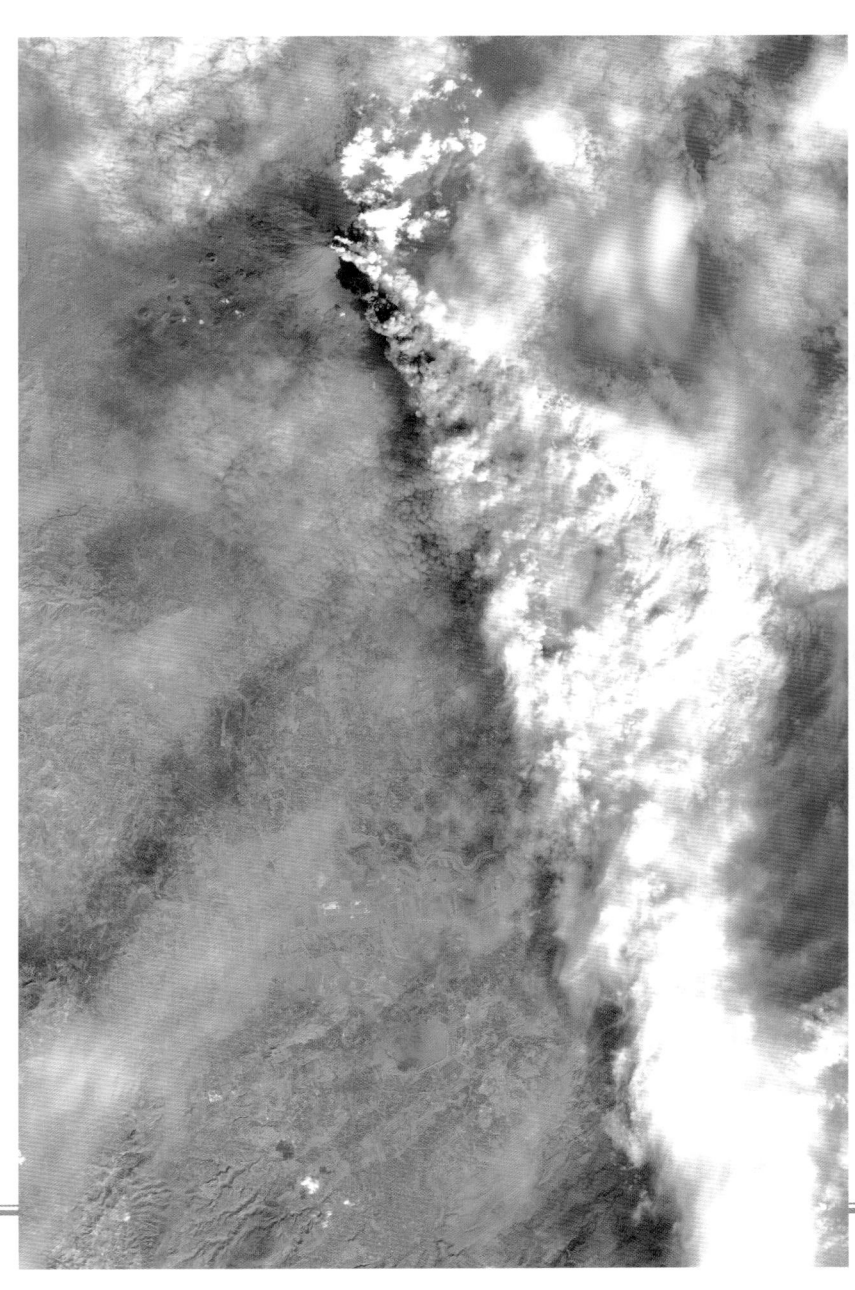

LAND AND ENVIRONMENT

Covering over 3.8 million square miles (9.8 million sq km), Europe is the second-smallest continent. It is separated from Asia by the Ural Mountains of Russia and bounded by sea to the north, west, and south. A chain of mountain ranges, including the Pyrenees, Alps, and Carpathian Mountains, stretches across the continent from west to east. It separates the rugged lands that fringe the island-studded Mediterranean Sea from the North European Plain, a belt of flat land that extends from the English Channel to the Urals. Farther north lie the broad, glacier-carved Scandinavian Peninsula and the large islands of Great Britain, Ireland, and Iceland.

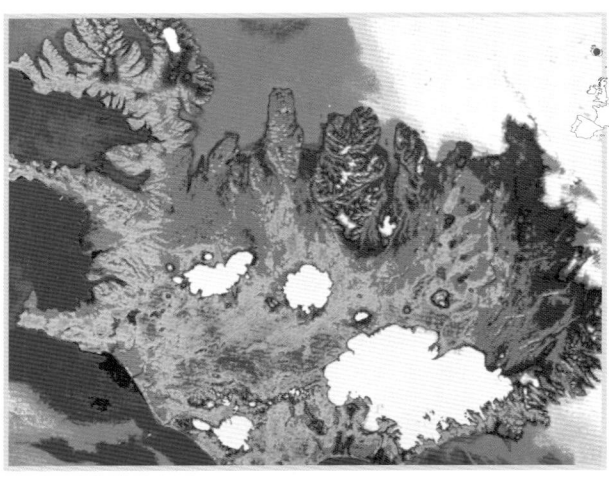

Above: As its name suggests, much of the isolated volcanic island of Iceland is covered by ice. The island's largest ice sheet, Vatnajökull, clearly visible at the bottom right of this satellite image, is bigger than all of mainland Europe's glaciers combined.
Below: The Alps stretch for 650 miles (1,000 km) from southeastern France, through Italy, Switzerland, and Austria to Slovenia. This satellite photograph shows the western end of the chain.

SCALE 1:20,000,000
Lamberts Conformal Conic Projection

NATURAL HAZARDS

Earthquakes

Europe is located on the western side of the Eurasian Plate. Beneath the Mediterranean Sea, this plate is colliding with the African Plate and the smaller Anatolian Plate. Sudden movements along the plate boundaries create shock waves that are felt regularly in parts of southern Europe as earthquakes. Over the centuries, earthquakes have caused massive destruction and many deaths.

Along the plate boundaries that run through the Mediterranean, the thinner African Plate is forced under the thicker Eurasian Plate, buckling the land above and forcing magma to the surface. This creates volcanoes such as Mounts Etna and Vesuvius in Italy.

A woman salvages belongings from the remains of her home following the 1980 earthquake in southern Italy.

Eurasian Plate

African Plate

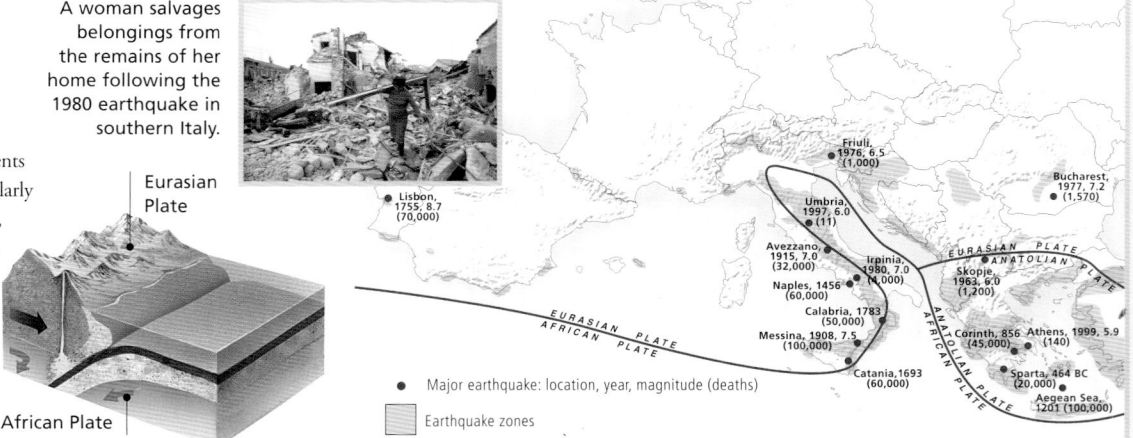

● Major earthquake: location, year, magnitude (deaths)

   Earthquake zones

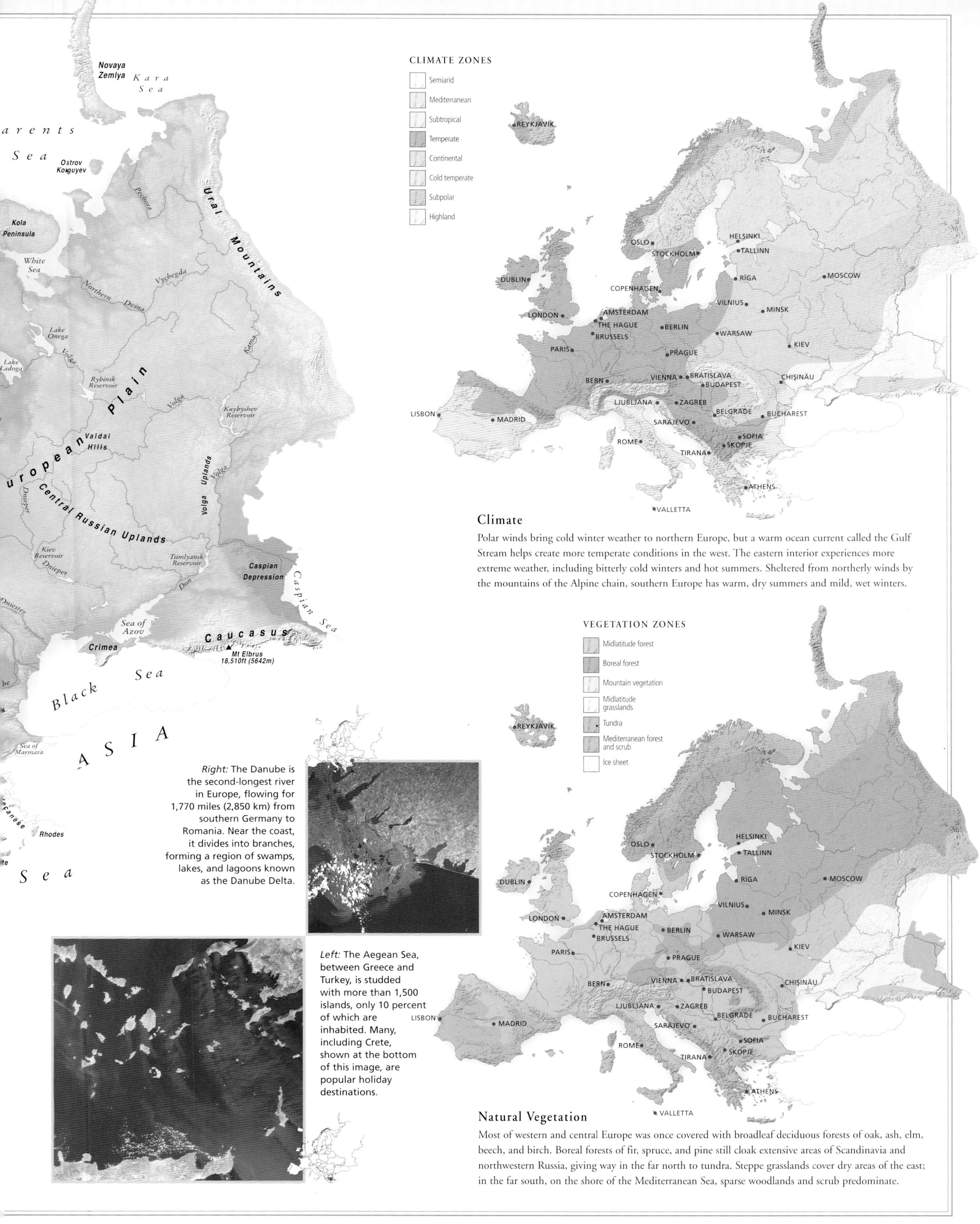

CLIMATE ZONES

- Semiarid
- Mediterranean
- Subtropical
- Temperate
- Continental
- Cold temperate
- Subpolar
- Highland

Climate

Polar winds bring cold winter weather to northern Europe, but a warm ocean current called the Gulf Stream helps create more temperate conditions in the west. The eastern interior experiences more extreme weather, including bitterly cold winters and hot summers. Sheltered from northerly winds by the mountains of the Alpine chain, southern Europe has warm, dry summers and mild, wet winters.

VEGETATION ZONES

- Midlatitude forest
- Boreal forest
- Mountain vegetation
- Midlatitude grasslands
- Tundra
- Mediterranean forest and scrub
- Ice sheet

Right: The Danube is the second-longest river in Europe, flowing for 1,770 miles (2,850 km) from southern Germany to Romania. Near the coast, it divides into branches, forming a region of swamps, lakes, and lagoons known as the Danube Delta.

Left: The Aegean Sea, between Greece and Turkey, is studded with more than 1,500 islands, only 10 percent of which are inhabited. Many, including Crete, shown at the bottom of this image, are popular holiday destinations.

Natural Vegetation

Most of western and central Europe was once covered with broadleaf deciduous forests of oak, ash, elm, beech, and birch. Boreal forests of fir, spruce, and pine still cloak extensive areas of Scandinavia and northwestern Russia, giving way in the far north to tundra. Steppe grasslands cover dry areas of the east; in the far south, on the shore of the Mediterranean Sea, sparse woodlands and scrub predominate.

PEOPLES AND NATIONS

Europe has a population of about 720 million and has long been one of the most densely inhabited parts of the world. It is home to a great diversity of peoples, languages, and cultures—the result of thousands of years of migrations, invasions, wars, and changing allegiances—and its cities are rich in historical, architectural, and artistic treasures. Today, Europe encompasses 42 nations as well as the Eastern Thrace region of Turkey and the eastern part of the Russian Federation, which are sometimes referred to as European Turkey and European Russia. Most European nations have substantial natural resources, and the inhabitants of northwestern Europe, especially, enjoy a high standard of living.

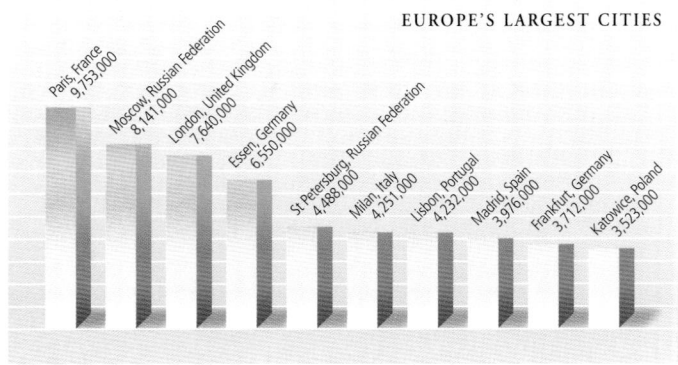

Paris, France 9,753,000
Moscow, Russian Federation 8,147,000
London, United Kingdom 7,640,000
Essen, Germany 6,550,000
St Petersburg, Russian Federation 4,488,000
Milan, Italy 4,251,000
Lisbon, Portugal 4,222,000
Madrid, Spain 3,976,000
Frankfurt, Germany 3,712,000
Katowice, Poland 3,523,000

Urbanization

Until the 18th century, relatively few Europeans lived in cities. Following the Industrial Revolution, however, urban areas expanded rapidly. Toward the end of the 18th century, London became the first city in the world to reach a population of 1 million, a figure attained by nine other cities by 1900. Today, approximately 74 percent of Europeans live in urban areas.

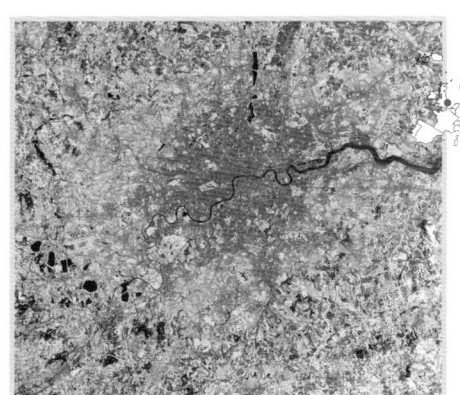

Right: In this false-color satellite image of London, urban areas appear blue, with commercial areas darker than the lighter residential areas. Pale green and orange areas are parklands, and dark orange and red areas indicate arable land. The River Thames is clearly visible as a dark, snaking line.

Population Patterns

Europe's early population growth centered on strategically important ports and major rivers. Industrial development in the 19th century attracted large numbers of workers to major manufacturing centers, such as central England, Germany's Ruhr Valley, and northern Italy, and these urban areas are still the most densely populated regions. The least densely populated parts of Europe are the high peaks of the central mountain ranges and the far north, most notably northern Scandinavia, and the Scottish Highlands.

POPULATION DENSITY

- Uninhabited
- Less than 2.6 persons per sq mile/1 per sq km
- 2.6–26 per sq mile/ 1–10 per sq km
- 26–65 per sq mile/ 10–25 per sq km
- 65–130 per sq mile/ 25–50 per sq km
- 130–260 per sq mile/ 50–100 per sq km
- 260–520 per sq mile/ 100–200 per sq km

The European Union

Twenty-five European nations belong to the European Union (EU), which seeks to establish common economic, social, and judicial policies across the continent. The EU began to take shape in the early 1950s, when Belgium, France, Germany, Italy, Luxembourg, and the Netherlands agreed to establish a common trading market, the European Economic Community (EEC). Its success led other countries to apply for membership. The EU's major institutions include the Council of the EU, the principal decision-making body located in Brussels, Belgium, and the European Parliament, based in Strasbourg, France.

- EU members
- Applicant members
- Seeking membership

FLASHPOINTS

With so many nations, peoples, and cultures living in close proximity to each other, it is not surprising that Europe is the site of several longstanding disputes.

Basqueland

The Basque people of northern Spain and southwestern France have a distinct culture and unique language. Since the 1970s, in an attempt to gain independence for their homeland from Spain, Basques belonging to a group called ETA, or Euzkada Ta Askatasuna (Basque Homeland and Liberty), have resorted to terrorism.

Northern Ireland

In 1921, Ireland became self-governing and the six counties of Northern Ireland were incorporated into the United Kingdom (U.K.). Since then, Northern Ireland has been the site of violent conflict between Protestants, who want to remain part of the U.K., and Catholics, who wish to unite with Ireland.

Percentage of Total Population
Catholic 100 80 60 40 20 0
Protestant 0 20 40 60 80 100

Kosovo

About 90 percent of the inhabitants of the Serbian province of Kosovo are ethnic Albanians, most of whom would like their region to be autonomous or independent. Serbia has violently resisted Kosovar moves toward independence, partly because it fears the unification of Kosovo with neighboring Albania.

Nations of Europe

The political outlines of Europe have been modified repeatedly over hundreds of years, but most of the changes occurred in the 20th century. Of the continent's 42 nations, 22 were formed in the 1900s. Among the oldest states are Andorra and Monaco, both founded in the late 13th century.

SCALE 1:20,000,000
Lamberts Conformal Conic Projection
0   500 miles
0   500 kilometers

EUROPE IN 1100

EUROPE IN 1500

EUROPE IN 1914

THE HUMAN IMPACT

Along with eastern and southern Asia, Europe was the focus of early population growth. Large-scale modification of the landscape began with the development of subsistence farming around 4000 BC, increased with the introduction of the iron plow and commercial farming in the Middle Ages, then accelerated rapidly with the advent of industry in the 18th century. Humans have now removed more than half of the continent's original forest, along with large areas of natural steppe grasslands. Urban areas, roadways, and railways form a tangled web of concrete, tarmac, and steel covering thousands of square miles. Mines have been excavated, rivers dammed, and swamps drained. Overall, humans are thought to have modified about 65 percent of Europe's surface—double the proportion of any other continent. These transformations have brought significant benefits and enabled Europeans to enjoy a high standard of living. But continuing prosperity could be undermined by damage to the environment caused by depletion of resources and the polluting effects of waste.

THE CHANGING FACE OF EUROPE

Forests

About 8,000 years ago, forests covered about 70 percent of Europe, flourishing almost everywhere except for especially high, exposed, or poorly drained land. As populations expanded and technology developed, Europeans cleared ever-larger numbers of trees to provide farmland, fuel, and building materials. Today, excluding Russia, 68 percent of the original forest has disappeared and only one percent of old-growth trees survive. Large stands of forest remain only in northern Europe, European Russia, and subalpine regions. On a more positive note, Europe has increased its forest cover in recent years by 4 percent—more than any other continent.

ORIGINAL FOREST COVER

CURRENT FOREST COVER

LAND USE AND RESOURCES

- Forest and woodland
- Arable land
- Grazing
- Marginal or nonproductive

Cereals	Oilseed rape	Pigs
Rice	Tobacco	Fishing
Flax	Sugar beet	Shellfish
Potatoes	Flowers	Industrial center
Fruit and vegetables	Olives	Mining
Fruit	Reindeer	Oil production
Vegetables	Beef cattle	Gas production
Citrus fruits	Dairy cattle	Tourism
Wine	Sheep	Timber
		Winter sports

Economic Profile

Europe's abundant resources include major reserves of fossil fuels, reliable supplies of fresh water, and sizable swathes of arable land. The fertile west, center, and southeast produce large amounts of cereals (20 percent of the world's supply), root crops (including two-thirds of the world's potatoes), fruit, and livestock products. Dairy and beef cattle predominate in the north; the south is better suited to the farming of olives, grapes, citrus fruits, sheep, and goats. European industries make half of the world's steel, one-third of its chemicals, and a plethora of consumer goods, the continent also accounts for half of the world's exports and imports.

Land Cover

Most of Europe's forests and woodlands lie in European Russia and Scandinavia. Western Europe has much higher proportions of arable land and pasture. Large parts of Europe are covered by urban and industrial areas, roads, and railways.

PROPORTIONS OF TOTAL LAND AREA

- Forest and woodland 33.6%
- Arable land 28.2%
- Grazing 16.4%
- Other land 21.8%

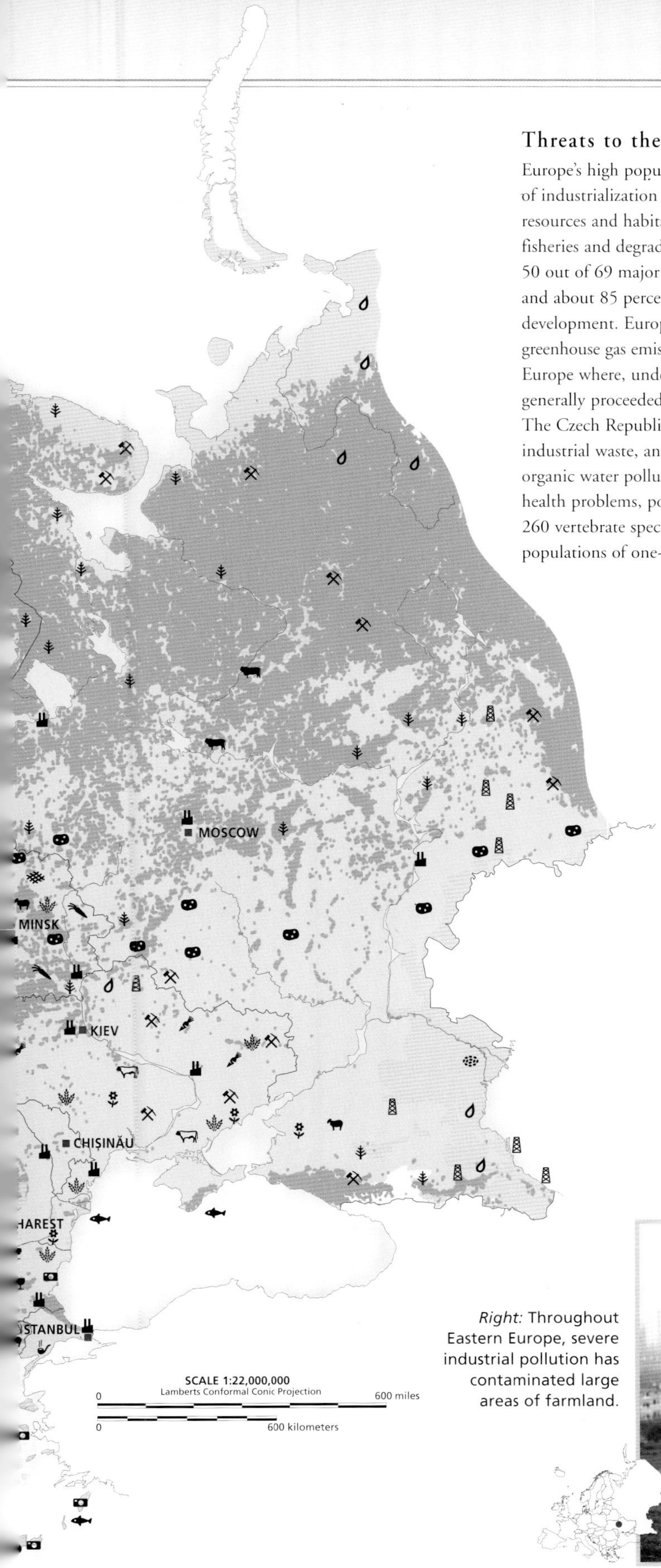

Threats to the Environment

Europe's high population density and high level of industrialization have placed great strain on its natural resources and habitats. Overexploitation has depleted fisheries and degraded soils. A recent assessment found 50 out of 69 major rivers to be of poor ecological quality, and about 85 percent of the coastline is threatened by development. Europe is responsible for one-third of global greenhouse gas emissions; pollution is especially bad in Eastern Europe where, under Soviet control, industrialization generally proceeded unchecked by environmental restrictions. The Czech Republic now has the continent's highest levels of industrial waste, and Moldova has the highest levels of organic water pollutants. As well as giving rise to human health problems, pollution has decimated wildlife—about 260 vertebrate species are on the brink of extinction and the populations of one-third of bird species are in decline.

Right: On November 19, 2002, the *Prestige* oil tanker ran aground off the northwest coast of Spain, releasing 24,500 tons (25,000 t) of oil. The spill decimated wildlife and local fishing industries.

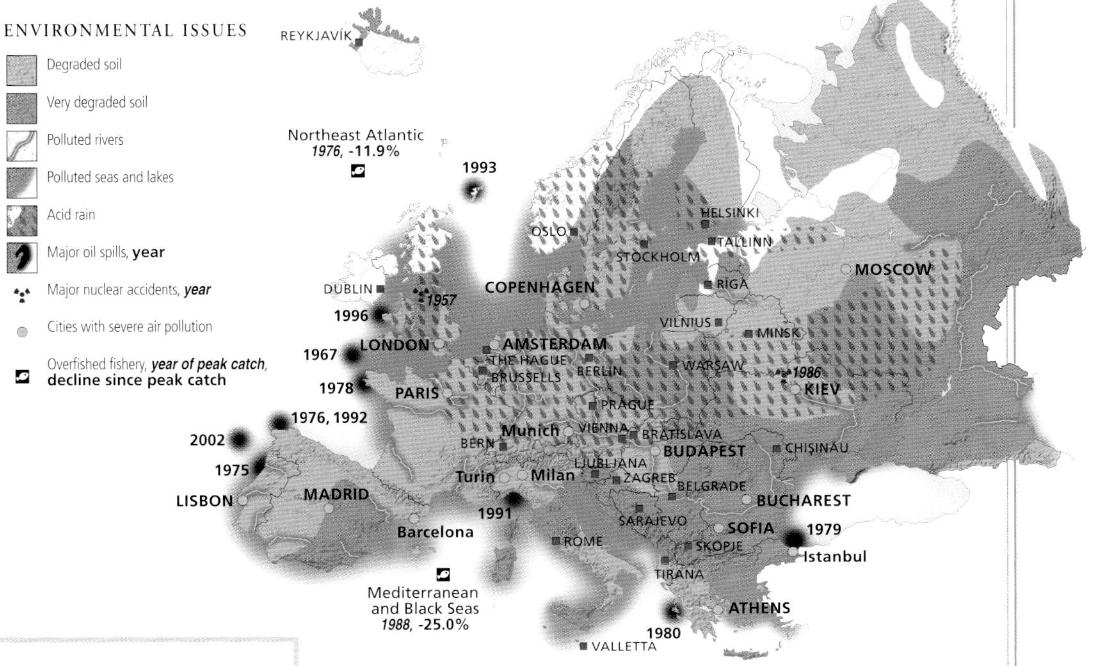

ENVIRONMENTAL ISSUES

- Degraded soil
- Very degraded soil
- Polluted rivers
- Polluted seas and lakes
- Acid rain
- Major oil spills, **year**
- Major nuclear accidents, **year**
- Cities with severe air pollution
- Overfished fishery, **year of peak catch**, **decline since peak catch**

Northeast Atlantic *1976*, -11.9%

Mediterranean and Black Seas *1988*, -25.0%

SCALE 1:22,000,000
Lamberts Conformal Conic Projection

0   600 miles

0   600 kilometers

Right: Throughout Eastern Europe, severe industrial pollution has contaminated large areas of farmland.

Right: Chernobyl in the Soviet Union (now Ukraine) was the site of the worst-ever nuclear disaster, in April 1986. It killed 32 people and spread radioactive fallout throughout Europe.

Protecting the Environment

The implementation of recent international legislation has resulted in significant progress in reducing pollution, with greenhouse-gas emissions falling 2 percent between 1990 and 1998, and carbon dioxide emissions declining 8 percent in Eastern Europe between 1990 and 2000. The use of pesticides has dwindled in Eastern Europe, and phosphorous discharges have dropped by 50 to 80 percent in Western Europe in the past 20 years. Levels of the heavy metals cadmium, lindane, and mercury in seas fell by 80 percent in the 1990s. The number of protected areas grows every year and in Western Europe legislation designed to protect biodiversity now covers over 54 million acres (22 million ha) of farmland. However, environmental groups fear that the level of protection offered by many preserves is inadequate.

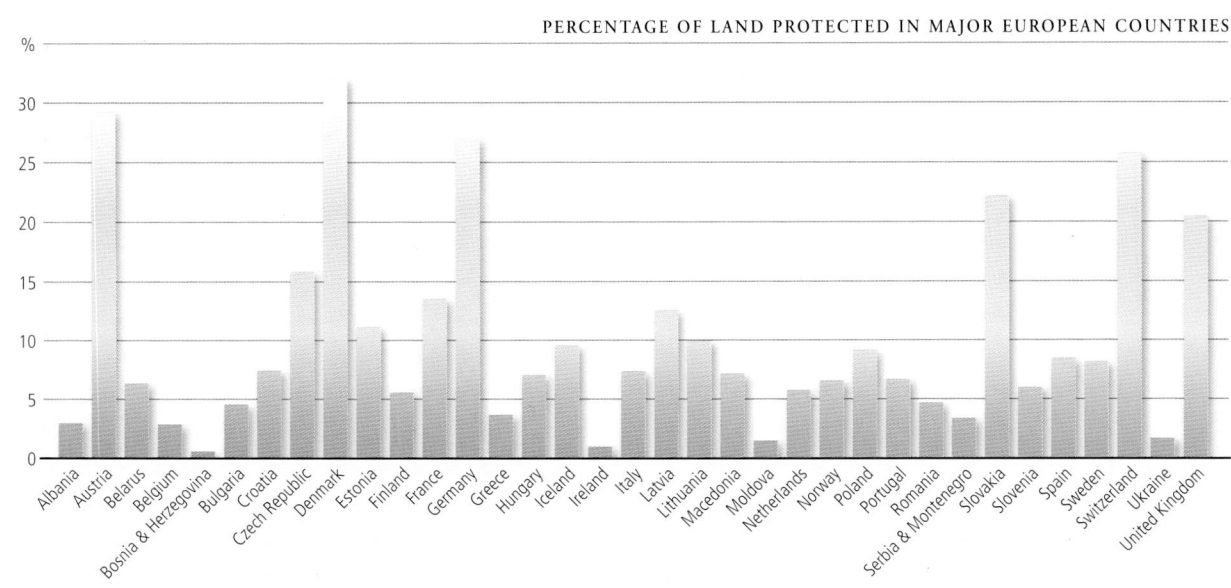

PERCENTAGE OF LAND PROTECTED IN MAJOR EUROPEAN COUNTRIES

(Bar chart with vertical axis labeled % and values 0, 5, 10, 15, 20, 25, 30. Countries along horizontal axis: Albania, Austria, Belarus, Belgium, Bosnia & Herzegovina, Bulgaria, Croatia, Czech Republic, Denmark, Estonia, Finland, France, Germany, Greece, Hungary, Iceland, Ireland, Italy, Latvia, Lithuania, Macedonia, Moldova, Netherlands, Norway, Poland, Portugal, Romania, Serbia & Montenegro, Slovakia, Slovenia, Spain, Sweden, Switzerland, Ukraine, United Kingdom)

THE BRITISH ISLES
Republic of Ireland, United Kingdom

The British Isles consist of two large islands, Great Britain and Ireland, and numerous smaller islands located off the northwest coast of mainland Europe.

Together with the troubled province of Northern Ireland, the once-independent nations of England, Scotland, and Wales make up the United Kingdom (U.K.). The southern part of the island of Ireland became self-governing in 1921. Most of southeastern Britain is low, gently undulating terrain, becoming almost entirely flat in the east-coast Fens region. To the north and west, the land is more rugged, with hills and mountains dominating central northern England, much of Wales, southern and northern Scotland, and parts of Northern Ireland. In southern Ireland, a well-watered central plain is studded with lakes and peat bogs and ringed by coastal uplands. Both the U.K. and Ireland have recently developed closer social and economic ties with other European nations, and a physical link between Britain and the rest of the continent was forged in 1994 with the completion of the Channel Tunnel.

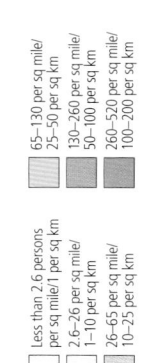

POPULATION PATTERNS

The U.K.'s highly urbanized population—about 90 percent inhabit towns and cities—is heavily concentrated in the southeast and around the industrial centers of Birmingham, Manchester, Leeds, Glasgow, and Belfast. The least densely populated areas are the Scottish Highlands, where sheep far outnumber people, and the uplands of northwest England and Wales. Ireland's population is more evenly distributed, with about 60 percent living in urban areas.

less than 2.6 persons per sq mile/1 per sq km
2.6–26 per sq mile/1–10 per sq km
26–65 per sq mile/10–25 per sq km
65–130 per sq mile/25–50 per sq km
130–260 per sq mile/50–100 per sq km
260–520 per sq mile/100–200 per sq km

ECONOMIC PROFILE

The decline of the U.K.'s manufacturing industries has been paralleled by the growth in services, which now employ three-quarters of workers. Still-important industries include engineering, chemicals and chemical products, metals, and food and beverages. The nation's most abundant food crops are cereals (especially wheat and barley), potatoes, sugar beet, and oilseed rape. Ireland's farming sector is more dependent on livestock. Its industries experienced a boom in the late 20th century, led by textiles, chemicals, machinery, and computer hardware and software.

Cereals
Potatoes
Sugar beet
Oilseed rape
Beef cattle
Dairy cattle
Sheep

Industrial center
Fishing
Oil production
Gas production
Shellfish
Timber

Forest and woodland
Arable land
Grazing

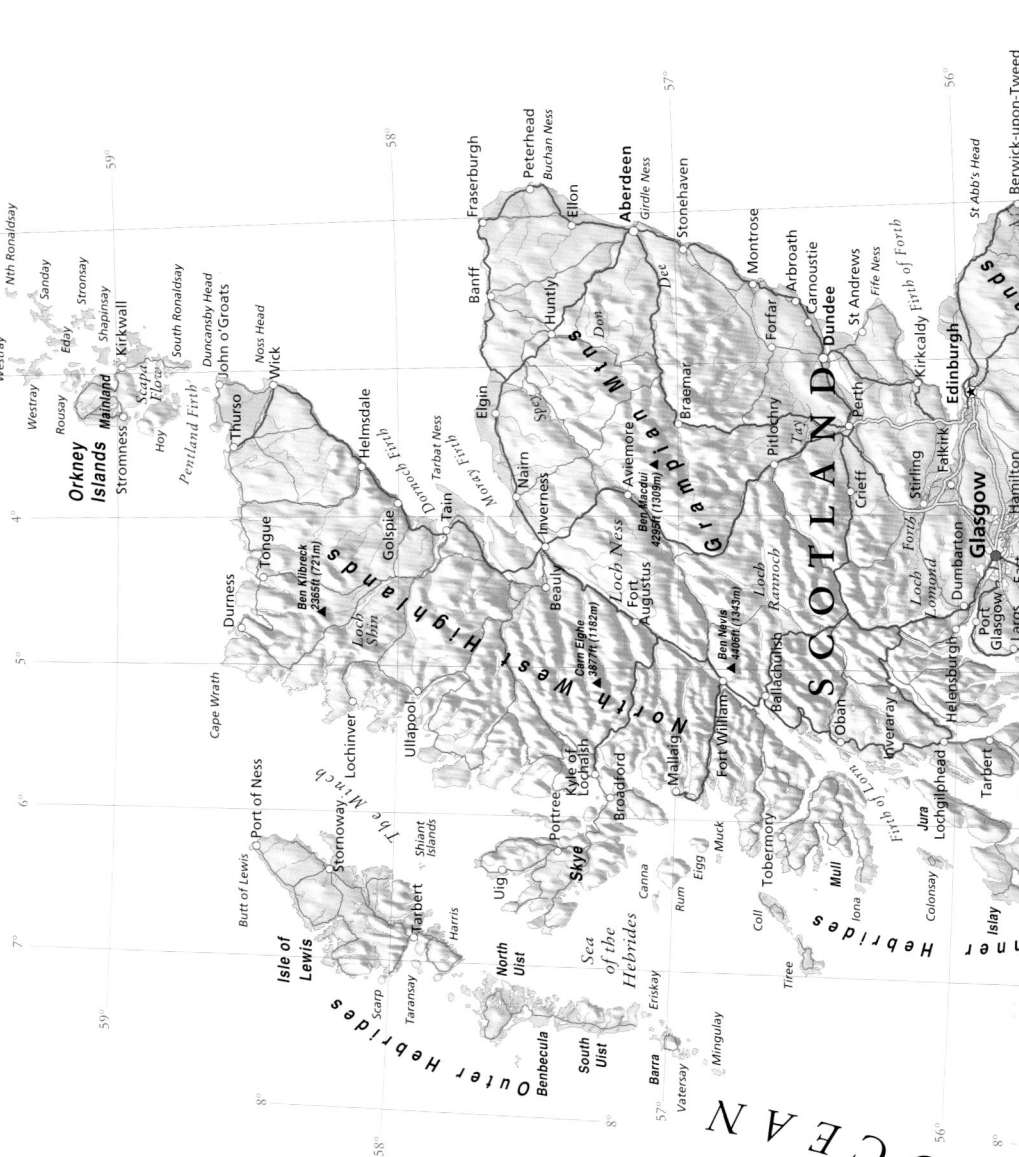

Oxford, England, is a manufacturing center, noted for automobile production. But it is best known as the site of the U.K.'s oldest university, founded in the 12th century.

On the west coast of Ireland, uplands abut the Atlantic Ocean, forming dramatic coastal landforms such as the spectacular Cliffs of Moher, near Hag's Head.

North Sea oil and gas fields have made the U.K. virtually self-sufficient in fossil fuels.

THE HIGHLANDS

The highest part of the British Isles, the Scottish Highlands rise from the Central Lowlands along the Highland Boundary Fault, which extends from Helensburgh in the southwest to Stonehaven in the northeast. They are split in two by another major fault, the Great Glen, which is partially filled by lakes including Loch Ness.

SCALE 1:3,000,000
Lambert's Conformal Conic Projection

100 miles
100 kilometers

ELEVATION
Feet / Meters
6562 2000
4921 1500
3281 1000
2461 750
1640 500
1312 400
984 300
656 200
328 100
0 Below sea level
656 200
3281 1000
6562 2000
13,123 4000
19,685 6000
26,246 8000
32,808 10,000

125

SOUTHERN GREAT BRITAIN

From the southern flanks of the Pennines, a broad belt of roads, towns, and cities runs southeastward through the low-lying heart of England, the region known as the Midlands, to London, the capital of the U.K. and its largest city. This corridor is by far the most developed part of the country, encompassing the majority of its industrial and commercial centers, the bulk of its freeways, and more than half of its population.

The urban sprawl is, however, broken by sizable tracts of fertile farmland—most notably in the East Midlands—remnants of forests, and scenic ranges of hills, including the Cotswolds and the Chilterns. On the eastern and western fringes lie quieter, culturally and geographically distinctive areas. The Cambrian Mountains dominate the interior of the Celtic nation of Wales, descending to a long, heavily indented coastline. In the east, the formerly swampy Fens isolate the tranquil agricultural plains of East Anglia, and in the far southwest, a picturesque, rocky coastline bounds the narrow, traditionally Celtic enclave of Cornwall and the rolling pastures and moorlands of Devon.

Made of chalk, the famous white cliffs of Dover border the English Channel.

The Royal Liver Building, a Liverpool landmark, was completed in 1911.

Snowdon in northwest Wales has five peaks. The tallest, Yr Wyddfa, is the highest point in England and Wales.

POPULATION PATTERNS

This region has more than two-thirds of the U.K. population, with the highest concentrations occurring in London (home to 7.6 million people), Birmingham, and the cluster of cities between Liverpool and Leeds. Population growth is relatively low and due mainly to natural increase. In the late 20th century, the demise of heavy industry and coal mining in the northwest, Wales, and Scotland accelerated migration to London. However, a concurrent trend saw many people and businesses move out of the capital to peripheral areas such as the East Midlands, East Anglia, and the southwest. One-quarter of people in Wales speak Welsh; the region's other Celtic language, Cornish, has all but died out.

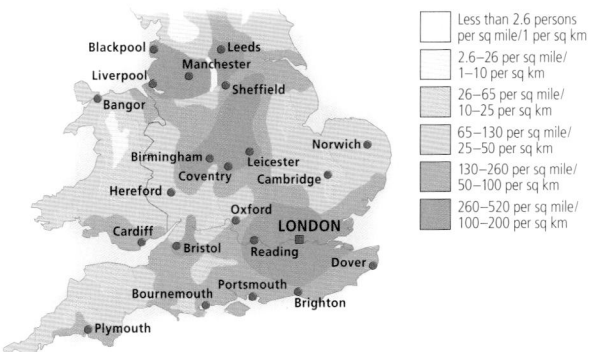

	Less than 2.6 persons per sq mile/1 per sq km
	2.6–26 per sq mile/1–10 per sq km
	26–65 per sq mile/10–25 per sq km
	65–130 per sq mile/25–50 per sq km
	130–260 per sq mile/50–100 per sq km
	260–520 per sq mile/100–200 per sq km

ECONOMIC PROFILE

The economy is dominated by services, particularly finance, retailing, health care, and tourism. While the northwest and Wales have suffered due to the collapse of coal mining and heavy industries, the east and southeast have thrived due to the boom in services and success in attracting light, high-tech industries to areas such as Cambridge and Reading. Southern England has most of the U.K.'s best farmland. The highly mechanized cultivation of wheat, oilseed rape, and sugar beet takes place in the east; dairy and beef cattle are reared in the west; and market gardening (the small-scale cultivation of fruit and vegetables) predominates in the southeast.

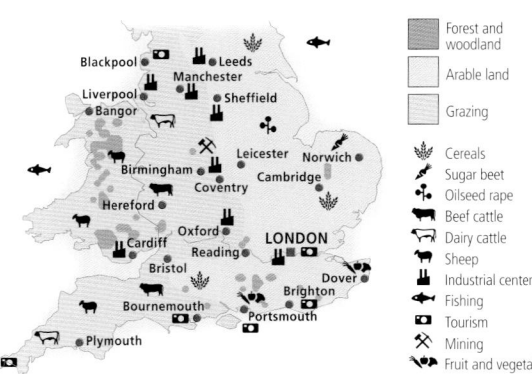

	Forest and woodland
	Arable land
	Grazing
	Cereals
	Sugar beet
	Oilseed rape
	Beef cattle
	Dairy cattle
	Sheep
	Industrial center
	Fishing
	Tourism
	Mining
	Fruit and vegetables

London The Romans founded Londinium, as they named it, on the banks of the Thames in the first century AD. After being all but abandoned in the fifth century, the town flourished again under the Saxons and the Normans, whose king, William I (the Conqueror), built a fortress to control local trade. Known as the White Fort and later the Tower of London, it was expanded by several monarchs over the following centuries, becoming a royal residence and, notoriously, a prison and place of execution. The city grew with it, attaining a population of 1 million by 1800 and 6.5 million a century later. Now a popular tourist attraction, the tower still hosts a military garrison and is patrolled by guards, known as "beefeaters," who dress in distinctive Tudor uniforms.

ELEVATION

Feet	Meters
6562	2000
4921	1500
3281	1000
2461	750
1640	500
1312	400
984	300
656	200
328	100
0	0
Below sea level	
0	0
656	200
3281	1000
6562	2000
13,123	4000
19,685	6000
26,246	8000
32,808	10,000

SCALE 1:1,500,000
Lamberts Conformal Conic Projection

0 ——— 50 miles

0 ——— 50 kilometers

From the early 18th century, windmills like this one near Holt, Norfolk, were used to drain marshes in East Anglia.

The precise function of the stone circles at Stonehenge, near Salisbury, begun around 2700 BC, remains uncertain.

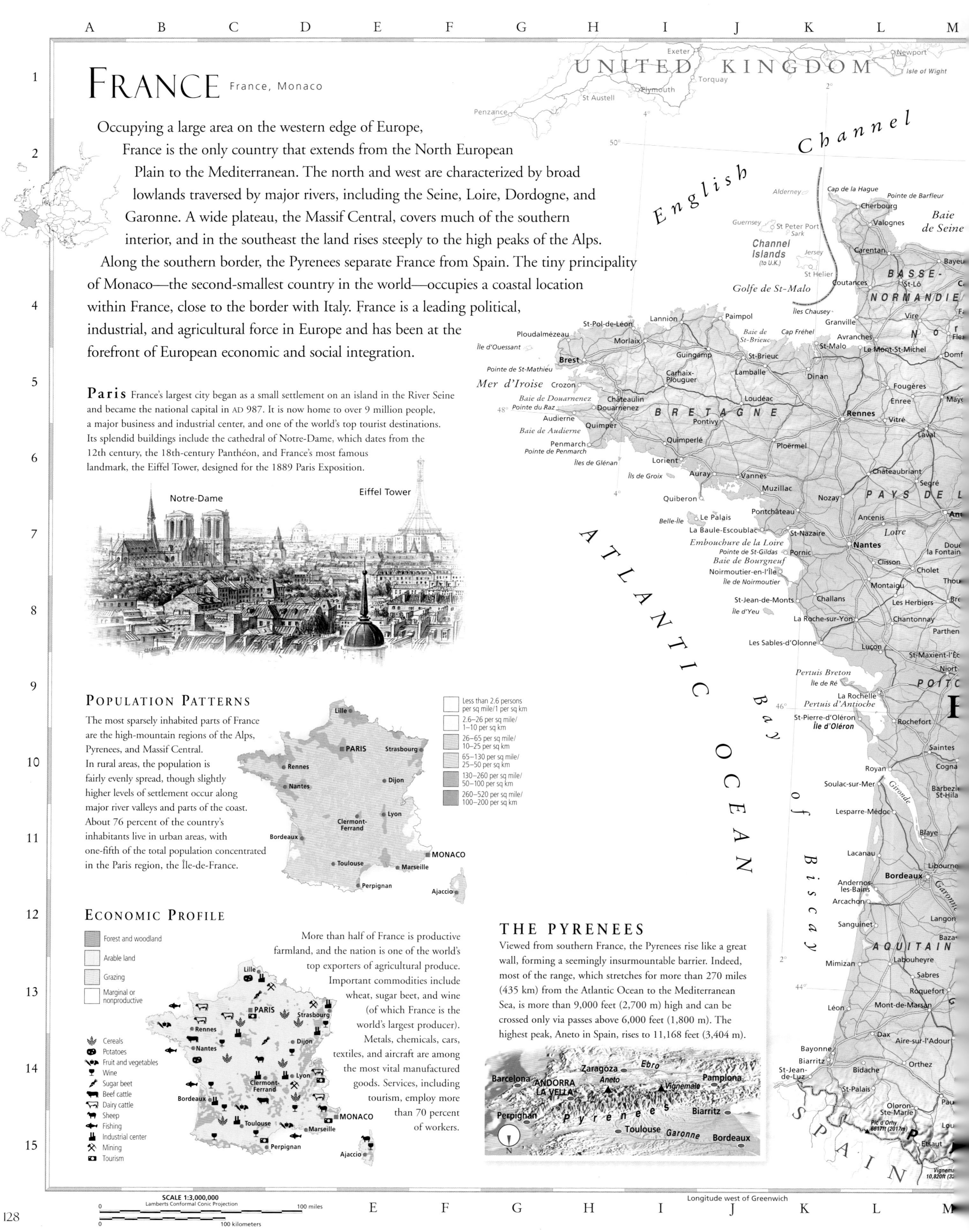

FRANCE
France, Monaco

Occupying a large area on the western edge of Europe, France is the only country that extends from the North European Plain to the Mediterranean. The north and west are characterized by broad lowlands traversed by major rivers, including the Seine, Loire, Dordogne, and Garonne. A wide plateau, the Massif Central, covers much of the southern interior, and in the southeast the land rises steeply to the high peaks of the Alps. Along the southern border, the Pyrenees separate France from Spain. The tiny principality of Monaco—the second-smallest country in the world—occupies a coastal location within France, close to the border with Italy. France is a leading political, industrial, and agricultural force in Europe and has been at the forefront of European economic and social integration.

Paris France's largest city began as a small settlement on an island in the River Seine and became the national capital in AD 987. It is now home to over 9 million people, a major business and industrial center, and one of the world's top tourist destinations. Its splendid buildings include the cathedral of Notre-Dame, which dates from the 12th century, the 18th-century Panthéon, and France's most famous landmark, the Eiffel Tower, designed for the 1889 Paris Exposition.

Notre-Dame

Eiffel Tower

POPULATION PATTERNS

The most sparsely inhabited parts of France are the high-mountain regions of the Alps, Pyrenees, and Massif Central. In rural areas, the population is fairly evenly spread, though slightly higher levels of settlement occur along major river valleys and parts of the coast. About 76 percent of the country's inhabitants live in urban areas, with one-fifth of the total population concentrated in the Paris region, the Île-de-France.

Less than 2.6 persons per sq mile/1 per sq km
2.6–26 per sq mile/ 1–10 per sq km
26–65 per sq mile/ 10–25 per sq km
65–130 per sq mile/ 25–50 per sq km
130–260 per sq mile/ 50–100 per sq km
260–520 per sq mile/ 100–200 per sq km

ECONOMIC PROFILE

Forest and woodland
Arable land
Grazing
Marginal or nonproductive

Cereals
Potatoes
Fruit and vegetables
Wine
Sugar beet
Beef cattle
Dairy cattle
Sheep
Fishing
Industrial center
Mining
Tourism

More than half of France is productive farmland, and the nation is one of the world's top exporters of agricultural produce. Important commodities include wheat, sugar beet, and wine (of which France is the world's largest producer). Metals, chemicals, cars, textiles, and aircraft are among the most vital manufactured goods. Services, including tourism, employ more than 70 percent of workers.

THE PYRENEES

Viewed from southern France, the Pyrenees rise like a great wall, forming a seemingly insurmountable barrier. Indeed, most of the range, which stretches for more than 270 miles (435 km) from the Atlantic Ocean to the Mediterranean Sea, is more than 9,000 feet (2,700 m) high and can be crossed only via passes above 6,000 feet (1,800 m). The highest peak, Aneto in Spain, rises to 11,168 feet (3,404 m).

SCALE 1:3,000,000
Lamberts Conformal Conic Projection
0   100 miles
0   100 kilometers

Longitude west of Greenwich

The Arc de Triomphe in Paris was commissioned by Napoleon in 1806 to celebrate his military victories.

Located on the French–Italian border, Mont Blanc, at 15,771 feet (4,807 m), is the Alps' highest peak.

Monaco measures a mere 0.75 square miles (1.95 sq km). Its tourist facilities and casino are among its principal sources of revenue.

The mountainous island of Corsica was purchased by France from the city-state of Genoa in 1768.

THE IBERIAN PENINSULA

Andorra, Portugal, Spain

Located at the southwestern edge of Europe, the wide, almost square-shaped Iberian Peninsula is flanked by the Atlantic Ocean to the west and by the Mediterranean Sea to the east. It is separated from France by the Pyrenees, and from Africa by the Strait of Gibraltar, which is just 8 miles (12.8 km) wide at its narrowest point. Spain occupies more than 80 percent of the landmass, Portugal almost all of the remainder; the tiny principality of Andorra nestles in the eastern Pyrenees. A large plateau, the Meseta, extends across much of the peninsula. It is bisected by the Sistema Central mountain chain and fringed by other ranges. Between the 15th and 17th centuries, Spain and Portugal ruled vast empires. But their 20th-century histories were marred by war and repressive regimes, and their economies are still recovering.

Completed in 1521, the Torre de Belém was built to protect the city of Lisbon.

In Spain's Castilla-La Mancha region, medieval windmills dot flat, semiarid plains.

POPULATION PATTERNS

In Spain, rapid industrial growth in the late 20th century led to significant urbanization, with the result that 78 percent of the population now live in cities—17 percent in Madrid and Barcelona. The temperate coastal areas are generally more densely inhabited than the less fertile Meseta. In Portugal, the south is more sparsely populated than the north, with the exception of Lisbon and the crowded coastal region of the Algarve.

Less than 2.6 persons per sq mile/1 per sq km
2.6–26 per sq mile/1–10 per sq km
26–65 per sq mile/10–25 per sq km
65–130 per sq mile/25–50 per sq km
130–260 per sq mile/50–100 per sq km

ECONOMIC PROFILE

Investment in agriculture is low relative to the European average and small farms are the norm. The region is renowned for its abundant fruit and vegetables; other major crops include cereals, wine grapes, and olives. About one-third of the land is forested, and Portugal is the world's foremost supplier of cork. Textiles and footwear, paper and paper products, chemicals, metals, wine, and tourism are the leading industries; automobile production is also important in Spain. Andorra relies heavily on tourism and its duty-free retail trade.

Cereals
Citrus fruits
Wine
Olives
Beef cattle
Sheep
Industrial center
Mining
Timber
Tourism
Fishing

Forest and woodland
Arable land
Grazing

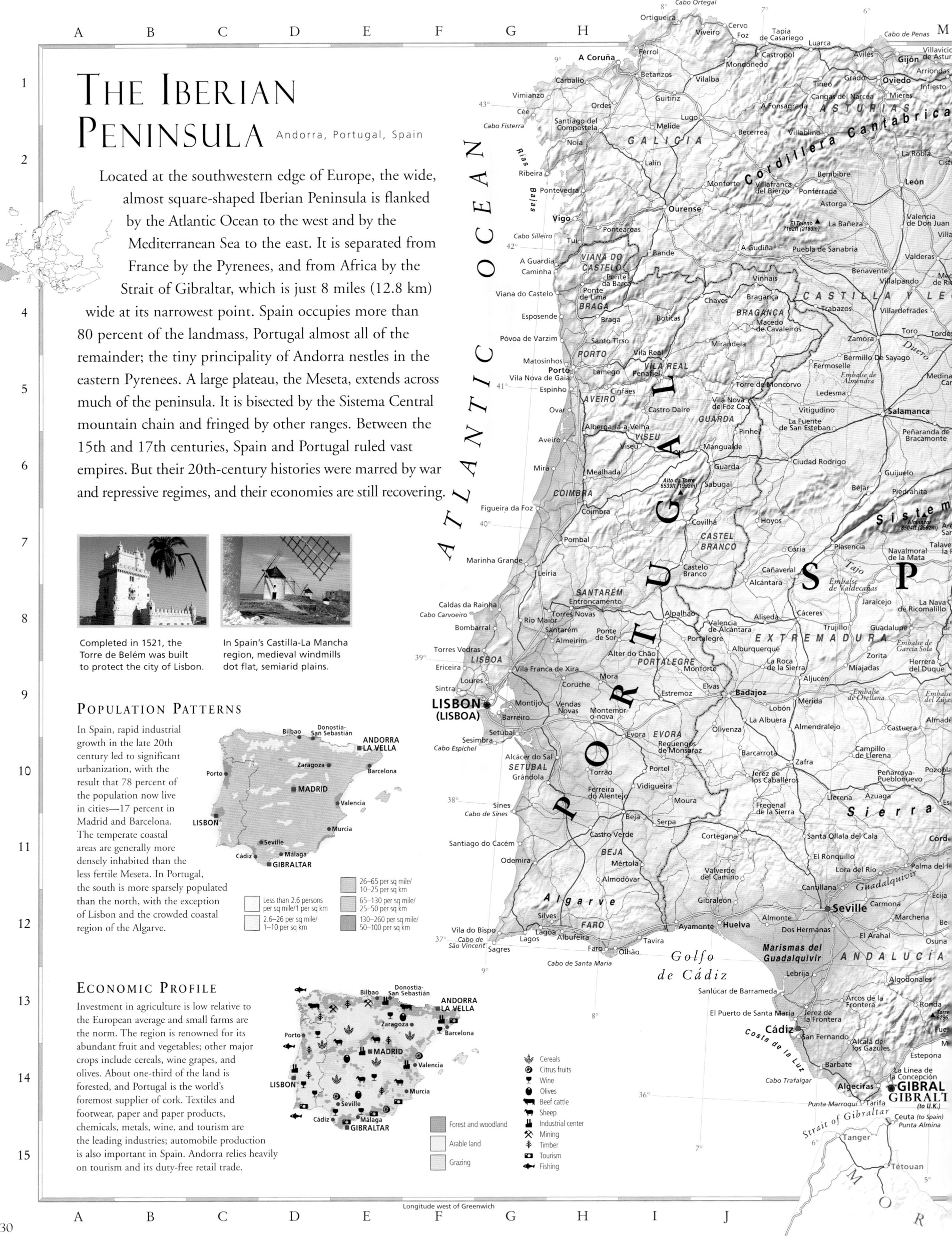

THE SISTEMAS BÉTICOS

In southeastern Spain, a mountain chain, known as the Sistemas Béticos or Baetic Cordillera, extends from Punta Marroquí on the Strait of Gibraltar to Cabo de la Nao on the Costa Blanca. Incorporating numerous small ranges, it rises to its highest point of 11,421 feet (3,481 m) at Mulhacén, northwest of Almería. East of Cabo de la Nao, the chain continues beneath the Mediterranean Sea—the Balearic Islands of Ibiza, Majorca, and Minorca are the summits of its submerged slopes.

ELEVATION	
Feet	Meters
6562	2000
4921	1500
3281	1000
2461	750
1640	500
1312	400
984	300
656	200
328	100
Below sea level	0
656	200
3281	1000
6562	2000
13,123	4000
19,685	6000
26,246	8000
32,808	10,000

Longitude east of Greenwich

SCALE 1:3,000,000
Lamberts Conformal Conic Projection
100 miles
100 kilometers

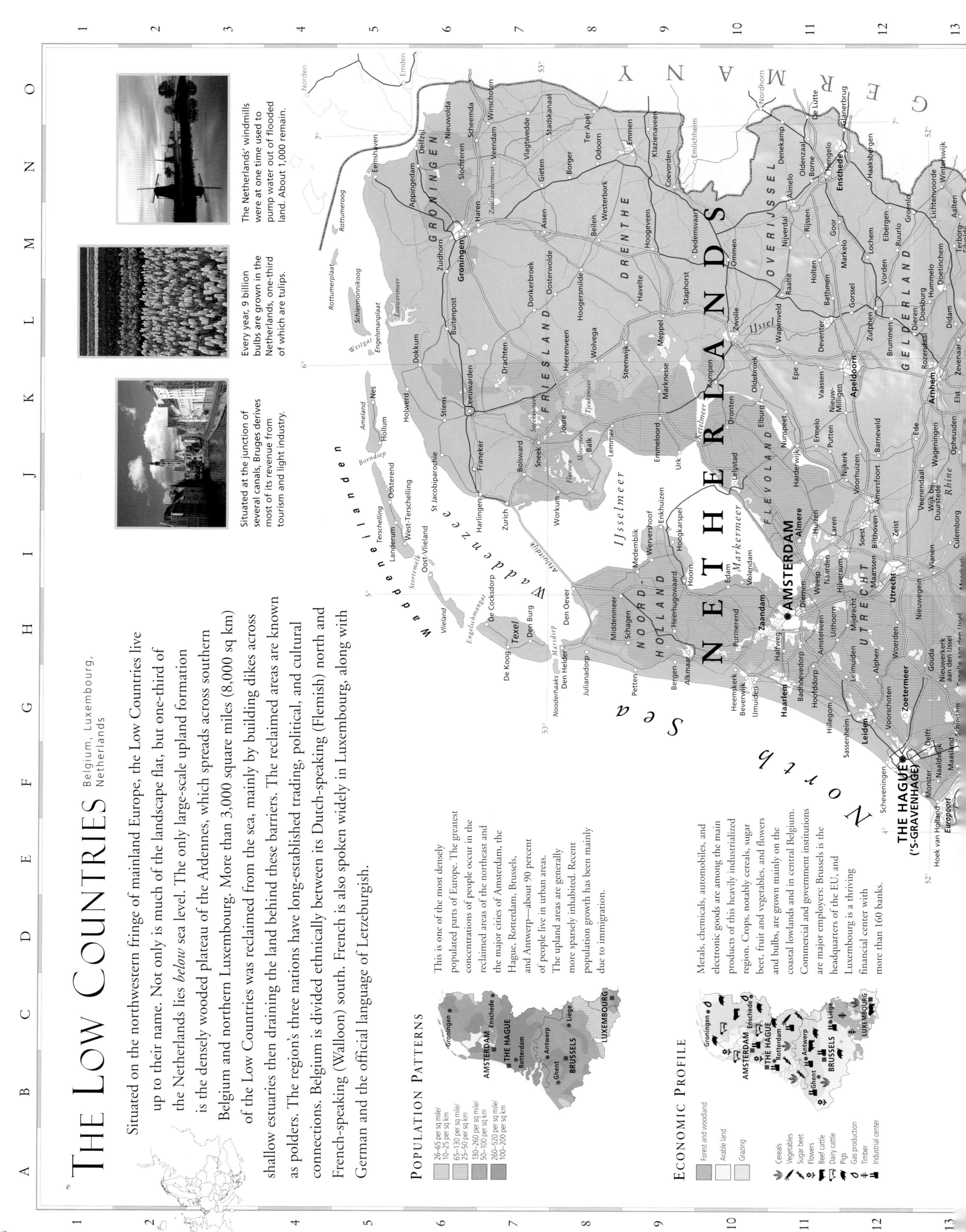

THE LOW COUNTRIES
Belgium, Luxembourg, Netherlands

Situated on the northwestern fringe of mainland Europe, the Low Countries live up to their name. Not only is much of the landscape flat, but one-third of the Netherlands lies *below* sea level. The only large-scale upland formation is the densely wooded plateau of the Ardennes, which spreads across southern Belgium and northern Luxembourg. More than 3,000 square miles (8,000 sq km) of the Low Countries was reclaimed from the sea, mainly by building dikes across shallow estuaries then draining the land behind these barriers. The reclaimed areas are known as polders. The region's three nations have long-established trading, political, and cultural connections. Belgium is divided ethnically between its Dutch-speaking (Flemish) north and French-speaking (Walloon) south. French is also spoken widely in Luxembourg, along with German and the official language of Letzeburgish.

The Netherlands' windmills were at one time used to pump water out of flooded land. About 1,000 remain.

Every year, 9 billion bulbs are grown in the Netherlands, one-third of which are tulips.

Situated at the junction of several canals, Bruges derives most of its revenue from tourism and light industry.

POPULATION PATTERNS

This is one of the most densely populated parts of Europe. The greatest concentrations of people occur in the reclaimed areas of the northeast and the major cities of Amsterdam, the Hague, Rotterdam, Brussels, and Antwerp—about 90 percent of people live in urban areas. The upland areas are generally more sparsely inhabited. Recent population growth has been mainly due to immigration.

26–65 per sq mile / 10–25 per sq km
65–130 per sq mile / 25–50 per sq km
130–260 per sq mile / 50–100 per sq km
260–520 per sq mile / 100–200 per sq km

ECONOMIC PROFILE

Metals, chemicals, automobiles, and electronic goods are among the main products of this heavily industrialized region. Crops, notably cereals, sugar beet, fruit and vegetables, and flowers and bulbs, are grown mainly on the coastal lowlands and in central Belgium. Commercial and government institutions are major employers: Brussels is the headquarters of the EU, and Luxembourg is a thriving financial center with more than 160 banks.

Forest and woodland
Arable land
Grazing

Cereals
Vegetables
Sugar beet
Flowers
Beef cattle
Dairy cattle
Pigs
Gas production
Timber
Industrial center

The European Parliament meets at this building in Brussels, as well as others in Luxembourg and in Strasbourg, France.

Luxembourg's Grand Ducal Palace has been the home of the head of state (the Grand Duke) since the 1890s.

Amsterdam

In the 13th century, Amsterdam was a fishing village on the Amstel River. By the late 16th century, following an influx of people and funds from other parts of war-ravaged Europe, it had become the world's foremost financial and commercial center. Now one of the Netherlands' two capitals (the Hague is the seat of national government), Amsterdam spreads across 90 islands linked by more than 1,000 bridges. Elegant churches and gabled houses line the canals, which are plied by tourist boats and traditional wooden barges.

SCALE 1:1,100,000
Lambert's Conformal Conic Projection

Longitude east of Greenwich

GERMANY

FRANCE

BELGIUM

LUXEMBOURG

NOORD-BRABANT

LIMBURG

ANTWERPEN

OOST-VLAANDEREN

WEST-VLAANDEREN

VLAAMS BRABANT

BRABANT WALLON

HAINAUT

NAMUR

LIÈGE

LUXEMBOURG

Ardennes

ZEELAND

Flanders

BRUSSELS (BRUSSEL/BRUXELLES)

Antwerp

Ghent

Bruges

Eindhoven

Tilburg

Breda

Maastricht

Liège

Charleroi

LUXEMBOURG

ELEVATION

Feet	Meters
6562	2000
4921	1500
3281	1000
2461	750
1640	500
1312	400
984	300
656	200
328	100
0	0 Below sea level
656	200
3281	1000
6562	2000
13,123	4000
19,685	6000
26,246	8000
32,808	10,000

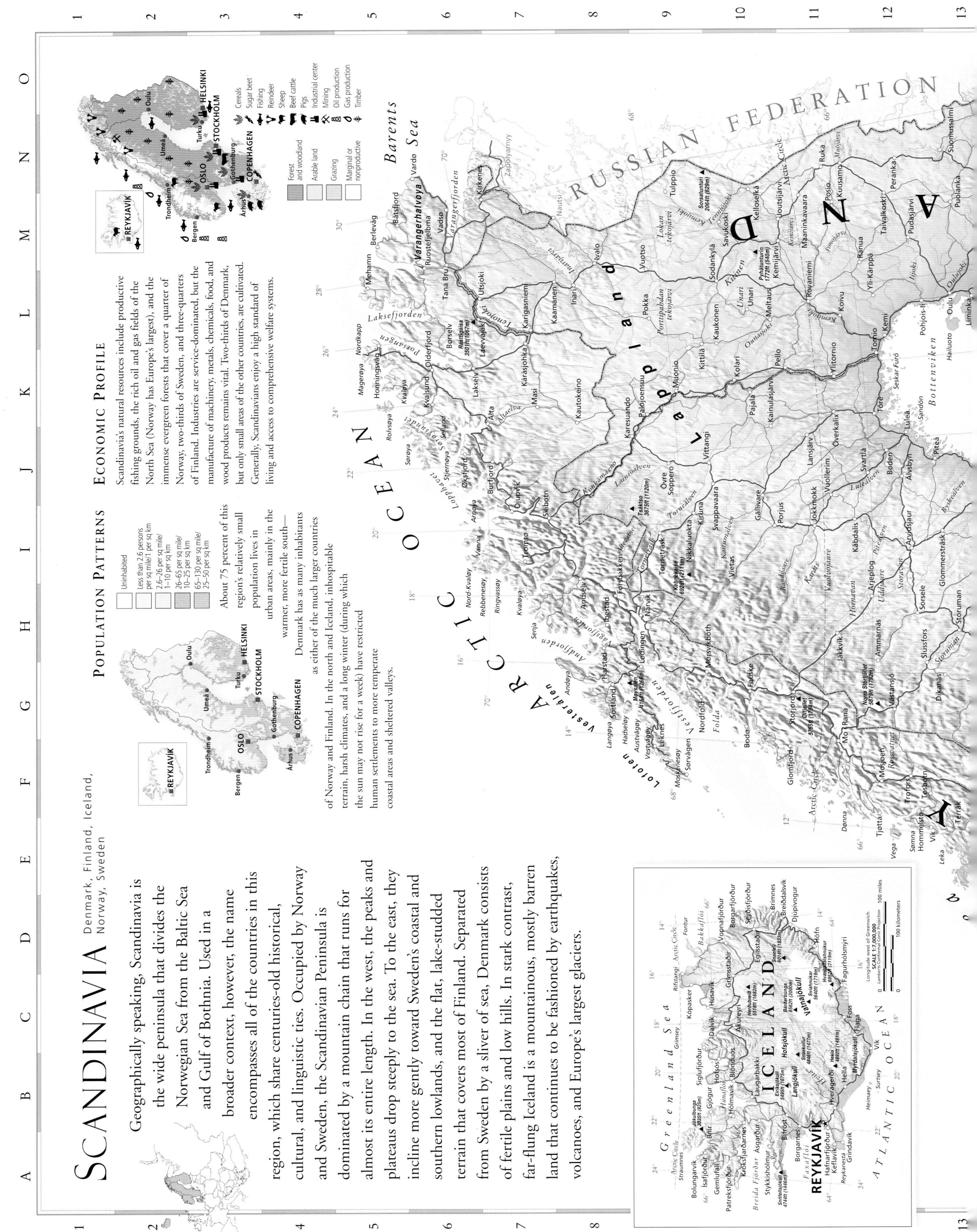

SCANDINAVIA

Denmark, Finland, Iceland, Norway, Sweden

Geographically speaking, Scandinavia is the wide peninsula that divides the Norwegian Sea from the Baltic Sea and Gulf of Bothnia. Used in a broader context, however, the name encompasses all of the countries in this region, which share centuries-old historical, cultural, and linguistic ties. Occupied by Norway and Sweden, the Scandinavian Peninsula is dominated by a mountain chain that runs for almost its entire length. In the west, the peaks and plateaus drop steeply to the sea. To the east, they incline more gently toward Sweden's coastal and southern lowlands, and the flat, lake-studded terrain that covers most of Finland. Separated from Sweden by a sliver of sea, Denmark consists of fertile plains and low hills. In stark contrast, far-flung Iceland is a mountainous, mostly barren land that continues to be fashioned by earthquakes, volcanoes, and Europe's largest glaciers.

ECONOMIC PROFILE

Scandinavia's natural resources include productive fishing grounds, the rich oil and gas fields of the North Sea (Norway has Europe's largest), and the immense evergreen forests that cover a quarter of Norway, two-thirds of Sweden, and three-quarters of Finland. Industries are service-dominated, but the manufacture of machinery, metals, chemicals, food, and wood products remains vital. Two-thirds of Denmark, but only small areas of the other countries, are cultivated. Generally, Scandinavians enjoy a high standard of living and access to comprehensive welfare systems.

POPULATION PATTERNS

Uninhabited
Less than 2.6 persons per sq mile/1 per sq km
2.6–26 per sq mile/1–10 per sq km
26–65 per sq mile/10–25 per sq km
65–130 per sq mile/25–50 per sq km

About 75 percent of this region's relatively small population lives in urban areas, mainly in the warmer, more fertile south—Denmark has as many inhabitants as either of the much larger countries of Norway and Finland. In the north and Iceland, inhospitable terrain, harsh climates, and a long winter (during which the sun may not rise for a week) have restricted human settlements to more temperate coastal areas and sheltered valleys.

Cereals
Sugar beet
Reindeer
Sheep
Beef cattle
Pigs
Industrial center
Mining
Oil production
Gas production
Timber

Forest and woodland
Arable land
Grazing
Marginal or nonproductive

SCALE 1:7,000,000
Lambert's Conformal Conic Projection
100 miles
100 kilometers
Longitude west of Greenwich

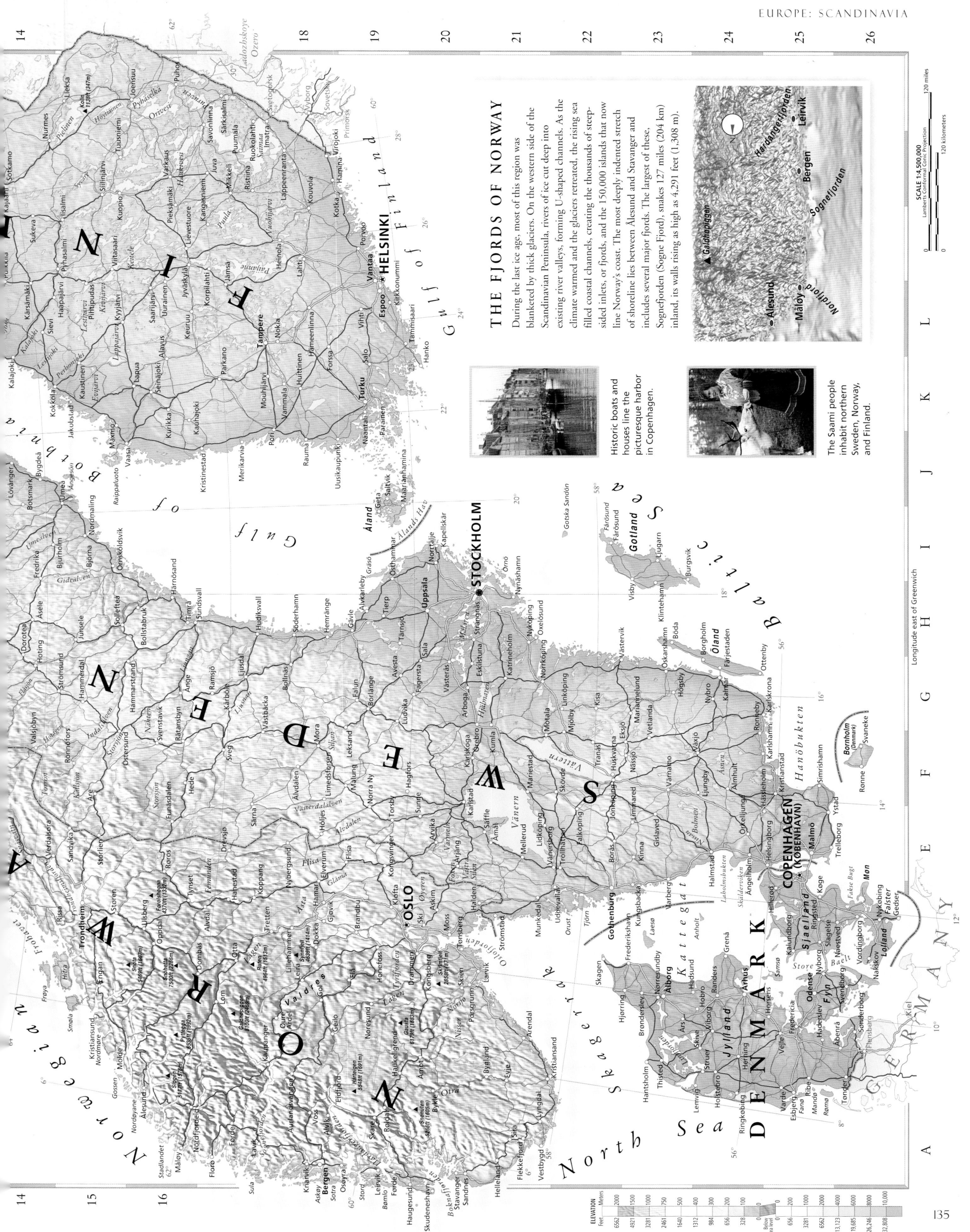

EUROPE: SCANDINAVIA

THE FJORDS OF NORWAY

During the last ice age, most of this region was blanketed by thick glaciers. On the western side of the Scandinavian Peninsula, rivers of ice cut deep into existing river valleys, forming U-shaped channels. As the climate warmed and the glaciers retreated, the rising sea filled coastal channels, creating the thousands of steep-sided inlets, or fjords, and the 150,000 islands that now line Norway's coast. The most deeply indented stretch of shoreline lies between Ålesund and Stavanger and includes several major fjords. The largest of these, Sognefjorden (Sogne Fjord), snakes 127 miles (204 km) inland, its walls rising as high as 4,291 feet (1,308 m).

Historic boats and houses line the picturesque harbor in Copenhagen.

The Saami people inhabit northern Sweden, Norway, and Finland.

SCALE 1:4,500,000
Lambert's Conformal Conic Projection

135

GERMANY

When East Germany and West Germany merged in October 1990, the reunified nation became the most populous country in Europe. More than 80 million people dwell in this broad land, which stretches south from the North and Baltic seas to the northern flank of the Alps. Germany can be divided into three main physical regions. In the northern lowlands, wide rivers, including the Elbe and Weser, meander seaward across expansive, sandy plains. A complex series of basins, partially wooded plateaus, and mountains extends across the center of the country. In the south, beyond the valley of the Main, stand the nation's highest ranges: the Black Forest, Swabian Alp, and Bavarian Alps. The great Rhine River, a historic artery of trade, defines the nation's southwestern boundaries. Continuing north, it cuts through the central uplands before veering westward across the plains to the Netherlands. Despite the economic and social challenges posed by reunification, Germany has retained its position as Europe's leading industrial power.

Construction of Cologne Cathedral, the largest Gothic church in Northern Europe, began in 1248 but was not completed until 1880.

POPULATION PATTERNS

Until the 19th century, Germany was divided into numerous small states with their own capitals and trading centers. As a result, its population is highly urbanized but fairly evenly distributed. Dense concentrations of inhabitants occur at the confluence of the Rhine and Ruhr rivers—the industrial heartland—and around Leipzig and Dresden in the east. Immigration has been the main contributor to recent population growth—10 million incomers settled in West Germany between 1950 and 1990.

2.6–26 per sq mile/ 1–10 per sq km	130–260 per sq mile/ 50–100 per sq km
26–65 per sq mile/ 10–25 per sq km	260–520 per sq mile/ 100–200 per sq km
65–130 per sq mile/ 25–50 per sq km	

ECONOMIC PROFILE

West Germany staged a remarkable economic recovery after the Second World War, and Germany is now the third-largest industrial power after the U.S.A. and Japan. The mainstays of manufacturing are machinery, automobiles, iron and steel, chemicals, electrical goods, and food and beverages. Two of the most significant agricultural products are wine and beer; cereals, potatoes, and sugar beet are also grown widely. The largest pastures are in the northwest, but dairying takes place throughout the country.

Cereals
Potatoes
Sugar beet
Wine
Beef cattle
Dairy cattle

Sheep
Pigs
Industrial center
Mining
Timber

Forest and woodland
Arable land
Grazing

GERMANY

Berlin

Established in the 13th century as a trading post on the Spree River, Berlin first became the capital of Germany in 1871. Though repeatedly ravaged by conflict, the city retains prominent buildings and landmarks from most periods of its history, including the 19th-century Victory Column.

Linked to the North Sea by the Elbe, Hamburg is one of the world's largest container ports.

A typical Rhine Valley town, Bacharach is crowned by a castle and surrounded by vineyards.

SCALE 1:2,250,000
Lambert's Conformal Conic Projection

0   60 miles
0   60 kilometers

Longitude east of Greenwich

Countries and regions
BRANDENBURG, SACHSEN, THÜRINGEN, HESSEN, BAYERN, BADEN-WÜRTTEMBERG, NORDRHEIN-WESTFALEN, RHEINLAND-PFALZ, SAARLAND

CZECH REPUBLIC, AUSTRIA, SWITZERLAND, FRANCE, BELGIUM, LUXEMBOURG

Selected cities and towns
Cottbus, Görlitz, Zittau, Löbau, Bautzen, Niesky, Weisswasser, Hoyerswerda, Senftenberg, Dresden, Meissen, Riesa, Freiberg, Chemnitz, Zwickau, Plauen, Hof, Gera, Jena, Erfurt, Weimar, Gotha, Eisenach, Kassel, Göttingen, Halle, Leipzig, Dessau, Magdeburg, Wittenberg, Braunschweig, Wolfsburg, Hannover, Hildesheim, Paderborn, Bielefeld, Münster, Dortmund, Essen, Duisburg, Düsseldorf, Köln (Cologne), Bonn, Aachen, Koblenz, Mainz, Wiesbaden, Frankfurt am Main, Offenbach, Darmstadt, Mannheim, Heidelberg, Heilbronn, Stuttgart, Pforzheim, Karlsruhe, Baden-Baden, Freiburg im Breisgau, Reutlingen, Ulm, Augsburg, Ingolstadt, Nuremberg, Fürth, Erlangen, Bamberg, Würzburg, Regensburg, Passau, Landshut, Munich, Rosenheim, Salzburg

Physical features
Harz, Thüringer Wald, Erzgebirge, Bayerischer Wald, Bohemian Forest, Oberpfälzer Wald, Fichtelgebirge, Schwäbische Alb, Black Forest, Allgäuer Alpen
Elbe, Saale, Weser, Leine, Werra, Fulda, Main, Rhine, Mosel, Neckar, Danube, Kyll, Lippe, Ruhr

Zugspitze 9721ft (2963m)
Wasserkuppe 3117ft (950m)

Elevation
Feet	Meters
32,808	10,000
26,246	8000
19,685	6000
13,123	4000
6562	2000
3281	1000
1640	500
984	300
656	200
328	100
Below sea level	Below sea level

137

THE ALPINE NATIONS Austria, Liechtenstein, Switzerland

Arcing northeastward from France, the countless peaks and valleys of the Alps sprawl across more than half of Switzerland, the tiny monarchy of Liechtenstein, and two-thirds of Austria. These nations occupy a continental crossroads, their mountain passes permitting the flow of people and goods between north and south, the Danube Valley forming a natural corridor between eastern and western Europe. Despite its strategic importance, Switzerland has remained politically neutral for almost 200 years. This, along with its prosperity and secretive banking practices, has made it a haven for international organizations, businesses, and funds. Austria's more tempestuous past includes periods as the heart of the powerful Holy Roman and Austro-Hungarian empires; its present boundaries were defined after the First World War. Liechtenstein established its independence, and neutrality, in 1866.

Millions of people visit the Alps each year to holiday at winter-sports resorts.

The spectacular Jet d'Eau, a 460-foot (140-m) fountain, is Geneva's best-known landmark.

THE CENTRAL ALPS

The Central Alps extend from Lake Geneva in the west to the Rhine Valley in the east. They encompass several ranges including the Bernese Alps—Switzerland's highest—and the valleys of two of Europe's great rivers, the Rhône and Rhine, which form a deep, straight, almost continuous gouge through the mountains. The northern flank of the Central Alps descends to Switzerland's Central Plateau, which is hemmed in to the north by the peaks of the Jura.

POPULATION PATTERNS

Rugged terrain has always limited the settlement of mountainous areas, so most of the population is concentrated in valleys and lowlands, most notably Switzerland's Central Plateau, site of the nation's major urban centers, and the Danube Valley, where Vienna accommodates one-fifth of the Austrian population. Postindustrial depopulation of upland areas has been slowed by the boom in tourism, which has brought jobs and funds to remote communities.

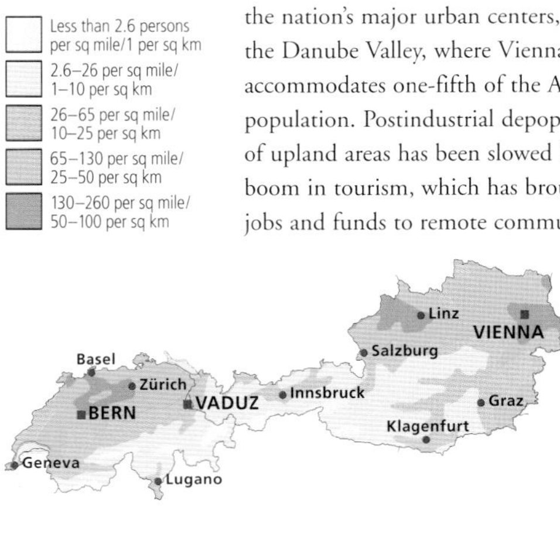

Less than 2.6 persons per sq mile/1 per sq km
2.6–26 per sq mile/ 1–10 per sq km
26–65 per sq mile/ 10–25 per sq km
65–130 per sq mile/ 25–50 per sq km
130–260 per sq mile/ 50–100 per sq km

The Matterhorn's distinctive faceted peak was shaped by intersecting glaciers.

ECONOMIC PROFILE

The resources of this affluent region include the forests that cover a quarter of Switzerland and two-fifths of Austria; deposits of magnesite, iron, and coal in Austria; and water—hydroelectricity provides 60 percent of energy. Services dominate the economy, but the engineering, machinery, and chemicals industries are significant employers. Switzerland is renowned for precision instruments, especially clocks. Crops are grown mainly on the lowlands; dairy and beef cattle graze upland pastures.

Forest and woodland
Arable land
Grazing
Marginal or nonproductive

Cereals
Wine
Sugar beet
Beef cattle
Dairy cattle
Pigs
Industrial center
Mining
Timber
Winter sports

Vienna Renowned for its architecture and art collections, music and theater, cafés and parks, Austria's capital has a population of just over 2 million. Originally a Celtic stronghold, it was taken over by the Romans in the first century AD. It subsequently developed as a trading center under the House of Babenberg before being seized in 1278 by the Habsburgs, who remained in power for more than 600 years. During that time, Vienna became capital of the Holy Roman Empire (1558–1806) and then of the Austro-Hungarian Empire (1806–1918). Its many grand buildings include the early-18th-century St Peter's, the early-17th-century University Church, and the city's major landmark, the Gothic cathedral of St Stephen's, which dates from the 12th century but was entirely rebuilt between the 14th and mid-16th centuries.

St Peter's Church
University Church
St Stephen's Cathedral

ELEVATION

Feet	Meters
6562	2000
4921	1500
3281	1000
2461	750
1640	500
1312	400
984	300
656	200
328	100
Below sea level	0
656	200
3281	1000
6562	2000
13,123	4000
19,685	6000
26,246	8000
32,808	10,000

SCALE 1:1,750,000
Lamberts Conformal Conic Projection
50 miles
50 kilometers

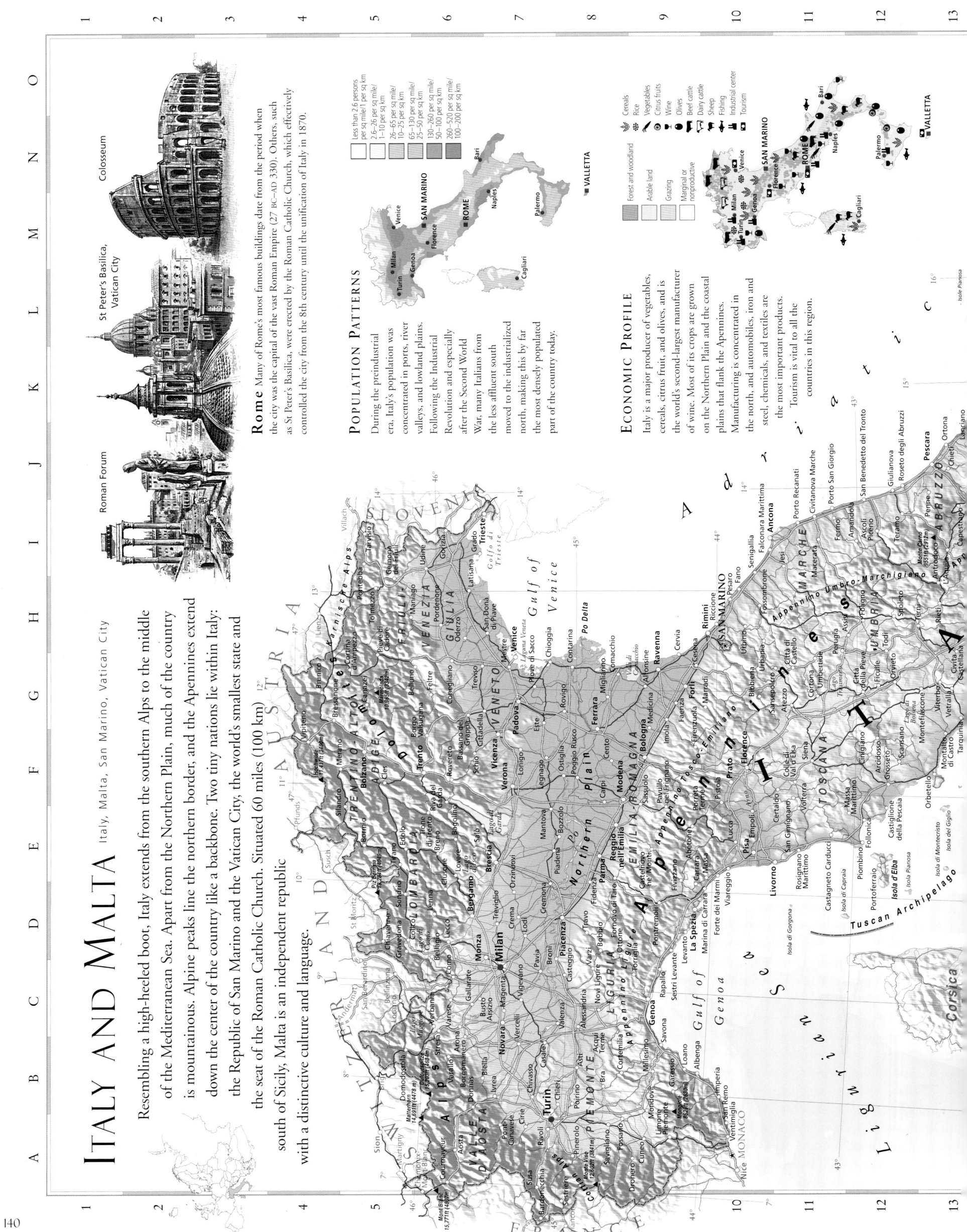

ITALY AND MALTA

Italy, Malta, San Marino, Vatican City

Resembling a high-heeled boot, Italy extends from the southern Alps to the middle of the Mediterranean Sea. Apart from the Northern Plain, much of the country is mountainous. Alpine peaks line the northern border, and the Apennines extend down the center of the country like a backbone. Two tiny nations lie within Italy: the Republic of San Marino and the Vatican City, the world's smallest state and the seat of the Roman Catholic Church. Situated 60 miles (100 km) south of Sicily, Malta is an independent republic with a distinctive culture and language.

Roman Forum

St Peter's Basilica, Vatican City

Colosseum

Rome Many of Rome's most famous buildings date from the period when the city was the capital of the vast Roman Empire (27 BC–AD 330). Others, such as St Peter's Basilica, were erected by the Roman Catholic Church, which effectively controlled the city from the 8th century until the unification of Italy in 1870.

POPULATION PATTERNS

During the preindustrial era, Italy's population was concentrated in ports, river valleys, and lowland plains. Following the Industrial Revolution and especially after the Second World War, many Italians from the less affluent south moved to the industrialized north, making this by far the most densely populated part of the country today.

Less than 2.6 persons per sq mile/1 per sq km
2.6–26 per sq mile/1–10 per sq km
65–130 per sq mile/25–50 per sq km
130–260 per sq mile/50–100 per sq km
260–520 per sq mile/100–200 per sq km

ECONOMIC PROFILE

Italy is a major producer of vegetables, cereals, citrus fruit, and olives, and is the world's second-largest manufacturer of wine. Most of its crops are grown on the Northern Plain and the coastal plains that flank the Apennines. Manufacturing is concentrated in the north, and automobiles, iron and steel, chemicals, and textiles are the most important products. Tourism is vital to all the countries in this region.

Cereals
Rice
Vegetables
Citrus fruits
Wine
Olives
Beef cattle
Dairy cattle
Sheep
Fishing
Industrial center
Tourism

Forest and woodland
Arable land
Grazing
Marginal or nonproductive

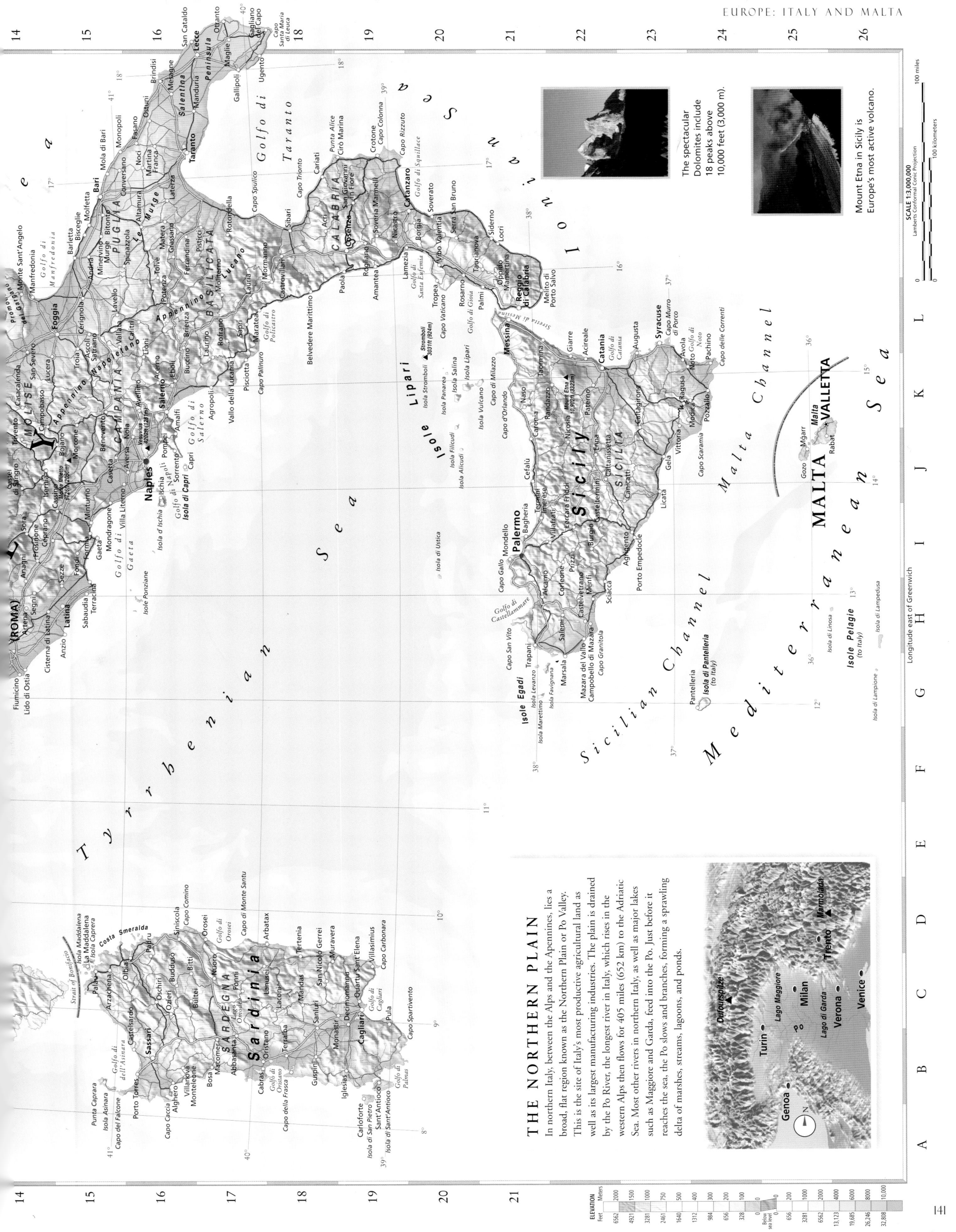

THE NORTHERN PLAIN

In northern Italy, between the Alps and the Apennines, lies a broad, flat region known as the Northern Plain or Po Valley. This is the site of Italy's most productive agricultural land as well as its largest manufacturing industries. The plain is drained by the Po River, the longest river in Italy, which rises in the western Alps then flows for 405 miles (652 km) to the Adriatic Sea. Most other rivers in northern Italy, as well as major lakes such as Maggiore and Garda, feed into the Po. Just before it reaches the sea, the Po slows and branches, forming a sprawling delta of marshes, streams, lagoons, and ponds.

The spectacular Dolomites include 18 peaks above 10,000 feet (3,000 m).

Mount Etna in Sicily is Europe's most active volcano.

SCALE 1:3,000,000
Lamberts Conformal Conic Projection

ELEVATION

Feet	Meters
6562	2000
4921	1500
3281	1000
2461	750
1640	500
1312	400
984	300
656	200
328	100
	Below sea level
656	200
3281	1000
6562	2000
13,123	4000
19,685	6000
26,246	8000
32,808	10,000

NORTHERN CENTRAL EUROPE

Czech Republic, Hungary, Poland, Slovakia

The Bohemian Massif and the Carpathian Mountains bisect this region from west to east, separating the flatlands of the North European Plain from those of the Great Hungarian Plain in the south. A ring of mountain ranges around a broad central basin, the Bohemian Massif covers most of the Czech Republic. The heavily forested Carpathians—a continuation of the Alps—occupy northern and central Slovakia, giving way to plains in the south and east.

Separated from these two nations by the peaks that line its southern border, Poland otherwise has little high land. Rivers meander across its central lowlands and lake-studded coastal plains, many, notably the Oder and Vistula, flowing all the way to the Baltic Sea. Hungary, too, is mostly flat, the Great Hungarian Plain spreading across more than half of its territory. All of these independent, democratic nations were part of the Eastern bloc until the collapse of communism in 1989. In 1992, Czechoslovakia split into two nations, the Czech Republic and Slovakia.

POPULATION PATTERNS

Key:
- 2.6–26 per sq mile / 1–10 per sq km
- 26–65 per sq mile / 10–25 per sq km
- 65–130 per sq mile / 25–50 per sq km
- 130–260 per sq mile / 50–100 per sq km
- 260–520 per sq mile / 100–200 per sq km

About 65 percent of the region's inhabitants are urban dwellers, with the highest levels in the Czech Republic and the lowest in less-developed Slovakia (which has half the population of its northwestern neighbor). The most densely populated areas are Poland's industrialized south and its capital Warsaw, the northern Czech Republic, and the Budapest region, home to one-quarter of Hungary's people. Settlements are more scattered in the Slovakian mountains and on the windswept and relatively infertile Baltic Sea coast. More than 5 percent of Hungary's population are ethnic Roma (Gypsy) people.

ECONOMIC PROFILE

Key:
- Forest and woodland
- Arable land
- Grazing

Symbols: Cereals, Potatoes, Dairy cattle, Pigs, Industrial center, Mining, Timber, Wine, Sugar beet

Significant natural resources in this region include Poland's rich Silesian coal fields, and the more modest but vital mineral reserves of Slovakia's Ore Mountains, and Hungary's large swathes of arable land. Cereals and potatoes are the major crops, along with sugar beet in Poland and Hungary. Leading industries include engineering and the production of automobiles, chemicals, textiles, and food and beverages—the Czech Republic is renowned for its beer and Hungary has a thriving wine industry.

In the mid-18th century, Gdańsk was the largest city in Eastern Europe. Still Poland's main port, it is also a center of shipbuilding.

The jagged Tatra Mountains of northern Slovakia and southern Poland are a refuge for rare animals such as bears and wolves.

Map labels

LITHUANIA

BELARUS

RUSSIAN FEDERATION

POLAND

WARSAW (WARSZAWA)

Baltic Sea

Gulf of Gdańsk

Zatoka Pomorska

Cities and towns: Hrodna, Lipsk, Sejny, Suwałki, Augustów, Sokółka, Bobrowniki, Białystok, Hajnówka, Bielsk Podlaski, Brańsk, Siemiatycze, Kleszczele, Janów Podlaski, Terespol, Biała Podlaska, Międzyrzec, Olecko, Gołdap, Węgorzewo, Gizycko, Ełk, Szczytno, Grajewo, Kolno, Mońki, Zambrów, Szczuczyn, Stawiski, Łomża, Ostrów Mazowiecki, Sokołów Podlaski, Łosice, Siedlce, Łuków, Stoczek Łukowski, Wegrów, Chełmiak, Kętrzyn, Mrągowo, Biskupiec, Pisz, Orzysz, Ruciane, Pasym, Wielbark, Chorzele, Przasnysz, Różan, Pułtusk, Ciechanów, Maków Mazowiecki, Wyszków, Nowy Dwór Mazowiecki, Pruszków, Piaseczno, Minsk Mazowiecki, Otwock, Kaliningrad, Bagrationovsk, Chernyakhovsk, Braniewo, Pieniężno, Lidzbark Warmiński, Dobre Miasto, Bartoszyce, Orneta, Morag, Olsztyn, Ostróda, Iława, Działdowo, Mława, Żuromin, Sierpc, Płońsk, Zakroczym, Płock, Gostynin, Sochaczew, Żyrardów, Grodzisk, Łowicz, Kutno, Łęczyca, Gąbin, Sannik, Gostynin, Lipno, Rypin, Brodnica, Chełmno, Chełmża, Toruń, Inowrocław, Strzelno, Mogilno, Gniezno, Września, Środa Wielkopolska, Poznań, Oborniki, Szamotuły, Pniewy, Międzychód, Skwierzyna, Międzyrzecz, Świebodzin, Sulechów, Krosno, Gubin, Słubice, Frankfurt an der Oder, Schwedt, Szczecin, Police, Świnoujście, Wolin, Kamień Pomorski, Gryfice, Trzebiatów, Kołobrzeg, Ustronie Morskie, Darłowko, Koszalin, Słupsk, Ustka, Leba, Władysławowo, Gdynia, Sopot, Gdańsk, Hel, Wejherowo, Krokowa, Puck, Lębork, Bytów, Kartuzy, Kościerzyna, Starogard Gdański, Tczew, Malbork, Elbląg, Kwidzyn, Grudziądz, Świecie, Chojnice, Tuchola, Brusy, Miastko, Bobolice, Białogard, Świdwin, Łobez, Nowogard, Goleniów, Stargard Szczeciński, Pyrzyce, Myślibórz, Dębno, Kostrzyn, Gorzów Wielkopolski, Skwierzyna, Drezdenko, Dobiegniew, Choszczno, Barlinek, Czaplinek, Wałcz, Piła, Czarnków, Chodzież, Wągrowiec, Żnin, Szubin, Nakło nad Notecią, Kcynia, Bydgoszcz, Wyrzysk, Złotów, Jastrowie, Mirosławiec, Kalisz Pomorski, Złocieniec

Rivers/lakes: Narew, Bug, Biebrza, Liwiec, Wkra, Noteć, Drawa, Warta, Obra, Odra, Oder, Vistula (Wisła), Brda, Wda, Gwda, Parsęta, Rega, Drawa, Reda, Łyna, Pisa, Wieprz, Bzura

Latitudes/longitudes: 54°, 53°, 52°, 14°, 15°, 16°, 17°, 18°, 19°, 20°, 21°, 22°, 23°

NORTHERN CENTRAL EUROPE

Czech Republic, Hungary, Poland, Slovakia

The Bohemian Massif and the Carpathian Mountains bisect this region from west to east, separating the flatlands of the North European Plain from those of the Great Hungarian Plain in the south. A ring of mountain ranges around a broad central basin, the Bohemian Massif covers most of the Czech Republic. The heavily forested Carpathians—a continuation of the Alps—occupy northern and central Slovakia, giving way to plains in the south and east. Separated from these two nations by the peaks that line its southern border, Poland otherwise has little high land. Rivers meander across its central lowlands and lake-studded coastal plains, many, notably the Oder and Vistula, flowing all the way to the Baltic Sea. Hungary, too, is mostly flat, the Great Hungarian Plain spreading across more than half of its territory. All of these independent, democratic nations were part of the Eastern bloc until the collapse of communism in 1989. In 1992, Czechoslovakia split into two nations, the Czech Republic and Slovakia.

POPULATION PATTERNS

	people per sq mile / people per sq km
	2.6–26 per sq mile / 1–10 per sq km
	26–65 per sq mile / 10–25 per sq km
	65–130 per sq mile / 25–50 per sq km
	130–260 per sq mile / 50–100 per sq km
	260–520 per sq mile / 100–200 per sq km

About 65 percent of the region's inhabitants are urban dwellers, with the highest levels in the Czech Republic and the lowest in less-developed Slovakia (which has half the population of its northwestern neighbor). The most densely populated areas are Poland's industrialized south and its capital Warsaw, the northern Czech Republic, and the Budapest region, home to one-quarter of Hungary's people. Settlements are more scattered in the Slovakian mountains and on the windswept and relatively infertile Baltic Sea coast. More than 5 percent of Hungary's population are ethnic Roma (Gypsy) people.

ECONOMIC PROFILE

- Forest and woodland
- Arable land
- Grazing

Significant natural resources in this region include Poland's rich Silesian coal fields, the more modest but vital mineral reserves of Slovakia's Ore Mountains, and Hungary's large swathes of arable land. Cereals and potatoes are the major crops, along with sugar beet in Poland and Hungary. Leading industries include engineering and the production of automobiles, chemicals, textiles, and food and beverages—the Czech Republic is renowned for its beer and Hungary has a thriving wine industry.

Economic Profile map symbols:
- Cereals
- Potatoes
- Pigs
- Industrial center
- Dairy cattle
- Mining
- Timber
- Wine
- Sugar beet

In the mid-18th century, Gdańsk was the largest city in Eastern Europe. Still Poland's main port, it is also a center of shipbuilding.

The jagged Tatra Mountains of northern Slovakia and southern Poland are a refuge for rare animals such as bears and wolves.

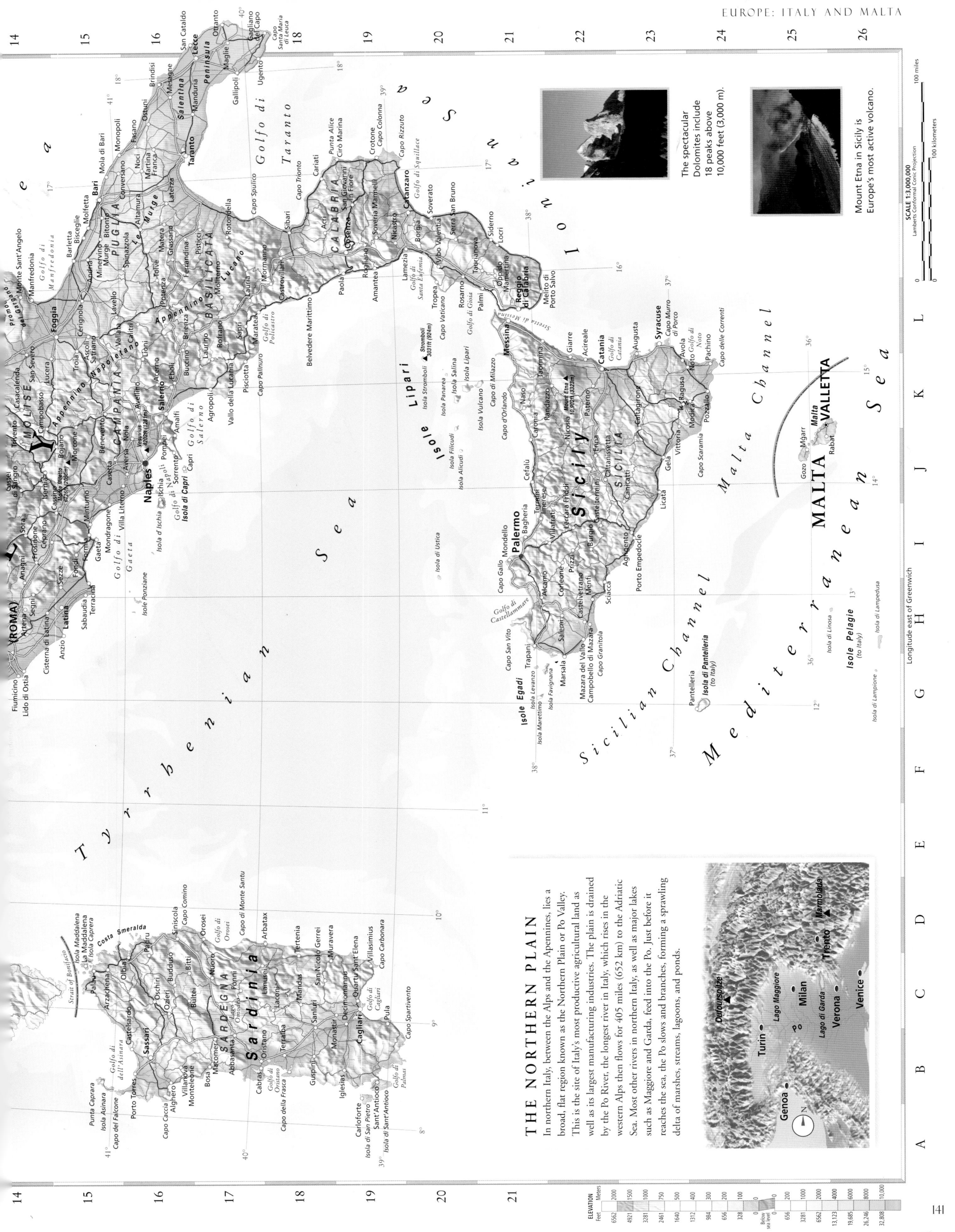

THE NORTHERN PLAIN

In northern Italy, between the Alps and the Apennines, lies a broad, flat region known as the Northern Plain or Po Valley. This is the site of Italy's most productive agricultural land as well as its largest manufacturing industries. The plain is drained by the Po River, the longest river in Italy, which rises in the western Alps then flows for 405 miles (652 km) to the Adriatic Sea. Most other rivers in northern Italy, as well as major lakes such as Maggiore and Garda, feed into the Po. Just before it reaches the sea, the Po slows and branches, forming a sprawling delta of marshes, streams, lagoons, and ponds.

The spectacular Dolomites include 18 peaks above 10,000 feet (3,000 m).

Mount Etna in Sicily is Europe's most active volcano.

SCALE 1:3,000,000
Lamberts Conformal Conic Projection

ELEVATION

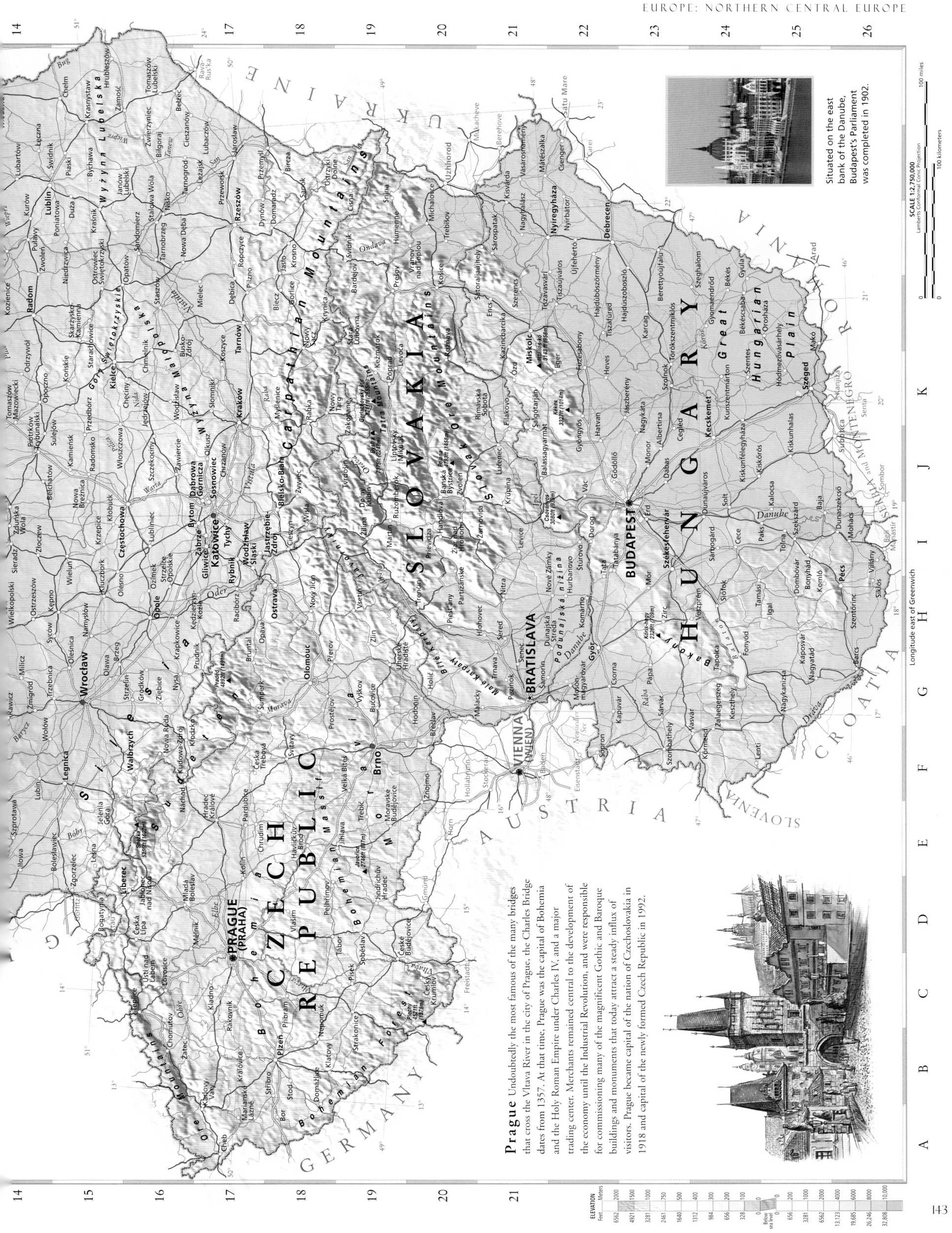

Situated on the east bank of the Danube, Budapest's Parliament was completed in 1902.

Prague Undoubtedly the most famous of the many bridges that cross the Vltava River in the city of Prague, the Charles Bridge dates from 1357. At that time, Prague was the capital of Bohemia and the Holy Roman Empire under Charles IV, and a major trading center. Merchants remained central to the development of the economy until the Industrial Revolution, and were responsible for commissioning many of the magnificent Gothic and Baroque buildings and monuments that today attract a steady influx of visitors. Prague became capital of the nation of Czechoslovakia in 1918 and capital of the newly formed Czech Republic in 1992.

SCALE 1:2,750,000
Lambert's Conformal Conic Projection

Longitude east of Greenwich

ELEVATION

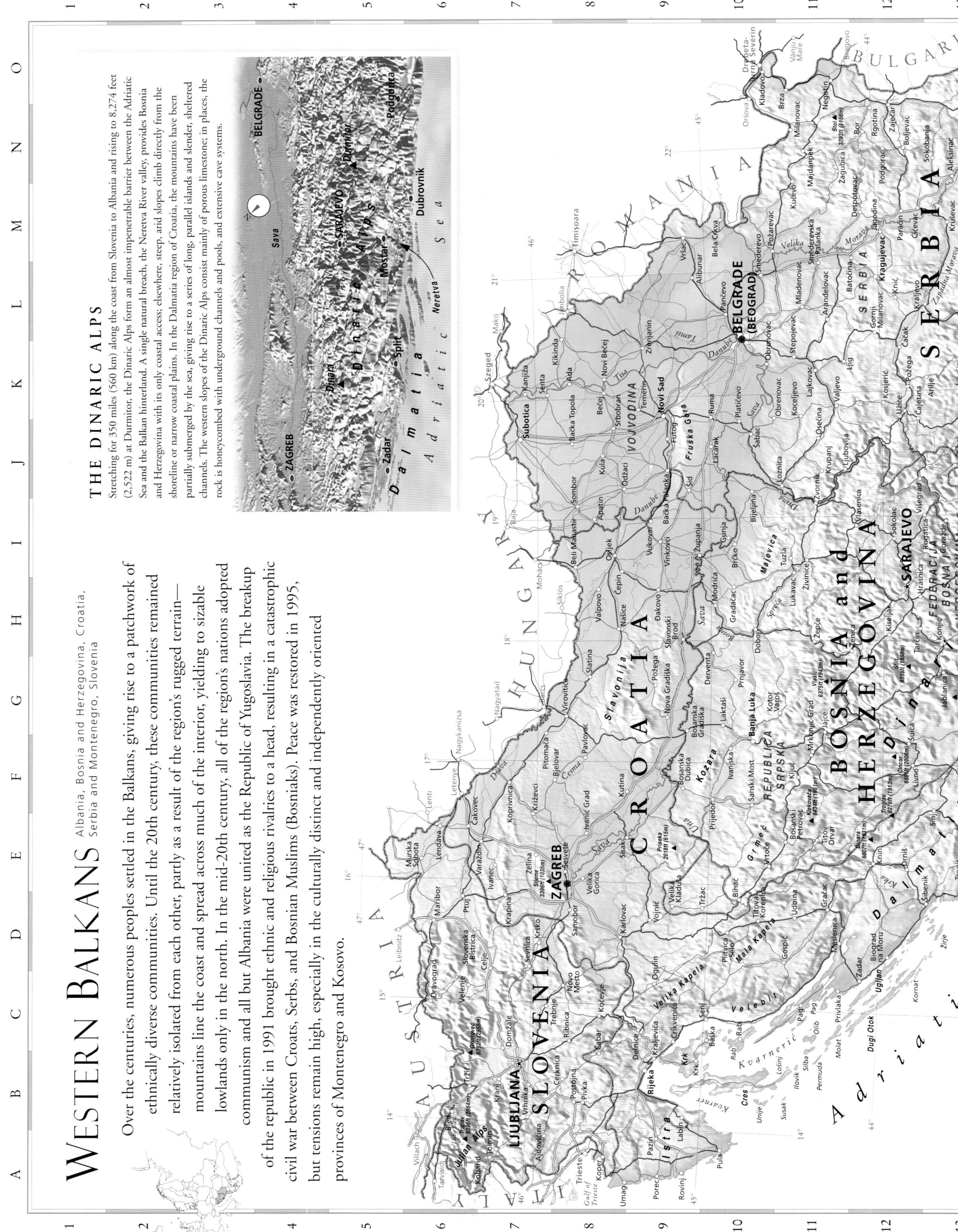

WESTERN BALKANS

Albania, Bosnia and Herzegovina, Croatia, Serbia and Montenegro, Slovenia

Over the centuries, numerous peoples settled in the Balkans, giving rise to a patchwork of ethnically diverse communities. Until the 20th century, these communities remained relatively isolated from each other, partly as a result of the region's rugged terrain—mountains line the coast and spread across much of the interior, yielding to sizable lowlands only in the north. In the mid-20th century, all of the region's nations adopted communism and all but Albania were united as the Republic of Yugoslavia. The breakup of the republic in 1991 brought ethnic and religious rivalries to a head, resulting in a catastrophic civil war between Croats, Serbs, and Bosnian Muslims (Bosniaks). Peace was restored in 1995, but tensions remain high, especially in the culturally distinct and independently oriented provinces of Montenegro and Kosovo.

THE DINARIC ALPS

Stretching for 350 miles (560 km) along the coast from Slovenia to Albania and rising to 8,274 feet (2,522 m) at Durmitor, the Dinaric Alps form an almost impenetrable barrier between the Adriatic Sea and the Balkan hinterland. A single natural breach, the Neretva River valley, provides Bosnia and Herzegovina with its only coastal access; elsewhere, steep, arid slopes climb directly from the shoreline or narrow coastal plains. In the Dalmatia region of Croatia, the mountains have been partially submerged by the sea, giving rise to a series of long, parallel islands and slender, sheltered channels. The western slopes of the Dinaric Alps consist mainly of porous limestone; in places, the rock is honeycombed with underground channels and pools, and extensive cave systems.

144

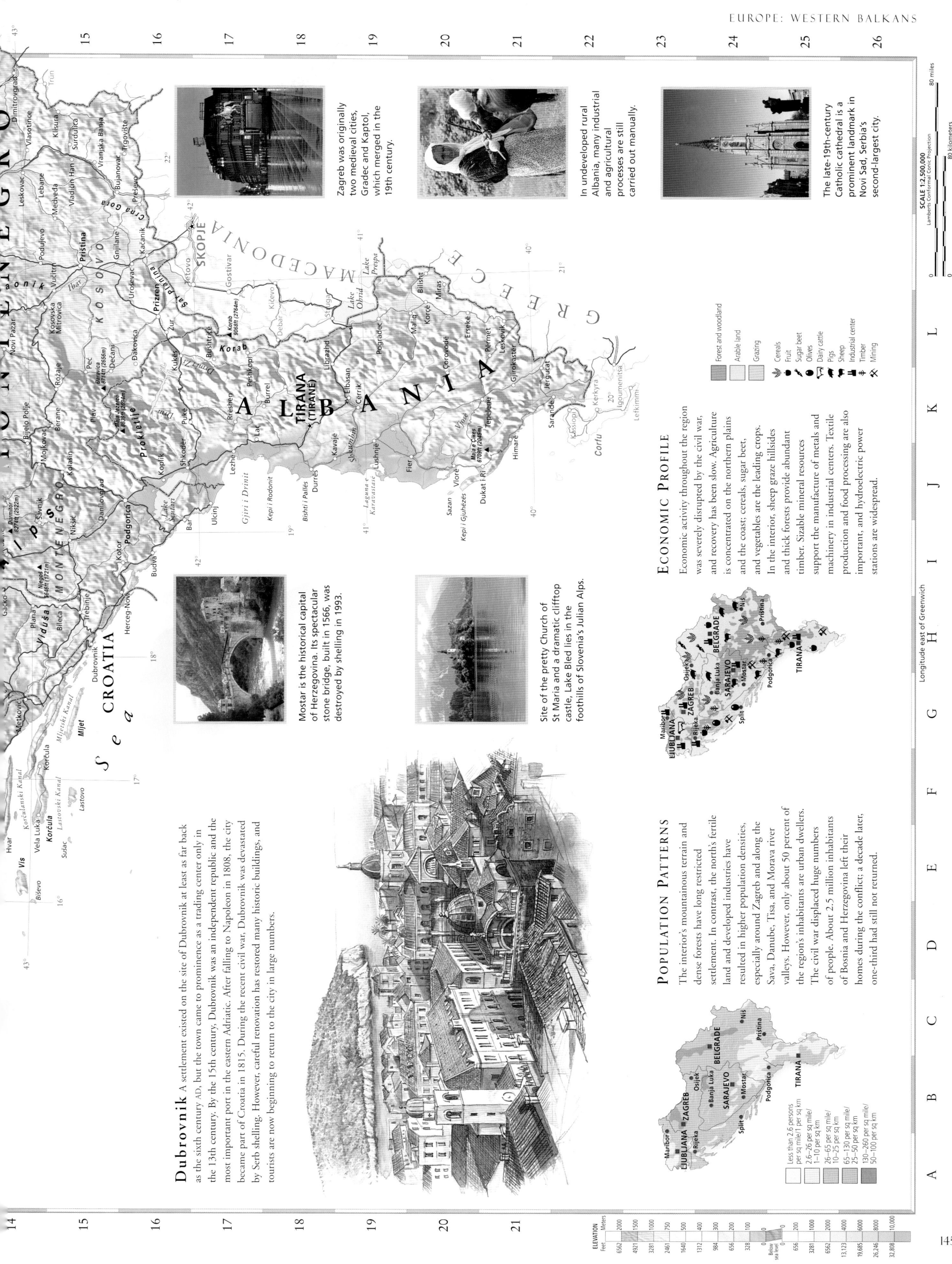

Zagreb was originally two medieval cities, Gradec and Kaptol, which merged in the 19th century.

In undeveloped rural Albania, many industrial and agricultural processes are still carried out manually.

The late-19th-century Catholic cathedral is a prominent landmark in Novi Sad, Serbia's second-largest city.

SCALE 1:2,500,000
Lamberts Conformal Conic Projection

Mostar is the historical capital of Herzegovina. Its spectacular stone bridge, built in 1566, was destroyed by shelling in 1993.

Site of the pretty Church of St Maria and a dramatic clifftop castle, Lake Bled lies in the foothills of Slovenia's Julian Alps.

ECONOMIC PROFILE

Economic activity throughout the region was severely disrupted by the civil war, and recovery has been slow. Agriculture is concentrated on the northern plains and the coast; cereals, sugar beet, and vegetables are the leading crops. In the interior, sheep graze hillsides and thick forests provide abundant timber. Sizable mineral resources support the manufacture of metals and machinery in industrial centers. Textile production and food processing are also important, and hydroelectric power stations are widespread.

Forest and woodland
Arable land
Grazing

Cereals
Fruit
Sugar beet
Olives
Dairy cattle
Pigs
Sheep
Industrial center
Timber
Mining

Dubrovnik

A settlement existed on the site of Dubrovnik at least as far back as the sixth century AD, but the town came to prominence as a trading center only in the 13th century. By the 15th century, Dubrovnik was an independent republic and the most important port in the eastern Adriatic. After falling to Napoleon in 1808, the city became part of Croatia in 1815. During the recent civil war, Dubrovnik was devastated by Serb shelling. However, careful renovation has restored many historic buildings, and tourists are now beginning to return to the city in large numbers.

POPULATION PATTERNS

The interior's mountainous terrain and dense forests have long restricted settlement. In contrast, the north's fertile land and developed industries have resulted in higher population densities, especially around Zagreb and along the Sava, Danube, Tisa, and Morava river valleys. However, only about 50 percent of the region's inhabitants are urban dwellers. The civil war displaced huge numbers of people. About 2.5 million inhabitants of Bosnia and Herzegovina left their homes during the conflict; a decade later, one-third had still not returned.

Less than 2.6 persons per sq mile/1 per sq km
2.6–26 per sq mile/1–10 per sq km
26–65 per sq mile/10–25 per sq km
65–130 per sq mile/25–50 per sq km
130–260 per sq mile/50–100 per sq km

ELEVATION

Feet	Meters
6562	2000
4921	1500
3281	1000
2461	750
1640	500
1312	400
994	300
656	200
328	100
0	0

Below sea level	
656	200
3281	1000
6562	2000
13,123	4000
19,685	6000
26,246	8000
32,808	10,000

80 miles
80 kilometers

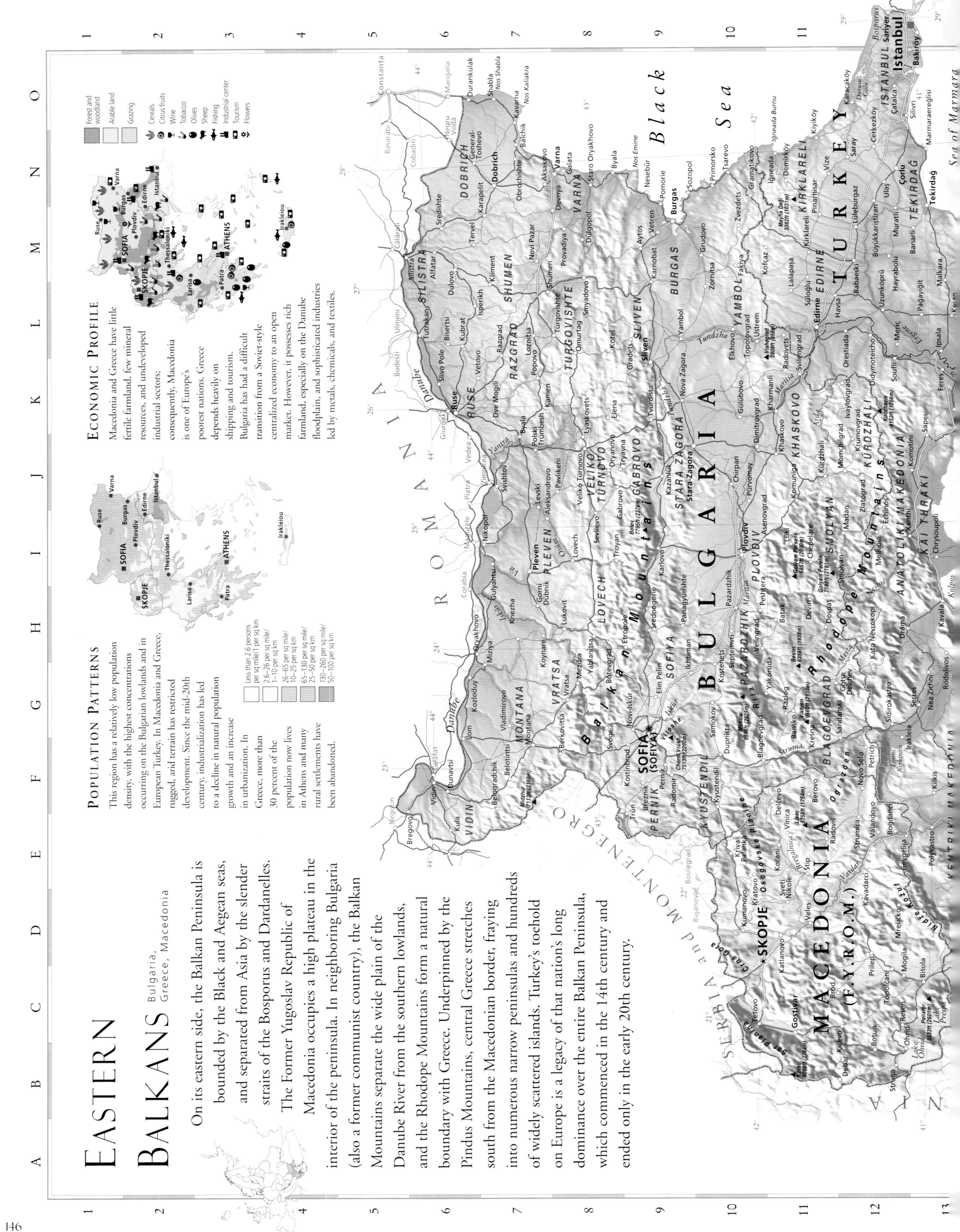

EASTERN BALKANS

Bulgaria, Greece, Macedonia

On its eastern side, the Balkan Peninsula is bounded by the Black and Aegean seas, and separated from Asia by the slender straits of the Bosporus and Dardanelles. The Former Yugoslav Republic of Macedonia occupies a high plateau in the interior of the peninsula. In neighboring Bulgaria (also a former communist country), the Balkan Mountains separate the wide plain of the Danube River from the southern lowlands, and the Rhodope Mountains form a natural boundary with Greece. Underpinned by the Pindus Mountains, central Greece stretches south from the Macedonian border, fraying into numerous narrow peninsulas and hundreds of widely scattered islands. Turkey's toehold on Europe is a legacy of that nation's long dominance over the entire Balkan Peninsula, which commenced in the 14th century and ended only in the early 20th century.

POPULATION PATTERNS

This region has a relatively low population density, with the highest concentrations occurring on the Bulgarian lowlands and in European Turkey. In Macedonia and Greece, rugged, arid terrain has restricted development. Since the mid-20th century, industrialization has led to a decline in natural population growth and an increase in urbanization. In Greece, more than 30 percent of the population now lives in Athens and many rural settlements have been abandoned.

Less than 2.6 persons per sq mile/1 per sq km	26–65 per sq mile/ 10–25 per sq km
2.6–26 per sq mile/ 1–10 per sq km	65–130 per sq mile/ 25–50 per sq km
	130–260 per sq mile/ 50–100 per sq km

ECONOMIC PROFILE

Macedonia and Greece have little fertile farmland, few mineral resources, and undeveloped industrial sectors; consequently, Macedonia is one of Europe's poorest nations. Greece depends heavily on shipping and tourism. Bulgaria has had a difficult transition from a Soviet-style centralized economy to an open market. However, it possesses rich farmland, especially on the Danube floodplain, and sophisticated industries led by metals, chemicals, and textiles.

Forest and woodland
Arable land
Grazing

Cereals
Citrus fruits
Wine
Tobacco
Olives
Sheep
Fishing
Industrial center
Tourism
Flowers

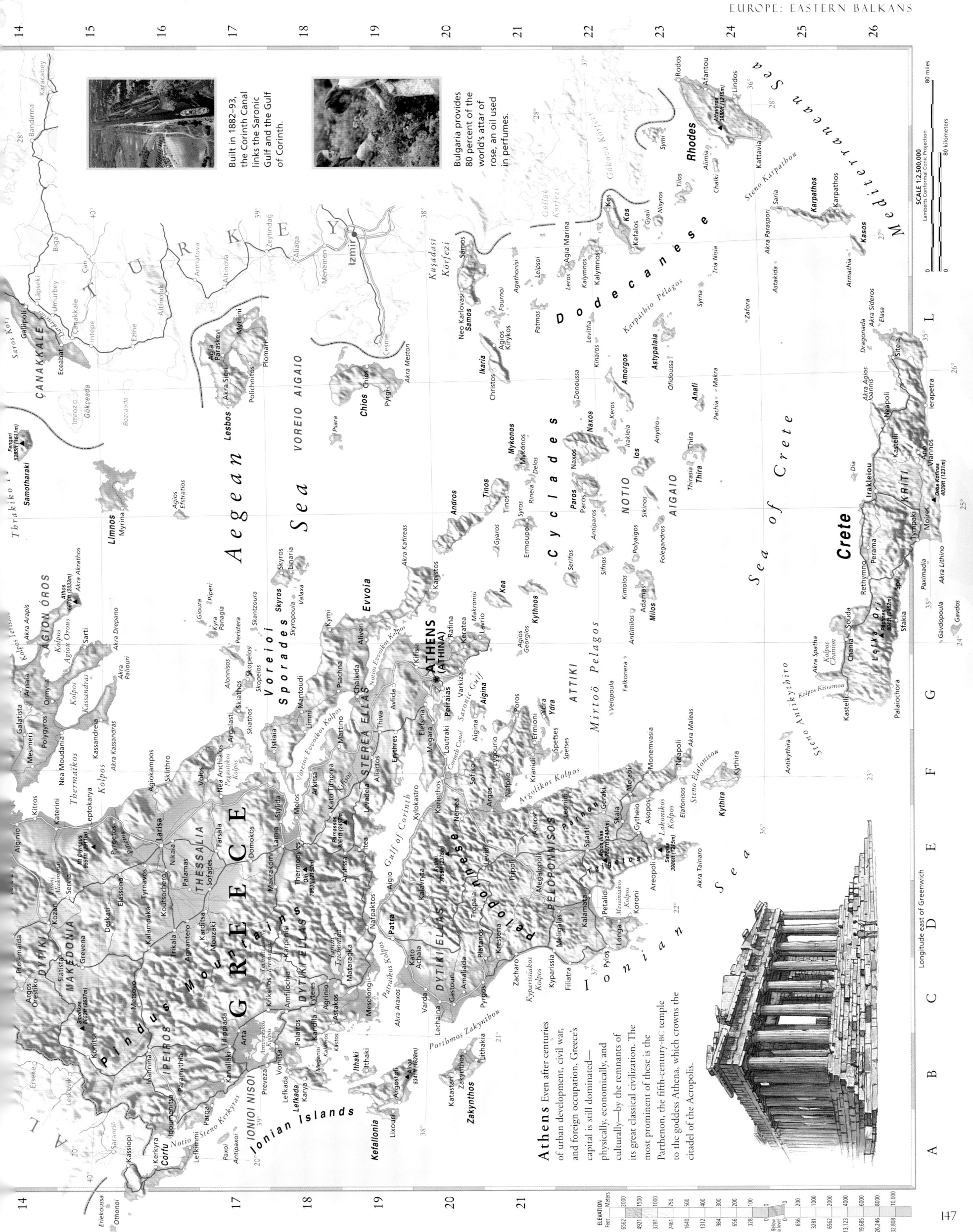

14 15 16 17 18 19 20 21 22 23 24 25 26

Built in 1882–93, the Corinth Canal links the Saronic Gulf and the Gulf of Corinth.

Bulgaria provides 80 percent of the world's attar of rose, an oil used in perfumes.

SCALE 1:2,500,000
Lambert Conformal Conic Projection
80 miles
80 kilometers

Athens Even after centuries of urban development, civil war, and foreign occupation, Greece's capital is still dominated—physically, economically, and culturally—by the remnants of its great classical civilization. The most prominent of these is the Parthenon, the fifth-century-BC temple to the goddess Athena, which crowns the citadel of the Acropolis.

Longitude east of Greenwich

ELEVATION
Feet   Meters
32,808 10,000
26,246 8000
19,685 6000
13,123 4000
6562   2000
3281   1000
1640   500
984   300
656   200
328   100
Below   sea
sea   level
level
328   100
656   200
3281   1000
6562   2000
13,123 4000
19,685 6000
26,246 8000
32,808 10,000

147

NORTHEASTERN EUROPE
Belarus, Estonia, Latvia, Lithuania

Much of Northeastern Europe's low-lying landscape was fashioned during the last ice age. Across the region, extensive plains, scoured flat by ice, are separated by hills and ridges originally deposited by the wide snouts of glaciers. Innumerable lakes fill hollows, and winding rivers have given rise to some of Europe's largest wetlands. Due to their proximity to the Baltic Sea, the nations of Estonia, Latvia, and Lithuania are often referred to as the Baltic States, even though the three countries are ethnically and linguistically distinct. In common with their southern neighbor Belarus, the Baltic States were, for long periods of their histories, controlled by more powerful nations, including Poland, Russia, Germany, Denmark, and Sweden. In the mid-20th century, all four countries became part of the Soviet Union, but all reasserted their independence soon after the collapse of the Eastern bloc in 1989. The Russian enclave around Kaliningrad is a remnant of the Soviet empire, and a vital Baltic port for the Russian Federation.

POPULATION PATTERNS

Northeastern Europe's population is fairly evenly spread, though it thins out in northern Latvia and on Estonia's chilly Baltic coast—only 14 of Estonia's 1,541 islands are inhabited. About 60 percent of people in Latvia and 70 percent in the other countries are urban dwellers; in both Estonia and Latvia roughly one-third inhabit the capital city. People of Russian origin live throughout the region, but make up 30 percent of the population in Estonia and Latvia, the result of a Soviet policy of encouraging workers from the U.S.S.R. to settle in these states.

	per sq mile / per sq km
	2.6–26 per sq mile / 1–10 per sq km
	26–65 per sq mile / 10–25 per sq km
	65–130 per sq mile / 25–50 per sq km
	130–260 per sq mile / 50–100 per sq km

ECONOMIC PROFILE

These nations are still dealing with the transition to a market economy, and are still dependent to some extent (especially Belarus) on Russian raw materials and sales. Much of Belarus's arable land was contaminated by fallout from Chernobyl, but it remains a significant supplier of flax as well as potash (widely used for fertilizers), and peat (from its marshlands); its heavy industries produce machinery, tools, tractors, and trucks. Estonia's oil-shale provides much of the Baltic States' energy. The Baltic States are also noted for wood products and textiles, and Lithuania is a major source of amber.

Forest and woodland
Arable land

Cereals
Flax
Potatoes
Vegetables
Dairy cattle
Sugar beet
Pigs
Industrial center
Timber

Gulf of Finland

Gulf of Riga

RUSSIAN FEDERATION

ESTONIA

LATVIA

Baltic Sea

TALLINN
RĪGA
Šiauliai
Kaliningrad
Liepāja
Klaipėda
Narva
Tartu
Pärnu
Daugavpils

Lake Peipus

Map labels

Grid/Longitude markers (top): 14 15 16 17 18 19 20 21 22 23 24 25 26

LITHUANIA

RUSSIAN FEDERATION

KALININGRADSKAYA OBLAST'

Kaliningrad

Courland Lagoon

Kuršskaya

POLAND

B E L A R U S

U K R A I N E

Pripet Marshes

Cities and towns (selection):

Vitsyebsk, Lyozna, Batsyshewsk, Dubrowna, Orsha, Shklow, Mahilyow, Kapyl, Klimavichy, Kastsyukovichy, Mstsislaw, Khotsimsk, Krychaw, Cherykaw, Krasnapollye, Slawharad, Bykhaw, Novy Bykhaw, Dowsk, Chachersk, Karma, Rahachow, Dobrush, Zhlobin, Buda-Kashalyova, Uvaravichy, Homyel', Rechytsa, Loyew, Brahin

Minsk, Barysaw, Smalyavichy, Zhodzina, Maladzyechna, Radashkovichy, Zaslawye, Dzyarzhynsk, Stowbtsy, Uzda, Mar'ina Horka, Asipovichy, Babruysk, Klichaw, Kirawsk, Svyetlahorsk, Mazyr, Kalinkavichy, Pyetrykaw, Zhlobin, Mikashevichy, Luninyets, Pinsk, Stolin, Drahichyn, Ivatsevichy, Baranavichy, Lyakhavichy, Slonim, Navahrudak, Lida, Radun', Shchuchyn, Skidal', Hrodna, Masty, Vawkavysk, Zelva, Ruzhany, Pruzhany, Byaroza, Kobryn, Brest, Malaryta, Vysokaye, Kamyanyets

Vilnius, Kaunas, Alytus, Varėna, Druskininkai, Marijampolė, Prienai, Jurbarkas, Tauragė, Šakiai, Panevėžys

Physical features:

Western Dvina, Dnieper, Berazina, Pripet, Neman, Vilija, Sož, Ptsich, Sluch, Lake Narach

Dzyarzhynskaya Hara (1132ft (346m))

Voblasts labels: VITSYEBSKAYA VOBLASTS', MAHILYOWSKAYA VOBLASTS', MINSKAYA VOBLASTS', HOMEL'SKAYA VOBLASTS', HRODZYENSKAYA VOBLASTS', BRESTSKAYA VOBLASTS'

Photo captions

Latvia's capital and principal port, Riga, was founded in 1201. The adjacent Gulf of Riga usually freezes solid for much of winter.

Workers in southern Belarus mark the harvest by wearing traditional dress. Many Belarusians work on large collective or state farms.

Tallinn Estonia's capital has one of the best-preserved medieval town centers in northern Europe. The city took shape around a fort founded by Danes in 1219. Sold to the Teutonic Knights in 1346, it became a trading post of the Hanseatic League. Increasing affluence resulted in the construction of some majestic buildings, including St Olaf's Church (founded in the 12th century and the tallest church in medieval Europe), the magnificent Town Hall (the current building dates from the early 15th century) and its fine square, and the imposing 16th-century city ramparts.

St Olaf's Church

City ramparts

Situated on Lake Galve near Vilnius, Trakai Castle became the residence of the Grand Dukes of Lithuania in the 15th century.

SCALE 1:2,750,000
Lamberts Conformal Conic Projection

0   80 miles

0   80 kilometers

Longitude east of Greenwich

ELEVATION

Feet	Meters
6562	2000
4921	1500
3281	1000
2461	750
1640	500
1312	400
984	300
656	200
328	100
0	0
	Below sea level
656	200
3281	1000
6562	2000
13,123	4000
19,685	6000
26,246	8000
32,808	10,000

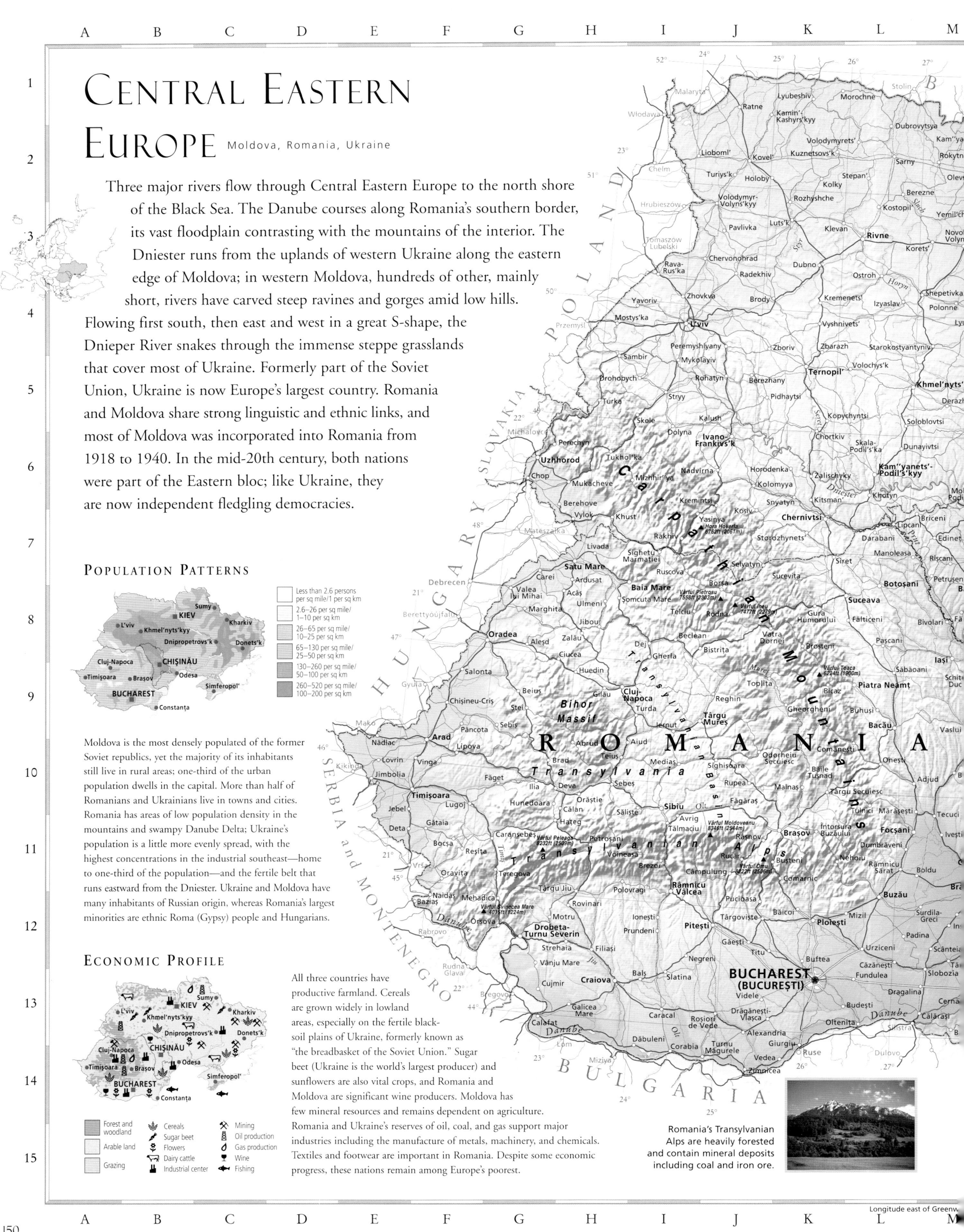

CENTRAL EASTERN EUROPE
Moldova, Romania, Ukraine

Three major rivers flow through Central Eastern Europe to the north shore of the Black Sea. The Danube courses along Romania's southern border, its vast floodplain contrasting with the mountains of the interior. The Dniester runs from the uplands of western Ukraine along the eastern edge of Moldova; in western Moldova, hundreds of other, mainly short, rivers have carved steep ravines and gorges amid low hills. Flowing first south, then east and west in a great S-shape, the Dnieper River snakes through the immense steppe grasslands that cover most of Ukraine. Formerly part of the Soviet Union, Ukraine is now Europe's largest country. Romania and Moldova share strong linguistic and ethnic links, and most of Moldova was incorporated into Romania from 1918 to 1940. In the mid-20th century, both nations were part of the Eastern bloc; like Ukraine, they are now independent fledgling democracies.

POPULATION PATTERNS

	Less than 2.6 persons per sq mile/1 per sq km
	2.6–26 per sq mile/1–10 per sq km
	26–65 per sq mile/10–25 per sq km
	65–130 per sq mile/25–50 per sq km
	130–260 per sq mile/50–100 per sq km
	260–520 per sq mile/100–200 per sq km

Moldova is the most densely populated of the former Soviet republics, yet the majority of its inhabitants still live in rural areas; one-third of the urban population dwells in the capital. More than half of Romanians and Ukrainians live in towns and cities. Romania has areas of low population density in the mountains and swampy Danube Delta; Ukraine's population is a little more evenly spread, with the highest concentrations in the industrial southeast—home to one-third of the population—and the fertile belt that runs eastward from the Dniester. Ukraine and Moldova have many inhabitants of Russian origin, whereas Romania's largest minorities are ethnic Roma (Gypsy) people and Hungarians.

ECONOMIC PROFILE

	Forest and woodland
	Arable land
	Grazing

Cereals	Mining
Sugar beet	Oil production
Flowers	Gas production
Dairy cattle	Wine
Industrial center	Fishing

All three countries have productive farmland. Cereals are grown widely in lowland areas, especially on the fertile black-soil plains of Ukraine, formerly known as "the breadbasket of the Soviet Union." Sugar beet (Ukraine is the world's largest producer) and sunflowers are also vital crops, and Romania and Moldova are significant wine producers. Moldova has few mineral resources and remains dependent on agriculture. Romania and Ukraine's reserves of oil, coal, and gas support major industries including the manufacture of metals, machinery, and chemicals. Textiles and footwear are important in Romania. Despite some economic progress, these nations remain among Europe's poorest.

Romania's Transylvanian Alps are heavily forested and contain mineral deposits including coal and iron ore.

In the Soviet era, Ukraine produced one-fifth of the U.S.S.R.'s agricultural goods.

Chişinău's buildings reflect Turkish and Soviet influences.

Kiev The Ukrainian capital's best-known landmark is golden-domed St Sophia Cathedral, which dates from 1037. At that time Kiev was the center of the powerful independent state of Kievan Rus. The city was razed by Mongol invaders in the 13th century and subsequently ruled by Poland, Lithuania, and Russia. It became the capital of newly independent Ukraine in 1991.

TRANSYLVANIA

Viewed from Romania's western border, the Carpathian Mountains and Transylvanian Alps form a vast amphitheater of mountains encompassing the region of Transylvania. Formerly autonomous but also ruled by Hungary for long periods, Transylvania was entirely ceded to Romania only in 1947.

SCALE 1:3,500,000
Lamberts Conformal Conic Projection
0   100 miles
0   100 kilometers

THE RUSSIAN FEDERATION

Spanning 11 time zones and most of the Eastern Hemisphere, the Russian Federation is the largest country on Earth. It is divided into European Russia and Asian Russia, or Siberia, by the Ural Mountains, which stretch from the shore of the Kara Sea to Kazakhstan. In European Russia, the site of the nation's largest cities, major rivers divide plains and ranges of low, rolling hills. East of the Urals, an immense, swampy plain stretches to the Yenisey River, where the land climbs to the wide Central Siberian Plateau. High mountains line the Mongolian border and skirt the east coast. An almost unbroken band of boreal forest crosses the entire country, dividing the tundra of the far north from the woodlands and steppe grasslands of the south.

In 1917, after a bloody revolution, Russia became a communist state known as the Soviet Union, or Union of Soviet Socialist Republics (U.S.S.R.). Following the collapse of communism in 1991, ten Soviet republics declared independence. The remainder of the union, about 75 percent of its land area, became the Russian Federation.

St Petersburg's Winter Palace is one of a series of buildings constructed in the mid-18th century by Peter the Great.

Local fishermen harvest more than 50 species of fish from Lake Baikal, the deepest lake in the world.

The Chukchi of northeastern Russia live mainly by herding reindeer, fishing, and hunting whales, seals, and walruses.

Moscow The focal point of Russia's capital city, Red Square, dates from the late 15th century and acquired its present name —the Russian word for "red" also means "beautiful"—in the 17th century. It is the site of some of the nation's most important buildings, including the Kremlin, Lenin's Tomb, and the 12-domed Cathedral of St Basil the Blessed (below). The cathedral was built between 1554 and 1560 by Ivan IV ("the Terrible") to celebrate his victory over the Mongols. Legend has it that Ivan then had the architect blinded to prevent him ever building anything to surpass this extraordinary work.

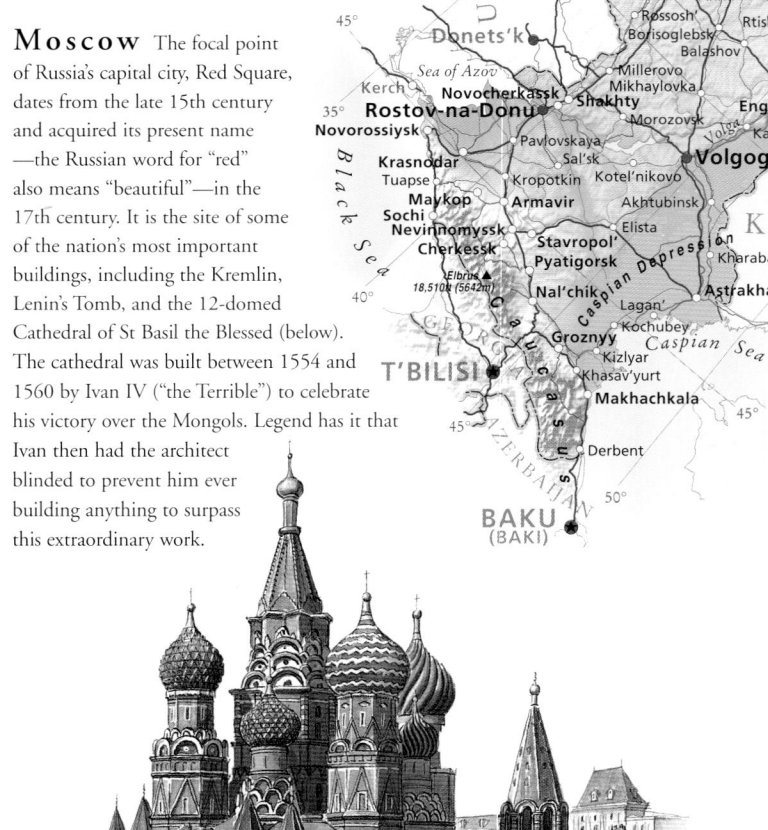

THE KAMCHATKA PENINSULA

Remote, cold, and desolate, the Kamchatka Peninsula extends for 750 miles (1,200 km) southwestward from the eastern edge of Russia, dividing the Sea of Okhotsk from the Bering Sea. Its forbidding landscape is characterized by forest-studded tundra, few towns or roads, hot springs, and more than 120 steep-sided volcanic peaks, including 15,584-foot (4,750-m) Sopka Klyuchevskaya, Siberia's highest mountain. No fewer than 22 of these volcanoes are still active.

Longitude east of Greenwich

POPULATION PATTERNS

European Russia constitutes one-quarter of the country but is home to four-fifths of its inhabitants. Settlement is especially dense around Moscow, along the River Volga, and in the southwest. East of the Urals, Russians cluster around the industrial centers of Omsk and Novosibirsk, the towns strung along the Trans-Siberian railway, and far-flung northern ports and mining centers. Over the past century, Russians have steadily abandoned the countryside for cities; 73 percent now live in urban areas. More than four-fifths are ethnic Russians; the remainder consists of a large number of other ethnic groups, including Ukrainians, Tatars, and Bashkirs.

ECONOMIC PROFILE

Much of the Soviet Union's best arable land was located in the now-independent republics of Ukraine and Belarus. Less than one-sixth of the Russian Federation is farmland; wheat, barley, and sugar beet are among the major crops. Russia has the world's largest forests and plentiful supplies of minerals, including coal, oil, gas, gold, copper, and nickel. These support the processing of metals and fossil fuels, and the manufacturing of chemicals and machinery. Communist rule accelerated industrialization, but ultimately stifled development. A shift toward privatization and a more open market is under way.

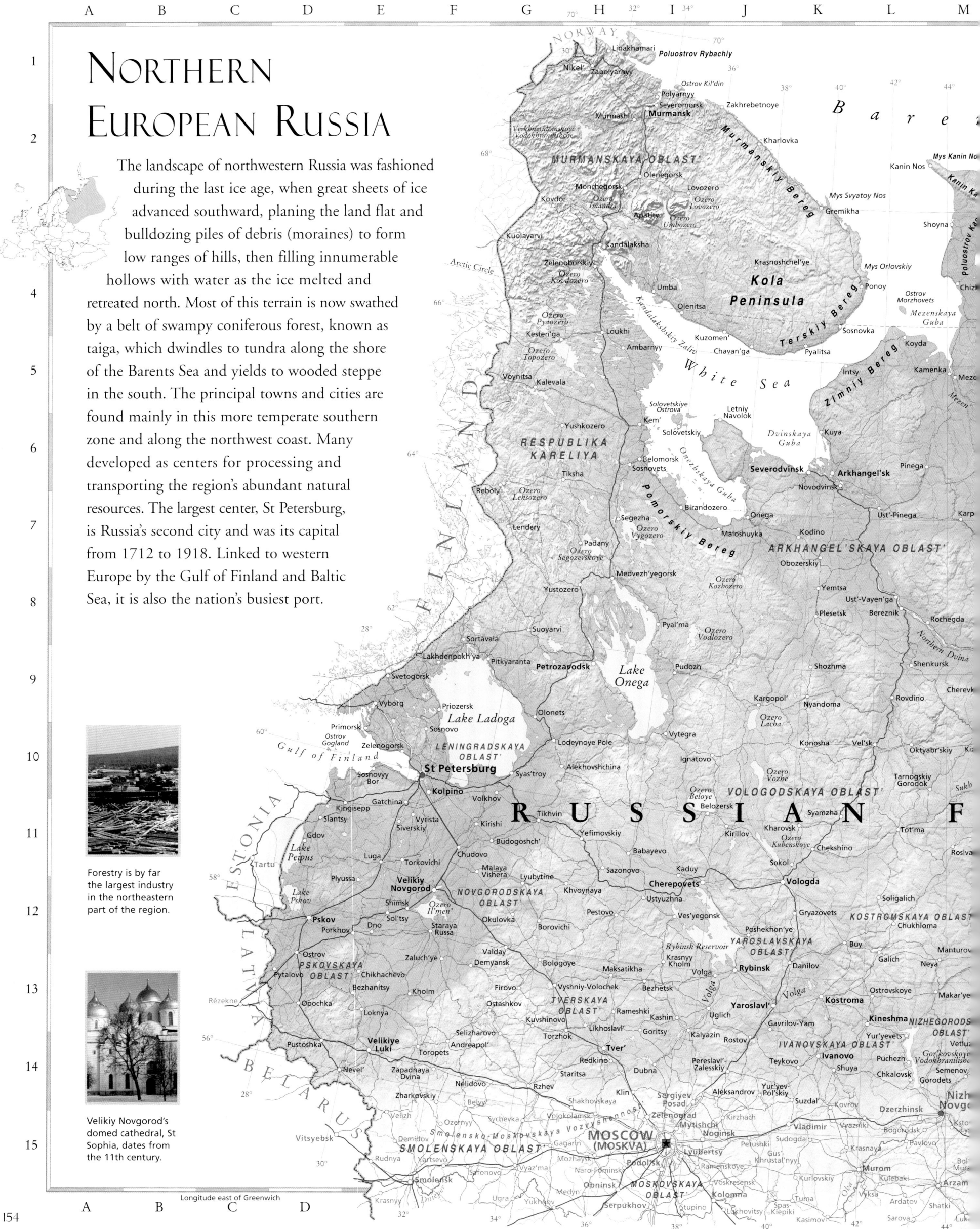

NORTHERN EUROPEAN RUSSIA

The landscape of northwestern Russia was fashioned during the last ice age, when great sheets of ice advanced southward, planing the land flat and bulldozing piles of debris (moraines) to form low ranges of hills, then filling innumerable hollows with water as the ice melted and retreated north. Most of this terrain is now swathed by a belt of swampy coniferous forest, known as taiga, which dwindles to tundra along the shore of the Barents Sea and yields to wooded steppe in the south. The principal towns and cities are found mainly in this more temperate southern zone and along the northwest coast. Many developed as centers for processing and transporting the region's abundant natural resources. The largest center, St Petersburg, is Russia's second city and was its capital from 1712 to 1918. Linked to western Europe by the Gulf of Finland and Baltic Sea, it is also the nation's busiest port.

Forestry is by far the largest industry in the northeastern part of the region.

Velikiy Novgorod's domed cathedral, St Sophia, dates from the 11th century.

Longitude east of Greenwich

Map labels

N O P Q R S T U V W X Y Z

1 2 3 4 5 6 7 8 9 10 11

Guba Dolgaya
Ostrov Vaygach
Ostrov Dolgiy
Amderma
Yugorskiy Poluostrov
Khrebet Pay-Khoy
Varandey
Khal'mer-Yu
S e a
Ostrov Kolguyev
Bugrino
Tobseda
Chernaya
Severnyy
Vorkuta
Pomorskiy Proliv
Pechorskaya Guba
Nosovaya
Yeletskiy
Indiga
Nar'yan-Mar
Khorey-Ver
Chum
Gora Payyer 4829ft (1472m)
Malozemel'skaya Tundra
Oksino
NENETSKIY AVTONOMNYY OKRUG
Bol'shezemel'skaya Tundra
Abez'
Novyy Bor
Usa
Adz'vavom
Adz'va
Arctic Circle
Krestovka
Usinsk
Inta
Timanskiy Kryazh
Ust'-Tsil'ma
Myla
Pechora
Synya
Pechora
Gora Narodnaya 6217ft (1895m)
Ural Mountains
Polyarnyy Ural
Vozhgora
Irayel'
RESPUBLIKA KOMI
Dutovo
Vuktyl'
Gora Tel'pos-Iz 5305ft (1617m)
Sosnogorsk
Mezen'
Vodnyy
Ukhta
Gora Kozhim-Iz 3920ft (1195m)
Usogorsk
Voyvozh
Troitsko-Pechorsk
Severnyy Ural
Vendinga
Sindor
Puzla
Yemva
Vol'dino
Mikun'
Kur'ya
Yarensk
Storozhevsk
Chasovo
Ust'-Nem
Gora Isherim 4367ft (1331m)
Ust'-Kulom
Syktyvkar
Srednyy Ural
Koryazhma
Nyrob
Gora Denezhkin Kamen' 4895ft (1492m)
Kotlas
Vizinga
Krasnovishersk
KOMI-PERMYATSKIY AVTONOMNYY OKRUG
Cherdyn'
Velikiy Ustyug
Luza
Ob"yachevo
Gayny
Gora Konzhakovskiy Kamen' 5148ft (1569m)
D E R A T I O N
Solikamsk
Kama
Oparino
Berezniki
Aleksandrovsk
Kizel
Yurla
Kamskoye Vodokhranilishche
Gubakha
chmengskiy Gorodok
Nagorsk
Kirs
Kudymkar
Chermoz
Murashi
Dobryanka
Southern Ural Mountains
Yur'ya
Slobodskoy
Il'inskiy
Chusovoy
Omutninsk
Krasnokamsk
Perm'
Lys'va
Kirov
Kirovo-Chepetsk
Glazov
Ocher
Okhansk
PERMSKAYA OBLAST'
Leninskoye
Balezino
Kungur
Kotel'nich
Igra
Osa
Suksun
Suna
KIROVSKAYA OBLAST'
Nolinsk
Selty
Barda
Uinskoye
Kiknur
Yaransk
Urzhum
UDMURTSKAYA RESPUBLIKA
Votkinsk
Votkinskoye Vodokhranilishche
Chaykovskiy
Krasnoufimsk
Vetluga
Shakhun'ya
Sovetsk
Kil'mez'
Izhevsk
Chernushka
ya
Kil'mez'
Askino
Sanchursk
Sernur
Malmyzh
Kuyeda
RESPUBLIKA MARIY EL
Mozhga
Agryz
Yanaul
Duvan
Yoshkar-Ola
UDMURTSKAYA RESPUBLIKA
Neftekamsk
Vyatskiye Polyany
Sarapul
Koz'modem'yansk
Cheboksary
Novocheboksarsk
Mendeleyevsk
Yelabuga
Menzelinsk
Birsk
Zlatoust
Tsivil'sk
Volzhsk
Kazan'
RESPUBLIKA TATARSTAN
Nizhnekamsk
Naberezhnyye Chelny
Dyurtyuli
HUVASHSKAYA RESPUBLIKA
Shumerlya
Kanash
Laishevo
Chistopol'
Zainsk
Bakaly
Kushnarenkovo
Blagoveshchensk
Sim
Ufa
Kazan'skoye
Ust'ye
Kushbyshevsk Reservoir
Al'met'yevsk
Chishmy
Inzer
Alatyr'
Buinsk
Bolgar
Al'met'yevsk

One of Russia's biggest ports, Murmansk is the largest city in the world north of the Arctic Circle.

These 18th-century churches lie on an island in Lake Onega, Europe's second-largest lake.

POPULATION PATTERNS

The north's inhospitable subarctic climate has confined settlement to sheltered harbors and river valleys, though small groups of Arctic peoples, including the Komi and Nenets, are scattered across the northeast. By far the most populous area is the south, where the highest densities of settlement occur around the industrial centers of Perm' and Kirov in the east, and St Petersburg in the west. St Petersburg alone accommodates almost 4.5 million people.

Uninhabited

Less than 2.6 persons per sq mile/1 per sq km

2.6–26 per sq mile/ 1–10 per sq km

26–65 per sq mile/ 10–25 per sq km

65–130 per sq mile/ 25–50 per sq km

130–260 per sq mile/ 50–100 per sq km

Murmansk
Vorkuta
Pechora
Arkangel'sk
Kotlas
St Petersburg
Kirov
Perm'
Yaroslavl'

ECONOMIC PROFILE

The processing of resources dominates the economy. Local forests provide one-third of Russia's wood products. Oil, gas, and coal reserves are exploited around Pechora, and metal production is also important, notably in Vologda, where it accounts for two-thirds of industrial output. The White and Barents seas yield one-quarter of Russia's fish. Dairying and the cultivation of fodder crops, oats, and rye take place in the southwest. Engineering, chemical production, printing, and food processing are the leading industries in St Petersburg.

Forest and woodland

Arable land

Grazing

Murmansk
Vorkuta
Pechora
Arkangel'sk
Kotlas
St Petersburg
Kirov
Perm'
Yaroslavl'

Cereals
Industrial center
Mining
Reindeer
Fishing
Dairy cattle
Gas production
Oil production
Timber
Flax
Tourism
Coal

ELEVATION

Feet	Meters
6562	2000
4921	1500
3281	1000
2461	750
1640	500
1312	400
984	300
656	200
328	100
Below sea level	0
656	200
3281	1000
6562	2000
13,123	4000
19,685	6000
26,246	8000
32,808	10,000

Large quantities of crude oil from western Siberia are piped to Perm' for refining.

SCALE 1:5,500,000
Lamberts Conformal Conic Projection
0   150 miles
0   150 kilometers

W

Southern European Russia

Europe's second-largest urban center, Moscow is not only the capital of the Russian Federation, but the heart of its most densely populated, developed, and productive region. The city lies on the wide valley of the Moskva River, a tributary of the Oka, which in turn flows east into the Volga, Europe's longest river. A chain of cities lines these waterways, running eastward and veering south with the Volga through Samara to Volgograd. West of the river, the Volga Hills roll down to the banks of the Don, Europe's fifth-longest waterway, which forms the eastern boundary of the Central Russian Uplands, a low plateau. Near Volgograd, the two rivers almost meet and are linked by the Volga–Don Canal. Turning away from each other, the Don and the Volga then drain across arid lowlands into, respectively, the Sea of Azov and the Caspian Sea. In the far south, where the mighty Caucasus range forms Russia's southern frontier and a natural boundary with Asia, a mere 200 miles (320 km) or so divides Europe's lowest point, in the Caspian Depression, from its highest, the towering summit of Elbrus.

THE CASPIAN DEPRESSION

Covering 77,000 square miles (200,000 sq km), the Caspian Depression is a vast lowland on the northwestern edge of the Caspian Sea. Part of an immense downward fold caused by crumpling of Earth's crust, it descends to 92 feet (28 m) below sea level at the shoreline. In the north, the depression is traversed by the Volga River, which forms Russia's largest delta. Elsewhere, the depression is mainly barren, although beneath its surface lie large deposits of oil and salt.

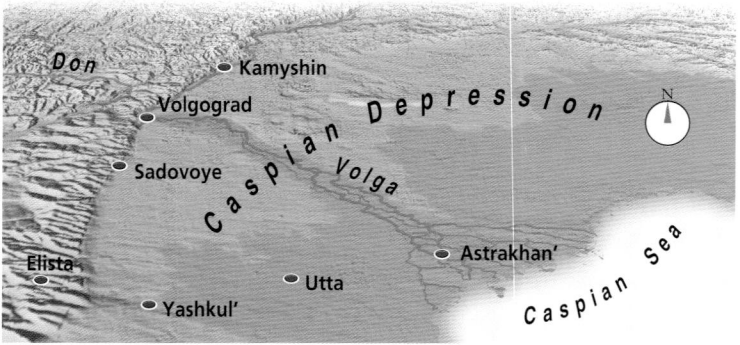

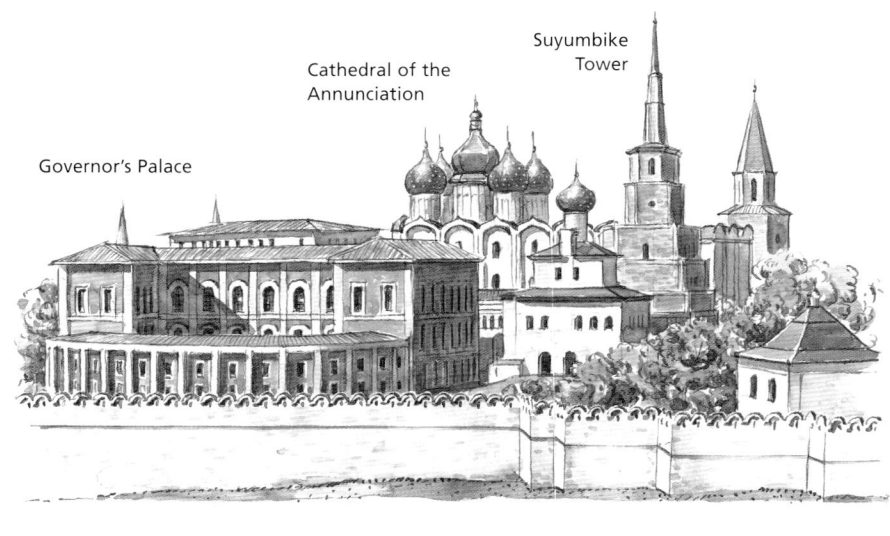

Governor's Palace

Cathedral of the Annunciation

Suyumbike Tower

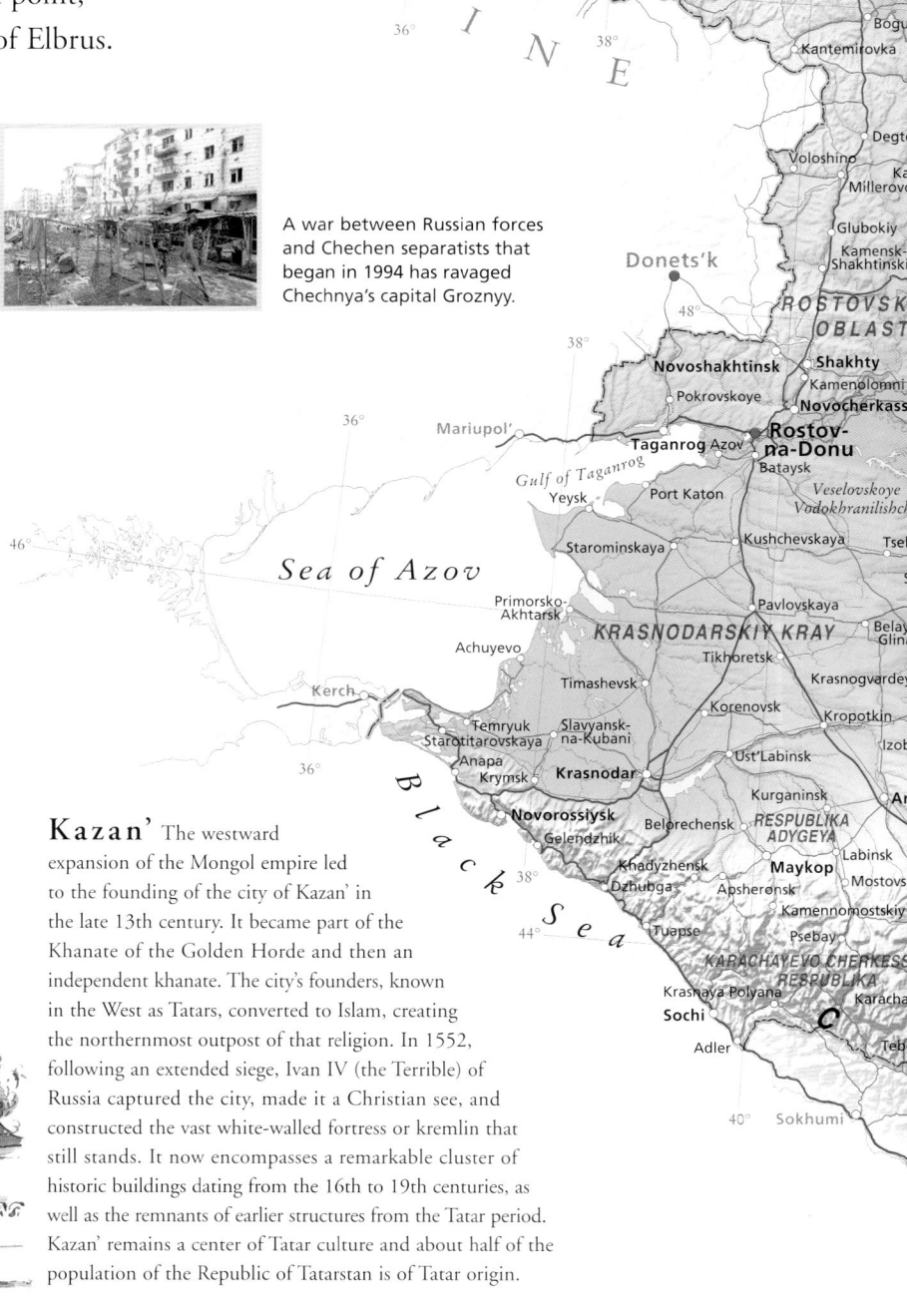

A war between Russian forces and Chechen separatists that began in 1994 has ravaged Chechnya's capital Groznyy.

Kazan' The westward expansion of the Mongol empire led to the founding of the city of Kazan' in the late 13th century. It became part of the Khanate of the Golden Horde and then an independent khanate. The city's founders, known in the West as Tatars, converted to Islam, creating the northernmost outpost of that religion. In 1552, following an extended siege, Ivan IV (the Terrible) of Russia captured the city, made it a Christian see, and constructed the vast white-walled fortress or kremlin that still stands. It now encompasses a remarkable cluster of historic buildings dating from the 16th to 19th centuries, as well as the remnants of earlier structures from the Tatar period. Kazan' remains a center of Tatar culture and about half of the population of the Republic of Tatarstan is of Tatar origin.

Longitude east of Greenwich

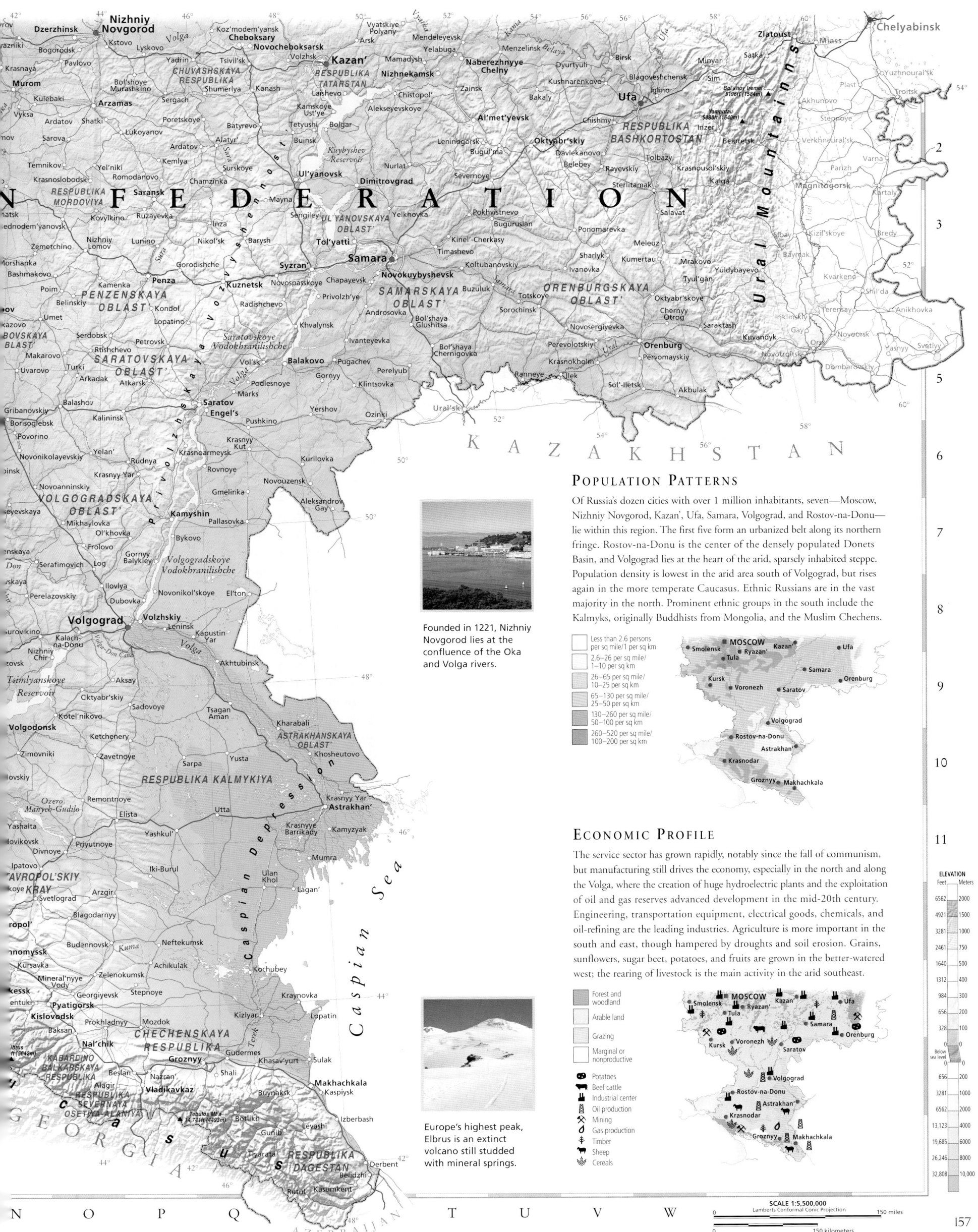

POPULATION PATTERNS

Of Russia's dozen cities with over 1 million inhabitants, seven—Moscow, Nizhniy Novgorod, Kazan', Ufa, Samara, Volgograd, and Rostov-na-Donu— lie within this region. The first five form an urbanized belt along its northern fringe. Rostov-na-Donu is the center of the densely populated Donets Basin, and Volgograd lies at the heart of the arid, sparsely inhabited steppe. Population density is lowest in the arid area south of Volgograd, but rises again in the more temperate Caucasus. Ethnic Russians are in the vast majority in the north. Prominent ethnic groups in the south include the Kalmyks, originally Buddhists from Mongolia, and the Muslim Chechens.

Founded in 1221, Nizhniy Novgorod lies at the confluence of the Oka and Volga rivers.

Less than 2.6 persons per sq mile/1 per sq km
2.6–26 per sq mile/1–10 per sq km
26–65 per sq mile/10–25 per sq km
65–130 per sq mile/25–50 per sq km
130–260 per sq mile/50–100 per sq km
260–520 per sq mile/100–200 per sq km

ECONOMIC PROFILE

The service sector has grown rapidly, notably since the fall of communism, but manufacturing still drives the economy, especially in the north and along the Volga, where the creation of huge hydroelectric plants and the exploitation of oil and gas reserves advanced development in the mid-20th century. Engineering, transportation equipment, electrical goods, chemicals, and oil-refining are the leading industries. Agriculture is more important in the south and east, though hampered by droughts and soil erosion. Grains, sunflowers, sugar beet, potatoes, and fruits are grown in the better-watered west; the rearing of livestock is the main activity in the arid southeast.

Forest and woodland
Arable land
Grazing
Marginal or nonproductive

Potatoes
Beef cattle
Industrial center
Oil production
Mining
Gas production
Timber
Sheep
Cereals

Europe's highest peak, Elbrus is an extinct volcano still studded with mineral springs.

ELEVATION
Feet / Meters
6562 / 2000
4921 / 1500
3281 / 1000
2461 / 750
1640 / 500
1312 / 400
984 / 300
656 / 200
328 / 100
Below sea level
656 / 200
3281 / 1000
6562 / 2000
13,123 / 4000
19,685 / 6000
26,246 / 8000
32,808 / 10,000

SCALE 1:5,500,000
Lamberts Conformal Conic Projection
150 miles
150 kilometers

157

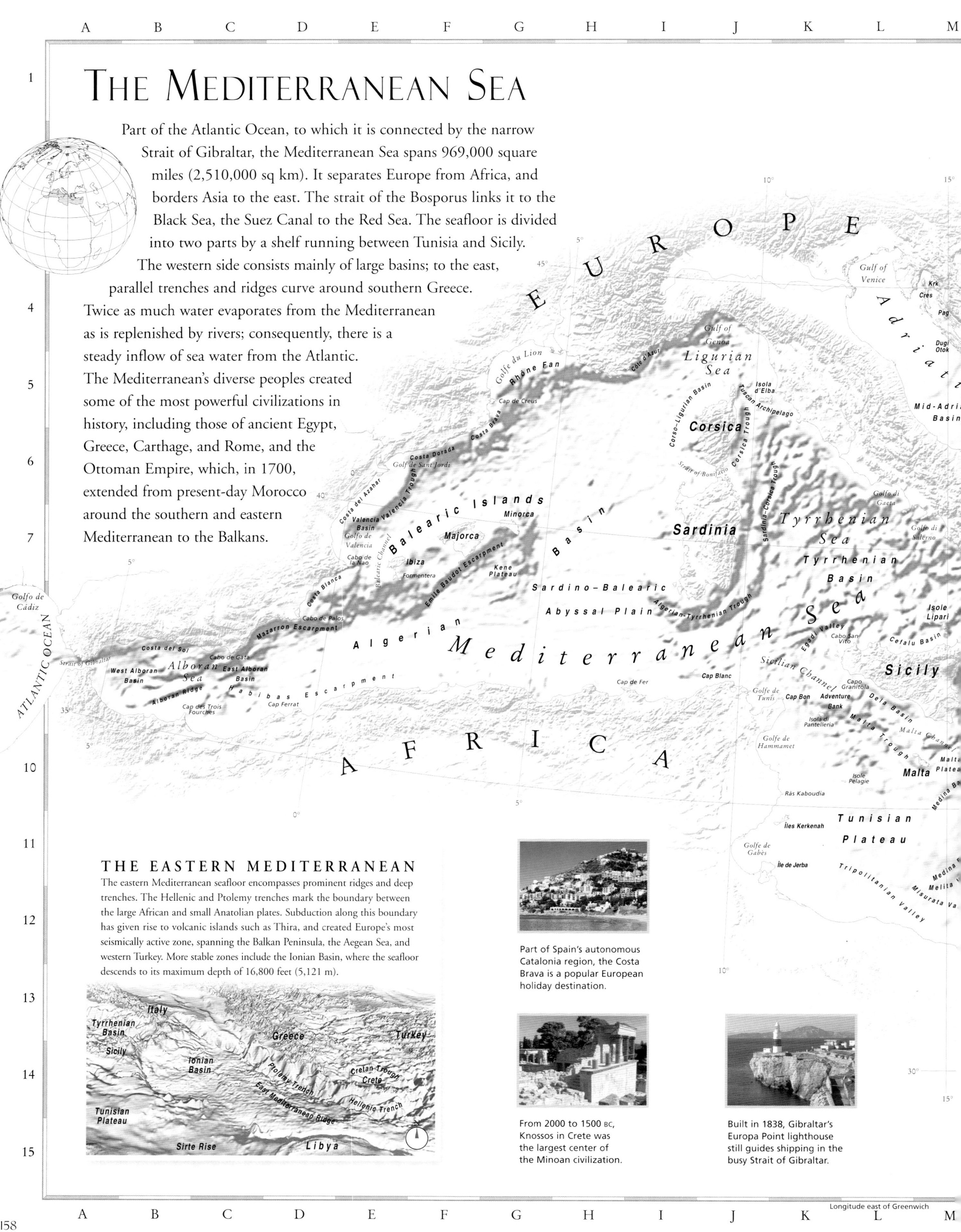

THE MEDITERRANEAN SEA

Part of the Atlantic Ocean, to which it is connected by the narrow Strait of Gibraltar, the Mediterranean Sea spans 969,000 square miles (2,510,000 sq km). It separates Europe from Africa, and borders Asia to the east. The strait of the Bosporus links it to the Black Sea, the Suez Canal to the Red Sea. The seafloor is divided into two parts by a shelf running between Tunisia and Sicily. The western side consists mainly of large basins; to the east, parallel trenches and ridges curve around southern Greece.

Twice as much water evaporates from the Mediterranean as is replenished by rivers; consequently, there is a steady inflow of sea water from the Atlantic. The Mediterranean's diverse peoples created some of the most powerful civilizations in history, including those of ancient Egypt, Greece, Carthage, and Rome, and the Ottoman Empire, which, in 1700, extended from present-day Morocco around the southern and eastern Mediterranean to the Balkans.

THE EASTERN MEDITERRANEAN

The eastern Mediterranean seafloor encompasses prominent ridges and deep trenches. The Hellenic and Ptolemy trenches mark the boundary between the large African and small Anatolian plates. Subduction along this boundary has given rise to volcanic islands such as Thira, and created Europe's most seismically active zone, spanning the Balkan Peninsula, the Aegean Sea, and western Turkey. More stable zones include the Ionian Basin, where the seafloor descends to its maximum depth of 16,800 feet (5,121 m).

Part of Spain's autonomous Catalonia region, the Costa Brava is a popular European holiday destination.

From 2000 to 1500 BC, Knossos in Crete was the largest center of the Minoan civilization.

Built in 1838, Gibraltar's Europa Point lighthouse still guides shipping in the busy Strait of Gibraltar.

Longitude east of Greenwich

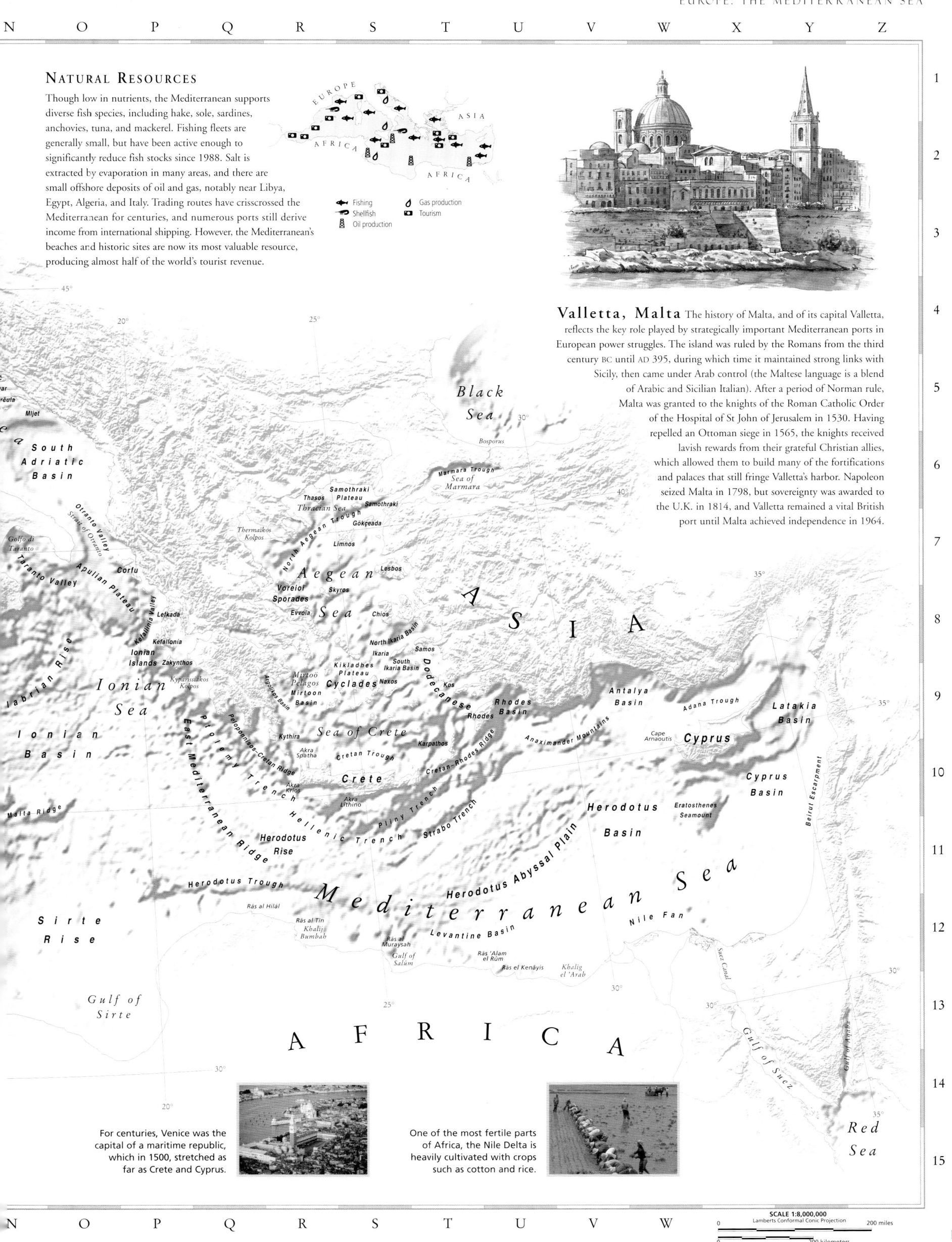

NATURAL RESOURCES

Though low in nutrients, the Mediterranean supports diverse fish species, including hake, sole, sardines, anchovies, tuna, and mackerel. Fishing fleets are generally small, but have been active enough to significantly reduce fish stocks since 1988. Salt is extracted by evaporation in many areas, and there are small offshore deposits of oil and gas, notably near Libya, Egypt, Algeria, and Italy. Trading routes have crisscrossed the Mediterranean for centuries, and numerous ports still derive income from international shipping. However, the Mediterranean's beaches and historic sites are now its most valuable resource, producing almost half of the world's tourist revenue.

EUROPE
AFRICA
ASIA
AFRICA

Fishing
Shellfish
Oil production
Gas production
Tourism

Valletta, Malta The history of Malta, and of its capital Valletta, reflects the key role played by strategically important Mediterranean ports in European power struggles. The island was ruled by the Romans from the third century BC until AD 395, during which time it maintained strong links with Sicily, then came under Arab control (the Maltese language is a blend of Arabic and Sicilian Italian). After a period of Norman rule, Malta was granted to the knights of the Roman Catholic Order of the Hospital of St John of Jerusalem in 1530. Having repelled an Ottoman siege in 1565, the knights received lavish rewards from their grateful Christian allies, which allowed them to build many of the fortifications and palaces that still fringe Valletta's harbor. Napoleon seized Malta in 1798, but sovereignty was awarded to the U.K. in 1814, and Valletta remained a vital British port until Malta achieved independence in 1964.

For centuries, Venice was the capital of a maritime republic, which in 1500, stretched as far as Crete and Cyprus.

One of the most fertile parts of Africa, the Nile Delta is heavily cultivated with crops such as cotton and rice.

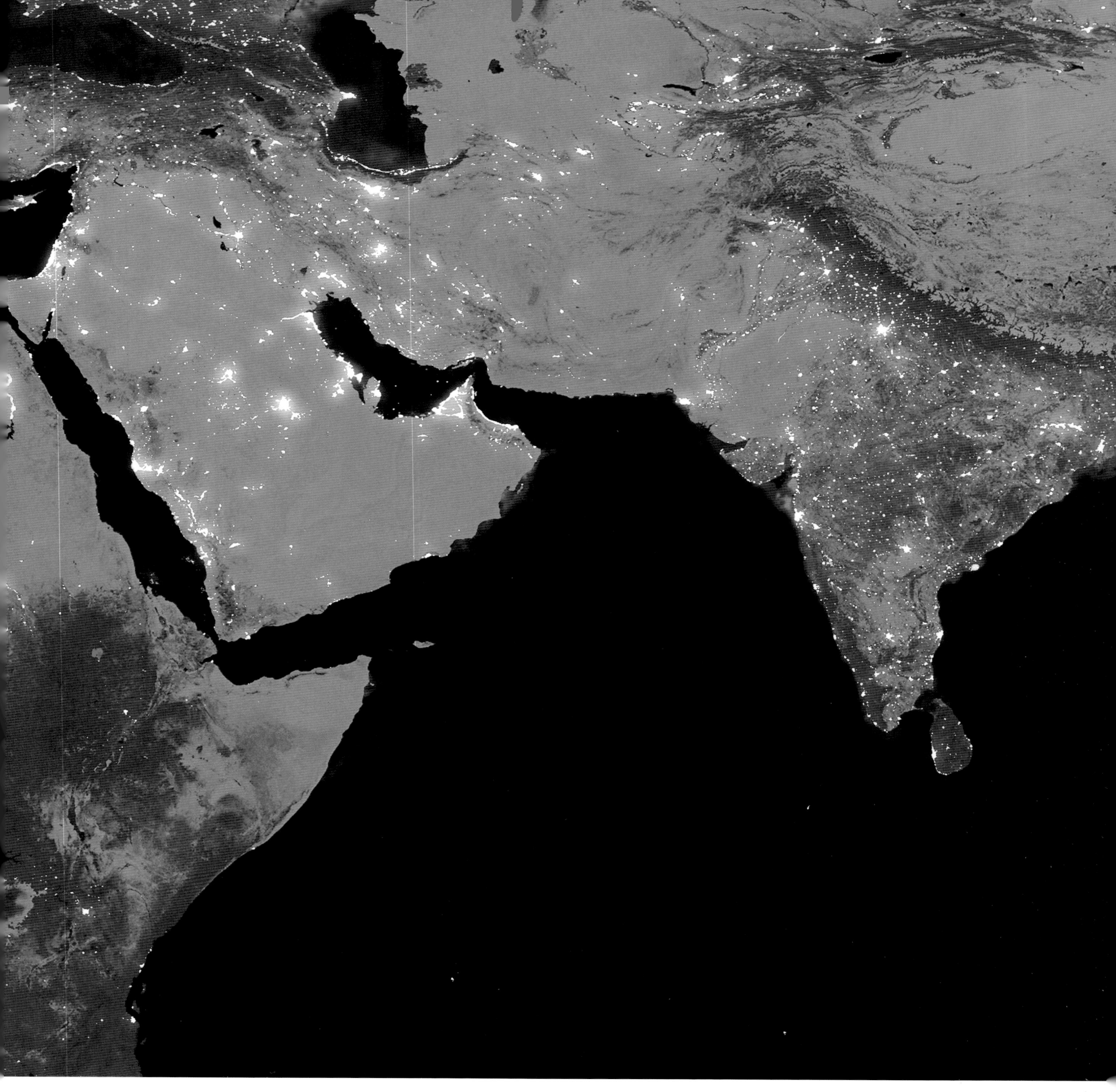

The intensity of light from Japan reflects that nation's high population density and considerable urbanization. The Indian subcontinent and eastern China stand out at night. The Himalayan mountains and the Gobi Desert remain mostly dark.

ASIA

ABOVE ASIA

Asia's eastern and southern fringes lie near the edge of a mighty tectonic plate called the Eurasian plate. It is one of the constantly shifting pieces of Earth's crust that make up the surface of the planet. The collision zone where the Eurasian plate converges with other plates is marked by the upthrust of massive mountain ranges such as the Himalayas, recurring earthquakes, and numerous active volcanoes, including the chain that runs from Sumatra through Java and north to Japan. Satellites have captured dramatic images of both current activity and the results of past upheavals. Also visible is evidence of climate change. Radar images of China's Taklimakan Desert reveal ancient alluvial fans laid down in wetter times, and changed landforms caused by the Kunlun Shan on the edge of the desert being pushed north by the continuing collision of the Eurasian plate with the Indian plate.

Gunung Merbabu and Merapi, Indonesia
Below: This false-color image shows part of the volcanic chain that crosses the Indonesian island of Java. Old lava flows appear in shades of yellow and green on Gunung Merbabu, center, and Gunung Merapi, lower right. In November 1994, six weeks after this image was collected, Gunung Merapi erupted, killing more than 60 people.

Taklimakan Desert, China
Bottom: The veined patterns in the center of this radar image of China's Taklimakan Desert are gravel deposits that accumulated at the base of the Kunlun Shan when the climate was wetter. They mark ancient alluvial fans. The large lavender triangles are the modern fans. Yellow areas on the modern fans are vegetated oases.

The Bosporus, Istanbul, Turkey
Left: This false-color view of the Turkish city of Istanbul displays urban areas as blue-green and vegetation as red. The busy shipping channel of the Bosporus divides the city and links the Black Sea in the north with the Sea of Marmara in the south. This image also indicates water temperature, with colder waters shown in deeper shades of blue.

Desert, northern Oman
Below: This radar image of a desert area in northern Oman, on the Arabian Peninsula, was collected by the space shuttle Endeavour in 1994. The bright arcs are limestone, formed on the bed of a shallow sea, and worn away into hills after sea levels dropped. The branching patterns are ancient drainage channels cut in wetter times.

LAND AND ENVIRONMENT

Asia covers 17.4 million square miles (45 million sq km), one-third of the world's landmass. The mainland is separated from Europe by Russia's Ural and Caucasus mountains and the narrow straits of the Bosporus in Turkey, from Africa by the Red Sea and Suez Canal, and from North America by the Bering Strait. Its center is dominated by an immense plateau region ringed by high mountain ranges. The northern ranges ripple across eastern Siberia to the Bering Sea. To the west, the uplands stretch through Afghanistan, Iran, and Turkey, dividing the arid Arabian Peninsula from the plains bordering the Caspian sea. The southern peaks are crowned by the world's highest mountain chain, the Himalaya, which falls steeply to the Gangetic Plain of the Indian Subcontinent but slopes more gently toward the Indochina Peninsula. Islands and archipelagoes fringe Asia's south and east coasts, including Sri Lanka, Japan, and the sprawling Malay Archipelago.

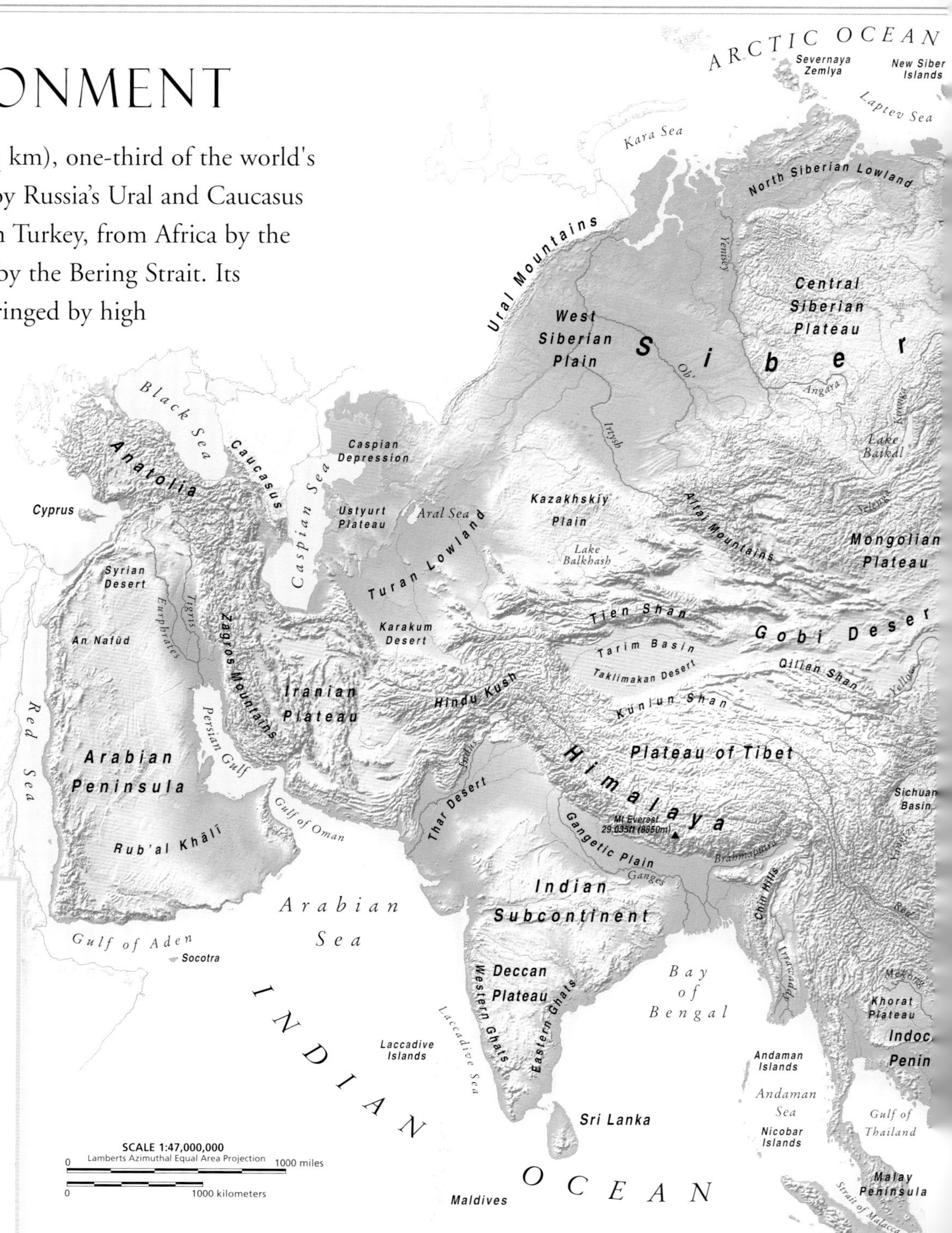

NATURAL HAZARDS

Hurricanes

Known in the western Pacific as typhoons (from the Cantonese *tai-fung*, meaning "great wind") and around the Indian Ocean as tropical cyclones, hurricanes regularly bring devastation to many parts of southern and eastern Asia. They occur when a large cluster of thunderstorms forms over open ocean and begins to spin as a result of Earth's rotation—something that occurs only if the storm system is more than five degrees from the Equator. Once the system starts spinning, it may intensify and grow. It qualifies as a hurricane when its wind speeds reach 74 mph (119 km/h), and it can generate wind gusts of up to 190 mph (305 km/h). One of its most destructive side-effects is a storm surge, a huge wave that can swamp low-lying areas.

HURRICANE DISTRIBUTION

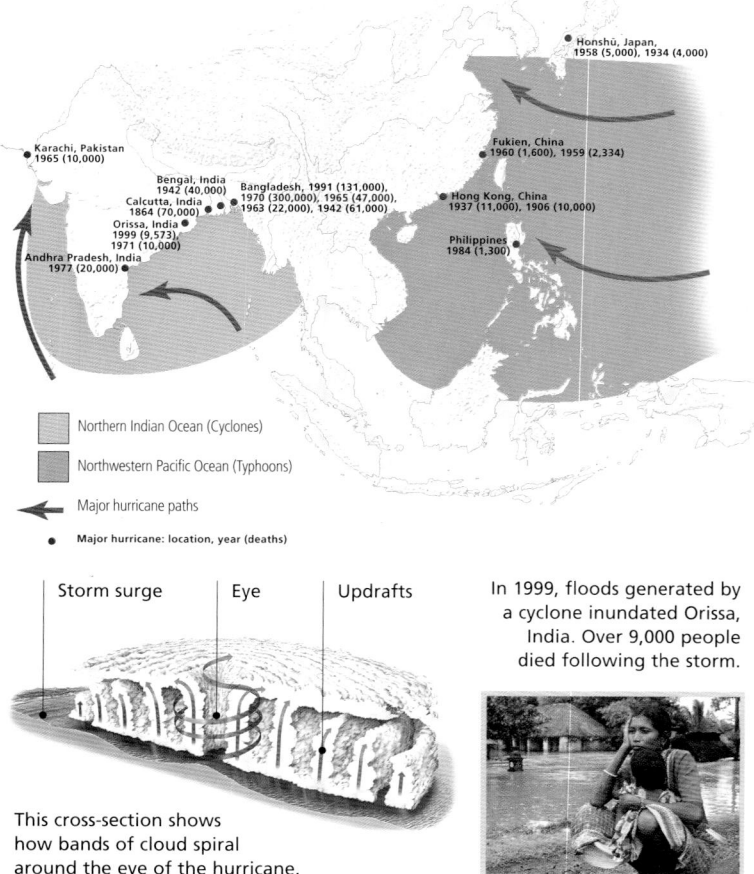

- Honshū, Japan, 1958 (5,000), 1934 (4,000)
- Karachi, Pakistan 1965 (10,000)
- Fukien, China 1960 (1,600), 1959 (2,334)
- Bengal, India 1942 (40,000)
- Bangladesh, 1991 (131,000), 1970 (300,000), 1965 (47,000), 1963 (22,000), 1942 (61,000)
- Calcutta, India 1864 (70,000)
- Orissa, India 1999 (9,573), 1971 (10,000)
- Hong Kong, China 1937 (11,000), 1906 (10,000)
- Philippines 1984 (1,300)
- Andhra Pradesh, India 1977 (20,000)

Northern Indian Ocean (Cyclones)

Northwestern Pacific Ocean (Typhoons)

Major hurricane paths

Major hurricane: location, year (deaths)

Storm surge   Eye   Updrafts

This cross-section shows how bands of cloud spiral around the eye of the hurricane.

In 1999, floods generated by a cyclone inundated Orissa, India. Over 9,000 people died following the storm.

SCALE 1:47,000,000
Lamberts Azimuthal Equal Area Projection
0 — 1000 miles
0 — 1000 kilometers

Right: The Himalaya divides the vast Plateau of Tibet from the low-lying Gangetic Plain. The gray veil that covers most of the plain in this image is air pollution.

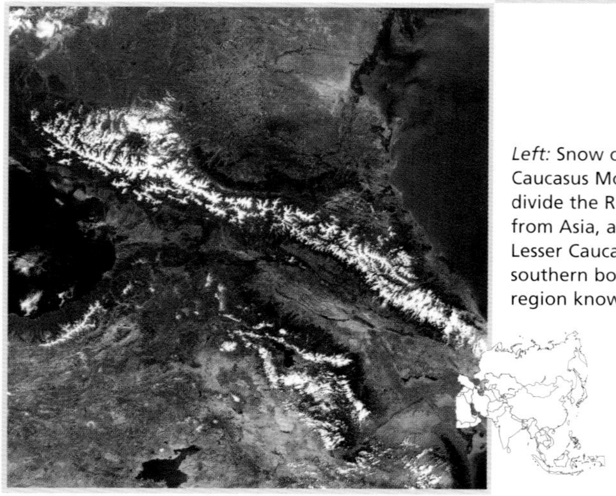

Left: Snow cover highlights the Caucasus Mountains, which divide the Russian Federation from Asia, and the associated Lesser Caucasus, which form the southern boundary of the region known as Transcaucasia.

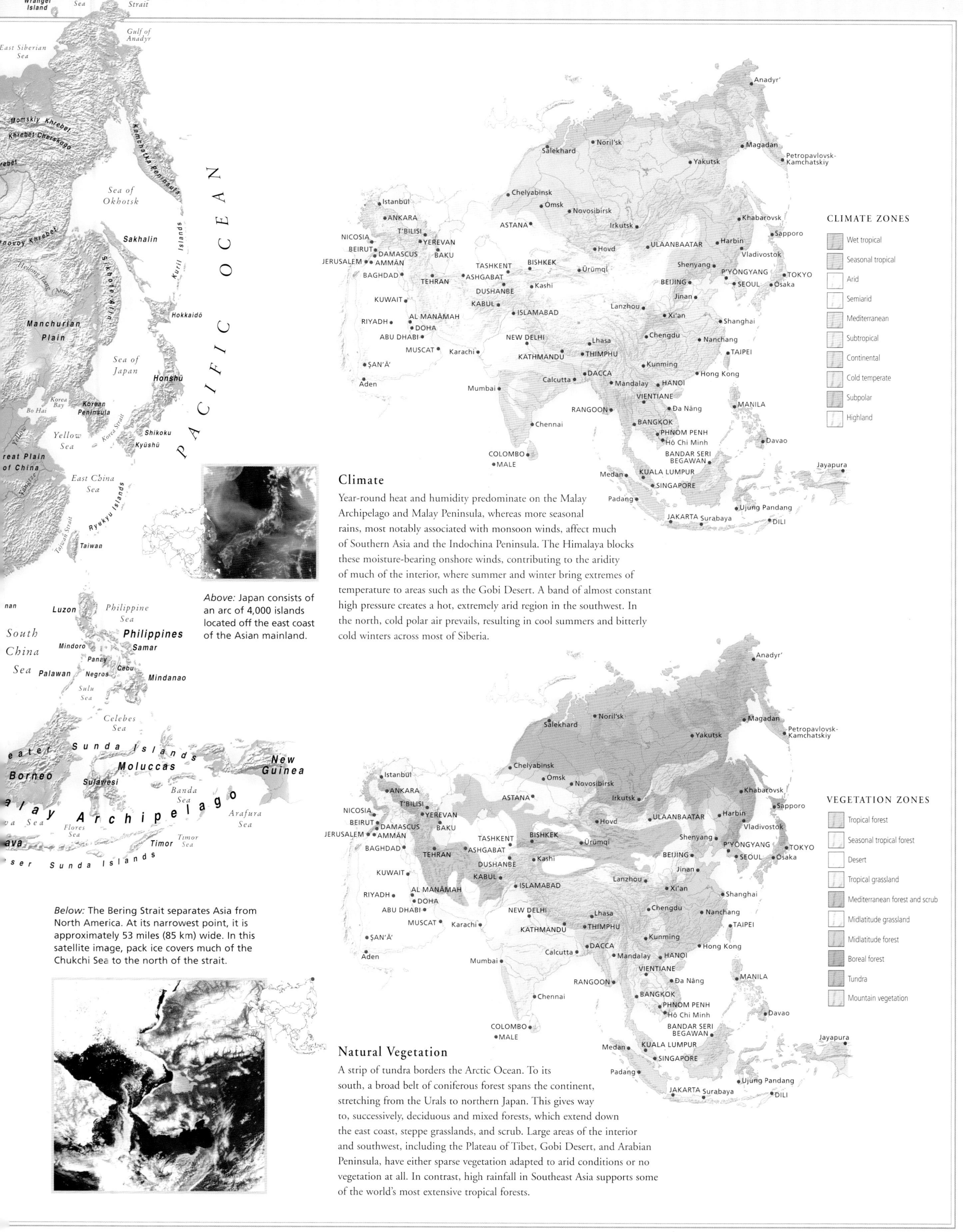

Above: Japan consists of an arc of 4,000 islands located off the east coast of the Asian mainland.

Below: The Bering Strait separates Asia from North America. At its narrowest point, it is approximately 53 miles (85 km) wide. In this satellite image, pack ice covers much of the Chukchi Sea to the north of the strait.

CLIMATE ZONES

- Wet tropical
- Seasonal tropical
- Arid
- Semiarid
- Mediterranean
- Subtropical
- Continental
- Cold temperate
- Subpolar
- Highland

Climate

Year-round heat and humidity predominate on the Malay Archipelago and Malay Peninsula, whereas more seasonal rains, most notably associated with monsoon winds, affect much of Southern Asia and the Indochina Peninsula. The Himalaya blocks these moisture-bearing onshore winds, contributing to the aridity of much of the interior, where summer and winter bring extremes of temperature to areas such as the Gobi Desert. A band of almost constant high pressure creates a hot, extremely arid region in the southwest. In the north, cold polar air prevails, resulting in cool summers and bitterly cold winters across most of Siberia.

VEGETATION ZONES

- Tropical forest
- Seasonal tropical forest
- Desert
- Tropical grassland
- Mediterranean forest and scrub
- Midlatitude grassland
- Midlatitude forest
- Boreal forest
- Tundra
- Mountain vegetation

Natural Vegetation

A strip of tundra borders the Arctic Ocean. To its south, a broad belt of coniferous forest spans the continent, stretching from the Urals to northern Japan. This gives way to, successively, deciduous and mixed forests, which extend down the east coast, steppe grasslands, and scrub. Large areas of the interior and southwest, including the Plateau of Tibet, Gobi Desert, and Arabian Peninsula, have either sparse vegetation adapted to arid conditions or no vegetation at all. In contrast, high rainfall in Southeast Asia supports some of the world's most extensive tropical forests.

PEOPLES AND NATIONS

In Asia, more than three-fifths of Earth's population—3.7 billion people—occupy one-third of its land. They inhabit 50 nations, ranging in size from the tiny city-state of Singapore to the world's largest country, the Russian Federation. The majority of these are developing nations, and many people lack ready access to clean water, reliable food supplies, and adequate health services. However, several nations, including Japan, South Korea, Singapore, Brunei, the Russian Federation, and Israel, have advanced economies and a relatively high standard of living. Asia has a great diversity of ethnic groups, and was the birthplace of all the world's major religions.

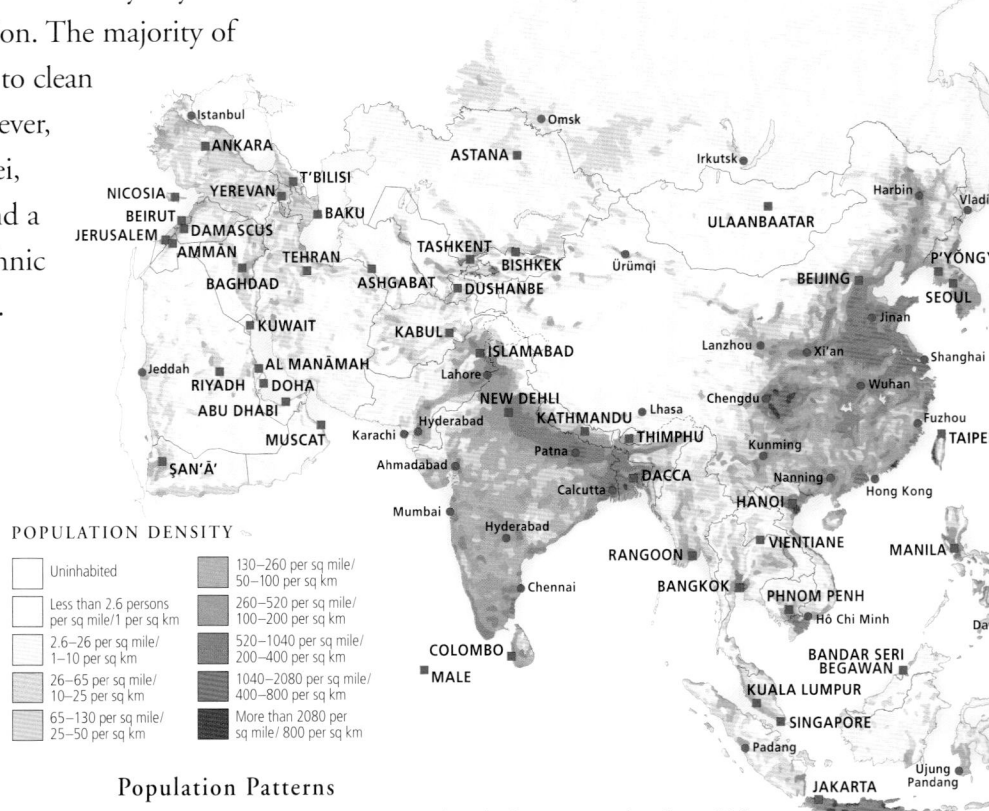

ASIA'S LARGEST CITIES

POPULATION DENSITY

Uninhabited	
Less than 2.6 persons per sq mile/1 per sq km	
2.6–26 per sq mile/ 1–10 per sq km	
26–65 per sq mile/ 10–25 per sq km	
65–130 per sq mile/ 25–50 per sq km	

130–260 per sq mile/ 50–100 per sq km	
260–520 per sq mile/ 100–200 per sq km	
520–1040 per sq mile/ 200–400 per sq km	
1040–2080 per sq mile/ 400–800 per sq km	
More than 2080 per sq mile/ 800 per sq km	

Urbanization

Most Asians are still dependent on subsistence farming and three-fifths live in rural areas. But many regions are becoming rapidly urbanized and industrialized. Singapore, Japan, and Israel are already among the world's most urbanized nations; South Korea's urban population was 21 percent in 1950, has passed 80 percent, and may reach 90 percent around 2025. By then, over half of all Asians are likely to be city dwellers. Already, six of the world's ten largest cities are located in Asia, three of them in India.

Population Patterns

Improvements in agricultural output and medical services greatly enhanced life expectancy in Asia during the 20th century, resulting in a population explosion. Between 1950 and the beginning of the 21st century, the population almost tripled, and it is expected to reach close to 5 billion by 2030. Despite this, great swathes of Asia remain virtually uninhabited, including Siberia, the barren Plateau of Tibet, and the deserts of Central Asia and the Arabian Peninsula. The bulk of the population is concentrated in the south and east, with especially high densities occurring along major rivers such as the Ganges, Yangtze, and Yellow, along the south and east coasts, and on the principal islands of the Japanese and Indonesian archipelagoes. Populations are also dense in fertile pockets of the southwest.

FLASHPOINTS

Religious rivalries underpin many conflicts in Asia. Other causes include ideological schisms, such as the one that divides Korea in two; territorial disputes; independence movements; and internal rebellions against authoritarian governments.

Palestine

Proclaimed in 1948 in predominantly Arab Palestine, the Jewish state of Israel expanded as a result of territorial gains made in a series of wars (in 1948, 1967, and 1973). This displaced thousands of Palestinian people and has led to almost continuous conflict. Palestinians seek restoration of occupied territories and the creation of their own state. Israel has used military might to quash uprisings and often-violent protests.

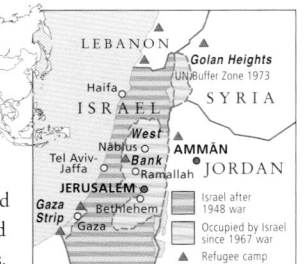

Kashmir

In 1947, the partition of British India created the Islamic state of Pakistan and the predominantly Hindu nation of India. The mainly Muslim state of Kashmir became part of India, but has been claimed by Pakistan ever since, resulting in two wars (1947–48 and 1967) and regular border skirmishes. A Kashmiri separatist movement, opposed by both India and Pakistan, has also conducted a guerilla campaign in recent years.

Korea

The Korean War of 1950–53 led to the creation of communist North Korea and democratic South Korea, and the demilitarized zone (DMZ) that separates them. About 151 miles (243 km) long and 2.5 miles (4 km) wide, it is guarded by 1.1 million soldiers on the North Korean side and, to the south, by 650,000 South Korean and 37,000 U.S. troops. Regular military exercises in the area keep tensions high.

Association of Southeast Asian Nations

Founder members

Subsequent members

Since the mid-19th century, Asian countries have been heavily reliant on exports to Western nations and have often competed for lucrative markets. Greater intraregional economic cooperation has developed only since the 1960s. Aside from international associations formed by traders in the same commodities, few formal bodies have emerged. By far the most significant is the Association of Southeast Asian Nations, or ASEAN. Founded in 1967, it now has ten members—Indonesia, Thailand, Malaysia, the Philippines, Singapore, Brunei, Vietnam, Laos, Myanmar (Burma), and Cambodia. It aims to promote trade between members in order to strengthen economic growth and political stability.

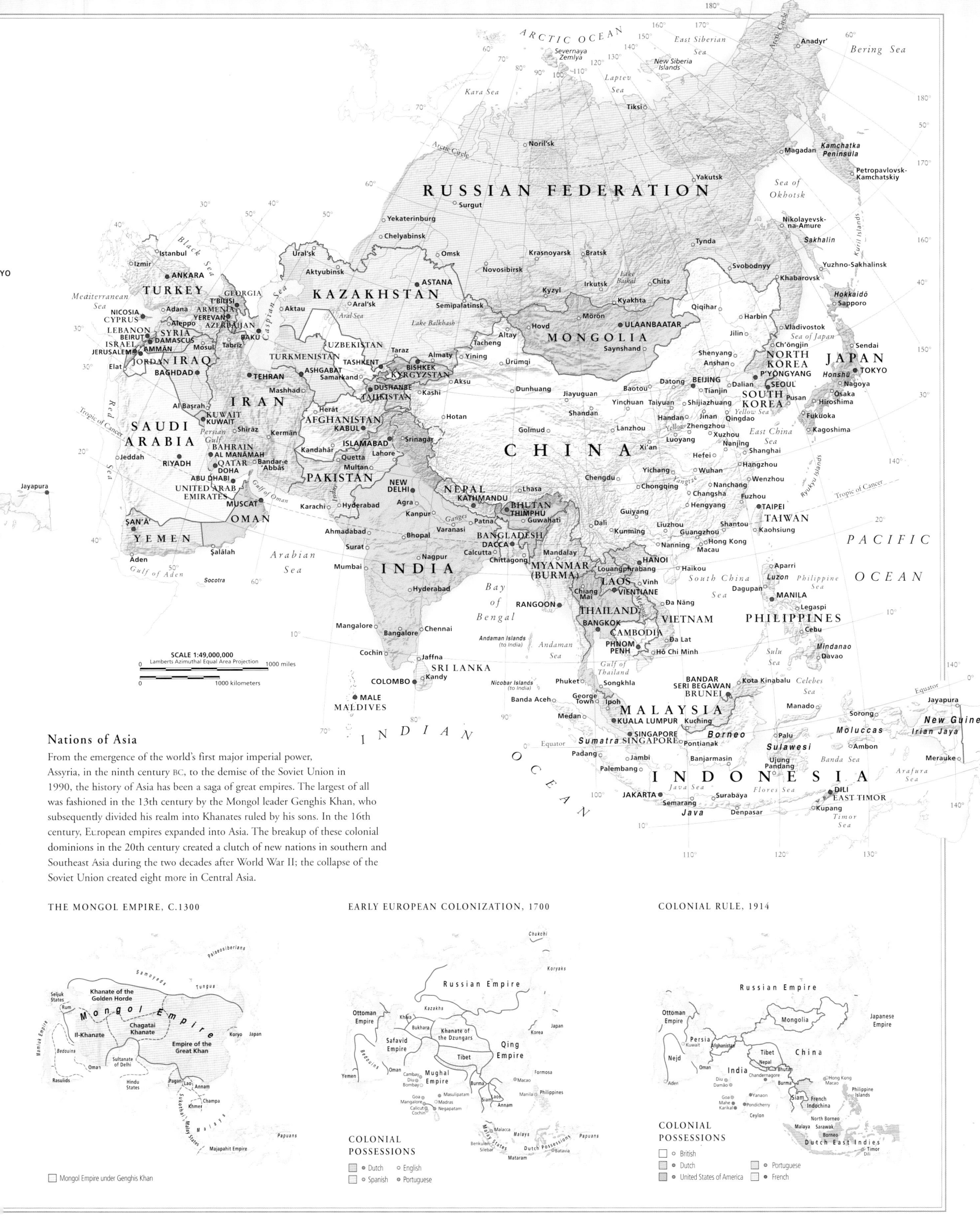

Nations of Asia

From the emergence of the world's first major imperial power, Assyria, in the ninth century BC, to the demise of the Soviet Union in 1990, the history of Asia has been a saga of great empires. The largest of all was fashioned in the 13th century by the Mongol leader Genghis Khan, who subsequently divided his realm into Khanates ruled by his sons. In the 16th century, European empires expanded into Asia. The breakup of these colonial dominions in the 20th century created a clutch of new nations in southern and Southeast Asia during the two decades after World War II; the collapse of the Soviet Union created eight more in Central Asia.

THE MONGOL EMPIRE, C.1300

EARLY EUROPEAN COLONIZATION, 1700

COLONIAL RULE, 1914

Mongol Empire under Genghis Khan

COLONIAL POSSESSIONS
Dutch   English
Spanish   Portuguese

COLONIAL POSSESSIONS
British   Portuguese
Dutch   French
United States of America

The Human Impact

Human transformation of the landscape and harnessing of natural resources first occurred on a large scale in Asia. The world's earliest agricultural settlements evolved in the Fertile Crescent region of Southwest Asia, where wheat, olives, peas, goats, and sheep were domesticated more than 10,000 years ago. About 9,000 years ago, farmers in eastern China began to cultivate rice and millet and rear pigs and silkworms. In turn, these settlements became the world's first cities. Southwest Asia and China remained centers of innovation, and from antiquity until the 15th century the flow of ideas and technology was mainly from Asia to Europe. Western interest in Asian technology led to the establishment of arteries of trade such as the Silk Road and the eventual European colonization of much of the continent. The colonial rulers accelerated land clearance, principally to permit the cultivation of plantation crops for export to the West. Steady industrialization and explosive population growth in the 20th century exerted even greater pressure on land and resources, resulting in widespread deforestation, land degradation, and pollution.

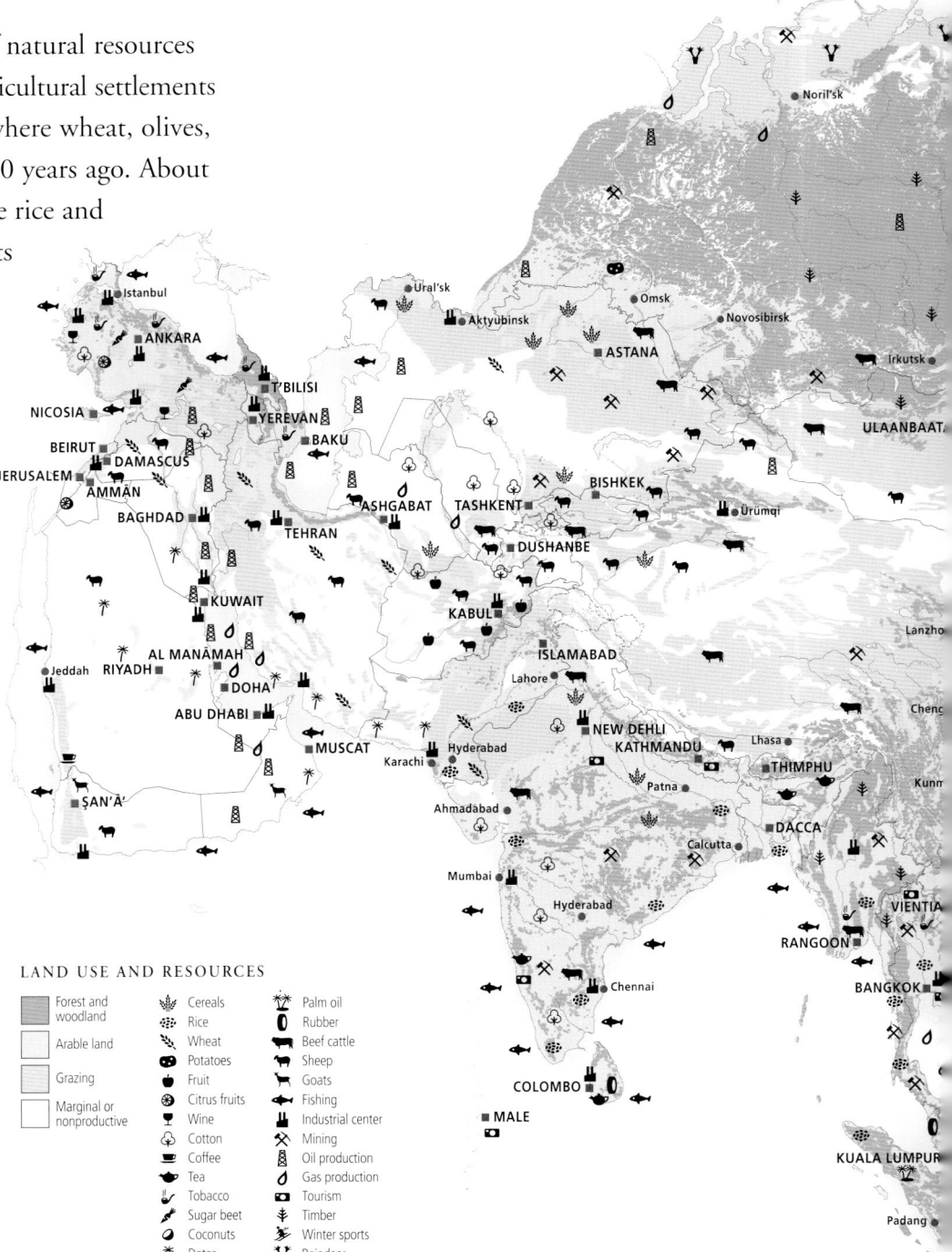

LAND USE AND RESOURCES

- Forest and woodland
- Arable land
- Grazing
- Marginal or nonproductive

- Cereals
- Rice
- Wheat
- Potatoes
- Fruit
- Citrus fruits
- Wine
- Cotton
- Coffee
- Tea
- Tobacco
- Sugar beet
- Coconuts
- Dates

- Palm oil
- Rubber
- Beef cattle
- Sheep
- Goats
- Fishing
- Industrial center
- Mining
- Oil production
- Gas production
- Tourism
- Timber
- Winter sports
- Reindeer

The Changing Face of Asia

The Aral Sea

About 85 percent of Asia's water is used for farming and the continent has two-thirds of all irrigated land. The creation of vast irrigation systems has had a catastrophic effect on river basins, most notably in Central Asia. The Aral Sea was once the world's fourth-largest inland sea and had a thriving fishing industry. In the 1960s, the Soviet Union began diverting the rivers that fed the sea, the Amudar'ya and Syrdar'ya, to irrigate cotton fields. Since then, the sea has shrunk to 15 percent of its former volume. Evaporation has raised salinity levels, and pesticides used by farmers have contaminated the remaining waters, decimating marine life. Salt- and chemical-laden sands from the shore have been blown across surrounding land, poisoning plants, animals, and humans. Efforts have been made to raise the sea's water level, but the damage is thought to be irreversible.

DEPLETION OF THE ARAL SEA, 1960–2002

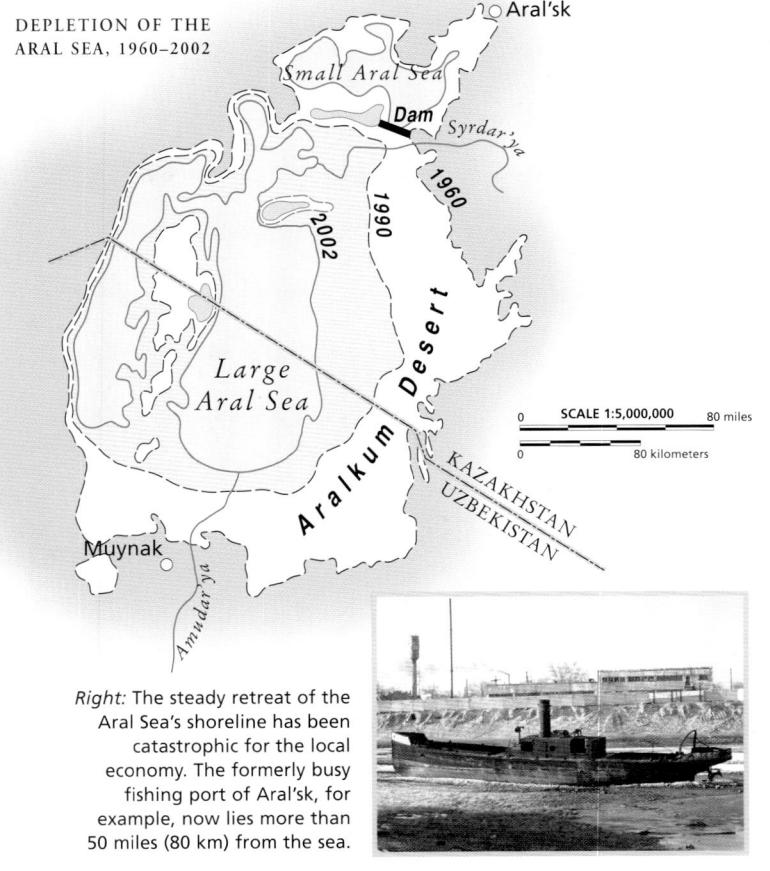

SCALE 1:5,000,000

Right: The steady retreat of the Aral Sea's shoreline has been catastrophic for the local economy. The formerly busy fishing port of Aral'sk, for example, now lies more than 50 miles (80 km) from the sea.

Economic Profile

From the subsistence-agriculture economies of Afghanistan, Bhutan, and Nepal to the sophisticated, technology-driven societies of Japan and South Korea, Asian countries have attained disparate levels of development. These have been determined by a range of factors, including resource distribution, foreign investment, conflicts, and governing ideologies. Asia harbors two-thirds of the world's known reserves of oil and gas, concentrated in Siberia and the Arabian Peninsula, and 60 percent of the world's coal, found mainly in China, Siberia, and India. It also supplies 60 percent of the world's tin, most of it coming from Southeast Asia. Russia has immense stands of timber and Southeast Asia is endowed with valuable hardwoods such as teak and mahogany, though supplies are dwindling. More than half of the population, however, still depends on farming. Rice is the main staple crop, though wheat predominates in the north. Services and industries are becoming more significant, but heavy industry is confined mainly to Japan, China, and India. More widespread light industries are based on food processing, the manufacture of textiles and pharmaceuticals, and tourism.

Land Cover

The world's largest conifer forests still cloak much of Siberia, though huge swathes of forest have been cleared elsewhere. Arable land covers a large area, but has to support some of the highest population densities on Earth. Extensive barren areas, including the Plateau of Tibet, the deserts of Central Asia, and the arctic shoreline, make a large proportion of the continent unproductive.

PROPORTIONS OF TOTAL LAND AREA

- Forest and woodland — 28.6%
- Arable land — 18.0%
- Grazing — 17.6%
- Other land — 35.8%

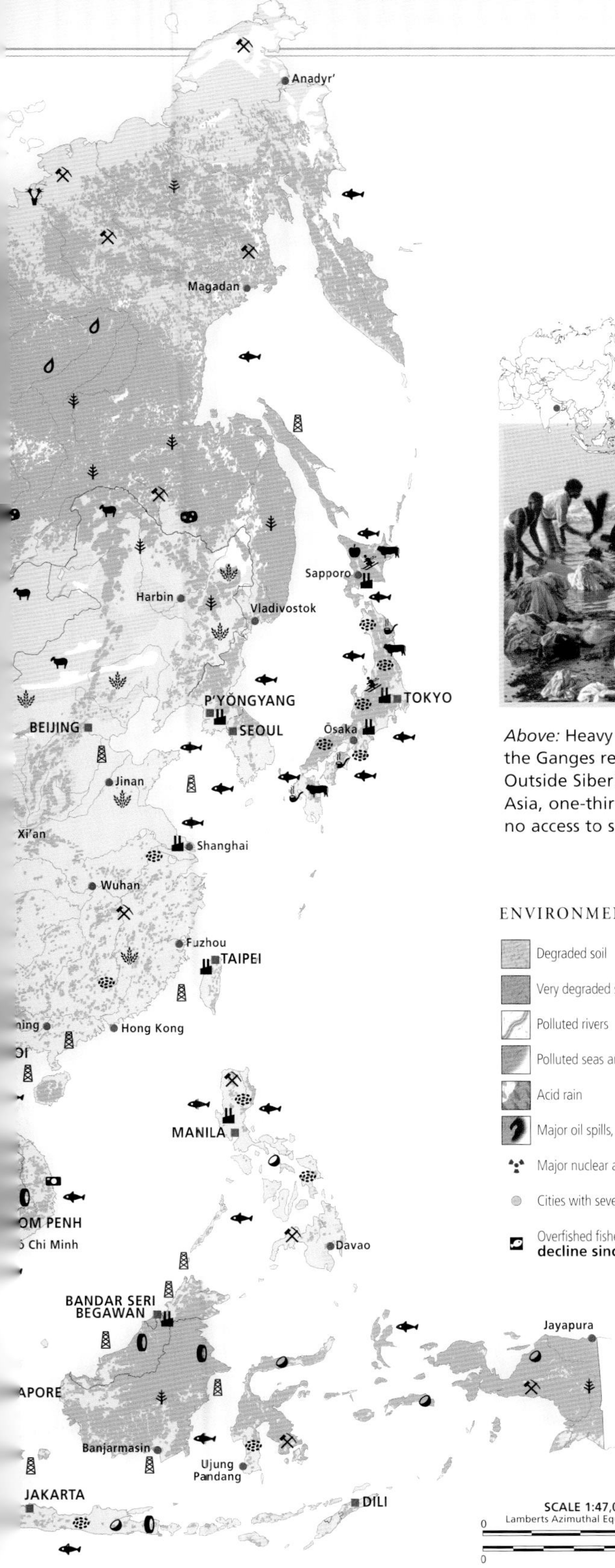

Right: Russia has decommissioned over 150 nuclear submarines. But few have been dismantled and most lie rusting in Arctic and eastern ports, posing a potential threat to the environment.

Above: The growth of aquaculture has led to habitat loss. About 60 percent of Asia's mangroves have been converted to shrimp ponds.

Above: Heavy use of rivers such as the Ganges reduces water quality. Outside Siberia and Southwest Asia, one-third of people have no access to safe drinking water.

ENVIRONMENTAL ISSUES

- Degraded soil
- Very degraded soil
- Polluted rivers
- Polluted seas and lakes
- Acid rain
- Major oil spills, **year**
- Major nuclear accidents, *year*
- Cities with severe air pollution
- Overfished fishery, *year of peak catch*, **decline since peak catch**

SCALE 1:47,000,000
Lamberts Azimuthal Equal Area Projection

0   1000 miles

0   1000 kilometers

Threats to the Environment

A desire to cater for impoverished, rapidly expanding populations is at the root of much recent environmental degradation in Asia, which has been compounded by neglect and failure to implement protective legislation. Intensive farming practices have increased agricultural output dramatically, but have also led to severe land degradation and water pollution. About 20 percent of vegetated land is degraded and more than half of drylands are affected by desertification. The continent also has some of the world's most polluted rivers. Demand for cultivable land has resulted in the virtual disappearance of Southeast Asia's species-rich lowland rain forests, while heavy logging has begun to threaten the integrity of Siberia's vast frontier forests (which could in turn contribute to global warming). Industrialization has invigorated local economies, especially in Japan, South Korea, Russia, China, Malaysia, Thailand, and India, but has also created some of the world's worst levels of air pollution and given rise to widespread acid rain.

Protecting the Environment

In western and Central Asia, a range of strategies has been implemented to combat the widespread problems of land degradation and desertification, including reforestation, sand-dune stabilization, and soil-fertility restoration programs. Japan has had notable success in reducing air pollution, and other governments are following its lead. In Nepal and Pakistan, for instance, users of gas- or battery-operated vehicles receive tax rebates, and the Indian city of Delhi has converted all its public transport to gas. Asian countries are at the forefront of reforestation: for example, China increased its forest coverage by more than 3.5 percent between 1993 and 2000. Large World Heritage areas have recently been designated in Siberia, and the number of protected areas is growing. However the overall proportion of land protected (3.7%) is low.

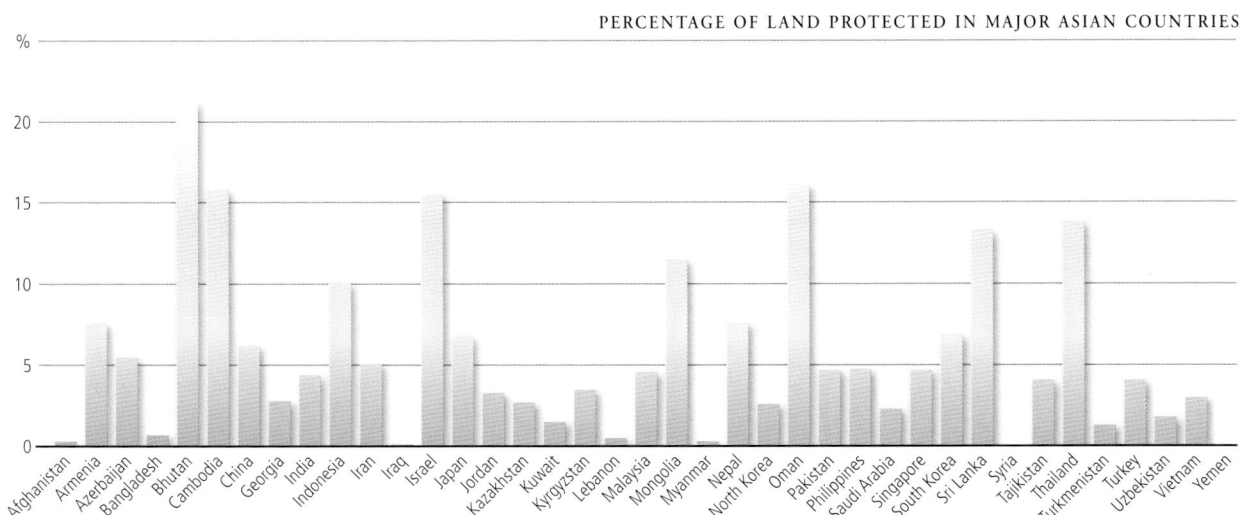

PERCENTAGE OF LAND PROTECTED IN MAJOR ASIAN COUNTRIES

TURKEY, CYPRUS, AND TRANSCAUCASIA

Armenia, Azerbaijan, Cyprus, Georgia, Turkey

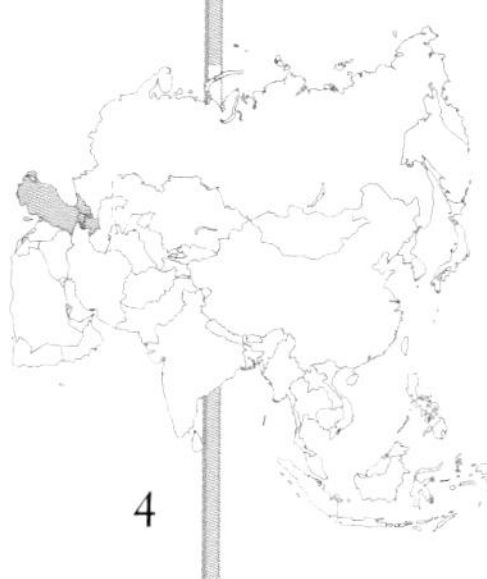

Projecting westward from the Middle East, Turkey forms a land bridge between Europe and Asia. Divided by the Bosporus, it straddles the two continents, its small region of Eastern Thrace lying within Europe and the remainder of the country, Anatolia, forming Asia's westernmost edge. An arid plateau covers much of Anatolia's interior, giving way in the east to a series of ranges that extends into Transcaucasia. Here, the towering Caucasus form another natural boundary between Asia and Europe. Three nations occupy Transcaucasia: Armenia, Azerbaijan, and Georgia. All became Soviet republics in the 20th century before attaining independence in 1991. Turkey was the heart of the Ottoman Empire, which endured from the 12th century to the early 20th century, and from 1573 to 1878 included the mainly Greek island of Cyprus.

THE CAUCASUS

The Caucasus and the associated Lesser Caucasus mountains isolate and define the region known as Transcaucasia. The much higher Caucasus peaks form a great wall that runs from the Black Sea to the shores of the Caspian Sea and reaches Europe's highest point of 18,510 feet (5,642 m) at Elbrus in Russia. The Lesser Caucasus spread to the south across Armenia, merging with the ranges of eastern Turkey. In-between are lowlands and major river valleys, including the Kür–Aras lowlands of Azerbaijan, parts of which lie below sea level.

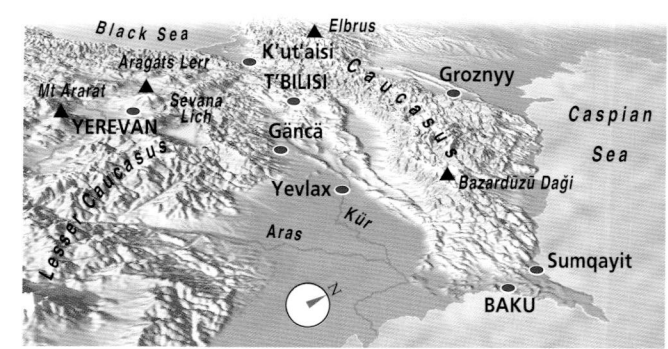

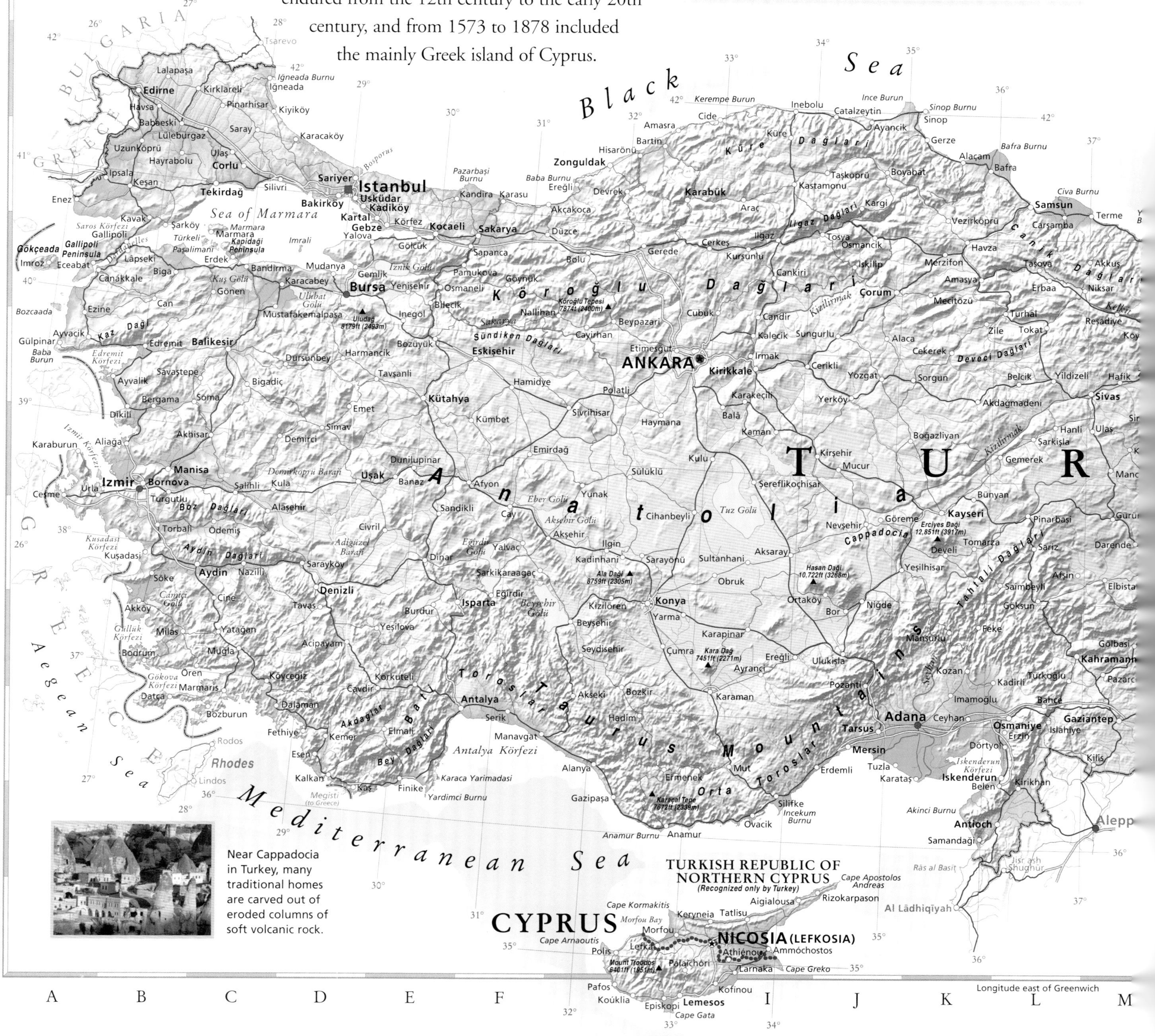

Near Cappadocia in Turkey, many traditional homes are carved out of eroded columns of soft volcanic rock.

TURKISH REPUBLIC OF NORTHERN CYPRUS
(Recognized only by Turkey)

CYPRUS

NICOSIA (LEFKOSIA)

Longitude east of Greenwich

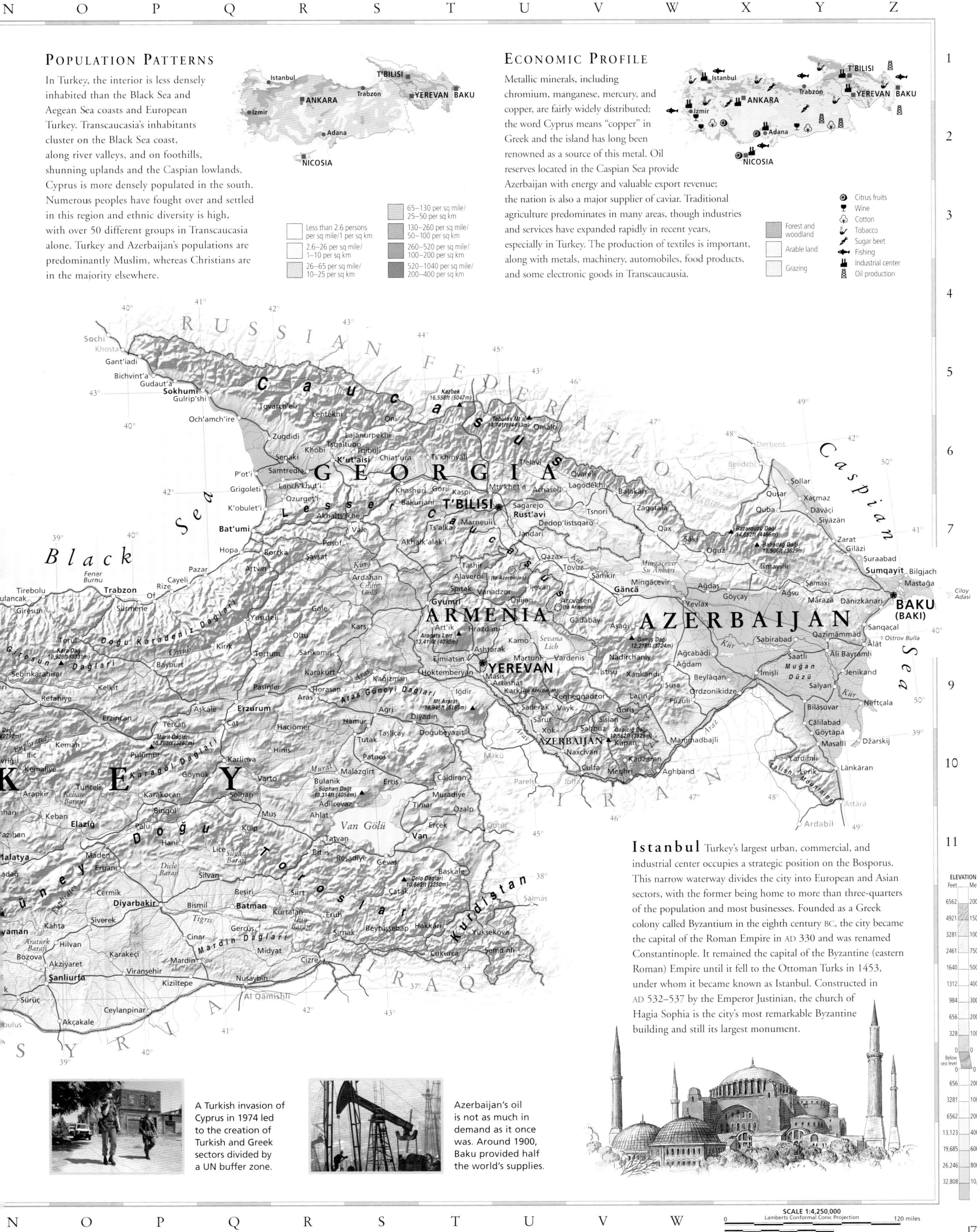

N O P Q R S T U V W X Y Z

POPULATION PATTERNS

In Turkey, the interior is less densely inhabited than the Black Sea and Aegean Sea coasts and European Turkey. Transcaucasia's inhabitants cluster on the Black Sea coast, along river valleys, and on foothills, shunning uplands and the Caspian lowlands. Cyprus is more densely populated in the south. Numerous peoples have fought over and settled in this region and ethnic diversity is high, with over 50 different groups in Transcaucasia alone. Turkey and Azerbaijan's populations are predominantly Muslim, whereas Christians are in the majority elsewhere.

Istanbul
ANKARA   T'BILISI
Trabzon   YEREVAN BAKU
İzmir
Adana
NICOSIA

Less than 2.6 persons per sq mile/1 per sq km
2.6–26 per sq mile/ 1–10 per sq km
26–65 per sq mile/ 10–25 per sq km
65–130 per sq mile/ 25–50 per sq km
130–260 per sq mile/ 50–100 per sq km
260–520 per sq mile/ 100–200 per sq km
520–1040 per sq mile/ 200–400 per sq km

ECONOMIC PROFILE

Metallic minerals, including chromium, manganese, mercury, and copper, are fairly widely distributed; the word Cyprus means "copper" in Greek and the island has long been renowned as a source of this metal. Oil reserves located in the Caspian Sea provide Azerbaijan with energy and valuable export revenue; the nation is also a major supplier of caviar. Traditional agriculture predominates in many areas, though industries and services have expanded rapidly in recent years, especially in Turkey. The production of textiles is important, along with metals, machinery, automobiles, food products, and some electronic goods in Transcaucausia.

Istanbul   T'BILISI
ANKARA   YEREVAN BAKU
İzmir   Trabzon
Adana
NICOSIA

Forest and woodland
Arable land
Grazing

Citrus fruits
Wine
Cotton
Tobacco
Sugar beet
Fishing
Industrial center
Oil production

Istanbul

Istanbul Turkey's largest urban, commercial, and industrial center occupies a strategic position on the Bosporus. This narrow waterway divides the city into European and Asian sectors, with the former being home to more than three-quarters of the population and most businesses. Founded as a Greek colony called Byzantium in the eighth century BC, the city became the capital of the Roman Empire in AD 330 and was renamed Constantinople. It remained the capital of the Byzantine (eastern Roman) Empire until it fell to the Ottoman Turks in 1453, under whom it became known as Istanbul. Constructed in AD 532–537 by the Emperor Justinian, the church of Hagia Sophia is the city's most remarkable Byzantine building and still its largest monument.

A Turkish invasion of Cyprus in 1974 led to the creation of Turkish and Greek sectors divided by a UN buffer zone.

Azerbaijan's oil is not as much in demand as it once was. Around 1900, Baku provided half the world's supplies.

ELEVATION
Feet	Meters
6562	2000
4921	1500
3281	1000
2461	750
1640	500
1312	400
984	300
656	200
328	100
0	0
Below sea level	
656	200
3281	1000
6562	2000
13,123	4000
19,685	6000
26,246	8000
32,808	10,000

SCALE 1:4,250,000
Lamberts Conformal Conic Projection
0   120 miles
0   120 kilometers

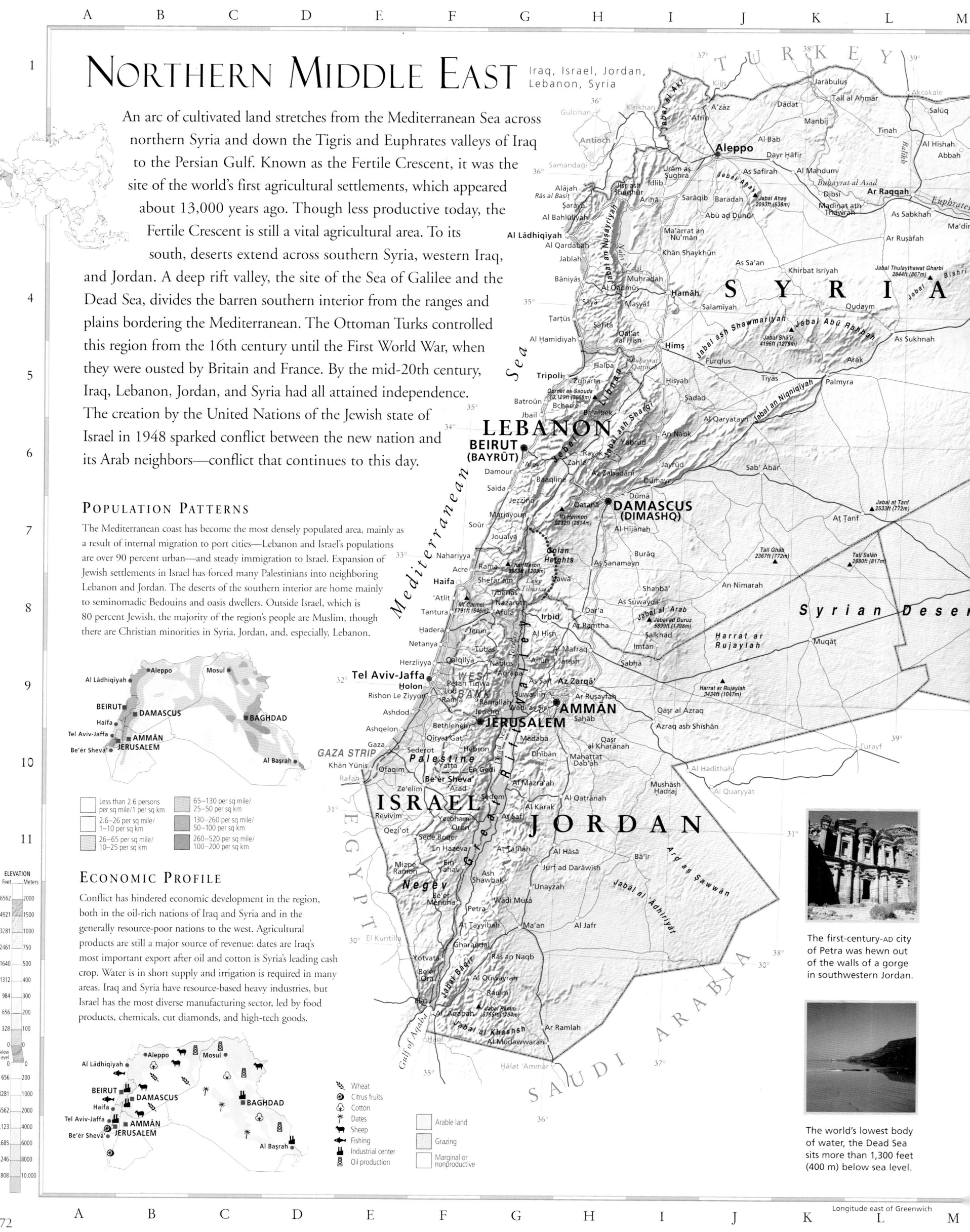

NORTHERN MIDDLE EAST

Iraq, Israel, Jordan, Lebanon, Syria

An arc of cultivated land stretches from the Mediterranean Sea across northern Syria and down the Tigris and Euphrates valleys of Iraq to the Persian Gulf. Known as the Fertile Crescent, it was the site of the world's first agricultural settlements, which appeared about 13,000 years ago. Though less productive today, the Fertile Crescent is still a vital agricultural area. To its south, deserts extend across southern Syria, western Iraq, and Jordan. A deep rift valley, the site of the Sea of Galilee and the Dead Sea, divides the barren southern interior from the ranges and plains bordering the Mediterranean. The Ottoman Turks controlled this region from the 16th century until the First World War, when they were ousted by Britain and France. By the mid-20th century, Iraq, Lebanon, Jordan, and Syria had all attained independence. The creation by the United Nations of the Jewish state of Israel in 1948 sparked conflict between the new nation and its Arab neighbors—conflict that continues to this day.

POPULATION PATTERNS

The Mediterranean coast has become the most densely populated area, mainly as a result of internal migration to port cities—Lebanon and Israel's populations are over 90 percent urban—and steady immigration to Israel. Expansion of Jewish settlements in Israel has forced many Palestinians into neighboring Lebanon and Jordan. The deserts of the southern interior are home mainly to seminomadic Bedouins and oasis dwellers. Outside Israel, which is 80 percent Jewish, the majority of the region's people are Muslim, though there are Christian minorities in Syria, Jordan, and, especially, Lebanon.

Less than 2.6 persons per sq mile/1 per sq km
2.6–26 per sq mile/ 1–10 per sq km
26–65 per sq mile/ 10–25 per sq km
65–130 per sq mile/ 25–50 per sq km
130–260 per sq mile/ 50–100 per sq km
260–520 per sq mile/ 100–200 per sq km

ECONOMIC PROFILE

Conflict has hindered economic development in the region, both in the oil-rich nations of Iraq and Syria and in the generally resource-poor nations to the west. Agricultural products are still a major source of revenue: dates are Iraq's most important export after oil and cotton is Syria's leading cash crop. Water is in short supply and irrigation is required in many areas. Iraq and Syria have resource-based heavy industries, but Israel has the most diverse manufacturing sector, led by food products, chemicals, cut diamonds, and high-tech goods.

ELEVATION
Feet / Meters
6562 / 2000
4921 / 1500
3281 / 1000
2461 / 750
1640 / 500
1312 / 400
984 / 300
656 / 200
328 / 100
0 / 0
Below sea level
656 / 200
3281 / 1000
6562 / 2000
13,123 / 4000
19,685 / 6000
26,246 / 8000
32,808 / 10,000

Wheat
Citrus fruits
Cotton
Dates
Sheep
Fishing
Industrial center
Oil production

Arable land
Grazing
Marginal or nonproductive

The first-century-AD city of Petra was hewn out of the walls of a gorge in southwestern Jordan.

The world's lowest body of water, the Dead Sea sits more than 1,300 feet (400 m) below sea level.

Longitude east of Greenwich

N O P 41° 42° Q 43° R 44° S T U 45° V W X 46° Y Z

TURKEY

Cizre

Nusaybin

Al Qāmishlī
Jāghir Bazār
Ra's al 'Ayn
Tall Baydar
Tall Tamir
bal Abd al Azīz
3018ft (920m)
Ghūnā
Ash Shaddādah
Fedghāmī
Al Hasakah
Kubaybāt
Khān as Sūr
Al Bādī
Al Ba'āj
Wardiyah
Al Hadr

Zākhō
Al Amādīyah
Amādiyah
Dahūk
Summēl
Zibār
Zēbār
Birkim
'Aqrah
Rawāndiz
Sar-i Kōrawa
16,994ft (3351m)
Safahuddīn
Rānya
Qala Dīza
Kuh-e Dalī Ebrāhīm
11,811ft (3600m)

Mosul
Arbīl
Guwēr
Qosh Tepe
Koi Sanjaq
Qayyārah
Makhmūr
Ash Sharqāt
Altin Köprü
Taqtaq
Sūrdāsh

As Sulaymānīyah
Penjwin
Chamchamal
Kirkūk
Arbat
Halabja
Tāza Khurmātū
Qādir Karam
Dāqūq

Al Malikīyah
Qaratshuk
Tall Kūjik
Tall 'Uwaynāt
Tall Huqnah
Tall Kayf
Tall 'Afar
Hammān al 'Alīl
Sinjār

Jabal Sinjār

Al Jazīrah

Wadi ath Tharthar
Little Zab
Great Zab
Tigris

Al Fathah
Pārapāra
Jabal Hamrīn
Tūz Khurmātū
Sulaymān Beg
Kifrī
Kalār

Bayjī
Sāmarrā'
Balad
Ad Dawr
Tikrīt
Qara Tepe
Jalawlā
Khanaqīn

Qasr-e Shirin

Sābiyah
Tibnī
Dayr az Zawr
Al Buşayrah
Al Mayādīn
Al 'Ashārah
Abū Hardan
As Sayyāl
Abū Kamāl
Anka
Rāwah
'Anah
Al Qā'im
Fuhaymī
Al Hadīthah
Tharthar
Khān al Baghdādī
Saniyah
Hīt
Kubaysah
Muhaywir
Ubaylah
Ar Rutbah
Akāshat
'Ab

Euphrates

Wadi Hawrān

I R A Q

Buhayrat ath Tharthar

Ar Ramādī
Al Habbānīyah
Kādhimain
Khān al Mashāhidah
Al Fallūjah
Hawr al Habbānīyah
Abū al Jir
Al Mahmūdīyah

BAGHDAD (BAGHDĀD)
Husayn al Ghafūs
Salmān Pāk
Sarābādī

Al Muqdādīyah
Diltāwa
Al Khālis
Ba'qūbah
Mandalī
Balad Rūz
Imām Hamid
Shandrūkh
Badrah
Mehrān

IRAN

Tursāq
Jaşşān

Bagsaya
Mūlat al Mashkhūr
Shaykh Sa'd
'Ali al Gharbī
Shaykh Jūwī
Marhaj Kahlīl
Al Kumayt
Someydeh
Al Halfāyah
Al 'Amārah

Ar Raḥḥālīyah
Buhayrat ar Razāzah
Saddat al Hindīyah
Karbalā'
Al Hindīyah
Al Hillah
Bi'r Sābil
Al Hāshimīyah
Khān al Muşallā
Al Kifl
An Nukhayb
At Taqtaqānah
Al Kūfah
Khān Jadwal
An Najaf
Abū Sukhayr
Al Ghammās
Khān ar Rahbah
Judaidat al Hamir

As Suwayrah
An Nu'mānīyah
'Alī
Hājī Muhsin
Arab Abdullah
Al Kūt
Ishaq
Ad Daghgharah
'Afak
Ad Dīwānīyah
Tahrīr
Fajīr
Imām al Hamzah
Ash Shanāfiyah
Ar Rumaythah
An Naşr
Tarād al Kahf
Telloh
Ar Rifā'ī
An Naşr
Ash Shatrah
Al Muwaffaqīyah
Al Hayy
Musallam
Qal'at Sukkār
Qal'at Şālih

Hawr as Sa'dīyah

Tigris
Sūsangerd

Al 'Uzayr

Al Ma'ānīyah
Ash Shabakah
As Samāwah
Al Khidr
As Salmān
Al Qusayr
Qal'at Abū Ghar
Nişāb

Ar Rihab
Euphrates
An Nāşirīyah
Al Qurnah
Kharfīyah
Aradah
Al Muzayri'ah
Sūq ash Shuyūkh
Ad Dayr
Tall al Lahm
Jalībah
Al Ma'qil
Al Başrah
Shu'aiba
Az Zubayr
Rumaila
Safwān
Umm Qasr
Al Busayyah

Khorramshahr
Abādān
Shatt al Arab

Sahrā' al Hijāra
Zahrat al Batn
Al Haniyah
Wadi al Bātin

SAUDI ARABIA

KUWAIT
KUWAIT (AL KUWAYT)

Raudhatain
Bubiyān Island
Al Fāw
Persian Gulf

Ash Shu'bah

29° 30° 31° 32° 33° 34° 35° 36° 37°

1 2 3 4 5 6 7 8 9 10 11 12 13 14 15

Elat in Israel is a popular center for divers exploring the wonders of the Red Sea's extensive coral reefs.

The capital of Lebanon, Beirut was ravaged by civil war between 1975 and 1990, and is just starting to recover.

The Great Ziggurat of Ur is one of the best-preserved parts of the ancient city of Ur, near An Nāşirīyah in Iraq.

Jerusalem

Situated in a river valley linking the Mediterranean coast and the Dead Sea, the ancient city of Jerusalem is a place of pilgrimage for the adherents of three major faiths: Judaism, Christianity, and Islam. The Old City's many shrines reflect this diversity of beliefs, most notably around the Dome of the Rock. The oldest remaining Islamic temple and said to be the scene of Muhammad's ascension to heaven, it backs onto the Western Wall, the remains of a temple that constitute the most sacred site of Judaism. Nearby is the Church of the Holy Sepulchre, where Jesus is said to have been entombed before rising again.

Dome of the Rock

SCALE 1:3,250,000
Lamberts Conformal Conic Projection
0   100 miles
0   100 kilometers

THE ARABIAN PENINSULA

Bahrain, Kuwait, Oman, Qatar, Saudi Arabia, United Arab Emirates, Yemen

Consisting of a broad plateau that slopes downward from a western coastal escarpment to low-lying eastern plains, the Arabian Peninsula is bounded by the Red Sea to the west, the Persian Gulf and Gulf of Oman to the northeast, and the Gulf of Aden and Arabian Sea to the south. Its interior is one of the most arid areas on Earth. Treeless, stony plains and vast sand deserts cover thousands of square miles. Rainfall is meager, and water flows only after seasonal showers along otherwise dry stream beds known as wadis. The Ottoman Turks occupied the western fringe of the peninsula from the 16th century until the early 20th century; by then Britain had established several protectorates on the east coast. An Islamic sect called the Wahhabis, led by the Saudi dynasty, held the interior from the 18th century, eventually founding Saudi Arabia in 1932. The discovery of oil has brought great wealth to that nation, as well as to the so-called Gulf States of Kuwait, Bahrain, Qatar, the United Arab Emirates, and, to a lesser extent, Oman.

Mecca The birthplace of the prophet Muhammad, Mecca is the most sacred site for Muslims, who are obliged by their faith to make at least one visit to the city, a pilgrimage known as the hajj. Two million pilgrims arrive each year, thronging the city and its temples, especially the Al-Haram Mosque. It encircles the Kaaba, a cubic stone shrine said to have been built originally by Abraham and Ishmael as a representation of God's house in heaven.

POPULATION PATTERNS

The population is concentrated along the shoreline and in the marginally better-watered coastal ranges, with the fertile uplands of Yemen being the most densely inhabited zone. With the exception of the area around the Saudi capital of Riyadh, interior settlements are small and widely dispersed; most center on oases. The urban population is small in Yemen (26 percent) but large elsewhere, ranging from 78 percent in Oman to 96 percent in Kuwait. Culturally, the peninsula is homogenous, the vast majority of the inhabitants being Arab peoples who speak Arabic and follow Islam, which originated here.

Uninhabited

Less than 2.6 persons per sq mile/1 per sq km

2.6–26 per sq mile/1–10 per sq km

26–65 per sq mile/10–25 per sq km

65–130 per sq mile/25–50 per sq km

130–260 per sq mile/50–100 per sq km

ECONOMIC PROFILE

The Arabian Peninsula holds the world's largest petroleum reserves and enormous deposits of natural gas, and the oil and gas industries dominate the local economy. As well as a wide range of services including banking and printing, they support the manufacturing of metals, plastics, fertilizers, cement, and other products. Fossil fuels aside, however, the region is resource-poor. Only small pockets can be cultivated and many of these require irrigation. The major crops are dates and other fruits, coffee, and wheat. Sheep, goats, and camels are widely distributed, but have to graze over large areas to obtain sufficient food.

Arable land

Grazing

Marginal or nonproductive

Coffee
Dates
Sheep
Goats
Fishing
Industrial center
Oil production
Gas production

Petroleum was first located in Bahrain in 1932, and soon after in Saudi Arabia.

Longitude east of Greenwich

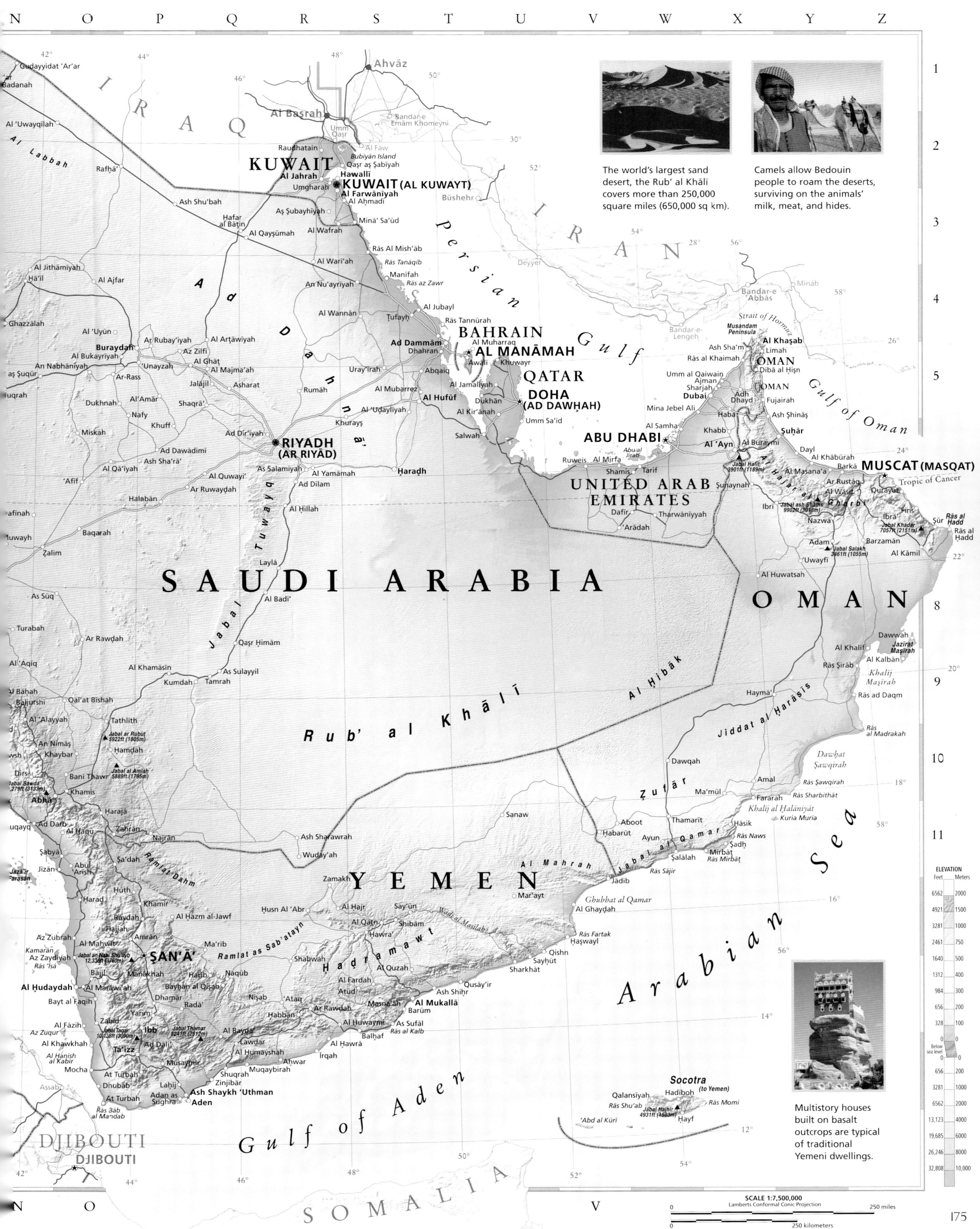

The world's largest sand desert, the Rub' al Khālī covers more than 250,000 square miles (650,000 sq km).

Camels allow Bedouin people to roam the deserts, surviving on the animals' milk, meat, and hides.

Multistory houses built on basalt outcrops are typical of traditional Yemeni dwellings.

SCALE 1:7,500,000
Lamberts Conformal Conic Projection

AFGHANISTAN, IRAN, AND PAKISTAN

A high, mainly barren plateau dominates the western half of this region, occupying most of Iran and extending into Afghanistan and Pakistan. It is bounded in the northwest by the forested Elburz Mountains and in the west by the Zagros Mountains. In northeastern Afghanistan, it rises to the lofty summits of the Hindu Kush and the Karakorams, offshoots of the Himalaya; in Pakistan, its crumpled eastern fringe abuts the broad, low valley of the Indus River. More than 97 percent of the inhabitants of this rugged and mostly arid land are Muslims, and their religion has profoundly influenced the region's history. Pakistan was founded in 1947 as a home for India's Muslims; Iran has been ruled by Islamic clerics since a revolution in 1979; and in the late 1990s Afghanistan was run by the Taliban, a fundamentalist Islamic regime that was toppled by a U.S.-led invasion in 2001.

Iran's Dasht-e Kavīr is characterized by vast stony plains and low-lying salt pans (*kavirs*).

Iranian carpets, most of which are still woven by hand, are much in demand overseas.

At 28,251 feet (8,611m), K2, in the Karakoram range, is the world's second-highest peak.

Thriving around 2500 BC, Mohenjo Daro, near Sukkur, Pakistan, was one of Indus Valley's first cities.

THE KHYBER PASS

One of just a few passes permitting travel between Central Asia and the Indian Subcontinent, the Khyber Pass has long been of strategic importance to locals and foreign powers, from the Persians, who used it to reach the Indus in the fifth century BC, to the British, who made it the focus of local operations in the late 19th century. Consisting of a narrow opening in the Safed Koh Range, the pass reaches its highest point of 3,543 feet (1,080 m) at Landi Kotal. Its road and rail links facilitate travel between Kabul in Afghanistan and Peshawar in Pakistan.

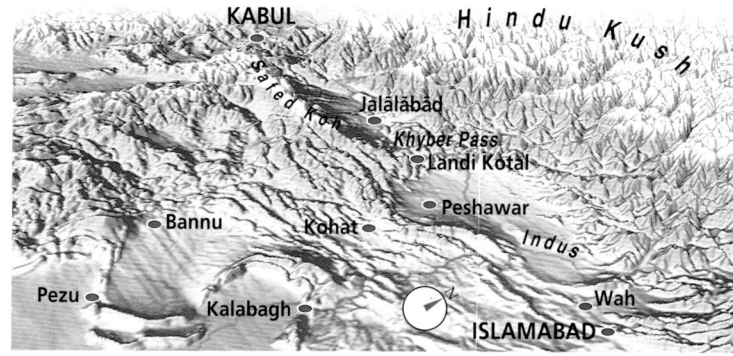

Longitude east of Greenwich

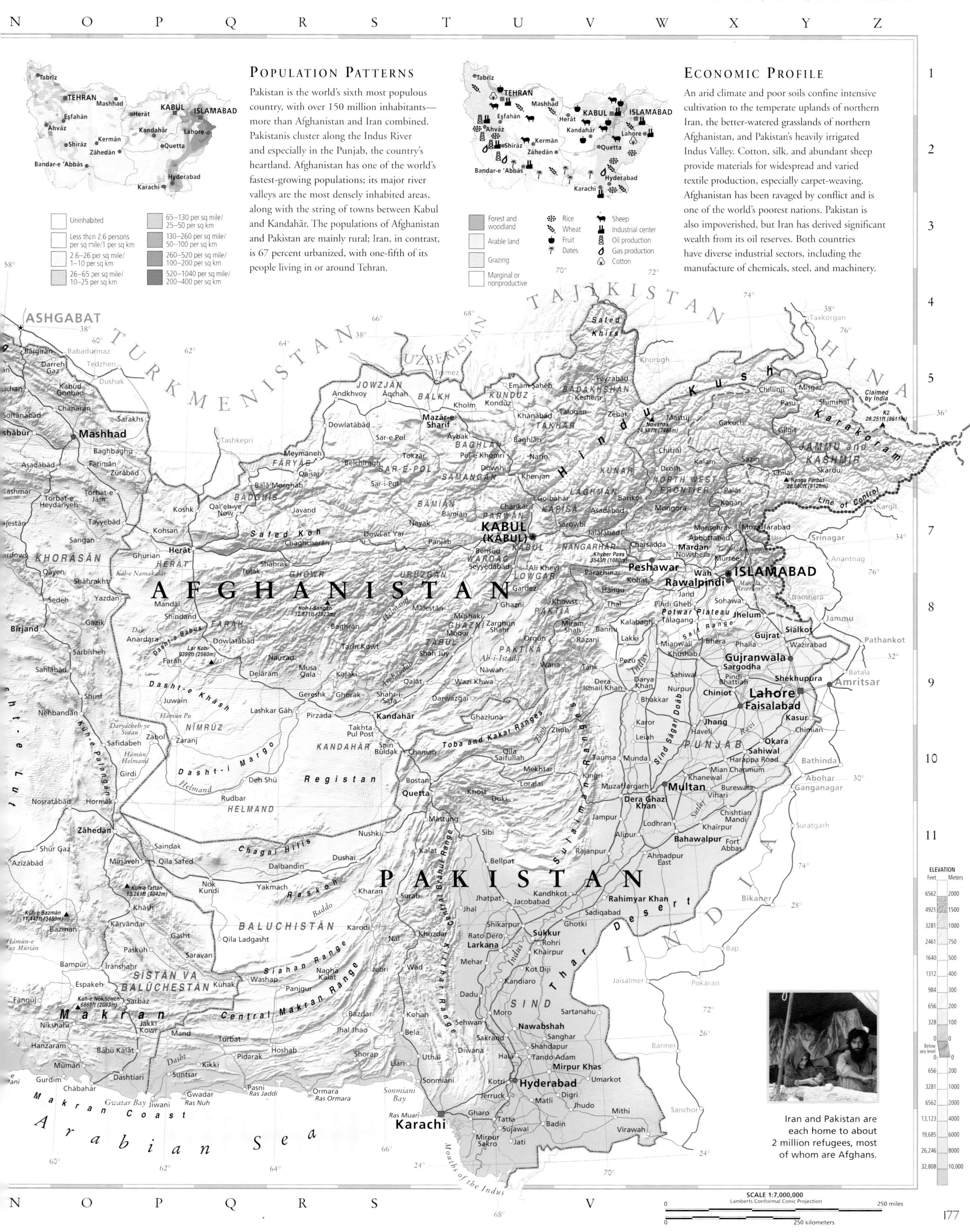

POPULATION PATTERNS

Pakistan is the world's sixth most populous country, with over 150 million inhabitants—more than Afghanistan and Iran combined. Pakistanis cluster along the Indus River and especially in the Punjab, the country's heartland. Afghanistan has one of the world's fastest-growing populations; its major river valleys are the most densely inhabited areas, along with the string of towns between Kabul and Kandahār. The populations of Afghanistan and Pakistan are mainly rural; Iran, in contrast, is 67 percent urbanized, with one-fifth of its people living in or around Tehran.

Uninhabited
Less than 2.6 persons per sq mile/1 per sq km
2.6–26 per sq mile/1–10 per sq km
26–65 per sq mile/10–25 per sq km
65–130 per sq mile/25–50 per sq km
130–260 per sq mile/50–100 per sq km
260–520 per sq mile/100–200 per sq km
520–1040 per sq mile/200–400 per sq km

ECONOMIC PROFILE

An arid climate and poor soils confine intensive cultivation to the temperate uplands of northern Iran, the better-watered grasslands of northern Afghanistan, and Pakistan's heavily irrigated Indus Valley. Cotton, silk, and abundant sheep provide materials for widespread and varied textile production, especially carpet-weaving. Afghanistan has been ravaged by conflict and is one of the world's poorest nations. Pakistan is also impoverished, but Iran has derived significant wealth from its oil reserves. Both countries have diverse industrial sectors, including the manufacture of chemicals, steel, and machinery.

Forest and woodland
Arable land
Grazing
Marginal or nonproductive
Rice
Wheat
Fruit
Dates
Sheep
Industrial center
Oil production
Gas production
Cotton

Iran and Pakistan are each home to about 2 million refugees, most of whom are Afghans.

ELEVATION
Feet / Meters
6562 / 2000
4921 / 1500
3281 / 1000
2461 / 750
1640 / 500
1312 / 400
984 / 300
656 / 200
328 / 100
0 / 0
Below sea level
656 / 200
3281 / 1000
6562 / 2000
13,123 / 4000
19,685 / 6000
26,246 / 8000
32,808 / 10,000

SCALE 1:7,000,000
Lamberts Conformal Conic Projection
250 miles
250 kilometers

CENTRAL ASIA
Kazakhstan, Kyrgyzstan, Tajikistan, Turkmenistan, Uzbekistan

The peoples of Central Asia have long been linked by a shared Islamic religious and cultural heritage, traditionally pastoral and seminomadic lifestyles, and related, mainly Turkic languages. During the 19th century, they were brought even closer together when their lands were annexed by the Russian Empire. Subsequent Soviet control transformed an undeveloped region, rapidly industrializing farming, manufacturing, and mining, turning several villages into cities, and creating separate republics for each of the major ethnic groups—the Uzbeks, Kazaks, Tajiks, Turkmens, and Kyrgyz. After the fall of communism in 1991, all five republics became independent states. These nations occupy a wide, mainly arid and low-lying region. The grasslands of the Kazakh Steppe stretch across its northern third, spreading into Russia. South of the Aral Sea, deserts cover the Turan Lowland. In the east, a series of ranges climbs toward the Pamir and Tien Shan ranges, whose soaring peaks divide Central Asia from China.

Cotton is Turkmenistan's principal crop. Production centers on irrigated areas along the Amudar'ya River.

Russia's spacecraft-launching center is near Baykonur in Kazakhstan.

POPULATION PATTERNS

The scarcity of fresh water has restricted dense settlement to upland areas and the banks of major rivers, leaving the deserts and grasslands sparsely inhabited. During the Soviet era, Central Asia's population grew rapidly, due partly to an influx of Russians and Ukrainians and partly to improvements in medical services. Despite this, Central Asian society remains predominantly rural; indeed, with the departure of many Russians after the demise of the Soviet Union, the continuing focus on cotton production, and high birth rates in country areas, rural populations have grown recently, against the prevailing world trend.

Less than 2.6 persons per sq mile/1 per sq km	130–260 per sq mile/ 50–100 per sq km
2.6–26 per sq mile/ 1–10 per sq km	260–520 per sq mile/ 100–200 per sq km
26–65 per sq mile/ 10–25 per sq km	520–1040 per sq mile/ 200–400 per sq km
65–130 per sq mile/ 25–50 per sq km	

ECONOMIC PROFILE

Central Asia's mineral reserves include oil and gas deposits near the Caspian Sea and supplies of coal, iron ore, and chromium in Kazakhstan; these support a variety of heavy industries. Three-fifths of the land is desert, and large areas are used for grazing. Crops can be grown only in fertile upland pockets and irrigated areas. Soviet emphasis on the production of coal and oil in Kazakhstan and cotton elsewhere not only created severe environmental problems, but left these nations dependent on just a few commodities. Recent expansion of the gas industry (Turkmenistan has the world's fifth-largest reserves) is part of an attempt to diversify produce and alleviate widespread poverty.

- Cereals
- Cotton
- Beef cattle
- Sheep
- Fishing
- Industrial center
- Mining
- Oil production
- Gas production
- Fruit and vegetables

- Forest and woodland
- Arable land
- Grazing
- Marginal or nonproductive

RUSSIAN FEDERATION

Ozinki · Kamenka · Ural'sk · Burlin · Ilek · Sol'-Iletsk · Orsk · Shil'da
Novouzensk · Kushum · Aksay · Chingirlau · Kransoyar · Martuk · Aktyubinsk · Komsomol'sk
ZAPADNYY KAZAKHSTAN · Bitik · Chapayevo · Zhympity · Khobda · Khromtau
Dzhanybek · Kaztalovka · Zhalpaktal · Dzhangala · Karatobe · Bestamak · Kandyagash · Zhuryn · Karabutak
Saykhin · Ozero Aralsor · Leninskoye · Taypak · Miyaly · Uil · Shubarkuduk
Ozero Itmurinkol' · Inderborskiy · Bayganin · Emba · Shakhty · Gory Mugodzhary
Kharabali · Ozero Inder · Sagiz · Zharkamys · Chelkar · Tog
Makhambet · Zhanterek · AKTYUBINSK
Novobogatinskoye · Dossor · Makat
Zhanbay · Atyrau · ATYRAU
Astrakhan' · Ganyushkino · Balykshi · Kul'sary
Karaton
Opornyy
Zaliv Komsomolets · Sarykamys
Ostrova Tyulen'i
Ostrov Kulaly · Beyneu
Mangyshlakskiy Zaliv · Kyushe
Mys Tyub-Karagan · Fort-Shevchenko · Karakalpakiya · Ostrov Vozrozhdeniya
Tauchik · Say-Utes · Aral Sea
Shetpe · Gora Besshoky 1821ft (555m)
Aktau · Ustyurt
Munayshy · QORAQALPOGHISTON RESPUBLIKASI
Mys Peschanyy · Kyzylsay · Plateau
Kuryk · Zhanaozen · Muynak · Kungrad
Fetisovo · MANGISTAU · Shumanay · Nukus
Kazakhskiy Zaliv · Keneurgench · Boldumsaz
Mys Sengirli · Akdepe · Dashkhovuz
Mys Suz · Sarykamyshskoye Ozero · DASHKHOVUZSKIY VELAYAT · Urge
Bekdash · Zaliv Kara-Bogaz-Gol · Gory Koymatdag · Chink Kaplankyr
Karabogazkel' · Karshi · Gory Akkyr
Darta · TURKMENISTA · Darvaza
Turkmenbashi · Gora Arlang 6168ft (1880m)
Krasnovodskiy Zaliv · Dzhebel · BALKANSKIY VELAYAT
Cheleken · Nebitdag · Gazandzhyk · Karakum Desert
Ostrov Ogurchinskiy · Gumdag · Danata · Yerbent
Turkmenskiy Zaliv · Bami · Bakhardok
Bugdayli · Gora Khasardag 5302ft (1616m) · AKHALSKIY VELAYA
Okarem · Madau · Kopetdag · Bakherden
Gora Tagarev 7358ft (2243m) · ASHGABAT
Esenguly · Gyzyletrek · Bojnurd · Babadurmaz · Tec
Gorgan · IRAN · Quchan · Dushak
Mashhad

Caspian Depression

Caspian Sea

Turan Lowland

Population map cities: Petropavlovsk · Ural'sk · Aktyubinsk · ASTANA · Ust'-Kamenogorsk · Kyzylorda · Dashkhovuz · TASHKENT · BISHKEK · ASHGABAT · DUSHANBE

Economic map cities: Petropavlovsk · Ural'sk · Aktyubinsk · ASTANA · Ust'-Kamenogorsk · Kyzylorda · Dashkhovuz · TASHKENT · BISHKEK · DUSHANBE · ASHGABAT

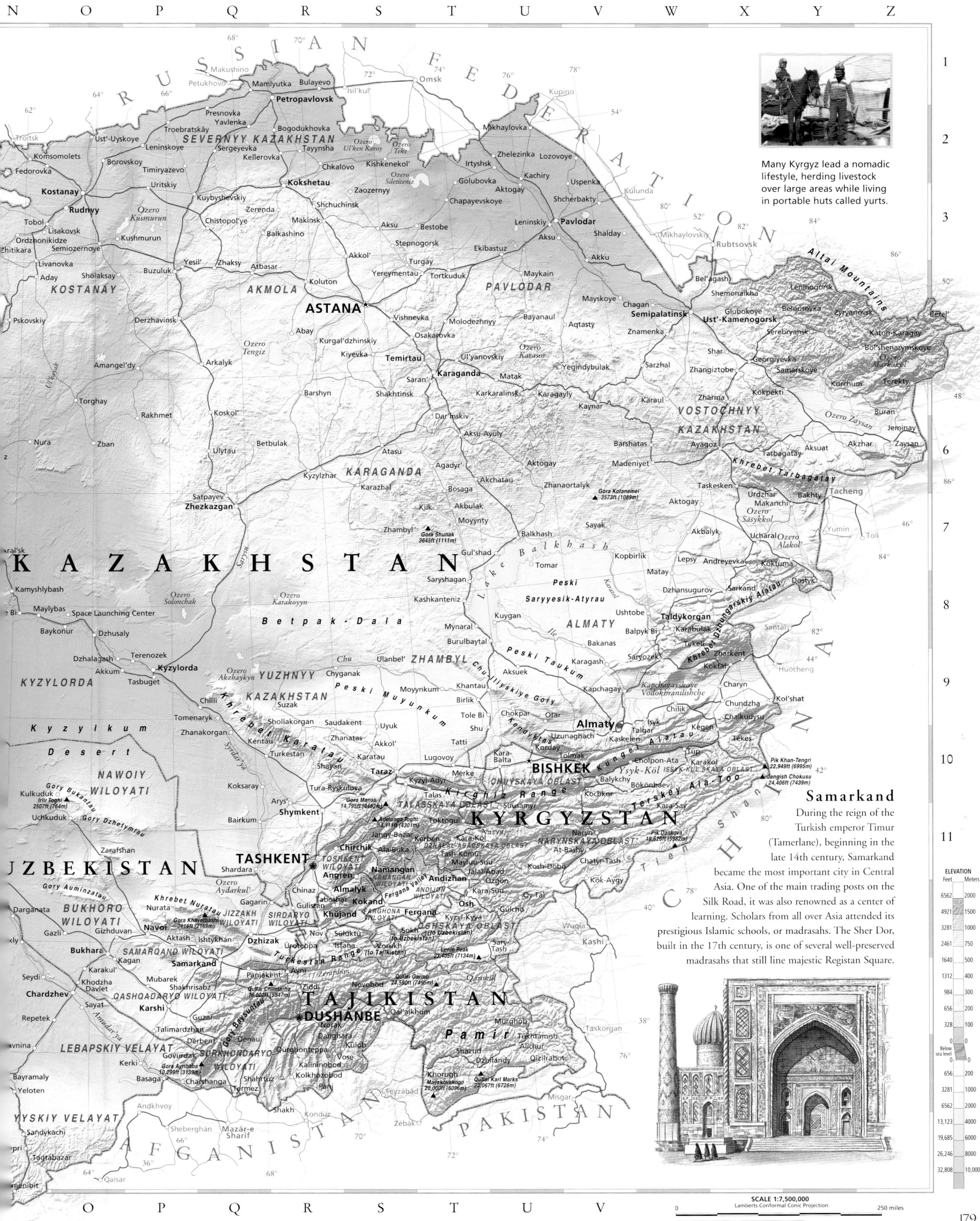

Many Kyrgyz lead a nomadic lifestyle, herding livestock over large areas while living in portable huts called yurts.

Samarkand

During the reign of the Turkish emperor Timur (Tamerlane), beginning in the late 14th century, Samarkand became the most important city in Central Asia. One of the main trading posts on the Silk Road, it was also renowned as a center of learning. Scholars from all over Asia attended its prestigious Islamic schools, or madrasahs. The Sher Dor, built in the 17th century, is one of several well-preserved madrasahs that still line majestic Registan Square.

SCALE 1:7,500,000
Lamberts Conformal Conic Projection

SOUTHERN ASIA
Bangladesh, Bhutan, India, Maldives, Nepal, Sri Lanka

Sometimes referred to as the Subcontinent, this region is dominated by India, the world's seventh-largest and second-most populous country. It also includes the Himalayan kingdoms of Nepal and Bhutan, low-lying Bangladesh, and the island nations of Sri Lanka and the Maldives. From their dizzy heights, the mountains of the Himalaya drop steeply to the wide, low plain of the Ganges River. West of the Gangetic Plain, the Thar Desert spreads into Pakistan; to the south, the triangular Deccan Plateau occupies most of central and southern India. In the early 16th century, much of Southern Asia was united by the Muslim Mughal dynasty, which ruled until it was undermined by the rise of the Hindu Marathas in the 18th century. Britain controlled most of the region from the early 19th century until 1948; before withdrawing, it created the states of West Pakistan and East Pakistan, which later became Pakistan and Bangladesh, and granted independence to Ceylon, now Sri Lanka.

POPULATION PATTERNS

More than one-sixth of the world's population lives in this region. India alone has more than 1 billion inhabitants and, given its growth rate—48,000 babies are born there every day—could surpass China as the world's most populous nation by 2050. High population densities occur on the Gangetic Plain and in the northeast—Bangladesh is one of the world's most densely populated countries—but only one-quarter of people live in cities. Most Indians and Nepalis are Hindu, whereas the majority of Bangladeshis are Muslim; Bhutan and Sri Lanka are predominantly Buddhist. Indigenous languages are many and varied, and English functions as a lingua franca.

ECONOMIC PROFILE

The region's enormous population places great strain on its resources, which include large tracts of arable land (including 50 percent of India), forests, and minerals—India has the world's fourth-largest coal reserves, and oil and gas fields have been tapped in many areas. Most people are dependent on agriculture, yet output is insufficient to support the population: half of all Nepalis live below the poverty line and one-quarter of Indians are undernourished. The industrial sector is little developed in Bhutan, Bangladesh, and Nepal, but becoming increasingly sophisticated in India and Sri Lanka, where products include textiles, chemicals, computer software, and machinery.

Tea is native to northeastern India. In the 19th century, the British greatly expanded its commercial cultivation.

In Sri Lanka, Tamil separatists have been waging war on the government since the 1980s.

Population density legend
- Uninhabited
- Less than .6 persons per sq mile/ per sq km
- 2.6–26 per sq mile/ 1–10 per sq km
- 26–65 per sq mile/ 10–25 per sq km
- 65–130 per sq mile/ 25–50 per sq km
- 130–260 per sq mile/ 50–100 per sq km
- 260–520 per sq mile/ 100–200 per sq km
- 520–1040 per sq mile/ 200–400 per sq km
- 1040–2080 per sq mile/ 400–800 per sq km
- More than 2080 per sq mile/800 per sq km

Land use / economic legend
- Forests and woodland
- Arable land
- Grazing
- Marginal or nonproductive
- Cereals
- Rice
- Cotton
- Tea
- Rubber
- Beef cattle
- Fishing
- Industrial center
- Mining
- Tourism

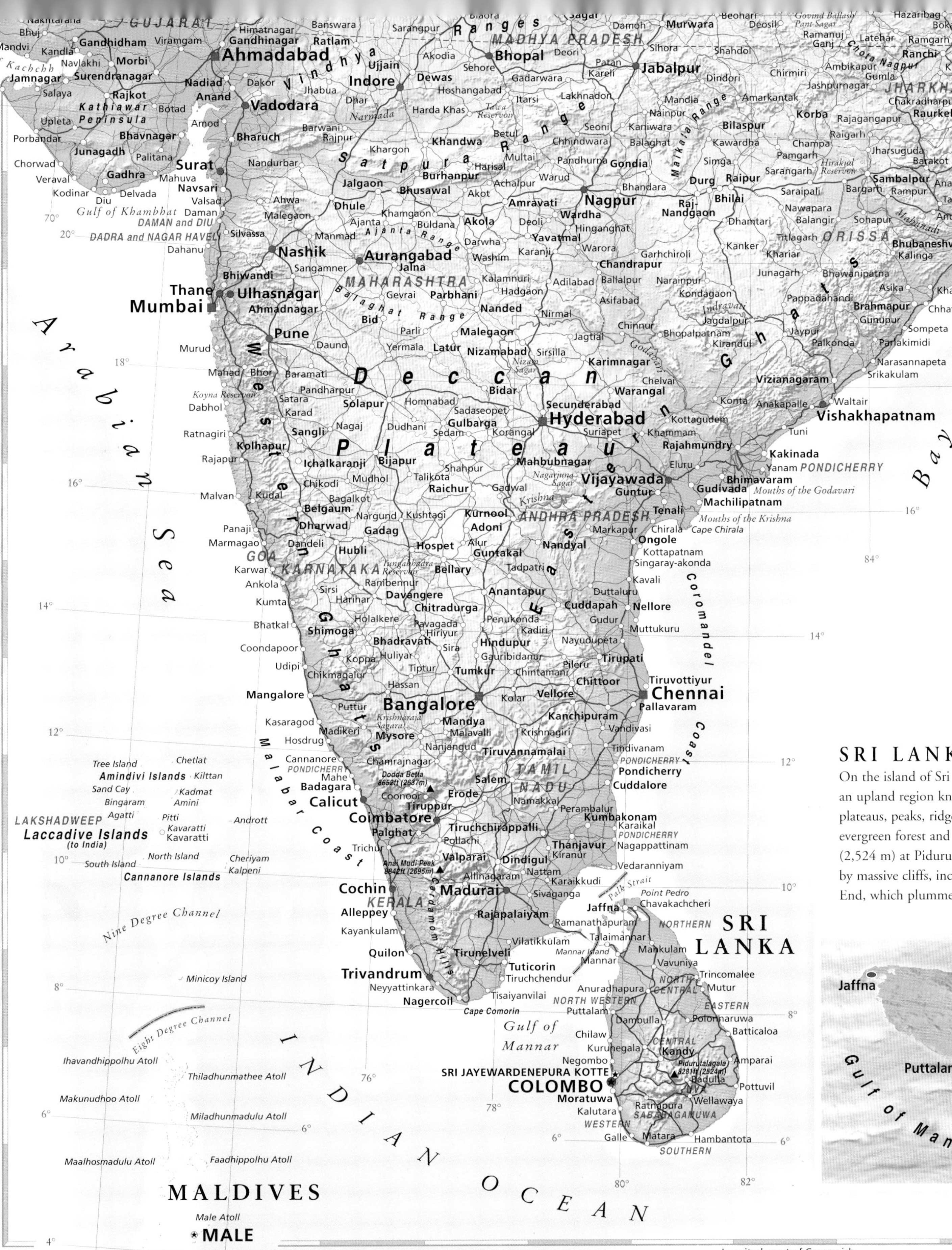

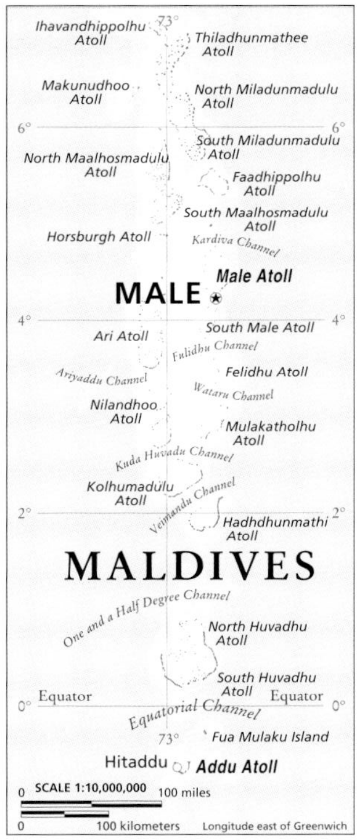

SRI LANKA'S CENTRAL HIGHLANDS

On the island of Sri Lanka, low plains surround the country's mountainous core, an upland region known as the Central Highlands. Consisting of a series of plateaus, peaks, ridges, and basins cut by steep-sided gorges and cloaked with evergreen forest and grasses, the highlands reach their highest point of 8,281 feet (2,524 m) at Pidurutalagala. Much of the perimeter of the highlands is marked by massive cliffs, including one escarpment south of Nuwara Eliya called World's End, which plummets almost 4,000 feet (1,200 m) to the plains below.

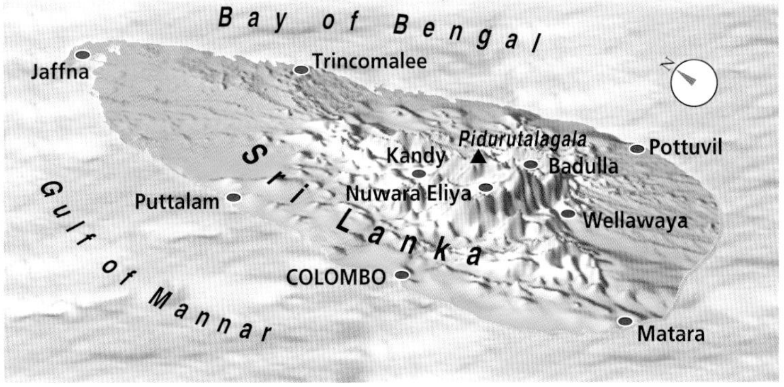

The streets of Delhi are typical of India's densely populated urban centers.

MALDIVES

Thiladhunmathee Atoll
North Miladunmadulu Atoll
South Miladunmadulu Atoll
North Maalhosmadulu Atoll
South Maalhosmadulu Atoll
Ari Atoll
Nilandhoo Atoll
Kolhumadulu Atoll
Horsburgh Atoll
North Male Atoll
MALE
Male Atoll
South Male Atoll
Felidhu Atoll
Mulakatholhu Atoll
North Huvadhu Atoll
Hadhdhunmathi Atoll
South Huvadhu Atoll
Fua Mulaku Island
Addu Atoll
Hitaddu
Equator

SCALE 1:10,000,000

SCALE 1:9,000,000
Lambert's Conformal Conic Projection

MALDIVES
MALE

INDIAN OCEAN

Arabian Sea

Bay of Bengal

Gulf of Mannar

SRI LANKA

COLOMBO
SRI JAYEWARDENEPURA KOTTE

Chennai

Mumbai

Bangalore

Hyderabad

Nagpur

Pune

DACCA (DHAKA)

Calcutta

ELEVATION
Meters / Feet

THE HIMALAYA AND THE GANGETIC PLAIN

Bangladesh, Bhutan, Nepal, Northern India

The world's tallest mountain range, the Himalaya forms a colossal barrier between the Subcontinent and Central Asia. Rising to the highest point on Earth, 29,035-foot (8,850-m) Mount Everest, it stretches for 1,550 miles (2,500 km) along the northern edge of India. Its southern flank yields abruptly to the densely populated and intensively farmed plain of the Ganges River. From its source in the western Himalaya, the Ganges flows south then east across northern India and into Bangladesh, branching repeatedly as it nears the Bay of Bengal to create one of the world's largest deltas. Cohesive states first took shape on the Gangetic Plain 3,000 years ago, and the valley was the heart of powerful Indian dynasties such as the Gupta (AD 300–550), the Mamluks (1206–1526), and the Mughals (1526–1761). Physical isolation helped preserve the autonomy of the kingdoms of Nepal, Sikkim, and Bhutan, though all were British protectorates during the 19th century, and in 1975 Sikkim acceded to India.

Up to 1,000 climbers a year now attempt an ascent of Mount Everest, which was first conquered in 1953.

Hindus view the Ganges as a holy river and visit places such as Varanasi to bathe in its waters.

The orchards of the fertile Kashmir Valley are one of India's most important sources of fruit and nuts.

POPULATION PATTERNS

This region includes the Subcontinent's least and most crowded areas. Above 16,000 feet (5,000 m), the Himalaya is virtually uninhabited. In contrast, population densities are among the world's highest in Bangladesh, which averages 2,000 people per square mile (770 per sq km); in Calcutta, where up to 100,000 people occupy each square mile of the city (40,000 per sq km); and in irrigated parts of the Gangetic Plain. The majority of people live in rural areas—Bhutan had no towns until the 1960s—and population growth rates are high. The region's peoples are a mix of Indo-European and Tibeto-Burman groups, with the latter, who include the Newar and Sherpa, generally occupying the higher land.

Uninhabited	
Less than 2.6 persons per sq mile/1 per sq km	
2.6–26 per sq mile/ 1–10 per sq km	
26–65 per sq mile/ 10–25 per sq km	
65–130 per sq mile/ 25–50 per sq km	
130–260 per sq mile/ 50–100 per sq km	
260–520 per sq mile/ 100–200 per sq km	
520–1040 per sq mile/ 200–400 per sq km	
1040–2080 per sq mile/ 400–800 per sq km	
More than 2080 per sq mile/800 per sq km	

ECONOMIC PROFILE

The region includes many large cities, but is little developed and its people mainly poor. On the Gangetic Plain, irrigation is used to grow wheat, cotton, and sugar. In the wetter Brahmaputra Valley and Bangladesh, tea is cultivated on the hillsides, rice on the plains. Despite its rugged terrain, the Himalaya has extensive arable land—mainly in foothills, basins, and river valleys—which produces wheat, corn, millet, and potatoes. On the upper slopes, sheep, goats, and yaks are herded between seasonal pastures. Minerals, including gold, sapphires, copper, and iron ore, are widespread, though difficult to access. The Himalaya and cities such as Agra, Delhi, and Varanasi are major tourist attractions.

Forest and woodland		
Arable land		
Grazing		
Marginal or nonproductive		
Cereals	Tea	
Rice	Dairy cattle	
Wheat	Fishing	
Fruit	Industrial center	
Cotton	Tourism	

Longitude east of Greenwich

N O P Q R S T U V W X Y Z

THE HIMALAYAN RANGES

The Himalaya climbs from the Gangetic Plain in a series of great steps formed by parallel, increasingly elevated ranges. From the Tarai Plain in Nepal, for example, an escarpment ascends to the 4,000-foot (1,200-m) summits of the Churia Ghati Hills. To the north rise the yet-loftier Mahabharat Range and Lesser Himalaya, which enclose the Kathmandu and Pokhara valleys. The highest part of the system is the Great Himalayan Range, which in Nepal includes 9 of the world's 14 tallest peaks.

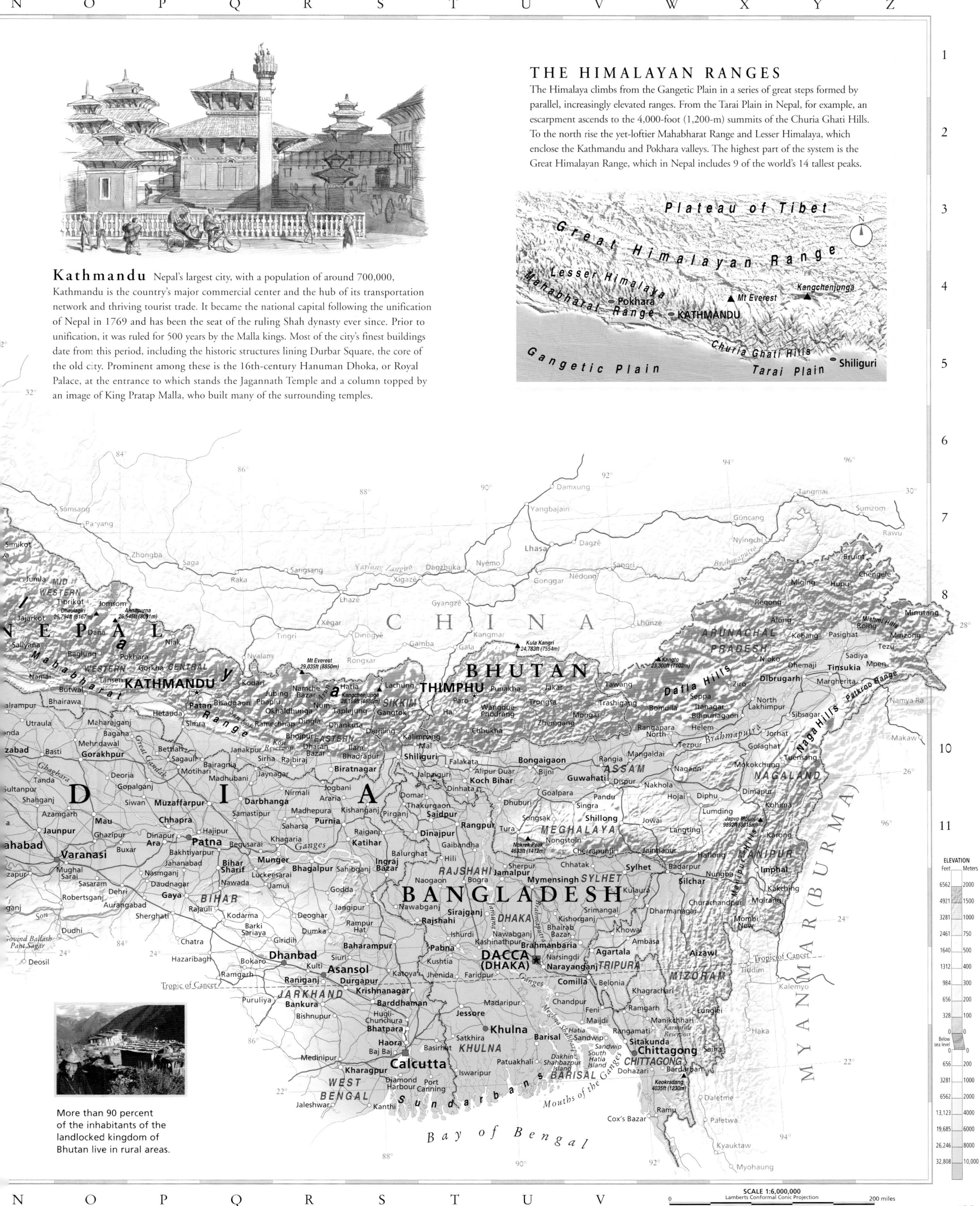

Kathmandu Nepal's largest city, with a population of around 700,000, Kathmandu is the country's major commercial center and the hub of its transportation network and thriving tourist trade. It became the national capital following the unification of Nepal in 1769 and has been the seat of the ruling Shah dynasty ever since. Prior to unification, it was ruled for 500 years by the Malla kings. Most of the city's finest buildings date from this period, including the historic structures lining Durbar Square, the core of the old city. Prominent among these is the 16th-century Hanuman Dhoka, or Royal Palace, at the entrance to which stands the Jagannath Temple and a column topped by an image of King Pratap Malla, who built many of the surrounding temples.

More than 90 percent of the inhabitants of the landlocked kingdom of Bhutan live in rural areas.

ELEVATION		
Feet		Meters
32,808		10,000
26,246		8000
19,685		6000
13,123		4000
6562		2000
3281		1000
1640		500
656		200
0		0
Below sea level		Below sea level
656		200
3281		1000
6562		2000
13,123		4000
19,685		6000
26,246		8000
32,808		10,000

SCALE 1:6,000,000
Lamberts Conformal Conic Projection

0 — 200 miles
0 — 200 kilometers

EASTERN ASIA

China, Mongolia, North Korea, South Korea, Taiwan

In both size and population, China dwarfs not only its neighbors, but most other countries. The world's third-largest and most populous country, it occupies 3.7 million square miles (9.6 million sq km) and is home to 1.3 billion people. From the Plateau of Tibet, which covers one-quarter of the country, major rivers, including the Yellow and the Yangtze, run eastward through the central ranges to the intensely cultivated coastal plains. Northward-flowing rivers quickly peter out in the belt of arid land that spans northern China and Mongolia. In the northeast, the forested Changbai Mountains separate China from the Korean Peninsula. Early Chinese civilizations led the world in technology, becoming the first to develop products such as paper, cast iron, silk, and gunpowder. The 20th century saw a power struggle within China between the Nationalist Party and the Communist Party. The latter won out, proclaiming the People's Republic of China in 1949, while the Nationalists repaired to Taiwan. That island's subsequent declaration of independence has yet to be recognized by China.

Cities such as Seoul have absorbed most of the rapid population growth that has occurred in South Korea.

Near Guilin in southeastern China, rice fields form a patchwork between steep, jagged limestone outcrops.

POPULATION PATTERNS

China's population increases by 10 million every year, a situation that helps explain the government's controversial policy of permitting each family to have only one child. Most Chinese live in small villages and two-thirds occupy the eastern lowlands, which constitute less than one-third of the country. The population dwindles in northern and western China—just 2 million or so inhabit the vast Plateau of Tibet—and in Mongolia. The latter is one of the world's least densely populated countries: its 2.5 million people live in an area bigger than Alaska, with an average of just four people occupying each square mile (1.6 per sq km). Tiny Taiwan has almost ten times the population of Mongolia and, like the similarly crowded Korean Peninsula, is highly urbanized.

Uninhabited	130–260 per sq mile/ 50–100 per sq km
Less than 2.6 persons per sq mile/1 per sq km	260–520 per sq mile/ 100–200 per sq km
2.6–26 per sq mile/ 1–10 per sq km	520–1040 per sq mile/ 200–400 per sq km
26–65 per sq mile/ 10–25 per sq km	1040–2080 per sq mile/ 400–800 per sq km
65–130 per sq mile/ 25–50 per sq km	More than 2080 per sq mile/800 per sq km

ECONOMIC PROFILE

With the world's largest workforce, abundant resources including coal, oil, iron ore, and hydroelectric power, and diverse, developed industries, China has huge economic potential. Until the late 1970s, this was held in check by strict government controls, but recent years have seen a degree of liberalization of production and trade, and consequent rises in productivity. A contrasting reluctance to relax state control has led to recession and food shortages in North Korea. South Korea and Taiwan have taken advantage of U.S. assistance to develop strong, technologically advanced industrial sectors, and both nations are now major producers of electronic goods. Though it has significant mineral reserves, including copper, coal, and oil, Mongolia is still dependent on its pastoral industry.

	Forest and woodland
	Arable land
	Grazing
	Marginal or nonproductive
🌾	Cereals
	Rice
🐂	Beef cattle
🐑	Sheep
	Fishing
🏭	Industrial center
⛏	Mining
	Oil production
	Timber

Immense dams are being built on the Three Gorges section of the Yangtze River.

About 70 percent of farming in Mongolia involves the rearing of domestic animals.

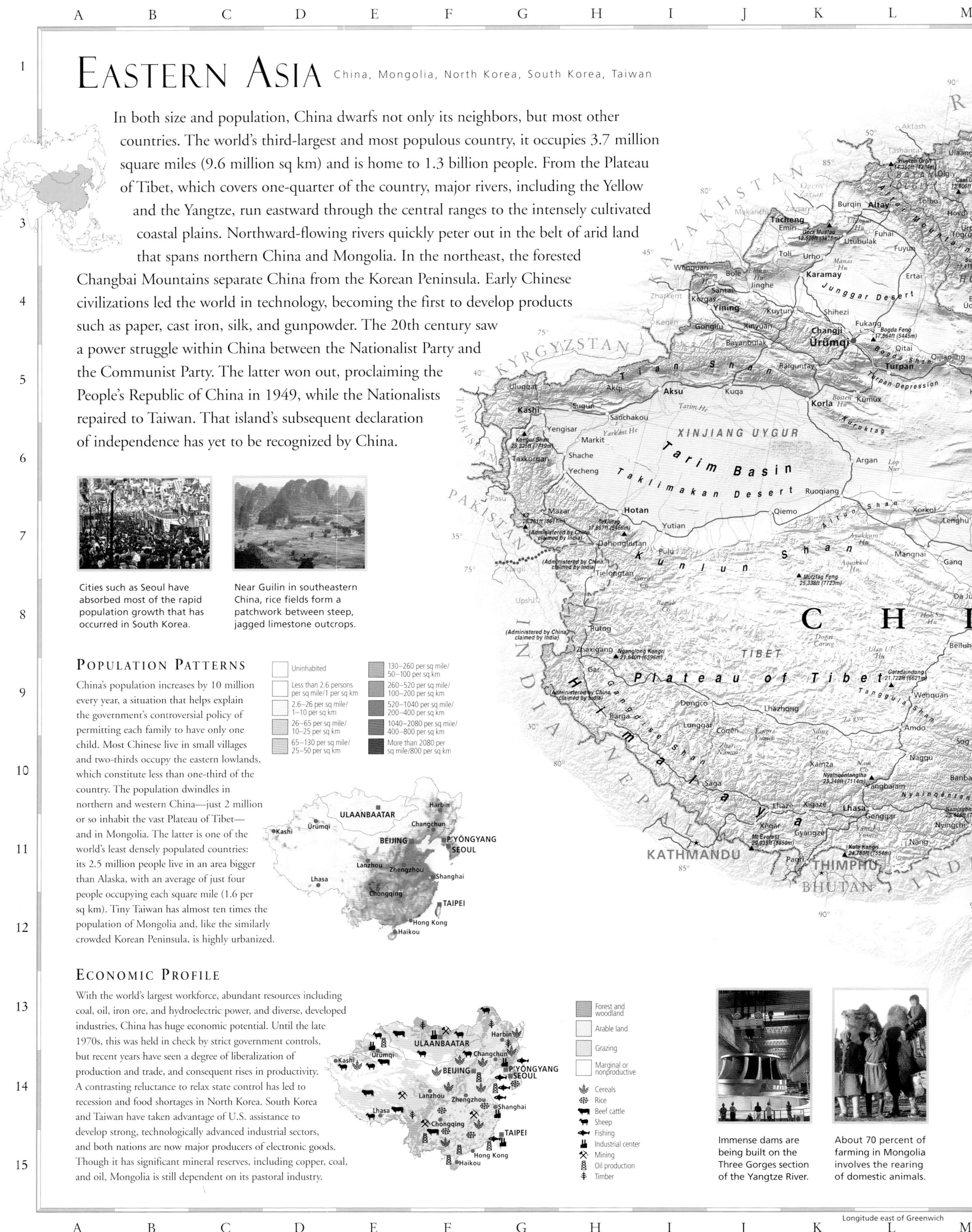

Longitude east of Greenwich

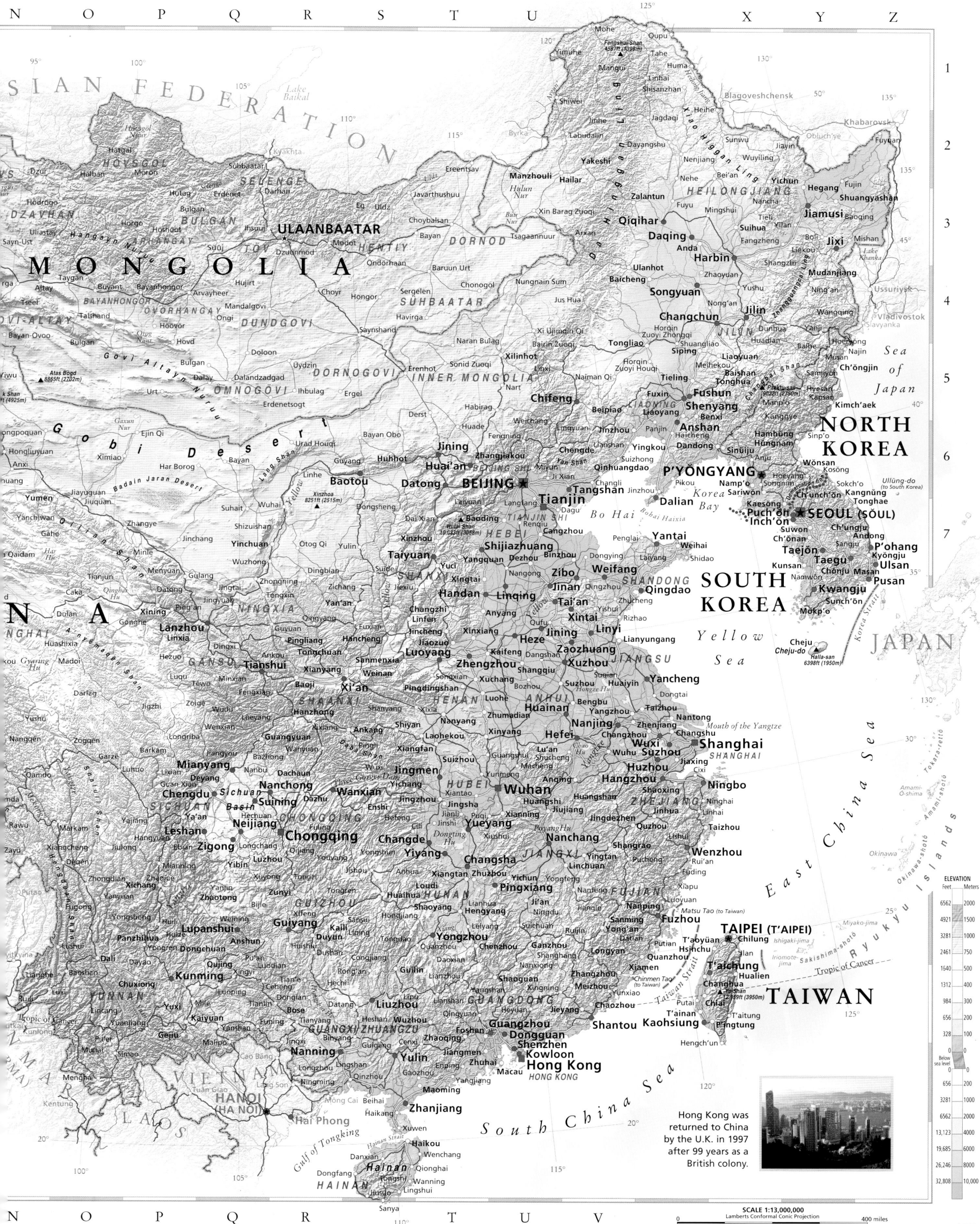

Hong Kong was
returned to China
by the U.K. in 1997
after 99 years as a
British colony.

ELEVATION	
Feet	Meters
6562	2000
4921	1500
3281	1000
2461	750
1640	500
1312	400
984	300
656	200
328	100
Below sea level	0
656	200
3281	1000
6562	2000
13,123	4000
19,685	6000
26,246	8000
32,808	10,000

SCALE 1:13,000,000
Lamberts Conformal Conic Projection

0 _____ 400 miles

0 _____ 400 kilometers

185

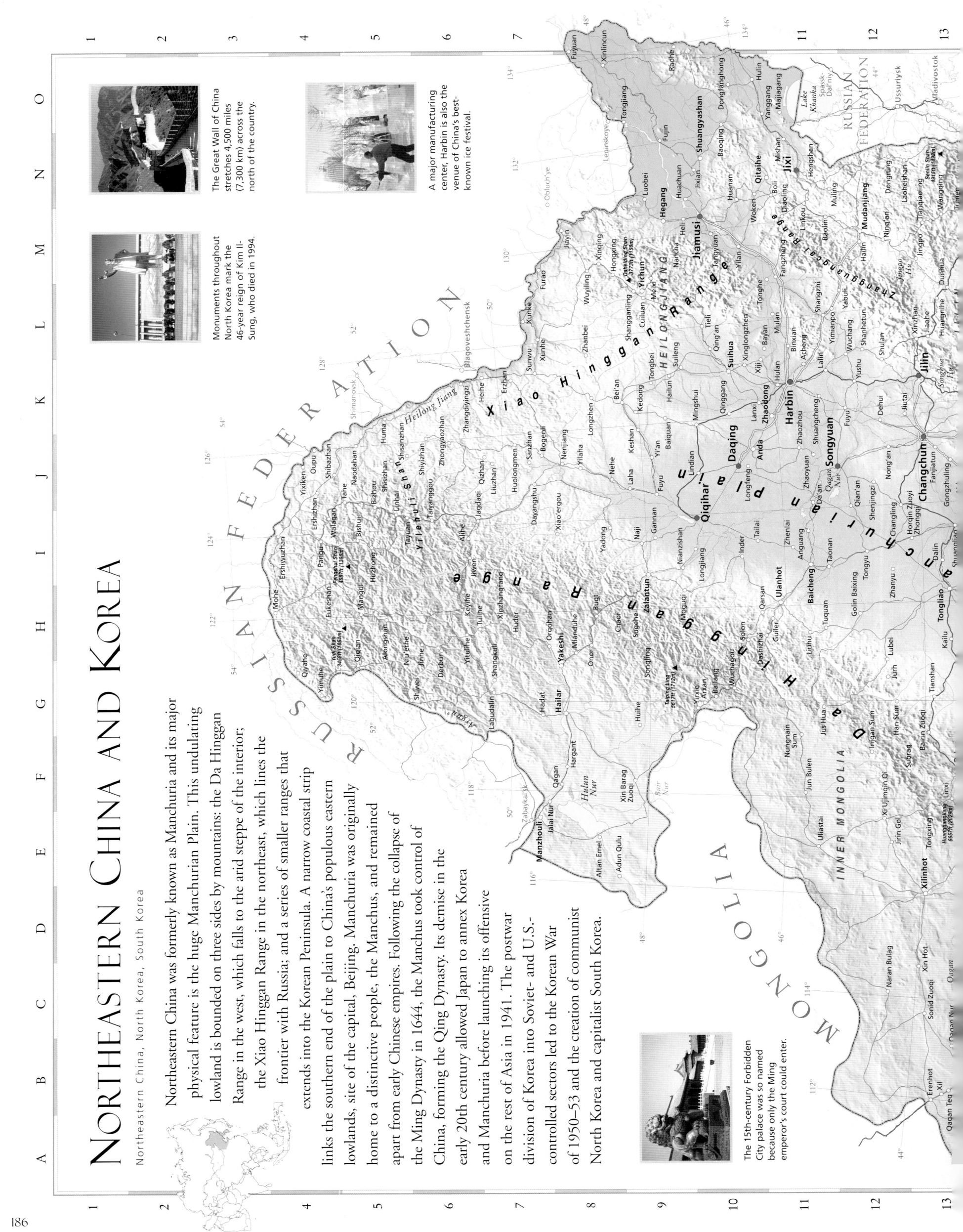

NORTHEASTERN CHINA AND KOREA

Northeastern China, North Korea, South Korea

Northeastern China was formerly known as Manchuria and its major physical feature is the huge Manchurian Plain. This undulating lowland is bounded on three sides by mountains: the Da Hinggan Range in the west, which falls to the arid steppe of the interior; the Xiao Hinggan Range in the northeast, which lines the frontier with Russia; and a series of smaller ranges that extends into the Korean Peninsula. A narrow coastal strip links the southern end of the plain to China's populous eastern lowlands, site of the capital, Beijing. Manchuria was originally home to a distinctive people, the Manchus, and remained apart from early Chinese empires. Following the collapse of the Ming Dynasty in 1644, the Manchus took control of China, forming the Qing Dynasty. Its demise in the early 20th century allowed Japan to annex Korea and Manchuria before launching its offensive on the rest of Asia in 1941. The postwar division of Korea into Soviet- and U.S.-controlled sectors led to the Korean War of 1950–53 and the creation of communist North Korea and capitalist South Korea.

The Great Wall of China stretches 4,500 miles (7,300 km) across the north of the country.

Monuments throughout North Korea mark the 46-year reign of Kim Il-Sung, who died in 1994.

A major manufacturing center, Harbin is also the venue of China's best-known ice festival.

The 15th-century Forbidden City palace was so named because only the Ming emperor's court could enter.

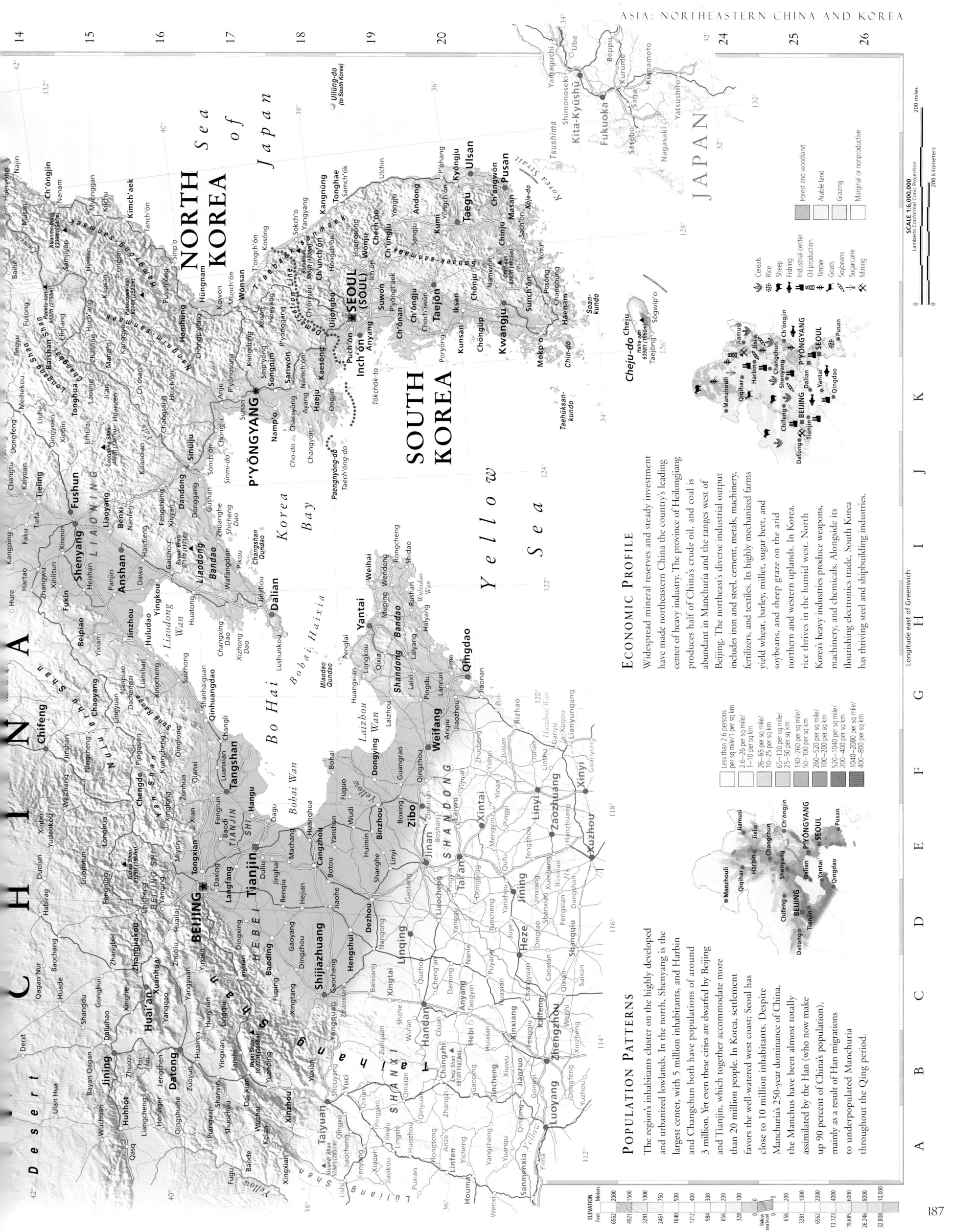

POPULATION PATTERNS

The region's inhabitants cluster on the highly developed and urbanized lowlands. In the north, Shenyang is the largest center, with 5 million inhabitants, and Harbin and Changchun both have populations of around 3 million. Yet even these cities are dwarfed by Beijing and Tianjin, which together accommodate more than 20 million people. In Korea, settlement favors the well-watered west coast; Seoul has close to 10 million inhabitants. Despite Manchuria's 250-year dominance of China, the Manchus have been almost totally assimilated by the Han (who now make up 90 percent of China's population), mainly as a result of Han migrations to underpopulated Manchuria throughout the Qing period.

ECONOMIC PROFILE

Widespread mineral reserves and steady investment have made northeastern China the country's leading center of heavy industry. The province of Heilongjiang produces half of China's crude oil, and coal is abundant in Manchuria and the ranges west of Beijing. The northeast's diverse industrial output includes iron and steel, cement, metals, machinery; fertilizers, and textiles. Its highly mechanized farms yield wheat, barley, millet, sugar beet, and soybeans, and sheep graze on the arid northern and western uplands. In Korea, rice thrives in the humid west. North Korea's heavy industries produce weapons, machinery, and chemicals. Alongside its flourishing electronics trade, South Korea has thriving steel and shipbuilding industries.

SCALE 1:6,000,000
Lambert's Conformal Conic Projection

Longitude east of Greenwich

187

SOUTHEASTERN CHINA AND TAIWAN

The valleys of the Yellow and Yangtze rivers were the cradles of Chinese civilization, giving rise to China's first agricultural societies, around 9,000 years ago, and its first urban society, the Shang Dynasty, around 1800 BC. They remained the center of development under the Han, who united most of this region in 221 BC. The Han gradually expanded their territory westward beyond the broad Sichuan Basin to the plateaus of modern-day Gansu and the deep valleys and steep slopes of Yunnan, and southward through the eroded limestone hills of present-day Guangdong to the humid lowlands lining the South China Sea. The Yellow and Yangtze valleys, and the plains that divide them, are still the cultural and economic heart of modern China, and were developed intensively by the communist government during the second half of the 20th century. Taiwan also underwent dramatic economic growth in the 20th century, initially under Japanese rule (1895–1943) and then under the leadership of the Chinese Nationalist Party, which controlled the island until 2000.

An ancient system of waterways dating from the 7th century, China's Grand Canal links Beijing with Hangzhou.

About 6,000 life-size terra-cotta warriors guard the tomb of Emperor Qin Shi Huang (259–210 BC), at Xi'an in Shaanxi province.

POPULATION PATTERNS

The plains between the lower Yellow and Yangtze valleys now encompass 20 or so cities with more than 1 million inhabitants, including Shanghai, the nation's largest city, which has almost 13 million people. Other centers of population include the fertile Sichuan Basin, and the Pearl River Valley in the south. The Han are by far the largest ethnic group, but China's second-largest ethnic group, the Zhuang, cluster in the autonomous region of Guangxi Zhuangzu. Taiwan's mountainous terrain concentrates its large population on the northern and western coastal lowlands. Its indigenous Malayo-Polynesian inhabitants have, for the most part, been assimilated by Chinese immigrants, who began arriving in the 17th century.

	Population density legend
Uninhabited	65–130 per sq mile/ 25–50 per sq km	520–1040 per sq mile/ 200–400 per sq km
Less than 2.6 persons per sq mile/1 per sq km	130–260 per sq mile/ 50–100 per sq km	1040–2080 per sq mile/ 400–800 per sq km
2.6–26 per sq mile/ 1–10 per sq km	260–520 per sq mile/ 100–200 per sq km	More than 2080 per sq mile/800 per sq km
26–65 per sq mile/ 10–25 per sq km		

ECONOMIC PROFILE

The rich loess soils of the Yellow River have long provided wheat, millet, and cotton. Intensive farming of the fertile southeast and Sichuan Basin yields up to three crops a year, mainly of rice (of which China is the world's largest producer) and vegetables. Coal is abundant in Shanxi and Sichuan, which also has half of the nation's gas reserves; these resources underpin heavy industries in the interior. However, port cities such as Guangzhou and Shanghai have become the most prosperous centers, thanks to their long-established links with other Asian and Western trading partners and a recent influx of foreign investment. China is now the largest market for the exports—mainly electrical goods, metals, textiles, and plastics—that power Taiwan's thriving economy.

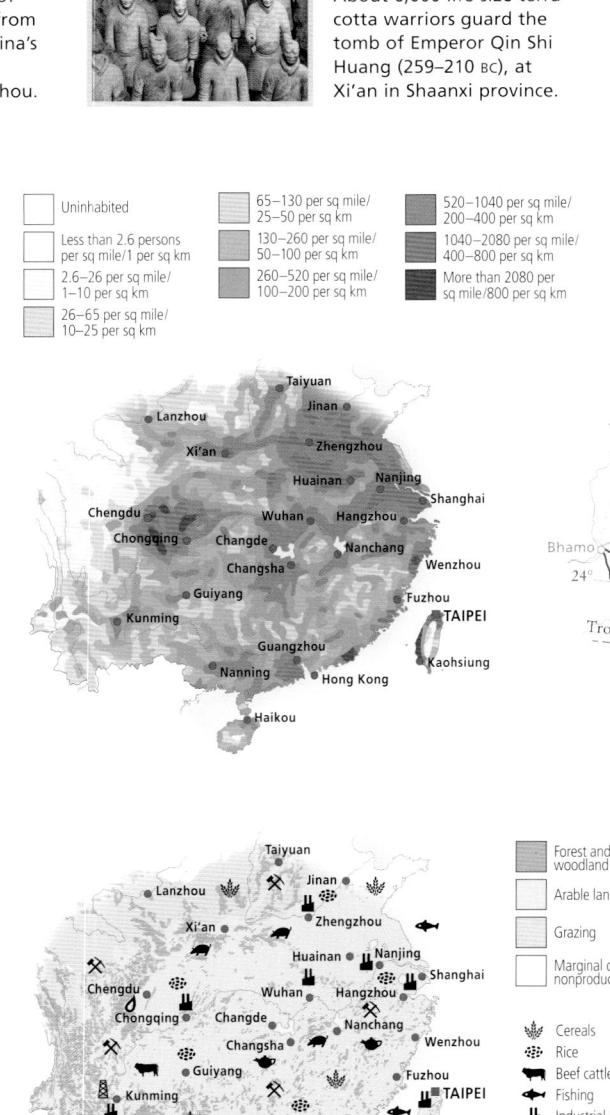

	Land use legend
	Forest and woodland
	Arable land
	Grazing
	Marginal or nonproductive

Cereals
Rice
Beef cattle
Fishing
Industrial center
Mining
Oil production
Pigs
Gas production
Tea

ELEVATION

Feet	Meters
6562	2000
4921	1500
3281	1000
2461	750
1640	500
1312	400
984	300
656	200
328	100
0 Below sea level	0
656	200
3281	1000
6562	2000
13,123	4000
19,685	6000
26,246	8000
32,808	10,000

Though resource-rich, the island of Hainan remains relatively undeveloped. Most of its people live by farming and fishing.

Longitude east of Greenwich

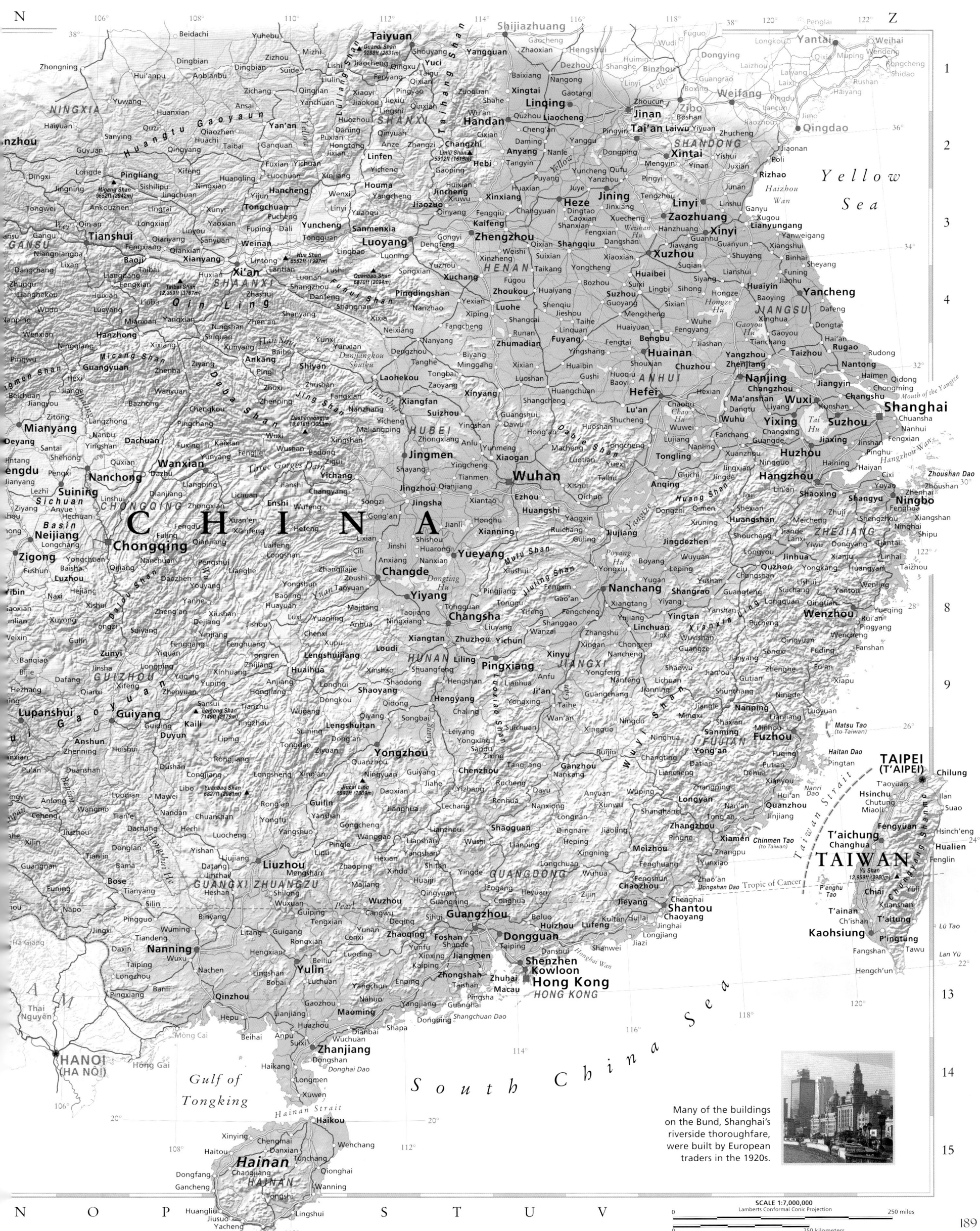

Many of the buildings on the Bund, Shanghai's riverside thoroughfare, were built by European traders in the 1920s.

SCALE 1:7,000,000
Lamberts Conformal Conic Projection

0   250 miles

0   250 kilometers

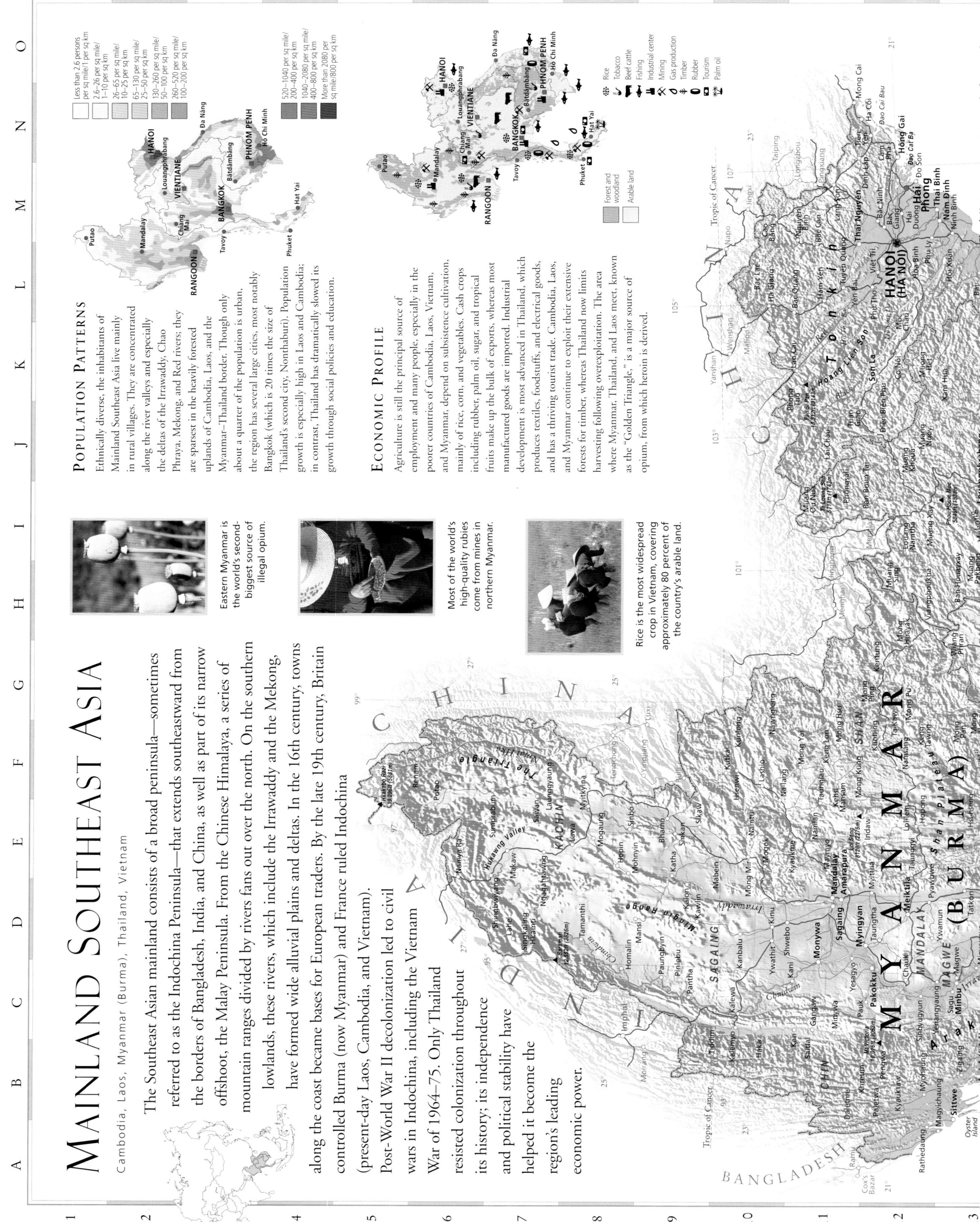

MAINLAND SOUTHEAST ASIA

Cambodia, Laos, Myanmar (Burma), Thailand, Vietnam

The Southeast Asian mainland consists of a broad peninsula—sometimes referred to as the Indochina Peninsula—that extends southeastward from the borders of Bangladesh, India, and China, as well as part of its narrow offshoot, the Malay Peninsula. From the Chinese Himalaya, a series of mountain ranges divided by rivers fans out over the north. On the southern lowlands, these rivers, which include the Irrawaddy and the Mekong, have formed wide alluvial plains and deltas. In the 16th century, towns along the coast became bases for European traders. By the late 19th century, Britain controlled Burma (now Myanmar) and France ruled Indochina (present-day Laos, Cambodia, and Vietnam). Post-World War II decolonization led to civil wars in Indochina, including the Vietnam War of 1964–75. Only Thailand resisted colonization throughout its history; its independence and political stability have helped it become the region's leading economic power.

POPULATION PATTERNS

Ethnically diverse, the inhabitants of Mainland Southeast Asia live mainly in rural villages. They are concentrated along the river valleys and especially the deltas of the Irrawaddy, Chao Phraya, Mekong, and Red rivers; they are sparsest in the heavily forested uplands of Cambodia, Laos, and the Myanmar–Thailand border. Though only about a quarter of the population is urban, the region has several large cities, most notably Bangkok (which is 20 times the size of Thailand's second city, Nonthaburi). Population growth is especially high in Laos and Cambodia; in contrast, Thailand has dramatically slowed its growth through social policies and education.

Eastern Myanmar is the world's second-biggest source of illegal opium.

ECONOMIC PROFILE

Agriculture is still the principal source of employment and many people, especially in the poorer countries of Cambodia, Laos, Vietnam, and Myanmar, depend on subsistence cultivation, mainly of rice, corn, and vegetables. Cash crops including rubber, palm oil, sugar, and tropical fruits make up the bulk of exports, whereas most manufactured goods are imported. Industrial development is most advanced in Thailand, which produces textiles, foodstuffs, and electrical goods, and has a thriving tourist trade. Cambodia, Laos, and Myanmar continue to exploit their extensive forests for timber, whereas Thailand now limits harvesting following overexploitation. The area where Myanmar, Thailand, and Laos meet, known as the "Golden Triangle," is a major source of opium, from which heroin is derived.

Most of the world's high-quality rubies come from mines in northern Myanmar.

Rice is the most widespread crop in Vietnam, covering approximately 80 percent of the country's arable land.

Less than 2.6 persons per sq mile/1 per sq km
2.6–26 per sq mile/1–10 per sq km
26–65 per sq mile/10–25 per sq km
65–130 per sq mile/25–50 per sq km
130–260 per sq mile/50–100 per sq km
260–520 per sq mile/100–200 per sq km
520–1040 per sq mile/200–400 per sq km
1040–2080 per sq mile/400–800 per sq km
More than 2080 per sq mile/800 per sq km

Rice
Tobacco
Beef cattle
Fishing
Industrial center
Mining
Gas production
Timber
Rubber
Tourism
Palm oil

Forest and woodland
Arable land

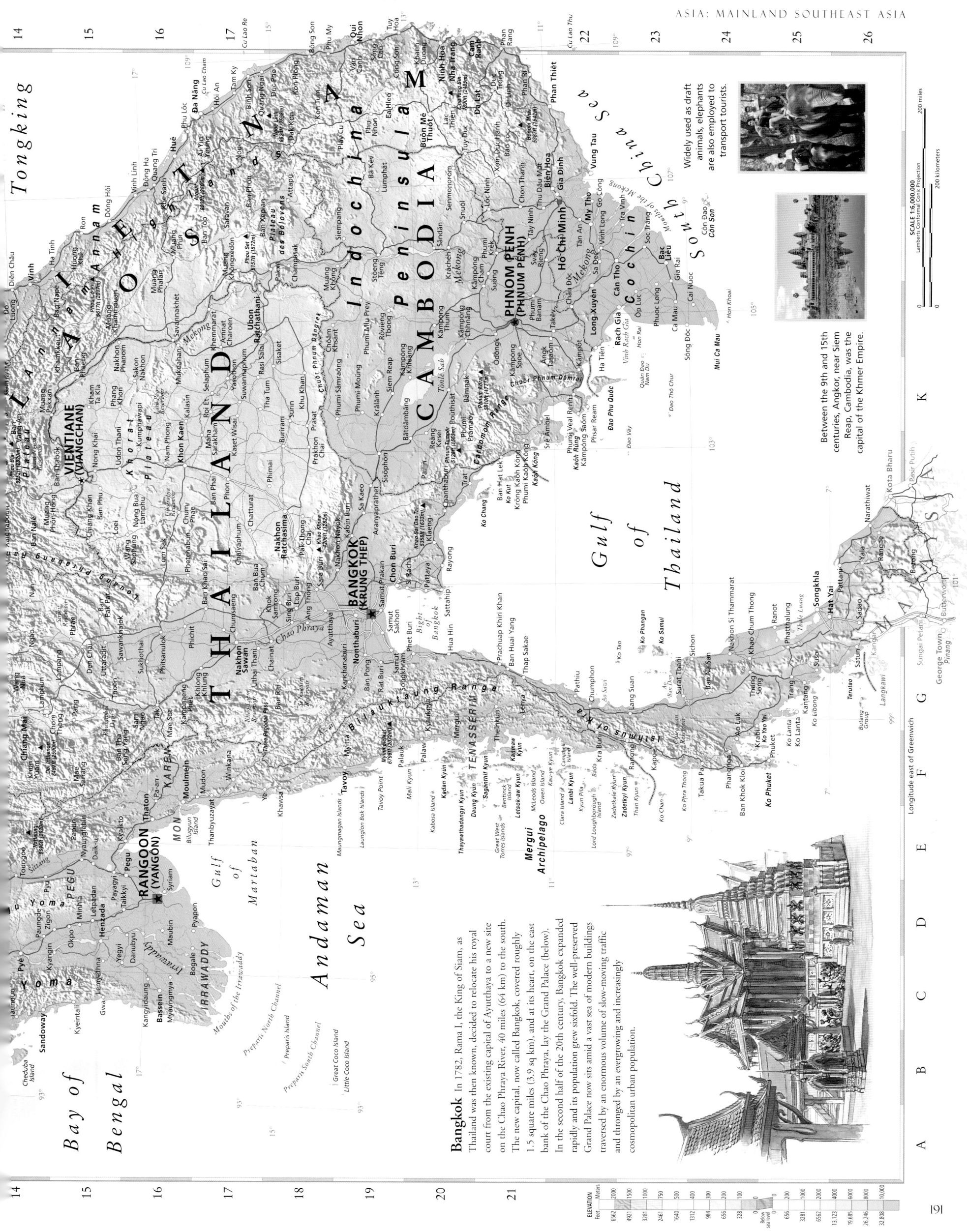

Widely used as draft animals, elephants are also employed to transport tourists.

Between the 9th and 15th centuries, Angkor, near Siem Reap, Cambodia, was the capital of the Khmer Empire.

SCALE 1:6,000,000
Lamberts Conformal Conic Projection

0   200 miles
0   200 kilometers

Bangkok In 1782, Rama I, the King of Siam, as Thailand was then known, decided to relocate his royal court from the existing capital of Ayutthaya to a new site on the Chao Phraya River, 40 miles (64 km) to the south. The new capital, now called Bangkok, covered roughly 1.5 square miles (3.9 sq km), and at its heart, on the east bank of the Chao Phraya, lay the Grand Palace (below). In the second half of the 20th century, Bangkok expanded rapidly and its population grew sixfold. The well-preserved Grand Palace now sits amid a vast sea of modern buildings traversed by an enormous volume of slow-moving traffic and thronged by an evergrowing and increasingly cosmopolitan urban population.

ELEVATION

MARITIME SOUTHEAST ASIA

Brunei, East Timor, Indonesia, Malaysia, Philippines, Singapore

Scattered around the southeastern fringe of the Asian mainland are more than 20,000 islands. Ranging from the massive, rain-forest-cloaked landmass of Borneo—the world's third-largest island—to the tiny atolls of the Banda Sea, they form the largest island group on Earth, the Malay Archipelago. Divided mainly between the large countries of Malaysia (which includes the southern part of the Malay Peninsula), the Philippines, and Indonesia, it is also the site of the small states of Singapore, East Timor, and Brunei. Beginning in the 16th century, intense competition for control of the lucrative spice trade led various European powers to colonize large areas of the region. The Dutch seized most of present-day Indonesia, the British gradually gained control of Malaysia, the Portuguese established a foothold in Timor, and the Spanish occupied the Philippines (from where they were ousted by the U.S.A. in 1898). Since decolonization in the second half of the 20th century, Indonesia and Malaysia, in particular, have become major regional powers.

JAVA'S VOLCANOES

The islands of southern Indonesia formed as a result of subduction of the Indo-Australian Plate beneath the Eurasian Plate. This process continues to fuel the country's 76 volcanoes (more than any other nation), 22 of which are on Java. Sporadic and sometimes destructive volcanic activity takes place at Gunung Semeru in the east, Gunung Merapi near Yogyakarta, and Galunggung in the west. But the largest recorded eruption occurred on August 28, 1883, when Krakatau (Krakatoa) exploded, unleashing a tidal wave that killed 36,000 people.

Krakatau JAKARTA — Galunggung — *Java Sea* — Semarang — Surabaya — *Java* — Gunung Merapi — Gunung Semeru — Yogyakarta — *Indian Ocean*

Native to Borneo and Sumatra, the orangutan has become endangered due to habitat loss.

East Timor attained independence in 2002, following almost 25 years of Indonesian rule.

Controlled by the Dutch from 1619 to 1941, Jakarta became the capital of Indonesia in 1949.

Christmas Island (to Australia)

Longitude east of Greenwich

192

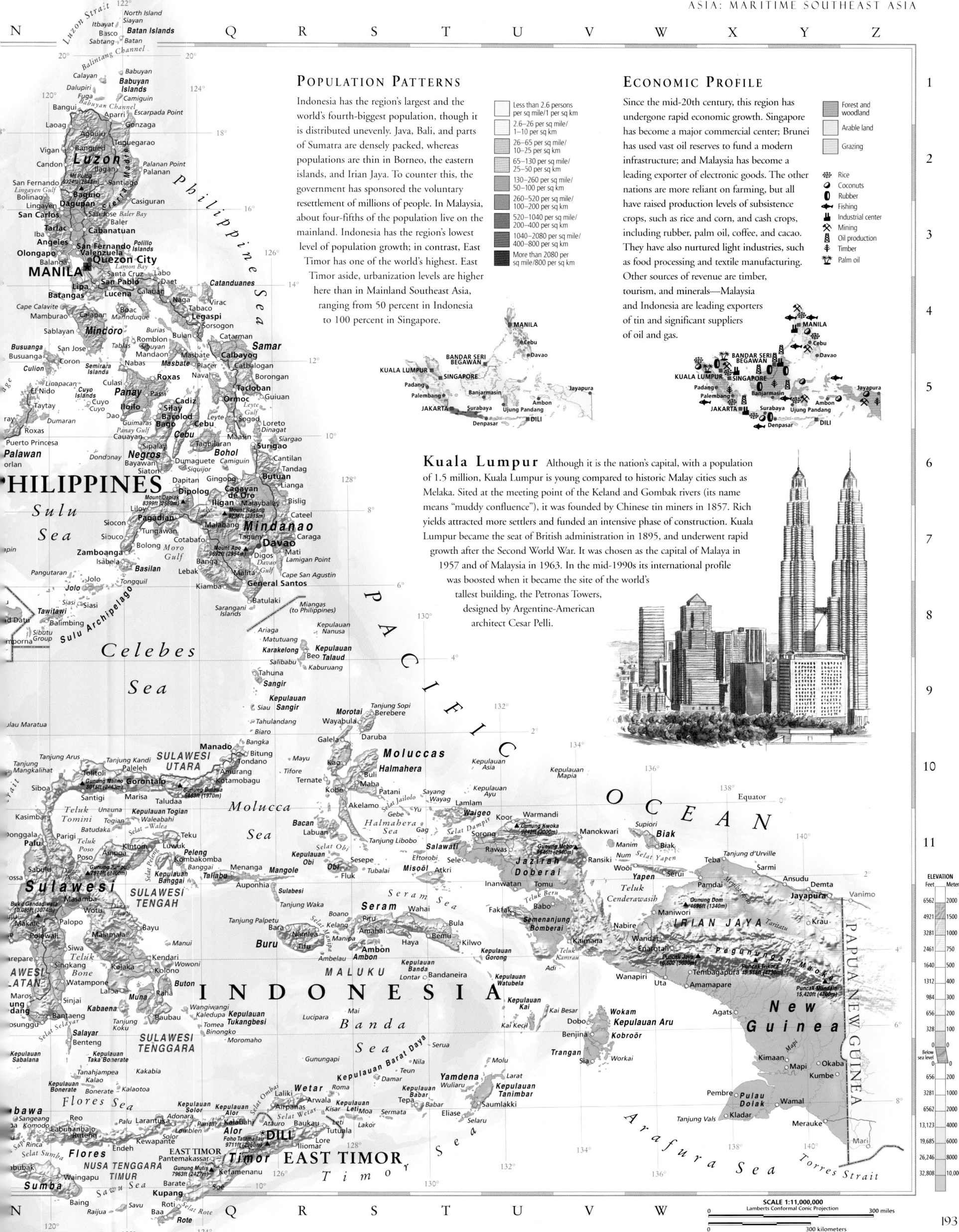

POPULATION PATTERNS

Indonesia has the region's largest and the world's fourth-biggest population, though it is distributed unevenly. Java, Bali, and parts of Sumatra are densely packed, whereas populations are thin in Borneo, the eastern islands, and Irian Jaya. To counter this, the government has sponsored the voluntary resettlement of millions of people. In Malaysia, about four-fifths of the population live on the mainland. Indonesia has the region's lowest level of population growth; in contrast, East Timor has one of the world's highest. East Timor aside, urbanization levels are higher here than in Mainland Southeast Asia, ranging from 50 percent in Indonesia to 100 percent in Singapore.

Less than 2.6 persons per sq mile/1 per sq km
2.6–26 per sq mile/1–10 per sq km
26–65 per sq mile/10–25 per sq km
65–130 per sq mile/25–50 per sq km
130–260 per sq mile/50–100 per sq km
260–520 per sq mile/100–200 per sq km
520–1040 per sq mile/200–400 per sq km
1040–2080 per sq mile/400–800 per sq km
More than 2080 per sq mile/800 per sq km

ECONOMIC PROFILE

Since the mid-20th century, this region has undergone rapid economic growth. Singapore has become a major commercial center; Brunei has used vast oil reserves to fund a modern infrastructure; and Malaysia has become a leading exporter of electronic goods. The other nations are more reliant on farming, but all have raised production levels of subsistence crops, such as rice and corn, and cash crops, including rubber, palm oil, coffee, and cacao. They have also nurtured light industries, such as food processing and textile manufacturing. Other sources of revenue are timber, tourism, and minerals—Malaysia and Indonesia are leading exporters of tin and significant suppliers of oil and gas.

Forest and woodland
Arable land
Grazing
Rice
Coconuts
Rubber
Fishing
Industrial center
Mining
Oil production
Timber
Palm oil

Kuala Lumpur

Although it is the nation's capital, with a population of 1.5 million, Kuala Lumpur is young compared to historic Malay cities such as Melaka. Sited at the meeting point of the Keland and Gombak rivers (its name means "muddy confluence"), it was founded by Chinese tin miners in 1857. Rich yields attracted more settlers and funded an intensive phase of construction. Kuala Lumpur became the seat of British administration in 1895, and underwent rapid growth after the Second World War. It was chosen as the capital of Malaya in 1957 and of Malaysia in 1963. In the mid-1990s its international profile was boosted when it became the site of the world's tallest building, the Petronas Towers, designed by Argentine-American architect Cesar Pelli.

SCALE 1:11,000,000
Lamberts Conformal Conic Projection
300 miles
300 kilometers

ELEVATION

Feet	Meters
6562	2000
4921	1500
3281	1000
2461	750
1640	500
1312	400
984	300
656	200
328	100
0	0
Below sea level	
656	200
3281	1000
6562	2000
13,123	4000
19,685	6000
26,246	8000
32,808	10,000

BRUNEI, MALAYSIA, AND SINGAPORE

Malaysia comprises the southern third of the Malay Peninsula and the northern third of the island of Borneo. Divided by the South China Sea, these territories are known, respectively, as West (or Peninsular) Malaysia and East Malaysia (which is made up of the states of Sabah and Sarawak). Nestled on their fringes are two small independent states: Singapore, a tiny island republic on the southern tip of West Malaysia, and Brunei, a sultanate consisting of two enclaves on the north shore of East Malaysia. When the Portuguese arrived in the early 16th century, the Malay Peninsula and northern Borneo were divided into autonomous Islamic sultanates. In the 19th century, most of these states were brought under British control. Following Japanese occupation during the Second World War, the sultanates of the Malay Peninsula gained independence from Britain as Malaya in 1957; in 1963, they invited Singapore, Sabah, Sarawak, and Brunei to unite with them as Malaysia. All but Brunei accepted, though Singapore seceded peacefully in 1965. Today, these three states are among the most prosperous in Southeast Asia.

The jagged summit of Mount Kinabalu, Malaysia's highest peak, looms above a mosque near Kota Kinabalu.

Malaysia's largest port, George Town, occupies a sheltered position on the east side of the island of Pinang.

THAILAND

Pattani
Satun
Terutao
Langkawi
Dayang Bunting
PERLIS
Kangar
Jitra
Rangae
Narathiwat
Tumpat
Kota Bharu
Pasir Mas
Perhentian Besar
Tanah Merah
Pasir Putih
Macang
Redang
Kuala Terengganu

KEDAH
Alor Setar
Sungei Petani
PINANG
George Town
Pinang
Butterworth
Gunung Bintang 6109ft (1862m)
Jeli
Kuala Kerai
Gunung Noring 6197ft (1889m)
Gunung Lawit 4977ft (1517m)
Tasik Temengor
Gunung Camah 7118ft (2170m)
Tasik Kenyir

Bukit Merah
Taiping
Port Weld
KELANTAN
Gua Musang
Gunung Tahan 7182ft (2189m)
TERENGGANU
Gunung Mandi Angin 4787ft (1459m)
Dungun
Tenggul

Kuala Kangsar
Ipoh
Batu Gajah
Bidor
Cameron Highlands
Gunung Batu Puteh 6998ft (2130m)
Kuala Lipis
Cukai

PERAK
Pantai Remis
Pangkor
Kampung Koh
Tanjung Beras Basah
Teluk Anson
Gunung Liang Timur 6335ft (1932m)
Gunung Benum 6913ft (2107m)
Gunung Tapis 4957ft (1511m)
Tanjung Gelang

MALAYSIA
Malay Peninsula

Sungai Besar
SELANGOR
Baub
PAHANG
Maran
Pekan

Kuala Selangor
Karak
Temerloh
Tanjung Pertandangan

KUALA LUMPUR
Kelang
Genting Highlands
Nenasi

Pelabuhan Kelang
Shah Alam
★ KUALA LUMPUR
Morib
Sepang
NEGERI SEMBILAN
Bahau
Seremban
Tanjung Senebui
Port Dickson
Gemas
Tampin
Segamat
Labis
JOHOR
Endau
Seri Buat
Pemanggil

Bagansiapiapi
Tanjung Tuan
MELAKA
Gunung Ledang 4186ft (1276m)
Mersing
Tanjung Resang
Babi Besar
Aur

Rupat
Melaka
Muar
Yong Peng
Keluang
Gunung Belumut 3314ft (1010m)
Sibu
Tinggi

Dumai
Batu Pahat
Ayer Hitam
Benut
Kota Tinggi
Kampong Sedili Kechil

Bengkalis
Bengkalis
Duri
Pontian Kechil
Kukup
Johor Bahru
SINGAPORE

RIAU
Sekodi
Padang
SINGAPORE ★
Jurong
Changi

Rangsang
Karimun
Batam
Bintan
Kepulauan Riau
Selatpanjang
Tanjungbalai
Bulan
Bagam
Mapor
Rantau
Sugi
Combol
Rempang
Tanjungpinang

Buatan
Kundur
Galang
Gin Besar

Sawang
Durian
Mendol
Durai

Pelalawan
Mendung
Sungaiguntung
Mesanak
Temiyang
Sebangka
Limas

Sungaiguntung
Bakung
Senayang
Tanjung Datuk
Lingga
Kelumu
Kepulauan Lingga

Tembilahan
Baso
Basu
Cukas
Dabo
Singkep
Labu

Niur
Kualatungal
Selat Berhala
Tanjung Buku

Simpang
Tanjung Jabung
Kepulauan Tujuh

JAMBI
Jambi
Belinyu
Tanjung Samak
Sungailiat
Pangkalpinang

SUMATERA SELATAN
Mentok
Kalapa
Bangka
Koba

Bayunglincir
Tanjung Carat
Selat
Tanjung Berikat

Payung

Liat
Lepar
Mendanau
Manggar
Tanjungpandan
Belitung
Dendang

Toboali
Mebalong
Seliu

INDONESIA

Natuna Besar
Telukbutun
Seluan
Kepulauan Natuna
Binjai
Panarik
Lagong

Kepulauan Anambas
Mubur
Matak
Siantan
Bajau
Subi Kecil
Subi Besar

Jemaja
Letung
Air
Midai
Seraya
Panjang
Serasan

Natuna
St Petrus
Tanjung Datu
Selat Serasan

Sea
Tanjung Mungguresak
Liku
Sekura
Sambas

Kepulauan Tambelan
Mendarik
Dumdam
Uwi
Tambelan Besar
Benua
Tanjung Gunung Pemangkat
Singkawang

Kepulauan Badas
Lemukutan
Temaju
Mempawah
Tanjung Bangkai
Sungaipinyuh

Pengiki
Datu
Pejantan
Pontianak

Tanjungsaleh
Laut
Sungaikakap

Kertamulia

Padangtikar
Padangtikar
Jawi
Telukbatang
Maya
Suka

Kepulauan Karimata
Penebangan
Pelapis
Padang
Karimata

Tanjung Baw
Tel Saka

INDONESIA

Singapore inset map

MALAYSIA
Johor Bahru
Sembawang
Yishun
Mandai
Sungei Seletar Reservoir
Ubin
Punggol
Changi

Kranji Reservoir
Mukti Reservoir
Bukit Panjang
Seletar Reservoir
Hougang
Toa Payoh
Tampines

Poyang Reservoir
Bukit Gombak 436ft (133m)
Peirce Reservoir
Katong

Jurong
Clementi
Tanglin
Geylang

Jurong Island
Telok Blangah
Sentosa
SINGAPORE
Tuas
SINGAPORE

Bukum Kechil
Semakau
Pawai
Sebarok
Senang

SCALE 1:800,000
Mercator Projection
0   10 miles
0   10 kilometers
Longitude east of Greenwich

Longitude east of Greenwich

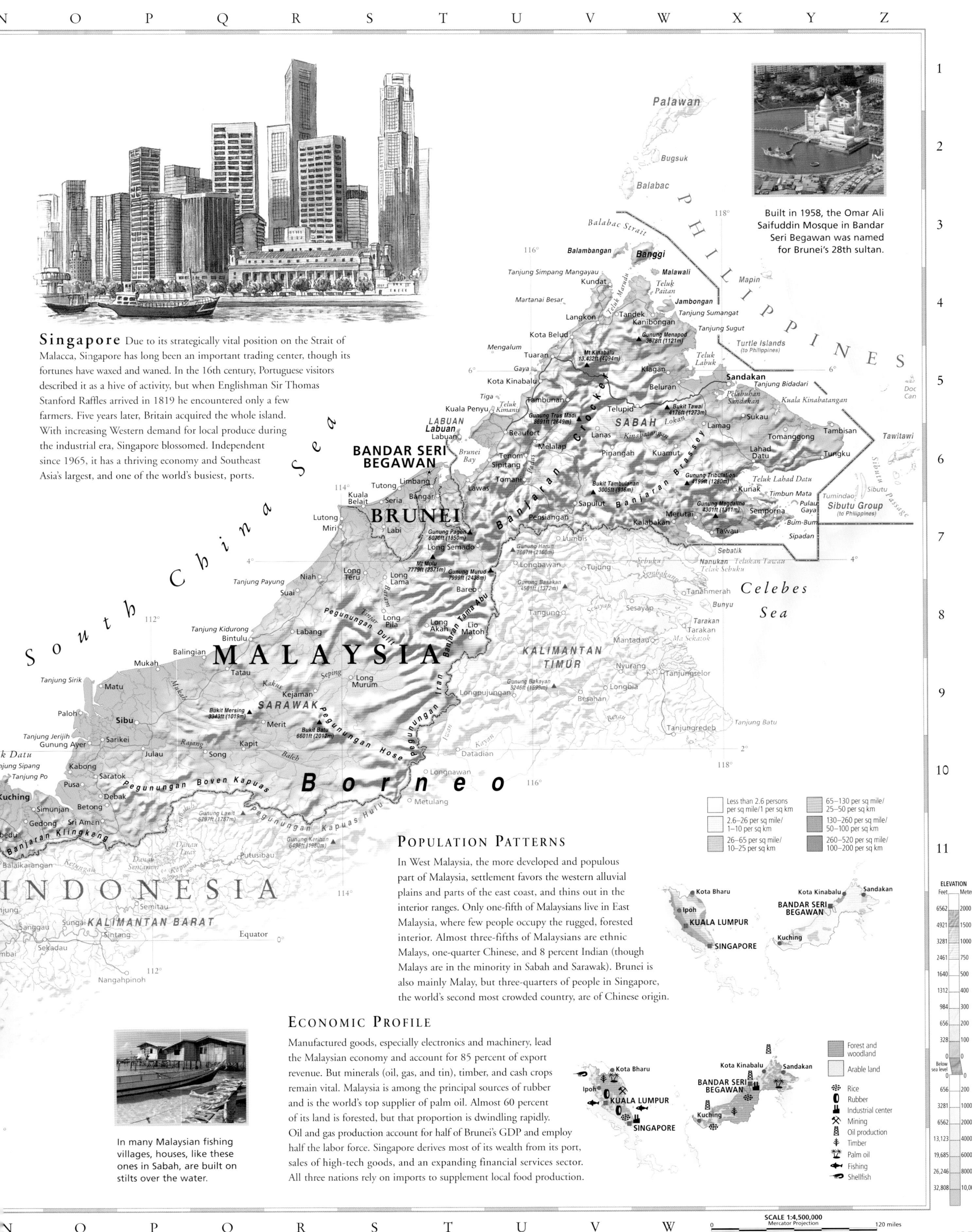

Singapore Due to its strategically vital position on the Strait of Malacca, Singapore has long been an important trading center, though its fortunes have waxed and waned. In the 16th century, Portuguese visitors described it as a hive of activity, but when Englishman Sir Thomas Stanford Raffles arrived in 1819 he encountered only a few farmers. Five years later, Britain acquired the whole island. With increasing Western demand for local produce during the industrial era, Singapore blossomed. Independent since 1965, it has a thriving economy and Southeast Asia's largest, and one of the world's busiest, ports.

Built in 1958, the Omar Ali Saifuddin Mosque in Bandar Seri Begawan was named for Brunei's 28th sultan.

In many Malaysian fishing villages, houses, like these ones in Sabah, are built on stilts over the water.

POPULATION PATTERNS

In West Malaysia, the more developed and populous part of Malaysia, settlement favors the western alluvial plains and parts of the east coast, and thins out in the interior ranges. Only one-fifth of Malaysians live in East Malaysia, where few people occupy the rugged, forested interior. Almost three-fifths of Malaysians are ethnic Malays, one-quarter Chinese, and 8 percent Indian (though Malays are in the minority in Sabah and Sarawak). Brunei is also mainly Malay, but three-quarters of people in Singapore, the world's second most crowded country, are of Chinese origin.

ECONOMIC PROFILE

Manufactured goods, especially electronics and machinery, lead the Malaysian economy and account for 85 percent of export revenue. But minerals (oil, gas, and tin), timber, and cash crops remain vital. Malaysia is among the principal sources of rubber and is the world's top supplier of palm oil. Almost 60 percent of its land is forested, but that proportion is dwindling rapidly. Oil and gas production account for half of Brunei's GDP and employ half the labor force. Singapore derives most of its wealth from its port, sales of high-tech goods, and an expanding financial services sector. All three nations rely on imports to supplement local food production.

Population density legend

Less than 2.6 persons per sq mile/1 per sq km	65–130 per sq mile/25–50 per sq km
2.6–26 per sq mile/1–10 per sq km	130–260 per sq mile/50–100 per sq km
26–65 per sq mile/10–25 per sq km	260–520 per sq mile/100–200 per sq km

ELEVATION

Feet	Meters
6562	2000
4921	1500
3281	1000
2461	750
1640	500
1312	400
984	300
656	200
328	100
Below sea level	0
656	200
3281	1000
6562	2000
13,123	4000
19,685	6000
26,246	8000
32,808	10,000

Forest and woodland
Arable land

Rice
Rubber
Industrial center
Mining
Oil production
Timber
Palm oil
Fishing
Shellfish

SCALE 1:4,500,000
Mercator Projection

120 miles
120 kilometers

The Philippines

A physically fractured country made up of more than 7,000 mainly volcanic islands, the Philippines encompasses 116,000 square miles (300,000 sq km) of land between China and Indonesia. Its two largest islands, Luzon in the north and Mindanao in the south, account for two-thirds of the country's area. Most of the islands are mountainous with narrow coastal plains. The indigenous inhabitants, the Filipinos, are of Malay origin, but modern Philippine society displays conspicuous colonial influences. Following Ferdinand Magellan's visit in 1521, Spain controlled the archipelago (naming it after its king, Philip II) from 1565 until 1898, when it was ceded to the U.S.A. Under Spanish rule, most of the population converted to Catholicism; under the Americans, English became the colony's lingua franca. The Second World War, during which Japan occupied the islands, delayed independence, which was achieved in 1946. In 1986, the repressive, 21-year rule of Ferdinand Marcos was ended by a popular uprising. A fragile democracy has since held, despite attempted coups, economic crises, and violence perpetrated by Muslim separatists, particularly on the islands of Mindanao and Basilan.

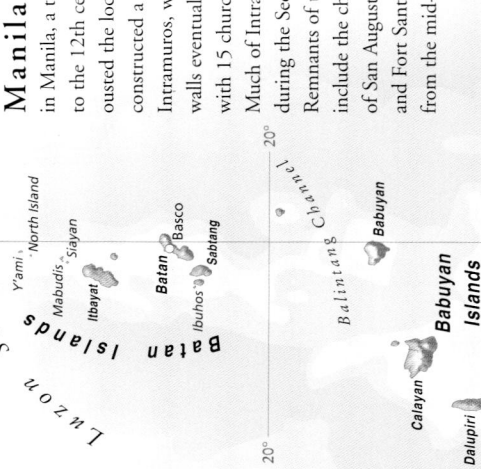

These rice terraces near Banaue, Luzon, were first built by the local Ifugao people 2,000 years ago.

Mayon in southeastern Luzon is a highly active volcano that poses a threat to nearby towns.

Manila

Spanish forces arrived in Manila, a trading post dating back to the 12th century, in 1571. Having ousted the local Muslim ruler, they constructed a fortress called Intramuros, whose 20-foot (6-m) walls eventually enclosed a town with 15 churches and 6 monasteries. Much of Intramuros was obliterated during the Second World War. Remnants of the Spanish colony include the church and monastery of San Augustin, built in 1599, and Fort Santiago, which dates from the mid-17th century.

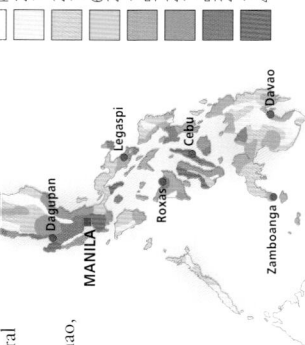

San Augustin Church

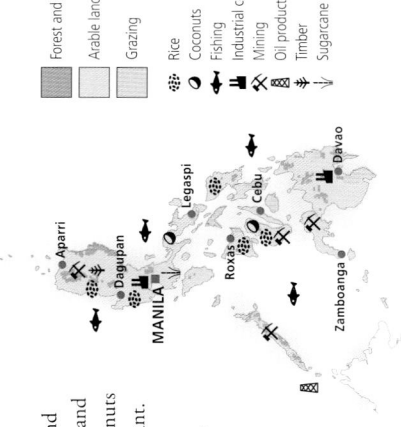

Fort Santiago

Population Patterns

The archipelago is densely though unevenly populated. The most developed area is central Luzon: Manila alone is home to 10 million people. Other areas, such as central Mindanao, Palawan, and northern Luzon, are sparsely inhabited. The population growth rate is high. Significant migration takes place, to the cities—urbanization has risen from 20 percent in 1900 to 63 percent in 2000—and overseas. More than 70 native languages are spoken; the official languages are Filipino (the Tagalog language of southern Luzon) and English.

Economic Profile

About 20 percent of the land is arable and agriculture is the biggest employer. Rice and corn are the staple crops, sugar and coconuts the main exports. Fishing is also important. Abundant minerals include some of the world's largest deposits of nickel, copper, and chromite. Electronic goods, mainly assembled in foreign-owned factories using imported parts, account for over half of exports. Other industrial products include textiles, metals, chemicals, and foodstuffs. Substantial income is also derived from tourism.

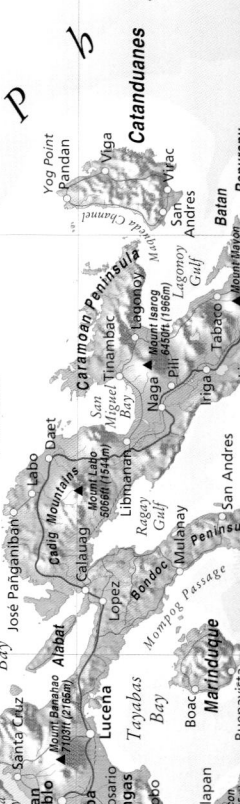

Less than 2.6 persons per sq mile/1 per sq km
2.6–26 per sq mile/ 1–10 per sq km
26–65 per sq mile/ 10–25 per sq km
65–130 per sq mile/ 25–50 per sq km
130–260 per sq mile/ 50–100 per sq km
260–520 per sq mile/ 100–200 per sq km
520–1040 per sq mile/ 200–400 per sq km
1040–2080 per sq mile/ 400–800 per sq km

Forest and woodland
Arable land
Grazing

Rice
Coconuts
Fishing
Industrial center
Mining
Oil production
Timber
Sugarcane

PHILIPPINES

INDONESIA

MALAYSIA

Mindanao

Samar

Leyte

Cebu

Negros

Panay

Masbate

Bohol

Palawan

Sulu Sea

Bohol Sea

Visayan Sea

Sibuyan Sea

Panay Gulf

Leyte Gulf

Moro Gulf

Davao Gulf

Celebes Sea

Mindoro Strait

Balabac Strait

Sulu Archipelago

Calamian Group

Cuyo Islands

Camotes Islands

Sarangani Islands

Samales Group

Tapul Group

Lugus

Pangutaran Group

Sibutu Group

Tawitawi

Basilan

Siargao

Dinagat

Homonhon

Ticao

Romblon

Tablas

Siquijor

Camiguin

Guimaras

Samal

Balut

Davao

Cagayan de Oro

Butuan

Surigao

Tacloban

Calbayog

Ormoc

Cadiz

Bacolod

Bago

San Carlos

Silay

Lapu-Lapu

Mandaue

Cebu

Dumaguete

Tagbilaran

Roxas

Iloilo

Zamboanga

Pagadian

Dipolog

Cotabato

General Santos

Puerto Princesa

A distinctively Filipino mode of transport, jeepneys were originally modified U.S.-Army-surplus jeeps.

Up to 25 typhoons strike the Philippines each year. They are most common in the east around Samar and Leyte.

SCALE 1:4,000,000
Lambert's Conformal Conic Projection

120 miles

120 kilometers

ELEVATION

Longitude east of Greenwich

197

JAPAN

Although it occupies a strategically important position off the northeast coast of Asia, Japan remained isolated from outside influences for long periods of its history. It limited relations with its neighbors from the ninth century and adopted an official policy of isolation in 1639, soon after the arrival of the first Western missionaries and explorers. Only in the mid-19th century did it open up to foreign influences and trade.

Its subsequent attempts to expand its empire led to international conflicts and a devastating defeat in the Second World War. Yet the nation recovered spectacularly to become the world's second-strongest industrial power after the United States and wield an economic and political influence far out of proportion to its small size. Occupying a land area smaller than California, Japan consists of about 4,000 islands, dominated by the large islands of Hokkaidō, Honshū, Shikoku, and Kyūshū. In the interiors of these islands, mountain ranges are separated by river valleys and bounded by narrow coastal plains. Being situated on the Pacific Rim of Fire, the country experiences regular earthquakes and volcanic eruptions, which periodically wreak havoc on the land and its people.

POPULATION PATTERNS

About 80 percent of Japan is mountainous and has low-to-moderate levels of population density; the other 20 percent, however—mainly valleys and coastal plains—supports the bulk of the population and includes some of the world's most densely inhabited areas. Urban dwellers account for 80 percent of the inhabitants and the capital, Tokyo, is the world's largest urban center. The population is ethnically homogenous, with 99 percent being Japanese. About 84% follow both Buddhist and Shinto traditions. In recent years, a declining birth rate and rapidly aging population have heightened concerns about labor shortages and the cost of maintaining social services.

Less than 2.6 persons per sq mile/1 per sq km
2.6–26 per sq mile/1–10 per sq km
26–65 per sq mile/10–25 per sq km
65–130 per sq mile/25–50 per sq km
130–260 per sq mile/50–100 per sq km
260–520 per sq mile/100–200 per sq km
520–1040 per sq mile/200–400 per sq km
1040–2080 per sq mile/400–800 per sq km
More than 2080 per sq mile/800 per sq km

ECONOMIC PROFILE

Japan is an economic superpower despite having only a small area of cultivable land and modest mineral resources (small deposits of copper, coal, and iron ore and meager reserves of oil and gas). Its success is due mainly to government support and innovation: large subsidies and intensive farming practices have helped it become virtually self-sufficient in rice and produce large quantities of fruit and vegetables; heavy investment in education, research, and technology have created a sophisticated industrial sector renowned for machinery and electronic goods. Even the nation's impressive fish catches, accounting for 15 percent of world totals, are due in part to the use of technology-loaded, wide-ranging fishing boats. This industrial success has greatly increased export revenue; however, a recession in the late 1990s cast a shadow over the nation's economic future.

Forest and woodland
Arable land

Rice
Fruit
Tobacco
Beef cattle
Fishing
Industrial center
Winter sports

In winter, mountain-dwelling macaque monkeys stay warm by sitting in pools fed by hot springs.

Bullet trains began operating in 1964. They now have a top speed of 160 mph (260 km/h).

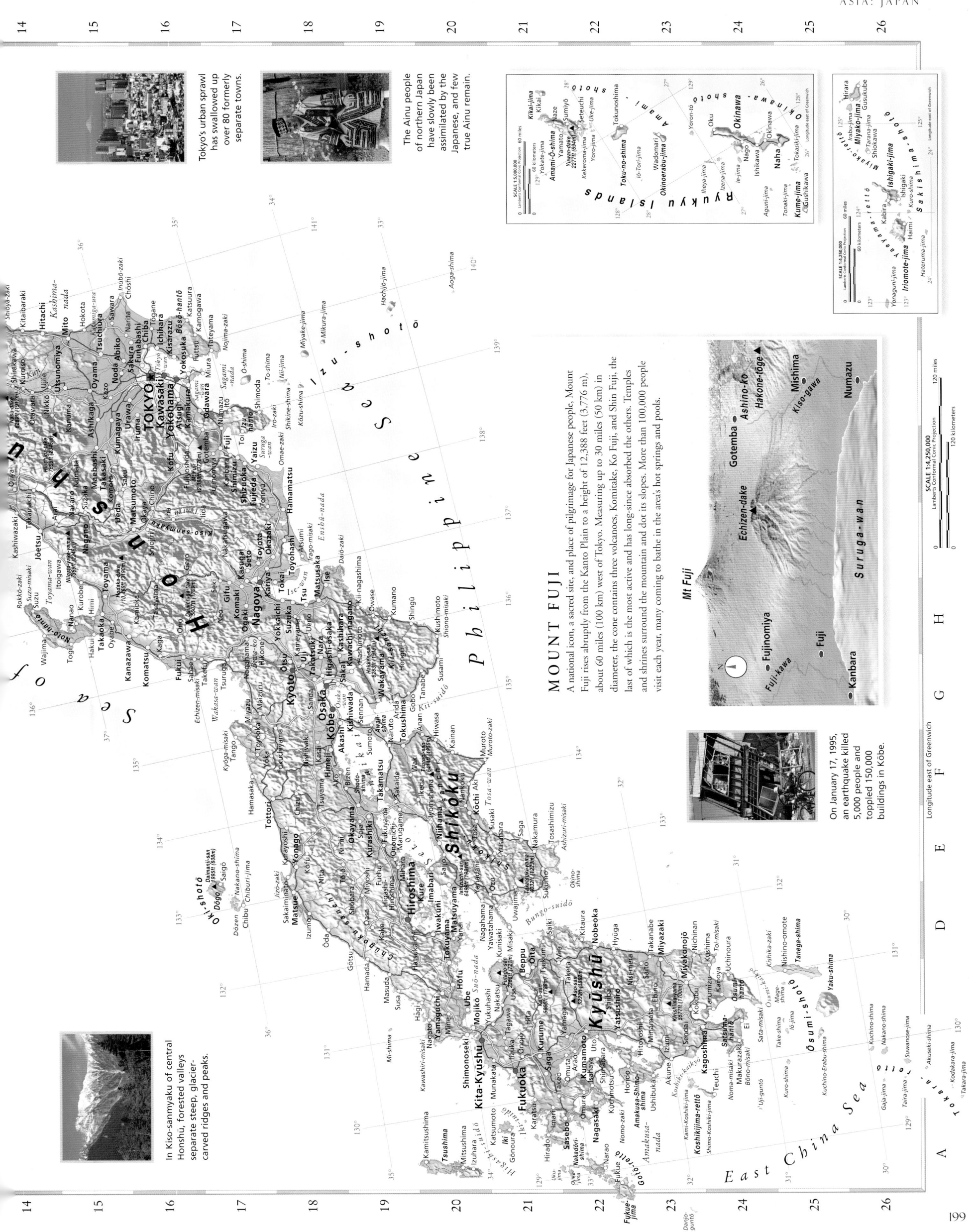

Tokyo's urban sprawl has swallowed up over 80 formerly separate towns.

The Ainu people of northern Japan have slowly been assimilated by the Japanese, and few true Ainu remain.

In Kiso-sanmyaku of central Honshū, forested valleys separate steep, glacier-carved ridges and peaks.

On January 17, 1995, an earthquake killed 5,000 people and toppled 150,000 buildings in Kōbe.

MOUNT FUJI

A national icon, a sacred site, and place of pilgrimage for Japanese people, Mount Fuji rises abruptly from the Kanto Plain to a height of 12,388 feet (3,776 m), about 60 miles (100 km) west of Tokyo. Measuring up to 30 miles (50 km) in diameter, the cone contains three volcanoes, Komitake, Ko Fuji, and Shin Fuji, the last of which is the most active and has long-since absorbed the others. Temples and shrines surround the mountain and dot its slopes. More than 100,000 people visit each year, many coming to bathe in the area's hot springs and pools.

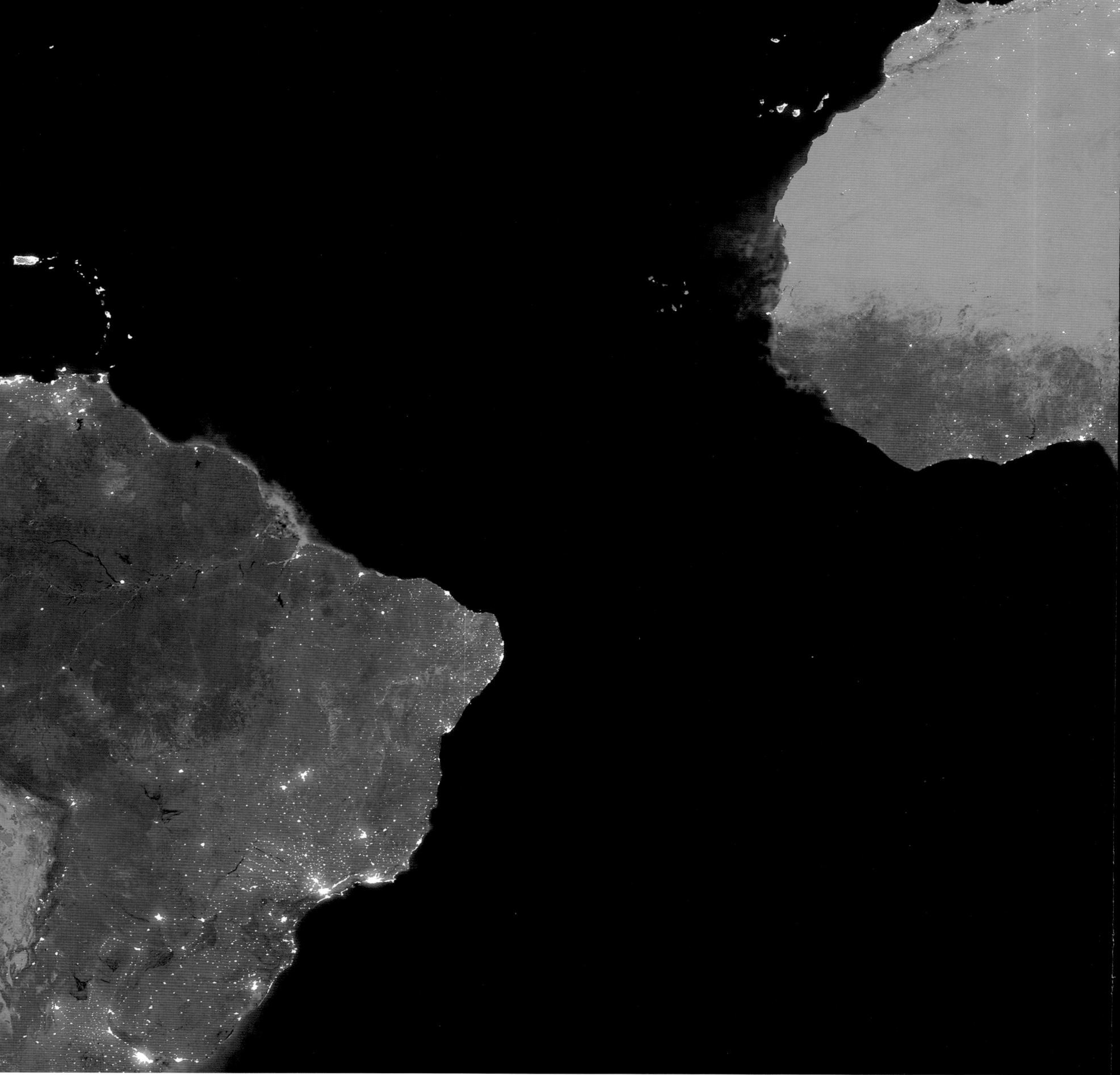

The Nile River, from the Aswan Dam to the Mediterranean, is illuminated at night.
This bright thread and the pockets of lights in the north and south indicate urbanized
areas. The Sahara and the tropical forests of the Congo Basin show little light.

AFRICA

ABOVE AFRICA

Dominating the top third of the continent of Africa is the mighty Sahara, the largest region of dry land on the planet. Using radar imaging that can penetrate the Sahara's dry sands, satellites can "see" geological features that chronicle past climate changes and events that are not visible at ground level. Revealed are ancient drainage channels, scoured out in wetter times when forests and grasslands covered the region, and long valleys carved by wind-driven sand. Satellites also record ongoing change, such as the effects of the prolonged drought that sent huge clouds of dust billowing across the Atlantic. Africa's few volcanoes are concentrated in the Great Rift Valley, in the east of the continent, where two tectonic plates are slowly pulling apart. The Virunga volcanic chain lies near the southwestern end of the valley, straddling the borders of Rwanda, the Democratic Republic of Congo, and Uganda.

Namib Sand Sea, Namibia
Below: Land and ocean seem reversed in this false-color image of the vast Namib Sand Sea, on the west coast of southern Africa. The magenta areas are fields of high, steep sand dunes, while the orange area at the bottom is the South Atlantic Ocean. The bright green features in the upper right are rocky hills poking above the sand sea.

The Sahara Desert, northern Africa
Above right: A comet slamming into the Sahara Desert millions of years ago left the circular scars seen in this radar image. The concentric ring structure left of center is the main impact crater, with a diameter of 10.5 miles (17 km). Scientists believe the comet broke apart before impact, and to the right are two similar, but less distinct, scars.

Virunga Mountains, Central Africa
Below: The rugged Virunga volcanic chain in Central Africa is home to the endangered mountain gorilla. This false-color image, centered on Mount Karisimbi, graphically illustrates the threat to the gorilla's forest habitat, shown as green, by farmlands, shown as purple. The thin green lines are thought to be agricultural terracing.

Cape Verde and the Canary Islands
Right: A dust plume over 1,000 miles (1,600 km) long sweeps past the islands of Cape Verde (lower left), north to the Canary Islands (top center). The dust comes from the savanna lands just south of the Sahara, where long-term drought and overgrazing has stripped the dry soil bare, leading to erosion and catastrophic dust storms.

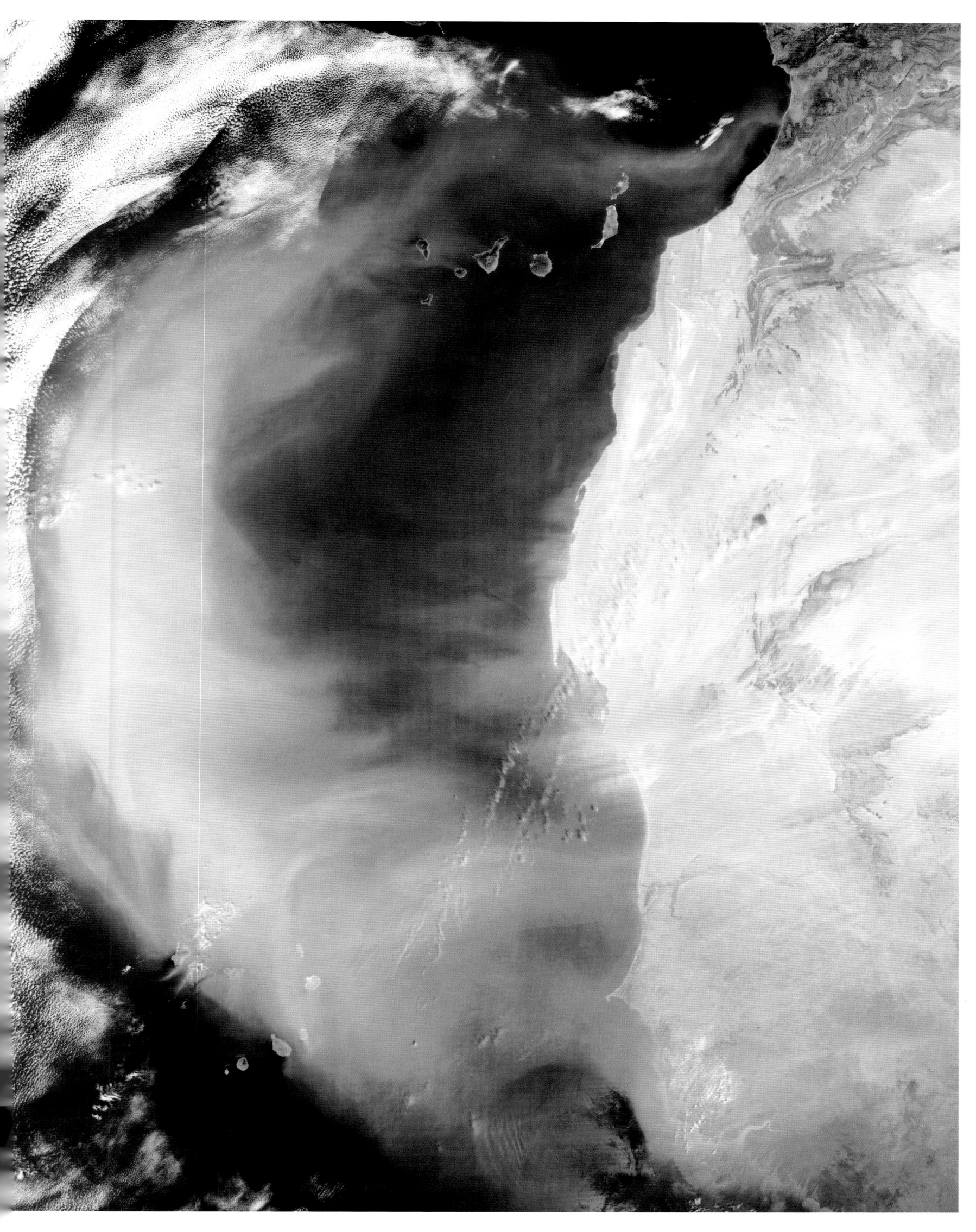

LAND AND ENVIRONMENT

The second-largest continent after Asia, Africa encompasses 11.7 million square miles (30 million sq km), almost one-fifth of Earth's land. It is separated from Europe by the Mediterranean Sea and from Asia by the Red Sea and Gulf of Aden. From Cap Blanc in the far north, it stretches about 5,000 miles (8,000 km) south to Cape Agulhas in South Africa. The northern half of the continent is far wider than the south, spanning 4,600 miles (7,360 km) between Cap Vert in Senegal and Rās Xaafuun in Somalia. Relative to the other continents, Africa has few extensive lowlands or high mountain ranges. It consists mainly of a huge plateau, rimmed by narrow coastal plains, which slopes gently from southeast to northwest. The highest areas are the Ethiopian Highlands and the East African Plateau, site of Africa's highest peak, Kilimanjaro. These uplands are riven by the Great Rift Valley, an extensive fault that runs for 4,000 miles (6,400 km) from the Red Sea to the Zambezi River.

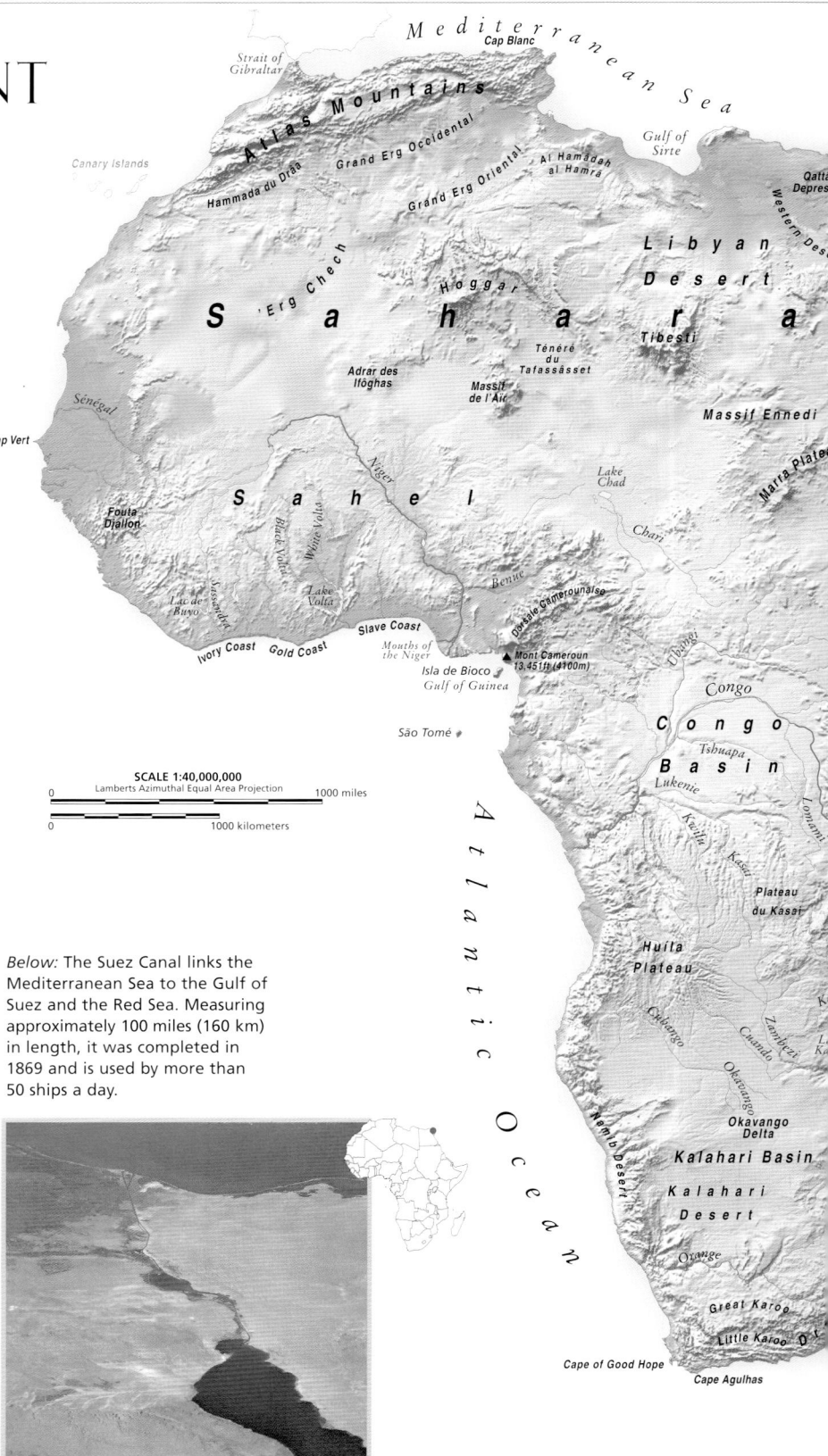

SCALE 1:40,000,000
Lamberts Azimuthal Equal Area Projection

0   1000 miles

0   1000 kilometers

Left: The Atlas Mountains, which run from southwest to northeast across the center of this image, stretch for 1,200 miles (2,000 km), isolating the temperate northwest coast from the Sahara Desert.

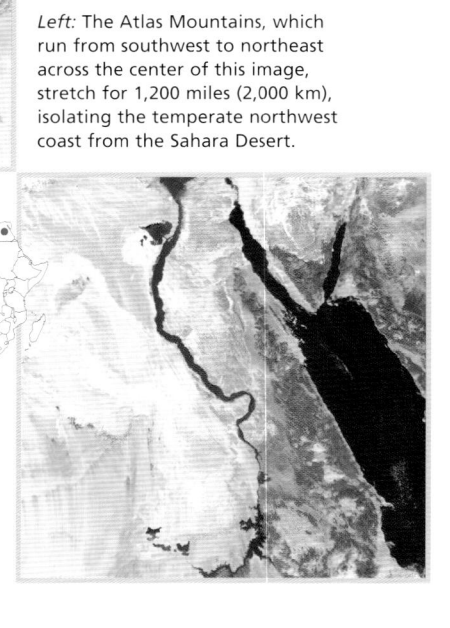

Right: The dark green line at center here is the 4,160-mile (6,695-km) Nile, the world's longest river. Rising in the Ethiopian Highlands, it flows north through Sudan and Egypt to the Mediterranean Sea.

Below: The Suez Canal links the Mediterranean Sea to the Gulf of Suez and the Red Sea. Measuring approximately 100 miles (160 km) in length, it was completed in 1869 and is used by more than 50 ships a day.

NATURAL HAZARDS

Drought

Many parts of Africa receive rain only during an annual wet season. Fluctuations in this seasonal rainfall can result in drought—periods of rainfall well below the long-term average. With so many of the inhabitants of these regions dependent on subsistence agriculture, drought can, in turn, cause great hardship and loss of life. Sometimes, the losses are due to a misreading of natural long-term climatic patterns. In the Sahel region in the 1960s, for example, a succession of years of above-average rainfall (see graph, right) encouraged farmers to cultivate this normally arid region. When rainfall levels returned to the norm, the crops soon failed. By 1973, an estimated 100,000 people had starved to death.

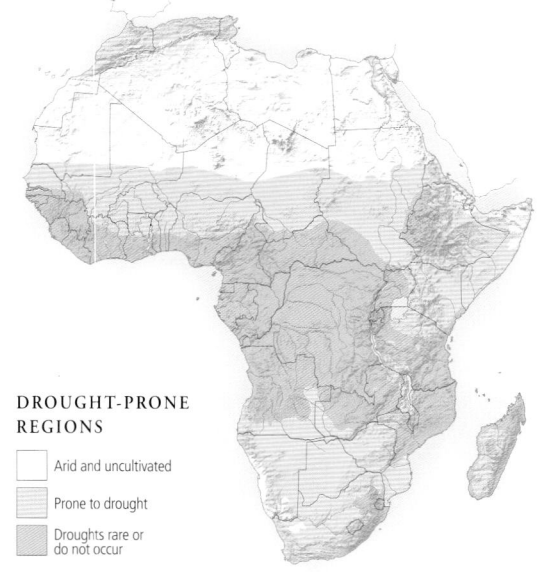

DROUGHT-PRONE REGIONS

    Arid and uncultivated

    Prone to drought

    Droughts rare or do not occur

RAINFALL IN THE SAHEL AND SUDAN, 1960–93

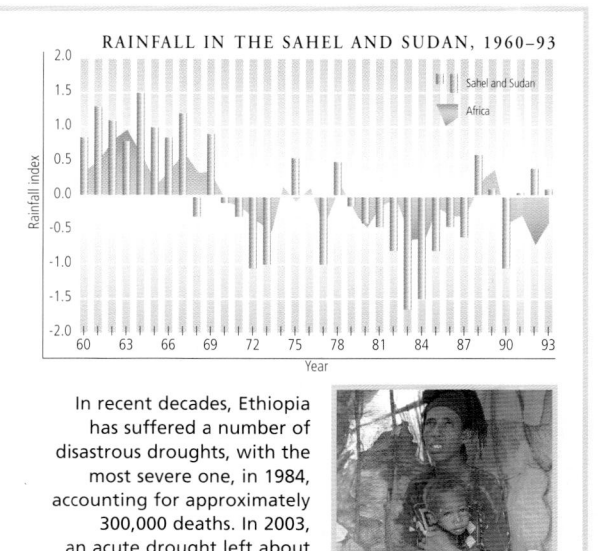

In recent decades, Ethiopia has suffered a number of disastrous droughts, with the most severe one, in 1984, accounting for approximately 300,000 deaths. In 2003, an acute drought left about 11 million people facing severe food shortages.

Climate

Africa's climate zones broadly mirror each other on either side of the Equator. Regular, abundant rainfall occurs at the Equator. Farther east, north, and south, rainfall is seasonal, the wet season decreasing in length with distance from the Equator. High pressure creates arid zones at 30 degrees north and south. The latter is limited to the southwest; the former spans the continent, creating the Sahara Desert. In the far north and far south, narrow Mediterranean zones line the coast. The irregularities in this otherwise symmetrical pattern are the tropical and subtropical zones of the southeast, created, respectively, by moist onshore air masses and a more pronounced southern shift of seasonal tropical rains.

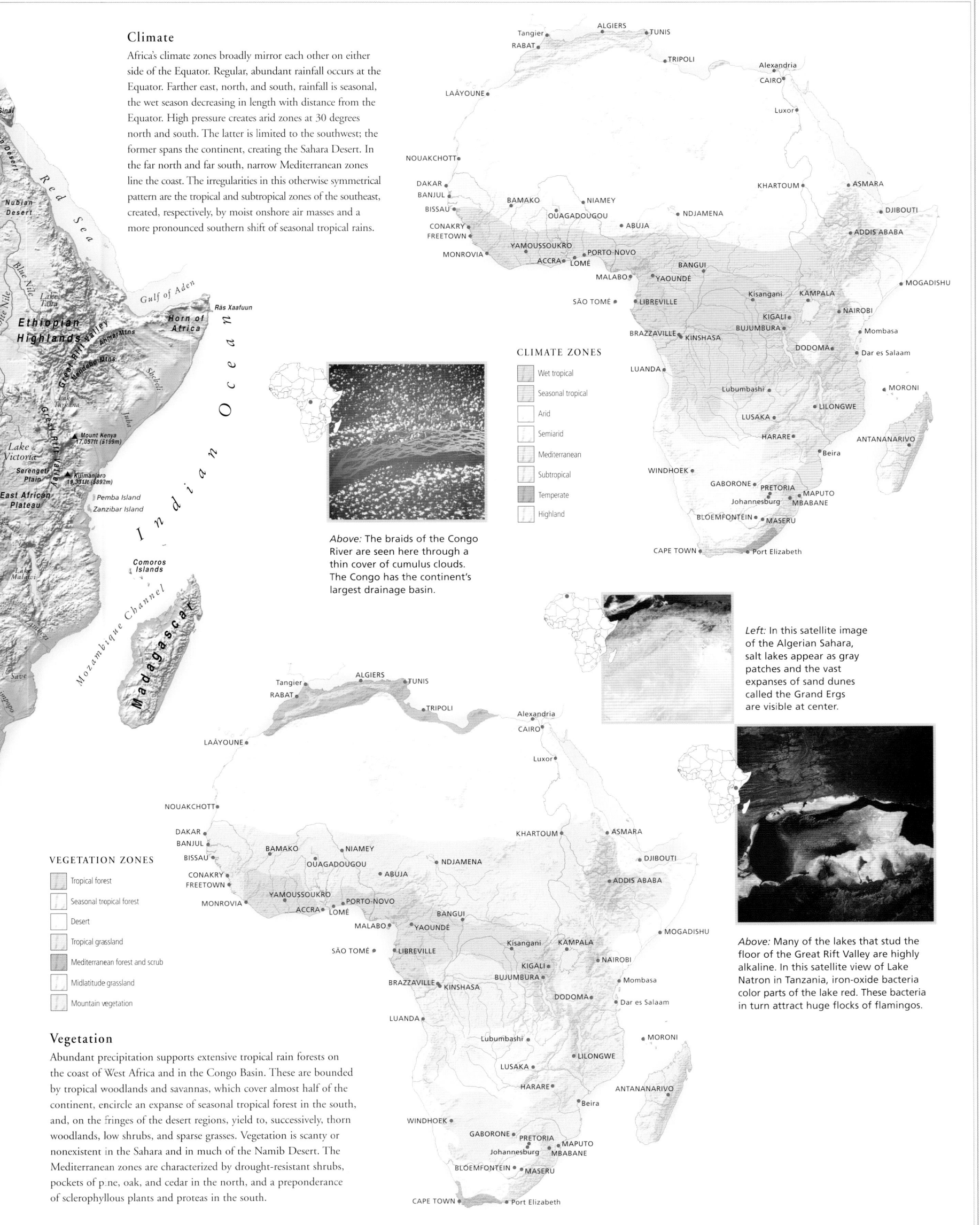

CLIMATE ZONES
- Wet tropical
- Seasonal tropical
- Arid
- Semiarid
- Mediterranean
- Subtropical
- Temperate
- Highland

Above: The braids of the Congo River are seen here through a thin cover of cumulus clouds. The Congo has the continent's largest drainage basin.

Left: In this satellite image of the Algerian Sahara, salt lakes appear as gray patches and the vast expanses of sand dunes called the Grand Ergs are visible at center.

Above: Many of the lakes that stud the floor of the Great Rift Valley are highly alkaline. In this satellite view of Lake Natron in Tanzania, iron-oxide bacteria color parts of the lake red. These bacteria in turn attract huge flocks of flamingos.

VEGETATION ZONES
- Tropical forest
- Seasonal tropical forest
- Desert
- Tropical grassland
- Mediterranean forest and scrub
- Midlatitude grassland
- Mountain vegetation

Vegetation

Abundant precipitation supports extensive tropical rain forests on the coast of West Africa and in the Congo Basin. These are bounded by tropical woodlands and savannas, which cover almost half of the continent, encircle an expanse of seasonal tropical forest in the south, and, on the fringes of the desert regions, yield to, successively, thorn woodlands, low shrubs, and sparse grasses. Vegetation is scanty or nonexistent in the Sahara and in much of the Namib Desert. The Mediterranean zones are characterized by drought-resistant shrubs, pockets of pine, oak, and cedar in the north, and a preponderance of sclerophyllous plants and proteas in the south.

PEOPLES AND NATIONS

The continent-spanning Sahara Desert divides Africa's 800 million or so people into two major groups: the culturally homogenous, predominantly Arabic and Islamic peoples of the north; and the numerous, and culturally and linguistically diverse, indigenous peoples of the south. Other ethnic groups include the descendants of European colonists, found mainly in the far north and far south, and the Malagasy of Madagascar, whose ancestors migrated from Indonesia. The late-20th-century decolonization of Africa resulted in the creation of numerous states—now 53 countries in all—some of whose borders, especially in sub-Saharan Africa, cut across traditional ethnic territories. Resulting conflicts hinder attempts to alleviate poverty.

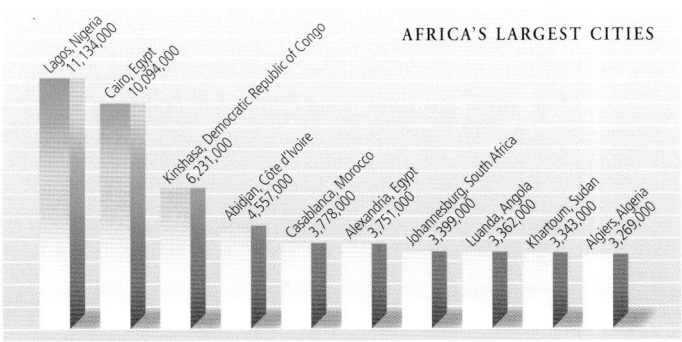

Urbanization

Africa had few large towns or cities until the 20th century, and its proportion of urban dwellers remains low relative to other continents—approximately 40 percent. Yet recently urbanization has occurred more rapidly here than anywhere else: in 1950, just 15 percent of Africans lived in towns and cities. North Africa is considerably more urbanized than sub-Saharan Africa, though Lagos in Nigeria is the continent's biggest city. Africa's largest urban areas tend to be on the coast, and many are ports established by former colonial powers.

Right: Population growth in Lagos, Nigeria, is due mainly to rural–urban migration. In an effort to slow the city's expansion, the government recently moved the national capital from Lagos to Abuja.

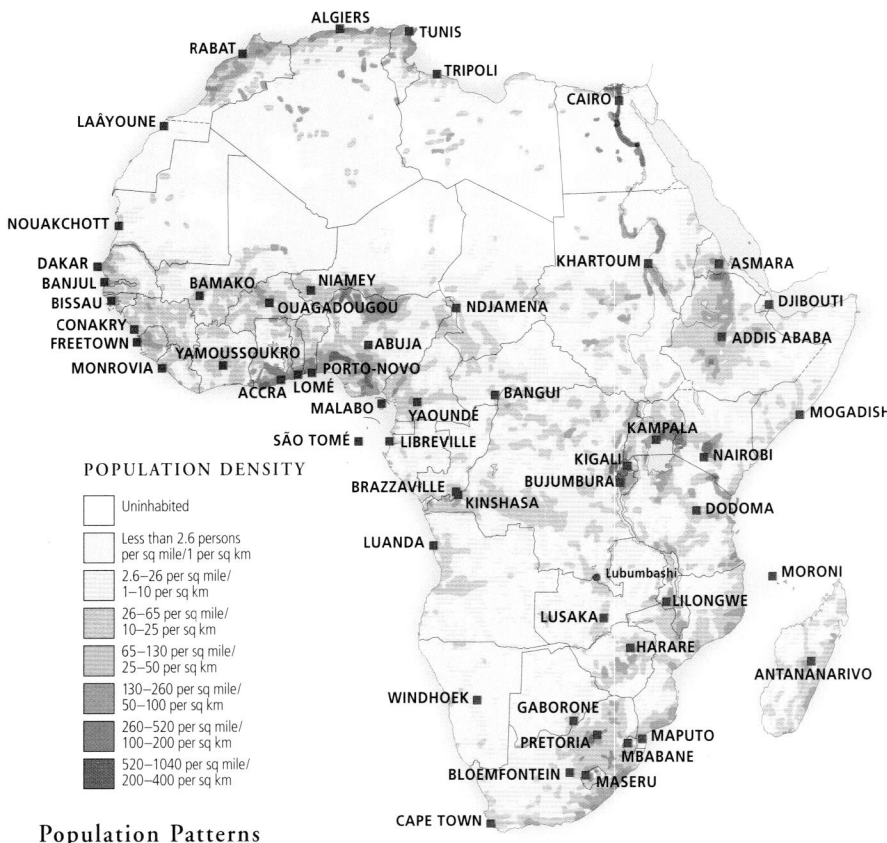

POPULATION DENSITY

- Uninhabited
- Less than 2.6 persons per sq mile/1 per sq km
- 2.6–26 per sq mile/ 1–10 per sq km
- 26–65 per sq mile/ 10–25 per sq km
- 65–130 per sq mile/ 25–50 per sq km
- 130–260 per sq mile/ 50–100 per sq km
- 260–520 per sq mile/ 100–200 per sq km
- 520–1040 per sq mile/ 200–400 per sq km

Population Patterns

Relative to most other continents, Africa is underpopulated, having just 13 percent of the world's people but more than 20 percent of its land. This is due in part to the high proportion of arid land, which precludes widespread permanent settlement, but also to the effects of disease and conflict. The greatest population densities occur on the coasts of North and West Africa, along major rivers and around large lakes, and in well-watered upland areas such as the highlands of the Great Rift Valley. Despite its low density, Africa's population is growing rapidly and is likely to reach almost 1.5 billion by 2030 (during that time, its growth rate will probably stay high while rates on other continents decline steeply). About 40 percent of the current population is under 15.

Trade Organizations

Intraregional trade has long been hampered by poor communications and a limited variety of commodities. However, the Abuja Treaty of 1991 established the African Economic Community, which aims to create an African common market by uniting the following regional organizations: the Economic Community of West African States (ECOWAS), the Economic Community of Central African States (ECCAS), the Southern African Development Community (SADC), the Common Market for Eastern and Southern Africa (COMESA), and the Arab Maghreb Union (AMU).

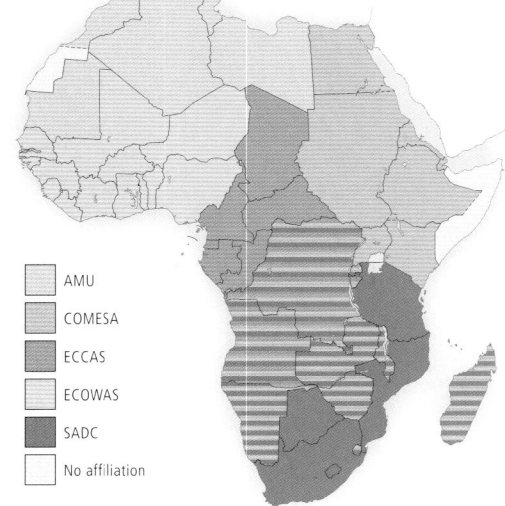

- AMU
- COMESA
- ECCAS
- ECOWAS
- SADC
- No affiliation

FLASHPOINTS

Many of Africa's numerous and frequently violent regional disputes have centered on the control of lucrative natural resources and been stoked by interethnic rivalries.

Western Sahara

As soon as Spain left its colony of Western Sahara in 1976, Morocco annexed the territory, encouraging Moroccans to settle there and forcing native Saharawi people into Algeria. It then built a fortified wall, the so-called Berm, to keep out the Saharawi and their independence fighters, the Polisario Front. UN attempts to broker peace have so far failed.

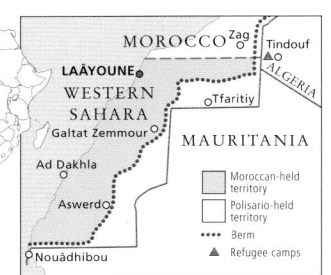

Democratic Republic of Congo

Ethnic disputes have fueled a civil war in the Democratic Republic of Congo that has claimed 3 million lives since 1998. Despite the formation in 2003 of a coalition government including the main rebel groups—the Movement for the Liberation of Congo (MLC) and the Rally for Congolese Democracy (RCD)—violence continues.

West Africa's Diamond Wars

In 1990, the rebel National Patriotic Front (NPF) took control of Liberia and began aiding Sierra Leone insurgents the Revolutionary United Front (RUF) in return for diamonds. This led to civil wars that have killed 300,000 people. The U.K. helped disarm the RUF in 2002, and the NPF was ousted in 2003, but the situation remains volatile.

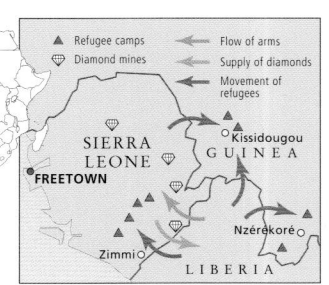

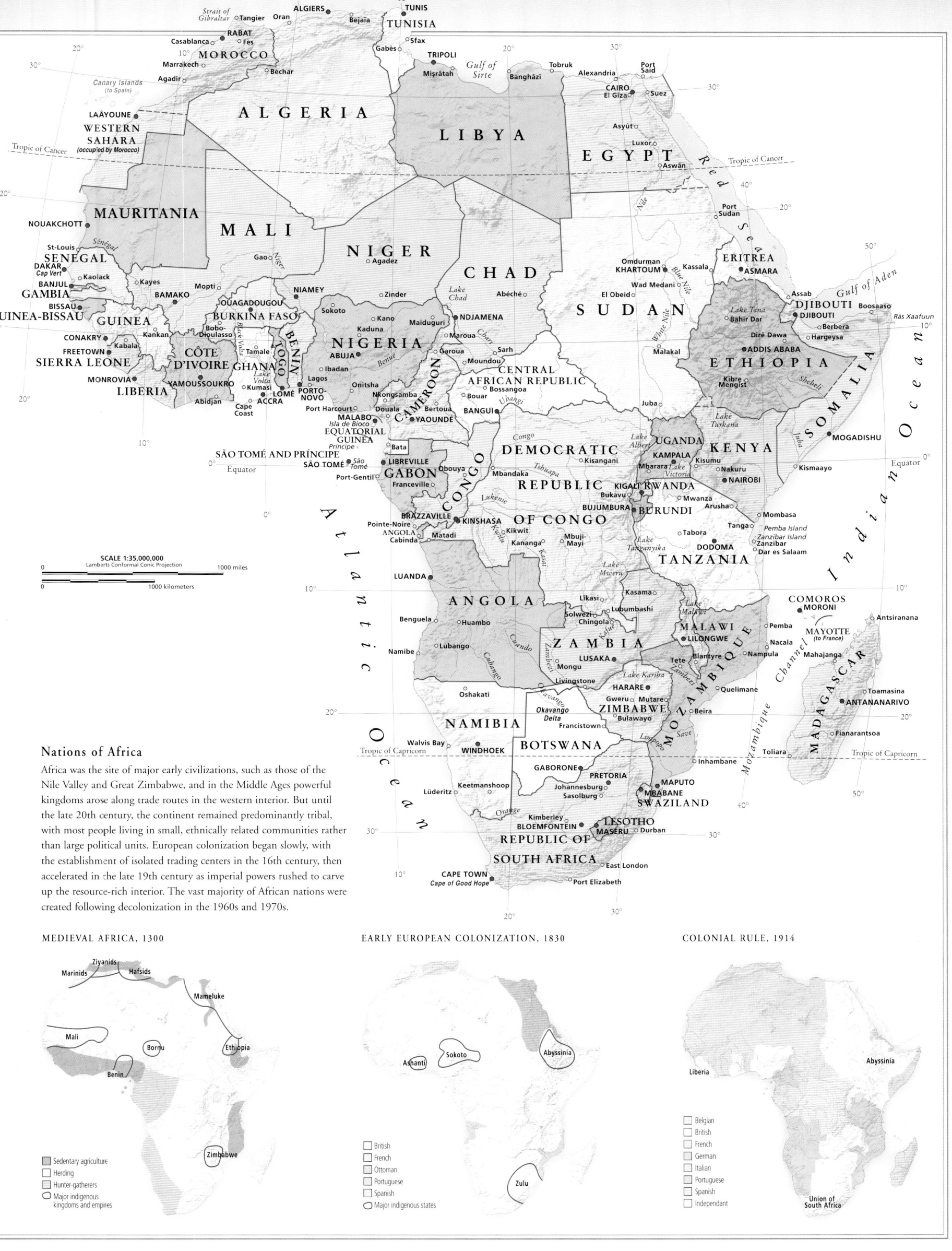

Nations of Africa

Africa was the site of major early civilizations, such as those of the Nile Valley and Great Zimbabwe, and in the Middle Ages powerful kingdoms arose along trade routes in the western interior. But until the late 20th century, the continent remained predominantly tribal, with most people living in small, ethnically related communities rather than large political units. European colonization began slowly, with the establishment of isolated trading centers in the 16th century, then accelerated in the late 19th century as imperial powers rushed to carve up the resource-rich interior. The vast majority of African nations were created following decolonization in the 1960s and 1970s.

MEDIEVAL AFRICA, 1300

EARLY EUROPEAN COLONIZATION, 1830

COLONIAL RULE, 1914

THE HUMAN IMPACT

Africa is where humans first evolved, and modification of the land to facilitate hunting and farming, as well as the excavation of minerals, have been happening there for thousands of years. As on most other continents, however, it was the arrival of European colonists that precipitated industrial-scale exploitation of natural resources—including people. An estimated 10 million Africans were deported as slaves between the 16th and 19th centuries. In addition, vast amounts of timber and huge quantities of minerals were shipped to foreign markets. Since decolonization, governments have faced the difficult balancing act of providing for impoverished populations while guarding against the exhaustion of resources. Environmental problems are exacerbated by population growth, inequitable land distribution, foreign penetration of local markets, corruption, weak institutions, and violent conflicts.

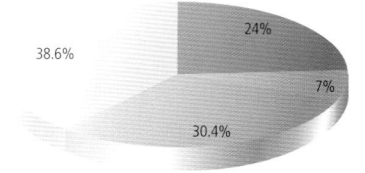

Land Cover

Two-thirds of Africa is arid or semiarid; much of this land is used, appropriately, for nomadic grazing. The proportion of arable land is low relative to other continents. Its quality varies, from fertile volcanic and alluvial soils to poor, leached soils in zones of high rainfall. Africa's forests represent 17 percent of global forest cover; one-fifth lies within the Democratic Republic of Congo.

PROPORTIONS OF TOTAL LAND AREA

24%
38.6%
7%
30.4%

- Forest and woodland
- Arable land
- Grazing
- Other land

THE CHANGING FACE OF AFRICA

Desertification

Significant fluctuations in rainfall, including prolonged droughts, periodically reduce vegetation cover in semiarid areas of Africa. The impact of this natural cycle has been intensified by human modification of the land, especially the cultivation and grazing of marginal areas. These activities remove the natural vegetation that binds light soils together, making them vulnerable to erosion, and in turn inhibiting the regeneration of plants. Desertification, as this process is widely known, now threatens 46 percent of Africa, and more than half of this land is at high or very high risk. Around 485 million Africans are affected.

AREAS AT RISK OF DESERTIFICATION

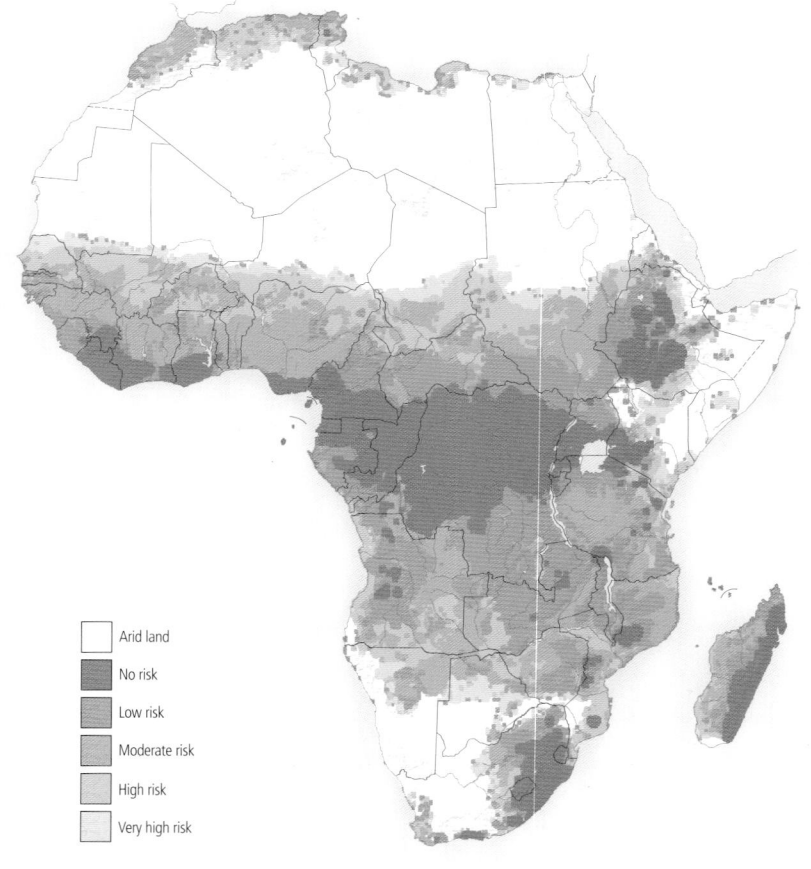

- Arid land
- No risk
- Low risk
- Moderate risk
- High risk
- Very high risk

Economic Profile

Africa is resource-wealthy, but due to its historical development and the uneven distribution of resources, Africans are not. About 44 percent live on the equivalent of less than US$1 a day, and almost 60 percent rely on subsistence farming. Yet minerals are abundant. Most North African nations, as well as Nigeria and Cameroon, have substantial oil and gas reserves. The Democratic Republic of Congo, Sierra Leone, and South Africa are important sources of diamonds. Uranium and gold are widespread in southern Africa, and the continent has a large part of the world's iron ore. Products from Africa's still-vast forests supply a higher proportion of GDP than on any other continent. The expansion of hydroelectric power has boosted energy output. Despite this, the industrial sector remains undeveloped. This is due in part to economic programs that have encouraged developing nations to focus on the export of only a few primary commodities. Such exporters are highly vulnerable in times of oversupply and falling prices. The current terms of world trade also prevent these countries from adding value to their raw products by processing them.

Protecting the Environment

Actions being taken to ameliorate land degradation include a return to the diverse farming systems used by many African farmers before industrial techniques were introduced. Some reforestation is taking place, but mainly in the form of monocultural plantations, which do not support the biological diversity of natural forests. More than 3,000 protected areas have, however, been created, covering 5.2 percent of the continent. Few more are likely to be established in the near future due to pressure on land, but increasing involvement of local people in the management of existing protected areas is helping to improve their effectiveness. Some 48 African countries have signed the Convention on International Trade in Endangered Species (CITES), which strictly controls trade in commodities such as ivory. However, some countries, notably in southern Africa where parks are well managed and elephants consequently abundant, contend that profits from a carefully controlled ivory trade could be used to fund the management of protected areas. Although air pollution is increasing in many cities, Africa emits just 3.5 percent of the world's carbon dioxide and a mere 7 percent of total greenhouse-gas emissions. Leaded petrol has been phased out in Egypt, Sudan, Libya, and Mauritius, and another 22 countries aim to follow suit by 2006.

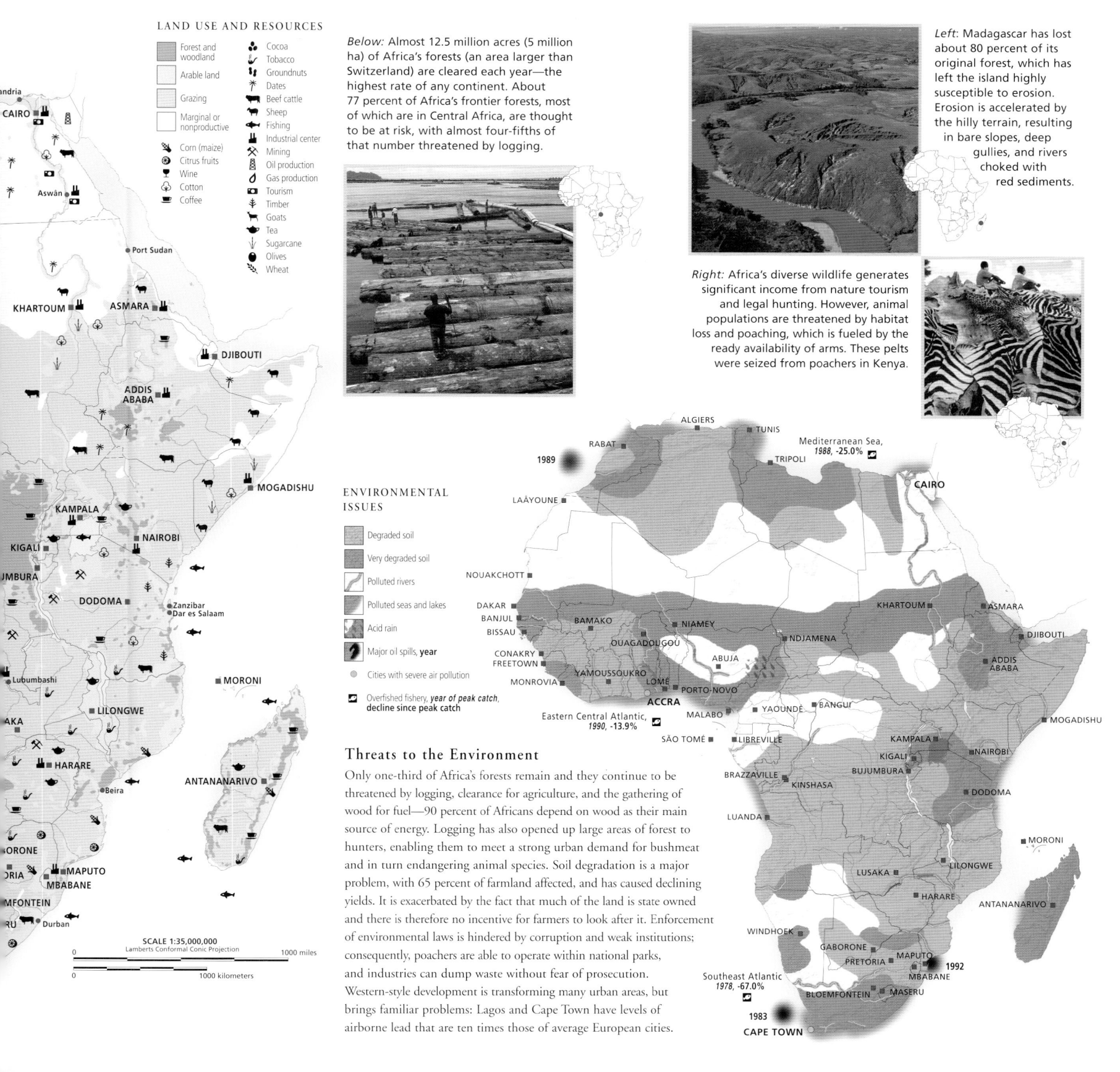

LAND USE AND RESOURCES

- Forest and woodland
- Arable land
- Grazing
- Marginal or nonproductive

- Cocoa
- Tobacco
- Groundnuts
- Dates
- Beef cattle
- Sheep
- Fishing
- Industrial center
- Mining
- Oil production
- Gas production
- Tourism
- Timber
- Goats
- Tea
- Sugarcane
- Olives
- Wheat

- Corn (maize)
- Citrus fruits
- Wine
- Cotton
- Coffee

Below: Almost 12.5 million acres (5 million ha) of Africa's forests (an area larger than Switzerland) are cleared each year—the highest rate of any continent. About 77 percent of Africa's frontier forests, most of which are in Central Africa, are thought to be at risk, with almost four-fifths of that number threatened by logging.

Left: Madagascar has lost about 80 percent of its original forest, which has left the island highly susceptible to erosion. Erosion is accelerated by the hilly terrain, resulting in bare slopes, deep gullies, and rivers choked with red sediments.

Right: Africa's diverse wildlife generates significant income from nature tourism and legal hunting. However, animal populations are threatened by habitat loss and poaching, which is fueled by the ready availability of arms. These pelts were seized from poachers in Kenya.

ENVIRONMENTAL ISSUES

- Degraded soil
- Very degraded soil
- Polluted rivers
- Polluted seas and lakes
- Acid rain
- Major oil spills, **year**
- Cities with severe air pollution
- Overfished fishery, *year of peak catch*, decline since peak catch

Mediterranean Sea, *1988, -25.0%*

Eastern Central Atlantic, *1990, -13.9%*

Southeast Atlantic *1978, -67.0%*

Threats to the Environment

Only one-third of Africa's forests remain and they continue to be threatened by logging, clearance for agriculture, and the gathering of wood for fuel—90 percent of Africans depend on wood as their main source of energy. Logging has also opened up large areas of forest to hunters, enabling them to meet a strong urban demand for bushmeat and in turn endangering animal species. Soil degradation is a major problem, with 65 percent of farmland affected, and has caused declining yields. It is exacerbated by the fact that much of the land is state owned and there is therefore no incentive for farmers to look after it. Enforcement of environmental laws is hindered by corruption and weak institutions; consequently, poachers are able to operate within national parks, and industries can dump waste without fear of prosecution. Western-style development is transforming many urban areas, but brings familiar problems: Lagos and Cape Town have levels of airborne lead that are ten times those of average European cities.

SCALE 1:35,000,000
Lamberts Conformal Conic Projection
0   1000 miles
0   1000 kilometers

PERCENTAGE OF LAND PROTECTED IN MAJOR AFRICAN COUNTRIES

Angola, Benin, Botswana, Burkina Faso, Burundi, Cameroon, Central African Republic, Chad, Congo, Côte d'Ivoire, Democratic Republic of Congo, Egypt, Equatorial Guinea, Eritrea, Ethiopia, Gabon, Gambia, Ghana, Guinea, Guinea-Bissau, Kenya, Lesotho, Liberia, Libya, Madagascar, Malawi, Mali, Mauritania, Morocco, Mozambique, Namibia, Niger, Nigeria, Rwanda, Senegal, Sierra Leone, Somalia, South Africa, Sudan, Tanzania, Togo, Tunisia, Uganda, Zambia, Zimbabwe

Northwestern Africa

Algeria, Libya, Morocco, Tunisia

Isolated from the rest of the continent by the Sahara Desert, Northwestern Africa is a transitional zone, between sea and remote interior, Europe and Africa, the West and the Middle East. Its distinctive and relatively homogenous culture was flavored by classical European civilizations and its original, nomadic Berber inhabitants, but derives mainly from the Arab peoples who invaded and settled here in the seventh century AD. This Arabic, Islamic heritage not only withstood subsequent occupation by the Ottoman Empire (between the 16th and 19th centuries), European colonial rule, and a torrid phase of decolonization, but also permeated almost every part of a vast, inhospitable region. Bounded by the Atlas Mountains in the northwest, the Sahara Desert occupies more than 80 percent of the land, confining major population centers and communications routes, sedentary farming, and industries to a narrow coastal strip.

The seminomadic Tuareg people roam the desert lands of Algeria, Libya, Mali, and Niger.

The Atlas Mountains are home to large numbers of Berbers, the region's original inhabitants.

POPULATION PATTERNS

The Sahara contains just a few isolated towns, scattered oases, and groups of nomadic pastoralists; the vast majority of the region's inhabitants dwell on the north coast. The population soared in the 20th century (Algeria's population doubled between 1960 and 1990), due to improving health services and persistent high fertility (even today, each woman has an average of four children). Migration to cities began under European rule and accelerated with industrialization, making this the most urbanized part of Africa. Libya is distinctly underpopulated and has to import skilled workers, whereas there is a steady outward flow of migrants from the other countries.

- Uninhabited
- Less than 2.6 persons per sq mile/1 per sq km
- 2.6–26 per sq mile/ 1–10 per sq km
- 26–65 per sq mile/ 10–25 per sq km
- 65–130 per sq mile/ 25–50 per sq km
- 130–260 per sq mile/ 50–100 per sq km
- 260–520 per sq mile/ 100–200 per sq km

Tangier Befitting a port that has at various times been ruled by the Phoenicians, Romans, Arabs, Spanish, Portuguese, and British, Tangier was for much of the 20th century designated an international zone. Since it became part of Morocco in 1956, many foreign residents have departed, but the city retains a cosmopolitan atmosphere. Encircled by 15th-century ramparts and surmounted by the Great Mosque, its whitewashed buildings climb a craggy limestone outcrop.

Great Mosque

ELEVATION

Feet	Meters
6562	2000
4921	1500
3281	1000
2461	750
1640	500
1312	400
984	300
656	200
328	100
0	Below sea level
656	200
3281	1000
6562	2000
13,123	4000
19,685	6000
26,246	8000
32,808	10,000

Longitude west of Greenwich

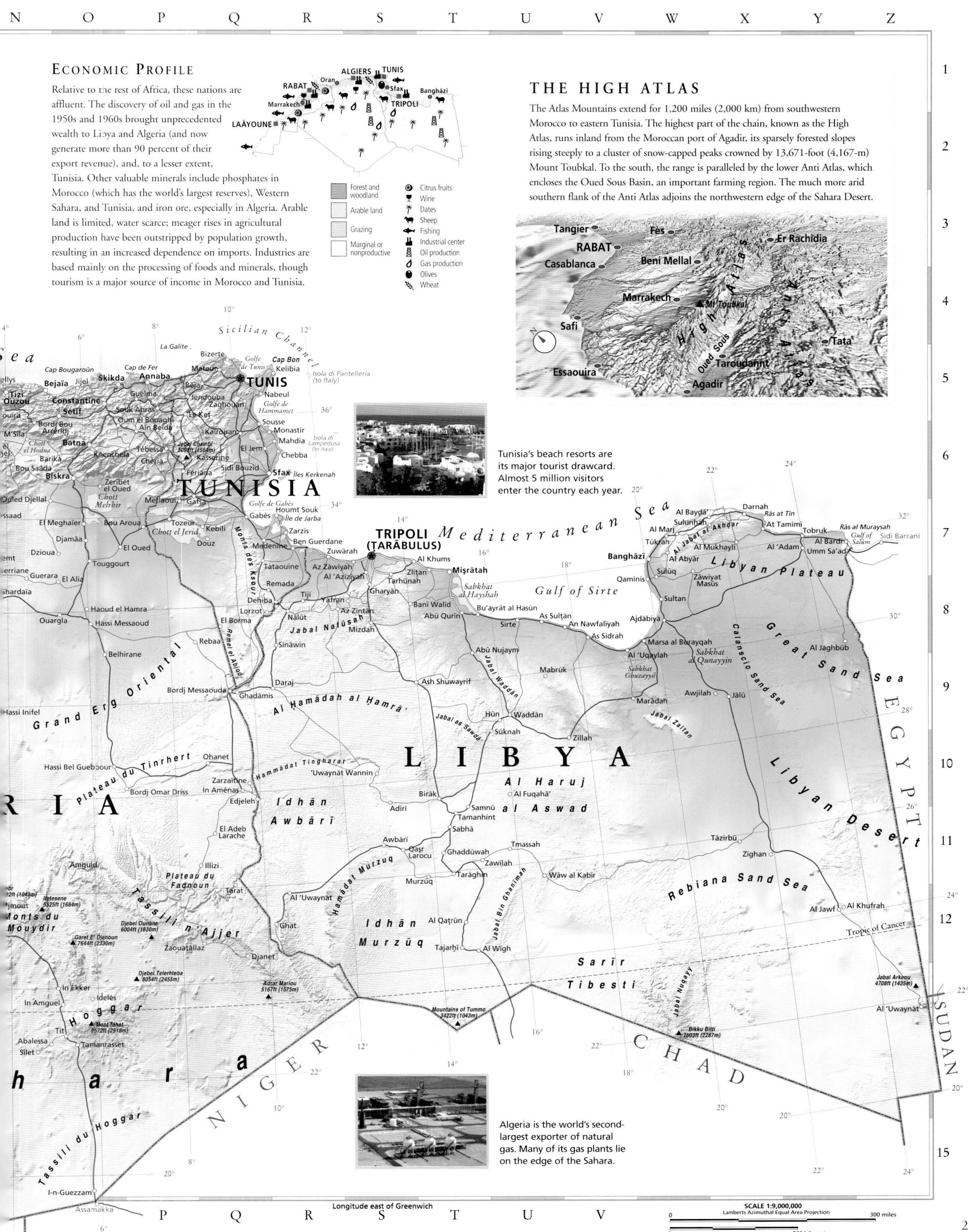

ECONOMIC PROFILE

Relative to the rest of Africa, these nations are affluent. The discovery of oil and gas in the 1950s and 1960s brought unprecedented wealth to Libya and Algeria (and now generate more than 90 percent of their export revenue), and, to a lesser extent, Tunisia. Other valuable minerals include phosphates in Morocco (which has the world's largest reserves), Western Sahara, and Tunisia, and iron ore, especially in Algeria. Arable land is limited, water scarce; meager rises in agricultural production have been outstripped by population growth, resulting in an increased dependence on imports. Industries are based mainly on the processing of foods and minerals, though tourism is a major source of income in Morocco and Tunisia.

ALGIERS TUNIS
RABAT Oran Banghāzī
Marrakech Sfax
LAÂYOUNE TRIPOLI

Forest and woodland
Arable land
Grazing
Marginal or nonproductive

Citrus fruits
Wine
Dates
Sheep
Fishing
Industrial center
Oil production
Gas production
Olives
Wheat

THE HIGH ATLAS

The Atlas Mountains extend for 1,200 miles (2,000 km) from southwestern Morocco to eastern Tunisia. The highest part of the chain, known as the High Atlas, runs inland from the Moroccan port of Agadir, its sparsely forested slopes rising steeply to a cluster of snow-capped peaks crowned by 13,671-foot (4,167-m) Mount Toubkal. To the south, the range is paralleled by the lower Anti Atlas, which encloses the Oued Sous Basin, an important farming region. The much more arid southern flank of the Anti Atlas adjoins the northwestern edge of the Sahara Desert.

Tangier Fès Er Rachidia
RABAT
Casablanca Beni Mellal
Marrakech ▲ Mt Toubkal High Atlas Anti Atlas
Safi Oued Sous Tata
Essaouira Taroudannt
Agadir

Tunisia's beach resorts are its major tourist drawcard. Almost 5 million visitors enter the country each year.

Algeria is the world's second-largest exporter of natural gas. Many of its gas plants lie on the edge of the Sahara.

Sicilian Channel
La Galite
Bizerte
Cap Bougaroûn Cap de Fer Mateur Golfe de Tunis Cap Bon Kelibia
Bejaïa Jijel Skikda Annaba Béja Isola di Pantelleria (to Italy)
Tizi Ouzou Guelma TUNIS Nabeul
Constantine Souk Ahras Jendouba Zaghouan Golfe de Hammamet
Sétif Oum el Bouaghi Aïn Beïda Le Kef Sousse
M'Sila Batna Khenchela Tébessa Kairouan Monastir Mahdia Isola di Lampedusa (to Italy)
Bordj Bou Arréridj Chéria Jebel Chambi 5098ft (1554m) Kasserine El Jem Chebba
Bou Saâda Barika Fériana Sidi Bouzid Sfax Îles Kerkenah
Biskra Zeribèt el Oued Meflaoui TUNISIA
Ouled Djellal Chott Melrhir Gafsa Golfe de Gabès Houmt Souk Île de Jerba
El Meghaïer Bou Aroua Tozeur Gabès Zarzis
Djamâa Chott el Jerid Kebili Medenine Ben Guerdane Zuwārah
Dzioua El Oued Douz Tataouine Az Zāwiyah Al ʿAzīzīyah
Guerara El Alia Touggourt Remada Yafran Gharyān
Ghardaïa Haoud el Hamra Dehiba Tiji Az Zintan Abū Qurīn
Ouargla Hassi Messaoud Lorzot Nālūt Jabal Nafūsah Mizdah Banī Walīd
Belhirane El Borma Rebaa Sināwin Daraj
Hassi Inifel Bordj Messaouda Ghadāmis Al Hamādah al Ḥamrāʾ
Grand Erg Oriental Remel el Abiod
Hassi Bel Guebbour Plateau du Tinrhert Ohanet Hammādat Tingharat ʿUwaynāt Wannin Jabal as Sawdāʾ Hūn
Zarzaïtine In Amenas Edjeleh Idhān Awbārī Sūknah Zillah
Bordj Omar Driss El Adeb Larache Birāk Al Haruj al Aswad Al Fuqahāʾ
Amguid Illizi Adirī Samnū Tamanhint Sabhā
Plateau du Fadnoun Awbārī Qaşr Larocu Ghaddūwah Tmassah Zawīlah
Tiltesene 5525ft (1684m) Tarat Qaşr Murzūq Tarāghin Wāw al Kabīr
Tassili nʿAjjer Ghat Hamādat Murzūq Idhān Murzūq Al Qatrūn Jabal Bin Ghanīmah
Garet E' Djenoun 7644ft (2330m) Djebel Ounane 6004ft (1830m) Zaouatallaz Djanet Tajarhī Al Wīgh
Djebel Telerhteba 8054ft (2455m) Adrar Mariou 5167ft (1575m) Sarīr Tibesti
In Ekker Idelès Mountains of Tummo 3422ft (1043m)
Hoggar Mont Tahat 9572ft (2918m) Jabal Nuqayy
In Amguel Bikku Bitti 7503ft (2287m)
Tit Tamanrasset
Abalessa Tassili du Hoggar
Silet
I-n-Guezzam
Assamakka

LIBYA
ALGERIA
NIGER
CHAD
SUDAN
EGYPT

Mediterranean Sea
TRIPOLI (ṬARĀBULUS) Al Khums Zlītan Mişrātah Banghāzī
Tarhūnah Sabkhat al Hayshah Gulf of Sirte Al Bayḍāʾ Darnah Rās at Tīn
Al Marj Sulunṭah At Tamimi Tobruk Rās al Murayṣah
Tūkrah Al Jabal al Akhḍar Al ʿAdam Al Bardī Sidi Barrani
Qaminis Al Mukhaylī Umm Saʿad Gulf of Salum
Sirte As Sultān An Nawfaliyah Sulūq Al Abyār Zāwiyat Masūs
Abū Nujaym As Sidrah Ajdābiyā Marsa al Burayqah Libyan Plateau
Bani Walīd Bu'ayrāt al Ḥasūn Al ʿUqaylah Sabkhat al Qunayyin
Mabrūk Sabkhat Ghuzayyil Al Jāghbūb
Ash Shuwayrif Marādah Awjilah Jālū Calanscio Sand Sea Great Sand Sea
Waddān Jabal Zaltan Rebiana Sand Sea
Tāzirbū Zighan Libyan Desert
Al Jawf Al Khufrah Jabal Arkenu 4708ft (1435m) Al ʿUwaynāt

36° 34° 32° 30° 28° 26° 24° 22° 20°
Tropic of Cancer

Longitude east of Greenwich

SCALE 1:9,000,000
Lamberts Azimuthal Equal Area Projection
0 300 miles
0 300 kilometers

211

NORTHEASTERN AFRICA

Djibouti, Egypt, Eritrea, Ethiopia, Somalia, Sudan

At the northern end of the Great Rift Valley, the Ethiopian Highlands divides the Horn of Africa in the east from the barren expanses of the Sahara in the west. Rivers that descend from the highlands, and from the East African Plateau to the south, are the lifeblood of this predominantly arid and impoverished land.

The Shebeli and Juba are the only permanent rivers in Somalia and supply most of the nation's water. From Lake Tana, the Blue Nile flows east then west to join the White Nile at Khartoum; continuing north, the Nile forms a riverine oasis that constitutes Egypt's only fertile zone.

Since decolonization took place after the Second World War, the southern part of this region has been crippled by famines and political instability, including a long civil war that saw Eritrea secede from Ethiopia in 1993.

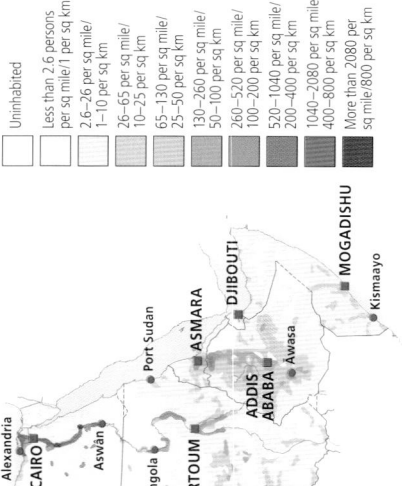

ECONOMIC PROFILE

The regional economy is undeveloped, and most people rely on subsistence farming of cereals, fruit and vegetables, sheep, cattle, goats, and camels—80 percent of Somalians are dependent on livestock. Cash crops include cotton and sugarcane, grown in the Nile Valley, and coffee from the Ethiopian Highlands (from whose Kaffa region the word "coffee" derives). Only Egypt has a developed industrial sector, based on engineering and the manufacture of metals and electronic goods. It also benefits from modest oil reserves, tourism, and revenue from the Suez Canal.

Forest and woodland
Arable land
Grazing
Marginal or nonproductive

Cotton
Coffee
Dates
Sugarcane
Beef cattle
Sheep
Industrial center
Oil production
Tourism

POPULATION PATTERNS

The highest population densities occur in the fertile Ethiopian Highlands and along the major rivers—99 percent of Egyptians live in the Nile Valley, an area that constitutes just 3 percent of the country. The deserts of the eastern Sahara, northern Ethiopia, and Somalia, and the swamps of southern Sudan deter settlement. In semiarid zones, many people, including 70 percent of Somalians, maintain a nomadic lifestyle. The Sahara separates the mainly Arabic peoples of the north from the diverse African groups of the south; however, the Middle East has influenced the entire region and most inhabitants are adherents of Islam.

Uninhabited
Less than 2.6 persons per sq mile/1 per sq km
2.6–26 per sq mile/ 1–10 per sq km
26–65 per sq mile/ 10–25 per sq km
65–130 per sq mile/ 25–50 per sq km
130–260 per sq mile/ 50–100 per sq km
260–520 per sq mile/ 100–200 per sq km
520–1040 per sq mile/ 200–400 per sq km
1040–2080 per sq mile/ 400–800 per sq km
More than 2080 per sq mile/800 per sq km

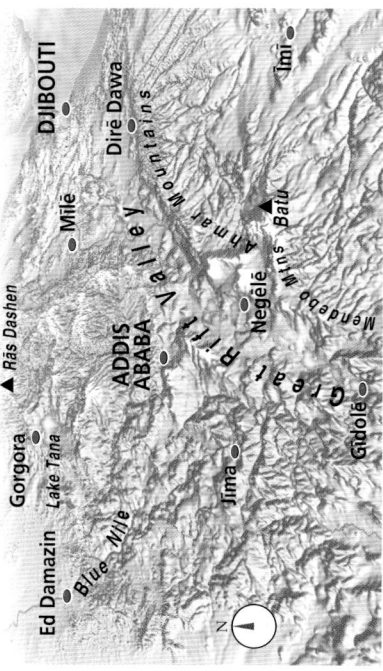

THE ETHIOPIAN HIGHLANDS

An enormous plateau, the Ethiopian Highlands cover most of Ethiopia and are bisected by the Great Rift Valley. The western highlands encompass the region's highest peak, 14,872-foot (4,533-m) Rās Dashen, Lake Tana, and Ethiopia's capital Addis Ababa, which sits about 8,000 feet (2,500 m) above sea level. The eastern highlands are narrower but almost as high, reaching 14,176 feet (4,321 m) at Batu. South of Addis Ababa, lakes and volcanic peaks stud the floor of the Great Rift Valley; northeast of the capital, the valley widens, the western wall forming a great escarpment that runs north to the Red Sea, the eastern side arcing toward the Gulf of Aden.

Completed in 1971, the Aswān Dam supplies half of Egypt's electricity.

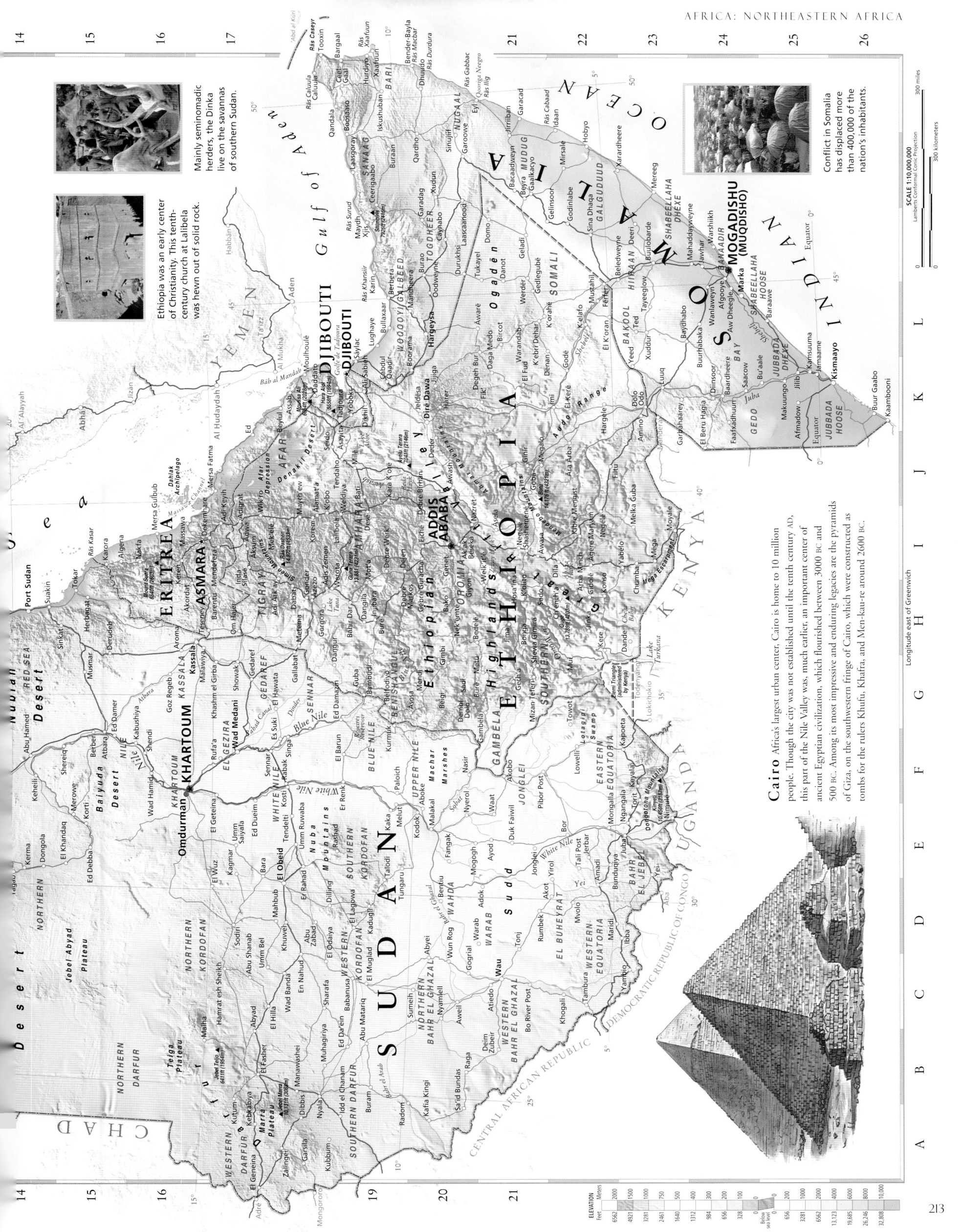

Mainly seminomadic herders, the Dinka live on the savannas of southern Sudan.

Ethiopia was an early center of Christianity. This tenth-century church at Lalibela was hewn out of solid rock.

Conflict in Somalia has displaced more than 400,000 of the nation's inhabitants.

Cairo Africa's largest urban center, Cairo is home to 10 million people. Though the city was not established until the tenth century AD, this part of the Nile Valley was, much earlier, an important center of ancient Egyptian civilization, which flourished between 3000 BC and 500 BC. Among its most impressive and enduring legacies are the pyramids of Giza, on the southwestern fringe of Cairo, which were constructed as tombs for the rulers Khufu, Khafra, and Men-kau-re around 2600 BC.

SCALE 1:10,000,000
Lambert's Conformal Conic Projection

WEST AFRICA

Benin, Burkina Faso, Cameroon, Chad, Côte d'Ivoire, Equatorial Guinea, Gambia, Ghana, Guinea, Guinea-Bissau, Liberia, Mali, Mauritania, Niger, Nigeria, Senegal, Sierra Leone, Togo

Isolated ranges and plateaus dot the West African landscape, but most of the terrain is low-lying. Distinctive environments and populations, however, divide the region into northern and southern sectors. Inhabited mainly by Muslim peoples, including Berbers and Arabs, the more arid northern two-thirds, sometimes called the Western Sudan, includes the western edge of the Sahara Desert, part of the scrubby Sahel, and wide savanna grasslands. The wetter southern third, the Guinea coast, is characterized by tropical rain forest and is home to diverse African peoples. In the Middle Ages, thriving trans-Saharan trade created prosperous kingdoms in the north. From the 16th century, the economic focus shifted to the coast with the arrival of European traders. European powers gradually took control of the region, relinquishing their hold only in the late 20th century.

Most inhabitants of the Sahel live near their livestock in traditional villages.

Djenné In the 14th century, Mali, located in the present-day country of the same name and centered on the cities of Djenné, Timbuktu, and Gao, was Africa's most powerful state. Larger than any contemporary state in Europe, it derived much of its wealth and power from its control of trans-Saharan trade in gold, salt, and slaves. Following its adoption of Islam, Mali became a center of Muslim scholarship and the site of several large mosques. The Great Mosque of Djenné was built in the 14th century, destroyed in 1896, and rebuilt in 1909. Made of sun-baked earth, it is the world's biggest mud-brick structure.

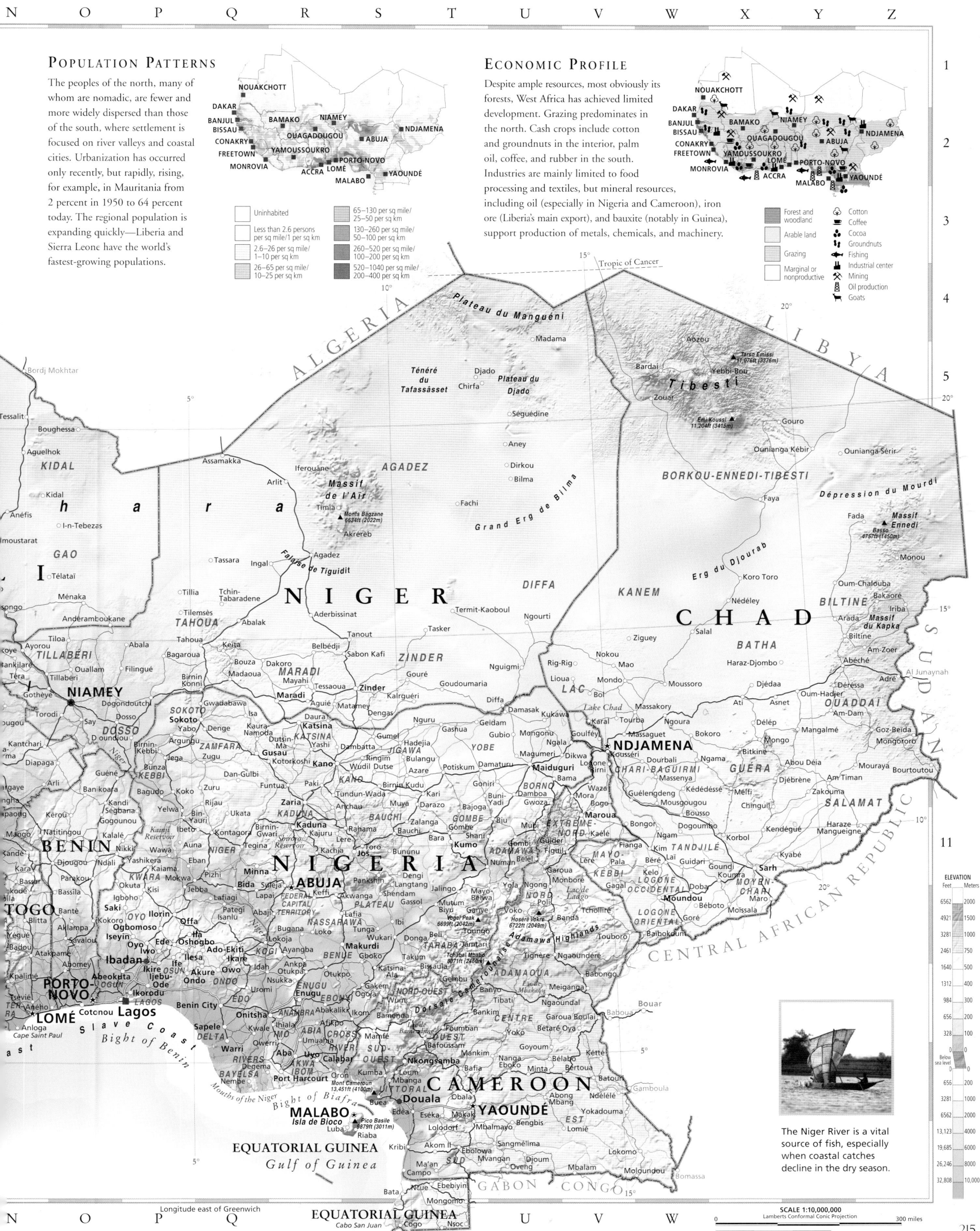

POPULATION PATTERNS

The peoples of the north, many of whom are nomadic, are fewer and more widely dispersed than those of the south, where settlement is focused on river valleys and coastal cities. Urbanization has occurred only recently, but rapidly, rising, for example, in Mauritania from 2 percent in 1950 to 64 percent today. The regional population is expanding quickly—Liberia and Sierra Leone have the world's fastest-growing populations.

Uninhabited

Less than 2.6 persons per sq mile/1 per sq km

2.6–26 per sq mile/ 1–10 per sq km

26–65 per sq mile/ 10–25 per sq km

65–130 per sq mile/ 25–50 per sq km

130–260 per sq mile/ 50–100 per sq km

260–520 per sq mile/ 100–200 per sq km

520–1040 per sq mile/ 200–400 per sq km

ECONOMIC PROFILE

Despite ample resources, most obviously its forests, West Africa has achieved limited development. Grazing predominates in the north. Cash crops include cotton and groundnuts in the interior, palm oil, coffee, and rubber in the south. Industries are mainly limited to food processing and textiles, but mineral resources, including oil (especially in Nigeria and Cameroon), iron ore (Liberia's main export), and bauxite (notably in Guinea), support production of metals, chemicals, and machinery.

Forest and woodland

Arable land

Grazing

Marginal or nonproductive

Cotton
Coffee
Cocoa
Groundnuts
Fishing
Industrial center
Mining
Oil production
Goats

The Niger River is a vital source of fish, especially when coastal catches decline in the dry season.

ELEVATION

Feet	Meters
6562	2000
4921	1500
3281	1000
2461	750
1640	500
1312	400
984	300
656	200
328	100
	Below sea level
656	200
3281	1000
6562	2000
13,123	4000
19,685	6000
26,246	8000
32,808	10,000

SCALE 1:10,000,000
Lamberts Conformal Conic Projection

0   300 miles

0   300 kilometers

Longitude east of Greenwich

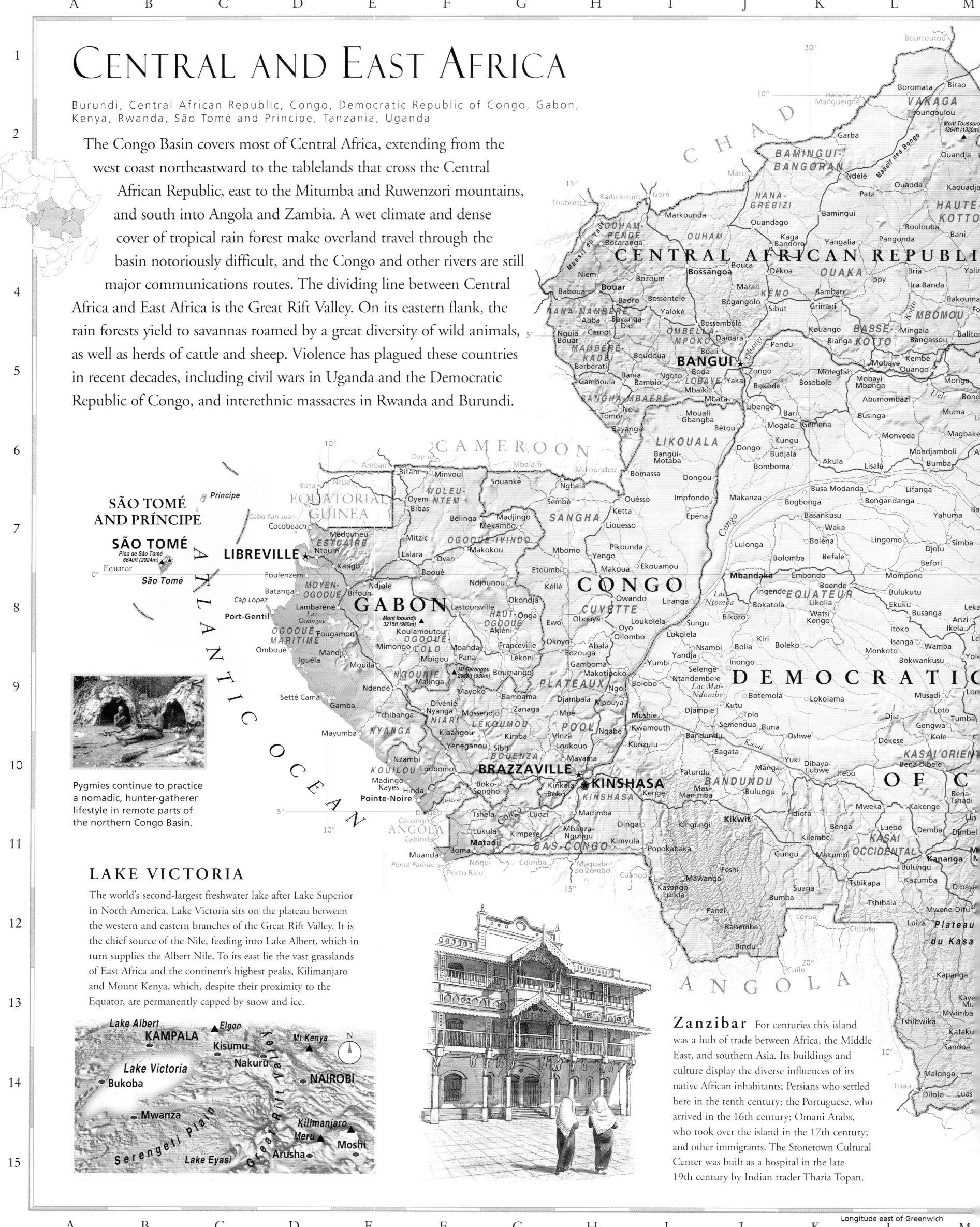

CENTRAL AND EAST AFRICA

Burundi, Central African Republic, Congo, Democratic Republic of Congo, Gabon, Kenya, Rwanda, São Tomé and Príncipe, Tanzania, Uganda

The Congo Basin covers most of Central Africa, extending from the west coast northeastward to the tablelands that cross the Central African Republic, east to the Mitumba and Ruwenzori mountains, and south into Angola and Zambia. A wet climate and dense cover of tropical rain forest make overland travel through the basin notoriously difficult, and the Congo and other rivers are still major communications routes. The dividing line between Central Africa and East Africa is the Great Rift Valley. On its eastern flank, the rain forests yield to savannas roamed by a great diversity of wild animals, as well as herds of cattle and sheep. Violence has plagued these countries in recent decades, including civil wars in Uganda and the Democratic Republic of Congo, and interethnic massacres in Rwanda and Burundi.

Pygmies continue to practice a nomadic, hunter-gatherer lifestyle in remote parts of the northern Congo Basin.

LAKE VICTORIA

The world's second-largest freshwater lake after Lake Superior in North America, Lake Victoria sits on the plateau between the western and eastern branches of the Great Rift Valley. It is the chief source of the Nile, feeding into Lake Albert, which in turn supplies the Albert Nile. To its east lie the vast grasslands of East Africa and the continent's highest peaks, Kilimanjaro and Mount Kenya, which, despite their proximity to the Equator, are permanently capped by snow and ice.

Zanzibar For centuries this island was a hub of trade between Africa, the Middle East, and southern Asia. Its buildings and culture display the diverse influences of its native African inhabitants; Persians who settled here in the tenth century; the Portuguese, who arrived in the 16th century; Omani Arabs, who took over the island in the 17th century; and other immigrants. The Stonetown Cultural Center was built as a hospital in the late 19th century by Indian trader Tharia Topan.

Longitude east of Greenwich

POPULATION PATTERNS

Communities in the heart of the Congo Basin are small and scattered; larger populations live on its upland fringes and near the river mouth. The most crowded areas in the east are the shores of Lake Victoria and the Great Rift Valley uplands. Though little urbanized, Rwanda and Burundi are Africa's most densely populated countries. Bantu is the most widely spoken native language; French is widely used in the west, English in the east. Tribal rivalries remain strong and have been a source of conflict. Across the region, birth rates are high.

Less than 2.6 persons per sq mile/1 per sq km
2.6–26 per sq mile/ 1–10 per sq km
26–65 per sq mile/ 10–25 per sq km
65–130 per sq mile/ 25–50 per sq km
130–260 per sq mile/ 50–100 per sq km
260–520 per sq mile/ 100–200 per sq km
520–1040 per sq mile/ 200–400 per sq km

ECONOMIC PROFILE

Central Africa's abundant minerals and huge forests are its most valuable resources. Congo and Gabon have plentiful oil, and the Democratic Republic of Congo is a leading producer of industrial diamonds and cobalt; it also has immense hydroelectric potential. Tropical hardwoods are lucrative exports, though foreign companies often absorb the profits. East Africa is more dependent on its land, with the savannas providing feed for cattle and the fertile uplands supporting the cultivation of coffee, tea, and other cash crops. Tourism is also vital in the east.

Forest and woodland
Arable land
Grazing
Marginal or nonproductive

Cotton
Coffee
Cocoa
Tobacco
Fishing
Industrial center
Mining
Oil production
Timber
Beef cattle
Tea

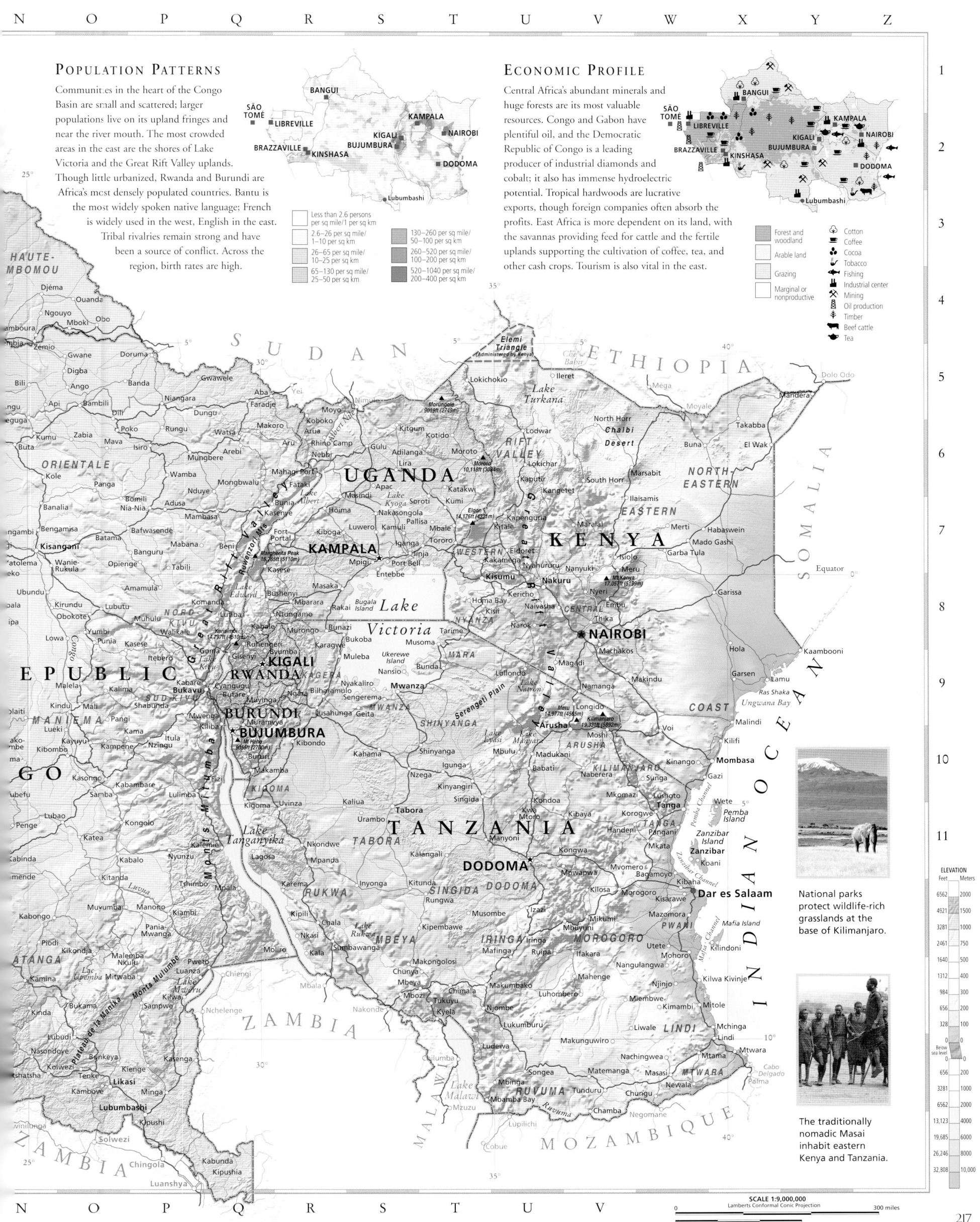

National parks protect wildlife-rich grasslands at the base of Kilimanjaro.

The traditionally nomadic Masai inhabit eastern Kenya and Tanzania.

ELEVATION
Feet	Meters
6562	2000
4921	1500
3281	1000
2461	750
1640	500
1312	400
984	300
656	200
328	100
Below sea level	0
656	200
6562	2000
13,123	4000
19,685	6000
26,246	8000
32,808	10,000

SCALE 1:9,000,000
Lamberts Conformal Conic Projection
0 300 miles
0 300 kilometers

SOUTHERN AFRICA

Angola, Botswana, Comoros, Lesotho, Madagascar, Malawi, Mozambique, Namibia, Republic of South Africa, Swaziland, Zambia, Zimbabwe

Consisting of an undulating tableland rimmed by escarpments and narrow coastal plains, the southern African mainland takes in contrasting environments, including the Namib and Kalahari deserts, the tropical forests of northern Mozambique, and the "Highveld" grasslands of South Africa. About 250 miles (400 km) off its east coast lie the culturally and ecologically distinct island of Madagascar and the small Comoros archipelago. As in other parts of Africa, colonialism left the region a legacy of instability and inequality. Portugal's efforts to retain Mozambique and Angola initiated devastating wars from the 1960s to the early 1990s. White-minority rule sparked conflict in postcolonial Zimbabwe, in Namibia, and in South Africa, where racial segregation was enshrined in law in 1948 as the system of apartheid, and formally abolished only in 1994.

POPULATION PATTERNS

The east is more densely populated than the west, with heavy settlement occurring in southern Mozambique, central and southern Zimbabwe, and between Pretoria, Durban, and Port Elizabeth in South Africa. Few people live in the western deserts, and Namibia and Botswana are two of Africa's least densely populated countries. Urbanization remains between 30 and 50 percent in most countries, but reaches 60 percent in South Africa. Most southern Africans belong to Bantu-speaking groups, such as the Zulu, Swazi, and Ndebele (Matabele), but Madagascar's Malagasy peoples originated in Indonesia.

ECONOMIC PROFILE

South Africa has by far the most developed and diversified industrial sector in Africa. Led by iron and steel, transport equipment, and chemicals, it accounts for one-third of the continent's total manufacturing output. The country also has huge mineral reserves, including diamonds, gold (half of world reserves), uranium, and iron ore. Uranium and diamonds are also found in Namibia, gold in Zimbabwe. Angola has sizable oil reserves, Madagascar deposits of graphite. The best arable land lies in the east. Cash crops include tobacco, coffee, tea, and citrus fruits—South Africa is the world's largest producer of grapefruit.

218

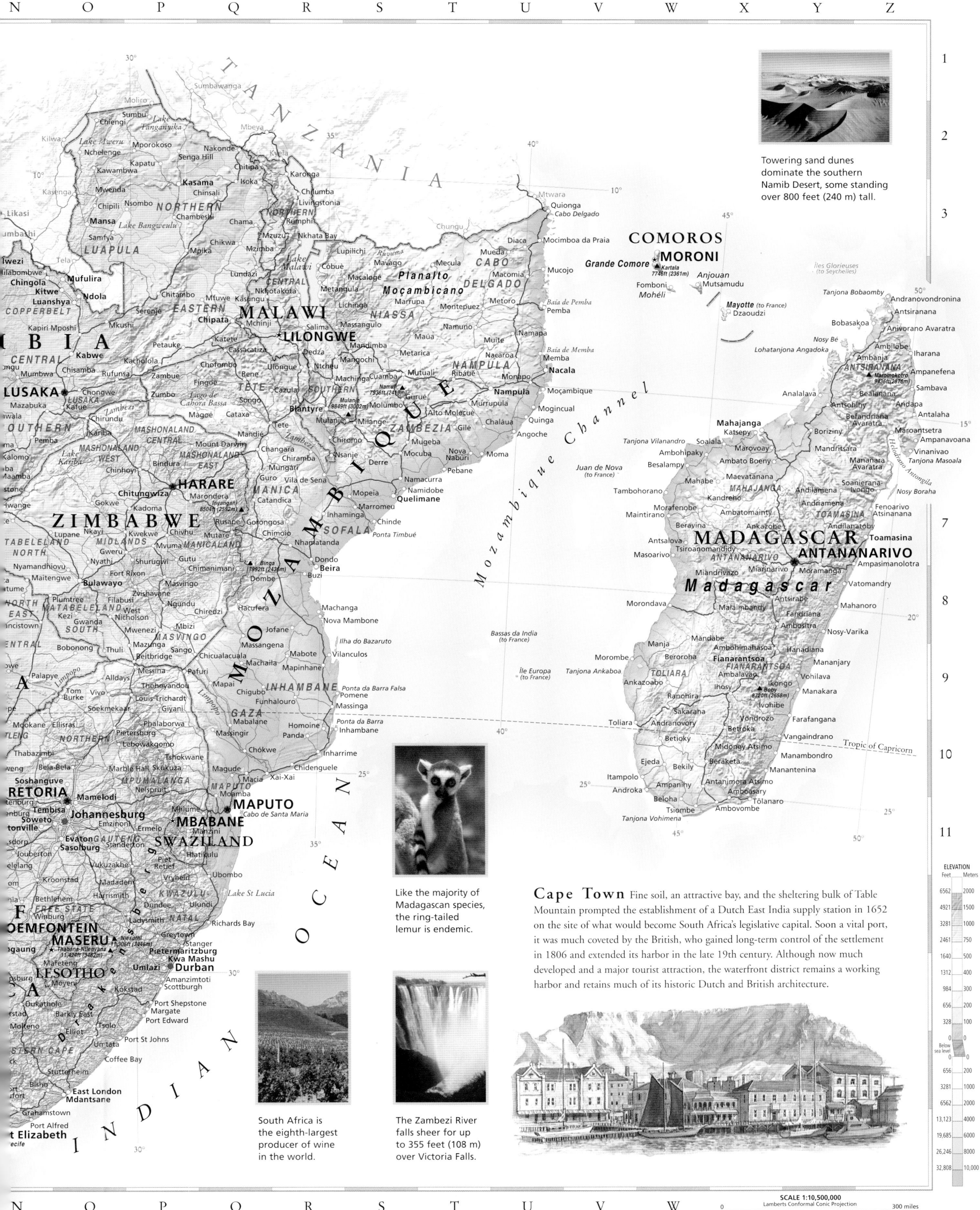

Towering sand dunes dominate the southern Namib Desert, some standing over 800 feet (240 m) tall.

Like the majority of Madagascan species, the ring-tailed lemur is endemic.

South Africa is the eighth-largest producer of wine in the world.

The Zambezi River falls sheer for up to 355 feet (108 m) over Victoria Falls.

Cape Town Fine soil, an attractive bay, and the sheltering bulk of Table Mountain prompted the establishment of a Dutch East India supply station in 1652 on the site of what would become South Africa's legislative capital. Soon a vital port, it was much coveted by the British, who gained long-term control of the settlement in 1806 and extended its harbor in the late 19th century. Although now much developed and a major tourist attraction, the waterfront district remains a working harbor and retains much of its historic Dutch and British architecture.

ELEVATION
Feet	Meters
6562	2000
4921	1500
3281	1000
2461	750
1640	500
1312	400
984	300
656	200
328	100
0	0
	Below sea level
656	200
3281	1000
6562	2000
13,123	4000
19,685	6000
26,246	8000
32,808	10,000

SCALE 1:10,500,000
Lamberts Conformal Conic Projection
300 miles
300 kilometers

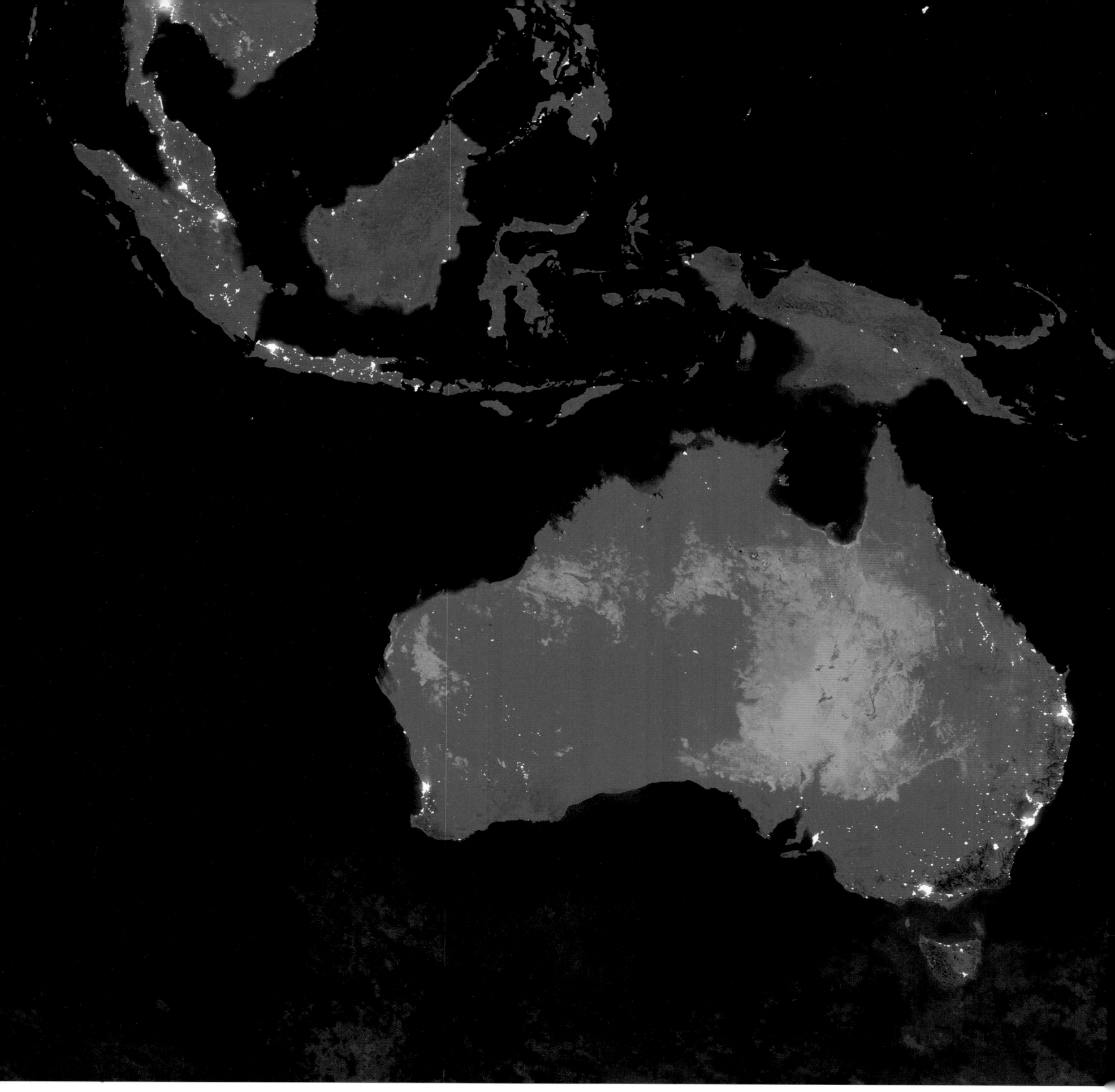

Australia's eastern seaboard is illuminated at night while the sparsely populated interior remains dark. The north and south islands of New Zealand are clearly visible. The dots of light smattered throughout the Pacific are island nations such as Fiji.

OCEANIA

ABOVE OCEANIA

Satellites can record grand-scale natural happenings, from the calving of a huge iceberg on Antarctica's slowly diminishing Ross Ice Shelf, to devastating wildfires raging across the southeast of Australia. From space, the relative stability of the ancient landmass of Australia is in stark contrast to continuing geological activity in its near neighbors. New Zealand lies in the collision zone between the Indo-Australian and Pacific tectonic plates. Movement of these plates caused the volcanic activity that shaped much of the North Island, and the country's fertile pastures are a legacy of layers of volcanic ash. In the image of Mount Taranaki (Mt Egmont), above, simulated natural color emphasizes the contrast between the lush forests preserved within the circular boundary of Egmont National Park, which extends in a 6-mile (10-km) radius from the volcano's summit, and the bright-colored dairy pastures beyond.

Egmont National Park, New Zealand
Above: The snow-capped, symmetrical peak of Mount Taranaki (Mt Egmont), 8,261 feet (2,518 m), towers over the forests of Egmont National Park in the west of New Zealand's North Island. Taranaki began forming 70,000 years ago and last erupted in 1755. Nearby are two older volcanoes. The gray area, top right, is the city of New Plymouth.

Southeastern Australia and the Tasman Sea
Right: In January 2003 nearly 100 wildfires were burning in southeastern Australia. This satellite image, gathered on 10 January, shows smoke from fires near Sydney, center, and northeastern Victoria, lower left, streaking the skies above the Tasman Sea. Ten days after this image was taken, the smoke and haze reached beyond New Zealand.

Uluru and Kata Tjuta, Australia
Top: Shown in blue in this false-color image, Uluru, center right, and Kata Tjuta, 30 miles (50 km) to the west, poke through the dry plains of Central Australia. Both are part of an ancient bed of sedimentary rock that has been folded and pushed upward. Uluru is the weathered end of the bed, now standing vertically.

Ross Ice Shelf, Antarctica
Above: A huge iceberg, center, broke off the Ross Ice Shelf at the end of the Antarctic summer in March 2000, calving along pre-existing cracks in the ice shelf. At 180 miles (300 km) long and 25 miles (40 km) wide it is one of the largest known. It was locked in sea ice until the spring thaw, but began to drift soon after this image was taken.

LAND AND ENVIRONMENT

Extending from the Indian Ocean to the eastern Pacific, and from the Tropic of Cancer to the remote subantarctic territory of Macquarie Island, Oceania covers a vast area of ocean and about 3.4 million square miles (8.8 million sq km) of land. Of this, almost 3 million square miles (7.7 million sq km) is encompassed by the island continent of Australia; the remainder consists of the eastern half of New Guinea, the large island group of New Zealand, and about 10,000 smaller islands. Oceania is traditionally divided into four subregions named for the ethnic groups that first inhabited them: Australia, Melanesia, Micronesia, and Polynesia (which includes New Zealand). These subregions encompass diverse landscapes. Located in the middle of the Indo-Australian Plate, Australia is an ancient, stable land, with few high mountains and an arid interior. More recently formed, the islands of Melanesia and New Zealand lie on plate margins and have high, young peaks and active volcanoes. Elsewhere in Polynesia, and in Micronesia, most islands are the summits of undersea volcanoes, or tiny atolls.

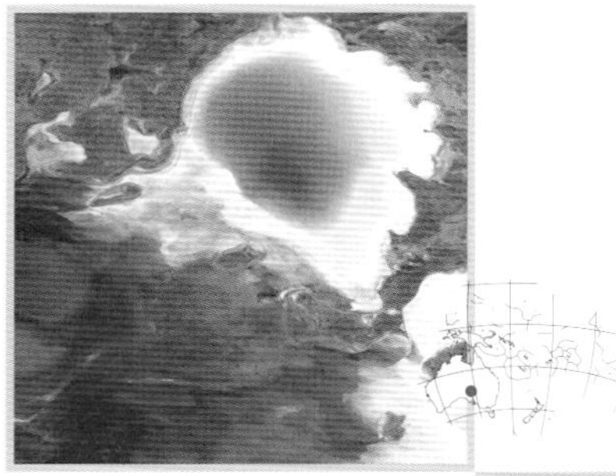

NATURAL HAZARDS

Wildfires

Long spells of dry weather combined with inflammable oils produced by widespread eucalypts and acacias make much of Australia highly susceptible to wildfires, or bushfires as they are known locally. Fire is part of the ecology of most Australian environments: many native plants are not only adapted to drought but can also withstand fire; indeed, some require fire to trigger germination. Wildfires are started naturally by lightning strikes. Increasingly, they are also caused by human carelessness or mischief, with the result that they occur regularly in urban areas. In dry, windy conditions, bushfires can move with astonishing speed, rapidly consuming vegetation, leaping roads and waterways, and, in severe cases, causing significant loss of life and property.

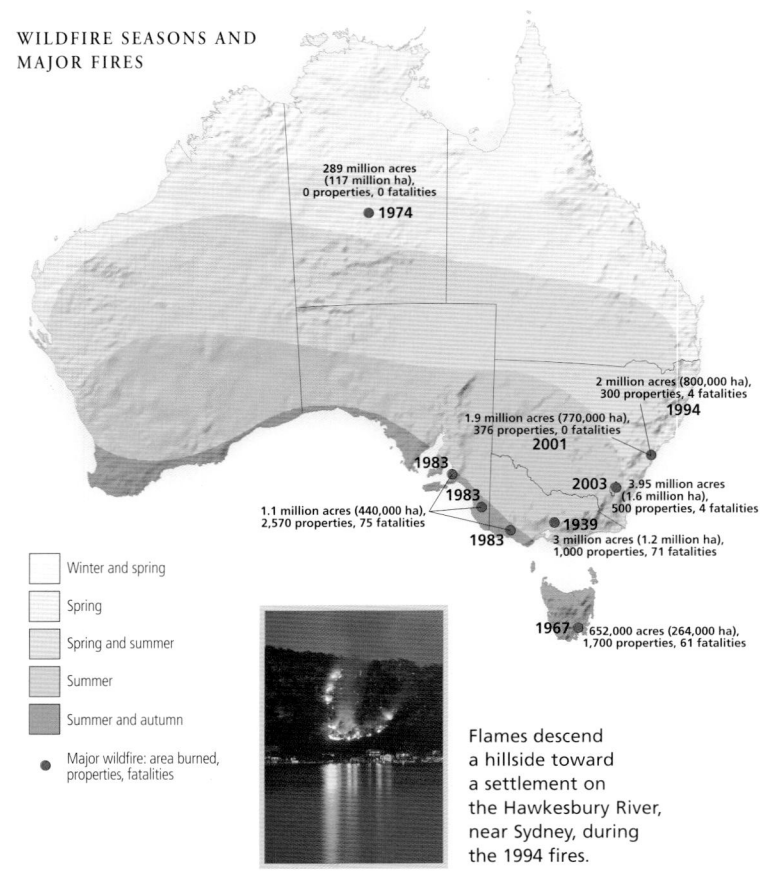

WILDFIRE SEASONS AND MAJOR FIRES

289 million acres (117 million ha), 0 properties, 0 fatalities
● 1974

2 million acres (800,000 ha), 300 properties, 4 fatalities
1994

1.9 million acres (770,000 ha), 376 properties, 0 fatalities
2001

1983

1983

2003 ● 3.95 million acres (1.6 million ha), 500 properties, 4 fatalities

1.1 million acres (440,000 ha), 2,570 properties, 75 fatalities

1983 ● 1939 3 million acres (1.2 million ha), 1,000 properties, 71 fatalities

Winter and spring
Spring
Spring and summer
Summer
Summer and autumn
● Major wildfire: area burned, properties, fatalities

1967 ● 652,000 acres (264,000 ha), 1,700 properties, 61 fatalities

Flames descend a hillside toward a settlement on the Hawkesbury River, near Sydney, during the 1994 fires.

Right: The largest lake in Australia, Lake Eyre is part of a system that drains one-sixth of the continent. But only rarely does the lake fill with water; most of the time, it is dry and encrusted with salt.

Right: This chain of coral reefs is part of the northern end of Australia's Great Barrier Reef. The world's largest coral reef, it extends for over 1,200 miles (2,000 km) down the northeast coast of the continent.

Agrihan
Pagan
Alamagan Mariana
Guguan Islands
Anatahan
Saipan
Tinian
Rota
Guam

M i c r o n e s i a

Hall Islands
Yap
Chuuk Islands
Pohnpei
Kosrae

C a r o l i n e   I s l a n d s

Palau Islands

Taraw
Gilbe
Islan
Banaba

Nauru

M e l a n e s i a

Admiralty Islands
Mussau Island
Manus Island
Tabar Islands
Lihir Group

Bismarck Sea
New Ireland
New Britain
Green Islands

Mt Wilhelm 14,793ft (4509m)
New Guinea
Bougainville
Choiseul
Santa Isabel
Malaita
San Cristobal
Ndeni
Santa Cruz Islands

S o l o m o n   I s l a n d s
Guadalcanal
Rennell

Solomon Sea

Torres Strait
Badu Island Moa Island
Cape York

Arafura Sea
Coral Sea

Torres Islands
Banks Islands
Espiritu Santo
Pentecost
Malakula
Epi
Éfaté
Erromango
Ouvéa
Lifou
Maré
Tanna
Île des Pins

Melville Island
Bathurst Island
Arnhem Land
Gulf of Carpentaria

Timor Sea

Great Barrier Reef

Fraser Island

New Caledonia

P A C I F I

Kimberley
Barkly Tableland

Great Dividing Range

Norfolk Island

Tanami Desert
Bartle Frere 5322ft (1622m)

Lord Howe Island

Great Sandy Desert
Mt Zeil 5023ft (1531m)
Simpson Desert
Great Artesian Basin

Barrow Island
North West Cape
Gibson Desert
Pilbara
Mt Meharry 4111ft (1253m)
Australia
Mt Woodroffe 4708ft (1435m)
Lake Eyre

Great Victoria Desert
Lake Torrens
Lake Gairdner
Lake Frome
Flinders Ranges

Great Dividing Range
Mount Kosciuszko 7310ft (2228m)

North Island

New Zealand

I N D I A N   O C E A N

Nullarbor Plain
Great Australian Bight
Murray
Lachlan
Darling

Tasman Sea

South Island

Cape Leeuwin
Kangaroo Island

Bass Strait
King Island
Flinders Island
Cape Barren Island
Mt Ossa 5305ft (1617m)
Tasmania

Mount Cook 12,316ft (3754m)

S O U T H E R N   O C E A N

Snares Islands
Stewart Island
Bounty
Antipodes

Macquarie Island

224

Climate

Most of the countries and territories of Oceania lie close to the Equator and therefore experience warm, humid conditions year-round. Rainfall varies little from month to month at the Equator, but farther north and south pronounced wet and dry seasons occur. During the Southern-Hemisphere summer, hurricanes (known locally as cyclones) occur above 5 degrees north and south. Seasonal tropical conditions—and cyclones—extend to the northern fringe of Australia. In middle latitudes, conditions are cooler, and moist onshore winds keep New Zealand and the east coast of Australia well-watered. The interior of Australia is, however, one of the most arid regions on Earth, and about half of the continent receives less than 12 inches (300 mm) of rain a year. Dry spells occasionally turn to droughts, especially in eastern Australia during El Niño episodes.

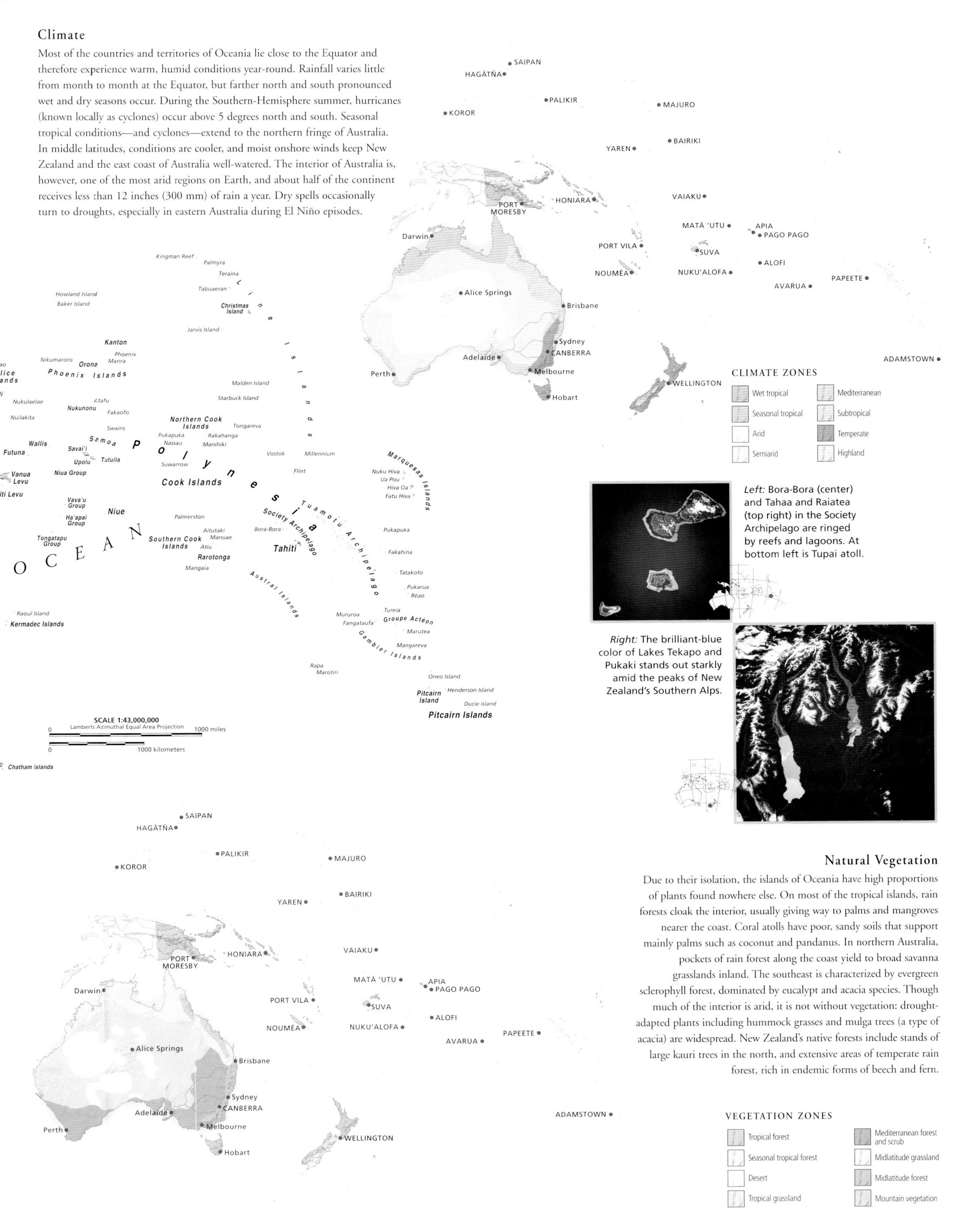

SCALE 1:43,000,000
Lamberts Azimuthal Equal Area Projection

CLIMATE ZONES

Wet tropical	Mediterranean
Seasonal tropical	Subtropical
Arid	Temperate
Semiarid	Highland

Left: Bora-Bora (center) and Tahaa and Raiatea (top right) in the Society Archipelago are ringed by reefs and lagoons. At bottom left is Tupai atoll.

Right: The brilliant-blue color of Lakes Tekapo and Pukaki stands out starkly amid the peaks of New Zealand's Southern Alps.

Natural Vegetation

Due to their isolation, the islands of Oceania have high proportions of plants found nowhere else. On most of the tropical islands, rain forests cloak the interior, usually giving way to palms and mangroves nearer the coast. Coral atolls have poor, sandy soils that support mainly palms such as coconut and pandanus. In northern Australia, pockets of rain forest along the coast yield to broad savanna grasslands inland. The southeast is characterized by evergreen sclerophyll forest, dominated by eucalypt and acacia species. Though much of the interior is arid, it is not without vegetation: drought-adapted plants including hummock grasses and mulga trees (a type of acacia) are widespread. New Zealand's native forests include stands of large kauri trees in the north, and extensive areas of temperate rain forest, rich in endemic forms of beech and fern.

VEGETATION ZONES

Tropical forest	Mediterranean forest and scrub
Seasonal tropical forest	Midlatitude grassland
Desert	Midlatitude forest
Tropical grassland	Mountain vegetation

225

PEOPLES AND NATIONS

Home to about 32 million people, Oceania encompasses 14 nations and numerous dependencies. Its indigenous peoples form four major groups—Australian Aboriginal peoples, Melanesians, Micronesians, and Polynesians—who speak a huge variety of languages. Since the 18th century, large numbers of immigrants have settled in the region, particularly in Australia and New Zealand. Most came from Europe, especially the United Kingdom, making English the most widely spoken language in Australia and New Zealand.

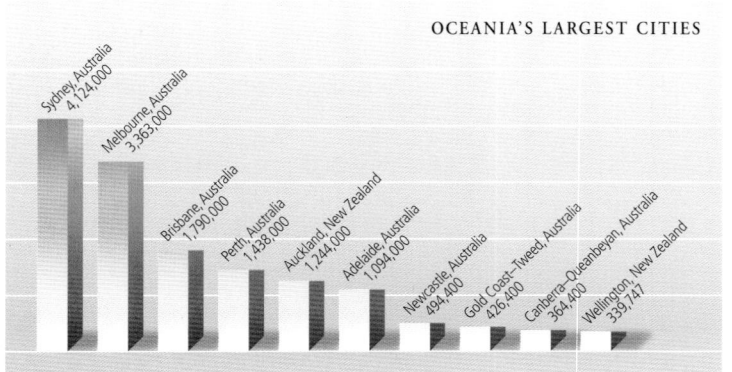

OCEANIA'S LARGEST CITIES

Urbanization

There is a stark contrast between Australia and New Zealand, where cities and towns accommodate around 90 percent of the inhabitants, and most of the rest of Oceania, where there are no major cities and the urban population is generally under 60 percent. An exception is the French territory of New Caledonia, where 82 percent of the inhabitants live in urban areas. In Papua New Guinea, just 19 percent of people live in towns and cities, but even here significant change has occurred in recent decades: in 1950, the urban population accounted for less than one percent of the total.

POPULATION DENSITY

Uninhabited	2.6–26 per sq mile/ 1–10 per sq km
Less than 2.6 persons per sq mile/1 per sq km	26–65 per sq mile/ 10–25 per sq km

Population Patterns

Australia accounts for most of Oceania's population, with about 20 million people. Another 5 million people inhabit New Guinea and about 4 million live in New Zealand. The remainder of Oceania's population is scattered across thousands of small islands. Population density is generally low but varies greatly. The highest concentrations of inhabitants occur on the southeast coast of Australia, in northern New Zealand and the Papua New Guinea highlands, and on the tiny islands of Nauru, the Cook Islands, and Tuvalu (where 11,000 people occupy just 10 square miles [26 sq km] of land). In contrast, the interior of Australia is one of the world's most sparsely populated regions, and many small Pacific islands are uninhabited. Growth rates are high in Micronesia and in Papua New Guinea, where the population is expected to double by 2030.

FLASHPOINTS

Oceania has no major international boundary disputes, but ethnic rivalries have undermined political and economic stability in some countries and sparked a number of regional conflicts.

Fiji

Almost half of the people of Fiji are the descendants of Indian laborers brought to the islands by the British. The accession of a democratically elected, Indo-Fijian-dominated government prompted a military coup in 1987 led by indigenous Fijians, and the introduction of laws to ensure indigenous rule. Continuing Indo-Fijian participation in politics prompted another failed coup by indigenous Fijians in May 2000.

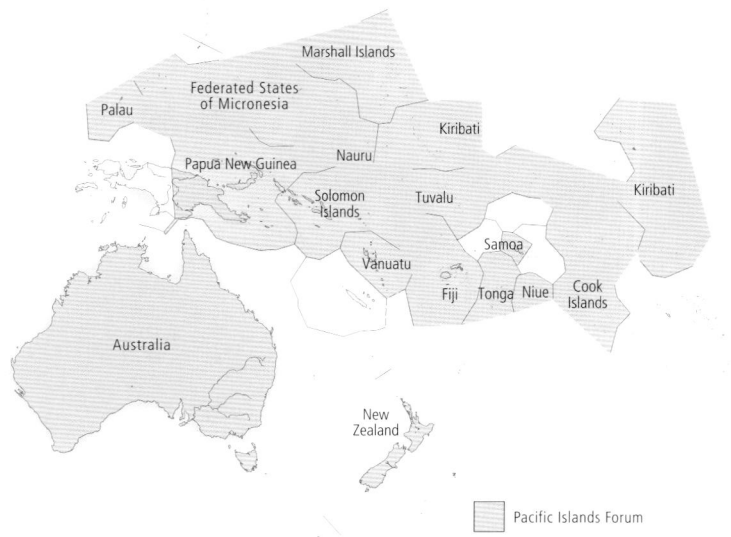

Solomon Islands

In 1998, inhabitants of Guadalcanal, resentful of the growing influence of immigrants from neighboring Malaita, founded the Isatabu Freedom Movement (IFM). It began a campaign to oust Malaitans, who responded by setting up the Malaita Eagle Force (MEF). Armed conflict between these groups claimed dozens of lives and wrecked the islands' economy. A degree of order was restored by the arrival of Australian security forces in 2003.

Bougainville

Politically, Bougainville is part of Papua New Guinea, but its inhabitants have strong cultural connections with the people of the Solomon Islands. Discontent among the islanders regarding the distribution of income from mineral reserves led to an armed secessionist revolt that lasted from 1988 to 2001. A peace accord reached in that year, providing an option of independence for Bougainville by 2011–16, has so far held.

Pacific Islands Forum

The Pacific Islands Forum was founded as the South Pacific Forum in 1971 by Australia, the Cook Islands, Fiji, Nauru, New Zealand, Tonga, and the former Western Samoa (now Samoa) to facilitate trade and economic development in the Oceania region and provide a strong political voice for its member states in international affairs. The forum, which changed its name to the Pacific Islands Forum in October 1999, now includes a total of 16 independent and self-governing states. Its secretariat is based in Suva, Fiji, but annual meetings are hosted by each of the member countries and territories in turn.

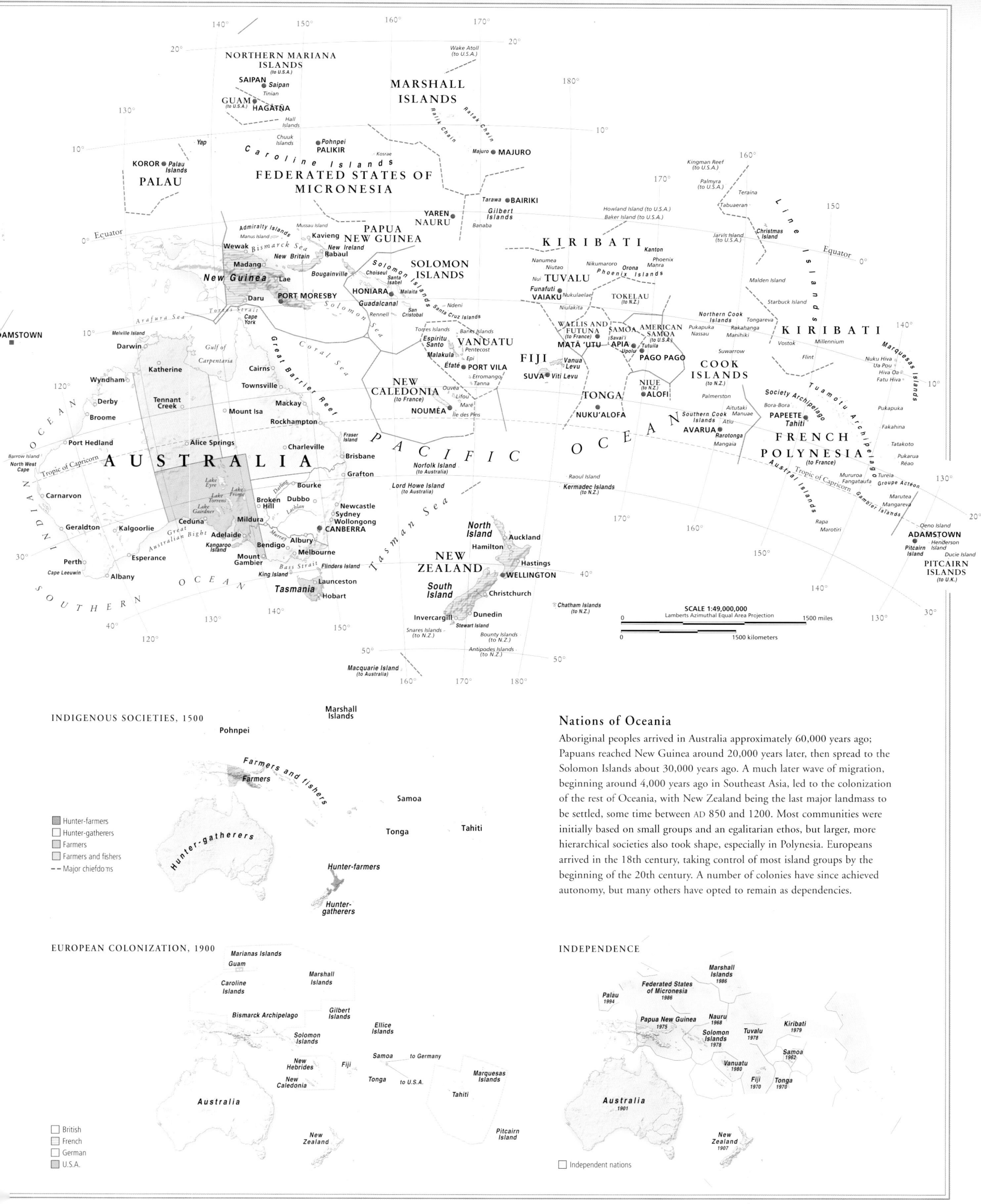

Nations of Oceania

Aboriginal peoples arrived in Australia approximately 60,000 years ago; Papuans reached New Guinea around 20,000 years later, then spread to the Solomon Islands about 30,000 years ago. A much later wave of migration, beginning around 4,000 years ago in Southeast Asia, led to the colonization of the rest of Oceania, with New Zealand being the last major landmass to be settled, some time between AD 850 and 1200. Most communities were initially based on small groups and an egalitarian ethos, but larger, more hierarchical societies also took shape, especially in Polynesia. Europeans arrived in the 18th century, taking control of most island groups by the beginning of the 20th century. A number of colonies have since achieved autonomy, but many others have opted to remain as dependencies.

INDIGENOUS SOCIETIES, 1500

- Hunter-farmers
- Hunter-gatherers
- Farmers
- Farmers and fishers
- – – Major chiefdoms

EUROPEAN COLONIZATION, 1900

- British
- French
- German
- U.S.A.

INDEPENDENCE

- Independent nations

THE HUMAN IMPACT

In well-watered New Guinea, agriculture began as early as 9,000 years ago; by 5,000 years ago, farmers there were clearing forest and digging extensive drainage systems. In Australia, by contrast, an arid climate and poor soils inhibited the development of sedentary agricultural societies. Mainly hunter-gatherers, early Aboriginal peoples did, however, divert waterways to trap fish, and burn woodlands to facilitate hunting, and may have contributed to the extinction of large mammal species, or megafauna. Some of the larger islands export cash crops such as sugar, palm oil, and cocoa, and many Melanesian islands have sizable mineral resources and forests. Europeans arriving in Oceania in the late 18th century imported the livestock, seeds, and technologies to permit rapid conversion of much larger tracts of land to agriculture. Their limited understanding of local conditions meant that they were often unaware of the havoc they were wreaking. In the industrial age, some problems have become acute. Dryland salinity threatens Australian water tables and soil; nuclear testing has contaminated land and ocean; and rising sea levels due to global warming threaten the livelihoods of entire island communities.

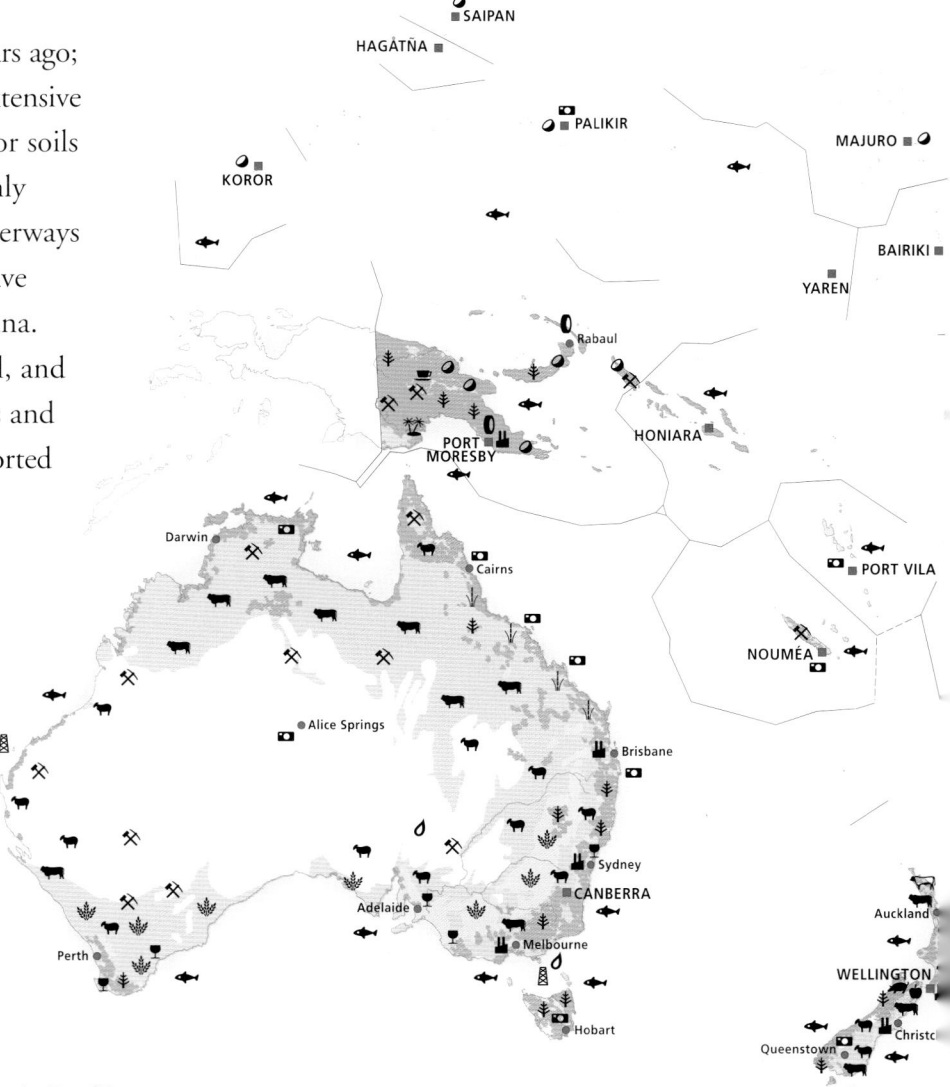

THE CHANGING FACE OF OCEANIA

Nuclear Testing

To foreign powers, the isolation and sparse populations of many parts of Oceania made them ideal for testing powerful weapons. In 1946, the U.S.A. relocated the inhabitants of Bikini and Enewetak to other other parts of the Marshall Islands, and for the next 12 years used the atolls for setting off nuclear explosions. The U.K. detonated 21 nuclear devices in Australia and the Pacific between 1952 and 1958, and France carried out 193 nuclear tests between 1966 and 1996 in French Polynesia. These tests contaminated the atmosphere and large tracts of land, and exposed service personnel and local people to fallout. Few residents of Bikini and Enewetak have been able to return home, and only in 2000 was the Maralinga site in Australia declared safe enough for its traditional owners to live there. In 1999, a French independent commission reported that radioactivity from French test sites continues to seep into fresh-water supplies, lagoons, and the sea.

NUCLEAR TEST SITES

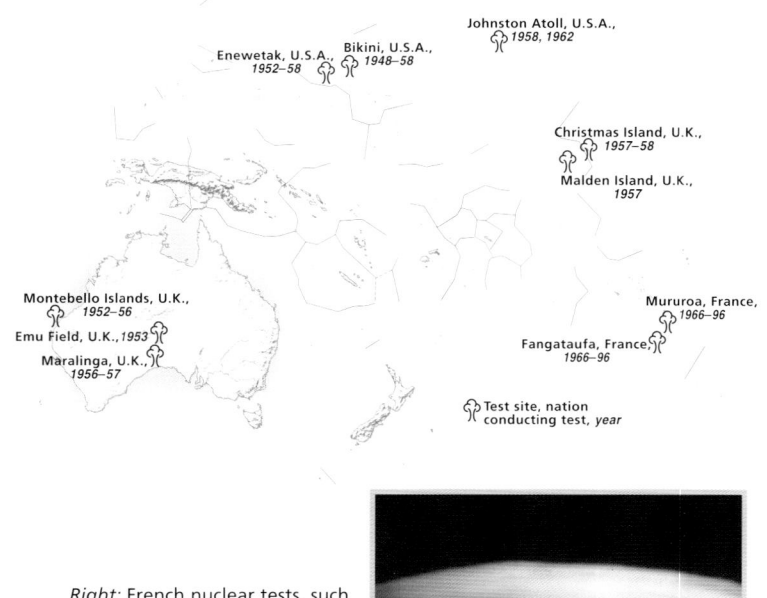

Johnston Atoll, U.S.A., 1958, 1962

Enewetak, U.S.A., 1952–58   Bikini, U.S.A., 1948–58

Christmas Island, U.K., 1957–58

Malden Island, U.K., 1957

Montebello Islands, U.K., 1952–56

Emu Field, U.K.,1953

Maralinga, U.K., 1956–57

Mururoa, France, 1966–96

Fangataufa, France, 1966–96

Test site, nation conducting test, year

Right: French nuclear tests, such as this detonation on Mururoa on October 1, 1977, have scattered plutonium particles over adjacent atolls and lagoons. These areas will remain contaminated for centuries.

Economic Profile

Australia and New Zealand have developed economies, with strong and diverse manufacturing sectors. However, most workers in these countries are employed in services such as the retail trade, banking, and tourism. Primary industries remain important: Australia's top exports are coal, crude oil, iron ore, gold, and wheat; New Zealand relies heavily on sales of dairy produce, meat, and timber. Elsewhere, the industrial sector is little developed, consisting mainly of the processing of raw materials. Many Melanesian islands have sizable mineral reserves and forests, and cash crops such as sugar, palm oil, and cocoa are exported by some of the larger islands. Tourism is a vital source of income for many Pacific communities, and some small islands have benefited from the sale of fishing rights to their disporportionately large maritime zones. However, most people outside Australia and New Zealand make a living from subsistence or small-scale commercial farming and fishing.

Land Cover

Abundant rainfall and volcanic soils make parts of Melanesia agriculturally productive, but arable land is scarce elsewhere. In Australia and New Zealand, in particular, most of the land is better suited to grazing, and in Australia livestock has to roam over large areas to find sufficient food. Though they are still being felled, forests cover almost one-quarter of Oceania. Australia's immense deserts account for much other land cover.

Australia has about 110 million sheep—down from a peak of 180 million in 1970—and their grazing contributes to land degradation. But wool remains an important export.

PROPORTIONS OF TOTAL LAND AREA

Forest and woodland — 23.6%

Arable land — 6.6%

Grazing — 49.4%

Other land — 20.4%

SAIPAN
HAGÅTÑA
PALIKIR
MAJURO
KOROR
Western Central Pacific
1995, -0.9%
BAIRIKI
YAREN
Banana
Rabaul
HONIARA
VAIAKU
PORT
MORESBY
MATÄ 'UTU
APIA
PAGO PAGO
Darwin
Atuona
Cairns
PORT VILA
SUVA
NOUMÉA
ALOFI
Alice
Springs
NUKU'ALOFA
AVARUA
PAPEETE
Brisbane
Southwest Pacific
1992, -8.7%
Sydney
CANBERRA
Auckland
ADAMSTOWN
Adelaide
Melbourne
Perth
WELLINGTON
Christchurch
Hobart
Queenstown

SCALE 1:47,500,000
Lamberts Azimuthal Equal Area Projection
0   1000 miles
0   1000 kilometers

Banana

VAIAKU

MATÄ 'UTU
APIA
PAGO PAGO
SUVA
ALOFI
NUKU'ALOFA
AVARUA
PAPEETE

Atuona

ADAMSTOWN

ENVIRONMENTAL ISSUES

- Degraded soil
- Very degraded soil
- Polluted rivers
- Polluted seas and lakes
- Cities with severe air pollution
- Overfished fishery, *year of peak catch*, **decline since peak catch**

LAND USE AND RESOURCES

- Forest and woodland
- Arable land
- Grazing
- Marginal or nonproductive

- Cereals
- Wine
- Sugarcane
- Beef cattle
- Sheep
- Fishing
- Industrial center
- Mining
- Tourism

- Timber
- Gas production
- Coconuts
- Rubber
- Coffee
- Palm oil
- Fruit
- Pigs
- Dairy cattle
- Oil production

Threats to the Environment

Environmental damage increased greatly following the arrival of Europeans. Forest clearance and the hooves of livestock acclerated erosion; intensive farming of fragile soils resulted in plummeting fertility; and introduced species decimated native ecosystems. Australia now has the world's highest rate of mammalian extinctions; many New Zealand native species survive only on isolated islands; and introduced plant species predominate on many Pacific islands. Since Europeans arrived, more than 40 percent of Australia's original forests have been cleared, and forest cover in New Zealand has fallen from 70 to 16 percent. As a result of corruption, most notably in Papua New Guinea, foreign logging companies have been able to illegally harvest ancient rain forests. Waterways throughout Melanesia have been contaminated by waste from mining operations. Human waste disposal is problematic on remote, densely populated islands: water-borne diseases are the leading cause of death on Kiribati, and in Ebey Lagoon in the Marshall Islands pollution levels are 25,000 times higher than standard safety levels. Due to depletion of stratospheric ozone, ultraviolet levels in Australia and New Zealand are rising by about 10 percent each decade, significantly increasing the risk of skin cancer.

Left: Toxic waste from the Australian-operated Ok Tedi gold mine in Papua New Guinea has destroyed large areas of rain forest and poisoned fish and plants in the Fly, the country's longest river.

Left: Sea levels could rise by up to 3 feet (1 m) over the next century. This would spell disaster for densely inhabited, low-lying island groups such as Tuvalu, which rises just 12 feet (4 m) above sea level.

Right: Over 40 percent of Pacific coral reefs are threatened by pollution, urban development, tourism, and destructive exotic species such as the crown-of-thorns starfish.

Protecting the Environment

In the 1990s, Australian conservation and farming organizations established a coordinated farmland-management program called Landcare, designed to halt degradation. It has now been extended to cover other environments, including bushland, rivers, sand dunes, and coastline. Sustainable forestry practices are now the norm in Australia and New Zealand, and plantation forests are a major source of timber, providing, for example, 99 percent of annual roundwood output in New Zealand. The Pacific Islands Forum Fisheries Agency has had notable success in promoting sustainable fisheries throughout the region. Interest in alternative energy is growing: Vanuatu has declared it will switch to renewable sources by 2020. Overall, Oceania has the lowest proportion of human-dominated land after Antarctica, and the number of protected areas has grown sevenfold since 1960—the proportion of protected land, 7.1 percent, is just above the world average. The majority of states and territories in Oceania have also declared their waters to be whale sanctuaries.

PERCENTAGE OF LAND PROTECTED IN MAJOR COUNTRIES OF OCEANIA

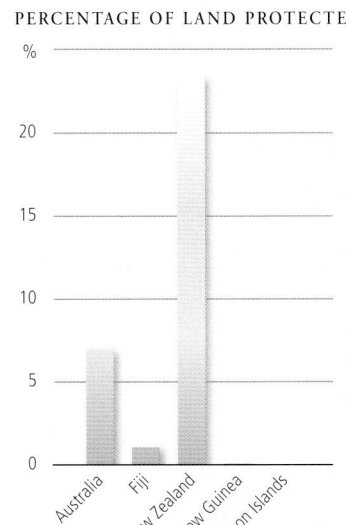

%
20
15
10
5
0

Australia · Fiji · New Zealand · Papua New Guinea · Solomon Islands

New Zealand's national parks help protect remnant populations of native flightless bird species, which have been easy prey for introduced predators. The ground-dwelling kakapo, the world's heaviest parrot, survives only on two small island reserves. As of 2003, just 86 kakapo remained.

AUSTRALIA

The world's sixth-largest country by area, Australia constitutes an entire continent—the world's smallest, flattest, and (after Antarctica) driest. Its massive landmass consists of an ancient western plateau joined by broad sedimentary lowlands to heavily eroded eastern ranges. Known as the Great Dividing Range, the ranges parallel the Pacific coast, separating the better-watered eastern seaboard from the vast, arid interior or "outback." Despite the continent's poor soils and harsh climate, Aboriginal peoples lived off the land for 60,000 years, developing one of the world's most enduring societies. Europeans began arriving only in the late 18th century after the founding of a British penal colony at Port Jackson, now Sydney, in 1788. This and other British colonies drew increasing numbers of free settlers, especially after the discovery of gold in the southeast in the mid-19th century. In 1901, the colonies agreed to federation, resulting in the creation of the independent nation of Australia.

POPULATION PATTERNS

Recent settlers have shunned the interior, clustering along the temperate east and southwest coasts, where 84 percent of Australians occupy one percent of the land. In the outback, vast areas are devoid of people. Although immigration from Asia has risen in the last 30 years, the majority of Australians are still of European, especially British, origin and English is the official language. Aboriginal and Torres Strait Islander peoples constitute just 2.4 percent of the population. Birth rates are low, and it is estimated that by 2035 immigration will be the country's only source of growth.

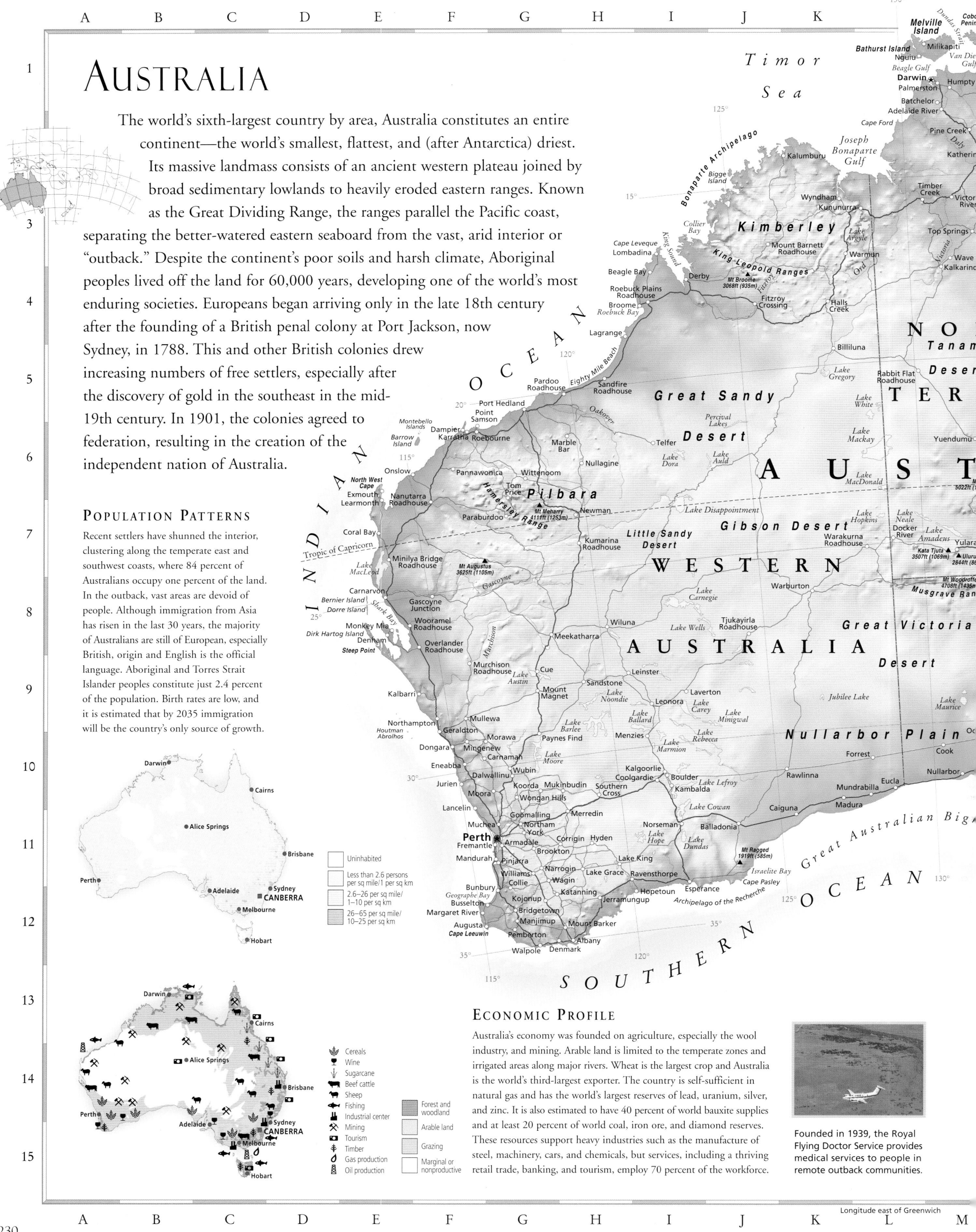

Uninhabited
Less than 2.6 persons per sq mile/1 per sq km
2.6–26 per sq mile/1–10 per sq km
26–65 per sq mile/10–25 per sq km

Cereals
Wine
Sugarcane
Beef cattle
Sheep
Fishing
Industrial center
Mining
Tourism
Timber
Gas production
Oil production

Forest and woodland
Arable land
Grazing
Marginal or nonproductive

ECONOMIC PROFILE

Australia's economy was founded on agriculture, especially the wool industry, and mining. Arable land is limited to the temperate zones and irrigated areas along major rivers. Wheat is the largest crop and Australia is the world's third-largest exporter. The country is self-sufficient in natural gas and has the world's largest reserves of lead, uranium, silver, and zinc. It is also estimated to have 40 percent of world bauxite supplies and at least 20 percent of world coal, iron ore, and diamond reserves. These resources support heavy industries such as the manufacture of steel, machinery, cars, and chemicals, but services, including a thriving retail trade, banking, and tourism, employ 70 percent of the workforce.

Founded in 1939, the Royal Flying Doctor Service provides medical services to people in remote outback communities.

Longitude east of Greenwich

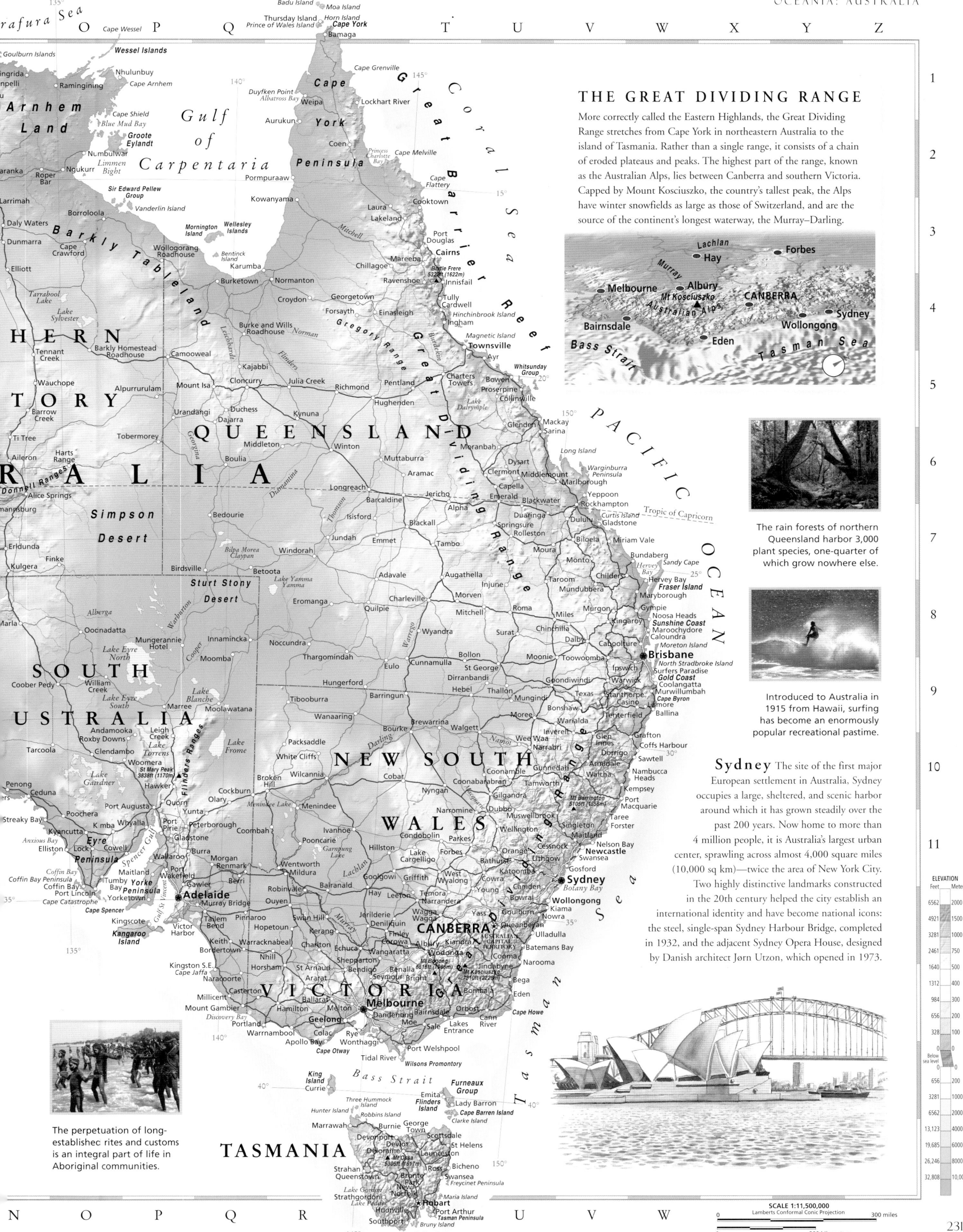

THE GREAT DIVIDING RANGE

More correctly called the Eastern Highlands, the Great Dividing Range stretches from Cape York in northeastern Australia to the island of Tasmania. Rather than a single range, it consists of a chain of eroded plateaus and peaks. The highest part of the range, known as the Australian Alps, lies between Canberra and southern Victoria. Capped by Mount Kosciuszko, the country's tallest peak, the Alps have winter snowfields as large as those of Switzerland, and are the source of the continent's longest waterway, the Murray–Darling.

The rain forests of northern Queensland harbor 3,000 plant species, one-quarter of which grow nowhere else.

Introduced to Australia in 1915 from Hawaii, surfing has become an enormously popular recreational pastime.

Sydney The site of the first major European settlement in Australia, Sydney occupies a large, sheltered, and scenic harbor around which it has grown steadily over the past 200 years. Now home to more than 4 million people, it is Australia's largest urban center, sprawling across almost 4,000 square miles (10,000 sq km)—twice the area of New York City. Two highly distinctive landmarks constructed in the 20th century helped the city establish an international identity and have become national icons: the steel, single-span Sydney Harbour Bridge, completed in 1932, and the adjacent Sydney Opera House, designed by Danish architect Jørn Utzon, which opened in 1973.

The perpetuation of long-established rites and customs is an integral part of life in Aboriginal communities.

ELEVATION	
Feet	Meters
6562	2000
4921	1500
3281	1000
2461	750
1640	500
1312	400
984	300
656	200
328	100
Below sea level	
656	200
3281	1000
6562	2000
13,123	4000
19,685	6000
26,246	8000
32,808	10,000

SCALE 1:11,500,000
Lamberts Conformal Conic Projection
0 — 300 miles
0 — 300 kilometers

NEW ZEALAND

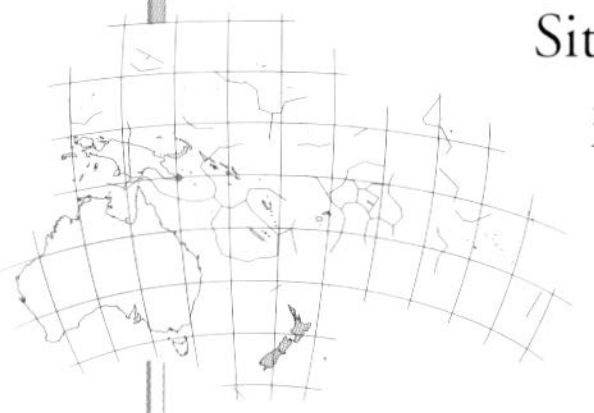

Situated 1,000 miles (1,600 km) southeast of Australia, its nearest neighbor, New Zealand consists of two large islands and several smaller ones. Both main islands straddle fault lines between the Indo-Australian and Pacific tectonic plates. Movement along these faults causes sporadic earthquakes and has formed active volcanoes and geysers in the North Island; over millions of years, it has also pushed up the steep-sided peaks of the Southern Alps, which form the backbone of the South Island. This rugged interior and the South Island's generally cold, wet climate concentrated the development of modern infrastructure in the North Island and along the drier, more fertile east coast of the South Island. Annexed by Britain in 1840, New Zealand became a self-governing colony in 1856 and a dominion in 1907, but did not achieve full independence until 1947. The descendants of British colonists now far outnumber the indigenous Maori, but Maori remains an official language and in recent years the government has made some reparations to Maori peoples for loss of traditional lands.

VOLCANO COUNTRY

Volcanic activity has fashioned the landscape of the North Island's central plateau and still has the potential to modify it further. Lake Taupo, the country's largest lake, occupies a crater formed by a massive volcanic explosion thought to have taken place in AD 186. To its south stretches a line of active volcanoes—Tongariro, Ngauruhoe, and Ruapehu—all of which erupted in the 20th century. In 1996, in the country's largest eruption in 400 years, Ruapehu spewed great clouds of steam and ash over the surrounding skifields; fortunately, there were no casualties. Farther west, the huge cone of Mount Taranaki (Mount Egmont) looms over the southwestern corner of the island. Now dormant, it last erupted in the 18th century.

Wellington Though Auckland is by far the largest city in New Zealand, Wellington is the country's national capital and major business center. The city occupies a large sheltered harbor—the flooded crater of an ancient volcano—at the southern end of the North Island. Europeans arrived in 1840 and moved their seat of government here in 1865. The foreshore, much of it reclaimed land, is the site of the commercial district and major government buildings including the parliament, with its distinctive executive office building, widely known as the Beehive. Designed by British architect Sir Basil Spence, it was begun in 1969 and completed in 1980.

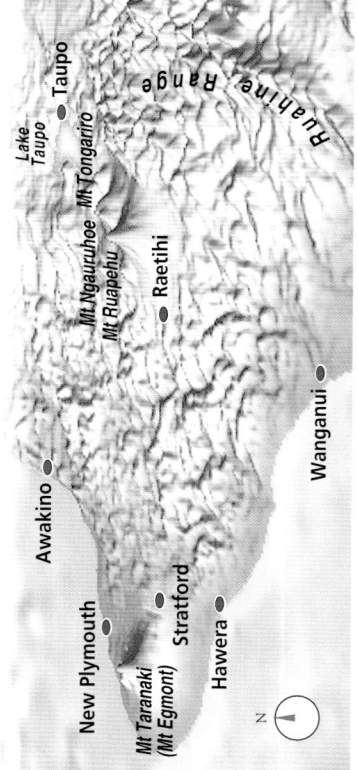

Geothermal activity is concentrated around Rotorua in the North Island.

Home to approximately 1 million people, Auckland occupies an isthmus between two broad harbors.

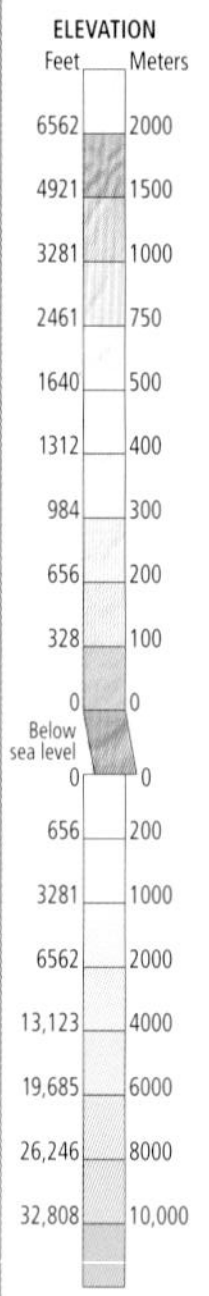

NEW ZEALAND

POPULATION PATTERNS

The North Island constitutes 42 percent of the country but is home to more than three-quarters of the population; indeed, more than 30 percent of New Zealanders live in the Auckland region. About 75 percent of inhabitants live in towns and cities. People of European extraction make up 80 percent of the population, and one in seven New Zealanders is Maori. Ethnic diversity is increasing. The number of residents of Asian origin, for example, climbed 140 percent between 1991 and 2001. Many Pacific Islander people have settled in New Zealand, and Auckland is recognized as the world's largest Polynesian city.

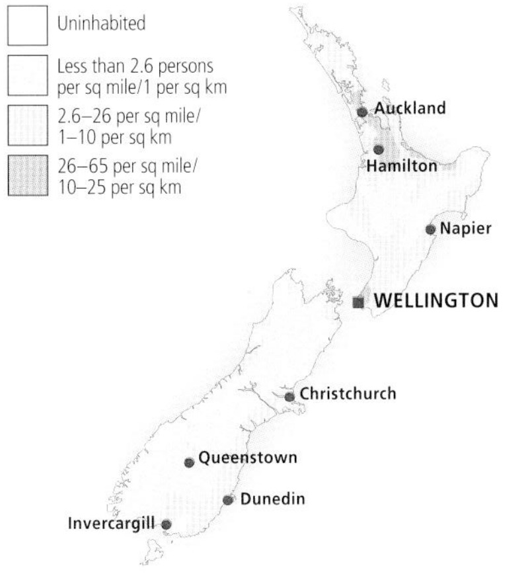

Uninhabited
Less than 2.6 persons per sq mile/1 per sq km
2.6–26 per sq mile/ 1–10 per sq km
26–65 per sq mile/ 10–25 per sq km

Forest and woodland
Arable land
Grazing
Marginal or nonproductive

Fruit
Wine
Beef cattle
Sheep
Pigs
Fishing
Industrial center
Timber
Dairy cattle
Tourism

SCALE 1:3,250,000
Lambert's Conformal Conic Projection

Cathedral Square is the heart of the South Island's largest city, Christchurch.

ECONOMIC PROFILE

New Zealand has a long association with wool, which was the country's leading agricultural product until the late 1970s. But the sheep population has declined, and dairy products and meat are now the nation's most valuable exports. Forests cover 30 percent of the country and forest products, overwhelmingly from plantations, constitute the third most lucrative export. New Zealand is self-sufficient in all energy sources except oil; two-thirds of its electricity comes from hydroelectric power and over 6 percent from geothermal power. Leading industries include foods and beverages (notably wine), machinery, metals, and textiles. However, services employ 65 percent of workers, with tourism alone generating 10 percent of GDP and supporting one in ten jobs.

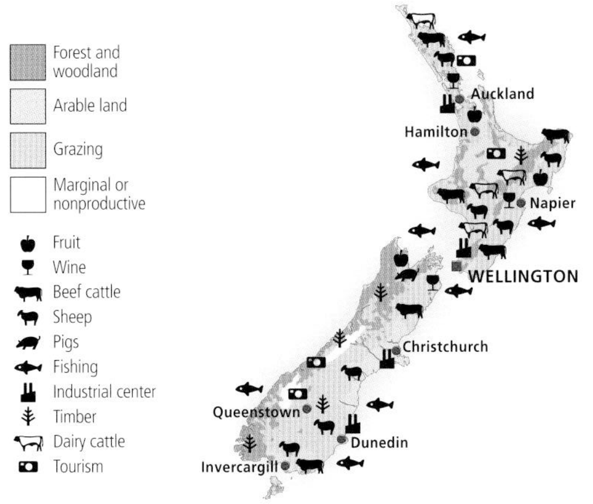

In the western South Island, Franz Josef Glacier (above) and Fox Glacier descend as far as the coastal lowlands.

The traditional welcome dance, or powhiri, is still performed for visitors to Maori meeting houses.

The southwest coast of the South Island is characterized by deep fjords, including spectacular Milford Sound.

233

MELANESIA
Fiji, Papua New Guinea, Solomon Islands, Vanuatu

The islands of Melanesia arc around the northeast coast of Australia, extend south toward the Tropic of Capricorn and spread east to the edge of the Western Hemisphere. They lie close to the boundary between the Indo-Australian and Pacific plates and have been shaped by relatively recent tectonic activity. Most are mountainous and many have active volcanoes and dark volcanic soil—the word Melanesia derives from the Greek terms *melas* (meaning "black") and *nesoi* ("islands"). Almost all are blanketed with a dense covering of tropical rain forest, though parts of this forest have been cleared. Independence has been achieved by all of the island groups except New Caledonia, which chose to remain part of France. However, many parts of Melanesia have been politically volatile in recent years. In New Caledonia in the 1980s, indigenous Kanak people began a campaign for independence that led to sporadic violence. Coups took place in Fiji in 1987 and 2000, and in Bougainville an armed independence movement fought a war against the Papua New Guinea government from 1988 to 2001.

In the Papua New Guinea highlands, men attending festivals called sing-sings wear paint and headdresses.

Bougainville's giant Panguna copper mine was closed down during the secessionist war and has not reopened.

Fiji's picturesque islands and highly developed tourist facilities attract up to 400,000 visitors a year.

Villagers on the island of Tanna in Vanuatu perform a traditional dance in sight of Yasur, a highly active volcano.

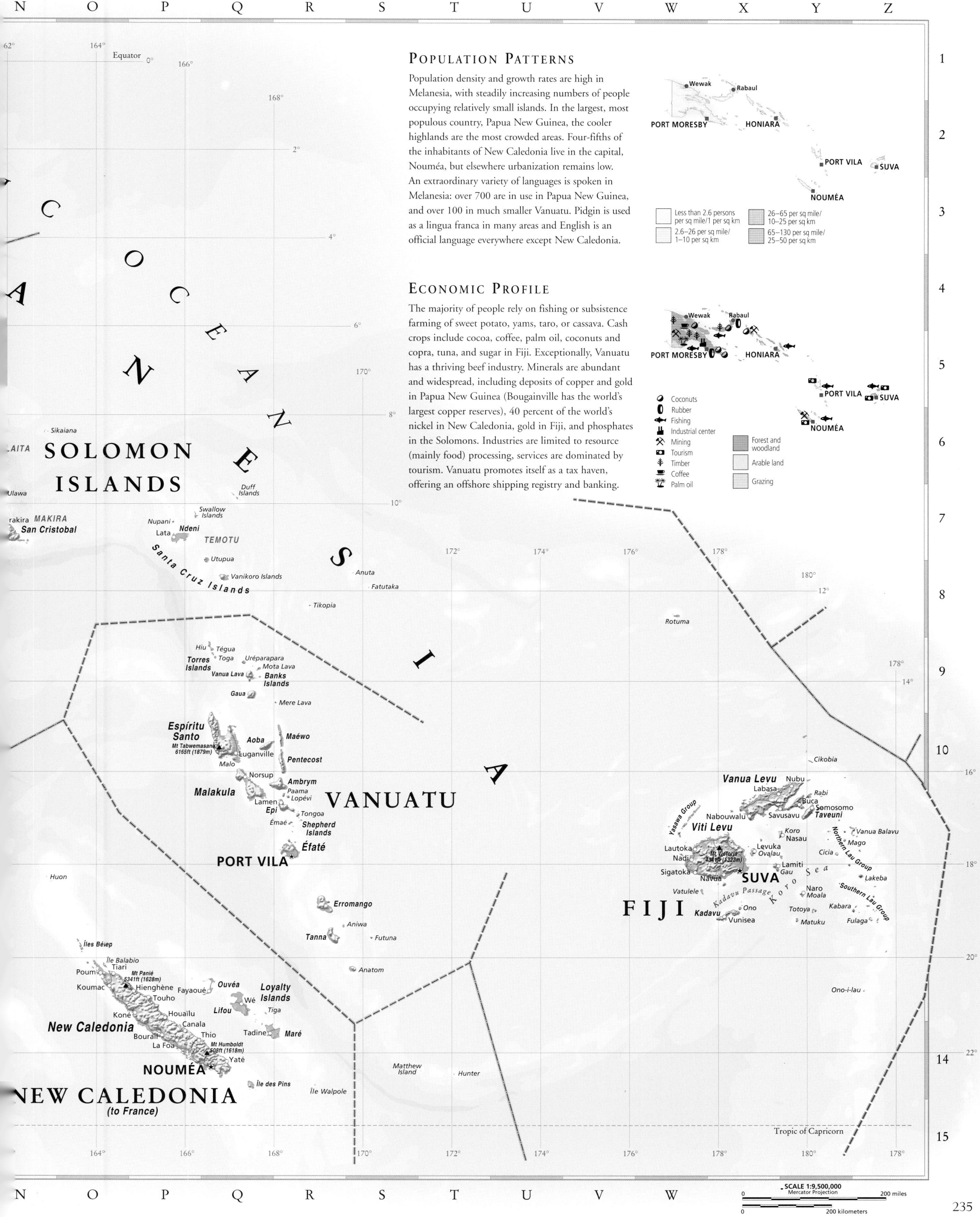

POPULATION PATTERNS

Population density and growth rates are high in Melanesia, with steadily increasing numbers of people occupying relatively small islands. In the largest, most populous country, Papua New Guinea, the cooler highlands are the most crowded areas. Four-fifths of the inhabitants of New Caledonia live in the capital, Nouméa, but elsewhere urbanization remains low. An extraordinary variety of languages is spoken in Melanesia: over 700 are in use in Papua New Guinea, and over 100 in much smaller Vanuatu. Pidgin is used as a lingua franca in many areas and English is an official language everywhere except New Caledonia.

Wewak Rabaul
PORT MORESBY HONIARA
PORT VILA SUVA
NOUMÉA

- Less than 2.6 persons per sq mile/1 per sq km
- 2.6–26 per sq mile/ 1–10 per sq km
- 26–65 per sq mile/ 10–25 per sq km
- 65–130 per sq mile/ 25–50 per sq km

ECONOMIC PROFILE

The majority of people rely on fishing or subsistence farming of sweet potato, yams, taro, or cassava. Cash crops include cocoa, coffee, palm oil, coconuts and copra, tuna, and sugar in Fiji. Exceptionally, Vanuatu has a thriving beef industry. Minerals are abundant and widespread, including deposits of copper and gold in Papua New Guinea (Bougainville has the world's largest copper reserves), 40 percent of the world's nickel in New Caledonia, gold in Fiji, and phosphates in the Solomons. Industries are limited to resource (mainly food) processing, services are dominated by tourism. Vanuatu promotes itself as a tax haven, offering an offshore shipping registry and banking.

Wewak Rabaul
PORT MORESBY HONIARA
PORT VILA SUVA
NOUMÉA

- Coconuts
- Rubber
- Fishing
- Industrial center
- Mining
- Tourism
- Timber
- Coffee
- Palm oil
- Forest and woodland
- Arable land
- Grazing

Equator
Sikaiana
LAITA
Ulawa
rakira MAKIRA
San Cristobal

SOLOMON ISLANDS

Duff Islands
Nupani Swallow Islands
Lata Ndeni
TEMOTU
Utupua
Vanikoro Islands
Anuta
Fatutaka
Tikopia
Rotuma

Santa Cruz Islands

Hiu Tégua
Toga Uréparapara
Torres Islands Mota Lava
Vanua Lava Banks Islands
Gaua
Mere Lava

Espíritu Santo
Mt Tabwemasana
6165ft (1879m) Aoba Maéwo
Luganville Pentecost
Malo
Norsup Ambrym
Malakula Paama
Lamen Lopévi
Epi
Émaé Tongoa
Shepherd Islands
Éfaté
PORT VILA

VANUATU

Erromango
Aniwa
Tanna Futuna

Anatom

Cikobia

Vanua Levu Nubu
Labasa
Rabi
Buca
Somosomo
Nabouwalu Savusavu Taveuni
Yasawa Group
Viti Levu Koro
Nasau Vanua Balavu
Lautoka Levuka Mago
Nadi Ovalau Northern Lau Group
Mt Victoria Lamiti Cicia
4341ft (1323m) Gau
Sigatoka Lakeba
Navua Naro
Vatulele SUVA Moala Southern Lau Group
Koro Sea
Kadavu Passage Ono Totoya Kabara
FIJI Kadavu Matuku Fulaga
Vunisea

Huon

Îles Bélep
Île Balabio
Poum Tiari
Mt Panié
5341ft (1628m)
Koumac Hienghène Fayaoué Ouvéa
Touho Loyalty Islands
Kone Wé
Houaïlu Lifou
Canala Tiga
Bourail Thio Tadine Maré
Mt Humboldt
La Foa 608ft (1618m)
NOUMÉA Yaté

NEW CALEDONIA
(to France)

Île des Pins
Île Walpole
Matthew Island Hunter

Ono-i-lau

Tropic of Capricorn

SCALE 1:9,500,000
Mercator Projection
0   200 miles
0   200 kilometers

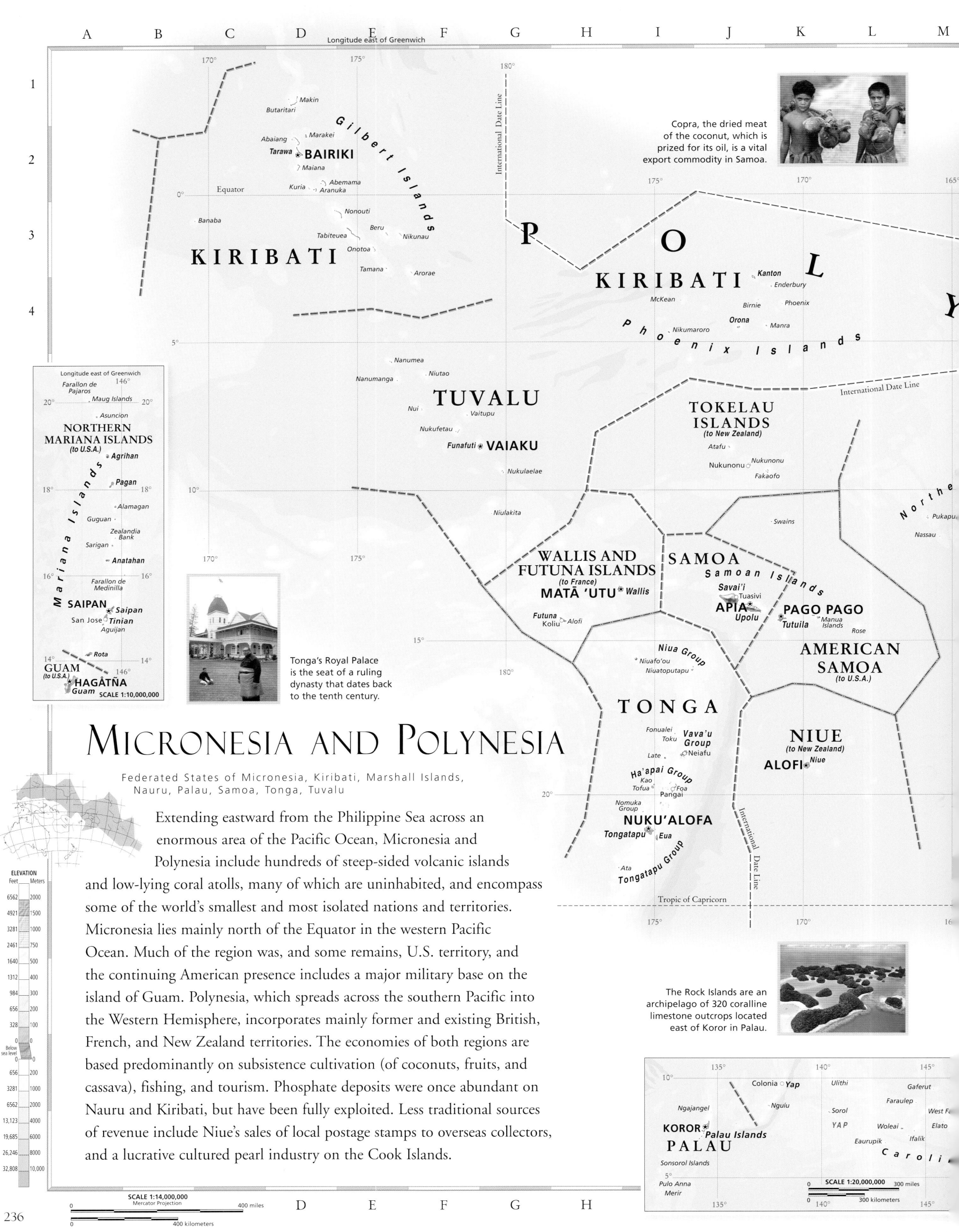

MICRONESIA AND POLYNESIA

Federated States of Micronesia, Kiribati, Marshall Islands, Nauru, Palau, Samoa, Tonga, Tuvalu

Extending eastward from the Philippine Sea across an enormous area of the Pacific Ocean, Micronesia and Polynesia include hundreds of steep-sided volcanic islands and low-lying coral atolls, many of which are uninhabited, and encompass some of the world's smallest and most isolated nations and territories. Micronesia lies mainly north of the Equator in the western Pacific Ocean. Much of the region was, and some remains, U.S. territory, and the continuing American presence includes a major military base on the island of Guam. Polynesia, which spreads across the southern Pacific into the Western Hemisphere, incorporates mainly former and existing British, French, and New Zealand territories. The economies of both regions are based predominantly on subsistence cultivation (of coconuts, fruits, and cassava), fishing, and tourism. Phosphate deposits were once abundant on Nauru and Kiribati, but have been fully exploited. Less traditional sources of revenue include Niue's sales of local postage stamps to overseas collectors, and a lucrative cultured pearl industry on the Cook Islands.

Copra, the dried meat of the coconut, which is prized for its oil, is a vital export commodity in Samoa.

Tonga's Royal Palace is the seat of a ruling dynasty that dates back to the tenth century.

The Rock Islands are an archipelago of 320 coralline limestone outcrops located east of Koror in Palau.

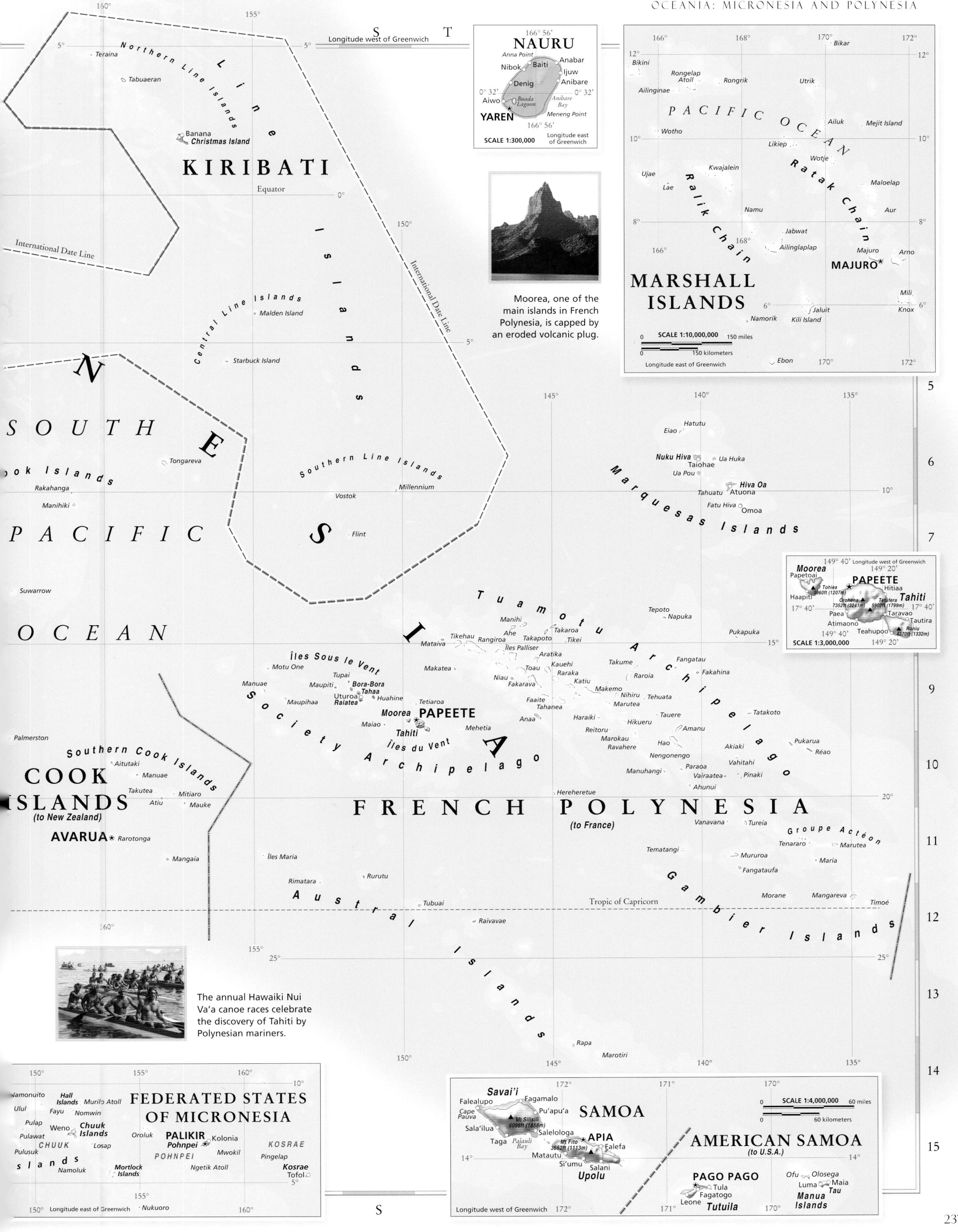

KIRIBATI

Northern Line Islands

Teraina
Tabuaeran
Banana
Christmas Island

Equator 0°

Central Line Islands
Malden Island
Starbuck Island
Vostok
Millennium
Flint

Southern Line Islands

International Date Line

Longitude west of Greenwich

S T

NAURU

Anna Point
Nibok   Baiti   Anabar
Denig   Ijuw   Anibare
Aiwo   Buada   Anibare Bay
Lagoon
YAREN   Meneng Point

166° 56'
0° 32'   0° 32'
166° 56'

SCALE 1:300,000
Longitude east of Greenwich

Moorea, one of the main islands in French Polynesia, is capped by an eroded volcanic plug.

MARSHALL ISLANDS

PACIFIC OCEAN

Ratak Chain
Ralik Chain

Bikar
Bikini
Rongelap Atoll   Rongrik   Utrik
Ailinginae
Wotho   Ailuk   Mejit Island
Likiep   Wotje
Ujae   Kwajalein
Lae   Maloelap
Namu   Aur
Jabwat
Ailinglaplap   Majuro   Arno
MAJURO
Mili
Namorik   Jaluit   Knox
Kili Island
Ebon

12° 10° 8° 6°
166° 168° 170° 172°

SCALE 1:10,000,000
150 miles
150 kilometers
Longitude east of Greenwich

MICRONESIA

SOUTHE

S

PACIFIC

OCEAN

ook Islands
Rakahanga
Manihiki
Tongareva
Suwarrow

Palmerston

Southern Cook Islands

COOK ISLANDS
(to New Zealand)

Aitutaki
Manuae
Takutea   Mitiaro
Atiu   Mauke
AVARUA   Rarotonga
Mangaia

Îles Maria
Rimatara   Rurutu
Raivavae
Tubuai

Austral Islands

Tropic of Capricorn

Marquesas Islands

Hatutu
Eiao
Nuku Hiva   Ua Huka
Ua Pou   Taiohae
Tahuata   Hiva Oa
Fatu Hiva   Atuona
Omoa

PAPEETE / Tahiti inset

Moorea   Papetoai   149° 40' 149° 20'
Papetoai   PAPEETE
Tohiea   Hitiaa
3660ft (1207m)
Haapiti   Orohena   Tetufera   Tahiti
7352ft (2241m) 5902ft (1799m)
Paea   Taravao
Atimaono   Taautira
Peahupoo   Raiui
4370ft (1332m)
17° 40'   17° 40'
149° 40'   149° 20'
SCALE 1:3,000,000

Tuamotu Archipelago

Mataiva   Tikehau   Rangiroa   Ahe   Takapoto
Îles Palliser   Takaroa
Tikei
Manihi
Tepoto   Napuka
Pukapuka
Niau   Toau   Kauehi
Fakarava   Raraka   Takume
Katiu   Raroia
Makemo   Fangatau
Faaite   Nihiru   Fakahina
Tahanea   Marutea   Tehuata
Anaa   Haraiki   Tauere   Takatoto
Reitoru   Hikueru   Amanu
Marokau   Akiaki
Mehetia   Ravahere   Hao   Pukarua
Nengonengo   Réao
Paraoa   Vahitahi
Manuhangi   Vairaatea   Pinaki
Ahunui

Society Archipelago / Îles Sous le Vent

Motu One
Tupai
Manuae   Maupiti   Bora-Bora
Tahaa
Maupihaa   Uturoa   Huahine   Tetiaroa
Raiatea
Maiao   Moorea   PAPEETE
Tahiti
Maiao   Îles du Vent
Hereheretue

FRENCH POLYNESIA
(to France)

Vanavana   Tureia   Groupe Actéon
Tenararo   Marutea
Tematangi   Maria
Mururoa
Fangataufa   Morane   Mangareva
Timoé

Gambier Islands

Rapa
Marotiri

The annual Hawaiki Nui Va'a canoe races celebrate the discovery of Tahiti by Polynesian mariners.

FEDERATED STATES OF MICRONESIA

Namonuito   Hall Islands   Murilo Atoll
Ulul   Nomwin
Fayu
Pulap   Weno   Chuuk Islands   Oroluk   Kolonia
Pulusuk   CHUUK   Losap   PALIKIR   Mwokil
Puluwat   Pohnpei   Pingelap
slands   POHNPEI   Ngetik Atoll   KOSRAE
Namoluk   Mortlock Islands   Kosrae
Tofol
Nukuoro

150° 155° 160° 10° 5°
Longitude east of Greenwich

SAMOA

Savai'i
Falealupo   Fagamalo
Cape   Pu'apu'a
Pauva
Sala'ilua   Mt Silisili
6096ft (1858m)
Taga   Salelologa   SAMOA
Palauli   APIA
Bay   Mt Fito   Falefa
Matautu   3652ft (1113m)
Si'umu   Salani
Upolu

14° 172° 171° 170°
SCALE 1:4,000,000
60 miles
60 kilometers

AMERICAN SAMOA
(to U.S.A.)

PAGO PAGO
Tula
Fagatogo   Ofu   Olosega
Leone   Luma   Maia
Tutuila   Tau
Manua Islands

14°
Longitude west of Greenwich   172°   171°   170°

S

237

Taken from NASA's Landsat 7 satellite, this image shows part of the Transantarctic Mountains. The glaciers visible at center and center right flow off the Antarctic plateau to the Ross Ice Shelf. The brown areas at left are the McMurdo Dry Valleys.

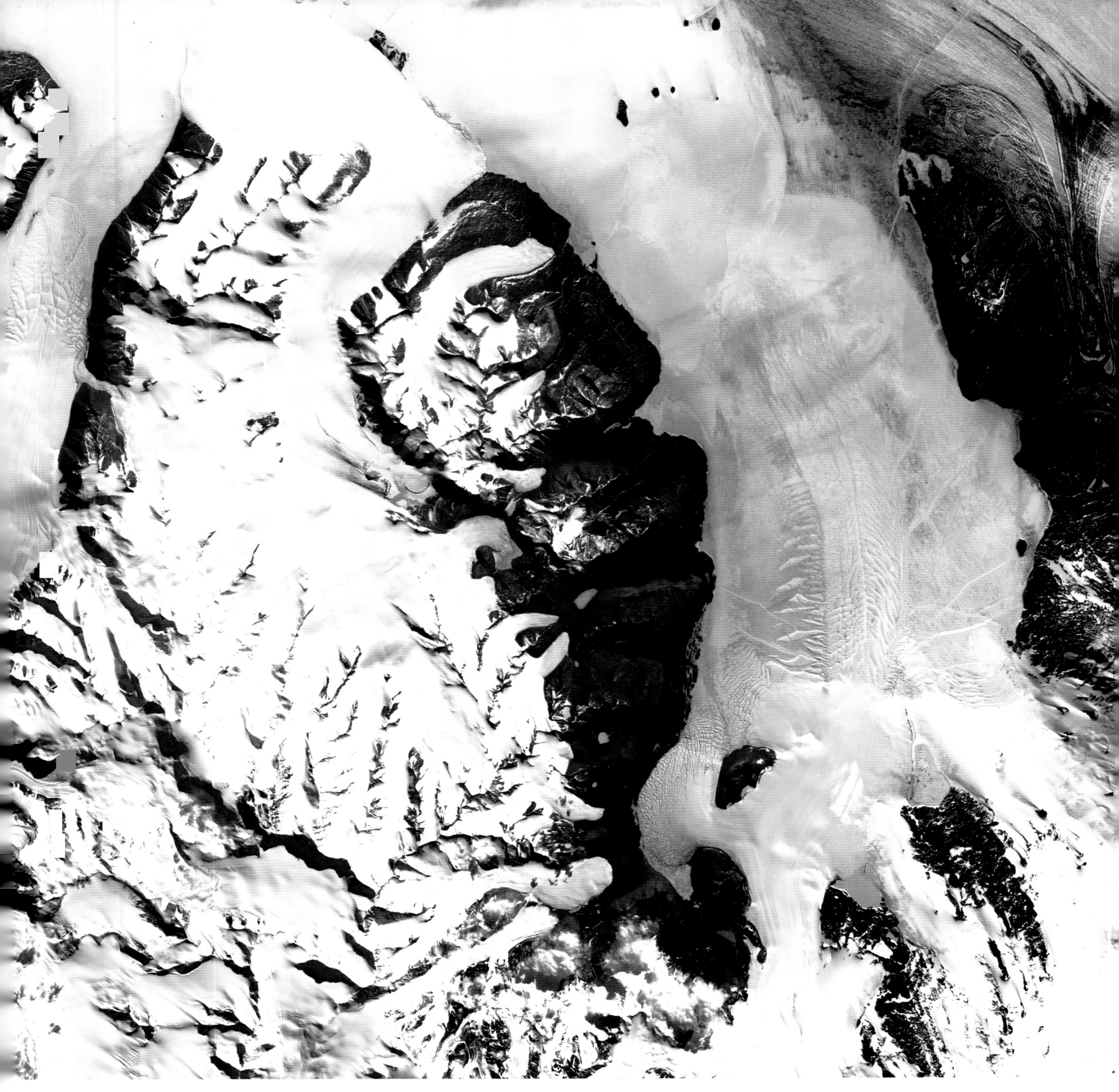

ANTARCTICA

Antarctica

An almost circular landmass centered on the South Pole, Antarctica is the world's fifth-largest as well as its coldest, windiest, driest, and, on average, highest continent. A vast ice sheet covers 98 percent of the land. Among the few topographical features not totally obscured by the ice are the Transantarctic Mountains, which divide the continent into East and West Antarctica. In the east, the ice sheet hides a high plateau; to the west, it conceals a mountainous archipelago. Much of the surrounding ocean freezes in winter, effectively doubling the size of Antarctica, and for much of that season the sun does not rise. These severe conditions drastically restrict animal and plant distribution, and have prohibited permanent human occupation. Nevertheless, Antarctica is home to a fluctuating population of scientists and support staff based at a total of 42 research stations. Their numbers swell annually from around 1,000 in winter to approximately 4,000 in summer.

THE ANTARCTIC PENINSULA

The roughly circular outline of Antarctica is interrupted by the narrow Antarctic Peninsula, which extends 800 miles (1,300 km) toward the southern tip of South America. The peninsula is mountainous—rising to 13,747 feet (4,190 m) at Mount Jackson—capped by ice sheets and glaciers, and fringed by numerous islands, slender channels, and ice shelves. Nevertheless, it experiences the continent's mildest conditions and includes most of its few patches of ice-free land. From the end of the peninsula, an undersea ridge known as the Scotia Arc runs east then west, forming a great loop that eventually connects with Cape Horn in South America.

THE ANTARCTIC TREATY

Seven countries—Argentina, Australia, Chile, France, New Zealand, Norway, and the United Kingdom—have at one time or other asserted sovereignty over parts of Antarctica. However, by becoming signatories to the Antarctic Treaty of 1959, they and 38 other nations have since agreed to suspend territorial claims and preserve the continent for nonmilitary scientific research. The Antarctic Treaty arose out of a worldwide scientific project called the International Geophysical Year, which began in 1957 and saw 12 nations establish numerous research stations across Antarctica.

NATURAL RESOURCES

Early sealers and whalers almost wiped out the continent's originally abundant marine mammals, but populations of seals and whales have recovered in recent years, especially since the International Whaling Commission declared most of the Southern Ocean a whale sanctuary in 1994. Although 23 countries have agreed to manage Antarctic fisheries for sustainability, illegal fishing is steadily depleting stocks of Antarctic cod, finfish, and toothfish. Geologists concur that Antarctica may harbor great mineral wealth, including copper, gold, platinum, and oil. No economically exploitable reserves have been found, however, and, in any case, mining is banned under the Antarctic Treaty. Tourism is proving a more viable economic activity, with visitor numbers rising steadily.

Icebergs abound in coastal waters, often providing a place for penguins to roost.

Completed in 1975, the U.S. Amundsen–Scott Base at the South Pole is covered by a huge aluminum dome.

Fishing
Gas
Tourism
Coal
Precious metals and minerals
Metallic minerals
Whales

Marginal or nonproductive

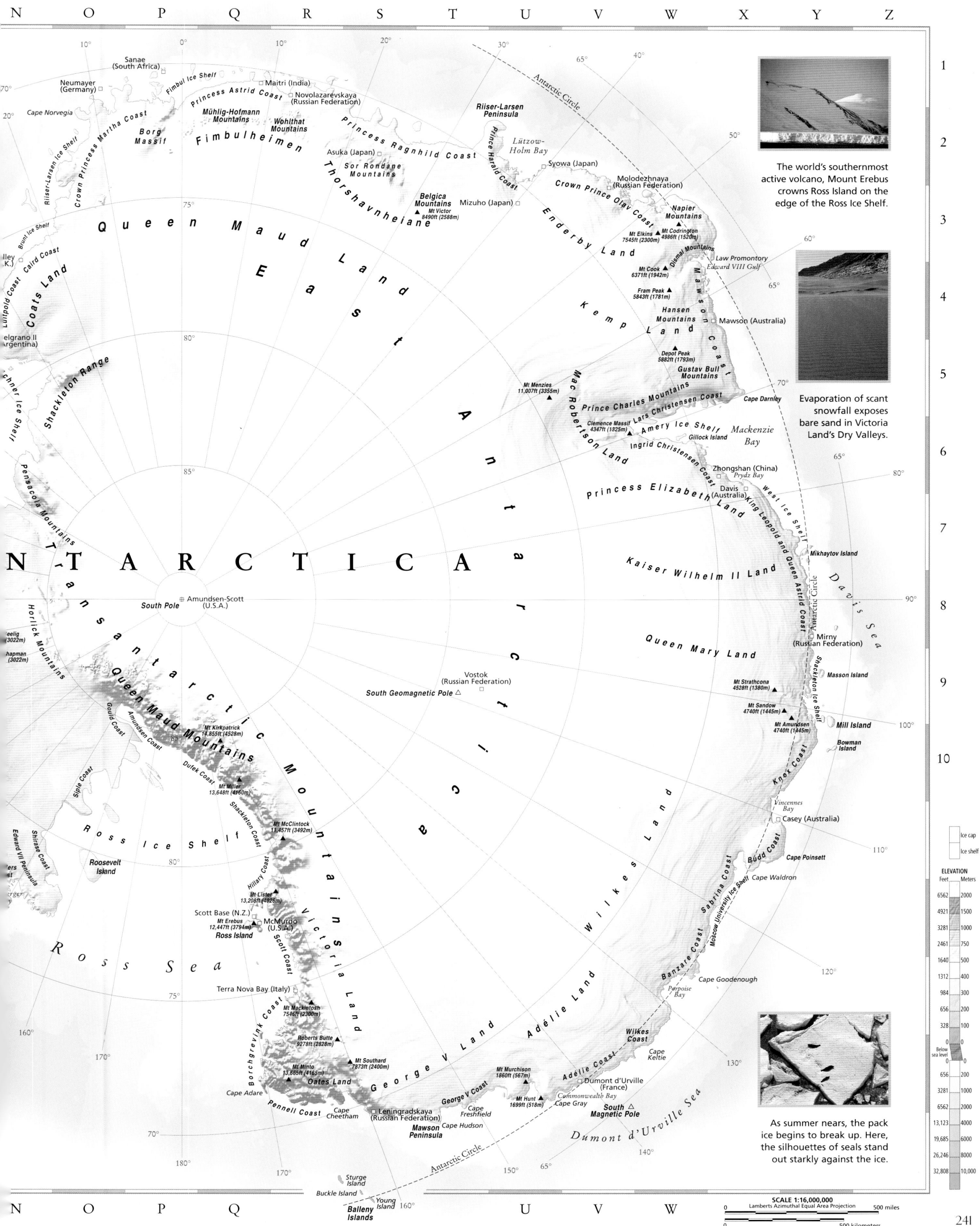

The world's southernmost active volcano, Mount Erebus crowns Ross Island on the edge of the Ross Ice Shelf.

Evaporation of scant snowfall exposes bare sand in Victoria Land's Dry Valleys.

As summer nears, the pack ice begins to break up. Here, the silhouettes of seals stand out starkly against the ice.

SCALE 1:16,000,000
Lamberts Azimuthal Equal Area Projection

ANTARCTICA IN FOCUS

Until the 20th century, Antarctica remained virtually unexplored. Although James Cook crossed the Antarctic Circle in 1773, he was blocked by ice, and it took another 65 years for the existence of a continent to be confirmed. The first human to set foot on this continent may have been the American John Davis in 1821, but it was 1899 before anyone spent a winter, and 1958 before a team crossed the icy expanse from one coast to the other.

The early 19th century saw sealers venture into the region, setting up bases on islands and almost destroying the fur seal populations. They were followed by 20th-century whalers, who killed 99 percent of blue whales, 97 percent of humpbacks, and 80 percent of fin whales before international agreements largely halted the practice.

The first permanent scientific bases were built in Antarctica in the 1950s. By studying the untouched ice layers, scientists have built up a picture of Earth's climate over the past 420,000 years. Fossil discoveries have shown that the continent was once lushly vegetated and had similar fauna to South America and Australia, providing evidence for the theory of continental drift, which states that Antarctica, Africa, India, South America, and Australia were once part of the supercontinent Gondwana. Current efforts are monitoring the ozone hole and the impact of global warming on Antarctic ice.

The lack of human impact that has made Antarctica a pristine laboratory for scientists has also made it a lure for adventurous tourists, whose numbers grew remarkably during the 1990s.

SCALE 1:48,000,000
Lambert Azimuthal Equal Area Projection

Tourism Boom

In 1956, the first plane carrying tourists flew over Antarctica without landing, a method of viewing the icy continent that remains popular today. It was not until the late 1960s, however, that tourist cruise ships began regular visits. In 1991–92, tourists outnumbered scientific personnel for the first time, and tourist numbers continued to grow dramatically throughout the decade that followed. The vast majority of tourists visit by cruise ship, but several dozen fly to Antarctica for a land-based adventure.

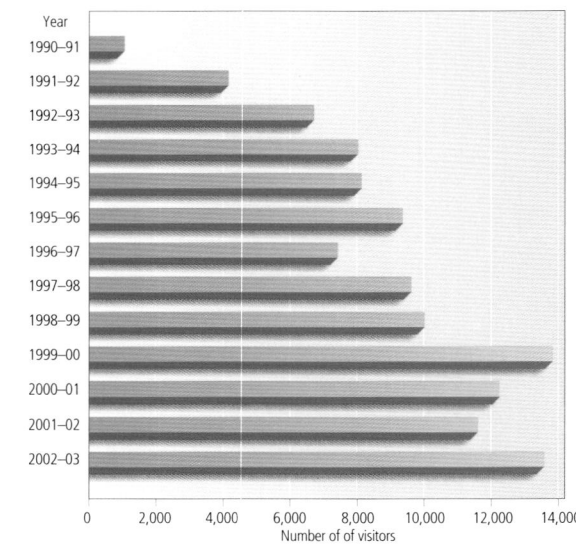

Number of visitors

Most current tourism in Antarctica is ship-based, with visitors living aboard cruise liners and using inflatable craft to reach the shore. Land-based tourism would have a greater environmental impact.

The pristine layers of Antarctica's ice preserve a record of Earth's changing climate. Cores drilled out of the ice can reveal centuries of varying precipitation, temperature, and atmospheric composition.

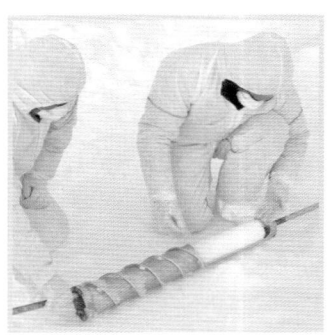

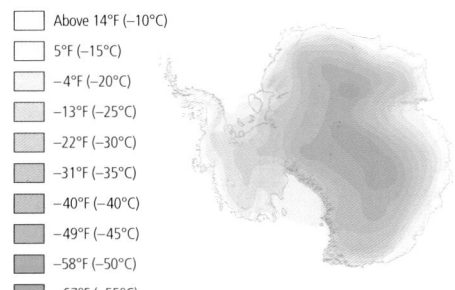

ANNUAL MEAN TEMPERATURE

Above 14°F (−10°C)
5°F (−15°C)
−4°F (−20°C)
−13°F (−25°C)
−22°F (−30°C)
−31°F (−35°C)
−40°F (−40°C)
−49°F (−45°C)
−58°F (−50°C)
−67°F (−55°C)

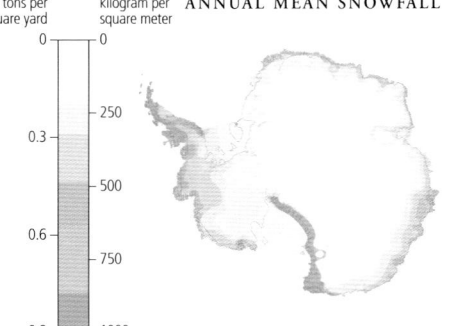

tons per square yard
kilogram per square meter

ANNUAL MEAN SNOWFALL

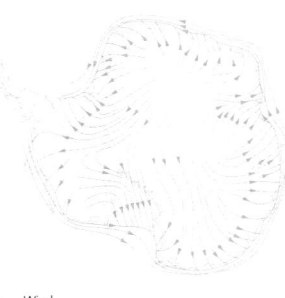

KATABATIC WINDS

Wind

Cold, Dry, and Windy

Because of both its high elevation and its distance from the moderating effects of the ocean, Antarctica's eastern interior has by far the lowest temperatures. The continent receives little precipitation because the air is usually too cold to hold water vapor. Driven by gravity rather than pressure differences, katabatic winds blow constantly and become exceptionally strong near the coast.

Antarctic Exploration

In search of a great southern land, James Cook crossed the Antarctic Circle three times on his voyage of 1772–75. Although he did not see land, his descriptions of the rich marine life encouraged sealers and explorers to follow him. In 1820, Bellingshausen and Palmer both investigated the Antarctic Peninsula region, while later explorers revealed more southerly areas of the continent. Scott and Amundsen raced each other to the South Pole, with Amundsen reaching it first in 1911. More than 45 years later, a joint Commonwealth team made the first overland crossing of Antarctica.

Led by Robert Falcon Scott, a British team reached the South Pole on January 17, 1912, only to discover that Roald Amundsen's Norwegian team had arrived a month earlier, on December 14, 1911. All members of Scott's team perished on the return journey.

The plankton-rich Antarctic waters support vast swarms of small crustaceans known as krill, which are the main food of baleen whales, three seal species, penguins and other birds, and many fishes.

THE OZONE HOLE

High in the stratosphere, a layer containing a small amount of the gas known as ozone absorbs most of the Sun's harmful ultraviolet rays. Since the 1980s, scientists have been monitoring Antarctica's ozone hole, an area of depleted ozone that forms every September. Their work showed that the hole was growing dramatically, and industrial pollutants such as chlorofluorocarbons (CFCs) were identified as the culprit. As each southern spring begins, the atmospheric conditions trap these ozone-destroying chlorine compounds above Antarctica. Most countries agreed to phase out the use of CFCs under the 1987 Montreal Protocol, but the pollutants linger in the atmosphere. The 2000 ozone hole (shown in the image below) was the largest ever recorded, measuring about 11 million square miles (29 million sq km)—roughly three times the size of the United States.

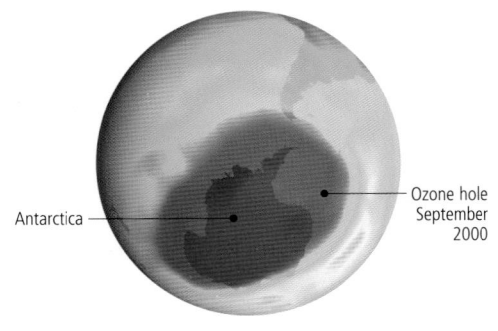

Antarctica — Ozone hole September 2000

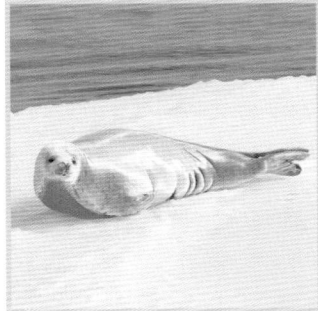

Insulated by thick layers of blubber, the Weddell seal spends the many months of winter darkness under the ice, using sonar to locate its food and breathing holes. It breeds on sea ice or land in summer.

POLAR OCEAN LIFE

Antarctic Polar Frontal Zone
Summer pack ice limit
Winter pack ice limit
Ice shelf
High zooplankton concentration
Medium zooplankton concentration
Low zooplankton concentration
Krill distribution
Humpback whale migratory route
Sei, blue, and fin whale distribution
Penguin breeding colonies

Antarctic Animals

The only true land animals on Antarctica are tiny wingless midges and microscopic species that live in summer ponds. Some of the waters that surround the continent, however, are teeming, with blooms of phytoplankton and swarms of krill forming the center of a vast food web supporting fish, penguins, seabirds, seals, and whales. The Antarctic Polar Frontal Zone, where warm northern waters meet cold southern waters, acts as an oceanographic and biological barrier.

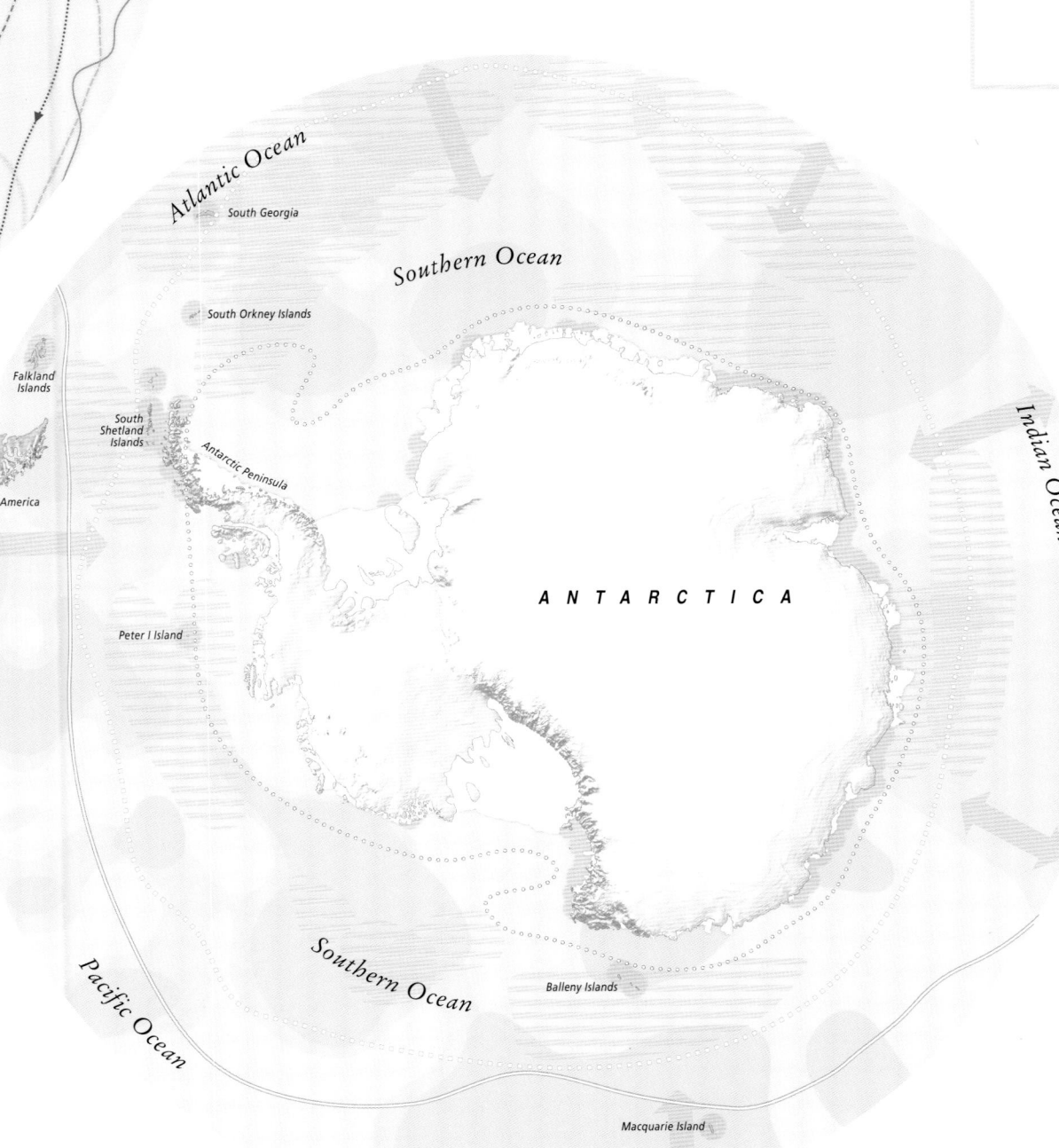

James Cook (U.K.) 1772–73

Thaddeus von Bellingshausen (Russia) 1819–1821

Charles Wilkes (U.S.A.) 1839–40

John Balleny (U.K.) 1839

To Australia

Atlantic Ocean

South Georgia

Southern Ocean

South Orkney Islands

Falkland Islands

South Shetland Islands

Antarctic Peninsula

South America

Peter I Island

ANTARCTICA

Indian Ocean

Pacific Ocean

Southern Ocean

Balleny Islands

Macquarie Island

SCALE 1:48,000,000
Lambert Azimuthal Equal Area Projection

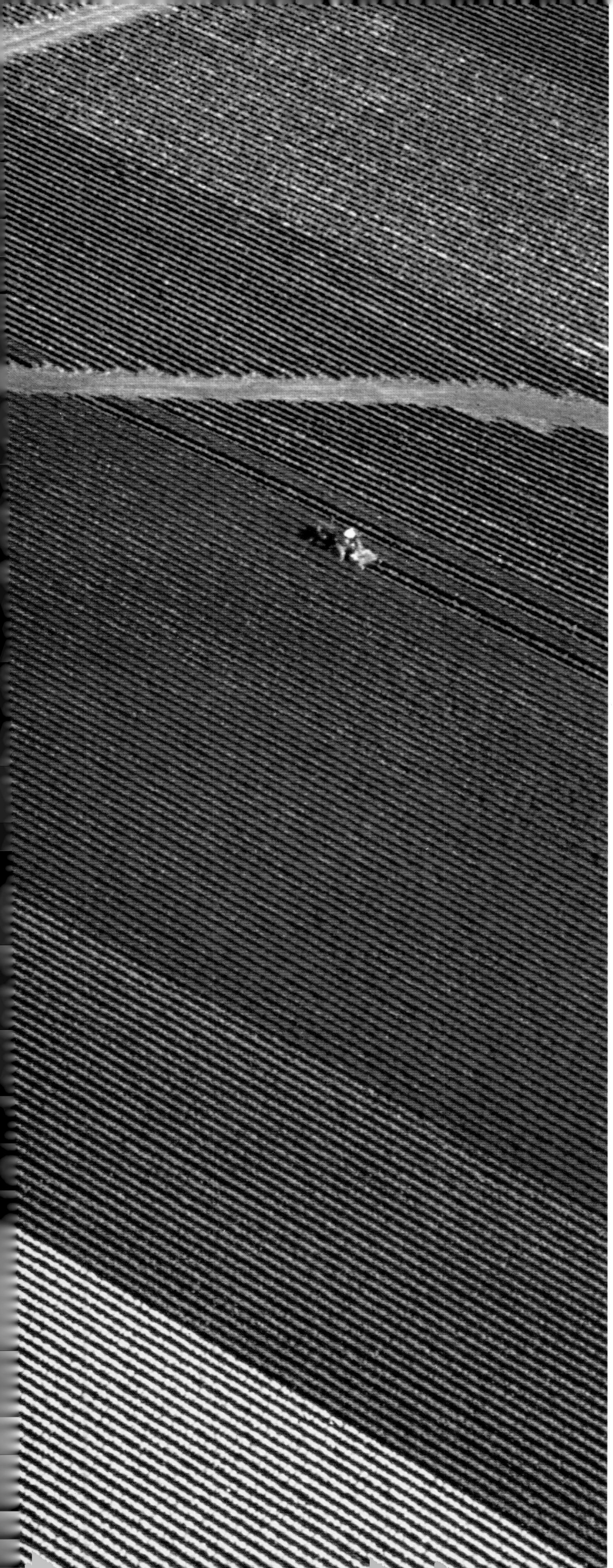

REFERENCE

These tulip fields, picturesque and colorful in April bloom, are located in the Skagit River delta, south of Mount Vernon in western Washington, U.S.A. The area boasts some of the state's most productive land, much of which, including these agricultural flats, was reclaimed from swampland. The tractor gives perspective to the large scale of the tulip plantation.

Geographical Comparisons

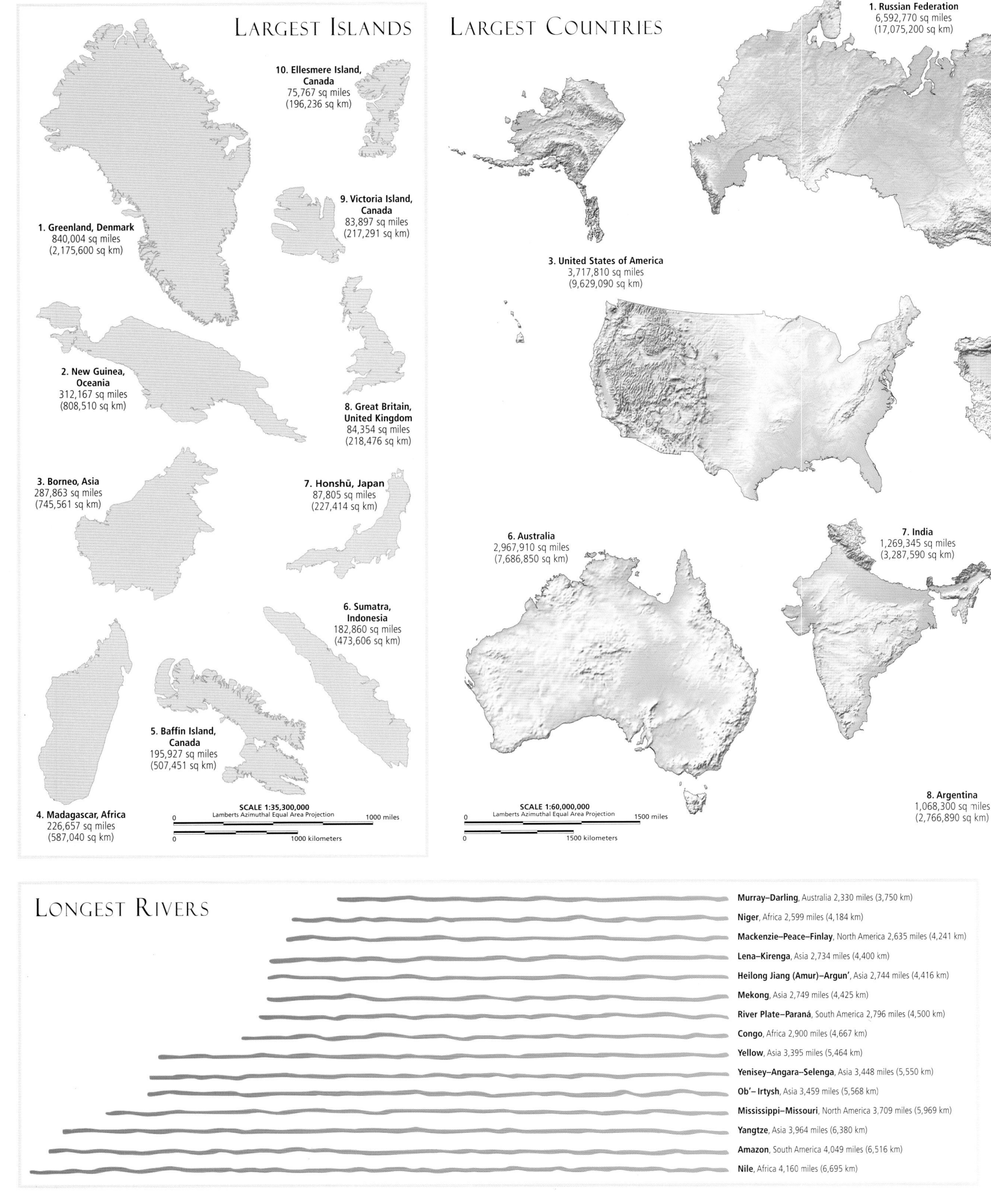

Largest Islands

Largest Countries

10. Ellesmere Island, Canada
75,767 sq miles
(196,236 sq km)

9. Victoria Island, Canada
83,897 sq miles
(217,291 sq km)

1. Greenland, Denmark
840,004 sq miles
(2,175,600 sq km)

2. New Guinea, Oceania
312,167 sq miles
(808,510 sq km)

8. Great Britain, United Kingdom
84,354 sq miles
(218,476 sq km)

3. Borneo, Asia
287,863 sq miles
(745,561 sq km)

7. Honshū, Japan
87,805 sq miles
(227,414 sq km)

6. Sumatra, Indonesia
182,860 sq miles
(473,606 sq km)

5. Baffin Island, Canada
195,927 sq miles
(507,451 sq km)

4. Madagascar, Africa
226,657 sq miles
(587,040 sq km)

SCALE 1:35,300,000
Lamberts Azimuthal Equal Area Projection
0 — 1000 miles
0 — 1000 kilometers

1. Russian Federation
6,592,770 sq miles
(17,075,200 sq km)

3. United States of America
3,717,810 sq miles
(9,629,090 sq km)

6. Australia
2,967,910 sq miles
(7,686,850 sq km)

7. India
1,269,345 sq miles
(3,287,590 sq km)

8. Argentina
1,068,300 sq miles
(2,766,890 sq km)

SCALE 1:60,000,000
Lamberts Azimuthal Equal Area Projection
0 — 1500 miles
0 — 1500 kilometers

Longest Rivers

Murray–Darling, Australia 2,330 miles (3,750 km)

Niger, Africa 2,599 miles (4,184 km)

Mackenzie–Peace–Finlay, North America 2,635 miles (4,241 km)

Lena–Kirenga, Asia 2,734 miles (4,400 km)

Heilong Jiang (Amur)–Argun', Asia 2,744 miles (4,416 km)

Mekong, Asia 2,749 miles (4,425 km)

River Plate–Paraná, South America 2,796 miles (4,500 km)

Congo, Africa 2,900 miles (4,667 km)

Yellow, Asia 3,395 miles (5,464 km)

Yenisey–Angara–Selenga, Asia 3,448 miles (5,550 km)

Ob'–Irtysh, Asia 3,459 miles (5,568 km)

Mississippi–Missouri, North America 3,709 miles (5,969 km)

Yangtze, Asia 3,964 miles (6,380 km)

Amazon, South America 4,049 miles (6,516 km)

Nile, Africa 4,160 miles (6,695 km)

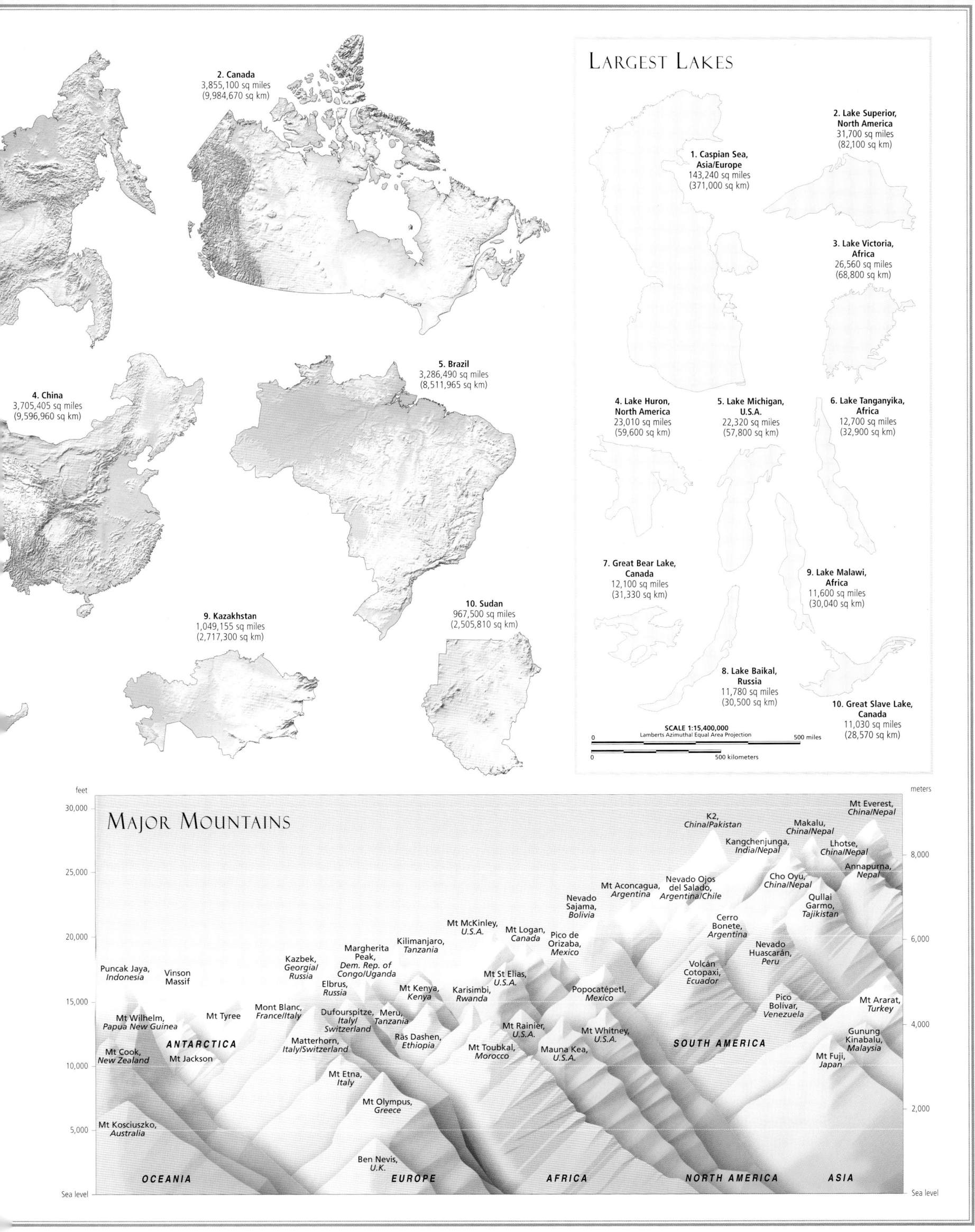

2. Canada
3,855,100 sq miles
(9,984,670 sq km)

4. China
3,705,405 sq miles
(9,596,960 sq km)

5. Brazil
3,286,490 sq miles
(8,511,965 sq km)

9. Kazakhstan
1,049,155 sq miles
(2,717,300 sq km)

10. Sudan
967,500 sq miles
(2,505,810 sq km)

LARGEST LAKES

**1. Caspian Sea,
Asia/Europe**
143,240 sq miles
(371,000 sq km)

**2. Lake Superior,
North America**
31,700 sq miles
(82,100 sq km)

**3. Lake Victoria,
Africa**
26,560 sq miles
(68,800 sq km)

**4. Lake Huron,
North America**
23,010 sq miles
(59,600 sq km)

**5. Lake Michigan,
U.S.A.**
22,320 sq miles
(57,800 sq km)

**6. Lake Tanganyika,
Africa**
12,700 sq miles
(32,900 sq km)

**7. Great Bear Lake,
Canada**
12,100 sq miles
(31,330 sq km)

**9. Lake Malawi,
Africa**
11,600 sq miles
(30,040 sq km)

**8. Lake Baikal,
Russia**
11,780 sq miles
(30,500 sq km)

**10. Great Slave Lake,
Canada**
11,030 sq miles
(28,570 sq km)

SCALE 1:15,400,000
Lamberts Azimuthal Equal Area Projection

0   500 miles

0   500 kilometers

MAJOR MOUNTAINS

feet

30,000

25,000

20,000

15,000

10,000

5,000

Sea level

meters

8,000

6,000

4,000

2,000

Sea level

Mt Everest,
China/Nepal

K2,
China/Pakistan

Makalu,
China/Nepal

Kangchenjunga,
India/Nepal

Lhotse,
China/Nepal

Annapurna,
Nepal

Cho Oyu,
China/Nepal

Qullai
Garmo,
Tajikistan

Mt Aconcagua,
Argentina

Nevado Ojos
del Salado,
Argentina/Chile

Cerro
Bonete,
Argentina

Nevado
Sajama,
Bolivia

Mt McKinley,
U.S.A.

Mt Logan,
Canada

Pico de
Orizaba,
Mexico

Nevado
Huascarán,
Peru

Kilimanjaro,
Tanzania

Volcán
Cotopaxi,
Ecuador

Puncak Jaya,
Indonesia

Vinson
Massif

Kazbek,
*Georgial
Russia*

Margherita
Peak,
Italy

Mt St Elias,
U.S.A.

Popocatépetl,
Mexico

Pico
Bolívar,
Venezuela

Mt Ararat,
Turkey

Elbrus,
Russia

Mt Kenya,
Kenya

Karisimbi,
Rwanda

Mt Wilhelm,
Papua New Guinea

Mt Tyree

Mont Blanc,
France/Italy

Dufourspitze,
*Italy/
Switzerland*

Meru,
Tanzania

Mt Rainier,
U.S.A.

Mt Whitney,
U.S.A.

SOUTH AMERICA

Gunung
Kinabalu,
Malaysia

Mt Fuji,
Japan

Mt Cook,
New Zealand

ANTARCTICA

Mt Jackson

Matterhorn,
Italy/Switzerland

Räs Dashen,
Ethiopia

Mt Toubkal,
Morocco

Mauna Kea,
U.S.A.

Mt Kosciuszko,
Australia

Mt Etna,
Italy

Mt Olympus,
Greece

Ben Nevis,
U.K.

OCEANIA

EUROPE

AFRICA

NORTH AMERICA

ASIA

TIME ZONES

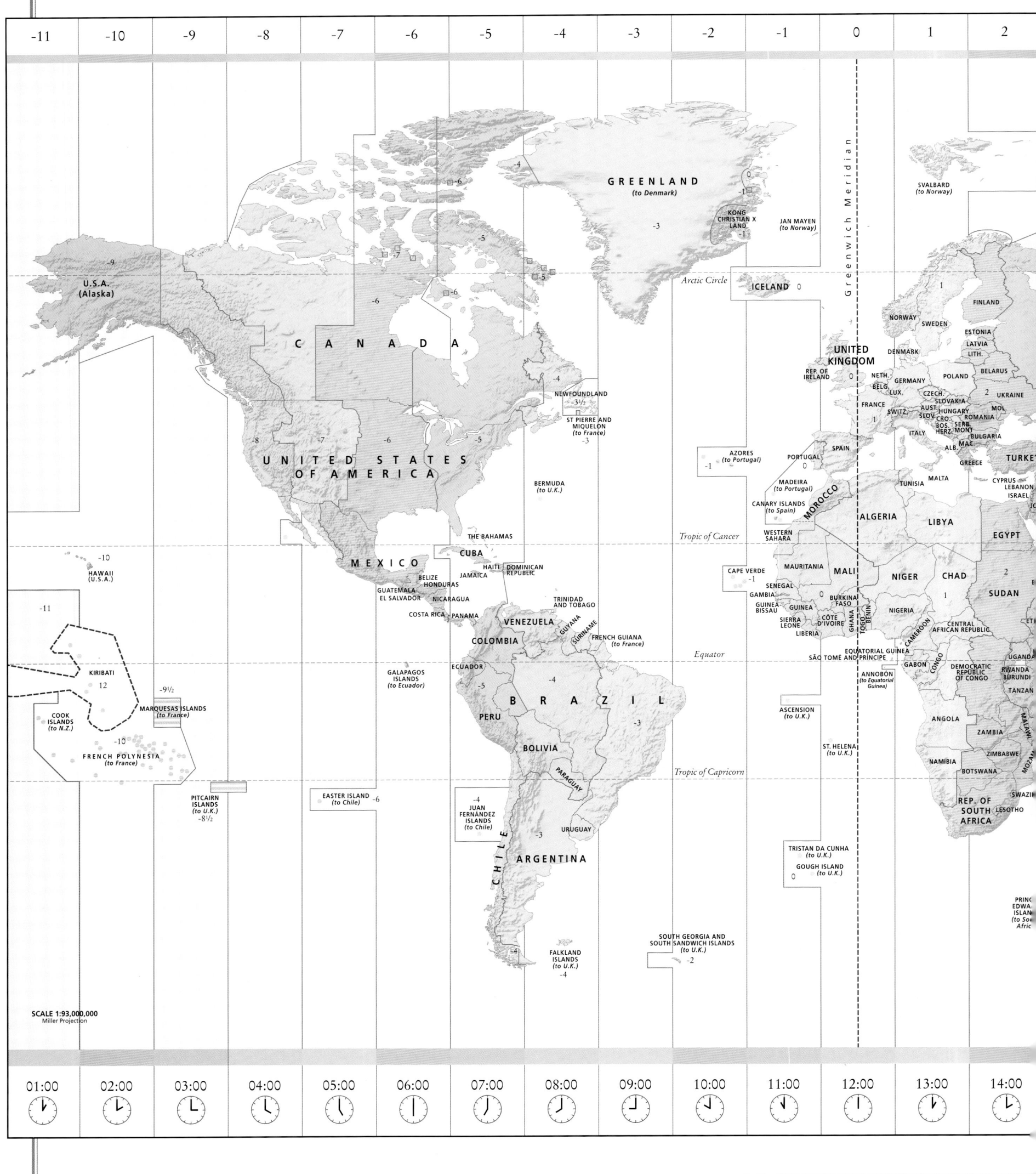

-11 -10 -9 -8 -7 -6 -5 -4 -3 -2 -1 0 1 2

GREENLAND
(to Denmark)

SVALBARD
(to Norway)

-4

KONG
CHRISTIAN X
LAND

JAN MAYEN
(to Norway)

-3

Arctic Circle

ICELAND 0

FINLAND

U.S.A.
(Alaska)

-9

NORWAY SWEDEN

ESTONIA
LATVIA
LITH.

-6

-7

-5

DENMARK

UNITED
KINGDOM

REP. OF
IRELAND

NETH.
BELG. GERMANY
LUX.

POLAND

BELARUS

C A N A D A

-5

FRANCE
SWITZ.

CZECH.
SLOVAKIA
AUST HUNGARY
SLOV
CRO.
BOS. SERB.
HERZ. MONT.

UKRAINE
MOL.

ROMANIA
BULGARIA

-4

NEWFOUNDLAND
-3½

ST PIERRE AND
MIQUELON
(to France)
-3

ITALY

SPAIN

ALB.
MAC.
GREECE

TURKEY

CYPRUS
LEBANON
ISRAEL

AZORES
(to Portugal)
-1

PORTUGAL

-8

-7

-6

UNITED STATES
OF AMERICA

-5

MADEIRA
(to Portugal)

CANARY ISLANDS
(to Spain)

MOROCCO

ALGERIA

TUNISIA

LIBYA

MALTA

EGYPT

BERMUDA
(to U.K.)

Tropic of Cancer

WESTERN
SAHARA

Tropic of Cancer

THE BAHAMAS

-10

HAWAII
(U.S.A.)

CUBA

MEXICO

HAITI DOMINICAN
REPUBLIC
JAMAICA

CAPE VERDE
-1

MAURITANIA

MALI

NIGER

CHAD

SUDAN

BELIZE
HONDURAS
GUATEMALA
EL SALVADOR NICARAGUA

SENEGAL
GAMBIA
GUINEA-
BISSAU

BURKINA
FASO

GUINEA
SIERRA CÔTE
LEONE D'IVOIRE

NIGERIA

CENTRAL
AFRICAN REPUBLIC

-11

COSTA RICA PANAMA

VENEZUELA

TRINIDAD
AND TOBAGO

GUYANA

LIBERIA

GHANA
TOGO
BENIN

CAMEROON

KIRIBATI

12

COLOMBIA

SURINAME

FRENCH GUIANA
(to France)

Equator

EQUATORIAL GUINEA
SÃO TOMÉ AND PRÍNCIPE

GABON

CONGO

UGANDA

DEMOCRATIC
REPUBLIC
OF CONGO

RWANDA
BURUNDI

TANZAN

-9½

GALAPAGOS
ISLANDS
(to Ecuador)

ECUADOR

ANNOBÓN
(to Equatorial
Guinea)

COOK
ISLANDS
(to N.Z.)

MARQUESAS ISLANDS
(to France)

-5

B R A Z I L

-4

ASCENSION
(to U.K.)

ANGOLA

ZAMBIA

MALAWI

-10

FRENCH POLYNESIA
(to France)

PERU

-3

ST. HELENA
(to U.K.)

NAMIBIA

ZIMBABWE

MOZA

BOLIVIA

Tropic of Capricorn

BOTSWANA

SWAZI

EASTER ISLAND
(to Chile)
-6

PARAGUAY

-4

JUAN
FERNÁNDEZ
ISLANDS
(to Chile)

URUGUAY

TRISTAN DA CUNHA
(to U.K.)

GOUGH ISLAND
(to U.K.)
0

REP. OF
SOUTH
AFRICA

LESOTHO

PITCAIRN
ISLANDS
(to U.K.)
-8½

CHILE

-3

ARGENTINA

PRINC
EDWA
ISLAN
(to Sou
Afric

-4

FALKLAND
ISLANDS
(to U.K.)
-4

SOUTH GEORGIA AND
SOUTH SANDWICH ISLANDS
(to U.K.)
-2

SCALE 1:93,000,000
Miller Projection

01:00 02:00 03:00 04:00 05:00 06:00 07:00 08:00 09:00 10:00 11:00 12:00 13:00 14:00

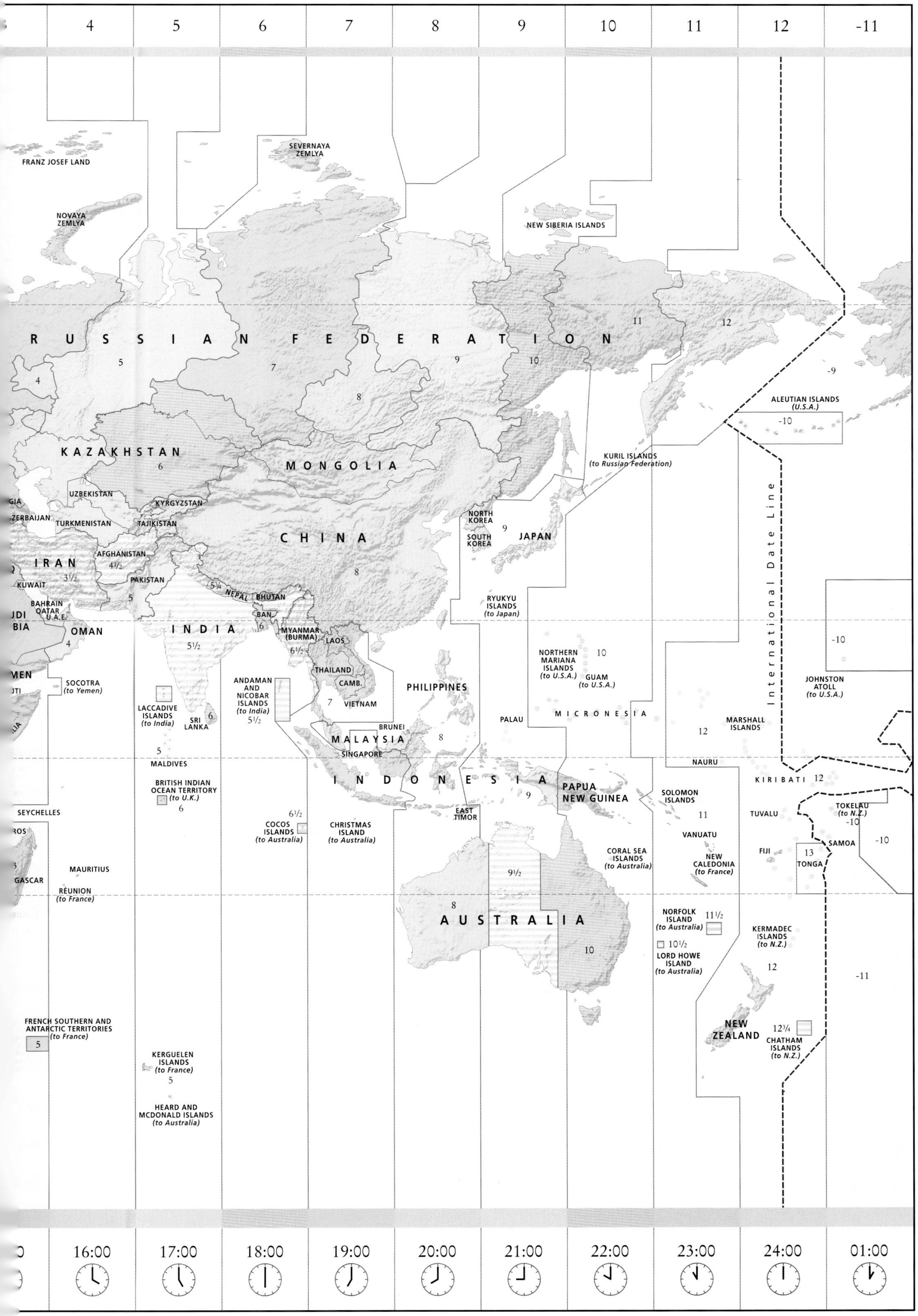

| | 4 | 5 | 6 | 7 | 8 | 9 | 10 | 11 | 12 | -11 |

FRANZ JOSEF LAND

NOVAYA
ZEMLYA

SEVERNAYA
ZEMLYA

NEW SIBERIA ISLANDS

R U S S I A N   F E D E R A T I O N

4

5

7

8

9

11

10

12

-9

ALEUTIAN ISLANDS
(U.S.A.)
-10

KAZAKHSTAN

6

M O N G O L I A

KURIL ISLANDS
(to Russian Federation)

UZBEKISTAN

KYRGYZSTAN

ZERBAIJAN
TURKMENISTAN

TAJIKISTAN

NORTH
KOREA

9

SOUTH
KOREA
JAPAN

GIA

IRAN

AFGHANISTAN

4½
PAKISTAN

C H I N A

RYUKYU
ISLANDS
(to Japan)

KUWAIT

3½

5

5½
NEPAL BHUTAN
BAN.

8

BAHRAIN
QATAR
U.A.E.

JDI
BIA

OMAN

4

I N D I A

5½

MYANMAR
(BURMA)

6

LAOS

NORTHERN
MARIANA
ISLANDS
(to U.S.A.)

10

THAILAND

CAMB.

GUAM
(to U.S.A.)

JOHNSTON
ATOLL
(to U.S.A.)

SOCOTRA
(to Yemen)

LACCADIVE
ISLANDS
(to India)

SRI
LANKA

6

ANDAMAN
AND
NICOBAR
ISLANDS
(to India)

5½

7

VIETNAM

PHILIPPINES

M I C R O N E S I A

PALAU

5

BRUNEI

International Date Line

MALDIVES

BRITISH INDIAN
OCEAN TERRITORY
(to U.K.)

6

6½

M A L A Y S I A

8

SINGAPORE

MARSHALL
ISLANDS

12

SEYCHELLES

I N D O N E S I A

PAPUA
NEW GUINEA

NAURU

ROS

COCOS
ISLANDS
(to Australia)

CHRISTMAS
ISLAND
(to Australia)

9

SOLOMON
ISLANDS

KIRIBATI

12

MAURITIUS

6½

EAST
TIMOR

VANUATU

TUVALU

TOKELAU
(to N.Z.)
-10

MASCAR

REUNION
(to France)

CORAL SEA
ISLANDS
(to Australia)

11

NEW
CALEDONIA
(to France)

FIJI

SAMOA

-10

9½

13

TONGA

3

A U S T R A L I A

8

NORFOLK
ISLAND
(to Australia)

11½

KERMADEC
ISLANDS
(to N.Z.)

FRENCH SOUTHERN AND
ANTARCTIC TERRITORIES
(to France)

5

10½
LORD HOWE
ISLAND
(to Australia)

10

12

-11

KERGUELEN
ISLANDS
(to France)

5

NEW
ZEALAND

12¾

CHATHAM
ISLANDS
(to N.Z.)

HEARD AND
MCDONALD ISLANDS
(to Australia)

| | 16:00 | 17:00 | 18:00 | 19:00 | 20:00 | 21:00 | 22:00 | 23:00 | 24:00 | 01:00 |

The standard time zone system is based on the theoretical division of the world into 24 zones of 15° of longitude. Each zone represents one hour of time. The middle meridian of each zone sets the time for that zone. The zero time zone is 7½° east and 7½° west of 0° longitude, the Greenwich (or prime) meridian. The time at this meridian is refered to as Greenwich mean time (GMT). Time zones to the west of the Greenwich meridian are earlier and zones to the east are later. The International Date Line has been designated at 180° longitude. The time is the same on both sides of this line but east of the International Date Line is one day earlier than it is to the west of the line.

Individual nations set their legal time based on this standard time zone system. For convenience certain islands or frontiers may be kept in a different time zone to the one in which they are physically located. For example, the South Island of New Zealand maintains the same time as the North Island despite its location in a different time zone. The time in certain nations or territories may differ from the rest of a zone by a fraction of an hour (for example India). This is indicated on the map by the striped areas. Some countries adjust the legal time for part of the year, particularly summer. They often advance their time by one hour to maximize the use of daylight hours.

On this map each zone is assigned a color. The numbers at the top of the map, and on each zone, signify the number of hours the zone is ahead or behind GMT. The 24-hour time and clocks at the bottom of the map indicate the time in each zone when it is 12:00 noon GMT.

The Greenwich meridian, located in London, England marks 0° longitude and the zero time zone.

COUNTRIES OF THE WORLD

NORTH AMERICA

Country	Area sq miles (sq km)	Population	Capital	Currency	Official Languages	Other Languages	Main Religions	Life Expectancy	Literacy Rate	Economy
Antigua and Barbuda	171 (443)	68,720	Saint John's	East Caribbean dollar (XCD)	English	Local dialects	✝, ✚	71.02	89% (1960)	✿ 3.9%, ⚒ 19.1%, ☰ 77%
The Bahamas	5,380 (13,940)	301,790	Nassau	Bahamian dollar (BSD)	English	Creole	✝ 70%, ✚ 19%, ∝ 6%, ✳ 5%	69.87	95.6%	✿ 3%, ⚒ 7%, ☰ 90%
Barbados	166 (431)	279,250	Bridgetown	Barbadian dollar (BBD)	English		✝ 67%, ✚ 4%, ✳ 29%	73.49	97.4% (1995)	✿ 6%, ⚒ 16%, ☰ 78%
Belize	8,870 (22,970)	279,460	Belmopan	Belizean dollar (BZD)	English	Spanish, Mayan, Garifuna (Carib), Creole	✚ 49.6%, ✝ 27%, ✳ 23.4%	71.46	94.1%	✿ 18%, ⚒ 24%, ☰ 58%
Canada	3,474,920 (9,984,670)	32,805,040	Ottawa	Canadian dollar (CAD)	English, French		✚ 46%, ✝ 36%, ✳ 18%	79.69	97% (1986)	✿ 2%, ⚒ 29%, ☰ 69%
Costa Rica	19,730 (51,100)	4,016,170	San José	Costa Rican colon (CRC)	Spanish	English	✚ 76.3%, ✝ 15.7%, ✳ 8%	76.22	96%	✿ 11%, ⚒ 37%, ☰ 52%
Cuba	42,800 (110,860)	11,339,890	Havana	Cuban peso (CUP)	Spanish		✚, ✝, ✡, ✳	76.6	96.9%	✿ 7.6%, ⚒ 34.5%, ☰ 57.9%
Dominica	291 (754)	69,030	Roseau	East Caribbean dollar (XCD)	English	French patois	✚ 77%, ✝ 15%, ✳ 8%	73.86	94%	NA
Dominican Republic	18,810 (48,730)	8,950,030	Santo Domingo	Dominican peso (DOP)	Spanish		✚ 95%	73.68	84.7%	✿ 11.1%, ⚒ 34.1%, ☰ 54.8%
El Salvador	8,120 (21,040)	6,704,930	San Salvador	Salvadoran colon (SVC), U.S. dollar (USD)	Spanish	Nahua	✚ 83% ✝	70.32	80.2%	✿ 10%, ⚒ 30%, ☰ 60%
Grenada	133 (344)	89,500	St George's	East Caribbean dollar (XCD)	English	French patois	✚ 53%, ✝ 47%	64.52	98% (1970)	✿ 7.7%, ⚒ 23.9%, ☰ 68.4%
Guatemala	42,040 (108,890)	14,655,190	Guatemala	quetzal (GTQ), U.S. dollar (USD)	Spanish	Amerindian languages	✚, ✝, O	66.85	70.6%	✿ 23%, ⚒ 20%, ☰ 57%
Haiti	10,710 (27,750)	7,790,340	Port-au-Prince	gourde (HTG)	French, Creole		✚ 80%, ✝ 16%, ✳ 4%	49.55	52.9%	✿ 30%, ⚒ 20%, ☰ 50%
Honduras	43,280 (112,090)	6,975,200	Tegucigalpa	lempira (HNL)	Spanish	Amerindian dialects	✚ 97%, ✝	68.77	76.2%	✿ 18%, ⚒ 32%, ☰ 50%
Jamaica	4,240 (10,990)	2,731,830	Kingston	Jamaican dollar (JMD)	English	Patois English	✝ 61.3%, ✚ 4%, ✳ 34.7%	75.64	87.9%	✿ 7%, ⚒ 28%, ☰ 65%
Mexico	761,610 (1,972,550)	107,869,840	Mexico City	Mexican peso (MXN)	Spanish	Mayan, Nahuatl, other indigenous languages	✚ 89%, ✝ 6%, ✳ 5%	72.03	92.2%	✿ 5%, ⚒ 26%, ☰ 69%
Nicaragua	50,000 (129,490)	5,334,680	Managua	gold cordoba (NIO)	Spanish	English, indigenous languages	✚ 85%, ✝	69.37	67.5%	✿ 33%, ⚒ 23%, ☰ 44%
Panama	30,190 (78,200)	3,039,150	Panama City	balboa (PAB), U.S. dollar (USD)	Spanish	English	✚ 85%, ✝ 15%	75.89	92.6%	✿ 7%, ⚒ 17%, ☰ 76%
St Kitts and Nevis	101 (261)	38,960	Basseterre	East Caribbean dollar (XCD)	English		✝, ✚	71.29	97% (1980)	✿ 3.5%, ⚒ 25.8%, ☰ 70.7%
St Lucia	238 (616)	166,310	Castries	East Caribbean dollar (XCD)	English	French patois	✚ 90%, ✝ 10%	72.82	67% (1980)	✿ 7.9%, ⚒ 19.6%, ☰ 72.5%
St Vincent and the Grenadines	150 (389)	117,530	Kingstown	East Caribbean dollar (XCD)	English	French patois	✝ 75%, ✚ 13%, ✳ 12%	72.82	96% (1970)	✿ 10%, ⚒ 26%, ☰ 64%
Trinidad and Tobago	1,980 (5,130)	1,088,640	Port of Spain	Trinidad and Tobago dollar (TTD)	English	Hindi, French, Spanish, Chinese	✚ 29.4%, ☸ 23.8%, ✝ 14.3%, ☪ 5.8%, ✳ 26.7%	68.59	98.6%	✿ 1.6%, ⚒ 43.2%, ☰ 55.2%
United States of America	3,717,810 (9,629,090)	295,734,130	Washington, D.C.	U.S. dollar (USD)	English	Spanish	✝ 56%, ✚ 28%, ✡ 2%, ✳ 14%	77.4	97% (1979)	✿ 2%, ⚒ 18%, ☰ 80%

SOUTH AMERICA

Country	Area sq miles (sq km)	Population	Capital	Currency	Official Languages	Other Languages	Main Religions	Life Expectancy	Literacy Rate	Economy
Argentina	1,068,300 (2,766,890)	39,537,940	Buenos Aires	Argentine peso (ARS)	Spanish	English, Italian, German, French	✚ 92%, ✝ 2%, ✡ 2%, ✳ 4%	75.48	97.1%	✿ 6%, ⚒ 28%, ☰ 66%
Bolivia	424,160 (1,098,580)	8,857,870	La Paz, Sucre	boliviano (BOB)	Spanish, Quechua, Aymara		✚ 95%, ✝	64.42	87.2%	✿ 14%, ⚒ 31%, ☰ 55%

Key to symbols: ∝ Christian ✚ Catholic ✚ Orthodox ✝ Protestant ☸ Buddhist ☸ Hindu ✡ Jewish ☪ Muslim ≡ Atheist O Indigenous ✳ Other ✿ Agriculture ⚒ Industry ☰ Services NA Not Available
Note: All literacy statistics are for 2003 unless otherwise stated.

250

Area sq miles (sq km)	Population	Capital	Currency	Official Languages	Other Languages	Main Religions	Life Expectancy	Literacy Rate	Economy		Country
3,286,490 (8,511,970)	186,112,790	Brasília	real (BRL)	Portuguese	Spanish, English, French	✟ 80%	63.55	86.4%	⚒ 9%, ⚓ 32%, ⚕ 59%		Brazil
292,260 (756,950)	15,984,780	Santiago	Chilean peso (CLP)	Spanish		✟ 89%, ✝ 11%, ✡ less than 1%	76.14	96.2%	⚒ 8%, ⚓ 38%, ⚕ 54%		Chile
439,740 (1,138,910)	42,954,280	Bogotá	Colombian peso (COP)	Spanish		✟ 90%, ✲ 10%	70.85	92.5%	⚒ 19%, ⚓ 26%, ⚕ 55%		Colombia
109,480 (283,560)	14,231,760	Quito	U.S. dollar (USD)	Spanish		✟ 95%, ✲ 5%	71.61	92.5%	⚒ 11%, ⚓ 25%, ⚕ 64%		Ecuador
83,000 (214,970)	710,660	Georgetown	Guyanese dollar (GYD)	English	Amerindian dialects, Creole, Hindi, Urdu	∝ 50%, ☣ 35%, ☾ 10%, ✲ 5%	62.59	98.8%	⚒ 36.1%, ⚓ 31.8%, ⚕ 32.1%		Guyana
157,050 (406,750)	6,347,880	Asunción	guarani (PYG)	Spanish, Guarani		✟ 90%, ✲ 10%	74.16	94%	⚒ 29%, ⚓ 26%, ⚕ 45%		Paraguay
496,230 (1,285,220)	29,309,290	Lima	nuevo sol (PEN)	Spanish, Quechua	Aymara	✟ 90%, ✲ 10%	70.59	90.9%	⚒ 10%, ⚓ 35%, ⚕ 55%		Peru
63,040 (163,270)	438,140	Paramaribo	Surinamese guilder (SRG)	Dutch	English, Sranang Tongo, Hindustani, Javanese	☣ 27.4%, ☾ 19.6%, ✟ 22.8%, ✝ 25.2%, ⊙ 5%	71.9	93% (1995)	⚒ 13%, ⚓ 22%, ⚕ 65%		Suriname
68,040 (176,220)	3,467,070	Montevideo	Uruguayan peso (UYU)	Spanish, Portunol, Brazilero		✟ 66%, ✝ 2%, ✡ 1%, ✲ 31%	75.66	98%	⚒ 6%, ⚓ 29%, ⚕ 65%		Uruguay
352,140 (912,050)	25,375,280	Caracas	bolivar (VEB)	Spanish	Indigenous dialects	✟ 96%, ✝ 2%, ✲ 2%	73.56	93.4%	⚒ 5%, ⚓ 40%, ⚕ 55%		Venezuela
11,100 (28,750)	3,654,960	Tirana	lek (ALL)	Albanian (Tosk is the official dialect)	Greek	☾ 70%, ✠ 20%, ✟ 10%	72.1	86.5%,	⚒ 52%, ⚓ 21%, ⚕ 27%		Albania
180 (470)	70,550	Andorra la Vella	euro (EUR)	Catalan	French, Castilian Spanish	✟	83.48	100%	NA		Andorra
32,380 (83,860)	8,221,260	Vienna	euro (EUR)	German		✟ 78%, ✝ 5%, ☾ and ✲ 17%	78	98%	⚒ 2%, ⚓ 29%, ⚕ 69%		Austria
80,150 (207,600)	10,300,480	Minsk	Belarusian ruble (BYB/BYR)	Belarusian	Russian	✠ 80%, ✲ 20%	68.28	99.6%	⚒ 13%, ⚓ 42%, ⚕ 45%		Belarus
11,780 (30,510)	10,313,490	Brussels	euro (EUR)	Dutch, French, German		✟ 75%, ✝ or ✲ 25%	78.13	98%	⚒ 1.4%, ⚓ 24%, ⚕ 74.6%		Belgium
19,740 (51,130)	4,025,480	Sarajevo	marka (BAM)	Croatian, Serbian, Bosnian		☾ 40%, ✠ 31%, ✟ 15%, ✝ 4%, ✲ 10%	72.02	NA	⚒ 16%, ⚓ 28%, ⚕ 56%		Bosnia and Herzegovina
42,820 (110,910)	7,377,370	Sofia	lev (BGL)	Bulgarian		✠ 83.8%, ☾ 12.1%, ✟ 1.7%, ✡ 0.8%, ✝ and ✲ 1.6%	71.5	98.6%	⚒ 14.5%, ⚓ 27.8%, ⚕ 57.7%		Bulgaria
21,830 (56,540)	4,449,290	Zagreb	kuna (HRK)	Croatian	Italian, Hungarian, Czech, Slovak, German	✟ 76.5%, ✠ 11.1%, ☾ 1.2%, ✝ 0.4%, ✲ 10.8%	74.13	98.5%	⚒ 10%, ⚓ 33%, ⚕ 57%		Croatia
30,450 (78,870)	10,230,740	Prague	Czech koruna (CZK)	Czech		≡ 39.8%, ✟ 39.2%, ✝ 4.6%, ✠ 3%, ✲ 13.4%	74.95	99.9% (1999)	⚒ 5%, ⚓ 41%, ⚕ 54%		Czech Republic
16,640 (43,090)	5,413,720	Copenhagen	Danish krone (DKK)	Danish	English, Faroese, Greenlandic, German	✝ 95%, ∝ 3%, ☾ 2%	76.91	100%	⚒ 3%, ⚓ 22%, ⚕ 75%		Denmark
17,460 (45,230)	1,395,850	Tallinn	Estonian kroon (EEK)	Estonian	Russian, Ukrainian, Finnish, other	✝, ✠, ✟, ✡, ∝	70.02	99.8%	⚒ 6%, ⚓ 28%, ⚕ 66%,		Estonia
130,130 (337,030)	5,203,940	Helsinki	euro (EUR)	Finnish	Swedish, Lapp, Russian	✝ 89%, ✠ 1%, ✲ 9%	77.75	100% (1980)	⚒ 3%, ⚓ 28%, ⚕ 69%		Finland
211,210 (547,030)	60,656,180	Paris	euro (EUR)	French	Provencal, Breton, Alsatian, Corsican, Basque, Flemish	✟ 83%-88%, ✝ 2%, ✡ 1%, ☾ 5%-10%, ✲ 4%	79.05	99% (1980)	⚒ 3.3%, ⚓ 25.7%, ⚕ 71%		France
137,850 (357,020)	82,431,390	Berlin	euro (EUR)	German		✝ 34%, ✟ 34%, ☾ 3.7%, ✲ 28.3%	77.78	99% (1977)	⚒ 1%, ⚓ 28%, ⚕ 71%		Germany
50,940 (131,940)	10,703,500	Athens	euro (EUR)	Greek	English, French	✠ 98%, ☾ 1.3%, ✲ 0.7%	78.74	97.5%	⚒ 8.3%, ⚓ 27.3%, ⚕ 64.4%		Greece

EUROPE

Key to symbols: ∝ Christian ✟ Catholic ✠ Orthodox ✝ Protestant ◉ Buddhist ☣ Hindu ✡ Jewish ☾ Muslim ≡ Atheist ⊙ Indigenous ✲ Other ⚒ Agriculture ⚓ Industry ⚕ Services NA Not Available

Note: All literacy statistics are for 2003 unless otherwise stated.

	Area sq miles (sq km)	Population	Capital	Currency	Official Languages	Other Languages	Main Religions	Life Expectancy	Literacy Rate	Economy
Hungary	35,920 (93,030)	9,986,520	Budapest	forint (HUF)	Hungarian		✠ 67.5%, ✝ 25%, ≡ and ✱ 7.5%	71.9	99.4%	⚘ 6%, ⚒ 34%, ⚙ 60%
Iceland	39,770 (103,000)	283,440	Reykjavík	Icelandic krona (ISK)	Icelandic		✝ 93%, ∝ and ✱ 7%	79.66	99.9% (1997)	⚘ 15% (includes fishing 13%), ⚒ 21%, ⚙ 64%
Ireland, Republic of	27,140 (70,280)	4,001,530	Dublin	euro (EUR)	English, Irish (Gaelic)		✠ 91.6%, ✝ 2.5%, ✱ 5.9%	77.17	98% (1981)	⚘ 4%, ⚒ 38%, ⚙ 58%
Italy	116,310 (301,230)	58,103,030	Rome	euro (EUR)	Italian	German, French, Slovene, Albanian, Greek	✠, ✝, ✡, ☪	79.25	98.6%	⚘ 2.4%, ⚒ 30%, ⚙ 67.6%
Latvia	24,940 (64,590)	2,316,420	Rīga	Latvian lat (LVL)	Latvian	Lithuanian, Russian	✠, ✝, ✞	69	99.8%	⚘ 5%, ⚒ 24%, ⚙ 71%
Liechtenstein	62 (160)	33,720	Vaduz	Swiss franc (CHF)	German	Alemannic dialect	✠ 80%, ✝ 7.4%, ✱ 12.6%	79.1	100%	NA
Lithuania	25,170 (65,200)	3,577,950	Vilnius	litas (LTL)	Lithuanian	Polish, Russian	✠, ✝, ✞, ☪, ✡	69.42	99.6% (1981)	⚘ 9%, ⚒ 32%, ⚙ 59%
Luxembourg	1,000 (2,590)	465,250	Luxembourg	euro (EUR)	Luxembourgish	German, French	✠ (predominantly), ✝, ✡, ☪	77.48	100%	⚘ 1%, ⚒ 30%, ⚙ 69%
Macedonia (F.Y.R.O.M.)	9,780 (25,330)	2,079,060	Skopje	Macedonian denar (MKD)	Macedonian	Albanian, Turkish, Serbo-Croatian	✞ 67%, ☪ 30%, ✱ 3%	74.26	NA	⚘ 10%, ⚒ 32%, ⚙ 58%
Malta	122 (316)	406,260	Valletta	Maltese lira (MTL)	Maltese, English		✠ 91%	78.26	92.8%	⚘ 2.8%, ⚒ 25.5%, ⚙ 71.7%
Moldova	13,070 (33,840)	4,455,420	Chişinău	Moldovan leu (MDL)	Moldovan, Russian	Gagauz (a Turkish dialect)	✞ 98.5%, ✡ 1.5%	64.74	99.1%	⚘ 28%, ⚒ 21%, ⚙ 51%
Monaco	0.75 (1.95)	32,410	Monaco	euro (EUR)	French	English, Italian, Monegasque	✠ 90%	79.12	99%	NA
Netherlands	16,030 (41,530)	16,304,210	Amsterdam, The Hague	euro (EUR)	Dutch		✠ 31%, ✝ 21%, ☪ 4.4%, ✱ 43.6%	78.58	99% (2000)	⚘ 3.3%, ⚒ 26.3%, ⚙ 70.4%
Norway	125,180 (324,220)	4,586,160	Oslo	Norwegian krone (NOK)	Norwegian	Saami, Finnish	✝ 86%, ∝ 3%, ✱ 11%	78.94	100%	⚘ 2%, ⚒ 31%, ⚙ 67%
Poland	120,730 (312,690)	38,635,140	Warsaw	zloty (PLN)	Polish		✠ 95%, ✞, ✝ and ✱ 5%	73.66	99.8%	⚘ 4%, ⚒ 32%, ⚙ 64%
Portugal	35,670 (92,390)	10,135,380	Lisbon	euro (EUR)	Portuguese		✠ 94%, ✝	76.14	93.3%	⚘ 3.8%, ⚒ 30.5%, ⚙ 65.7%
Romania	91,700 (237,500)	22,178,400	Bucharest	leu (ROL)	Romanian	Hungarian, German	✞ 70%, ✠ 6%, ✝ 6%, ✱ 18%	70.39	98.4%	⚘ 15%, ⚒ 30%, ⚙ 55%
Russian Federation	6,592,770 (17,075,200)	143,736,790	Moscow	Russian ruble (RUR)	Russian		✞, ☪, ✱	67.5	99.6%	⚘ 7%, ⚒ 37%, ⚙ 56%
San Marino	24 (61)	28,880	San Marino	euro (EUR)	Italian		✠	81.33	96% (1976)	NA
Serbia and Montenegro	39,520 (102,350)	10,668,570	Belgrade	new Yugoslav dinar (YUM), euro (EUR)	Serbian, Albanian		✞ 65%, ☪ 19%, ✠ 4%, ✝ 1%, ✱ 11%	73.72	93% (1991)	⚘ 26%, ⚒ 36%, ⚙ 38%
Slovakia	18,860 (48,850)	5,444,900	Bratislava	Slovak koruna (SKK)	Slovak	Hungarian	✠ 60.3%, ≡ 9.7%, ✝ 8.4%, ✞ 4.1%, ✱ 17.5%	74.2	NA	⚘ 4%, ⚒ 32%, ⚙ 64%
Slovenia	7,830 (20,720)	1,940,630	Ljubljana	tolar (SIT)	Slovenian, Serbo-Croatian		✠ 70.8%, ✝ 1%, ☪ 1%, ≡ 4.3%, ✱ 22.9%	75.29	99.7%	⚘ 4%, ⚒ 35%, ⚙ 61%
Spain	194,900 (504,780)	40,341,460	Madrid	euro (EUR))	Castilian Spanish	Catalan, Galician, Basque	✠ 94%, ✱ 6%	79.08	97.9%	⚘ 4%, ⚒ 28%, ⚙ 68%
Sweden	173,730 (449,960)	8,879,790	Stockholm	Swedish krona (SEK)	Swedish	Saami, Finnish	✝ 87%, ✞, ☪, ✡, and ☸ 13%	79.84	99% (1979)	⚘ 2%, ⚒ 28.7%, ⚙ 69.3%
Switzerland	15,940 (41,290)	7,346,070	Bern	Swiss franc (CHF)	German, French, Italian	Romansch, other	✠ 46.1%, ✝ 40%, ✱ 13.9%	79.86	99% (1980)	⚘ 2%, ⚒ 34%, ⚙ 64%

Key to symbols: ∝ Christian ✠ Catholic ✞ Orthodox ✝ Protestant ⊕ Buddhist ☸ Hindu ✡ Jewish ☪ Muslim ≡ Atheist ○ Indigenous ✱ Other ⚘ Agriculture ⚒ Industry ⚙ Services NA Not Available
Note: All literacy statistics are for 2003 unless otherwise stated.

ASIA

Area SQ MILES (SQ KM)	Population	Capital	Currency	Official Languages	Other Languages	Main Religions	Life Expectancy	Literacy Rate	Economy		Country
233,090 (603,700)	47,425,340	Kiev	hryvnia (UAH)	Ukrainian	Russian, Romanian, Polish, Hungarian	✡, ✠, ✝, ✢	66.33	99.7%	NA		Ukraine
94,530 (244,820)	60,441,460	London	British pound (GBP)	English, Welsh, Scottish (Gaelic)		✡, ✝, ∝, ✾, ✢, ✻	77.99	99% (2000)	☙ 1.7%, ⚒ 24.9%, ⚑ 73.4%		United Kingdom
0.17 (0.44)	900	Vatican City	euro (EUR)	Italian, Latin, French		✡		NA	NA		Vatican City
250,000 (647,500)	30,241,190	Kabul	afghani (AFA)	Pashtu, Afghan Persian (Dari)	Turkic languages, other languages	☾ 99%, ✻ 1%	46.6	36% (1999)	☙ 60%, ⚒ 20%, ⚑ 20% (1990 est.)		Afghanistan
11,510 (29,800)	3,326,830	Yerevan	dram (AMD)	Armenian, Russian		∝ 98%, ✻ 2%	66.59	98.6%	☙ 29%, ⚒ 32%, ⚑ 39%		Armenia
33,440 (86,600)	7,911,970	Baku	Azerbaijani manat (AZM)	Azerbaijani (Azeri), Russian	Armenian, other	☾ 93.4%, ✠ 4.8%, ✻ 1.8%	63.06	97% (1989)	☙ 22%, ⚒ 33%, ⚑ 45%		Azerbaijan
257 (665)	688,350	Al Manāmah	Bahraini dinar (BHD)	Arabic, English, Farsi, Urdu		☾ 100%	73.47	89.1%	☙ 1%, ⚒ 35%, ⚑ 64%		Bahrain
55,600 (144,000)	144,319,630	Dacca	taka (BDT)	Bangla (also known as Bengali)	English	☾ 83%, ✽ 16%, ✻ 1%	60.92	43.1%	☙ 30%, ⚒ 18%, ⚑ 52%		Bangladesh
18,147 (47,000)	2,232,290	Thimphu	ngultrum (BTN), Indian rupee (INR)	Dzongkha	Tibetan dialects, Nepalese dialects	◉ 75%, ✽ 25%	53.19	42.2% (1995)	☙ 45%, ⚒ 20%, ⚑ 35%		Bhutan
2,230 (5,770)	372,360	Bandar Seri Begawan	Bruneian dollar (BND)	Malay	English, Chinese	☾ 67%, ◉ 13%, ∝ 10%, O and ✻ 10%	74.06	91.8%	☙ 5%, ⚒ 45%, ⚑ 50%		Brunei
69,900 (181,040)	13,607,070	Phnom Penh	riel (KHR)	Khmer	French, English	◉ 95%, ✻ 5%	57.1	69.9%	☙ 50%, ⚒ 15%, ⚑ 35%		Cambodia
3,705,410 (9,569,960)	1,302,207,990	Beijing	yuan (CNY)	Mandarin, Cantonese, Shanghaiese	Fuzhou, Hokkien-Taiwanese, Xiang, Gan, Hakka, other	☾ 1%-2%, ∝ 3%-4%, ◉, ✻	71.86	86%	☙ 17.7%, ⚒ 49.3%, ⚑ 33%		China
3,570 (9,250)	780,130	Nicosia	Cypriot pound (CYP), Turkish lira (TRL)	Greek, Turkish, English		✠ 78%, ☾ 18%, ✻ 4%	77.08	97.6%	Gr: ☙4.6%, ⚒19.9%, ⚑75.5%, Tk: ☙8.3%, ⚒20.7%, ⚑71.0%		Cyprus
5,800 (15,010)	1,040,880	Dili	U.S. dollar (USD)	Tetum, Portuguese	Indonesian, English, Tetum, Galole, Mambae, Kemak	✡ 90%, ☾ 4%, ✝ 3%, ✽ 0.5%, ◉, O	64.85	48% (2001)	☙ 25.4%, ⚒ 17.2%, ⚑ 57.4%		East Timor
26,910 (69,700)	4,886,720	T'bilisi	lari (GEL)	Georgian	Russian, Armenian, Azeri	✡ 75%, ☾ 11%, ✻ 14%	64.67	99% (1999)	☙ 25%, ⚒ 20%, ⚑ 55%		Georgia
1,269,345 (3,287,590)	1,080,264,390	New Delhi	Indian rupee (INR)	Hindi	English, Bengali, Telugu, Marathi, Tamil, Urdu, other	✽ 81.3%, ☾ 12%, ∝ 2.3%, ✻ 4.4%	63.23	59.5%	☙ 25%, ⚒ 26%, ⚑ 49%		India
741,100 (1,919,440)	241,973,880	Jakarta	Indonesian rupiah (IDR)	Bahasa Indonesia	English, Dutch, Javanese, local dialects	☾ 88%, ✝ 5%, ✡ 3%, ✽ 2%, ◉ 1%, ✻ 1%	68.63	88.5%	☙ 17%, ⚒ 41%, ⚑ 42%		Indonesia
636,300 (1,648,000)	69,765,580	Tehran	Iranian rial (IRR)	Persian	Turkic, Kurdish, Luri, Balochi, Arabic, Turkish	☾ 99%, ✻ 1%	70.25	79.4%	☙ 20%, ⚒ 24%, ⚑ 56%		Iran
168,750 (437,070)	26,074,910	Baghdad	Iraqi dinar (IQD)	Arabic, Kurdish	Assyrian, Armenian	☾ 97%, ∝ or ✻ 3%	67.38	40.4%	☙ 6%, ⚒ 13%, ⚑ 81% (1993 est.)		Iraq
8,020 (20,070)	6,276,880	Jerusalem	new Israeli shekel (ILS)	Hebrew	Arabic, English	✢ 80.1%, ☾ 14.6%, ∝ 2.1%, ✻ 3.2%	78.86	95.4%	☙ 4%, ⚒ 37%, ⚑ 59%		Israel
145,880 (377,840)	127,417,240	Tokyo	yen (JPY)	Japanese		◉ 84%, ✻ 16%	80.91	99% (1995)	☙ 2%, ⚒ 36%, ⚑ 62%		Japan
35,640 (92,300)	5,759,730	Ammān	Jordanian dinar (JOD)	Arabic	English	☾ 92%, ∝ 6%, ✻ 2%	77.71	91.3%	☙ 3.7%, ⚒ 26%, ⚑ 70.3%		Jordan
1,049,155 (2,717,300)	16,846,390	Astana	tenge (KZT)	Kazakh, Russian		☾ 47%, ✡ 44%, ✝ 2%, ✻ 7%	63.38	98.4% (1999)	☙ 10%, ⚒ 30%, ⚑ 60%		Kazakhstan
6,880 (17,820)	2,335,650	Kuwait	Kuwaiti dinar (KD)	Arabic	English	☾ 85%, ∝, ✽, and ✻ 15%	76.46	83.5%	⚒ 60%, ⚑ 39.7%, ☙ 0.3%		Kuwait
76,640 (198,500)	5,039,210	Bishkek	Kyrgyzstani som (KGS)	Kyrgyz, Russian		☾ 75%, ✡ 20%, ✻ 5%	63.56	97% (1989)	☙ 38%, ⚒ 27%, ⚑ 35%		Kyrgyzstan

Key to symbols: ∝ Christian ✡ Catholic ✠ Orthodox ✝ Protestant ◉ Buddhist ✽ Hindu ✢ Jewish ☾ Muslim ≡ Atheist O Indigenous ✻ Other ☙ Agriculture ⚒ Industry ⚑ Services NA Not Available
Note: All literacy statistics are for 2003 unless otherwise stated.

		AREA SQ MILES (SQ KM)	POPULATION	CAPITAL	CURRENCY	OFFICIAL LANGUAGES	OTHER LANGUAGES	MAIN RELIGIONS	LIFE EXPECTANCY	LITERACY RATE	ECONOMY
Laos		91,430 (236,800)	6,217,140	Vientiane	kip (LAK)	Lao	French, English, other	◉ 60%, ✳ 40%	53.88	52.8%	⟱ 53%, ⚒ 22%, ⚕ 25%
Lebanon		4,020 (10,400)	3,826,020	Beirut	Lebanese pound (LBP)	Arabic	French, English, Armenian	☾ 70%, ∝ 30%, ✡ less than 1%	71.79	87.4%	⟱ 12%, ⚒ 21%, ⚕ 67%
Malaysia		127,320 (329,750)	23,953,140	Kuala Lumpur	ringgit (MYR)	Bahasa Melayu	English, Chinese dialects, Iban, Kadazan	☾, ◉, ☸, ∝, ✳	71.39	88.9%	⟱ 12%, ⚒ 40%, ⚕ 48%
Maldives		116 (300)	349,110	Male	rufiyaa (MVR)	Maldivian Dhivehi (dialect of Sinhala)	English	☾	62.93	97.2%	⟱ 20%, ⚒ 18%, ⚕ 62%
Mongolia		604,250 (1,565,000)	2,791,270	Ulaanbaatar	ogrog/tugrik (MNT)	Khalkha Mongol, Turkic, Russian		◉ 96%, ☾ and ∝ 4%	64.62	99.1%	⟱ 32%, ⚒ 30%, ⚕ 38%
Myanmar (Burma)		261,970 (678,500)	42,909,460	Rangoon	kyat (MMK)	Burmese	Minority ethnic groups have their own languages	◉ 89%, ∝ 4%, ☾ 4%, ✳ 3%	55.41	30% (1999)	⟱ 42%, ⚒ 17%, ⚕ 41%
Nepal		54,360 (140,800)	27,676,550	Kathmandu	Nepalese rupee (NPR)	Nepali	English, 12 other languages, about 30 major dialects	☸ 86.2%, ◉ 7.8%, ☾ 3.8%, ✳ 2.2%	58.61	45.2%	⟱ 41%, ⚒ 22%, ⚕ 37%
North Korea		46,540 (120,540)	22,912,180	P'yŏngyang	North Korean won (KPW)	Korean		◉, ∝, ✳	71.3	99%	⟱ 30%, ⚒ 42%, ⚕ 28%
Oman		82,030 (212,460)	3,001,580	Muscat	Omani rial (OMR)	Arabic	English, Baluchi, Urdu, Indian dialects	☾ 75%,	72.31	75.8%	⟱ 3%, ⚒ 40%, ⚕ 57%
Pakistan		310,400 (803,940)	156,689,150	Islamabad	Pakistani rupee (PKR)	Urdu, English	Punjabi, Sindhi, Siraiki, Pashtu, Balochi, other	☾ 97%, ∝, ☸, ✳ 3%	61.82	45.7%	⟱ 26%, ⚒ 24%, ⚕ 50%
Philippines		115,830 (300,000)	87,857,470	Manila	Philippine peso (PHP)	Filipino (based on Tagalog), English	Tagalog, Cebuano, Ilocan, Hiligaynon, Bicol, Waray, other	✟ 83%, ✚ 9%, ☾ 5%, ◉ and ✳ 3%	68.12	95.9%	⟱ 17%, ⚒ 30%, ⚕ 53%
Qatar		4,420 (11,440)	863,050	Doha	Qatari rial (QAR)	Arabic	English	☾ 95%	72.88	82.5%	⟱ 1%, ⚒ 49%, ⚕ 50%
Saudi Arabia		756,980 (1,960,580)	25,934,590	Riyadh	Saudi riyal (SAR)	Arabic		☾ 100%	68.4	78.8%	⟱ 7%, ⚒ 48%, ⚕ 45%
Singapore		268 (693)	4,930,860	Singapore	Singapore dollar (SGD)	Chinese, Malay, Tamil, English		◉, ☾, ∝, ☸, ✳	80.29	93.2%	⚒ 33%, ⚕ 67%
South Korea		38,020 (98,480)	48,893,070	Seoul	South Korean won (KRW)	Korean	English	∝ 49%, ◉ 47%, ✳ 4%	74.88	98.1%	⟱ 5%, ⚒ 44%, ⚕ 51%
Sri Lanka		25,330 (65,610)	20,064,780	Colombo, Sri Jayewardenepura Kotte	Sri Lankan rupee (LKR)	Sinhala	Tamil	◉ 70%, ☸ 15%, ∝ 8%, ☾ 7%	72.35	92.3%	⟱ 21%, ⚒ 27%, ⚕ 52%
Syria		71,500 (185,180)	18,448,750	Damascus	Syrian pound (SYP)	Arabic	Kurdish, Armenian, Aramaic, Circassian, French, English	☾ 90%, ∝ 10%, ✡ less than 1%	69.08	76.9%	⟱ 27%, ⚒ 23%, ⚕ 50%
Taiwan		13,980 (35,980)	22,894,380	Taipei	new Taiwan dollar (TWD)	Mandarin Chinese	Taiwanese (Min), Hakka dialects	◉ 93%, ∝ 4.5%, ✳ 2.5%	76.74	86% (1980)	⟱ 2%, ⚒ 32%, ⚕ 66%
Tajikistan		55,250 (143,100)	7,163,510	Dushanbe	somoni (TJS)	Tajik	Russian	☾ 90%	64.28	99.4%	⟱ 19%, ⚒ 25%, ⚕ 56%
Thailand		198,460 (514,000)	65,444,370	Bangkok	baht (THB)	Thai	English, ethnic and regional dialects	◉ 95%, ☾ 3.8%, ∝ 0.5%, ☸ 0.1%, ✳ 0.6%	69.18	96%	⟱ 11%, ⚒ 40%, ⚕ 49%
Turkey		301,380 (780,580)	69,660,560	Ankara	Turkish lira (TRL)	Turkish	Kurdish, Arabic, Armenian, Greek	☾ 99.8%, ✳ 0.2%	71.52	86.5%	⟱ 14.5%, ⚒ 28.4%, ⚕ 57.1%
Turkmenistan		188,460 (488,100)	4,952,080	Ashgabat	Turkmen manat (TMM)	Turkmen, Russian, Uzbek		☾ 89%, ✚ 9%, ✳ 2%	61.1	98%	⟱ 27%, ⚒ 45%, ⚕ 28%
United Arab Emirates		32,000 (82,880)	2,563,210	Abu Dhabi	Emirati dirham (AED)	Arabic	Persian, English, Hindi, Urdu	☾ 96%, ∝, ☸, and ✳ 4%	74.52	77.9%	⟱ 3%, ⚒ 46%, ⚕ 51%
Uzbekistan		172,740 (447,400)	26,851,200	Tashkent	Uzbekistani sum (UZS)	Uzbek, Russian, Tajik		☾ 88%, ✚ 9%, ✳ 3%	63.9	99.3%	⟱ 33%, ⚒ 24%, ⚕ 43%
Vietnam		127,240 (329,560)	83,769,670	Hanoi	dong (VND)	Vietnamese	English, French, Chinese, Khmer	◉, ∝, ○, ☾	69.86	94%	⟱ 25%, ⚒ 35%, ⚕ 40%

Key to symbols: ∝ Christian ✟ Catholic ○ Orthodox ✚ Protestant ◉ Buddhist ☸ Hindu ✡ Jewish ☾ Muslim ≡ Atheist ○ Indigenous ✳ Other ⟱ Agriculture ⚒ Industry ⚕ Services NA Not Available
Note: All literacy statistics are for 2003 unless otherwise stated.

254

AREA SQ MILES (SQ KM)	POPULATION	CAPITAL	CURRENCY	OFFICIAL LANGUAGES	OTHER LANGUAGES	MAIN RELIGIONS	LIFE EXPECTANCY	LITERACY RATE	ECONOMY		
203,850 (527,970)	20,727,060	Şan'ā'	Yemeni rial (YER)	Arabic		ᴳ, ✿, ∝, ☪	60.59	50.2%	🌾 17%, ⚒ 40%, ⚕ 43%		Yemen
919,590 (2,381,740)	33,892,390	Algiers	Algerian dinar (DZD)	Arabic	French, Berber dialects	ᴳ 99%, ∝ and ✿ 1%	70.24	70%	🌾 17%, ⚒ 33%, ⚕ 50%		Algeria
481,350 (1,246,700)	11,190,790	Luanda	kwanza (AOA)	Portuguese	Bantu and African languages	○ 47%, ∝ 38%, ✝ 15%	38.87	42% (1998)	🌾 6%, ⚒ 70%, ⚕ 24%		Angola
43,480 (112,620)	7,460,030	Porto-Novo	Communaute Financiere Africaine franc (XOF)	French	Fon, Yoruba, tribal languages	○ 50%, ∝ 30%, ᴳ 20%	49.69	40.9% (2000)	🌾 36%, ⚒ 14%, ⚕ 50%		Benin
231,800 (600,370)	1,545,290	Gaborone	pula (BWP)	English	Setswana	○ 85%, ∝ 15%	35.29	79.8%	🌾 4%, ⚒ 44% (including 36% mining), ⚕ 52%		Botswana
105,870 (274,200)	13,925,310	Ouagadougou	Communaute Financiere Africaine franc (XOF)	French	African languages (belonging to Sudanic family)	○ 40%, ᴳ 50%, ∝ 10%	46.11	26.6%	🌾 31%, ⚒ 28%, ⚕ 41%		Burkina Faso
10,750 (27,830)	6,370,610	Bujumbura	Burundi franc (BIF)	Kirundi, French	Swahili	∝ 67%, ○ 23%, ᴳ 10%	45.94	51.6%	🌾 50%, ⚒ 18%, ⚕ 32%		Burundi
183,570 (475,440)	16,380,010	Yaoundé	Communaute Financiere Africaine franc (XAF)	English, French	24 major African language groups	○ 40%, ∝ 40%, ᴳ 20%	54.36	79%	🌾 44%, ⚒ 20%, ⚕ 36%		Cameroon
1,560 (4,030)	418,220	Praia	Cape Verdean escudo (CVE)	Portuguese, Crioulo		✝, ✝	69.52	76.6%	🌾 11%, ⚒ 17%, ⚕ 72%		Cape Verde
240,530 (622,980)	3,799,900	Bangui	Communaute Financiere Africaine franc (XAF)	French	Sangho, tribal languages	○ 35%, ✝ 25%, ✝ 25%, ᴳ 15%	43.58	51%	🌾 55%, ⚒ 20%, ⚕ 25%		Central African Republic
495,760 (1,284,000)	9,826,420	Ndjamena	Communaute Financiere Africaine franc (XAF)	French, Arabic	Sara, more than 120 languages and dialects	ᴳ 51%, ∝ 35%, ✱ 14%	51.27	47.5%	🌾 38%, ⚒ 13%, ⚕ 49%		Chad
838 (2,170)	671,250	Moroni	Comoran franc (KMF)	Arabic, French	Shikomoro (a blend of Swahili and Arabic)	ᴳ 98%, ✝ 2%	60.79	56.5%	🌾 40%, ⚒ 4%, ⚕ 56%		Comoros
132,050 (342,000)	3,039,130	Brazzaville	Communaute Financiere Africaine franc (XAF)	French	Monokutuba, Lingala, other language/dialects	∝ 50%, ○ 48%, ᴳ 2%	47.71	83.8%	🌾 10%, ⚒ 48%, ⚕ 42%		Congo
124,500 (322,460)	17,693,380	Yamoussoukro	Communaute Financiere Africaine franc (XOF)	French	60 native dialects (Dioula the most widely spoken)	∝ 20-30%, ᴳ 35-40%, ○ 25-40%	44.72	50.9%	🌾 28%, ⚒ 29%, ⚕ 43%		Côte d'Ivoire
909,040 (2,354,410)	60,085,000	Kinshasa	Congolese franc (CDF)	French	Lingala, Kingwana, Kikongo, Tshiluba	✝ 50%, ✝ 20%, ✱ 10%, ᴳ 10%, ○ 10%	49.13	65.5%	🌾 54%, ⚒ 9%, ⚕ 37%		Democratic Republic of Congo
8,880 (23,000)	476,700	Djibouti	Djiboutian franc (DJF)	French, Arabic	Somali, Afar	ᴳ 94%, ∝ 6%	51.6	67.9%	🌾 3%, ⚒ 10%, ⚕ 87%		Djibouti
386,660 (1,001,450)	77,505,760	Cairo	Egyptian pound (EGP)	Arabic	English, French	ᴳ 94%, ∝ and ✱ 6%	64.05	57.7%	🌾 14%, ⚒ 30%, ⚕ 56%		Egypt
10,830 (28,050)	535,880	Malabo	Communaute Financiere Africaine franc (XAF)	Spanish, French	Pidgin English, Fang, Bubi, Ibo	∝, ✱	54.35	85.7%	🌾 20%, ⚒ 60%, ⚕ 20%		Equatorial Guinea
46,840 (121,320)	4,561,600	Asmara	nakfa (ERN)	Afar, Arabic, Tigre, Kunama, Tigrinya, Cushitic languages		ᴳ, ∝, ✝, ✝	56.57	58.6%	🌾 17%, ⚒ 29%, ⚕ 54%		Eritrea
435,190 (1,127,130)	69,113,730	Addis Ababa	birr (ETB)	Amharic, Tigrinya, Oromigna, Somali Guaragigna, Arabic	English, other local languages	ᴳ 45%-50%, ✝ 35%-40%, ○ 12%, ✱ 3%-8%	44.21	42.7%	🌾 52.3%, ⚒ 11.1%, ⚕ 36.6%		Ethiopia
103,350 (267,670)	1,389,200	Libreville	Communaute Financiere Africaine franc (XAF)	French	Fang, Myene, Nzebi, Bapounou/Eschira, Bandjabi	∝ 55%-75%, ○ and ᴳ less than 1%	49.11	63.2% (1995)	🌾 10%, ⚒ 60%, ⚕ 30%		Gabon
4,360 (11,300)	1,593,260	Banjul	dalasi (GMD)	English	Mandinka, Wolof, Fula, other indigenous languages	ᴳ 90%, ∝ 9%, ○ 1%	53.98	40.1%	🌾 21%, ⚒ 12%, ⚕ 67%		Gambia
92,460 (239,460)	21,029,850	Accra	cedi (GHC)	English	African languages (e.g. Akan, Moshi-Dagomba, Ewe, Ga)	○ 21%, ᴳ 16%, ∝ 63%	57.06	74.8%	🌾 36%, ⚒ 25%, ⚕ 39%		Ghana
94,930 (245,860)	9,467,870	Conakry	Guinean franc (GNF)	French	Each ethinic group has its own language	ᴳ 85%, ∝ 8%, ○ 7%	46.28	35.9% (1995)	🌾 24%, ⚒ 38%, ⚕ 38%		Guinea
13,950 (36,120)	1,416,030	Bissau	Communaute Financiere Africaine franc (XOF)	Portuguese	Crioulo, African languages	○ 50%, ᴳ 45%, ∝ 5%	49.8	42.4%	🌾 54%, ⚒ 15%, ⚕ 31%		Guinea-Bissau

Key to symbols: ∝ Christian   ✝ Catholic   ✝ Orthodox   ✝ Protestant   ◉ Buddhist   ☪ Hindu   ✿ Jewish   ᴳ Muslim   ≡ Atheist   ○ Indigenous   ✱ Other   🌾 Agriculture   ⚒ Industry   ⚕ Services   NA Not Available

Note: All literacy statistics are for 2003 unless otherwise stated.

		Area sq miles (sq km)	Population	Capital	Currency	Official Languages	Other Languages	Main Religions	Life Expectancy	Literacy Rate	Economy
Kenya		224,960 (582,650)	32,368,100	Nairobi	Kenyan shilling (KES)	English, Kiswahili	Indigenous languages	✝ 45%, ✚ 33%, O 10%, ☾ 10%, ✱ 2%	47.02	85.1%	⚘ 24%, ⛏ 13%, ⚒ 63%
Lesotho		11,720 (30,360)	1,867,040	Maseru	loti (LSL), South African rand (ZAR)	English	Sesotho (southern Sotho), Zulu, Xhosa	∝ 80%, O 20%	47	84.8%	⚘ 18%, ⛏ 38%, ⚒ 44%
Liberia		43,000 (111,370)	3,482,210	Monrovia	Liberian dollar (LRD)	English	20 ethnic group languages	O 40%, ∝ 40%, ☾ 20%	51.8	57.5%	⚘ 60%, ⛏ 10%, ⚒ 30%
Libya		679,360 (1,759,540)	5,765,560	Tripoli	Libyan dinar (LYD)	Arabic, Italian, English		☾ 97%	75.86	82.6%	⚘ 7%, ⛏ 47%, ⚒ 46%
Madagascar		226,660 (587,040)	18,040,340	Antananarivo	Malagasy franc (MGF)	French, Malagasy		O 52%, ∝ 41%, ☾ 7%	55.74	68.9%	⚘ 34%, ⛏ 11%, ⚒ 55%
Malawi		45,750 (118,480)	12,158,920	Lilongwe	Malawian kwacha (MWK)	English, Chichewa	Other regional languages	✝ 55%, ✚ 20%, ☾ 20%, O 3%, ✱ 2%	36.59	62.7%	⚘ 40%, ⛏ 19%, ⚒ 41%
Mali		478,770 (1,240,000)	12,291,530	Bamako	Communaute Financiere Africaine franc (XOF)	French	Bambara, African languages	☾ 90%, O 9%, ∝ 1%	47.39	46.4%	⚘ 45%, ⛏ 17%, ⚒ 38%
Mauritania		397,960 (1,030,700)	3,086,860	Nouakchott	ouguiya (MRO)	Hassaniya Arabic, Wolof	Pulaar, Soninke, French	☾ 100%	51.53	41.7%	⚘ 25%, ⛏ 29%, ⚒ 46%
Mauritius		788 (2,040)	1,230,600	Port Louis	Mauritian rupee (MUR)	English, French	Creole, Hindi, Urdu, Hakka, Bhojpuri	ॐ 52%, ∝ 28.3%, ☾ 16.6%, ✱ 3.1%	71.53	85.6%	⚘ 6%, ⛏ 33%, ⚒ 61%
Morocco		172,410 (446,550)	32,725,850	Rabat	Moroccan dirham (MAD)	Arabic	Berber dialects, French	☾ 98.7%, ∝ 1.1%, ✡ 0.2%	69.73	51.7%	⚘ 15%, ⛏ 33%, ⚒ 52%
Mozambique		309,500 (801,590)	17,710,040	Maputo	metical (MZM)	Portuguese	Indigenous dialects	O 50%, ∝ 30%, ☾ 20%	35.46	47.8%	⚘ 33%, ⛏ 25%, ⚒ 42%
Namibia		318,700 (825,420)	1,975,850	Windhoek	Namibian dollar (NAD), South African rand (ZAR)	English	Afrikaans, German, Oshivambo, Herero, Nama	∝ 80%-90%, O 10%-20%	38.97	84%	⚘ 11%, ⛏ 28%, ⚒ 61%
Niger		489,190 (1,267,000)	11,665,940	Niamey	Communaute Financiere Africaine franc (XOF)	French	Hausa, Djerma	☾ 80%, O and ∝ 20%	41.91	17.6%	⚘ 41%, ⛏ 17%, ⚒ 42%
Nigeria		356,670 (923,770)	140,601,620	Abuja	naira (NGN)	English	Hausa, Yoruba, Igbo (Ibo), Fulani	☾ 50%, ∝ 40%, O 10%	50.59	68%	⚘ 39%, ⛏ 33%, ⚒ 28%
Rwanda		10,170 (26,340)	8,098,620	Kigali	Rwandan franc (RWF)	Kinyarwanda, French, English	Bantu, Kiswahili (Swahili)	✚ 56.5%, ✝ 37.1%, ☾ 4.6%, O 0.1%, ✱ 1.7%	38.66	70.4%	⚘ 46%, ⛏ 20%, ⚒ 34%
São Tomé and Príncipe		386 (1,000)	187,410	São Tomé	dobra (STD)	Portuguese		∝ 80%	65.93	79.3% (1991)	⚘ 25%, ⛏ 10%, ⚒ 65%
Senegal		75,750 (196,190)	11,126,830	Dakar	Communaute Financiere Africaine franc (XOF)	French	Wolof, Pulaar, Jola, Mandinka	☾ 94%, ∝ 5%, O 1%	62.93	40.2%	⚘ 18.5%, ⛏ 20.7%, ⚒ 60.8%
Seychelles		176 (455)	81,190	Victoria	Seychelles rupee (SCR)	English, French	Creole	✚ 86.6%, ✝ 6.8%, ∝ 2.5%, ✱ 4.1%	70.97	58% (1971)	⚘ 3.1%, ⛏ 26.3%, ⚒ 70.6%
Sierra Leone		27,700 (71,740)	6,017,640	Freetown	leone (SLL)	English	Mende, Temne, Krio	☾ 60%, O 30%, ∝ 10%	45.96	31.4% (1995)	⚘ 43%, ⛏ 27%, ⚒ 30%
Somalia		246,200 (637,660)	8,591,630	Mogadishu	Somali shilling (SOS)	Somali	Arabic, Italian, English	☾	46.96	37.8% (2001)	⚘ 65%, ⛏ 10%, ⚒ 25%
South Africa, Republic of		471,010 (1,219,910)	42,552,330	Bloemfontein, Cape Town, Pretoria	rand (ZAR)	Afrikaans, English, Ndebele, Pedi, Sotho, Swazi, Tsonga, Tswana,	Official: Venda, Xhosa, Zulu	∝ 68%, ☾ 2%, ॐ 1.5%, O 28.5%	45.43	86.4%	⚘ 3%, ⛏ 31%, ⚒ 66%
Sudan		967,500 (2,505,810)	40,187,490	Khartoum	Sudanese dinar (SDD)	Arabic	Nubian, Ta Bedawie, Nilotic, Nilo-Hamitic, Sudanic, English	☾ 70%, O 25%, ∝ 5%	57.33	61.1%	⚘ 43%, ⛏ 17%, ⚒ 40%
Swaziland		6,700 (17,360)	1,173,900	Mbabane	lilangeni (SZL)	English, siSwati		∝ and O 40%, ✚ 20%, ☾ 10%, ✝, ✡, and ✱ 30%	37	81.6%	⚘ 10%, ⛏ 43%, ⚒ 47%
Tanzania		364,900 (945,090)	37,322,700	Dodoma	Tanzanian shilling (TZS)	Kiswahili, Swahili	Kiunguju, English, Arabic	mainland: ∝ 30%, ☾ 35%, O 35%, Zanzibar: ☾ 99%	51.7	78.2%	⚘ 48.4%, ⛏ 16.7%, ⚒ 34.9%
Togo		21,930 (56,790)	5,681,520	Lomé	Communaute Financiere Africaine franc (XOF)	French	Ewe, Mina, Kabye, Dagomba	O 51%, ∝ 29%, ☾ 20%	54.02	60.9%	⚘ 42%, ⛏ 21%, ⚒ 37%

Key to symbols: ∝ Christian ✚ Catholic O Orthodox ✝ Protestant Buddhist ॐ Hindu ✡ Jewish ☾ Muslim ≡ Atheist O Indigenous ✱ Other ⚘ Agriculture ⛏ Industry ⚒ Services NA Not Available
Note: All literacy statistics are for 2003 unless otherwise stated.

Area sq miles (sq km)	Population	Capital	Currency	Official Languages	Other Languages	Main Religions	Life Expectancy	Literacy Rate	Economy		Country
63,170 (163,610)	10,137,250	Tunis	Tunisian dinar (TND)	Arabic	French	☾ 98%, ∝ 1%, ✡ and ✳ 1%	74.16	74.2%	⇟ 13%, ⚒ 33%, ⬤ 54%		Tunisia
91,140 (236,040)	27,202,150	Kampala	Ugandan shilling (UGX)	English	Niger-Congo/Nilo-Saharan languages Swahili, Arabic	✚ 33%, ✝ 33%, ☾ 16%, ○ 18%	43.81	69.9%	NA		Uganda
290,580 (752,610)	10,613,620	Lusaka	Zambian kwacha (ZMK)	English	Bemba, Kaonda, Lozi, Lunda, Luvale, Nyanja, Tonga, other	∝ 50%-75%, ☾ and ⚛ 24%-49%, ○ 1%	37.35	80.6%	⇟ 24%, ⚒ 25%, ⬤ 51%		Zambia
150,800 (390,580)	12,746,990	Harare	Zimbabwean dollar (ZWD)	English	Shona, Sindebele, minor tribal dialects	syncretic (blend of ∝ and ○) 50%, ∝ 25%, ○ 24%, ☾ and ✳ 1%	36.5	90.7%	⇟ 11%, ⚒ 14%, ⬤ 75%		Zimbabwe
2,967,910 (7,686,850)	20,090,440	Canberra	Australian dollar (AUD)	English	Indigenous languages	✝ 26.1%, ✚ 26%, ∝ 24.3%, ✳ 33.6%	80	100% (1980)	⇟ 3%, ⚒ 25%, ⬤ 72%		Australia
7,050 (18,270)	893,350	Suva	Fijian dollar (FJD)	English	Fijian, Hindustani	∝ 52%, ⚛ 38%, ☾ 8%, ✳ 2%	68.56	93.7%	⇟ 17%, ⚒ 25%, ⬤ 58%		Fiji
313 (811)	103,090	Bairiki	Australian dollar (AUD)	English	I-Kiribati	✝ 52%, ✚ 40%, ☾ and ✳ 8%	60.54	NA	⇟ 30%, ⚒ 7%, ⬤ 63%		Kiribati
70 (181)	59,070	Majuro	U.S. dollar (USD)	Marshallese, English	Marshallese dialects (Malayo-Polynesian family), Japanese	∝	66.18	93.7% (1999)	⇟ 14%, ⚒ 16%, ⬤ 70%		Marshall Islands
271 (702)	138,740	Palikir	U.S. dollar (USD)	English	Trukese, Pohnpeian, Yapese, Kosrean, Ulithian, other	✝ 50%, ✚ 47%	NA	89% (1980)	⇟ 50%, ⚒ 4%, ⬤ 46%		Micronesia, Federated States of
8 (21)	13,050	Yaren	Australian dollar (AUD)	Nauruan	English	∝	61.57	NA	NA		Nauru
103,740 (268,680)	4,035,460	Wellington	New Zealand dollar (NZD)	English, Maori		✚ 52%, ✝ 15%, ✳ 33%	78.15	99% (1980)	⇟ 8%, ⚒ 23%, ⬤ 69%		New Zealand
177 (458)	20,300	Koror	U.S. dollar (USD)	English, Palauan, Tobi, Angaur, Japanese, Sonsoralese		∝ 49%, ○	69.19	92% (1980)	NA		Palau
178,700 (462,840)	5,545,270	Port Moresby	kina (PGK)	English, pidgin English, Motu	715 indigenous languages	✝ 22%, ✚ 44%, ○ 34%	63.83	66%	⇟ 30.4%, ⚒ 36.8%, ⬤ 32.8%		Papua New Guinea
1,140 (2,940)	177,290	Apia	tala (WST)	Samoan (Polynesian), English		∝ 99.7%, ✳ 0.3%	69.8	99.7%	⇟ 16%, ⚒ 18%, ⬤ 66%		Samoa
10,980 (28,450)	538,030	Honiara	Solomon Islands dollar (SBD)	Melanesian pidgin, English	120 indigenous languages	✚ 78%, ✝ 18%, ○ 4%	71.82	NA	⇟ 42%, ⚒ 11%, ⬤ 47%		Solomon Islands
289 (748)	112,420	Nuku'alofa	pa'anga (TOP)	Tongan, English		∝	68.56	98.5% (1996)	⇟ 30%, ⚒ 10%, ⬤ 60%		Tonga
10 (26)	11,640	Vaiaku	Australian dollar (AUD), Tuvaluan dollar	Tuvaluan, English, Samoan, I-Kiribati		✚ 98.4%, ✳ 1.6%	66.98	NA	NA		Tuvalu
4,710 (12,200)	205,750	Port Vila	vatu (VUV)	English, French, Pidgin	more than 100 local languages	✚ 61.7%, ✝ 15%, ○ 7.6%, ✳ 15.7%	61.33	53% (1979)	⇟ 26%, ⚒ 12%, ⬤ 62%		Vanuatu
77 (199)	73,320	Pago Pago	U.S. dollar (USD)	Samoan (Polynesian), English		∝ 50%, ✝ 20%, ✚ and ✳ 30%	75.53	97% (1980)	NA		American Samoa (U.S.A.)
39 (102)	13,250	The Valley	East Caribbean dollar (XCD)	English		✚ 85%, ✝ 3%, ✳ 12%	76.5	95%	⇟ 4%, ⚒ 18%, ⬤ 78%		Anguilla (U.K.)
75 (193)	71,570	Oranjestad	Aruban guilder/florin (AWG)	Dutch	Papiamento, English, Spanish	✝ 82%, ✚ 8%, ✳ 10%	78.67	97%	NA		Aruba (Netherlands)
2 (5)	no indigenous inhabitants										Ashmore Reef and Cartier Islands (Australia)
0.54 (1.4)	no indigenous inhabitants										Baker Island (U.S.A.)
21 (53)	65,370	Hamilton	Bermudian dollar (BMD)	English	Portuguese	✚ 66%, ✝ 15%, ✳ 19%	77.3	98% (1970)	⇟ 1%, ⚒ 10%, ⬤ 89%		Bermuda (U.K.)
23 (59)	uninhabited										Bouvetøya (Norway)

Key to symbols: ∝ Christian ✝ Catholic ✚ Orthodox ✚ Protestant ◉ Buddhist ⚛ Hindu ✡ Jewish ☾ Muslim ≡ Atheist ○ Indigenous ✳ Other ⇟ Agriculture ⚒ Industry ⬤ Services NA Not Available

Note: All literacy statistics are for 2003 unless otherwise stated.

		AREA SQ MILES (SQ KM)	POPULATION	CAPITAL	CURRENCY	OFFICIAL LANGUAGES	OTHER LANGUAGES	MAIN RELIGIONS	LIFE EXPECTANCY	LITERACY RATE	ECONOMY
British Indian Ocean Territory (U.K.)		23 (60)	no indigenous inhabitants								
British Virgin Islands (U.K.)		59 (153)	22,640	Road Town	U.S. dollar (USD)	English		✝ 86%, ✚ 10%, ✳ 4%	75.85	97.8% (1991)	↯ 1.8%, ⚒ 6.2%, ⊕ 92%
Cayman Islands (U.K.)		101 (262)	44,270	George Town	Caymanian dollar (KYD)	English		✝, ✚	79.18	98% (1970)	↯ 1.4%, ⚒ 3.2%, ⊕ 95.4%
Christmas Island (Australia)		52 (135)	470	The Settlement	Australian dollar (AUD)	English	Chinese, Malay	◉ 36%, ☪ 25%, ∝ 18%, ✳ 21%	NA	NA	NA
Clipperton Island (France)		2 (6)	uninhabited								
Cocos Islands (Australia)		5 (14)	630		Australian dollar (AUD)	Malay (Cocos dialect), English		☪ 80%, ✳ 20%	NA	NA	NA
Cook Islands (N.Z.)		93 (240)	21,340	Avarua	New Zealand dollar (NZD)	English	Maori	∝	NA	95%	↯ 17%, ⚒ 7.8%, ⊕ 75.2%
Coral Sea Islands Territory (Australia)		1.1 (2.9)	no indigenous inhabitants								
Falkland Islands (U.K.)		4,700 (12,170)	2,970	Stanley	Falkland pound (FKP)	English		✝, ✚	NA	NA	NA
Faroe Islands (Denmark)		540 (1,400)	46,960	Torshavn	Danish krone (DKK)	Faroese, Danish		✝	78.74	NA	↯ 27%, ⚒ 11%, ⊕ 62%
French Guiana (France)		35,140 (91,000)	195,510	Cayenne	euro (EUR)	French		✚	76.69	83% (1982)	NA
French Polynesia (France)		1,610 (4,170)	270,490	Papeete	Comptoirs Français du Pacifique franc (XPF)	French, Tahitian		✝ 54%, ✚ 30%, ✳ 16%	75.23	98% (1977)	↯ 6%, ⚒ 18%, ⊕ 76%
French Southern and Antarctic Lands (France)		3,020 (7,830)	no indigenous inhabitants								
Gibraltar (U.K.)		2.5 (6.5)	27,880	Gibraltar	Gibraltar pound (GIP)	English	Spanish, Italian, Portuguese, Russian	✚ 76.9%, ✝ 6.9%, ☪ 6.9%, ✡ 2.3%, ✳ 7%	79.23	above 80%	NA
Greenland (Denmark)		836,330 (2,166,090)	56,380	Nuuk	Danish krone (DKK)	Greenlandic (East Inuit), Danish, English		✝	68.69	NA	NA
Guadeloupe (France)		690 (1,780)	448,710	Basse-Terre	euro (EUR)	French	Creole patois	✚ 95%, 🕉 and ⊙ 4%, ✝ 1%	77.35	90% (1982)	NA
Guam (U.S.A.)		212 (549)	169,970	Hagåtña	U.S. dollar (USD)	English, Chamorro, Japanese		✚ 85%, ✳ 15%	78.11	99% (1990)	↯ 7%, ⚒ 15%, ⊕ 78%
Guernsey (U.K.)		30 (78)	65,230	St Peter Port	British pound (GBP), Guernsey pound	English, French, Norman-French dialect		✝, ✚	79.9	NA	↯ 3%, ⚒ 10%, ⊕ 87%
Heard and McDonald Islands (Australia)		159 (412)	uninhabited								
Howland Island (U.S.A.)		0.6 (1.6)	uninhabited								
Isle of Man (U.K.)		221 (572)	75,050	Douglas	British pound (GBP), Manx pound	English, Manx Gaelic		✝, ✚, ∝	77.81	NA	↯ 1%, ⚒ 13%, ⊕ 86%
Jan Mayen (Norway)		144 (373)	no indigenous inhabitants								
Jarvis Island (U.S.A.)		1.7 (4.5)	uninhabited								
Jersey (U.K.)		45 (116)	90,810	St Helier	British pound (GBP), Jersey pound	English, French	Norman-French dialect	✝, ✚	78.78	NA	↯ 5%, ⚒ 2%, ⊕ 93%
Johnston Atoll (U.S.A.)		1.1 (2.8)	no indigenous inhabitants								

Key to symbols: ∝ Christian ✚ Catholic ✝ Orthodox ✝ Protestant ◉ Buddhist 🕉 Hindu ✡ Jewish ☪ Muslim ≡ Atheist ⊙ Indigenous ✳ Other ↯ Agriculture ⚒ Industry ⊕ Services **NA** Not Available

Note: All literacy statistics are for 2003 unless otherwise stated.

AREA SQ MILES (SQ KM)	POPULATION	CAPITAL	CURRENCY	OFFICIAL LANGUAGES	OTHER LANGUAGES	MAIN RELIGIONS	LIFE EXPECTANCY	LITERACY RATE	ECONOMY		
0.4 (1.0)	uninhabited										Kingman Reef (U.S.A.)
420 (1,100)	432,900	Fort-de-France	euro (EUR)	French, Creole patois		✟ 95%, ⚕ and O 5%	78.56	97.7%	⚘ 6%, ⚒ 11%, ⚓ 83%		Martinique (France)
140 (374)	193,630	Dzadaoudzi	euro (EUR)	French	Mahorian (a Swahili dialect)	☾ 97%, ∝ 3%	60.21	NA	NA		Mayotte (France)
2.4 (6.2)	no indigenous inhabitants										Midway Islands (U.S.A.)
39 (102)	9,340	Plymouth	East Caribbean dollar (XCD)	English		✠, ✟, ∝	78.2	97% (1970)	⚘ 5.4%, ⚒ 13.6%, ⚓ 81%		Montserrat (U.K.)
2.0 (5.2)	uninhabited										Navassa Island (U.S.A.)
371 (960)	219,960	Willemstad	Netherlands Antillean guilder (ANG)	Dutch	Papiamento, English, Spanish	✟, ✠, ✶	75.15	96.7%	⚘ 1%, ⚒ 15%, ⚓ 84%		Netherlands Antilles (Netherlands)
7,360 (19,060)	216,490	Nouméa	Comptoirs Francais du Pacifique franc (XPF)	French	33 Melanesian-Polynesian dialects	✟ 60%, ✠ 30%, ✲ 10%	73.27	91% (1976)	⚘ 5%, ⚒ 30%, ⚓ 65%		New Caledonia (France)
100 (260)	2,130	Alofi	New Zealand dollar (NZD)	Niuean, English		✠ 85%, ✲ 15%	NA	95%	⚘ NA, ⚒ NA, ⚓ 55%		Niue (N.Z.)
13 (34)	1,870	Kingston	Australian dollar (AUD)	English	Norfolk (mixture of 18th century English and ancient Tahitian)	✠ 55%, ✟ 11.5%, ✲ 33.5%	NA	NA	NA		Norfolk Island (Australia)
184 (477)	85,370	Saipan	U.S. dollar (USD)	English, Chamorro, Carolinian		∝	75.95	97% (1980)	NA		Northern Mariana Islands (U.S.A.)
5 (12)	no indigenous inhabitants										Palmyra Atoll (U.S.A.)
NA	no indigenous inhabitants										Paracel Islands (Occupied by China)
18 (47)	50	Adamstown	New Zealand dollar (NZD)	English	Pitcairnese	✠ 100%	NA	NA	NA		Pitcairn Islands (U.K.)
3,510 (9,100)	3,929,510	San Juan	U.S. dollar (USD)	Spanish, English		✟ 85%, ✠ and ✲ 15%	75.96	93.8% (2001)	⚘ 1%, ⚒ 45%, ⚓ 54%		Puerto Rico (U.S.A.)
970 (2,520)	776,950	Saint-Denis	euro (EUR), French franc (FRF)	French	Creole widely used	✟ 86%, ⚕, ☾, ◉	73.18	88.9%	⚘ 8%, ⚒ 19%, ⚓ 73%		Réunion (France)
158 (410)	7,460	Jamestown	Saint Helenian pound (SHP)	English		✠, ✟	77.2	97% (1987)	NA		St Helena (U.K.)
93 (242)	7,010	St-Pierre	euro (EUR)	French		✟ 99%	77.93	99% (1982)	NA		St Pierre and Miquelon (France)
1,510 (3,900)	no indigenous inhabitants										South Georgia and Sandwich Islands (U.K.)
1,510 (62,050)	2,870	Longyearbyen	Norwegian krone (NOK)	Russian, Norwegian		NA	NA	NA	NA		Svalbard (Norway)
4 (10)	1,430	administrative center on each atoll	New Zealand dollar (NZD)	Tokelauan (a Polynesian language), English		✠ 70%, ✟ 28%, ✲ 2%	NA	NA	NA		Tokelau Islands (N.Z.)
166 (430)	20,560	Cockburn Town	U.S. dollar (USD)	English		✠ 86%, ✲ 14%	73.76	98% (1970)	NA		Turks and Caicos Islands (U.K.)
136 (352)	127,310	Charlotte Amalie	U.S. dollar (USD)	English	Spanish, Creole	✠ 59%, ✟ 34%, ✲ 7%	78.43	NA	NA		U.S. Virgin Islands (U.S.A.)
2.5 (6.5)	no indigenous inhabitants										Wake Atoll (U.S.A.)
106 (274)	16,030	Matā'Utu	Comptoirs Francais du Pacifique franc (XPF)	French, Wallisian (indigenous Polynesian language)		✟ 100%	NA	50% (1969)	NA		Wallis and Futuna Islands (France)

Key to symbols: ∝ Christian   ✟ Catholic   ✠ Orthodox   ✠ Protestant   ◉ Buddhist   ⚕ Hindu   ✶ Jewish   ☾ Muslim   ≡ Atheist   O Indigenous   ✲ Other   ⚘ Agriculture   ⚒ Industry   ⚓ Services   NA Not Available

Note: All literacy statistics are for 2003 unless otherwise stated.

WORLD FACT FILE

Planet Earth Vital Statistics

DIAMETER: 7,926 miles (12,756 km)

AVERAGE DISTANCE FROM THE SUN: 93 million miles (150 million km)

ORBIT PERIOD: 365.25 days

ROTATION PERIOD: 23 hours 56 minutes

TOTAL SURFACE AREA: 196,940,000 sq miles (510,072,000 sq km)

TOTAL LAND AREA: 57,506,000 sq miles (148,940,000 sq km)

TOTAL WATER AREA: 139,434,000 sq miles (361,132,000 sq km)

†**TOTAL WORLD POPULATION:** 6,448,780,202

†**WORLD POPULATION GROWTH RATE:** 1.12% p.a.

AVERAGE LIFE EXPECTANCY: 63.95 years

AVERAGE LITERACY RATE: 77%

AVERAGE GDP PER CAPITA: US$7,900

† 2005 population figures

Largest Countries by Population

COUNTRY	POPULATION
1. China	1,302,207,990
2. India	1,080,264,390
3. United States	295,734,130
4. Indonesia	241,973,880
5. Brazil	186,112,790
6. Pakistan	156,689,150
7. Bangladesh	144,319,630
8. Russian Fed.	143,736,790
9. Nigeria	140,601,620
10. Japan	127,417,240

Smallest Countries by Population

COUNTRY	POPULATION
1. Vatican City	900
2. Tuvalu	11,640
3. Nauru	13,050
4. Palau	20,300
5. San Marino	28,880
6. Monaco	32,410
7. Liechtenstein	33,720
8. St Kitts and Nevis	38,960
9. Marshall Islands	59,070
10. Antigua and Barbuda	68,720

Largest Countries by Area

COUNTRY	TOTAL AREA
1. Russian Federation	6,592,770 sq miles (17,075,200 sq km)
2. Canada	3,474,920 sq miles (9,984,670 sq km)
3. United States of America	3,717,810 sq miles (9,629,090 sq km)
4. China	3,705,405 sq miles (9,596,960 sq km)
5. Brazil	3,286,490 sq miles (8,511,965 sq km)
6. Australia	2,967,910 sq miles (7,686,850 sq km)
7. India	1,269,345 sq miles (3,287,590 sq km)
8. Argentina	1,068,300 sq miles (2,766,890 sq km)
9. Kazakhstan	1,049,155 sq miles (2,717,300 sq km)
10. Sudan	967,500 sq miles (2,505,810 sq km)

Smallest Countries by Area

COUNTRY	TOTAL AREA
1. Vatican City	0.17 sq mile (0.44 sq km)
2. Monaco	0.75 sq mile (1.95 sq km)
3. Nauru	8 sq miles (21 sq km)
4. Tuvalu	10 sq miles (26 sq km)
5. San Marino	24 sq miles (61 sq km)
6. Liechtenstein	62 sq miles (160 sq km)
7. Marshall Islands	70 sq miles (181 sq km)
8. St Kitts and Nevis	101 sq miles (261 sq km)
9. Maldives	116 sq miles (300 sq km)
10. Malta	122 sq miles (316 sq km)

Largest Urban Agglomerations

AGGLOMERATION	COUNTRY	POPULATION
1. Tokyo	Japan	26,849,000
2. São Paulo	Brazil	19,591,000
3. Mexico City	Mexico	18,934,000
4. Mumbai	India	18,337,000
5. New York	United States	17,147,000
6. Dacca	Bangladesh	15,921,000
7. Delhi	India	15,335,000
8. Calcutta	India	14,299,000
9. Los Angeles	United States	13,766,000
10. Jakarta	Indonesia	13,156,000
11. Rhein-Ruhr*	Germany	12,944,000
12. Shanghai	China	12,665,000
13. Buenos Aires	Argentina	12,439,000
14. Karachi	Pakistan	11,830,000
15. Rio de Janeiro	Brazil	11,170,000
16. Lagos	Nigeria	11,134,000
17. Ōsaka	Japan	11,013,000
18. Manila	Philippines	10,864,000
19. Beijing	China	10,849,000
20. Cairo	Egypt	10,094,000

* Rhein-Ruhr includes Düsseldorf, Essen, Bonn, and Cologne.

Most Crowded Countries

COUNTRY	INHABITANTS
1. Monaco	26,784 per sq mile (16,620 per sq km)
2. Singapore	11,629 per sq mile (7,219 per sq km)
3. Vatican City	5,015 per sq mile (3,111 per sq km)
4. Malta	2,073 per sq mile (1,286 per sq km)
5. Maldives	1,877 per sq mile (1,164 per sq km)
6. Bangladesh	1,735 per sq mile (1,078 per sq km)
7. Bahrain	1,667 per sq mile (1,035 per sq km)
8. Taiwan	1,143 per sq mile (710 per sq km)
9. Barbados	1,042 per sq mile (648 per sq km)
10. Nauru	1,004 per sq mile (621 per sq km)

Least Crowded Countries

COUNTRY	INHABITANTS
1. Mongolia	2.9 per sq mile (1.8 per sq km)
2. Namibia	3.9 per sq mile (2.4 per sq km)
3. Australia	4.2 per sq mile (2.6 per sq km)
4. Botswana	4.3 per sq mile (2.6 per sq km)
5. Suriname	4.4 per sq mile (2.7 per sq km)
6. Iceland	4.6 per sq mile (2.8 per sq km)
7. Mauritania	4.8 per sq mile (3.0 per sq km)
8. Libya	5.3 per sq mile (3.3 per sq km)
9. Canada	5.8 per sq mile (3.6 per sq km)
10. Guyana	5.8 per sq mile (3.6 per sq km)

Most Widely Spoken Languages

LANGUAGE	NATIVE SPEAKERS
1. Mandarin Chinese	874 million
2. Hindi	366 million
3. English	341 million
4. Spanish	340 million
5. Bengali	207 million
6. Portuguese	176 million
7. Russian	167 million
8. Arabic	150 million
9. Japanese	125 million
10. German	100 million
11. Korean	78 million
12. French	77 million
13. Shanghainese (Wu)	77 million
14. Javanese	75 million
15. Cantonese (Yue)	71 million

Fastest Growing Populations*

COUNTRY	ANNUAL POPULATION GROWTH
1. Liberia	5.53%
2. Sierra Leone	4.54%
3. Eritrea	4.22%
4. Somalia	4.21%
5. Yemen	4.07%
6. Afghanistan	3.68%
7. Niger	3.63%
8. Democratic Republic of Congo	3.34%
9. Oman	3.27%
10. Uganda	3.11%

Fastest Shrinking Populations

COUNTRY	ANNUAL POPULATION GROWTH
1. Estonia	−1.14%
2. Bulgaria	−0.98%
3. Ukraine	−0.94%
4. Russian Federation	−0.64%
5. Latvia	−0.56%
6. Georgia	−0.53%
7. Hungary	−0.50%
8. Belarus	−0.40%
9. Kazakhstan	−0.37%
10. Romania	−0.26%

Major Classical Religions

RELIGION	ADHERENTS
1. Christianity	2 billion
2. Islam	1.3 billion
3. Hinduism	900 million
4. Buddhism	360 million
5. Confucianism	350 million
6. Taoism	187 million
7. Sikhism	23 million
8. Judaism	14 million
9. Baha'i	6 million
10. Jainism	4 million
11. Shinto	4 million
12. Zoroastrianism	500,000

* Countries with more than 1 million inhabitants

Richest Countries by GDP

COUNTRY	GDP PER CAPITA*
1. Luxembourg	US$44,000
2. United States	US$37,600
3. San Marino	US$34,600
4. Norway	US$31,800
5. Switzerland	US$31,700
6. Ireland	US$30,500
7. Canada	US$29,400
8. Belgium	US$29,000
9. Denmark	US$29,000
10. Japan	US$28,000

Poorest Countries by GDP

COUNTRY	GDP PER CAPITA*
1. East Timor	US$500
2. Somalia	US$550
3. Sierra Leone	US$580
4. Burundi	US$600
5. Democratic Republic of Congo	US$610
6. Tanzania	US$630
7. Malawi	US$670
8. Afghanistan	US$700
9. Comoros	US$720
10. Eritrea	US$740

Richest Countries by HDI

COUNTRY	HDI VALUE*
1. Norway	0.944
2. Iceland	0.942
3. Sweden	0.941
4. Australia	0.939
5. Netherlands	0.938
6. Belgium	0.937
7. United States	0.937
8. Canada	0.937
9. Japan	0.932
10. Switzerland	0.932

Poorest Countries by HDI

COUNTRY	HDI VALUE*
1. Sierra Leone	0.275
2. Niger	0.292
3. Burkina Faso	0.330
4. Mali	0.337
5. Burundi	0.337
6. Mozambique	0.356
7. Ethiopia	0.359
8. Central African Republic	0.363
9. Democratic Republic of Congo	0.363
10. Guinea-Bissau	0.373

GDP (Gross Domestic Product) is the total value of all the goods and services produced each year. All GDP figures are in PPP (Purchasing Power Parity), which takes into account price differences between countries.

HDI (Human Development Index) takes into account Gross Domestic Product (GDP), life expectancy, adult literacy rates, and education enrollments.

Most Educated Countries

COUNTRY	SCHOOL LIFE EXPECTANCY* (YEARS)
1. Norway	16.9
2. Finland	16.7
3. Australia	16.6
4. United Kingdom	16.4
5. New Zealand	16.2
6. Sweden	16.0
7. Netherlands	15.9
8. Belgium	15.8
9. Iceland	15.8
10. Denmark	15.6

Least Educated Countries

COUNTRY	SCHOOL LIFE EXPECTANCY* (YEARS)
1. Mali	2.1
2. Niger	2.3
3. Burkina Faso	2.8
4. Djibouti	3.4
5. Chad	3.9
6. Democratic Republic of Congo	4.3
7. Ethiopia	4.3
8. Eritrea	4.6
9. Burundi	4.9
10. Tanzania	5.0

School life expectancy is the total number of years of schooling a child can expect to receive.

Hottest Places: Highest Temperatures by Continent

CONTINENT	LOCATION	DATE	TEMPERATURE
1. Africa	Al 'Azīzīyah, Libya	13 Sept. 1922	136°F (57.3°C)
2. North America	Death Valley, California	10 July 1913	134°F (56.7°C)
3. Asia	Tirat Tsvi, Israel	21 June 1942	129°F (53.9°C)
4. Oceania	Cloncurry, Australia	16 Jan. 1889	128°F (53.3°C)
5. Europe	Seville, Spain	4 Aug. 1881	122°F (50°C)
6. South America	Rivadavia, Argentina	11 Dec. 1905	120°F (48.9°C)
7. Antarctica	Vanda Station, Scott Coast	5 Jan. 1974	59°F (15°C)

Coldest Places: Lowest Temperatures by Continent

CONTINENT	LOCATION	DATE	TEMPERATURE
1. Antarctica	Vostok Station	21 July 1983	−129°F (−89°C)
2a. Asia	Oymyakon, Russian Federation	6 Feb. 1933	−90°F (−68°C)
2b. Asia	Verkhoyanskiy Khrebet, Russian Fed.	7 Feb. 1892	−90°F (−68°C)
3. North America	Northice, Greenland	9 Jan.1954	−87°F (−66°C)
4. Europe	Ust'-Shchuger, Russian Federation	Not known	−67°F (−55°C)
5. South America	Sarmiento, Argentina	1 June 1907	−27°F (−33°C)
6. Africa	Ifrane, Morocco	11 Feb. 1935	−11°F (−24°C)
7. Oceania	Charlotte Pass, Australia	29 June 1994	−9.4°F (−23°C)

Top Rail Networks

COUNTRY	LENGTH
1. United States	121,000 miles (194,700 km)
2. Russian Fed.	54,200 miles (87,200 km)
3. China	44,500 miles (71,600 km)
4. Canada	40,400 miles (65,000 km)
5. India	39,500 miles (63,500 km)
6. Germany	28,300 miles (45,500 km)
7. Australia	25,800 miles (41,600 km)
8. Argentina	21,400 miles (34,500 km)
9. France	20,300 miles (32,700 km)
10. Brazil	19,600 miles (31,500 km)

Top Road Networks

COUNTRY	LENGTH
1. United States	3,958,000 miles (6,370,000 km)
2. India	2,063,000 miles (3,320,000 km)
3. Brazil	1,230,000 miles (1,980,000 km)
4. China	870,000 miles (1,400,000 km)
5. Japan	716,000 miles (1,152,000 km)
6. Russian Fed.	592,000 miles (952,000 km)
7. Australia	567,000 miles (913,000 km)
8. Canada	561,000 miles (902,000 km)
9. France	555,000 miles (893,000 km)
10. Italy	416,000 miles (669,000 km)

Wettest Places: Highest Average Annual Precipitation by Continent

CONTINENT	LOCATION	PRECIPITATION
1. Asia	Mawsynram, India	467 in (11,862 mm)
2. Oceania	Mt Waialeale, Hawaii	460 in (11,684 mm)
3. Africa	Debundscha, Cameroon	405 in (10,287 mm)
4. South America	Quibdó, Colombia	354 in (8,992 mm)
5. North America	Henderson Lake, Canada	256 in (6,502 mm)
6. Europe	Crkvica, Bosnia-Herzegovina	183 in (4,648 mm)

Driest Places: Lowest Average Annual Precipitation by Continent

CONTINENT	LOCATION	PRECIPITATION
1. South America	Quillagua, Chile	0.02 in (0.5 mm)
2. Africa	Wadi Halfa, Sudan	<0.1 in (<2.5 mm)
3. Antarctica	South Pole	0.8 in (20 mm)
4. North America	Batagues, Mexico	1.2 in (31 mm)
5. Asia	Aden, Yemen	1.8 in (46 mm)
6. Oceania	Mulka, Australia	4.1 in (104 mm)
7. Europe	Astrakhan, Russian Federation	6.4 in (163 mm)

Deadliest Earthquakes

LOCATION	DATE	DEATHS
1. Shanxi, China	1556	830,000
2. Tangshan, China	1976	255,000
3. Ḥalab (Aleppo), Syria	1138	230,000
4. near Xining, China	1927	200,000
5. Damghan, Iran	856	200,000
6. Gansu, China	1920	200,000
7. Ardabīl, Iran	893	150,000
8. Kwanto, Japan	1923	143,000
9. Ashgabat, Turkmenistan	1948	110,000
10. Messina, Italy	1908	100,000

Deadliest Volcanic Eruptions

LOCATION	DATE	DEATHS
1. Tambora, Indonesia	1815	92,000
2. Krakatau, Indonesia	1883	36,417
3. Mt Pelée, Martinique	1902	29,025
4. Ruiz, Colombia	1985	25,000
5. Unzen, Japan	1792	14,300
6. Laki, Iceland	1783	9,350
7. Kelut, Indonesia	1919	5,110
8. Galunggung, Indonesia	1882	4,011
9. Vesuvius, Italy	1631	3,500
10. Vesuvius, Italy	79	3,360

Geographic Terms

A

Abyssal plain
Flat area of the ocean floor generally extending from the base of the continental slope to the mid-ocean ridge.

Acid rain
Wet and dry deposition of oxides of nitrogen and sulfur derived from burning fossil fuels, smelting metals, and motor vehicle exhaust fumes. Results in damage to the natural and built environment.

Air mass
A large body of air of relatively constant temperature and humidity.

Alluvial fan
A deposit that radiates downslope from the point where a stream leaves a confined channel. Typically found along mountain fronts.

Alpine
High-altitude, high-relative-relief terrain that is actively affected by frost action, lies above the tree line, and has been subjected to glacial erosion.

Altitude
Height above sea level.

Antarctic Circle
Line of latitude at 66.5°S, poleward of which the Sun does not set at the summer solstice (21–22 December) and does not rise at the winter solstice (21–22 June).

Anticyclone
Area of high atmospheric pressure, generally stable and slow-moving, around which light winds spiral outward (clockwise in the Northern Hemisphere, anti clockwise in the Southern).

Arable
Strictly, a system of land use involving plowing. Usually refers to land that is tilled for crops.

Archipelago
Either a sea studded with islands or, nowadays, a group of islands.

Arctic Circle
Line of latitude at 66.5°N, poleward of which the Sun does not set at the summer solstice (21–22 June) and does not rise at the winter solstice (21–22 December).

Arid
Dry, either because of low precipitation or high evapotranspiration with respect to precipitation.

Asthenosphere
Part of Earth's mantle extending from the base of the lithosphere (at depths of 30–185 miles [50–300 km]) to depths of around 430 miles (700 km). It is in a partially molten state and is less resistant to deformation than the over- and underlying zones.

Atmosphere
Layer of air that envelops Earth. Dry air contains roughly 78% nitrogen, 21% oxygen, 1% argon, and 0.03% carbon dioxide.

Atmospheric pressure
The pressure exerted by the weight of the atmosphere above a point.

Atoll
Low, subcircular coral reef enclosing a lagoon. Found mainly in the Indian and Pacific oceans.

Avalanche
Sudden and rapid movement of ice, snow, and/or debris down a slope.

Axis
An imaginary line connecting the North and South poles, tilted at about 66.5° to the plane of Earth's orbit, around which Earth rotates.

B

Basin
1. The total area of land drained by a river and its tributaries. 2. Depression within which deposition occurs, ranging from a small hollow to a major structural feature. 3. Hollow in the ground, with a multitude of possible origins including subsidence, glacial erosion, and tectonics.

Bedrock
Consolidated, relatively unweathered rock either exposed at the ground surface or underlying the regolith.

Biodiversity
The range of flora and fauna present in an ecosystem.

Biomass
The total mass of organisms in an area.

Biome
A major ecological community of plants and animals that occupies a particular terrestrial or, less commonly, marine environment.

Biosphere
The zone in which life occurs on Earth, normally conceived as a zone of interaction with the lithosphere, atmosphere, and hydrosphere.

Border
An imaginary line that separates one administrative and/or political unit from another.

Boreal forest
The Northern Hemisphere coniferous forest, lying between approximately 55°N and 65°N.

C

Caldera
A large crater-like, steep-walled basin created by the collapse of a volcano. May contain a crater lake and subsidiary volcanoes.

Canal
An artificial waterway cut to carry irrigation water or to provide a route for shipping.

Carbon cycle
The carbon occurring as carbon dioxide in the atmosphere is absorbed and stored by plants. The plants, some animals, and bacteria obtain nourishment from the carbon and return some back to the atmosphere as carbon dioxide.

Cash crop
A crop grown for sale, by contrast with a subsistence crop grown for use by the grower.

Channel
1. A natural or artificial course for running water. 2. A narrow stretch of water between two landmasses. 3. A natural or dredged navigable waterway in an area of generally shallower water.

City
A very large permanent settlement lacking self-sufficiency in the production of food and usually dependent on manufacturing and commerce. The combined population of a city and its suburbs is known as an urban agglomeration. All city population statistics quoted in this atlas are of urban agglomerations.

Climate
The average pattern of weather that occurs in a place over an extended period of time. Several schemes divide Earth into distinct climatic zones.

Coniferous forest
A forest comprised mainly of cone-bearing, often evergreen trees that usually have needle-shaped or scaly leaves.

Continent
1. One of Earth's seven principal landmasses: Africa, Antarctica, Asia, Australia, Europe, North America, South America. 2. That part of Earth's crust composed of ancient, thick, low-density material.

Continental drift
The theory that the present distribution of the continents is a result of the fragmentation of one or more pre-existing supercontinents that have drifted apart. Subsequently subsumed within the plate tectonics model.

Continental shelf
The part of the continental crust below sea level. Usually very gently sloping. Terminated by the steeper continental slope, which forms the true edge of the continents.

Coral
A porous, calcareous rock consisting of the continuous skeleton secreted by coral polyps, bottom-dwelling marine invertebrates common at shallow depth in clear intertropical seas.

Coral reef
An extensive, solidified accumulation of coral; divided into atolls, fringing, and barrier.

Cordillera
A linear mountain chain.

Core
The central part of Earth, 2,200 miles (3,500 km) in diameter. Composed of nickel–iron alloys, solid in the inner core (800 miles [1,300 km] in diameter) and liquid in the outer.

Coriolis effect
Earth's rotation means that bodies moving over its surface such as air (winds) and water (ocean currents) are deflected to the right in the Northern Hemisphere and to the left in the Southern.

Crust
The outermost layer of Earth, 3.75–43 miles (6–70 km) thick and composed of low-density rocks.

Cyclone
An area of relatively low atmospheric pressure, typically 620–1,200 miles (1,000–2,000 km) across, into which low-level winds spiral anti clockwise in the Northern Hemisphere and clockwise in the Southern.

D

Deciduous forest
An area dominated by woody perennial plants that shed their leaves at a particular time, season, or growth stage, such as before the cold or dry season.

Deforestation
The removal of trees from an area. May occur naturally, but the main cause is clearance for timber, agriculture, and urbanization. The practice may cause significant environmental damage.

Delta
An accumulation of river-borne sediment deposited where a stream enters a body of standing water and its strength is reduced by the sudden decrease in flow velocity.

Dependency
A territory and its population governed or held in trust by another nation.

Desert
An area of moisture deficiency where precipitation is low relative to losses by evapotranspiration.

Desertification
Land degradation in arid areas resulting from factors including climatic variation and human activities such as deforestation, overgrazing, and cultivation of marginal land.

Distributary
A stream channel that splits from the main line of flow.

Drainage basin
An area drained by a river system.

Drought
May be defined meteorologically as a relatively long period of relatively low precipitation or, in human terms, taking account of impacts on agriculture, water supply, etc.

Dune
A mound or ridge of windblown sand found most commonly in deserts and coastal environments.

E

Earthquake
A shock or series of shocks in Earth's crust caused by a sudden release of pressure in the crust or upper mantle.

Ecosystem
An interacting system of organisms and the environment to which they are adapted.

El Niño
The replacement of cold upwelling waters along the west coast of South America by warm currents from the west and north. Occurs irregularly at intervals of 2–7 years. Associated with changes in global atmospheric and ocean circulation that cause major shifts in climate worldwide.

Endangered species
A plant or animal species in danger of extinction whose survival is unlikely if the factors causing its vulnerability continue operating.

Environment
Simply, the surroundings. These may be natural (e.g. biological or physical environments) or artificial (e.g. built or social environments).

Eon
1. The longest period of geological time, such as the Phanerozoic, the last 590 million years. 2. A thousand million years.

Epicenter
The point on Earth's surface that lies directly above the focus of an earthquake.

Equator
An imaginary line that is at right angles to Earth's axis of rotation lying midway between the two poles. It divides the world into the Northern and Southern hemispheres.

Era
A division of geological time. The Phanerozoic (see Eon) is divided into three eras: Paleozoic, Mesozoic, and Cenozoic.

Erosion
The process whereby material is loosened or dissolved and moved from at or near Earth's surface.

Estuary
That section of a river where it enters the sea and is influenced by marine processes, such as tides and marine water quality.

Evapotranspiration
Total water loss from the soil, including evaporation and transpiration from plant surfaces.

Evergreen
A woody perennial plant that retains its foliage throughout the year by continuously shedding and replacing a few leaves at a time.

F

Fault
A planar fracture surface in rock along which relative motion has occurred. The fracturing is an adjustment to stresses in the rock.

Fauna
A group of animals particular to a region or a period of time.

Floodplain
That part of a river valley that is inundated in times of flood.

Flora
A group of plants particular to a region or a period of time.

Forest
A large area of trees whose crowns touch to form a continuous canopy.

Fossil
The remains of an organism preserved within rock.

Fossil fuel
Combustible material derived from the fossilized remains of plants and animals. Includes coal, gas, and oil.

G

Geothermal energy
Anomalously hot zones in Earth's crust may give rise to hot springs, steam, and hot rocks at the surface. Such energy may be employed for human use.

Geyser
A spring or fountain of geothermally heated water that erupts intermittently.

Glaciation
1. An episode of marked extension of ice sheets and glaciers. 2. The occupation of an area by ice sheets or glaciers. 3. The action of ice on the landscape.

Glacier
A mass of ice sufficiently large to deform and flow under its own weight.

Global warming
The possibility that Earth is warming as a consequence of human activity over the past century or more.

Grassland
A region in which the vegetation is dominated by grasses and other herbs.

Grazing
1. An area where livestock feed on growing grass or other herbs. 2. The act of feeding livestock on such areas.

Greenhouse effect
A natural phenomenon that occurs when short-wave solar radiation passes through Earth's atmosphere, is absorbed at the surface, and is re-radiated as longer wavelength thermal radiation. This maintains Earth's average temperature at a point warm enough to sustain life. It is argued that an increase in the incidence of greenhouse gases such as carbon dioxide, as a result of fossil fuel combustion, is enhancing the greenhouse effect and causing global temperatures to rise.

Greenwich mean time (GMT)
The official time at the Greenwich meridian (0°) in Greenwich, U.K. from which all time is calculated.

Greenwich meridian
A theoretical line, extending from the North to the South Pole, that

runs through Greenwich, U.K. This is the prime meridian, the 0° of longitude, from which all other meridians are measured.

H

Habitat
The environment in which an organism lives.

Hemisphere
Earth's surface is bisected by the Equator, producing the Northern and Southern hemispheres. Less precisely, the continents of North and South America are referred to as the Western Hemisphere.

High latitude
Broadly, the areas poleward of the Arctic and Antarctic circles.

Humidity
The water vapor content of the atmosphere.

Hurricane
An intense cyclonic vortex that occurs mainly over tropical oceans. Around 400 miles (650 km) in diameter and 90–185 miles (150–300 km) high, with maximum wind speeds of 330 feet per second (100 m/s). Also known in various parts of the world as typhoon, tropical cyclone, and cyclone.

Hydroelectricity
Electricity generated using the power of running water to turn turbines.

Hydrosphere
The component of Earth's system pertaining to water in its fresh or saline, and its solid, liquid, or gaseous state.

I

Ice age
A period in Earth's history when ice is found relatively extensively on the surface. There have been at least six ice ages. The present one, the Cenozoic, began perhaps 42 million years ago. The latest advance in the present ice age ended around 13,000 years ago.

Ice cap
A large, dome-shaped body of ice displaying a generally outward and radial flow.

Indigenous
Indigenous plants and animals are those that occur naturally in a region. Indigenous people are descendants of the people who inhabited a territory before the formation of modern nation states.

International Date Line
A theoretical line at approximately 180° of longitude. Places just west of the line are 12 hours ahead of GMT; points just east are 12 hours behind. East of the line the date is one day earlier than to the west.

Irrigation
The supply of water by artificial means to assist plant growth.

Island
A landmass smaller than a continent that is enclosed by water.

L

Latitude
The distance north and south of the Equator. Latitude is given by the angle formed between a line from the center of Earth to the Equator and a line from the center of Earth to the relevant point on Earth's surface. The latitude of the Equator is thus 0° and that of the North Pole is 90°N.

Lava
Magma that is extruded from volcanic fissures and vents. The term is also applied to the cooled and solidified form of this material.

Lithosphere
Earth's crust and part of the upper mantle form a strong layer relative to the underlying and more easily deformable asthenosphere. Varies from a few miles thick over the mid-ocean ridge to over 180 miles (300 km) thick below some continents.

Longitude
The distance east and west of the Greenwich meridian. Longitude is given by the angle formed between a line from the axis of Earth to the Greenwich meridian and a line from the axis of Earth to the relevant point on Earth's surface. The angles are measured both east and west of the Greenwich meridian. 180°W thus coincides with 180°E.

M

Magma
Molten or partly molten rock generated by partial melting within Earth's crust or upper mantle. Magma may be intruded into the crust where it cools and solidifies to form intrusive rock or it may be extruded onto Earth's surface where it cools and solidifies to form volcanic rock.

Mantle
That part of Earth's interior between the core and the crust.

Map projection
A means of allowing the whole or part of the spherical surface of Earth to be represented on a flat map. Earth's lines of latitude and longitude are transformed into a net on a plane surface, the map projection. There are many ways in which this may be undertaken, but all introduce some form of distortion onto the resultant map.

Meridian
A line of longitude linking the North and South poles.

Mesa
An isolated, flat-topped hill bounded by steep slopes or cliffs.

Midlatitudes
Broadly, those areas of Earth lying between the tropics and the poles.

Mid-ocean ridge
A linear mountain chain rising 0.5–1.75 miles (1–3 km) from the ocean floor, developed where upwelling basaltic magma forms new ocean crust along a margin between divergent tectonic plates.

Mineral
1. A natural, inorganic substance of definite chemical composition, almost always in crystalline form, that cannot be physically separated into simpler compounds. 2. A loose term for inorganic material.

Monsoon
A markedly seasonal wind. The term has been extended to cover the rains that accompany these winds.

Mountain
A high-altitude, high-relative-relief topographic feature with a summit small in proportion to its base.

N

Northern Hemisphere
Refers to the half of Earth north of the Equator (0°).

North Pole
The northernmost geographical point on Earth. It marks the northern axis of Earth's rotation.

O

Oasis
An area in a hot desert where there is sufficient water to sustain plant life.

Ocean
1. The body of salt water that covers 71% of Earth's surface. 2. One of Earth's large bodies of salt water (the Arctic, Atlantic, Indian, Pacific, and Southern oceans).

Ozone layer
An ozone-enriched region of the stratosphere 9–21 miles (15–35 km) above Earth's surface. Absorbs much of the Sun's ultraviolet radiation, preventing the damaging radiation from reaching Earth's surface.

P

Pangaea
The name given to the supercontinent postulated by continental drift theory. This split to produce the northern and southern continents of Laurasia and Gondwana.

Pasture
1. A place with growing grass or other herbs on which livestock are grazed. 2. The growing grass or other herbs on which livestock are grazed.

Peninsula
A narrow neck of land projecting into a body of water.

Plain
An area of flat or rolling land devoid of prominent elevations or depressions.

Plate tectonics
The theory that the lithosphere is divided into seven major (and several minor) segments or plates that are being formed along the mid-ocean ridges and reworked down into the mantle along the deep-sea trenches. The plates carry the continents on them, explaining their movement over time. The zones of interaction between plates are often characterized by earthquakes, volcanoes, and tectonic activity.

Plateau
A broad, elevated area of flat or rolling land.

R

Rain forest
Largely evergreen forest characteristic of permanently wet regions of the tropics and midlatitudes.

Rain shadow
The leeward side of a topographic barrier where precipitation is low. Moist air is forced upward on the windward slopes. This causes rain, reducing the moisture content of the air, which is warmed and dried further as it descends the leeward slopes.

Reef
1. A narrow area of rock or sediment (including coral) usually covered at high tide, but often exposed at low tide. 2. A coral reef.

Regolith
The mantle or layer of rock fragments, alluvium, soil, blown sand, etc, that rests on bedrock. It forms almost all of the surface of Earth's land.

Renewable energy
Energy from (in practical terms) inexhaustible sources. Includes hydroelectricity, solar and geothermal energy, and wind power.

Resource
An element of the environment that may be used to meet human needs. Resources may be natural (such as water or minerals) or human (such as the entrepreneurial talents of a population).

Rift valley
A long, linear trough formed by faulting due to tension in the lithosphere.

Ring of Fire
A belt of volcanoes and associated tectonic activity found around the perimeter of the Pacific Ocean. Also known as the Rim of Fire.

S

Savanna
An area of open grassland with some trees and shrubs found in the tropics and subtropics. Characterized by seasonal wet and dry climates.

Sea
1. The body of salt water that covers 71% of Earth's surface. 2. A large body of salt water wholly or partly enclosed by the land.

Sea ice
Ice that forms on the sea surface at temperatures below around 30°F (-2°C). Covers large areas of the polar oceans. Known as fast ice when attached to land and pack ice when floating free.

Sea level
The elevation of the ocean surface. The term is often used synonymously with mean sea level, which varies slightly from place to place.

Seamount
An isolated submarine hill or mountain, usually of volcanic origin.

Solstice
Either of the two times of the year (21–22 June or 21–22 December) when the Sun is at its greatest distance from the Equator. At these times of year, there are the longest hours of either day or night.

Southern Hemisphere
Refers to the half of Earth south of the Equator (0°).

South Pole
The southernmost geographical point on Earth. It marks the southern axis of Earth's rotation.

State
1. A territorial unit with clearly defined and internationally accepted boundaries, having an independent existence and responsible for its own legal system. 2. A unit of regional government with some independence in relation to internal affairs.

Steppe
A midlatitude grassland biome stretching from Austria to China.

Strait
A narrow passage of water connecting two larger water bodies.

Subduction
Where tectonic plates collide, one of the plates may be drawn down into the mantle in a process known as subduction. The subducted plate is almost invariably that composed of denser, ocean crust. Friction along the surface of the subducting slab may give rise to earthquakes or melting, and thus volcanic activity.

Subsistence agriculture
Farming in which the products grown or raised are primarily for the support of the farmer and dependents.

T

Tectonic plate
One of the seven large and several smaller segments into which the lithosphere is divided.

Temperate
A climate without extremes of temperature.

Territory
1. The land, sea, and air ruled by a sovereign authority. 2. An area dependent upon a sovereign state, but having some authority. 3. A large tract of land with undefined boundaries. 4. In Australia, Canada, and the U.S.A., an area without full rights as a state or province.

Time zone
A division of Earth's surface selected so that standard time is the same across the whole area. Adjacent time zones usually differ by an hour. Each time zone should theoretically cover 15° of longitude.

Topography
The surface features of an area. Strictly refers not only to physical, but also to human features.

Tornado
A violent rotating storm with winds of high speed circulating round a funnel cloud around 330 feet (100 m) in diameter.

Trench (deep-sea)
A narrow, elongated, steep-sided depression 10,000 feet (3,000 m) or more deeper than the adjacent deep-sea floor. Thought to mark the zone along which one tectonic plate is subducted beneath another.

Tributary
A stream or river that flows into a larger river.

Tropic of Cancer
An imaginary line encircling Earth at 23.5°N that marks the most northerly point at which the noonday Sun is directly overhead at some stage of the year (21–22 June, the summer solstice). Denotes the northern limit of the tropics.

Tropic of Capricorn
An imaginary line encircling Earth at 23.5°S that marks the most southerly point at which the noonday Sun is directly overhead at some stage of the year (21–22 December, the summer solstice). Denotes the southern limit of the tropics.

Tundra
Vast, level, treeless, marshy regions, usually with permanently frozen subsoil, supporting mosses, lichens, herbs, and dwarf shrubs. Classically the northern part of Eurasia, but the term has been expanded to include similar terrains in the Arctic, Antarctica, and at high altitude.

V

Vegetation
The plant cover of an area.

Volcano
1. An opening or vent in Earth's crust through which lava, gas, pumice, and ash is emitted. 2. The landform produced by the accumulation of lava and other volcanic materials around a vent.

W

Weathering
The in-situ alteration of materials at or near Earth's surface by physical, chemical, and biological processes.

Wilderness
An extensive area of land that exists in a natural or nearly natural state.

Woodland
A vegetation community of widely spaced, mature trees.

1

83	G 20	**100 Mile House**, British Columbia, Canada

A

130	H 1	**A Coruña**, Spain
130	J 1	**A Fonsagrada**, Spain
130	G 3	**A Guardia**, Spain
130	J 3	**A Gudiña**, Spain
137	B 17	**Aachen**, Germany
137	H 22	**Aalen**, Germany
133	J 16	**Aalst**, Netherlands
133	E 18	**Aalst**, Luxembourg
132	M 13	**Aalten**, Netherlands
133	D 17	**Aalter**, Belgium
138	F 6	**Aarau**, Switzerland
138	F 6	**Aare**, Switzerland ↳
133	H 18	**Aarschot**, Belgium
133	F 17	**Aartselaar**, Belgium
177	T 9	**Ab-i-Istada**, Afghanistan ↳
215	R 14	**Aba**, Nigeria
217	Q 5	**Aba**, Democratic Republic of Congo
188	L 4	**Aba**, China
176	G 9	**Ābādān**, Iran
176	J 9	**Abādeh**, Iran
210	J 8	**Abadla**, Algeria
236	D 2	**Abaiang**, Kiribati ≈
215	R 12	**Abaji**, Nigeria
74	M 6	**Abajo Peak**, Utah, U.S.A. ▲
215	R 13	**Abakaliki**, Nigeria
153	N 13	**Abakan**, Russian Federation
215	P 8	**Abala**, Niger
216	H 8	**Abala**, Congo
215	Q 8	**Abalak**, Niger
211	N 14	**Abalessa**, Algeria
107	F 17	**Abancay**, Peru
176	J 9	**Abarqū**, Iran
198	L 3	**Abashiri**, Japan
198	L 4	**Abashiri-ko**, Japan ↳
234	F 7	**Abau**, Papua New Guinea
179	R 4	**Abay**, Kazakhstan
213	I 22	**Ābaya Hāyk'**, Ethiopia ↳
153	N 13	**Abaza**, Russian Federation
216	H 4	**Abba**, Central African Republic
172	M 2	**Abbah**, Syria
141	B 17	**Abbasanta**, Italy
129	P 2	**Abbeville**, France
60	M 12	**Abbeville**, South Carolina, U.S.A.
62	J 8	**Abbeville**, Louisiana, U.S.A.
63	R 6	**Abbeville**, Alabama, U.S.A.
63	U 5	**Abbeville**, Georgia, U.S.A.
125	B 20	**Abbeyfeale**, Republic of Ireland
240	J 8	**Abbot Ice Shelf**, Antarctica ◇
127	P 14	**Abbotsbury**, United Kingdom
64	E 11	**Abbotsford**, Wisconsin, U.S.A.
83	G 22	**Abbotsford**, British Columbia, Canada
177	X 7	**Abbottabad**, Pakistan
175	V 15	**'Abd al Kūrī**, Yemen ≈
215	Y 9	**Abéché**, Chad
133	A 19	**Abele**, Belgium
236	D 2	**Abemama**, Kiribati ≈
214	L 13	**Abengourou**, Côte d'Ivoire
135	B 26	**Åbenrå**, Denmark
215	P 13	**Abeokuta**, Nigeria
126	M 8	**Aberaeron**, United Kingdom
127	O 10	**Aberdare**, United Kingdom
126	L 6	**Aberdaron**, United Kingdom
218	M 14	**Aberdeen**, Republic of South Africa
124	J 10	**Aberdeen**, United Kingdom
61	V 2	**Aberdeen**, Maryland, U.S.A.
61	Q 10	**Aberdeen**, North Carolina, U.S.A.
63	N 3	**Aberdeen**, Mississippi, U.S.A.
66	M 7	**Aberdeen**, South Dakota, U.S.A.
76	F 7	**Aberdeen**, Washington, U.S.A.
84	K 2	**Aberdeen Lake**, Nunavut, Canada ↳
126	M 7	**Aberdyfi**, United Kingdom
127	P 9	**Abergavenny**, United Kingdom
126	L 8	**Aberporth**, United Kingdom
126	L 6	**Abersoch**, United Kingdom
127	O 10	**Abertillery**, United Kingdom
126	M 7	**Aberystwyth**, United Kingdom
140	E 9	**Abetone**, Italy
155	T 3	**Abez'**, Russian Federation
175	N 11	**Abhā**, Saudi Arabia
176	H 5	**Abhar**, Iran
215	R 13	**Abia**, Nigeria □
214	K 14	**Abidjan**, Côte d'Ivoire
199	K 15	**Abiko**, Japan
70	M 6	**Abilene**, Texas, U.S.A.
127	T 10	**Abingdon**, United Kingdom
60	M 7	**Abingdon**, Virginia, U.S.A.
58	I 13	**Abington**, Pennsylvania, U.S.A.
75	P 8	**Abiquia Reservoir**, New Mexico, U.S.A. ↳
212	E 10	**Abnûb**, Egypt
182	G 7	**Abohar**, India
214	L 13	**Aboisso**, Côte d'Ivoire
213	E 20	**Aboke**, Sudan
215	O 13	**Abomey**, Benin
215	U 14	**Abong Mbang**, Cameroon
175	V 11	**Aboot**, Oman
197	C 19	**Aborlan**, Philippines
215	V 10	**Abou Déia**, Chad
175	T 5	**Abqaiq**, Saudi Arabia
196	F 7	**Abra**, Philippines ↳
110	I 5	**Abra Pampa**, Argentina
93	O 4	**Abraham's Bay**, The Bahamas
212	D 13	**'Abri**, Sudan
43	H 16	**Abrolhos Bank**, Atlantic Ocean ◇
150	H 10	**Abrud**, Romania
148	D 8	**Abruka**, Estonia ≈
140	I 13	**Abruzzo**, Italy □
56	K 6	**Absaroka Range**, Montana/Wyoming, U.S.A. ▲▲
139	R 6	**Abtenau**, Austria
172	I 3	**Abū aḍ Ḍuhūr**, Syria
173	R 7	**Abū al Jīr**, Iraq
175	W 6	**Abu al Jirab**, United Arab Emirates ≈
175	O 11	**Abū 'Arīsh**, Saudi Arabia
175	W 6	**Abu Dhabi**, United Arab Emirates ◆
212	D 8	**Abu Haggag**, Egypt
213	F 14	**Abu Hamed**, Sudan
173	O 5	**Abū Ḥardān**, Syria
173	O 5	**Abū Kamāl**, Syria
213	B 19	**Abu Matariq**, Sudan
176	K 13	**Abu Musa**, Iran ≈
211	T 8	**Abū Nujaym**, Libya
211	T 8	**Abū Qurīn**, Libya
174	M 6	**Abū Rubayq**, Saudi Arabia
213	C 17	**Abu Shanab**, Sudan
212	E 12	**Abu Simbel**, Egypt
173	T 9	**Abū Ṣukhayr**, Iraq
213	D 18	**Abu Zabad**, Sudan
212	F 9	**Abu Zenîma**, Egypt
215	R 12	**Abuja**, Nigeria □
196	G 5	**Abulog**, Philippines
216	L 5	**Abumombazi**, Democratic Republic of Congo
108	D 13	**Abunã**, Brazil
198	J 6	**Abuta**, Japan
213	C 17	**Abyad**, Sudan
213	C 20	**Abyei**, Sudan
108	N 11	**Açailândia**, Brazil
90	I 7	**Acajutla**, El Salvador
131	P 6	**Acalá de Henares**, Spain
89	Q 11	**Acambaro**, Mexico
88	M 10	**Acaponeta**, Mexico
89	Q 14	**Acapulco**, Mexico
108	K 10	**Acará**, Brazil
108	N 11	**Acaraú**, Brazil
108	F 9	**Acari Mountains**, Brazil ▲▲
104	M 3	**Acarigua**, Venezuela
150	H 8	**Acâş**, Romania
89	S 13	**Acatlan**, Mexico
89	S 12	**Acatzingo**, Mexico
61	W 5	**Accomac**, Virginia, U.S.A.
192	B 8	**Aceh**, Indonesia □
141	K 16	**Acerno**, Italy
105	N 4	**Achaguas**, Venezuela
181	E 16	**Achalpur**, India
171	U 6	**Achaseli**, Georgia
186	N 11	**Acheng**, China
139	N 6	**Achenkirch**, Austria
157	P 13	**Achikulak**, Russian Federation
125	A 16	**Achill Island**, Republic of Ireland ≈
153	N 12	**Achinsk**, Russian Federation
156	J 11	**Achuyevo**, Russian Federation
170	D 12	**Acipayam**, Turkey
141	K 22	**Acireale**, Italy
70	K 6	**Ackerly**, Texas, U.S.A.
93	N 4	**Acklins Island**, The Bahamas ≈
127	Z 6	**Acle**, United Kingdom
64	J 11	**Acme**, Michigan, U.S.A.
91	P 9	**Acoyapa**, Nicaragua
140	C 8	**Acqui Terme**, Italy
108	B 13	**Acre**, Brazil □
172	F 7	**Acre**, Israel
141	M 18	**Acri**, Italy
89	R 11	**Actopan**, Mexico
108	O 12	**Açu**, Brazil
215	T 15	**Acurenam**, Equatorial Guinea
175	N 7	**Ad Dafinah**, Saudi Arabia
173	U 9	**Ad Daghgharah**, Iraq
175	P 4	**Ad Dahnā'**, Saudi Arabia ✱
210	B 12	**Ad Dakhla**, Western Sahara
175	P 14	**Aḍ Ḍāli'**, Yemen
175	T 5	**Ad Dammām**, Saudi Arabia
175	N 11	**Ad Darb**, Saudi Arabia
175	P 6	**Ad Dawādimī**, Saudi Arabia
173	S 5	**Ad Dawr**, Iraq
173	Y 1	**Ad Dayr**, Iraq
175	R 6	**Ad Dilam**, Saudi Arabia
175	Q 6	**Ad Dir'īyah**, Saudi Arabia
173	U 9	**Ad Dīwānīyah**, Iraq
173	T 6	**Ad Dujayl**, Iraq
144	K 8	**Ada**, Serbia and Montenegro
69	O 11	**Ada**, Oklahoma, U.S.A.
78	F 14	**Adak**, Alaska, U.S.A.
78	F 14	**Adak Island**, Alaska, U.S.A. ≈
175	Y 7	**Adam**, Oman
215	U 13	**Adamaoua**, Cameroon □
147	H 23	**Adamas**, Greece
215	U 11	**Adamawa**, Nigeria □
215	U 12	**Adamawa Highlands**, Cameroon ▲▲
58	H 7	**Adams**, New York, U.S.A.
41	Y 15	**Adam's Rock**, Pitcairn Island ▶
41	Y 14	**Adamstown**, Pitcairn Island ◆
175	P 14	**Adan as Sughra**, Yemen
170	K 13	**Adana**, Turkey
159	W 9	**Adana Trough**, Mediterranean Sea ◇
198	K 13	**Adatara-san**, Japan ▲
231	S 7	**Adavale**, Queensland, Australia
77	M 19	**Adaven**, Nevada, U.S.A.
179	N 4	**Aday**, Kazakhstan
213	I 20	**Addis Ababa**, Ethiopia ◆
181	L 20	**Addu Atoll**, Maldives ≈
63	U 6	**Adel**, Georgia, U.S.A.
231	P 12	**Adelaide**, South Australia, Australia
240	H 5	**Adelaide Island**, Antarctica ≈
230	M 2	**Adelaide River**, Northern Territory, Australia
241	U 14	**Adélie Coast**, Antarctica ◇
241	U 14	**Adélie Land**, Antarctica ◇
193	X 13	**Agats**, Indonesia
181	B 22	**Agatti**, India ≈
78	B 12	**Agattu Island**, Alaska, U.S.A. ≈
78	B 12	**Agattu Strait**, Alaska, U.S.A. ≈
215	R 8	**Aderbissinat**, Niger
175	X 5	**Adh Dhayd**, United Arab Emirates
193	U 13	**Adi**, Indonesia ≈
213	I 18	**Ādī Ārk'ay**, Ethiopia
213	I 17	**Adi Keyih**, Eritrea
213	I 17	**Ādīgrat**, Ethiopia
170	D 11	**Adigüzel Baraji**, Turkey ↳
181	F 17	**Adilabad**, India
217	T 6	**Adilanga**, Uganda
171	S 10	**Adilcevaz**, Turkey
77	H 15	**Adin**, California, U.S.A.
133	A 18	**Adinkerke**, Belgium
58	J 8	**Adirondack Mountains**, New York, U.S.A. ▲▲
213	H 18	**Ādīs Zemen**, Ethiopia
171	N 12	**Adiyaman**, Turkey
150	L 10	**Adjud**, Romania
156	L 14	**Adler**, Russian Federation
138	G 7	**Adliswil**, Switzerland
76	G 6	**Admiralty Inlet**, Washington, U.S.A. ≈
79	X 11	**Admiralty Island**, Alaska, U.S.A. ≈
234	D 2	**Admiralty Islands**, Papua New Guinea ≈
215	Q 12	**Ado-Ekiti**, Nigeria
213	D 21	**Adok**, Sudan
193	P 15	**Adonara**, Indonesia ≈
181	E 19	**Adoni**, India
131	P 13	**Adra**, Spain
210	K 11	**Adrar**, Algeria
214	H 5	**Adrar**, Mauritania □
211	R 13	**Adrar Mariou**, Algeria ▲
210	B 14	**Adrar Souttouf**, Western Sahara ▲
215	Z 9	**Adré**, Chad
65	L 16	**Adrian**, Michigan, U.S.A.
70	I 2	**Adrian**, Texas, U.S.A.
140	I 9	**Adriatic Sea**, Europe ⌇
186	E 8	**Adun Qulu**, China
217	P 7	**Adusa**, Democratic Republic of Congo
149	H 14	**Adutiškis**, Lithuania
158	K 9	**Adventure Bank**, Mediterranean Sea ◇
213	I 17	**Ādwa**, Ethiopia
214	K 13	**Adzopé**, Côte d'Ivoire
155	S 4	**Adz'va**, Russian Federation ↳
155	S 4	**Adz'vavom**, Russian Federation
147	I 17	**Aegean Sea**, Greece ⌇
148	G 6	**Aegviidu**, Estonia
173	V 9	**'Afak**, Iraq
147	O 24	**Afantou**, Greece
213	J 18	**Afar**, Ethiopia □
213	J 17	**Afar Depression**, Ethiopia ◇
177	R 8	**Afghanistan**, Asia □
213	M 24	**Afgooye**, Somalia
175	O 6	**'Afif**, Saudi Arabia
215	R 13	**Afikpo**, Nigeria
210	M 7	**Aflou**, Algeria
213	K 25	**Afmadow**, Somalia
79	Q 11	**Afognak Island**, Alaska, U.S.A. ≈
108	M 13	**Afrânio**, Brazil
38	G 10	**Africana Seamount**, Indian Ocean ▲
172	J 2	**'Afrīn**, Syria
170	L 11	**Afşin**, Turkey
132	I 8	**Afsluitdijk**, Netherlands ◇
108	I 9	**Afuá**, Brazil
172	G 8	**'Afula**, Israel
170	F 10	**Afyon**, Turkey
215	R 7	**Agadez**, Niger
215	S 6	**Agadez**, Niger □
210	F 9	**Agadir**, Morocco
42	K 9	**Agadir Canyon**, Atlantic Ocean ◇
179	T 6	**Agadyr'**, Kazakhstan
183	V 13	**Agartala**, India
41	T 12	**Agassiz Fracture Zone**, Pacific Ocean ◇
147	M 21	**Agathonisi**, Greece ≈
215	R 8	**Agadez**, Niger
214	K 13	**Agboville**, Côte d'Ivoire
196	G 6	**Agbulu**, Philippines
171	W 9	**Ağcabädi**, Azerbaijan
171	W 9	**Ağdam**, Azerbaijan
171	W 8	**Ağdaş**, Azerbaijan
129	R 14	**Agde**, France
129	N 13	**Agen**, France
213	I 22	**Āgere Maryam**, Ethiopia
171	W 10	**Ağhband**, Azerbaijan
147	M 22	**Agia Marina**, Greece
147	K 17	**Agia Paraskevi**, Greece
153	R 14	**Aginskoye**, Russian Federation
147	M 21	**Agiokampos**, Greece
147	H 14	**Ágion Óros**, Greece □
147	I 16	**Agios Efstratios**, Greece ≈
147	H 21	**Agios Georgios**, Greece ≈
147	E 22	**Ágios Ilias**, Greece ▲
147	L 21	**Agios Kirykos**, Greece
147	D 16	**Agnantero**, Greece
76	E 13	**Agness**, Oregon, U.S.A.
214	K 13	**Agnibilékrou**, Côte d'Ivoire
196	E 9	**Agno**, Philippines
182	J 10	**Agra**, India
131	R 4	**Ágreda**, Spain
171	S 9	**Ağri**, Turkey
141	I 23	**Agrigento**, Italy
236	B 6	**Agrihan**, Northern Mariana Islands ≈
147	C 18	**Agrinio**, Greece
141	K 17	**Agropoli**, Italy
155	R 14	**Agryz**, Russian Federation
171	X 8	**Ağsu**, Azerbaijan
196	H 11	**Agta Point**, Philippines ▶
88	J 3	**Agua Prieta**, Mexico
111	I 16	**Aguada Cecilio**, Argentina
93	T 8	**Aguadilla**, Puerto Rico
91	V 14	**Aguadulce**, Panama
91	N 4	**Agúan**, Honduras ↳
89	O 10	**Aguascalientes**, Mexico
89	O 10	**Aguascalientes**, Mexico □
112	J 6	**Agudos**, Brazil
215	R 9	**Aguié**, Niger
236	B 8	**Aguijan**, Northern Mariana Islands ≈
74	I 12	**Aguila**, Arizona, U.S.A.
131	N 2	**Aguilar de Campóo**, Spain
90	I 7	**Aguilares**, El Salvador
131	R 12	**Águilas**, Spain
89	O 12	**Aguililla**, Mexico
43	N 18	**Agulhas Bank**, Atlantic Ocean/Indian Ocean ◇
43	O 19	**Agulhas Basin**, Atlantic Ocean ◇
38	G 10	**Agulhas Basin Plateau**, Indian Ocean ◇
112	M 6	**Agulhas Negras**, Brazil ▲
38	G 10	**Agulhas Plateau**, Indian Ocean ◇
43	M 19	**Agulhas Ridge**, Atlantic Ocean ▲▲
199	N 24	**Aguni-jima**, Japan ≈
197	M 20	**Agusan**, Philippines
197	G 16	**Agutaya**, Philippines
176	G 3	**Ahar**, Iran
233	G 18	**Ahaura**, New Zealand
137	C 14	**Ahaus**, Germany
232	I 5	**Ahipara**, New Zealand
232	I 5	**Ahipara Bay**, New Zealand ≈
232	J 12	**Ahititi**, New Zealand
79	O 13	**Ahklun Mountains**, Alaska, U.S.A. ▲▲
171	R 11	**Ahlat**, Turkey
137	E 15	**Ahlen**, Germany
181	C 14	**Ahmadabad**, India
181	C 17	**Ahmadnagar**, India
177	W 11	**Ahmadpur East**, Pakistan
213	J 21	**Ahmar Mountains**, Ethiopia ▲▲
88	J 7	**Ahome**, Mexico
176	G 9	**Āhū**, Iran
90	I 7	**Ahuachapán**, El Salvador
176	G 9	**Ahvāz**, Iran
181	C 16	**Ahwa**, India
175	R 14	**Aḩwar**, Yemen
191	N 17	**Ai Yin Young**, Vietnam
234	A 5	**Aiambak**, Papua New Guinea
137	J 23	**Aichach**, Germany
139	S 2	**Aigen**, Austria
170	I 15	**Aigialousa**, Cyprus
147	G 21	**Aigina**, Greece ≈
147	G 20	**Aigina**, Greece
147	E 14	**Aiginio**, Greece
147	D 19	**Aigio**, Greece
138	C 10	**Aigle**, Switzerland
113	F 15	**Aiguá**, Uruguay
198	I 13	**Aikawa**, Japan
188	K 11	**Ailao Shan**, China ▲▲
231	N 6	**Aileron**, Northern Territory, Australia
91	Z 13	**Ailigandi**, Panama
237	W 1	**Ailinginae**, Marshall Islands ≈
237	Y 3	**Ailinglaplap**, Marshall Islands ≈
237	Y 2	**Ailuk**, Marshall Islands ≈
110	H 8	**Aimogasta**, Argentina
211	P 6	**Aïn Beïda**, Algeria
214	I 2	**Aïn Ben Tili**, Mauritania
210	J 7	**Aïn Beni Mathar**, Morocco
210	M 5	**Aïn Defla**, Algeria
210	M 6	**Aïn Deheb**, Algeria
211	N 6	**Aïn el Hadjel**, Algeria
210	K 8	**Aïn Sefra**, Algeria
210	K 6	**Aïn Temouchent**, Algeria
148	F 9	**Ainaži**, Latvia
147	B 19	**Ainos**, Greece ▲
131	U 3	**Ainsa**, Spain
66	K 12	**Ainsworth**, Nebraska, U.S.A.
107	K 20	**Aiquile**, Bolivia
192	G 9	**Air**, Indonesia ≈
85	Q 1	**Air Force Island**, Nunavut, Canada ≈
192	D 10	**Airbangis**, Indonesia
128	M 14	**Aire-sur-l'Adour**, France
138	G 9	**Airolo**, Switzerland
193	R 14	**Airpanas**, Indonesia
111	F 20	**Aisén**, Chile □
131	T 9	**Aitana**, Spain ▲
234	B 3	**Aitape**, Papua New Guinea
67	R 5	**Aitkin**, Minnesota, U.S.A.
237	P 10	**Aitutaki**, Cook Islands ≈
150	I 10	**Aiud**, Romania
148	H 13	**Aivieskste**, Latvia ↳
237	U 1	**Aiwo**, Nauru
129	U 14	**Aix-en-Provence**, France
129	V 10	**Aix-les-Bains**, France
183	W 13	**Aizawl**, India
148	G 11	**Aizkraukle**, Latvia
148	C 11	**Aizpute**, Latvia
198	K 13	**Aizu-Wakamatsu**, Japan
129	X 15	**Ajaccio**, France
182	L 12	**Ajaigarh**, India
181	D 16	**Ajanta**, India
181	D 16	**Ajanta Range**, India ▲▲
211	W 8	**Ajdābiyā**, Libya
144	A 7	**Ajdovščina**, Slovenia
172	G 9	**'Ajlūn**, Jordan
175	X 5	**Ajman**, United Arab Emirates
180	D 12	**Ajmer**, India
182	H 5	**Ajnala**, India
74	I 14	**Ajo**, Arizona, U.S.A.
198	K 5	**Akabira**, Japan
210	L 11	**Akabli**, Algeria
213	I 20	**Āk'ak'ī**, Ethiopia
233	H 21	**Akaroa**, New Zealand
233	I 21	**Akaroa Harbour**, New Zealand ≈
173	N 6	**Akāshat**, Iraq
199	G 18	**Akashi**, Japan
179	W 3	**Akbalyk**, Kazakhstan
157	W 5	**Akbulak**, Russian Federation
179	T 7	**Akbulak**, Kazakhstan
171	N 11	**Akçadağ**, Turkey
171	O 13	**Akşakale**, Turkey
170	G 7	**Akşakoca**, Turkey
214	F 5	**Akchâr**, Mauritania ▲▲

Akchatau – Alimia

179 T 6 Akchatau, Kazakhstan
170 D 13 Akdağlar, Turkey
170 K 10 Akdağmadeni, Turkey
178 L 11 Akdepe, Turkmenistan
193 S 10 Akelamo, Indonesia
216 M 6 Aketi, Democratic Republic of Congo
171 S 7 Akhalk'alak'i, Georgia
178 L 13 Akhalskiy Velayat, Turkmenistan
171 S 7 Akhalts'ikhe, Georgia
170 C 10 Akhisar, Turkey
212 E 10 Akhmîm, Egypt
182 H 4 Akhnoor, India
157 Q 9 Akhtubinsk, Russian Federation
199 F 20 Aki, Japan
216 G 8 Akiéni, Gabon
85 O 9 Akimiski Island, Québec, Canada
170 K 14 Akinci Burnu, Turkey
198 J 10 Akita, Japan
214 F 5 Akjoujt, Mauritania
210 G 9 Akka, Morocco
198 M 5 Akkeshi, Japan
198 M 5 Akkeshi-wan, Japan
179 S 10 Akkol', Kazakhstan
179 S 3 Akkol', Kazakhstan
170 B 12 Akköy, Turkey
179 V 3 Akku, Kazakhstan
179 O 9 Akkum, Kazakhstan
170 M 8 Akkuş, Turkey
215 O 12 Aklampa, Benin
82 B 9 Aklavik, Northwest Territories, Canada
179 R 4 Akmola, Kazakhstan
148 H 12 Akniste, Latvia
199 F 18 Akō, Japan
213 F 21 Akobo, Sudan
181 E 14 Akodia, India
181 E 16 Akola, India
215 T 15 Akom II, Cameroon
213 H 16 Akordat, Eritrea
213 D 22 Akot, Sudan
181 E 16 Akot, India
85 S 5 Akpatok Island, Nunavut, Canada
184 H 5 Akqi, China
47 K 26 Akra Agios Ioannis, Greece
47 H 15 Akra Akrathos, Greece
47 H 14 Akra Arapis, Greece
47 C 19 Akra Araxos, Greece
47 H 15 Akra Drepano, Greece
47 I 19 Akra Kafireas, Greece
47 G 15 Akra Kassandras, Greece
59 R 10 Akra Krios, Mediterranean Sea
47 I 26 Akra Lithino, Greece
47 F 23 Akra Maleas, Greece
47 K 19 Akra Meston, Greece
47 G 15 Akra Paliouri, Greece
47 M 25 Akra Paraspori, Greece
47 L 26 Akra Sideros, Greece
47 K 17 Akra Sigri, Greece
47 G 25 Akra Spatha, Greece
47 E 24 Akra Tainaro, Greece
15 S 7 Akrérèb, Niger
5 N 17 Akron, Ohio, U.S.A.
32 L 3 Aksai Chin, India
46 N 7 Aksakovo, Bulgaria
70 I 11 Aksaray, Turkey
57 O 9 Aksay, Russian Federation
78 J 4 Aksay, Kazakhstan
70 G 11 Akşehir, Turkey
70 F 11 Aksehir Gölü, Turkey
70 G 13 Akseki, Turkey
79 S 3 Aksu, Kazakhstan
79 U 3 Aksu, Kazakhstan
34 I 5 Aksu, China
79 T 6 Aksu-Ayuly, Kazakhstan
79 Y 6 Aksuat, Kazakhstan
79 U 9 Aksuek, Kazakhstan
3 I 17 Āksum, Ethiopia
79 P 12 Aktash, Uzbekistan
8 H 9 Aktau, Kazakhstan
9 U 3 Aktogay, Kazakhstan
9 U 6 Aktogay, Kazakhstan
9 W 7 Aktogay, Kazakhstan
9 K 20 Aktsyabrski, Belarus
178 L 6 Aktyubinsk, Kazakhstan
178 L 5 Aktyubinsk, Kazakhstan
216 K 6 Akula, Democratic Republic of Congo
85 P 5 Akulivik, Québec, Canada
199 B 23 Akune, Japan
215 Q 13 Akure, Nigeria
134 C 10 Akureyri, Iceland
199 B 26 Akuseki-shima, Japan
78 K 13 Akutan Island, Alaska, U.S.A.
215 R 14 Akwa Ibom, Nigeria
215 R 12 Akwanga, Nigeria
179 Y 6 Akzhar, Kazakhstan
171 O 12 Akziyaret, Turkey
211 W 7 Al Abyār, Libya
211 Y 7 Al 'Adam, Libya
175 S 3 Al Aḩmadī, Kuwait
175 O 4 Al Ajfar, Saudi Arabia
175 N 9 Al 'Alayyah, Saudi Arabia
173 S 1 Al Amādīyah, Iraq
173 Y 9 Al 'Amārah, Iraq
172 F 13 Al 'Aqabah, Jordan
175 N 9 Al 'Aqīq, Saudi Arabia
210 B 12 Al Argoub, Western Sahara
175 Q 4 Al Arţāwīyah, Saudi Arabia
173 O 4 Al 'Ashārah, Syria
175 X 6 Al 'Ayn, United Arab Emirates
211 S 8 Al 'Azīzīyah, Libya
173 U 8 Al 'Azīzīyah, Iraq
173 P 2 Al Ba'āj, Iraq
172 J 2 Al Bāb, Syria
173 P 3 Al Bādī, Iraq
175 Q 8 Al Badī', Saudi Arabia
175 N 9 Al Bāḩah, Saudi Arabia
172 H 3 Al Bahlūlīyah, Syria
211 Y 7 Al Bardī, Libya
173 Z 11 Al Başrah, Iraq
211 W 7 Al Bayḑā', Libya
175 Q 13 Al Bayḑā', Yemen
174 M 7 Al Bi'ār, Saudi Arabia
174 K 3 Al Bi'r, Saudi Arabia
175 N 11 Al Birk, Saudi Arabia
175 O 5 Al Bukayrīyah, Saudi Arabia
175 X 6 Al Buraymī, Oman
173 N 4 Al Buşayrah, Syria
173 W 12 Al Buşayyah, Iraq
173 S 7 Al Fallūjah, Iraq
175 S 13 Al Fardah, Yemen
175 S 3 Al Farwānīyah, Kuwait
173 S 4 Al Fatḩah, Iraq
173 Z 12 Al Fāw, Iraq
175 O 13 Al Fāzih, Yemen
211 U 10 Al Fuqahā', Libya
173 U 10 Al Ghammās, Iraq
175 P 5 Al Ghāţ, Saudi Arabia
175 V 12 Al Ghayḑah, Yemen
173 S 7 Al Ḩabbānīyah, Iraq
173 Q 6 Al Ḩadīthah, Iraq
173 R 3 Al Ḩaḑr, Iraq
210 E 10 Al Haggounia, Western Sahara
175 X 6 Al Hajar'al Gharbī, Oman
175 R 12 Al Ḩajr, Yemen
173 Y 9 Al Ḩalfāyah, Iraq
174 L 1 Al Hamād, Saudi Arabia
211 Q 9 Al Ḩamādah al Ḩamrā', Libya
172 H 4 Al Ḩamīdīyah, Syria
174 M 6 Al Ḩanākīyah, Saudi Arabia
175 O 14 Al Ḩanīsh al Kabīr, Yemen
173 W 14 Al Haniyah, Iraq
175 O 11 Al Haqū, Saudi Arabia
211 U 10 Al Haruj al Aswad, Libya
172 G 11 Al Ḩasā, Jordan
173 O 2 Al Ḩasakah, Syria
173 U 9 Al Hāshimīyah, Iraq
173 O 2 Al Hawl, Syria
175 R 14 Al Ḩawrā, Yemen
173 W 9 Al Ḩayy, Iraq
175 P 12 Al Ḩazm al-Jawf, Yemen
175 V 9 Al Ḩibāk, Saudi Arabia
172 H 7 Al Ḩijānah, Syria
173 T 8 Al Ḩillah, Iraq
175 R 7 Al Ḩillah, Saudi Arabia
173 T 8 Al Hindīyah, Iraq
172 L 2 Al Hishah, Syria
172 G 8 Al Ḩişn, Jordan
210 J 6 Al Hoceima, Morocco
175 O 13 Al Ḩudaydah, Yemen
175 T 5 Al Hufūf, Saudi Arabia
175 Q 14 Al Ḩumayshah, Yemen
175 X 8 Al Huwatsah, Oman
175 S 13 Al Ḩuwaymi, Yemen
174 L 1 Al 'Īsāwīyah, Saudi Arabia
211 W 7 Al Jabal al Akhḑar, Libya
172 H 12 Al Jafr, Jordan
211 Y 8 Al Jaghbūb, Libya
175 R 2 Al Jahrah, Kuwait
175 U 5 Al Jamalīyah, Qatar
211 Y 12 Al Jawf, Libya
174 M 2 Al Jawf, Saudi Arabia
173 N 2 Al Jazīrah, Syria
175 N 4 Al Jithāmīyah, Saudi Arabia
175 T 4 Al Jubayl, Saudi Arabia
174 M 8 Al Jumūm, Saudi Arabia
175 Z 9 Al Kalbān, Oman
172 G 11 Al Karak, Jordan
212 F 11 Al Karnak, Egypt
175 Y 6 Al Khābūrah, Oman
175 Z 9 Al Khalīf, Oman
173 U 6 Al Khāliş, Iraq
175 P 9 Al Khamāsīn, Saudi Arabia
175 Y 5 Al Khaşab, Oman
175 O 14 Al Khawkhah, Yemen
173 V 10 Al Khiḑr, Iraq
211 Y 12 Al Khufrah, Libya
211 T 7 Al Khums, Libya
173 T 9 Al Kifl, Iraq
175 U 5 Al Kir'ānah, Qatar
173 T 9 Al Kūfah, Iraq
173 X 9 Al Kumayt, Iraq
173 W 8 Al Kūt, Iraq
175 N 2 Al Labbah, Saudi Arabia
172 H 3 Al Lādhiqīyah, Syria
174 M 9 Al Līth, Saudi Arabia
173 R 11 Al Ma'ānīyah, Iraq
172 H 8 Al Mafraq, Jordan
210 F 10 Al Mahbas, Western Sahara
172 K 2 Al Mahdum, Syria
173 T 7 Al Maḩmūdīyah, Iraq
175 U 11 Al Mahrah, Yemen
175 O 12 Al Maḩwīt, Yemen
175 Q 5 Al Majma'ah, Saudi Arabia
173 Q 1 Al Mālikīyah, Syria
175 T 5 Al Manāmah, Bahrain
173 Z 11 Al Ma'qil, Iraq
175 O 13 Al Marāwi'ah, Yemen
211 W 7 Al Marj, Libya
175 Y 6 Al Masana'a, Oman
173 N 4 Al Mayādīn, Syria
172 G 10 Al Mazra'ah, Jordan
175 V 6 Al Mirfa, United Arab Emirates
175 T 5 Al Mubarrez, Saudi Arabia
172 G 14 Al Mudawwarah, Jordan
175 T 5 Al Muharraq, Bahrain
175 T 13 Al Mukallā, Yemen
211 X 7 Al Mukhaylī, Libya
173 U 6 Al Muqdādīyah, Iraq
174 L 6 Al Musayjīd, Saudi Arabia
173 W 9 Al Muwaffaqīyah, Iraq
175 N 7 Al Muwayh, Saudi Arabia
174 J 3 Al Muwayliḩ, Saudi Arabia
173 Y 11 Al Muzayri'ah, Iraq
172 H 4 Al Qadmūs, Syria
173 P 5 Al Qā'im, Iraq
175 O 6 Al Qā'īyah, Saudi Arabia
174 L 3 Al Qalībah, Saudi Arabia
173 O 1 Al Qāmishlī, Syria
172 H 3 Al Qardābah, Syria
172 I 5 Al Qaryatayn, Syria
175 S 12 Al Qaţn, Yemen
172 H 10 Al Qaţrānah, Jordan
211 T 12 Al Qaţrūn, Libya
175 Q 3 Al Qayşūmah, Saudi Arabia
174 M 10 Al Qunfidhah, Saudi Arabia
173 Y 11 Al Qurnah, Iraq
173 W 11 Al Qusayr, Iraq
175 Q 6 Al Quwayi', Saudi Arabia
172 F 13 Al Quwayrah, Jordan
175 S 13 Al Quzah, Yemen
175 W 6 Al Samha, United Arab Emirates
175 S 5 Al 'Uḑaylīyah, Saudi Arabia
174 L 4 Al 'Ulā, Saudi Arabia
211 V 9 Al 'Uqaylah, Libya
211 R 12 Al 'Uwaynāt, Libya
211 Z 13 Al 'Uwaynāt, Libya
175 O 2 Al 'Uwayqīlah, Saudi Arabia
174 M 6 Al 'Uyūn, Saudi Arabia
175 O 4 Al 'Uyūn, Saudi Arabia
173 Y 10 Al 'Uzayr, Iraq
175 S 3 Al Wafrah, Kuwait
174 J 4 Al Wajh, Saudi Arabia
175 S 4 Al Wannān, Saudi Arabia
175 R 3 Al Wari'ah, Saudi Arabia
175 Y 6 Al Wāsiţ, Oman
211 T 12 Al Wīgh, Libya
175 R 6 Al Yamāmah, Saudi Arabia
179 S 11 Ala-Buka, Kyrgyzstan
170 G 11 Ala Dağl, Turkey
63 O 4 Alabama, U.S.A.
63 O 5 Alabama, Alabama, U.S.A.
196 H 12 Alabat, Philippines
170 J 9 Alaca, Turkey
170 K 7 Alaşşam, Turkey
63 V 8 Alachua, Florida, U.S.A.
157 O 14 Alagir, Russian Federation
108 O 13 Alagoas, Brazil
109 N 14 Alagoinhas, Brazil
131 S 4 Alagón, Spain
197 L 22 Alah, Philippines
172 H 3 Alājah, Syria
91 P 12 Alajuela, Costa Rica
236 B 7 Alamagan, Northern Mariana Islands
175 P 5 Al'Amār, Saudi Arabia
213 I 18 Ālamat'ā, Ethiopia
91 Q 7 Alamicamba, Nicaragua
196 E 9 Alaminos, Philippines
77 M 20 Alamo, Nevada, U.S.A.
74 H 11 Alamo Lake, Arizona, U.S.A.
75 Q 13 Alamogordo, New Mexico, U.S.A.
75 Q 7 Alamosa, Colorado, U.S.A.
135 I 19 Åland, Finland
135 I 19 Ålands Hav, Finland
170 G 13 Alanya, Turkey
170 C 11 Alaşehir, Turkey
79 P 6 Alaska, U.S.A.
79 P 9 Alaska Range, Alaska, U.S.A.
78 L 13 Alaskan Peninsula, Alaska, U.S.A.
171 Z 8 Älät, Azerbaijan
157 Q 2 Alatyr', Russian Federation
106 B 10 Alausí, Ecuador
171 T 8 Alaverdi, Armenia
135 K 16 Alavus, Finland
153 V 7 Alazeya, Russian Federation
131 R 9 Albacete, Spain
145 K 17 Albania, Europe
230 H 12 Albany, Western Australia, Australia
232 K 8 Albany, New Zealand
58 K 9 Albany, New York, U.S.A.
60 H 7 Albany, Kentucky, U.S.A.
63 S 6 Albany, Georgia, U.S.A.
71 N 6 Albany, Texas, U.S.A.
76 G 10 Albany, Oregon, U.S.A.
84 L 10 Albany, Ontario, Canada
132 G 13 Albasserdam, Netherlands
231 R 1 Albatross Bay, Queensland, Australia
232 K 10 Albatross Point, New Zealand
196 K 13 Albay Gulf, Philippines
61 P 10 Albemarle, North Carolina, U.S.A.
61 V 8 Albemarle Sound, North Carolina, U.S.A.
140 B 9 Albenga, Italy
109 G 20 Alberdi, Paraguay
231 O 8 Alberga, South Australia, Australia
130 H 5 Albergaria-a-Velha, Portugal
129 Q 2 Albert, France
67 S 10 Albert Lea, Minnesota, U.S.A.
217 R 6 Albert Nile, Uganda
61 T 7 Alberta, Virginia, U.S.A.
83 I 16 Alberta, Canada
143 J 23 Albertirsa, Hungary
129 V 10 Albertville, France
63 R 2 Albertville, Alabama, U.S.A.
129 Q 13 Albi, France
58 A 10 Albion, Pennsylvania, U.S.A.
65 K 15 Albion, Michigan, U.S.A.
67 N 13 Albion, Nebraska, U.S.A.
158 B 9 Alboran Ridge, Mediterranean Sea
131 O 14 Alboran Sea, Africa/Spain
135 C 23 Ålborg, Denmark
130 H 12 Albufeira, Portugal
138 I 9 Albula Alpen, Switzerland
75 Q 10 Albuquerque, New Mexico, U.S.A.
130 J 8 Alburquerque, Spain
231 T 12 Albury, New South Wales, Australia
130 H 10 Alcácer do Sal, Portugal
196 H 6 Alcala, Philippines
130 L 13 Alcalá de los Gazules, Spain
131 O 12 Alcalá la Real, Spain
141 H 22 Alcamo, Italy
131 T 5 Alcañiz, Spain
130 J 8 Alcántara, Spain
131 Q 10 Alcaraz, Spain
131 N 12 Alcaudete, Spain
131 P 8 Alcázar de San Juan, Spain
127 S 8 Alcester, United Kingdom
151 Y 6 Alchevs'k, Ukraine
131 T 6 Alcorisa, Spain
113 B 15 Alcorta, Argentina
131 U 7 Alcossebre, Spain
73 W 12 Alcova, Wyoming, U.S.A.
131 T 9 Alcoy, Spain
131 Y 7 Alcúdia, Spain
38 K 5 Aldabra Islands, Seychelles
89 S 9 Aldama, Mexico
153 U 11 Aldan, Russian Federation
153 T 12 Aldan, Russian Federation
127 Z 8 Aldeburgh, United Kingdom
58 I 7 Alder Creek, New York, U.S.A.
125 J 25 Alderney, United Kingdom
127 U 11 Aldershot, United Kingdom
65 D 17 Aledo, Illinois, U.S.A.
214 F 7 Aleg, Mauritania
42 O 11 Alegranza, Canary Islands
112 O 5 Alegre, Brazil
112 E 12 Alegrete, Brazil
154 H 10 Alekhovshchina, Russian Federation
154 J 14 Aleksandrov, Russian Federation
157 R 7 Aleksandrov Gay, Russian Federation
146 I 7 Aleksandrovo, Bulgaria
155 T 11 Aleksandrovsk, Russian Federation
153 X 13 Aleksandrovsk-Sakhalinskiy, Russian Federation
156 L 6 Alekseyevka, Russian Federation
157 N 7 Alekseyevskaya, Russian Federation
157 S 1 Alekseyevskoye, Russian Federation
156 K 2 Aleksin, Russian Federation
144 N 13 Aleksinac, Serbia and Montenegro
112 N 6 Além Paraíba, Brazil
129 N 5 Alençon, France
108 H 10 Alenquer, Brazil
78 D 8 Alenuihaha Channel, Hawaii, U.S.A.
172 J 2 Aleppo, Syria
129 Z 15 Aléria, France
81 P 1 Alert, Nunavut, Canada
107 G 15 Alerta, Peru
129 S 13 Alès, France
150 G 8 Aleşd, Romania
140 C 8 Alessandria, Italy
135 B 16 Ålesund, Norway
41 P 2 Aleutian Basin, Pacific Ocean
78 E 13 Aleutian Islands, Alaska, U.S.A.
79 N 12 Aleutian Range, Alaska, U.S.A.
41 O 2 Aleutian Trench, Pacific Ocean
79 W 11 Alexander Archipelago, Alaska, U.S.A.
218 I 12 Alexander Bay, Republic of South Africa
63 Q 4 Alexander City, Alabama, U.S.A.
240 I 6 Alexander Island, Antarctica
233 D 23 Alexandra, New Zealand
212 D 7 Alexandria, Egypt
150 J 13 Alexandria, Romania
61 U 3 Alexandria, Virginia, U.S.A.
62 I 6 Alexandria, Louisiana, U.S.A.
67 P 6 Alexandria, Minnesota, U.S.A.
86 J 10 Alexandria, Ontario, Canada
58 H 6 Alexandria Bay, New York, U.S.A.
146 K 13 Alexandroupoli, Greece
172 G 6 'Aley, Lebanon
152 L 13 Aleysk, Russian Federation
146 M 6 Alfatar, Bulgaria
112 L 5 Alfenas, Brazil
140 G 9 Alfonsine, Italy
127 W 4 Alford, United Kingdom
127 S 5 Alfreton, United Kingdom
178 I 4 Algabas, Kazakhstan
130 G 12 Algarve, Portugal
130 L 14 Algeciras, Spain
213 I 15 Algena, Eritrea
210 K 11 Algeria, Africa
158 D 8 Algerian Basin, Mediterranean Sea
158 I 8 Algerian–Tyrrhenian Trough, Mediterranean Sea
141 A 16 Alghero, Italy
210 M 5 Algiers, Algeria
131 T 9 Alginet, Spain
130 L 13 Algodonales, Spain
64 H 11 Algoma, Wisconsin, U.S.A.
67 R 11 Algona, Iowa, U.S.A.
173 V 8 'Alī, Iraq
173 X 8 'Alī al Gharbī, Iraq
171 Y 9 Äli Bayramli, Azerbaijan
177 V 7 'Alī Kheyl, Afghanistan
213 K 19 Ali Sabieh, Djibouti
170 B 10 Aliağa, Turkey
147 F 19 Aliartos, Greece
144 L 10 Alibunar, Serbia and Montenegro
131 T 10 Alicante, Spain
71 P 13 Alice, Texas, U.S.A.
92 J 10 Alice Shoal, Jamaica
231 O 6 Alice Springs, Northern Territory, Australia
92 J 2 Alice Town, The Bahamas
63 O 4 Aliceville, Alabama, U.S.A.
179 U 14 Alichur, Tajikistan
182 J 9 Aligarh, India
186 I 6 Alihe, China
147 N 24 Alimia, Greece

Country · Internal administrative region: State/Province/Territory/Dependent territory · Capital city · Mountain range/Undersea ridge · Mountain peak/Volcano/Seamount · Geographic feature · Headland/Point/Cape/Peninsula · Desert · Island/Island group · Antarctic base · Ocean · Sea · Bay/Gulf/Channel/Strait · Lake · Salt pan/Dry/Intermittent lake · River

105 W 8 **Alimimuni Peak**, Suriname ▲
197 H 22 **Alimpaya Point**, Philippines ▶
177 W 11 **Alipur**, Pakistan
183 T 10 **Alipur Duar**, India
130 J 8 **Aliseda**, Spain
147 H 19 **Aliveri**, Greece
130 K 9 **Aljucén**, Spain
77 M 19 **Alkali Flat**, Nevada, U.S.A. ⅃
132 H 9 **Alkmaar**, Netherlands
183 N 11 **Allahabad**, India
79 Q 5 **Allakaket**, Alaska, U.S.A.
153 V 10 **Allakh-Yun'**, Russian Federation
219 O 9 **Alldays**, Republic of South Africa
58 E 10 **Allegeny Plateau**, New York, U.S.A. ◇
58 C 14 **Allegheny Mountains**, Pennsylvania/West Virginia, U.S.A. ▲
197 K 14 **Allen**, Philippines
61 O 14 **Allendale**, South Carolina, U.S.A.
89 P 5 **Allende**, Mexico
89 Q 7 **Allende**, Mexico
58 H 13 **Allentown**, Pennsylvania, U.S.A.
181 D 23 **Alleppey**, India
138 K 7 **Allgäuer Alpen**, Austria/Germany ▲
66 H 12 **Alliance**, Nebraska, U.S.A.
181 E 23 **Allinagaram**, India
63 V 6 **Alma**, Georgia, U.S.A.
64 K 13 **Alma**, Michigan, U.S.A.
66 L 15 **Alma**, Nebraska, U.S.A.
86 M 6 **Alma**, Québec, Canada
131 U 4 **Almacelles**, Spain
130 M 9 **Almadén**, Spain
131 O 9 **Almagro**, Spain
179 S 12 **Almalyk**, Uzbekistan
131 S 9 **Almansa**, Spain
130 M 7 **Almanzor**, Spain ▲
109 K 14 **Almas**, Brazil
179 V 8 **Almaty**, Kazakhstan ▣
179 V 10 **Almaty**, Kazakhstan
131 Q 4 **Almazán**, Spain
108 I 10 **Almeirim**, Brazil
130 H 8 **Almeirim**, Portugal
132 N 11 **Almelo**, Netherlands
131 Q 4 **Almenar de Soria**, Spain
130 K 9 **Almendralejo**, Spain
132 I 11 **Almere**, Netherlands
131 Q 13 **Almería**, Spain
157 T 2 **Al'met'yevsk**, Russian Federation
135 F 24 **Älmhult**, Sweden
91 S 13 **Almirante**, Panama
130 H 11 **Almodôvar**, Portugal
130 J 12 **Almonte**, Spain
182 L 7 **Almora**, India
131 O 13 **Almuñécar**, Spain
125 J 14 **Alnwick**, United Kingdom
236 J 10 **Alofi**, Niue ♣
236 H 8 **Alofi**, Wallis and Futuna Islands ♣
148 G 9 **Aloja**, Latvia
183 X 8 **Along**, India
186 G 5 **Alongshan**, China
147 G 17 **Alonnisos**, Greece ⇄
193 Q 15 **Alor**, Indonesia ⇄
194 A 5 **Alor Setar**, Malaysia
234 G 7 **Alotau**, Papua New Guinea
130 I 8 **Alpalhao**, Portugal
64 L 11 **Alpena**, Michigan, U.S.A.
231 T 7 **Alpha**, Queensland, Australia
45 R 7 **Alpha Ridge**, Arctic Ocean ▲
65 E 17 **Alphe**, Illinois, U.S.A.
132 G 12 **Alphen**, Netherlands
70 H 9 **Alpine**, Texas, U.S.A.
74 M 12 **Alpine**, Arizona, U.S.A.
140 A 6 **Alps**, Europe ▲
231 P 5 **Alpurrurulam**, Northern Territory, Australia
129 W 5 **Alsace**, France ▣
131 Q 2 **Alsasua**, Spain
137 G 17 **Alsfeld**, Germany
148 C 11 **Alsunga**, Latvia

134 K 7 **Alta**, Norway
110 J 10 **Alta Gracia**, Argentina
91 O 10 **Alta Gracia**, Nicaragua
134 K 7 **Altaelva**, Norway ⅃
105 O 3 **Altagracia de Orituco**, Venezuela
184 L 2 **Altai Mountains**, Asia ▲
63 V 5 **Altamaha**, Georgia, U.S.A. ⅃
108 I 10 **Altamira**, Brazil
110 G 7 **Altamira**, Chile
91 P 11 **Altamira**, Costa Rica
141 M 16 **Altamura**, Italy
186 E 8 **Altan Emel**, China
61 Q 7 **Altavista**, Virginia, U.S.A.
184 L 3 **Altay**, China
185 N 4 **Altay**, Mongolia
138 G 8 **Altdorf**, Switzerland
131 U 10 **Altea**, Spain
137 N 17 **Altenberg**, Germany
137 L 17 **Altenburg**, Germany
130 I 8 **Alter do Chão**, Portugal
134 I 8 **Altevatnet**, Norway ⅃
139 Q 4 **Altheim**, Austria
173 T 3 **Altin Köprü**, Iraq
107 H 20 **Altiplano**, Bolivia ◇
71 T 7 **Alto**, Texas, U.S.A.
109 H 16 **Alto Araguaia**, Brazil
218 J 3 **Alto Chicapa**, Angola
90 F 4 **Alto Cuchumatanes**, Guatemala ▲
130 I 6 **Alto da Torre**, Portugal ▲
104 I 4 **Alto de Tamar**, Colombia ▲
109 H 16 **Alto Garças**, Brazil
219 T 6 **Alto Molócuè**, Mozambique
104 G 5 **Alto Musinga**, Colombia ▲
108 K 13 **Alto Parnaíba**, Brazil
107 G 15 **Alto Purús**, Peru ⅃
111 G 19 **Alto Rio Senguerr**, Argentina
127 U 12 **Alton**, United Kingdom
69 W 8 **Alton**, Missouri, U.S.A.
58 D 13 **Altoona**, Pennsylvania, U.S.A.
137 L 24 **Altötting**, Germany
127 Q 4 **Altrincham**, United Kingdom
184 K 7 **Altun Shan**, China ▲
77 I 15 **Alturas**, California, U.S.A.
68 K 11 **Altus**, Oklahoma, U.S.A.
151 S 2 **Altynivka**, Ukraine
148 I 10 **Alūksne**, Latvia
151 U 13 **Alupka**, Ukraine
181 E 19 **Alur**, India
151 U 12 **Alushta**, Ukraine
68 L 8 **Alva**, Oklahoma, U.S.A.
71 Q 6 **Alvarado**, Texas, U.S.A.
89 T 12 **Alvarado**, Mexico
108 D 11 **Alvarães**, Brazil
135 D 17 **Alvdal**, Norway
135 E 18 **Alvdalen**, Sweden ⅃
135 F 18 **Älvdalen**, Sweden
135 A 18 **Alvik**, Norway
71 T 11 **Alvin**, Texas, U.S.A.
135 H 19 **Alvkarleby**, Sweden
134 J 12 **Älvsbyn**, Sweden
182 I 9 **Alwar**, India
149 F 16 **Alytus**, Lithuania
73 Z 8 **Alzada**, Montana, U.S.A.
137 E 20 **Alzey**, Germany
215 Y 9 **Am-Dam**, Chad
215 Y 10 **Am Timan**, Chad
215 Z 8 **Am-Zoer**, Chad
213 D 22 **Amadi**, Sudan
173 S 1 **Amādīyah**, Iraq
85 Q 3 **Amadjuak Lake**, Nunavut, Canada ⅃
193 S 12 **Amahai**, Indonesia
199 A 23 **Amakusa-nada**, Japan ≈
199 B 23 **Amakusa-Shimo-shima**, Japan ⇄
175 X 10 **Amal**, Oman
135 E 21 **Åmål**, Sweden
141 K 16 **Amalfi**, Italy
147 C 20 **Amaliada**, Greece
193 X 13 **Amamapare**, Indonesia
109 H 19 **Amambaí**, Brazil
199 N 21 **Amami-Ō-shima**, Japan ⇄
199 N 23 **Amami shotō**, Japan ⇄

217 P 8 **Amamula**, Democratic Republic of Congo
234 A 3 **Amanab**, Papua New Guinea
140 I 12 **Amandola**, Italy
179 P 5 **Amangel'dy**, Kazakhstan
141 M 19 **Amantea**, Italy
219 P 13 **Amanzimtoti**, Republic of South Africa
108 I 8 **Amapá**, Brazil
108 I 9 **Amapá**, Brazil ▣
190 D 11 **Amarapura**, Myanmar
77 L 21 **Amargosa Valley**, Nevada, U.S.A.
70 J 2 **Amarillo**, Texas, U.S.A.
181 H 15 **Amarkantak**, India
170 H 7 **Amasra**, Turkey
170 K 8 **Amasya**, Turkey
108 C 11 **Amatauá**, Brazil
133 I 20 **Amay**, Belgium
108 F 11 **Amazon**, Brazil/Peru ⅃
108 C 11 **Amazon Basin**, Brazil ◇
42 F 13 **Amazon Cone**, Atlantic Ocean ▲
104 L 11 **Amazonas**, Colombia ▣
105 O 8 **Amazonas**, Venezuela ▣
106 C 11 **Amazonas**, Peru ▣
108 D 11 **Amazonas**, Brazil ▣
182 I 7 **Ambala**, India
219 X 9 **Ambalavao**, Madagascar
219 Z 5 **Ambanja**, Madagascar
153 W 7 **Ambarchik**, Russian Federation
154 H 5 **Ambarnyy**, Russian Federation
183 V 12 **Ambāsa**, India
106 B 9 **Ambato**, Ecuador
219 X 6 **Ambato Boeny**, Madagascar
219 X 7 **Ambatomainty**, Madagascar
193 R 12 **Ambelau**, Indonesia ⇄
137 K 21 **Amberg**, Germany
64 G 10 **Amberg**, Wisconsin, U.S.A.
90 L 1 **Ambergris Cay**, Belize ⇄
129 U 9 **Ambérieu-en-Bugey**, France
233 H 19 **Amberley**, New Zealand
86 C 12 **Amberley**, Ontario, Canada
181 H 14 **Ambikapur**, India
196 F 12 **Ambil**, Philippines ⇄
219 Z 5 **Ambilobe**, Madagascar
79 O 5 **Ambler**, Alaska, U.S.A.
107 D 15 **Ambo**, Peru
219 X 10 **Amboasary**, Madagascar
219 X 9 **Ambohimahasoa**, Madagascar
219 W 6 **Ambohipaky**, Madagascar
193 S 12 **Ambon**, Indonesia
193 S 12 **Ambon**, Indonesia ▣
219 X 8 **Ambositra**, Madagascar
219 X 11 **Ambovombe**, Madagascar
77 M 24 **Amboy**, California, U.S.A.
218 F 2 **Ambriz**, Angola
235 R 10 **Ambrym**, Vanuatu ⇄
78 D 13 **Amchitka Island**, Alaska, U.S.A. ⇄
78 E 14 **Amchitka Islands**, Alaska, U.S.A. ⇄
78 D 14 **Amchitka Pass**, Alaska, U.S.A. ≈
155 S 1 **Amderma**, Russian Federation
184 L 9 **Amdo**, China
89 N 11 **Ameca**, Mexico
132 K 5 **Ameland**, Netherlands ⇄
61 S 6 **Amelia Court House**, Virginia, U.S.A.
73 O 12 **American Falls**, Idaho, U.S.A.
73 O 12 **American Falls Reservoir**, Idaho, U.S.A. ⅃
236 L 9 **American Samoa**, U.S.A. ▣
43 J 22 **American–Antarctic Ridge**, Atlantic Ocean ▲
63 S 5 **Americus**, Georgia, U.S.A.
132 J 12 **Amersfoort**, Netherlands
127 V 10 **Amersham**, United Kingdom
241 W 6 **Amery Ice Shelf**, Antarctica ◇

127 S 12 **Amesbury**, United Kingdom
147 C 18 **Amfilochia**, Greece
147 E 19 **Amfissa**, Greece
153 T 11 **Amga**, Russian Federation ⅃
153 U 11 **Amga**, Russian Federation
153 W 15 **Amgu**, Russian Federation
153 Z 6 **Amguema**, Russian Federation
211 O 11 **Amguid**, Algeria
153 V 13 **Amgun**, Russian Federation
213 I 19 **Amhara**, Ethiopia ▣
58 M 9 **Amherst**, Massachusetts, U.S.A.
87 U 9 **Amherst**, Nova Scotia, Canada
129 Q 2 **Amiens**, France
181 A 22 **Amindivi Islands**, India ⇄
181 B 22 **Amini**, India ⇄
213 K 23 **Amino**, Ethiopia
218 J 10 **Aminuis**, Namibia
38 K 5 **Amirante Islands**, Seychelles ⇄
38 K 5 **Amirante Trench**, Indian Ocean ◇
83 N 16 **Amisk Lake**, Saskatchewan, Canada ⅃
62 L 7 **Amite**, Louisiana, U.S.A.
78 G 14 **Amlia Island**, Alaska, U.S.A. ⇄
126 L 4 **Amlwch**, United Kingdom
172 H 9 **Ammān**, Jordan ♣
68 M 9 **Ammanford**, United Kingdom
134 H 12 **Ammarnäs**, Sweden
45 N 13 **Ammassalik**, Greenland
137 J 25 **Ammersee**, Germany ⅃
170 I 15 **Ammóchostos**, Cyprus
191 L 17 **Amnat Charoen**, Thailand
181 C 15 **Amod**, India
176 J 5 **Amol**, Iran
131 Q 1 **Amorebieta**, Spain
147 K 23 **Amorgos**, Greece ⇄
63 N 2 **Amory**, Mississippi, U.S.A.
86 G 6 **Amos**, Québec, Canada
135 B 20 **Åmot**, Norway
214 J 8 **Amourj**, Mauritania
90 L 8 **Ampala**, Honduras
219 Z 6 **Ampanavoana**, Madagascar
219 Z 5 **Ampanefena**, Madagascar
219 W 10 **Ampanihy**, Madagascar
181 H 25 **Amparai**, Sri Lanka
219 Z 8 **Ampasimanolotra**, Madagascar
42 K 9 **Ampere Seamount**, Atlantic Ocean ▲
193 O 11 **Ampoa**, Indonesia
131 U 6 **Amposta**, Spain
127 V 8 **Ampthill**, United Kingdom
87 R 6 **Amqui**, Québec, Canada
175 P 12 **Amrân**, Yemen
181 E 16 **Amravati**, India
182 H 5 **Amritsar**, India
136 E 7 **Amrum**, Germany ⇄
132 H 11 **Amstelveen**, Netherlands
132 H 11 **Amsterdam**, Netherlands ♣
39 N 10 **Amsterdam Fracture Zone**, Indian Ocean ◇
39 O 10 **Amsterdam Island**, Indian Ocean ⇄
139 U 4 **Amstetten**, Austria
179 O 13 **Amudar'ya**, Turkmenistan ⅃
78 H 15 **Amukta Pass**, Alaska, U.S.A. ≈
45 P 8 **Amund Ringnes Island**, Canada ⇄
81 O 3 **Amund Ringnes Island**, Nunavut, Canada ⇄
41 S 15 **Amundsen Abyssal Plain**, Pacific Ocean ◇
241 P 9 **Amundsen Coast**, Antarctica ◇
39 R 3 **Amundsen Gulf**, Arctic Ocean ⇄
82 D 7 **Amundsen Gulf**, Northwest Territories, Canada ⇄
241 Q 8 **Amundsen-Scott**, Antarctica

240 I 9 **Amundsen Sea**, Antarctica ⌐
192 L 12 **Amuntai**, Indonesia
153 U 14 **Amur**, Russian Federation
193 Q 10 **Amurang**, Indonesia
131 P 2 **Amurrio**, Spain
153 V 13 **Amursk**, Russian Federation
147 B 17 **Amvrakikos Kolpos**, Greece ≈
151 Y 7 **Amvrosiyivka**, Ukraine
175 O 5 **An Nabhānīyah**, Saudi Arabia
172 I 6 **An Nabk**, Syria
174 L 2 **An Nafūd**, Saudi Arabia ◇
173 T 9 **An Najaf**, Iraq
173 W 11 **An Nāşirīyah**, Iraq
173 W 10 **An Naşr**, Iraq
211 V 8 **An Nawfalīyah**, Libya
172 J 8 **An Nimarah**, Syria
175 N 10 **An Nimāş**, Saudi Arabia
175 S 4 **An Nu'ayrīyah**, Saudi Arabia
173 Q 9 **An Nukhayb**, Iraq
173 U 8 **An Nu'māniyah**, Iraq
173 U 8 **An Nu'māniyah**, Iraq
237 V 1 **Anabar**, Nauru
105 Q 3 **Anaco**, Venezuela
73 O 6 **Anaconda**, Montana, U.S.A.
153 Z 7 **Anadyr'**, Russian Federation
147 K 24 **Anafi**, Greece ⇄
109 M 15 **Anagé**, Brazil
141 I 14 **Anagni**, Italy
173 P 5 **'Ānah**, Iraq
77 K 25 **Anaheim**, California, U.S.A.
89 Q 6 **Anáhuac**, Mexico
181 D 23 **Anai Mudi Peak**, India ▲
181 H 18 **Anakapalle**, India
219 Y 5 **Analalava**, Madagascar
108 E 11 **Anamã**, Brazil
215 R 13 **Anambra**, Nigeria ▣
170 H 14 **Anamur**, Turkey
170 H 14 **Anamur Burnu**, Turkey ▶
199 G 20 **Anan**, Japan
181 C 15 **Anand**, India
181 J 16 **Anandapur**, India
181 E 20 **Anantapur**, India
182 H 4 **Anantnag**, India
156 J 12 **Anapa**, Russian Federation
109 J 16 **Anápolis**, Brazil
176 K 10 **Anār**, Iran
176 K 8 **Anārak**, Iran
177 P 8 **Anardara**, Afghanistan
236 A 7 **Anatahan**, Northern Mariana Islands ⇄
170 D 10 **Anatolia**, Turkey ◇
146 I 12 **Anatoliki Makedonia Kai Thraki**, Greece ▣
235 S 13 **Anatom**, Vanuatu ⇄
110 K 8 **Añatuya**, Argentina
159 U 9 **Anaximander Mountains**, Mediterranean Sea ▲
189 P 1 **Anbianbu**, China
107 C 14 **Ancash**, Peru ▣
128 L 7 **Ancenis**, France
215 R 11 **Anchau**, Nigeria
79 R 9 **Anchorage**, Alaska, U.S.A. ▣
107 C 16 **Ancón**, Peru
140 I 11 **Ancona**, Italy
111 E 17 **Ancud**, Chile
186 J 10 **Anda**, China
196 E 8 **Anda**, Philippines
107 E 17 **Andahuaylas**, Peru
110 I 8 **Andalgalá**, Argentina
130 L 12 **Andalucía**, Spain ▣
63 Q 6 **Andalusia**, Alabama, U.S.A.
181 O 23 **Andaman and Nicobar Islands**, India ▣
39 R 3 **Andaman Basin**, Indian Ocean ◇
181 O 21 **Andaman Islands**, India ⇄
191 D 18 **Andaman Sea**, Asia ⌐
231 P 9 **Andamooka**, South Australia, Australia
219 Z 5 **Andapa**, Madagascar

138 I 9 **Andeer**, Switzerland
133 I 21 **Andenne**, Belgium
133 F 21 **Anderlues**, Belgium
138 G 9 **Andermatt**, Switzerland
128 L 12 **Andernos-les-Bains**, France
60 L 11 **Anderson**, South Carolina, U.S.A.
65 J 18 **Anderson**, Indiana, U.S.A.
69 S 8 **Anderson**, Missouri, U.S.A.
79 R 7 **Anderson**, Alaska, U.S.A.
82 C 9 **Anderson**, Northwest Territories, Canada ⅃
110 G 13 **Andes**, South America ▲
134 G 8 **Andfjorden**, Norway ≈
181 F 19 **Andhra Pradesh**, India ▣
179 T 12 **Andijon Wiloyati**, Uzbekistan ▣
219 Y 7 **Andilamena**, Madagascar
219 Y 7 **Andilanatoby**, Madagascar
176 G 3 **Andimeshk**, Iran
179 T 12 **Andizhan**, Uzbekistan
177 R 5 **Andkhvoy**, Afghanistan
106 D 10 **Andoas**, Peru
187 M 20 **Andong**, South Korea
131 W 2 **Andorra**, Europe ▣
131 W 2 **Andorra La Vella**, Andorra ♣
127 S 11 **Andover**, United Kingdom
134 G 8 **Andøya**, Norway ≈
112 H 5 **Andradina**, Brazil
219 Z 4 **Andranovondronina**, Madagascar
219 W 10 **Andranovory**, Madagascar
131 X 8 **Andratx**, Spain
78 E 14 **Andreanof Islands**, Alaska, U.S.A. ⇄
154 F 14 **Andreapol'**, Russian Federation
112 M 6 **Andrelândia**, Brazil
38 K 3 **Andrew Tablemount**, Indian Ocean ▲
70 J 6 **Andrews**, Texas, U.S.A.
179 X 7 **Andreyevka**, Kazakhstan
141 M 15 **Andria**, Italy
219 Y 7 **Andriamena**, Madagascar
151 X 8 **Andriyivka**, Ukraine
219 W 10 **Androka**, Madagascar
147 I 20 **Andros**, Greece ⇄
92 K 3 **Andros Island**, The Bahamas ⇄
92 K 2 **Andros Town**, The Bahamas
157 S 4 **Androsovka**, Russian Federation
181 C 22 **Andrott**, India ⇄
134 I 8 **Andselv**, Norway
131 N 11 **Andújar**, Spain
218 H 4 **Andulo**, Angola
93 W 7 **Anegada**, Virgin Islands, United Kingdom ⇄
215 N 13 **Aného**, Togo
197 C 18 **Anepahan**, Philippines
131 U 2 **Aneto**, Spain ▲
215 U 6 **Aney**, Niger
189 U 9 **Anfu**, China
191 H 18 **Ang Thong**, Thailand
153 O 11 **Angara**, Russian Federation ⅃
153 P 13 **Angarsk**, Russian Federation
135 G 16 **Ånge**, Sweden
105 R 6 **Angel Falls**, Venezuela ◀
196 F 10 **Angeles**, Philippines
135 E 24 **Ängelholm**, Sweden
136 N 12 **Angermünde**, Germany
128 M 7 **Angers**, France
135 J 15 **Ängesön**, Sweden
191 L 21 **Ångk Tasaôm**, Cambodia
126 L 4 **Anglesey**, United Kingdom ⇄
71 S 11 **Angleton**, Texas, U.S.A.
217 O 5 **Ango**, Democratic Republic of Congo
219 U 6 **Angoche**, Mozambique
176 M 13 **Angohrān**, Iran
111 F 15 **Angol**, Chile
218 H 3 **Angola**, Africa ▣
43 M 16 **Angola Basin**, Atlantic Ocean ◇
234 C 3 **Angoram**, Papua New Guinea
129 N 10 **Angoulême**, France

■ Country   ▣ Internal administrative region: State/Province/Territory/Dependent territory   ♣ Capital city   ▲ Mountain range/Undersea ridge   ▲ Mountain peak/Volcano/Seamount   ◇ Geographic feature   ▶ Headland/Point/Cape/Peninsula   ▲ Desert   ⇄ Island/Island group   ⇌ Antarctic base   ⊘ Ocean   ⌐ Sea   ≈ Bay/Gulf/Channel/Strait   ▭ Lake   ⅃ Salt pan/Dry/Intermittent lake   Ri... River

Angra do Heroísmo – Arriaga

42 N 1 **Angra do Heroísmo**, Azores
112 M 7 **Angra dos Reis**, Brazil
179 S 11 **Angren**, Uzbekistan
217 N 5 **Angu**, Democratic Republic of Congo
186 I 11 **Anguang**, China
131 T 3 **Angüés**, Spain
93 X 7 **Anguilla**, United Kingdom, United Kingdom
92 J 3 **Anguilla Cay**, The Bahamas
135 D 24 **Anholt**, Denmark
189 S 8 **Anhua**, China
189 W 5 **Anhui**, China
109 H 16 **Anhumas**, Brazil
198 J 10 **Ani**, Japan
79 N 9 **Aniak**, Alaska, U.S.A.
237 V 1 **Anibare**, Nauru
237 V 1 **Anibare Bay**, Nauru
75 N 15 **Animas Peak**, New Mexico, U.S.A.
197 M 15 **Anitaguipan Point**, Philippines
219 Z 4 **Anivorano Avaratra**, Madgascar
235 S 12 **Aniwa**, Vanuatu
189 R 9 **Anjiang**, China
219 W 4 **Anjouan**, Comoros
187 K 17 **Anju**, North Korea
173 O 5 **Anka**, Iraq
189 Q 5 **Ankang**, China
170 H 9 **Ankara**, Turkey
219 V 9 **Ankazoabo**, Madgascar
219 Y 7 **Ankazobe**, Madgascar
57 S 13 **Ankeny**, Iowa, U.S.A.
136 M 9 **Anklam**, Germany
181 C 20 **Ankola**, India
185 R 9 **Ankou**, China
89 P 3 **Ankouzhen**, China
15 R 13 **Ankpa**, Nigeria
189 N 10 **Anlong**, China
89 T 6 **Anlu**, China
5 L 15 **Ann Arbor**, Michigan, U.S.A.
56 M 5 **Anna**, Russian Federation
5 F 22 **Anna**, Illinois, U.S.A.
37 U 1 **Anna Point**, Nauru
11 P 5 **Annaba**, Algeria
91 M 15 **Annam**, Vietnam
91 K 14 **Annam Highlands**, Laos
1 V 3 **Annapolis**, Maryland, U.S.A.
7 T 11 **Annapolis Royal**, Nova Scotia, Canada
83 P 8 **Annapurna**, Nepal
29 V 9 **Annecy**, France
88 L 11 **Anning**, China
3 R 3 **Anniston**, Alabama, U.S.A.
29 T 11 **Annonay**, France
47 J 26 **Ano Viannos**, Greece
89 R 14 **Anpu**, China
89 W 6 **Anqing**, China
87 F 20 **Anqiu**, China
83 J 20 **Ans**, Belgium
89 Q 1 **Ansai**, China
37 I 21 **Ansbach**, Germany
A 10 **Anse à la Mouche**, Seychelles
B 10 **Anse Royal**, Seychelles
7 H 16 **Anshan**, China
89 O 10 **Anshun**, China
2 F 13 **Ansina**, Uruguay
L 14 **Ansley**, Nebraska, U.S.A.
M 6 **Anson**, Texas, U.S.A.
3 Y 11 **Ansudu**, Indonesia
7 F 18 **Antabamba**, Peru
9 Z 6 **Antalaha**, Madgascar
0 F 13 **Antalya**, Turkey
9 V 9 **Antalya Basin**, Mediterranean Sea
0 F 13 **Antalya Körfezi**, Turkey
9 Y 7 **Antananarivo**, Madgascar
9 X 7 **Antananarivo**, Madgascar
9 W 10 **Antanimora Atsimo**, Madgascar
0 H 4 **Antarctic Peninsula**, Antarctica
241 Q 7 **Antarctica**
131 N 13 **Antequera**, Spain
75 Q 14 **Anthony**, New Mexico, U.S.A.
210 F 9 **Anti Atlas**, Morocco
129 X 14 **Antibes**, France
64 F 11 **Antigo**, Wisconsin, U.S.A.
87 W 9 **Antigonish**, Nova Scotia, Canada
90 H 6 **Antigua**, Guatemala
93 Y 9 **Antigua**, Antigua and Barbuda
93 Z 8 **Antigua and Barbuda**, North America
147 F 25 **Antikythira**, Greece
147 H 23 **Antimilos**, Greece
170 L 14 **Antioch**, Turkey
104 H 5 **Antioquia**, Colombia
147 I 22 **Antiparos**, Greece
147 A 17 **Antipaxoi**, Greece
152 M 8 **Antipayuta**, Russian Federation
41 P 13 **Antipodes Islands**, New Zealand
110 F 5 **Antofagasta**, Chile
110 F 5 **Antofagasta**, Chile
110 H 7 **Antofagasta de la Sierra**, Argentina
111 I 21 **Antonio de Biedma**, Argentina
125 F 15 **Antrim**, United Kingdom
140 H 13 **Antrodoco**, Italy
219 W 7 **Antsalova**, Madgascar
219 X 8 **Antsirabe**, Madgascar
219 Z 4 **Antsiranana**, Madgascar
219 Z 5 **Antsiranana**, Madgascar
148 H 9 **Antsla**, Estonia
219 Y 5 **Antsohihy**, Madgascar
187 M 14 **Antu**, China
111 F 14 **Antuco**, Chile
133 G 17 **Antwerp**, Belgium
133 G 17 **Antwerpen**, Belgium
181 I 16 **Anugul**, India
180 C 11 **Anupgarh**, India
181 G 24 **Anuradhapura**, Sri Lanka
235 S 8 **Anuta**, Solomon Islands
240 H 4 **Anvers Island**, Antarctica
185 N 6 **Anxi**, China
189 S 7 **Anxiang**, China
231 O 11 **Anxious Bay**, South Australia, Australia
187 L 19 **Anyang**, South Korea
189 U 2 **Anyang**, China
147 K 23 **Anydro**, Greece
185 O 8 **A'nyêmaqên Shan**, China
149 G 14 **Anykščiai**, Lithuania
189 V 10 **Anyuan**, China
189 N 7 **Anyue**, China
189 S 2 **Anze**, China
133 D 19 **Anzegem**, Belgium
216 M 8 **Anzi**, Democratic Republic of Congo
141 H 15 **Anzio**, Italy
105 Q 4 **Anzoátegui**, Venezuela
191 G 23 **Ao Ban Don**, Thailand
191 F 24 **Ao Luk**, Thailand
191 G 22 **Ao Sawi**, Thailand
235 Q 10 **Aoba**, Vanuatu
199 L 20 **Aoga-shima**, Japan
234 M 7 **Aola**, Solomon Islands
198 J 9 **Aomori**, Japan
182 K 9 **Aonla**, India
140 A 6 **Aosta**, Italy
210 C 11 **Aoufist**, Western Sahara
214 G 7 **Aoukâr**, Mauritania
210 L 11 **Aoulef**, Algeria
215 W 5 **Aozou**, Chad
217 S 6 **Apac**, Uganda
68 M 11 **Apache**, Oklahoma, U.S.A.
74 L 15 **Apache Peak**, Arizona, U.S.A.
63 T 8 **Apalachee Bay**, Florida, U.S.A.
63 S 8 **Apalachicola**, Florida, U.S.A.
112 H 4 **Aparecida do Taboado**, Brazil
196 H 5 **Aparri**, Philippines
144 I 8 **Apatin**, Serbia and Montenegro
154 H 3 **Apatity**, Russian Federation
89 O 12 **Apatzingán**, Mexico
148 I 9 **Ape**, Latvia
132 L 12 **Apeldoorn**, Netherlands
140 D 9 **Apennines**, Italy
217 N 5 **Api**, Democratic Republic of Congo
182 M 7 **Api**, Nepal
236 J 8 **Apia**, Samoa
107 F 19 **Aplao**, Peru
108 N 12 **Apodi**, Brazil
105 V 6 **Apoera**, Suriname
231 R 14 **Apollo Bay**, Victoria, Australia
107 I 18 **Apolo**, Bolivia
112 H 3 **Aporé**, Brazil
112 H 4 **Aporé**, Brazil
64 E 7 **Apostle Islands**, Wisconsin, U.S.A.
44 M 14 **Apostolens Tommefinger**, Greenland
112 E 10 **Apóstoles**, Argentina
151 T 8 **Apostolove**, Ukraine
57 U 11 **Appalachian Mountains**, Georgia, U.S.A.
140 I 13 **Appennino Abruzzese**, Italy
140 B 9 **Appennino Ligure**, Italy
141 L 16 **Appennino Lucano**, Italy
141 K 15 **Appennino Napoletano**, Italy
140 E 9 **Appennino Tosco-Emiliano**, Italy
140 H 11 **Appennino Umbro-Marchigiano**, Italy
138 I 7 **Appenzell**, Switzerland
132 N 6 **Appingedam**, Netherlands
64 G 12 **Appleton**, Wisconsin, U.S.A.
61 S 6 **Appomattox**, Virginia, U.S.A.
156 L 13 **Apsheronsk**, Russian Federation
129 U 13 **Apt**, France
112 H 7 **Apucarana**, Brazil
159 O 7 **Apulian Plateau**, Mediterranean Sea
105 N 5 **Apure**, Venezuela
105 N 4 **Apure**, Venezuela
107 F 18 **Apurímac**, Peru
107 E 16 **Apurímac**, Peru
177 S 5 **Āqchah**, Afghanistan
176 K 8 **Āqdā**, Iran
184 K 7 **Aqqikkol Hu**, China
172 G 9 **'Aqraba**, Israel
173 S 1 **'Aqrah**, Iraq
179 V 4 **Aqtasty**, Kazakhstan
109 G 18 **Aquidauana**, Brazil
128 L 12 **Aquitaine**, France
173 S 8 **Ar Raḥḥālīyah**, Iraq
173 S 7 **Ar Ramādī**, Iraq
172 G 13 **Ar Ramlah**, Jordan
172 H 8 **Ar Ramtha**, Jordan
172 L 3 **Ar Raqqah**, Syria
174 L 8 **Ar Rās al Aswad**, Saudi Arabia
175 O 5 **Ar-Rass**, Saudi Arabia
175 O 8 **Ar Rawḍah**, Saudi Arabia
175 R 13 **Ar Rawḍah**, Yemen
173 W 10 **Ar Rifā'ī**, Iraq
173 V 10 **Ar Rihab**, Iraq
175 P 5 **Ar Rubay'iyah**, Saudi Arabia
173 V 10 **Ar Rumaythah**, Iraq
172 L 3 **Ar Ruṣāfah**, Syria
172 H 9 **Ar Ruṣayfah**, Jordan
175 Z 6 **Ar Rustāq**, Oman
173 N 8 **Ar Ruṭbah**, Iraq
175 P 6 **Ar Ruwayḍah**, Saudi Arabia
183 P 11 **Ara**, India
213 J 22 **Āra Ārba**, Ethiopia
63 Q 2 **Arab**, Alabama, U.S.A.
173 V 8 **Arab Abdullah**, Iraq
38 M 2 **Arabian Basin**, Indian Ocean
175 V 13 **Arabian Sea**, Asia
170 I 7 **Araş**, Turkey
109 O 14 **Aracaju**, Brazil
108 O 11 **Aracati**, Brazil
112 I 5 **Araçatuba**, Brazil
172 F 10 **'Arad**, Israel
150 F 10 **Arad**, Romania
215 Y 8 **Arada**, Chad
175 V 7 **'Arādah**, United Arab Emirates
173 Y 11 **Aradah**, Iraq
193 V 14 **Arafura Sea**, Asia/Oceania
40 K 9 **Arafura Shelf**, Pacific Ocean
171 T 8 **Aragats Lerr**, Armenia
131 S 5 **Aragón**, Spain
105 O 3 **Aragua**, Venezuela
109 J 14 **Araguaçu**, Brazil
108 J 13 **Araguaia**, Brazil
108 J 12 **Araguaína**, Brazil
109 J 17 **Araguari**, Brazil
199 I 14 **Arai**, Japan
176 H 7 **Arāk**, Iran
211 N 12 **Arak**, Algeria
172 L 5 **Arak**, Syria
190 B 13 **Arakan**, Myanmar
190 B 12 **Arakan Yoma**, Myanmar
178 L 9 **Aral Sea**, Kazakhstan/Uzbekistan
179 N 7 **Aral'sk**, Kazakhstan
231 S 6 **Aramac**, Queensland, Australia
234 B 6 **Aramia**, Papua New Guinea
127 N 6 **Aran Fawddwy**, United Kingdom
125 A 18 **Aran Islands**, Republic of Ireland
131 O 4 **Aranda de Duero**, Spain
144 L 11 **Aranđelovac**, Serbia and Montenegro
131 O 7 **Aranjuez**, Spain
218 J 10 **Aranos**, Namibia
236 D 2 **Aranuka**, Kiribati
191 J 19 **Aranyaprathet**, Thailand
199 B 22 **Arao**, Japan
66 K 15 **Arapahoe**, Nebraska, U.S.A.
233 J 16 **Arapawa Island**, New Zealand
108 O 13 **Arapiraca**, Brazil
171 N 10 **Arapkir**, Turkey
112 H 7 **Arapongas**, Brazil
175 N 1 **'Ar'ar**, Saudi Arabia
104 K 10 **Araracuara**, Colombia
112 I 11 **Araranguá**, Brazil
112 J 6 **Araraquara**, Brazil
108 H 12 **Araras**, Brazil
231 R 13 **Ararat**, Victoria, Australia
183 R 11 **Araria**, India
171 R 9 **Aras**, Turkey
171 S 9 **Aras**, Azerbaijan/Turkey
171 R 10 **Aras Güneyi Dağlari**, Turkey
171 N 12 **Aratürk Baraji**, Turkey
104 K 5 **Arauca**, Colombia
104 L 5 **Arauca**, Colombia
104 M 5 **Arauca**, Venezuela
111 F 15 **Araucania**, Chile
111 E 14 **Arauco**, Chile
180 C 13 **Aravalli Range**, India
109 K 17 **Araxá**, Brazil
171 W 10 **Araz**, Azerbaijan
213 H 22 **Ārba Minch**, Ethiopia
173 V 4 **Arbat**, Iraq
141 D 18 **Arbatax**, Italy
139 U 3 **Arbesbach**, Austria
173 T 2 **Arbīl**, Iraq
135 G 20 **Arboga**, Sweden
104 G 4 **Arboletes**, Colombia
138 I 6 **Arbon**, Switzerland
124 I 12 **Arbroath**, United Kingdom
128 L 12 **Arcachon**, France
58 D 9 **Arcade**, New York, U.S.A.
62 I 4 **Arcadia**, Louisiana, U.S.A.
63 W 11 **Arcadia**, Florida, U.S.A.
105 T 8 **Arcarai Mountains**, Guyana
77 E 15 **Arcata**, California, U.S.A.
89 Q 13 **Arcelia**, Mexico
230 I 12 **Archipelago of the Recherche**, Western Australia, Australia
91 S 12 **Archipiélago de Bocas del Toro**, Panama
92 J 4 **Archipiélago de Camagüey**, Cuba
111 E 23 **Archipiélago de la Reina Adelaida**, Chile
91 X 15 **Archipiélago de las Perlas**, Panama
92 G 4 **Archipiélago de los Canarreros**, Cuba
111 E 20 **Archipiélago de los Chonos**, Chile
92 J 5 **Archipiélago de los Jardines de la Reina**, Cuba
92 H 3 **Archipiélago de Sabana**, Cuba
91 Y 12 **Archipiélago de San Blas**, Panama
91 P 10 **Archipiélago de Solentiname**, Nicaragua
41 W 2 **Archipiélago Juan Fernández**, Juan Fernández Islands
140 F 12 **Arcidosso**, Italy
73 N 11 **Arco**, Idaho, U.S.A.
130 L 13 **Arcos de la Frontera**, Spain
81 Q 4 **Arctic Bay**, Nunavut, Canada
45 Q 8 **Arctic Ocean**
240 G 3 **Arctowski**, Antarctica
171 U 8 **Arcvašen**, Armenia
172 I 11 **Arḍ aş Ṣawwān**, Jordan
146 J 11 **Arda**, Bulgaria
176 H 3 **Ardabīl**, Iran
176 H 3 **Ardabīl**, Iran
171 S 8 **Ardahan**, Turkey
176 K 8 **Ardakān**, Iran
157 Q 2 **Ardatov**, Russian Federation
86 E 10 **Ardbeg**, Ontario, Canada
125 E 17 **Ardee**, Republic of Ireland
133 H 23 **Ardennes**, Belgium
176 J 7 **Ardestān**, Iran
69 N 12 **Ardmore**, Oklahoma, U.S.A.
150 H 7 **Ardusat**, Romania
135 F 15 **Åre**, Sweden
217 Q 6 **Arebi**, Democratic Republic of Congo
93 U 7 **Arecibo**, Puerto Rico
197 F 19 **Arena**, Philippines
91 P 11 **Arenal**, Costa Rica
109 G 15 **Arenápolis**, Brazil
130 M 7 **Arenas de San Pedro**, Spain
135 B 21 **Arendal**, Norway
133 H 16 **Arendonk**, Belgium
147 E 23 **Areopoli**, Greece
107 G 19 **Arequipa**, Peru
107 F 20 **Arequipa**, Peru
140 G 11 **Arezzo**, Italy
147 F 17 **Argalasti**, Greece
184 L 6 **Argan**, China
131 O 7 **Arganda**, Spain
129 N 4 **Argentan**, France
110 J 11 **Argentina**, South America
110 J 9 **Argentina**, Argentina
43 F 19 **Argentine Abyssal Plain**, Atlantic Ocean
43 G 18 **Argentine Basin**, Atlantic Ocean
177 S 9 **Arghandab**, Afghanistan
159 Q 9 **Argolikos Basin**, Mediterranean Sea
147 E 21 **Argolikos Kolpos**, Greece
147 E 21 **Argos**, Greece
147 C 14 **Argos Orestiko**, Greece
147 B 19 **Argostoli**, Greece
186 G 6 **Argun'**, China
215 P 10 **Argungu**, Nigeria
87 T 12 **Argyle**, Nova Scotia, Canada
185 P 3 **Arhangay**, Mongolia
135 C 24 **Århus**, Denmark
181 L 18 **Ari Atoll**, Maldives
193 Q 8 **Ariaga**, Indonesia
218 J 12 **Ariamsvlei**, Namibia
113 B 15 **Arias**, Argentina
104 K 11 **Arica**, Colombia
106 D 9 **Arica**, Peru
110 F 2 **Arica**, Chile
199 G 19 **Arida**, Japan
172 I 3 **Arīḥā**, Syria
144 K 13 **Arilje**, Serbia and Montenegro
109 G 14 **Arinos**, Brazil
108 F 12 **Aripuanã**, Brazil
108 E 13 **Ariquemes**, Brazil
105 N 4 **Arismendi**, Venezuela
181 K 18 **Ariyaddu Channel**, Maldives
131 Q 5 **Ariza**, Spain
74 H 11 **Arizona**, U.S.A.
135 E 20 **Årjäng**, Sweden
134 H 12 **Arjeplog**, Sweden
157 O 5 **Arkadak**, Russian Federation
69 U 12 **Arkadelphia**, Arkansas, U.S.A.
179 Q 5 **Arkalyk**, Kazakhstan
69 T 11 **Arkansas**, U.S.A.
69 O 8 **Arkansas**, U.S.A., U.S.A.
69 N 7 **Arkansas City**, Kansas, U.S.A.
154 K 6 **Arkhangel'sk**, Russian Federation
154 L 7 **Arkhangel'skaya Oblast'**, Russian Federation
153 P 6 **Arkhipelag Nordenshel'da**, Russian Federation
147 F 18 **Arkitsa**, Greece
125 F 19 **Arklow**, Republic of Ireland
129 T 14 **Arles**, France
61 U 3 **Arlington**, District of Columbia, U.S.A.
67 O 9 **Arlington**, South Dakota, U.S.A.
71 Q 6 **Arlington**, Texas, U.S.A.
215 Q 6 **Arlit**, Niger
133 K 25 **Arlon**, Belgium
230 G 11 **Armadale**, Western Australia, Australia
125 E 16 **Armagh**, United Kingdom
212 F 11 **Armant**, Egypt
147 M 26 **Armathia**, Greece
156 M 12 **Armavir**, Russian Federation
104 H 7 **Armenia**, Colombia
171 T 8 **Armenia**, Asia
231 V 10 **Armidale**, New South Wales, Australia
73 Q 4 **Armington**, Montana, U.S.A.
84 L 10 **Armstrong**, Ontario, Canada
147 G 14 **Arnaia**, Greece
85 R 5 **Arnaud**, Québec, Canada
133 D 15 **Arnemuiden**, Netherlands
68 J 9 **Arnett**, Oklahoma, U.S.A.
132 K 13 **Arnhem**, Netherlands
231 N 1 **Arnhem Land**, Northern Territory, Australia
146 D 13 **Arnissa**, Greece
237 Z 3 **Arno**, Marshall Islands
140 E 10 **Arno**, Italy
134 I 6 **Arnøya**, Norway
137 I 17 **Arnstadt**, Germany
218 K 11 **Aroab**, Namibia
84 M 11 **Aroland**, Ontario, Canada
213 H 16 **Aroma**, Sudan
42 M 12 **Arona**, Canary Islands
140 C 6 **Arona**, Italy
236 F 3 **Arorae**, Kiribati
197 J 14 **Aroroy**, Philippines
138 I 8 **Arosa**, Switzerland
214 D 10 **Arquipélago dos Bijagós**, Guinea-Bissau
124 G 13 **Arran**, United Kingdom
129 Q 2 **Arras**, France
129 N 15 **Arreau**, France
42 O 11 **Arrecife**, Canary Islands
113 C 15 **Arrecifes**, Argentina
89 P 10 **Arriaga**, Mexico
89 V 14 **Arriaga**, Mexico

Country | Internal administrative region: State/Province/Territory/Dependent territory | Capital city | Mountain range/Undersea ridge | Mountain peak/Volcano/Seamount | Geographic feature | Headland/Point/Cape/Peninsula | Desert | Island/Island group | Antarctic base | Ocean | Sea | Bay/Gulf/Channel/Strait | Lake | Salt pan/Dry/Intermittent lake | River

Arriondas – 'Azīzābād

130 M 1 **Arriondas**, Spain
113 G 14 **Arroio Grande**, Brazil
77 H 23 **Arroyo Grande**, California, U.S.A.
135 C 23 **Års**, Denmark
157 S 1 **Arsk**, Russian Federation
147 C 17 **Arta**, Greece
131 Z 8 **Artà**, Spain
171 U 9 **Artashat**, Armenia
89 O 13 **Arteaga**, Mexico
92 G 4 **Artemisa**, Cuba
151 X 6 **Artemivs'k**, Ukraine
141 H 14 **Artena**, Italy
137 J 15 **Artern**, Germany
131 V 4 **Artesa de Segre**, Spain
75 S 13 **Artesia**, New Mexico, U.S.A.
66 I 13 **Arthur**, Nebraska, U.S.A.
233 G 19 **Arthur's Pass**, New Zealand
82 C 10 **Artic Red**, Northwest Territories, Canada
112 E 12 **Artigas**, Uruguay
112 E 12 **Artigas**, Uruguay
171 T 8 **Art'ik**, Armenia
151 O 10 **Artsyz**, Ukraine
171 Q 7 **Artvin**, Turkey
217 R 6 **Aru**, Democratic Republic of Congo
217 R 6 **Arua**, Uganda
109 I 15 **Aruanã**, Brazil
93 R 12 **Aruba**, The Netherlands, The Netherlands
108 E 11 **Arumã**, Brazil
183 R 9 **Arun**, Nepal
183 X 8 **Arunachal Pradesh**, India
127 V 13 **Arundel**, United Kingdom
217 V 10 **Arusha**, Tanzania
217 V 10 **Arusha**, Tanzania
75 R 4 **Arvada**, Colorado, U.S.A.
185 P 4 **Arvayheer**, Mongolia
82 N 11 **Arviat**, Nunavut, Canada
84 L 4 **Arviat**, Nunavut, Canada
134 I 12 **Arvidsjaur**, Sweden
135 E 20 **Arvika**, Sweden
193 R 14 **Arwala**, Indonesia
186 G 10 **Arxan**, China
179 R 11 **Arys'**, Kazakhstan
141 C 15 **Arzachena**, Italy
157 O 1 **Arzamas**, Russian Federation
210 L 6 **Arzew**, Algeria
157 O 12 **Arzgir**, Russian Federation
172 J 3 **As Sa'an**, Syria
172 M 3 **As Sabkhah**, Syria
172 G 11 **Aş Şafi**, Jordan
173 N 1 **Aş Şafiḩ**, Syria
172 J 2 **As Safirah**, Syria
175 R 6 **As Salamiyah**, Saudi Arabia
173 U 12 **As Salmān**, Iraq
172 G 13 **As Salţ**, Jordan
173 V 10 **As Samāwah**, Iraq
172 H 7 **Aş Şanamayn**, Syria
174 J 3 **Aş Şawrah**, Saudi Arabia
173 O 5 **As Sayyāl**, Syria
211 V 8 **As Sidrah**, Libya
175 R 3 **Aş Şubayhīyah**, Kuwait
175 S 13 **As Sufāl**, Yemen
172 L 4 **As Sukhnah**, Syria
173 U 3 **As Sulaymānīyah**, Iraq
175 Q 9 **As Sulayyil**, Saudi Arabia
211 U 8 **As Sulţān**, Libya
175 O 8 **As Sūq**, Saudi Arabia
173 O 3 **Aş Şuwār**, Syria
172 H 8 **As Suwaydā'**, Syria
173 T 8 **As Suwayrah**, Iraq
176 G 6 **Asadābād**, Iran
177 O 6 **Asadābād**, Iran
177 V 7 **Asadābād**, Afghanistan
171 V 8 **Asaği**, Azerbaijan
198 K 4 **Asahi-dake**, Japan
198 K 4 **Asahikawa**, Japan
176 H 4 **Asālem**, Iran
183 R 13 **Asansol**, India
213 J 19 **Āsayita**, Ethiopia
58 J 13 **Asbury Park**, New Jersey, U.S.A.
43 K 25 **Ascension**, U.K.
88 L 3 **Ascensión**, Mexico
137 F 19 **Aschaffenburg**, Germany
140 I 12 **Ascoli Piceno**, Italy
141 L 15 **Ascoli Satriano**, Italy
213 I 21 **Āsela**, Ethiopia
135 H 14 **Åsele**, Sweden
146 I 10 **Asenovgrad**, Bulgaria
134 B 10 **Ásgarður**, Iceland
69 W 9 **Ash Flat**, Arkansas, U.S.A.
74 J 10 **Ash Fork**, Arizona, U.S.A.
173 S 11 **Ash Shabakah**, Iraq
173 O 2 **Ash Shaddādah**, Syria
175 X 5 **Ash Sha'm**, United Arab Emirates
173 V 12 **Ash Shāmīyah**, Iraq
173 U 10 **Ash Shanāfīyah**, Iraq
175 P 6 **Ash Sha'rā'**, Saudi Arabia
175 R 11 **Ash Sharawrah**, Saudi Arabia
173 S 3 **Ash Sharqāţ**, Iraq
173 W 10 **Ash Shaţrah**, Iraq
172 G 11 **Ash Shawbak**, Jordan
175 P 14 **Ash Shaykh 'Uthman**, Yemen
175 T 13 **Ash Shiḩr**, Yemen
175 X 5 **Ash Şhināş**, Oman
175 P 3 **Ash Shu'bah**, Saudi Arabia
175 N 11 **Ash Shuqayq**, Saudi Arabia
211 T 9 **Ash Shuwayrif**, Libya
175 Q 5 **Asharat**, Saudi Arabia
127 S 5 **Ashbourne**, United Kingdom
233 G 21 **Ashburton**, New Zealand
127 S 6 **Ashby de la Zouch**, United Kingdom
172 E 9 **Ashdod**, Israel
69 S 13 **Ashdown**, Arkansas, U.S.A.
61 Q 9 **Asheboro**, North Carolina, U.S.A.
69 O 11 **Asher**, Oklahoma, U.S.A.
60 M 9 **Asheville**, North Carolina, U.S.A.
127 Y 12 **Ashford**, United Kingdom
178 L 14 **Ashgabat**, Turkmenistan
198 K 5 **Ashibetsu**, Japan
199 J 15 **Ashikaga**, Japan
198 K 10 **Ashiro**, Japan
199 E 22 **Ashizuri-misaki**, Japan
59 R 1 **Ashland**, Maine, U.S.A.
60 L 4 **Ashland**, Kentucky, U.S.A.
64 E 8 **Ashland**, Wisconsin, U.S.A.
65 N 17 **Ashland**, Ohio, U.S.A.
68 J 7 **Ashland**, Kansas, U.S.A.
77 G 14 **Ashland**, Oregon, U.S.A.
66 L 6 **Ashley**, North Dakota, U.S.A.
149 H 16 **Ashmyany**, Belarus
198 L 5 **Ashoro**, Japan
172 E 10 **Ashqelon**, Israel
65 O 15 **Ashtabula**, Ohio, U.S.A.
171 T 8 **Ashtarak**, Armenia
73 Q 10 **Ashton**, Idaho, U.S.A.
197 J 15 **Asid Gulf**, Philippines
181 F 17 **Asifabad**, India
181 I 17 **Asika**, India
210 I 6 **Asilah**, Morocco
152 M 12 **Asino**, Russian Federation
149 K 18 **Asipovichy**, Belarus
171 P 9 **Aşkale**, Turkey
127 T 3 **Askern**, United Kingdom
135 D 20 **Askim**, Norway
155 T 14 **Askino**, Russian Federation
135 A 18 **Askøy**, Norway
176 G 2 **Aşlāndūz**, Iran
213 I 17 **Asmara**, Eritrea
135 F 24 **Åsnen**, Sweden
215 X 9 **Asnet**, Chad
199 C 22 **Aso-san**, Japan
147 F 23 **Asopos**, Greece
213 G 20 **Āsosa**, Ethiopia
139 X 5 **Aspang-Markt**, Austria
75 P 5 **Aspen**, Colorado, U.S.A.
70 M 5 **Aspermont**, Texas, U.S.A.
213 K 18 **Assab**, Eritrea
214 G 7 **Assaba**, Mauritania
183 V 10 **Assam**, India
215 Q 6 **Assamakka**, Niger
61 X 5 **Assateague Island**, Virginia, U.S.A.
133 F 18 **Asse**, Belgium
132 M 7 **Assen**, Netherlands
133 I 21 **Assesse**, Belgium
84 H 10 **Assiniboine**, Manitoba, Canada
112 I 6 **Assis**, Brazil
109 B 14 **Assis Brasil**, Brazil
140 H 12 **Assisi**, Italy
135 D 18 **Åsta**, Norway
147 M 25 **Astakida**, Greece
147 C 18 **Astakos**, Greece
179 R 4 **Astana**, Kazakhstan
176 H 3 **Āstārā**, Iran
133 K 16 **Asten**, Netherlands
140 B 8 **Asti**, Italy
107 H 17 **Astillero**, Peru
127 T 4 **Aston**, United Kingdom
130 L 3 **Astorga**, Spain
76 F 8 **Astoria**, Oregon, U.S.A.
157 R 11 **Astrakhan'**, Russian Federation
151 V 9 **Astrakhanka**, Ukraine
157 R 10 **Astrakhanskaya Oblast'**, Russian Federation
43 N 23 **Astrid Ridge**, Atlantic Ocean
234 D 4 **Astrolabe Bay**, Papua New Guinea
147 E 21 **Astros**, Greece
149 F 18 **Astryna**, Belarus
130 L 1 **Asturias**, Spain
147 L 23 **Astypalaia**, Greece
241 S 2 **Asuka**, Antarctica
236 A 5 **Asuncion**, Northern Mariana Islands
107 I 16 **Asunción**, Bolivia
109 G 20 **Asunción**, Paraguay
90 I 6 **Asunción Mita**, Guatemala
148 J 13 **Asvyeya**, Belarus
212 F 12 **Aswân**, Egypt
212 E 10 **Asyût**, Egypt
179 U 11 **At-Bashy**, Kyrgyzstan
172 G 13 **Aţ Ţafilah**, Jordan
174 M 8 **Aţ Ţā'if**, Saudi Arabia
211 X 7 **At Tamīmī**, Libya
172 L 7 **Aţ Ţanf**, Syria
173 T 9 **Aţ Ţaqţaqānah**, Iraq
172 G 12 **Aţ Ţayyibah**, Jordan
173 N 3 **At Tibnī**, Syria
174 K 2 **Aţ Ţubayq**, Saudi Arabia
175 O 14 **At Turbah**, Yemen
175 P 14 **At Turbah**, Yemen
236 H 11 **Ata**, Tonga
110 F 8 **Atacama**, Chile
110 F 2 **Atacama Desert**, Chile
236 J 6 **Atafu**, Tokelau Islands
215 N 12 **Atakpamé**, Togo
107 E 15 **Atalaya**, Peru
175 R 13 **'Ataq**, Yemen
214 G 5 **Atâr**, Mauritania
185 O 5 **Atas Bogd**, Mongolia
179 S 6 **Atasu**, Kazakhstan
193 Q 15 **Atauro**, Indonesia
213 F 15 **Atbara**, Sudan
213 G 16 **Atbara**, Sudan
179 Q 4 **Atbasar**, Kazakhstan
62 J 9 **Atchafalaya Bay**, Louisiana, U.S.A.
69 Q 3 **Atchison**, Kansas, U.S.A.
133 E 20 **Ath**, Belgium
83 I 18 **Athabasca**, Alberta, Canada
147 G 20 **Athens**, Greece
60 I 10 **Athens**, Tennessee, U.S.A.
63 U 2 **Athens**, Georgia, U.S.A.
65 N 19 **Athens**, Ohio, U.S.A.
71 R 6 **Athens**, Texas, U.S.A.
170 H 15 **Athiénou**, Cyprus
125 D 18 **Athlone**, Republic of Ireland
58 M 9 **Athol**, Massachusetts, U.S.A.
147 H 15 **Athos**, Greece
215 X 9 **Ati**, Chad
107 E 19 **Atico**, Peru
213 C 21 **Atiedo**, Sudan
131 P 5 **Atienza**, Spain
84 K 11 **Atikokan**, Ontario, Canada
90 I 7 **Atiquizaya**, El Salvador
90 G 6 **Atitlán**, Guatemala
237 P 10 **Atiu**, Cook Islands
153 X 10 **Atka**, Russian Federation
78 G 14 **Atka**, Alaska, U.S.A.
78 G 14 **Atka Island**, Alaska, U.S.A.
157 P 5 **Atkarsk**, Russian Federation
193 T 11 **Atkri**, Indonesia
63 S 3 **Atlanta**, Georgia, U.S.A.
64 K 11 **Atlanta**, Michigan, U.S.A.
72 L 10 **Atlanta**, Idaho, U.S.A.
61 V 10 **Atlantic**, North Carolina, U.S.A.
67 R 13 **Atlantic**, Iowa, U.S.A.
58 J 15 **Atlantic City**, New Jersey, U.S.A.
38 J 14 **Atlantic–Indian–Antarctic Basin**, Southern Ocean
43 K 20 **Atlantic–Indian Ridge**, Atlantic Ocean/Indian Ocean
42 G 10 **Atlantic Ocean**
104 H 2 **Atlantico**, Colombia
42 F 9 **Atlantis Fracture Zone**, Atlantic Ocean
210 H 9 **Atlas Mountains**, Morocco
210 L 7 **Atlas Saharien**, Algeria
83 B 15 **Atlin Lake**, British Columbia, Canada
172 F 8 **'Atlit**, Israel
63 P 6 **Atmore**, Alabama, U.S.A.
107 J 22 **Atocha**, Bolivia
69 P 12 **Atoka**, Oklahoma, U.S.A.
191 N 17 **Atouat**, Laos
176 M 4 **Atrak**, Iran
199 K 16 **Atsugi**, Japan
198 J 12 **Atsumi**, Japan
199 I 18 **Atsumi**, Japan
198 J 5 **Atsuta**, Japan
191 N 18 **Attapu**, Laos
147 O 24 **Attavyros**, Greece
84 M 10 **Attawapiskat**, Ontario, Canada
85 O 9 **Attawapiskat**, Ontario, Canada
84 L 9 **Attawapiskat Lake**, Ontario, Canada
139 R 5 **Attersee**, Austria
133 K 25 **Attert**, Belgium
58 D 8 **Attica**, New York, U.S.A.
65 H 18 **Attica**, Indiana, U.S.A.
147 G 22 **Attiki**, Greece
127 Y 7 **Attleborough**, United Kingdom
78 B 11 **Attu Island**, Alaska, U.S.A.
175 S 13 **Atūd**, Yemen
111 H 14 **Atuel**, Argentina
178 I 7 **Atyrau**, Kazakhstan
178 I 7 **Atyrau**, Kazakhstan
64 L 12 **Au Sable Point**, Michigan, U.S.A.
234 B 2 **Aua Island**, Papua New Guinea
133 K 26 **Aubange**, Belgium
129 S 12 **Aubenas**, France
129 Q 7 **Aubigny-sur-Nère**, France
129 Q 12 **Aubin**, France
58 G 8 **Auburn**, New York, U.S.A.
59 N 10 **Auburn**, Massachusetts, U.S.A.
63 R 4 **Auburn**, Alabama, U.S.A.
65 E 19 **Auburn**, Illinois, U.S.A.
67 Q 15 **Auburn**, Nebraska, U.S.A.
76 G 7 **Auburn**, Washington, U.S.A.
77 H 18 **Auburn**, California, U.S.A.
129 Q 9 **Aubusson**, France
148 D 12 **Auce**, Latvia
129 N 14 **Auch**, France
232 K 8 **Auckland**, New Zealand
232 J 8 **Auckland**, New Zealand
41 O 13 **Auckland Islands**, New Zealand
128 H 5 **Audierne**, France
213 J 22 **Audo Range**, Ethiopia
137 L 18 **Aue**, Germany
137 L 18 **Auerbach**, Germany
231 T 7 **Augathella**, Queensland, Australia
137 I 24 **Augsburg**, Germany
148 H 13 **Augšzemes Augstiene**, Latvia
230 F 12 **Augusta**, Western Australia, Australia
141 L 23 **Augusta**, Italy
59 P 6 **Augusta**, Maine, U.S.A.
63 V 3 **Augusta**, Georgia, U.S.A.
64 D 11 **Augusta**, Wisconsin, U.S.A.
65 D 18 **Augusta**, Illinois, U.S.A.
73 P 4 **Augusta**, Montana, U.S.A.
110 G 6 **Augusta Victoria**, Chile
142 N 9 **Augustów**, Poland
234 M 6 **Auki**, Solomon Islands
75 R 2 **Ault**, Colorado, U.S.A.
215 P 11 **Auna**, Nigeria
85 S 6 **Aupaluk**, Québec, Canada
193 R 12 **Auponhia**, Indonesia
237 Z 3 **Aur**, Marshall Islands
192 F 9 **Aur**, Malaysia
64 G 8 **Aura**, Michigan, U.S.A.
182 L 10 **Auraiya**, India
183 P 12 **Aurangabad**, India
128 J 6 **Auray**, France
136 D 10 **Aurich**, Germany
129 Q 11 **Aurillac**, France
135 B 18 **Aurlandsvangen**, Norway
196 H 8 **Aurora**, Philippines
65 G 16 **Aurora**, Illinois, U.S.A.
75 R 4 **Aurora**, Colorado, U.S.A.
108 K 10 **Aurora do Pará**, Brazil
231 R 2 **Aurukun**, Queensland, Australia
218 I 11 **Aus**, Namibia
67 T 10 **Austin**, Minnesota, U.S.A.
71 P 9 **Austin**, Texas, U.S.A.
77 L 17 **Austin**, Nevada, U.S.A.
41 T 10 **Austral Fracture Zone**, Pacific Ocean
41 S 10 **Austral Islands**, French Polynesia
231 N 6 **Australia**, Oceania
231 U 12 **Australian Capital Territory**, Australia
139 P 7 **Austria**, Europe
134 G 9 **Austvågøy**, Norway
108 F 11 **Autazes**, Brazil
89 N 11 **Autlán**, Mexico
129 S 8 **Autun**, France
129 Q 10 **Auvergne**, France
129 R 6 **Auxerre**, France
105 R 6 **Auyan Tepuí**, Venezuela
69 U 7 **Ava**, Missouri, U.S.A.
129 S 7 **Avallon**, France
58 I 15 **Avalon**, New Jersey, U.S.A.
85 Z 10 **Avalon Peninsula**, Newfoundland and Labrador, Canada
112 J 7 **Avaré**, Brazil
237 N 11 **Avarua**, Cook Islands
127 R 11 **Avebury**, United Kingdom
108 H 11 **Aveiro**, Brazil
130 H 5 **Aveiro**, Portugal
130 H 6 **Aveiro**, Portugal
141 K 16 **Avellino**, Italy
141 J 16 **Aversa**, Italy
72 K 4 **Avery**, Idaho, U.S.A.
42 E 12 **Aves Ridge**, Atlantic Ocean
129 S 2 **Avesnes-sur-Helpe**, France
135 G 19 **Avesta**, Sweden
110 L 7 **Aviá Terai**, Argentina
112 C 10 **Avia Teray**, Argentina
124 H 10 **Aviemore**, United Kingdom
129 T 13 **Avignon**, France
131 N 6 **Ávila**, Spain
130 L 1 **Avilés**, Spain
148 I 6 **Avinurme**, Estonia
147 G 19 **Avlida**, Greece
141 K 23 **Avola**, Italy
127 R 9 **Avon**, United Kingdom
58 E 8 **Avon**, New York, U.S.A.
63 W 11 **Avon Park**, Florida, U.S.A.
74 I 12 **Avondale**, Arizona, U.S.A.
128 L 4 **Avranches**, France
150 I 11 **Avrig**, Romania
213 L 24 **Aw Dheegle**, Somalia
198 J 12 **Awa-shima**, Japan
199 G 19 **Awaji-shima**, Japan
232 K 11 **Awakino**, New Zealand
175 T 5 **Awālī**, Bahrain
232 I 5 **Awanui**, New Zealand
213 L 21 **Āwarē**, Ethiopia
232 J 6 **Awarua**, New Zealand
233 B 21 **Awarua Point**, New Zealand
213 I 21 **Āwasa**, Ethiopia
213 J 20 **Āwash**, Ethiopia
213 J 19 **Āwash**, Ethiopia
233 I 17 **Awatere**, New Zealand
211 S 11 **Awbārī**, Libya
213 C 20 **Aweil**, Sudan
63 P 5 **Awin**, Alabama, U.S.A.
211 X 9 **Awjilah**, Libya
210 C 13 **Awserd**, Western Sahara
81 O 2 **Axel Heiberg Island**, Nunavut, Canada
146 E 13 **Axios**, Greece
127 O 13 **Axminster**, United Kingdom
107 E 17 **Ayacucho**, Peru
107 E 18 **Ayacucho**, Peru
113 D 18 **Ayacucho**, Argentina
179 X 6 **Ayagoz**, Kazakhstan
184 L 7 **Ayakkum Hu**, China
130 I 12 **Ayamonte**, Spain
153 V 12 **Ayan**, Russian Federation
170 J 7 **Ayancik**, Turkey
187 K 18 **Ayang**, North Korea
105 T 6 **Ayanganna Mountain**, Guyana
215 R 12 **Ayangba**, Nigeria
107 G 18 **Ayaviri**, Peru
177 T 6 **Āybak**, Afghanistan
151 Y 5 **Aydar**, Ukraine
170 C 11 **Aydin**, Turkey
170 B 11 **Aydin Dağlari**, Turkey
213 J 19 **Āyelu Terara**, Ethiopia
194 E 10 **Ayer Hitam**, Malaysia
131 S 3 **Ayerbe**, Spain
153 R 10 **Aykhal**, Russian Federation
233 H 20 **Aylesbury**, New Zealand
127 U 9 **Aylesbury**, United Kingdom
131 P 5 **Ayllón**, Spain
82 J 10 **Aylmer Lake**, Northwest Territories, Canada
127 Z 6 **Aylsham**, United Kingdom
179 R 13 **Ayni**, Tajikistan
213 E 21 **Ayod**, Sudan
131 S 9 **Ayora**, Spain
215 N 8 **Ayorou**, Niger
214 H 7 **'Ayoûn el 'Atroûs**, Mauritania
231 U 5 **Ayr**, Queensland, Australia
125 G 14 **Ayr**, United Kingdom
170 I 12 **Ayranci**, Turkey
179 N 8 **Ayteke Bi**, Kazakhstan
146 M 9 **Aytos**, Bulgaria
175 W 11 **Ayun**, Oman
191 H 18 **Ayutthaya**, Thailand
170 A 9 **Ayvacik**, Turkey
170 B 9 **Ayvalik**, Turkey
172 H 6 **Az Zabadānī**, Syria
172 H 9 **Az Zarqā'**, Jordan
211 S 7 **Az Zāwīyah**, Libya
175 O 13 **Az Zaydīyah**, Yemen
175 P 5 **Az Zilfī**, Saudi Arabia
211 R 8 **Az Zintān**, Libya
173 Z 12 **Az Zubayr**, Iraq
175 O 12 **Az Zuhrah**, Yemen
175 O 14 **Az Zuqur**, Yemen
91 N 6 **Azacualpa**, Honduras
76 F 13 **Azalea**, Oregon, U.S.A.
183 O 11 **Azamgarh**, India
176 F 4 **Āzarbāyjān-e Gharbī**, Iran
176 G 3 **Āzarbāyjān-e Sharqī**, Iran
215 S 10 **Azare**, Nigeria
149 L 20 **Azarychy**, Belarus
172 J 1 **A'zāz**, Syria
210 G 7 **Azemmour**, Morocco
171 V 10 **Azerbaijan**, Asia
213 H 18 **Āzezo**, Ethiopia
210 H 8 **Azilal**, Morocco
177 N 11 **'Azīzābād**, Iran

Country · Internal administrative region: State/Province/Territory/Dependent territory · Capital city · Mountain range/Undersea ridge · Mountain peak/Volcano/Seamount · Geographic feature · Headland/Point/Cape/Peninsula · Desert · Island/Island group · Antarctic base · Ocean · Sea · Bay/Gulf/Channel/Strait · Lake · Salt pan/Dry/Intermittent lake · R

42 O 1 **Azores**, Portugal □
42 J 8 **Azores-Biscay Rise**, Atlantic Ocean ▲
156 L 10 **Azov**, Russian Federation
172 I 9 **Azraq ash Shīshān**, Jordan
210 I 7 **Azrou**, Morocco
74 H 13 **Aztec**, Arizona, U.S.A.
75 O 8 **Aztec**, New Mexico, U.S.A.
93 Q 8 **Azua**, Dominican Republic
130 L 10 **Azuaga**, Spain
106 B 10 **Azuay**, Ecuador □
113 C 17 **Azul**, Argentina
214 E 5 **Azzeffâl**, Mauritania ▲

B

61 R 9 **B. Everett Jordan Reservoir**, North Carolina, U.S.A.
191 N 19 **Bă Kêv**, Cambodia
193 P 15 **Baa**, Indonesia
172 H 5 **Ba'albek**, Lebanon
172 G 6 **Baaqline**, Lebanon
213 L 24 **Baardheere**, Somalia
213 K 17 **Bāb al Mandab**, Africa/Asia ≈
170 G 7 **Baba Burnu**, Turkey ▶
170 A 9 **Baba Burun**, Turkey ▶
151 N 12 **Babadag**, Romania
171 X 7 **Babadağ Dağı**, Azerbaijan ▲
178 L 14 **Babadurmaz**, Turkmenistan
170 B 7 **Babaeski**, Turkey
213 C 19 **Babanusa**, Sudan
193 T 14 **Babar**, Indonesia ≈
217 U 10 **Babati**, Tanzania
154 I 11 **Babayevo**, Russian Federation
73 O 2 **Babb**, Montana, U.S.A.
127 N 14 **Babbacombe Bay**, United Kingdom ≈
194 F 9 **Babi Besar**, Malaysia ≈
33 E 18 **Babine Lake**, British Columbia, Canada
193 U 12 **Babo**, Indonesia
76 J 5 **Bābol**, Iran
?15 V 13 **Babongo**, Cameroon
?4 K 15 **Baboquivari Peak**, Arizona, U.S.A. ▲
16 G 4 **Baboua**, Central African Republic
49 L 19 **Babruysk**, Belarus
96 H 4 **Babuyan**, Philippines ≈
97 D 18 **Babuyan**, Philippines
96 G 5 **Babuyan Channel**, Philippines ≈
96 H 4 **Babuyan Islands**, Philippines ≈
90 M 11 **Băc Can**, Vietnam
90 M 12 **Băc Giang**, Vietnam
90 L 10 **Bac Lac**, Vietnam
91 M 23 **Bac Liêu**, Vietnam
90 M 12 **Băc Ninh**, Vietnam
90 L 11 **Băc Quang**, Vietnam
13 N 21 **Bacaadweyn**, Somalia
08 L 11 **Bacabal**, Brazil
08 I 11 **Bacajá**, Brazil
3 Z 12 **Bacalar**, Mexico
93 R 11 **Bacan**, Indonesia ≈
06 F 6 **Bacarra**, Philippines
60 L 9 **Bacău**, Romania
29 V 5 **Baccarat**, France
48 K 7 **Bach**, Austria
47 D 19 **Bacharach**, Germany
? K 1 **Back**, Nunavut, Canada
-4 J 9 **Bačka Palanka**, Serbia and Montenegro
44 J 8 **Bačka Topola**, Serbia and Montenegro
7 G 22 **Backnang**, Germany
7 J 17 **Bacolod**, Philippines
J 6 **Bácum**, Mexico
9 S 6 **Bad Aussee**, Austria
D 22 **Bad Bergzabern**, Germany
6 H 9 **Bad Bramstedt**, Germany
6 N 12 **Bad Freienwalde**, Germany
9 R 6 **Bad Goisern**, Austria
9 Q 7 **Bad Hofgastein**, Austria
7 E 14 **Bad Iburg**, Germany
9 R 5 **Bad Ischl**, Austria
9 S 8 **Bad Kleinkirchheim**, Austria

137 D 20 **Bad Kreuznach**, Germany
137 I 17 **Bad Langensalza**, Germany
139 T 3 **Bad Leonfelden**, Austria
137 H 21 **Bad Mergentheim**, Germany
137 H 19 **Bad Neustadt an der Saale**, Germany
136 H 10 **Bad Oldesloe**, Germany
139 X 8 **Bad Radkersburg**, Austria
137 L 25 **Bad Reichenhall**, Germany
137 H 17 **Bad Salzungen**, Germany
136 H 9 **Bad Segeberg**, Germany
139 U 7 **Bad St Leonhard**, Austria
137 J 25 **Bad Tölz**, Germany
137 G 25 **Bad Waldsee**, Germany
191 F 22 **Bada**, Myanmar ≈
181 D 22 **Badagara**, India
189 N 11 **Badahe**, China
185 O 7 **Badain Jaran Desert**, China ◇
130 J 9 **Badajoz**, Spain
177 V 5 **Badakhshān**, Afghanistan □
175 N 1 **Badanah**, Saudi Arabia
180 F 9 **Badarinath Peaks**, India ▲
183 W 11 **Badarpur**, India
87 X 8 **Baddeck**, Nova Scotia, Canada
177 R 12 **Baddo**, Pakistan ⌇
139 X 4 **Baden**, Austria
137 E 22 **Baden Baden**, Germany
137 E 23 **Baden-wurttemberg**, Germany □
139 Q 7 **Badgastein**, Austria
177 Q 7 **Bādghīs**, Afghanistan □
132 H 11 **Badhoevedorp**, Netherlands
131 Z 7 **Badia d'Alcúdia**, Spain ≈
131 X 8 **Badia di Palma**, Spain ≈
177 U 15 **Badin**, Pakistan
66 G 6 **Badlands**, North Dakota, U.S.A. ◇
196 F 6 **Badoc**, Philippines
189 R 6 **Badong**, China
215 N 12 **Badou**, Togo
174 L 6 **Badr Ḩunayn**, Saudi Arabia
173 W 7 **Badrah**, Iraq
182 L 6 **Badrinath Peaks**, India ▲
231 R 1 **Badu Island**, Queensland, Australia
181 G 25 **Badulla**, Sri Lanka
131 N 12 **Baena**, Spain
131 O 11 **Baeza**, Spain
214 E 10 **Bafatá**, Guinea-Bissau
45 O 9 **Baffin Basin**, Arctic Ocean ≈
45 N 10 **Baffin Bay**, Arctic Ocean ≈
85 Q 1 **Baffin Island**, Nunavut, Canada
215 T 14 **Bafia**, Cameroon
215 T 14 **Bafoussam**, Cameroon
176 L 9 **Bāfq**, Iran
170 K 7 **Bafra**, Turkey
170 L 7 **Bafra Burnu**, Turkey ▶
217 P 7 **Bafwasende**, Democratic Republic of Congo
196 G 8 **Bagabag**, Philippines
196 F 11 **Bagac**, Philippines
196 F 11 **Bagac Bay**, Philippines ≈
91 O 11 **Bagaces**, Costa Rica
183 O 10 **Bagaha**, India
181 D 19 **Bagalkot**, India
217 W 11 **Bagamoyo**, Tanzania
197 N 21 **Baganga**, Philippines
218 K 7 **Bagani**, Namibia
197 J 22 **Baganian Peninsula**, Philippines ▶
192 D 9 **Bagansiapiapi**, Indonesia
215 P 9 **Bagaroua**, Niger
216 J 10 **Bagata**, Democratic Republic of Congo
112 F 13 **Bagé**, Brazil
182 L 7 **Bageshwar**, India
73 V 15 **Baggs**, Wyoming, U.S.A.
126 M 12 **Baggy Point**, United Kingdom ▶
177 O 6 **Baghbaghū**, Iran
173 T 7 **Baghdad**, Iraq ■
141 I 21 **Bagheria**, Italy

176 L 10 **Bāghīn**, Iran
177 T 6 **Baghlān**, Afghanistan □
177 U 6 **Baghlān**, Afghanistan
177 R 8 **Baghrān**, Afghanistan
183 O 9 **Baglung**, Nepal
197 I 17 **Bago**, Philippines
140 E 6 **Bagolino**, Italy
149 B 16 **Bagrationovsk**, Russian Federation
108 J 10 **Bagre**, Brazil
173 W 8 **Bagsaya**, Iraq
127 U 11 **Bagshot**, United Kingdom
106 B 12 **Bagua**, Peru
215 P 10 **Bagudo**, Nigeria
196 F 8 **Baguio**, Philippines
196 H 6 **Baguio Point**, Philippines ▶
92 K 1 **Bahamas, The**, North America □
183 R 13 **Baharampur**, India
212 D 9 **Bahariya Oasis**, Egypt ◇
151 W 7 **Bahatyr**, Ukraine
194 D 9 **Bahau**, Malaysia
177 W 11 **Bahawalpur**, Pakistan
170 L 13 **Bahşşe**, Turkey
109 M 14 **Bahia**, Brazil □
111 K 16 **Bahía Anegada**, Argentina ≈
88 G 6 **Bahía Asunción**, Mexico
113 B 19 **Bahía Blanca**, Argentina ≈
113 B 19 **Bahía Blanca**, Argentina
111 I 19 **Bahía Bustamante**, Argentina ≈
111 I 19 **Bahía Camarones**, Argentina ≈
89 Z 12 **Bahía Chetumal**, Mexico ≈
90 J 4 **Bahía de Amatique**, Guatemala ≈
106 B 7 **Bahía de Ancón de Sardinas**, Ecuador ≈
88 G 6 **Bahía de Ballenas**, Mexico ≈
88 M 11 **Bahía de Banderas**, Mexico ≈
91 R 10 **Bahía de Bluefields**, Nicaragua ≈
89 V 11 **Bahía de Campeche**, Mexico ≈
106 A 9 **Bahía de Caráquez**, Ecuador ≈
90 L 1 **Bahía de Chetumal**, Belize ≈
111 G 26 **Bahía de Cook**, Chile ≈
91 Q 14 **Bahía de Coronado**, Costa Rica ≈
89 Z 11 **Bahía de Espíritu Santo**, Mexico ≈
90 K 8 **Bahía de Jiquilisco**, El Salvador ≈
89 Z 11 **Bahía de la Ascensión**, Mexico ≈
88 I 8 **Bahía de La Paz**, Mexico ≈
88 G 4 **Bahía de los Ángeles**, Mexico
106 A 9 **Bahía de Mania**, Ecuador ≈
91 X 14 **Bahía de Panamá**, Panama ≈
91 W 15 **Bahía de Parita**, Panama ≈
89 P 13 **Bahía de Petacalco**, Mexico ≈
93 R 7 **Bahía de Samaná**, Dominican Republic ≈
91 R 10 **Bahía de San Juan del Norte**, Nicaragua ≈
111 H 24 **Bahía de San Sebastián**, Argentina ≈
106 A 9 **Bahía de Santa Elena**, Ecuador ≈
88 K 7 **Bahía de Santa María**, Mexico ≈
106 A 12 **Bahía de Sechura**, Peru ≈
91 N 4 **Bahía de Trujillo**, Honduras ≈
93 R 7 **Bahía Escocesa**, Dominican Republic ≈
111 H 23 **Bahía Grande**, Argentina ≈
88 I 4 **Bahía Kino**, Mexico
111 I 21 **Bahía Laura**, Argentina
104 G 7 **Bahía Magdalena**, Colombia ≈

88 H 8 **Bahía Magdalena**, Mexico ≈
111 I 26 **Bahía Nassau**, Chile ≈
109 G 18 **Bahía Negra**, Paraguay
111 F 25 **Bahía Otway**, Chile ≈
110 F 8 **Bahía Salada**, Chile ≈
111 E 23 **Bahía Salvación**, Chile ≈
113 E 16 **Bahía Samborombón**, Argentina ≈
107 E 18 **Bahía San Nicolás**, Peru ≈
88 G 5 **Bahía Sebastián Vizcaíno**, Mexico ≈
111 I 19 **Bahía Solano**, Argentina ≈
88 F 5 **Bahía Tortugas**, Mexico
113 B 20 **Bahía Unión**, Argentina ≈
213 H 19 **Bahir Dar**, Ethiopia
213 A 19 **Bahr el Arab**, Sudan ◇
213 D 20 **Bahr el Ghazal**, Sudan ◇
213 E 23 **Bahr el Jebel**, Sudan □
182 M 9 **Bahraich**, India
175 U 4 **Bahrain**, Asia □
177 P 14 **Bāhū Kālāt**, Iran
149 M 15 **Bahushewsk**, Belarus
190 L 13 **Bai Thurong**, Vietnam
151 N 12 **Baia**, Romania
108 J 10 **Baía de Marajó**, Brazil ≈
219 U 5 **Baía de Memba**, Mozambique ≈
219 U 4 **Baía de Pemba**, Mozambique ≈
108 L 10 **Baía de São Marcos**, Brazil ≈
218 F 6 **Baía dos Tigres**, Angola
218 F 4 **Baía Farta**, Angola
150 I 8 **Baia Mare**, Romania
108 J 10 **Baião**, Brazil
176 L 8 **Baiazeh**, Iran
215 W 12 **Baïbokoum**, Chad
186 H 11 **Baicheng**, China
150 K 12 **Băicoi**, Romania
87 Q 5 **Baie-Comeau**, Québec, Canada
128 H 6 **Baie de Audierne**, France ≈
128 K 7 **Baie de Bourgneuf**, France ≈
128 H 5 **Baie de Douarnenez**, France ≈
128 M 3 **Baie de Seine**, France ≈
128 J 4 **Baie de St-Brieuc**, France ≈
87 N 7 **Baie-St-Paul**, Québec, Canada
87 R 5 **Baie-Trinité**, Québec, Canada
85 X 9 **Baie Verte**, Newfoundland and Labrador, Canada
187 M 14 **Baihe**, China
189 R 5 **Baihe**, China
186 G 10 **Bailang**, China
150 K 10 **Băile Tuşnad**, Romania
131 O 11 **Bailén**, Spain
108 J 9 **Bailique**, Brazil
133 J 22 **Baillonville**, Belgium
218 H 4 **Bailundo**, Angola
188 K 4 **Baima**, China
234 C 5 **Baimuru**, Papua New Guinea
63 S 6 **Bainbridge**, Georgia, U.S.A.
193 O 15 **Baing**, Indonesia
186 K 9 **Baiquan**, China
172 I 11 **Bā'ir**, Jordan
184 I 8 **Bairab Co**, China ⌇
183 Q 10 **Bairagnia**, India
79 O 5 **Baird Mountains**, Alaska, U.S.A. ▲
236 D 2 **Bairiki**, Kiribati ▪
186 F 13 **Bairin Qiao**, China
186 F 13 **Bairin Zuoqi**, China
179 Q 11 **Bairkum**, Kazakhstan
231 T 13 **Bairnsdale**, Victoria, Australia
189 O 7 **Baisha**, China
187 K 14 **Baishan**, China
187 L 14 **Baishan**, China
182 M 8 **Baitadi**, Nepal
188 I 4 **Baitang**, China
237 U 1 **Baiti**, Nauru
189 U 1 **Baixiang**, China

218 J 6 **Baixo-Longa**, Angola
188 J 5 **Baiyü**, China
213 F 15 **Baiyuda Desert**, Sudan ◇
183 S 14 **Baj Baj**, India
143 I 25 **Baja**, Hungary
88 F 2 **Baja California**, Mexico ▶
88 F 2 **Baja California Norte**, Mexico □
88 G 7 **Baja California Sur**, Mexico □
182 M 8 **Bajang**, Nepal
192 G 9 **Bajau**, Indonesia ≈
177 N 7 **Bajestān**, Iran
177 O 5 **Bājgīrān**, Iran
175 O 13 **Bājil**, Yemen
91 S 14 **Bajo Boquete**, Panama
111 G 21 **Bajo Caracoles**, Argentina
215 T 11 **Bajoga**, Nigeria
157 U 1 **Bakaly**, Russian Federation
179 V 8 **Bakanas**, Kazakhstan
215 Z 8 **Bakaoré**, Chad
214 G 8 **Bakel**, Senegal
73 Z 6 **Baker**, Montana, U.S.A.
76 K 11 **Baker**, Oregon, U.S.A.
77 L 23 **Baker**, California, U.S.A.
41 P 7 **Baker Island**, U.S.A. □
84 K 3 **Baker Lake**, Nunavut, Canada
77 J 23 **Bakersfield**, California, U.S.A.
127 S 4 **Bakewell**, United Kingdom
178 L 13 **Bakhardok**, Turkmenistan
151 T 12 **Bakhcyisaray**, Ukraine
178 K 13 **Bakherden**, Turkmenistan
151 S 2 **Bakhmach**, Ukraine
153 N 10 **Bakhta**, Russian Federation
183 Q 11 **Bakhtiyarpur**, India
179 Y 7 **Bakhty**, Kazakhstan
170 D 7 **Bakirköy**, Turkey
146 O 13 **Bakiröy**, Turkey
134 D 10 **Bakkaflói**, Iceland ≈
182 H 5 **Bakloh**, India
213 H 20 **Bako**, Ethiopia
214 I 11 **Bako**, Côte d'Ivoire
143 G 24 **Bakony**, Hungary ▲
213 L 23 **Bakool**, Somalia □
234 H 4 **Bakop**, Papua New Guinea
216 M 4 **Bakouma**, Central African Republic
157 O 13 **Baksan**, Russian Federation
171 Z 8 **Baku**, Azerbaijan ▪
171 S 7 **Bakuriani**, Georgia
240 K 10 **Bakutis Coast**, Antarctica ◇
127 N 5 **Bala**, United Kingdom
170 H 10 **Balâ**, Turkey
177 Q 6 **Bālā Morghāb**, Afghanistan
197 B 21 **Balabac**, Philippines
197 A 21 **Balabac**, Philippines ≈
197 A 21 **Balabac Strait**, Philippines ≈
151 U 7 **Balabyne**, Ukraine
173 T 6 **Balad**, Iraq
173 U 6 **Balad Rūz**, Iraq
181 G 15 **Balaghat**, India
181 D 17 **Balaghat Range**, India ▲
131 V 4 **Balaguer**, Spain
171 V 6 **Balakän**, Azerbaijan
151 T 13 **Balaklava**, Ukraine
151 W 5 **Balakliya**, Ukraine
157 R 5 **Balakovo**, Russian Federation
195 V 3 **Balambangan**, Malaysia ≈
196 F 11 **Balanga**, Philippines
181 H 16 **Balangir**, India
157 O 5 **Balashov**, Russian Federation
143 J 21 **Balassagyarmat**, Hungary
143 G 24 **Balaton**, Hungary ⌇
196 G 7 **Balbalan**, Philippines
108 F 10 **Balbina**, Brazil
91 W 13 **Balboa**, Panama
125 F 17 **Balbriggan**, Republic of Ireland
113 D 18 **Balcarce**, Argentina
146 N 7 **Balchik**, Bulgaria

233 E 25 **Balclutha**, New Zealand
70 N 10 **Balcones Escarpment**, Texas, U.S.A. ▲
61 T 12 **Bald Head Island**, North Carolina, U.S.A. ▶
69 W 10 **Bald Knob**, Arkansas, U.S.A.
63 W 7 **Baldwin**, Florida, U.S.A.
64 C 11 **Baldwin**, Wisconsin, U.S.A.
64 J 13 **Baldwin**, Michigan, U.S.A.
58 G 8 **Baldwinsville**, New York, U.S.A.
73 S 3 **Baldy Mountain**, Montana, U.S.A. ▲
84 H 9 **Baldy Mountain**, Manitoba, Canada ▲
74 M 12 **Baldy Peak**, Arizona, U.S.A. ▲
158 E 8 **Balearic Channel**, Mediterranean Sea ≈
131 V 9 **Balearic Islands**, Spain ≈
195 R 10 **Baleh**, Malaysia ⌇
196 H 9 **Baler**, Philippines
196 H 9 **Baler Bay**, Philippines ≈
181 K 16 **Baleshwar**, India
155 Q 13 **Balezino**, Russian Federation
184 K 5 **Balguntay**, China
175 S 14 **Balḩaf**, Yemen
180 C 13 **Bali**, India
192 L 14 **Bali**, Indonesia ≈
192 L 15 **Bali**, Indonesia ≈
192 K 14 **Bali Sea**, Indonesia ≈
192 D 9 **Balige**, Indonesia
170 C 9 **Balikesir**, Turkey
172 L 2 **Balikh**, Syria ⌇
192 M 11 **Balikpapan**, Indonesia
197 E 25 **Balimbing**, Philippines
197 L 20 **Balingasag**, Philippines
137 F 24 **Balingen**, Germany
195 P 8 **Balingian**, Malaysia
197 L 19 **Balingoon**, Philippines
196 G 3 **Balintang Channel**, Philippines ≈
216 M 5 **Balitondo**, Central African Republic
175 N 9 **Baljurshi**, Saudi Arabia
132 J 8 **Balk**, Netherlands
146 F 8 **Balkan Mountains**, Bulgaria ▲
178 J 12 **Balkanskiy Velayat**, Turkmenistan
179 Q 3 **Balkashino**, Kazakhstan
177 T 5 **Balkh**, Afghanistan □
179 U 7 **Balkhash**, Kazakhstan
124 G 11 **Ballachulish**, United Kingdom
230 J 11 **Balladonia**, Western Australia, Australia
125 C 17 **Ballaghaderreen**, Republic of Ireland
181 F 17 **Ballalpur**, India
125 G 14 **Ballantrae**, United Kingdom
231 R 13 **Ballarat**, Victoria, Australia
241 S 15 **Balleny Islands**, Antarctica ≈
231 W 9 **Ballina**, New South Wales, Australia
125 B 16 **Ballina**, Republic of Ireland
125 C 18 **Ballinasloe**, Republic of Ireland
70 M 7 **Ballinger**, Texas, U.S.A.
125 F 15 **Ballymena**, United Kingdom
125 C 16 **Ballysadare**, Republic of Ireland
111 G 20 **Balmaceda**, Chile
70 H 8 **Balmorhea**, Texas, U.S.A.
218 G 4 **Balombo**, Angola
180 B 13 **Balotra**, India
179 W 8 **Balpyk Bi**, Kazakhstan
181 N 11 **Balrampur**, India
231 R 11 **Balranald**, New South Wales, Australia
150 I 13 **Balş**, Romania
91 P 12 **Balsa**, Costa Rica ⌇
106 C 13 **Balsas**, Peru
108 K 12 **Balsas**, Brazil
89 R 13 **Balsas**, Mexico ⌇
138 E 7 **Balsthal**, Switzerland
151 O 7 **Balta**, Ukraine

Balta Berilovac – Battle Creek

144 O 13 **Balta Berilovac**, Serbia and Montenegro
150 M 8 **Bălţi**, Moldova
135 G 26 **Baltic Sea**, Europe
61 U 2 **Baltimore**, Maryland, U.S.A.
149 A 15 **Baltiysk**, Russian Federation
177 R 12 **Baluchistān**, Pakistan
197 J 15 **Balud**, Philippines
183 S 11 **Balurghat**, India
197 M 25 **Balut**, Philippines
148 I 10 **Balvi**, Latvia
179 V 10 **Balykchy**, Kyrgyzstan
178 I 7 **Balykshi**, Kazakhstan
177 N 11 **Bam**, Iran
215 U 10 **Bama**, Nigeria
189 P 11 **Bama**, China
231 R 1 **Bamaga**, Queensland, Australia
216 G 9 **Bambama**, Congo
218 K 6 **Bambangando**, Angola
216 K 4 **Bambari**, Central African Republic
137 I 20 **Bamberg**, Germany
61 O 14 **Bamberg**, South Carolina, U.S.A.
217 O 5 **Bambili**, Democratic Republic of Congo
216 I 5 **Bambio**, Central African Republic
213 G 19 **Bambudi**, Ethiopia
109 K 17 **Bambuí**, Brazil
188 I 6 **Bamda**, China
215 S 13 **Bamenda**, Cameroon
83 F 22 **Bamfield**, British Columbia, Canada
178 K 13 **Bami**, Turkmenistan
177 T 7 **Bāmīān**, Afghanistan
177 T 7 **Bāmīān**, Afghanistan
186 J 13 **Bamiancheng**, China
216 K 3 **Bamingui**, Central African Republic
216 K 2 **Bamingui-Bangoran**, Central African Republic
191 K 20 **Bâmnak**, Cambodia
127 N 12 **Bampton**, United Kingdom
177 O 13 **Bampūr**, Iran
190 K 13 **Ban Ban**, Laos
190 I 12 **Ban Boun Tai**, Laos
191 I 17 **Ban Bua Chum**, Thailand
191 J 21 **Ban Hat Lek**, Thailand
190 H 13 **Ban Houayxay**, Laos
191 G 21 **Ban Huai Yang**, Thailand
191 H 17 **Ban Khao Sai**, Thailand
191 E 24 **Ban Khok Kloi**, Thailand
191 G 24 **Ban Na San**, Thailand
191 I 14 **Ban Nalè**, Laos
191 L 15 **Ban Napè**, Laos
191 H 15 **Ban Pak Pat**, Thailand
191 K 15 **Ban Phaeng**, Laos
191 J 17 **Ban Phai**, Thailand
191 M 17 **Ban Phon**, Laos
191 J 15 **Ban Phu**, Thailand
191 G 19 **Ban Pong**, Thailand
191 G 18 **Ban Rai**, Thailand
191 F 15 **Ban Tha Song Yang**, Thailand
191 J 15 **Ban Thabôk**, Laos
191 M 17 **Ban Tôp**, Laos
191 K 14 **Ban Vang-An**, Laos
191 M 18 **Ban Xepian**, Laos
213 M 24 **Banaadir**, Somalia
236 C 3 **Banaba**, Kiribati
217 N 7 **Banalia**, Democratic Republic of Congo
237 P 2 **Banana**, Kiribati
181 O 25 **Bananga**, India
146 M 13 **Banarli**, Turkey
180 D 13 **Banas**, India
196 G 8 **Banaue**, Philippines
170 E 10 **Banaz**, Turkey
184 M 10 **Banbar**, China
125 F 16 **Banbridge**, United Kingdom
127 S 8 **Banbury**, United Kingdom
89 Z 12 **Banco Chinchorro**, Mexico
92 G 10 **Banco Gorda**, Jamaica
197 D 21 **Bancoran**, Philippines
86 G 11 **Bancroft**, Ontario, Canada
215 U 12 **Banda**, Cameroon
217 P 5 **Banda**, Democratic Republic of Congo
182 L 11 **Banda**, India
192 B 8 **Banda Aceh**, Indonesia
39 V 5 **Banda Sea**, Indian Ocean
193 S 13 **Banda Sea**, Indonesia
193 T 13 **Bandaneira**, Indonesia
176 L 12 **Bandar-e 'Abbās**, Iran
176 H 4 **Bandar-e Anzalī**, Iran
176 G 9 **Bandar-e Emām Khomeynī**, Iran
176 K 13 **Bandar-e Lengeh**, Iran
176 J 13 **Bandar-e Moghūyeh**, Iran
192 G 13 **Bandar Lampung**, Indonesia
195 S 6 **Bandar Seri Begawan**, Brunei
130 I 3 **Bande**, Spain
110 K 9 **Bandera**, Argentina
71 N 10 **Bandera**, Texas, U.S.A.
182 H 3 **Bandipur**, India
170 C 8 **Bandirma**, Turkey
76 E 12 **Bandon**, Oregon, U.S.A.
216 J 10 **Bandundu**, Democratic Republic of Congo
216 I 10 **Bandundu**, Democratic Republic of Congo
192 H 14 **Bandung**, Indonesia
150 M 13 **Băneasa**, Romania
92 M 6 **Banes**, Cuba
124 I 9 **Banff**, United Kingdom
83 I 20 **Banff**, Alberta, Canada
216 K 11 **Banga**, Democratic Republic of Congo
197 L 23 **Banga**, Philippines
197 N 21 **Bangai Point**, Philippines
181 D 21 **Bangalore**, India
195 T 6 **Bangar**, Malaysia
216 M 5 **Bangassou**, Central African Republic
193 P 11 **Banggai**, Indonesia
195 W 3 **Banggi**, Malaysia
211 W 7 **Banghāzī**, Libya
192 G 11 **Bangka**, Indonesia
193 Q 10 **Bangka**, Indonesia
192 K 14 **Bangkalan**, Indonesia
192 D 10 **Bangkinang**, Indonesia
192 F 11 **Bangko**, Indonesia
191 I 19 **Bangkok**, Thailand
183 U 12 **Bangladesh**, Asia
126 M 4 **Bangor**, United Kingdom
59 R 5 **Bangor**, Maine, U.S.A.
196 F 7 **Bangued**, Philippines
216 J 5 **Bangui**, Central African Republic
196 F 5 **Bangui**, Philippines
216 I 6 **Bangui-Motaba**, Congo
217 P 7 **Banguru**, Democratic Republic of Congo
216 M 3 **Bani**, Central African Republic
196 E 10 **Bani Point**, Philippines
175 O 10 **Banī Thawr**, Saudi Arabia
211 S 8 **Banī Walīd**, Libya
216 H 5 **Bania**, Central African Republic
234 G 7 **Baniara**, Papua New Guinea
215 O 10 **Banikoara**, Benin
172 H 4 **Bāniyās**, Syria
144 G 10 **Banja Luka**, Bosnia and Herzegovina
195 V 7 **Banjaran Brassey**, Malaysia
195 U 7 **Banjaran Crocker**, Malaysia
195 N 11 **Banjaran Klingkang**, Malaysia
195 T 9 **Banjaran Tama Abu**, Malaysia
192 L 12 **Banjarmasin**, Indonesia
214 D 9 **Banjul**, Gambia
215 N 9 **Bankilaré**, Niger
215 T 13 **Bankim**, Cameroon
72 K 9 **Banks**, Idaho, U.S.A.
82 E 5 **Banks Island**, Northwest Territories, Canada
235 R 9 **Banks Islands**, Vanuatu
76 J 6 **Banks Lake**, Washington, U.S.A.
233 I 20 **Banks Peninsula**, New Zealand
183 R 13 **Bankura**, India
189 P 13 **Banli**, China
177 V 8 **Bannu**, Pakistan
189 N 9 **Banqiao**, China
143 J 20 **Banská Bystrica**, Slovakia
146 G 11 **Bansko**, Bulgaria
181 C 14 **Banswara**, India
193 O 13 **Bantaeng**, Indonesia
197 K 16 **Bantayan**, Philippines
197 J 16 **Bantayan**, Philippines
215 O 12 **Bantè**, Benin
125 A 21 **Bantry Bay**, Republic of Ireland
215 U 13 **Banyo**, Cameroon
192 K 14 **Banyuwangi**, Indonesia
241 W 13 **Banzare Coast**, Antarctica
39 O 13 **Banzare Seamount**, Indian Ocean
191 N 21 **Bao Lôc**, Vietnam
187 C 15 **Baochang**, China
187 A 17 **Baode**, China
187 E 17 **Baodi**, China
187 D 18 **Baoding**, China
189 P 3 **Baoji**, China
189 R 8 **Baojing**, China
186 M 11 **Baolin**, China
186 O 10 **Baoqing**, China
216 H 4 **Baoro**, Central African Republic
188 J 10 **Baoshan**, China
185 S 6 **Baotou**, China
189 V 5 **Baoyi**, China
189 X 4 **Baoying**, China
180 C 12 **Bap**, India
175 O 7 **Baqarah**, Saudi Arabia
173 U 6 **Ba'qūbah**, Iraq
145 I 17 **Bar**, Serbia and Montenegro
150 M 6 **Bar**, Ukraine
59 S 6 **Bar Harbor**, Maine, U.S.A.
129 T 4 **Bar-le-Duc**, France
213 E 17 **Bara**, Sudan
215 T 11 **Bara**, Nigeria
193 R 12 **Bara**, Indonesia
182 M 10 **Bara Banki**, India
213 L 25 **Baraawe**, Somalia
172 J 3 **Baradah**, Syria
113 C 15 **Baradero**, Argentina
93 Q 8 **Barahona**, Dominican Republic
181 I 15 **Barakot**, India
195 S 7 **Baram**, Malaysia
181 C 18 **Baramati**, India
182 H 3 **Baramula**, India
149 H 19 **Baranavichy**, Belarus
79 W 11 **Baranof Island**, Alaska, U.S.A.
133 J 22 **Baraque de Fraiture**, Belgium
193 P 15 **Barate**, Indonesia
109 L 18 **Barbacena**, Brazil
112 M 5 **Barbacena**, Brazil
93 Z 11 **Barbados**, North America
131 U 3 **Barbastro**, Spain
130 K 14 **Barbate**, Spain
81 P 1 **Barbeau Peak**, Nunavut, Canada
128 M 10 **Barbezieux-St-Hilaire**, France
104 J 6 **Barbosa**, Colombia
93 Y 8 **Barbuda**, Antigua and Barbuda
231 S 6 **Barcaldine**, Queensland, Australia
130 J 10 **Barcarrota**, Spain
105 P 3 **Barcelona**, Venezuela
131 X 5 **Barcelona**, Spain
108 E 10 **Barcelos**, Brazil
143 G 26 **Barcs**, Hungary
155 T 13 **Barda**, Russian Federation
215 W 5 **Bardai**, Chad
183 W 14 **Bardarban**, Bangladesh
134 C 11 **Bárðarbunga**, Iceland
110 G 13 **Bardas Blancas**, Argentina
183 S 13 **Barddhaman**, India
143 L 19 **Bardejov**, Slovakia
140 A 7 **Bardonecchia**, Italy
126 K 6 **Bardsey Island**, United Kingdom
126 K 6 **Bardsey Sound**, United Kingdom
125 G 19 **Bardsley Island**, United Kingdom
60 H 5 **Bardstown**, Kentucky, U.S.A.
182 L 9 **Bareilly**, India
45 T 10 **Barents Plain**, Arctic Ocean
134 N 5 **Barents Sea**, Europe
45 U 13 **Barents Trough**, Arctic Ocean
213 H 17 **Barentu**, Eritrea
195 T 8 **Bareo**, Malaysia
184 H 9 **Barga**, China
213 O 19 **Bargaal**, Somalia
181 I 16 **Bargarh**, India
127 Z 11 **Barham**, United Kingdom
213 O 19 **Bari**, Somalia
216 K 6 **Bari**, Democratic Republic of Congo
141 N 15 **Bari**, Italy
211 O 6 **Barika**, Algeria
177 W 7 **Barikoi**, Afghanistan
104 L 4 **Barinas**, Venezuela
104 L 4 **Barinas**, Venezuela
212 E 11 **Bârîs**, Egypt
183 U 14 **Barisal**, Bangladesh
183 V 14 **Barisal**, Bangladesh
192 L 11 **Barito**, Indonesia
175 Y 6 **Barkā**, Oman
188 L 5 **Barkam**, China
148 I 11 **Barkava**, Latvia
183 Q 12 **Barki Sariaya**, India
60 D 7 **Barkley Lake**, Kentucky, U.S.A.
219 O 13 **Barkly East**, Republic of South Africa
231 P 5 **Barkly Homestead Roadhouse**, Northern Territory, Australia
231 O 3 **Barkly Tableland**, Northern Territory, Australia
184 M 5 **Barkol**, China
150 M 10 **Bârlad**, Romania
141 M 15 **Barletta**, Italy
142 E 11 **Barlinek**, Poland
180 B 13 **Barmer**, India
126 M 6 **Barmouth**, United Kingdom
126 M 6 **Barmouth Bay**, United Kingdom
43 N 25 **Barn Long Point**, St Helena
152 M 13 **Barnaul**, Russian Federation
127 V 10 **Barnet**, United Kingdom
132 J 12 **Barneveld**, Netherlands
70 K 8 **Barnhart**, Texas, U.S.A.
127 S 3 **Barnsley**, United Kingdom
59 P 11 **Barnstable**, Massachusetts, U.S.A.
126 M 12 **Barnstaple**, United Kingdom
61 N 14 **Barnwell**, South Carolina, U.S.A.
104 L 3 **Barquisimeto**, Venezuela
109 L 14 **Barra**, Brazil
124 D 11 **Barra**, United Kingdom
108 G 12 **Barra de São Manuel**, Brazil
109 G 15 **Barra do Bugres**, Brazil
108 L 12 **Barra do Corda**, Brazil
109 I 16 **Barra do Garças**, Brazil
112 H 12 **Barra do Ribeiro**, Brazil
89 S 8 **Barra Jesús María**, Mexico
91 S 5 **Barra Kruta**, Honduras
42 F 11 **Barracuda Fracture Zone**, Atlantic Ocean
42 F 11 **Barracuda Ridge**, Atlantic Ocean
108 L 13 **Barragem de Sobradinho**, Brazil
109 J 17 **Barragen de São Simão**, Brazil
104 J 3 **Barranca**, Venezuela
107 C 15 **Barranca**, Peru
105 R 4 **Barrancas**, Venezuela
104 I 2 **Barranquilla**, Colombia
58 M 9 **Barre**, Massachusetts, U.S.A.
110 G 11 **Barreal**, Argentina
109 L 14 **Barreiras**, Brazil
108 E 12 **Barreirinha do Baeta**, Brazil
130 G 9 **Barreiro**, Portugal
181 O 21 **Barren Island**, India
112 K 5 **Barretos**, Brazil
86 E 12 **Barrie**, Ontario, Canada
87 T 12 **Barrington**, Nova Scotia, Canada
231 S 9 **Barringun**, New South Wales, Australia
125 E 19 **Barrow**, Republic of Ireland
79 O 2 **Barrow**, Alaska, U.S.A.
231 N 5 **Barrow Creek**, Northern Territory, Australia
127 O 1 **Barrow-in-Furness**, United Kingdom
230 E 6 **Barrow Island**, Western Australia, Australia
127 O 11 **Barry**, United Kingdom
86 H 10 **Barrys Bay**, Ontario, Canada
179 W 6 **Barshatas**, Kazakhstan
179 R 5 **Barshyn**, Kazakhstan
77 L 23 **Barstow**, California, U.S.A.
148 C 12 **Bārta**, Latvia
136 L 8 **Barth**, Germany
105 U 5 **Bartica**, Guyana
170 H 7 **Bartin**, Turkey
231 T 3 **Bartle Frere**, Queensland, Australia
69 P 8 **Bartlesville**, Oklahoma, U.S.A.
60 A 10 **Bartlett**, Tennessee, U.S.A.
66 M 13 **Bartlett**, Nebraska, U.S.A.
58 M 5 **Barton**, Vermont, U.S.A.
127 U 3 **Barton-upon-Humber**, United Kingdom
142 K 8 **Bartoszyce**, Poland
63 W 11 **Bartow**, Florida, U.S.A.
175 S 13 **Barūm**, Yemen
192 M 10 **Barung**, Indonesia
192 K 15 **Barung**, Indonesia
192 C 9 **Barus**, Indonesia
185 T 4 **Baruun Urt**, Mongolia
181 C 15 **Barwani**, India
143 F 14 **Barycz**, Poland
149 K 16 **Barysaw**, Belarus
157 Q 3 **Barysh**, Russian Federation
175 Z 7 **Barzamān**, Oman
216 H 11 **Bas-Congo**, Democratic Republic of Congo
179 P 14 **Basaga**, Turkmenistan
110 L 8 **Basail**, Argentina
77 J 19 **Basalt**, Nevada, U.S.A.
216 K 7 **Basankusu**, Democratic Republic of Congo
196 H 2 **Basco**, Philippines
137 D 26 **Basel**, Germany
138 D 6 **Basel**, Switzerland
157 O 4 **Bashmakovo**, Russian Federation
176 H 10 **Bāsht**, Iran
151 S 8 **Bashtanka**, Ukraine
197 H 23 **Basilan**, Philippines
197 H 23 **Basilan Strait**, Philippines
127 X 10 **Basildon**, United Kingdom
141 M 17 **Basilicata**, Italy
73 U 9 **Basin**, Wyoming, U.S.A.
127 T 11 **Basingstoke**, United Kingdom
183 T 14 **Basirhat**, India
171 T 11 **Başkale**, Turkey
216 M 7 **Basoko**, Democratic Republic of Congo
77 K 14 **Basque**, Oregon, U.S.A.
231 S 14 **Bass Strait**, Tasmania, Australia
140 G 6 **Bassano del Grappa**, Italy
215 N 11 **Bassar**, Togo
219 U 8 **Bassas da India**, France
216 L 4 **Basse-Kotto**, Central African Republic
128 L 4 **Basse-Normandie**, France
93 Y 9 **Basse-Terre**, Guadeloupe
191 C 16 **Bassein**, Myanmar
131 V 3 **Bassella**, Spain
93 X 8 **Basseterre**, St Kitts and Nevis
66 L 12 **Bassett**, Nebraska, U.S.A.
215 O 12 **Bassila**, Benin
215 Z 7 **Basso**, Chad
67 U 3 **Basswood Lake**, Minnesota, U.S.A.
176 K 12 **Bastak**, Iran
176 G 3 **Bastānābād**, Iran
183 N 10 **Basti**, India
129 Z 14 **Bastia**, France
133 K 23 **Bastogne**, Belgium
62 J 4 **Bastrop**, Louisiana, U.S.A.
71 Q 10 **Bastrop**, Texas, U.S.A.
215 S 15 **Bata**, Equatorial Guinea
196 F 11 **Bataan Peninsula**, Philippines
196 F 6 **Batac**, Philippines
153 T 9 **Batagay**, Russian Federation
112 H 5 **Bataguassu**, Brazil
146 H 11 **Batak**, Bulgaria
192 L 13 **Batakan**, Indonesia
182 H 5 **Batala**, India
192 F 10 **Batam**, Indonesia
217 O 7 **Batama**, Democratic Republic of Congo
153 T 10 **Batamay**, Russian Federation
196 H 2 **Batan**, Philippines
196 K 13 **Batan**, Philippines
196 H 3 **Batan Islands**, Philippines
188 J 7 **Batang**, China
216 D 8 **Batanga**, Gabon
196 G 12 **Batangas**, Philippines
197 E 16 **Batas**, Philippines
58 D 8 **Batavia**, New York, U.S.A.
39 S 8 **Batavia Seamount**, Indian Ocean
156 L 10 **Bataysk**, Russian Federation
197 H 16 **Batbatan**, Philippines
230 M 1 **Batchelor**, Northern Territory, Australia
191 J 20 **Bătdâmbâng**, Cambodia
231 U 12 **Batemans Bay**, New South Wales, Australia
61 N 12 **Batesburg**, South Carolina, U.S.A.
62 M 2 **Batesville**, Mississippi, U.S.A.
69 W 9 **Batesville**, Arkansas, U.S.A.
71 N 12 **Batesville**, Texas, U.S.A.
127 Q 11 **Bath**, United Kingdom
58 F 9 **Bath**, New York, U.S.A.
59 P 6 **Bath**, Maine, U.S.A.
87 R 9 **Bath**, New Brunswick, Canada
215 X 8 **Batha**, Chad
182 H 7 **Bathinda**, India
132 L 11 **Bathmen**, Netherlands
231 U 11 **Bathurst**, New South Wales, Australia
87 S 7 **Bathurst**, New Brunswick, Canada
45 O 7 **Bathurst Island**, Canada
82 H 9 **Bathurst Inlet**, Nunavut, Canada
82 I 8 **Bathurst Inlet**, Nunavut, Canada
230 L 1 **Bathurst Island**, Northern Territory, Australia
81 O 3 **Bathurst Island**, Nunavut, Canada
213 J 19 **Batī**, Ethiopia
170 E 13 **Bati Toroslar**, Turkey
171 Q 12 **Batman**, Turkey
211 O 6 **Batna**, Algeria
144 L 12 **Batočina**, Serbia and Montenegro
62 K 7 **Baton Rouge**, Louisiana, U.S.A.
182 H 4 **Batote**, India
215 V 14 **Batouri**, Cameroon
172 G 5 **Batroûn**, Lebanon
134 M 5 **Båtsfjord**, Norway
181 N 24 **Batti Malv**, India
181 G 24 **Batticaloa**, Sri Lanka
127 X 12 **Battle**, United Kingdom
65 J 15 **Battle Creek**, Michigan, U.S.A.

Country · Internal administrative region: State/Province/Territory/Dependent territory · Capital city · Mountain range/Undersea ridge · Mountain peak/Volcano/Seamount · Geographic feature · Headland/Point/Cape/Peninsula · Desert · Island/Island group · Antarctic base · Ocean · Sea · Bay/Gulf/Channel/Strait · Lake · Salt pan/Dry/Intermittent lake · Ri

■ Country □ Internal administrative region: State/Province/Territory/Dependent territory ▲ Capital city ▲ Mountain range/Undersea ridge ▲ Mountain peak/Volcano/Seamount ◇ Geographic feature ▶ Headland/Point/Cape/Peninsula ⊛ Desert ≥ Island/Island group ▦ Antarctic base ⊚ Ocean ≈ Sea ≈ Bay/Gulf/Channel/Strait ≈ Lake ↘ Salt pan/Dry/Intermittent lake ▶ River

■ Country ▣ Internal administrative region: State/Province/Territory/Dependent territory ▲ Capital city ▲▲ Mountain range/ Undersea ridge ▲ Mountain peak/ Volcano/Seamount ◇ Geographic feature ▶ Headland/Point/ Cape/Peninsula ▼ Desert ⌑ Island/Island group ▣ Antarctic base ⌐ Ocean ⌐ Sea ≈ Bay/Gulf/Channel/Strait ⌇ Lake ⌊ Salt pan/ Intermittent lake ⌇ River

272

Country ▢ Internal administrative region: State/Province/Territory/Dependent territory ▲ Capital city ▲ Mountain range/Undersea ridge ▲ Mountain peak/Volcano/Seamount ◇ Geographic feature ► Headland/Point/Cape/Peninsula ▲ Desert ⌇ Island/Island group ⊞ Antarctic base ◇ Ocean ≈ Sea ≈ Bay/Gulf/Channel/Strait ⌇ Lake ⌇ Salt pan/Dry/Intermittent lake ⌇ River

235	P 14	**Bourail**, New Caledonia
129	U 9	**Bourg-en-Bresse**, France
129	W 10	**Bourg-St-Maurice**, France
129	P 10	**Bourganeuf**, France
129	Q 7	**Bourges**, France
129	R 7	**Bourgogne**, France ▣
129	T 10	**Bourgoin-Jallieu**, France
231	S 9	**Bourke**, New South Wales, Australia
127	V 6	**Bourne**, United Kingdom
127	R 13	**Bournemouth**, United Kingdom
133	L 24	**Bourscheid**, Luxembourg
215	Z 10	**Bourtoutou**, Chad
74	H 12	**Bouse**, Arizona, U.S.A.
215	W 11	**Bousso**, Chad
133	H 19	**Boutersem**, Belgium
214	F 7	**Boutilimit**, Mauritania
43	M 21	**Bouvetøya**, Norway ▣
215	Q 9	**Bouza**, Niger
127	N 14	**Bovey Tracey**, United Kingdom
72	K 5	**Bovill**, Idaho, U.S.A.
112	C 13	**Bovril**, Argentina
66	I 2	**Bowbells**, North Dakota, U.S.A.
231	U 5	**Bowen**, Queensland, Australia
71	P 5	**Bowie**, Texas, U.S.A.
74	M 14	**Bowie**, Arizona, U.S.A.
60	F 7	**Bowling Green**, Kentucky, U.S.A.
61	T 5	**Bowling Green**, Virginia, U.S.A.
65	L 17	**Bowling Green**, Ohio, U.S.A.
69	W 3	**Bowling Green**, Missouri, U.S.A.
66	G 6	**Bowman**, North Dakota, U.S.A.
81	S 6	**Bowman Bay**, Nunavut, Canada ≈
240	H 4	**Bowman Coast**, Antarctica ◇
241	Y 10	**Bowman Island**, Antarctica ⌓
231	U 12	**Bowral**, New South Wales, Australia
187	F 19	**Boxing**, China
133	K 15	**Boxmeer**, Netherlands
133	I 15	**Boxtel**, Netherlands
170	J 7	**Boyabat**, Turkey
104	J 6	**Boyaca**, Colombia ▣
189	W 7	**Boyang**, China
62	I 6	**Boyce**, Louisiana, U.S.A.
73	T 7	**Boyd**, Montana, U.S.A.
125	C 16	**Boyle**, Republic of Ireland
83	J 17	**Boyle**, Alberta, Canada
107	L 22	**Boyuibe**, Bolivia
170	B 11	**Boz Dağlari**, Turkey
170	C 13	**Bozburun**, Turkey
170	A 9	**Bozcaada**, Turkey ⌓
73	Q 7	**Bozeman**, Montana, U.S.A.
189	V 4	**Bozhou**, China
170	G 13	**Bozkir**, Turkey
216	I 4	**Bozoum**, Central African Republic
171	N 12	**Bozova**, Turkey
170	E 9	**Bozüyük**, Turkey
140	E 8	**Bozzolo**, Italy
140	B 8	**Bra**, Italy
240	H 4	**Brabant Island**, Antarctica ⌓
133	F 19	**Brabant Wallon**, Belgium ▣
159	N 5	**Brač**, Mediterranean Sea ⌓
86	F 11	**Bracebridge**, Ontario, Canada
127	T 9	**Brackley**, United Kingdom
127	U 11	**Bracknell**, United Kingdom
150	G 10	**Brad**, Romania
63	V 11	**Bradenton**, Florida, U.S.A.
127	S 2	**Bradford**, United Kingdom
127	Q 11	**Bradford-on-Avon**, United Kingdom
71	N 8	**Brady**, Texas, U.S.A.
124	J 4	**Brae**, United Kingdom
124	I 11	**Braemar**, United Kingdom
130	H 4	**Braga**, Portugal ▣
130	H 4	**Braga**, Portugal
113	C 16	**Bragado**, Argentina
108	K 10	**Bragança**, Brazil
130	J 4	**Bragança**, Portugal ▣
130	K 4	**Bragança**, Portugal
149	M 21	**Brahin**, Belarus
183	V 13	**Brahmanbaria**, Bangladesh
181	I 17	**Brahmapur**, India
183	W 10	**Brahmaputra**, India ∿
126	K 6	**Braich y Pwll**, United Kingdom ▶
150	M 11	**Brăila**, Romania
133	F 20	**Braine-l'Alleud**, Belgium
67	R 6	**Brainerd**, Minnesota, U.S.A.
127	X 9	**Braintree**, United Kingdom
136	E 11	**Brake**, Germany
214	F 7	**Brâkna**, Mauritania ▣
127	Z 7	**Brampton**, United Kingdom
86	E 13	**Brampton**, Ontario, Canada
136	E 13	**Bramsche**, Germany
43	A 16	**Branco**, Cape Verde ⌓
108	E 9	**Branco**, Brazil ∿
218	G 9	**Brandberg**, Namibia ▲
135	D 19	**Brandbu**, Norway
137	M 14	**Brandenburg**, Germany ▣
136	L 13	**Brandenburg**, Germany
127	X 7	**Brandon**, United Kingdom
84	H 10	**Brandon**, Manitoba, Canada
218	K 13	**Brandvlei**, Republic of South Africa
63	U 8	**Branford**, Florida, U.S.A.
142	J 8	**Braniewo**, Poland
240	H 3	**Bransfield Strait**, Antarctica ≈
142	N 11	**Brańsk**, Poland
69	T 8	**Branson**, Missouri, U.S.A.
86	E 13	**Brantford**, Ontario, Canada
63	Q 6	**Brantley**, Alabama, U.S.A.
87	Y 9	**Bras d'Or Lake**, Nova Scotia, Canada ∽
108	A 11	**Brasil**, Brazil
109	C 14	**Brasiléia**, Brazil
109	J 16	**Brasília**, Brazil ⌂
149	I 14	**Braslaw**, Belarus
150	K 11	**Braşov**, Romania
133	G 17	**Brasschaat**, Belgium
63	T 1	**Brasstown Bald**, Georgia, U.S.A. ▲
143	G 21	**Bratislava**, Slovakia ⌂
153	P 12	**Bratsk**, Russian Federation
153	P 12	**Bratskoye Vodokhranilishche**, Russian Federation ∽
58	M 9	**Brattleboro**, Vermont, U.S.A.
151	O 11	**Braţul Chilia**, Romania ∿
151	N 12	**Braţul Sfântu Gheorghe**, Romania ∿
151	O 12	**Braţul Sulina**, Romania ∿
139	Q 4	**Braunau am Inn**, Austria
137	I 15	**Braunlage**, Germany
136	I 13	**Braunschweig**, Germany
126	M 12	**Braunton**, United Kingdom
43	A 17	**Brava**, Cape Verde ⌓
77	M 26	**Brawley**, California, U.S.A.
85	P 1	**Bray Island**, Nunavut, Canada ⌓
108	H 13	**Brazil**, South America □
65	H 19	**Brazil**, Indiana, U.S.A.
43	I 18	**Brazil Basin**, Atlantic Ocean ◇
109	K 16	**Brazilian Highlands**, Brazil ⛰
71	Q 7	**Brazos**, Texas, U.S.A. ∿
216	H 10	**Brazzaville**, Congo ⌂
144	I 10	**Brčko**, Bosnia and Herzegovina
142	H 10	**Brda**, Poland ∿
41	Y 15	**Break im Hip**, Pitcairn Island ▶
233	A 24	**Breaksea Island**, New Zealand ⌓
232	K 6	**Bream Bay**, New Zealand ≈
133	G 16	**Brecht**, Belgium
71	N 6	**Breckenridge**, Texas, U.S.A.
143	F 20	**Břeclav**, Czech Republic
127	O 9	**Brecon**, United Kingdom
127	N 9	**Brecon Beacons**, United Kingdom ⛰
133	H 15	**Breda**, Netherlands
218	K 15	**Bredasdorp**, Republic of South Africa
136	F 7	**Bredstedt**, Germany
133	J 17	**Bree**, Belgium
146	E 11	**Bregalnica**, Macedonia (F.Y.R.O.M.) ∿
137	G 26	**Bregenz**, Germany
138	J 6	**Bregenz**, Austria
146	F 6	**Bregovo**, Bulgaria
134	A 10	**Breida Fjörður**, Iceland ≈
134	D 11	**Breiðdalsvík**, Iceland
66	J 6	**Breien**, North Dakota, U.S.A.
108	M 11	**Brejo**, Brazil
136	F 11	**Bremen**, Germany ▣
136	F 11	**Bremen**, Germany
136	F 10	**Bremerhaven**, Germany
76	G 7	**Bremerton**, Washington, U.S.A.
136	G 10	**Bremervörde**, Germany
71	R 9	**Brenham**, Texas, U.S.A.
138	M 8	**Brenner**, Austria
140	E 6	**Breno**, Italy
127	W 10	**Brentwood**, United Kingdom
140	E 7	**Brescia**, Italy
133	D 16	**Breskens**, Netherlands
140	G 4	**Bressanone**, Italy
124	K 5	**Bressay**, United Kingdom ⌓
128	M 8	**Bressuire**, France
128	H 5	**Brest**, France
149	E 21	**Brest**, Belarus
149	G 20	**Brestskaya Voblasts'**, Belarus ▣
128	I 5	**Bretagne**, France ▣
129	Q 3	**Breteuil**, France
62	M 8	**Breton Sound**, Louisiana, U.S.A. ≈
137	F 22	**Bretten**, Germany
60	L 10	**Brevard**, North Carolina, U.S.A.
108	J 10	**Breves**, Brazil
78	L 6	**Brevig Mission**, Alaska, U.S.A.
231	T 9	**Brewarrina**, New South Wales, Australia
59	R 5	**Brewer**, Maine, U.S.A.
76	J 6	**Brewster**, Washington, U.S.A.
63	P 6	**Brewton**, Alabama, U.S.A.
146	F 9	**Breznik**, Bulgaria
150	I 11	**Brezoi**, Romania
216	L 4	**Bria**, Central African Republic
129	W 11	**Briançon**, France
91	S 13	**Bribri**, Costa Rica
150	M 7	**Briceni**, Moldova
127	N 10	**Bridgend**, United Kingdom
58	L 12	**Bridgeport**, Connecticut, U.S.A.
66	G 13	**Bridgeport**, Nebraska, U.S.A.
77	I 19	**Bridgeport**, California, U.S.A.
73	T 8	**Bridger**, Montana, U.S.A.
58	I 15	**Bridgeton**, New Jersey, U.S.A.
230	G 12	**Bridgetown**, Western Australia, Australia
93	Z 12	**Bridgetown**, Barbados ⌂
87	U 11	**Bridgewater**, Nova Scotia, Canada
127	P 7	**Bridgnorth**, United Kingdom
59	O 6	**Bridgton**, Maine, U.S.A.
127	P 12	**Bridgwater**, United Kingdom
127	O 11	**Bridgwater Bay**, United Kingdom ≈
127	V 1	**Bridlington**, United Kingdom
127	V 1	**Bridlington Bay**, United Kingdom ≈
127	P 13	**Bridport**, United Kingdom
138	H 8	**Briel**, Switzerland
129	T 5	**Brienne-le-Château**, France
138	F 8	**Brienz**, Switzerland
141	L 16	**Brienza**, Italy
138	E 8	**Brienzer See**, Switzerland ∽
138	E 10	**Brig**, Switzerland
127	V 3	**Brigg**, United Kingdom
74	J 1	**Brigham City**, Utah, U.S.A.
231	S 13	**Bright**, Victoria, Australia
233	E 25	**Brighton**, New Zealand
127	W 13	**Brighton**, United Kingdom
63	X 11	**Brighton**, Florida, U.S.A.
65	L 15	**Brighton**, Michigan, U.S.A.
75	R 3	**Brighton**, Colorado, U.S.A.
214	D 9	**Brikama**, Gambia
134	D 10	**Brimnes**, Iceland
141	O 16	**Brindisi**, Italy
69	X 11	**Brinkley**, Arkansas, U.S.A.
129	R 11	**Brioude**, France
231	W 9	**Brisbane**, Queensland, Australia
127	P 11	**Bristol**, United Kingdom
60	M 8	**Bristol**, Tennessee, U.S.A.
63	S 7	**Bristol**, Florida, U.S.A.
79	N 11	**Bristol Bay**, Alaska, U.S.A. ≈
126	M 11	**Bristol Channel**, United Kingdom ≈
77	M 24	**Bristol Lake**, California, U.S.A. ∽
83	E 17	**British Columbia**, Canada ▣
129	P 11	**Brive-la-Gaillarde**, France
131	P 2	**Briviesca**, Spain
127	N 14	**Brixham**, United Kingdom
143	F 19	**Brno**, Czech Republic
126	J 9	**Broad Haven**, United Kingdom
124	F 10	**Broadford**, United Kingdom
127	Z 11	**Broadstairs**, United Kingdom
73	X 7	**Broadus**, Montana, U.S.A.
83	O 19	**Broadview**, Saskatchewan, Canada
127	R 9	**Broadway**, United Kingdom
84	I 6	**Brochet**, Manitoba, Canada
59	O 10	**Brockton**, Massachusetts, U.S.A.
86	I 12	**Brockville**, Ontario, Canada
58	D 11	**Brockway**, Pennsylvania, U.S.A.
146	C 11	**Brod**, Macedonia (F.Y.R.O.M.)
81	P 5	**Brodeur Peninsula**, Nunavut, Canada ▶
142	J 10	**Brodnica**, Poland
150	J 4	**Brody**, Ukraine
76	K 11	**Brogan**, Oregon, U.S.A.
69	Q 9	**Broken Arrow**, Oklahoma, U.S.A.
69	R 13	**Broken Bow**, Oklahoma, U.S.A.
69	R 12	**Broken Bow Reservoir**, Oklahoma, U.S.A. ∽
231	R 10	**Broken Hill**, New South Wales, Australia
39	Q 8	**Broken Plateau**, Indian Ocean ◇
105	X 6	**Brokopondo**, Suriname
127	W 11	**Bromley**, United Kingdom
127	R 7	**Bromsgrove**, United Kingdom
135	C 23	**Brønderslev**, Denmark
140	C 7	**Broni**, Italy
70	M 7	**Bronte**, Texas, U.S.A.
231	T 15	**Bronte Park**, Tasmania, Australia
197	C 20	**Brooke's Point**, Philippines
69	T 2	**Brookfield**, Missouri, U.S.A.
62	L 6	**Brookhaven**, Mississippi, U.S.A.
67	P 9	**Brookings**, South Dakota, U.S.A.
77	E 14	**Brookings**, Oregon, U.S.A.
61	R 7	**Brookneal**, Virginia, U.S.A.
79	O 4	**Brooks Range**, Alaska, U.S.A. ⛰
63	V 10	**Brooksville**, Florida, U.S.A.
230	G 11	**Brookton**, Western Australia, Australia
65	K 19	**Brookville Lake**, Indiana, U.S.A. ∽
230	I 4	**Broome**, Western Australia, Australia
150	K 8	**Broşteni**, Romania
181	N 22	**Brothers**, India ⌓
129	O 5	**Brou**, France
151	Q 3	**Brovary**, Ukraine
70	K 5	**Brownfield**, Texas, U.S.A.
73	O 2	**Browning**, Montana, U.S.A.
65	I 20	**Brownstown**, Indiana, U.S.A.
60	A 9	**Brownsville**, Tennessee, U.S.A.
71	Q 15	**Brownsville**, Texas, U.S.A.
71	N 7	**Brownwood**, Texas, U.S.A.
149	L 19	**Brozha**, Belarus
62	M 2	**Bruce**, Mississippi, U.S.A.
64	D 10	**Bruce**, Wisconsin, U.S.A.
64	G 8	**Bruce Crossing**, Michigan, U.S.A.
86	C 11	**Bruce Peninsula**, Ontario, Canada ▶
137	F 22	**Bruchsal**, Germany
139	Q 7	**Bruck**, Austria
139	Y 4	**Bruck an der Leitha**, Austria
139	V 6	**Bruck an der Mur**, Austria
192	A 8	**Brueuh**, Indonesia ⌓
133	C 17	**Bruges**, Belgium
183	Z 7	**Bruint**, India
64	D 8	**Brule**, Wisconsin, U.S.A.
133	G 24	**Brûly**, Belgium
109	M 15	**Brumado**, Brazil
132	L 12	**Brummen**, Netherlands
63	R 5	**Brundidge**, Alabama, U.S.A.
195	T 7	**Brunei**, Asia □
195	T 6	**Brunei Bay**, Malaysia ≈
140	G 4	**Brunico**, Italy
136	F 9	**Brunsbüttel**, Germany
59	P 7	**Brunswick**, Maine, U.S.A.
63	W 6	**Brunswick**, Georgia, U.S.A.
69	T 3	**Brunswick**, Missouri, U.S.A.
241	N 3	**Brunt Ice Shelf**, Antarctica ◇
143	G 17	**Bruntál**, Czech Republic
231	T 15	**Bruny Island**, Tasmania, Australia ⌓
144	M 13	**Brus**, Serbia and Montenegro
91	P 4	**Brus Laguna**, Honduras ∽
75	T 3	**Brush**, Colorado, U.S.A.
138	K 10	**Brusio**, Switzerland
133	E 19	**Brussels**, Belgium ⌂
142	H 9	**Brusy**, Poland
151	O 4	**Brusyliv**, Ukraine
65	K 16	**Bryan**, Ohio, U.S.A.
71	R 9	**Bryan**, Texas, U.S.A.
240	J 8	**Bryan Coast**, Antarctica ◇
151	Y 6	**Bryanka**, Ukraine
156	I 3	**Bryansk**, Russian Federation
156	H 4	**Bryanskaya Oblast'**, Russian Federation ▣
127	N 9	**Brynamman**, United Kingdom
232	J 7	**Brynderwyn**, New Zealand
60	K 10	**Bryson City**, North Carolina, U.S.A.
144	O 11	**Brza**, Serbia and Montenegro
143	G 15	**Brzeg**, Poland
213	K 25	**Bu'aale**, Somalia
237	U 1	**Buada Lagoon**, Nauru ∽
234	L 6	**Buala**, Solomon Islands
211	T 8	**Bu'ayrāt al Hasūn**, Libya
214	E 10	**Buba**, Guinea-Bissau
175	S 2	**Bubīyān Island**, Kuwait ⌓
235	Y 11	**Buca**, Fiji
104	J 5	**Bucaramanga**, Colombia
197	N 19	**Bucas Grande**, Philippines ⌓
141	K 16	**Buccino**, Italy
124	J 10	**Buchan Ness**, United Kingdom ▶
214	H 13	**Buchanan**, Liberia
61	Q 6	**Buchanan**, Virginia, U.S.A.
85	X 10	**Buchans**, Newfoundland and Labrador, Canada
150	J 13	**Bucharest**, Romania ⌂
127	N 14	**Buckfastleigh**, United Kingdom
61	P 3	**Buckhannon**, West Virginia, U.S.A.
61	S 6	**Buckingham**, Virginia, U.S.A.
79	N 6	**Buckland**, Alaska, U.S.A.
241	S 15	**Buckle Island**, Antarctica ⌓
68	K 6	**Bucklin**, Kansas, U.S.A.
143	G 19	**Bučovice**, Czech Republic
65	M 17	**Bucyrus**, Ohio, U.S.A.
149	M 20	**Buda-Kashelyova**, Belarus
143	I 23	**Budapest**, Hungary ⌂
182	K 9	**Budaun**, India
241	X 11	**Budd Coast**, Antarctica ◇
141	C 16	**Buddusò**, Italy
126	L 13	**Bude**, United Kingdom
62	K 6	**Bude**, Mississippi, U.S.A.
126	K 13	**Bude Bay**, United Kingdom ≈
133	J 17	**Budel**, Netherlands
157	O 12	**Budennovsk**, Russian Federation
150	L 13	**Budeşti**, Romania
216	K 6	**Budjala**, Democratic Republic of Congo
154	G 11	**Budogoshch'**, Russian Federation
145	I 16	**Budva**, Serbia and Montenegro
215	S 14	**Buea**, Cameroon
111	H 19	**Buen Pasto**, Argentina
110	I 12	**Buena Esperanza**, Argentina
77	I 23	**Buena Vista Lake Bed**, California, U.S.A. ∽
104	G 7	**Buenaventura**, Colombia
88	L 4	**Buenaventura**, Mexico
196	H 13	**Buenavista**, Philippines
88	J 8	**Buenavista**, Mexico
113	D 16	**Buenos Aires**, Argentina ⌂
113	C 17	**Buenos Aires**, Argentina ▣
91	R 13	**Buenos Aires**, Costa Rica
88	M 6	**Búfalo**, Mexico
58	D 8	**Buffalo**, New York, U.S.A.
60	D 9	**Buffalo**, Tennessee, U.S.A.
66	G 7	**Buffalo**, South Dakota, U.S.A.
68	J 8	**Buffalo**, Oklahoma, U.S.A.
69	U 6	**Buffalo**, Missouri, U.S.A.
71	R 8	**Buffalo**, Texas, U.S.A.
73	W 9	**Buffalo**, Wyoming, U.S.A.
83	K 16	**Buffalo Narrows**, Saskatchewan, Canada
150	K 12	**Buftea**, Romania
142	N 12	**Bug**, Poland ∿
104	H 7	**Buga**, Colombia
217	S 8	**Bugala Island**, Uganda ⌓
215	R 12	**Bugana**, Nigeria
197	H 16	**Bugasong**, Philippines
178	I 13	**Bugdayli**, Turkmenistan
42	O 5	**Bugio**, Madeira ⌓
155	O 2	**Bugrino**, Russian Federation
197	B 20	**Bugsuk**, Philippines ⌓
186	H 8	**Bugt**, China
197	J 14	**Bugui Point**, Philippines ▶
157	U 2	**Bugul'ma**, Russian Federation
157	U 3	**Buguruslan**, Russian Federation
172	K 2	**Buḩayrat al Asad**, Syria ∽
173	S 8	**Buḩayrat ar Razāzah**, Iraq ∽
173	S 6	**Buḩayrat ath Tharthār**, Iraq ∽
172	I 5	**Buḩayrat Qaţţīnah**, Syria ∽
72	L 12	**Buhl**, Idaho, U.S.A.
150	L 9	**Buhuşi**, Romania
127	O 8	**Builth Wells**, United Kingdom
234	J 5	**Buin**, Papua New Guinea
157	R 2	**Buinsk**, Russian Federation
185	U 3	**Buir Nur**, China ∽

□ Country ▣ Internal administrative region: State/Province/Territory/Dependent territory ⌂ Capital city ⛰ Mountain range/Undersea ridge ▲ Mountain peak/Volcano/Seamount ◇ Geographic feature ▶ Headland/Point/Cape/Peninsula ◭ Desert ⌓ Island/Island group ⁙ Antarctic base ◌ Ocean ≋ Sea ≈ Bay/Gulf/Channel/Strait ∽ Lake ⚑ Salt pan/Dry/Intermittent lake ∿ Riv

132 L 6 Buitenpost, Netherlands
218 K 9 Buitepos, Namibia
145 N 15 Bujanovac, Serbia and Montenegro
131 T 4 Bujaraloz, Spain
217 Q 10 Bujumbura, Burundi ⚓
234 B 6 Buk, Papua New Guinea
234 I 4 Buka, Papua New Guinea
217 O 13 Bukama, Democratic Republic of Congo
217 Q 9 Bukavu, Democratic Republic of Congo
179 O 12 Bukhara, Uzbekistan
179 O 12 Bukhoro Wiloyati, Uzbekistan
195 R 9 Bukit Batu, Malaysia ▲
193 N 12 Bukit Gandadiwata, Indonesia ▲
194 A 14 Bukit Gombak, Singapore ▲
192 L 10 Bukit Liangpran, Indonesia ▲
192 E 12 Bukit Masurai, Indonesia ▲
194 A 6 Bukit Merah, Malaysia
195 Q 9 Bukit Mersing, Malaysia ▲
194 A 14 Bukit Panjang, Singapore
192 K 11 Bukit Raya, Indonesia ▲
195 V 6 Bukit Tambulanan, Malaysia ▲
195 W 5 Bukit Tawai, Malaysia ▲
192 D 11 Bukittinggi, Indonesia
217 S 8 Bukoba, Tanzania
194 A 15 Bukum, Singapore ⇄
194 A 15 Bukum Kechil, Singapore ⇄
193 T 12 Bula, Indonesia
138 G 6 Bülach, Switzerland
197 K 14 Bulan, Philippines
197 H 24 Bulan, Philippines
171 N 8 Bulancak, Turkey
215 S 10 Bulangu, Nigeria
171 R 10 Bulanik, Turkey
212 E 11 Bûlâq, Egypt
219 O 8 Bulawayo, Zimbabwe
179 R 1 Bulayevo, Kazakhstan
181 D 16 Buldana, India
78 C 12 Buldir Island, Alaska, U.S.A.
185 P 3 Bulgan, Mongolia ◙
185 O 5 Bulgan, Mongolia
185 P 3 Bulgan, Mongolia
185 Q 5 Bulgan, Mongolia
146 G 10 Bulgaria, Europe ◙
193 S 10 Buli, Indonesia
69 U 8 Bull Shoals Lake, Arkansas, U.S.A. ⤙
213 L 19 Bullaxaar, Somalia
138 C 9 Bulle, Switzerland
233 Q 17 Buller, New Zealand ⤚
233 K 14 Bulls, New Zealand
61 Q 14 Bulls Bay, South Carolina, U.S.A. ≈
234 D 5 Bulolo, Papua New Guinea
141 C 17 Bultei, Italy
216 L 8 Bulukutu, Democratic Republic of Congo
153 S 8 Bulun, Russian Federation
216 J 10 Bulungu, Democratic Republic of Congo
216 L 11 Bulungu, Democratic Republic of Congo
197 K 14 Bulusan, Philippines
195 Y 7 Bum-Bum, Malaysia
216 J 12 Bumba, Democratic Republic of Congo
216 L 6 Bumba, Democratic Republic of Congo
216 J 9 Buna, Democratic Republic of Congo
217 W 6 Buna, Kenya
217 R 8 Bunazi, Tanzania
230 G 12 Bunbury, Western Australia, Australia
17 T 9 Bunda, Tanzania
231 W 7 Bundaberg, Queensland, Australia
80 D 13 Bundi, India
213 D 22 Bunduqiya, Sudan
127 Z 7 Bungay, United Kingdom
218 H 2 Bungo, Angola

199 D 21 Bungo-suidō, Japan ≈
215 T 10 Buni-Yadi, Nigeria
217 R 7 Bunia, Democratic Republic of Congo
217 O 14 Bunkeya, Democratic Republic of Congo
62 J 6 Bunkie, Louisiana, U.S.A.
63 X 8 Bunnell, Florida, U.S.A.
215 S 11 Bununu, Nigeria
170 K 10 Bünyan, Turkey
215 P 10 Bunza, Nigeria
191 N 20 Buôn Mê Thuôt, Vietnam
153 S 7 Buorkhaya Guba, Russian Federation ≈
212 G 10 Bûr Safâga, Egypt
213 N 19 Buraan, Somalia
213 B 19 Buram, Sudan
179 Z 5 Buran, Kazakhstan
213 M 20 Burao, Somalia
172 I 7 Burāq, Syria
175 P 5 Buraydah, Saudi Arabia
127 S 11 Burbage, United Kingdom
77 J 24 Burbank, California, U.S.A.
231 T 4 Burdekin, Queensland, Australia ⤚
133 I 20 Burdinne, Belgium
170 E 12 Burdur, Turkey
43 E 21 Burdwood Bank, Atlantic Ocean ◇
213 G 21 Burē, Ethiopia
213 H 19 Burē, Ethiopia
177 X 10 Burewala, Pakistan
134 J 7 Burfjord, Norway
127 S 9 Burford, United Kingdom
136 K 13 Burg, Germany
146 M 9 Burgas, Bulgaria ◙
146 M 9 Burgas, Bulgaria
61 T 11 Burgaw, North Carolina, U.S.A.
138 E 7 Burgdorf, Switzerland
72 K 8 Burgdorf, Idaho, U.S.A.
139 X 8 Burgenland, Austria ◙
85 X 11 Burgeo, Newfoundland and Labrador, Canada
127 W 12 Burgess Hill, United Kingdom
133 D 14 Burgh-Haamstede, Netherlands
137 L 24 Burghausen, Germany
141 I 22 Burgio, Italy
131 O 3 Burgos, Spain
135 I 23 Burgsvik, Sweden
181 E 16 Burhanpur, India
196 I 13 Burias, Philippines
191 J 18 Buriram, Thailand
197 M 19 Butuan, Philippines
188 L 8 Butuo, China
231 R 4 Burke and Wills Roadhouse, Queensland, Australia
240 J 9 Burke Island, Antarctica ⤚
231 Q 4 Burketown, Queensland, Australia
214 M10 Burkina Faso, Africa ◙
73 N 12 Burley, Idaho, U.S.A.
178 I 4 Burlin, Kazakhstan
58 L 6 Burlington, Vermont, U.S.A.
61 Q 8 Burlington, North Carolina, U.S.A.
67 V 14 Burlington, Iowa, U.S.A.
69 P 5 Burlington, Kansas, U.S.A.
75 U 4 Burlington, Colorado, U.S.A.
86 F 13 Burlington, Ontario, Canada
69 R 1 Burlington Junction, Missouri, U.S.A.
71 P 6 Burlson, Texas, U.S.A.
233 H 17 Burnbrae, New Zealand
71 O 9 Burnet, Texas, U.S.A.
77 G 15 Burney, California, U.S.A.
127 Y 10 Burnham-on-Crouch, United Kingdom
127 O 11 Burnham-on-Sea, United Kingdom
231 S 15 Burnie, Tasmania, Australia
127 Q 2 Burnley, United Kingdom
76 J 12 Burns, Oregon, U.S.A.
76 K 13 Burns Junction, Oregon, U.S.A.
184 L 3 Burqin, China

231 P 11 Burra, South Australia, Australia
145 K 18 Burrel, Albania
131 T 7 Burriana, Spain
131 U 6 Burriana, Spain
170 D 8 Bursa, Turkey
127 S 6 Burton upon Trent, United Kingdom
193 Q 12 Buru, Indonesia ⇄
179 T 8 Burulbaytal, Kazakhstan
217 Q 9 Burundi, Africa ◙
217 Q 10 Bururi, Burundi
127 Q 3 Bury, United Kingdom
127 Y 8 Bury St Edmunds, United Kingdom
151 T 2 Buryn', Ukraine
216 K 6 Busa Modanda, Democratic Republic of Congo
197 I 21 Busan Bay, Philippines ≈
216 L 8 Busanga, Democratic Republic of Congo
176 I 11 Būshehr, Iran ◙
176 H 11 Būshehr, Iran
216 L 6 Businga, Democratic Republic of Congo
143 K 16 Busko-Zdrój, Poland
230 F 12 Busselton, Western Australia, Australia
150 K 11 Bușteni, Romania
140 C 7 Busto Arsizio, Italy
197 E 15 Busuanga, Philippines
197 I 15 Busuanga, Philippines ⇄
136 F 9 Büsum, Germany
217 N 6 Buta, Democratic Republic of Congo
64 D 9 Cable, Wisconsin, U.S.A.
191 G 26 Butang Group, Thailand ⇄
217 Q 9 Butare, Rwanda
236 D 1 Butaritari, Kiribati ⇄
58 B 12 Butler, Pennsylvania, U.S.A.
63 O 5 Butler, Alabama, U.S.A.
63 S 4 Butler, Georgia, U.S.A.
69 S 5 Butler, Missouri, U.S.A.
193 P 13 Buton, Indonesia ⇄
124 F 8 Butt of Lewis, United Kingdom ▶
73 O 6 Butte, Montana, U.S.A.
194 A 6 Butterworth, Malaysia
84 K 5 Button Bay, Manitoba, Canada ≈
85 T 5 Button Islands, Nunavut, Canada ⇄
197 M 19 Butuan, Philippines
188 L 8 Butuo, China
156 M 6 Buturlinovka, Russian Federation
183 O 9 Butwal, Nepal
137 F 18 Butzbach, Germany
213 M 23 Buulobarde, Somalia
213 K 26 Buur Gaabo, Somalia
213 L 24 Buurhabaka, Somalia
183 O 11 Buxar, India
127 R 4 Buxton, United Kingdom
76 G 9 Buxton, Oregon, U.S.A.
154 K 12 Buy, Russian Federation
185 O 4 Buyant, Mongolia
157 R 14 Buynaksk, Russian Federation
149 K 21 Buynavichy, Belarus
146 M 12 Büyükkarıştıran, Turkey
187 I 16 Buyun Shan, China ▲
150 L 12 Buzău, Romania
219 R 8 Buzi, Mozambique
157 U 4 Buzuluk, Russian Federation
179 P 4 Buzuluk, Kazakhstan
59 O 11 Buzzards Bay, Massachusetts, U.S.A. ≈
149 J 15 Byahoml', Belarus
146 J 7 Byala, Bulgaria
146 N 8 Byala, Bulgaria
149 L 19 Byalynichy, Belarus
81 N 4 Byam Martin Island, Nunavut, Canada ⇄
127 Q 2 Burnley, United Kingdom
149 L 19 Byarezina, Belarus ⤙
149 G 20 Byaroza, Belarus
143 N 15 Bychawa, Poland
142 H 11 Bydgoszcz, Poland
149 J 15 Byerazino, Belarus

149 K 17 Byerazino, Belarus
149 L 15 Byeshankovichy, Belarus
135 J 14 Bygdeå, Sweden
135 B 21 Bygland, Norway
149 M 18 Bykhaw, Belarus
135 B 20 Bykle, Norway
157 P 7 Bykovo, Russian Federation
74 L 13 Bylas, Arizona, U.S.A.
81 Q 4 Bylot Island, Nunavut, Canada ⇄
134 L 13 Byskeälven, Sweden ⤙
143 J 19 Bystra, Slovakia ▲
143 I 17 Bytom, Poland
142 G 8 Bytów, Poland
217 Q 9 Byumba, Rwanda
142 K 12 Bzura, Poland ⤙

C

191 L 23 Ca Mau, Vietnam
218 H 4 Caala, Angola
109 G 20 Caazapá, Paraguay
107 D 18 Caballas, Peru
75 P 13 Caballo Reservoir, New Mexico, U.S.A. ⤙
106 H 11 Caballococha, Peru
196 G 10 Cabanatuan, Philippines
87 P 7 Cabano, Québec, Canada
144 C 8 Čabar, Slovenia
213 K 19 Cabdul Qaadir, Somalia
107 L 21 Cabezas, Bolivia
104 K 3 Cabimas, Venezuela
218 F 1 Cabinda, Angola
218 F 1 Cabinda, Angola
72 K 2 Cabinet Mountains, Montana, U.S.A. ▲
111 I 20 Cabo Blanco, Argentina
110 F 9 Cabo Bascuñán, Chile ▶
93 Q 8 Cabo Beata, Dominican Republic ▶
111 I 23 Cabo Buen Tiempo, Argentina ▶
93 R 7 Cabo Cabron, Dominican Republic ▶
91 P 4 Cabo Camarón, Honduras ▶
130 F 8 Cabo Carvoeiro, Portugal ▶
89 Z 9 Cabo Catoche, Mexico ▶
88 F 3 Cabo Colonet, Mexico ▶
104 G 6 Cabo Corrientes, Colombia ▶
113 E 18 Cabo Corrientes, Argentina ▶
88 M 11 Cabo Corrientes, Mexico ▶
92 F 5 Cabo Corrientes, Cuba ▶
92 K 7 Cabo Cruz, Cuba ▶
111 I 22 Cabo Dañoso, Argentina ▶
158 C 9 Cabo de Gata, Mediterranean Sea ▶
131 U 9 Cabo de la Nao, Spain ▶
104 J 1 Cabo de la Vela, Colombia ▶
131 T 11 Cabo de Palos, Spain ▶
130 L 1 Cabo de Penas, Spain ▶
131 U 9 Cabo de San Antonio, Spain ▶
219 Q 11 Cabo de Santa Maria, Mozambique ▶
130 H 12 Cabo de Santa Maria, Portugal ▶
218 F 5 Cabo de Santa Marta, Angola ▶
112 J 11 Cabo de Santa Marta Grande, Brazil ▶
108 O 13 Cabo de Santo Agostinho, Brazil ▶
109 M 18 Cabo de São Tomé, Brazil ▶
130 G 12 Cabo de São Vincent, Portugal ▶
130 G 11 Cabo de Sines, Portugal ▶
219 U 3 Cabo Delgado, Mozambique ▶
219 U 4 Cabo Delgado, Mozambique ◙
111 I 19 Cabo Dos Bahías, Argentina ▶

93 S 7 Cabo Engaño, Dominican Republic ▶
130 G 10 Cabo Espichel, Portugal ▶
91 R 5 Cabo Falso, Honduras ▶
93 P 8 Cabo Falso, Dominican Republic ▶
130 G 2 Cabo Fisterra, Spain ▶
112 N 7 Cabo Frio, Brazil ▶
112 O 7 Cabo Frio, Brazil ▶
91 R 5 Cabo Gracias á Dios, Nicaragua/Honduras ▶
131 T 10 Cabo Huertas, Spain ▶
110 F 13 Cabo Humos, Chile ▶
93 Q 6 Cabo Isabela, Dominican Republic ▶
92 M 5 Cabo Lucrecia, Cuba ▶
131 P 1 Cabo Machichaco, Spain ▶
104 G 5 Cabo Marzo, Colombia ▶
91 R 14 Cabo Matapalo, Costa Rica ▶
131 O 1 Cabo Mayor, Spain ▶
108 J 8 Cabo Norte, Brazil ▶
108 I 7 Cabo Orange, Brazil ▶
130 I 1 Cabo Ortegal, Spain ▶
106 E 9 Cabo Pantoja, Peru
111 F 24 Cabo Pilar, Chile ▶
88 E 2 Cabo Punta Banda, Mexico ▶
111 E 17 Cabo Quedal, Chile ▶
111 E 18 Cabo Quilán, Chile ▶
111 J 19 Cabo Raso, Argentina
41 Z 4 Cabo Roggewein, Easter Island ▶
89 S 10 Cabo Rojo, Mexico ▶
131 O 13 Cabo Sacratif, Spain ▶
113 E 17 Cabo San Antonio, Argentina ▶
92 E 5 Cabo San Antonio, Cuba ▶
111 I 25 Cabo San Diego, Argentina ▶
111 H 22 Cabo San Francisco de Paula, Argentina ▶
215 S 15 Cabo San Juan, Equatorial Guinea ▶
88 H 8 Cabo San Lázaro, Mexico ▶
88 J 9 Cabo San Lucas, Mexico ▶
88 F 3 Cabo San Quintín, Mexico ▶
158 L 8 Cabo San Vito, Mediterranean Sea ▶
91 N 11 Cabo Santa Elena, Costa Rica ▶
113 G 16 Cabo Santa Maria, Uruguay ▶
111 E 23 Cabo Santiago, Chile ▶
130 H 3 Cabo Silleiro, Spain ▶
41 Y 5 Cabo Sur, Easter Island ▶
130 K 14 Cabo Trafalgar, Spain ▶
111 I 20 Cabo Tres Puntas, Argentina ▶
91 N 12 Cabo Vélas, Costa Rica ▶
111 H 24 Cabo Virgenes, Argentina ▶
69 V 7 Cabool, Missouri, U.S.A.
231 W 8 Caboolture, Queensland, Australia
88 I 3 Caborca, Mexico
85 W 11 Cabot Strait, Nova Scotia, Canada ≈
196 E 12 Cabra, Philippines ⤙
141 B 17 Cabras, Italy
131 Y 9 Cabrera, Spain ⇄
93 R 7 Cabrera, Dominican Republic
83 L 20 Cabri, Saskatchewan, Canada
108 N 13 Cabrobó, Brazil
105 O 5 Cabruta, Venezuela
196 F 6 Cabugao, Philippines
197 F 16 Cabulauan, Philippines ⤙
196 H 6 Cabutunan Point, Philippines ▶
112 H 9 Caçador, Brazil
144 K 12 Čačak, Serbia and Montenegro
112 G 12 Cacapava do Sul, Brazil
112 F 12 Cacequi, Brazil
109 G 16 Cáceres, Brazil
130 K 8 Cáceres, Spain
214 D 9 Cacheu, Guinea-Bissau

110 I 6 Cachi, Argentina
108 H 13 Cachimbo, Brazil
218 I 4 Cachingues, Angola
112 I 3 Cachoeira Alta, Brazil
112 G 12 Cachoeira do Sul, Brazil
108 H 11 Cachoeirinha, Brazil
112 O 5 Cachoeiro de Itapemirim, Brazil
107 J 15 Cachuela Esperanza, Bolivia
214 E 10 Cacine, Guinea-Bissau
218 J 3 Cacolo, Angola
218 F 1 Cacongo, Angola
109 I 17 Caçu, Brazil
218 G 2 Cacuaco, Angola
127 N 6 Cadair Idris, United Kingdom ▲
131 Y 3 Cadaqués, Spain
71 U 5 Caddo Lake, Texas, U.S.A. ⤙
196 I 12 Cadig Mountains, Philippines ▲
64 K 12 Cadillac, Michigan, U.S.A.
86 G 6 Cadillac, Québec, Canada
197 J 16 Cadiz, Philippines
60 D 7 Cadiz, Kentucky, U.S.A.
130 K 13 Cádiz, Spain
77 M 24 Cadiz Lake, California, U.S.A. ⤙
128 M 4 Caen, France
126 M 4 Caernarfon, United Kingdom
126 L 5 Caernarfon Bay, United Kingdom ≈
127 O 10 Caerphilly, United Kingdom
109 M 15 Caetité, Brazil
110 I 7 Cafayate, Argentina
196 H 7 Cagayan, Philippines ⤚
197 L 20 Cagayan de Oro, Philippines
197 G 19 Cagayan Islands, Philippines ⇄
141 B 19 Cagliari, Italy
93 U 8 Caguas, Puerto Rico
218 G 6 Cahama, Angola
125 D 20 Caher, Republic of Ireland
125 A 20 Cahersiveen, Republic of Ireland
125 F 19 Cahore Point, Republic of Ireland ▶
129 P 12 Cahors, France
106 C 12 Cahuapanas, Peru
191 N 10 Cahul, Moldova
191 L 24 Cai Nuoc, Vietnam
218 L 3 Caianda, Angola
109 I 16 Caiapônia, Brazil
92 J 4 Caibarién, Cuba
108 O 12 Caicó, Brazil
93 P 5 Caicos Islands, Turks and Caicos Islands ⇄
93 O 5 Caicos Passage, The Bahamas ≈
230 K 10 Caiguna, Western Australia, Australia
108 H 11 Caima, Brazil
196 E 9 Caiman Point, Philippines ▶
188 L 5 Cainnyigoin, China
241 N 4 Caird Coast, Antarctica ◇
231 T 3 Cairns, Queensland, Australia
212 F 8 Cairo, Egypt ⚓
63 S 7 Cairo, Georgia, U.S.A.
65 F 23 Cairo, Illinois, U.S.A.
127 V 3 Caistor, United Kingdom
218 G 5 Caitou, Angola
218 I 6 Caiundo, Angola
106 B 13 Cajamarca, Peru
106 B 12 Cajamarca, Peru ◙
108 N 12 Cajazeiras, Brazil
144 K 12 Čajetina, Serbia and Montenegro
197 I 14 Cajidiocan, Philippines
185 O 6 Caka, China
215 R 14 Calabar, Nigeria
105 N 4 Calabozo, Venezuela
141 M 19 Calabria, Italy ◙
159 N 9 Calabrian Rise, Mediterranean Sea ◇
107 I 20 Calacoto, Bolivia
150 G 13 Calafat, Romania
111 G 23 Calafate, Argentina

◙ Country · ◙ Internal administrative region: State/Province/Territory/Dependent territory · ⚓ Capital city · ▲ Mountain range/ Undersea ridge · ▲ Mountain peak/ Volcano/Seamount · ◇ Geographic feature · ▶ Headland/Point/ Cape/Peninsula · ⇌ Desert · ⇄ Island/Island group · ▲ Antarctic base · ⊘ Ocean · ⊃ Sea · ≈ Bay/Gulf/Channel/Strait · ⤙ Lake · ⤚ Salt pan/Dry/ Intermittent lake · ⤚ River

275

▣ Country   ▣ Internal administrative region: State/Province/Territory/Dependent territory   ▰ Capital city   ▲ Mountain range/ Undersea ridge   ▲ Mountain peak/ Volcano/Seamount   ◇ Geographic feature   ▶ Headland/Point/ Cape/Peninsula   ◈ Desert   ⚐ Island/Island group   ● Antarctic base   ◉ Ocean   ≈ Sea   ≈ Bay/Gulf/Channel/Strait   ⌇ Lake   ⌇ Salt pan/Dry/ Intermittent lake   ⌇ River

230 I 3 **Cape Leveque**, Western Australia, Australia ▶
39 V 6 **Cape Leveque**, Indian Ocean ▶
61 V 11 **Cape Lookout**, North Carolina, U.S.A. ▶
240 K 5 **Cape Mackintosh**, Antarctica ▶
38 B 11 **Cape Malheureux**, Mauritius ▶
232 H 4 **Cape Maria van Diemen**, New Zealand ▶
58 I 15 **Cape May**, New Jersey, U.S.A. ▶
58 I 15 **Cape May**, New Jersey, U.S.A.
231 S 2 **Cape Melville**, Queensland, Australia ▶
197 A 21 **Cape Melville**, Philippines ▶
77 E 16 **Cape Mendocino**, California, U.S.A. ▶
85 T 2 **Cape Mercy**, Nunavut, Canada ▶
111 K 24 **Cape Meredith**, Falkland Islands ▶
78 K 9 **Cape Mohican**, Alaska, U.S.A. ▶
39 W 15 **Cape Morse**, Indian Ocean ▶
234 F 6 **Cape Nelson**, Papua New Guinea ▶
78 M 11 **Cape Newenham**, Alaska, U.S.A. ▶
78 M 7 **Cape Nome**, Alaska, U.S.A. ▶
87 Y 7 **Cape North**, Nova Scotia, Canada ▶
241 O 2 **Cape Norvegia**, Antarctica ▶
218 J 15 **Cape of Good Hope**, Republic of South Africa ▶
43 N 18 **Cape of Good Hope**, Atlantic Ocean ▶
231 R 14 **Cape Otway**, Victoria, Australia ▶
233 L 17 **Cape Palliser**, New Zealand ▶
214 I 14 **Cape Palmas**, Côte d'Ivoire ▶
82 E 7 **Cape Parry**, Northwest Territories, Canada ▶
230 J 11 **Cape Pasley**, Western Australia, Australia ▶
39 Q 15 **Cape Penck**, Indian Ocean ▶
241 Y 11 **Cape Poinsett**, Antarctica ▶
80 L 4 **Cape Prince Alfred**, Northwest Territories, Canada ▶
233 A 25 **Cape Providence**, New Zealand ▶
219 N 15 **Cape Recife**, Republic of South Africa ▶
232 H 4 **Cape Reinga**, New Zealand ▶
61 R 14 **Cape Romain**, South Carolina, U.S.A. ▶
63 W 13 **Cape Romano**, Florida, U.S.A. ▶
232 O 10 **Cape Runaway**, New Zealand ▶
42 E 8 **Cape Sable**, Atlantic Ocean ▶
3 X 14 **Cape Sable**, Florida, U.S.A. ▶
87 T 13 **Cape Sable Island**, Nova Scotia, Canada ▶
97 N 23 **Cape San Agustin**, Philippines ▶
3 D 21 **Cape Scott**, British Columbia, Canada ▶
18 M 15 **Cape Seal**, Republic of South Africa ▶
31 O 1 **Cape Shield**, Northern Territory, Australia ▶
34 F 2 **Cape Siemens**, Papua New Guinea ▶
34 I 8 **Cape Siri**, Papua New Guinea ▶
5 N 4 **Cape Southampton**, Nunavut, Canada ▶
31 P 12 **Cape Spencer**, South Australia, Australia ▶
34 H 4 **Cape St George**, Papua New Guinea ▶
233 J 15 **Cape Stephens**, New Zealand ▶
84 L 7 **Cape Tatnam**, Manitoba, Canada ▶
233 J 16 **Cape Terawhiti**, New Zealand ▶
218 J 15 **Cape Town**, Republic of South Africa 🏛
233 M 15 **Cape Turnagain**, New Zealand ▶
85 U 6 **Cape Uivak**, Newfoundland and Labrador, Canada ▶
43 A 16 **Cape Verde**, Atlantic Ocean □
42 I 12 **Cape Verde Basin**, Atlantic Ocean ◇
42 J 11 **Cape Verde Plateau**, Atlantic Ocean ◇
241 X 12 **Cape Waldron**, Antarctica ▶
234 E 6 **Cape Ward Hunt**, Papua New Guinea ▶
231 O 1 **Cape Wessel**, Northern Territory, Australia ▶
85 O 2 **Cape Wilson**, Nunavut, Canada ▶
124 G 8 **Cape Wrath**, United Kingdom ▶
231 R 1 **Cape York**, Queensland, Australia ▶
231 R 1 **Cape York Peninsula**, Queensland, Australia ▶
109 M 16 **Capelinha**, Brazil
231 U 6 **Capella**, Queensland, Australia
132 G 13 **Capelle aan den IJssel**, Netherlands
133 L 25 **Capellen**, Luxembourg
218 I 2 **Capenda-Camulemba**, Angola
140 I 13 **Capestrano**, Italy
75 R 12 **Capitan Peak**, New Mexico, U.S.A. ▲
197 G 17 **Capnoyan**, Philippines 🏝
141 A 16 **Capo Caccia**, Italy ▶
141 C 19 **Capo Carbonara**, Italy ▶
141 N 19 **Capo Colonna**, Italy ▶
141 D 16 **Capo Comino**, Italy ▶
141 B 15 **Capo del Falcone**, Italy ▶
141 B 18 **Capo della Frasca**, Italy ▶
141 K 24 **Capo delle Correnti**, Italy ▶
141 K 21 **Capo di Milazzo**, Italy ▶
141 D 17 **Capo di Monte Santu**, Italy ▶
141 K 21 **Capo d'Orlando**, Italy ▶
141 I 21 **Capo Gallo**, Italy ▶
158 L 9 **Capo Granitola**, Mediterranean Sea ▶
141 L 23 **Capo Murro di Porco**, Italy ▶
141 L 17 **Capo Palinuro**, Italy ▶
141 N 20 **Capo Rizzuto**, Italy ▶
141 H 21 **Capo San Vito**, Italy ▶
141 O 18 **Capo Santa Maria di Leuca**, Italy ▶
141 J 24 **Capo Scaramia**, Italy ▶
141 B 20 **Capo Spartivento**, Italy ▶
141 N 17 **Capo Spulico**, Italy ▶
141 N 18 **Capo Trionto**, Italy ▶
141 L 20 **Capo Vaticano**, Italy ▶
218 G 3 **Capolo**, Angola
170 J 11 **Cappadocia**, Turkey ◇
141 J 16 **Capri**, Italy
218 L 7 **Caprivi**, Namibia ▣
218 K 7 **Caprivi Strip**, Namibia ◇
78 D 9 **Captain Cook**, Hawaii, U.S.A.
104 I 9 **Caquetá**, Colombia ▣
104 J 10 **Caquetá**, Colombia 〰
181 N 23 **Car Nicobar**, India 🏝
197 H 15 **Carabao**, Philippines 🏝
105 N 3 **Carabobo**, Venezuela ▣
105 S 5 **Carabobo**, Venezuela
150 I 13 **Caracal**, Romania
108 E 8 **Caracaraí**, Brazil
105 O 2 **Caracas**, Venezuela 🏛
108 L 13 **Caracol**, Brazil
107 I 20 **Caracollo**, Bolivia
197 N 22 **Caraga**, Philippines
111 F 15 **Carahue**, Chile
196 J 12 **Caramoan Peninsula**, Philippines ▶
112 M 5 **Carandaí**, Brazil
150 G 11 **Caransebeș**, Romania
87 T 7 **Caraquet**, New Brunswick, Canada
106 A 9 **Caráquez**, Ecuador
91 Q 5 **Caratasca**, Honduras
91 R 14 **Carate**, Costa Rica
108 C 11 **Carauari**, Brazil
131 R 11 **Caravaca de la Cruz**, Spain
109 N 17 **Caravelas**, Brazil
112 G 11 **Carazinho**, Brazil
130 H 1 **Carballo**, Spain
58 H 11 **Carbondale**, Pennsylvania, U.S.A.
65 F 22 **Carbondale**, Illinois, U.S.A.
75 P 4 **Carbondale**, Colorado, U.S.A.
131 R 13 **Carboneras**, Spain
131 R 7 **Carboneras de Guadazaón**, Spain
113 B 15 **Carcaraña**, Argentina 〰
129 Q 14 **Carcassonne**, France
106 B 8 **Carchi**, Ecuador ▣
181 E 22 **Cardamom Hills**, India ⛰
89 T 12 **Cardel**, Mexico
131 N 10 **Cárdena**, Spain
89 V 13 **Cárdenas**, Mexico
92 H 4 **Cárdenas**, Cuba
127 O 11 **Cardiff**, United Kingdom
126 K 8 **Cardigan**, United Kingdom
126 L 7 **Cardigan Bay**, United Kingdom ≈
191 J 21 **Cardomom Range**, Cambodia ⛰
113 E 15 **Cardona**, Uruguay
233 D 23 **Cardrona**, New Zealand
83 K 21 **Cardston**, Alberta, Canada
231 T 4 **Cardwell**, Queensland, Australia
150 G 7 **Carei**, Romania
128 L 3 **Carentan**, France
72 M 11 **Carey**, Idaho, U.S.A.
38 L 6 **Cargados Carajos Bank**, Indian Ocean ◇
38 M 6 **Cargados Carajos Islands**, Mauritius 🏝
128 I 5 **Carhaix-Plouguer**, France
112 O 5 **Cariacica**, Brazil
105 Q 2 **Cariaco**, Venezuela
106 B 11 **Cariamanga**, Ecuador
141 N 18 **Cariati**, Italy
92 I 13 **Caribbean Sea**, North America 🌊
59 R 1 **Caribou**, Maine, U.S.A.
83 H 15 **Caribou Mountains**, Alberta, Canada ⛰
197 L 16 **Carigara**, Philippines
131 S 5 **Cariñena**, Spain
109 L 15 **Carinhanha**, Brazil
105 R 3 **Caripito**, Venezuela
86 I 11 **Carleton Place**, Ontario, Canada
219 N 11 **Carletonville**, Republic of South Africa
77 M 16 **Carlin**, Nevada, U.S.A.
65 E 20 **Carlinville**, Illinois, U.S.A.
125 I 15 **Carlisle**, United Kingdom
58 F 13 **Carlisle**, Pennsylvania, U.S.A.
141 B 19 **Carloforte**, Italy
113 B 16 **Carlos Casares**, Argentina
125 E 19 **Carlow**, Republic of Ireland
75 T 14 **Carlsbad**, New Mexico, U.S.A.
38 K 2 **Carlsberg Ridge**, Indian Ocean ⛰
83 O 19 **Carlyle**, Saskatchewan, Canada
65 F 21 **Carlyle Lake**, Illinois, U.S.A. 💧
82 B 13 **Carmacks**, Yukon Territory, Canada
126 L 9 **Carmarthen**, United Kingdom
126 L 10 **Carmarthen Bay**, United Kingdom ≈
129 P 13 **Carmaux**, France
126 L 3 **Carmel Head**, United Kingdom ▶
90 I 2 **Carmelita**, Guatemala
113 D 15 **Carmelo**, Uruguay
104 I 3 **Carmen**, Colombia
110 G 7 **Carmen**, Chile
74 K 15 **Carmen**, Arizona, U.S.A.
110 G 5 **Carmen Alto**, Chile
113 B 20 **Carmen de Patagones**, Argentina
110 H 13 **Carmensa**, Argentina
65 G 22 **Carmi**, Illinois, U.S.A.
130 L 12 **Carmona**, Spain
91 O 12 **Carmona**, Costa Rica
124 G 10 **Carn Eighe**, United Kingdom ▲
230 G 10 **Carnamah**, Western Australia, Australia
218 L 13 **Carnarvon**, Republic of South Africa
230 E 8 **Carnarvon**, Western Australia, Australia
240 K 11 **Carney Island**, Antarctica 🏝
127 P 1 **Carnforth**, United Kingdom
216 H 4 **Carnot**, Central African Republic
124 I 12 **Carnoustie**, United Kingdom
125 F 20 **Carnsore Point**, Republic of Ireland ▶
63 Y 13 **Carol City**, Florida, U.S.A.
108 K 12 **Carolina**, Brazil
236 L 15 **Caroline Islands**, Federated States of Micronesia 🏝
141 J 21 **Caronia**, Italy
143 J 18 **Carpathian Mountains**, Europe ⛰
129 T 13 **Carpentras**, France
140 F 8 **Carpi**, Italy
77 I 24 **Carpinteria**, California, U.S.A.
63 S 8 **Carrabelle**, Florida, U.S.A.
140 D 9 **Carrara**, Italy
131 P 7 **Carrascosa del Campo**, Spain
125 A 20 **Carrauntuohil**, Republic of Ireland ▲
93 Y 12 **Carriacou**, Grenada 🏝
89 N 6 **Carrillo**, Mexico
66 L 4 **Carrington**, North Dakota, U.S.A.
110 F 8 **Carrizal Bajo**, Chile
70 M 12 **Carrizo Springs**, Texas, U.S.A.
75 R 12 **Carrizozo**, New Mexico, U.S.A.
67 R 12 **Carroll**, Iowa, U.S.A.
63 S 3 **Carrollton**, Georgia, U.S.A.
170 L 8 **Carșamba**, Turkey
140 I 13 **Carsoli**, Italy
77 I 18 **Carson City**, Nevada, U.S.A.
104 H 2 **Cartagena**, Colombia
131 S 12 **Cartagena**, Spain
104 H 6 **Cartago**, Colombia
91 Q 12 **Cartago**, Costa Rica
60 G 8 **Carthage**, Tennessee, U.S.A.
62 M 4 **Carthage**, Mississippi, U.S.A.
71 T 6 **Carthage**, Texas, U.S.A.
91 X 13 **Carti Suitupo**, Panama
84 H 10 **Cartwright**, Manitoba, Canada
85 W 8 **Cartwright**, Newfoundland and Labrador, Canada
108 O 13 **Caruarú**, Brazil
105 Q 2 **Carúpano**, Venezuela
197 D 17 **Caruray**, Philippines
108 K 10 **Carutapera**, Brazil
77 K 18 **Carvers**, Nevada, U.S.A.
112 K 6 **Casa Branca**, Brazil
74 J 13 **Casa Grande**, Arizona, U.S.A.
210 H 7 **Casablanca**, Morocco
141 K 14 **Casacalenda**, Italy
140 B 7 **Casale**, Italy
104 K 6 **Casanare**, Colombia ▣
91 N 10 **Casares**, Nicaragua
88 L 3 **Casas Grandes**, Mexico
131 R 9 **Casas Ibáñez**, Spain
112 H 11 **Casca**, Brazil
38 A 9 **Cascade**, Seychelles
72 K 9 **Cascade**, Idaho, U.S.A.
233 C 21 **Cascade Point**, New Zealand ▶
76 G 13 **Cascade Range**, Canada/U.S.A. ⛰
72 K 9 **Cascade Reservoir**, Idaho, U.S.A. 💧
41 U 3 **Cascadia Basin**, Pacific Ocean ◇
108 N 11 **Cascavel**, Brazil
112 G 8 **Cascavel**, Brazil
59 P 7 **Casco Bay**, Maine, U.S.A. ≈
141 J 15 **Caserta**, Italy
64 L 13 **Caseville**, Michigan, U.S.A.
241 Y 11 **Casey**, Antarctica ⁂
65 G 20 **Casey**, Illinois, U.S.A.
196 I 9 **Casiguran**, Philippines
196 H 9 **Casiguran Sound**, Philippines ≈
113 B 15 **Casilda**, Argentina
231 W 9 **Casino**, New South Wales, Australia
107 B 15 **Casma**, Peru
131 T 5 **Caspe**, Spain
73 W 12 **Casper**, Wyoming, U.S.A.
178 G 6 **Caspian Depression**, Kazakhstan/Russian Federation ◇
157 S 14 **Caspian Sea**, Asia/Europe 🌊
64 M 13 **Cass City**, Michigan, U.S.A.
219 Q 5 **Cassacatiza**, Mozambique
218 J 4 **Cassamba**, Angola
83 D 15 **Cassiar**, British Columbia, Canada
83 C 14 **Cassiar Mountains**, Yukon Territory, Canada ⛰
109 I 17 **Cassilândia**, Brazil
218 H 5 **Cassinga**, Angola
141 I 15 **Cassino**, Italy
218 H 4 **Cassongue**, Angola
184 M 2 **Cast Uul**, Mongolia ▲
140 D 11 **Castagneto Carducci**, Italy
108 F 12 **Castanha**, Brazil
108 K 10 **Castanhal**, Brazil
110 G 10 **Castaño**, Argentina
138 I 10 **Castasegna**, Switzerland
140 C 8 **Casteggio**, Italy
130 J 7 **Castel Branco**, Portugal ▣
141 J 14 **Castél di Sangro**, Italy
129 V 13 **Castellane**, France
110 L 7 **Castelli**, Argentina
113 D 17 **Castelli**, Argentina
131 U 7 **Castelló de la Plana**, Spain
129 P 14 **Castelnaudary**, France
140 E 9 **Castelnovo ne' Monti**, Italy
130 I 7 **Castelo Branco**, Portugal
141 B 16 **Castelsardo**, Italy
141 I 22 **Casteltermini**, Italy
141 H 22 **Castelvetrano**, Italy
231 Q 13 **Casterton**, Victoria, Australia
140 E 12 **Castiglione della Pescaia**, Italy
110 F 8 **Castilla**, Chile
131 Q 8 **Castilla-La Mancha**, Spain ▣
130 K 4 **Castilla Y Leõn**, Spain ▣
113 G 15 **Castillos**, Uruguay
127 P 12 **Castle Cary**, United Kingdom
74 L 5 **Castle Dale**, Utah, U.S.A.
74 H 13 **Castle Dome Peak**, Arizona, U.S.A. ▲
127 S 6 **Castle Donnington**, United Kingdom
125 H 15 **Castle Douglas**, United Kingdom
42 B 7 **Castle Harbour**, Bermuda ≈
72 M 10 **Castle Peak**, Idaho, U.S.A. ▲
75 R 4 **Castle Rock**, Colorado, U.S.A.
43 N 26 **Castle Rock Point**, St Helena ▶
125 B 17 **Castlebar**, Republic of Ireland
127 T 2 **Castleford**, United Kingdom
83 I 21 **Castlegar**, British Columbia, Canada
129 Q 14 **Castres**, France
93 Z 11 **Castries**, St Lucia 🏛
111 F 18 **Castro**, Chile
112 I 8 **Castro**, Brazil
130 I 5 **Castro Daire**, Portugal
130 H 11 **Castro Verde**, Portugal
130 J 1 **Castropol**, Spain
141 M 18 **Castrovillari**, Italy
130 L 9 **Castuera**, Spain
233 A 23 **Caswell Sound**, New Zealand ≈
171 Q 9 **Cat**, Turkey
92 L 3 **Cat Island**, The Bahamas 🏝
84 K 10 **Cat Lake**, Ontario, Canada 💧
91 N 5 **Catacamas**, Honduras
62 J 6 **Catahoula Lake**, Louisiana, U.S.A. 💧
171 S 12 **Çatak**, Turkey
109 J 17 **Catalão**, Brazil
146 O 12 **Çatalca**, Turkey
131 W 4 **Cataluña**, Spain ▣
170 J 6 **Catalzeytin**, Turkey
110 I 8 **Catamarca**, Argentina
110 H 7 **Catamarca**, Argentina ▣
111 G 16 **Catán Lil**, Argentina
219 Q 7 **Catandica**, Mozambique
196 L 12 **Catanduanes**, Philippines 🏝
141 K 22 **Catania**, Italy
141 M 20 **Catanzaro**, Italy
71 N 12 **Catarina**, Texas, U.S.A.
197 L 14 **Catarman**, Philippines
219 Q 6 **Cataxa**, Mozambique
197 L 15 **Catbalogan**, Philippines
197 N 21 **Cateel**, Philippines
214 E 10 **Catió**, Guinea-Bissau
233 D 25 **Catlins**, New Zealand ⛰
89 Q 8 **Catorce**, Mexico
111 H 15 **Catriel**, Argentina
110 J 13 **Catriló**, Argentina
58 K 10 **Catskill**, New York, U.S.A.
58 I 10 **Catskill Mountains**, New York, U.S.A. ⛰
196 H 8 **Cauayan**, Philippines
197 I 18 **Cauayan**, Philippines
104 G 8 **Cauca**, Colombia ▣
104 I 4 **Cauca**, Colombia 〰
104 H 4 **Caucasia**, Colombia
156 L 13 **Caucasus**, Russian Federation ⛰
171 Q 5 **Caucasus**, Georgia ⛰
110 H 10 **Caucete**, Argentina
197 N 19 **Cauit Point**, Philippines ▶
218 I 2 **Caungula**, Angola
110 F 13 **Cauquenes**, Chile
105 Q 6 **Caura**, Venezuela 〰
87 R 6 **Causapscal**, Québec, Canada
67 N 2 **Cavalier**, North Dakota, U.S.A.
232 J 5 **Cavalli Islands**, New Zealand 🏝
214 I 13 **Cavally**, Liberia 〰
125 D 16 **Cavan**, Republic of Ireland
170 E 13 **Cavdir**, Turkey
233 F 21 **Cave**, New Zealand
60 K 5 **Cave Run Lake**, Kentucky, U.S.A. 💧
197 G 19 **Cavili**, Philippines 🏝
196 G 11 **Cavite**, Philippines
108 L 11 **Caxias**, Brazil
112 H 11 **Caxias do Sul**, Brazil
218 G 2 **Caxito**, Angola
170 F 11 **Cay**, Turkey
92 I 3 **Cay Sal**, The Bahamas 🏝
106 C 8 **Cayambe**, Ecuador ▲
171 P 8 **Cayeli**, Turkey
105 Z 6 **Cayenne**, French Guiana 🏛
170 G 9 **Cayirhan**, Turkey
92 I 7 **Cayman Brac**, Cayman Islands 🏝
92 I 7 **Cayman Islands**, United Kingdom, United Kingdom ▣
42 B 11 **Cayman Trench**, Atlantic Ocean ◇
92 H 8 **Cayman Trench**, Cayman Islands ≈
213 M 20 **Caynabo**, Somalia
92 G 5 **Cayo del Rosario**, Cuba 🏝
92 H 5 **Cayo Largo**, Cuba 🏝
92 K 4 **Cayo Romano**, Cuba 🏝

□ Country ▣ Internal administrative region: State/Province/Territory/Dependent territory 🏛 Capital city ⛰ Mountain range/Undersea ridge ▲ Mountain peak/Volcano/Seamount ◇ Geographic feature ▶ Headland/Point/Cape/Peninsula ⏶ Desert 🏝 Island/Island group ⁂ Antarctic base ◎ Ocean 🌊 Sea ≈ Bay/Gulf/Channel/Strait 💧 Lake ⚑ Salt pan/Dry/Intermittent lake 〰 River

92 K 5 **Cayo Sabinal**, Cuba 🏝
91 S 6 **Cayos Miskitos**, Nicaragua 🏝
150 L 12 **Căzănești**, Romania
129 O 14 **Cazères**, France
218 L 4 **Cazombo**, Angola
219 R 5 **Cazula**, Mozambique
108 N 12 **Ceará**, Brazil ▣
43 H 14 **Ceara Abyssal Plain**, Atlantic Ocean ◇
42 G 13 **Ceara Ridge**, Atlantic Ocean ⛰
89 N 6 **Ceballos**, Mexico
131 P 4 **Cebollera**, Spain ▲
197 K 18 **Cebu**, Philippines
197 K 17 **Cebu**, Philippines 🏝
143 I 24 **Cece**, Hungary
67 T 11 **Cedar**, Iowa, U.S.A. ∿
74 I 7 **Cedar City**, Utah, U.S.A.
67 T 11 **Cedar Falls**, Iowa, U.S.A.
69 X 4 **Cedar Hill**, Missouri, U.S.A.
61 W 5 **Cedar Island**, Virginia, U.S.A. 🏝
63 U 9 **Cedar Key**, Florida, U.S.A.
84 H 8 **Cedar Lake**, Manitoba, Canada 💧
67 U 12 **Cedar Rapids**, Iowa, U.S.A.
63 S 2 **Cedartown**, Georgia, U.S.A.
90 L 8 **Cedeño**, Honduras
41 V 4 **Cedros Trench**, Pacific Ocean ◇
231 N 10 **Ceduna**, South Australia, Australia
142 D 11 **Cedynia**, Poland
130 G 1 **Cée**, Spain
213 O 19 **Ceel Gaal**, Somalia
213 N 19 **Ceerigaabo**, Somalia
141 J 21 **Cefalù**, Italy
158 L 8 **Cefalu Basin**, Mediterranean Sea ◇
143 J 23 **Cegléd**, Hungary
189 O 11 **Ceheng**, China
170 K 9 **Cekerek**, Turkey
89 Q 11 **Celaya**, Mexico
40 J 7 **Celebes Sea**, Pacific Ocean 🌊
193 P 8 **Celebes Sea**, Asia 🌊
89 X 10 **Celestún**, Mexico
60 H 8 **Celina**, Tennessee, U.S.A.
65 K 18 **Celina**, Ohio, U.S.A.
144 D 7 **Celje**, Slovenia
136 H 13 **Celle**, Germany
133 D 20 **Celles**, Belgium
171 T 11 **Çelo Daglari**, Turkey ▲
125 D 21 **Celtic Sea**, Republic of Ireland 🌊
42 K 7 **Celtic Shelf**, Atlantic Ocean ◇
60 G 9 **Center Hill Lake**, Tennessee, U.S.A. 💧
63 P 4 **Centerville**, Alabama, U.S.A.
67 T 14 **Centerville**, Iowa, U.S.A.
69 X 6 **Centerville**, Missouri, U.S.A.
71 R 8 **Centerville**, Texas, U.S.A.
140 F 8 **Cento**, Italy
217 V 8 **Central**, Kenya ▣
219 N 5 **Central**, Zambia ▣
219 N 9 **Central**, Botswana ▣
219 Q 4 **Central**, Malawi ▣
234 E 7 **Central**, Papua New Guinea ▣
234 L 6 **Central**, Solomon Islands ▣
234 M 8 **Central**, Solomon Islands ▣
181 G 24 **Central**, Sri Lanka ▣
183 P 9 **Central**, Nepal ▣
216 H 4 **Central African Republic**, Africa □
138 E 9 **Central Alps**, Switzerland ◇
40 K 5 **Central Basin**, Pacific Ocean ◇
177 T 12 **Central Brāhui Range**, Pakistan ⛰
60 F 6 **Central City**, Kentucky, U.S.A.
148 H 11 **Central Highlands of Vidzemes**, Latvia ⛰
237 Q 5 **Central Line Islands**, Kiribati 🏝
177 Q 13 **Central Makran Range**, Pakistan ⛰
41 P 6 **Central Pacific Basin**, Pacific Ocean ◇
138 D 7 **Central Plateau**, Switzerland ◇
234 A 4 **Central Range**, Papua New Guinea ⛰
153 Q 9 **Central Siberian Plateau**, Russian Federation ◇
111 F 14 **Central Valley**, Chile ◇
77 H 16 **Central Valley**, California, U.S.A. ◇
65 F 21 **Centralia**, Illinois, U.S.A.
76 G 8 **Centralia**, Washington, U.S.A.
215 U 13 **Centre**, Cameroon ▣
129 P 7 **Centre**, France ▣
38 B 12 **Centre de Flacq**, Mauritius
233 B 25 **Centre Island**, New Zealand 🏝
189 R 12 **Cenxi**, China
141 I 14 **Ceprano**, Italy
110 K 9 **Ceres**, Argentina
141 L 15 **Cerignola**, Italy
170 I 9 **Cerikli**, Turkey
170 H 8 **Cerkeş**, Turkey
146 N 12 **Cerkezköy**, Turkey
144 B 8 **Cerknica**, Slovenia
171 O 12 **Cermik**, Turkey
151 N 12 **Cerna**, Romania
150 M 13 **Cernavodă**, Romania
89 Q 7 **Cerralvo**, Mexico
145 K 19 **Cërrik**, Albania
89 Q 10 **Cerritos**, Mexico
110 G 11 **Cerro Amarillo**, Argentina ▲
111 F 21 **Cerro Arenales**, Chile ▲
107 A 19 **Cerro Azol**, Ecuador ▲
112 J 8 **Cerro Azul**, Brazil
89 S 10 **Cerro Azul**, Mexico
107 J 23 **Cerro Bonete**, Bolivia ▲
110 G 8 **Cerro Bonete**, Argentina ▲
113 F 15 **Cerro Catedral**, Uruguay ▲
111 F 23 **Cerro Cervantes**, Argentina ▲
110 J 11 **Cerro Champaqui**, Argentina ▲
91 R 13 **Cerro Chirripó Grande**, Costa Rica ▲
111 H 20 **Cerro Cojudo Blanco**, Argentina ▲
88 F 2 **Cerro de La Encantada**, Mexico ▲
110 G 10 **Cerro de Olivares**, Chile ▲
107 D 15 **Cerro de Pasco**, Peru
110 G 8 **Cerro de Petro**, Chile ▲
93 U 8 **Cerro de Punta**, Puerto Rico ▲
110 H 6 **Cerro del Rincón**, Argentina ▲
89 R 9 **Cerro del Tigre**, Mexico ▲
105 P 7 **Cerro Duida**, Venezuela ▲
104 I 7 **Cerro El Nevado**, Colombia ▲
88 H 6 **Cerro Encantado**, Mexico ▲
111 F 22 **Cerro Fitz Roy**, Argentina ▲
110 H 7 **Cerro Galán**, Argentina ▲
105 Q 6 **Cerro Guaiquinima**, Venezuela ▲
111 F 20 **Cerro Hudson**, Chile ▲
88 L 8 **Cerro Huehueto**, Mexico ▲
112 F 13 **Cerro Largo**, Uruguay ▣
90 K 6 **Cerro Las Minas**, Honduras ▲
110 F 9 **Cerro Las Tórtolas**, Chile ▲
111 F 22 **Cerro Lautaro**, Chile ▲
105 O 7 **Cerro Marahuaca**, Venezuela ▲
111 F 21 **Cerro Mellizo Sur**, Chile ▲
107 I 22 **Cerro Milliri**, Bolivia/Chile ▲
111 F 22 **Cerro Murallón**, Chile ▲
110 H 13 **Cerro Nevado**, Argentina ▲
105 O 7 **Cerro Ovana**, Venezuela ▲
111 F 23 **Cerro Paine**, Chile ▲
105 O 6 **Cerro Paraque**, Venezuela ▲
111 H 14 **Cerro Payún**, Argentina ▲
89 R 8 **Cerro Peña Nevada**, Mexico ▲
110 H 6 **Cerro Pular**, Chile ▲
91 S 13 **Cerro Punta**, Panama
111 F 21 **Cerro San Lorenzo**, Argentina ▲
109 G 20 **Cerro San Rafael**, Paraguay ▲
111 F 20 **Cerro San Valentín**, Chile ▲
91 O 7 **Cerro Saslaya**, Nicaragua ▲
88 J 5 **Cerro Seberi**, Mexico ▲
89 U 12 **Cerro Sta Martha**, Mexico ▲
89 O 12 **Cerro Tancitaro**, Mexico ▲
113 B 19 **Cerro Tres Picos**, Argentina ▲
110 G 12 **Cerro Tupungato**, Argentina ▲
88 H 3 **Cerro Viejo**, Mexico ▲
107 C 15 **Cerro Yerupaja**, Peru ▲
140 F 11 **Certaldo**, Italy
131 V 4 **Cervera**, Spain
140 H 9 **Cervia**, Italy
130 J 1 **Cervo**, Spain
104 J 3 **Cesar**, Colombia ▣
140 G 9 **Cesena**, Italy
148 G 10 **Cēsis**, Latvia
143 D 16 **Česká Lípa**, Czech Republic
143 F 17 **Česká Třebová**, Czech Republic
143 C 19 **České Budějovice**, Czech Republic
143 C 20 **Český Krumlov**, Czech Republic
170 A 11 **Çeşme**, Turkey
231 V 11 **Cessnock**, New South Wales, Australia
148 H 11 **Cesvaine**, Latvia
130 L 14 **Ceuta**, Spain
138 G 10 **Cevio**, Switzerland
170 K 13 **Ceyhan**, Turkey
171 P 13 **Ceylanpinar**, Turkey
39 P 4 **Ceylon Plain**, Indian Ocean ◇
177 O 14 **Chābahār**, Iran
106 C 12 **Chachapoyas**, Peru
149 N 19 **Chachersk**, Belarus
110 K 7 **Chaco**, Argentina ▣
215 W 8 **Chad**, Africa □
61 R 12 **Chadbourn**, North Carolina, U.S.A.
111 I 14 **Chadileo**, Argentina ∿
66 H 11 **Chadron**, Nebraska, U.S.A.
187 K 18 **Chaeryŏng**, North Korea
177 P 11 **Chagai Hills**, Pakistan ⛰
179 W 4 **Chagan**, Kazakhstan
177 R 7 **Chaghcharān**, Afghanistan
39 N 5 **Chagos Archipelago**, British Indian Ocean Territory 🏝
39 N 5 **Chagos Trench**, Indian Ocean ◇
39 N 4 **Chagos–Laccadive Ridge**, Indian Ocean ⛰
176 I 8 **Chahār Mahall Va Bakhtīārī**, Iran ▣
181 J 15 **Chaibasa**, India
38 K 4 **Chain Ridge**, Indian Ocean ⛰
191 H 18 **Chainat**, Thailand
111 F 18 **Chaitén**, Chile
191 I 17 **Chaiyaphum**, Thailand
112 D 13 **Chajarí**, Argentina
181 J 15 **Chakradharpur**, India
182 J 6 **Chakrata**, India
217 R 12 **Chala**, Tanzania
107 E 19 **Chala**, Peru
129 N 11 **Chalais**, France
90 J 6 **Chalatenango**, El Salvador
219 T 6 **Chaláua**, Mozambique
217 V 6 **Chalbi Desert**, Kenya ◇
127 T 14 **Chale**, United Kingdom
87 S 7 **Chaleur Bay**, New Brunswick, Canada ≈
189 T 9 **Chaling**, China
147 N 24 **Chalki**, Greece 🏝
147 G 19 **Chalkida**, Greece
179 X 9 **Chalkudysu**, Kazakhstan
128 K 8 **Challans**, France
107 J 21 **Challapata**, Bolivia
40 L 6 **Challenger Deep**, Pacific Ocean ▲
41 V 11 **Challenger Fracture Zone**, Pacific Ocean ◇
41 O 12 **Challenger Plateau**, Pacific Ocean ◇
72 M 9 **Challis**, Idaho, U.S.A.
129 T 8 **Chalon-sur-Saône**, France
129 S 4 **Châlons-en-Champagne**, France
176 I 5 **Chālūs**, Iran
137 L 21 **Cham**, Germany
219 Q 3 **Chama**, Zambia
177 S 10 **Chaman**, Pakistan
217 V 15 **Chamba**, Tanzania
182 I 5 **Chamba**, India
66 L 10 **Chamberlain**, South Dakota, U.S.A.
59 Q 2 **Chamberlain Lake**, Maine, U.S.A. 💧
74 M 10 **Chambers**, Arizona, U.S.A.
58 E 14 **Chambersburg**, Pennsylvania, U.S.A.
129 V 10 **Chambéry**, France
219 P 3 **Chambeshi**, Zambia
173 U 3 **Chamchamāl**, Iraq
91 W 14 **Chame**, Panama
90 J 5 **Chamelec**, Honduras ∿
110 I 10 **Chamical**, Argentina
182 L 7 **Chamoli**, India
129 W 9 **Chamonix-Mont-Blanc**, France
181 H 15 **Champa**, India
129 T 4 **Champagne-Ardenne**, France ▣
65 G 18 **Champaign**, Illinois, U.S.A.
191 L 18 **Champasak**, Laos
58 K 5 **Champlain**, New York, U.S.A.
89 X 12 **Champotón**, Mexico
181 D 22 **Chamrajnagar**, India
157 P 2 **Chamzinka**, Russian Federation
110 F 7 **Chañaral**, Chile
177 O 5 **Chanārān**, Iran
110 F 10 **Chanco**, Chile
182 K 8 **Chandausi**, India
181 J 16 **Chandbali**, India
63 N 8 **Chandeleur Islands**, Mississippi, U.S.A. 🏝
63 N 8 **Chandeleur Sound**, Mississippi, U.S.A. ≈
180 E 13 **Chanderi**, India
182 J 6 **Chandigarh**, India
74 J 13 **Chandler**, Arizona, U.S.A.
87 T 6 **Chandler**, Québec, Canada
183 U 13 **Chandpur**, Bangladesh
181 F 17 **Chandrapur**, India
219 Q 6 **Changara**, Mozambique
187 K 15 **Changbai Shan**, China ⛰
186 J 13 **Changchun**, China
189 S 8 **Changde**, China
189 Z 11 **Changhua**, Taiwan
187 L 22 **Changhŭng**, South Korea
194 C 14 **Changi**, Singapore
184 K 4 **Changji**, China
189 Q 15 **Changjiang**, China
187 F 17 **Changli**, China
186 I 12 **Changling**, China
189 T 8 **Changsha**, China
189 X 8 **Changshan**, China
187 I 17 **Changshan Qundao**, China 🏝
189 Y 5 **Changshu**, China
187 J 16 **Changsong**, North Korea
189 W 10 **Changting**, China
187 J 14 **Changtu**, China
91 S 13 **Changuinola**, Panama
187 N 21 **Ch'angwŏn**, South Korea
189 Y 6 **Changxing**, China
187 H 17 **Changxing Dao**, China 🏝
189 S 6 **Changyang**, China
187 J 18 **Changyŏn**, North Korea
189 U 3 **Changyuan**, China
189 T 2 **Changzhi**, China
189 Y 5 **Changzhou**, China
147 H 26 **Chania**, Greece
125 J 26 **Channel Islands**, United Kingdom 🏝
77 I 24 **Channel Islands**, California, U.S.A. 🏝
85 X 11 **Channel-Port-aux-Basques**, Newfoundland and Labrador, Canada
127 Z 12 **Channel Tunnel**, France/United Kingdom ◇
70 J 2 **Channing**, Texas, U.S.A.
153 Z 6 **Chantal'skiy**, Russian Federation ▲
191 I 20 **Chanthaburi**, Thailand
128 L 8 **Chantonnay**, France
181 N 24 **Chanumla**, India
69 Q 6 **Chanute**, Kansas, U.S.A.
107 B 14 **Chao**, Peru
189 W 5 **Chao Hu**, China 💧
191 G 17 **Chao Phraya**, Thailand ∿
189 W 5 **Chaohu**, China
186 H 8 **Chaor**, China
210 I 6 **Chaouèn**, Morocco
187 G 15 **Chaoyang**, China
189 W 12 **Chaoyang**, China
189 W 12 **Chaozhou**, China
104 H 7 **Chaparral**, Colombia
178 I 4 **Chapayevo**, Kazakhstan
157 S 4 **Chapayevsk**, Russian Federation
179 T 3 **Chapayevskoye**, Kazakhstan
112 G 10 **Chapecó**, Brazil
127 R 4 **Chapel-en-le-Frith**, United Kingdom
86 B 7 **Chapleau**, Ontario, Canada
83 M 19 **Chaplin**, Saskatchewan, Canada
156 M 4 **Chaplygin**, Russian Federation
151 T 10 **Chaplynka**, Ukraine
60 M 5 **Chapmanville**, West Virginia, U.S.A.
107 L 22 **Charagua**, Bolivia
107 H 20 **Charana**, Bolivia
110 K 8 **Charata**, Argentina
89 P 9 **Charcas**, Mexico
240 I 6 **Charcot Island**, Antarctica 🏝
127 P 13 **Chard**, United Kingdom
179 O 13 **Chardzhev**, Turkmenistan
215 W 10 **Chari-Baguirmi**, Chad ▣
177 U 7 **Chārīkār**, Afghanistan
67 T 14 **Chariton**, Iowa, U.S.A.
105 U 5 **Charity**, Guyana
64 L 12 **Charity Island**, Michigan, U.S.A. 🏝
182 I 8 **Charkhi Dadri**, India
133 G 21 **Charleroi**, Belgium
67 T 11 **Charles City**, Iowa, U.S.A.
65 E 15 **Charles Mound**, Illinois, U.S.A. ▲
87 N 8 **Charlesbourg**, Québec, Canada
233 F 17 **Charleston**, New Zealand
61 Q 15 **Charleston**, South Carolina, U.S.A.
61 N 4 **Charleston**, West Virginia, U.S.A.
77 M 21 **Charleston Peak**, Nevada, U.S.A. ▲
231 T 8 **Charleville**, Queensland, Australia
129 S 3 **Charleville-Mézières**, France
64 J 10 **Charlevoix**, Michigan, U.S.A.
42 G 6 **Charlie–Gibbs Fracture Zone**, Atlantic Ocean ◇
61 O 10 **Charlotte**, North Carolina, U.S.A.
65 K 14 **Charlotte**, Michigan, U.S.A.
93 V 8 **Charlotte Amalie**, Virgin Islands, U.S.A. 🏛
63 W 12 **Charlotte Harbor**, Florida, U.S.A. ≈
61 S 5 **Charlottesville**, Virginia, U.S.A.
87 V 8 **Charlottetown**, Prince Edward Island, Canada
93 Z 13 **Charlotteville**, Trinidad and Tobago
231 R 12 **Charlton**, Victoria, Australia
81 T 11 **Charlton Island**, Nunavut, Canada 🏝
129 V 5 **Charmes**, France
127 P 13 **Charmouth**, United Kingdom
177 W 7 **Charsadda**, Pakistan
179 P 14 **Charshanga**, Turkmenistan
231 T 5 **Charters Towers**, Queensland, Australia
129 P 5 **Chartres**, France
179 X 9 **Charyn**, Kazakhstan
113 D 16 **Chascomús**, Argentina
149 K 15 **Chashniki**, Belarus
67 S 8 **Chaska**, Minnesota, U.S.A.
187 K 15 **Chasŏng**, North Korea
155 P 9 **Chasovo**, Russian Federation
79 S 6 **Chatanika**, Alaska, U.S.A.
129 S 7 **Château-Chinon**, France
129 N 6 **Château-du-Loir**, France
129 R 4 **Château-Thierry**, France
128 L 6 **Châteaubriant**, France
129 O 6 **Châteaudun**, France
86 L 11 **Châteauguay**, Québec, Canada
128 H 5 **Châteaulin**, France
129 P 8 **Châteauroux**, France
129 N 8 **Châtellerault**, France
127 X 11 **Chatham**, United Kingdom
86 B 14 **Chatham**, Ontario, Canada
87 T 8 **Chatham**, New Brunswick, Canada
41 P 12 **Chatham Islands**, Pacific Ocean 🏝
79 X 11 **Chatham Strait**, Alaska, U.S.A. ≈
129 O 8 **Châtillon-sur-Indre**, France
129 T 6 **Châtillon-sur-Seine**, France
183 P 12 **Chatra**, India
60 H 10 **Chattanooga**, Tennessee, U.S.A.
63 S 7 **Chattaoochee**, Florida, U.S.A.
127 W 7 **Chatteris**, United Kingdom
191 I 17 **Chatturat**, Thailand
179 V 11 **Chatyr-Tash**, Kyrgyzstan
191 L 22 **Châu Đôc**, Vietnam
190 C 12 **Chauk**, Myanmar
182 L 9 **Chauka**, India ∿
129 T 5 **Chaumont**, France
181 G 23 **Chavakachcheri**, Sri Lanka
154 J 5 **Chavan'ga**, Russian Federation
108 J 9 **Chaves**, Brazil
130 J 4 **Chaves**, Portugal
218 L 4 **Chavuma**, Zambia
149 N 17 **Chavusy**, Belarus
155 P 14 **Chaykovskiy**, Russian Federation
110 J 11 **Chazón**, Argentina
63 Q 3 **Cheaha Mountain**, Alabama, U.S.A. ▲
143 A 17 **Cheb**, Czech Republic
211 R 6 **Chebba**, Tunisia
157 R 1 **Cheboksary**, Russian Federation
64 K 10 **Cheboygan**, Michigan, U.S.A.
157 P 13 **Chechenskaya Respublika**, Russian Federation ▣
187 M 19 **Chech'ŏn**, South Korea
143 K 16 **Chęciny**, Poland
69 Q 10 **Checotah**, Oklahoma, U.S.A.
127 P 11 **Cheddar**, United Kingdom
191 B 14 **Cheduba Island**, Myanmar 🏝
78 L 9 **Chefornak**, Alaska, U.S.A.
214 K 3 **Chegga**, Mauritania
76 G 8 **Chehalis**, Washington, U.S.A.
187 L 23 **Cheju**, South Korea
187 L 23 **Cheju-do**, South Korea 🏝
154 K 11 **Chekshino**, Russian Federation
178 I 12 **Cheleken**, Turkmenistan
111 I 15 **Chelforó**, Argentina

□ Country ▣ Internal administrative region: State/Province/Territory/Dependent territory 🏛 Capital city ⛰ Mountain range/Undersea ridge ▲ Mountain peak/Volcano/Seamount ◇ Geographic feature ▶ Headland/Point/Cape/Peninsula ◮ Desert 🏝 Island/Island group ⁘ Antarctic base 🌀 Ocean 🌊 Sea ≈ Bay/Gulf/Channel/Strait 💧 Lake ◩ Salt pan/Dry/Intermittent lake ∿ Riv

■ Country   ▣ Internal administrative region: State/Province/Territory/Dependent territory   ★ Capital city   ▲ Mountain range/Undersea ridge   ▲ Mountain peak/Volcano/Seamount   ◇ Geographic feature   ▶ Headland/Point/Cape/Peninsula   ▨ Desert   ☷ Island/Island group   ▥ Antarctic base   ◈ Ocean   ≈ Sea   ≈ Bay/Gulf/Channel/Strait   ↘ Lake   ▤ Salt pan/Dry/Intermittent lake   ↘ River

279

Key: ■ Country □ Internal administrative region: State/Province/Territory/Dependent territory ▲ Capital city ▲ Mountain range/Undersea ridge ▲ Mountain peak/Volcano/Seamount ◇ Geographic feature ▶ Headland/Point/Cape/Peninsula ▲ Desert ≈ Island/Island group ▦ Antarctic base ≋ Ocean ➘ Sea ≈ Bay/Gulf/Channel/Strait Lake Salt pan/Dry/Intermittent lake

Comstock – Cuchilla Grande Inferior

70 L 10 **Comstock**, Texas, U.S.A.
41 R 3 **Comstock Seamount**, Pacific Ocean
191 M 24 **Côn Đao**, Vietnam
191 M 24 **Côn Son**, Vietnam
111 H 17 **Cona Niyeu**, Argentina
214 F 11 **Conakry**, Guinea
109 M 17 **Conceição da Barra**, Brazil
108 J 12 **Conceição do Araguaia**, Brazil
107 J 16 **Concepción**, Bolivia
109 G 19 **Concepción**, Paraguay
110 I 8 **Concepción**, Argentina
111 E 14 **Concepción**, Chile
89 P 8 **Concepción**, Mexico
91 S 14 **Concepción**, Panama
113 D 14 **Concepción del Uruguay**, Argentina
112 J 7 **Conchas**, Brazil
75 S 10 **Conchas**, New Mexico, U.S.A.
75 S 9 **Conchas Lake**, New Mexico, U.S.A.
129 O 4 **Conches-en-Ouche**, France
110 G 4 **Conchi**, Chile
88 L 6 **Conchos**, Mexico
59 N 8 **Concord**, New Hampshire, U.S.A.
59 N 9 **Concord**, Massachusetts, U.S.A.
61 P 10 **Concord**, North Carolina, U.S.A.
77 G 19 **Concord**, California, U.S.A.
106 E 11 **Concordia**, Peru
112 D 13 **Concordia**, Argentina
129 Q 11 **Condat**, France
231 T 11 **Condobolin**, New South Wales, Australia
129 N 13 **Condom**, France
76 I 10 **Condon**, Oregon, U.S.A.
140 G 6 **Conegliano**, Italy
89 N 7 **Conejos**, Mexico
234 H 7 **Conflict Group**, Papua New Guinea
151 N 10 **Congaz**, Moldova
189 U 12 **Conghua**, China
189 Q 10 **Congjiang**, China
27 R 4 **Congleton**, United Kingdom
16 H 8 **Congo**, Africa
16 J 7 **Congo**, Democratic Republic of Congo/Angola
3 M 14 **Congo Cone**, Atlantic Ocean
4 I 11 **Congress**, Arizona, U.S.A.
27 V 5 **Coningsby**, United Kingdom
27 O 1 **Coniston**, United Kingdom
6 D 9 **Coniston**, Ontario, Canada
3 J 17 **Conklin**, Alberta, Canada
25 B 17 **Connaught**, Republic of Ireland
5 O 15 **Conneaut**, Ohio, U.S.A.
8 K 11 **Connecticut**, U.S.A.
8 L 11 **Connecticut**, Connecticut, U.S.A.
6 J 8 **Connell**, Washington, U.S.A.
4 C 10 **Connorsville**, Wisconsin, U.S.A.
3 P 3 **Conrad**, Montana, U.S.A.
8 K 12 **Conrad Rise**, Indian Ocean
S 9 **Conroe**, Texas, U.S.A.
K 1 **Consejo**, Belize
12 N 5 **Conselheiro Lafaiete**, Brazil
51 N 13 **Constanța**, Romania
1 O 5 **Constantine**, Algeria
31 O 8 **Consuegra**, Spain
L 20 **Consul**, Saskatchewan, Canada
0 G 8 **Contarina**, Italy
6 B 13 **Contumazá**, Peru
I 10 **Contwoyto Lake**, Nunavut, Canada
1 N 16 **Conversano**, Italy
N 6 **Conway**, New Hampshire, U.S.A.
R 12 **Conway**, South Carolina, U.S.A.
V 11 **Conway**, Arkansas, U.S.A.
127 N 4 **Conwy**, United Kingdom
231 N 9 **Coober Pedy**, South Australia, Australia
230 M 10 **Cook**, South Australia, Australia
67 S 3 **Cook**, Minnesota, U.S.A.
45 O 1 **Cook Inlet**, Arctic Ocean
79 P 10 **Cook Inlet**, Alaska, U.S.A.
237 O 10 **Cook Islands**, New Zealand
41 Q 9 **Cook Islands**, New Zealand
233 J 15 **Cook Strait**, New Zealand
60 H 8 **Cookeville**, Tennessee, U.S.A.
231 T 3 **Cooktown**, Queensland, Australia
231 W 9 **Coolangatta**, Queensland, Australia
230 I 10 **Coolgardie**, Western Australia, Australia
231 U 12 **Cooma**, New South Wales, Australia
231 Q 11 **Coombah**, New South Wales, Australia
67 S 7 **Coon Rapids**, Minnesota, U.S.A.
231 T 10 **Coonabarabran**, New South Wales, Australia
231 U 10 **Coonamble**, New South Wales, Australia
181 C 20 **Coondapoor**, India
181 D 22 **Coonoor**, India
231 P 9 **Cooper**, South Australia, Australia
71 S 5 **Cooper**, Texas, U.S.A.
92 L 1 **Cooper's Town**, The Bahamas
76 E 12 **Coos Bay**, Oregon, U.S.A.
110 H 8 **Copacabana**, Argentina
89 R 14 **Copala**, Mexico
135 D 25 **Copenhagen**, Denmark
110 F 8 **Copiapó**, Chile
64 H 7 **Copper Harbor**, Michigan, U.S.A.
219 N 4 **Copperbelt**, Zambia
127 N 13 **Copplestone**, United Kingdom
184 J 9 **Coqên**, China
110 F 10 **Coquimbo**, Chile
110 F 10 **Coquimbo**, Chile
150 I 14 **Corabia**, Romania
107 E 18 **Coracora**, Peru
230 E 7 **Coral Bay**, Western Australia, Australia
63 Y 13 **Coral Gables**, Florida, U.S.A.
85 O 3 **Coral Harbour**, Nunavut, Canada
234 C 6 **Coral Sea**, Oceania
40 M 9 **Coral Sea Basin**, Pacific Ocean
40 M 9 **Coral Sea Islands**, New Zealand
113 B 17 **Corbett**, Argentina
60 J 7 **Corbin**, Kentucky, U.S.A.
127 U 7 **Corby**, United Kingdom
111 G 18 **Corcovado**, Argentina
63 T 5 **Cordele**, Georgia, U.S.A.
130 J 2 **Cordillera Cantabrica**, Spain
104 H 8 **Cordillera Central**, Colombia
196 F 8 **Cordillera Central**, Philippines
91 T 14 **Cordillera Central**, Panama
91 O 11 **Cordillera de Guanacaste**, Costa Rica
91 Y 13 **Cordillera de San Blas**, Panama
91 R 13 **Cordillera de Talamanca**, Costa Rica
91 P 10 **Cordillera de Yolaina**, Nicaragua
110 G 6 **Cordillera Domeyko**, Chile
91 N 7 **Cordillera Entre Rios**, Honduras
91 O 8 **Cordillera Isabelia**, Nicaragua
89 Q 12 **Cordillera Neo-Volcánica**, Mexico
107 C 14 **Cordillera Occidental**, South America
107 D 15 **Cordillera Oriental**, South AmericaņF817
197 H 17 **Cordilleras Range**, Philippines
104 H 4 **Córdoba**, Colombia
110 K 11 **Córdoba**, Argentina
130 M 11 **Córdoba**, Spain
89 T 12 **Córdoba**, Mexico
110 J 10 **Córdoba**, Argentina
79 S 9 **Cordova**, Alaska, U.S.A.
127 R 14 **Corfe Castle**, United Kingdom
147 A 16 **Corfu**, Greece
130 K 7 **Coria**, Spain
60 I 4 **Corinth**, Kentucky, U.S.A.
63 N 1 **Corinth**, Mississippi, U.S.A.
147 F 20 **Corinth Canal**, Greece
90 M 9 **Corinto**, Nicaragua
109 F 16 **Corixa Grande**, Brazil
125 C 21 **Cork**, Republic of Ireland
125 C 21 **Cork Harbour**, Republic of Ireland
141 I 22 **Corleone**, Italy
170 C 7 **Corlu**, Turkey
146 N 12 **Çorlu**, Turkey
112 I 7 **Cornélio Procópio**, Brazil
64 D 11 **Cornell**, Wisconsin, U.S.A.
85 X 10 **Corner Brook**, Newfoundland and Labrador, Canada
42 G 8 **Corner Seamounts**, Atlantic Ocean
58 F 10 **Corning**, New York, U.S.A.
69 Y 8 **Corning**, Arkansas, U.S.A.
77 G 17 **Corning**, California, U.S.A.
86 J 11 **Cornwall**, Ontario, Canada
92 L 1 **Cornwall**, The Bahamas
81 O 3 **Cornwall Island**, Nunavut, Canada
81 O 4 **Cornwallis Island**, Nunavut, Canada
104 M 2 **Coro**, Venezuela
197 G 16 **Coroco**, Philippines
107 I 19 **Coroico**, Bolivia
232 L 8 **Coromandel**, New Zealand
181 G 20 **Coromandel Coast**, India
232 L 8 **Coromandel Peninsula**, New Zealand
232 L 8 **Coromandel Range**, New Zealand
197 F 15 **Coron**, Philippines
197 F 15 **Coron**, Philippines
75 R 11 **Corona**, New Mexico, U.S.A.
197 H 21 **Coronado Bay**, Philippines
82 H 8 **Coronation Gulf**, Nunavut, Canada
240 H 1 **Coronation Island**, South Orkney Islands
113 B 14 **Coronda**, Argentina
113 C 19 **Coronel Dorrego**, Argentina
109 H 20 **Coronel Oviedo**, Paraguay
113 B 18 **Coronel Pringles**, Argentina
109 H 19 **Coronel Sapucaia**, Brazil
113 B 18 **Coronel Suárez**, Argentina
113 E 18 **Coronel Vidal**, Argentina
233 C 23 **Coronet Peak**, New Zealand
145 K 20 **Çorovodë**, Albania
231 S 12 **Corowa**, New South Wales, Australia
90 K 1 **Corozal**, Belize
111 H 22 **Corpen Aike**, Argentina
71 Q 13 **Corpus Christi**, Texas, U.S.A.
107 I 21 **Corque**, Bolivia
42 O 11 **Corralejo**, Canary Islands
196 F 11 **Corregidor**, Philippines
109 L 14 **Corrente**, Brazil
109 H 16 **Correntes**, Brazil
109 L 15 **Correntina**, Brazil
112 C 10 **Corrientes**, Argentina
112 D 11 **Corrientes**, Argentina
71 T 8 **Corrigan**, Texas, U.S.A.
230 G 11 **Corrigin**, Western Australia, Australia
127 Q 11 **Corsham**, United Kingdom
129 X 14 **Corsica**, France
158 J 6 **Corsica Trough**, Mediterranean Sea
71 R 7 **Corsicana**, Texas, U.S.A.
158 I 6 **Corso–Ligurian Basin**, Mediterranean Sea
130 J 11 **Cortegana**, Spain
140 B 8 **Cortemilia**, Italy
75 N 7 **Cortez**, Colorado, U.S.A.
140 H 5 **Cortina d'Ampezzo**, Italy
58 G 9 **Cortland**, New York, U.S.A.
140 G 11 **Cortona**, Italy
130 H 9 **Coruche**, Portugal
171 P 9 **Coruh**, Turkey
170 J 8 **Çorum**, Turkey
109 G 17 **Corumbá**, Brazil
109 O 14 **Corurípe**, Brazil
76 F 11 **Corvallis**, Oregon, U.S.A.
42 L 1 **Corvo**, Azores
88 L 8 **Cosalá**, Mexico
89 T 12 **Cosamaloapan**, Mexico
110 G 3 **Coscaya**, Chile
141 M 19 **Cosenza**, Italy
65 N 18 **Coshocton**, Ohio, U.S.A.
129 R 7 **Cosne-cours-sur-Loire**, France
110 J 10 **Cosquín**, Argentina
131 T 11 **Costa Blanca**, Spain
131 X 4 **Costa Brava**, Spain
130 J 13 **Costa de la Luz**, Spain
131 T 8 **Costa del Azahar**, Spain
131 N 14 **Costa del Sol**, Spain
131 V 6 **Costa Dorada**, Spain
109 D 14 **Costa Marques**, Brazil
88 L 8 **Costa Rica**, Mexico
91 Q 13 **Costa Rica**, North America
141 D 15 **Costa Smeralda**, Italy
131 N 1 **Costa Verde**, Spain
137 K 15 **Coswig**, Germany
197 K 22 **Cotabato**, Philippines
107 J 22 **Cotagaita**, Bolivia
107 F 18 **Cotahuasi**, Peru
129 W 15 **Côte d'Azur**, France
214 K 12 **Côte d'Ivoire**, Africa
91 R 14 **Coto Brus**, Costa Rica
215 O 13 **Cotonou**, Benin
106 B 9 **Cotopaxi**, Ecuador
127 R 10 **Cotswold Hills**, United Kingdom
137 N 15 **Cottbus**, Germany
69 V 8 **Cotter**, Arkansas, U.S.A.
140 A 8 **Cottian Alps**, Italy
72 K 6 **Cottonwood**, Idaho, U.S.A.
77 G 16 **Cottonwood**, California, U.S.A.
71 N 12 **Cotulla**, Texas, U.S.A.
58 E 10 **Coudersport**, Pennsylvania, U.S.A.
76 J 7 **Coulee City**, Washington, U.S.A.
129 Q 4 **Coulommiers**, France
65 F 21 **Coulterville**, Illinois, U.S.A.
72 J 8 **Council**, Idaho, U.S.A.
78 M 6 **Council**, Alaska, U.S.A.
67 Q 14 **Council Bluffs**, Iowa, U.S.A.
105 U 7 **Courantyne**, Suriname
133 F 21 **Courcelles**, Belgium
149 B 15 **Courland Lagoon**, Russian Federation
140 A 6 **Courmayeur**, Italy
62 H 5 **Coushatta**, Louisiana, U.S.A.
38 B 8 **Cousin**, Seychelles
38 B 9 **Cousine**, Seychelles
128 L 4 **Coutances**, France
83 K 21 **Coutts**, Alberta, Canada
133 G 23 **Couvin**, Belgium
127 S 7 **Coventry**, United Kingdom
74 J 14 **Covered Wells**, Arizona, U.S.A.
130 J 7 **Covilhã**, Portugal
60 A 9 **Covington**, Tennessee, U.S.A.
62 L 7 **Covington**, Louisiana, U.S.A.
63 T 3 **Covington**, Georgia, U.S.A.
231 P 11 **Cowell**, South Australia, Australia
127 T 13 **Cowes**, United Kingdom
231 T 11 **Cowra**, New South Wales, Australia
112 G 12 **Coxilha Grande**, Brazil
109 H 17 **Coxim**, Brazil
183 W 15 **Cox's Bazar**, Bangladesh
214 F 11 **Coyah**, Guinea
91 P 12 **Coyolar**, Costa Rica
89 Z 10 **Cozumel**, Mexico
38 E 8 **Crab Island**, Rodrigues Island
219 N 14 **Cradock**, Republic of South Africa
232 K 7 **Cradock Channel**, New Zealand
75 O 3 **Craig**, Colorado, U.S.A.
137 H 22 **Crailsheim**, Germany
150 H 13 **Craiova**, Romania
84 H 7 **Cranberry Portage**, Manitoba, Canada
127 X 12 **Cranbrook**, United Kingdom
83 I 21 **Cranbrook**, British Columbia, Canada
64 G 10 **Crandon**, Wisconsin, U.S.A.
70 J 8 **Crane**, Texas, U.S.A.
76 J 12 **Crane**, Oregon, U.S.A.
240 L 10 **Crary Mountains**, Antarctica
76 G 13 **Crater Lake**, Oregon, U.S.A.
234 H 4 **Crater Point**, Papua New Guinea
108 M 11 **Crateús**, Brazil
127 P 7 **Craven Arms**, United Kingdom
104 L 5 **Cravo Norte**, Colombia
66 G 12 **Crawford**, Nebraska, U.S.A.
71 P 8 **Crawford**, Texas, U.S.A.
43 K 18 **Crawford Seamount**, Atlantic Ocean
65 I 19 **Crawfordsville**, Indiana, U.S.A.
63 S 8 **Crawfordville**, Florida, U.S.A.
127 V 12 **Crawley**, United Kingdom
61 O 5 **Crawley**, West Virginia, U.S.A.
73 R 6 **Crazy Mtns**, Montana, U.S.A.
127 N 13 **Crediton**, United Kingdom
83 K 15 **Cree Lake**, Saskatchewan, Canada
88 L 5 **Creel**, Mexico
140 D 7 **Crema**, Italy
140 D 7 **Cremona**, Italy
62 L 2 **Crenshaw**, Mississippi, U.S.A.
158 M 4 **Cres**, Mediterranean Sea
76 H 12 **Crescent**, Oregon, U.S.A.
63 W 8 **Crescent City**, Florida, U.S.A.
77 E 14 **Crescent City**, California, U.S.A.
63 W 8 **Crescent Lake**, Florida, U.S.A.
76 G 12 **Crescent Lake**, Oregon, U.S.A.
113 C 14 **Crespo**, Argentina
129 T 12 **Crest**, France
67 R 14 **Creston**, Iowa, U.S.A.
73 V 14 **Creston**, Wyoming, U.S.A.
83 I 21 **Creston**, British Columbia, Canada
63 Q 7 **Crestview**, Florida, U.S.A.
159 R 10 **Cretan Trough**, Mediterranean Sea
159 T 10 **CretanŠRhodes Ridge**, Mediterranean Sea
147 I 26 **Crete**, Greece
127 Q 5 **Crewe**, United Kingdom
61 S 6 **Crewe**, Virginia, U.S.A.
127 P 13 **Crewkerne**, United Kingdom
112 J 11 **Criciúma**, Brazil
127 O 9 **Crickhowell**, United Kingdom
124 H 12 **Crieff**, United Kingdom
151 U 11 **Crimea**, Ukraine
108 L 13 **Cristino Castro**, Brazil
91 W 13 **Cristóbal**, Panama
151 O 8 **Criuleni**, Moldova
109 J 15 **Crixás**, Brazil
145 M 16 **Crna Gora**, Macedonia (F.Y.R.O.M.)/Serbia and Montenegro
144 E9 **Croatia**, Europe
71 S 8 **Crockett**, Texas, U.S.A.
127 Z 5 **Cromer**, United Kingdom
233 D 23 **Cromwell**, New Zealand
93 N 4 **Crooked Island**, The Bahamas
67 O 3 **Crookston**, Minnesota, U.S.A.
63 U 8 **Cross City**, Florida, U.S.A.
125 J 15 **Cross Fell**, United Kingdom
59 T 5 **Cross Island**, Maine, U.S.A.
84 J 8 **Cross Lake**, Manitoba, Canada
71 N 6 **Cross Plains**, Texas, U.S.A.
215 R 13 **Cross River**, Nigeria
64 J 10 **Cross Village**, Michigan, U.S.A.
69 V 14 **Crossett**, Arkansas, U.S.A.
60 H 9 **Crossville**, Tennessee, U.S.A.
64 M 13 **Croswell**, Michigan, U.S.A.
141 N 19 **Crotone**, Italy
73 V 7 **Crow Agency**, Montana, U.S.A.
64 G 8 **Covington**, Michigan, U.S.A.
73 P 6 **Crow Peak**, Montana, U.S.A.
127 W 12 **Crowborough**, United Kingdom
62 I 7 **Crowley**, Louisiana, U.S.A.
65 H 16 **Crown Point**, Indiana, U.S.A.
241 U 3 **Crown Prince Olav Coast**, Antarctica
241 O 3 **Crown Princess Martha Coast**, Antarctica
75 O 9 **Crownpoint**, New Mexico, U.S.A.
126 M 12 **Croyde**, United Kingdom
231 R 4 **Croydon**, Queensland, Australia
127 W 11 **Croydon**, United Kingdom
38 M 9 **Crozet Basin**, Indian Ocean
38 K 11 **Crozet Islands**, Indian Ocean
38 J 11 **Crozet Plateau**, Indian Ocean
128 H 5 **Crozon**, France
42 I 9 **Cruiser Tablemount**, Atlantic Ocean
112 G 11 **Cruz Alta**, Brazil
112 L 6 **Cruzeiro**, Brazil
108 A 13 **Cruzeiro do Sul**, Brazil
126 L 9 **Crymych**, United Kingdom
64 G 9 **Crystal Falls**, Michigan, U.S.A.
143 N 22 **Csenger**, Hungary
143 G 22 **Csorna**, Hungary
143 I 22 **Csóványos**, Hungary
191 O 17 **Cu Lao Cham**, Vietnam
191 O 17 **Cu Lao Re**, Vietnam
191 O 22 **Cu Lao Thu**, Vietnam
219 S 5 **Cuamba**, Mozambique
218 K 6 **Cuando Cubango**, Angola
218 J 7 **Cuangar**, Angola
218 G 2 **Cuanza Norte**, Angola
218 H 3 **Cuanza Sul**, Angola
112 E 12 **Cuareim**, Brazil
89 O 6 **Cuatro Ciénegas**, Mexico
88 L 5 **Cuauhtémoc**, Mexico
65 E 18 **Cuba**, Illinois, U.S.A.
75 P 9 **Cuba**, New Mexico, U.S.A.
92 I 5 **Cuba**, North America
218 G 4 **Cubal**, Angola
218 I 6 **Cubango**, Angola
170 H 9 **Cubuk**, Turkey
90 H 5 **Cubulco**, Guatemala
218 I 5 **Cuchi**, Angola
113 F 15 **Cuchilla Grande**, Uruguay
113 D 15 **Cuchilla Grande Inferior**, Uruguay

Country · Internal administrative region: State/Province/Territory/Dependent territory · Capital city · Mountain range/Undersea ridge · Mountain peak/Volcano/Seamount · Geographic feature · Headland/Point/Cape/Peninsula · Desert · Island/Island group · Antarctic base · Ocean · Sea · Bay/Gulf/Channel/Strait · Lake · Salt pan/Dry/Intermittent lake · River

111 I 15 **Cuchillo-Có**, Argentina
108 C 9 **Cucuí**, Brazil
218 J 3 **Cucumbi**, Angola
104 J 4 **Cúcuta**, Colombia
181 F 22 **Cuddalore**, India
181 F 20 **Cuddapah**, India
230 G 9 **Cue**, Western Australia, Australia
131 N 5 **Cuéllar**, Spain
218 I 4 **Cuemba**, Angola
106 B 10 **Cuenca**, Ecuador
131 Q 7 **Cuenca**, Spain
196 G 12 **Cuenca**, Philippines
89 N 8 **Cuencamé**, Mexico
89 R 12 **Cuernavaca**, Mexico
71 Q 11 **Cuero**, Texas, U.S.A.
92 M 6 **Cueto**, Cuba
108 F 12 **Cuiaba**, Brazil
109 G 16 **Cuiabá**, Brazil
90 H 6 **Cuilapa**, Guatemala
90 F 4 **Cuilco**, Guatemala ʃ
218 J 2 **Cuilo**, Angola
186 L 9 **Cuiluan**, China
218 G 1 **Cuimba**, Angola
218 J 5 **Cuito Cuanavale**, Angola
150 G 13 **Cujmir**, Romania
194 E 7 **Cukai**, Malaysia
171 T 12 **Cukurca**, Turkey
197 H 16 **Culasi**, Philippines
73 Y 3 **Culbertson**, Montana, U.S.A.
107 C 15 **Culebras**, Peru
132 I 13 **Culemborg**, Netherlands
171 V 10 **Culfa**, Azerbaijan
88 L 8 **Culiacán**, Mexico
197 E 15 **Culion**, Philippines
197 E 15 **Culion**, Philippines 🏝
131 Q 12 **Cúllar-Baza**, Spain
131 T 9 **Cullera**, Spain
63 Q 2 **Cullman**, Alabama, U.S.A.
127 O 13 **Cullompton**, United Kingdom
61 S 4 **Culpeper**, Virginia, U.S.A.
105 Q 2 **Cumaná**, Venezuela
60 E 8 **Cumberland**, Tennessee/Kentucky, U.S.A. ʃ
61 R 2 **Cumberland**, Maryland, U.S.A.
83 N 16 **Cumberland Lake**, Saskatchewan, Canada ◣
85 S 1 **Cumberland Peninsula**, Nunavut, Canada ▶
60 G 10 **Cumberland Plateau**, Tennessee, U.S.A. ◇
64 F 6 **Cumberland Point**, Michigan, U.S.A. ▶
85 S 2 **Cumberland Sound**, Nunavut, Canada ≈
108 H 9 **Cuminapanema**, Brazil ʃ
125 H 14 **Cumnock**, United Kingdom
88 J 4 **Cumpas**, Mexico
170 H 12 **Çumra**, Turkey
90 G 5 **Cunén**, Guatemala
218 H 6 **Cunene**, Angola ▣
218 F 7 **Cunene**, Angola ʃ
140 A 9 **Cuneo**, Italy
191 O 19 **Cung Son**, Vietnam
231 T 9 **Cunnamulla**, Queensland, Australia
108 N 13 **Curaçá**, Brazil
108 A 12 **Curaçá**, Brazil ʃ
93 R 13 **Curaçao**, Netherlands Antilles 🏝
111 F 15 **Curacautín**, Chile
106 E 9 **Curaray**, Peru/Ecuador ʃ
38 B 12 **Curepipe**, Mauritius
110 F 13 **Curicó**, Chile
38 B 8 **Curieuse**, Seychelles 🏝
104 I 10 **Curiplaya**, Colombia
112 J 8 **Curitiba**, Brazil
112 I 10 **Curitibanos**, Brazil
43 C 16 **Curral Velho**, Cape Verde
77 M 18 **Currant**, Nevada, U.S.A.
231 R 14 **Currie**, Tasmania, Australia
77 N 16 **Currie**, Nevada, U.S.A.
61 W 7 **Currituck**, North Carolina, U.S.A.
61 W 7 **Currituck Sound**, North Carolina, U.S.A. ≈
79 Q 8 **Curry**, Alaska, U.S.A.
76 F 12 **Curtin**, Oregon, U.S.A.
231 V 7 **Curtis Island**, Queensland, Australia 🏝
108 H 9 **Curuá**, Brazil ʃ
108 I 10 **Curumu**, Brazil
107 G 17 **Cusco**, Peru ▣
63 S 5 **Cusseta**, Georgia, U.S.A.
66 G 10 **Custer**, South Dakota, U.S.A.
73 V 6 **Custer**, Montana, U.S.A.
73 P 2 **Cut Bank**, Montana, U.S.A.
62 L 8 **Cut Off**, Louisiana, U.S.A.
63 S 5 **Cuthbert**, Georgia, U.S.A.
63 Y 14 **Cutler Ridge**, Florida, U.S.A.
111 G 15 **Cutral-Co**, Argentina
181 J 16 **Cuttack**, India
218 H 6 **Cuvelai**, Angola
216 H 8 **Cuvette**, Congo ▣
39 T 7 **Cuvier Basin**, Indian Ocean ◇
39 S 7 **Cuvier Plateau**, Indian Ocean ◇
136 F 9 **Cuxhaven**, Germany
110 F 2 **Cuya**, Chile
196 F 9 **Cuyapo**, Philippines
197 G 17 **Cuyo**, Philippines
197 G 17 **Cuyo**, Philippines 🏝
197 G 15 **Cuyo East Passage**, Philippines ≈
197 G 15 **Cuyo Islands**, Philippines 🏝
197 F 16 **Cuyo West Passage**, Philippines ≈
105 S 5 **Cuyuni**, Guyana ʃ
107 G 17 **Cuzco**, Peru
217 Q 9 **Cyangugu**, Rwanda
147 I 22 **Cyclades**, Greece 🏝
60 J 4 **Cynthiana**, Kentucky, U.S.A.
159 X 10 **Cyprus**, Mediterranean Sea 🏝
170 G 15 **Cyprus**, Asia ◻
170 I 14 **Cyprus (Turkish Republic Of Northern Cyprus)**, Asia ◻
159 X 10 **Cyprus Basin**, Mediterranean Sea ◇
142 F 10 **Czaplinek**, Poland
83 K 19 **Czar**, Alberta, Canada
142 F 11 **Czarnków**, Poland
143 C 18 **Czech Republic**, Europe ◻
142 H 9 **Czersk**, Poland
143 I 16 **Częstochowa**, Poland
142 F 11 **Człopa**, Poland
142 G 10 **Człuchów**, Poland

D

185 V 3 **Da Hinggan Ling**, China ⛰
186 G 11 **Da Hinggan Range**, China ⛰
184 M 8 **Da Juh**, China
191 O 21 **Đa Lat**, Vietnam
191 O 17 **Đa Nẵng**, Vietnam
185 N 7 **Da Qaidam**, China
186 J 11 **Da'an**, China
197 K 16 **Daanbantayan**, Philippines
189 Q 5 **Daba Shan**, China ⛰
104 L 2 **Dabajuro**, Venezuela
214 K 12 **Dabakala**, Côte d'Ivoire
186 F 13 **Daban**, China
143 J 23 **Dabas**, Hungary
213 H 18 **Dabat**, Ethiopia
104 G 5 **Dabeiba**, Colombia
181 C 18 **Dabhol**, India
189 U 6 **Dabie Shan**, China ⛰
214 G 11 **Dabola**, Guinea
214 K 14 **Dabou**, Côte d'Ivoire
143 J 17 **Dąbrowa Górnicza**, Poland
150 I 13 **Dăbuleni**, Romania
183 U 13 **Dacca**, Bangladesh ♜
189 P 11 **Dachang**, China
137 J 24 **Dachau**, Germany
185 R 10 **Dachaun**, China
187 G 16 **Dachengzi**, China
189 P 6 **Dachuan**, China
42 J 10 **Dacia Seamount**, Atlantic Ocean ▲
233 C 25 **Dacre**, New Zealand
172 K 1 **Dādāt**, Syria
213 K 18 **Daddato**, Djibouti
63 V 10 **Dade City**, Florida, U.S.A.
181 C 16 **Dadra and Nagar Haveli**, India ▣
177 T 13 **Dadu**, Pakistan
196 J 12 **Daet**, Philippines
189 N 9 **Dafang**, China
189 Y 4 **Dafeng**, China
175 V 7 **Dafīr**, United Arab Emirates
183 W 9 **Dafla Hills**, India ⛰
213 L 21 **Daga Medo**, Ethiopia
148 I 13 **Dagda**, Latvia
187 E 18 **Dagu**, China
188 M 8 **Daguan**, China
196 F 9 **Dagupan**, Philippines
174 L 8 **Dahabān**, Saudi Arabia
181 B 16 **Dahanu**, India
186 M 9 **Daheiding Shan**, China ▲
213 J 16 **Dahlak Archipelago**, Eritrea 🏝
137 M 14 **Dahme**, Germany
184 H 7 **Dahongliutan**, China
173 R 1 **Dahūk**, Iraq
234 M 6 **Dai**, Solomon Islands 🏝
187 B 16 **Dai Hai**, China ◣
187 B 17 **Dai Xian**, China
191 E 15 **Daik-u**, Myanmar
199 E 17 **Daimanji-san**, Japan ▲
131 O 9 **Daimiel**, Spain
71 T 5 **Daingerfield**, Texas, U.S.A.
199 H 16 **Dainichiga-take**, Japan ▲
188 I 4 **Dainkog**, China
199 I 18 **Daiō-zaki**, Japan ▶
113 B 17 **Daireaux**, Argentina
212 E 9 **Dairût**, Egypt
64 C 9 **Dairyland**, Wisconsin, U.S.A.
231 Q 5 **Dajarra**, Queensland, Australia
177 P 8 **Dak**, Afghanistan ◣
191 N 18 **Dak Kon**, Vietnam
214 D 8 **Dakar**, Senegal ♜
183 U 14 **Dakhin Shahbazpur Island**, Bangladesh 🏝
212 D 11 **Dakhla Oasis**, Egypt ◇
214 E 5 **Dakhlet Nouâdhibou**, Mauritania ▣
181 O 25 **Dakoank**, India
181 C 15 **Dakor**, India
215 Q 9 **Dakoro**, Niger
67 O 12 **Dakota City**, Nebraska, U.S.A.
145 L 16 **Đakovica**, Serbia and Montenegro
218 J 3 **Dala**, Angola
214 G 11 **Dalaba**, Guinea
197 J 18 **Dalaguete**, Philippines
186 E 13 **Dalai Nur**, China ◣
170 D 13 **Dalaman**, Turkey
185 Q 5 **Dalandzadgad**, Mongolia
197 F 17 **Dalanganem Islands**, Philippines 🏝
185 P 5 **Dalay**, Mongolia
177 R 11 **Dalbandin**, Pakistan
231 V 8 **Dalby**, Queensland, Australia
60 H 8 **Dale Hollow Lake**, Tennessee, U.S.A. ◣
151 S 11 **Daleke**, Ukraine
190 B 11 **Daletme**, Myanmar
70 I 1 **Dalhart**, Texas, U.S.A.
87 S 6 **Dalhousie**, Québec, Canada
188 J 10 **Dali**, China
189 R 3 **Dali**, China
187 H 18 **Dalian**, China
186 I 13 **Dalin**, China
187 B 15 **Daliuhao**, China
71 Q 6 **Dallas**, Texas, U.S.A.
76 F 10 **Dallas**, Oregon, U.S.A.
153 W 15 **Dal'negorsk**, Russian Federation
214 J 13 **Daloa**, Côte d'Ivoire
189 O 8 **Dalou Shan**, China ⛰
181 I 14 **Daltenganj**, India
63 S 1 **Dalton**, Georgia, U.S.A.
86 A 6 **Dalton**, Ontario, Canada
127 O 1 **Dalton-in-Furness**, United Kingdom
196 G 4 **Dalupiri**, Philippines 🏝
134 C 10 **Dalvík**, Iceland
230 G 10 **Dalwallinu**, Western Australia, Australia
230 M 2 **Daly**, Northern Territory, Australia ʃ
231 N 3 **Daly Waters**, Northern Territory, Australia
181 B 16 **Daman**, India
181 B 16 **Daman and Diu**, India ▣
212 E 7 **Damanhûr**, Egypt
193 S 14 **Damar**, Indonesia 🏝
216 J 5 **Damara**, Central African Republic
218 J 8 **Damaraland**, Namibia ◇
215 U 9 **Damasak**, Nigeria
172 H 7 **Damascus**, Syria ♜
215 T 10 **Damaturu**, Nigeria
218 G 1 **Damba**, Angola
215 R 10 **Dambatta**, Nigeria
215 U 10 **Damboa**, Nigeria
181 G 24 **Dambulla**, Sri Lanka
176 K 6 **Damghan**, Iran
189 U 2 **Daming**, China
181 F 14 **Damoh**, India
172 G 6 **Damour**, Lebanon
230 F 6 **Dampier**, Western Australia, Australia
234 E 4 **Dampier Strait**, Papua New Guinea ≈
215 Q 10 **Dan-Gulbi**, Nigeria
183 O 8 **Dana**, Nepal
214 I 13 **Danané**, Côte d'Ivoire
197 K 17 **Danao**, Philippines
178 J 13 **Danata**, Turkmenistan
192 K 10 **Danau Luar**, Indonesia ◣
193 O 11 **Danau Poso**, Indonesia ◣
192 F 13 **Danau Ranau**, Indonesia ◣
192 L 10 **Danau Semayang**, Indonesia ◣
192 J 12 **Danau Sembulu**, Indonesia ◣
192 C 9 **Danau Toba**, Indonesia ◣
193 O 12 **Danau Towuti**, Indonesia ◣
188 L 6 **Danba**, China
58 K 11 **Danbury**, Connecticut, U.S.A.
64 C 9 **Danbury**, Wisconsin, U.S.A.
77 M 24 **Danby Lake**, California, U.S.A. ◣
213 H 23 **Dande**, Ethiopia
181 C 19 **Dandeli**, India
231 S 13 **Dandenong**, Victoria, Australia
187 J 16 **Dandong**, China
45 Q 12 **Daneborg**, Greenland
189 R 4 **Danfeng**, China
59 S 3 **Danforth**, Maine, U.S.A.
189 N 4 **Dangchang**, China
218 G 2 **Dange**, Angola
179 R 14 **Danghara**, Tajikistan
213 H 19 **Dangila**, Ethiopia
90 K 3 **Dangriga**, Belize
189 V 3 **Dangshan**, China
189 X 5 **Dangtu**, China
213 G 19 **Dangur**, Ethiopia
73 R 12 **Daniel**, Wyoming, U.S.A.
85 X 9 **Daniel's Harbour**, Newfoundland and Labrador, Canada
154 K 13 **Danilov**, Russian Federation
145 I 15 **Danilovgrad**, Serbia and Montenegro
189 R 2 **Daning**, China
171 Z 8 **Dänizkänari**, Azerbaijan
189 S 5 **Danjiangkou Shuiku**, China ◣
199 A 23 **Danjo-guntō**, Japan 🏝
156 L 3 **Dankov**, Russian Federation
136 I 11 **Dannenberg**, Germany
213 M 21 **Danot**, Ethiopia
189 U 12 **Danshui**, China
58 E 9 **Dansville**, New York, U.S.A.
137 G 24 **Danube**, Europe ʃ
191 D 16 **Danubyu**, Myanmar
60 I 6 **Danville**, Kentucky, U.S.A.
61 Q 7 **Danville**, Virginia, U.S.A.
65 G 18 **Danville**, Illinois, U.S.A.
65 I 19 **Danville**, Indiana, U.S.A.
189 Q 15 **Danxian**, China
197 H 17 **Dao**, Philippines
190 N 12 **Đao Cai Bau**, Vietnam 🏝
190 M 12 **Đao Cat Ba**, Vietnam 🏝
191 K 22 **Đao Phu Quôc**, Vietnam 🏝
191 K 23 **Đao Thô Chur**, Vietnam 🏝
191 J 23 **Đao Vây**, Vietnam 🏝
189 S 10 **Daoxian**, China
189 P 8 **Daozhen**, China
197 M 18 **Dapa**, Philippines
215 N 11 **Dapaong**, Togo
197 J 20 **Dapitan**, Philippines
186 J 10 **Daqing**, China
173 T 4 **Dāqūq**, Iraq
217 W 12 **Dar Es Salaam**, Tanzania
172 H 8 **Dar'a**, Syria
214 E 8 **Dara**, Senegal
176 K 11 **Dārāb**, Iran
150 L 7 **Darabani**, Romania
196 J 13 **Daraga**, Philippines
211 R 9 **Daraj**, Libya
176 H 8 **Dārān**, Iran
145 K 15 **Đaravica**, Serbia and Montenegro ▲
212 F 11 **Daraw**, Egypt
215 T 10 **Darazo**, Nigeria
176 M 9 **Darband**, Iran
183 Q 11 **Darbhanga**, India
72 M 6 **Darby**, Montana, U.S.A.
170 B 8 **Dardanelles**, Turkey ≈
170 M 11 **Darende**, Turkey
213 A 18 **Darfur**, Sudan ◇
179 N 12 **Darganata**, Turkmenistan
232 J 7 **Dargaville**, New Zealand
185 Q 3 **Darhan**, Mongolia
63 W 6 **Darien**, Georgia, U.S.A.
179 T 6 **Dar'inskiy**, Kazakhstan
91 N 8 **Darío**, Nicaragua
183 S 10 **Darjiling**, India
188 K 4 **Darlag**, China
231 S 10 **Darling**, New South Wales, Australia ʃ
125 J 15 **Darlington**, United Kingdom
142 F 8 **Darłowka**, Poland
137 F 20 **Darmstadt**, Germany
211 X 7 **Darnah**, Libya
82 E 8 **Darnley Bay**, Northwest Territories, Canada ≈
131 R 5 **Daroca**, Spain
177 O 5 **Darreh Gaz**, Iran
136 K 8 **Darss**, Germany 🏝
178 H 12 **Darta**, Turkmenistan
127 W 11 **Dartford**, United Kingdom
126 M 14 **Dartmeet**, United Kingdom
126 M 14 **Dartmoor**, United Kingdom ◇
127 N 15 **Dartmouth**, United Kingdom
87 V 11 **Dartmouth**, Nova Scotia, Canada
234 B 6 **Daru**, Papua New Guinea
193 S 10 **Daruba**, Indonesia
178 K 12 **Darvaza**, Turkmenistan
177 T 9 **Darwazgai**, Afghanistan
127 Q 3 **Darwen**, United Kingdom
181 E 16 **Darwha**, India
230 L 1 **Darwin**, Northern Territory, Australia
111 L 23 **Darwin**, Falkland Islands
65 N 20 **Darwin**, Ohio, U.S.A.
177 W 9 **Darya Khan**, Pakistan
176 J 11 **Daryācheh-ye Bakhtegan**, Iran ◣
176 J 6 **Daryācheh-ye Namak**, Iran ◣
177 P 10 **Daryācheh-ye Sistau**, Iran ◣
176 J 10 **Daryācheh-ye Tashk**, Iran ◣
176 M 11 **Dārzīn**, Iran
189 R 6 **Dashennongjia**, China ▲
186 H 10 **Dashizhai**, China
178 M 11 **Dashkhovuz**, Turkmenistan
178 L 11 **Dashkhovuzskiy Velayat**, Turkmenistan ▣
176 M 5 **Dasht**, Iran
177 P 14 **Dasht**, Pakistan ʃ
177 P 9 **Dasht-e Babus**, Afghanistan ◇
176 J 7 **Dasht-e Kavīr**, Iran ◇
177 O 9 **Dasht-e Khāsh**, Afghanistan ◇
176 M 8 **Dasht-e Lut**, Iran ◇
177 P 10 **Dasht-i Margo**, Afghanistan ◇
177 O 14 **Dashtiari**, Iran
188 M 9 **Dashuijing**, China
197 G 23 **Dassalan**, Philippines 🏝
182 H 1 **Dastegil Sar**, India ▲
189 Q 11 **Datang**, China
170 B 13 **Datşşa**, Turkey
198 J 7 **Date**, Japan
189 X 10 **Datian**, China
75 O 11 **Datil**, New Mexico, U.S.A.
185 P 8 **Datong**, China
187 B 16 **Datong**, China
183 P 12 **Daudnagar**, India
149 F 16 **Daugai**, Lithuania
148 H 13 **Daugavpils**, Latvia
181 C 17 **Daund**, India
191 F 20 **Daung Kyun**, Myanmar 🏝
84 H 9 **Dauphin**, Manitoba, Canada
63 O 8 **Dauphin Island**, Alabama, U.S.A. 🏝
215 R 9 **Daura**, Nigeria
171 Y 7 **Däväşşi**, Azerbaijan
181 D 20 **Davangere**, India
197 N 22 **Davao**, Philippines
193 R 7 **Davao Gulf**, Philippines ≈
67 W 13 **Davenport**, Iowa, U.S.A.
76 K 7 **Davenport**, Washington, U.S.A.
127 T 8 **Daventry**, United Kingdom
91 S 14 **David**, Panama
83 M 19 **Davidson**, Saskatchewan, Canada
38 J 6 **Davie Ridge**, Indian Ocean ⛰
241 X 6 **Davis**, Antarctica ⊞
69 N 12 **Davis**, Oklahoma, U.S.A.
77 G 18 **Davis**, California, U.S.A.
74 G 10 **Davis Dam**, Arizona, U.S.A.
85 V 7 **Davis Inlet**, Newfoundland and Labrador, Canada
70 H 9 **Davis Mountains**, Texas, U.S.A. ⛰
241 Y 8 **Davis Sea**, Antarctica ◗
85 T 1 **Davis Strait**, Nunavut, Canada ≈
157 U 2 **Davlekanovo**, Russian Federation
138 J 8 **Davos**, Switzerland
83 K 14 **Davy Lake**, Saskatchewan, Canada ◣
151 S 8 **Davydiv Brid**, Ukraine
187 H 16 **Dawa**, China
175 Y 10 **Dawḩat Şawqirah**, Oman ≈
149 I 16 **Dawhinava**, Belarus
174 M 9 **Dawqah**, Saudi Arabia
175 W 10 **Dawqah**, Oman
210 D 10 **Dawra**, Western Sahara
63 S 5 **Dawson**, Georgia, U.S.A.
66 K 5 **Dawson**, North Dakota, U.S.A.
82 A 12 **Dawson**, Yukon Territory, Canada
83 G 17 **Dawson Creek**, British Columbia, Canada
60 E 6 **Dawson Springs**, Kentucky, U.S.A.
188 K 6 **Dawu**, China
189 U 6 **Dawu**, China
175 Z 8 **Dawwah**, Oman
128 L 13 **Dax**, France
189 P 12 **Daxin**, China
187 D 17 **Daxing**, China
188 L 6 **Daxue Shan**, China ⛰
194 A 5 **Dayang Bunting**, Malaysia 🏝
185 W 2 **Dayangshu**, China
186 J 7 **Dayangshu**, China
188 K 10 **Dayao**, China
188 M 6 **Dayi**, China
175 Y 6 **Dayl**, Oman

◻ Country ▣ Internal administrative region: State/Province/Territory/Dependent territory ♜ Capital city ⛰ Mountain range/Undersea ridge ▲ Mountain peak/Volcano/Seamount ◇ Geographic feature ▶ Headland/Point/Cape/Peninsula ◒ Desert 🏝 Island/Island group ⊞ Antarctic base ◌ Ocean ◗ Sea ≈ Bay/Gulf/Channel/Strait ◣ Lake ⚑ Salt pan/Dry/Intermittent lake ʃ R…

173 N 4 **Dayr az Zawr**, Syria
172 J 2 **Dayr Ḩāfir**, Syria
60 H 10 **Dayton**, Tennessee, U.S.A.
65 L 19 **Dayton**, Ohio, U.S.A.
71 T 10 **Dayton**, Texas, U.S.A.
76 K 9 **Dayton**, Washington, U.S.A.
63 X 9 **Daytona Beach**, Florida, U.S.A.
189 U 10 **Dayu**, China
76 J 11 **Dayville**, Oregon, U.S.A.
189 P 6 **Dazhu**, China
218 M 13 **De Aar**, Republic of South Africa
132 H 7 **De Cocksdorp**, Netherlands
63 Q 7 **De Funiak Springs**, Florida, U.S.A.
133 B 16 **De Haan**, Belgium
65 G 16 **De Kalb**, Illinois, U.S.A.
71 T 4 **De Kalb**, Texas, U.S.A.
153 W 13 **De-Kastri-Nysh**, Russian Federation
132 H 7 **De Koog**, Netherlands
79 N 4 **De Long Mountains**, Alaska, U.S.A. ⛰
132 O 11 **De Lutte**, Netherlands
133 A 17 **De Panne**, Belgium
64 G 12 **De Pere**, Wisconsin, U.S.A.
69 S 13 **De Queen**, Arkansas, U.S.A.
62 H 7 **De Ridder**, Louisiana, U.S.A.
67 S 13 **De Soto**, Iowa, U.S.A.
64 L 9 **De Tour Village**, Michigan, U.S.A.
67 W 12 **De Witt**, Iowa, U.S.A.
69 X 12 **De Witt**, Arkansas, U.S.A.
172 G 10 **Dead Sea**, Israel 💧
92 M 4 **Deadman's Cay**, The Bahamas
127 Z 11 **Deal**, United Kingdom
55 M 15 **Dearborn**, Michigan, U.S.A.
33 D 16 **Dease Lake**, British Columbia, Canada
32 I 8 **Dease Strait**, Nunavut, Canada ≈
7 L 21 **Death Valley**, California, U.S.A.
7 K 21 **Death Valley**, California, U.S.A. ◇
95 O 10 **Debak**, Malaysia
51 Y 6 **Debal'tseve**, Ukraine
46 B 12 **Debar**, Macedonia (F.Y.R.O.M.)
43 L 17 **Dębica**, Poland
53 X 9 **Debin**, Russian Federation
43 M 14 **Dęblin**, Poland
42 D 11 **Dębno**, Poland
13 I 20 **Debre Birhan**, Ethiopia
13 H 19 **Debre Markos**, Ethiopia
13 I 19 **Debre Werk'**, Ethiopia
43 M 22 **Debrecen**, Hungary
45 K 15 **Dečani**, Serbia and Montenegro
3 P 2 **Decatur**, Alabama, U.S.A.
3 S 3 **Decatur**, Georgia, U.S.A.
5 F 19 **Decatur**, Illinois, U.S.A.
5 K 17 **Decatur**, Indiana, U.S.A.
P 12 **Decatur**, Nebraska, U.S.A.
1 P 5 **Decatur**, Texas, U.S.A.
31 E 18 **Deccan Plateau**, India ◇
40 H 3 **Deception Island**, Antarctica 🏝
41 C 19 **Decimomannu**, Italy
29 R 8 **Decize**, France
U 10 **Decorah**, Iowa, U.S.A.
32 M 9 **Dedemsvaart**, Netherlands
3 J 20 **Deder**, Ethiopia
2 K 8 **Dedo de Deus**, Brazil ▲
1 V 7 **Dedop'listsqaro**, Georgia
9 R 5 **Dedza**, Malawi
4 I 11 **Dee**, United Kingdom ∿
H 10 **Deep River**, Ontario, Canada
S 11 **Deer Island**, New Brunswick, Canada 🏝
R 6 **Deer Isle**, Maine, U.S.A. 🏝
X 10 **Deer Lake**, Newfoundland and Labrador, Canada
76 K 6 **Deer Park**, Washington, U.S.A.
63 Y 12 **Deerfield Beach**, Florida, U.S.A.
213 M 23 **Deeri**, Somalia
79 N 6 **Deering**, Alaska, U.S.A.
65 K 17 **Defiance**, Ohio, U.S.A.
188 I 5 **Dêgê**, China
213 L 21 **Degeh Bur**, Ethiopia
87 P 7 **Dégelis**, Québec, Canada
215 R 14 **Degema**, Nigeria
137 L 22 **Deggendorf**, Germany
156 M 8 **Degtevo**, Russian Federation
176 J 10 **Deh Bīd**, Iran
177 Q 10 **Deh Shū**, Afghanistan
211 Q 8 **Dehiba**, Tunisia
176 F 7 **Dehlorān**, Iran
182 J 7 **Dehra Dun**, India
183 O 12 **Dehri**, India
189 X 10 **Dehua**, China
186 K 12 **Dehui**, China
213 B 21 **Deim Zubeir**, Sudan
133 D 18 **Deinze**, Belgium
150 I 8 **Dej**, Romania
213 I 19 **Dejen**, Ethiopia
189 P 8 **Dejiang**, China
213 I 17 **Dekemhare**, Eritrea
216 L 10 **Dekese**, Democratic Republic of Congo
216 J 4 **Dékoa**, Central African Republic
38 I 11 **Del Cano Rise**, Indian Ocean ⛰
70 L 11 **Del Rio**, Texas, U.S.A.
158 L 9 **Dela Basin**, Mediterranean Sea ◇
77 I 22 **Delano**, California, U.S.A.
177 Q 9 **Delārām**, Afghanistan
218 M 11 **Delareyville**, Republic of South Africa
58 I 10 **Delaware**, New York, U.S.A. ∿
61 W 3 **Delaware**, U.S.A. ◘
65 M 18 **Delaware**, Ohio, U.S.A.
61 X 2 **Delaware Bay**, Delaware, U.S.A. ≈
70 G 7 **Delaware Mountains**, Texas, U.S.A. ⛰
146 E 11 **Delčevo**, Macedonia (F.Y.R.O.M.)
61 S 12 **Delco**, North Carolina, U.S.A.
138 D 6 **Delémont**, Switzerland
215 X 9 **Délép**, Chad
132 F 13 **Delft**, Netherlands
132 N 6 **Delfzijl**, Netherlands
213 E 14 **Delgo**, Sudan
182 J 8 **Delhi**, India
182 J 8 **Delhi**, India ◘
176 I 7 **Delījān**, Iran
82 E 11 **Déline**, Northwest Territories, Canada
137 K 15 **Delitzsch**, Germany
211 N 5 **Dellys**, Algeria
136 E 12 **Delmenhorst**, Germany
231 S 15 **Deloraine**, Tasmania, Australia
147 J 21 **Delos**, Greece 🏝
63 Y 12 **Delray Beach**, Florida, U.S.A.
215 Q 13 **Delta**, Nigeria ◘
74 J 4 **Delta**, Utah, U.S.A.
75 O 5 **Delta**, Colorado, U.S.A.
105 S 3 **Delta Amacuro**, Venezuela ◘
79 S 7 **Delta Junction**, Alaska, U.S.A.
63 X 9 **Deltona**, Florida, U.S.A.
181 B 16 **Delvada**, India
216 L 11 **Demba**, Democratic Republic of Congo
213 G 20 **Dembī Dolo**, Ethiopia
217 N 5 **Dembia**, Central African Republic
42 G 12 **Demerara Abyssal Plain**, Atlantic Ocean ◇
42 F 12 **Demerara Plateau**, Atlantic Ocean ◇
156 H 1 **Demidov**, Russian Federation
75 O 14 **Deming**, New Mexico, U.S.A.
170 D 10 **Demirci**, Turkey
170 C 10 **Demirköprü Baraji**, Turkey 💧
146 N 11 **Demirköy**, Turkey
136 L 9 **Demmin**, Germany
216 M 9 **Democratic Republic Of Congo**, Africa ◘
63 O 4 **Demopolis**, Alabama, U.S.A.
193 Y 12 **Demta**, Indonesia
154 F 13 **Demyansk**, Russian Federation
132 H 7 **Den Burg**, Netherlands
191 H 15 **Den Chai**, Thailand
132 H 8 **Den Helder**, Netherlands
132 I 8 **Den Oever**, Netherlands
213 J 18 **Denakil Desert**, Ethiopia ◇
79 R 8 **Denali**, Alaska, U.S.A.
213 L 22 **Denan**, Ethiopia
179 Q 14 **Denau**, Uzbekistan
127 O 4 **Denbigh**, United Kingdom
86 H 11 **Denbigh**, Ontario, Canada
192 H 12 **Dendang**, Indonesia
214 J 8 **Dendâra**, Mauritania
133 E 19 **Denderleeuw**, Belgium
133 F 18 **Dendermonde**, Belgium
240 J 8 **Dendtler Island**, Antarctica 🏝
132 N 11 **Denekamp**, Netherlands
215 S 9 **Dengas**, Niger
215 Q 10 **Denge**, Nigeria
189 T 3 **Dengfeng**, China
215 S 11 **Dengi**, Nigeria
189 S 5 **Dengzhou**, China
230 E 8 **Denham**, Western Australia, Australia
131 U 9 **Denia**, Spain
237 U 1 **Denig**, Nauru
231 S 12 **Deniliquin**, New South Wales, Australia
77 J 14 **Denio**, Nevada, U.S.A.
67 Q 12 **Denison**, Iowa, U.S.A.
71 Q 4 **Denison**, Texas, U.S.A.
170 D 12 **Denizli**, Turkey
230 G 12 **Denmark**, Western Australia, Australia
135 C 25 **Denmark**, Europe ◘
61 N 13 **Denmark**, South Carolina, U.S.A.
45 O 14 **Denmark Strait**, Arctic Ocean ≈
127 Z 8 **Dennington**, United Kingdom
192 L 15 **Denpasar**, Indonesia
61 V 3 **Denton**, Maryland, U.S.A.
71 Q 5 **Denton**, Texas, U.S.A.
234 G 6 **D'Entrecasteaux Islands**, Papua New Guinea 🏝
75 R 4 **Denver**, Colorado, U.S.A.
180 C 13 **Deogarh**, India
183 R 12 **Deoghar**, India
181 F 16 **Deoli**, India
181 F 14 **Deori**, India
183 P 10 **Deoria**, India
183 N 13 **Deosil**, India
86 H 8 **Depot-Forbes**, Québec, Canada
241 W 5 **Depot Peak**, Antarctica ▲
215 Y 6 **Dépression Du Mourdi**, Chad ◇
153 U 8 **Deputatskiy**, Russian Federation
188 J 8 **Dêqên**, China
189 S 12 **Deqing**, China
177 W 11 **Dera Ghazi Khan**, Pakistan
177 V 9 **Dera Ismail Khan**, Pakistan
150 M 5 **Derazhnya**, Ukraine
157 S 15 **Derbent**, Russian Federation
179 Q 14 **Derbent**, Uzbekistan
87 V 10 **Derbert**, Nova Scotia, Canada
186 H 6 **Derbur**, China
230 I 4 **Derby**, Western Australia, Australia
127 S 5 **Derby**, United Kingdom
69 N 6 **Derby**, Kansas, U.S.A.
215 Y 9 **Déréssa**, Chad
151 T 6 **Deriyivka**, Ukraine
151 Z 6 **Derkul**, Ukraine ∿
188 J 8 **Dêrong**, China
219 S 6 **Derre**, Mozambique
59 N 8 **Derry**, New Hampshire, U.S.A.
127 X 6 **Dersingham**, United Kingdom
187 B 14 **Derst**, China
213 H 15 **Derudeb**, Sudan
144 H 10 **Derventa**, Bosnia and Herzegovina
179 P 4 **Derzhavinsk**, Kazakhstan
65 H 16 **Des Plains**, Illinois, U.S.A.
67 S 13 **Des Moines**, Iowa, U.S.A.
67 S 12 **Des Moines**, Iowa/Missouri, U.S.A. ∿
75 T 8 **Des Moines**, New Mexico, U.S.A.
110 H 11 **Desaguadero**, Argentina ∿
88 E 2 **Descanso**, Mexico
213 I 19 **Desē**, Ethiopia
111 I 21 **Deseado**, Argentina
111 H 20 **Deseado**, Argentina ∿
88 H 3 **Desemboque**, Mexico
74 I 3 **Deseret Peak**, Utah, U.S.A. ▲
77 M 25 **Desert Center**, California, U.S.A.
74 I 2 **Desert Peak**, Utah, U.S.A. ▲
74 K 9 **Desert View**, Arizona, U.S.A.
42 O 5 **Deserta Grande**, Madeira 🏝
110 I 10 **Desiderio Tello**, Argentina
147 D 15 **Deskati**, Greece
151 Q 3 **Desna**, Ukraine ∿
197 M 17 **Desolation Point**, Philippines ▶
144 M 12 **Despotovac**, Serbia and Montenegro
137 K 15 **Dessau**, Germany
133 E 18 **Destelbergen**, Belgium
150 E 11 **Deta**, Romania
219 N 7 **Dete**, Zimbabwe
137 F 14 **Detmold**, Germany
65 M 15 **Detroit**, Michigan, U.S.A.
87 S 4 **Détroit de Jacques-Cartier**, Québec, Canada ≈
87 T 4 **Détroit d'Honguedo**, Québec, Canada ≈
67 P 5 **Detroit Lakes**, Minnesota, U.S.A.
133 K 16 **Deurne**, Netherlands
139 Y 5 **Deutschkreutz**, Austria
139 V 8 **Deutschlandsberg**, Austria
150 H 10 **Deva**, Romania
170 K 9 **Deveci Dağlari**, Turkey
170 K 11 **Develi**, Turkey
132 L 11 **Deventer**, Netherlands
180 B 12 **Devikot**, India
233 H 15 **Devil River Peak**, New Zealand ▲
64 D 8 **Devil's Island**, Wisconsin, U.S.A. 🏝
66 L 3 **Devil's Lake**, North Dakota, U.S.A.
66 L 3 **Devil's Lake**, North Dakota, U.S.A. 💧
73 Y 8 **Devil's Tower**, Wyoming, U.S.A. ▲
146 H 11 **Devin**, Bulgaria
71 O 11 **Devine**, Texas, U.S.A.
231 S 15 **Deviot**, Tasmania, Australia
127 R 11 **Devizes**, United Kingdom
146 M 8 **Devnya**, Bulgaria
81 P 4 **Devon Island**, Nunavut, Canada 🏝
231 S 15 **Devonport**, Tasmania, Australia
170 G 7 **Devrek**, Turkey
181 E 15 **Dewas**, India
127 S 3 **Dewsbury**, United Kingdom
189 N 6 **Deyang**, China
176 M 8 **Deyhuk**, Iran
176 I 12 **Deyyer**, Iran
176 G 8 **Dezfūl**, Iran
187 D 19 **Dezhou**, China
175 T 5 **Dhahran**, Saudi Arabia
183 U 12 **Dhaka**, Bangladesh ◘
175 P 13 **Dhamār**, Yemen
181 G 16 **Dhamtari**, India
183 R 13 **Dhanbad**, India
182 M 8 **Dhangadhi**, Nepal
183 R 10 **Dhankuta**, Nepal
181 D 15 **Dhar**, India
183 R 10 **Dharan Bazar**, Nepal
183 W 12 **Dharmanagar**, India
181 C 19 **Dharwad**, India
183 O 8 **Dhaulagiri**, Nepal ▲
183 Y 9 **Dhemaji**, India
172 G 10 **Dhībān**, Jordan
175 O 14 **Dhubāb**, Yemen
183 U 11 **Dhuburi**, India
181 D 16 **Dhule**, India
213 O 20 **Dhuudo**, Somalia
191 O 21 **Di Linh**, Vietnam
147 J 26 **Dia**, Greece 🏝
77 G 21 **Diablo Range**, California, U.S.A. ⛰
219 U 3 **Diaca**, Mozambique
214 F 9 **Dialakoto**, Senegal
113 C 14 **Diamante**, Argentina
231 Q 7 **Diamantina**, Queensland, Australia ∿
39 S 9 **Diamantina Deep**, Indian Ocean ▲
39 R 9 **Diamantina Fracture Zone**, Indian Ocean ◇
183 S 14 **Diamond Harbour**, India
75 N 2 **Diamond Peak**, Colorado, U.S.A. ▲
73 R 14 **Diamondville**, Wyoming, U.S.A.
214 F 8 **Diamounguél**, Senegal
43 N 25 **Diana's Peak**, St Helena ▲
189 S 13 **Dianbai**, China
188 K 10 **Diancang Shan**, China ▲
189 P 6 **Dianjiang**, China
186 M 11 **Diaoling**, China
218 H 11 **Diaz Point**, Namibia ▶
175 X 5 **Dibā al Ḩişn**, Oman
216 M 11 **Dibaya**, Democratic Republic of Congo
216 K 10 **Dibaya-Lubwe**, Democratic Republic of Congo
213 A 18 **Dibbis**, Sudan
218 L 12 **Dibeng**, Republic of South Africa
183 X 9 **Dibrugarh**, India
172 K 3 **Dibsī**, Syria
70 L 5 **Dickens**, Texas, U.S.A.
66 H 5 **Dickinson**, North Dakota, U.S.A.
60 E 8 **Dickson**, Tennessee, U.S.A.
171 P 11 **Dicle Baraji**, Turkey 💧
132 L 13 **Didam**, Netherlands
127 T 10 **Didcot**, United Kingdom
180 D 12 **Didwana**, India
146 L 12 **Didymoteicho**, Greece
129 U 12 **Die**, France
137 F 20 **Dieburg**, Germany
39 N 5 **Diego Garcia**, British Indian Ocean Territory 🏝
214 H 12 **Diéké**, Guinea
133 K 23 **Diekirch**, Luxembourg ◘
133 L 24 **Diekirch**, Luxembourg
132 H 11 **Diemen**, Netherlands
190 J 12 **Điên Biên Phu**, Vietnam
191 L 14 **Diên Châu**, Vietnam
148 G 12 **Dienvidsusēja**, Latvia ∿
136 E 13 **Diepholz**, Germany
129 O 2 **Dieppe**, France
132 L 12 **Dieren**, Netherlands
69 S 12 **Dierks**, Arkansas, U.S.A.
133 I 18 **Diest**, Belgium
215 U 9 **Diffa**, Niger
215 U 8 **Diffa**, Niger ◘
217 O 5 **Digba**, Democratic Republic of Congo
87 T 11 **Digby**, Nova Scotia, Canada
68 I 4 **Dighton**, Kansas, U.S.A.
129 V 13 **Digne-les-Baines**, France
129 S 9 **Digoin**, France
197 M 23 **Digos**, Philippines
177 V 14 **Digri**, Pakistan
213 K 24 **Diinsoor**, Somalia
129 T 7 **Dijon**, France
134 G 13 **Dikanäs**, Sweden
213 K 19 **Dikhil**, Djibouti
170 B 10 **Dikili**, Turkey
153 S 11 **Dikimdya**, Russian Federation
214 J 12 **Dikodougou**, Côte d'Ivoire
133 B 18 **Diksmuide**, Belgium
153 N 6 **Dikson**, Russian Federation
215 V 10 **Dikwa**, Nigeria
213 I 22 **Dīla**, Ethiopia
217 O 5 **Dili**, Democratic Republic of Congo
193 Q 15 **Dili**, East Timor 🏛
171 U 8 **Dilijan**, Armenia
71 N 12 **Dilley**, Texas, U.S.A.
137 C 21 **Dilligen**, Germany
213 D 18 **Dilling**, Sudan
137 I 23 **Dillingen**, Germany
79 N 11 **Dillingham**, Alaska, U.S.A.
61 R 11 **Dillon**, South Carolina, U.S.A.
73 O 8 **Dillon**, Montana, U.S.A.
216 L 14 **Dilolo**, Democratic Republic of Congo
133 K 18 **Dilsen**, Belgium
173 T 6 **Diltāwa**, Iraq
183 X 11 **Dimapur**, India
216 M 11 **Dimbelenge**, Democratic Republic of Congo
214 K 13 **Dimbokro**, Côte d'Ivoire
146 J 10 **Dimitrovgrad**, Bulgaria
157 S 2 **Dimitrovgrad**, Russian Federation
145 O 14 **Dimitrovgrad**, Serbia and Montenegro
70 J 3 **Dimmit**, Texas, U.S.A.
197 M 18 **Dinagat**, Philippines
197 M 18 **Dinagat**, Philippines 🏝
183 T 11 **Dinajpur**, Bangladesh
128 K 5 **Dinan**, France
133 H 22 **Dinant**, Belgium
183 P 11 **Dinapur**, India
170 E 11 **Dinar**, Turkey
144 E 11 **Dinaric Alps**, Bosnia and Herzegovina ⛰
213 G 18 **Dinder**, Sudan ∿
181 E 23 **Dindigul**, India
181 G 15 **Dindori**, India
216 I 11 **Dinga**, Democratic Republic of Congo
196 G 10 **Dingalan Bay**, Philippines ≈
189 P 1 **Dingbian**, China
189 Q 1 **Dingbian**, China
218 F 1 **Dinge**, Angola
183 R 10 **Dingla**, Nepal
125 A 20 **Dingle**, Republic of Ireland
125 A 20 **Dingle Bay**, Republic of Ireland ≈
58 I 11 **Dingmans Ferry**, Pennsylvania, U.S.A.
189 U 11 **Dingnan**, China
137 L 23 **Dingolfing**, Germany
189 V 3 **Dingtao**, China
214 G 10 **Dinguiraye**, Guinea
87 Y 7 **Dingwall**, Nova Scotia, Canada
189 N 2 **Dingxi**, China
187 D 17 **Dingxing**, China
187 C 18 **Dingzhou**, China
190 N 12 **Dinh Lâp**, Vietnam
183 T 10 **Dinhata**, India
137 H 22 **Dinkelsbühl**, Germany
75 N 3 **Dinosaur**, Colorado, U.S.A.
133 F 15 **Dinteloord**, Netherlands
132 M 13 **Dinxperlo**, Netherlands
112 G 9 **Dionísio Cerqueira**, Brazil
109 I 20 **Dioníso Cerqueira**, Brazil
214 D 9 **Diouloulou**, Senegal
215 P 10 **Dioundiou**, Niger
214 E 8 **Diourbel**, Senegal
182 M 8 **Dipayal**, Nepal
183 W 11 **Diphu**, India
197 J 20 **Dipolog**, Philippines
133 L 25 **Dippach**, Luxembourg
213 K 20 **Dirē Dawa**, Ethiopia
39 Z 1 **Direction Island**, Cocos Islands 🏝
91 N 9 **Diriamba**, Nicaragua
218 K 7 **Dirico**, Angola
230 E 8 **Dirk Hartog Island**, Western Australia, Australia 🏝
215 U 6 **Dirkou**, Niger

Country ◘ Internal administrative region: State/Province/Territory/Dependent territory 🏛 Capital city ⛰ Mountain range/ Undersea ridge ▲ Mountain peak/ Volcano/Seamount ◇ Geographic feature ▶ Headland/Point/ Cape/Peninsula 🏜 Desert 🏝 Island/Island group ⛺ Antarctic base 🌊 Ocean 〰 Sea ≈ Bay/Gulf/Channel/Strait 💧 Lake ▦ Salt pan/Dry/ Intermittent lake ∿ River

Dirranbandi – Dunmore

231 U 9 Dirranbandi, Queensland, Australia
175 N 10 Ḍirs, Saudi Arabia
231 Q 13 Discovery Bay, South Australia, Australia
43 L 19 Discovery Seamount, Atlantic Ocean
138 H 9 Disentis, Switzerland
45 N 11 Disko, Greenland
241 W 4 Dismal Mountains, Antarctica
183 V 10 Dispur, India
87 N 10 Disraëli, Québec, Canada
127 Y 7 Diss, United Kingdom
61 U 3 District of Columbia, U.S.A.
197 G 16 Dit, Philippines
181 A 16 Diu, India
197 M 19 Diuata Mountains, Philippines
197 L 19 Diuata Point, Philippines
176 G 5 Dīvān Darreh, Iran
216 F 9 Divénié, Congo
73 O 7 Divide, Montana, U.S.A.
196 I 7 Divilacan Bay, Philippines
109 K 18 Divinópolis, Brazil
91 V 15 Divisa, Panama
157 N 11 Divnoye, Russian Federation
214 J 13 Divo, Côte d'Ivoire
171 N 10 Divriği, Turkey
177 T 14 Diwana, Pakistan
65 F 16 Dixon, Illinois, U.S.A.
83 B 18 Dixon Entrance, British Columbia, Canada
93 N 3 Dixon's, The Bahamas
171 S 9 Diyadin, Turkey
171 P 12 Diyarbakir, Turkey
215 T 5 Djado, Niger
211 O 7 Djamâa, Algeria
216 H 9 Djambala, Congo
216 J 9 Djampie, Democratic Republic of Congo
211 Q 12 Djanet, Algeria
234 G 3 Djaul Island, Papua New Guinea
210 L 7 Djebel Aïssa, Algeria
211 P 12 Djebel Ounane, Algeria
211 P 13 Djebel Telerhteba, Algeria
211 N 12 Djebr, Algeria
215 X 10 Djébrène, Chad
215 X 9 Djédaa, Chad
210 K 11 Djedid, Algeria
210 M 6 Djelfa, Algeria
217 N 4 Djéma, Central African Republic
216 L 9 Djia, Democratic Republic of Congo
213 K 19 Djibouti, Djibouti
213 L 18 Djibouti, Africa
214 I 8 Djiguéni, Mauritania
216 L 7 Djolu, Democratic Republic of Congo
215 O 11 Djougou, Benin
215 U 15 Djoum, Cameroon
134 D 11 Djúpivogur, Iceland
134 I 7 Djupvik, Norway
151 U 7 Dmytrivka, Ukraine
151 W 6 Dmytrivka, Ukraine
151 Q 4 Dnieper, Europe
150 K 6 Dniester, Moldova/Ukraine
151 U 6 Dniprodzerzhyns'k, Ukraine
151 U 6 Dnipropetrovs'k, Ukraine
151 Q 9 Dniprovs'kyy Lyman, Ukraine
151 P 10 Dnistrov'ky Lyman, Ukraine
154 E 12 Dno, Russian Federation
149 F 21 Dnyaprowski Buhski Kanal, Belarus
191 L 14 Đô Luong, Vietnam
190 M 12 Đo Son, Vietnam
87 S 8 Doaktown, New Brunswick, Canada
192 M 13 Doangdoangan Kecil, Indonesia
215 W 12 Doba, Chad
149 L 19 Dobasna, Belarus
148 E 11 Dobele, Latvia
137 L 16 Döbeln, Germany
139 V 1 Dobersberg, Austria
142 E 11 Dobiegniew, Poland
193 V 13 Dobo, Indonesia
144 H 10 Doboj, Bosnia and Herzegovina
142 K 9 Dobre Miasto, Poland
146 N 6 Dobrich, Bulgaria
146 N 7 Dobrich, Bulgaria
156 M 5 Dobrinka, Russian Federation
149 D 15 Dobrovol'sk, Russian Federation
149 N 20 Dobrush, Belarus
151 Q 1 Dobryanka, Ukraine
155 T 12 Dobryanka, Russian Federation
197 E 24 Doc Can, Philippines
230 L 7 Docker River, Northern Territory, Australia
182 I 4 Doda, India
181 D 22 Dodda Betta, India
147 L 21 Dodecanese, Greece
68 J 6 Dodge City, Kansas, U.S.A.
65 E 14 Dodgeville, Wisconsin, U.S.A.
126 K 15 Dodman Point, United Kingdom
217 U 11 Dodoma, Tanzania
217 U 12 Dodoma, Tanzania
73 U 2 Dodson, Montana, U.S.A.
132 L 13 Doesburg, Netherlands
132 L 13 Doetinchem, Netherlands
63 S 8 Dog Island, Florida, U.S.A.
86 B 6 Dog Lake, Ontario, Canada
184 K 8 Dogai Coring, China
199 D 17 Dōgo, Japan
215 P 9 Dogondoutchi, Niger
215 W 11 Dogoumbo, Chad
171 O 8 Doğu Karadeniz Dağlari, Turkey
171 T 10 Doğubeyazit, Turkey
175 U 5 Doha, Qatar
183 W 14 Dohazari, Bangladesh
191 F 14 Doi Inthanon, Thailand
135 D 18 Dokka, Norway
132 K 6 Dokkum, Netherlands
149 J 15 Dokshytsy, Belarus
151 X 7 Dokuchayevs'k, Ukraine
111 I 18 Dolavón, Argentina
86 M 6 Dolbeau, Québec, Canada
42 G 12 Doldrums Fracture Zone, Atlantic Ocean
129 U 7 Dôle, France
91 S 14 Dolega, Panama
127 N 6 Dolgellau, United Kingdom
153 X 14 Dolinsk, Russian Federation
145 N 14 Doljevac, Serbia and Montenegro
136 D 11 Dollart, Germany
136 J 13 Dolle, Germany
240 J 4 Dolleman Island, Antarctica
143 J 19 Dolný Kubín, Slovakia
213 K 23 Dolo Odo, Ethiopia
140 F 5 Dolomites, Italy
185 Q 5 Doloon, Mongolia
113 D 15 Dolores, Uruguay
113 D 17 Dolores, Argentina
90 J 3 Dolores, Guatemala
82 F 8 Dolphin and Union Strait, Nunavut, Canada
218 H 11 Dolphin Head, Namibia
150 I 6 Dolyna, Ukraine
151 S 7 Dolyns'ka, Ukraine
112 F 13 Dom Pedrito, Brazil
183 T 11 Domar, Bangladesh
143 M 18 Domaradz, Poland
143 B 18 Domažlice, Czech Republic
135 C 17 Dombås, Norway
219 Q 8 Dombe, Mozambique
143 H 25 Dombóvár, Hungary
83 G 19 Dome Creek, British Columbia, Canada
110 F 9 Domeyko, Chile
128 M 5 Domfront, France
93 Y 10 Dominica, North America
91 Q 13 Dominical, Costa Rica
93 R 8 Dominican Republic, North America
213 M 21 Domo, Ethiopia
140 B 5 Domodossola, Italy
147 E 17 Domokos, Greece
193 N 15 Dompu, Indonesia
144 C 7 Domžale, Slovenia
124 I 10 Don, United Kingdom
156 M 9 Don, Russian Federation
88 K 6 Don, Mexico
62 K 8 Donaldsonville, Louisiana, U.S.A.
63 S 6 Donalsonville, Georgia, U.S.A.
137 E 25 Donaueschingen, Germany
137 I 23 Donauwörth, Germany
127 T 3 Doncaster, United Kingdom
218 G 3 Dondo, Angola
219 R 7 Dondo, Mozambique
197 G 19 Dondonay, Philippines
125 D 15 Donegal, Republic of Ireland
125 C 15 Donegal Bay, Republic of Ireland
151 X 7 Donets'k, Ukraine
191 N 16 Đông Ha, Vietnam
191 M 15 Đông Hôi, Vietnam
215 S 12 Donga, Nigeria
189 R 10 Dong'an, China
230 F 10 Dongara, Western Australia, Australia
188 M 10 Dongchuan, China
184 J 9 Dongco, China
189 Q 15 Dongfang, China
186 O 10 Dongfanghong, China
187 K 14 Dongfeng, China
193 N 11 Donggala, Indonesia
187 J 17 Donggang, China
189 U 12 Dongguan, China
189 R 14 Donghai Dao, China
189 R 9 Dongkou, China
189 P 11 Donglan, China
186 N 12 Dongning, China
188 K 8 Dongnyi, China
216 J 6 Dongo, Democratic Republic of Congo
218 H 5 Dongo, Angola
213 E 14 Dongola, Sudan
213 E 23 Dongotona Mountains, Sudan
216 J 6 Dongou, Congo
189 S 13 Dongping, China
189 V 2 Dongping, China
189 R 14 Dongshan, China
189 W 12 Dongshan Dao, China
185 S 7 Dongsheng, China
189 Y 4 Dongtai, China
189 T 8 Dongting Hu, China
189 Y 7 Dongyang, China
187 F 19 Dongying, China
189 W 7 Dongzhi, China
132 L 7 Donkerbroek, Netherlands
134 F 11 Dønna, Norway
86 M 9 Donnacona, Québec, Canada
140 B 6 Donnas, Italy
83 H 17 Donnelly, Alberta, Canada
139 T 6 Donnersbach, Austria
131 Q 1 Donostia-San Sebastián, Spain
147 K 22 Donoussa, Greece
157 N 12 Donskoye, Russian Federation
197 J 14 Donsol, Philippines
64 H 11 Door Peninsula, Wisconsin, U.S.A.
127 Q 13 Dorchester, United Kingdom
218 I 9 Dordabis, Namibia
129 N 12 Dordogne, France
133 G 14 Dordrecht, Netherlands
127 V 11 Dorking, United Kingdom
138 J 6 Dornbirn, Austria
124 H 9 Dornoch Firth, United Kingdom
185 T 3 Dornod, Mongolia
185 R 5 Dornogovi, Mongolia
143 I 22 Dorog, Hungary
135 H 14 Dorotea, Sweden
230 E 8 Dorre Island, Western Australia, Australia
231 V 10 Dorrigo, New South Wales, Australia
215 S 13 Dorsale Camerounaise, Cameroon
137 D 15 Dortmund, Germany
170 L 13 Dörtyol, Turkey
217 P 5 Doruma, Democratic Republic of Congo
176 M 7 Dorūneh, Iran
130 K 12 Dos Hermanas, Spain
90 I 1 Dos Lagunos, Guatemala
111 I 18 Dos Pozos, Argentina
146 H 11 Dospat, Bulgaria
215 O 9 Dosso, Niger
215 O 10 Dosso, Niger
178 I 6 Dossor, Kazakhstan
179 Y 8 Dostyk, Kazakhstan
79 S 7 Dot Lake, Alaska, U.S.A.
63 R 6 Dothan, Alabama, U.S.A.
129 R 2 Douai, France
215 S 14 Douala, Cameroon
128 H 5 Douarnenez, France
233 D 23 Double Cone, New Zealand
63 P 2 Double Springs, Alabama, U.S.A.
233 A 23 Doubtful Sound, New Zealand
232 I 5 Doubtless Bay, New Zealand
128 M 7 Doué-la Fontaine, France
218 M 12 Douglas, Republic of South Africa
125 G 16 Douglas, United Kingdom
63 U 6 Douglas, Georgia, U.S.A.
73 Y 12 Douglas, Wyoming, U.S.A.
74 M 15 Douglas, Arizona, U.S.A.
60 K 9 Douglas Lake, Tennessee, U.S.A.
129 Q 2 Doullens, France
109 H 18 Dourados, Brazil
215 W 10 Dourbali, Chad
211 P 7 Douz, Tunisia
127 Z 12 Dover, United Kingdom
58 J 12 Dover, New Jersey, U.S.A.
59 O 8 Dover, New Hampshire, U.S.A.
60 D 8 Dover, Tennessee, U.S.A.
61 W 2 Dover, Delaware, U.S.A.
176 H 7 Dow Rūd, Iran
177 S 7 Dowl at Yār, Afghanistan
177 Q 8 Dowlatābād, Afghanistan
177 R 6 Dowlatābād, Afghanistan
73 P 13 Downey, Idaho, U.S.A.
127 X 6 Downham Market, United Kingdom
58 I 10 Downsville, New York, U.S.A.
177 U 6 Dowshī, Afghanistan
149 M 19 Dowsk, Belarus
199 D 17 Dōzen, Japan
151 R 4 Drabiv, Ukraine
112 H 5 Dracena, Brazil
132 L 7 Drachten, Netherlands
150 M 13 Dragalina, Romania
150 J 13 Drăgănești-Vlașca, Romania
147 K 26 Dragonada, Greece
149 G 21 Drahichyn, Belarus
43 D 21 Drake Passage, Atlantic Ocean
111 G 26 Drake Passage, Chile
219 N 14 Drakensberg, Republic of South Africa
146 H 12 Drama, Greece
135 D 20 Drammen, Norway
143 F 25 Dráva, Hungary
144 C 6 Dravograd, Slovenia
142 E 10 Drawa, Poland
83 I 19 Drayton Valley, Alberta, Canada
132 M 9 Drenthe, Netherlands
137 N 17 Dresden, Germany
60 C 8 Dresden, Tennessee, U.S.A.
148 K 13 Dretun', Belarus
129 O 4 Dreux, France
135 E 17 Drevsjø, Norway
76 K 12 Drewsey, Oregon, U.S.A.
233 L 15 Dreyers Rock, New Zealand
145 K 16 Drin, Albania
144 I 11 Drina, Bosnia and Herzegovina
145 K 17 Drini i Zi, Albania
62 I 5 Driskill Mountain, Louisiana, U.S.A.
150 G 12 Drobeta-Turnu Severin, Romania
125 E 17 Drogheda, Republic of Ireland
150 I 5 Drohobych, Ukraine
127 R 8 Droitwich, United Kingdom
140 A 9 Dronero, Italy
45 N 12 Dronning Ingrid Land, Greenland
132 K 10 Dronten, Netherlands
139 V 2 Drosendorf, Austria
177 W 6 Drosh, Pakistan
83 K 19 Drumheller, Alberta, Canada
64 L 9 Drummond, Michigan, U.S.A.
73 N 5 Drummond, Montana, U.S.A.
64 L 9 Drummond Island, Michigan, U.S.A.
86 M 10 Drummondville, Québec, Canada
149 E 17 Druskininkai, Lithuania
149 L 17 Druts', Belarus
148 I 13 Druya, Belarus
153 V 8 Druzhina, Russian Federation
142 I 11 Drwęca, Poland
63 V 15 Dry Tortugas, Florida, U.S.A.
146 J 8 Dryanovo, Bulgaria
84 J 11 Dryden, Ontario, Canada
148 K 13 Drysa, Belarus
58 C 12 Du Bois, Pennsylvania, U.S.A.
65 F 22 Du Quoin, Illinois, U.S.A.
189 O 10 Duanshan, China
231 U 7 Duaringa, Queensland, Australia
174 J 4 Ḍubā, Saudi Arabia
175 X 5 Dubai, United Arab Emirates
151 O 8 Dubăsari, Moldova
151 O 8 Dubăsari Reservoir, Moldova
84 J 3 Dubawnt Lake, Nunavut, Canada
231 U 11 Dubbo, New South Wales, Australia
125 F 18 Dublin, Republic of Ireland
63 U 4 Dublin, Georgia, U.S.A.
154 I 14 Dubna, Russian Federation
150 K 3 Dubno, Ukraine
73 P 10 Dubois, Idaho, U.S.A.
73 S 11 Dubois, Wyoming, U.S.A.
157 P 8 Dubovka, Russian Federation
150 L 2 Dubrovytsya, Ukraine
149 M 16 Dubrowna, Belarus
67 W 11 Dubuque, Iowa, U.S.A.
191 O 18 Đuc Pho, Vietnam
191 O 21 Duc Trong, Vietnam
74 L 3 Duchesne, Utah, U.S.A.
231 Q 5 Duchess, Queensland, Australia
60 I 10 Ducktown, Tennessee, U.S.A.
151 T 8 Dudchany, Ukraine
133 L 26 Dudelange, Luxembourg
181 E 18 Dudhani, India
183 O 12 Dudhi, India
153 N 8 Dudinka, Russian Federation
127 R 7 Dudley, United Kingdom
214 I 13 Duékoué, Côte d'Ivoire
131 N 4 Dueñas, Spain
130 L 4 Duero, Spain
241 P 10 Dufek Coast, Antarctica
235 Q 7 Duff Islands, Solomon Islands
140 B 6 Dufourspitze, Italy/Switzerland
158 M 4 Dugi Otok, Mediterranean Sea
137 C 16 Duisburg, Germany
213 E 21 Duk Faiwil, Sudan
145 J 21 Dukat i Ri, Albania
219 N 13 Dukathole, Republic of South Africa
175 U 5 Dukhān, Qatar
175 O 5 Dukhnah, Saudi Arabia
177 U 11 Duki, Pakistan
149 H 14 Dūkštas, Lithuania
185 O 8 Dulan, China
110 K 9 Dulce, Argentina
75 P 8 Dulce, New Mexico, U.S.A.
91 O 5 Dulce Nombre de Culmí, Honduras
146 M 8 Dŭlgopol, Bulgaria
187 E 18 Duliu, China
197 K 17 Duljugan Point, Philippines
137 D 15 Dülmen, Germany
146 M 6 Dulovo, Bulgaria
231 V 7 Dululu, Queensland, Australia
67 T 5 Duluth, Minnesota, U.S.A.
127 N 12 Dulverton, United Kingdom
172 H 6 Dūmā, Syria
197 J 19 Dumaguete, Philippines
192 E 10 Dumai, Indonesia
197 E 17 Dumaran, Philippines
69 W 13 Dumas, Arkansas, U.S.A.
70 J 1 Dumas, Texas, U.S.A.
172 I 6 Ḍumayr, Syria
124 G 13 Dumbarton, United Kingdom
150 L 11 Dumbrăveni, Romania
182 K 4 Dumchele, India
125 H 15 Dumfries, United Kingdom
61 T 4 Dumfries, Virginia, U.S.A.
183 R 12 Dumka, India
241 V 14 Dumont d'Urville, Antarctica
241 U 15 Dumont d'Urville Sea, Antarctica
212 F 7 Dumyât, Egypt
143 H 22 Dunajská Streda, Slovakia
143 I 26 Dunaszekcső, Hungary
143 I 24 Dunaújváros, Hungary
146 F 6 Dunavtsi, Bulgaria
150 L 6 Dunayivtsi, Ukraine
68 M 12 Duncan, Oklahoma, U.S.A.
75 N 13 Duncan, Arizona, U.S.A.
181 N 22 Duncan Passage, India
124 J 7 Duncansby Head, United Kingdom
148 D 9 Dundaga, Latvia
125 E 17 Dundalk, Republic of Ireland
61 V 2 Dundalk, Maryland, U.S.A.
125 E 17 Dundalk Bay, Republic of Ireland
86 E 13 Dundas, Ontario, Canada
230 M 1 Dundas Strait, Northern Territory, Australia
219 P 12 Dundee, Republic of South Africa
124 I 12 Dundee, United Kingdom
240 H 3 Dundee Island, Antarctica
185 Q 4 Dundgovi, Mongolia
233 E 24 Dunedin, New Zealand
181 C 14 Dungarpur, India
125 D 20 Dungarvan, Republic of Ireland
127 Y 13 Dungeness, United Kingdom
217 P 5 Dungu, Democratic Republic of Congo
194 E 6 Dungun, Malaysia
212 H 13 Dungunab, Sudan
186 L 13 Dunhua, China
185 N 6 Dunhuang, China
170 E 10 Dunilupinar, Turkey
129 Q 1 Dunkerque, France
127 N 12 Dunkery Beacon, United Kingdom
58 C 9 Dunkirk, New York, U.S.A.
67 Q 13 Dunlap, Iowa, U.S.A.
231 N 3 Dunmarra, Northern Territory, Australia
58 H 11 Dunmore, Pennsylvania, U.S.A.

Country · Internal administrative region: State/Province/Territory/Dependent territory · Capital city · Mountain range/Undersea ridge · Mountain peak/Volcano/Seamount · Geographic feature · Headland/Point/Cape/Peninsula · Desert · Island/Island group · Antarctic base · Ocean · Sea · Bay/Gulf/Channel/Strait · Lake · Salt pan/Dry/Intermittent lake · R

Country ▣ Internal administrative region: State/Province/Territory/Dependent territory   ▲ Capital city   ▲ Mountain range/Undersea ridge   ▲ Mountain peak/Volcano/Seamount   ◇ Geographic feature   ▶ Headland/Point/Cape/Peninsula   ▲ Desert   ⊞ Island/Island group   ⊞ Antarctic base   ◇ Ocean   ◇ Sea   ≈ Bay/Gulf/Channel/Strait   ↘ Lake   ↘ Salt pan/Dry/Intermittent lake   ↘ River

285

147 E 15 **Elassona**, Greece
172 F 13 **Elat**, Israel
236 M 15 **Elato**, Federated States of Micronesia ⚓
171 O 11 **Elazığ**, Turkey
63 Q 6 **Elba**, Alabama, U.S.A.
145 K 19 **Elbasan**, Albania
136 I 11 **Elbe**, Czech Republic/Germany ↘
76 H 8 **Elbe**, Washington, U.S.A.
63 U 2 **Elberton**, Georgia, U.S.A.
170 M 11 **Elbistan**, Turkey
142 J 8 **Elbląg**, Poland
83 M 19 **Elbow**, Saskatchewan, Canada
157 N 14 **Elbrus**, Russian Federation ▲
132 K 10 **Elburg**, Netherlands
176 I 5 **Elburz Mountains**, Iran ⛰
131 S 10 **Elche**, Spain
131 R 10 **Elche de la Sierra**, Spain
131 S 10 **Elda**, Spain
153 U 11 **El'dikan**, Russian Federation
69 U 5 **Eldon**, Missouri, U.S.A.
112 F 9 **Eldorado**, Argentina
65 G 22 **Eldorado**, Illinois, U.S.A.
70 L 9 **Eldorado**, Texas, U.S.A.
108 J 12 **Eldorado dos Carajás**, Brazil
217 U 7 **Eldoret**, Kenya
147 G 20 **Elefsina**, Greece
148 E 12 **Eleja**, Latvia
217 U 4 **Elemi Triangle**, Kenya ◇
146 K 8 **Elena**, Bulgaria
75 P 13 **Elephant Butte Reservoir**, New Mexico, U.S.A. ↘
240 G 2 **Elephant Island**, Antarctica ⚓
92 L 2 **Eleuthera**, The Bahamas ⚓
124 I 9 **Elgin**, United Kingdom
65 G 16 **Elgin**, Illinois, U.S.A.
66 I 6 **Elgin**, North Dakota, U.S.A.
71 Q 9 **Elgin**, Texas, U.S.A.
76 K 10 **Elgin**, Oregon, U.S.A.
217 T 7 **Elgon**, Kenya ▲
193 T 13 **Eliase**, Indonesia
75 T 12 **Elida**, New Mexico, U.S.A.
146 G 9 **Elin Pelin**, Bulgaria
217 N 8 **Elipa**, Democratic Republic of Congo
108 L 13 **Eliseu Martins**, Brazil
157 O 11 **Elista**, Russian Federation
58 J 13 **Elizabeth**, New Jersey, U.S.A.
61 W 8 **Elizabeth City**, North Carolina, U.S.A.
60 L 8 **Elizabethton**, Tennessee, U.S.A.
60 G 6 **Elizabethtown**, Kentucky, U.S.A.
61 S 11 **Elizabethtown**, North Carolina, U.S.A.
142 M 9 **Ełk**, Poland
68 J 10 **Elk City**, Oklahoma, U.S.A.
72 L 7 **Elk City**, Idaho, U.S.A.
83 K 18 **Elk Point**, Alberta, Canada
67 S 7 **Elk River**, Minnesota, U.S.A.
65 J 15 **Elkhart**, Indiana, U.S.A.
68 G 7 **Elkhart**, Kansas, U.S.A.
65 G 14 **Elkhorn**, Wisconsin, U.S.A.
146 L 10 **Elkhovo**, Bulgaria
61 O 8 **Elkin**, North Carolina, U.S.A.
61 P 3 **Elkins**, West Virginia, U.S.A.
77 M 16 **Elko**, Nevada, U.S.A.
83 J 21 **Elko**, British Columbia, Canada
60 F 10 **Elkton**, Tennessee, U.S.A.
61 R 4 **Elkton**, Virginia, U.S.A.
63 S 5 **Ellaville**, Georgia, U.S.A.
81 N 2 **Ellef Ringnes Island**, Nunavut, Canada ⚓
66 M 6 **Ellendale**, North Dakota, U.S.A.
76 I 8 **Ellensburg**, Washington, U.S.A.
127 P 6 **Ellesmere**, United Kingdom

81 P 1 **Ellesmere Island**, Nunavut, Canada ⚓
127 P 4 **Ellesmere Port**, United Kingdom
63 S 1 **Ellijay**, Georgia, U.S.A.
219 O 14 **Elliot**, Republic of South Africa
86 C 9 **Elliot Lake**, Ontario, Canada
231 N 3 **Elliott**, Northern Territory, Australia
61 Q 5 **Elliott Knob**, Virginia, U.S.A. ▲
219 N 10 **Ellisras**, Republic of South Africa
231 O 11 **Elliston**, South Australia, Australia
124 J 10 **Ellon**, United Kingdom
59 R 5 **Ellsworth**, Maine, U.S.A.
64 C 11 **Ellsworth**, Wisconsin, U.S.A.
240 J 8 **Ellsworth Land**, Antarctica ◇
240 L 8 **Ellsworth Mountains**, Antarctica ⛰
137 H 22 **Ellwangen**, Germany
76 G 7 **Elma**, Washington, U.S.A.
170 E 13 **Elmali**, Turkey
138 K 7 **Elmen**, Austria
58 F 10 **Elmira**, New York, U.S.A.
87 W 8 **Elmira**, Prince Edward Island, Canada
136 G 10 **Elmshorn**, Germany
68 I 8 **Elmwood**, Oklahoma, U.S.A.
74 K 13 **Eloy**, Arizona, U.S.A.
132 K 13 **Elst**, Netherlands
137 M 16 **Elsterwerda**, Germany
41 S 13 **Eltanin Fracture Zone**, Pacific Ocean ◇
232 J 13 **Eltham**, New Zealand
157 Q 8 **El'ton**, Russian Federation
181 G 19 **Eluru**, India
148 H 8 **Elva**, Estonia
130 J 9 **Elvas**, Portugal
135 E 18 **Elverum**, Norway
108 A 12 **Elvira**, Brazil
65 J 18 **Elwood**, Indiana, U.S.A.
127 W 7 **Ely**, United Kingdom
77 N 18 **Ely**, Nevada, U.S.A.
65 N 16 **Elyria**, Ohio, U.S.A.
137 G 14 **Elze**, Germany
235 R 11 **Émaé**, Vanuatu ⚓
177 U 5 **Emām Şāḩeb**, Afghanistan
178 K 7 **Emba**, Kazakhstan ↘
178 L 6 **Emba**, Kazakhstan
90 J 7 **Embalse Cerrón Grande**, El Salvador ↘
111 H 15 **Embalse Cerros Colorados**, Argentina ↘
90 H 5 **Embalse Chixoy**, Guatemala ↘
131 Q 8 **Embalse de Alarcón**, Spain ↘
130 L 5 **Embalse de Almendra**, Spain ↘
131 Q 6 **Embalse de Buendía**, Spain ↘
130 M 8 **Embalse de Cijara**, Spain ↘
130 M 8 **Embalse de Garcia Sola**, Spain ↘
105 R 4 **Embalse de Guri**, Venezuela ↘
131 N 12 **Embalse de Iznajar**, Spain ↘
130 L 9 **Embalse de Orellana**, Spain ↘
130 K 8 **Embalse de Valdecañas**, Spain ↘
130 M 9 **Embalse del Zújar**, Spain ↘
111 H 15 **Embalse Ezequiel Ramos Mexia**, Argentina ↘
111 H 18 **Embalse Florentino Ameghino**, Argentina ↘
110 J 5 **Embarcación**, Argentina
216 K 8 **Embondo**, Democratic Republic of Congo
128 K 7 **Embouchure de la Loire**, France ↘
217 V 8 **Embu**, Kenya
136 D 10 **Emden**, Germany
188 M 7 **Emei**, China
231 U 6 **Emerald**, Queensland, Australia

74 K 5 **Emery**, Utah, U.S.A.
170 D 10 **Emet**, Turkey
234 B 6 **Emeti**, Papua New Guinea
215 X 6 **Emi Koussi**, Chad ▲
158 F 8 **Emile Baudot Escarpment**, Mediterranean Sea ◇
140 F 9 **Emilia-Romagna**, Italy □
89 X 13 **Emiliano Zapata**, Mexico
184 J 3 **Emin**, China
234 F 2 **Emirau Island**, Papua New Guinea ⚓
170 F 10 **Emirdağ**, Turkey
231 T 14 **Emita**, Tasmania, Australia
136 C 13 **Emlichheim**, Germany
148 D 7 **Emmaste**, Estonia
132 K 9 **Emmeloord**, Netherlands
132 N 9 **Emmen**, Netherlands
137 B 14 **Emmerich**, Germany
231 S 7 **Emmet**, Queensland, Australia
67 R 11 **Emmetsburg**, Iowa, U.S.A.
78 L 8 **Emmonak**, Alaska, U.S.A.
70 I 11 **Emory Peak**, Texas, U.S.A. ▲
88 I 5 **Empalme**, Mexico
112 C 10 **Empedrado**, Argentina
41 O 3 **Emperor Trough**, Pacific Ocean ◇
140 E 10 **Empoli**, Italy
61 T 7 **Emporia**, Virginia, U.S.A.
69 P 5 **Emporia**, Kansas, U.S.A.
58 D 11 **Emporium**, Pennsylvania, U.S.A.
136 D 12 **Ems**, Germany ↘
86 F 10 **Emsdale**, Ontario, Canada
219 P 11 **Emzinoni**, Republic of South Africa
172 F 10 **En Gedi**, Israel
172 F 11 **'En Hazeva**, Israel
213 C 18 **En Nahud**, Sudan
193 W 12 **Enarotali**, Indonesia
109 G 20 **Encarnación**, Paraguay
71 N 13 **Encinal**, Texas, U.S.A.
77 K 26 **Encinitas**, California, U.S.A.
75 R 11 **Encino**, New Mexico, U.S.A.
110 H 11 **Encón**, Argentina
112 H 12 **Encruzilhada do Sul**, Brazil
143 L 21 **Encs**, Hungary
194 E 9 **Endau**, Malaysia
41 T 3 **Endeavour Seamount**, Pacific Ocean ▲
193 O 15 **Endeh**, Indonesia
236 K 4 **Enderbury**, Kiribati ⚓
38 H 14 **Enderby Abyssal Plain**, Indian Ocean ◇
241 U 3 **Enderby Land**, Antarctica ◇
58 H 10 **Endicott**, New York, U.S.A.
79 P 4 **Endicott Mountains**, Alaska, U.S.A. ⛰
230 F 10 **Eneabba**, Western Australia, Australia
113 D 19 **Energía**, Argentina
146 K 13 **Enez**, Turkey
170 A 7 **Enez**, Turkey
127 W 10 **Enfield**, United Kingdom
58 L 10 **Enfield**, Connecticut, U.S.A.
61 T 8 **Enfield**, North Carolina, U.S.A.
87 V 10 **Enfield**, Nova Scotia, Canada
234 B 4 **Enga**, Papua New Guinea □
64 J 9 **Engadine**, Michigan, U.S.A.
135 C 15 **Engan**, Norway
198 L 4 **Engaru**, Japan
138 G 8 **Engelberg**, Switzerland
139 R 3 **Engelhartszell**, Austria
157 Q 5 **Engel's**, Russian Federation
132 H 6 **Engelschmangat**, Netherlands ≈
132 L 5 **Engelsmanplaat**, Netherlands ≈
192 E 13 **Enggano**, Indonesia ⚓
133 E 20 **Enghien**, Belgium
125 I 19 **Enghien**, United Kingdom
69 W 12 **England**, Arkansas, U.S.A.

85 X 9 **Englee**, Newfoundland and Labrador, Canada
86 E 7 **Englehart**, Ontario, Canada
43 K 25 **English Bay**, Ascension ≈
127 Q 14 **English Channel**, France/United Kingdom ↘
240 J 6 **English Coast**, Antarctica ◇
148 E 10 **Engure**, Latvia
148 E 10 **Engures ezers**, Latvia ↘
68 M 8 **Enid**, Oklahoma, U.S.A.
198 J 6 **Eniwa**, Japan
132 I 9 **Enkhuizen**, Netherlands
141 J 22 **Enna**, Italy
82 L 12 **Ennadai Lake**, Nunavut, Canada ↘
125 B 19 **Ennis**, Republic of Ireland
73 P 8 **Ennis**, Montana, U.S.A.
125 E 19 **Enniscorthy**, Republic of Ireland
125 D 16 **Enniskillen**, United Kingdom
139 T 4 **Enns**, Austria
189 S 13 **Enping**, China
128 L 5 **Enree**, France
132 N 11 **Enschede**, Netherlands
88 F 2 **Ensenada**, Mexico
189 Q 7 **Enshi**, China
199 I 18 **Enshū-nada**, Japan ≈
217 S 8 **Entebbe**, Uganda
63 R 6 **Enterprise**, Alabama, U.S.A.
74 H 7 **Enterprise**, Utah, U.S.A.
76 L 10 **Enterprise**, Oregon, U.S.A.
83 H 14 **Enterprise**, Northwest Territories, Canada
197 D 17 **Enterprise Point**, Philippines ▶
83 H 19 **Entrance**, Alberta, Canada
113 C 14 **Entre Ríos**, Argentina □
130 H 8 **Entroncamento**, Portugal
215 R 13 **Enugu**, Nigeria
215 R 13 **Enugu**, Nigeria □
153 Z 5 **Enurmino**, Russian Federation
108 B 12 **Envira**, Brazil
132 K 11 **Epe**, Netherlands
216 I 7 **Epéna**, Congo
129 S 4 **Épernay**, France
58 G 13 **Ephrata**, Pennsylvania, U.S.A.
76 J 7 **Ephrata**, Washington, U.S.A.
235 R 11 **Epi**, Vanuatu ⚓
129 V 5 **Épinal**, France
170 H 15 **Episkopi**, Cyprus
127 W 10 **Epping**, United Kingdom
127 V 11 **Epsom**, United Kingdom
111 J 14 **Epu-pel**, Argentina
127 U 3 **Epworth**, United Kingdom
216 K 8 **Equateur**, Democratic Republic of Congo □
181 L 20 **Equatorial Channel**, Maldives ↘
215 R 15 **Equatorial Guinea**, Africa □
210 I 8 **Er Rachidia**, Morocco
213 E 18 **Er Rahad**, Sudan
210 J 9 **Er Raoui**, Algeria ◇
213 F 19 **Er Renk**, Sudan
159 W 10 **Eratosthenes Seamount**, Mediterranean Sea ◇
234 C 5 **Erave**, Papua New Guinea
170 L 8 **Erbaa**, Turkey
171 T 11 **Erşşek**, Turkey
171 S 10 **Erciş**, Turkey
170 K 11 **Erciyes Dağı**, Turkey ▲
143 I 23 **Érd**, Hungary
170 C 8 **Erdek**, Turkey
170 J 13 **Erdemli**, Turkey
185 Q 3 **Erdenet**, Mongolia
185 Q 5 **Erdenetsogt**, Mongolia
137 K 24 **Erding**, Germany
112 H 10 **Erechim**, Brazil
185 T 2 **Ereentsav**, Mongolia
170 I 12 **Ereğli**, Turkey
170 G 7 **Ereğli**, Turkey
186 B 13 **Erenhot**, China
210 I 8 **Erfoud**, Morocco
137 I 17 **Erfurt**, Germany
210 H 13 **'Erg Chech**, Algeria ◇

215 W 8 **Erg du Djourab**, Chad ◇
210 I 10 **Erg Iabès**, Algeria ◇
210 G 11 **Erg Iguidi**, Algeria ◇
171 O 11 **Ergani**, Turkey
185 S 5 **Ergel**, Mongolia
146 L 13 **Ergene**, Turkey ↘
148 G 11 **Ērgļi**, Latvia
187 J 15 **Erhulai**, China
234 C 5 **Eri**, Papua New Guinea ⚓
43 N 18 **Erica Seamount**, Atlantic Ocean ▲
130 F 9 **Ericeira**, Portugal
58 B 10 **Erie**, Pennsylvania, U.S.A.
147 A 15 **Eriekoussa**, Greece ⚓
84 I 10 **Eriksdale**, Manitoba, Canada
198 L 6 **Erimo**, Japan
198 L 7 **Erimo-misaki**, Japan ▶
124 E 11 **Eriskay**, United Kingdom ⚓
213 H 16 **Eritrea**, Africa □
136 M 13 **Erkner**, Germany
137 I 20 **Erlangen**, Germany
231 N 7 **Erldunda**, Northern Territory, Australia
219 P 11 **Ermelo**, Republic of South Africa
132 J 11 **Ermelo**, Netherlands
170 H 13 **Ermenek**, Turkey
147 F 21 **Ermioni**, Greece
147 I 21 **Ermoupoli**, Greece
137 E 17 **Erndtebrück**, Germany
139 X 3 **Ernstbrunn**, Austria
181 E 22 **Erode**, India
231 R 8 **Eromanga**, Queensland, Australia
218 H 9 **Erongo**, Namibia □
133 F 22 **Erquelinnes**, Belgium
125 B 16 **Erris Head**, Republic of Ireland ▶
59 N 5 **Errol**, New Hampshire, U.S.A.
235 R 12 **Erromango**, Vanuatu ⚓
145 L 20 **Ersekë**, Albania
186 I 4 **Ershiwuzhan**, China
186 J 4 **Ershizhan**, China
67 P 4 **Erskine**, Minnesota, U.S.A.
184 L 4 **Ertai**, China
171 R 12 **Eruh**, Turkey
112 G 13 **Erval**, Brazil
137 F 15 **Erwitte**, Germany
147 F 19 **Erythres**, Greece
188 J 10 **Eryuan**, China
186 K 7 **Erzhan**, China
153 O 14 **Erzin**, Russian Federation
170 L 13 **Erzin**, Turkey
171 O 9 **Erzincan**, Turkey
171 Q 9 **Erzurum**, Turkey
149 D 14 **Eržvilkas**, Lithuania
210 E 11 **Es Semara**, Western Sahara
213 F 18 **Es Suki**, Sudan
234 G 7 **Esa-ala**, Papua New Guinea
198 J 7 **Esan-misaki**, Japan ▶
198 I 8 **Esashi**, Japan
198 K 3 **Esashi**, Japan
135 B 25 **Esbjerg**, Denmark
197 J 17 **Escalante**, Philippines
74 K 7 **Escalante**, Utah, U.S.A.
89 N 6 **Escalón**, Mexico
64 H 10 **Escanaba**, Michigan, U.S.A.
89 X 12 **Escárcega**, Mexico
196 I 5 **Escarpada Point**, Philippines ▶
133 F 16 **Escaut**, Belgium ↘
133 K 26 **Esch-sur-Alzette**, Luxembourg
137 H 16 **Eschwege**, Germany
107 H 19 **Escoma**, Bolivia
77 K 26 **Escondido**, California, U.S.A.
91 Q 9 **Escondido**, Nicaragua ↘
88 M 6 **Escuinapa**, Mexico
90 H 6 **Escuintla**, Guatemala
215 T 14 **Eséka**, Cameroon
170 D 13 **Esen**, Turkey
178 I 14 **Esenguly**, Turkmenistan
176 J 7 **Eşfahān**, Iran □
176 I 8 **Eşfahān**, Iran
176 M 5 **Esfarāyen**, Iran

85 T 8 **Esker**, Newfoundland and Labrador, Canada
135 G 21 **Eskilstuna**, Sweden
170 F 9 **Eskişehir**, Turkey
176 F 6 **Eslāmābād-e Gharb**, Iran
92 K 5 **Esmeralda**, Cuba
106 B 7 **Esmeraldas**, Ecuador
106 A 8 **Esmeraldas**, Ecuador □
177 O 13 **Espakeh**, Iran
129 Q 12 **Espalion**, France
75 Q 9 **Espanola**, New Mexico, U.S.A.
86 C 9 **Espanola**, Ontario, Canada
136 F 13 **Espelkamp**, Germany
230 I 12 **Esperance**, Western Australia, Australia
240 H 3 **Esperanza**, Antarctica ⛟
107 G 15 **Esperanza**, Peru
111 G 23 **Esperanza**, Argentina
88 J 5 **Esperanza**, Mexico
130 M 10 **Espiel**, Spain
104 I 7 **Espinal**, Colombia
130 G 5 **Espinho**, Portugal
109 M 17 **Espírito Santo**, Brazil □
235 P 10 **Espíritu Santo**, Vanuatu ⚓
109 N 14 **Esplanada**, Brazil
135 L 19 **Espoo**, Finland
130 H 4 **Esposende**, Portugal
111 G 18 **Esquel**, Argentina
112 C 12 **Esquina**, Argentina
210 F 8 **Essaouira**, Morocco
137 C 15 **Essen**, Germany
105 U 6 **Essequibo**, Guyana ↘
86 B 14 **Essex**, Ontario, Canada
153 Y 10 **Esso**, Russian Federation
215 V 15 **Est**, Cameroon □
196 I 7 **Estagno Point**, Philippines ▶
109 N 14 **Estância**, Brazil
140 G 7 **Este**, Italy
110 K 9 **Esteban Rams**, Argentina
91 N 8 **Estelí**, Nicaragua
131 Q 2 **Estella**, Spain
70 L 3 **Estelline**, Texas, U.S.A.
130 M 14 **Estepona**, Spain
79 R 7 **Ester**, Alaska, U.S.A.
67 Q 10 **Estherville**, Iowa, U.S.A.
61 N 15 **Estill**, South Carolina, U.S.A.
148 F 7 **Estonia**, Europe □
111 I 26 **Estrecho de Le Maire**, Argentina ↘
111 E 24 **Estrecho Nelson**, Chile ↘
130 I 9 **Estremoz**, Portugal
216 D 7 **Estuaire**, Gabon □
182 K 9 **Etah**, India
129 U 3 **Étain**, France
81 Y 9 **Etamamiou**, Québec, Canada
85 W 10 **Etamamoiu**, Québec, Canada
129 P 5 **Étampes**, France
182 K 10 **Etawah**, India
213 G 21 **Ethiopia**, Africa □
213 G 20 **Ethiopian Highlands**, Ethiopia ⛰
170 H 9 **Etimesğut**, Turkey
78 K 9 **Etolin Strait**, Alaska, U.S.A. ≈
216 H 7 **Etoumbi**, Congo
129 N 3 **Étretat**, France
146 H 9 **Etropole**, Bulgaria
128 M 15 **Etsaut**, France
133 L 24 **Ettelbruck**, Luxembourg
236 I 11 **Eua**, Tonga ⚓
230 L 10 **Eucla**, Western Australia, Australia
65 N 16 **Euclid**, Ohio, U.S.A.
63 R 5 **Eufaula**, Alabama, U.S.A.
69 Q 11 **Eufaula**, Oklahoma, U.S.A.
69 P 10 **Eufaula Lake**, Oklahoma, U.S.A. ↘
76 F 11 **Eugene**, Oregon, U.S.A.
231 S 9 **Eulo**, Queensland, Australia
62 J 7 **Eunice**, Louisiana, U.S.A.
75 U 14 **Eunice**, New Mexico, U.S.A.
133 L 20 **Eupen**, Belgium
172 L 3 **Euphrates**, Syria/Iraq ↘
62 M 3 **Eupora**, Mississippi, U.S.A.

□ Country   □ Internal administrative region: State/Province/Territory/Dependent territory   ⚓ Capital city   ▲ Mountain range/Undersea ridge   ▶ Mountain peak/Volcano/Seamount   ◇ Geographic feature   ▶ Headland/Point/Cape/Peninsula   ▲ Desert   ⚓ Island/Island group   ⛟ Antarctic base   ≋ Ocean   ≈ Sea   ≈ Bay/Gulf/Channel/Strait   ↘ Lake   ↘ Salt pan/Dry/Intermittent lake

72 M 2 Eureka, Montana, U.S.A.
74 J 4 Eureka, Utah, U.S.A.
77 E 15 Eureka, California, U.S.A.
77 M 17 Eureka, Nevada, U.S.A.
132 F 13 Europoort, Netherlands ◇
137 C 18 Euskirchen, Germany
63 W 9 Eustis, Florida, U.S.A.
63 O 4 Eutaw, Alabama, U.S.A.
83 E 19 Eutsuk Lake, British Columbia, Canada ➘
85 O 4 Evans Strait, Nunavut, Canada ≈
65 H 15 Evanston, Illinois, U.S.A.
73 Q 15 Evanston, Wyoming, U.S.A.
65 H 22 Evansville, Indiana, U.S.A.
71 O 8 Evant, Texas, U.S.A.
219 O 11 Evaton, Republic of South Africa
176 J 12 Evaz, Iran
153 Y 9 Evensk, Russian Federation
59 D 13 Everett, Pennsylvania, U.S.A.
72 H 6 Everett, Washington, U.S.A.
63 X 14 Everglades, Florida, U.S.A. ◇
63 P 6 Evergreen, Alabama, U.S.A.
127 R 8 Evesham, United Kingdom
135 K 15 Evijärvi, Finland ➘
135 B 21 Evje, Norway
130 I 10 Evora, Portugal ▣
130 I 9 Évora, Portugal
129 O 4 Évreux, France
146 K 13 Evros, Greece ➘
147 H 19 Evvoia, Greece ≈
78 B 7 Ewa Beach, Hawaii, U.S.A.
43 M 16 Ewing Seamount, Atlantic Ocean ▲
216 G 8 Ewo, Congo
69 S 3 Excelsior Springs, Missouri, U.S.A.
127 N 13 Exe, United Kingdom ➘
240 L 11 Executive Committee Range, Antarctica ▲
127 N 13 Exeter, United Kingdom
77 J 21 Exeter, California, U.S.A.
67 R 13 Exira, Iowa, U.S.A.
127 O 14 Exminster, United Kingdom
127 N 12 Exmoor, United Kingdom
61 W 5 Exmore, Virginia, U.S.A.
230 E 6 Exmouth, Western Australia, Australia
127 O 14 Exmouth, United Kingdom
39 T 7 Exmouth Plateau, Indian Ocean ◇
58 H 14 Exton, Pennsylvania, U.S.A.
130 K 8 Extremadura, Spain ▣
215 V 11 Extrême-Nord, Cameroon ▣
92 L 3 Exuma Cays, The Bahamas ≈
127 Y 7 Eye, United Kingdom
113 O 21 Eyl, Somalia
129 P 10 Eymoutiers, France
231 O 11 Eyre Peninsula, South Australia, Australia ▶
33 H 20 Eyreton, New Zealand
148 J 12 Ezernieki, Latvia
189 U 7 Ezhou, China
70 A 9 Ezine, Turkey

181 L 17 Faadhippolhu Atoll, Maldives ≈
113 J 24 Faafxadhuun, Somalia
70 E 7 Fabens, Texas, U.S.A.
215 T 7 Fachi, Niger
111 G 19 Facundo, Argentina
115 Y 7 Fada, Chad
140 G 9 Faenza, Italy
150 J 10 Făgăraş, Romania
135 G 20 Fagersta, Sweden
150 G 10 Făget, Romania
134 C 11 Fagurhólsmýri, Iceland
2 N 1 Faial, Azores ≈

138 G 9 Faido, Switzerland
124 J 6 Fair Isle, United Kingdom
79 R 7 Fairbanks, Alaska, U.S.A.
65 G 21 Fairfield, Illinois, U.S.A.
71 R 7 Fairfield, Texas, U.S.A.
72 L 11 Fairfield, Idaho, U.S.A.
77 G 19 Fairfield, California, U.S.A.
233 F 21 Fairlie, New Zealand
61 P 2 Fairmont, West Virginia, U.S.A.
67 N 15 Fairmont, Nebraska, U.S.A.
67 R 10 Fairmont, Minnesota, U.S.A.
75 Q 5 Fairplay, Colorado, U.S.A.
64 I 10 Fairport, Michigan, U.S.A.
68 L 9 Fairview, Oklahoma, U.S.A.
177 X 9 Faisalabad, Pakistan
66 I 8 Faith, South Dakota, U.S.A.
183 N 10 Faizabad, India
93 U 8 Fajardo, Puerto Rico
173 W 9 Fajir, Iraq
236 J 6 Fakaofo, Tokelau Islands ≈
127 Y 6 Fakenham, United Kingdom
193 U 12 Fakfak, Indonesia
146 M 10 Fakiya, Bulgaria
135 D 26 Fakse Bugt, Denmark ≈
187 I 14 Faku, China
128 M 4 Falaise, France
215 R 7 Falaise de Tiguidit, Niger ▲
183 T 10 Falakata, India
104 M 2 Falcón, Venezuela ▣
140 I 10 Falconara Marittima, Italy
150 M 8 Făleşti, Moldova
71 P 14 Falfurrias, Texas, U.S.A.
136 L 13 Falkensee, Germany
124 H 13 Falkirk, United Kingdom
43 F 20 Falkland Escarpment, Atlantic Ocean ◇
111 J 24 Falkland Islands, U.K. ▣
43 F 20 Falkland Plateau, Atlantic Ocean ◇
111 K 24 Falkland Sound, Falkland Islands ≈
147 G 23 Falkonera, Greece ≈
135 E 22 Falköping, Sweden
59 O 11 Fall River, Massachusetts, U.S.A.
77 J 17 Fallon, Nevada, U.S.A.
67 Q 15 Falls City, Nebraska, U.S.A.
61 S 8 Falls Lake Reserve, North Carolina, U.S.A. ➘
126 J 15 Falmouth, United Kingdom
60 J 4 Falmouth, Kentucky, U.S.A.
61 T 4 Falmouth, Virginia, U.S.A.
92 K 8 Falmouth, Jamaica
126 J 15 Falmouth Bay, United Kingdom ≈
218 J 15 False Bay, Republic of South Africa ≈
78 L 13 False Pass, Alaska, U.S.A.
181 J 16 False Point, India ▶
135 D 26 Falster, Denmark
150 L 8 Fălticeni, Romania
135 G 19 Falun, Sweden
110 H 9 Famatina, Argentina
176 H 6 Famenin, Iran
190 I 11 Fan Si Pan, Vietnam ▲
189 X 6 Fanchang, China
219 Y 8 Fandriana, Madagascar
190 G 13 Fang, Thailand
213 E 20 Fangak, Sudan
189 T 4 Fangcheng, China
189 Z 12 Fangshan, Taiwan
189 R 5 Fangxian, China
186 M 11 Fangzheng, China
186 J 13 Fanjiatun, China
177 N 13 Fannūj, Iran
140 H 10 Fano, Italy
135 B 25 Fanø, Denmark ≈
189 Y 8 Fanshan, China
187 B 17 Fanshi, China
182 M 8 Far Western, Nepal ▣
240 H 4 Faraday, Antarctica ▦

217 Q 5 Faradje, Democratic Republic of Congo
219 Y 10 Farafangana, Madagascar
177 Q 8 Farāh, Afghanistan ▣
177 P 9 Farāh, Afghanistan
236 A 8 Farallon de Medinilla, Northern Mariana Islands ≈
236 A 5 Farallon de Pajaros, Northern Mariana Islands ≈
214 H 11 Faranah, Guinea
175 X 10 Fararah, Oman
236 M 14 Faraulep, Federated States of Micronesia ≈
127 T 13 Fareham, United Kingdom
79 P 8 Farewell, Alaska, U.S.A.
233 H 15 Farewell Spit, New Zealand ▶
179 S 12 Farghona Wiloyati, Uzbekistan
63 V 7 Fargo, Georgia, U.S.A.
67 O 5 Fargo, North Dakota, U.S.A.
67 S 9 Faribault, Minnesota, U.S.A.
182 J 9 Faridabad, India
182 H 6 Faridkot, India
183 T 13 Faridpur, Bangladesh
177 O 6 Farīmān, Iran
127 S 10 Faringdon, United Kingdom
135 G 24 Färjestaden, Sweden
59 P 5 Farmington, Maine, U.S.A.
75 O 8 Farmington, New Mexico, U.S.A.
61 R 6 Farmville, Virginia, U.S.A.
127 U 11 Farnborough, United Kingdom
127 T 11 Farnham, United Kingdom
130 H 12 Faro, Portugal ▣
130 H 12 Faro, Portugal
82 C 13 Faro, Yukon Territory, Canada
45 R 15 Faroe Islands, Denmark ▣
45 Q 15 Faroe–Iceland Ridge, Arctic Ocean ▲
42 K 5 Faroe–Shetland Trough, Atlantic Ocean ◇
135 I 22 Fårösund, Sweden
135 I 22 Fårösund, Sweden
38 K 6 Farquhar Islands, Seychelles ≈
69 X 5 Farrington, Missouri, U.S.A.
176 J 10 Fārs, Iran ▣
147 E 17 Farsala, Greece
73 S 13 Farson, Wyoming, U.S.A.
70 I 3 Farwell, Texas, U.S.A.
240 J 8 Farwell Island, Antarctica
177 R 6 Fāryāb, Afghanistan ▣
176 J 11 Fasā, Iran
141 N 16 Fasano, Italy
151 P 4 Fastiv, Ukraine
217 R 6 Fataki, Democratic Republic of Congo
182 I 7 Fatehabad, India
182 L 9 Fatehgarh, India
182 M 11 Fatehpur, India
156 J 4 Fatezh, Russian Federation
214 D 8 Fatick, Senegal
216 I 10 Fatundu, Democratic Republic of Congo
235 S 8 Fatutaka, Solomon Islands ≈
134 G 10 Fauske, Norway
127 Y 11 Faversham, United Kingdom
134 A 11 Faxaflói, Iceland ≈
215 X 7 Faya, Chad
235 Q 13 Fayaoué, New Caledonia
62 K 5 Fayette, Mississippi, U.S.A.
63 O 3 Fayette, Alabama, U.S.A.
60 F 10 Fayetteville, Tennessee, U.S.A.
61 R 10 Fayetteville, North Carolina, U.S.A.
65 L 20 Fayetteville, Ohio, U.S.A.
69 S 9 Fayetteville, Arkansas, U.S.A.
214 G 4 Fdérik, Mauritania

129 N 3 Fécamp, France
144 H 13 Federacija Bosna Hercegovina, Bosnia and Herzegovina
112 D 13 Federación, Argentina
112 D 13 Federal, Argentina
215 R 12 Federal Capital Territory, Nigeria ▣
237 Q 14 Federated States of Micronesia, Oceania ▣
173 O 3 Fedghāmī, Syria
179 O 2 Fedorovka, Kazakhstan
136 I 8 Fehmarn, Germany ≈
136 I 7 Fehmarnbelt, Germany ≈
139 X 8 Fehring, Austria
B 13 Feijó, Brazil
109 N 14 Feira de Santana, Brazil
170 K 12 Feke, Turkey
131 Y 8 Felanitx, Spain
139 X 8 Feldbach, Austria
138 I 7 Feldkirch, Austria
139 S 8 Feldkirchen in Kärnten, Austria
38 C 8 Félicité, Seychelles ≈
181 L 18 Felidhu Atoll, Maldives ≈
89 Z 11 Felipe Carrillo Puerto, Mexico
127 Z 9 Felixstowe, United Kingdom
140 G 6 Feltre, Italy
135 E 17 Femunden, Norway ➘
170 O 8 Fener Burnu, Turkey ▶
147 J 14 Fengari, Greece ▲
187 I 16 Fengcheng, China
189 U 8 Fengcheng, China
189 P 7 Fengdu, China
189 P 8 Fenggang, China
189 Z 7 Fenghua, China
189 Q 8 Fenghuang, China
189 W 11 Fenghuang, China
189 Q 6 Fengjie, China
189 Z 11 Fenglin, Taiwan
187 E 15 Fengning, China
188 J 11 Fengqing, China
189 U 3 Fengqiu, China
187 F 17 Fengrun, China
186 I 4 Fengshui Shan, China ▲
189 V 11 Fengshun, China
189 V 5 Fengtai, China
189 O 4 Fengxian, China
189 V 3 Fengxian, China
189 Z 6 Fengxian, China
189 P 3 Fengxiang, China
189 W 4 Fengxin, China
189 W 4 Fengyang, China
189 Z 11 Fengyüan, Taiwan
187 B 16 Fengzhen, China
183 V 13 Feni, Bangladesh
234 I 3 Feni Islands, Papua New Guinea ≈
65 E 14 Fennimore, Wisconsin, U.S.A.
219 Z 7 Fenoarivo Atsinanana, Madagascar
237 N 14 Fayu, Federated States of Micronesia ≈
189 S 1 Fenyang, China
151 V 12 Feodosiya, Ukraine
65 I 21 Ferdinand, Indiana, U.S.A.
177 N 7 Ferdows, Iran
146 K 13 Feres, Greece
213 L 22 Fērfēr, Ethiopia
179 T 12 Fergana, Uzbekistan
179 S 12 Fergana Valley, Uzbekistan ◇
67 P 6 Fergus Falls, Minnesota, U.S.A.
234 G 6 Fergusson Island, Papua New Guinea ≈
211 P 6 Fériana, Tunisia
214 K 11 Ferkessédougou, Côte d'Ivoire
140 I 11 Fermo, Italy
130 K 5 Fermoselle, Spain
125 C 20 Fermoy, Republic of Ireland
110 J 8 Fernández, Argentina
63 W 7 Fernandina Beach, Florida, U.S.A.
43 I 14 Fernando de Noronha, Brazil ≈
112 I 4 Fernandópolis, Brazil
77 I 17 Fernley, Nevada, U.S.A.

141 M 16 Ferrandina, Italy
140 G 8 Ferrara, Italy
130 H 10 Ferreira do Alentejo, Portugal
62 K 6 Ferriday, Louisiana, U.S.A.
130 I 1 Ferrol, Spain
210 I 7 Fès, Morocco
216 J 11 Feshi, Democratic Republic of Congo
66 K 4 Fessenden, North Dakota, U.S.A.
69 Y 5 Festus, Missouri, U.S.A.
150 M 13 Feteşti-Gara, Romania
170 D 13 Fethiye, Turkey
178 I 10 Fetisovo, Kazakhstan
124 K 4 Fetlar, United Kingdom ≈
137 H 22 Feuchtwangen, Germany
129 S 10 Feurs, France
177 V 5 Feyzābād, Afghanistan
127 N 5 Ffestiniog, United Kingdom
110 H 8 Fiambalá, Argentina
219 X 9 Fianarantsoa, Madagascar
219 X 9 Fianarantsoa, Madagascar ▣
215 X 11 Fianga, Chad
213 I 20 Fichē, Ethiopia
137 J 20 Fichtelgebirge, Germany ▲
140 G 12 Ficulle, Italy
140 E 8 Fidenza, Italy
145 E 20 Fier, Albania
138 F 10 Fiesch, Switzerland
64 J 12 Fife Lake, Michigan, U.S.A.
124 I 12 Fife Ness, United Kingdom ▶
129 P 12 Figeac, France
130 G 7 Figueira da Foz, Portugal
131 Y 3 Figueres, Spain
210 K 8 Figuig, Morocco
215 V 11 Figuil, Cameroon
237 W 12 Fiji, Oceania ▣
213 K 21 Fik', Ethiopia
219 O 8 Filabusi, Zimbabwe
91 O 10 Filadelfia, Costa Rica
109 F 18 Filadélfia, Paraguay
143 K 21 Filakovo, Slovakia
241 N 5 Filchner Ice Shelf, Antarctica ◇
127 V 1 Filey, United Kingdom
127 V 1 Filey Head, United Kingdom ▶
150 H 12 Filiaşi, Romania
147 C 22 Filiatra, Greece
215 P 9 Filingué, Niger
147 B 17 Filippiada, Greece
74 I 5 Fillmore, Utah, U.S.A.
77 J 24 Fillmore, California, U.S.A.
213 J 23 Filtu, Ethiopia
241 P 1 Fimbul Ice Shelf, Antarctica ◇
241 P 2 Fimbulheimen, Antarctica ▲
131 P 12 Fiñana, Spain
65 L 17 Findlay, Ohio, U.S.A.
58 F 9 Finger Lakes, New York, U.S.A. ➘
219 P 5 Fingoè, Mozambique
170 E 14 Finike, Turkey
234 D 4 Finisterre Range, Papua New Guinea ▲
231 O 7 Finke, Northern Territory, Australia
135 L 18 Finland, Europe ▣
83 E 16 Finlay, British Columbia, Canada ➘
231 S 12 Finley, New South Wales, Australia
67 N 4 Finley, North Dakota, U.S.A.
175 Z 7 Fins, Oman
234 E 5 Finschhafen, Papua New Guinea
138 F 9 Finsteraarhorn, Switzerland ▲
233 A 25 Fiordland, New Zealand ◇
83 J 15 Firebag, Alberta, Canada ➘
140 F 9 Firenzuola, Italy
113 B 15 Firmat, Argentina
129 S 11 Firminy, France

154 G 13 Firovo, Russian Federation
182 K 10 Firozabad, India
182 H 6 Firozpur, India
125 G 14 Firth of Clyde, United Kingdom ≈
124 I 12 Firth of Forth, United Kingdom ≈
124 F 12 Firth of Lorn, United Kingdom ≈
232 L 8 Firth of Thames, New Zealand ≈
176 J 11 Fīrūzābād, Iran
176 J 6 Fīrūzkūh, Iran
39 Y 15 Fisher Bay, Indian Ocean ≈
85 N 4 Fisher Strait, Nunavut, Canada ≈
126 K 9 Fishguard, United Kingdom
126 J 8 Fishguard Bay, United Kingdom ≈
129 R 3 Fismes, France
124 J 5 Fitful Head, United Kingdom ▶
111 H 20 Fitz Roy, Argentina
107 F 16 Fitzcarrald, Peru
230 J 4 Fitzroy, Western Australia, Australia ➘
230 J 4 Fitzroy Crossing, Western Australia, Australia
86 C 10 Fitzwilliam Island, Ontario, Canada ≈
141 G 14 Fiumicino, Italy
140 D 9 Fivizzano, Italy
217 Q 10 Fizi, Democratic Republic of Congo
135 C 19 Flå, Norway
134 C 12 Flaga, Iceland
74 K 10 Flagstaff, Arizona, U.S.A.
43 N 25 Flagstaff Bay, St Helena ≈
59 O 4 Flagstaff Lake, Maine, U.S.A. ➘
85 P 8 Flaherty Island, Ontario, Canada ≈
127 V 1 Flamborough, United Kingdom
127 V 1 Flamborough Head, United Kingdom ▶
137 K 14 Fläming, Germany ▲
74 M 2 Flaming Gorge Reservoir, Utah/Wyoming, U.S.A. ➘
63 X 14 Flamingo, Florida, U.S.A.
133 C 19 Flanders, Belgium ◇
135 G 14 Flåsjön, Sweden ➘
38 B 11 Flat Island, Mauritius ≈
73 N 3 Flathead Lake, Montana, U.S.A. ➘
139 S 8 Flattnitz, Austria
42 B 7 Flatts Village, Bermuda
127 O 2 Fleetwood, United Kingdom
135 A 21 Flekkefjord, Norway
42 G 7 Flemish Cap, Atlantic Ocean ▲
135 B 26 Flensburg, Denmark
136 G 7 Flensburg, Germany
128 M 4 Flers, France
240 I 8 Fletcher Peninsula, Antarctica ◇
138 B 8 Fleurier, Switzerland
132 I 10 Flevoland, Netherlands ▣
84 H 7 Flin Flon, Manitoba, Canada
231 R 5 Flinders, Queensland, Australia ➘
231 T 14 Flinders Island, Tasmania, Australia ≈
231 P 10 Flinders Ranges, South Australia, Australia ▲
237 S 7 Flint, Kiribati ≈
127 O 4 Flint, United Kingdom
65 L 14 Flint, Michigan, U.S.A.
69 O 7 Flint Hills, Kansas, U.S.A.
135 E 18 Flisa, Norway ➘
135 E 19 Flisa, Norway
65 G 21 Flora, Illinois, U.S.A.
129 S 12 Florac, France
63 Q 6 Florala, Alabama, U.S.A.
140 F 10 Florence, Italy
58 A 13 Florence, Pennsylvania, U.S.A.
61 P 12 Florence, South Carolina, U.S.A.

▣ Country   ▣ Internal administrative region: State/Province/Territory/Dependent territory   ● Capital city   ▲ Mountain range/Undersea ridge   ▲ Mountain peak/Volcano/Seamount   ◇ Geographic feature   ▶ Headland/Point/Cape/Peninsula   ▲ Desert   ≈ Island/Island group   ▦ Antarctic base   ◇ Ocean   ≈ Sea   ≈ Bay/Gulf/Channel/Strait   ➘ Lake   ▪ Salt pan/Dry/Intermittent lake   ➚ River

Country ◻ Internal administrative region: State/Province/Territory/Dependent territory ◼ Capital city ▲ Mountain range/Undersea ridge ▲ Mountain peak/Volcano/Seamount ◇ Geographic feature ▶ Headland/Point/Cape/Peninsula ≡ Desert ⚓ Island/Island group ✪ Antarctic base ⚓ Ocean ⚓ Sea ⚓ Bay/Gulf/Channel/Strait ⚓ Lake ⚓ Salt pan/Dry/Intermittent lake ⚓ Riv

38 B 11 **Gabriel Island**, Mauritius 🏝
146 J 9 **Gabrovo**, Bulgaria ▣
146 J 8 **Gabrovo**, Bulgaria
214 F 9 **Gabú**, Guinea-Bissau
145 H 14 **Gacko**, Bosnia and Herzegovina
171 V 8 **Gädäbäy**, Azerbaijan
181 D 19 **Gadag**, India
181 F 15 **Gadarwara**, India
181 A 16 **Gadhra**, India
63 R 2 **Gadsden**, Alabama, U.S.A.
181 E 19 **Gadwal**, India
150 J 12 **Găești**, Romania
141 I 15 **Gaeta**, Italy
236 M 14 **Gaferut**, Federated States of Micronesia 🏝
61 N 10 **Gaffney**, South Carolina, U.S.A.
211 P 7 **Gafsa**, Tunisia
193 T 11 **Gag**, Indonesia 🏝
215 V 12 **Gagal**, Chad
156 J 1 **Gagarin**, Russian Federation
179 Q 12 **Gagarin**, Uzbekistan
141 O 17 **Gagliano del Capo**, Italy
214 J 13 **Gagnoa**, Côte d'Ivoire
85 T 9 **Gagnon**, Québec, Canada
185 O 7 **Gahe**, China
183 T 11 **Gaibandha**, Bangladesh
129 P 13 **Gaillac**, France
63 T 2 **Gainesville**, Georgia, U.S.A.
63 V 8 **Gainesville**, Florida, U.S.A.
69 V 8 **Gainesville**, Missouri, U.S.A.
71 Q 4 **Gainesville**, Texas, U.S.A.
127 U 4 **Gainsborough**, United Kingdom
187 I 16 **Gaizhou**, China
148 G 11 **Gaiziņkalns**, Latvia ▲
199 B 26 **Gaja-jima**, Japan 🏝
215 S 13 **Gakem**, Nigeria
79 S 8 **Gakona**, Alaska, U.S.A.
177 X 6 **Gakuch**, Pakistan
41 T 8 **Galapagos Fracture Zone**, Pacific Ocean ◇
107 A 17 **Galapagos Islands**, Ecuador 🏝
124 I 13 **Galashiels**, United Kingdom
146 N 8 **Galata**, Bulgaria
150 M 11 **Galați**, Romania
147 F 14 **Galatista**, Greece
42 M 12 **Gáldar**, Canary Islands
135 C 17 **Galdhøpiggen**, Norway ▲
38 L 4 **Galeana**, Mexico
193 S 10 **Galela**, Indonesia
55 E 15 **Galena**, Illinois, U.S.A.
79 O 7 **Galena**, Alaska, U.S.A.
93 Z 14 **Galeota Point**, Trinidad and Tobago ▶
93 Z 14 **Galera Point**, Trinidad and Tobago ▶
55 E 17 **Galesburg**, Illinois, U.S.A.
54 D 12 **Galesville**, Wisconsin, U.S.A.
58 E 10 **Galeton**, Pennsylvania, U.S.A.
13 N 22 **Galguduud**, Somalia ▣
50 H 13 **Galicea Mare**, Romania
154 L 13 **Galich**, Russian Federation
30 I 2 **Galicia**, Spain ▣
2 K 8 **Galicia Bank**, Atlantic Ocean ◇
13 H 18 **Gallabat**, Sudan
40 C 6 **Gallarate**, Italy
0 F 8 **Gallatin**, Tennessee, U.S.A.
81 F 25 **Galle**, Sri Lanka
11 G 24 **Gallegos**, Argentina ∿
41 O 17 **Gallipoli**, Italy
70 B 8 **Gallipoli**, Turkey
70 A 8 **Gallipoli Peninsula**, Turkey ▶
5 N 20 **Gallipolis**, Ohio, U.S.A.
34 J 10 **Gällivare**, Sweden
5 N 9 **Gallup**, New Mexico, U.S.A.
10 D 12 **Galtat Zemmour**, Western Sahara
1 T 11 **Galveston**, Texas, U.S.A.
1 T 10 **Galveston Bay**, Texas, U.S.A. ≈
110 K 11 **Gálvez**, Argentina
183 N 7 **Galwa**, Nepal
125 B 18 **Galway**, Republic of Ireland
125 B 18 **Galway Bay**, Republic of Ireland ≈
216 D 9 **Gamba**, Gabon
194 D 8 **Gambang**, Malaysia
213 G 21 **Gambēla**, Ethiopia
213 F 21 **Gambēla**, Ethiopia ▣
214 D 9 **Gambia**, Africa □
214 E 9 **Gambia**, Gambia ∿
42 J 12 **Gambia Abyssal Plain**, Atlantic Ocean ◇
216 H 9 **Gamboma**, Congo
216 H 5 **Gamboula**, Central African Republic
171 W 8 **Gamiş Dağl**, Azerbaijan ▲
188 J 5 **Gamtog**, China
189 V 9 **Gan**, China ∿
188 K 5 **Gana**, China
74 M 9 **Ganado**, Arizona, U.S.A.
86 I 12 **Gananoque**, Ontario, Canada
176 H 10 **Ganāveh**, Iran
171 V 8 **Gäncä**, Azerbaijan
189 Q 15 **Gancheng**, China
218 G 5 **Ganda**, Angola
85 Y 10 **Gander**, Newfoundland and Labrador, Canada
131 U 5 **Gandesa**, Spain
181 A 14 **Gandhidham**, India
181 C 14 **Gandhinagar**, India
131 T 9 **Gandía**, Spain
111 H 17 **Gangán**, Argentina
182 G 7 **Ganganagar**, India
180 E 12 **Gangapur**, India
190 C 11 **Gangaw**, Myanmar
184 H 9 **Gangdise Shan**, China ⛰
137 B 17 **Gangelt**, Germany
129 S 13 **Ganges**, France
182 K 9 **Ganges**, India/Bangladesh ∿
39 P 1 **Ganges Cone**, Indian Ocean ◇
180 G 12 **Gangetic Plain**, India ◇
183 S 10 **Gangtok**, India
189 O 3 **Gangu**, China
188 L 7 **Ganluo**, China
186 I 9 **Gannan**, China
129 R 9 **Gannat**, France
73 S 11 **Gannett Peak**, Wyoming, U.S.A. ▲
184 M 7 **Ganq**, China
189 Q 2 **Ganquan**, China
139 Y 3 **Gänserndorf**, Austria
189 N 3 **Gansu**, China
189 N 3 **Gansu**, China ▣
171 P 5 **Gant'iadi**, Georgia
215 T 12 **Ganye**, Nigeria
189 X 3 **Ganyu**, China
178 G 7 **Ganyushkino**, Kazakhstan
189 U 10 **Ganzhou**, China
189 V 8 **Gao'an**, China
187 C 18 **Gaocheng**, China
189 T 2 **Gaoping**, China
189 V 1 **Gaotang**, China
189 N 8 **Gaoxian**, China
187 D 18 **Gaoyang**, China
189 X 4 **Gaoyou**, China
189 X 4 **Gaoyou Hu**, China ◣
189 R 13 **Gaozhou**, China
129 V 12 **Gap**, France
196 G 10 **Gapan**, Philippines
184 H 9 **Gar**, China
213 O 21 **Garacad**, Somalia
91 Y 15 **Garachiné**, Panama
213 M 20 **Garadag**, Somalia
108 O 13 **Garanhuns**, Brazil
216 K 2 **Garba**, Central African Republic
217 W 7 **Garba Tula**, Kenya
213 K 23 **Garbahaarey**, Somalia
77 E 16 **Garberville**, California, U.S.A.
136 G 13 **Garbsen**, Germany
112 I 6 **Garça**, Brazil
136 J 13 **Gardelegen**, Germany
68 I 5 **Garden City**, Kansas, U.S.A.
64 J 9 **Garden Island**, Michigan, U.S.A. 🏝
177 U 8 **Gardez**, Afghanistan
73 R 8 **Gardiner**, Montana, U.S.A.
63 W 11 **Gardner**, Florida, U.S.A.
41 Q 5 **Gardner Pinnacles**, Hawaii 🏝
78 E 13 **Gareloi Island**, Alaska, U.S.A. 🏝
140 B 9 **Garessio**, Italy
211 O 12 **Garet El Djenoun**, Algeria ▲
75 Q 5 **Garfield**, Colorado, U.S.A.
127 S 2 **Garforth**, United Kingdom
148 B 13 **Gargždai**, Lithuania
181 G 16 **Garhchiroli**, India
112 H 11 **Garibaldi**, Brazil
218 J 13 **Garies**, Republic of South Africa
217 X 8 **Garissa**, Kenya
61 S 11 **Garland**, North Carolina, U.S.A.
71 Q 5 **Garland**, Texas, U.S.A.
149 E 15 **Garliava**, Lithuania
176 H 3 **Garmī**, Iran
137 I 26 **Garmisch-Partenkirchen**, Germany
176 J 6 **Garmsār**, Iran
69 Q 5 **Garnett**, Kansas, U.S.A.
231 R 11 **Garnpung Lake**, New South Wales, Australia ◣
128 M 11 **Garonne**, France ∿
213 N 20 **Garoowe**, Somalia
215 U 11 **Garoua**, Cameroon
215 V 13 **Garoua Boulai**, Cameroon
234 F 4 **Garove Island**, Papua New Guinea 🏝
73 O 6 **Garrison**, Montana, U.S.A.
84 K 1 **Garry Lake**, Nunavut, Canada ◣
217 X 9 **Garsen**, Kenya
213 A 18 **Garsila**, Sudan
127 P 2 **Garstang**, United Kingdom
127 O 8 **Garth**, United Kingdom
192 H 14 **Garut**, Indonesia
233 C 24 **Garvie Mountains**, New Zealand ⛰
181 I 14 **Garwa**, India
142 M 13 **Garwolin**, Poland
65 H 16 **Gary**, Indiana, U.S.A.
188 K 5 **Garzê**, China
104 H 8 **Garzón**, Colombia
128 M 13 **Gascony**, France ◇
230 F 8 **Gascoyne**, Western Australia, Australia ∿
230 F 8 **Gascoyne Junction**, Western Australia, Australia
39 S 7 **Gascoyne Plain**, Indian Ocean ◇
177 P 12 **Gasht**, Iran
215 T 10 **Gashua**, Nigeria
234 G 5 **Gasmata**, Papua New Guinea
87 T 5 **Gaspé**, Québec, Canada
198 K 12 **Gassan**, Japan ▲
215 T 12 **Gassol**, Nigeria
61 O 10 **Gastonia**, North Carolina, U.S.A.
147 C 20 **Gastouni**, Greece
111 G 17 **Gastre**, Argentina
150 F 11 **Gătaia**, Romania
154 E 11 **Gatchina**, Russian Federation
82 J 6 **Gateshead Island**, Nunavut, Canada 🏝
71 P 8 **Gatesville**, Texas, U.S.A.
86 I 10 **Gatineau**, Québec, Canada
60 K 9 **Gatlinburg**, Tennessee, U.S.A.
91 W 13 **Gatún**, Panama
235 Y 12 **Gau**, Fiji 🏝
235 Q 9 **Gaua**, Vanuatu 🏝
148 G 9 **Gauja**, Latvia ∿
181 E 21 **Gauribidanur**, India
135 C 19 **Gausta**, Norway ▲
219 O 11 **Gauteng**, Republic of South Africa ▣
176 I 12 **Gāvbandī**, Iran
147 H 26 **Gavdopoula**, Greece 🏝
147 H 26 **Gavdos**, Greece 🏝
108 C 12 **Gaviãozinho**, Brazil
135 H 19 **Gävle**, Sweden
154 J 13 **Gavrilov-Yam**, Russian Federation
231 P 11 **Gawler**, South Australia, Australia
185 P 6 **Gaxun Nur**, China ◣
183 P 12 **Gaya**, India
195 U 5 **Gaya**, Malaysia 🏝
64 K 11 **Gaylord**, Michigan, U.S.A.
155 R 10 **Gayny**, Russian Federation
219 Q 9 **Gaza**, Mozambique ▣
172 E 10 **Gaza**, Israel
172 E 10 **Gaza Strip**, Israel ◇
178 J 13 **Gazandzhyk**, Turkmenistan
217 X 10 **Gazi**, Kenya
170 M 13 **Gaziantep**, Turkey
177 O 8 **Gazīk**, Iran
170 G 14 **Gazipaşa**, Turkey
179 O 12 **Gazli**, Uzbekistan
214 H 12 **Gbarnga**, Liberia
214 H 13 **Gbatala**, Liberia
215 S 12 **Gboko**, Nigeria
142 I 8 **Gdańsk**, Poland
154 D 11 **Gdov**, Russian Federation
142 I 8 **Gdynia**, Poland
193 S 11 **Gebe**, Indonesia 🏝
212 G 11 **Gebel Hamâta**, Egypt ▲
212 F 9 **Gebel Katherîna**, Egypt ▲
213 I 20 **Gebre Guracha**, Ethiopia
170 E 8 **Gebze**, Turkey
213 G 21 **Gech'a**, Ethiopia
213 G 17 **Gedaref**, Sudan
213 G 18 **Gedaref**, Sudan ▣
213 L 21 **Gedlegubē**, Ethiopia
213 K 24 **Gedo**, Somalia ▣
195 N 11 **Gedong**, Malaysia
135 D 26 **Gedser**, Denmark
133 H 17 **Geel**, Belgium
231 S 13 **Geelong**, Victoria, Australia
215 T 9 **Geidam**, Nigeria
83 L 15 **Geikie**, Saskatchewan, Canada ∿
135 C 18 **Geilo**, Norway
217 S 9 **Geita**, Tanzania
188 L 12 **Gejiu**, China
141 J 23 **Gela**, Italy
184 L 9 **Geladaindong**, China ▲
213 M 21 **Geladī**, Ethiopia
132 K 12 **Gelderland**, Netherlands ▣
137 B 15 **Geldern**, Germany
133 J 16 **Geldrop**, Netherlands
133 K 18 **Geleen**, Netherlands
156 K 12 **Gelendzhik**, Russian Federation
213 M 22 **Gelinsoor**, Somalia
194 C 9 **Gemas**, Malaysia
133 G 20 **Gembloux**, Belgium
215 T 13 **Gembu**, Nigeria
216 K 6 **Gemena**, Democratic Republic of Congo
170 L 10 **Gemerek**, Turkey
170 D 8 **Gemlik**, Turkey
134 A 10 **Gemlufall**, Iceland
140 I 5 **Gemona del Friuli**, Italy
212 F 10 **Gemsa**, Egypt
111 J 14 **General Acha**, Argentina
110 H 13 **General Alvear**, Argentina
113 D 16 **General Belgrano**, Argentina
110 J 11 **General Cabrera**, Argentina
89 P 7 **General Cepreda**, Mexico
113 A 20 **General Conesa**, Argentina
112 C 9 **General José de San Martín**, Argentina
113 E 17 **General Juan Madariaga**, Argentina
113 C 18 **General La Madrid**, Argentina
110 G 1 **General Lagos**, Chile
113 E 17 **General Lavalle**, Argentina
197 M 16 **General MacArthur**, Philippines
110 I 6 **General Martín Miguel de Güemes**, Argentina
113 A 17 **General Pico**, Argentina
113 B 16 **General Pinto**, Argentina
111 H 15 **General Roca**, Argentina
197 M 23 **General Santos**, Philippines
146 N 6 **General-Toshevo**, Bulgaria
113 A 16 **General Villegas**, Argentina
65 E 16 **Geneseo**, Illinois, U.S.A.
213 I 20 **Genet**, Ethiopia
138 A 10 **Geneva**, Switzerland
58 F 8 **Geneva**, New York, U.S.A.
188 J 11 **Gengma**, China
216 M 9 **Gengwa**, Democratic Republic of Congo
133 J 18 **Genk**, Belgium
140 C 9 **Genoa**, Italy
192 G 14 **Genteng**, Indonesia
136 K 13 **Genthin**, Germany
194 C 8 **Genting Highlands**, Malaysia
230 G 12 **Geographe Bay**, Western Australia, Australia ≈
218 L 15 **George**, Republic of South Africa
85 T 6 **George**, Québec, Canada ∿
43 N 26 **George Island**, St Helena 🏝
233 A 23 **George Sound**, New Zealand ≈
231 T 15 **George Town**, Tasmania, Australia
194 A 6 **George Town**, Malaysia
92 H 7 **George Town**, Cayman Islands 🏛
92 M 3 **George Town**, The Bahamas
241 T 14 **George V Coast**, Antarctica ◇
241 S 14 **George V Land**, Antarctica ◇
240 I 5 **George VI Sound**, Antarctica ≈
71 P 12 **George West**, Texas, U.S.A.
214 E 9 **Georgetown**, Gambia
231 S 4 **Georgetown**, Queensland, Australia
43 K 25 **Georgetown**, Ascension 🏛
105 U 5 **Georgetown**, Guyana 🏛
60 I 5 **Georgetown**, Kentucky, U.S.A.
61 W 3 **Georgetown**, Delaware, U.S.A.
61 R 13 **Georgetown**, South Carolina, U.S.A.
93 Z 12 **Georgetown**, St Vincent and the Grenadines
171 T 6 **Georgia**, Asia □
63 S 4 **Georgia**, U.S.A. ▣
86 D 10 **Georgian Bay**, Ontario, Canada ≈
231 P 5 **Georgina**, Queensland, Australia ∿
179 X 5 **Georgiyevka**, Kazakhstan
157 O 13 **Georgiyevsk**, Russian Federation
136 D 10 **Georgsheil**, Germany
137 K 17 **Gera**, Germany
133 E 19 **Geraardsbergen**, Belgium
147 E 22 **Geraki**, Greece
69 X 5 **Gerald**, Missouri, U.S.A.
230 F 10 **Geraldton**, Western Australia, Australia
171 Q 12 **Gercüş**, Turkey
170 H 8 **Gerede**, Turkey
177 R 9 **Gereshk**, Afghanistan
131 Q 12 **Gérgal**, Spain
77 J 16 **Gerlach**, Nevada, U.S.A.
143 K 19 **Gerlachovský štít**, Slovakia ▲
137 H 17 **Germany**, Europe □
199 I 16 **Gero**, Japan
170 K 7 **Gerze**, Turkey
135 I 19 **Geta**, Finland
131 O 7 **Getafe**, Spain
58 F 14 **Gettysburg**, Pennsylvania, U.S.A.
66 K 8 **Gettysburg**, South Dakota, U.S.A.
240 K 10 **Getz Ice Shelf Range**, Antarctica ◇
171 S 11 **Gevaş**, Turkey
146 E 12 **Gevgelija**, Macedonia (F.Y.R.O.M.)
181 D 17 **Gevrai**, India
194 B 14 **Geylang**, Singapore
139 V 3 **Gföhl**, Austria
218 L 12 **Ghaap Plateau**, Republic of South Africa ◇
211 Q 9 **Ghadāmis**, Libya
211 T 11 **Ghaddūwah**, Libya
183 N 10 **Ghaghara**, India ∿
214 M12 **Ghana**, Africa □
218 K 9 **Ghanzi**, Botswana
218 L 9 **Ghanzi**, Botswana ▣
172 F 12 **Gharandal**, Jordan
211 N 8 **Ghardaïa**, Algeria
177 T 15 **Gharo**, Pakistan
211 S 8 **Gharyān**, Libya
211 R 12 **Ghāt**, Libya
210 K 6 **Ghazaouet**, Algeria
182 J 8 **Ghaziabad**, India
183 O 11 **Ghazipur**, India
177 T 9 **Ghazluna**, Pakistan
177 U 8 **Ghaznī**, Afghanistan
177 T 8 **Ghaznī**, Afghanistan ▣
175 N 4 **Ghazzālah**, Saudi Arabia
133 D 18 **Ghent**, Belgium
150 K 9 **Gheorgheni**, Romania
150 I 8 **Gherla**, Romania
177 R 9 **Ghorak**, Afghanistan
177 V 12 **Ghotki**, Pakistan
177 R 8 **Ghowr**, Afghanistan ▣
175 V 12 **Ghubbat al Qamar**, Yemen ≈
173 O 2 **Ghūnā**, Syria
177 P 7 **Ghurian**, Afghanistan
191 N 22 **Gia Đinh**, Vietnam
191 L 23 **Gia Rai**, Vietnam
146 E 13 **Giannitsa**, Greece
141 L 22 **Giarre**, Italy
73 N 7 **Gibbonsville**, Idaho, U.S.A.
42 A 8 **Gibb's Hill**, Bermuda ▲
218 I 10 **Gibeon**, Namibia
130 J 12 **Gibraleón**, Spain
130 L 14 **Gibraltar**, Gibraltar 🏛
130 L 14 **Gibraltar**, U.K. ▣
230 J 7 **Gibson Desert**, Western Australia, Australia ◇
71 Q 10 **Giddings**, Texas, U.S.A.
135 H 14 **Gideälven**, Sweden ∿
213 H 22 **Gīdolē**, Ethiopia
129 Q 6 **Gien**, France
137 F 18 **Giessen**, Germany
132 N 7 **Gieten**, Netherlands
76 K 6 **Gifford**, Washington, U.S.A.
136 H 13 **Gifhorn**, Germany
199 H 17 **Gifu**, Japan
130 L 1 **Gijón**, Spain
74 K 13 **Gila**, Arizona, U.S.A. ∿
74 I 13 **Gila Bend**, Arizona, U.S.A.
74 L 12 **Gila Mountains**, Arizona, U.S.A. ⛰
176 H 4 **Gīlān**, Iran ▣
150 H 9 **Gilău**, Romania
171 Y 7 **Gilăzi**, Azerbaijan
236 D 1 **Gilbert Islands**, Kiribati 🏝
108 K 13 **Gilbués**, Brazil
73 R 2 **Gildford**, Montana, U.S.A.
219 T 6 **Gilé**, Mozambique
212 B 12 **Gilf Kebir Plateau**, Egypt ◇
231 U 10 **Gilgandra**, New South Wales, Australia
177 Y 6 **Gilgit**, Pakistan
182 H 2 **Gilgit**, India
43 O 26 **Gill Point**, St Helena ▶
84 K 7 **Gillam**, Manitoba, Canada
73 X 9 **Gillette**, Wyoming, U.S.A.
127 Q 12 **Gillingham**, United Kingdom
127 X 11 **Gillingham**, United Kingdom
241 W 6 **Gillock Island**, Antarctica 🏝
65 G 17 **Gilman**, Illinois, U.S.A.
77 G 20 **Gilroy**, California, U.S.A.
213 G 20 **Gīmbī**, Ethiopia
197 L 20 **Gingoog**, Philippines
213 J 21 **Gīnīr**, Ethiopia
147 H 17 **Gioura**, Greece 🏝
177 P 10 **Girdi**, Iran
124 J 11 **Girdle Ness**, United Kingdom ▶
171 N 8 **Giresun**, Turkey

□ Country ▣ Internal administrative region: State/Province/Territory/Dependent territory 🏛 Capital city ⛰ Mountain range/Undersea ridge ▲ Mountain peak/Volcano/Seamount ◇ Geographic feature ▶ Headland/Point/Cape/Peninsula 🏜 Desert 🏝 Island/Island group ⁙ Antarctic base 🌊 Ocean ≋ Sea ≈ Bay/Gulf/Channel/Strait ◣ Lake ⛶ Salt pan/Dry/Intermittent lake ∿ River

◻ Country ◻ Internal administrative region: State/Province/Territory/Dependent territory ⅷ Capital city ▲ Mountain range/ Undersea ridge ▲ Mountain peak/ Volcano/Seamount ◇ Geographic feature ⅷ Headland/Point/ Cape/Peninsula ◇ Desert ⅷ Island/Island group ⅷ Antarctic base ⅷ Ocean ⅿ Sea ⋍ Bay/Gulf/Channel/Strait ◡ Lake ⅿ Salt pan/Dry/ Intermittent lake ⅿ River

291

152 M 8 **Guba**, Russian Federation ≈
155 R 1 **Guba Dolgaya**, Russian Federation
155 T 11 **Gubakha**, Russian Federation
142 D 13 **Gubin**, Poland
215 U 10 **Gubio**, Nigeria
171 P 5 **Gudaut'a**, Georgia
175 O 1 **Gudayyidat 'Ar'ar**, Saudi Arabia
157 Q 14 **Gudermes**, Russian Federation
41 X 15 **Gudgeon Harbour**, Pitcairn Island ≈
181 G 19 **Gudivada**, India
181 F 20 **Gudur**, India
214 H 12 **Guéckédou**, Guinea
215 V 10 **Guélengdeng**, Chad
211 P 5 **Guelma**, Algeria
210 F 9 **Guelmine**, Morocco
86 E 13 **Guelph**, Ontario, Canada
89 R 8 **Güémez**, Mexico
215 O 10 **Guéné**, Benin
215 X 10 **Guéra**, Chad ▣
211 N 8 **Guerara**, Algeria
210 J 7 **Guercif**, Morocco
129 P 9 **Guéret**, France
125 J 25 **Guernsey**, United Kingdom 🏝
73 Z 12 **Guernsey**, Wyoming, U.S.A.
214 G 7 **Guérou**, Mauritania
89 Q 6 **Guerrero**, Mexico
89 Q 13 **Guerrero**, Mexico ▣
88 G 5 **Guerrero Negro**, Mexico
214 J 13 **Guéyo**, Côte d'Ivoire
213 H 22 **Gugē**, Ethiopia ▲
236 A 7 **Guguan**, Northern Mariana Islands 🏝
42 G 13 **Guiana Basin**, Atlantic Ocean ◇
105 O 6 **Guiana Highlands**, South America ⛰
189 W 6 **Guichi**, China
113 E 14 **Guichón**, Uruguay
215 W 11 **Guidari**, Chad
215 V 11 **Guider**, Cameroon
214 G 8 **Guidimaka**, Mauritania ▣
189 P 10 **Guiding**, China
189 Q 12 **Guigang**, China
214 I 13 **Guiglo**, Côte d'Ivoire
130 L 6 **Guijuelo**, Spain
127 U 11 **Guildford**, United Kingdom
186 H 11 **Guiler**, China
59 Q 4 **Guilford**, Maine, U.S.A.
189 R 11 **Guilin**, China
129 W 12 **Guillestre**, France
42 M 12 **Güímar**, Canary Islands
197 I 17 **Guimaras**, Philippines 🏝
63 O 2 **Guin**, Alabama, U.S.A.
197 L 18 **Guindulman**, Philippines
214 F 10 **Guinea**, Africa □
43 L 14 **Guinea Basin**, Atlantic Ocean ◇
214 E 10 **Guinea-Bissau**, Africa □
214 I 12 **Guinée-Forestière**, Guinea ▣
214 F 10 **Guinée-Maritime**, Guinea ▣
92 H 4 **Güines**, Cuba
128 J 5 **Guingamp**, France
189 R 12 **Guiping**, China
127 Y 6 **Guist**, United Kingdom
130 I 1 **Guitiriz**, Spain
197 M 16 **Guiuan**, Philippines
189 O 9 **Guiyang**, China
189 T 10 **Guiyang**, China
189 O 9 **Guizhou**, China ▣
181 B 14 **Gujarat**, India ▣
177 Y 9 **Gujranwala**, Pakistan
177 Y 8 **Gujrat**, Pakistan
185 P 8 **Gulang**, China
181 E 18 **Gulbarga**, India
148 I 10 **Gulbene**, Latvia
179 U 12 **Gülchö**, Kyrgyzstan
234 C 6 **Gulf**, Papua New Guinea ▣
191 I 22 **Gulf of Thailand**, Thailand ≈
213 M 18 **Gulf of Aden**, Africa/Asia ≈
79 Q 11 **Gulf of Alaska**, Alaska, U.S.A. ≈
153 Z 6 **Gulf of Anadyr**, Russian Federation ≈
174 I 3 **Gulf of Aqaba**, Asia ≈
82 L 4 **Gulf of Boothia**, Nunavut, Canada ≈
135 I 19 **Gulf of Bothnia**, Sweden ≈
88 G 3 **Gulf of California**, Mexico ≈
231 Q 2 **Gulf of Carpentaria**, Queensland, Australia ≈
147 E 19 **Gulf of Corinth**, Greece ≈
104 G 3 **Gulf of Darién**, Colombia ≈
135 L 20 **Gulf of Finland**, Europe ≈
142 J 7 **Gulf of Gdańsk**, Europe ≈
140 C 10 **Gulf of Genoa**, Italy ≈
106 A 10 **Gulf of Guayaquil**, Ecuador ≈
215 R 15 **Gulf of Guinea**, Africa ≈
90 M 3 **Gulf of Honduras**, Honduras ≈
181 A 14 **Gulf of Kachchh**, India ≈
181 B 16 **Gulf of Khambhat**, India ≈
59 P 9 **Gulf of Maine**, Maine, U.S.A. ≈
181 F 24 **Gulf of Mannar**, Sri Lanka ≈
191 E 17 **Gulf of Martaban**, Myanmar ≈
57 R 15 **Gulf of Mexico**, North America ≈
175 Y 5 **Gulf of Oman**, Asia ≈
91 X 15 **Gulf of Panama**, Panama ≈
234 C 6 **Gulf of Papua**, Papua New Guinea ≈
105 R 3 **Gulf of Paria**, Venezuela ≈
148 E 9 **Gulf of Riga**, Estonia/Latvia ≈
212 C 7 **Gulf of Salûm**, Egypt/Libya ≈
211 V 8 **Gulf of Sirte**, Libya ≈
159 O 13 **Gulf of Sirte**, Mediterranean Sea ≈
87 W 5 **Gulf of St Lawrence**, Québec, Canada ≈
212 F 8 **Gulf of Suez**, Egypt ≈
151 Y 9 **Gulf of Taganrog**, Russian Federation/Ukraine ≈
39 S 3 **Gulf of Thailand**, Indian Ocean ≈
189 Q 14 **Gulf of Tongking**, China ≈
144 A 8 **Gulf of Trieste**, Slovenia ≈
104 K 2 **Gulf of Venezuela**, Venezuela ≈
140 H 7 **Gulf of Venice**, Italy ≈
63 O 8 **Gulf Shores**, Alabama, U.S.A.
231 P 12 **Gulf St Vincent**, South Australia, Australia ≈
57 T 13 **Gulfport**, Mississippi, U.S.A.
189 O 8 **Gulin**, China/Vietnam
189 V 7 **Guling**, China
179 R 12 **Gulistan**, Uzbekistan
170 B 12 **Güllük Körfezi**, Turkey ≈
170 A 9 **Gülpinar**, Turkey
171 Q 5 **Gulrip'shi**, Georgia
179 U 7 **Gul'shad**, Kazakhstan
217 S 6 **Gulu**, Uganda
146 K 10 **Gŭlŭbovo**, Bulgaria
146 I 7 **Gulyantsi**, Bulgaria
218 L 7 **Gumare**, Botswana
178 I 13 **Gumdag**, Turkmenistan
215 S 10 **Gumel**, Nigeria
181 I 15 **Gumla**, India
180 E 13 **Guna**, India
213 I 19 **Guna Terara**, Ethiopia ▲
139 Q 4 **Gundertshausen**, Austria
170 L 12 **Güney Doğu Toroslar**, Turkey ⛰
216 J 11 **Gungu**, Democratic Republic of Congo
157 R 15 **Gunib**, Russian Federation
45 P 13 **Gunnbjørn Fjeld**, Greenland ▲
231 U 10 **Gunnedah**, New South Wales, Australia
38 B 11 **Gunners Quoin**, Mauritius 🏝
74 K 5 **Gunnison**, Utah, U.S.A.
75 P 5 **Gunnison**, Colorado, U.S.A.
181 E 19 **Guntakal**, India
63 Q 2 **Guntersville Lake**, Alabama, U.S.A. 💧
181 G 19 **Guntur**, India
192 B 8 **Gunung Abongabong**, Indonesia ▲
195 O 10 **Gunung Ayer**, Malaysia
194 C 7 **Gunung Batu Puteh**, Malaysia ▲
194 E 10 **Gunung Belumut**, Malaysia ▲
194 C 7 **Gunung Benum**, Malaysia ▲
194 A 6 **Gunung Bintang**, Malaysia ▲
193 Q 10 **Gunung Bulawa**, Indonesia ▲
194 C 6 **Gunung Camah**, Malaysia ▲
193 W 12 **Gunung Dom**, Indonesia ▲
192 D 11 **Gunung Kerinci**, Indonesia ▲
193 U 11 **Gunung Kwoka**, Indonesia ▲
194 D 5 **Gunung Lawit**, Malaysia ▲
194 D 9 **Gunung Ledang**, Malaysia ▲
194 C 7 **Gunung Liang Timur**, Malaysia ▲
195 X 7 **Gunung Magdaline**, Malaysia ▲
193 O 10 **Gunung Malino**, Indonesia ▲
194 D 6 **Gunung Mandi Angin**, Malaysia ▲
193 V 11 **Gunung Mebo**, Indonesia ▲
195 W 4 **Gunung Menapod**, Malaysia ▲
195 T 7 **Gunung Murud**, Malaysia ▲
193 Q 15 **Gunung Mutis**, Indonesia ▲
194 C 5 **Gunung Noring**, Malaysia ▲
195 T 7 **Gunung Pagon**, Malaysia ▲
192 K 15 **Gunung Semeru**, Indonesia ▲
192 I 14 **Gunung Slamet**, Indonesia ▲
194 D 6 **Gunung Tahan**, Malaysia ▲
194 D 7 **Gunung Tapis**, Malaysia ▲
195 X 6 **Gunung Tribulation**, Malaysia ▲
195 U 5 **Gunung Trus Madi**, Malaysia ▲
193 P 11 **Gunung Tumpu**, Indonesia ▲
193 R 14 **Gunungapi**, Indonesia 🏝
192 C 10 **Gunungsitoli**, Indonesia
181 I 17 **Gunupur**, India
137 H 23 **Günzburg**, Germany
187 E 15 **Guojiatun**, China
189 V 4 **Guoyang**, China
150 K 8 **Gura Humorului**, Romania
182 H 3 **Gurais**, India
186 A 13 **Gurban Obo**, China
177 O 14 **Gurdim**, Iran
180 B 13 **Gurha**, India
112 I 4 **Gurinhatã**, Brazil
139 T 8 **Gurk**, Austria
219 Q 6 **Guro**, Mozambique
219 S 5 **Gurué**, Mozambique
170 M 11 **Gürün**, Turkey
108 I 10 **Gurupá**, Brazil
109 J 14 **Gurupi**, Brazil
156 M 1 **Gus'-Khrustal'nyy**, Russian Federation
215 Q 10 **Gusau**, Nigeria
149 C 16 **Gusev**, Russian Federation
187 I 17 **Gushan**, China
189 V 5 **Gushi**, China
199 M 25 **Gushikawa**, Japan
141 B 18 **Guspini**, Italy
139 X 7 **Güssing**, Austria
139 V 5 **Gusswerk**, Austria
241 W 5 **Gustav Bull Mountains**, Antarctica ⛰
79 W 10 **Gustavus**, Alaska, U.S.A.
199 O 26 **Gusukube**, Japan
137 E 14 **Gütersloh**, Germany
69 N 9 **Guthrie**, Oklahoma, U.S.A.
70 M 4 **Guthrie**, Texas, U.S.A.
74 M 13 **Guthrie**, Arizona, U.S.A.
189 X 9 **Gutian**, China
67 V 11 **Guttenberg**, Iowa, U.S.A.
219 P 7 **Gutu**, Zimbabwe
183 V 10 **Guwahati**, India
173 S 2 **Guwēr**, Iraq
105 S 6 **Guyana**, South America □
185 R 6 **Guyang**, China
68 G 8 **Guymon**, Oklahoma, U.S.A.
189 O 2 **Guyuan**, China
179 P 13 **Guzar**, Uzbekistan
149 B 16 **Gvardeysk**, Russian Federation
191 C 15 **Gwa**, Myanmar
215 Q 9 **Gwadabawa**, Nigeria
177 P 14 **Gwadar**, Pakistan
182 J 11 **Gwalior**, India
219 O 8 **Gwanda**, Zimbabwe
217 O 5 **Gwane**, Democratic Republic of Congo
177 P 14 **Gwatar Bay**, Iran ≈
217 Q 5 **Gwawele**, Democratic Republic of Congo
142 G 10 **Gwda**, Poland ∿
219 O 7 **Gweru**, Zimbabwe
218 M 8 **Gweta**, Botswana
64 H 9 **Gwinn**, Michigan, U.S.A.
215 U 10 **Gwoza**, Nigeria
147 M 23 **Gyali**, Greece 🏝
184 K 11 **Gyangzê**, China
185 N 9 **Gyaring Hu**, China 💧
147 I 21 **Gyaros**, Greece 🏝
188 K 7 **Gyawa**, China
153 N 7 **Gyda**, Russian Federation
153 N 7 **Gydanskiy Poluostrov**, Russian Federation ▶
188 I 6 **Gyitang**, China
231 W 8 **Gympie**, Queensland, Australia
143 L 24 **Gyomaendrőd**, Hungary
143 K 22 **Gyöngyös**, Hungary
143 H 22 **Győr**, Hungary
84 I 9 **Gypsumville**, Manitoba, Canada
147 E 23 **Gytheio**, Greece
143 L 24 **Gyula**, Hungary
171 T 8 **Gyumri**, Armenia
178 J 13 **Gyzylarbat**, Turkmenistan
178 I 14 **Gyzyletrek**, Turkmenistan

H

183 T 9 **Ha**, Bhutan
190 N 12 **Ha Côi**, Vietnam
190 L 10 **Ha Giang**, Vietnam
191 L 22 **Ha Tiên**, Vietnam
191 M 15 **Ha Tinh**, Vietnam
148 F 8 **Häädemeeste**, Estonia
137 K 24 **Haag in Oberbayern**, Germany
132 N 12 **Haaksbergen**, Netherlands
236 I 10 **Ha'apai Group**, Tonga 🏝
135 L 15 **Haapajärvi**, Finland
148 E 7 **Haapsalu**, Estonia
132 G 11 **Haarlem**, Netherlands
233 D 21 **Haast**, New Zealand
175 X 5 **Haba**, United Arab Emirates
175 V 11 **Ḩabarūt**, Oman
217 X 7 **Habaswein**, Kenya
133 J 25 **Habay-la-Neuve**, Belgium
175 R 13 **Ḩabbān**, Yemen
158 C 9 **Habibas Escarpment**, Mediterranean Sea ◇
187 D 14 **Habirag**, China
104 H 10 **Hacha**, Colombia
199 L 19 **Hachijō-jima**, Japan 🏝
198 K 9 **Hachinohe**, Japan
171 R 9 **Haciömer**, Turkey
58 J 12 **Hackensack**, New Jersey, U.S.A.
219 Q 8 **Hacufera**, Mozambique
186 G 7 **Hadat**, China
215 S 10 **Hadejia**, Nigeria
172 F 8 **Ḩadera**, Israel
135 B 25 **Haderslev**, Denmark
181 E 17 **Hadgaon**, India
181 L 19 **Hadhdhunmathi Atoll**, Maldives 🏝
175 W 14 **Hadībоh**, Yemen
170 H 13 **Hadim**, Turkey
127 Y 8 **Hadleigh**, United Kingdom
82 H 5 **Hadley Bay**, Nunavut, Canada ≈
175 R 13 **Ḩaḑramawt**, Yemen ⛰
134 G 8 **Hadseløy**, Norway 🏝
135 C 24 **Hadsund**, Denmark
151 T 3 **Hadyach**, Ukraine
187 K 18 **Haeju**, North Korea
187 L 22 **Haenam**, South Korea
175 Q 3 **Ḩafar al Bāţin**, Saudi Arabia
170 M 9 **Hafik**, Turkey
174 L 4 **Hafirat al'Aydā**, Saudi Arabia
183 W 11 **Haflong**, India
134 A 11 **Hafnarfjörður**, Iceland
236 A 9 **Hagåtña**, Guam 🏛
137 D 16 **Hagen**, Germany
72 L 12 **Hagerman**, Idaho, U.S.A.
61 T 2 **Hagerstown**, Maryland, U.S.A.
135 F 20 **Hagfors**, Sweden
199 C 20 **Hagi**, Japan
125 B 18 **Hag's Head**, Republic of Ireland ▶
129 X 4 **Haguenau**, France
190 M 12 **Hai Duong**, Vietnam
190 M 12 **Hai Phong**, Vietnam
189 Y 4 **Hai'an**, China
187 I 16 **Haicheng**, China
172 F 8 **Haifa**, Israel
189 R 14 **Haikang**, China
189 R 15 **Haikou**, China
175 N 4 **Ḩā'īl**, Saudi Arabia
186 G 8 **Hailar**, China
186 M 12 **Hailin**, China
127 W 13 **Hailsham**, United Kingdom
186 K 9 **Hailun**, China
134 L 13 **Hailuoto**, Finland 🏝
189 Z 5 **Haimen**, China
199 M 26 **Haimi**, Japan
189 Q 15 **Hainan**, China 🏝
189 Q 15 **Hainan**, China ▣
189 Q 15 **Hainan Strait**, China ≈
133 E 21 **Hainaut**, Belgium ▣
139 Z 4 **Hainburg an der Donau**, Austria
79 W 10 **Haines**, Alaska, U.S.A.
63 W 10 **Haines City**, Florida, U.S.A.
83 A 14 **Haines Junction**, Yukon Territory, Canada
139 W 4 **Hainfeld**, Austria
189 Y 6 **Haining**, China
189 Y 10 **Haitan Dao**, China 🏝
93 O 8 **Haiti**, North America □
189 Q 15 **Haitou**, China
189 Z 6 **Haiyan**, China
187 H 20 **Haiyang**, China
189 O 2 **Haiyuan**, China
189 X 3 **Haizhou Wan**, China ≈
143 M 22 **Hajdúböszörmény**, Hungary
143 M 23 **Hajdúszoboszló**, Hungary
173 V 8 **Hājī Muḩsin**, Iraq
198 I 13 **Hajiki-zaki**, Japan ▶
183 Q 11 **Hajipur**, India
175 O 12 **Ḩajjah**, Yemen
176 L 12 **Ḩājjīābād**, Iran
142 O 11 **Hajnówka**, Poland
190 B 10 **Haka**, Myanmar
171 T 12 **Hakkâri**, Turkey
199 G 19 **Hakken-san**, Japan ▲
198 K 9 **Hakkōda-san**, Japan ▲
198 K 3 **Hako-dake**, Japan ▲
198 J 8 **Hakodate**, Japan
199 H 15 **Hakui**, Japan
177 U 14 **Hala**, Pakistan
175 P 7 **Halabān**, Saudi Arabia
173 V 4 **Halabja**, Iraq
212 H 13 **Halaib**, Sudan
212 G 12 **Halaib Triangle**, Sudan ◇
174 J 2 **Ḩālat 'Ammār**, Saudi Arabia
172 H 5 **Halba**, Lebanon
185 O 2 **Halban**, Mongolia
137 I 14 **Halberstadt**, Germany
135 D 20 **Halden**, Norway
182 L 8 **Haldwani**, India
127 Q 4 **Hale**, United Kingdom
78 D 8 **Haleakala**, Hawaii, U.S.A. ▲
127 R 7 **Halesowen**, United Kingdom
127 Z 7 **Halesworth**, United Kingdom
77 I 19 **Half Dome**, California, U.S.A. ▲
171 N 13 **Halfeti**, Turkey
233 C 26 **Halfmoon Bay**, New Zealand
132 H 11 **Halfweg**, Netherlands
86 G 10 **Haliburton Highlands**, Ontario, Canada ⛰
127 R 2 **Halifax**, United Kingdom
87 V 11 **Halifax**, Nova Scotia, Canada
85 O 1 **Hall Beach**, Nunavut, Canada
139 N 7 **Hall in Tirol**, Austria
237 O 14 **Hall Islands**, Federated States of Micronesia 🏝
85 S 3 **Hall Peninsula**, Nunavut, Canada ▶
187 L 23 **Halla-san**, South Korea ▲
133 F 19 **Halle**, Belgium
137 K 16 **Halle**, Germany
139 Q 6 **Hallein**, Austria
71 Q 11 **Hallettsville**, Texas, U.S.A.
241 N 3 **Halley**, Antarctica ⁙
66 H4 **Halliday**, North Dakota, U.S.A.
230 K 4 **Halls Creek**, Western Australia, Australia
139 R 6 **Hallstatt**, Austria
138 F 7 **Hallwiler See**, Switzerland 💧
126 L 13 **Hallworthy**, United Kingdom
193 S 10 **Halmahera**, Indonesia 🏝
193 S 11 **Halmahera Sea**, Indonesia 🌊
135 E 24 **Halmstad**, Sweden
127 X 9 **Halstead**, United Kingdom
133 F 15 **Halsteren**, Netherlands
127 N 15 **Halwell**, United Kingdom
190 L 11 **Ham Yên**, Vietnam
199 C 19 **Hamada**, Japan
176 G 6 **Hamadān**, Iran ▣
176 G 6 **Hamadān**, Iran
211 R 12 **Hamādat Murzuq**, Libya ⛰
210 J 9 **Hamaguir**, Algeria
172 I 4 **Ḩamāh**, Syria
199 I 18 **Hamamatsu**, Japan
135 D 18 **Hamar**, Norway
199 F 17 **Hamasaka**, Japan
198 J 3 **Hamatonbetsu**, Japan
181 G 26 **Hambantota**, Sri Lanka
136 H 10 **Hamburg**, Germany
58 C 9 **Hamburg**, New York, U.S.A.
67 Q 15 **Hamburg**, Iowa, U.S.A.
175 O 10 **Ḩamḑah**, Saudi Arabia
174 M 9 **Ḩamdānah**, Saudi Arabia
135 L 18 **Hämeenlinna**, Finland
137 G 14 **Hameln**, Germany
230 F 6 **Hamersley Range**, Western Australia, Australia ⛰
187 L 16 **Hamgyŏng-sanmaek**, North Korea ⛰
187 L 16 **Hamhŭng**, North Korea
184 M 5 **Hami**, China
170 F 9 **Hamidye**, Turkey
231 R 13 **Hamilton**, Victoria, Australia
232 K 10 **Hamilton**, New Zealand
42 A 7 **Hamilton**, Bermuda 🏛
124 H 13 **Hamilton**, United Kingdom
63 O 2 **Hamilton**, Alabama, U.S.A.
65 D 18 **Hamilton**, Illinois, U.S.A.

□ Country ▣ Internal administrative region: State/Province/Territory/Dependent territory 🏛 Capital city ⛰ Mountain range/Undersea ridge ▲ Mountain peak/Volcano/Seamount ◇ Geographic feature ▶ Headland/Point/Cape/Peninsula ◓ Desert 🏝 Island/Island group ⁙ Antarctic base ◎ Ocean 🌊 Sea ≈ Bay/Gulf/Channel/Strait 💧 Lake ⚑ Salt pan/Dry/Intermittent lake ∿ River

▪ Country ◻ Internal administrative region: State/Province/Territory/Dependent territory ♦ Capital city ▲ Mountain range/ Undersea ridge ▲ Mountain peak/ Volcano/Seamount ◇ Geographic feature ▶ Headland/Point/ Cape/Peninsula ▦ Desert ± Island/Island group ⊠ Antarctic base ◎ Ocean ◢ Sea ≈ Bay/Gulf/Channel/Strait ━ Lake ↙ Salt pan/Dry/ Intermittent lake ↘ River

293

Henry – Hoshiarpur

65 F 17 Henry, Illinois, U.S.A.
69 P 10 Henryetta, Oklahoma, U.S.A.
218 H 9 Hentiesbaai, Namibia
185 S 3 Hentiy, Mongolia
191 D 15 Henzada, Myanmar
189 U 11 Heping, China
76 J 10 Heppner, Oregon, U.S.A.
189 Q 13 Hepu, China
177 P 7 Herāt, Afghanistan
177 P 7 Herāt, Afghanistan
213 H 15 Herbagat, Sudan
137 H 23 Herbrechtingen, Germany
145 I 16 Herceg-Novi, Serbia and Montenegro
134 C 10 Herðubreið, Iceland
91 Q 12 Heredia, Costa Rica
127 P 9 Hereford, United Kingdom
70 J 3 Hereford, Texas, U.S.A.
232 I 5 Herekino, New Zealand
131 O 8 Herencia, Spain
133 H 17 Herentals, Belgium
137 F 14 Herford, Germany
69 O 4 Herington, Kansas, U.S.A.
138 H 6 Herisau, Switzerland
124 K 3 Herma Ness, United Kingdom
139 R 9 Hermagor, Austria
89 P 6 Hermanas, Mexico
69 W 4 Hermann, Missouri, U.S.A.
231 N 7 Hermannsburg, Northern Territory, Australia
218 K 15 Hermanus, Republic of South Africa
76 J 9 Hermiston, Oregon, U.S.A.
234 C 2 Hermit Islands, Papua New Guinea
88 I 4 Hermosillo, Mexico
62 M 1 Hernando, Mississippi, U.S.A.
137 D 15 Herne, Germany
127 Z 11 Herne Bay, United Kingdom
135 B 24 Herning, Denmark
159 S 11 Herodotus Abyssal Plain, Mediterranean Sea
159 V 10 Herodotus Basin, Mediterranean Sea
159 R 11 Herodotus Rise, Mediterranean Sea
159 P 12 Herodotus Trough, Mediterranean Sea
112 C 9 Herradura, Argentina
137 F 23 Herrenberg, Germany
131 N 2 Herrera de Pisuerga, Spain
130 M 9 Herrera del Duque, Spain
82 A 8 Herschel Island, Yukon Territory, Canada
127 V 9 Hertford, United Kingdom
133 K 20 Herve, Belgium
231 W 7 Hervey Bay, Queensland, Australia
231 W 8 Hervey Bay, Queensland, Australia
137 H 15 Herzberg, Germany
137 M 15 Herzberg, Germany
172 F 9 Herzliyya, Israel
129 P 2 Hesdin, France
136 D 11 Hesel, Germany
189 Q 12 Heshan, China
41 P 6 Hess Tablemount, Pacific Ocean
137 G 18 Hessen, Germany
127 O 4 Heswall, United Kingdom
183 P 10 Hetauda, Nepal
66 H 6 Hettinger, North Dakota, U.S.A.
143 K 22 Heves, Hungary
188 L 8 Hexi, China
189 O 5 Hexi, China
189 S 11 Hexian, China
189 X 5 Hexian, China
127 P 1 Heysham, United Kingdom
189 U 12 Heyuan, China
189 U 3 Heze, China
189 N 9 Hezhang, China
185 P 9 Hezuo, China
63 Y 13 Hialeah, Florida, U.S.A.
69 Q 2 Hiawatha, Kansas, U.S.A.
67 T 4 Hibbing, Minnesota, U.S.A.
60 B 7 Hickman, Kentucky, U.S.A.
61 N 9 Hickory, North Carolina, U.S.A.
90 K 1 Hicks Cay, Belize
61 O 5 Hico, West Virginia, U.S.A.
71 P 7 Hico, Texas, U.S.A.
198 K 6 Hidaka, Japan
198 K 6 Hidaka-sanmyaku, Japan
89 Q 11 Hidalgo, Mexico
88 M 6 Hidalgo del Parral, Mexico
136 L 7 Hiddensee, Germany
139 U 6 Hieflau, Austria
235 P 13 Hienghène, New Caledonia
199 D 19 Higashi-Hiroshima, Japan
199 G 18 Higashi-ōsaka, Japan
199 A 21 Higashi-suidō, Japan
64 K 12 Higgins Lake, Michigan, U.S.A.
210 H 8 High Atlas, Morocco
64 J 10 High Island, Michigan, U.S.A.
71 U 10 High Island, Texas, U.S.A.
83 H 15 High Level, Alberta, Canada
196 F 10 High Peak, Philippines
70 K 1 High Plains, Texas, U.S.A.
58 J 11 High Point, New Jersey, U.S.A.
61 P 9 High Point, North Carolina, U.S.A.
63 V 8 High Springs, Florida, U.S.A.
126 M 13 High Willhays, United Kingdom
127 U 10 High Wycombe, United Kingdom
127 T 11 Highclere, United Kingdom
65 H 15 Highland Park, Illinois, U.S.A.
60 K 10 Highlands, North Carolina, U.S.A.
66 L 9 Highmore, South Dakota, U.S.A.
213 M 23 Hiiraan, Somalia
148 D 6 Hiiumaa, Estonia
174 K 3 Hijaz, Saudi Arabia
199 H 17 Hikone, Japan
232 J 6 Hikurangi, New Zealand
232 O 10 Hikurangi, New Zealand
137 I 18 Hildburghausen, Germany
137 H 14 Hildesheim, Germany
183 T 11 Hili, Bangladesh
90 K 2 Hill Bank, Belize
67 R 5 Hill City, Minnesota, U.S.A.
68 J 3 Hill City, Kansas, U.S.A.
72 L 11 Hill City, Idaho, U.S.A.
241 Q 12 Hillary Coast, Antarctica
132 G 11 Hillegom, Netherlands
135 D 25 Hillerød, Denmark
58 M 8 Hillsboro, New Hampshire, U.S.A.
64 E 13 Hillsboro, Wisconsin, U.S.A.
65 F 20 Hillsboro, Illinois, U.S.A.
65 L 20 Hillsboro, Ohio, U.S.A.
71 Q 7 Hillsboro, Texas, U.S.A.
93 Y 12 Hillsborough, Grenada
231 S 11 Hillston, New South Wales, Australia
61 P 7 Hillsville, Virginia, U.S.A.
78 E 8 Hilo, Hawaii, U.S.A.
197 L 17 Hilongos, Philippines
61 O 15 Hilton Head Island, South Carolina, U.S.A.
171 O 12 Hilvan, Turkey
132 I 11 Hilversum, Netherlands
182 J 5 Himachal Pradesh, India
182 I 4 Himalaya, India
145 K 21 Himarë, Albania
233 K 14 Himatangi, New Zealand
181 C 14 Himatnagar, India
199 F 18 Himeji, Japan
199 H 15 Himi, Japan
172 I 5 Ḩimş, Syria
197 N 20 Hinatuan, Philippines
151 N 9 Hîncești, Moldova
93 P 7 Hinche, Haiti
231 T 4 Hinchinbrook Island, Queensland, Australia
79 S 10 Hinchinbrook Island, Alaska, U.S.A.
127 S 7 Hinckley, United Kingdom
67 S 6 Hinckley, Minnesota, U.S.A.
216 F 10 Hinda, Congo
180 E 12 Hindaun, India
127 U 12 Hindhead, United Kingdom
233 G 21 Hinds, New Zealand
177 U 6 Hindu Kush, Afghanistan
181 E 20 Hindupur, India
181 F 16 Hinganghat, India
171 R 10 Hinis, Turkey
197 I 18 Hinobaan, Philippines
139 N 7 Hintertux, Austria
199 A 21 Hirado, Japan
181 H 15 Hirakud Reservoir, India
199 O 26 Hirara, Japan
181 E 20 Hiriyur, India
198 L 6 Hiroo, Japan
198 J 9 Hirosaki, Japan
199 D 19 Hiroshima, Japan
129 S 2 Hirson, France
182 H 8 Hisar, India
170 G 7 Hisarönü, Turkey
93 O 6 Hispaniola, Dominican Republic
172 I 5 Ḩisyah, Syria
173 R 6 Hīt, Iraq
199 C 21 Hita, Japan
199 L 14 Hitachi, Japan
181 L 20 Hitaddu, Maldives
127 V 9 Hitchin, United Kingdom
199 C 23 Hitoyoshi, Japan
135 C 15 Hitra, Norway
235 P 9 Hiu, Vanuatu
199 J 14 Hiuchiga-take, Japan
199 F 20 Hiwasa, Japan
82 I 13 Hjalmar Lake, Northwest Territories, Canada
135 G 21 Hjälmaren, Sweden
135 C 23 Hjørring, Denmark
190 F 5 Hkakabo Razi, Myanmar
219 P 11 Hlatikulu, Swaziland
151 S 5 Hlobyne, Ukraine
143 H 21 Hlohovec, Slovakia
151 T 1 Hlukhiv, Ukraine
149 K 19 Hlusk, Belarus
149 J 15 Hlybokaye, Belarus
191 M 22 Hô Chi Minh, Vietnam
190 K 12 Hô Sông Đa, Vietnam
190 K 11 Hô Thac Ba, Vietnam
190 L 12 Hoa Binh, Vietnam
190 K 11 Hoang Liên Son, Vietnam
231 T 15 Hobart, Tasmania, Australia
68 K 11 Hobart, Oklahoma, U.S.A.
75 U 13 Hobbs, New Mexico, U.S.A.
240 L 11 Hobbs Coast, Antarctica
63 Y 11 Hobe Sound, Florida, U.S.A.
135 C 24 Hobro, Denmark
213 N 22 Hobyo, Somalia
139 R 8 Hochalmspitze, Austria
138 F 7 Hochdorf, Switzerland
218 I 9 Hochfeld, Namibia
139 T 6 Hochreichart, Austria
139 U 5 Hochschwab, Austria
140 F 4 Hochwilde, Austria/Italy
199 H 15 Hodaka-dake, Japan
60 G 6 Hodgenville, Kentucky, U.S.A.
214 I 7 Hodh Ech Chargui, Mauritania
214 I 7 Hodh El Gharbi, Mauritania
143 K 25 Hódmezővásárhely, Hungary
143 G 20 Hodonín, Czech Republic
185 O 3 Hödrögö, Mongolia
132 F 13 Hoek van Holland, Netherlands
187 M 19 Hoengsŏng, South Korea
133 K 18 Hoensbroek, Netherlands
187 N 14 Hoeryŏng, North Korea
187 L 18 Hoeyang, North Korea
137 K 18 Hof, Germany
134 D 11 Höfn, Iceland
134 C 11 Hofsjökull, Iceland
134 B 10 Hofsós, Iceland
199 C 20 Hōfu, Japan
61 W 6 Hog Island, Virginia, U.S.A.
66 G 13 Hogback Mountain, Nebraska, U.S.A.
211 O 14 Hoggar, Algeria
135 G 23 Högsby, Sweden
184 M 8 Hoh Sai Hu, China
139 O 7 Hohe Tauern, Austria
139 Y 2 Hohenau an der March, Austria
139 S 6 Hoher Dachstein, Austria
151 Q 3 Hoholiv, Ukraine
191 O 17 Hôi An, Vietnam
190 L 13 Hôi Xuân, Vietnam
217 R 7 Hoima, Uganda
68 L 5 Hoisington, Kansas, U.S.A.
183 W 11 Hojai, India
232 H 6 Hokianga Harbour, New Zealand
233 F 19 Hokitika, New Zealand
198 K 5 Hokkaidō, Japan
199 L 15 Hokota, Japan
171 T 9 Hoktemberyan, Armenia
217 X 9 Hola, Kenya
151 S 10 Hola Prystan, Ukraine
181 D 20 Holalkere, India
107 K 18 Holanda, Bolivia
127 W 6 Holbeach, United Kingdom
73 O 13 Holbrook, Idaho, U.S.A.
74 L 10 Holbrook, Arizona, U.S.A.
74 J 5 Holden, Utah, U.S.A.
127 V 2 Holderness, United Kingdom
66 L 15 Holdrege, Nebraska, U.S.A.
92 L 6 Holguín, Cuba
143 G 20 Holíč, Slovakia
135 E 18 Höljes, Sweden
139 X 2 Hollabrunn, Austria
65 I 14 Holland, Michigan, U.S.A.
133 G 14 Hollands Diep, Netherlands
133 K 24 Hollange, Belgium
58 D 13 Hollidaysburg, Pennsylvania, U.S.A.
68 J 11 Hollis, Oklahoma, U.S.A.
77 G 21 Hollister, California, U.S.A.
132 J 5 Hollum, Netherlands
61 T 11 Holly Ridge, North Carolina, U.S.A.
62 L 1 Holly Springs, Mississippi, U.S.A.
63 Y 13 Hollywood, Florida, U.S.A.
134 B 10 Hólmavík, Iceland
127 T 2 Holme-upon-Spalding-Moor, United Kingdom
127 R 3 Holmfirth, United Kingdom
234 E 6 Holnicote Bay, Papua New Guinea
150 J 2 Holoby, Ukraine
172 F 9 Ḩolon, Israel
218 J 12 Holoog, Namibia
63 X 10 Holopaw, Florida, U.S.A.
135 B 24 Holstebro, Denmark
67 Q 12 Holstein, Iowa, U.S.A.
126 L 13 Holsworthy, United Kingdom
127 Y 5 Holt, United Kingdom
132 L 11 Holten, Netherlands
151 V 6 Holubivka, Ukraine
132 K 6 Holwerd, Netherlands
79 N 8 Holy Cross, Alaska, U.S.A.
126 L 4 Holy Island, United Kingdom
126 L 4 Holyhead, United Kingdom
126 L 4 Holyhead Bay, United Kingdom
58 L 10 Holyoke, Massachusetts, U.S.A.
75 U 3 Holyoke, Colorado, U.S.A.
127 O 4 Holywell, United Kingdom
137 J 25 Holzkirchen, Germany
137 G 15 Holzminden, Germany
217 T 8 Homa Bay, Kenya
190 C 8 Homalin, Myanmar
137 D 21 Homburg, Germany
85 R 1 Home Bay, Nunavut, Canada
39 Z 2 Home Island, Cocos Islands
39 Z 2 Home Island Settlement, Cocos Islands
149 L 20 Homel'skaya Voblasts', Belarus
62 I 4 Homer, Louisiana, U.S.A.
79 Q 10 Homer, Alaska, U.S.A.
63 U 6 Homerville, Georgia, U.S.A.
63 Y 14 Homestead, Florida, U.S.A.
134 F 12 Hommelstø, Norway
181 E 18 Homnabad, India
219 R 10 Homoine, Mozambique
197 M 17 Homonhon, Philippines
149 N 20 Homyel', Belarus
191 L 24 Hon Khoai, Vietnam
191 L 23 Hon Rai, Vietnam
104 I 6 Honda, Colombia
197 D 18 Honda Bay, Philippines
199 B 22 Hondo, Japan
71 N 11 Hondo, Texas, U.S.A.
75 R 12 Hondo, New Mexico, U.S.A.
90 J 1 Hondo, Belize
90 L 5 Honduras, North America
60 L 12 Honea Path, South Carolina, U.S.A.
135 D 19 Hønefoss, Norway
77 I 16 Honey Lake, California, U.S.A.
190 N 12 Hông Gai, Vietnam
189 U 13 Hong Kong, China
189 U 13 Hong Kong, China
189 U 6 Hong'an, China
187 M 18 Hongch'ŏn, South Korea
189 V 12 Honghai Wan, China
189 T 7 Honghu, China
189 R 9 Hongjiang, China
185 N 6 Hongliuyuan, China
185 S 4 Hongor, Mongolia
189 P 11 Hongshui He, China
189 S 2 Hongtong, China
199 H 19 Hongū, Japan
186 M 8 Hongxing, China
188 M 7 Hongya, China
188 M 5 Hongyuan, China
189 X 4 Hongze, China
189 X 4 Hongze Hu, China
234 L 6 Honiara, Solomon Islands
127 O 13 Honiton, United Kingdom
198 J 11 Honjō, Japan
134 K 5 Honningsvåg, Norway
78 E 8 Honokaa, Hawaii, U.S.A.
78 D 9 Honokohau, Hawaii, U.S.A.
78 C 7 Honolulu, Hawaii, U.S.A.
199 H 17 Honshū, Japan
132 G 11 Hoofddorp, Netherlands
136 F 7 Hooge, Germany
132 M 8 Hoogersmilde, Netherlands
132 M 9 Hoogeveen, Netherlands
132 I 9 Hoogkarspel, Netherlands
127 T 11 Hook, United Kingdom
125 E 20 Hook Head, Republic of Ireland
68 H 7 Hooker, Oklahoma, U.S.A.
79 W 10 Hoonah, Alaska, U.S.A.
78 L 8 Hooper Bay, Alaska, U.S.A.
132 I 9 Hoorn, Netherlands
65 K 19 Hoosier Hill, Indiana, U.S.A.
185 P 4 Höövör, Mongolia
171 Q 7 Hopa, Turkey
127 P 5 Hope, United Kingdom
69 T 13 Hope, Arkansas, U.S.A.
79 R 9 Hope, Alaska, U.S.A.
83 G 22 Hope, British Columbia, Canada
62 M 8 Hopedale, Louisiana, U.S.A.
85 V 7 Hopedale, Newfoundland and Labrador, Canada
89 Y 11 Hopelchén, Mexico
230 I 12 Hopetoun, Western Australia, Australia
231 R 12 Hopetoun, Victoria, Australia
218 M 13 Hopetown, Republic of South Africa
190 E 8 Hopin, Myanmar
60 E 7 Hopkinsville, Kentucky, U.S.A.
190 E 12 Hopong, Myanmar
76 F 7 Hoquiam, Washington, U.S.A.
150 J 7 Hora Hoverla, Ukraine
171 R 9 Horasan, Turkey
131 N 8 Horcajo de los Montes, Spain
185 O 3 Horgo, Mongolia
151 N 12 Horia, Romania
187 A 16 Horinger, China
41 P 10 Horizon Deep, Pacific Ocean
149 N 16 Horki, Belarus
241 N 8 Horlick Mountains, Antarctica
151 X 6 Horlivka, Ukraine
177 O 11 Hormak, Iran
176 L 13 Hormoz, Iran
176 L 12 Hormozgān, Iran
139 W 2 Horn, Austria
231 R 1 Horn Island, Queensland, Australia
63 N 8 Horn Island, Mississippi, U.S.A.
82 F 13 Horn Mountains, Northwest Territories, Canada
134 H 12 Hornavan, Sweden
77 G 14 Hornbrook, California, U.S.A.
127 V 4 Horncastle, United Kingdom
91 T 14 Hornconcitos, Panama
58 E 9 Hornell, New York, U.S.A.
85 N 11 Hornepayne, Ontario, Canada
127 V 2 Hornsea, United Kingdom
150 K 6 Horodenka, Ukraine
151 Q 1 Horodnya, Ukraine
151 Q 5 Horodyshche, Ukraine
198 J 3 Horonobe, Japan
198 K 6 Horoshiri-dake, Japan
232 K 10 Horotiu, New Zealand
185 W 4 Horqin Zouyi Zhongqi, China
187 H 14 Horqin Zuoyi Houqi, China
186 I 13 Horqin Zuoyi Zhongqi, China
181 L 17 Horsburgh Atoll, Maldives
39 Y 1 Horsburgh Island, Cocos Islands
135 C 25 Horsens, Denmark
72 K 10 Horseshoe Bend, Idaho, U.S.A.
42 J 9 Horseshoe Seamounts, Atlantic Ocean
231 R 13 Horsham, Victoria, Australia
127 V 12 Horsham, United Kingdom
133 L 16 Horst, Netherlands
42 N 1 Horta, Azores
69 Q 2 Horton, Kansas, U.S.A.
82 E 8 Horton, Northwest Territories, Canada
138 F 8 Horw, Switzerland
127 Q 3 Horwich, United Kingdom
150 L 4 Horyn, Ukraine
213 I 21 Hosa'ina, Ethiopia
181 D 21 Hosdrug, India
215 U 12 Hoséré Vokre, Cameroon
177 R 14 Hoshab, Pakistan
181 E 15 Hoshangabad, India
182 I 6 Hoshiarpur, India

Country · Internal administrative region: State/Province/Territory/Dependent territory · Capital city · Mountain range/Undersea ridge · Mountain peak/Volcano/Seamount · Geographic feature · Headland/Point/Cape/Peninsula · Desert · Island/Island group · Antarctic base · Ocean · Sea · Bay/Gulf/Channel/Strait · Lake · Salt pan/Dry/Intermittent lake · Riv

185	P 3	**Höshööt**, Mongolia
133	L 23	**Hosingen**, Luxembourg
234	G 4	**Hoskins**, Papua New Guinea
181	D 19	**Hospet**, India
66	G 10	**Hot Springs**, South Dakota, U.S.A.
69	U 12	**Hot Springs**, Arkansas, U.S.A.
135	F 14	**Hotagen**, Sweden 💧
184	H 7	**Hotan**, China
135	G 14	**Hoting**, Sweden
43	H 15	**Hotspur Seamount**, Atlantic Ocean ▲
82	G 11	**Hottah Lake**, Northwest Territories, Canada 💧
235	P 13	**Houaïlu**, New Caledonia
133	K 23	**Houffalize**, Belgium
194	B 14	**Hougang**, Singapore
64	G 8	**Houghton**, Michigan, U.S.A.
64	K 12	**Houghton Lake**, Michigan, U.S.A. 💧
232	I 4	**Houhora**, New Zealand
59	S 2	**Houlton**, Maine, U.S.A.
189	S 3	**Houma**, China
62	K 8	**Houma**, Louisiana, U.S.A.
211	R 7	**Houmt Souk**, Tunisia
232	N 10	**Houpoto**, New Zealand
63	N 2	**Houston**, Mississippi, U.S.A.
69	V 7	**Houston**, Missouri, U.S.A.
71	T 10	**Houston**, Texas, U.S.A.
83	E 18	**Houston**, British Columbia, Canada
133	J 18	**Houthalen**, Belgium
230	E 9	**Houtman Abrolhos**, Western Australia, Australia 🏝
184	M 4	**Hovd**, Mongolia ▣
184	M 3	**Hovd**, Mongolia
185	P 5	**Hovd**, Mongolia
127	V 13	**Hove**, United Kingdom
127	Z 6	**Hoveton**, United Kingdom
185	O 2	**Hövsgöl**, Mongolia ▣
185	P 2	**Hövsgöl Nuur**, Mongolia 💧
69	P 6	**Howard**, Kansas, U.S.A.
127	T 2	**Howden**, United Kingdom
5	L 14	**Howell**, Michigan, U.S.A.
6	I 9	**Howes**, South Dakota, U.S.A.
32	K 8	**Howick**, New Zealand
1	P 7	**Howland Island**, U.S.A. ▣
3	I 21	**Howser**, British Columbia, Canada
37	G 15	**Höxter**, Germany
24	H 7	**Hoy**, United Kingdom 🏝
37	N 15	**Hoyerswerda**, Germany
30	J 7	**Hoyos**, Spain
35	O 15	**Höytiäinen**, Finland 💧
43	E 17	**Hradec Králové**, Czech Republic
51	S 5	**Hradyz'k**, Ukraine
49	K 18	**Hradzyanka**, Belarus
44	H 12	**Hrasnica**, Bosnia and Herzegovina
71	U 8	**Hrazdan**, Armenia
51	R 4	**Hrebinka**, Ukraine
51	P 4	**Hrebinky**, Ukraine
49	E 18	**Hrodna**, Belarus
49	G 18	**Hrodzyenskaya Voblasts'**, Belarus ▣
43	O 15	**Hrubieszów**, Poland
90	F 10	**Hsenwi**, Myanmar
90	E 13	**Hsi-hseng**, Myanmar
39	Z 11	**Hsinch'eng**, Taiwan
39	Z 10	**Hsinchu**, Taiwan
91	H 20	**Hua Hin**, Thailand
39	R 3	**Hua Shan**, China ▲
39	P 2	**Huachi**, China
7	C 16	**Huacho**, Peru
6	N 9	**Huachuan**, China
7	C 14	**Huacrachuco**, Peru
7	C 15	**Huade**, China
7	K 14	**Huadian**, China
7	C 16	**Huai'an**, China
9	V 4	**Huaibei**, China
9	V 5	**Huaibin**, China
9	R 9	**Huaihua**, China
9	S 12	**Huaiji**, China
7	D 16	**Huailai**, China
9	W 5	**Huainan**, China
187	B 17	**Huairen**, China
189	U 4	**Huaiyang**, China
189	X 4	**Huaiyin**, China
189	V 4	**Huaiyuan**, China
89	S 13	**Huajuápan de León**, Mexico
74	H 10	**Hualapai Peak**, Arizona, U.S.A. ▲
189	Z 11	**Hualien**, Taiwan
107	D 14	**Huallaga**, Peru ⌇
106	C 13	**Huamachuco**, Peru
218	H 4	**Huambo**, Angola
218	G 4	**Huambo**, Angola ▣
186	N 10	**Huanan**, China
107	E 17	**Huancavelica**, Peru
107	E 17	**Huancavelica**, Peru ▣
107	E 16	**Huancayo**, Peru
189	W 7	**Huang Shan**, China ⛰
189	U 5	**Huangchuan**, China
186	E 13	**Huanggangliang**, China ▲
187	E 18	**Huanghua**, China
189	Q 2	**Huangling**, China
189	Q 15	**Huangliu**, China
186	L 13	**Huangnihe**, China
189	X 7	**Huangshan**, China
189	U 7	**Huangshi**, China
189	O 2	**Huangtu Gaoyuan**, China ◇
113	B 18	**Huanguelén**, Argentina
187	G 19	**Huangxian**, China
189	Y 7	**Huangyan**, China
187	K 15	**Huanren**, China
107	E 17	**Huanta**, Peru
107	D 15	**Huánuco**, Peru
107	D 15	**Huánuco**, Peru ▣
107	J 20	**Huanuni**, Bolivia
189	P 2	**Huanxian**, China
107	C 15	**Huaráz**, Peru
107	C 15	**Huari**, Peru
107	C 15	**Huarmey**, Peru
189	T 7	**Huarong**, China
110	F 9	**Huasco**, Chile
185	N 8	**Huashixia**, China
88	J 6	**Huatabampo**, Mexico
187	H 16	**Huatong**, China
189	U 3	**Huaxian**, China
107	C 14	**Huaylas**, Peru
189	Q 8	**Huayuan**, China
189	R 13	**Huazhou**, China
71	Q 7	**Hubbard**, Texas, U.S.A.
71	N 6	**Hubbard Creek Lake**, Texas, U.S.A. 💧
84	K 5	**Hubbart Point**, Manitoba, Canada ▶
189	T 6	**Hubei**, China ▣
181	D 19	**Hubli**, India
187	L 15	**Huch'ang**, North Korea
125	J 17	**Huddersfield**, United Kingdom
127	S 3	**Huddersfield**, United Kingdom
186	H 7	**Huder**, China
135	H 17	**Hudiksvall**, Sweden
58	K 9	**Hudson**, New York, U.S.A. ⌇
65	K 16	**Hudson**, Michigan, U.S.A.
85	N 5	**Hudson Bay**, Québec, Canada ≈
58	K 8	**Hudson Falls**, New York, U.S.A.
85	Q 4	**Hudson Strait**, Nunavut, Canada ≈
191	N 16	**Huê**, Vietnam
70	E 7	**Hueco Mountains**, Texas, U.S.A. ⛰
150	H 9	**Huedin**, Romania
90	G 5	**Huehuetenango**, Guatemala
89	R 12	**Huejotzingo**, Mexico
89	N 9	**Huejuqilla**, Mexico
89	R 10	**Huejutla**, Mexico
131	O 11	**Huelma**, Spain
130	J 12	**Huelva**, Spain
110	F 11	**Huentelauquén**, Chile
131	Q 12	**Huércal-Overa**, Spain
131	T 3	**Huesca**, Spain
131	Q 11	**Huéscar**, Spain
89	P 12	**Huétamo**, Mexico
231	S 5	**Hughenden**, Queensland, Australia
183	S 13	**Hugli-Chunchura**, India
69	Q 13	**Hugo**, Oklahoma, U.S.A.
68	H 7	**Hugoton**, Kansas, U.S.A.
187	A 16	**Huhhot**, China
189	X 10	**Hui'an**, China
189	P 1	**Hui'anpu**, China
232	M 12	**Huiarau Range**, New Zealand ⛰
187	K 16	**Huich'ŏn**, North Korea
188	L 9	**Huidong**, China
186	G 9	**Huihe**, China
104	H 8	**Huila**, Colombia ▣
218	G 5	**Huíla**, Angola ▣
218	H 6	**Huíla Plateau**, Angola ◇
189	V 12	**Huilai**, China
188	L 9	**Huili**, China
187	E 19	**Huimin**, China
110	I 5	**Huinahuaca**, Argentina
187	K 14	**Huinan**, China
110	J 12	**Huinca Renancó**, Argentina
189	O 10	**Huishui**, China
135	K 18	**Huittinen**, Finland
189	O 4	**Huixian**, China
189	T 2	**Huixian**, China
89	W 15	**Huixtla**, Mexico
188	M 10	**Huize**, China
132	I 11	**Huizen**, Netherlands
189	U 12	**Huizhou**, China
185	Q 4	**Hujirt**, Mongolia
190	D 6	**Hukawng Valley**, Myanmar ◇
218	K 10	**Hukuntsi**, Botswana
186	K 11	**Hulan**, China
174	M 5	**Ḩulayfah**, Saudi Arabia
186	O 10	**Hulin**, China
181	D 21	**Huliyar**, India
133	E 17	**Hulst**, Netherlands
187	H 16	**Huludao**, China
186	F 8	**Hulun Nur**, China 💧
151	W 7	**Hulyaypole**, Ukraine
186	K 5	**Huma**, China
93	U 8	**Humacao**, Puerto Rico
108	E 12	**Humaitá**, Brazil
127	V 3	**Humber**, United Kingdom ⌇
71	T 9	**Humble**, Texas, U.S.A.
77	J 16	**Humbold**, Nevada, U.S.A.
56	H 8	**Humboldt**, Nevada, U.S.A. ⌇
60	B 9	**Humboldt**, Tennessee, U.S.A.
67	R 11	**Humboldt**, Iowa, U.S.A.
113	B 17	**Humeda**, Argentina ◇
143	M 19	**Humenné**, Slovakia
132	L 13	**Hummelo**, Netherlands
218	F 6	**Humpata**, Angola
67	N 13	**Humphrey**, Nebraska, U.S.A.
74	J 10	**Humphreys Peak**, Arizona, U.S.A. ▲
230	M 1	**Humpty Doo**, Northern Territory, Australia
90	L 5	**Humuya**, Honduras ⌇
211	U 9	**Hūn**, Libya
134	B 10	**Húnaflói**, Iceland ≈
189	T 9	**Hunan**, China ▣
186	N 13	**Hunchun**, China
150	G 10	**Hunedoara**, Romania
137	G 18	**Hünfeld**, Germany
143	H 24	**Hungary**, Europe □
231	S 9	**Hungerford**, Queensland, Australia
127	S 11	**Hungerford**, United Kingdom
187	L 17	**Hŭngnam**, North Korea
127	U 1	**Hunmanby**, United Kingdom
137	C 20	**Hunsrück**, Germany ⛰
127	X 5	**Hunstanton**, United Kingdom
235	T 14	**Hunter**, Oceania 🏝
231	S 14	**Hunter Island**, Tasmania, Australia 🏝
65	I 21	**Huntingburg**, Indiana, U.S.A.
127	V 7	**Huntingdon**, United Kingdom
60	C 8	**Huntingdon**, Tennessee, U.S.A.
60	M 4	**Huntington**, West Virginia, U.S.A.
65	J 17	**Huntington**, Indiana, U.S.A.
77	J 25	**Huntington Beach**, California, U.S.A.
124	I 10	**Huntly**, United Kingdom
63	P 1	**Huntsville**, Alabama, U.S.A.
69	T 9	**Huntsville**, Arkansas, U.S.A.
71	S 9	**Huntsville**, Texas, U.S.A.
86	F 10	**Huntsville**, Ontario, Canada
187	C 17	**Hunyuan**, China
186	J 7	**Huolongmen**, China
235	N 12	**Huon**, New Caledonia 🏝
191	M 15	**Huong Khê**, Vietnam
231	S 15	**Huonville**, Tasmania, Australia
189	V 5	**Huoqiu**, China
189	V 6	**Huoshan**, China
189	S 2	**Huozhou**, China
183	Y 8	**Hupu**, India
143	H 22	**Hurbanovo**, Slovakia
213	O 19	**Hurdiyo**, Somalia
187	H 14	**Hure**, China
212	F 10	**Hurghada**, Egypt
66	M 9	**Huron**, South Dakota, U.S.A.
127	X 12	**Hurst Green**, United Kingdom
63	R 5	**Hurtsboro**, Alabama, U.S.A.
134	C 10	**Húsavík**, Iceland
173	U 7	**Ḩusayn al Ghafūs**, Iraq
127	T 7	**Husbands Bosworth**, United Kingdom
150	M 9	**Huşi**, Romania
135	F 22	**Huskvarna**, Sweden
79	O 6	**Huslia**, Alaska, U.S.A.
175	Q 12	**Ḩusn Al 'Abr**, Yemen
136	F 8	**Husum**, Germany
185	P 3	**Hutag**, Mongolia
67	R 8	**Hutchinson**, Minnesota, U.S.A.
68	M 5	**Hutchinson**, Kansas, U.S.A.
175	P 12	**Ḩūth**, Yemen
234	I 4	**Hutjena**, Papua New Guinea
138	E 7	**Huttwil**, Switzerland
189	Q 4	**Huxian**, China
133	I 21	**Huy**, Belgium
184	L 2	**Huyten Orgil**, Mongolia ▲
186	I 5	**Huzhong**, China
189	Y 6	**Huzhou**, China
134	C 11	**Hvannadalshnúkur**, Iceland ▲
159	N 5	**Hvar**, Mediterranean Sea 🏝
151	T 12	**Hvardiys'ke**, Ukraine
134	B 11	**Hveragerði**, Iceland
134	B 11	**Hvíta**, Iceland ⌇
219	N 7	**Hwange**, Zimbabwe
66	I 13	**Hyannis**, Nebraska, U.S.A.
185	N 3	**Hyargus Nuur**, Mongolia 💧
230	H 11	**Hyden**, Western Australia, Australia
177	U 14	**Hyderabad**, Pakistan
181	F 18	**Hyderabad**, India
129	V 15	**Hyères**, France
187	M 15	**Hyesan**, North Korea
73	V 6	**Hysham**, Montana, U.S.A.
127	Z 12	**Hythe**, United Kingdom
199	D 22	**Hyūga**, Japan

I

211	O 15	**I-n-Guezzam**, Algeria
109	M 15	**Iaçu**, Brazil
151	N 9	**Ialoveni**, Moldova
150	M 9	**Iaşi**, Romania
108	B 9	**Iauaretê**, Brazil
196	E 10	**Iba**, Philippines
215	P 12	**Ibadan**, Nigeria
104	I 7	**Ibagué**, Colombia
145	L 15	**Ibar**, Serbia and Montenegro ⌇
106	C 8	**Ibarra**, Ecuador
110	L 6	**Ibarreta**, Argentina
175	P 13	**Ibb**, Yemen
213	D 23	**Ibba**, Sudan
136	D 13	**Ibbenbüren**, Germany
106	E 12	**Iberia**, Peru
134	H 8	**Ibestad**, Norway
215	Q 11	**Ibeto**, Nigeria
215	S 12	**Ibi**, Nigeria
131	T 10	**Ibi**, Spain
112	O 5	**Ibiraçu**, Brazil
112	I 10	**Ibirama**, Brazil
131	W 9	**Ibiza**, Spain 🏝
109	L 14	**Ibotirama**, Brazil
175	Z 7	**Ibrā'**, Oman
175	X 7	**Ibrī**, Oman
196	H 2	**Ibuhos**, Philippines 🏝
107	D 18	**Ica**, Peru
107	D 18	**Ica**, Peru ▣
108	B 10	**Içá**, Brazil ⌇
108	C 9	**Içana**, Brazil
108	C 9	**Içana**, Brazil ⌇
134	C 10	**Iceland**, Europe □
42	I 6	**Iceland Basin**, Atlantic Ocean ◇
45	Q 14	**Icelandic Plateau**, Arctic Ocean ◇
181	D 19	**Ichalkaranji**, India
199	L 16	**Ichihara**, Japan
198	K 11	**Ichinoseki**, Japan
151	R 3	**Ichnya**, Ukraine
187	M 19	**Ich'ŏn**, South Korea
133	B 17	**Ichtegem**, Belgium
108	N 12	**Icó**, Brazil
42	M 11	**Icod de Los Vinos**, Canary Islands
79	N 3	**Icy Cape**, Alaska, U.S.A. ▶
67	Q 12	**Ida Grove**, Iowa, U.S.A.
213	O 22	**Idaan**, Somalia
69	R 13	**Idabel**, Oklahoma, U.S.A.
233	E 23	**Idaburn**, New Zealand
215	Q 13	**Idah**, Nigeria
72	L 10	**Idaho**, U.S.A. ▣
73	P 11	**Idaho Falls**, Idaho, U.S.A.
137	D 20	**Idar-Oberstein**, Germany
213	A 19	**Idd el Chanam**, Sudan
211	O 13	**Idelès**, Algeria
212	F 11	**Idfu**, Egypt
211	R 10	**Idhān Awbārī**, Libya ◇
211	S 12	**Idhān Murzūq**, Libya ◇
216	K 11	**Idiofa**, Democratic Republic of Congo
172	I 2	**Idlib**, Syria
199	N 24	**Ie-jima**, Japan 🏝
148	F 12	**Iecava**, Latvia
112	H 6	**Iepê**, Brazil
133	B 19	**Ieper**, Belgium
147	K 26	**Ierapetra**, Greece
150	I 9	**Iernut**, Romania
217	V 12	**Ifakara**, Tanzania
236	M 15	**Ifalik**, Federated States of Micronesia 🏝
219	Y 9	**Ifanadiana**, Madgascar
215	P 13	**Ife**, Nigeria
215	R 6	**Iferouâne**, Niger
211	N 12	**Ifetesene**, Algeria ▲
143	H 25	**Igal**, Hungary
217	T 7	**Iganga**, Uganda
112	K 4	**Igarapava**, Brazil
153	N 9	**Igarka**, Russian Federation
215	P 12	**Igboho**, Nigeria
171	T 9	**Iğdir**, Turkey
141	B 19	**Iglesias**, Italy
157	W 1	**Iglino**, Russian Federation
85	O 1	**Igloolik**, Nunavut, Canada
84	M 3	**Igluligaarjuk**, Nunavut, Canada
84	K 11	**Ignace**, Ontario, Canada
149	H 14	**Ignalina**, Lithuania
154	I 10	**Ignatovo**, Russian Federation
170	C 6	**Iğneada**, Turkey
170	C 6	**Iğneada Burnu**, Turkey ▶
181	N 22	**Ignoitijala**, India
147	A 16	**Igoumenitsa**, Greece
155	R 13	**Igra**, Russian Federation
152	K 9	**Igrim**, Russian Federation
112	I 9	**Iguaçu**, Brazil ⌇
112	F 9	**Iguaçu Falls**, Brazil ◇
89	R 13	**Iguala**, Mexico
112	K 8	**Iguape**, Brazil
112	F 7	**Iguatemi**, Brazil
108	N 12	**Iguatu**, Brazil
216	D 9	**Iguéla**, Gabon
217	T 10	**Igunga**, Tanzania
219	Z 5	**Iharana**, Madgascar
181	L 16	**Ihavandhippolhu Atoll**, Maldives 🏝
185	R 5	**Ihbulag**, Mongolia
199	N 24	**Iheya-jima**, Japan 🏝
215	R 13	**Ihiala**, Nigeria
219	X 9	**Ihosy**, Madgascar
185	Q 3	**Ihsuuj**, Mongolia
199	I 17	**Iida**, Japan
134	L 12	**Iijoki**, Finland ⌇
135	M 15	**Iisalmi**, Finland
199	B 21	**Iizuka**, Japan
215	P 13	**Ijebu-Ode**, Nigeria
171	U 8	**Ijevan**, Armenia
132	G 10	**IJmuiden**, Netherlands
132	L 10	**IJssel**, Netherlands ⌇
132	I 8	**IJsselmeer**, Netherlands ≈
112	G 11	**Ijuí**, Brazil
237	V 1	**Ijuw**, Nauru
133	B 17	**IJzer**, Belgium ⌇
82	E 6	**Ikaahuk**, Northwest Territories, Canada
233	G 18	**Ikamatua**, New Zealand
215	Q 12	**Ikare**, Nigeria
147	K 21	**Ikaria**, Greece 🏝
232	F 23	**Ikawai**, New Zealand
198	L 5	**Ikeda**, Japan
199	F 20	**Ikeda**, Japan
216	M 8	**Ikela**, Democratic Republic of Congo
146	G 9	**Ikhtiman**, Bulgaria
199	A 21	**Iki**, Japan 🏝
157	P 11	**Iki-Burul**, Russian Federation
199	A 21	**Iki-suidō**, Japan ≈
215	P 13	**Ikire**, Nigeria
215	S 13	**Ikom**, Nigeria
219	X 9	**Ikongo**, Madgascar
215	P 13	**Ikorodu**, Nigeria
187	L 20	**Iksan**, South Korea
215	P 12	**Ila**, Nigeria
196	H 7	**Ilagan**, Philippines
217	V 7	**Ilaisamis**, Kenya
176	F 7	**Īlām**, Iran ▣
176	F 7	**Īlām**, Iran
183	S 10	**Ilam**, Nepal
189	Z 10	**Ilan**, Taiwan
151	V 6	**Ilarionove**, Ukraine
142	J 10	**Iława**, Poland
127	P 12	**Ilchester**, United Kingdom
179	U 8	**Ile**, Kazakhstan ⌇
38	B 8	**Île Aride**, Seychelles 🏝
38	A 9	**Île au Cerf**, Seychelles 🏝
38	C 12	**Île aux Cerfs**, Mauritius 🏝
38	B 9	**Île aux Récifs**, Seychelles 🏝
38	D 7	**Île aux Sables**, Rodrigues Island 🏝
235	O 13	**Île Balabio**, New Caledonia 🏝
87	X 6	**Île Brion**, Québec, Canada 🏝
38	E 7	**Île Cocos**, Rodrigues Island 🏝
38	A 9	**Île Conception**, Seychelles 🏝
38	B 11	**Île d'Ambre**, Mauritius 🏝
87	V 4	**Île d'Anticosti**, Québec, Canada 🏝
129	P 5	**Île-de-France**, France ▣
211	R 7	**Île de Jarba**, Tunisia 🏝
158	K 11	**Île de Jerba**, Mediterranean Sea 🏝
93	N 7	**Île de la Gonâve**, Haiti 🏝
93	O 6	**Île de la Tortue**, Haiti 🏝
87	W 6	**Île de l'Est**, Québec, Canada 🏝
128	K 8	**Île de Noirmoutier**, France 🏝
129	V 15	**Île de Porquerolles**, France 🏝
128	K 9	**Île de Ré**, France 🏝
235	Q 14	**Île des Pins**, New Caledonia 🏝
128	L 9	**Île d'Oléron**, France 🏝
128	G 5	**Île d'Ouessant**, France 🏝
87	W 7	**Île du Harve Aubert**, Québec, Canada 🏝
128	J 8	**Île d'Yeu**, France 🏝
219	U 9	**Île Europa**, France 🏝
87	T 7	**Île Lamèque**, New Brunswick, Canada 🏝
38	A 10	**Île Thérèse**, Seychelles 🏝

□ Country ▣ Internal administrative region: State/Province/Territory/Dependent territory 🏛 Capital city ⛰ Mountain range/Undersea ridge ▲ Mountain peak/Volcano/Seamount ◇ Geographic feature ▶ Headland/Point/Cape/Peninsula 🏜 Desert 🏝 Island/Island group ⊞ Antarctic base 🌊 Ocean ≋ Sea ≈ Bay/Gulf/Channel/Strait 💧 Lake ⚑ Salt pan/Dry/Intermittent lake ⌇ River

□ Country | ■ Internal administrative region: State/Province/Territory/Dependent territory | ⚓ Capital city | ▲ Mountain range/Undersea ridge | ▲ Mountain peak/Volcano/Seamount | ◇ Geographic feature | ▶ Headland/Point/Cape/Peninsula | ▲ Desert | ⚏ Island/Island group | ⁑ Antarctic base | ◈ Ocean | ⌇ Sea | ≈ Bay/Gulf/Channel/Strait | ▭ Lake | ⸖ Salt pan/Dry/Intermittent lake

Isla Patricio Lynch – Jaşşān

111 E 22 **Isla Patricio Lynch**, Chile
111 I 26 **Isla Picton**, Chile
107 B 17 **Isla Pinta**, Ecuador
111 E 21 **Isla Prat**, Chile
106 A 10 **Isla Puná**, Ecuador
111 G 24 **Isla Riesco**, Chile
41 Z 2 **Isla Robinson Crusoe**, Juan Fernández Islands
41 Z 10 **Isla San Ambrosio**, Pacific Ocean
107 C 19 **Isla San Cristóbal**, Ecuador
88 H 5 **Isla San Esteban**, Mexico
41 Y 10 **Isla San Felix**, Pacific Ocean
88 I 7 **Isla San José**, Mexico
91 X 14 **Isla San José**, Panama
88 L 10 **Isla San Juanito**, Mexico
88 H 4 **Isla San Lorenzo**, Mexico
107 B 18 **Isla San Salvador**, Ecuador
88 I 7 **Isla Santa Catalina**, Mexico
41 Y 2 **Isla Santa Clara**, Juan Fernández Islands
107 B 18 **Isla Santa Cruz**, Ecuador
107 B 19 **Isla Santa Fé**, Ecuador
111 G 25 **Isla Santa Inés**, Chile
88 H 8 **Isla Santa Margarita**, Mexico
107 B 19 **Isla Santa María**, Ecuador
93 S 8 **Isla Saona**, Dominican Republic
91 S 14 **Isla Sevilla**, Panama
111 G 26 **Isla Stewart**, Chile
88 H 4 **Isla Tiburón**, Mexico
113 B 19 **Isla Trinidad**, Argentina
111 F 20 **Isla Victoria**, Chile
111 F 24 **Isla Vidal**, Chile
111 F 22 **Isla Wellington**, Chile
91 O 10 **Isla Zapatra**, Nicaragua
170 L 13 **Islahiye**, Turkey
177 Y 8 **Islamabad**, Pakistan
63 Y 14 **Islamorada**, Florida, U.S.A.
197 C 19 **Island Bay**, Philippines
34 J 8 **Island Lake**, Manitoba, Canada
4 J 8 **Island Lake**, Manitoba, Canada
3 Q 9 **Island Park**, Idaho, U.S.A.
8 I 14 **Islands of The Four Mountains**, Alaska, U.S.A.
31 V 7 **Islas Columbretes**, Spain
0 M 4 **Islas de la Bahía**, Honduras
1 S 9 **Islas del Maíz**, Nicaragua
11 H 26 **Islas Diego Ramirez**, Chile
05 O 2 **Islas Los Roques**, Venezuela
8 L 10 **Islas Marías**, Mexico
3 H 20 **Islas Orcadas Rise**, Atlantic Ocean
1 T 15 **Islas Secas**, Panama
11 I 26 **Islas Wollaston**, Chile
24 E 13 **Islay**, United Kingdom
9 R 6 **Isle au Haut**, Maine, U.S.A.
24 E 8 **Isle of Lewis**, United Kingdom
25 H 16 **Isle of Man**, United Kingdom
27 Q 14 **Isle of Portland**, United Kingdom
27 Y 11 **Isle of Sheppey**, United Kingdom
27 O 1 **Isle of Walney**, United Kingdom
27 S 14 **Isle of Wight**, United Kingdom
G 6 **Isle Royale**, Michigan, U.S.A.
K 9 **Isles Dernieres**, Louisiana, U.S.A.
5 E 24 **Isles of Scilly**, United Kingdom
212 F 8 **Ismâ'ilîya**, Egypt
171 X 7 **Ismayilli**, Azerbaijan
212 F 11 **Isna**, Egypt
219 Q 3 **Isoka**, Zambia
141 J 20 **Isola Alicudi**, Italy
141 B 15 **Isola Asinara**, Italy
141 C 15 **Isola Caprera**, Italy
140 D 12 **Isola d' Elba**, Italy
141 I 16 **Isola d' Ischia**, Italy
140 E 13 **Isola del Giglio**, Italy
158 J 5 **Isola d'Elba**, Mediterranean Sea
140 D 12 **Isola di Capraia**, Italy
141 J 16 **Isola di Capri**, Italy
140 D 11 **Isola di Gorgona**, Italy
141 H 26 **Isola di Lampedusa**, Italy
141 G 26 **Isola di Lampione**, Italy
141 H 26 **Isola di Linosa**, Italy
140 E 13 **Isola di Montecristo**, Italy
141 G 24 **Isola di Pantelleria**, Italy
141 B 19 **Isola di San Pietro**, Italy
141 B 19 **Isola di Sant'Antioco**, Italy
141 I 20 **Isola di Ustica**, Italy
141 G 22 **Isola Favignana**, Italy
141 J 20 **Isola Filicudi**, Italy
141 G 21 **Isola Levanzo**, Italy
141 K 20 **Isola Lipari**, Italy
141 C 15 **Isola Maddalena**, Italy
141 G 21 **Isola Marettimo**, Italy
141 K 20 **Isola Panarea**, Italy
140 D 12 **Isola Pianosa**, Italy
141 K 20 **Isola Salina**, Italy
141 K 20 **Isola Stromboli**, Italy
141 K 21 **Isola Vulcano**, Italy
141 F 21 **Isole Egadi**, Italy
141 G 26 **Isole Pelagie**, Italy
141 L 13 **Isole Pianosa**, Italy
141 H 16 **Isole Ponziane**, Italy
140 L 13 **Isole San Domino**, Italy
141 L 13 **Isole Tremiti**, Italy
170 F 12 **Isparta**, Turkey
146 L 7 **Isperikh**, Bulgaria
172 F 11 **Israel**, Asia
230 J 11 **Israelite Bay**, Western Australia, Australia
214 J 13 **Issia**, Côte d'Ivoire
179 W 10 **Issyk-Kul'skaya Oblast'**, Kyrgyzstan
143 K 21 **Istállós-kő**, Hungary
146 O 12 **Istanbul**, Turkey
170 D 7 **Istanbul**, Turkey
176 H 7 **Īstgāh-e Eznā**, Iran
191 F 23 **Isthmus of Kra**, Thailand
91 W 13 **Isthmus of Panama**, Panama
147 F 18 **Istiaia**, Greece
171 V 9 **Istisu**, Azerbaijan
89 V 13 **Istmo de Tehuantepec**, Mexico
183 T 14 **Iswaripur**, Bangladesh
179 W 9 **Isyk**, Kazakhstan
109 N 15 **Itabuna**, Brazil
108 F 10 **Itacoatiara**, Brazil
112 H 6 **Itaguajé**, Brazil
109 K 15 **Itaguari**, Brazil
108 G 11 **Itaituba**, Brazil
112 J 10 **Itajaí**, Brazil
112 L 6 **Itajubá**, Brazil
140 F 10 **Italy**, Europe
219 W 10 **Itampolo**, Madgascar
183 X 9 **Itanagar**, India
109 M 16 **Itaobim**, Brazil
112 I 4 **Itapagipe**, Brazil
109 N 16 **Itapebi**, Brazil
108 L 11 **Itapecuru Mirim**, Brazil
112 O 6 **Itaperuna**, Brazil
112 J 7 **Itapetininga**, Brazil
112 J 7 **Itapeva**, Brazil
108 B 12 **Itaquai**, Brazil
112 E 11 **Itaqui**, Brazil
112 J 7 **Itararé**, Brazil
181 E 15 **Itarsi**, India
112 H 3 **Itarumã**, Brazil
108 I 9 **Itaupã**, Brazil
196 H 2 **Itbayat**, Philippines
107 G 20 **Ite**, Peru
147 E 19 **Itea**, Greece
217 P 9 **Itebero**, Democratic Republic of Congo
58 G 9 **Ithaca**, New York, U.S.A.
147 B 19 **Ithaki**, Greece
147 B 19 **Ithaki**, Greece
109 M 16 **Itinga**, Brazil
109 G 16 **Itiquira**, Brazil
199 K 17 **Itō**, Japan
199 I 15 **Itoigawa**, Japan
216 L 8 **Itoko**, Democratic Republic of Congo
45 Q 13 **Ittoqqortoormiit**, Greenland
112 K 7 **Itu**, Brazil
108 B 11 **Ituí**, Brazil
112 J 3 **Ituitaba**, Brazil
109 J 17 **Ituiutaba**, Brazil
217 P 10 **Itula**, Democratic Republic of Congo
109 J 17 **Itumbiara**, Brazil
105 U 6 **Ituni**, Guyana
112 I 10 **Ituporanga**, Brazil
112 I 4 **Iturama**, Brazil
112 E 10 **Ituzaingo**, Argentina
110 N 8 **Ituzaingó**, Argentina
136 G 9 **Itzehoe**, Germany
153 Z 6 **Iul'tin**, Russian Federation
112 G 7 **Ivaí**, Brazil
134 M 8 **Ivalo**, Finland
149 G 21 **Ivanava**, Belarus
231 S 11 **Ivanhoe**, New South Wales, Australia
144 K 13 **Ivanjica**, Serbia and Montenegro
144 F 10 **Ivanjska**, Bosnia and Herzegovina
151 P 3 **Ivankiv**, Ukraine
150 J 6 **Ivano-Frankivs'k**, Ukraine
157 V 4 **Ivanovka**, Russian Federation
154 K 14 **Ivanovo**, Russian Federation
154 K 14 **Ivanovskaya Oblast'**, Russian Federation
157 S 4 **Ivanteyevka**, Russian Federation
151 S 3 **Ivanytsya**, Ukraine
149 G 20 **Ivatsevichy**, Belarus
146 K 12 **Ivaylovgrad**, Bulgaria
152 J 9 **Ivdel'**, Russian Federation
150 M 11 **Iveşti**, Romania
112 G 6 **Ivinheima**, Brazil
44 L 13 **Ivittuut**, Greenland
219 X 9 **Ivohibe**, Madgascar
214 J 14 **Ivory Coast**, Côte d'Ivoire
140 B 7 **Ivrea**, Italy
85 P 4 **Ivujivik**, Québec, Canada
149 I 17 **Ivyanyets**, Belarus
61 O 4 **Ivydale**, West Virginia, U.S.A.
198 L 10 **Iwaizumi**, Japan
199 L 14 **Iwaki**, Japan
198 J 9 **Iwaki-san**, Japan
199 D 20 **Iwakuni**, Japan
198 J 5 **Iwamizawa**, Japan
198 I 6 **Iwanai**, Japan
198 K 10 **Iwate-san**, Japan
215 P 12 **Iwo**, Nigeria
149 G 17 **Iwye**, Belarus
107 I 17 **Ixiamas**, Bolivia
89 N 10 **Ixtlán**, Mexico
89 T 13 **Ixtlán**, Mexico
127 Y 8 **Ixworth**, United Kingdom
199 E 20 **Iyomishima**, Japan
217 U 12 **Izazi**, Tanzania
157 R 15 **Izberbash**, Russian Federation
133 C 18 **Izegem**, Belgium
199 N 24 **Izena-jima**, Japan
155 R 14 **Izhevsk**, Russian Federation
151 N 11 **Izmayil**, Ukraine
170 B 10 **Izmir**, Turkey
170 A 10 **Izmir Körfezi**, Turkey
170 E 8 **Iznik Gölü**, Turkey
156 M 12 **Izobil'nyy**, Russian Federation
89 R 12 **Iztaccihuatl**, Mexico
90 H 7 **Iztapa**, Guatemala
199 K 17 **Izu-hantō**, Japan
199 K 18 **Izu-shotō**, Japan
40 L 4 **Izu Trench**, Pacific Ocean
89 R 12 **Izúcar de Matamoros**, Mexico
199 A 20 **Izuhara**, Japan
199 B 23 **Izumi**, Japan
199 D 18 **Izumo**, Japan
150 L 4 **Izyaslav**, Ukraine
151 X 5 **Izyum**, Ukraine

J

44 M 13 **J.A.D. Jenson Nunatakker**, Greenland
173 N 2 **Jabal 'Abd al 'Azīz**, Syria
173 N 2 **Jabal Abd al Aziz**, Syria
172 K 4 **Jabal Abū Raḥbah**, Syria
174 J 3 **Jabal ad Dubbagh**, Saudi Arabia
172 I 8 **Jabal ad Duruz**, Syria
172 J 3 **Jabal Aḥaṣ**, Syria
172 H 11 **Jabāl al 'Ādhiriyāt**, Jordan
172 I 2 **Jabal al Akr**, Syria
175 P 10 **Jabal al Amlaḥ**, Saudi Arabia
172 I 8 **Jabal al 'Arab**, Syria
172 F 13 **Jabal al Khashsh**, Jordan
174 J 3 **Jabal al Lawz**, Saudi Arabia
175 V 11 **Jabal al Qamar**, Oman
175 O 13 **Jabal an Nabī Shu'ayb**, Yemen
172 J 6 **Jabal an Niqniqīyah**, Syria
172 H 4 **Jabal an Nuṣayrīyah**, Syria
175 P 10 **Jabal ar Rubūţ**, Saudi Arabia
211 Z 13 **Jabal Arkenu**, Libya
211 S 9 **Jabal as Sawdā'**, Libya
175 Y 7 **Jabal ash Shāms**, Oman
172 H 6 **Jabal ash Sharqī**, Lebanon
172 I 5 **Jabal ash Shawmariyah**, Syria
174 J 3 **Jabal ash Shifa**, Saudi Arabia
172 L 7 **Jabal aţ Ţanf**, Syria
172 F 13 **Jabal Bāqir**, Jordan
211 U 13 **Jabal Bin Ghanīmah**, Libya
172 L 4 **Jabal Bishrī**, Syria
175 X 6 **Jabal Ḥafīt**, United Arab Emirates
175 W 15 **Jabal Ḥajhir**, Yemen
173 S 4 **Jabal Hamrin**, Iraq
175 Z 7 **Jabal Khadar**, Oman
211 R 8 **Jabal Nafūsah**, Libya
174 L 5 **Jabal Nahr**, Saudi Arabia
211 W 14 **Jabal Nuqayy**, Libya
174 M 8 **Jabal Qarnayţ**, Saudi Arabia
174 L 6 **Jabal Raḍwá**, Saudi Arabia
174 M 2 **Jabal Rāf**, Saudi Arabia
172 G 13 **Jabal Ramm**, Jordan
175 Z 7 **Jabal Salakh**, Oman
175 N 10 **Jabal Sawdá'**, Saudi Arabia
172 K 4 **Jabal Shā'īr**, Syria
173 O 2 **Jabal Sinjār**, Iraq
175 O 13 **Jabal Taqar**, Yemen
175 P 13 **Jabal Thamar**, Yemen
172 L 4 **Jabal Thulaythawat Gharbi**, Syria
175 Q 9 **Jabal Tuwayq**, Saudi Arabia
211 U 8 **Jabal Waddān**, Libya
211 V 9 **Jabal Zaltan**, Libya
181 G 15 **Jabalpur**, India
133 B 17 **Jabbeke**, Belgium
231 N 1 **Jabiru**, Northern Territory, Australia
172 H 3 **Jablah**, Syria
144 G 13 **Jablanica**, Bosnia and Herzegovina
143 E 16 **Jablonec nad Nisou**, Czech Republic
112 J 5 **Jaboticabal**, Brazil
237 Y 3 **Jabwat**, Marshall Islands
131 T 2 **Jaca**, Spain
89 R 11 **Jacala**, Mexico
90 F 4 **Jacaltenango**, Guatemala
108 G 12 **Jacareacanga**, Brazil
112 L 7 **Jacareí**, Brazil
110 H 9 **Jáchal**, Argentina
108 D 13 **Jaciparaná**, Brazil
59 P 3 **Jackman**, Maine, U.S.A.
71 O 5 **Jacksboro**, Texas, U.S.A.
60 C 9 **Jackson**, Tennessee, U.S.A.
62 L 5 **Jackson**, Mississippi, U.S.A.
63 O 6 **Jackson**, Alabama, U.S.A.
63 T 3 **Jackson**, Georgia, U.S.A.
65 K 15 **Jackson**, Michigan, U.S.A.
65 N 20 **Jackson**, Ohio, U.S.A.
73 R 11 **Jackson**, Wyoming, U.S.A.
77 H 19 **Jackson**, California, U.S.A.
233 C 21 **Jackson Bay**, New Zealand
233 C 21 **Jackson Bay**, New Zealand
73 R 10 **Jackson Lake**, Wyoming, U.S.A.
233 G 19 **Jacksons**, New Zealand
61 T 11 **Jacksonville**, North Carolina, U.S.A.
63 W 7 **Jacksonville**, Florida, U.S.A.
65 E 19 **Jacksonville**, Illinois, U.S.A.
69 V 11 **Jacksonville**, Arkansas, U.S.A.
71 S 7 **Jacksonville**, Texas, U.S.A.
63 W 7 **Jacksonville Beach**, Florida, U.S.A.
93 P 8 **Jacmel**, Haiti
91 P 13 **Jacó**, Costa Rica
177 U 12 **Jacobabad**, Pakistan
108 J 11 **Jacunda**, Brazil
112 J 8 **Jacupiranga**, Brazil
136 E 10 **Jadebusen**, Germany
175 V 12 **Jādib**, Yemen
131 P 6 **Jadraque**, Spain
106 B 12 **Jaén**, Peru
131 O 11 **Jaén**, Spain
181 F 23 **Jaffna**, Sri Lanka
58 M 9 **Jaffrey**, New Hampshire, U.S.A.
181 H 17 **Jagdalpur**, India
186 I 6 **Jagdaqi**, China
173 O 1 **Jāghir Bāzār**, Syria
144 M 12 **Jagodina**, Serbia and Montenegro
182 H 6 **Jagraon**, India
181 F 17 **Jagtial**, India
113 G 14 **Jaguarão**, Brazil
113 G 14 **Jaguarão**, Uruguay
110 H 8 **Jagüé**, Argentina
92 H 4 **Jagüey Grande**, Cuba
183 P 11 **Jahanabad**, India
176 J 11 **Jahrom**, Iran
108 M 12 **Jaicós**, Brazil
183 W 11 **Jaintiapur**, Bangladesh
180 D 12 **Jaipur**, India
180 B 12 **Jaisalmer**, India
183 N 8 **Jajarkot**, Nepal
144 G 11 **Jajce**, Bosnia and Herzegovina
183 U 9 **Jakar**, Bhutan
192 H 13 **Jakarta**, Indonesia
192 H 13 **Jakarta Raya**, Indonesia
83 B 14 **Jakes Corner**, Yukon Territory, Canada
177 P 13 **Jakkī**, Iran
134 H 11 **Jäkkvik**, Sweden
135 K 15 **Jakobstad**, Finland
186 E 7 **Jalai Nur**, China
175 Q 5 **Jalājil**, Saudi Arabia
179 T 11 **Jalal-Abad**, Kyrgyzstan
177 V 7 **Jalālābād**, Afghanistan
182 I 6 **Jalandhar**, India
90 I 6 **Jalapa**, Guatemala
91 N 7 **Jalapa**, Nicaragua
89 T 12 **Jalapa Enríquez**, Mexico
182 K 11 **Jalaun**, India
173 U 5 **Jalawlā**, Iraq
112 I 4 **Jales**, Brazil
183 R 15 **Jaleshwar**, India
181 D 16 **Jalgaon**, India
173 X 11 **Jalībah**, Iraq
215 T 12 **Jalingo**, Nigeria
88 M 11 **Jalisco**, Mexico
181 D 17 **Jalna**, India
180 C 13 **Jalor**, India
89 O 10 **Jalostotitlán**, Mexico
89 O 10 **Jalpa**, Mexico
183 S 10 **Jalpaiguri**, India
211 X 9 **Jālū**, Libya
237 Y 4 **Jaluit**, Marshall Islands
213 K 25 **Jamaame**, Somalia
92 K 8 **Jamaica**, North America
92 L 7 **Jamaica Channel**, Jamaica
183 U 12 **Jamalpur**, Bangladesh
192 F 9 **Jamaluang**, Malaysia
192 F 11 **Jambi**, Indonesia
192 E 11 **Jambi**, Indonesia
195 W 4 **Jambongan**, Malaysia
66 M 5 **James**, North Dakota/South Dakota, U.S.A.
81 T 10 **James Bay**, Nunavut, Canada
240 H 3 **James Ross Island**, Antarctica
43 N 25 **Jamestown**, St Helena
58 C 10 **Jamestown**, New York, U.S.A.
66 M 5 **Jamestown**, North Dakota, U.S.A.
182 H 4 **Jammu**, India
182 I 3 **Jammu and Kashmir**, India/Pakistan
181 A 15 **Jamnagar**, India
133 J 25 **Jamoigne**, Belgium
177 V 11 **Jampur**, Pakistan
135 L 17 **Jämsä**, Finland
181 J 15 **Jamshedpur**, India
215 T 12 **Jamtari**, Nigeria
183 Q 12 **Jamui**, India
183 T 12 **Jamuna**, Bangladesh
45 R 13 **Jan Mayen**, Norway
183 Q 10 **Janakpur**, Nepal
109 L 16 **Janaúba**, Brazil
177 W 8 **Jand**, Pakistan
176 K 7 **Jandaq**, Iran
171 U 7 **Jandari**, Georgia
42 O 12 **Jandía Playa**, Canary Islands
65 F 14 **Janesville**, Wisconsin, U.S.A.
192 M 12 **Jangeru**, Indonesia
183 R 12 **Jangipur**, India
179 S 11 **Jangy-Bazar**, Kyrgyzstan
88 K 3 **Janos**, Mexico
143 N 15 **Janów Lubelski**, Poland
142 N 12 **Janów Podlaski**, Poland
109 L 16 **Januária**, Brazil
198 I 11 **Japan**, Asia
40 L 3 **Japan Basin**, Pacific Ocean
40 L 4 **Japan Trench**, Pacific Ocean
136 E 7 **Japsand**, Germany
108 B 10 **Japurá**, Brazil
183 X 11 **Japvo Mount**, India
91 Z 15 **Jaqué**, Panama
172 K 1 **Jarābulus**, Syria
112 J 9 **Jaraguá do Sul**, Brazil
130 L 8 **Jaraicejo**, Spain
172 H 9 **Jarash**, Jordan
109 G 18 **Jardim**, Brazil
108 H 9 **Jari**, Brazil
183 R 13 **Jarkhand**, India
142 G 13 **Jarocin**, Poland
143 N 17 **Jarosław**, Poland
41 Q 8 **Jarvis Island**, U.S.A.
181 I 15 **Jashpurnagar**, India
149 G 16 **Jāšiūnai**, Lithuania
176 M 14 **Jāsk**, Iran
143 M 18 **Jasło**, Poland
240 I 4 **Jason Peninsula**, Antarctica
63 P 3 **Jasper**, Alabama, U.S.A.
63 S 2 **Jasper**, Georgia, U.S.A.
63 U 7 **Jasper**, Florida, U.S.A.
65 I 21 **Jasper**, Indiana, U.S.A.
69 U 9 **Jasper**, Arkansas, U.S.A.
71 U 8 **Jasper**, Texas, U.S.A.
81 H 19 **Jasper**, Alberta, Canada
173 W 7 **Jaşşān**, Iraq

Country ■ Internal administrative region: State/Province/Territory/Dependent territory ■ Capital city ▲ Mountain range/Undersea ridge ▲ Mountain peak/Volcano/Seamount ◆ Geographic feature ▶ Headland/Point/Cape/Peninsula ▲ Desert Island/Island group Antarctic base Ocean Sea Bay/Gulf/Channel/Strait Lake Salt pan/Dry/Intermittent lake River

142	G 10	**Jastrowie**, Poland
143	I 18	**Jastrzębie-Zdrój**, Poland
143	K 23	**Jászberény**, Hungary
109	I 17	**Jataí**, Brazil
108	F 9	**Jatapu**, Brazil 〰
177	U 15	**Jati**, Pakistan
112	J 6	**Jaú**, Brazil
107	D 16	**Jauja**, Peru
148	G 12	**Jaunjelgava**, Latvia
148	H 10	**Jaunpiebalga**, Latvia
148	D 11	**Jaunpils**, Latvia
183	N 11	**Jaunpur**, India
192	H 15	**Java**, Indonesia 🏝
39	R 5	**Java Ridge**, Indian Ocean ⛰
192	I 13	**Java Sea**, Indonesia 🌊
39	T 6	**Java Trench**, Indian Ocean ▲
177	R 7	**Javand**, Afghanistan
185	S 3	**Javarthushuu**, Mongolia
143	E 19	**Javořice**, Czech Republic ▲
143	H 19	**Javorníky**, Slovakia ⛰
192	G 14	**Jawa Barat**, Indonesia ▣
192	I 14	**Jawa Tengah**, Indonesia ▣
192	K 15	**Jawa Timur**, Indonesia ▣
213	M 24	**Jawhar**, Somalia
106	B 13	**Jayanca**, Peru
193	Y 12	**Jayapura**, Indonesia
183	Q 10	**Jaynagar**, India
181	H 17	**Jaypur**, India
172	I 6	**Jayrūd**, Syria
175	N 11	**Jazā'ir Farasān**, Saudi Arabia 🏝
193	U 11	**Jazirah Doberai**, Indonesia ▶
175	Z 8	**Jazīrat Maşīrah**, Oman 🏝
173	N 3	**Jazrah**, Syria
172	G 5	**Jbail**, Lebanon
210	J 7	**Jbel Bou Naceur**, Morocco ▲
210	F 10	**Jdiriya**, Western Sahara
172	J 2	**Jebal Aḩaş**, Syria ⛰
215	P 12	**Jebba**, Nigeria
150	E 10	**Jebel**, Romania
213	C 15	**Jebel Abyad Plateau**, Sudan ◇
211	P 6	**Jebel Chambi**, Tunisia ▲
172	G 6	**Jebel Libnan**, Lebanon ⛰
213	B 18	**Jebel Marra**, Sudan ▲
213	H 14	**Jebel Oda**, Sudan ▲
213	B 17	**Jebel Teljo**, Sudan ▲
213	B 13	**Jebel Uweinat**, Sudan ▲
177	S 13	**Jebri**, Pakistan
174	L 8	**Jeddah**, Saudi Arabia
143	K 16	**Jędrzejów**, Poland
67	R 12	**Jefferson**, Iowa, U.S.A.
69	V 4	**Jefferson City**, Missouri, U.S.A.
73	U 12	**Jeffrey City**, Wyoming, U.S.A.
218	M 15	**Jeffrey's Bay**, Republic of South Africa
215	P 10	**Jega**, Nigeria
148	H 12	**Jēkabpils**, Latvia
213	K 20	**Jeldēsa**, Ethiopia
143	E 15	**Jelenia Góra**, Poland
148	E 11	**Jelgava**, Latvia
194	C 5	**Jeli**, Malaysia
84	L 11	**Jellicoe**, Ontario, Canada
232	K 7	**Jellicoe Channel**, New Zealand ≈
192	G 9	**Jemaja**, Indonesia 🏝
192	K 15	**Jember**, Indonesia
133	G 21	**Jemeppe**, Belgium
179	Z 6	**Jeminay**, Kazakhstan
137	J 17	**Jena**, Germany
62	J 6	**Jena**, Louisiana, U.S.A.
211	P 5	**Jendouba**, Tunisia
179	Y 10	**Jengish Chokusu**, Kyrgyzstan ▲
171	Y 9	**Jenikand**, Azerbaijan
172	G 8	**Jenin**, Israel
60	L 6	**Jenkins**, Kentucky, U.S.A.
83	K 20	**Jenner**, Alberta, Canada
62	I 8	**Jennings**, Louisiana, U.S.A.
74	M 3	**Jensen**, Utah, U.S.A.
192	I 13	**Jepara**, Indonesia
109	M 15	**Jequié**, Brazil
213	E 22	**Jerbar**, Sudan
93	N 7	**Jérémie**, Haiti
89	O 9	**Jerez**, Mexico
130	K 13	**Jerez de la Frontera**, Spain
130	J 10	**Jerez de los Caballeros**, Spain
145	L 21	**Jergucat**, Albania
231	T 6	**Jericho**, Queensland, Australia
172	G 9	**Jericho**, Israel
231	S 12	**Jerilderie**, New South Wales, Australia
230	H 12	**Jerramungup**, Western Australia, Australia
177	U 14	**Jerruck**, Pakistan
125	J 26	**Jersey**, United Kingdom 🏝
58	J 13	**Jersey City**, New Jersey, U.S.A.
65	E 20	**Jerseyville**, Illinois, U.S.A.
172	G 9	**Jerusalem**, Israel ⌂
140	I 11	**Jesi**, Italy
183	T 13	**Jessore**, Bangladesh
63	W 5	**Jesup**, Georgia, U.S.A.
110	J 10	**Jesús María**, Argentina
68	J 5	**Jetmore**, Kansas, U.S.A.
136	E 10	**Jever**, Germany
142	J 9	**Jezioro Jeziorak**, Poland 💧
142	G 7	**Jezioro Łebsko**, Poland 💧
142	L 9	**Jezioro Mamry**, Poland 💧
142	L 9	**Jezioro Sniardwy**, Poland 💧
142	J 12	**Jezioro Włocławskie**, Poland 💧
142	L 12	**Jezioro Zegrzyńskie**, Poland 💧
172	G 7	**Jezzine**, Lebanon
181	D 15	**Jhabua**, India
177	T 12	**Jhal**, Pakistan
177	R 14	**Jhal Jhao**, Pakistan
177	X 9	**Jhang**, Pakistan
180	F 13	**Jhansi**, India
181	I 15	**Jharkhand**, India ▣
181	I 15	**Jharsuguda**, India
177	U 12	**Jhatpat**, Pakistan
177	X 8	**Jhelum**, Pakistan
183	T 13	**Jhenida**, Bangladesh
177	V 14	**Jhudo**, Pakistan
109	E 14	**Ji-Paraná**, Brazil
187	E 17	**Ji Xian**, China
189	T 10	**Jiahe**, China
189	O 5	**Jialing**, China 〰
186	M 10	**Jiamusi**, China
187	K 15	**Ji'an**, China
189	U 9	**Ji'an**, China
188	J 9	**Jianchuan**, China
189	X 7	**Jiande**, China
189	O 5	**Jiange**, China
189	S 11	**Jianghua**, China
189	W 9	**Jiangle**, China
189	T 12	**Jiangmen**, China
189	X 4	**Jiangsu**, China ▣
189	V 9	**Jiangxi**, China ▣
189	Y 5	**Jiangyin**, China
189	N 5	**Jiangyou**, China
189	X 4	**Jianhu**, China
189	T 7	**Jianli**, China
189	W 9	**Jianning**, China
189	X 9	**Jian'ou**, China
189	R 6	**Jianshi**, China
188	L 12	**Jianshui**, China
189	N 6	**Jianyang**, China
189	X 9	**Jianyang**, China
189	S 1	**Jiaocheng**, China
186	L 13	**Jiaohe**, China
187	D 19	**Jiaohe**, China
189	S 1	**Jiaokou**, China
189	V 11	**Jiaoling**, China
187	G 21	**Jiaonan**, China
189	X 2	**Jiaonan**, China
187	F 20	**Jiaozhou**, China
189	T 3	**Jiaozuo**, China
188	K 11	**Jiasa**, China
189	W 5	**Jiashan**, China
189	W 3	**Jiawang**, China
189	Y 6	**Jiaxing**, China
186	M 8	**Jiayin**, China
185	O 6	**Jiayuguan**, China
189	V 12	**Jiazi**, China
150	H 8	**Jibou**, Romania
175	X 10	**Jiddat al Ḩarāsīs**, Oman ◇
189	U 4	**Jieshou**, China
189	S 1	**Jiexiu**, China
189	W 12	**Jieyang**, China
149	F 16	**Jieznas**, Lithuania
215	S 10	**Jigawa**, Nigeria ▣
188	L 4	**Jigzhi**, China
143	E 19	**Jihlava**, Czech Republic
211	O 5	**Jijel**, Algeria
213	K 20	**Jijiga**, Ethiopia
213	K 25	**Jilib**, Somalia
186	K 13	**Jilin**, China
186	L 13	**Jilin**, China ▣
213	H 21	**Jīma**, Ethiopia
150	E 10	**Jimbolia**, Romania
197	K 20	**Jimenez**, Philippines
89	N 6	**Jiménez**, Mexico
187	G 20	**Jimo**, China
189	V 2	**Jinan**, China
189	Q 11	**Jinchai**, China
185	P 7	**Jinchang**, China
189	T 3	**Jincheng**, China
188	L 5	**Jinchuan**, China
182	I 8	**Jind**, India
231	T 13	**Jindabyne**, New South Wales, Australia
143	D 19	**Jindřichův Hradec**, Czech Republic
189	R 5	**Jing Shan**, China ⛰
189	P 3	**Jingchuan**, China
189	X 6	**Jingde**, China
189	W 7	**Jingdezhen**, China
188	J 12	**Jinggu**, China
187	D 18	**Jinghai**, China
189	W 12	**Jinghai**, China
184	J 4	**Jinghe**, China
188	K 13	**Jinghong**, China
189	T 6	**Jingmen**, China
189	O 3	**Jingning**, China
186	E 13	**Jingpeng**, China
186	M 13	**Jingpo**, China
186	M 12	**Jingpo Hu**, China 💧
189	S 7	**Jingsha**, China
185	Q 8	**Jingtai**, China
189	O 12	**Jingxi**, China
189	X 6	**Jingxian**, China
187	K 14	**Jingyu**, China
185	Q 8	**Jingyuan**, China
189	T 6	**Jingzhou**, China
189	Q 9	**Jingzhou**, China
186	H 6	**Jinhe**, China
189	X 7	**Jinhua**, China
189	V 3	**Jining**, China
187	B 15	**Jining**, China
217	S 7	**Jinja**, Uganda
188	K 10	**Jinjiang**, China
189	X 11	**Jinjiang**, China
213	H 22	**Jinka**, Ethiopia
188	L 7	**Jinkouhe**, China
91	N 8	**Jinotega**, Nicaragua
91	N 10	**Jinotepe**, Nicaragua
189	O 9	**Jinsha**, China
187	F 15	**Jinshan**, China
189	Z 6	**Jinshan**, China
189	S 7	**Jinshi**, China
189	N 6	**Jintang**, China
197	J 15	**Jintotolo**, Philippines 🏝
189	W 8	**Jinxi**, China
189	V 3	**Jinxiang**, China
187	H 16	**Jinzhou**, China
187	I 17	**Jinzhou**, China
106	A 9	**Jipijapa**, Ecuador
186	E 12	**Jirin Gol**, China
176	M 11	**Jīroft**, Iran
213	N 21	**Jirriiban**, Somalia
189	Q 8	**Jishou**, China
172	H 2	**Jisr Ash Shughūr**, Syria
194	A 5	**Jitra**, Malaysia
150	H 12	**Jiu**, Romania 〰
189	S 10	**Jiucai Ling**, China ▲
189	V 7	**Jiujiang**, China
189	U 8	**Jiuling Shan**, China ⛰
188	L 7	**Jiulong**, China
185	O 7	**Jiuquan**, China
189	Q 15	**Jiusuo**, China
186	K 12	**Jiutai**, China
189	O 11	**Jiuzhou**, China
177	P 14	**Jiwani**, Pakistan
186	I 6	**Jiwen**, China
186	N 11	**Jixi**, China
189	X 7	**Jixi**, China
186	N 10	**Jixian**, China
189	R 2	**Jixian**, China
175	O 11	**Jīzān**, Saudi Arabia
199	E 18	**Jizō-zaki**, Japan ▶
179	Q 12	**Jizzakh Wiloyati**, Uzbekistan ▣
112	H 10	**Joaçaba**, Brazil
108	O 12	**João Pessoa**, Brazil
109	K 17	**João Pinheiro**, Brazil
110	J 6	**Joaquín V. González**, Argentina
197	N 20	**Jobo Point**, Philippines ▶
180	C 12	**Jodhpur**, India
135	O 16	**Joensuu**, Finland
75	U 4	**Joes**, Colorado, U.S.A.
199	I 14	**Jōetsu**, Japan
219	R 8	**Jofane**, Mozambique
183	R 10	**Jogbani**, India
182	L 8	**Jogbura**, Nepal
148	H 7	**Jõgeva**, Estonia
148	I 6	**Jõgua**, Estonia
219	O 11	**Johannesburg**, Republic of South Africa
77	K 23	**Johannesburg**, California, U.S.A.
76	J 11	**John Day**, Oregon, U.S.A.
61	S 8	**John H. Kerr Reservoir**, North Carolina, U.S.A. 💧
75	U 6	**John Martin Reservoir**, Colorado, U.S.A. 💧
124	I 8	**John o'Groats**, United Kingdom
68	G 6	**Johnson**, Kansas, U.S.A.
60	M 8	**Johnson City**, Tennessee, U.S.A.
71	O 9	**Johnson City**, Texas, U.S.A.
41	Q 6	**Johnston Atoll**, U.S.A. ▣
194	E 10	**Johor**, Malaysia 〰
194	E 9	**Johor**, Malaysia ▣
194	E 10	**Johor Bahru**, Malaysia
148	I 6	**Jõhvi**, Estonia
112	J 9	**Joinville**, Brazil
129	T 5	**Joinville**, France
240	H 2	**Joinville Island**, Antarctica 🏝
134	I 11	**Jokkmokk**, Sweden
134	B 9	**Jökulbunga**, Iceland ▲
176	F 3	**Jolfa**, Iran
65	G 16	**Joliet**, Illinois, U.S.A.
86	L 10	**Joliette**, Québec, Canada
197	G 24	**Jolo**, Philippines
197	G 24	**Jolo**, Philippines 🏝
196	I 11	**Jomalig**, Philippines 🏝
183	O 8	**Jomsom**, Nepal
90	K 3	**Jonathán Point**, Belize ▶
149	F 15	**Jonava**, Lithuania
81	P 3	**Jones Sound**, Nunavut, Canada ≈
62	I 5	**Jonesboro**, Louisiana, U.S.A.
63	S 3	**Jonesboro**, Georgia, U.S.A.
69	X 9	**Jonesboro**, Arkansas, U.S.A.
61	N 11	**Jonesville**, South Carolina, U.S.A.
62	J 6	**Jonesville**, Louisiana, U.S.A.
213	E 21	**Jonglei**, Sudan
213	F 21	**Jonglei**, Sudan ▣
148	E 12	**Joniškis**, Lithuania
135	F 22	**Jönköping**, Sweden
87	N 6	**Jonquière**, Québec, Canada
69	R 7	**Joplin**, Missouri, U.S.A.
180	E 12	**Jora**, India
172	H 11	**Jordan**, Asia □
172	G 9	**Jordan**, Israel 〰
73	V 4	**Jordan**, Montana, U.S.A.
76	L 13	**Jordan Valley**, Oregon, U.S.A.
183	X 10	**Jorhat**, India
91	U 15	**Jorones**, Panama
215	S 11	**Jos**, Nigeria
107	J 17	**José Agustín Palacios**, Bolivia
111	G 18	**José de San Martin**, Argentina
196	I 12	**José Pañganiban**, Philippines
113	G 15	**José Pedro Varela**, Uruguay
230	L 2	**Joseph Bonaparte Gulf**, Western Australia, Australia ≈
234	C 4	**Josephstaal**, Papua New Guinea
172	G 7	**Jouaiya**, Lebanon
219	N 11	**Jouberton**, Republic of South Africa
132	K 8	**Joure**, Netherlands
134	M 11	**Joutsijärvi**, Finland
183	W 11	**Jowai**, India
177	S 5	**Jowzjān**, Afghanistan ▣
76	F 6	**Joyce**, Washington, U.S.A.
214	E 6	**Jreïda**, Mauritania
76	E 5	**Juan de Fuca Strait**, Washington, U.S.A. ≈
219	V 6	**Juan de Nova**, France 🏝
41	W 1	**Juan Fernández Islands**, Chile ▣
106	D 13	**Juanjuí**, Peru
108	M 13	**Juàzeiro**, Brazil
108	N 12	**Juázeiro do Norte**, Brazil
214	I 13	**Juazohn**, Liberia
213	E 23	**Juba**, Sudan
213	K 24	**Juba**, Somalia 〰
213	K 25	**Jubbada Dhexe**, Somalia ▣
213	K 26	**Jubbada Hoose**, Somalia ▣
230	K 9	**Jubilee Lake**, Western Australia, Australia 💧
183	R 9	**Jubing**, Nepal
131	Q 8	**Júcar**, Spain 〰
89	U 14	**Juchitán**, Mexico
89	N 11	**Juchitlán**, Mexico
173	P 10	**Judaidat al Hamir**, Iraq
139	U 7	**Judenburg**, Austria
188	J 9	**Judian**, China
91	O 9	**Juigalpa**, Nicaragua
109	F 14	**Juína**, Brazil
136	C 10	**Juist**, Germany 🏝
112	N 6	**Juiz de Fora**, Brazil
110	I 5	**Jujuy**, Argentina ▣
107	I 22	**Julaca**, Bolivia
195	P 10	**Julau**, Malaysia
107	H 19	**Juli**, Peru
231	R 5	**Julia Creek**, Queensland, Australia
107	H 19	**Juliaca**, Peru
144	A 6	**Julian Alps**, Slovenia ⛰
105	W 7	**Juliana Top**, Suriname ▲
132	H 8	**Julianadorp**, Netherlands
137	B 17	**Jülich**, Germany
131	S 10	**Jumilla**, Spain
183	N 8	**Jumla**, Nepal
186	F 11	**Jun Bulen**, China
181	A 15	**Junagadh**, India
181	H 17	**Junagarh**, India
189	X 3	**Junan**, China
70	M 9	**Junction**, Texas, U.S.A.
74	J 6	**Junction**, Utah, U.S.A.
62	I 4	**Junction City**, Louisiana, U.S.A.
69	O 4	**Junction City**, Kansas, U.S.A.
76	F 11	**Junction City**, Oregon, U.S.A.
231	R 7	**Jundah**, Queensland, Australia
112	K 7	**Jundiaí**, Brazil
79	X 10	**Juneau**, Alaska, U.S.A.
138	F 9	**Jungfrau**, Switzerland ▲
184	K 4	**Junggar Desert**, China ◇
107	D 16	**Junín**, Peru ▣
113	B 16	**Junín**, Argentina
189	N 8	**Junlian**, China
135	H 15	**Junsele**, Sweden
76	K 12	**Juntura**, Oregon, U.S.A.
149	G 16	**Juozapinės kalnas**, Lithuania ▲
112	K 8	**Juquiá**, Brazil
112	K 8	**Juquiá**, Brazil 〰
124	F 12	**Jura**, United Kingdom 🏝
129	U 9	**Jura**, France/Switzerland ⛰
104	F 5	**Juradó**, Colombia
149	D 15	**Jurbarkas**, Lithuania
172	G 11	**Jurf ad Darāwīsh**, Jordan
186	G 12	**Jurh**, China
230	F 10	**Jurien**, Western Australia, Australia
151	N 12	**Jurilovca**, Romania
148	E 11	**Jūrmala**, Latvia
194	A 14	**Jurong**, Singapore
194	A 14	**Jurong Island**, Singapore 🏝
108	C 11	**Juruá**, Brazil
108	C 11	**Juruá**, Brazil 〰
108	F 13	**Juruena**, Brazil 〰
186	F 11	**Jus Hua**, China
110	I 12	**Justo Daract**, Argentina
108	C 10	**Jutaí**, Brazil
108	C 11	**Jutaí**, Brazil 〰
137	L 14	**Jüterbog**, Germany
112	F 6	**Juti**, Brazil
90	I 6	**Jutiapa**, Guatemala
91	N 4	**Jutiapa**, Honduras
91	N 6	**Juticalpa**, Honduras
135	N 17	**Juva**, Finland
177	P 9	**Juwain**, Afghanistan
189	X 2	**Juxian**, China
189	V 3	**Juye**, China
176	J 12	**Jūyom**, Iran
135	C 24	**Jylland**, Denmark ◇
135	M 16	**Jyväskylä**, Finland

K

177	Z 5	**K2**, Pakistan ▲
78	E 9	**Ka Lae**, Hawaii, U.S.A. ▶
134	L 8	**Kaamanen**, Finland
213	K 26	**Kaambooni**, Somalia
217	Y 9	**Kaambooni**, Kenya
193	O 13	**Kabaena**, Indonesia 🏝
179	N 12	**Kabakly**, Turkmenistan
214	G 11	**Kabala**, Sierra Leone
217	Q 8	**Kabale**, Uganda
217	O 11	**Kabalo**, Democratic Republic of Congo
217	P 10	**Kabambare**, Democratic Republic of Congo
192	C 9	**Kabanjahe**, Indonesia
197	I 18	**Kabankalan**, Philippines
235	Y 12	**Kabara**, Fiji 🏝
157	O 14	**Kabardino Balkarskaya Respublika**, Russian Federation ▣
217	P 9	**Kabare**, Democratic Republic of Congo
197	I 21	**Kabasalan**, Philippines
134	I 12	**Kåbdalis**, Sweden
191	I 19	**Kabin Buri**, Thailand
86	B 5	**Kabinakagami Lake**, Ontario, Canada 💧
217	N 11	**Kabinda**, Democratic Republic of Congo
199	M 26	**Kabira**, Japan
195	O 10	**Kabong**, Malaysia
217	N 12	**Kabongo**, Democratic Republic of Congo
191	F 20	**Kabosa Island**, Myanmar 🏝
177	O 5	**Kabūd Gonbad**, Iran
176	G 6	**Kabūd Rāhang**, Iran
177	U 7	**Kābul**, Afghanistan ▣
177	U 7	**Kabul**, Afghanistan ⌂
217	Q 15	**Kabunda**, Democratic Republic of Congo
193	R 9	**Kaburuang**, Indonesia 🏝
213	F 16	**Kabushiya**, Sudan
219	O 5	**Kabwe**, Zambia
145	M 16	**Kačanik**, Serbia and Montenegro
215	R 11	**Kachia**, Nigeria
190	E 8	**Kachin**, Myanmar ▣
179	U 2	**Kachiry**, Kazakhstan
219	P 5	**Kacholola**, Zambia
153	Q 13	**Kachug**, Russian Federation
191	F 20	**Kadan Kyun**, Myanmar 🏝
235	W 12	**Kadavu**, Fiji 🏝
235	W 12	**Kadavu Passage**, Fiji ≈
173	T 7	**Kādhimain**, Iraq
170	D 7	**Kadiköy**, Turkey
170	G 11	**Kadinhani**, Turkey
181	E 20	**Kadiri**, India
170	L 12	**Kadirli**, Turkey
181	B 22	**Kadmat**, India 🏝
66	I 10	**Kadoka**, South Dakota, U.S.A.
219	P 7	**Kadoma**, Zimbabwe
213	D 19	**Kadugli**, Sudan
215	R 11	**Kaduna**, Nigeria
215	R 11	**Kaduna**, Nigeria ▣
154	I 11	**Kaduy**, Russian Federatio
171	V 10	**Kadžaran**, Armenia

□ Country ▣ Internal administrative region: State/Province/Territory/Dependent territory ⌂ Capital city ⛰ Mountain range/Undersea ridge ▲ Mountain peak/Volcano/Seamount ◇ Geographic feature ▶ Headland/Point/Cape/Peninsula ◒ Desert 🏝 Island/Island group ⁙ Antarctic base Ⓞ Ocean 🌊 Sea ≈ Bay/Gulf/Channel/Strait 💧 Lake ⚑ Salt pan/Dry/Intermittent lake 〰 Ri

214 F 7	Kaédi, Mauritania
215 V 11	Kaélé, Cameroon
232 J 5	Kaeo, New Zealand
187 K 18	Kaesŏng, North Korea
174 K 1	Kāf, Saudi Arabia
216 M 13	Kafakumba, Democratic Republic of Congo
214 E 9	Kaffrine, Senegal
213 A 20	Kafia Kingi, Sudan
219 O 5	Kafue, Zambia
219 H 16	Kaga, Japan
216 K 3	Kaga Bandoro, Central African Republic
177 X 7	Kagan, Pakistan
179 O 13	Kagan, Uzbekistan
217 R 9	Kagera, Tanzania □
171 S 9	Kağizman, Turkey
213 E 17	Kagmar, Sudan
199 C 24	Kagoshima, Japan
176 M 5	Kāhak, Iran
217 S 10	Kahama, Tanzania
151 Q 4	Kaharlyk, Ukraine
216 J 12	Kahemba, Democratic Republic of Congo
176 M 12	Kahnūj, Iran
214 I 14	Kahnwia, Liberia
232 I 5	Kahoe, New Zealand
69 V 1	Kahoka, Missouri, U.S.A.
78 C 8	Kahoolawe, Hawaii, U.S.A.
170 L 12	Kahramanmaraş, Turkey
171 N 12	Kahta, Turkey
193 U 13	Kai Besar, Indonesia ⇄
193 U 13	Kai Kecil, Indonesia ⇄
215 P 11	Kaiama, Nigeria
233 H 20	Kaiapoi, New Zealand
74 K 8	Kaibito, Arizona, U.S.A.
189 T 3	Kaifeng, China
232 J 6	Kaikohe, New Zealand
233 I 18	Kaikoura, New Zealand
233 I 18	Kaikoura Peninsula, New Zealand ▶
189 P 9	Kaili, China
186 H 13	Kailu, China
78 D 7	Kailua, Hawaii, U.S.A.
193 V 12	Kaimana, Indonesia
48 D 7	Käina, Estonia
99 F 20	Kainan, Japan
234 D 5	Kainantu, Papua New Guinea
139 X 7	Kaindorf, Austria
215 P 11	Kainji Reservoir, Nigeria ⇆
134 K 10	Kainulasjärvi, Sweden
32 I 7	Kaipara Harbour, New Zealand ≈
89 S 13	Kaiping, China
33 N 14	Kairakau Beach, New Zealand
34 B 3	Kairiru, Papua New Guinea ⇄
111 Q 6	Kairouan, Tunisia
34 D 6	Kairuku, Papua New Guinea
41 W 7	Kaiser Wilhelm II Land, Antarctica ◇
37 D 21	Kaiserslautern, Germany
49 F 15	Kaišiadorys, Lithuania
33 E 25	Kaitangata, New Zealand
34 I 10	Kaitumälven, Sweden ⇆
8 C 7	Kaiwi Channel, Hawaii, U.S.A. ≈
89 Q 6	Kaixian, China
87 J 14	Kaiyuan, China
88 M 11	Kaiyuan, China
45 M 14	Kajaani, Finland
81 Q 5	Kajabbi, Queensland, Australia
177 R 9	Kajaki, Afghanistan
194 C 8	Kajang, Malaysia
215 R 11	Kajuru, Nigeria
3 E 19	Kaka, Sudan
33 E 25	Kaka Point, New Zealand
193 P 14	Kakabia, Indonesia
197 K 23	Kakal, Philippines ⇆
218 K 12	Kakamas, Republic of South Africa
217 T 7	Kakamega, Kenya
181 N 23	Kakana, India
232 H 13	Kakaramea, New Zealand
214 H 13	Kakata, Liberia
232 K 13	Kakatahi, New Zealand

183 X 12	Kakching, India
199 D 19	Kake, Japan
216 L 10	Kakenge, Democratic Republic of Congo
151 T 9	Kakhovka Tavriys'k, Ukraine
151 T 8	Kakhovs'ke Vodoskhovyshche, Ukraine
176 I 11	Kākī, Iran
181 H 18	Kakinada, India
214 K 12	Kakpin, Côte d'Ivoire
79 S 3	Kaktovik, Alaska, U.S.A.
198 K 12	Kakuda, Japan
195 Q 9	Kakus, Malaysia ⇆
177 O 8	Kāl-e Namakasār, Afghanistan ⟂
217 R 12	Kala, Tanzania
177 V 8	Kalabagh, Pakistan
193 Q 15	Kalabahi, Indonesia
195 W 7	Kalabakan, Malaysia
218 L 5	Kalabo, Zambia
156 M 7	Kalach, Russian Federation
157 O 8	Kalach-na-Donu, Russian Federation
86 H 12	Kaladar, Ontario, Canada
218 K 9	Kalahari Desert, Botswana ◇
135 L 14	Kalajoki, Finland ⇆
135 K 14	Kalajoki, Finland
215 P 11	Kalalé, Benin
177 W 6	Kalam, Pakistan
147 F 14	Kalamaria, Greece
147 D 22	Kalamata, Greece
65 J 15	Kalamazoo, Michigan, U.S.A.
181 E 17	Kalamnuri, India
147 B 18	Kalamos, Greece ⇄
147 D 16	Kalampaka, Greece
151 T 12	Kalamyts'ka Zatoka, Ukraine ≈
151 S 10	Kalanchak, Ukraine
217 T 11	Kalangali, Tanzania
193 O 14	Kalao, Indonesia ⇄
193 O 14	Kalaotoa, Indonesia ⇄
173 V 5	Kalār, Iraq
191 K 16	Kalasin, Thailand
177 T 11	Kalat, Pakistan
197 K 21	Kalatungan Mountains, Philippines ▲▲
147 D 20	Kalavryta, Greece
230 F 9	Kalbarri, Western Australia, Australia
170 I 9	Kalecik, Turkey
193 Q 13	Kaledupa, Indonesia ⇄
217 N 10	Kalema, Democratic Republic of Congo
217 Q 11	Kalémié, Democratic Republic of Congo
190 C 10	Kalemyo, Myanmar
154 G 5	Kalevala, Russian Federation
190 C 10	Kalewa, Myanmar
157 X 2	Kalga, Russian Federation
230 I 10	Kalgoorlie, Western Australia, Australia
197 H 15	Kalibo, Philippines
217 O 9	Kalima, Democratic Republic of Congo
192 I 11	Kalimantan Barat, Indonesia □
192 M 12	Kalimantan Selatan, Indonesia □
192 J 12	Kalimantan Tengah, Indonesia □
192 L 10	Kalimantan Timur, Indonesia □
183 S 10	Kalimpang, India
181 I 16	Kalinga, India
149 B 15	Kaliningrad, Russian Federation
149 B 15	Kaliningradskaya Oblast', Russian Federation □
179 R 14	Kalininobod, Tajikistan
157 O 5	Kalininsk, Russian Federation
149 L 21	Kalinkavichy, Belarus
72 M 3	Kalispell, Montana, U.S.A.
143 H 14	Kalisz, Poland
142 F 10	Kalisz Pomorski, Poland
217 R 11	Kaliua, Tanzania
170 D 13	Kalkan, Turkey

230 M 4	Kalkarindji, Northern Territory, Australia
64 J 11	Kalkaska, Michigan, U.S.A.
218 I 8	Kalkfeld, Namibia
135 F 15	Kallsjön, Sweden ⇆
135 G 24	Kalmar, Sweden
148 F 11	Kalnciems, Latvia
143 I 25	Kalocsa, Hungary
219 N 6	Kalomo, Zambia
190 D 9	Kalon, Myanmar
182 K 6	Kalpa, India
181 C 23	Kalpeni, India ⇄
182 L 11	Kalpi, India
215 S 9	Kalrguéri, Niger
149 H 14	Kaltanėnai, Lithuania
156 J 2	Kaluga, Russian Federation
230 K 2	Kalumburu, Western Australia, Australia
135 D 25	Kalundborg, Denmark
150 I 5	Kalush, Ukraine
181 F 25	Kalutara, Sri Lanka
156 I 2	Kaluzhskaya Oblast', Russian Federation □
149 E 16	Kalvarija, Lithuania
154 I 14	Kalyazin, Russian Federation
147 M 22	Kalymnos, Greece
147 M 22	Kalymnos, Greece
151 N 5	Kalynivka, Ukraine
217 O 10	Kama, Democratic Republic of Congo
155 S 10	Kama, Russian Federation ⇆
191 C 14	Kama, Myanmar
198 L 10	Kamaishi, Japan
199 J 16	Kamakura, Japan
214 G 11	Kamakwie, Sierra Leone
170 I 10	Kaman, Turkey
218 G 8	Kamanjab, Namibia
175 O 12	Kamarān, Yemen ⇄
214 G 11	Kamaron, Sierra Leone
230 I 10	Kambalda, Western Australia, Australia
217 O 14	Kambove, Democratic Republic of Congo
153 Y 9	Kamchatka Peninsula, Russian Federation ▶
146 K 7	Kamen, Bulgaria
152 M 12	Kamen'-na-Obi, Russian Federation
217 N 11	Kamende, Democratic Republic of Congo
154 M 5	Kamenka, Russian Federation
157 O 4	Kamenka, Russian Federation
178 H 4	Kamenka, Kazakhstan
156 L 13	Kamennomostskiy, Russian Federation
156 L 9	Kamenolomni, Russian Federation
156 M 8	Kamensk-Shakhtinskiy, Russian Federation
152 J 10	Kamensk-Ural'skiy, Russian Federation
199 H 18	Kameyama, Japan
199 B 23	Kami-Koshiki-jima, Japan ⇄
142 D 9	Kamień Pomorski, Poland
143 J 15	Kamieńsk, Poland
198 K 4	Kamikawa, Japan
82 L 11	Kamilukuak Lake, Nunavut, Canada ⇆
150 K 1	Kamin'-Kashyrs'kyy, Ukraine
217 N 13	Kamina, Democratic Republic of Congo
199 H 16	Kamioka, Japan
199 A 20	Kamitsushima, Japan
83 H 21	Kamloops, British Columbia, Canada
41 O 4	Kammu Seamount, Pacific Ocean ▲
171 U 8	Kamo, Armenia
199 L 16	Kamogawa, Japan
217 S 7	Kampala, Uganda ●
192 E 8	Kampar, Malaysia
132 K 10	Kampen, Netherlands
217 O 10	Kampene, Democratic Republic of Congo
191 G 16	Kamphaeng Phet, Thailand

191 M 20	Kâmpóng Cham, Cambodia
191 L 20	Kâmpóng Chhnăng, Cambodia
191 K 19	Kâmpóng Khleăng, Cambodia
191 K 22	Kâmpóng Saôm, Cambodia
194 F 10	Kampong Sedili Kechil, Malaysia
191 K 21	Kâmpóng Spoe, Cambodia
191 L 20	Kâmpóng Thum, Cambodia
191 K 22	Kâmpôt, Cambodia
194 A 7	Kampung Koh, Malaysia
214 E 10	Kamsar, Guinea
157 R 1	Kamskoye Ust'ye, Russian Federation
155 S 11	Kamskoye Vodokhanilishche, Russian Federation ⇆
213 K 25	Kamsuuma, Somalia
198 L 6	Kamui-dake, Japan ▲
198 I 6	Kamui-misaki, Japan ▶
217 S 7	Kamuli, Uganda
150 M 2	Kam"yane, Ukraine
150 L 6	Kam"yanets'-Podil's'kyy, Ukraine
151 U 8	Kam"yanka, Ukraine
149 E 20	Kamyanyets, Belarus
176 F 6	Kāmyārān, Iran
149 K 15	Kamyen', Belarus
157 P 7	Kamyshin, Russian Federation
179 N 8	Kamyshlybash, Kazakhstan
157 R 11	Kamyzyak, Russian Federation
190 C 11	Kan, Myanmar
74 J 7	Kanab, Utah, U.S.A.
78 E 14	Kanaga Island, Alaska, U.S.A. ⇄
85 U 8	Kanairiktoktok, Newfoundland and Labrador, Canada ⇆
147 B 17	Kanallaki, Greece
216 L 11	Kananga, Democratic Republic of Congo
157 Q 1	Kanash, Russian Federation
199 H 15	Kanazawa, Japan
190 D 10	Kanbalu, Myanmar
199 J 17	Kanbara, Japan
191 G 19	Kanchanaburi, Thailand
181 F 21	Kanchipuram, India
177 S 10	Kandahār, Afghanistan
177 S 9	Kandahār, Afghanistan
154 H 3	Kandalaksha, Russian Federation
154 H 4	Kandalakshskiy Zaliv, Russian Federation ≈
215 N 11	Kandé, Togo
177 V 12	Kandhkot, Pakistan
215 O 10	Kandi, Benin
177 U 13	Kandiaro, Pakistan
147 B 18	Kandila, Greece
170 F 7	Kandıra, Turkey
181 A 14	Kandla, India
219 W 7	Kandreho, Madagascar
234 F 5	Kandrian, Papua New Guinea
181 G 25	Kandy, Sri Lanka
178 L 5	Kandyagash, Kazakhstan
58 C 11	Kane, Pennsylvania, U.S.A.
42 G 10	Kane Fracture Zone, Atlantic Ocean ◇
215 W 8	Kanem, Chad □
78 C 7	Kaneohe, Hawaii, U.S.A.
148 I 9	Kanepi, Estonia
218 L 10	Kang, Botswana
197 F 24	Kang Tipayan Dakula, Philippines ⇄
44 M 12	Kangaamiut, Greenland
170 M 10	Kangal, Turkey
176 M 14	Kangān, Iran
194 A 4	Kangar, Malaysia
231 P 12	Kangaroo Island, South Australia, Australia ⇄
135 M 17	Kangasniemi, Finland
183 S 9	Kangchenjunga, India/Nepal ▲
188 L 6	Kangding, China
187 K 17	Kangdong, North Korea

85 S 1	Kangeeak Point, Nunavut, Canada ▶
45 N 12	Kangerlussaq, Greenland
45 O 11	Kangersuatsiaq, Greenland
217 U 6	Kangetet, Kenya
187 L 16	Kanggye, North Korea
85 T 6	Kangiqsualujjuaq, Québec, Canada
85 R 4	Kangiqsujuaq, Québec, Canada
85 R 5	Kangirsuk, Québec, Canada
187 M 18	Kangnŭng, South Korea
216 E 7	Kango, Gabon
187 I 14	Kangping, China
182 I 5	Kangra, India
183 W 9	Kangto, India ▲
191 C 16	Kangyidaung, Myanmar
214 J 12	Kani, Côte d'Ivoire
190 C 11	Kani, Myanmar
195 W 4	Kanibongan, Malaysia
154 M 2	Kanin Kamen', Russian Federation ◇
154 L 2	Kanin Nos, Russian Federation
151 Q 4	Kaniv, Ukraine
181 F 15	Kaniwara, India
144 K 7	Kanjiža, Serbia and Montenegro
65 H 17	Kankakee, Illinois, U.S.A.
214 H 11	Kankan, Guinea
181 G 16	Kanker, India
191 F 21	Kanmaw Kyun, Myanmar ⇄
61 O 10	Kannapolis, North Carolina, U.S.A.
182 K 10	Kannauj, India
215 R 10	Kano, Nigeria
215 S 10	Kano, Nigeria □
199 C 24	Kanoya, Japan
182 M 10	Kanpur, India
68 L 5	Kansas, U.S.A. □
69 O 3	Kansas, Kansas, U.S.A. ⇆
69 R 3	Kansas City, Missouri, U.S.A.
153 O 12	Kansk, Russian Federation
191 G 25	Kantang, Thailand
156 L 7	Kantemirovka, Russian Federation
183 S 15	Kanthi, India
236 J 4	Kanton, Kiribati ⇄
199 K 15	Kanuma, Japan
182 H 9	Kanwat, India
218 M 10	Kanye, Botswana
236 I 10	Kao, Tonga ⇄
193 S 10	Kao, Indonesia
191 J 21	Kaôh Kông, Cambodia ⇄
191 J 22	Kaôh Rŭng, Cambodia ⇄
189 Z 12	Kaohsiung, Taiwan
218 G 7	Kaokoveld, Namibia ◇
214 E 8	Kaolack, Senegal
218 M 5	Kaoma, Zambia
216 M 3	Kaouadja, Central African Republic
136 M 7	Kap Arkona, Germany ▶
45 Q 13	Kap Brewster, Greenland ▶
44 M 14	Kap Farvel, Greenland ▶
45 R 9	Kap Morris Jesup, Greenland ▶
171 V 10	Kapan, Armenia
216 M 13	Kapanga, Democratic Republic of Congo
219 P 2	Kapatu, Zambia
179 V 9	Kapchagay, Kazakhstan
179 W 9	Kapchagayskoye Vodokhranilishche, Kazakhstan ⇆
133 E 16	Kapelle, Netherlands
133 G 16	Kapellen, Belgium
135 I 20	Kapellskär, Sweden
217 U 7	Kapenguria, Kenya
139 V 6	Kapfenberg, Austria
170 C 8	Kapidaği Peninsula, Turkey ▶
219 O 4	Kapiri Mposhi, Zambia
177 V 7	Kāpīsā, Afghanistan □
195 Q 10	Kapit, Malaysia
233 K 15	Kapiti Island, New Zealand ⇄
191 F 23	Kapoe, Thailand
213 F 23	Kapoeta, Sudan

143 H 25	Kaposvár, Hungary
137 D 19	Kappel, Germany
136 H 7	Kappeln, Germany
187 M 15	Kapsan, North Korea
192 I 11	Kapuas, Indonesia ⇆
86 C 5	Kapuskasing, Ontario, Canada
157 Q 8	Kapustin Yar, Russian Federation
217 U 6	Kaputir, Kenya
143 G 23	Kapuvár, Hungary
149 I 19	Kapyl', Belarus
215 N 11	Kara, Togo
179 U 10	Kara-Balta, Kyrgyzstan
170 H 12	Kara Dağ, Turkey ▲
171 O 8	Kara Dağ, Turkey ▲
179 T 11	Kara-Köl, Kyrgyzstan
213 J 19	Kara K'orē, Ethiopia
179 W 11	Kara-Say, Kyrgyzstan
152 M 6	Kara Sea, Russian Federation ⊕
179 T 12	Kara-Suu, Kyrgyzstan
178 I 11	Karabogazkel', Turkmenistan
170 H 7	Karabük, Turkey
179 W 8	Karabulak, Kazakhstan
170 A 10	Karaburun, Turkey
178 M 5	Karabutak, Kazakhstan
170 E 13	Karaca Yarimadasi, Turkey ▶
170 D 8	Karacabey, Turkey
170 D 7	Karacaköy, Turkey
170 H 14	Karaçal Tepe, Turkey ▲
156 M 13	Karachayevo Cherkesskaya Respublika, Russian Federation □
156 M 13	Karachayevsk, Russian Federation
156 I 3	Karachev, Russian Federation
177 T 15	Karachi, Pakistan
181 C 18	Karad, India
179 S 6	Karaganda, Kazakhstan □
179 T 5	Karaganda, Kazakhstan
179 V 9	Karagash, Kazakhstan
179 U 5	Karagayly, Kazakhstan
153 Z 9	Karaginskiy Zaliv, Russian Federation ≈
171 O 10	Karagöl Dağlari, Turkey ▲
217 R 8	Karagwe, Tanzania
181 F 22	Karaikal, India
181 F 23	Karaikkudi, India
176 I 6	Karaj, Iran
194 C 8	Karak, Malaysia
178 K 9	Karakalpakiya, Uzbekistan
171 O 12	Karakeşşi, Turkey
171 I 9	Karakeşşili, Turkey
193 R 8	Karakelong, Indonesia ⇄
171 P 10	Karakoşşan, Turkey
179 W 10	Karakol, Kyrgyzstan
177 Y 5	Karakoram, Pakistan ▲▲
180 Z 9	Karakoram Range, India ▲▲
179 O 13	Karakul', Uzbekistan
178 L 13	Karakum Desert, Turkmenistan ◇
171 R 9	Karakurt, Turkey
215 V 9	Kara, Chad
148 C 8	Karala, Estonia
170 H 13	Karaman, Turkey
184 K 4	Karamay, China
233 G 16	Karamea, New Zealand
233 G 17	Karamea Bight, New Zealand ≈
192 L 13	Karamian, Indonesia ⇄
232 K 10	Karamu, New Zealand
181 E 16	Karanji, India
146 M 7	Karapelit, Bulgaria
170 I 12	Karapinar, Turkey
218 I 11	Karas, Namibia □
218 J 12	Karasburg, Namibia
134 L 7	Kárášjohka, Norway
170 F 7	Karasu, Turkey
152 L 12	Karasuk, Russian Federation
170 K 13	Karataş, Turkey
179 S 10	Karatau, Kazakhstan
178 J 5	Karatobe, Kazakhstan
179 V 8	Karatol, Kazakhstan
178 I 7	Karaton, Kazakhstan
134 I 11	Karats, Sweden ⇆

□ Country ■ Internal administrative region: State/Province/Territory/Dependent territory ▲ Capital city ▲▲ Mountain range/Undersea ridge ▲ Mountain peak/Volcano/Seamount ◇ Geographic feature ▶ Headland/Point/Cape/Peninsula ▲ Desert ⇄ Island/Island group ⊞ Antarctic base ⊕ Ocean ≈ Sea ≈ Bay/Gulf/Channel/Strait ⇆ Lake ⟂ Salt pan/Dry/Intermittent lake ⇆ River

Kepulauan Nanusa – Kingston

193 R 8 **Kepulauan Nanusa**, Indonesia
192 H 8 **Kepulauan Natuna**, Indonesia
193 R 11 **Kepulauan Obi**, Indonesia
193 N 14 **Kepulauan Sabalana**, Indonesia
193 R 9 **Kepulauan Sangir**, Indonesia
193 P 14 **Kepulauan Solor**, Indonesia
193 O 14 **Kepulauan Taka'Bonerate**, Indonesia
193 R 8 **Kepulauan Talaud**, Indonesia
192 H 10 **Kepulauan Tambelan**, Indonesia
193 U 14 **Kepulauan Tanimbar**, Indonesia
192 M 14 **Kepulauan Tengah**, Indonesia
193 P 11 **Kepulauan Togian**, Indonesia
193 Q 13 **Kepulauan Tukangbesi**, Indonesia
193 U 13 **Kepulauan Watubela**, Indonesia
181 D 23 **Kerala**, India
231 R 12 **Kerang**, Victoria, Australia
147 H 20 **Keratea**, Greece
179 S 11 **Kerben**, Kyrgyzstan
151 W 11 **Kerch**, Ukraine
151 W 12 **Kerch Strait**, Ukraine
213 H 22 **Kere**, Ethiopia
234 C 6 **Kerema**, Papua New Guinea
170 I 6 **Kerempe Burun**, Turkey
213 I 16 **Keren**, Eritrea
39 N 11 **Kerguelen Islands**, France
38 M 11 **Kerguelen Plateau**, Indian Ocean
217 U 8 **Kericho**, Kenya
232 J 5 **Kerikeri**, New Zealand
179 P 14 **Kerki**, Turkmenistan
147 A 16 **Kerkyra**, Greece
213 E 14 **Kerma**, Sudan
41 P 11 **Kermadec Islands**, New Zealand
41 P 11 **Kermadec Ridge**, Pacific Ocean
41 P 11 **Kermadec Trench**, Pacific Ocean
76 M 11 **Kermān**, Iran
76 M 10 **Kermān**, Iran
76 F 6 **Kermānshāh**, Iran
76 F 6 **Kermānshāh**, Iran
0 I 7 **Kermit**, Texas, U.S.A.
47 K 22 **Keros**, Greece
15 O 11 **Kérou**, Benin
14 H 11 **Kérouané**, Guinea
3 L 19 **Kerrobert**, Saskatchewan, Canada
1 N 10 **Kerrville**, Texas, U.S.A.
25 A 19 **Kerry Head**, Republic of Ireland
1 P 11 **Kershaw**, South Carolina, U.S.A.
92 I 11 **Kertamulia**, Indonesia
70 H 15 **Keryneia**, Cyprus
10 K 9 **Kerzaz**, Algeria
38 D 8 **Kerzers**, Switzerland
70 B 7 **Keşan**, Turkey
36 K 9 **Keshan**, China
77 V 5 **Keshem**, Afghanistan
3 L 16 **Kessel**, Netherlands
54 G 5 **Kesten'ga**, Russian Federation
25 I 15 **Keswick**, United Kingdom
3 G 24 **Keszthely**, Hungary
2 M 11 **Ket'**, Russian Federation
2 I 11 **Ketapang**, Indonesia
7 O 10 **Ketchenery**, Russian Federation
Y 12 **Ketchikan**, Alaska, U.S.A.
M 10 **Ketchum**, Idaho, U.S.A.
2 J 10 **Ketelmeer**, Netherlands
2 L 9 **Kętrzyn**, Poland
5 H 7 **Ketta**, Congo
5 V 14 **Ketté**, Cameroon
127 U 7 **Kettering**, United Kingdom
65 L 19 **Kettering**, Ohio, U.S.A.
76 K 5 **Kettle Falls**, Washington, U.S.A.
135 L 16 **Keuruu**, Finland
65 E 17 **Kewanee**, Illinois, U.S.A.
193 P 15 **Kewapante**, Indonesia
64 G 8 **Keweenaw Bay**, Michigan, U.S.A.
64 H 7 **Keweenaw Peninsula**, Michigan, U.S.A.
64 H 7 **Keweenaw Point**, Michigan, U.S.A.
63 Y 13 **Key Biscayne**, Florida, U.S.A.
86 D 10 **Key Harbour**, Ontario, Canada
63 Y 14 **Key Largo**, Florida, U.S.A.
63 Y 14 **Key Largo**, Florida, U.S.A.
63 W 15 **Key West**, Florida, U.S.A.
213 F 23 **Keyala**, Sudan
68 G 7 **Keyes**, Oklahoma, U.S.A.
186 H 6 **Keyihe**, China
61 R 2 **Keyser**, West Virginia, U.S.A.
69 P 8 **Keystone Lake**, Oklahoma, U.S.A.
61 S 6 **Keysville**, Virginia, U.S.A.
69 U 3 **Keytesville**, Missouri, U.S.A.
219 O 8 **Kezi**, Zimbabwe
143 K 19 **Kežmarok**, Slovakia
218 K 10 **Kgalagadi**, Botswana
219 N 10 **Kgatleng**, Botswana
153 V 14 **Khabarovsk**, Russian Federation
175 X 6 **Khabb**, United Arab Emirates
156 L 12 **Khadyzhensk**, Russian Federation
151 P 9 **Khadzhybeys'kyy Lyman**, Ukraine
183 Q 11 **Khagaria**, India
183 V 13 **Khagrachari**, Bangladesh
177 U 12 **Khairpur**, Pakistan
177 X 11 **Khairpur**, Pakistan
212 D 7 **Khalig el 'Arab**, Egypt
175 Y 11 **Khalīj al Ḩalāniyāt**, Oman
159 R 12 **Khalīj Bumbah**, Mediterranean Sea
175 Z 9 **Khalīj Maşīrah**, Oman
181 I 17 **Khallikot**, India
155 U 2 **Khal'mer-Yu**, Russian Federation
149 K 16 **Khalopyenichy**, Belarus
191 K 15 **Kham Ta Kla**, Thailand
181 D 16 **Khamgaon**, India
176 K 13 **Khamīr**, Iran
175 P 12 **Khamir**, Yemen
175 O 10 **Khamis**, Saudi Arabia
191 K 15 **Khamkkeut**, Laos
181 G 18 **Khammam**, India
153 S 10 **Khampa**, Russian Federation
153 R 11 **Khamra**, Russian Federation
173 Q 6 **Khān al Baghdādī**, Iraq
173 T 8 **Khan al Maḩāwīl**, Iraq
173 T 7 **Khān al Mashāhīdah**, Iraq
173 T 9 **Khān al Muşallá**, Iraq
173 T 10 **Khān ar Rahbah**, Iraq
173 P 2 **Khān as Sūr**, Iraq
173 U 9 **Khān Jadwal**, Iraq
172 I 3 **Khān Shaykhūn**, Syria
172 E 10 **Khān Yūnis**, Israel
177 U 5 **Khānābād**, Afghanistan
173 V 5 **Khānaqīn**, Iraq
181 E 15 **Khandwa**, India
153 U 10 **Khandyga**, Russian Federation
177 W 10 **Khanewal**, Pakistan
191 O 20 **Khanh Duong**, Vietnam
153 S 12 **Khani**, Russian Federation
182 I 6 **Khanna**, India
179 T 9 **Khantau**, Kazakhstan
152 K 10 **Khanty-Mansiysk**, Russian Federation
191 H 24 **Khao Chum Thong**, Thailand
191 I 18 **Khao Khiaw**, Thailand
191 G 17 **Khao Laem Reservoir**, Thailand
191 I 20 **Khao Sai Dao Tai**, Thailand
182 I 2 **Khapalu**, India
157 R 9 **Kharabali**, Russian Federation
183 S 14 **Kharagpur**, India
177 S 12 **Kharan**, Pakistan
182 G 8 **Kharbara**, India
173 X 11 **Kharfiyah**, Iraq
176 H 10 **Khārg Islands**, Iran
181 D 15 **Khargon**, India
181 H 16 **Khariar**, India
151 V 4 **Kharkiv**, Ukraine
154 J 2 **Kharlovka**, Russian Federation
146 K 11 **Kharmanli**, Bulgaria
154 K 11 **Kharovsk**, Russian Federation
213 F 16 **Khartoum**, Sudan
213 F 16 **Khartoum**, Sudan
157 Q 14 **Khasav'yurt**, Russian Federation
177 P 12 **Khāsh**, Iran
152 L 8 **Khashgort**, Russian Federation
213 G 17 **Khashm el Girba**, Sudan
171 S 6 **Khashuri**, Georgia
146 K 11 **Khaskovo**, Bulgaria
146 J 11 **Khaskovo**, Bulgaria
153 P 8 **Khatanga**, Russian Federation
153 Q 8 **Khatanga**, Russian Federation
153 Q 7 **Khatangskiy Zaliv**, Russian Federation
153 Z 7 **Khatyrka**, Russian Federation
181 A 14 **Khavda**, India
191 F 18 **Khawsa**, Myanmar
175 N 10 **Khawsh**, Saudi Arabia
174 L 5 **Khaybar**, Saudi Arabia
175 O 10 **Khaybar**, Saudi Arabia
218 K 15 **Khayelitsha**, Republic of South Africa
155 S 2 **Khaypudyrskaya Guba**, Russian Federation
191 K 14 **Khê Bo**, Vietnam
191 N 16 **Khe Sanh**, Vietnam
182 M 7 **Khela**, India
210 I 7 **Khemisset**, Morocco
191 L 17 **Khemmarat**, Thailand
211 P 6 **Khenchela**, Algeria
210 I 7 **Khenifra**, Morocco
177 U 6 **Khenjan**, Afghanistan
151 S 9 **Kherson**, Ukraine
176 J 5 **Khezerābād**, Iran
153 R 14 **Khilok**, Russian Federation
172 K 4 **Khirbat Isrīyah**, Syria
191 G 17 **Khlong Khlung**, Thailand
150 M 5 **Khmel'nyts'kyy**, Ukraine
151 Q 6 **Khmel'ove**, Ukraine
151 N 5 **Khmil'nyk**, Ukraine
178 K 5 **Khobda**, Kazakhstan
171 R 6 **Khobi**, Georgia
151 O 4 **Khodorkiv**, Ukraine
179 O 13 **Khodzha Davlet**, Uzbekistan
213 C 22 **Khogali**, Sudan
191 H 18 **Khok Samrong**, Thailand
154 E 13 **Kholm**, Russian Federation
177 T 5 **Kholm**, Afghanistan
153 X 14 **Kholmsk**, Russian Federation
149 M 21 **Kholmyech**, Belarus
218 I 9 **Khomas**, Namibia
176 H 7 **Khomeyn**, Iran
176 I 8 **Khomeynīshahr**, Iran
191 J 16 **Khon Kaen**, Thailand
176 J 12 **Khonj**, Iran
153 V 9 **Khonuu**, Russian Federation
153 V 14 **Khor**, Russian Federation
177 O 7 **Khorāsān**, Iran
191 J 16 **Khorat Plateau**, Thailand
155 S 3 **Khorey-Ver**, Russian Federation
153 Q 13 **Khorinsk**, Russian Federation
218 H 8 **Khorixas**, Namibia
151 T 10 **Khorly**, Ukraine
151 T 3 **Khorol**, Ukraine
151 S 4 **Khorol**, Ukraine
176 G 7 **Khorramābād**, Iran
176 F 9 **Khorramshahr**, Iran
179 T 14 **Khorugh**, Tajikistan
157 R 10 **Khosheutovo**, Russian Federation
177 T 10 **Khost**, Pakistan
150 L 6 **Khotyn**, Ukraine
210 H 7 **Khouribga**, Morocco
183 V 12 **Khowai**, India
176 H 11 **Khowr-e Soltānī**, Iran
177 V 8 **Khowst**, Afghanistan
149 M 21 **Khoyniki**, Belarus
153 U 9 **Khrebet Cherskogo**, Russian Federation
153 U 12 **Khrebet Dzhugdzhur**, Russian Federation
179 W 9 **Khrebet Dzhungarskiy Alatau**, Kazakhstan
179 Q 9 **Khrebet Karatau**, Kazakhstan
153 P 14 **Khrebet Khamar-Daban**, Russian Federation
153 X 10 **Khrebet Kolymskiy**, Russian Federation
179 P 12 **Khrebet Nuratau**, Uzbekistan
153 T 8 **Khrebet Orulgan**, Russian Federation
155 S 1 **Khrebet Pay-Khoy**, Russian Federation
153 T 12 **Khrebet Synnagyn**, Russian Federation
179 X 6 **Khrebet Tarbagatay**, Kazakhstan
190 B 12 **Khreum**, Myanmar
178 L 5 **Khromtau**, Kazakhstan
191 K 18 **Khu Khan**, Thailand
175 P 6 **Khuff**, Saudi Arabia
179 R 12 **Khŭjand**, Tajikistan
174 L 7 **Khulays**, Saudi Arabia
183 T 14 **Khulna**, Bangladesh
183 T 14 **Khulna**, Bangladesh
191 F 14 **Khun Yuam**, Thailand
181 J 14 **Khunti**, India
175 R 6 **Khurayş**, Saudi Arabia
182 J 9 **Khurja**, India
177 W 9 **Khushab**, Pakistan
150 H 7 **Khust**, Ukraine
175 U 5 **Khuwayr**, Qatar
213 D 18 **Khuwei**, Sudan
177 T 12 **Khuzdar**, Pakistan
176 G 9 **Khūzestān**, Iran
157 R 4 **Khvalynsk**, Russian Federation
176 L 7 **Khvor**, Iran
176 I 11 **Khvormūj**, Iran
176 F 3 **Khvoy**, Iran
154 H 12 **Khvoynaya**, Russian Federation
177 V 7 **Khyber Pass**, Afghanistan
234 L 5 **Kia**, Solomon Islands
231 U 12 **Kiama**, New South Wales, Australia
197 L 24 **Kiamba**, Philippines
217 P 12 **Kiambi**, Democratic Republic of Congo
79 N 5 **Kiana**, Alaska, U.S.A.
231 T 12 **Kiandra**, New South Wales, Australia
217 W 12 **Kibaha**, Tanzania
216 F 10 **Kibangou**, Congo
197 L 21 **Kibawe**, Philippines
217 V 11 **Kibaya**, Tanzania
217 R 7 **Kiboga**, Uganda
217 O 10 **Kibombo**, Democratic Republic of Congo
217 R 10 **Kibondo**, Tanzania
213 I 22 **Kibre Mengist**, Ethiopia
146 C 12 **Kičevo**, Macedonia (F.Y.R.O.M.)
155 N 11 **Kichmengskiy Gorodok**, Russian Federation
197 L 22 **Kidapawan**, Philippines
127 Q 7 **Kidderminster**, United Kingdom
214 G 8 **Kidira**, Senegal
127 T 9 **Kidlington**, United Kingdom
127 R 5 **Kidsgrove**, United Kingdom
126 M 10 **Kidwelly**, United Kingdom
136 H 8 **Kiel**, Germany
64 G 12 **Kiel**, Wisconsin, U.S.A.
143 K 15 **Kielce**, Poland
136 H 8 **Kieler Bucht**, Germany
217 P 14 **Kienge**, Democratic Republic of Congo
234 J 5 **Kieta**, Papua New Guinea
151 P 3 **Kiev**, Ukraine
151 P 3 **Kiev Reservoir**, Ukraine
214 G 7 **Kiffa**, Mauritania
145 H 14 **Kifino Selo**, Bosnia and Herzegovina
147 G 20 **Kifisia**, Greece
147 E 18 **Kifisos**, Greece
173 U 5 **Kifrī**, Iraq
217 Q 9 **Kigali**, Rwanda
217 Q 10 **Kigoma**, Tanzania
217 Q 11 **Kigoma**, Tanzania
78 D 8 **Kihei**, Hawaii, U.S.A.
232 L 10 **Kihikihi**, New Zealand
148 F 8 **Kihnu**, Estonia
199 H 19 **Kii-nagashima**, Japan
199 G 19 **Kii-sanchi**, Japan
199 G 19 **Kii-suidō**, Japan
179 T 7 **Kiik**, Kazakhstan
199 O 21 **Kikai**, Japan
199 O 21 **Kikai-jima**, Japan
144 L 8 **Kikinda**, Serbia and Montenegro
177 Q 14 **Kikki**, Pakistan
159 S 9 **Kikladhes Plateau**, Mediterranean Sea
155 O 14 **Kiknur**, Russian Federation
217 O 12 **Kikondja**, Democratic Republic of Congo
234 C 5 **Kikori**, Papua New Guinea
234 C 5 **Kikori**, Papua New Guinea
216 J 11 **Kikwit**, Democratic Republic of Congo
78 A 6 **Kilauea**, Hawaii, U.S.A.
78 E 9 **Kilauea**, Hawaii, U.S.A.
187 M 15 **Kilchu**, North Korea
125 E 18 **Kilcock**, Republic of Ireland
125 E 18 **Kildare**, Republic of Ireland
216 K 11 **Kilembe**, Democratic Republic of Congo
71 T 6 **Kilgore**, Texas, U.S.A.
237 Y 4 **Kili Island**, Marshall Islands
217 Q 10 **Kiliba**, Democratic Republic of Congo
217 X 10 **Kilifi**, Kenya
217 V 9 **Kilimanjaro**, Tanzania
217 V 10 **Kilimanjaro**, Tanzania
217 X 12 **Kilindoni**, Tanzania
148 F 8 **Kilingi-Nõmme**, Estonia
170 M 13 **Kilis**, Turkey
172 J 1 **Kilis**, Syria
125 B 19 **Kilkee**, Republic of Ireland
125 D 19 **Kilkenny**, Republic of Ireland
126 K 13 **Kilkhampton**, United Kingdom
146 F 13 **Kilkis**, Greece
125 B 20 **Killarney**, Republic of Ireland
86 D 9 **Killarney**, Ontario, Canada
66 H 4 **Killdeer**, North Dakota, U.S.A.
71 P 8 **Killeen**, Texas, U.S.A.
85 T 5 **Killiniq**, Québec, Canada
124 G 13 **Kilmarnock**, United Kingdom
155 Q 14 **Kil'mez'**, Russian Federation
217 V 12 **Kilosa**, Tanzania
125 B 19 **Kilrush**, Republic of Ireland
181 B 22 **Kiltan**, India
217 P 13 **Kilwa**, Democratic Republic of Congo
217 W 13 **Kilwa Kivinje**, Tanzania
193 T 12 **Kilwo**, Indonesia
215 W 11 **Kim**, Chad
75 T 7 **Kim**, Colorado, U.S.A.
193 X 14 **Kimaan**, Indonesia
217 W 13 **Kimambi**, Tanzania
216 G 10 **Kimba**, Congo
231 O 11 **Kimba**, South Australia, Australia
66 G 14 **Kimball**, Nebraska, U.S.A.
234 G 4 **Kimbe**, Papua New Guinea
218 M 12 **Kimberley**, Republic of South Africa
230 K 3 **Kimberley**, Western Australia, Australia
187 M 16 **Kimch'aek**, North Korea
85 R 4 **Kimmirut**, Nunavut, Canada
147 I 23 **Kimolos**, Greece
216 G 11 **Kimpese**, Democratic Republic of Congo
198 I 13 **Kimpoku-san**, Japan
216 H 11 **Kimvula**, Democratic Republic of Congo
195 V 6 **Kinabatangan**, Malaysia
217 W 10 **Kinango**, Kenya
147 L 22 **Kinaros**, Greece
86 C 12 **Kincardine**, Ontario, Canada
217 N 13 **Kinda**, Democratic Republic of Congo
62 I 7 **Kinder**, Louisiana, U.S.A.
83 L 19 **Kindersley**, Saskatchewan, Canada
214 F 11 **Kindia**, Guinea
217 O 9 **Kindu**, Democratic Republic of Congo
157 T 3 **Kinel'-Cherkasy**, Russian Federation
154 L 13 **Kineshma**, Russian Federation
77 H 21 **King City**, California, U.S.A.
111 K 23 **King George Bay**, Falkland Islands
240 G 3 **King George Island**, Antarctica
81 S 9 **King George Islands**, Nunavut, Canada
231 R 14 **King Island**, Tasmania, Australia
241 X 7 **King Leopold and Queen Astrid Coast**, Antarctica
230 I 3 **King Leopold Ranges**, Western Australia, Australia
83 D 16 **King Mountain**, British Columbia, Canada
240 J 9 **King Peninsula**, Antarctica
230 I 3 **King Sound**, Western Australia, Australia
84 L 1 **King William Island**, Nunavut, Canada
231 W 8 **Kingaroy**, Queensland, Australia
68 M 9 **Kingfisher**, Oklahoma, U.S.A.
154 D 11 **Kingisepp**, Russian Federation
68 M 6 **Kingman**, Kansas, U.S.A.
74 G 10 **Kingman**, Arizona, U.S.A.
41 Q 7 **Kingman Reef**, U.S.A.
177 V 10 **Kingri**, Pakistan
125 M 19 **King's**, United Kingdom
127 X 6 **King's Lynn**, United Kingdom
58 L 12 **Kings Park**, New York, U.S.A.
74 L 2 **Kings Peak**, Utah, U.S.A.
127 T 12 **King's Worthy**, United Kingdom
127 N 15 **Kingsbridge**, United Kingdom
127 T 11 **Kingsclere**, United Kingdom
231 P 12 **Kingscote**, South Australia, Australia
63 W 6 **Kingsland**, Georgia, U.S.A.
60 L 8 **Kingsport**, Tennessee, U.S.A.
233 C 23 **Kingston**, New Zealand
58 J 10 **Kingston**, New York, U.S.A.
59 N 11 **Kingston**, Rhode Island, U.S.A.
65 D 19 **Kingston**, Illinois, U.S.A.

Country · Internal administrative region: State/Province/Territory/Dependent territory · Capital city · Mountain range/Undersea ridge · Mountain peak/Volcano/Seamount · Geographic feature · Headland/Point/Cape/Peninsula · Desert · Island/Island group · Antarctic base · Ocean · Sea · Bay/Gulf/Channel/Strait · Lake · Salt pan/Dry/Intermittent lake · River

86 I 12 **Kingston**, Ontario, Canada
92 L 8 **Kingston**, Jamaica 🏛
231 Q 13 **Kingston S.E.**, South Australia, Australia
127 V 2 **Kingston upon Hull**, United Kingdom
127 V 11 **Kingston upon Thames**, United Kingdom
93 Y 12 **Kingstown**, St Vincent and the Grenadines 🏛
71 P 13 **Kingsville**, Texas, U.S.A.
127 Q 11 **Kingswood**, United Kingdom
127 P 8 **Kington**, United Kingdom
216 J 11 **Kingungi**, Democratic Republic of Congo
198 L 12 **Kinka-san**, Japan ▶
216 G 10 **Kinkala**, Congo
232 L 11 **Kinloch**, New Zealand
135 E 23 **Kinna**, Sweden
133 K 17 **Kinrooi**, Belgium
216 H 10 **Kinshasa**, Democratic Republic of Congo 🏛
216 H 10 **Kinshasa**, Democratic Republic of Congo ▣
68 K 5 **Kinsley**, Kansas, U.S.A.
61 T 10 **Kinston**, North Carolina, U.S.A.
214 H 10 **Kintinian**, Guinea
193 P 11 **Kintom**, Indonesia
192 L 12 **Kintop**, Indonesia
125 F 14 **Kintyre**, United Kingdom 🏝
190 D 10 **Kinu**, Myanmar
217 T 10 **Kinyangiri**, Tanzania
213 F 23 **Kinyeti**, Sudan ▲
217 T 12 **Kipembawe**, Tanzania
217 R 12 **Kipili**, Tanzania
78 L 10 **Kipnuk**, Alaska, U.S.A.
217 P 15 **Kipushi**, Democratic Republic of Congo
217 Q 15 **Kipushia**, Democratic Republic of Congo
235 N 7 **Kirakira**, Solomon Islands
181 G 17 **Kirandul**, India
181 F 23 **Kiranur**, India
149 L 18 **Kirawsk**, Belarus
71 U 8 **Kirbyville**, Texas, U.S.A.
139 T 5 **Kirchdorf**, Austria
137 G 23 **Kirchheim**, Germany
153 Q 13 **Kirenga**, Russian Federation 〰
153 Q 12 **Kirensk**, Russian Federation
179 T 10 **Kirghiz Range**, Kyrgyzstan ⛰
216 J 8 **Kiri**, Democratic Republic of Congo
236 I 4 **Kiribati**, Oceania □
171 Q 8 **Kirik**, Turkey
170 L 13 **Kirikhan**, Turkey
170 I 9 **Kirikkale**, Turkey
154 J 11 **Kirillov**, Russian Federation
154 F 11 **Kirishi**, Russian Federation
199 C 23 **Kirishima-yama**, Japan ▲
232 K 11 **Kiritehere**, New Zealand
234 G 6 **Kiriwina Island**, Papua New Guinea 🏝
127 Q 1 **Kirkby Lonsdale**, United Kingdom
127 U 1 **Kirkbymoorside**, United Kingdom
124 I 12 **Kirkcaldy**, United Kingdom
134 M 6 **Kirkenes**, Norway
127 P 2 **Kirkham**, United Kingdom
135 L 19 **Kirkkonummi**, Finland
86 E 6 **Kirkland Lake**, Ontario, Canada
146 M 11 **Kirklareli**, Turkey
170 C 6 **Kirklareli**, Turkey
69 U 1 **Kirksville**, Missouri, U.S.A.
173 T 3 **Kirkūk**, Iraq
124 I 7 **Kirkwall**, United Kingdom
69 X 4 **Kirkwood**, Missouri, U.S.A.
137 D 20 **Kirn**, Germany
155 P 12 **Kirov**, Russian Federation
156 I 2 **Kirov**, Russian Federation
151 V 8 **Kirove**, Ukraine
155 P 12 **Kirovo-Chepetsk**, Russian Federation
151 R 6 **Kirovohrad**, Ukraine
155 P 13 **Kirovskaya Oblast'**, Russian Federation ▣
151 V 11 **Kirovs'ke**, Ukraine
155 Q 11 **Kirs**, Russian Federation
170 J 10 **Kirşehir**, Turkey
177 T 12 **Kirthar Range**, Pakistan ⛰
134 I 9 **Kiruna**, Sweden
217 N 8 **Kirundu**, Democratic Republic of Congo
156 L 1 **Kirzhach**, Russian Federation
135 G 22 **Kisa**, Sweden
217 N 7 **Kisangani**, Democratic Republic of Congo
193 R 14 **Kisar**, Indonesia 🏝
217 W 12 **Kisarawe**, Tanzania
199 K 16 **Kisarazu**, Japan
152 M 12 **Kiselevsk**, Russian Federation
144 H 12 **Kiseljak**, Bosnia and Herzegovina
183 R 11 **Kishanganj**, India
199 C 24 **Kishika-zaki**, Japan ▶
199 G 19 **Kishiwada**, Japan
179 S 2 **Kishkenekol'**, Kazakhstan
183 U 12 **Kishorganj**, Bangladesh
182 I 4 **Kishtwar**, India
215 P 12 **Kisi**, Nigeria
217 T 8 **Kisii**, Kenya
78 C 12 **Kiska Island**, Alaska, U.S.A. 🏝
143 J 25 **Kiskőrös**, Hungary
143 K 24 **Kiskunfélegyháza**, Hungary
143 J 25 **Kiskunhalas**, Hungary
157 O 13 **Kislovodsk**, Russian Federation
213 K 26 **Kismaayo**, Somalia
199 I 17 **Kiso-sanmyaku**, Japan ⛰
214 H 11 **Kissidougou**, Guinea
63 W 10 **Kissimmee**, Florida, U.S.A.
217 T 8 **Kisumu**, Kenya
143 N 21 **Kisvárda**, Hungary
75 U 5 **Kit Carson**, Colorado, U.S.A.
199 B 20 **Kita-Kyūshū**, Japan
199 L 14 **Kitaibaraki**, Japan
198 K 11 **Kitakami**, Japan
198 K 13 **Kitakata**, Japan
217 U 7 **Kitale**, Kenya
198 L 4 **Kitami**, Japan
198 J 3 **Kitami-sanchi**, Japan ⛰
217 O 11 **Kitanda**, Democratic Republic of Congo
199 D 22 **Kitaura**, Japan
86 D 13 **Kitchener**, Ontario, Canada
217 S 6 **Kitgum**, Uganda
83 D 19 **Kitimat**, British Columbia, Canada
134 L 10 **Kitinen**, Finland 〰
147 E 14 **Kitros**, Greece
150 K 6 **Kitsman'**, Ukraine
58 B 12 **Kittanning**, Pennsylvania, U.S.A.
134 K 10 **Kittilä**, Finland
61 W 8 **Kitty Hawk**, North Carolina, U.S.A.
217 S 12 **Kitunda**, Tanzania
219 O 4 **Kitwe**, Zambia
139 P 6 **Kitzbühel**, Austria
139 O 7 **Kitzbüheler Alpen**, Austria ⛰
234 A 5 **Kiunga**, Papua New Guinea
135 L 15 **Kivijärvi**, Finland 💧
148 I 6 **Kiviõli**, Estonia
234 C 6 **Kiwai Island**, Papua New Guinea 🏝
79 N 6 **Kiwalik**, Alaska, U.S.A.
179 S 5 **Kiyevka**, Kazakhstan
170 C 6 **Kiyiköy**, Turkey
155 T 11 **Kizel**, Russian Federation
154 M 10 **Kizema**, Russian Federation
170 I 9 **Kizilirmak**, Turkey 〰
170 G 12 **Kizilören**, Turkey
171 P 13 **Kiziltepe**, Turkey
157 Q 13 **Kizlyar**, Russian Federation
133 G 14 **Klaaswaal**, Netherlands
193 X 15 **Kladar**, Indonesia
143 C 17 **Kladno**, Czech Republic
144 O 10 **Kladovo**, Serbia and Montenegro
191 I 20 **Klaeng**, Thailand
195 W 5 **Klagan**, Malaysia
139 T 9 **Klagenfurt**, Austria
148 B 13 **Klaipėda**, Lithuania
77 E 14 **Klamath**, California, U.S.A.
77 H 14 **Klamath Falls**, Oregon, U.S.A.
143 B 18 **Klatovy**, Czech Republic
132 N 9 **Klazienaveen**, Netherlands
218 I 13 **Kleinsee**, Republic of South Africa
144 E 11 **Klekovača**, Bosnia and Herzegovina ▲
151 N 7 **Klembivka**, Ukraine
219 N 11 **Klerksdorp**, Republic of South Africa
142 N 12 **Kleszczele**, Poland
156 H 3 **Kletnya**, Russian Federation
150 L 3 **Klevan**, Ukraine
137 B 15 **Kleve**, Germany
149 L 18 **Klichaw**, Belarus
149 O 17 **Klimavichy**, Belarus
146 L 7 **Kliment**, Bulgaria
154 H 14 **Klin**, Russian Federation
135 H 23 **Klintehamn**, Sweden
157 S 5 **Klintsovka**, Russian Federation
156 G 3 **Klintsy**, Russian Federation
145 O 15 **Klisura**, Serbia and Montenegro
144 F 11 **Ključ**, Bosnia and Herzegovina
143 I 15 **Kłobuck**, Poland
143 F 17 **Kłodzko**, Poland
135 D 19 **Kløfta**, Norway
133 E 16 **Kloosterzande**, Netherlands
138 J 8 **Klosters**, Switzerland
143 H 15 **Kluczbork**, Poland
149 I 19 **Klyetsk**, Belarus
153 Y 10 **Klyuchi**, Russian Federation
127 S 1 **Knaresborough**, United Kingdom
135 A 18 **Knarvik**, Norway
146 H 7 **Knezha**, Bulgaria
144 L 12 **Knić**, Serbia and Montenegro
127 O 7 **Knighton**, United Kingdom
139 U 7 **Knittelfeld**, Austria
63 V 12 **Knob Island**, Florida, U.S.A. 🏝
133 C 16 **Knokke-Heist**, Belgium
127 T 2 **Knottingley**, United Kingdom
237 Z 4 **Knox**, Marshall Islands 🏝
65 I 17 **Knox**, Indiana, U.S.A.
241 X 10 **Knox Coast**, Antarctica ◇
60 J 9 **Knoxville**, Tennessee, U.S.A.
63 T 4 **Knoxville**, Georgia, U.S.A.
67 T 13 **Knoxville**, Iowa, U.S.A.
45 P 10 **Knud Rasmussen Land**, Greenland ◇
127 Q 4 **Knutsford**, United Kingdom
218 L 15 **Knysna**, Republic of South Africa
191 F 23 **Ko Chan**, Thailand 🏝
191 J 21 **Ko Chang**, Thailand 🏝
198 I 8 **Ko-jima**, Japan 🏝
191 J 21 **Ko Kut**, Thailand 🏝
191 F 25 **Ko Lanta**, Thailand 🏝
191 G 25 **Ko Lanta**, Thailand
191 G 25 **Ko Libong**, Thailand 🏝
191 H 23 **Ko Phangan**, Thailand 🏝
191 F 23 **Ko Phra Thong**, Thailand 🏝
191 F 25 **Ko Phuket**, Thailand 🏝
191 H 23 **Ko Samui**, Thailand 🏝
191 G 23 **Ko Tao**, Thailand 🏝
191 G 25 **Ko Yao Yai**, Thailand 🏝
217 W 11 **Koani**, Tanzania
192 G 12 **Koba**, Indonesia
144 A 7 **Kobarid**, Slovenia
199 F 18 **Kōbe**, Japan
193 R 10 **Kobe**, Indonesia
151 T 5 **Kobelyaky**, Ukraine
214 H 8 **Kobenni**, Mauritania
137 D 18 **Koblenz**, Germany
151 Q 9 **Kobleve**, Ukraine
213 I 18 **K'obo**, Ethiopia
217 R 6 **Koboko**, Uganda
193 V 13 **Kobroör**, Indonesia 🏝
149 F 21 **Kobryn**, Belarus
79 O 5 **Kobuk**, Alaska, U.S.A.
79 O 5 **Kobuk**, Alaska, U.S.A. 〰
171 Q 7 **K'obulet'i**, Georgia
170 E 8 **Kocaeli**, Turkey
146 E 11 **Kočani**, Macedonia (F.Y.R.O.M.)
144 K 11 **Koceljevo**, Serbia and Montenegro
144 C 8 **Kočevje**, Slovenia
183 T 10 **Koch Bihar**, India
199 E 20 **Kōchi**, Japan
179 V 10 **Kochkor**, Kyrgyzstan
157 R 13 **Kochubey**, Russian Federation
143 N 14 **Kock**, Poland
199 B 26 **Kodakara-jima**, Japan 🏝
183 Q 9 **Kodari**, Nepal
183 Q 12 **Kodarma**, India
79 Q 11 **Kodiak**, Alaska, U.S.A.
79 P 12 **Kodiak Island**, Alaska, U.S.A. 🏝
181 A 16 **Kodinar**, India
154 K 7 **Kodino**, Russian Federation
153 P 12 **Kodinsk**, Russian Federation
213 E 20 **Kodok**, Sudan
198 J 8 **Kodomari-misaki**, Japan ▶
146 K 12 **Kodzhaele**, Greece ▲
218 J 11 **Koës**, Namibia
146 M 11 **Kofşaz**, Turkey
170 H 15 **Kofinou**, Cyprus
139 V 7 **Köflach**, Austria
199 J 16 **Kōfu**, Japan
199 E 18 **Kōfu**, Japan
85 P 6 **Kogaluk**, Québec, Canada 〰
152 L 10 **Kogalym**, Russian Federation
135 D 25 **Køge**, Denmark
215 Q 12 **Kogi**, Nigeria ▣
177 R 8 **Koh-i-Sangān**, Afghanistan ▲
177 S 13 **Kohan**, Pakistan
177 W 8 **Kohat**, Pakistan
148 G 6 **Kohila**, Estonia
183 X 11 **Kohima**, India
176 H 9 **Kohkīlūyeh Va Būyeraḥmadī**, Iran ▣
177 P 7 **Kohsan**, Afghanistan
148 I 5 **Kohtla-Järve**, Estonia
173 T 2 **Koi Sanjaq**, Iraq
134 L 11 **Koivu**, Finland
187 N 21 **Kōje-do**, South Korea 🏝
230 G 12 **Kojonup**, Western Australia, Australia
179 V 12 **Kök-Aygy**, Kyrgyzstan
179 S 12 **Kokand**, Uzbekistan
214 E 8 **Koki**, Senegal
135 K 14 **Kokkola**, Finland
215 P 10 **Koko**, Nigeria
234 E 6 **Kokoda**, Papua New Guinea
65 I 18 **Kokomo**, Indiana, U.S.A.
233 E 23 **Kokonga**, New Zealand
234 H 4 **Kokopo**, Papua New Guinea
215 O 12 **Kokoro**, Benin
179 X 5 **Kokpekti**, Kazakhstan
179 Q 10 **Koksaray**, Kazakhstan
179 R 3 **Kokshetau**, Kazakhstan
133 A 17 **Koksijde**, Belgium
219 O 13 **Kokstad**, Republic of South Africa
179 X 9 **Koktal**, Kazakhstan
179 Y 7 **Koktuma**, Kazakhstan
199 C 23 **Kokubu**, Japan
154 J 4 **Kola Peninsula**, Russian Federation ▶
193 O 13 **Kolaka**, Indonesia
181 E 21 **Kolar**, India
180 E 13 **Kolaras**, India
134 K 10 **Kolari**, Finland
145 J 15 **Kolašin**, Serbia and Montenegro
180 C 11 **Kolayat**, India
214 E 9 **Kolda**, Senegal
216 M 10 **Kole**, Democratic Republic of Congo
217 N 6 **Kole**, Democratic Republic of Congo
148 H 7 **Kolga-Jaani**, Estonia
148 G 5 **Kolga laht**, Estonia ≈
181 C 18 **Kolhapur**, India
181 L 19 **Kolhumadulu Atoll**, Maldives 🏝
79 O 10 **Koliganek**, Alaska, U.S.A.
135 O 15 **Kolin**, Finland ▲
143 E 17 **Kolín**, Czech Republic
213 I 21 **K'olito**, Ethiopia
236 H 8 **Koliu**, Wallis and Futuna Islands
148 D 9 **Kolkasrags**, Latvia ▶
179 R 14 **Kolkhozobod**, Tajikistan
150 K 2 **Kolky**, Ukraine
139 S 3 **Kollerschlag**, Austria
142 M 10 **Kolno**, Poland
142 I 13 **Koło**, Poland
142 E 8 **Kołobrzeg**, Poland
234 K 6 **Kolombangara**, Solomon Islands 🏝
156 L 2 **Kolomna**, Russian Federation
150 J 6 **Kolomyya**, Ukraine
237 Q 15 **Kolonia**, Federated States of Micronesia
193 P 13 **Kolono**, Indonesia
152 M 11 **Kolpashevo**, Russian Federation
154 F 10 **Kolpino**, Russian Federation
147 H 15 **Kolpos Agiou Orous**, Greece ≈
147 H 25 **Kolpos Chanion**, Greece ≈
147 G 14 **Kolpos Ierissou**, Greece ≈
147 G 15 **Kolpos Kassandras**, Greece ≈
146 H 13 **Kolpos Kavalas**, Greece ≈
147 G 25 **Kolpos Kissamou**, Greece ≈
179 X 9 **Kol'shat**, Kazakhstan
157 T 3 **Koltubanovskiy**, Russian Federation
179 R 4 **Koluton**, Kazakhstan
217 N 14 **Kolwezi**, Democratic Republic of Congo
149 M 22 **Kolyban**, Belarus
153 W 8 **Kolyma**, Russian Federation 〰
212 F 11 **Kôm Ombo**, Egypt
199 H 17 **Komaki**, Japan
217 Q 8 **Komanda**, Democratic Republic of Congo
143 H 22 **Komárno**, Slovakia
199 H 16 **Komatsu**, Japan
193 P 11 **Kombakomba**, Indonesia
155 R 10 **Komi-Permyatskiy Avtonomnyy Okrug**, Russian Federation ▣
151 Q 9 **Kominternivs'ke**, Ukraine
143 H 25 **Komló**, Hungary
193 N 15 **Komodo**, Indonesia 🏝
214 H 11 **Komodou**, Guinea
199 J 15 **Komoro**, Japan
147 J 13 **Komotinì**, Greece
151 R 7 **Kompaniyivka**, Ukraine
218 M 14 **Kompasberg**, Republic of South Africa ▲
179 N 2 **Komsomolets**, Kazakhstan
153 W 13 **Komsomol'sk-na-Amure**, Russian Federation
153 Y 6 **Komsomol'skiy**, Russian Federation
178 M 5 **Komsomol'skoye**, Kazakhstan
146 J 11 **Komuniga**, Bulgaria
191 O 18 **Kon Plong**, Vietnam
191 O 18 **Kon Tum**, Vietnam
181 J 17 **Konarka**, India
182 K 11 **Konch**, India
181 H 17 **Kondagaon**, India
217 U 11 **Kondoa**, Tanzania
157 P 4 **Kondol**, Russian Federation
177 U 5 **Kondūz**, Afghanistan
235 P 13 **Koné**, New Caledonia
45 O 13 **Kong Christian IX Land**, Greenland ◇
45 P 12 **Kong Christian X Land**, Greenland ◇
45 N 12 **Kong Frederik IX Land**, Greenland ◇
45 Q 11 **Kong Frederik VIII Land**, Greenland ◇
45 Q 12 **Kong Wilhelm Land**, Greenland ◇
218 L 7 **Kongola**, Namibia
217 O 11 **Kongolo**, Democratic Republic of Congo
135 D 20 **Kongsberg**, Norway
135 E 19 **Kongsvinger**, Norway
184 G 6 **Kongur Shan**, China ▲
217 U 11 **Kongwa**, Tanzania
137 M 25 **Königssee**, Germany 〰
142 H 13 **Konin**, Poland
233 L 15 **Konini**, New Zealand
147 B 15 **Konitsa**, Greece
144 H 13 **Konjic**, Bosnia and Herzegovina
134 J 8 **Könkämäeno**, Finland 〰
234 G 3 **Konos**, Papua New Guinea
154 K 10 **Konosha**, Russian Federation
151 S 2 **Konotop**, Ukraine
143 K 15 **Końskie**, Poland
213 H 22 **Konso**, Ethiopia
137 F 25 **Konstanz**, Germany
181 G 18 **Konta**, India
215 Q 11 **Kontagora**, Nigeria
135 N 14 **Kontiomäki**, Finland
170 H 12 **Konya**, Turkey
193 U 11 **Koor**, Indonesia
230 G 10 **Koorda**, Western Australia, Australia
72 K 6 **Kooskia**, Idaho, U.S.A.
232 K 11 **Kopaki**, New Zealand
145 L 14 **Kopaonik**, Serbia and Montenegro ⛰
134 C 9 **Kópasker**, Iceland
179 V 7 **Kopbirlik**, Kazakhstan
144 A 8 **Koper**, Slovenia
178 J 13 **Kopet Dag**, Turkmenistan ⛰
145 J 16 **Koplik**, Albania
181 D 21 **Koppa**, India
135 D 17 **Koppang**, Norway
150 L 5 **Kopychyntsi**, Ukraine
145 L 17 **Korab**, Albania ▲
145 L 17 **Korab**, Albania ⛰
156 M 3 **Korablino**, Russian Federation
213 L 22 **K'orahē**, Ethiopia
181 E 18 **Korangal**, India
181 H 15 **Korba**, India
137 F 16 **Korbach**, Germany
215 X 11 **Korbol**, Chad
145 L 20 **Korçë**, Albania
159 N 5 **Korčula**, Mediterranean Sea 🏝
179 U 10 **Korday**, Kazakhstan
176 F 5 **Kordestān**, Iran ▣
187 I 18 **Korea Bay**, China/North Korea ≈
187 M 22 **Korea Strait**, Japan/South Korea ≈
213 I 18 **Korem**, Ethiopia
232 J 7 **Koremoa**, New Zealand
156 I 5 **Korenevo**, Russian Federation
156 L 11 **Korenovsk**, Russian Federation
150 L 3 **Korets'**, Ukraine
153 Z 9 **Korf**, Russian Federation
170 E 8 **Körfez**, Turkey
184 I 4 **Korgas**, China
214 J 11 **Korhogo**, Côte d'Ivoire
147 F 20 **Korinthos**, Greece
143 H 23 **Kőris-hegy**, Hungary ▲
198 K 13 **Kōriyama**, Japan
170 E 12 **Korkuteli**, Turkey
184 K 5 **Korla**, China
143 F 24 **Körmend**, Hungary
139 X 3 **Korneuburg**, Austria
235 Y 11 **Koro**, Fiji 🏝
235 X 12 **Koro Sea**, Fiji 🌊
215 X 8 **Koro Toro**, Chad

□ Country ▣ Internal administrative region: State/Province/Territory/Dependent territory 🏛 Capital city ⛰ Mountain range/Undersea ridge ▲ Mountain peak/Volcano/Seamount ◇ Geographic feature ▶ Headland/Point/Cape/Peninsula ◭ Desert 🏝 Island/Island group ⁙ Antarctic base ◎ Ocean 🌊 Sea ≈ Bay/Gulf/Channel/Strait 💧 Lake ⚑ Salt pan/Dry/Intermittent lake 〰 R

▣ Country | ▣ Internal administrative region: State/Province/Territory/Dependent territory | ♣ Capital city | ▲ Mountain range/Undersea ridge | ▲ Mountain peak/Volcano/Seamount | ◇ Geographic feature | ▶ Headland/Point/Cape/Peninsula | ⊐ Desert | ⊐ Island/Island group | ▲ Antarctic base | Ocean | ≈ Sea | ≈ Bay/Gulf/Channel/Strait | Lake | ↘ Salt pan/Dry/Intermittent lake | ↘ River

◻ Country ▣ Internal administrative region: State/Province/Territory/Dependent territory ◼ Capital city ▲ Mountain range/Undersea ridge ▲ Mountain peak/Volcano/Seamount ◇ Geographic feature ▸ Headland/Point/Cape/Peninsula ▲ Desert ◼ Island/Island group ⊕ Antarctic base ◡ Ocean ◡ Sea ≈ Bay/Gulf/Channel/Strait ◡ Lake ◼ Salt pan/Dry/Intermittent lake ◡ River

138 L 7 **Längenfeld**, Austria
139 W 3 **Langenlois**, Austria
138 E 7 **Langenthal**, Switzerland
136 D 10 **Langeoog**, Germany 🏝
152 L 10 **Langepas**, Russian Federation
187 E 17 **Langfang**, China
134 B 11 **Langjökull**, Iceland ◇
194 A 4 **Langkawi**, Malaysia 🏝
195 V 4 **Langkon**, Malaysia
64 G 10 **Langlade**, Wisconsin, U.S.A.
76 E 12 **Langlois**, Oregon, U.S.A.
138 E 8 **Langnau**, Switzerland
129 R 12 **Langogne**, France
128 M 12 **Langon**, France
134 G 8 **Langøya**, Norway 🏝
129 U 6 **Langres**, France
192 C 8 **Langsa**, Indonesia
133 M 25 **Langsur**, Luxembourg
215 S 12 **Langtang**, Nigeria
183 W 11 **Langting**, India
129 Q 14 **Languedoc-Roussillon**, France ▣
189 O 6 **Langzhong**, China
126 K 14 **Lanivet**, United Kingdom
171 Y 10 **Länkäran**, Azerbaijan
128 I 4 **Lannion**, France
58 I 13 **Lansdale**, Pennsylvania, U.S.A.
65 K 14 **Lansing**, Michigan, U.S.A.
134 J 11 **Lansjärv**, Sweden
189 Q 4 **Lantian**, China
141 C 18 **Lanusei**, Italy
186 K 10 **Lanxi**, China
189 Y 7 **Lanxi**, China
42 O 11 **Lanzarote**, Canary Islands 🏝
189 N 2 **Lanzhou**, China
190 K 11 **Lao Cai**, Vietnam
196 F 6 **Laoag**, Philippines
197 L 14 **Laoang**, Philippines
186 N 12 **Laoheishan**, China
189 S 5 **Laohekou**, China
187 K 15 **Laoling**, China
129 R 3 **Laon**, France
191 K 14 **Laos**, Asia □
186 M 13 **Laotougou**, China
187 J 15 **Laotuding Shan**, China ▲
112 I 9 **Lapa**, Brazil
197 F 24 **Lapac**, Philippines 🏝
112 C 10 **Lapachito**, Argentina
215 Q 12 **Lapai**, Nigeria
129 S 9 **Lapalisse**, France
197 E 24 **Laparan**, Philippines 🏝
135 K 15 **Lappajärvi**, Finland ◢
135 N 18 **Lappeenranta**, Finland
134 I 11 **Lappland**, Sweden ◇
170 B 8 **Lâpseki**, Turkey
153 R 6 **Laptev Sea**, Russian Federation 🌊
197 K 17 **Lapu-Lapu**, Philippines
135 K 16 **Lapua**, Finland
142 N 11 **Łapy**, Poland
140 I 13 **L'Aquila**, Italy
176 K 12 **Lār**, Iran
177 Q 9 **Lar Koh**, Afghanistan ▲
104 L 2 **Lara**, Venezuela ▣
210 H 6 **Larache**, Morocco
176 L 13 **Lārak**, Iran 🏝
73 Y 14 **Laramie**, Wyoming, U.S.A.
73 X 13 **Laramie**, Wyoming, U.S.A. 〰
73 W 12 **Laramie Mountains**, Wyoming, U.S.A. ⛰
112 G 8 **Laranjeiras do Sul**, Brazil
193 P 15 **Larantuka**, Indonesia
193 U 14 **Larat**, Indonesia 🏝
131 P 1 **Laredo**, Spain
71 N 13 **Laredo**, Texas, U.S.A.
132 I 11 **Laren**, Netherlands
63 V 11 **Largo**, Florida, U.S.A.
124 G 13 **Largs**, United Kingdom
176 G 3 **Lārī**, Iran
67 N 3 **Larimore**, North Dakota, U.S.A.
0 E 16 **Larisa**, Greece
177 U 12 **Larkana**, Pakistan
170 I 15 **Larnaka**, Cyprus
125 F 15 **Larne**, United Kingdom
68 K 5 **Larned**, Kansas, U.S.A.
231 N 3 **Larrimah**, Northern Territory, Australia
241 W 5 **Lars Christensen Coast**, Antarctica ◇
240 I 4 **Larsen Ice Shelf**, Antarctica ◇
82 J 6 **Larsen Sound**, Nunavut, Canada ≈
135 C 21 **Larvik**, Norway
75 T 6 **Las Animas**, Colorado, U.S.A.
105 P 4 **Las Bonitas**, Venezuela
75 P 14 **Las Cruces**, New Mexico, U.S.A.
113 D 17 **Las Flores**, Argentina
110 G 11 **Las Heras**, Argentina
88 M 7 **Las Herreras**, Mexico
111 G 21 **Las Horquetas**, Argentina
111 G 15 **Las Lajas**, Argentina
106 A 11 **Las Lomas**, Peru
110 L 6 **Las Lomitas**, Argentina
111 H 21 **Las Martinetas**, Argentina
91 U 15 **Las Palmas**, Panama
42 N 12 **Las Palmas de Gran Canaria**, Canary Islands
131 Q 8 **Las Pedroñeras**, Spain
113 E 16 **Las Piedras**, Uruguay
91 O 6 **Las Planchas**, Honduras
111 H 18 **Las Plumas**, Argentina
113 A 14 **Las Rosas**, Argentina
91 W 15 **Las Tablas**, Panama
110 I 8 **Las Termas**, Argentina
91 N 6 **Las Trojes**, Honduras
92 L 6 **Las Tunas**, Cuba
88 M 10 **Las Varas**, Mexico
113 A 14 **Las Varillas**, Argentina
75 R 9 **Las Vegas**, New Mexico, U.S.A.
77 M 22 **Las Vegas**, Nevada, U.S.A.
113 F 15 **Lascano**, Uruguay
190 F 10 **Lashio**, Myanmar
177 R 9 **Lashkar Gāh**, Afghanistan
143 I 14 **Łask**, Poland
77 H 16 **Lassen Peak**, California, U.S.A. ▲
240 K 5 **Lassiter Coast**, Antarctica ◇
75 T 4 **Last Chance**, Colorado, U.S.A.
216 F 8 **Lastoursville**, Gabon
235 P 7 **Lata**, Solomon Islands
106 B 9 **Latacunga**, Ecuador
240 I 6 **Lataday Island**, Antarctica 🏝
159 Y 9 **Latakia Basin**, Mediterranean Sea ◇
86 E 8 **Latchford**, Ontario, Canada
236 I 10 **Late**, Tonga 🏝
181 I 14 **Latehar**, India
141 N 16 **Laterza**, Italy
141 H 15 **Latina**, Italy
140 H 6 **Latisana**, Italy
181 E 17 **Latur**, India
148 F 10 **Latvia**, Europe □
134 B 10 **Laugarbakki**, Iceland
126 L 9 **Laugharne**, United Kingdom
148 C 13 **Laukuva**, Lithuania
231 T 15 **Launceston**, Tasmania, Australia
126 L 14 **Launceston**, United Kingdom
190 F 7 **Launggyaung**, Myanmar
191 F 19 **Launglon Bok Islands**, Myanmar 🏝
196 G 10 **Laur**, Philippines
231 S 3 **Laura**, Queensland, Australia
63 N 5 **Laurel**, Mississippi, U.S.A.
67 O 12 **Laurel**, Nebraska, U.S.A.
73 T 7 **Laurel**, Montana, U.S.A.
60 M 11 **Laurens**, South Carolina, U.S.A.
81 V 11 **Laurentian Mountains**, Québec, Canada ⛰
141 L 17 **Lauria**, Italy
240 I 1 **Laurie Island**, South Orkney Islands 🏝
61 Q 11 **Laurinburg**, North Carolina, U.S.A.
141 K 17 **Laurino**, Italy
233 G 21 **Lauriston**, New Zealand
138 B 9 **Lausanne**, Switzerland
192 H 8 **Laut**, Indonesia 🏝
192 M 13 **Laut**, Indonesia 🏝
235 W 11 **Lautoka**, Fiji
132 L 5 **Lauwersmeer**, Netherlands ◢
128 M 6 **Laval**, France
86 K 10 **Laval**, Québec, Canada
113 F 15 **Lavalleja**, Uruguay ▣
139 U 8 **Lavamünd**, Austria
176 H 11 **Lāvar**, Iran
141 L 15 **Lavello**, Italy
127 Y 8 **Lavenham**, United Kingdom
68 J 8 **Laverne**, Oklahoma, U.S.A.
230 I 9 **Laverton**, Western Australia, Australia
135 A 17 **Lavik**, Norway
73 T 6 **Lavina**, Montana, U.S.A.
240 H 5 **Lavoisier Island**, Antarctica 🏝
112 M 5 **Lavras**, Brazil
147 H 21 **Lavrio**, Greece
241 X 3 **Law Promontory**, Antarctica ▶
190 E 8 **Lawa**, Myanmar
195 T 6 **Lawas**, Malaysia
175 Q 14 **Lawdar**, Yemen
233 E 24 **Lawrence**, New Zealand
59 O 9 **Lawrence**, Massachusetts, U.S.A.
69 Q 4 **Lawrence**, Kansas, U.S.A.
60 E 10 **Lawrenceburg**, Tennessee, U.S.A.
61 S 7 **Lawrenceville**, Virginia, U.S.A.
65 H 20 **Lawrenceville**, Illinois, U.S.A.
68 L 12 **Lawton**, Oklahoma, U.S.A.
175 R 7 **Laylá**, Saudi Arabia
41 P 5 **Laysan Island**, Hawaii 🏝
77 F 17 **Laytonville**, California, U.S.A.
43 L 23 **Lazarev Sea**, Atlantic Ocean 🌊
89 O 13 **Lázaro Cárdenas**, Mexico
110 O 12 **Lazcano**, Uruguay
140 G 13 **Lazio**, Italy ▣
153 U 9 **Lazo**, Russian Federation
151 S 10 **Lazurne**, Ukraine
129 O 8 **Le Blanc**, France
129 Q 15 **Le Boulou**, France
138 B 9 **Le Brassus**, Switzerland
38 A 15 **Le Gros Morne**, Réunion ▲
129 N 3 **Le Havre**, France
211 P 5 **Le Kef**, Tunisia
138 C 7 **Le Locle**, Switzerland
129 N 6 **Le Mans**, France
67 P 11 **Le Mars**, Iowa, U.S.A.
128 L 5 **Le Mont-St-Michel**, France
141 M 15 **Le Murge**, Italy ⛰
128 J 7 **Le Palais**, France
38 A 14 **Le Port**, Réunion
129 S 11 **Le-Puy-en-Velay**, France
67 R 8 **Le Sueur**, Minnesota, U.S.A.
38 B 15 **Le Tampon**, Réunion
129 P 1 **Le Touquet-Paris-Plage**, France
129 O 2 **Le Tréport**, France
129 R 13 **Le Vigan**, France
127 U 5 **Leadenham**, United Kingdom
83 L 19 **Leader**, Saskatchewan, Canada
84 I 7 **Leaf Rapids**, Manitoba, Canada
86 B 15 **Leamington**, Ontario, Canada
71 P 9 **Leander**, Texas, U.S.A.
230 E 7 **Learmonth**, Western Australia, Australia
133 F 22 **L'Eau d'Heure**, Belgium ◢
69 R 3 **Leavenworth**, Kansas, U.S.A.
76 I 7 **Leavenworth**, Washington, U.S.A.
142 H 7 **Łeba**, Poland
197 K 23 **Lebak**, Philippines
145 N 14 **Lebane**, Serbia and Montenegro
172 H 6 **Lebanon**, Asia □
58 G 13 **Lebanon**, Pennsylvania, U.S.A.
58 M 7 **Lebanon**, New Hampshire, U.S.A.
60 G 8 **Lebanon**, Tennessee, U.S.A.
60 M 7 **Lebanon**, Virginia, U.S.A.
65 I 18 **Lebanon**, Indiana, U.S.A.
69 U 6 **Lebanon**, Missouri, U.S.A.
76 G 11 **Lebanon**, Oregon, U.S.A.
179 N 12 **Lebap**, Turkmenistan
179 O 14 **Lebapskiy Velayat**, Turkmenistan ▣
77 J 23 **Lebec**, California, U.S.A.
156 L 4 **Lebedyan'**, Russian Federation
151 T 3 **Lebedyn**, Ukraine
216 M 5 **Lebo**, Democratic Republic of Congo
142 H 8 **Lębork**, Poland
219 O 10 **Lebowakgomo**, Republic of South Africa
130 K 13 **Lebrija**, Spain
111 E 14 **Lebu**, Chile
141 O 17 **Lecce**, Italy
140 D 6 **Lecco**, Italy
138 J 7 **Lech**, Austria
147 C 20 **Lechaina**, Greece
189 T 11 **Lechang**, China
127 S 10 **Lechlade**, United Kingdom
138 K 7 **Lechtaler Alpen**, Austria ⛰
136 F 7 **Leck**, Germany
62 I 6 **Lecompte**, Louisiana, U.S.A.
143 N 14 **Łęczna**, Poland
142 I 13 **Łęczyca**, Poland
127 Q 9 **Ledbury**, United Kingdom
130 K 5 **Ledesma**, Spain
125 B 21 **Lee**, Republic of Ireland 〰
77 J 19 **Lee Vining**, California, U.S.A.
127 S 2 **Leeds**, United Kingdom
63 Q 3 **Leeds**, Alabama, U.S.A.
127 R 5 **Leek**, United Kingdom
136 D 11 **Leer**, Germany
132 I 13 **Leerdam**, Netherlands
69 S 4 **Lees Summit**, Missouri, U.S.A.
61 T 3 **Leesburg**, Virginia, U.S.A.
63 W 9 **Leesburg**, Florida, U.S.A.
148 G 5 **Leesi**, Estonia
62 H 6 **Leesville**, Louisiana, U.S.A.
231 T 12 **Leeton**, New South Wales, Australia
218 L 14 **Leeu-Gamka**, Republic of South Africa
132 K 6 **Leeuwarden**, Netherlands
93 W 7 **Leeward Islands**, Caribbean Sea 🏝
170 H 15 **Lefka**, Cyprus
147 G 26 **Lefka Ori**, Greece ⛰
147 B 18 **Lefkada**, Greece
147 B 18 **Lefkada**, Greece 🏝
147 A 16 **Lefkimmi**, Greece
196 K 13 **Legaspi**, Philippines
77 E 16 **Leggett**, California, U.S.A.
133 J 24 **Léglise**, Belgium
140 F 7 **Legnago**, Italy
143 F 15 **Legnica**, Poland
217 N 6 **Leguga**, Democratic Republic of Congo
182 J 3 **Leh**, India
58 G 12 **Lehighton**, Pennsylvania, U.S.A.
177 W 10 **Leiah**, Pakistan
139 W 8 **Leibnitz**, Austria
127 T 6 **Leicester**, United Kingdom
231 Q 4 **Leichhardt**, Queensland, Australia 〰
132 G 12 **Leiden**, Netherlands
232 K 7 **Leigh**, New Zealand
231 P 9 **Leigh Creek**, South Australia, Australia
127 U 9 **Leighton Buzzard**, United Kingdom
189 Q 9 **Leigong Shan**, China ▲
132 G 12 **Leimuiden**, Netherlands
137 G 14 **Leine**, Germany 〰
137 H 16 **Leinefelde**, Germany
230 H 9 **Leinster**, Western Australia, Australia
125 D 19 **Leinster**, Republic of Ireland ▣
147 L 21 **Leipsoi**, Greece 🏝
137 K 16 **Leipzig**, Germany
135 C 18 **Leira**, Norway
130 G 7 **Leiria**, Portugal
135 A 19 **Leirvik**, Norway
148 D 7 **Leisi**, Estonia
60 G 6 **Leitchfield**, Kentucky, U.S.A.
189 T 10 **Leiyang**, China
134 E 13 **Leka**, Norway 🏝
216 M 8 **Lekatero**, Democratic Republic of Congo
134 F 9 **Leknes**, Norway
216 G 9 **Lékoni**, Gabon
216 G 9 **Lékoumou**, Congo ▣
135 G 19 **Leksand**, Sweden
62 K 3 **Leland**, Mississippi, U.S.A.
132 J 10 **Lelystad**, Netherlands
234 I 4 **Lemankoa**, Papua New Guinea
170 H 15 **Lemesos**, Cyprus
137 F 14 **Lemgo**, Germany
85 T 3 **Lemieux Islands**, Nunavut, Canada 🏝
132 K 8 **Lemmer**, Netherlands
66 I 7 **Lemmon**, South Dakota, U.S.A.
135 B 24 **Lemvig**, Denmark
191 C 15 **Lemyethna**, Myanmar
153 S 11 **Lena**, Russian Federation 〰
109 M 15 **Lençóis**, Brazil
144 E 6 **Lendava**, Slovenia
154 G 7 **Lendery**, Russian Federation
184 M 7 **Lenghu**, China
189 S 9 **Lengshuijiang**, China
189 S 10 **Lengshuitan**, China
194 D 10 **Lenik**, Malaysia 〰
179 T 12 **Lenin Peak**, Kyrgyzstan ▲
151 W 11 **Lenine**, Ukraine
241 S 15 **Leningradskaya**, Antarctica ⁙
154 F 10 **Leningradskaya Oblast'**, Russian Federation ▣
153 Y 5 **Leningradskiy**, Russian Federation
157 T 2 **Leninogorsk**, Russian Federation
179 Y 4 **Leninogorsk**, Kazakhstan
157 P 8 **Leninsk**, Russian Federation
179 U 3 **Lenīnskīy**, Kazakhstan
155 N 12 **Leninskoye**, Russian Federation
178 H 5 **Leninskoye**, Kazakhstan
179 P 2 **Leninskoye**, Kazakhstan
140 D 6 **Lenna**, Italy
137 E 16 **Lennestadt**, Germany
61 N 9 **Lenoir**, North Carolina, U.S.A.
129 Q 1 **Lens**, France
133 E 20 **Lens**, Belgium
153 R 11 **Lensk**, Russian Federation
171 S 5 **Lentekhi**, Georgia
143 F 24 **Lenti**, Hungary
149 G 16 **Lentvaris**, Lithuania
152 G 7 **Lent'yevo**, Russian Federation
191 G 21 **Lenya**, Myanmar
139 V 6 **Leoben**, Austria
139 X 4 **Leobersdorf**, Austria
127 Q 8 **Leominster**, United Kingdom
130 L 2 **León**, Spain
89 P 10 **León**, Mexico
90 M 9 **León**, Nicaragua
128 L 13 **Léon**, France
71 R 5 **Leonard**, Texas, U.S.A.
147 F 22 **Leonidi**, Greece
230 I 9 **Leonora**, Western Australia, Australia
112 N 6 **Leopoldina**, Brazil
151 N 10 **Leova**, Moldova
219 N 9 **Lephepe**, Botswana
189 W 7 **Leping**, China
179 W 7 **Lepsy**, Kazakhstan
147 E 15 **Leptokarya**, Greece
141 I 22 **Lercara Friddi**, Italy
215 R 11 **Lere**, Nigeria
215 V 11 **Léré**, Chad
171 Y 10 **Lerik**, Azerbaijan
131 O 3 **Lerma**, Spain
138 L 6 **Lermoos**, Austria
147 M 22 **Leros**, Greece 🏝
124 J 4 **Lerwick**, United Kingdom
93 N 8 **Les Cayes**, Haiti
64 K 9 **Les Cheneaux Islands**, Michigan, U.S.A. 🏝
87 P 6 **Les Escoumins**, Québec, Canada
128 L 8 **Les Herbiers**, France
87 R 5 **Les Méchins**, Québec, Canada
129 V 13 **Les Mées**, France
128 K 8 **Les Sables-d'Olonne**, France
38 C 8 **Les Sšurs**, Seychelles 🏝
129 S 12 **Les Vans**, France
147 J 17 **Lesbos**, Greece 🏝
188 M 7 **Leshan**, China
155 N 6 **Leshukonskoye**, Russian Federation
145 N 14 **Leskovac**, Serbia and Montenegro
145 L 21 **Leskovik**, Albania
65 K 15 **Leslie**, Michigan, U.S.A.
73 N 10 **Leslie**, Idaho, U.S.A.
143 E 15 **Leśna**, Poland
153 O 12 **Lesosibirsk**, Russian Federation
219 N 13 **Lesotho**, Africa □
153 V 15 **Lesozavodsk**, Russian Federation
128 L 11 **Lesparre-Médoc**, France
93 S 12 **Lesser Antilles**, Caribbean Sea 🏝
171 R 7 **Lesser Caucasus**, Georgia ⛰
83 I 17 **Lesser Slave Lake**, Alberta, Canada ◢
39 T 5 **Lesser Sunda Islands**, Indonesia 🏝
133 E 20 **Lessines**, Belgium
135 L 15 **Lestijärvi**, Finland ◢
135 K 14 **Lestijoki**, Finland 〰
142 F 13 **Leszno**, Poland
83 K 21 **Lethbridge**, Alberta, Canada
105 T 7 **Lethem**, Guyana
193 R 15 **Leti**, Indonesia 🏝
104 L 13 **Leticia**, Colombia
154 J 5 **Letniy Navolok**, Russian Federation
191 D 15 **Letpadan**, Myanmar
191 F 21 **Letsok-aw Kyun**, Myanmar 🏝
218 J 4 **Léua**, Angola
137 H 25 **Leutkirch**, Germany
133 H 19 **Leuven**, Belgium
133 D 20 **Leuze-en-Hainaut**, Belgium
147 F 19 **Levadeia**, Greece
159 S 12 **Levantine Basin**, Mediterranean Sea ◇
140 D 9 **Levanto**, Italy
157 R 15 **Levashi**, Russian Federation
70 I 5 **Levelland**, Texas, U.S.A.
127 V 2 **Leven**, United Kingdom
137 C 17 **Leverkusen**, Germany
143 I 21 **Levice**, Slovakia
147 E 21 **Levidi**, Greece
147 L 22 **Levitha**, Greece 🏝
58 I 13 **Levittown**, Pennsylvania, U.S.A.
143 K 19 **Levoča**, Slovakia
146 J 7 **Levski**, Bulgaria
235 X 11 **Levuka**, Fiji
127 W 13 **Lewes**, United Kingdom
61 X 3 **Lewes**, Delaware, U.S.A.
67 N 11 **Lewis and Clark Lake**, South Dakota, U.S.A. ◢
72 M 2 **Lewis Range**, Montana, U.S.A. ⛰
63 P 2 **Lewis Smith Lake**, Alabama, U.S.A. ◢
60 E 7 **Lewisburg**, Kentucky, U.S.A.
60 F 10 **Lewisburg**, Tennessee, U.S.A.
61 P 5 **Lewisburg**, West Virginia, U.S.A.

□ Country ▣ Internal administrative region: State/Province/Territory/Dependent territory ♜ Capital city ⛰ Mountain range/Undersea ridge ▲ Mountain peak/Volcano/Seamount ◇ Geographic feature ▶ Headland/Point/Cape/Peninsula ◠ Desert 🏝 Island/Island group ⁙ Antarctic base 🌀 Ocean 🌊 Sea ≈ Bay/Gulf/Channel/Strait ◢ Lake ⚑ Salt pan/Dry/Intermittent lake 〰 Riv

180 C 12 **Lohawat**, India
190 E 12 **Loi-lem**, Myanmar
190 E 11 **Loi Sang**, Myanmar ▲
190 E 13 **Loikaw**, Myanmar
128 L 7 **Loire**, France 〰
106 B 11 **Loja**, Ecuador
106 A 11 **Loja**, Ecuador ▣
131 N 12 **Loja**, Spain
195 W 5 **Lokan**, Malaysia 〰
134 M 9 **Lokan tekojärvi**, Finland 💧
133 E 17 **Lokeren**, Belgium
151 S 4 **Lokhvytsya**, Ukraine
217 U 6 **Lokichar**, Kenya
217 T 5 **Lokichokio**, Kenya
154 E 13 **Loknya**, Russian Federation
215 R 12 **Loko**, Nigeria
216 M 8 **Lokofe**, Democratic Republic of Congo
215 R 12 **Lokoja**, Nigeria
216 K 9 **Lokolama**, Democratic Republic of Congo
215 V 15 **Lokomo**, Cameroon
85 T 4 **Loks Land**, Nunavut, Canada 🏝
218 G 5 **Lola**, Angola
135 D 26 **Lolland**, Denmark 🏝
217 U 9 **Lollondo**, Tanzania
73 N 5 **Lolo**, Montana, U.S.A.
72 M 5 **Lolo Hot Springs**, Montana, U.S.A.
234 G 4 **Lolobau Island**, Papua New Guinea 🏝
215 T 15 **Lolodorf**, Cameroon
135 C 17 **Lom**, Norway
146 F 6 **Lom**, Bulgaria
191 I 16 **Lom Sak**, Thailand
214 H 11 **Loma Mountains**, Sierra Leone ▲
107 E 19 **Lomas**, Peru
113 C 16 **Lomas de Zamora**, Argentina
230 I 3 **Lombadina**, Western Australia, Australia
140 E 6 **Lombardia**, Italy ▣
193 P 15 **Lomblen**, Indonesia 🏝
192 L 15 **Lombok**, Indonesia 🏝
39 T 5 **Lombok Basin**, Indian Ocean ◇
215 N 13 **Lomé**, Togo 🏛
216 M 9 **Lomela**, Democratic Republic of Congo
215 V 15 **Lomié**, Cameroon
133 I 17 **Lommel**, Belgium
45 R 9 **Lomonosov Ridge**, Arctic Ocean ⛰
77 H 24 **Lompoc**, California, U.S.A.
142 M 11 **Łomża**, Poland
111 G 15 **Loncopué**, Argentina
133 F 18 **Londerzeel**, Belgium
127 W 10 **London**, United Kingdom 🏛
60 J 7 **London**, Kentucky, U.S.A.
86 D 13 **London**, Ontario, Canada
125 D 15 **Londonderry**, United Kingdom
112 H 7 **Londrina**, Brazil
195 T 8 **Long Akah**, Malaysia
127 P 11 **Long Ashton**, United Kingdom
61 R 13 **Long Bay**, South Carolina, U.S.A. ≈
58 K 13 **Long Beach**, New York, U.S.A.
77 J 25 **Long Beach**, California, U.S.A.
58 J 14 **Long Beach Island**, New Jersey, U.S.A. 🏝
90 L 2 **Long Cay**, Belize 🏝
76 J 11 **Long Creek**, Oregon, U.S.A.
231 V 6 **Long Island**, Queensland, Australia 🏝
234 E 4 **Long Island**, Papua New Guinea 🏝
58 L 12 **Long Island**, New York, U.S.A. 🏝
81 T 10 **Long Island**, Nunavut, Canada 🏝
92 M 4 **Long Island**, The Bahamas 🏝
58 L 12 **Long Island Sound**, New York, U.S.A. ≈
195 S 7 **Long Lama**, Malaysia
195 S 9 **Long Murum**, Malaysia
195 S 8 **Long Pila**, Malaysia
197 C 18 **Long Point**, Philippines ►
84 I 8 **Long Point**, Manitoba, Canada ►
86 D 14 **Long Point**, Ontario, Canada
86 E 14 **Long Point**, Ontario, Canada ►
127 R 1 **Long Preston**, United Kingdom
85 X 10 **Long Range Mountains**, Newfoundland and Labrador, Canada ⛰
195 T 7 **Long Semado**, Malaysia
127 Y 7 **Long Stratton**, United Kingdom
195 S 7 **Long Teru**, Malaysia
74 J 7 **Long Valley Junction**, Utah, U.S.A.
191 L 22 **Long Xuyên**, Vietnam
218 I 5 **Longa**, Angola
147 D 22 **Longa**, Greece
187 K 15 **Longang Shan**, China ⛰
192 L 9 **Longbawan**, Indonesia
189 N 7 **Longchang**, China
189 V 11 **Longchuan**, China
189 O 2 **Longde**, China
186 J 10 **Longfeng**, China
125 D 17 **Longford**, Republic of Ireland
187 E 15 **Longhua**, China
189 S 9 **Longhui**, China
217 V 9 **Longido**, Tanzania
192 L 11 **Longiram**, Indonesia
186 I 10 **Longjiang**, China
189 W 12 **Longjiang**, China
187 G 19 **Longkou**, China
84 M 11 **Longlac**, Ontario, Canada
189 R 14 **Longmen**, China
189 N 5 **Longmen Shan**, China ⛰
75 R 3 **Longmont**, Colorado, U.S.A.
189 U 11 **Longnan**, China
192 L 10 **Longnawan**, Indonesia
189 P 9 **Longping**, China
189 X 8 **Longquan**, China
231 S 6 **Longreach**, Queensland, Australia
185 P 10 **Longriba**, China
189 Q 7 **Longshan**, China
189 R 10 **Longsheng**, China
87 T 3 **Longue-Pointe**, Québec, Canada
86 L 10 **Longueuil**, Québec, Canada
129 U 3 **Longuyon**, France
71 T 6 **Longview**, Texas, U.S.A.
76 G 8 **Longview**, Washington, U.S.A.
43 N 25 **Longwood**, St Helena
188 L 11 **Longwu**, China
133 K 26 **Longwy**, Belgium
189 P 3 **Longxian**, China
189 W 10 **Longyan**, China
45 T 11 **Longyearbyen**, Svalbard
189 X 7 **Longyou**, China
186 K 8 **Longzhen**, China
189 O 13 **Longzhou**, China
140 F 7 **Lonigo**, Italy
129 U 8 **Lons-le-Saunier**, France
193 S 13 **Lontar**, Indonesia 🏝
197 H 15 **Looc**, Philippines
65 H 21 **Loogootee**, Indiana, U.S.A.
125 A 19 **Loop Head**, Republic of Ireland ►
191 H 18 **Lop Buri**, Thailand
184 L 6 **Lop Nur**, China 💧
157 R 13 **Lopatin**, Russian Federation
157 P 4 **Lopatino**, Russian Federation
235 R 11 **Lopévi**, Vanuatu 🏝
196 H 12 **Lopez**, Philippines
134 I 6 **Lopphavet**, Norway ≈
130 L 11 **Lora del Río**, Spain
65 N 16 **Lorain**, Ohio, U.S.A.
177 U 10 **Loralai**, Pakistan
131 R 11 **Lorca**, Spain
41 N 11 **Lord Howe Island**, Australia 🏝
191 F 22 **Lord Loughborough Island**, Myanmar 🏝
75 N 14 **Lordsburg**, New Mexico, U.S.A.
193 R 15 **Lore**, East Timor
234 E 2 **Lorengau**, Papua New Guinea
176 G 7 **Lorestān**, Iran ▣
107 K 19 **Loreto**, Bolivia
106 E 11 **Loreto**, Peru ▣
108 K 12 **Loreto**, Brazil
197 M 17 **Loreto**, Philippines
88 I 7 **Loreto**, Mexico
104 H 3 **Lorica**, Colombia
128 I 6 **Lorient**, France
73 U 2 **Loring**, Montana, U.S.A.
61 R 12 **Loris**, South Carolina, U.S.A.
137 D 25 **Lörrach**, Germany
129 U 4 **Lorraine**, France ▣
211 Q 8 **Lorzot**, Tunisia
75 Q 9 **Los Alamos**, New Mexico, U.S.A.
77 H 23 **Los Alamos**, California, U.S.A.
112 C 11 **Los Amores**, Argentina
111 F 14 **Los Angeles**, Chile
77 J 24 **Los Angeles**, California, U.S.A.
77 J 23 **Los Angeles Aqueduct**, California, U.S.A. 〰
77 H 20 **Los Banos**, California, U.S.A.
110 K 5 **Los Blancos**, Argentina
91 P 11 **Los Chiles**, Costa Rica
107 K 19 **Los Cusis**, Bolivia
77 G 20 **Los Gatos**, California, U.S.A.
111 E 16 **Los Lagos**, Chile ▣
111 H 16 **Los Menucos**, Argentina
88 K 7 **Los Mochis**, Mexico
92 G 4 **Los Palacios**, Cuba
88 I 5 **Los Pocitos**, Mexico
106 B 10 **Los Ríos**, Ecuador ▣
110 J 9 **Los Telares**, Argentina
105 Q 2 **Los Testigos**, Venezuela 🏝
110 F 11 **Los Vilos**, Chile
237 O 15 **Losap**, Federated States of Micronesia 🏝
142 N 12 **Łosice**, Poland
77 I 22 **Lost Hills**, California, U.S.A.
126 L 14 **Lostwithiel**, United Kingdom
234 G 6 **Losuia**, Papua New Guinea
111 E 14 **Lota**, Chile
213 G 22 **Lotagipi Swamp**, Sudan ◇
216 M 9 **Loto**, Democratic Republic of Congo
190 I 12 **Louang Namtha**, Laos
191 H 16 **Louang Phrabang Range**, Thailand ⛰
190 I 13 **Louangphrabang**, Laos
216 F 10 **Loubomo**, Congo
128 J 5 **Loudéac**, France
189 S 9 **Loudi**, China
129 N 8 **Loudun**, France
214 D 8 **Louga**, Senegal
125 D 16 **Lough Allen**, Republic of Ireland 💧
125 C 16 **Lough Conn**, Republic of Ireland 💧
125 C 18 **Lough Corrib**, Republic of Ireland 💧
125 C 19 **Lough Derg**, Republic of Ireland 💧
125 B 17 **Lough Mask**, Republic of Ireland 💧
125 E 15 **Lough Neagh**, United Kingdom 💧
125 C 17 **Lough Ree**, Republic of Ireland 💧
127 T 6 **Loughborough**, United Kingdom
45 P 7 **Lougheed Island**, Arctic Ocean 🏝
81 N 3 **Lougheed Island**, Nunavut, Canada 🏝
125 C 18 **Loughrea**, Republic of Ireland
219 P 9 **Louis Trichardt**, Republic of South Africa
60 L 5 **Louisa**, Kentucky, U.S.A.
61 S 8 **Louisberg**, North Carolina, U.S.A.
87 Y 8 **Louisbourg**, Nova Scotia, Canada
234 H 7 **Louisiade Archipelago**, Papua New Guinea 🏝
62 I 7 **Louisiana**, U.S.A. ▣
60 G 5 **Louisville**, Kentucky, U.S.A.
63 N 4 **Louisville**, Mississippi, U.S.A.
154 H 4 **Loukhi**, Russian Federation
216 H 8 **Loukoléla**, Congo
216 G 10 **Loukouo**, Congo
215 S 14 **Loum**, Cameroon
128 M 15 **Lourdes**, France
108 I 8 **Lourenço**, Brazil
130 G 9 **Loures**, Portugal
127 W 4 **Louth**, United Kingdom
147 F 20 **Loutraki**, Greece
86 H 7 **Louvicourt**, Québec, Canada
129 O 4 **Louviers**, France
135 J 14 **Lövånger**, Sweden
146 H 8 **Lovech**, Bulgaria ▣
146 I 8 **Lovech**, Bulgaria
75 R 3 **Loveland**, Colorado, U.S.A.
73 U 9 **Lovell**, Wyoming, U.S.A.
77 J 16 **Lovelock**, Nevada, U.S.A.
140 E 6 **Lovere**, Italy
75 U 13 **Lovington**, New Mexico, U.S.A.
143 C 16 **Lovosice**, Czech Republic
154 I 3 **Lovozero**, Russian Federation
150 E 10 **Lovrin**, Romania
218 J 1 **Lóvua**, Angola
218 L 3 **Lôvua**, Angola
217 O 8 **Lowa**, Democratic Republic of Congo
59 N 9 **Lowell**, Massachusetts, U.S.A.
72 L 6 **Lowell**, Idaho, U.S.A.
213 F 22 **Lowelli**, Sudan
136 L 12 **Löwenberg**, Germany
233 K 16 **Lower Hutt**, New Zealand
125 D 15 **Lower Lough Erne**, United Kingdom 💧
67 Q 3 **Lower Red Lake**, Minnesota, U.S.A. 💧
127 Z 7 **Lowestoft**, United Kingdom
177 U 8 **Lowgar**, Afghanistan ▣
142 J 13 **Łowicz**, Poland
72 K 10 **Lowman**, Idaho, U.S.A.
58 H 7 **Lowville**, New York, U.S.A.
136 F 10 **Loxstedt**, Germany
188 K 5 **Loxur**, China
235 R 13 **Loyalty Islands**, New Caledonia 🏝
149 N 21 **Loyew**, Belarus
144 J 11 **Loznica**, Serbia and Montenegro
146 L 7 **Loznitsa**, Bulgaria
151 W 6 **Lozova**, Ukraine
179 V 2 **Lozovoye**, Kazakhstan
131 O 5 **Lozoyuela**, Spain
189 Z 12 **Lü Tao**, Taiwan 🏝
108 G 11 **Lua Nova**, Brazil
218 K 3 **Luacano**, Angola
189 V 5 **Lu'an**, China
218 F 2 **Luanda**, Angola 🏛
218 G 3 **Luanda**, Angola ▣
218 I 4 **Luando**, Angola
219 O 4 **Luanshya**, Zambia
187 F 17 **Luanxian**, China
217 P 13 **Luanza**, Democratic Republic of Congo
219 O 3 **Luapula**, Zambia ▣
130 K 1 **Luarca**, Spain
216 M 14 **Luashi**, Democratic Republic of Congo
218 K 3 **Luau**, Angola
215 S 15 **Luba**, Equatorial Guinea
143 O 17 **Lubaczów**, Poland
218 J 2 **Lubalo**, Angola
148 I 11 **Lubāna**, Latvia
148 I 11 **Lubānas ezers**, Latvia 💧
196 F 12 **Lubang**, Philippines 🏝
196 E 12 **Lubang Islands**, Philippines 🏝
218 G 5 **Lubango**, Angola
217 O 11 **Lubao**, Democratic Republic of Congo
143 N 14 **Lubartów**, Poland
142 J 10 **Lubawa**, Poland
70 K 5 **Lubbock**, Texas, U.S.A.
59 T 5 **Lubec**, Maine, U.S.A.
136 I 9 **Lübeck**, Germany
136 I 9 **Lübecker Bucht**, Germany ≈
217 N 10 **Lubefu**, Democratic Republic of Congo
186 H 12 **Lubei**, China
196 F 12 **Lubgan**, Philippines
197 F 16 **Lubic**, Philippines 🏝
143 F 14 **Lubin**, Poland
143 N 14 **Lublin**, Poland
143 I 16 **Lubliniec**, Poland
151 S 4 **Lubny**, Ukraine
196 G 7 **Lubuagan**, Philippines
217 O 14 **Lubudi**, Democratic Republic of Congo
217 P 14 **Lubumbashi**, Democratic Republic of Congo
219 N 5 **Lubungu**, Zambia
217 O 8 **Lubutu**, Democratic Republic of Congo
218 H 2 **Lucala**, Angola
218 K 2 **Lucapa**, Angola
67 S 14 **Lucas**, Iowa, U.S.A.
140 E 10 **Lucca**, Italy
63 N 7 **Lucedale**, Mississippi, U.S.A.
112 I 6 **Lucélia**, Brazil
131 N 12 **Lucena**, Spain
196 H 12 **Lucena**, Philippines
143 J 21 **Lučenec**, Slovakia
141 K 14 **Lucera**, Italy
107 H 16 **Lucerna**, Peru
188 L 9 **Luchang**, China
136 J 12 **Lüchow**, Germany
189 R 13 **Luchuan**, China
193 R 13 **Lucipara**, Indonesia 🏝
218 F 5 **Lucira**, Angola
137 M 14 **Luckau**, Germany
183 Q 12 **Luckeesarai**, India
137 M 14 **Luckenwalde**, Germany
182 M 10 **Lucknow**, India
62 I 5 **Lucky**, Louisiana, U.S.A.
128 L 8 **Luçon**, France
218 K 4 **Lucusse**, Angola
218 H 11 **Lüderitz**, Namibia
218 H 11 **Lüderitz Bay**, Namibia ≈
217 T 14 **Ludewa**, Tanzania
182 I 6 **Ludhiana**, India
188 M 9 **Ludian**, China
64 I 12 **Ludington**, Michigan, U.S.A.
127 P 7 **Ludlow**, United Kingdom
58 L 7 **Ludlow**, Vermont, U.S.A.
77 L 23 **Ludlow**, California, U.S.A.
63 W 5 **Ludowici**, Georgia, U.S.A.
135 G 19 **Ludvika**, Sweden
137 F 22 **Ludwigsburg**, Germany
136 M 13 **Ludwigsfelde**, Germany
136 J 11 **Ludwigslust**, Germany
148 J 12 **Ludza**, Latvia
216 L 11 **Luebo**, Democratic Republic of Congo
217 O 10 **Lueki**, Democratic Republic of Congo
218 J 4 **Luena**, Angola
189 O 4 **Lüeyang**, China
189 V 12 **Lufeng**, China
71 T 8 **Lufkin**, Texas, U.S.A.
154 E 11 **Luga**, Russian Federation
197 K 20 **Lugait**, Philippines
138 H 11 **Lugano**, Switzerland
235 Q 10 **Luganville**, Vanuatu
213 L 19 **Lughaye**, Somalia
130 J 1 **Lugo**, Spain
150 F 10 **Lugoj**, Romania
179 T 10 **Lugovoy**, Kazakhstan
197 G 24 **Lugus**, Philippines 🏝
151 Z 6 **Luhans'k**, Ukraine
217 V 13 **Luhombero**, Tanzania
188 K 6 **Luhuo**, China
218 L 6 **Luiana**, Angola
241 N 4 **Luitpold Coast**, Antarctica ◇
216 L 12 **Luiza**, Democratic Republic of Congo
110 G 11 **Luján de Cuyo**, Argentina
189 W 6 **Lujiang**, China
144 H 11 **Lukavac**, Bosnia and Herzegovina
156 L 2 **Lukhovitsy**, Russian Federation
146 I 11 **Lŭki**, Bulgaria
216 I 8 **Lukolela**, Democratic Republic of Congo
146 H 8 **Lukovit**, Bulgaria
142 M 13 **Łuków**, Poland
157 P 2 **Lukoyanov**, Russian Federation
216 F 11 **Lukula**, Democratic Republic of Congo
218 L 5 **Lukulu**, Zambia
217 U 13 **Lukumburu**, Tanzania
134 J 12 **Luleå**, Sweden
134 J 11 **Luleälven**, Sweden 〰
170 C 7 **Lüleburgaz**, Turkey
189 R 2 **Lüliang Shan**, China ⛰
217 P 10 **Lulimba**, Democratic Republic of Congo
216 J 7 **Lulonga**, Democratic Republic of Congo
218 K 4 **Lumbala Kaquengue**, Angola
218 K 5 **Lumbala N'guimbo**, Angola
61 R 11 **Lumberton**, North Carolina, U.S.A.
62 M 6 **Lumberton**, Mississippi, U.S.A.
110 I 6 **Lumbrera**, Argentina
183 X 11 **Lumding**, India
234 B 3 **Lumi**, Papua New Guinea
191 N 19 **Lumphăt**, Cambodia
233 C 24 **Lumsden**, New Zealand
218 I 2 **Lunda Norte**, Angola ▣
218 K 3 **Lunda Sul**, Angola ▣
219 Q 4 **Lundazi**, Zambia
194 M 10 **Lundu**, Malaysia
126 L 12 **Lundy Island**, United Kingdom 🏝
136 H 11 **Lüneburg**, Germany
137 D 15 **Lünen**, Germany
129 V 4 **Lunéville**, France
138 F 8 **Lungern**, Switzerland
184 I 9 **Lunggar**, China
214 F 12 **Lungi**, Sierra Leone
183 X 13 **Lunglei**, India
77 K 19 **Luning**, Nevada, U.S.A.
157 P 3 **Lunino**, Russian Federation
149 I 21 **Luninyets**, Belarus
182 G 8 **Lunkaransar**, India
214 F 12 **Lunsar**, Sierra Leone
139 U 5 **Lunz am See**, Austria
186 N 9 **Luobei**, China
189 Q 11 **Luocheng**, China
189 Q 2 **Luochuan**, China
189 O 10 **Luodian**, China
189 R 12 **Luoding**, China
189 U 4 **Luohe**, China
189 R 4 **Luonan**, China
189 S 3 **Luoning**, China
188 M 11 **Luoping**, China
189 U 5 **Luoshan**, China
189 V 6 **Luotian**, China
189 U 9 **Luoxiao Shan**, China ⛰
189 S 3 **Luoyang**, China
189 Y 9 **Luoyuan**, China
216 G 11 **Luozi**, Democratic Republic of Congo
219 O 7 **Lupane**, Zimbabwe
189 N 9 **Lupanshui**, China
219 R 3 **Lupilichi**, Mozambique
188 M 3 **Luqu**, China
218 I 2 **Luremo**, Angola
125 F 16 **Lurgan**, United Kingdom
107 D 17 **Lurín**, Peru
217 R 9 **Lusahunga**, Tanzania
219 O 5 **Lusaka**, Zambia 🏛
219 O 5 **Lusaka**, Zambia ▣
216 M 11 **Lusambo**, Democratic Republic of Congo
189 R 4 **Lushi**, China
145 J 19 **Lushnjë**, Albania
217 W 10 **Lushoto**, Tanzania
188 I 10 **Lushui**, China
187 H 18 **Lushunkou**, China

□ Country ▣ Internal administrative region: State/Province/Territory/Dependent territory 🏛 Capital city ⛰ Mountain range/Undersea ridge ▲ Mountain peak/Volcano/Seamount ◇ Geographic feature ► Headland/Point/Cape/Peninsula ☗ Desert 🏝 Island/Island group ⁙ Antarctic base 🌊 Ocean ◗ Sea ≈ Bay/Gulf/Channel/Strait 💧 Lake ⚑ Salt pan/Dry/Intermittent lake 〰 River

♣ Country ◻ Internal administrative region: State/Province/Territory/Dependent territory   ♣ Capital city ▲ Mountain range/Undersea ridge ▲ Mountain peak/Volcano/Seamount   ◇ Geographic feature ▶ Headland/Point/Cape/Peninsula ◇ Desert ⊻ Island/Island group ⊞ Antarctic base ≈ Ocean ≈ Sea ≈ Bay/Gulf/Channel/Strait ≈ Lake ↘ Salt pan/Dry/Intermittent lake ↘ River

309

105 X 7 **Maripasoula**, French Guiana
77 I 20 **Mariposa**, California, U.S.A.
193 P 10 **Marisa**, Indonesia
130 K 12 **Marismas del Guadalquivir**, Spain ◇
146 K 11 **Maritsa**, Bulgaria ↘
151 X 8 **Mariupol'**, Ukraine
196 F 11 **Mariveles**, Philippines
41 F 7 **Märjamaa**, Estonia
172 G 7 **Marjayoun**, Lebanon
69 W 3 **Mark Twain Lake**, Missouri, U.S.A. ↘
213 L 24 **Marka**, Somalia
188 J 7 **Markam**, China
181 F 19 **Markapur**, India
176 H 7 **Markazī**, Iran ▣
132 M 12 **Markelo**, Netherlands
132 I 10 **Markermeer**, Netherlands ≈
127 Q 6 **Market Drayton**, United Kingdom
127 T 7 **Market Harborough**, United Kingdom
127 V 4 **Market Rasen**, United Kingdom
127 U 2 **Market Weighton**, United Kingdom
86 F 12 **Markham**, Ontario, Canada
184 H 6 **Markit**, China
151 Z 4 **Markivka**, Ukraine
132 K 9 **Marknesse**, Netherlands
216 I 3 **Markounda**, Central African Republic
153 Y 7 **Markovo**, Russian Federation
157 Q 5 **Marks**, Russian Federation
62 J 6 **Marksville**, Louisiana, U.S.A.
137 K 19 **Marktredwitz**, Germany
231 N 8 **Marla**, South Australia, Australia
231 V 6 **Marlborough**, Queensland, Australia
233 I 17 **Marlborough**, New Zealand ▣
127 S 11 **Marlborough**, United Kingdom
127 S 10 **Marlborough Downs**, United Kingdom ◇
71 Q 8 **Marlin**, Texas, U.S.A.
61 P 4 **Marlinton**, West Virginia, U.S.A.
127 U 10 **Marlow**, United Kingdom
181 C 19 **Marmagao**, India
129 N 12 **Marmande**, France
170 C 8 **Marmara**, Turkey
170 C 8 **Marmara**, Turkey
159 T 6 **Marmara Trough**, Mediterranean Sea ◇
146 N 13 **Marmaraereğlisi**, Turkey
170 C 13 **Marmaris**, Turkey
140 G 5 **Marmolada**, Italy ▲
136 F 9 **Marne**, Germany
171 U 7 **Marneuli**, Georgia
215 X 12 **Maro**, Chad
105 N 8 **Maroa**, Venezuela
219 Z 6 **Maroantsetra**, Madagascar
219 Z 5 **Maromokotro**, Madagascar ▲
219 P 7 **Marondera**, Zimbabwe
105 X 8 **Maroni**, French Guiana ↘
231 W 8 **Maroochydore**, Queensland, Australia
75 O 5 **Maroon Peak**, Colorado, U.S.A. ▲
232 I 6 **Maropiu**, New Zealand
193 N 13 **Maros**, Indonesia
215 V 11 **Maroua**, Cameroon
219 X 6 **Marovoay**, Madagascar
14 S 9 **Marquesas Fracture Zone**, Pacific Ocean ◇
15 T 8 **Marquesas Islands**, French Polynesia
14 W 15 **Marquesas Keys**, Florida, U.S.A.
64 H 8 **Marquette**, Michigan, U.S.A.
71 R 8 **Marquez**, Texas, U.S.A.
213 A 17 **Marra Plateau**, Sudan ◇
140 G 10 **Marradi**, Italy
10 G 8 **Marrakech**, Morocco

231 S 15 **Marrawah**, Tasmania, Australia
231 P 9 **Marree**, South Australia, Australia
219 S 7 **Marromeu**, Mozambique
219 S 4 **Marrupa**, Mozambique
211 W 8 **Marsa al Burayqah**, Libya
212 G 11 **Marsa Alam**, Egypt
212 C 7 **Marsa Matrûh**, Egypt
217 V 6 **Marsabit**, Kenya
141 G 22 **Marsala**, Italy
132 H 8 **Marsdiep**, Netherlands ≈
129 U 14 **Marseille**, France
92 L 1 **Marsh Harbour**, The Bahamas
62 J 8 **Marsh Island**, Louisiana, U.S.A.
67 P 9 **Marshall**, Minnesota, U.S.A.
69 T 3 **Marshall**, Missouri, U.S.A.
69 U 9 **Marshall**, Arkansas, U.S.A.
71 T 6 **Marshall**, Texas, U.S.A.
237 W 4 **Marshall Islands**, Oceania
67 T 12 **Marshalltown**, Iowa, U.S.A.
64 E 11 **Marshfield**, Wisconsin, U.S.A.
195 V 4 **Martanai Besar**, Malaysia
192 L 12 **Martapura**, Indonesia
192 F 13 **Martapura**, Indonesia
133 K 24 **Martelange**, Belgium
86 F 8 **Marten River**, Ontario, Canada
59 O 11 **Martha's Vineyard**, Massachusetts, U.S.A. ☈
138 C 10 **Martigny**, Switzerland
143 I 19 **Martin**, Slovakia
60 C 8 **Martin**, Tennessee, U.S.A.
66 I 11 **Martin**, South Dakota, U.S.A.
240 K 10 **Martin Peninsula**, Antarctica
141 N 16 **Martina Franca**, Italy
233 L 16 **Martinborough**, New Zealand
89 S 11 **Martínez**, Mexico
93 Y 11 **Martinique**, France, France ▣
93 Y 10 **Martinique Passage**, Dominica ◇
147 F 19 **Martino**, Greece
65 O 18 **Martins Ferry**, Ohio, U.S.A.
61 S 2 **Martinsburg**, West Virginia, U.S.A.
61 Q 7 **Martinsville**, Virginia, U.S.A.
65 I 20 **Martinsville**, Indiana, U.S.A.
233 L 14 **Marton**, New Zealand
178 K 4 **Martuk**, Kazakhstan
171 U 9 **Martuni**, Armenia
199 E 19 **Marugame**, Japan
109 O 14 **Maruim**, Brazil
179 N 14 **Mary**, Turkmenistan
231 W 8 **Maryborough**, Queensland, Australia
61 T 3 **Maryland**, U.S.A. ▣
74 J 6 **Marysvale**, Utah, U.S.A.
65 L 18 **Marysville**, Ohio, U.S.A.
69 O 2 **Marysville**, Kansas, U.S.A.
74 H 6 **Marysville**, Washington, U.S.A.
77 G 18 **Marysville**, California, U.S.A.
60 J 9 **Maryville**, Tennessee, U.S.A.
69 R 1 **Maryville**, Missouri, U.S.A.
179 N 15 **Maryyskiy Velayat**, Turkmenistan ▣
90 G 6 **Masagua**, Guatemala
217 R 8 **Masaka**, Uganda
192 L 13 **Masalembu Besar**, Indonesia
192 L 13 **Masalembu Kecil**, Indonesia
171 Y 9 **Masalli**, Azerbaijan
193 O 12 **Masamba**, Indonesia
187 M 21 **Masan**, South Korea
217 W 14 **Masasi**, Tanzania
107 L 21 **Masavi**, Bolivia
91 N 9 **Masaya**, Nicaragua
197 J 14 **Masbate**, Philippines

197 J 15 **Masbate**, Philippines ≠
38 L 6 **Mascarene Basin**, Indian Ocean ◇
38 K 7 **Mascarene Plain**, Indian Ocean ◇
38 L 5 **Mascarene Ridge**, Indian Ocean ◇
219 N 12 **Maseru**, Lesotho ●
127 S 1 **Masham**, United Kingdom
177 O 6 **Mashhad**, Iran
176 L 10 **Mashīz**, Iran
219 P 6 **Mashonaland Central**, Zimbabwe
219 Q 6 **Mashonaland East**, Zimbabwe
219 O 6 **Mashonaland West**, Zimbabwe
134 K 7 **Masi**, Norway
216 J 10 **Masi-Manimba**, Democratic Republic of Congo
88 J 6 **Masiáca**, Mexico
217 R 7 **Masindi**, Uganda
171 T 9 **Masis**, Armenia
107 E 14 **Masisea**, Peru
176 G 8 **Masjed Soleymān**, Iran
175 S 13 **Masna'ah**, Yemen
219 W 7 **Masoarivo**, Madagascar
60 M 3 **Mason**, West Virginia, U.S.A.
71 N 9 **Mason**, Texas, U.S.A.
233 B 26 **Mason Bay**, New Zealand ≈
65 F 18 **Mason City**, Illinois, U.S.A.
67 T 10 **Mason City**, Iowa, U.S.A.
42 N 12 **Maspalomas**, Canary Islands
140 E 10 **Massa**, Italy
140 F 12 **Massa Marittimo**, Italy
59 N 9 **Massachusetts**, U.S.A. ▣
59 O 9 **Massachusetts Bay**, Massachusetts, U.S.A. ≈
215 V 10 **Massaguet**, Chad
215 W 9 **Massakory**, Chad
219 Q 9 **Massangena**, Mozambique
219 R 4 **Massangulo**, Mozambique
213 I 16 **Massawa**, Eritrea
213 I 16 **Massawa Channel**, Eritrea ≈
58 I 5 **Massena**, New York, U.S.A.
215 W 10 **Massenya**, Chad
83 C 19 **Masset**, British Columbia, Canada
86 C 9 **Massey**, Ontario, Canada
129 R 11 **Massif Central**, France ▲
93 N 8 **Massif de la Hotte**, Haiti ▲
215 S 6 **Massif de L'aïr**, Niger ▲
216 L 3 **Massif des Bongo**, Central African Republic ▲
215 Z 8 **Massif du Kapka**, Chad ▲
214 G 10 **Massif du Tamgué**, Guinea ▲
216 H 4 **Massif du Yadé**, Central African Republic ▲
215 Z 7 **Massif Ennedi**, Chad ▲
219 R 9 **Massinga**, Mozambique
219 Q 10 **Massingir**, Mozambique
241 Y 9 **Masson Island**, Antarctica ≠
174 L 8 **Mastābah**, Saudi Arabia
171 Z 8 **Mastağa**, Azerbaijan
233 L 15 **Masterton**, New Zealand
92 K 2 **Mastic Point**, The Bahamas
177 W 5 **Mastuj**, Pakistan
177 T 11 **Mastung**, Pakistan
174 L 7 **Mastūrah**, Saudi Arabia
199 C 19 **Masuda**, Japan
219 P 8 **Masvingo**, Zimbabwe
219 P 8 **Masvingo**, Zimbabwe ▣
172 H 4 **Maşyāf**, Syria
149 E 21 **Masyevichy**, Belarus
236 H 8 **Matā 'Utu**, Wallis and Futuna Islands ●
219 N 7 **Matabeleland North**, Zimbabwe
219 O 8 **Matabeleland South**, Zimbabwe
218 I 4 **Matala**, Angola
86 E 7 **Matachewan**, Ontario, Canada
91 N 9 **Masaya**, Nicaragua
216 G 11 **Matadi**, Democratic Republic of Congo

70 L 4 **Matador**, Texas, U.S.A.
91 N 8 **Matagalpa**, Nicaragua
85 P 11 **Matagami**, Québec, Canada
71 R 12 **Matagorda Bay**, Texas, U.S.A. ≈
71 R 12 **Matagorda Island**, Texas, U.S.A. ≠
71 R 12 **Matagorda Peninsula**, Texas, U.S.A. ▶
218 H 5 **Matala**, Angola
214 F 8 **Matam**, Senegal
232 L 10 **Matamata**, New Zealand
215 R 9 **Matamey**, Niger
89 S 7 **Matamoros**, Mexico
197 I 23 **Matanal Point**, Philippines ▶
87 Q 5 **Matane**, Québec, Canada
92 H 4 **Matanzas**, Cuba
181 G 25 **Matara**, Sri Lanka
147 C 19 **Mataragka**, Greece
192 L 15 **Mataram**, Indonesia
231 N 2 **Mataranka**, Northern Territory, Australia
131 X 4 **Mataró**, Spain
232 M 10 **Matata**, New Zealand
233 D 25 **Mataura**, New Zealand
233 C 24 **Mataura**, New Zealand ↘
41 Y 5 **Mataveri**, Easter Island
232 N 11 **Matawai**, New Zealand
179 W 8 **Matay**, Kazakhstan
107 L 17 **Mategua**, Bolivia
89 Q 9 **Matehuala**, Mexico
217 V 14 **Matemanga**, Tanzania
141 M 16 **Matera**, Italy
143 N 21 **Mátészalka**, Hungary
211 Q 5 **Mateur**, Tunisia
86 E 6 **Matheson**, Ontario, Canada
61 V 6 **Mathews**, Virginia, U.S.A.
71 P 13 **Mathis**, Texas, U.S.A.
182 I 9 **Mathura**, India
197 N 22 **Mati**, Philippines
109 L 15 **Matias Cardoso**, Brazil
85 T 8 **Matimekosh**, Québec, Canada
91 R 12 **Matina**, Costa Rica
148 G 9 **Matīši**, Latvia
177 U 14 **Matli**, Pakistan
127 S 5 **Matlock**, United Kingdom
197 K 14 **Matnog**, Philippines
109 H 14 **Mato Grosso**, Brazil ▣
112 F 6 **Mato Grosso do Sul**, Brazil ▣
130 H 5 **Matosinhos**, Portugal
139 P 8 **Matrei in Osttirol**, Austria
218 J 15 **Matroosberg**, Republic of South Africa ▲
189 Y 10 **Matsu Tao**, Taiwan ▶
199 D 18 **Matsue**, Japan
198 I 8 **Matsumae**, Japan
199 I 16 **Matsumoto**, Japan
199 H 18 **Matsusaka**, Japan
199 D 20 **Matsuyama**, Japan
86 F 9 **Mattawa**, Ontario, Canada
59 R 4 **Mattawamkeag**, Maine, U.S.A.
138 D 11 **Matterhorn**, Switzerland ▲
77 M 15 **Matterhorn**, Nevada, U.S.A. ▲
139 Y 5 **Mattersburg**, Austria
235 S 14 **Matthew Island**, Vanuatu ≠
93 N 6 **Matthew Town**, The Bahamas
139 Q 4 **Mattighofen**, Austria
65 G 19 **Mattoon**, Illinois, U.S.A.
195 O 9 **Matu**, Malaysia
107 D 16 **Matucana**, Peru
235 Y 12 **Matuku**, Fiji ≠
218 I 4 **Matumbo**, Angola
105 R 3 **Maturín**, Venezuela
193 O 11 **Matutuang**, Indonesia ≠
183 O 11 **Mau**, India
180 F 13 **Mau Rampur**, India

219 S 5 **Maúa**, Mozambique
129 S 2 **Maubeuge**, France
191 D 16 **Maubin**, Myanmar
43 L 23 **Maud Rise**, Atlantic Ocean ◇
182 L 11 **Maudaha**, India
108 G 11 **Maués**, Brazil
236 A 5 **Maug Islands**, Northern Mariana Islands ≠
183 N 12 **Mauganj**, India
78 D 7 **Maui**, Hawaii, U.S.A. ≠
192 G 9 **Matak**, Indonesia ≠
237 P 10 **Mauke**, Cook Islands ≠
110 F 13 **Maule**, Chile ▣
111 F 17 **Maullín**, Chile
65 L 16 **Maumee**, Ohio, U.S.A.
218 L 8 **Maun**, Botswana
78 E 8 **Mauna Kea**, Hawaii, U.S.A. ▲
78 E 9 **Mauna Loa**, Hawaii, U.S.A. ▲
232 J 6 **Maungatapere**, New Zealand
191 F 19 **Maungmagan Islands**, Myanmar ≠
76 H 10 **Maupin**, Oregon, U.S.A.
129 Q 11 **Mauriac**, France
214 F 6 **Mauritania**, Africa ▣
38 A 11 **Mauritius**, Indian Ocean ▣
38 K 8 **Mauritius Trench**, Indian Ocean ◇
42 I 6 **Maury Seachannel**, Atlantic Ocean ≈
139 R 7 **Mauterndorf**, Austria
217 O 6 **Mava**, Democratic Republic of Congo
219 S 4 **Mavago**, Mozambique
218 J 6 **Mavengue**, Angola
218 K 6 **Mavinga**, Angola
216 I 11 **Mawanga**, Democratic Republic of Congo
189 P 10 **Mawei**, China
241 X 4 **Mawson**, Antarctica ▦
241 W 4 **Mawson Coast**, Antarctica ◇
241 T 15 **Mawson Peninsula**, Antarctica ▶
66 J 4 **Max**, North Dakota, U.S.A.
110 I 8 **Maxán**, Argentina
89 Y 10 **Maxcanú**, Mexico
135 K 15 **Maxmo**, Finland
153 U 11 **Maya**, Russian Federation ↘
188 M 4 **Maya**, China
192 I 11 **Maya**, Indonesia ≠
90 I 4 **Maya Mountains**, Guatemala ▲
93 O 4 **Mayaguana Island**, The Bahamas ≠
93 T 8 **Mayagüez**, Puerto Rico
215 R 9 **Mayahi**, Niger
179 T 14 **Mayakovskogo**, Tajikistan ▲
216 H 10 **Mayama**, Congo
176 L 5 **Mayamey**, Iran
213 I 18 **Maych'ew**, Ethiopia
213 M 19 **Maydh**, Somalia
128 M 5 **Mayenne**, France
233 F 21 **Mayfield**, New Zealand
60 C 7 **Mayfield**, Kentucky, U.S.A. ↘
146 M 11 **Mayha Daĝi**, Turkey ▲
75 R 13 **Mayhill**, New Mexico, U.S.A.
179 U 4 **Maykain**, Kazakhstan
156 L 12 **Maykop**, Russian Federation
179 T 11 **Mayluu-Suu**, Kyrgyzstan
179 N 8 **Maylybas**, Kazakhstan
190 E 11 **Maymyo**, Myanmar
157 R 3 **Mayna**, Russian Federation
63 U 8 **Mayo**, Florida, U.S.A.
82 B 12 **Mayo**, Yukon Territory, Canada
215 T 12 **Mayo-Belwa**, Nigeria
215 V 11 **Mayo-Kébbi**, Chad ▣
216 F 9 **Mayoko**, Congo
232 M 9 **Mayor Island**, New Zealand ≠

109 F 17 **Mayor Pablo Lagerenza**, Paraguay
219 X 4 **Mayotte**, France ≠
196 G 5 **Mayraira Point**, Philippines ▶
139 N 7 **Mayrhofen**, Austria
153 U 13 **Mayskiy**, Russian Federation
179 V 4 **Mayskoye**, Kazakhstan
60 J 4 **Maysville**, Kentucky, U.S.A.
197 E 16 **Maytiguid**, Philippines ≠
193 R 10 **Mayu**, Indonesia ≠
216 E 10 **Mayumba**, Gabon
66 K 15 **Maywood**, Nebraska, U.S.A.
113 A 18 **Maza**, Argentina
219 N 5 **Mazabuka**, Zambia
76 I 5 **Mazama**, Washington, U.S.A.
129 Q 14 **Mazamet**, France
106 F 10 **Mazán**, Peru
176 J 5 **Māzandarān**, Iran ▣
184 G 7 **Mazar**, China
177 T 5 **Mazār-e Sharīf**, Afghanistan
141 G 22 **Mazara del Vallo**, Italy
131 R 12 **Mazarrón**, Spain
158 C 9 **Mazarron Escarpment**, Mediterranean Sea ◇
88 J 4 **Mazatán**, Mexico
90 F 6 **Mazatenango**, Guatemala
88 L 9 **Mazatlán**, Mexico
74 J 11 **Mazatzal Peak**, Arizona, U.S.A. ▲
148 D 12 **Mažeikiai**, Lithuania
148 D 9 **Mazirbe**, Latvia
88 J 4 **Mazocahui**, Mexico
217 W 12 **Mazomora**, Tanzania
219 P 9 **Mazunga**, Zimbabwe
149 L 21 **Mazyr**, Belarus
219 P 11 **Mbabane**, Swaziland ●
214 K 12 **Mbahiakro**, Côte d'Ivoire
216 J 5 **Mbaïki**, Central African Republic
215 V 15 **Mbalam**, Cameroon
217 T 7 **Mbale**, Uganda
215 T 15 **Mbalmayo**, Cameroon
234 M 7 **Mbambanakira**, Solomon Islands
217 T 14 **Mbamba Bay**, Tanzania
216 J 8 **Mbandaka**, Democratic Republic of Congo
215 S 14 **Mbanga**, Cameroon
218 G 1 **M'banza Congo**, Angola
216 H 11 **Mbanza-Ngungu**, Democratic Republic of Congo
217 R 8 **Mbarara**, Uganda
216 J 5 **Mbata**, Central African Republic
217 S 12 **Mbeya**, Tanzania
217 T 13 **Mbeya**, Tanzania ▣
216 F 9 **Mbigou**, Gabon
217 U 14 **Mbinga**, Tanzania
219 P 8 **Mbizi**, Zimbabwe
217 O 4 **Mboki**, Central African Republic
216 G 7 **Mbomo**, Congo
216 M 4 **Mbomou**, Central African Republic ▣
214 D 8 **Mbour**, Senegal
214 G 8 **Mbout**, Mauritania
217 S 13 **Mbozi**, Tanzania
216 M 11 **Mbuji-Mayi**, Democratic Republic of Congo
217 U 10 **Mbulu**, Tanzania
217 U 12 **Mbuyuni**, Tanzania
87 R 10 **McAdam**, New Brunswick, Canada
69 P 11 **McAlester**, Oklahoma, U.S.A.
71 P 15 **McAllen**, Texas, U.S.A.
61 P 11 **McBee**, South Carolina, U.S.A.
83 G 19 **McBride**, British Columbia, Canada
72 K 8 **McCall**, Idaho, U.S.A.
70 I 9 **McCamey**, Texas, U.S.A.
73 P 12 **McCammon**, Idaho, U.S.A.
82 I 5 **McClintock Channel**, Nunavut, Canada ≈
58 I 7 **McClure**, Pennsylvania, U.S.A.

80 L 4 **McClure Strait**, Northwest Territories, Canada ≈
45 O 6 **McClure Strait Gulf**, Arctic Ocean ≈
66 K 4 **McClusky**, North Dakota, U.S.A.
62 L 6 **McComb**, Mississippi, U.S.A.
66 K 15 **McCook**, Nebraska, U.S.A.
60 M 12 **McCormick**, South Carolina, U.S.A.
77 K 14 **McDermitt**, Nevada, U.S.A.
69 X 13 **McGehee**, Arkansas, U.S.A.
77 N 17 **McGill**, Nevada, U.S.A.
87 S 9 **McGivney**, New Brunswick, Canada
79 P 8 **McGrath**, Alaska, U.S.A.
217 X 13 **Mchinga**, Tanzania
219 Q 4 **Mchinji**, Malawi
66 J 7 **McIntosh**, South Dakota, U.S.A.
236 I 4 **McKean**, Kiribati ⌓
60 C 8 **McKenzie**, Tennessee, U.S.A.
79 R 7 **McKinley Park**, Alaska, U.S.A.
71 Q 5 **McKinney**, Texas, U.S.A.
66 J 7 **McLaughlin**, South Dakota, U.S.A.
65 G 21 **McLeansboro**, Illinois, U.S.A.
83 F 18 **McLeod Lake**, British Columbia, Canada
191 F 21 **McLeods Island**, Myanmar ⌓
64 J 9 **McMillan**, Michigan, U.S.A.
60 H 9 **McMinnville**, Tennessee, U.S.A.
76 F 10 **McMinnville**, Oregon, U.S.A.
241 R 12 **McMurdo**, Antarctica ⁙
69 N 5 **Mcpherson**, Kansas, U.S.A.
63 U 5 **McRae**, Georgia, U.S.A.
219 O 14 **Mdantsane**, Republic of South Africa
68 I 7 **Meade**, Kansas, U.S.A.
79 O 3 **Meade**, Alaska, U.S.A. ∫
83 L 17 **Meadow Lake**, Saskatchewan, Canada
58 B 10 **Meadville**, Pennsylvania, U.S.A.
130 H 6 **Mealhada**, Portugal
85 V 8 **Mealy Mountains**, Newfoundland and Labrador, Canada ⛰
129 Q 4 **Meaux**, France
174 M 8 **Mecca**, Saudi Arabia
77 L 25 **Mecca**, California, U.S.A.
133 G 18 **Mechelen**, Belgium
210 L 7 **Mecheria**, Algeria
170 K 8 **Mecitözü**, Turkey
136 K 10 **Mecklenburg-Vorpommern**, Germany ▣
136 J 8 **Mecklenburger Bucht**, Germany ≈
219 T 4 **Mecula**, Mozambique
192 C 9 **Medan**, Indonesia
113 B 19 **Médanos**, Argentina
210 M 5 **Médéa**, Algeria
104 G 5 **Medellín**, Colombia
132 I 9 **Medemblik**, Netherlands
211 R 7 **Medenine**, Tunisia
214 E 7 **Mederdra**, Mauritania
64 E 11 **Medford**, Wisconsin, U.S.A.
76 F 13 **Medford**, Oregon, U.S.A.
110 I 12 **Media Luna**, Argentina
150 I 10 **Mediaș**, Romania
140 G 9 **Medicina**, Italy
73 X 13 **Medicine Bow**, Wyoming, U.S.A.
83 K 20 **Medicine Hat**, Alberta, Canada
68 L 7 **Medicine Lodge**, Kansas, U.S.A.
174 M 6 **Medina**, Saudi Arabia
58 D 8 **Medina**, New York, U.S.A.
66 L 5 **Medina**, North Dakota, U.S.A.
158 M 11 **Medina Bank**, Mediterranean Sea ◇
130 M 4 **Medina de Rioseco**, Spain
130 M 5 **Medina del Campo**, Spain
158 M 11 **Medina Escarpment**, Mediterranean Sea ◇
214 F 9 **Medina Gounas**, Senegal
131 Q 5 **Medinaceli**, Spain
183 R 14 **Medinipur**, India
158 F 8 **Mediterranean Sea**, Europe/Africa 〰
149 G 16 **Mednininkai**, Lithuania
216 E 7 **Médouneu**, Gabon
145 M 15 **Medveđa**, Serbia and Montenegro
154 H 8 **Medvezh'yegorsk**, Russian Federation
156 J 2 **Medyn'**, Russian Federation
230 G 8 **Meekatharra**, Western Australia, Australia
75 N 4 **Meeker**, Colorado, U.S.A.
133 H 16 **Meer**, Belgium
132 I 13 **Meerkerk**, Netherlands
133 J 19 **Meerssen**, Belgium
182 J 8 **Meerut**, India
73 T 10 **Meeteetse**, Wyoming, U.S.A.
213 I 23 **Mēga**, Ethiopia
213 H 23 **Mega Escarpment**, Ethiopia ⛰
213 J 21 **Megalo**, Ethiopia
147 D 21 **Megalopoli**, Greece
147 B 18 **Meganisi**, Greece ⌓
147 G 20 **Megara**, Greece
183 V 11 **Meghalaya**, India ▣
183 U 13 **Meghna Shahbazpur**, Bangladesh ∫
171 V 10 **Meghri**, Azerbaijan
170 D 14 **Megisti**, Greece ⌓
150 G 12 **Mehadica**, Romania
134 L 5 **Mehamn**, Norway
177 U 13 **Mehar**, Pakistan
183 O 10 **Mehndawal**, India
176 L 8 **Mehr Jān**, Iran
176 F 7 **Mehrān**, Iran
189 Y 7 **Meicheng**, China
215 U 13 **Meiganga**, Cameroon
188 M 8 **Meigu**, China
187 K 14 **Meihekou**, China
190 D 12 **Meiktila**, Myanmar
137 H 18 **Meiningen**, Germany
188 M 7 **Meishan**, China
137 M 16 **Meissen**, Germany
186 M 9 **Meixi**, China
189 V 11 **Meizhou**, China
110 H 9 **Mejicana**, Argentina ▲
110 F 5 **Mejillones**, Chile
237 Z 2 **Mejit Island**, Marshall Islands ⌓
216 G 7 **Mékambo**, Gabon
213 I 18 **Mek'elē**, Ethiopia
214 D 8 **Mékhé**, Senegal
177 U 10 **Mekhtar**, Pakistan
210 I 7 **Meknès**, Morocco
191 L 20 **Mekong**, Asia ∫
194 C 10 **Melaka**, Malaysia
194 C 9 **Melaka**, Malaysia ▣
195 U 6 **Melalap**, Malaysia
234 H 2 **Melanesia**, Oceania ◇
40 M 7 **Melanesian Basin**, Pacific Ocean ◇
231 S 13 **Melbourne**, Victoria, Australia
63 X 10 **Melbourne**, Florida, U.S.A.
69 W 9 **Melbourne**, Arkansas, U.S.A.
90 J 2 **Melchor de Mencos**, Guatemala
86 B 9 **Meldrum Bay**, Ontario, Canada
157 W 3 **Meleuz**, Russian Federation
215 X 10 **Mélfi**, Chad
83 M 17 **Melfort**, Saskatchewan, Canada
130 I 2 **Melide**, Spain
147 D 22 **Meligalas**, Greece
131 P 15 **Melilla**, Spain
110 F 12 **Melipilla**, Chile
84 H 10 **Melita**, Manitoba, Canada
158 M 12 **Melita Valley**, Mediterranean Sea ◇
141 L 22 **Melito di Porto Salvo**, Italy
151 V 9 **Melitopol'**, Ukraine
146 I 12 **Melivoia**, Greece
139 V 4 **Melk**, Austria
213 I 23 **Melka Guba**, Ethiopia
127 R 11 **Melksham**, United Kingdom
138 J 7 **Mellau**, Austria
133 E 18 **Melle**, Belgium
64 E 9 **Mellen**, Wisconsin, U.S.A.
135 E 21 **Mellerud**, Sweden
66 M 8 **Mellette**, South Dakota, U.S.A.
136 E 10 **Mellum**, Germany ⌓
143 D 17 **Mělník**, Czech Republic
113 G 14 **Melo**, Uruguay
73 O 7 **Melrose**, Montana, U.S.A.
73 U 5 **Melstone**, Montana, U.S.A.
134 L 10 **Meltaus**, Finland
231 S 13 **Melton**, Victoria, Australia
127 U 6 **Melton Mowbray**, United Kingdom
129 Q 5 **Melun**, France
213 E 19 **Melut**, Sudan
83 O 18 **Melville**, Saskatchewan, Canada
230 M 1 **Melville Island**, Northern Territory, Australia ⌓
81 N 4 **Melville Island**, Nunavut, Canada ⌓
85 O 1 **Melville Peninsula**, Nunavut, Canada ▶
192 J 11 **Memala**, Indonesia
219 U 5 **Memba**, Mozambique
193 X 11 **Memberamo**, Indonesia ∫
137 H 25 **Memmingen**, Germany
192 I 10 **Mempawah**, Indonesia
60 A 10 **Memphis**, Tennessee, U.S.A.
70 L 3 **Memphis**, Texas, U.S.A.
151 R 2 **Mena**, Ukraine
69 S 12 **Mena**, Arkansas, U.S.A.
126 M 4 **Menai Bridge**, United Kingdom
193 Q 11 **Menanga**, Indonesia
41 T 12 **Menard Fracture Zone**, Pacific Ocean ◇
129 R 12 **Mende**, France
213 I 22 **Mendebo Mountains**, Ethiopia ⛰
213 I 17 **Mendefera**, Eritrea
45 S 6 **Mendeleyev Ridge**, Arctic Ocean ⛰
157 T 1 **Mendeleyevsk**, Russian Federation
62 M 5 **Mendenhall**, Mississippi, U.S.A.
89 R 7 **Méndez**, Mexico
213 G 20 **Mendī**, Ethiopia
234 B 5 **Mendi**, Papua New Guinea
127 P 11 **Mendip Hills**, United Kingdom ⛰
77 E 17 **Mendocino**, California, U.S.A.
41 Q 4 **Mendocino Fracture Zone**, Pacific Ocean ◇
65 F 16 **Mendota**, Illinois, U.S.A.
110 H 11 **Mendoza**, Argentina
110 H 12 **Mendoza**, Argentina ▣
133 B 19 **Menen**, Belgium
237 U 1 **Meneng Point**, Nauru ▶
141 H 22 **Menfi**, Italy
195 U 5 **Mengalum**, Malaysia ⌓
189 V 4 **Mengcheng**, China
192 G 13 **Menggala**, Indonesia
188 J 13 **Menghai**, China
188 K 13 **Mengla**, China
189 R 11 **Mengshan**, China
189 W 2 **Mengyin**, China
188 J 13 **Mengzhe**, China
188 M 12 **Mengzi**, China
231 R 10 **Menindee**, New South Wales, Australia
231 R 10 **Menindee Lake**, New South Wales, Australia ⋃
153 S 9 **Menkere**, Russian Federation
65 G 14 **Menomonee Falls**, Wisconsin, U.S.A.
218 I 5 **Menongue**, Angola
192 G 12 **Mentok**, Indonesia
185 P 7 **Menyuan**, China
157 U 1 **Menzelinsk**, Russian Federation
230 I 10 **Menzies**, Western Australia, Australia
132 L 9 **Meppel**, Netherlands
136 D 12 **Meppen**, Germany
128 G 5 **Mer d'Iroise**, France 〰
192 G 13 **Merak**, Indonesia
140 F 5 **Merano**, Italy
193 Y 15 **Merauke**, Indonesia
104 F 8 **Mercaderes**, Colombia
77 H 20 **Merced**, California, U.S.A.
112 D 11 **Mercedes**, Argentina
113 D 15 **Mercedes**, Uruguay
58 A 11 **Mercer**, Pennsylvania, U.S.A.
64 E 9 **Mercer**, Wisconsin, U.S.A.
232 L 8 **Mercury Bay**, New Zealand ≈
232 L 8 **Mercury Islands**, New Zealand ⌓
235 R 9 **Mere Lava**, Vanuatu ⌓
213 N 23 **Mereeg**, Somalia
232 K 9 **Meremere**, New Zealand
191 F 20 **Mergui**, Myanmar
191 E 21 **Mergui Archipelago**, Myanmar ⌓
146 L 12 **Meriş**, Turkey
104 K 4 **Mérida**, Venezuela ▣
104 L 4 **Mérida**, Venezuela
130 K 9 **Mérida**, Spain
89 Y 10 **Mérida**, Mexico
58 L 11 **Meriden**, Connecticut, U.S.A.
63 N 5 **Meridian**, Mississippi, U.S.A.
210 J 8 **Meridja**, Algeria
135 J 17 **Merikarvia**, Finland
137 I 24 **Mering**, Germany
236 I 15 **Merir**, Palau ⌓
195 R 9 **Merit**, Malaysia
179 T 10 **Merke**, Kazakhstan
149 F 17 **Merkinė**, Lithuania
213 E 15 **Merowe**, Sudan
230 H 11 **Merredin**, Western Australia, Australia
64 F 10 **Merrill**, Wisconsin, U.S.A.
66 I 11 **Merriman**, Nebraska, U.S.A.
83 G 21 **Merritt**, British Columbia, Canada
63 X 10 **Merritt Island**, Florida, U.S.A. ⌓
213 J 17 **Mersa Fatma**, Eritrea
213 I 16 **Mersa Gulbub**, Eritrea
133 L 25 **Mersch**, Luxembourg
127 Y 9 **Mersea Island**, United Kingdom ⌓
127 P 4 **Mersey**, United Kingdom ∫
170 J 13 **Mersin**, Turkey
194 E 9 **Mersing**, Malaysia
148 E 10 **Mērsrags**, Latvia
180 C 12 **Merta**, India
127 O 10 **Merthyr Tydfil**, United Kingdom
217 W 7 **Merti**, Kenya
130 I 11 **Mértola**, Portugal
217 V 9 **Meru**, Tanzania ▲
217 V 7 **Meru**, Kenya
195 W 7 **Merutai**, Malaysia
170 K 8 **Merzifon**, Turkey
137 B 21 **Merzig**, Germany
74 J 12 **Mesa**, Arizona, U.S.A.
75 S 12 **Mesa**, New Mexico, U.S.A.
89 P 9 **Mesa Central**, Mexico ⛰
67 S 4 **Mesabi Range**, Minnesota, U.S.A. ⛰
141 O 16 **Mesagne**, Italy
137 E 16 **Meschede**, Germany
64 J 12 **Mesick**, Michigan, U.S.A.
147 F 14 **Mesimeri**, Greece
138 H 10 **Mesocco**, Switzerland
147 C 19 **Mesolongi**, Greece
112 D 13 **Mesopotamia**, Argentina ◇
71 Q 6 **Mesquite**, Texas, U.S.A.
77 N 21 **Mesquite**, Nevada, U.S.A.
211 N 7 **Messaad**, Algeria
219 P 9 **Messina**, Republic of South Africa
141 L 21 **Messina**, Italy
147 D 22 **Messiniakos Kolpos**, Greece ≈
146 G 11 **Mesta**, Bulgaria ∫
140 G 7 **Mestre**, Italy
104 J 7 **Meta**, Colombia ▣
104 M 6 **Meta**, Colombia ∫
85 R 3 **Meta Incognita Peninsula**, Nunavut, Canada ▶
86 M 6 **Métabetchouan**, Québec, Canada
62 L 8 **Metairie**, Louisiana, U.S.A.
110 I 6 **Metán**, Argentina
219 R 4 **Metangula**, Mozambique
90 I 6 **Metapan**, El Salvador
219 S 5 **Metarica**, Mozambique
87 S 12 **Meteghan**, Nova Scotia, Canada
213 H 18 **Metema**, Ethiopia
234 G 3 **Meteran**, Papua New Guinea
233 G 20 **Methven**, New Zealand
211 P 7 **Metlaoui**, Tunisia
219 U 4 **Metoro**, Mozambique
192 G 13 **Metro**, Indonesia
65 F 23 **Metropolis**, Illinois, U.S.A.
147 C 16 **Metsovo**, Greece
213 G 21 **Metu**, Ethiopia
129 V 4 **Metz**, France
133 H 21 **Meuse**, Belgium ∫
126 K 15 **Mevagissey**, United Kingdom
71 R 7 **Mexia**, Texas, U.S.A.
88 F 2 **Mexicali**, Mexico
74 L 7 **Mexican Hat**, Utah, U.S.A.
58 G 7 **Mexico**, New York, U.S.A.
69 V 3 **Mexico**, Missouri, U.S.A.
89 N 8 **Mexico**, North America ◘
89 Q 12 **México**, Mexico ▣
89 R 12 **Mexico City**, Mexico ♜
177 R 6 **Meymaneh**, Afghanistan
176 I 7 **Meymeh**, Iran
89 V 13 **Mezcalapa**, Mexico ∫
146 G 8 **Mezdra**, Bulgaria
154 M 5 **Mezen'**, Russian Federation ∫
154 M 5 **Mezen'**, Russian Federation
154 M 4 **Mezenskaya Guba**, Russian Federation ≈
89 S 7 **Mezquital**, Mexico
219 Q 4 **Mfuwe**, Zambia
141 K 25 **Mgarr**, Malta
219 Q 11 **Mhlume**, Swaziland
199 C 19 **Mi-shima**, Japan ⌓
197 H 17 **Miagao**, Philippines
89 T 14 **Miahuatlán**, Mexico
130 L 9 **Miajadas**, Spain
63 Y 13 **Miami**, Florida, U.S.A.
69 R 7 **Miami**, Oklahoma, U.S.A.
63 Y 13 **Miami Beach**, Florida, U.S.A.
177 X 10 **Mian Chanmum**, Pakistan
176 F 4 **Miandowāb**, Iran
219 X 8 **Miandrivazo**, Madgascar
186 H 8 **Mianduhe**, China
176 G 4 **Mīāneh**, Iran
193 R 8 **Miangas**, Indonesia ⌓
197 O 24 **Miangas**, Philippines ⌓
188 L 8 **Mianning**, China
142 G 8 **Mianowice**, Poland
177 W 8 **Mianwali**, Pakistan
189 O 4 **Mianxian**, China
189 N 6 **Mianyang**, China
187 G 18 **Miaodao Qundao**, China ⌓
189 Z 11 **Miaoli**, Taiwan
219 Y 8 **Miarinarivo**, Madgascar
152 I 11 **Miass**, Russian Federation
142 G 9 **Miastko**, Poland
189 O 5 **Micang Shan**, China ⛰
143 M 20 **Michalovce**, Slovakia
64 J 12 **Michigan**, U.S.A. ▣
65 I 16 **Michigan City**, Indiana, U.S.A.
86 A 7 **Michipicoten Bay**, Ontario, Canada ≈
84 M 12 **Michipicoten Island**, Ontario, Canada ⌓
86 A 6 **Michipicoten River**, Ontario, Canada
89 O 12 **Michoacán**, Mexico ▣
156 M 4 **Michurinsk**, Russian Federation
91 P 9 **Mico**, Nicaragua ∫
93 Z 11 **Micoud**, St Lucia
158 M 5 **Mid-Adriatic Basin**, Mediterranean Sea ◇
39 P 5 **Mid-Indian Basin**, Indian Ocean ◇
38 L 3 **Mid-Indian Ridge**, Indian Ocean ⛰
183 O 8 **Mid Western**, Nepal ▣
192 H 9 **Midai**, Indonesia ⌓
218 M 14 **Middelburg**, Republic of South Africa
133 D 15 **Middelburg**, Netherlands
132 H 8 **Middenmeer**, Netherlands
41 X 6 **Middle America Trench**, Pacific Ocean ◇
181 N 21 **Middle Andaman**, India ⌓
43 O 16 **Middle Island**, Tristan da Cunha ⌓
233 E 24 **Middlemarch**, New Zealand
231 U 6 **Middlemount**, Queensland, Australia
60 K 7 **Middlesboro**, Kentucky, U.S.A.
125 K 15 **Middlesbrough**, United Kingdom
90 K 2 **Middlesex**, Belize
231 Q 6 **Middleton**, Queensland, Australia
60 B 10 **Middleton**, Tennessee, U.S.A.
87 T 10 **Middleton**, Nova Scotia, Canada
58 J 11 **Middletown**, New York, U.S.A.
58 J 13 **Middletown**, New Jersey, U.S.A.
58 L 11 **Middletown**, Connecticut, U.S.A.
61 W 2 **Middletown**, Delaware, U.S.A.
127 Q 4 **Middlewich**, United Kingdom
210 I 7 **Midelt**, Morocco
127 U 12 **Midhurst**, United Kingdom
129 O 14 **Midi-Pyrénées**, France ▣
64 K 13 **Midland**, Michigan, U.S.A.
70 J 7 **Midland**, Texas, U.S.A.
86 E 11 **Midland**, Ontario, Canada
219 O 7 **Midlands**, Zimbabwe ▣
71 Q 6 **Midlothian**, Texas, U.S.A.
219 X 10 **Midongy Atsimo**, Madgascar
43 K 20 **Mid–Atlantic Ridge**, Atlantic Ocean ⛰
197 L 22 **Midsayap**, Philippines
41 P 5 **Midway Islands**, U.S.A. ◘
73 X 11 **Midwest**, Wyoming, U.S.A.
69 N 10 **Midwest City**, Oklahoma, U.S.A.
90 K 1 **Midwinters Lagoon**, Belize ⋃
171 Q 12 **Midyat**, Turkey
146 F 7 **Midzhur**, Bulgaria ▲
199 D 21 **Mie**, Japan
142 F 12 **Międzychód**, Poland
142 N 13 **Międzyrzec Podlaski**, Poland
142 E 12 **Międzyrzecz**, Poland
143 L 17 **Mielec**, Poland
217 V 13 **Miembwe**, Tanzania
130 L 1 **Mieres**, Spain
133 J 16 **Mierlo**, Netherlands
142 I 7 **Mierzeja Helska**, Poland ▶
142 I 8 **Mierzeja Wiślana**, Poland ▶
189 O 3 **Migang Shan**, China ▲
183 Y 8 **Miging**, India
140 G 8 **Migliarino**, Italy
89 O 8 **Miguel Auza**, Mexico
91 V 13 **Miguel de la Borda**, Panama
190 C 13 **Migyaunye**, Myanmar
199 E 19 **Mihara**, Japan
132 H 12 **Mijdrecht**, Netherlands
149 I 21 **Mikashevichy**, Belarus
156 L 2 **Mikhaylov**, Russian Federation
157 O 7 **Mikhaylovka**, Russian Federation

◘ Country ▣ Internal administrative region: State/Province/Territory/Dependent territory ♜ Capital city ⛰ Mountain range/Undersea ridge ▲ Mountain peak/Volcano/Seamount ◇ Geographic feature ▶ Headland/Point/Cape/Peninsula ◭ Desert ⌓ Island/Island group ⁙ Antarctic base ∿ Ocean 〰 Sea ≈ Bay/Gulf/Channel/Strait ⋃ Lake ⊻ Salt pan/Dry/Intermittent lake ∫ Ri

Mikhaylovka – Mongu

179 U 2 **Mikhaylovka**, Kazakhstan
152 L 13 **Mikhaylovskiy**, Russian Federation
241 Y 7 **Mikhaytov Island**, Antarctica
135 N 17 **Mikkeli**, Finland
217 V 12 **Mikumi**, Tanzania
155 P 8 **Mikun'**, Russian Federation
199 L 18 **Mikura-jima**, Japan
67 S 6 **Milaca**, Minnesota, U.S.A.
181 B 25 **Miladhunmadulu Atoll**, Maldives
140 C 7 **Milan**, Italy
60 B 8 **Milan**, Tennessee, U.S.A.
69 T 1 **Milan**, Missouri, U.S.A.
219 S 6 **Milange**, Mozambique
144 N 11 **Milanovac**, Serbia and Montenegro
170 B 12 **Milas**, Turkey
149 H 19 **Milavidy**, Belarus
67 O 8 **Milbank**, South Dakota, U.S.A.
59 R 5 **Milbridge**, Maine, U.S.A.
127 W 7 **Mildenhall**, United Kingdom
231 R 11 **Mildura**, Victoria, Australia
213 J 19 **Mīlē**, Ethiopia
188 M 11 **Mile**, China
231 V 8 **Miles**, Queensland, Australia
73 X 6 **Miles City**, Montana, U.S.A.
58 I 11 **Milford**, Pennsylvania, U.S.A.
58 L 12 **Milford**, Connecticut, U.S.A.
59 N 10 **Milford**, Massachusetts, U.S.A.
59 N 8 **Milford**, New Hampshire, U.S.A.
61 W 3 **Milford**, Delaware, U.S.A.
74 I 6 **Milford**, Utah, U.S.A.
126 K 9 **Milford Haven**, United Kingdom
69 N 3 **Milford Lake**, Kansas, U.S.A.
233 A 22 **Milford Sound**, New Zealand
233 B 22 **Milford Sound**, New Zealand
237 Z 4 **Mili**, Marshall Islands
143 G 14 **Milicz**, Poland
230 M 1 **Milikapiti**, Northern Territory, Australia
153 Z 11 **Mil'kovo**, Russian Federation
241 Y 10 **Mill Island**, Antarctica
5 P 3 **Mill Island**, Nunavut, Canada
29 R 13 **Millau**, France
57 R 6 **Mille Lacs**, Minnesota, U.S.A.
3 U 4 **Milledgeville**, Georgia, U.S.A.
37 S 6 **Millennium**, Kiribati
56 M 8 **Millerovo**, Russian Federation
8 F 13 **Millersburg**, Pennsylvania, U.S.A.
5 N 17 **Millersburg**, Ohio, U.S.A.
40 B 9 **Millesimo**, Italy
31 Q 13 **Millicent**, South Australia, Australia
9 R 3 **Millinocket**, Maine, U.S.A.
3 O 3 **Millport**, Alabama, U.S.A.
2 G 13 **Mills Lake**, Northwest Territories, Canada
7 R 10 **Milltown**, New Brunswick, Canada
5 B 19 **Milltown Malbay**, Republic of Ireland
I 15 **Millville**, New Jersey, U.S.A.
M 18 **Millwood**, Ohio, U.S.A.
T 13 **Millwood Lake**, Arkansas, U.S.A.
4 G 7 **Milne Bay**, Papua New Guinea
4 H 7 **Milne Bay**, Papua New Guinea
7 P 1 **Milnthorpe**, United Kingdom
Q 4 **Milo**, Maine, U.S.A.
7 H 23 **Milos**, Greece
151 Z 4 **Milove**, Ukraine
233 E 25 **Milton**, New Zealand
58 F 12 **Milton**, Pennsylvania, U.S.A.
63 P 7 **Milton**, Florida, U.S.A.
76 K 9 **Milton-Freewater**, Oregon, U.S.A.
127 U 9 **Milton Keynes**, United Kingdom
69 N 3 **Miltonvale**, Kansas, U.S.A.
65 H 14 **Milwaukee**, Wisconsin, U.S.A.
42 E 11 **Milwaukee Deep**, Atlantic Ocean
128 L 13 **Mimizan**, France
216 F 8 **Mimongo**, Gabon
188 M 7 **Min**, China
77 K 19 **Mina**, Nevada, U.S.A.
175 W 5 **Mina Jebel Ali**, United Arab Emirates
175 S 3 **Minā' Sa'ūd**, Kuwait
176 M 13 **Mīnāb**, Iran
199 B 23 **Minamata**, Japan
113 F 15 **Minas**, Uruguay
92 K 5 **Minas**, Cuba
87 U 10 **Minas Basin**, Nova Scotia, Canada
87 T 10 **Minas Channel**, Nova Scotia, Canada
112 F 13 **Minas de Corrales**, Uruguay
92 F 4 **Minas de Matahambre**, Cuba
109 L 16 **Minas Gerais**, Brazil
89 V 13 **Minatitlán**, Mexico
190 C 13 **Minbu**, Myanmar
214 I 11 **Mininian**, Côte d'Ivoire
111 F 18 **Minchinmávida**, Chile
197 M 21 **Mindanao**, Philippines
197 K 22 **Mindanao**, Philippines
137 H 24 **Mindelheim**, Germany
43 A 15 **Mindelo**, Cape Verde
136 F 13 **Minden**, Germany
62 H 4 **Minden**, Louisiana, U.S.A.
86 F 11 **Minden**, Ontario, Canada
196 G 13 **Mindoro**, Philippines
197 F 14 **Mindoro Strait**, Philippines
199 C 20 **Mine**, Japan
125 D 20 **Mine Head**, Republic of Ireland
127 N 11 **Minehead**, United Kingdom
71 S 6 **Mineola**, Texas, U.S.A.
71 O 6 **Mineral Wells**, Texas, U.S.A.
157 O 13 **Mineral'nyye Vody**, Russian Federation
74 I 6 **Minersville**, Utah, U.S.A.
141 M 15 **Minervino Murge**, Italy
217 P 14 **Minga**, Democratic Republic of Congo
171 W 8 **Mingäçevir**, Azerbaijan
171 W 7 **Mingäçevir Su Anbari**, Azerbaijan
216 L 4 **Mingala**, Central African Republic
230 G 10 **Mingenew**, Western Australia, Australia
189 T 5 **Minggang**, China
190 D 9 **Mingin Range**, Myanmar
186 K 10 **Mingshui**, China
124 D 11 **Mingulay**, United Kingdom
189 W 9 **Mingxi**, China
191 D 15 **Minhla**, Myanmar
189 X 10 **Minhou**, China
181 B 24 **Minicoy Island**, India
73 N 12 **Minidoka**, Idaho, U.S.A.
230 F 7 **Minilya Bridge Roadhouse**, Western Australia, Australia
182 H 2 **Minimarg**, India
185 P 7 **Minle**, China
215 Q 11 **Minna**, Nigeria
67 R 8 **Minneapolis**, Minnesota, U.S.A.
68 J 6 **Minneola**, Kansas, U.S.A.
67 O 6 **Minnesota**, U.S.A.
67 R 8 **Minnesota**, Minnesota, U.S.A.
131 Z 7 **Minorca**, Spain
66 J 3 **Minot**, North Dakota, U.S.A.
149 J 17 **Minsk**, Belarus
142 L 13 **Mińsk Mazowiecki**, Poland
149 J 18 **Minskaya Voblasts'**, Belarus
215 U 14 **Minta**, Cameroon
79 Q 7 **Minto**, Alaska, U.S.A.
87 S 9 **Minto**, New Brunswick, Canada
82 F 7 **Minto Inlet**, Northwest Territories, Canada
83 N 20 **Minton**, Saskatchewan, Canada
141 J 15 **Minturno**, Italy
183 Z 8 **Minutang**, India
216 F 6 **Minvoul**, Gabon
185 Q 9 **Minxian**, China
157 X 1 **Minyar**, Russian Federation
183 Z 9 **Minzong**, India
64 L 11 **Mio**, Michigan, U.S.A.
149 H 18 **Mir**, Belarus
130 H 6 **Mira**, Portugal
108 J 13 **Miracema do Tocantins**, Brazil
177 V 8 **Miram Shah**, Pakistan
113 D 18 **Miramar**, Argentina
87 T 7 **Miramichi Bay**, New Brunswick, Canada
129 N 12 **Miramont-de-Guyenne**, France
105 O 3 **Miranda**, Venezuela
109 G 17 **Miranda**, Brazil
131 P 2 **Miranda de Ebro**, Spain
130 J 4 **Mirandela**, Portugal
112 H 5 **Mirandópolis**, Brazil
145 M 20 **Miras**, Albania
175 X 11 **Mirbāţ**, Oman
195 R 7 **Miri**, Malaysia
231 V 7 **Miriam Vale**, Queensland, Australia
177 P 11 **Mirjāveh**, Iran
241 Y 8 **Mirny**, Antarctica
153 R 11 **Mirnyy**, Russian Federation
142 F 10 **Mirosławiec**, Poland
177 U 14 **Mirpur Khas**, Pakistan
177 U 15 **Mirpur Sakro**, Pakistan
213 N 22 **Mirsale**, Somalia
147 F 22 **Mirtoö Pelagos**, Greece
159 R 9 **Mirtoon Basin**, Mediterranean Sea
183 N 12 **Mirzapur**, India
199 D 21 **Misaki**, Japan
198 K 9 **Misawa**, Japan
87 U 6 **Miscou Island**, New Brunswick, Canada
177 Y 5 **Misgar**, Pakistan
182 H 1 **Misgar**, India
181 O 24 **Misha**, India
186 N 11 **Mishan**, China
183 Z 8 **Mishmi Hills**, India
234 C 5 **Misiki**, Papua New Guinea
112 F 10 **Misiones**, Argentina
175 O 6 **Miskah**, Saudi Arabia
143 L 21 **Miskolc**, Hungary
193 T 11 **Misoöl**, Indonesia
211 T 7 **Mişrātah**, Libya
66 J 11 **Mission**, South Dakota, U.S.A.
85 N 9 **Missisa Lake**, Ontario, Canada
86 E 13 **Mississauga**, Ontario, Canada
57 S 11 **Mississippi**, U.S.A., U.S.A.
62 K 3 **Mississippi**, U.S.A.
62 M 9 **Mississippi Delta**, Louisiana, U.S.A.
62 M 7 **Mississippi Sound**, Mississippi, U.S.A.
73 N 5 **Missoula**, Montana, U.S.A.
210 J 7 **Missour**, Morocco
56 M 5 **Missouri**, U.S.A., U.S.A.
69 S 5 **Missouri**, U.S.A.
71 S 10 **Missouri City**, Texas, U.S.A.
67 P 12 **Missouri Valley**, Iowa, U.S.A.
85 R 11 **Mistassini**, Québec, Canada
139 Y 2 **Mistelbach**, Austria
92 F 7 **Misteriosa Bank**, Cayman Islands
151 Y 5 **Mistky**, Ukraine
158 L 11 **Misurata Valley**, Mediterranean Sea
108 H 8 **Mitaraka**, Brazil
231 R 3 **Mitchell**, Queensland, Australia
231 T 8 **Mitchell**, Queensland, Australia
67 N 10 **Mitchell**, South Dakota, U.S.A.
76 I 11 **Mitchell**, Oregon, U.S.A.
125 C 20 **Mitchelstown**, Republic of Ireland
177 V 15 **Mithi**, Pakistan
237 P 10 **Mitiaro**, Cook Islands
199 L 15 **Mito**, Japan
217 W 13 **Mitole**, Tanzania
198 K 6 **Mitsuishi**, Japan
199 A 20 **Mitsushima**, Japan
138 J 7 **Mittelberg**, Austria
138 L 8 **Mittelberg**, Austria
139 P 7 **Mittersill**, Austria
137 M 26 **Mittlespitze**, Germany
104 L 9 **Mitú**, Colombia
217 P 13 **Mitwaba**, Democratic Republic of Congo
216 E 7 **Mitzic**, Gabon
199 K 17 **Miura**, Japan
199 L 18 **Miyake-jima**, Japan
198 L 10 **Miyako**, Japan
199 O 26 **Miyako-jima**, Japan
199 N 26 **Miyako-rettō**, Japan
199 C 23 **Miyakonojō**, Japan
178 J 5 **Miyaly**, Kazakhstan
199 D 23 **Miyazaki**, Japan
199 G 17 **Miyazu**, Japan
199 D 19 **Miyoshi**, Japan
187 E 16 **Miyun**, China
213 G 21 **Mizan Teferī**, Ethiopia
211 S 8 **Mizdah**, Libya
125 A 21 **Mizen Head**, Republic of Ireland
150 I 6 **Mizhhir"ya**, Ukraine
189 R 1 **Mizhi**, China
150 L 12 **Mizil**, Romania
146 G 7 **Miziya**, Bulgaria
190 W 13 **Mizoram**, India
172 E 11 **Mizpe Ramon**, Israel
241 T 3 **Mizuho**, Antarctica
135 F 22 **Mjölby**, Sweden
217 W 11 **Mkata**, Tanzania
217 W 10 **Mkomazi**, Tanzania
219 O 4 **Mkushi**, Zambia
143 D 16 **Mladá Boleslav**, Czech Republic
144 L 11 **Mladenovac**, Serbia and Montenegro
142 K 11 **Mława**, Poland
159 N 5 **Mljet**, Mediterranean Sea
134 F 11 **Mo i Rana**, Norway
193 S 14 **Moa**, Indonesia
93 N 6 **Moa**, Cuba
231 R 1 **Moa Island**, Queensland, Australia
74 M 5 **Moab**, Utah, U.S.A.
235 Y 12 **Moala**, Fiji
219 Q 10 **Moamba**, Mozambique
233 G 18 **Moana**, New Zealand
216 F 8 **Moanda**, Gabon
176 I 8 **Mobārakeh**, Iran
216 L 5 **Mobaye**, Central African Republic
216 L 5 **Mobayi-Mbongo**, Democratic Republic of Congo
69 U 3 **Moberly**, Missouri, U.S.A.
63 O 7 **Mobile**, Alabama, U.S.A.
63 O 7 **Mobile Bay**, Alabama, U.S.A.
66 K 7 **Mobridge**, South Dakota, U.S.A.
190 L 12 **Môc Châu**, Vietnam
93 Q 7 **Moca**, Dominican Republic
219 U 5 **Moçambique**, Mozambique
175 O 14 **Mocha**, Yemen
41 X 12 **Mocha Fracture Zone**, Pacific Ocean
219 U 3 **Mocimboa da Praia**, Mozambique
218 H 4 **Môco**, Angola
104 G 9 **Mocoa**, Colombia
112 K 5 **Mococa**, Brazil
88 M 4 **Moctezuma**, Mexico
219 S 6 **Mocuba**, Mozambique
129 W 11 **Modane**, France
140 F 8 **Modena**, Italy
74 H 6 **Modena**, Utah, U.S.A.
77 H 20 **Modesto**, California, U.S.A.
90 J 4 **Modesto Méndez**, Guatemala
141 K 24 **Modica**, Italy
139 X 4 **Mödling**, Austria
185 R 3 **Modot**, Mongolia
144 H 10 **Modriča**, Bosnia and Herzegovina
231 S 13 **Moe**, Victoria, Australia
232 K 7 **Moehau**, New Zealand
105 X 6 **Moengo**, Suriname
137 C 15 **Moers**, Germany
182 H 6 **Moga**, India
213 M 24 **Mogadishu**, Somalia
216 J 6 **Mogalo**, Democratic Republic of Congo
198 J 12 **Mogami**, Japan
190 E 8 **Mogaung**, Myanmar
112 J 5 **Mogi-Guaçu**, Brazil
146 C 12 **Mogila**, Macedonia (F.Y.R.O.M.)
142 H 12 **Mogilno**, Poland
219 U 5 **Mogincual**, Mozambique
153 S 13 **Mogocha**, Russian Federation
213 E 20 **Mogogh**, Sudan
190 E 10 **Mogok**, Myanmar
91 N 7 **Mogotón**, Nicaragua
186 H 9 **Moguqi**, China
143 I 26 **Mohács**, Hungary
210 H 7 **Mohammedia**, Morocco
58 J 8 **Mohawk**, New York, U.S.A.
186 H 4 **Mohe**, China
219 W 4 **Mohéli**, Comoros
218 K 7 **Mohembo**, Botswana
45 R 13 **Mohns Ridge**, Arctic Ocean
190 E 9 **Mohnyin**, Myanmar
107 H 18 **Moho**, Peru
217 W 13 **Mohoro**, Tanzania
150 M 6 **Mohyliv-Podil's'kyy**, Ukraine
183 X 12 **Moirang**, India
147 I 26 **Moires**, Greece
112 B 13 **Moisés Ville**, Argentina
87 S 3 **Moisie**, Québec, Canada
215 X 12 **Moïssala**, Chad
77 J 23 **Mojave**, California, U.S.A.
77 K 23 **Mojave Desert**, California, U.S.A.
188 K 12 **Mojiang**, China
199 C 20 **Mojikō**, Japan
145 J 14 **Mojkovac**, Serbia and Montenegro
183 X 10 **Mokokchung**, India
233 D 25 **Mokoreta**, New Zealand
187 L 21 **Mokp'o**, South Korea
215 P 11 **Mokwa**, Nigeria
133 I 17 **Mol**, Belgium
141 N 15 **Mola di Bari**, Italy
89 R 11 **Molango**, Mexico
147 F 23 **Molaoi**, Greece
135 B 15 **Molde**, Norway
151 N 9 **Moldova**, Europe
87 T 11 **Molega Lake**, Nova Scotia, Canada
216 K 5 **Molegbe**, Democratic Republic of Congo
218 M 10 **Molepolole**, Botswana
149 G 14 **Molėtai**, Lithuania
141 M 15 **Molfetta**, Italy
131 R 6 **Molina de Aragón**, Spain
65 E 16 **Moline**, Illinois, U.S.A.
69 P 7 **Moline**, Kansas, U.S.A.
217 R 12 **Moliro**, Democratic Republic of Congo
141 K 14 **Molise**, Italy
141 L 17 **Moliterno**, Italy
139 Q 8 **Möll**, Austria
107 F 20 **Mollendo**, Peru
131 V 4 **Mollerussa**, Spain
136 I 10 **Mölln**, Germany
151 V 8 **Molochans'k**, Ukraine
151 V 9 **Molochnyy Lyman**, Ukraine
241 V 2 **Molodezhnaya**, Antarctica
179 T 4 **Molodezhnyy**, Kazakhstan
78 D 7 **Molokai**, Hawaii, U.S.A.
41 R 5 **Molokai Fracture Zone**, Pacific Ocean
147 E 18 **Molos**, Greece
215 V 15 **Moloundou**, Cameroon
219 N 13 **Molteno**, Republic of South Africa
193 U 14 **Molu**, Indonesia
193 Q 11 **Molucca Sea**, Indonesia
193 T 10 **Moluccas**, Indonesia
219 S 5 **Molumbo**, Mozambique
219 T 6 **Moma**, Mozambique
217 X 10 **Mombasa**, Kenya
183 X 12 **Mombi New**, India
146 J 12 **Momchilgrad**, Bulgaria
196 H 12 **Mompog Passage**, Philippines
216 L 8 **Mompono**, Democratic Republic of Congo
104 I 3 **Mompós**, Colombia
153 U 8 **Momskiy Khrebet**, Russian Federation
191 E 16 **Mon**, Myanmar
135 E 26 **Møn**, Denmark
129 X 13 **Monaco**, Monaco
129 W 13 **Monaco**, Europe
42 J 9 **Monaco Basin**, Atlantic Ocean
105 R 3 **Monagas**, Venezuela
70 I 8 **Monahans**, Texas, U.S.A.
219 U 5 **Monapo**, Mozambique
211 R 6 **Monastir**, Tunisia
141 B 19 **Monastir**, Italy
198 K 6 **Monbetsu**, Japan
215 U 11 **Monboré**, Cameroon
154 H 3 **Monchegorsk**, Russian Federation
137 B 16 **Mönchengladbach**, Germany
139 Y 4 **Mönchhof**, Austria
61 Q 14 **Moncks Corner**, South Carolina, U.S.A.
89 P 6 **Monclova**, Mexico
87 U 9 **Moncton**, New Brunswick, Canada
141 I 21 **Mondello**, Italy
216 L 6 **Mondjamboli**, Democratic Republic of Congo
215 V 9 **Mondo**, Chad
130 J 1 **Mondoñedo**, Spain
140 A 9 **Mondovì**, Italy
141 I 15 **Mondragone**, Italy
139 R 5 **Mondsee**, Austria
147 F 23 **Monemvasia**, Greece
58 B 13 **Monessen**, Pennsylvania, U.S.A.
130 J 2 **Monforte**, Spain
130 I 9 **Monforte**, Portugal
190 N 11 **Mong Cai**, Vietnam
190 F 13 **Mong Hang**, Myanmar
190 H 12 **Mong Hpayak**, Myanmar
190 F 11 **Mong Hsu**, Myanmar
190 F 11 **Mong Kung**, Myanmar
190 E 10 **Möng Mir**, Myanmar
190 F 13 **Mong Pan**, Myanmar
190 G 12 **Mong Ping**, Myanmar
190 G 12 **Mong Pu**, Myanmar
190 F 11 **Mong Yai**, Myanmar
216 M 5 **Monga**, Democratic Republic of Congo
213 E 22 **Mongalla**, Sudan
183 V 10 **Mongar**, Bhutan
217 Q 6 **Mongbwalu**, Democratic Republic of Congo
140 A 9 **Mongioie**, Italy
215 X 10 **Mongo**, Chad
185 N 4 **Mongolia**, Asia
215 T 15 **Mongomo**, Equatorial Guinea
215 U 10 **Mongonu**, Nigeria
177 W 7 **Mongora**, Pakistan
215 Z 10 **Mongororo**, Chad
218 L 5 **Mongu**, Zambia

Country · Internal administrative region: State/Province/Territory/Dependent territory · Capital city · Mountain range/Undersea ridge · Mountain peak/Volcano/Seamount · Geographic feature · Headland/Point/Cape/Peninsula · Desert · Island/Island group · Antarctic base · Ocean · Sea · Bay/Gulf/Channel/Strait · Lake · Salt pan/Dry/Intermittent lake · River

64 F 10 **Monico**, Wisconsin, U.S.A.
90 I 6 **Monjas**, Guatemala
230 E 8 **Monkey Mia**, Western Australia, Australia
197 N 21 **Monkeyo**, Philippines
142 N 10 **Mońki**, Poland
216 L 9 **Monkoto**, Democratic Republic of Congo
127 P 9 **Monmouth**, United Kingdom
65 E 17 **Monmouth**, Illinois, U.S.A.
77 J 19 **Mono Lake**, California, U.S.A. 💧
59 Q 11 **Monomoy Island**, Massachusetts, U.S.A. 🏝
141 N 15 **Monopoli**, Italy
143 J 23 **Monor**, Hungary
215 Z 7 **Monou**, Chad
129 O 12 **Monpazier**, France
131 S 6 **Monreal del Campo**, Spain
58 J 11 **Monroe**, New York, U.S.A.
61 P 10 **Monroe**, North Carolina, U.S.A.
62 J 4 **Monroe**, Louisiana, U.S.A.
65 L 15 **Monroe**, Michigan, U.S.A.
65 F 15 **Monroe**, Wisconsin, U.S.A.
69 V 2 **Monroe City**, Missouri, U.S.A.
65 I 20 **Monroe Lake**, Indiana, U.S.A. 💧
58 B 13 **Monroeville**, Pennsylvania, U.S.A.
63 P 6 **Monroeville**, Alabama, U.S.A.
214 G 13 **Monrovia**, Liberia 🏛
133 E 21 **Mons**, Belgium
137 B 18 **Monschau**, Germany
132 F 13 **Monster**, Netherlands
129 W 9 **Mont Blanc**, France/Switzerland ▲
215 S 14 **Mont Cameroun**, Cameroon ▲
38 B 12 **Mont Cocotte**, Mauritius ▲
85 S 10 **Mont de Babel**, Québec, Canada ▲
128 M 13 **Mont-de-Marsan**, France
45 O 13 **Mont Forel**, Greenland ▲
216 E 8 **Mont Iboundji**, Gabon ▲
87 S 5 **Mont Jacques Cartier**, Québec, Canada ▲
87 Q 6 **Mont-Joli**, Québec, Canada
86 J 9 **Mont-Laurier**, Québec, Canada
87 S 5 **Mont Louis**, Québec, Canada
129 W 12 **Mont Pelat**, France ▲
105 Y 8 **Mont St-Marcel**, French Guiana ▲
211 O 13 **Mont Tahat**, Algeria ▲
129 W 11 **Mont Thabor**, France ▲
216 M 2 **Mont Toussoro**, Central African Republic ▲
129 U 13 **Mont Ventoux**, France ▲
85 T 9 **Mont Wright**, Québec, Canada ▲
85 R 9 **Mont Yapeitso**, Québec, Canada ▲
79 S 10 **Montague Island**, Alaska, U.S.A. 🏝
128 L 8 **Montaigu**, France
131 S 6 **Montalbán**, Spain
140 F 13 **Montalto di Castro**, Italy
106 C 10 **Montalvo**, Ecuador
146 G 7 **Montana**, Bulgaria ▣
146 F 7 **Montana**, Bulgaria
73 Q 5 **Montana**, U.S.A. ▣
91 P 5 **Montañas de Colón**, Honduras ⛰
129 Q 6 **Montargis**, France
129 O 13 **Montauban**, France
58 M 12 **Montauk**, New York, U.S.A.
59 N 12 **Montauk Point**, New York, U.S.A. ▶
129 S 6 **Montbard**, France
129 V 6 **Montbéliard**, France
131 V 5 **Montblanc**, Spain
129 S 8 **Montceau-les-Mines**, France
108 H 10 **Monte Alegre**, Brazil
140 J 13 **Monte Amaro**, Italy ▲
109 M 16 **Monte Azul**, Brazil
106 E 12 **Monte Bello**, Peru
111 F 24 **Monte Burney**, Chile ▲
129 X 13 **Monte Carlo**, Monaco
140 I 13 **Monte Carno**, Italy ▲
112 D 12 **Monte Caseros**, Argentina
129 Y 14 **Monte Cinto**, France ▲
93 P 6 **Monte Cristi**, Dominican Republic
111 H 25 **Monte Darwin**, Chile ▲
111 H 24 **Monte Dinero**, Argentina
129 Y 15 **Monte Incudine**, France ▲
111 F 19 **Monte Macá**, Chile ▲
111 F 18 **Monte Melimoyu**, Chile ▲
141 J 15 **Monte Miletto**, Italy ▲
109 N 16 **Monte Pascoal**, Brazil ▲
110 K 7 **Monte Quemado**, Argentina
129 Y 15 **Monte Rotondo**, France ▲
141 L 14 **Monte Sant'Angelo**, Italy
109 N 14 **Monte Santo**, Brazil
140 A 8 **Monte Viso**, Italy ▲
75 Q 7 **Monte Vista**, Colorado, U.S.A.
86 J 10 **Montebello**, Québec, Canada
230 F 6 **Montebello Islands**, Western Australia, Australia 🏝
112 F 9 **Montecarlo**, Argentina
140 F 13 **Montefiascone**, Italy
92 K 8 **Montego Bay**, Jamaica
129 T 12 **Montélimar**, France
64 F 13 **Montello**, Wisconsin, U.S.A.
130 H 9 **Montemor-o-nova**, Portugal
89 Q 7 **Montemorelos**, Mexico
112 G 12 **Montenegro**, Brazil
145 I 15 **Montenegro**, Serbia and Montenegro ▣
219 T 4 **Montepuez**, Mozambique
61 Q 4 **Monterey**, Virginia, U.S.A.
77 G 21 **Monterey**, California, U.S.A.
77 G 21 **Monterey Bay**, California, U.S.A. ≈
104 H 4 **Montería**, Colombia
107 L 20 **Montero**, Bolivia
89 Q 7 **Monterrey**, Mexico
109 L 16 **Montes Claros**, Brazil
113 E 16 **Montevideo**, Uruguay 🏛
67 P 8 **Montevideo**, Minnesota, U.S.A.
68 I 6 **Montezuma**, Kansas, U.S.A.
127 O 7 **Montgomery**, United Kingdom
63 R 5 **Montgomery**, Alabama, U.S.A.
138 C 10 **Monthey**, Switzerland
58 I 11 **Monticello**, New York, U.S.A.
60 I 7 **Monticello**, Kentucky, U.S.A.
62 L 6 **Monticello**, Mississippi, U.S.A.
67 V 11 **Monticello**, Iowa, U.S.A.
69 V 2 **Monticello**, Missouri, U.S.A.
69 W 13 **Monticello**, Arkansas, U.S.A.
74 M 6 **Monticello**, Utah, U.S.A.
130 G 9 **Montijo**, Portugal
129 P 9 **Montluçon**, France
129 R 4 **Montmirail**, France
231 V 7 **Monto**, Queensland, Australia
131 N 11 **Montoro**, Spain
58 L 6 **Montpelier**, Vermont, U.S.A.
73 Q 13 **Montpelier**, Idaho, U.S.A.
129 S 14 **Montpellier**, France
86 L 10 **Montréal**, Québec, Canada
83 M 17 **Montreal Lake**, Saskatchewan, Canada
83 M 17 **Montreal Lake**, Saskatchewan, Canada 💧
86 A 8 **Montreal River**, Ontario, Canada
138 C 9 **Montreux**, Switzerland
124 J 11 **Montrose**, United Kingdom
58 H 10 **Montrose**, Pennsylvania, U.S.A.
69 W 14 **Montrose**, Arkansas, U.S.A.
75 O 6 **Montrose**, Colorado, U.S.A.
215 S 7 **Monts Bagzane**, Niger ▲
211 Q 7 **Monts des Ksour**, Tunisia ⛰
211 N 12 **Monts du Mouydir**, Algeria ◇
217 Q 12 **Monts Mitumba**, Democratic Republic of Congo ⛰
217 O 13 **Monts Mulumbe**, Democratic Republic of Congo ⛰
87 P 8 **Monts Notre Dame**, Québec, Canada ⛰
93 X 9 **Montserrat**, United Kingdom, United Kingdom ▣
131 N 5 **Montuenga**, Spain
74 M 7 **Monument Valley**, Utah, U.S.A. ◇
216 L 6 **Monveda**, Democratic Republic of Congo
190 O 11 **Monywa**, Myanmar
140 C 6 **Monza**, Italy
107 O 14 **Monzón**, Peru
131 J 4 **Monzón**, Spain
219 N 10 **Mookane**, Botswana
231 Q 9 **Moolawatana**, South Australia, Australia
231 Q 9 **Moomba**, South Australia, Australia
231 J 9 **Moonie**, Queensland, Australia
230 G 10 **Moora**, Western Australia, Australia
71 N 11 **Moore**, Texas, U.S.A.
73 N 10 **Moore**, Idaho, U.S.A.
73 S 5 **Moore**, Montana, U.S.A.
61 R 3 **Moorefield**, West Virginia, U.S.A.
67 O 5 **Moorhead**, Minnesota, U.S.A.
73 R 11 **Moose**, Wyoming, U.S.A.
85 O 10 **Moose**, Ontario, Canada ∿
79 R 10 **Moose Pass**, Alaska, U.S.A.
59 Q 3 **Moosehead Lake**, Maine, U.S.A. 💧
85 O 10 **Moosonee**, Ontario, Canada
219 S 7 **Mopeia**, Mozambique
177 T 8 **Moqor**, Afghanistan
107 G 20 **Moquegua**, Peru
107 H 19 **Moquegua**, Peru ▣
143 H 23 **Mór**, Hungary
215 V 10 **Mora**, Cameroon
130 H 9 **Mora**, Portugal
135 F 18 **Mora**, Sweden
131 O 8 **Mora**, Spain
75 R 9 **Mora**, New Mexico, U.S.A.
182 K 8 **Moradabad**, India
219 W 7 **Morafenobe**, Madgascar
142 L 9 **Morąg**, Poland
90 L 5 **Morales**, Guatemala
219 Y 8 **Moramanga**, Madgascar
73 R 10 **Moran**, Wyoming, U.S.A.
231 U 6 **Moranbah**, Queensland, Australia
181 F 25 **Moratuwa**, Sri Lanka
143 G 17 **Morava**, Czech Republic ∿
143 E 19 **Moravia**, Czech Republic ◇
143 E 19 **Moravské Budějovice**, Czech Republic
230 F 10 **Morawa**, Western Australia, Australia
124 H 9 **Moray Firth**, United Kingdom ≈
90 L 5 **Morazán**, Honduras
137 C 20 **Morbach**, Germany
181 B 14 **Morbi**, India
139 Y 5 **Mörbisch**, Austria
141 J 15 **Morcone**, Italy
156 M 5 **Mordovo**, Russian Federation
66 I 8 **Moreau**, South Dakota, U.S.A. ∿
127 P 1 **Morecambe**, United Kingdom
127 P 1 **Morecambe Bay**, United Kingdom ≈
231 U 9 **Moree**, New South Wales, Australia
234 A 6 **Morehead**, Papua New Guinea
60 K 5 **Morehead**, Kentucky, U.S.A.
61 U 11 **Morehead City**, North Carolina, U.S.A.
89 P 11 **Morelia**, Mexico
131 T 6 **Morella**, Spain
89 R 12 **Morelos**, Mexico ▣
182 J 10 **Morena**, India
83 C 20 **Moresby Island**, British Columbia, Canada 🏝
127 S 9 **Moreton- in-Marsh**, United Kingdom
231 W 8 **Moreton Island**, Queensland, Australia 🏝
129 V 8 **Morez**, France
170 H 15 **Morfou**, Cyprus
170 G 15 **Morfou Bay**, Cyprus ≈
231 Q 11 **Morgan**, South Australia, Australia
62 K 8 **Morgan City**, Louisiana, U.S.A.
77 G 20 **Morgan Hill**, California, U.S.A.
61 V 8 **Morgans Corner**, North Carolina, U.S.A.
61 N 9 **Morganton**, North Carolina, U.S.A.
61 P 2 **Morgantown**, West Virginia, U.S.A.
138 B 9 **Morges**, Switzerland
198 J 7 **Mori**, Japan
75 Q 10 **Moriarty**, New Mexico, U.S.A.
194 B 9 **Morib**, Malaysia
214 H 11 **Moribaya**, Guinea
104 L 8 **Morichal**, Colombia
198 K 10 **Morioka**, Japan
128 I 4 **Morlaix**, France
141 M 18 **Mormanno**, Italy
38 A 9 **Morne Seychellois**, Seychelles ▲
41 X 13 **Mornington Abyssal Plain**, Pacific Ocean ◇
231 P 3 **Mornington Island**, Queensland, Australia 🏝
177 U 13 **Moro**, Pakistan
197 J 22 **Moro Gulf**, Philippines ≈
234 E 5 **Morobe**, Papua New Guinea
234 E 5 **Morobe**, Papua New Guinea ▣
210 F 8 **Morocco**, Africa □
65 H 17 **Morocco**, Indiana, U.S.A.
150 K 1 **Morochne**, Ukraine
217 V 12 **Morogoro**, Tanzania ▣
217 V 12 **Morogoro**, Tanzania
89 P 11 **Moroleón**, Mexico
193 Q 14 **Moromaho**, Indonesia 🏝
219 V 9 **Morombe**, Madgascar
92 J 5 **Morón**, Cuba
185 P 2 **Mörön**, Mongolia
106 C 10 **Morona**, Ecuador
106 C 10 **Morona-Santiago**, Ecuador ▣
219 W 8 **Morondava**, Madgascar
214 J 11 **Morondo**, Côte d'Ivoire
219 W 4 **Moroni**, Comoros 🏛
193 S 9 **Morotai**, Indonesia 🏝
217 T 6 **Moroto**, Uganda ▲
217 T 6 **Moroto**, Uganda
157 N 9 **Morozovsk**, Russian Federation
109 L 14 **Morpara**, Brazil
232 L 10 **Morrinsville**, New Zealand
67 P 7 **Morris**, Minnesota, U.S.A.
84 I 11 **Morris**, Manitoba, Canada
58 J 12 **Morristown**, New Jersey, U.S.A.
60 K 8 **Morristown**, Tennessee, U.S.A.
77 H 22 **Morro Bay**, California, U.S.A.
109 M 14 **Morro do Chapéu**, Brazil
157 N 3 **Morshanka**, Russian Federation
134 G 10 **Mørsvikboth**, Norway
129 N 5 **Mortagne-au-Perche**, France
126 M 12 **Morte Bay**, United Kingdom ≈
112 B 13 **Morteros**, Argentina
93 N 4 **Mortimer's**, The Bahamas
237 P 15 **Mortlock Islands**, Federated States of Micronesia 🏝
70 I 4 **Morton**, Texas, U.S.A.
76 G 8 **Morton**, Washington, U.S.A.
217 T 5 **Morungole**, Uganda ▲
231 T 8 **Morven**, Queensland, Australia
156 J 2 **Mosal'sk**, Russian Federation
73 U 5 **Mosby**, Montana, U.S.A.
156 K 1 **Moscow**, Russian Federation 🏛
60 B 10 **Moscow**, Tennessee, U.S.A.
72 J 5 **Moscow**, Idaho, U.S.A.
241 X 12 **Moscow University Ice Shelf**, Antarctica ◇
137 C 19 **Mosel**, Germany ∿
76 J 8 **Moses Lake**, Washington, U.S.A. 💧
217 V 10 **Moshi**, Tanzania
151 R 5 **Moshny**, Ukraine
142 G 13 **Mosina**, Poland
134 F 12 **Mosjøen**, Norway
134 F 9 **Moskenesøy**, Norway 🏝
156 K 1 **Moskovskaya Oblast'**, Russian Federation ▣
143 G 22 **Moson-magyaróvár**, Hungary
85 P 5 **Mosquito Bay**, Québec, Canada ≈
91 R 8 **Mosquito Coast**, Nicaragua ◇
63 X 9 **Mosquito Lagoon**, Florida, U.S.A. 💧
135 D 20 **Moss**, Norway
233 C 24 **Mossburn**, New Zealand
218 L 15 **Mossel Bay**, Republic of South Africa
216 F 9 **Mossendjo**, Congo
108 O 12 **Mossoró**, Brazil
210 L 6 **Mostaganem**, Algeria
145 G 14 **Mostar**, Bosnia and Herzegovina
112 I 13 **Mostardas**, Brazil
151 Q 8 **Mostove**, Ukraine
156 M 13 **Mostovskoy**, Russian Federation
150 H 4 **Mostys'ka**, Ukraine
173 R 2 **Mosul**, Iraq
213 I 19 **Mot'a**, Ethiopia
131 P 8 **Mota del Cuervo**, Spain
235 Q 9 **Mota Lava**, Vanuatu 🏝
90 I 5 **Motagua**, Guatemala ∿
149 G 21 **Motal'**, Belarus
135 F 21 **Motala**, Sweden
182 K 11 **Moth**, India
183 P 10 **Motihari**, India
131 R 8 **Motilla del Palancar**, Spain
232 M 10 **Motiti Island**, New Zealand 🏝
131 Q 1 **Motrico**, Spain
150 G 12 **Motru**, Romania
198 I 7 **Motsuta-misaki**, Japan ▶
66 H 6 **Mott**, North Dakota, U.S.A.
232 N 11 **Motu**, New Zealand ∿
41 X 5 **Motu Nui**, Easter Island 🏝
233 H 16 **Motueka**, New Zealand
232 J 12 **Motunui**, New Zealand
234 I 5 **Motupena Point**, Papua New Guinea ▶
216 I 6 **Mouali Gbangba**, Congo
214 G 7 **Moudjéria**, Mauritania
135 K 17 **Mouhijärvi**, Finland
216 E 9 **Mouila**, Gabon
213 K 18 **Moulhoulê**, Djibouti
129 R 8 **Moulins**, France
191 F 16 **Moulmein**, Myanmar
63 O 2 **Moulton**, Alabama, U.S.A.
63 T 6 **Moultrie**, Georgia, U.S.A.
65 F 23 **Mound City**, Illinois, U.S.A.
69 Q 1 **Mound City**, Missouri, U.S.A.
215 W 12 **Moundou**, Chad
61 O 2 **Moundsville**, West Virginia, U.S.A.
110 G 11 **Mount Aconcagua**, Argentina ▲
111 K 23 **Mt Adam**, Falkland Islands ▲
76 H 8 **Mt Adams**, Washington, U.S.A. ▲
61 O 8 **Mount Airy**, North Carolina, U.S.A.
234 E 6 **Mt Albert Edward**, Papua New Guinea ▲
241 Y 10 **Mt Amundsen**, Antarctica ▲
233 C 26 **Mt Anglem**, New Zealand ▲
197 M 22 **Mount Apo**, Philippines ▲
171 T 9 **Mt Ararat**, Turkey ▲
233 F 20 **Mt Arrowsmith**, New Zealand ▲
64 G 8 **Mt Arvon**, Michigan, U.S.A. ▲
233 C 22 **Mt Aspiring**, New Zealand ▲
83 J 20 **Mt Assiniboine**, British Columbia, Canada ▲
230 F 7 **Mt Augustus**, Western Australia, Australia ▲
197 G 14 **Mount Baco**, Philippines ▲
76 H 5 **Mt Baker**, Washington, U.S.A. ▲
234 I 4 **Mt Balbi**, Papua New Guinea ▲
196 H 12 **Mount Banahao**, Philippines ▲
234 E 5 **Mt Bangeta**, Papua New Guinea ▲
74 H 8 **Mt Bangs**, Arizona, U.S.A. ▲
230 H 12 **Mount Barker**, Western Australia, Australia
230 K 3 **Mount Barnett Roadhouse**, Western Australia, Australia
231 V 10 **Mt Barrington**, New South Wales, Australia ▲
85 V 7 **Mt Benedict**, Newfoundland and Labrador, Canada ▲
240 M 11 **Mt Berlin**, Antarctica ▲
216 F 9 **Mt Berongou**, Congo ▲
79 T 8 **Mt Blackburn**, Alaska, U.S.A. ▲
231 T 12 **Mt Bogong**, Victoria, Australia ▲
79 T 9 **Mt Bona**, Alaska, U.S.A. ▲
234 B 5 **Mt Bosavi**, Papua New Guinea ▲
230 J 4 **Mt Broome**, Western Australia, Australia ▲
197 I 17 **Mount Canlaon**, Philippines ▲
197 L 14 **Mount Capotoah**, Philippines ▲
233 C 22 **Mt Cardrona**, New Zealand ▲
81 X 11 **Mt Carleton**, New Brunswick, Canada ▲
65 I 21 **Mount Carmel**, Indiana, U.S.A.
172 F 8 **Mt Carmel**, Israel ▲
85 U 5 **Mt Caubvick**, Newfoundland and Labrador, Canada ▲
241 N 9 **Mt Chapman**, Antarctica ▲
73 N 2 **Mount Cleveland**, Montana, U.S.A. ▲
241 W 3 **Mt Codrington**, Antarctica ▲
83 H 19 **Mt Columbia**, British Columbia/Alberta, Canada ▲
240 K 5 **Mt Coman**, Antarctica ▲
233 E 20 **Mount Cook**, New Zealand
233 E 20 **Mt Cook**, New Zealand ▲
241 W 4 **Mt Cook**, Antarctica ▲
197 J 20 **Mount Dapiak**, Philippines ▲
219 P 6 **Mount Darwin**, Zimbabw
58 C 14 **Mt Davis**, Pennsylvania, U.S.A. ▲
59 R 6 **Mount Desert Island**, Maine, U.S.A. 🏝

□ Country ▣ Internal administrative region: State/Province/Territory/Dependent territory 🏛 Capital city ⛰ Mountain range/Undersea ridge ▲ Mountain peak/Volcano/Seamount ◇ Geographic feature ▶ Headland/Point/Cape/Peninsula ⏶ Desert 🏝 Island/Island group ⁘ Antarctic base 🌊 Ocean ⛵ Sea ≈ Bay/Gulf/Channel/Strait 💧 Lake ⚑ Salt pan/Dry/Intermittent lake ∿ Ri

Mt Doonerak – Mungerannie Hotel

79 Q 5 Mt Doonerak, Alaska, U.S.A. ▲
79 P 11 Mt Douglas, Alaska, U.S.A. ▲
234 E 2 Mt Dremsel, Papua New Guinea ▲
233 C 22 Mt Earnslaw, New Zealand ▲
75 Q 4 Mount Elbert, Colorado, U.S.A. ▲
241 W 3 Mt Elkins, Antarctica ▲
74 L 6 Mt Ellen, Utah, U.S.A. ▲
241 Q 12 Mt Erebus, Antarctica ▲
234 D 5 Mt Eruki, Papua New Guinea ▲
141 K 22 Mount Etna, Italy ▲
73 N 6 Mount Evans, Montana, U.S.A. ▲
183 R 9 Mt Everest, China/Nepal ▲
80 H 8 Mt Fairweather, Canada/U.S.A. ▲
43 A 17 Mt Fogo, Cape Verde ▲
86 D 12 Mount Forest, Ontario, Canada
240 L 10 Mt Frakes, Antarctica ▲
199 J 16 Mt Fuji, Japan ▲
231 Q 13 Mount Gambier, South Australia, Australia
234 C 5 Mt Giluwe, Papua New Guinea ▲
74 M 14 Mt Graham, Arizona, U.S.A. ▲
58 L 9 Mount Greylock, Massachusetts, U.S.A. ▲
197 I 14 Mount Guitinguitin, Philippines ▲
60 L 9 Mt Guyot, Tennessee, U.S.A. ▲
234 C 4 Mount Hagen, Papua New Guinea
196 G 13 Mount Halcon, Philippines ▲
79 S 7 Mt Harper, Alaska, U.S.A. ▲
75 P 5 Mt Harvard, Colorado, U.S.A. ▲
83 A 15 Mt Hay, British Columbia, Canada ▲
79 S 7 Mt Hayes, Alaska, U.S.A. ▲
233 K 15 Mt Hector, New Zealand ▲
217 Q 10 Mt Hehan, Burundi ▲
233 H 20 Mt Herbert, New Zealand ▲
172 H 7 Mt Hermon, Syria ▲
197 M 19 Mount Hilonghilong, Philippines ▲
76 H 10 Mt Hood, Oregon, U.S.A. ▲
65 F 14 Mount Horeb, Wisconsin, U.S.A.
235 Q 14 Mt Humboldt, New Caledonia ▲
241 U 14 Mt Hunt, Antarctica ▲
233 G 20 Mount Hutt, New Zealand ▲
233 F 20 Mt Hutt, New Zealand ▲
231 Q 5 Mount Isa, Queensland, Australia
196 J 12 Mount Isarog, Philippines ▲
240 K 5 Mt Jackson, Antarctica ▲
76 H 10 Mt Jefferson, Oregon, U.S.A. ▲
77 L 18 Mt Jefferson, Nevada, U.S.A. ▲
59 Q 3 Mt Katahdin, Maine, U.S.A. ▲
79 P 11 Mt Katmai, Alaska, U.S.A. ▲
217 V 8 Mt Kenya, Kenya ▲
195 V 5 Mt Kinabalu, Malaysia ▲
241 Q 10 Mt Kirkpatrick, Antarctica ▲
231 T 13 Mt Kosciuszko, New South Wales, Australia ▲
196 I 12 Mount Labo, Philippines ▲
241 Q 12 Mt Lister, Antarctica ▲
H 9 Mt Livermore, Texas, U.S.A. ▲
83 A 14 Mt Logan, Yukon Territory, Canada ▲
233 B 23 Mt Lyall, New Zealand ▲
241 R 13 Mt Mackintosh, Antarctica ▲
230 G 9 Mount Magnet, Western Australia, Australia
197 J 20 Mount Malindang, Philippines ▲
58 L 5 Mt Mansfield, Vermont, U.S.A. ▲
197 B 19 Mount Mantalingajan, Philippines ▲
79 R 9 Mt Marcus Baker, Alaska, U.S.A. ▲
58 J 6 Mt Marcy, New York, U.S.A. ▲
74 K 5 Mt Marvine, Utah, U.S.A. ▲
197 L 23 Mount Matutum, Philippines ▲
232 M 10 Mount Maunganui, New Zealand
196 K 13 Mount Mayon, Philippines ▲
241 R 11 Mt McClintock, Antarctica ▲
72 M 8 Mount McGuire, Idaho, U.S.A. ▲
79 Q 8 Mt McKinley, Alaska, U.S.A. ▲
230 G 7 Mt Meharry, Western Australia, Australia ▲
241 U 5 Mt Menzies, Antarctica ▲
79 S 3 Mt Michelson, Alaska, U.S.A. ▲
241 Q 10 Mt Miller, Antarctica ▲
241 R 14 Mt Minto, Antarctica ▲
60 M 9 Mt Mitchell, North Carolina, U.S.A. ▲
240 M 8 Mt Moore, Antarctica ▲
58 A 14 Mount Morris, Pennsylvania, U.S.A.
58 E 9 Mount Morris, New York, U.S.A.
195 T 7 Mt Mulu, Malaysia ▲
241 U 14 Mt Murchison, Antarctica ▲
83 D 14 Mt Murray, Yukon Territory, Canada ▲
232 L 12 Mt Ngauruhoe, New Zealand ▲
61 T 10 Mount Olive, North Carolina, U.S.A.
147 E 15 Mt Olympus, Greece ▲
76 F 6 Mt Olympus, Washington, U.S.A. ▲
233 F 22 Mt Orr, New Zealand ▲
231 S 15 Mt Ossa, Tasmania, Australia ▲
235 P 13 Mt Panié, New Caledonia ▲
196 F 10 Mount Pinatubo, Philippines ▲
77 I 23 Mt Pinos, California, U.S.A. ▲
58 B 13 Mount Pleasant, Pennsylvania, U.S.A.
61 Q 14 Mount Pleasant, South Carolina, U.S.A.
64 K 13 Mount Pleasant, Michigan, U.S.A.
67 V 13 Mount Pleasant, Iowa, U.S.A.
71 S 5 Mount Pleasant, Texas, U.S.A.
74 K 4 Mount Pleasant, Utah, U.S.A.
234 M 7 Mt Popomanaseu, Solomon Islands ▲
196 G 8 Mount Pulog, Philippines ▲
83 F 20 Mt Queen Bess, British Columbia, Canada ▲
197 L 21 Mount Ragang, Philippines ▲
230 J 11 Mt Ragged, Western Australia, Australia ▲
76 H 7 Mt Rainier, Washington, U.S.A. ▲
83 C 16 Mt Ratz, British Columbia, Canada ▲
83 H 19 Mt Robson, British Columbia, Canada ▲
61 N 7 Mt Rogers, Virginia, U.S.A. ▲
233 F 19 Mt Rolleston, New Zealand ▲
105 S 6 Mt Roraima, Brazil/Guyana ▲
233 L 16 Mt Ross, New Zealand ▲
232 K 12 Mt Ruapehu, New Zealand ▲
66 G 10 Mt Rushmore, South Dakota, U.S.A. ▲
241 X 9 Mt Sandow, Antarctica ▲
83 E 20 Mt Saugstad, British Columbia, Canada ▲
68 L 11 Mt Scott, Oklahoma, U.S.A. ▲
76 G 13 Mt Scott, Oregon, U.S.A. ▲
241 N 8 Mt Seelig, Antarctica ▲
77 G 15 Mount Shasta, California, U.S.A.
77 G 15 Mt Shasta, California, U.S.A. ▲
196 G 6 Mount Sicapoo, Philippines ▲
240 L 10 Mt Sidley, Antarctica ▲
234 G 7 Mt Simpson, Papua New Guinea ▲
234 H 4 Mt Sinewit, Papua New Guinea ▲
240 K 11 Mt Siple, Antarctica ▲
82 D 13 Mt Sir James MacBrian, Northwest Territories, Canada ▲
234 B 5 Mt Sisa, Papua New Guinea ▲
233 B 24 Mt Solitary, New Zealand ▲
241 S 14 Mt Southard, Antarctica ▲
79 T 9 Mt St Elias, Alaska, U.S.A. ▲
76 G 8 Mt St Helens, Washington, U.S.A. ▲
233 D 22 Mt St Mary, New Zealand ▲
60 K 5 Mount Sterling, Kentucky, U.S.A.
233 J 16 Mt Stokes, New Zealand ▲
241 X 9 Mt Strathcona, Antarctica ▲
234 E 5 Mt Strong, Papua New Guinea ▲
213 H 16 Mount Suara, Eritrea ▲
68 G 3 Mount Sunflower, Kansas, U.S.A. ▲
83 E 16 Mt Sylvia, British Columbia, Canada ▲
234 D 5 Mt Tabletop, Papua New Guinea ▲
235 P 10 Mt Tabwemasana, Vanuatu ▲
234 J 5 Mt Takuan, Papua New Guinea ▲
232 J 12 Mt Taranaki (Mt Egmont), New Zealand ▲
75 O 10 Mt Taylor, New Mexico, U.S.A. ▲
74 H 9 Mt Tipton, Arizona, U.S.A. ▲
232 L 12 Mt Tongariro, New Zealand ▲
79 Q 9 Mt Torbert, Alaska, U.S.A. ▲
210 G 8 Mt Toubkal, Morocco ▲
170 G 15 Mount Troödos, Cyprus ▲
74 I 8 Mt Trumbull, Arizona, U.S.A. ▲
240 L 7 Mt Tyree, Antarctica ▲
234 G 4 Mt Ulawun, Papua New Guinea ▲
233 H 18 Mt Una, New Zealand ▲
58 E 13 Mt Union, Pennsylvania, U.S.A.
111 L 23 Mt Usborne, Falkland Islands ▲
79 N 12 Mt Veniaminof, Alaska, U.S.A. ▲
63 O 6 Mount Vernon, Alabama, U.S.A.
65 F 21 Mount Vernon, Illinois, U.S.A.
65 G 22 Mount Vernon, Indiana, U.S.A.
69 S 7 Mount Vernon, Missouri, U.S.A.
76 H 6 Mount Vernon, Washington, U.S.A.
65 M 18 Mt Vernon, Ohio, U.S.A.
241 T 3 Mt Victor, Antarctica ▲
234 E 6 Mt Victoria, Papua New Guinea ▲
235 X 11 Mt Victoria, Fiji ▲
190 C 12 Mt Victoria, Myanmar ▲
234 F 6 Mt Victory, Papua New Guinea ▲
80 I 12 Mt Waddington, British Columbia, Canada ▲
59 N 6 Mt Washington, New Hampshire, U.S.A. ▲
77 K 21 Mt Whitney, California, U.S.A. ▲
64 E 9 Mt Whittlesey, Wisconsin, U.S.A. ▲
234 C 4 Mt Wilhelm, Papua New Guinea ▲
83 D 16 Mt Will, British Columbia, Canada ▲
75 O 7 Mt Wilson, Colorado, U.S.A. ▲
230 M 8 Mt Woodroffe, South Australia, Australia ▲
240 M 8 Mt Woollard, Antarctica ▲
79 T 8 Mt Wrangell, Alaska, U.S.A. ▲
230 M 6 Mt Zeil, Northern Territory, Australia ▲
75 P 2 Mt Zirkel, Colorado, U.S.A. ▲
72 K 11 Mountain Home, Idaho, U.S.A.
69 V 9 Mountain View, Arkansas, U.S.A.
211 T 13 Mountains of Tummo, Libya ⛰
126 J 15 Mount's Bay, United Kingdom ≈
231 V 7 Moura, Queensland, Australia
108 E 10 Moura, Brazil
130 I 10 Moura, Portugal
215 Z 10 Mouraya, Chad
232 M 10 Mourea, New Zealand
133 C 19 Mouscron, Belgium
215 W 10 Mousgougou, Chad
213 K 18 Moussa Ali, Djibouti ▲
215 W 9 Moussoro, Chad
131 V 6 Mouth of the Ebro, Spain ◇
125 A 19 Mouth of the Shannon, Republic of Ireland ◇
189 Z 5 Mouth of the Yangtze, China ◇
108 J 9 Mouths of the Amazon, Brazil ◇
183 U 15 Mouths of the Ganges, Bangladesh ◇
181 H 19 Mouths of the Godavari, India ◇
177 T 15 Mouths of the Indus, Pakistan ◇
191 B 17 Mouths of the Irrawaddy, Myanmar ◇
181 G 19 Mouths of the Krishna, India ◇
191 M 23 Mouths of the Mekong, Vietnam ◇
215 Q 14 Mouths of the Niger, Nigeria ◇
138 D 7 Moutier, Switzerland
129 V 10 Moûtiers, France
147 D 17 Mouzaki, Greece
218 J 5 Moxico, Angola ◘
213 I 23 Moyale, Ethiopia
210 H 8 Moyen Atlas, Morocco ⛰
215 X 11 Moyen-Chari, Chad ◘
216 D 8 Moyen-Ogooué, Gabon ◘
219 N 13 Moyeni, Lesotho
214 F 10 Moyenne-Guinée, Guinea ◘
217 R 5 Moyo, Uganda
192 M 15 Moyo, Indonesia ✱
106 C 12 Moyobamba, Peru
134 G 9 Møysalen, Norway ▲
179 T 9 Moyynkum, Kazakhstan
179 T 7 Moyynty, Kazakhstan
219 Q 9 Mozambique, Africa ◘
219 T 8 Mozambique Channel, Mozambique ≈
38 I 10 Mozambique Escarpment, Indian Ocean ⛰
38 I 9 Mozambique Ridge, Indian Ocean ⛰
157 P 13 Mozdok, Russian Federation
156 J 1 Mozhaysk, Russian Federation
155 R 14 Mozhga, Russian Federation
217 Q 12 Mpala, Democratic Republic of Congo
217 R 11 Mpanda, Tanzania
218 M 7 Mpandamatenga, Botswana
216 H 9 Mpé, Congo
183 Z 9 Mpen, India
217 S 7 Mpigi, Uganda
219 P 3 Mpika, Zambia
219 P 2 Mporokoso, Zambia
216 H 9 Mpouya, Congo
219 O 10 Mpumalanga, Republic of South Africa ◘
217 U 11 Mpwapwa, Tanzania
142 L 9 Mrągowo, Poland
157 W 3 Mrakovo, Russian Federation
146 D 12 Mrešičko, Macedonia (F.Y.R.O.M.)
144 F 11 Mrkonjić-Grad, Bosnia and Herzegovina
151 Q 2 Mryn, Ukraine
211 N 6 M'sila, Algeria
149 N 17 Mstsislaw, Belarus
217 W 14 Mtama, Tanzania
156 J 3 Mtsensk, Russian Federation
171 T 6 Mts'khet'a, Georgia
217 W 14 Mtwara, Tanzania ◘
217 X 14 Mtwara, Tanzania
216 F 11 Muanda, Democratic Republic of Congo
191 L 15 Muang Khammouan, Laos
191 M 18 Muang Không, Laos
191 L 17 Muang Khôngxédôn, Laos
190 J 12 Muang Khoua, Laos
190 J 12 Muang Ngoy, Laos
190 I 11 Muang Ou Nua, Laos
190 H 13 Muang Pakbeng, Laos
191 K 14 Muang Pakxan, Laos
191 L 16 Muang Phalan, Laos
191 M 16 Muang Phin, Laos
191 I 14 Muang Phôn-Hông, Laos
190 H 12 Muang Sing, Laos
190 J 13 Muang Souy, Laos
191 I 14 Muang Xaignabouri, Laos
190 I 12 Muang Xay, Laos
194 C 10 Muar, Malaysia
194 D 9 Muar, Malaysia ʃ
192 E 12 Muaraaman, Indonesia
192 F 12 Muarabeliti, Indonesia
192 E 11 Muarabungo, Indonesia
192 F 13 Muaradua, Indonesia
192 F 12 Muaraenim, Indonesia
192 C 11 Muarasiberut, Indonesia
179 P 13 Mubarek, Uzbekistan
215 U 11 Mubi, Nigeria
127 P 7 Much Wenlock, United Kingdom
230 G 11 Muchea, Western Australia, Australia
188 M 8 Muchuan, China
124 F 11 Muck, United Kingdom ✱
219 U 4 Mucojo, Mozambique
218 K 3 Muconda, Angola
218 H 6 Mucope, Angola
170 J 10 Mucur, Turkey
109 N 17 Mucuri, Brazil
66 H 8 Mud Butte, South Dakota, U.S.A.
194 A 5 Muda, Malaysia ʃ
186 M 12 Mudanjiang, China
170 D 8 Mudanya, Turkey
73 V 13 Muddy Gap, Wyoming, U.S.A.
181 D 19 Mudhol, India
191 F 17 Mudon, Myanmar
213 N 21 Mudug, Somalia ◘
219 U 3 Mueda, Mozambique
189 U 7 Mufu Shan, China ⛰
219 O 4 Mufulira, Zambia
218 M 4 Mufumbwe, Zambia
171 Y 9 Muğan Düzü, Azerbaijan ◇
219 S 6 Mugeba, Mozambique
183 O 12 Mughal Sarai, India
176 J 7 Mūghār, Iran
170 C 12 Muğla, Turkey
213 B 18 Muhagiriya, Sudan
212 G 13 Muhammad Qol, Sudan
173 O 7 Muḩaywīr, Iraq
241 Q 2 Mühlig-Hofmann Mountains, Antarctica ⛰
139 S 3 Mühlviertel, Austria ⛰
172 H 4 Muḩradah, Syria
148 E 7 Muhu, Estonia ✱
217 P 8 Muhulu, Democratic Republic of Congo
213 G 22 Mui, Ethiopia
191 L 24 Mui Ca Mau, Vietnam ▶
219 T 5 Muite, Mozambique
150 H 6 Mukacheve, Ukraine
195 P 9 Mukah, Malaysia
195 P 9 Mukah, Malaysia ʃ
191 L 16 Mukdahan, Thailand
230 G 10 Mukinbudin, Western Australia, Australia
192 E 12 Mukomuko, Indonesia
182 G 6 Muktsar, India
188 K 7 Mula, China
91 Z 13 Mula-tupo, Panama
181 L 18 Mulakatholhu Atoll, Maldives ✱
186 L 11 Mulan, China
196 I 13 Mulanay, Philippines
219 R 6 Mulanje, Malawi
219 S 5 Mulanje, Malawi ▲
173 W 8 Mūlat al Mashkhūr, Iraq
182 I 3 Mulbekh, India
79 O 10 Mulchatna, Alaska, U.S.A. ʃ
111 F 14 Mulchén, Chile
73 Z 10 Mule Creek, Wyoming, U.S.A.
217 S 9 Muleba, Tanzania
88 I 6 Mulegé, Mexico
70 I 4 Muleshoe, Texas, U.S.A.
131 P 12 Mulhacén, Spain ▲
129 W 6 Mulhouse, France
186 M 11 Muling, China
124 F 12 Mull, United Kingdom ✱
125 G 15 Mull of Galloway, United Kingdom ▶
125 F 14 Mull of Kintyre, United Kingdom ▶
124 F 13 Mull of Oa, United Kingdom ▶
230 F 9 Mullewa, Western Australia, Australia
137 D 25 Müllheim, Germany
125 D 17 Mullingar, Republic of Ireland
126 J 15 Mullion, United Kingdom
218 M 6 Mulobezi, Zambia
181 F 15 Multai, India
177 W 10 Multan, Pakistan
216 M 5 Muma, Democratic Republic of Congo
177 O 14 Mūmān, Iran
181 B 17 Mumbai, India
218 L 5 Mumbeji, Zambia
218 G 3 Mumbondo, Angola
219 N 5 Mumbwa, Zambia
234 E 5 Mumeng, Papua New Guinea
157 R 11 Mumra, Russian Federation
193 P 13 Muna, Indonesia ✱
89 Y 11 Muna, Mexico
180 A 12 Munabao, India
188 J 12 Munai, China
199 B 21 Munakata, Japan
178 H 9 Munayshy, Kazakhstan
83 E 15 Muncho Lake, British Columbia, Canada
187 L 17 Munch'ŏn, North Korea
65 J 18 Muncie, Indiana, U.S.A.
58 F 11 Muncy, Pennsylvania, U.S.A.
177 W 10 Munda, Pakistan
70 M 5 Munday, Texas, U.S.A.
127 X 7 Mundford, United Kingdom
112 F 7 Mundo Novo, Brazil
230 K 10 Mundrabilla, Western Australia, Australia
231 V 8 Mundubbera, Queensland, Australia
131 Q 9 Munera, Spain
60 G 6 Munfordville, Kentucky, U.S.A.
219 Q 6 Mungári, Mozambique
217 P 6 Mungbere, Democratic Republic of Congo
183 R 11 Munger, India
231 P 8 Mungerannie Hotel, South Australia, Australia

Country ◘ Internal administrative region: State/Province/Territory/Dependent territory ■ Capital city ⛰ Mountain range/Undersea ridge ▲ Mountain peak/Volcano/Seamount ◇ Geographic feature ▶ Headland/Point/Cape/Peninsula ∴ Desert ✱ Island/Island group ⁂ Antarctic base ≋ Ocean ∼ Sea ≈ Bay/Gulf/Channel/Strait ⌇ Lake ⌐ Salt pan/Dry/Intermittent lake ʃ River

Mungindi – Nanpiao

231 U 9 Mungindi, New South Wales, Australia
137 J 24 Munich, Germany
64 I 9 Munising, Michigan, U.S.A.
135 D 21 Munkedal, Sweden
125 B 20 Munster, Republic of Ireland
136 H 12 Münster, Germany
138 F 9 Münster, Switzerland
137 D 14 Münster, Germany
196 F 11 Muntinglupa, Philippines
134 H 11 Muojärvi, Finland
190 K 12 Muong Het, Laos
134 K 9 Muonio, Finland
187 H 19 Muping, China
172 K 8 Muqāţ, Jordan
175 Q 14 Muqaybirah, Yemen
171 T 10 Muradiye, Turkey
182 J 8 Muradnagar, India
194 A 13 Murai Reservoir, Singapore
198 J 13 Murakami, Japan
217 Q 9 Muramvya, Burundi
155 P 11 Murashi, Russian Federation
129 Q 11 Murat, France
171 R 10 Murat, Turkey
146 M 12 Muratli, Turkey
139 T 7 Murau, Austria
141 C 18 Muravera, Italy
176 I 8 Murchek-Khort, Iran
230 F 9 Murchison, Western Australia, Australia
233 H 17 Murchison, New Zealand
230 F 9 Murchison Roadhouse, Western Australia, Australia
131 R 11 Murcia, Spain
131 S 11 Murcia, Spain
66 J 10 Murdo, South Dakota, U.S.A.
87 S 5 Murdochville, Québec, Canada
139 W 8 Mureck, Austria
150 J 9 Mureș, Romania
129 O 14 Muret, France
60 F 9 Murfreesboro, Tennessee, U.S.A.
61 U 8 Murfreesboro, North Carolina, U.S.A.
179 U 13 Murghob, Tajikistan
231 V 8 Murgon, Queensland, Australia
138 F 7 Muri, Switzerland
112 N 5 Muriaé, Brazil
218 K 3 Muriege, Angola
237 O 14 Murilo Atoll, Federated States of Micronesia
171 P 10 Mürit Dağlari, Turkey
136 L 10 Müritz, Germany
232 O 12 Muriwai, New Zealand
154 I 2 Murmansk, Russian Federation
45 U 12 Murmansk Rise, Arctic Ocean
154 H 2 Murmanskaya Oblast', Russian Federation
154 I 2 Murmanskiy Bereg, Russian Federation
154 H 2 Murmashi, Russian Federation
157 N 1 Murom, Russian Federation
217 R 8 Murongo, Tanzania
198 J 7 Muroran, Japan
199 F 20 Muroto, Japan
199 F 21 Muroto-zaki, Japan
60 J 10 Murphy, North Carolina, U.S.A.
72 J 11 Murphy, Idaho, U.S.A.
231 R 12 Murray, New South Wales, Australia
60 C 7 Murray, Kentucky, U.S.A.
231 Q 12 Murray Bridge, South Australia, Australia
41 R 4 Murray Fracture Zone, Pacific Ocean
87 W 9 Murray Harbour, Prince Edward Island, Canada
38 M 2 Murray Ridge, Indian Ocean
65 E 19 Murrayville, Illinois, U.S.A.
177 X 7 Murree, Pakistan
219 T 5 Murrupula, Mozambique
144 E 6 Murska Sobota, Slovenia
83 G 19 Murtle Lake, British Columbia, Canada
181 B 17 Murud, India
232 M 11 Murupara, New Zealand
181 G 14 Murwara, India
231 W 9 Murwillumbah, New South Wales, Australia
211 S 11 Murzūq, Libya
139 W 5 Mürzzuschlag, Austria
171 Q 11 Muş, Turkey
148 E 12 Mūša, Lithuania
177 R 9 Musa Qala, Afghanistan
216 M 9 Musadi, Democratic Republic of Congo
146 G 10 Musala, Bulgaria
173 X 9 Musallam, Iraq
187 M 14 Musan, North Korea
175 X 4 Musandam Peninsula, Oman
175 P 14 Musaymir, Yemen
175 Z 6 Muscat, Oman
67 V 13 Muscatine, Iowa, U.S.A.
85 Y 9 Musgrave Harbour, Newfoundland and Labrador, Canada
230 L 8 Musgrave Ranges, South Australia, Australia
177 U 8 Mūshakī, Afghanistan
172 I 10 Mushāsh Ḩadraj, Jordan
216 I 9 Mushie, Democratic Republic of Congo
234 C 3 Mushu, Papua New Guinea
65 I 14 Muskegon, Michigan, U.S.A.
69 Q 10 Muskogee, Oklahoma, U.S.A.
83 F 15 Muskwa, British Columbia, Canada
213 G 15 Musmar, Sudan
217 T 8 Musoma, Tanzania
217 T 12 Musombe, Tanzania
85 W 10 Musquaro, Québec, Canada
234 F 2 Mussau Island, Papua New Guinea
73 U 4 Musselshell, Montana, U.S.A.
218 H 3 Mussende, Angola
129 N 11 Mussidan, France
170 C 9 Mustafakemalpaşa, Turkey
213 L 22 Mustahīl, Ethiopia
138 K 9 Müstair, Switzerland
93 Z 12 Mustique, St Vincent and the Grenadines
148 D 7 Mustjala, Estonia
148 H 8 Mustla, Estonia
148 I 7 Mustvee, Estonia
231 V 11 Muswellbrook, New South Wales, Australia
212 D 11 Mut, Egypt
170 I 13 Mut, Turkey
219 Q 7 Mutare, Zimbabwe
104 G 5 Mutis, Colombia
219 W 4 Mutsamudu, Comoros
217 N 14 Mutshatsha, Democratic Republic of Congo
198 K 8 Mutsu, Japan
198 J 8 Mutsu-wan, Japan
231 S 6 Muttaburra, Queensland, Australia
233 B 26 Muttonbird Islands, New Zealand
181 F 20 Muttukuru, India
219 S 5 Mutuali, Mozambique
215 T 12 Mutum Biyu, Nigeria
181 G 24 Mutur, Sri Lanka
184 K 8 Mutztag Feng, China
218 H 2 Muxaluando, Angola
218 F 3 Muxima, Angola
215 S 10 Muya, Nigeria
217 R 9 Muyinga, Burundi
178 L 10 Muynak, Uzbekistan
217 O 12 Muyumba, Democratic Republic of Congo
177 X 7 Muzaffarabad, Pakistan
177 W 10 Muzaffargarh, Pakistan
182 K 8 Muzaffarnagar, India
183 P 11 Muzaffarpur, India
128 J 6 Muzillac, France
89 P 5 Múzquiz, Mexico
215 T 15 Mvangan, Cameroon
213 D 22 Mvolo, Sudan
217 V 11 Mvomero, Tanzania
219 P 7 Mvuma, Zimbabwe
217 S 9 Mwanza, Tanzania
217 S 9 Mwanza, Tanzania
216 L 10 Mweka, Democratic Republic of Congo
219 O 3 Mwenda, Zambia
216 M 12 Mwene-Ditu, Democratic Republic of Congo
219 P 8 Mwenezi, Zimbabwe
217 P 9 Mwenga, Democratic Republic of Congo
216 M 13 Mwimba, Democratic Republic of Congo
218 M 3 Mwinilunga, Zambia
237 Q 15 Mwokil, Federated States of Micronesia
191 M 22 My Tho, Vietnam
149 I 15 Myadzyel, Belarus
63 V 11 Myakka City, Florida, U.S.A.
190 C 12 Myanmar (Burma), Asia
191 C 16 Myaungmya, Myanmar
190 D 12 Myingyan, Myanmar
191 F 19 Myinmoletkat, Myanmar
190 E 8 Myitkyina, Myanmar
191 F 19 Myitta, Myanmar
190 D 12 Myittha, Myanmar
151 V 8 Mykhaylivka, Ukraine
151 R 9 Mykolayiv, Ukraine
150 I 5 Mykolayiv, Ukraine
147 J 21 Mykonos, Greece
147 J 21 Mykonos, Greece
155 P 5 Myla, Russian Federation
183 U 12 Mymensingh, Bangladesh
179 T 8 Mynaral, Kazakhstan
190 B 12 Myohaung, Myanmar
187 M 15 Myŏnggan, North Korea
148 J 13 Myory, Belarus
134 B 12 Myrdalsjökull, Iceland
151 T 4 Myrhorod, Ukraine
147 I 15 Myrina, Greece
151 Q 4 Myrne, Ukraine
151 X 8 Myrne, Ukraine
61 R 13 Myrtle Beach, South Carolina, U.S.A.
76 F 12 Myrtle Creek, Oregon, U.S.A.
76 E 12 Myrtle Point, Oregon, U.S.A.
153 X 10 Mys Alevina, Russian Federation
153 X 14 Mys Aniva, Russian Federation
151 T 13 Mys Ayya, Ukraine
153 Y 5 Mys Blossom, Russian Federation
151 W 12 Mys Chauda, Ukraine
153 R 5 Mys Chelyuskin, Russian Federation
153 W 10 Mys Duga-Zapadnaya, Russian Federation
153 W 12 Mys Elizavety, Russian Federation
153 Z 9 Mys Govena, Russian Federation
154 M 2 Mys Kanin Nos, Russian Federation
151 W 11 Mys Kazantip, Ukraine
151 S 13 Mys Khersones, Ukraine
153 X 14 Mys Kril'on, Russian Federation
153 Y 5 Mys Litke, Russian Federation
153 V 7 Mys Lopatka, Russian Federation
153 Z 12 Mys Lopatka, Russian Federation
153 Z 7 Mys Navarin, Russian Federation
154 L 4 Mys Orlovskiy, Russian Federation
178 H 10 Mys Peschanyy, Kazakhstan
178 H 10 Mys Sengirli, Kazakhstan
153 X 6 Mys Shelagskiy, Russian Federation
153 Y 5 Mys Shmidta, Russian Federation
178 H 11 Mys Suz, Kazakhstan
154 K 3 Mys Svyatoy Nos, Russian Federation
153 X 13 Mys Terpeniya, Russian Federation
153 X 10 Mys Tolstoy, Russian Federation
178 G 8 Mys Tyub-Karagan, Kazakhstan
151 S 12 Mys Yevpatoriys'kyy, Ukraine
153 Y 10 Mys Yuzhnyy, Russian Federation
153 N 5 Mys Zhelaniya, Russian Federation
143 K 18 Myślenice, Poland
142 D 11 Myślibórz, Poland
181 D 21 Mysore, India
147 L 17 Mytilini, Greece
156 L 1 Mytishchi, Russian Federation
74 M 3 Myton, Utah, U.S.A.
219 Q 3 Mzimba, Malawi
219 Q 3 Mzuzu, Malawi

N

190 F 10 Na-lang, Myanmar
132 F 13 Naaldwijk, Netherlands
78 E 9 Naalehu, Hawaii, U.S.A.
210 K 7 Naama, Algeria
135 K 19 Naantali, Finland
132 I 11 Naarden, Netherlands
197 H 15 Nabas, Philippines
217 V 10 Naberera, Tanzania
157 U 1 Naberezhnyye Chelny, Russian Federation
79 T 8 Nabesna, Alaska, U.S.A.
211 Q 5 Nabeul, Tunisia
182 I 7 Nabha, India
193 W 12 Nabire, Indonesia
172 G 9 Nāblus, Israel
235 X 11 Nabouwalu, Fiji
219 U 5 Nacala, Mozambique
90 L 7 Nacaome, Honduras
219 U 5 Nacaroa, Mozambique
189 P 13 Nachen, China
217 W 14 Nachingwea, Tanzania
180 B 11 Nachna, India
143 F 16 Náchod, Czech Republic
181 N 22 Nachuge, India
71 T 7 Nacogdoches, Texas, U.S.A.
88 J 3 Nacozari de García, Mexico
235 W 11 Nadi, Fiji
181 C 15 Nadiad, India
171 V 9 Nadirchanly, Azerbaijan
150 E 10 Nădlac, Romania
210 J 6 Nador, Morocco
150 J 6 Nadvirna, Ukraine
152 L 8 Nadym, Russian Federation
135 D 26 Naestved, Denmark
147 D 19 Nafpaktos, Greece
147 F 21 Nafplio, Greece
175 P 5 Nafy, Saudi Arabia
212 F 11 Nag' Hammadi, Egypt
196 J 12 Naga, Philippines
183 Y 10 Naga Hills, India
199 D 20 Nagahama, Japan
199 H 17 Nagahama, Japan
181 D 18 Nagaj, India
183 Y 10 Nagaland, India
199 I 15 Nagano, Japan
199 J 14 Nagaoka, Japan
183 W 10 Nagaon, India
181 F 22 Nagappattinam, India
181 F 19 Nagarjuna Sagar, India
199 B 22 Nagasaki, Japan
199 C 20 Nagato, Japan
180 C 12 Nagaur, India
181 E 24 Nagercoil, India
177 R 13 Nagha Kalat, Pakistan
182 K 8 Nagina, India
199 N 24 Nago, Japan
182 L 12 Nagod, India
137 F 23 Nagold, Germany
155 Q 11 Nagorsk, Russian Federation
199 H 17 Nagoya, Japan
181 F 16 Nagpur, India
184 L 10 Nagqu, China
152 M 3 Nagurskoye, Russian Federation
143 G 25 Nagyatád, Hungary
143 M 21 Nagyhalász, Hungary
143 G 25 Nagykanizsa, Hungary
143 J 23 Nagykáta, Hungary
199 N 25 Naha, Japan
172 F 7 Nahariyya, Israel
64 I 10 Nahma Junction, Michigan, U.S.A.
172 H 3 Nahr al Āşī, Syria
173 U 7 Nahr Diyālá, Iraq
189 S 13 Nahuo, China
88 M 5 Naica, Mexico
150 F 12 Naidăș, Romania
127 R 10 Nailsworth, United Kingdom
187 G 14 Naiman Qi, China
176 J 8 Nā'īn, Iran
85 U 7 Nain, Newfoundland and Labrador, Canada
181 G 15 Nainpur, India
124 H 10 Nairn, United Kingdom
217 V 8 Nairobi, Kenya
148 F 5 Naissaar, Estonia
217 U 8 Naivasha, Kenya
176 I 8 Najafābād, Iran
186 I 9 Naji, China
182 K 7 Najibabad, India
187 N 14 Najin, North Korea
175 P 11 Najrān, Saudi Arabia
199 A 22 Nakadōri-shima, Japan
199 E 21 Nakamura, Japan
199 I 15 Nakano, Japan
199 B 26 Nakano-shima, Japan
199 D 17 Nakano-shima, Japan
198 M 4 Nakashibetsu, Japan
217 S 7 Nakasongola, Uganda
199 C 21 Nakatsu, Japan
199 I 17 Nakatsugawa, Japan
213 I 16 Nakfa, Eritrea
212 F 8 Nakhl, Egypt
176 I 12 Nakhl-e Taqī, Iran
153 V 15 Nakhodka, Russian Federation
183 W 10 Nakhola, India
191 I 19 Nakhon Nayok, Thailand
191 K 15 Nakhon Phanom, Thailand
191 I 18 Nakhon Ratchasima, Thailand
191 G 17 Nakhon Sawan, Thailand
191 H 24 Nakhon Si Thammarat, Thailand
181 A 14 Nakhtarana, India
142 G 11 Nakło nad Notecią, Poland
79 O 11 Naknek, Alaska, U.S.A.
79 O 11 Naknek Lake, Alaska, U.S.A.
182 H 6 Nakodar, India
219 Q 2 Nakonde, Zambia
135 D 26 Nakskov, Denmark
135 F 16 Näkten, Sweden
217 U 8 Nakuru, Kenya
83 I 21 Nakusp, British Columbia, Canada
177 S 12 Nal, Pakistan
157 O 14 Nal'chik, Russian Federation
181 A 14 Naliya, India
170 G 9 Nallihan, Turkey
211 R 8 Nālūt, Libya
184 L 10 Nam Co, China
190 M 13 Nam Đinh, Vietnam
191 J 14 Nam Ngum Reservoir, Laos
191 J 16 Nam Phong, Thailand
218 H 7 Namacunde, Angola
219 S 6 Namacurra, Mozambique
183 N 9 Namai, Nepal
67 S 2 Namakan Lake, Minnesota, U.S.A.
181 E 22 Namakkal, India
217 V 9 Namanga, Kenya
179 S 11 Namangan, Uzbekistan
179 S 11 Namangan Wiloyati, Uzbekistan
219 U 5 Namapa, Mozambique
218 J 11 Namaqualand, Namibia
234 G 3 Namatanai, Papua New Guinea
231 W 10 Nambucca Heads, New South Wales, Australia
183 R 9 Namche Bazar, Nepal
187 K 18 Namch'ŏn, North Korea
218 G 8 Namib Desert, Namibia
218 F 6 Namibe, Angola
218 F 6 Namibe, Angola
218 H 9 Namibia, Africa
43 M 17 Namibia Abyssal Plain, Atlantic Ocean
219 S 7 Namidobe, Mozambique
184 M 10 Namjagbarwa, China
190 E 11 Namlan, Myanmar
193 R 12 Namlea, Indonesia
231 T 10 Namoi, New South Wales, Australia
237 O 15 Namoluk, Federated States of Micronesia
237 N 14 Namonuito, Federated States of Micronesia
237 X 4 Namorik, Marshall Islands
72 J 10 Nampa, Idaho, U.S.A.
187 J 18 Namp'o, North Korea
219 U 5 Nampula, Mozambique
219 T 5 Nampula, Mozambique
190 F 12 Namsang, Myanmar
135 E 14 Namsos, Norway
153 T 10 Namtsy, Russian Federation
190 E 10 Namtu, Myanmar
237 X 3 Namu, Marshall Islands
219 S 5 Namuli, Mozambique
219 T 4 Namuno, Mozambique
133 H 22 Namur, Belgium
133 H 21 Namur, Belgium
218 I 7 Namutoni, Namibia
219 N 6 Namwala, Zambia
187 L 21 Namwŏn, South Korea
190 E 6 Namya Ra, Myanmar
143 H 15 Namysłów, Poland
191 H 14 Nan, Thailand
216 J 3 Nana-Grébizi, Central African Republic
216 H 4 Nana-Mambéré, Central African Republic
83 F 22 Nanaimo, British Columbia, Canada
187 N 15 Nanam, North Korea
189 X 11 Nan'an, China
199 H 15 Nanao, Japan
189 O 6 Nanbu, China
186 M 9 Nancha, China
189 V 8 Nanchang, China
189 W 9 Nancheng, China
189 O 6 Nanchong, China
189 P 7 Nanchuan, China
181 O 24 Nancowry, India
129 V 4 Nancy, France
182 L 7 Nanda Devi, India
189 P 11 Nandan, China
181 E 17 Nanded, India
181 C 15 Nandurbar, India
181 F 19 Nandyal, India
187 I 16 Nanfen, China
189 V 9 Nanfeng, China
184 L 11 Nang, China
215 U 14 Nanga Eboko, Cameroon
177 Y 6 Nanga Parbat, Pakistan
197 F 16 Nangalao, Philippines
177 V 7 Nangarhār, Afghanistan
192 J 11 Nangatayap, Indonesia
187 K 17 Nangnim-sanmaek, North Korea
189 U 1 Nangong, China
188 H 5 Nangqên, China
217 W 13 Nangulangwa, Tanzania
188 K 10 Nanhua, China
189 Z 6 Nanhui, China
181 E 21 Nanjangud, India
189 X 5 Nanjing, China
189 U 10 Nankang, China
199 F 20 Nankoku, Japan
218 J 6 Nankova, Angola
189 U 2 Nanle, China
189 X 6 Nanling, China
189 P 12 Nanning, China
44 M 14 Nanortalik, Greenland
189 N 11 Nanpan, China
187 G 16 Nanpiao, China

Country · Internal administrative region: State/Province/Territory/Dependent territory · Capital city · Mountain range/Undersea ridge · Mountain peak/Volcano/Seamount · Geographic feature · Headland/Point/Cape/Peninsula · Desert · Island/Island group · Antarctic base · Ocean · Sea · Bay/Gulf/Channel/Strait · Lake · Salt pan/Dry/Intermittent lake · Ri

189 N 4 Nanping, China
189 Y 10 Nanri Dao, China ⚓
45 T 9 Nansen Basin, Arctic Ocean ◇
45 S 10 Nansen Cordillera, Arctic Ocean ▲
81 O 1 Nansen Sound, Nunavut, Canada ≈
217 S 9 Nansio, Tanzania
128 L 7 Nantes, France
86 E 14 Nanticoke, Ontario, Canada
83 J 20 Nanton, Alberta, Canada
189 Y 5 Nantong, China
59 P 11 Nantucket, Massachusetts, U.S.A.
59 P 11 Nantucket Island, Massachusetts, U.S.A. ⚓
59 P 11 Nantucket Sound, Massachusetts, U.S.A. ≈
127 Q 5 Nantwich, United Kingdom
236 E 5 Nanumanga, Tuvalu ⚓
236 E 5 Nanumea, Tuvalu ⚓
230 E 6 Nanutarra Roadhouse, Western Australia, Australia
189 S 7 Nanxian, China
189 U 11 Nanxiong, China
189 T 5 Nanyang, China
198 K 13 Nanyo, Japan
217 V 7 Nanyuki, Kenya
189 S 5 Nanzhang, China
189 S 4 Nanzhao, China
186 J 5 Naodahan, China
183 T 12 Naogaon, Bangladesh
182 H 4 Naoshera, India
77 G 19 Napa, California, U.S.A.
82 H 9 Napaktulik Lake, Nunavut, Canada ⌐
232 N 13 Napier, New Zealand
241 W 3 Napier Mountains, Antarctica ▲
141 J 16 Naples, Italy
63 W 13 Naples, Florida, U.S.A.
72 K 2 Naples, Idaho, U.S.A.
106 B 8 Napo, Ecuador □
106 D 9 Napo, Ecuador/Peru ⌐
189 O 12 Napo, China
65 L 16 Napoleon, Ohio, U.S.A.
66 K 6 Napoleon, North Dakota, U.S.A.
175 Q 13 Naqūb, Yemen
199 H 18 Nara, Japan
75 U 9 Nara Visa, New Mexico, U.S.A.
149 I 15 Narach, Belarus
231 Q 13 Naracoorte, South Australia, Australia
181 G 17 Narainpur, India
186 C 12 Naran Bulag, China
106 B 10 Naranjal, Ecuador
106 D 11 Naranjal, Peru
89 S 10 Naranjos, Mexico
199 A 22 Narao, Japan
181 I 18 Narasannapeta, India
191 I 26 Narathiwat, Thailand
183 U 13 Narayanganj, Bangladesh
129 R 15 Narbonne, France
181 O 20 Narcondam Island, India ⚓
112 C 13 Naré, Argentina
42 D 10 Nares Abyssal Plain, Atlantic Ocean ◇
42 F 10 Nares Deep, Atlantic Ocean ◇
81 Q 1 Nares Strait, Nunavut, Canada ≈
142 L 11 Narew, Poland ⌐
81 D 19 Nargund, India
18 J 10 Narib, Namibia
77 U 6 Narin, Afghanistan
104 F 9 Nariño, Colombia □
199 L 16 Narita, Japan
182 J 6 Narkanda, India
181 D 15 Narmada, India ⌐
235 Y 12 Naro, Fiji
156 K 1 Naro-Fominsk, Russian Federation
217 U 8 Narok, Kenya
231 U 13 Narooma, New South Wales, Australia
231 U 13 Narrabri, New South Wales, Australia

231 T 12 Narrandera, New South Wales, Australia
230 G 11 Narrogin, Western Australia, Australia
231 T 11 Narromine, New South Wales, Australia
61 O 6 Narrows, Virginia, U.S.A.
44 M 13 Narsarsuaq, Greenland
183 U 13 Narsingdi, Bangladesh
187 D 14 Nart, China
199 F 19 Naruto, Japan
148 J 5 Narva, Estonia
148 J 5 Narva Bay, Estonia ≈
196 F 7 Narvacan, Philippines
134 H 9 Narvik, Norway
155 P 3 Nar'yan-Mar, Russian Federation
179 T 11 Naryn, Kyrgyzstan ⌐
179 V 11 Naryn, Kyrgyzstan
179 V 11 Narynskaya Oblast', Kyrgyzstan
156 J 4 Naryshkino, Russian Federation
235 Y 11 Nasau, Fiji
76 G 8 Naselle, Washington, U.S.A.
181 C 16 Nashik, India
59 N 9 Nashua, New Hampshire, U.S.A.
73 W 3 Nashua, Montana, U.S.A.
60 F 8 Nashville, Tennessee, U.S.A.
65 F 21 Nashville, Illinois, U.S.A.
69 T 13 Nashville, Arkansas, U.S.A.
42 F 10 Nashville Seamount, Atlantic Ocean ▲
213 F 20 Nasir, Sudan
85 U 8 Naskaupi, Newfoundland and Labrador, Canada ⌐
183 P 12 Nasmganj, India
141 K 21 Naso, Italy
217 N 14 Nasondoye, Democratic Republic of Congo
215 R 12 Nassarawa, Nigeria □
236 M 7 Nassau, Cook Islands ⚓
92 L 2 Nassau, The Bahamas ◆
135 F 23 Nässjö, Sweden
85 Q 7 Nastapoca, Québec, Canada ⌐
85 P 7 Nastapoka Islands, Ontario, Canada ⚓
199 K 14 Nasu-dake, Japan ▲
196 F 12 Nasugbu, Philippines
219 N 8 Nata, Botswana
104 H 7 Natagaima, Colombia
108 O 12 Natal, Brazil
192 C 10 Natal, Indonesia
38 I 9 Natal Basin, Indian Ocean ◇
38 H 9 Natal Valley, Indian Ocean ◇
176 I 7 Natanz, Iran
87 V 3 Natashquan, Québec, Canada
62 K 6 Natchez, Mississippi, U.S.A.
62 I 5 Natchitoches, Louisiana, U.S.A.
234 D 7 National Capital District, Papua New Guinea □
215 N 11 Natitingou, Benin
198 K 12 Natori, Japan
58 B 12 Natrona Heights, Pennsylvania, U.S.A.
181 E 23 Nattam, India
191 E 14 Nattaung, Myanmar ▲
192 H 9 Natuna Besar, Indonesia
39 S 9 Naturaliste Fracture Zone, Indian Ocean ◇
39 T 9 Naturaliste Plateau, Indian Ocean ◇
218 I 10 Nauchas, Namibia
138 K 8 Nauders, Austria
136 L 13 Nauen, Germany
180 C 11 Naukh, India
237 U 1 Nauru, Oceania □
106 E 11 Nauta, Peru
89 T 11 Nautla, Mexico
177 R 9 Nauzad, Afghanistan
131 N 8 Navahermosa, Spain
149 H 18 Navahrudak, Belarus
75 O 8 Navajo Lake, New Mexico, U.S.A. ⌐

74 L 7 Navajo Mount, Utah, U.S.A. ▲
197 K 16 Naval, Philippines
130 L 7 Navalmoral de la Mata, Spain
149 K 14 Navapolatsk, Belarus
131 R 2 Navarra, Spain □
93 N 7 Navassa Island, U.S.A., U.S.A.
149 G 18 Navavel'nya, Belarus
110 F 12 Navidad, Chile
181 A 14 Navlakhi, India
156 I 4 Navlya, Russian Federation
179 P 12 Navoi, Uzbekistan
88 J 6 Navojoa, Mexico
181 C 16 Navsari, India
235 W 12 Navua, Fiji
172 H 8 Nawá, Syria
183 S 12 Nawabganj, Bangladesh
183 U 12 Nawabganj, Bangladesh
177 U 13 Nawabshah, Pakistan
183 Q 12 Nawada, India
177 T 9 Nāwah, Afghanistan
182 H 9 Nawalgarh, India
181 H 16 Nawapara, India
190 F 10 Nawngleng, Myanmar
179 O 10 Nawoiy Wiloyati, Uzbekistan
171 V 10 Naxçivan, Azerbaijan
189 N 8 Naxi, China
147 J 22 Naxos, Greece
147 J 22 Naxos, Greece ⚓
104 G 7 Naya, Colombia
177 T 7 Nayak, Afghanistan
89 N 10 Nayar, Mexico
88 M 10 Nayarit, Mexico □
181 F 20 Nayudupeta, India
172 G 8 Nazareth, Israel
38 L 6 Nazareth Bank, Indian Ocean ◇
107 E 18 Nazca, Peru
199 O 22 Naze, Japan
170 C 11 Nazilli, Turkey
157 P 14 Nazran', Russian Federation
213 I 20 Nazrēt, Ethiopia
175 Y 7 Nazwá, Oman
219 O 2 Nchelenge, Zambia
218 K 9 Ncojane, Botswana
215 T 15 Ncue, Equatorial Guinea
218 G 3 N'dalatando, Angola
215 O 11 Ndali, Benin
216 K 3 Ndélé, Central African Republic
215 V 14 Ndélélé, Cameroon
216 E 9 Ndendé, Gabon
235 P 7 Ndeni, Solomon Islands ⚓
215 V 10 Ndjamena, Chad ◆
216 E 8 Ndjolé, Gabon
216 G 8 Ndjounou, Gabon
219 O 4 Ndola, Zambia
217 Q 6 Nduye, Democratic Republic of Congo
147 F 17 Nea Anchialos, Greece
147 F 15 Nea Moudania, Greece
146 G 13 Nea Zichni, Greece
76 F 6 Neah Bay, Washington, U.S.A.
147 F 23 Neapoli, Greece
147 K 26 Neapoli, Greece
78 B 11 Near Islands, Alaska, U.S.A. ⚓
127 N 10 Neath, United Kingdom
217 R 6 Nebbi, Uganda
178 I 12 Nebitdag, Turkmenistan
66 H 13 Nebraska, U.S.A. □
67 P 15 Nebraska City, Nebraska, U.S.A.
64 E 12 Necedah, Wisconsin, U.S.A.
71 T 7 Neches, Texas, U.S.A. ⌐
137 F 21 Neckar, Germany ⌐
113 D 19 Necochea, Argentina
215 X 8 Nédéley, Chad
133 K 17 Nederweert, Netherlands
151 T 3 Nedryhayliv, Ukraine
73 T 10 Needle Mountain, Wyoming, U.S.A. ▲
77 N 24 Needles, California, U.S.A.

84 H 10 Neepawa, Manitoba, Canada
171 Z 9 Neftçala, Azerbaijan
155 S 14 Neftekamsk, Russian Federation
157 P 12 Neftekumsk, Russian Federation
152 L 10 Nefteyugansk, Russian Federation
126 L 5 Nefyn, United Kingdom
218 G 2 Negage, Angola
192 L 15 Negara, Indonesia
213 I 21 Negēlē, Ethiopia
213 I 22 Negēlē, Ethiopia
194 C 9 Negeri Sembilan, Malaysia
172 E 12 Negev, Israel ◇
217 W 15 Negomane, Tanzania
181 F 25 Negombo, Sri Lanka
144 O 11 Negotin, Serbia and Montenegro
150 I 12 Negreni, Romania
106 A 11 Negritos, Peru
111 H 15 Negro, South America ⌐
197 I 18 Negros, Philippines ⚓
151 N 14 Negru Vodă, Romania
177 O 9 Nehbandān, Iran
186 J 8 Nehe, China
150 K 11 Nehoiu, Romania
218 H 6 Nehone, Angola
236 J 10 Neiafu, Tonga
93 P 8 Neiba, Dominican Republic
189 N 7 Neijiang, China
181 N 22 Neill Island, India ⚓
104 H 8 Neiva, Colombia
189 S 4 Neixiang, China
89 T 14 Nejapa Tequisistlán, Mexico
213 H 20 Nek'emtē, Ethiopia
154 F 14 Nelidovo, Russian Federation
67 N 12 Neligh, Nebraska, U.S.A.
181 G 20 Nellore, India
233 I 16 Nelson, New Zealand
233 I 16 Nelson, New Zealand □
83 I 21 Nelson, British Columbia, Canada
231 V 11 Nelson Bay, New South Wales, Australia
219 P 10 Nelspruit, Republic of South Africa
197 S 16 Nelyan Point, Philippines ▶
214 J 7 Néma, Mauritania
149 D 15 Neman, Lithuania
149 C 15 Neman, Russian Federation ⌐
215 Q 14 Nembe, Nigeria
147 E 20 Nemea, Greece
149 G 15 Nemenčinė, Lithuania
198 N 4 Nemuro, Japan
198 N 4 Nemuro-hantō, Japan ▶
198 M 3 Nemuro-kaikyō, Japan ≈
198 N 4 Nemuro-wan, Japan ≈
151 N 6 Nemyriv, Ukraine
79 R 7 Nenana, Alaska, U.S.A.
194 E 8 Nenasi, Malaysia
155 R 2 Nenetskiy Avtonomnyy Okrug, Russian Federation □
189 J 8 Nenjiang, China
199 H 17 Neo, Japan
147 L 20 Neo Karlovasi, Greece
67 Q 13 Neola, Iowa, U.S.A.
183 O 8 Nepal, Asia □
182 M 9 Nepalganj, Nepal
86 I 11 Nepean, Ontario, Canada
143 B 18 Nepomuk, Czech Republic
153 S 14 Nerchinsk, Russian Federation
148 G 12 Nereta, Latvia
145 G 14 Neretva, Bosnia and Herzegovina ⌐
218 K 6 Neriquinha, Angola
149 F 15 Neris, Lithuania ⌐
131 N 13 Nerja, Spain
153 T 12 Neryungri, Russian Federation
132 K 5 Nes, Netherlands
146 N 9 Nesebŭr, Bulgaria
68 J 5 Ness City, Kansas, U.S.A.

149 D 15 Nesterov, Russian Federation
84 J 11 Nestor Falls, Ontario, Canada
146 H 12 Nestos, Greece ⌐
172 F 8 Netanya, Israel
132 H 10 Netherlands, Europe □
93 S 12 Netherlands Antilles, The Netherlands, The Netherlands □
85 Q 2 Nettilling Lake, Nunavut, Canada ⌐
137 J 23 Neuberg, Germany
136 M 10 Neubrandenburg, Germany
136 J 9 Neubukow, Germany
138 C 7 Neuchâtel, Switzerland
136 M 13 Neuenhagen, Germany
129 U 5 Neufchâteau, France
133 J 24 Neufchâteau, Belgium
129 O 2 Neufchâtel-en-Bray, France
139 S 3 Neufelden, Austria
139 W 4 Neulengbach, Austria
137 J 21 Neumarkt, Germany
241 O 1 Neumayer, Antarctica ⊞
136 H 9 Neumünster, Germany
129 P 6 Neung-sur-Beuvron, France
137 C 21 Neunkirchen, Germany
139 W 5 Neunkirchen, Austria
111 H 15 Neuquén, Argentina
111 G 15 Neuquén, Argentina □
111 G 14 Neuquén, Argentina ⌐
136 L 12 Neuruppin, Germany
139 Y 5 Neusiedler See, Austria ⌐
137 C 16 Neuss, Germany
137 J 17 Neustadt, Germany
137 K 22 Neustadt, Germany
136 G 13 Neustadt, Germany
136 I 9 Neustadt, Germany
137 E 21 Neustadt, Germany
137 I 20 Neustadt an der Aisch, Germany
136 L 11 Neustrelitz, Germany
136 F 9 Neuwerk, Germany
137 D 18 Neuwied, Germany
69 S 6 Nevada, Missouri, U.S.A.
77 J 18 Nevada, U.S.A., U.S.A. □
77 H 17 Nevada City, California, U.S.A.
89 N 12 Nevada de Colima, Mexico ▲
107 F 19 Nevado Ampato, Peru ▲
110 G 13 Nevado Campanario, Argentina ▲
107 F 18 Nevado Coropuna, Peru ▲
110 H 5 Nevado de Chañi, Argentina ▲
110 H 5 Nevado de Poquis, Chile ▲
89 Q 12 Nevado de Toluca, Mexico ▲
104 H 8 Nevado del Huila, Colombia ▲
104 I 6 Nevado del Ruiz, Colombia ▲
107 C 14 Nevado Huascarán, Peru ▲
107 I 19 Nevado Illampu, Bolivia ▲
110 H 8 Nevado Ojos del Salado, Argentina ▲
107 I 20 Nevado Sajama, Bolivia ▲
110 H 6 Nevados de Cachi, Argentina ▲
154 E 14 Nevel', Russian Federation
129 R 8 Nevers, France
157 N 12 Nevinnomyssk, Russian Federation
93 X 8 Nevis, St Kitts and Nevis ⚓
170 J 11 Nevşehir, Turkey
63 N 2 New Albany, Mississippi, U.S.A.
65 J 21 New Albany, Indiana, U.S.A.
127 T 12 New Alresford, United Kingdom
105 V 5 New Amsterdam, Guyana
59 O 11 New Bedford, Massachusetts, U.S.A.

61 U 10 New Bern, North Carolina, U.S.A.
71 T 4 New Boston, Texas, U.S.A.
71 P 10 New Braunfels, Texas, U.S.A.
234 F 4 New Britain, Papua New Guinea ⚓
87 S 8 New Brunswick, Canada □
235 N 14 New Caledonia, New Caledonia ⚓
235 O 15 New Caledonia, France ⚓
41 N 10 New Caledonia Trough, Pacific Ocean ◇
87 T 6 New Carlisle, Québec, Canada
58 A 11 New Castle, Pennsylvania, U.S.A.
60 H 4 New Castle, Kentucky, U.S.A.
58 J 12 New City, New York, U.S.A.
182 J 8 New Delhi, India ◆
61 N 13 New Ellenton, South Carolina, U.S.A.
59 N 9 New England, New Hampshire, U.S.A. ◇
42 E 8 New England Seamounts, Atlantic Ocean ▲
127 S 12 New Forest, United Kingdom ◇
234 K 6 New Georgia, Solomon Islands ⚓
234 J 6 New Georgia Islands, Solomon Islands ⚓
234 K 5 New Georgia Sound, Solomon Islands ≈
87 W 9 New Glasgow, Nova Scotia, Canada
234 A 4 New Guinea, Indonesia/Papua New Guinea ⚓
59 N 7 New Hampshire, U.S.A. □
234 G 2 New Hanover, Papua New Guinea ⚓
58 L 11 New Haven, Connecticut, U.S.A.
83 D 18 New Hazelton, British Columbia, Canada
41 O 10 New Hebrides Trench, Pacific Ocean ◇
62 J 8 New Iberia, Louisiana, U.S.A.
234 G 3 New Ireland, Papua New Guinea ⚓
234 H 2 New Ireland, Papua New Guinea ⚓
58 I 14 New Jersey, U.S.A. □
65 N 19 New Lexington, Ohio, U.S.A.
86 F 7 New Liskeard, Ontario, Canada
58 M 11 New London, Connecticut, U.S.A.
64 G 12 New London, Wisconsin, U.S.A.
61 R 4 New Market, Virginia, U.S.A.
72 J 8 New Meadows, Idaho, U.S.A.
75 O 11 New Mexico, U.S.A. □
231 S 15 New Norfolk, Tasmania, Australia
62 L 8 New Orleans, Louisiana, U.S.A.
65 N 18 New Philadelphia, Ohio, U.S.A.
77 I 14 New Pine Creek, California, U.S.A.
232 J 12 New Plymouth, New Zealand
92 K 2 New Providence, The Bahamas ⚓
126 L 8 New Quay, United Kingdom
87 S 6 New Richmond, Québec, Canada
62 K 7 New Roads, Louisiana, U.S.A.
58 K 12 New Rochelle, New York, U.S.A.
66 L 4 New Rockford, North Dakota, U.S.A.
127 Y 12 New Romney, United Kingdom
125 E 20 New Ross, Republic of Ireland
87 U 11 New Ross, Nova Scotia, Canada

Legend:
■ Country □ Internal administrative region: State/Province/Territory/Dependent territory ◆ Capital city ▲ Mountain range/Undersea ridge ▲ Mountain peak/Volcano/Seamount ◇ Geographic feature ▶ Headland/Point/Cape/Peninsula ◆ Desert ⚓ Island/Island group ⊞ Antarctic base ◎ Ocean ≈ Sea ≈ Bay/Gulf/Channel/Strait ⌐ Lake ◆ Salt pan/Dry/Intermittent lake ⌐ River

■ Country **▣** Internal administrative region: State/Province/Territory/Dependent territory **♣** Capital city **▲** Mountain range/ Undersea ridge **▲** Mountain peak/ Volcano/Seamount **◇** Geographic feature **▸** Headland/Point/ Cape/Peninsula **●** Desert **⇄** Island/Island group **▦** Antarctic base **⊙** Ocean **⊃** Sea **≈** Bay/Gulf/Channel/Strait **◣** Lake **⇂** Salt pan/Dry/ Intermittent lake **⇂** Riv

232 J 7 North Head, New Zealand ▶
217 V 6 North Horr, Kenya
181 L 20 North Huvadhu Atoll, Maldives ⇄
159 S 8 North Ikaria Basin, Mediterranean Sea ◇
232 M 11 North Island, New Zealand ⇄
38 A 9 North Island, Seychelles ⇄
181 B 23 North Island, India ⇄
196 H 1 North Island, Philippines ⇄
197 E 20 North Islet, Philippines ⇄
39 Q 5 North Keeling Island, Cocos Islands ⇄
187 M 17 North Korea, Asia ⊡
183 X 9 North Lakhimpur, India
181 L 17 North Maalhosmadulu Atoll, Maldives ⇄
81 N 2 North Magnetic Pole, Nunavut, Canada ◇
181 L 16 North Miladunmadulu Atoll, Maldives ⇄
66 G 13 North Platte, Nebraska, U.S.A. ꞥ
38 A 9 North Point, Seychelles ▶
43 K 25 North Point, Ascension ▶
43 N 16 North Point, Tristan da Cunha ▶
64 L 11 North Point, Michigan, U.S.A. ▶
45 S 8 North Pole, Arctic Ocean ◇
79 R 7 North Pole, Alaska, U.S.A. ◇
76 K 10 North Powder, Oregon, U.S.A.
181 N 21 North Reef Island, India ⇄
74 J 9 North Rim, Arizona, U.S.A.
124 I 6 North Ronaldsay, United Kingdom ⇄
83 K 18 North Saskatchewan, Saskatchewan, Canada ꞥ
42 M 6 North Sea, Atlantic Ocean ꞕ
181 N 22 North Sentinel Island, India ⇄
234 J 4 North Solomons, Papua New Guinea ⊡
127 W 3 North Somercotes, United Kingdom
231 W 9 North Stradbroke Island, Queensland, Australia ⇄
232 J 12 North Taranaki Bight, New Zealand ꞕ
85 O 9 North Twin Island, Québec, Canada ⇄
197 F 23 North Ubian, Philippines ⇄
124 E 10 North Uist, United Kingdom ⇄
197 D 18 North Verde, Philippines ⇄
65 J 20 North Vernon, Indiana, U.S.A.
127 Z 5 North Walsham, United Kingdom
218 L 11 North West, Republic of South Africa ⊡
230 E 6 North West Cape, Western Australia, Australia ▶
177 W 6 North West Frontier, Pakistan ⊡
124 G 11 North West Highlands, United Kingdom ▲
181 F 24 North Western, Sri Lanka ⊡
218 M 4 North-Western, Zambia ⊡
86 F 13 North York, Ontario, Canada
127 S 1 Northallerton, United Kingdom
230 G 11 Northam, Western Australia, Australia
230 E 9 Northampton, Western Australia, Australia
127 U 8 Northampton, United Kingdom
58 L 9 Northampton, Massachusetts, U.S.A.
78 K 7 Northeast Cape, Alaska, U.S.A. ▶
41 R 3 Northeast Pacific Basin, Pacific Ocean ◇

137 H 15 Northeim, Germany
213 D 14 Northern, Sudan ⊡
214 G 11 Northern, Sierra Leone ⊡
219 O 10 Northern, Republic of South Africa
219 P 3 Northern, Zambia ⊡
219 Q 3 Northern, Malawi ⊡
234 F 6 Northern, Papua New Guinea ⊡
181 G 23 Northern, Sri Lanka ⊡
213 C 20 Northern Bahr el Ghazal, Sudan
218 K 13 Northern Cape, Republic of South Africa ⊡
90 L 2 Northern Cay, Belize ⇄
236 L 7 Northern Cook Islands, Cook Islands ⇄
213 B 15 Northern Darfur, Sudan
154 L 8 Northern Dvina, Russian Federation ꞥ
125 E 15 Northern Ireland, United Kingdom ⊡
213 D 16 Northern Kordofan, Sudan
90 K 2 Northern Lagoon, Belize ꞥ
235 Y 11 Northern Lau Group, Fiji ⇄
236 A 6 Northern Mariana Islands, U.S.A.
140 D 8 Northern Plain, Italy ◇
231 N 4 Northern Territory, Australia ⊡
67 S 8 Northfield, Minnesota, U.S.A.
232 J 6 Northland, New Zealand ⊡
87 U 8 Northumberland Strait, Prince Edward Island, Canada ꞕ
58 J 8 Northville, New York, U.S.A.
42 E 5 Northwest Atlantic Mid-Ocean Channel, Atlantic Ocean ꞕ
78 K 7 Northwest Cape, Alaska, U.S.A. ▶
41 N 3 Northwest Pacific Basin, Pacific Ocean ◇
82 H 11 Northwest Territories, Canada ⊡
127 Q 4 Northwich, United Kingdom
45 R 4 Northwind Plain, Arctic Ocean ◇
68 J 2 Norton, Kansas, U.S.A.
78 M 7 Norton Sound, Alaska, U.S.A. ꞕ
60 E 6 Nortonville, Kentucky, U.S.A.
58 K 12 Norwalk, Connecticut, U.S.A.
65 M 17 Norwalk, Ohio, U.S.A.
135 B 19 Norway, Europe ⊡
84 J 8 Norway House, Manitoba, Canada
45 S 15 Norwegian Basin, Arctic Ocean ◇
135 A 16 Norwegian Sea, Norway ꞕ
127 Z 6 Norwich, United Kingdom
58 M 11 Norwich, Connecticut, U.S.A.
146 N 9 Nos Emine, Bulgaria ▶
146 O 7 Nos Kaliakra, Bulgaria ▶
146 O 7 Nos Shabla, Bulgaria ▶
198 N 4 Nosapu-misaki, Japan ▶
198 I 2 Noshappu-misaki, Japan ▶
198 J 10 Noshiro, Japan
155 Q 2 Nosovaya, Russian Federation
177 O 11 Noṣratābād, Iran
124 I 8 Noss Head, United Kingdom ▶
219 Y 5 Nosy Be, Madagascar ⇄
219 Z 7 Nosy Boraha, Madagascar ⇄
219 Y 8 Nosy-Varika, Madagascar
74 I 4 Notch Peak, Utah, U.S.A. ▲
142 E 11 Noteć, Poland ꞥ
147 J 23 Notio Aigaio, Greece
147 A 16 Notio Steno Kerkyras, Greece ꞕ

147 G 19 Notios Evvoïkos Kolpos, Greece ꞕ
141 K 24 Noto, Italy
199 H 15 Noto-hantō, Japan ▶
198 M 3 Notoro-ko, Japan ꞥ
85 Y 9 Notre Dame Bay, Newfoundland and Labrador, Canada ꞕ
86 E 11 Nottawasaga Bay, Ontario, Canada ꞕ
85 P 10 Nottaway, Québec, Canada ꞥ
127 T 5 Nottingham, United Kingdom
85 P 4 Nottingham Island, Nunavut, Canada ⇄
210 A 14 Nouâdhibou, Western Sahara
214 D 5 Nouâdhibou, Mauritania
214 E 6 Nouakchott, Mauritania ●
214 E 6 Nouâmghâr, Mauritania
191 N 17 Nouei, Vietnam
235 Q 14 Nouméa, New Caledonia ▣
179 R 12 Nov, Tajikistan
109 J 15 Nova, Brazil
112 G 5 Nova Alvorada, Brazil
218 F 2 Nova Caipemba, Angola
112 N 6 Nova Friburgo, Brazil
112 M 6 Nova Iguaçu, Brazil
219 R 8 Nova Mambone, Mozambique
219 T 6 Nova Nabúri, Mozambique
151 R 8 Nova Odesa, Ukraine
87 W 10 Nova Scotia, Canada ⊡
41 P 8 Nova Trough, Pacific Ocean ◇
144 K 13 Nova Varoš, Serbia and Montenegro
146 K 9 Nova Zagora, Bulgaria
140 B 7 Novara, Italy
77 F 19 Novato, California, U.S.A.
152 L 6 Novaya Zemlya, Russian Federation ⇄
143 H 22 Nové Zámky, Slovakia
154 G 12 Novgorodskaya Oblast', Russian Federation
151 S 1 Novhorod-Sivers'kyy, Ukraine
151 S 7 Novhorodka, Ukraine
144 K 8 Novi Bečej, Serbia and Montenegro
146 G 9 Novi-Iskŭr, Bulgaria
140 C 8 Novi Ligure, Italy
145 L 14 Novi Pazar, Serbia and Montenegro
146 M 7 Novi Pazar, Bulgaria
144 K 9 Novi Sad, Serbia and Montenegro
108 E 10 Novo Airão, Brazil
108 F 11 Novo Aripuanã, Brazil
112 N 12 Novo Hamburgo, Brazil
144 C 8 Novo Mesto, Slovenia
146 F 12 Novo Selo, Macedonia (F.Y.R.O.M.)
157 N 6 Novoanninskiy, Russian Federation
151 Q 6 Novoarkhanhel's'k, Ukraine
151 Y 8 Novoazovs'k, Ukraine
179 S 13 Novobod, Tajikistan
178 H 6 Novobogatinskoye, Kazakhstan
151 V 8 Novobohdanivka, Ukraine
157 Q 1 Novocheboksarsk, Russian Federation
156 L 9 Novocherkassk, Russian Federation
154 K 6 Novodvinsk, Russian Federation
150 M 3 Novohrad-Volyns'kyy, Ukraine
156 M 6 Novokhopersk, Russian Federation
157 S 4 Novokuybyshevsk, Russian Federation
152 M 13 Novokuznetsk, Russian Federation
241 R 1 Novolazarevskaya, Antarctica ⊞
151 V 6 Novomoskovs'k, Ukraine
156 L 3 Novomoskovsk, Russian Federation

157 N 6 Novonikolayevskiy, Russian Federation
157 P 8 Novonikol'skoye, Russian Federation
151 U 10 Novoolekisiyivka, Ukraine
151 U 7 Novopokrovka, Ukraine
151 Z 4 Novopskov, Ukraine
156 K 12 Novorossiysk, Russian Federation
153 Q 7 Novorybnaya, Russian Federation
151 T 11 Novoselivs'ke, Ukraine
157 V 4 Novosergiyevka, Russian Federation
156 L 9 Novoshakhtinsk, Russian Federation
152 M 12 Novosibirsk, Russian Federation
157 R 4 Novospasskoye, Russian Federation
151 U 10 Novotroyits'ke, Ukraine
151 Q 7 Novoukrayinka, Ukraine
157 R 6 Novouzensk, Russian Federation
156 G 4 Novozybkov, Russian Federation
149 M 18 Novy Bykhaw, Belarus
143 H 18 Nový Jičín, Czech Republic
155 P 4 Novyy Bor, Russian Federation
151 S 8 Novyy Buh, Ukraine
151 R 3 Novyy Bykiv, Ukraine
156 K 6 Novyy Oskol, Russian Federation
152 M 8 Novyy Port, Russian Federation
152 M 9 Novyy Urengoy, Russian Federation
153 V 13 Novyy Urgal, Russian Federation
143 I 15 Nowa, Poland
143 M 16 Nowa Dęba, Poland
143 F 16 Nowa Ruda, Poland
142 E 10 Nowogard, Poland
231 U 12 Nowra, New South Wales, Australia
177 W 6 Nowshak, Pakistan ▲
177 W 7 Nowshera, Pakistan
142 K 12 Nowy Dwór Mazowiecki, Poland
143 L 18 Nowy Sącz, Poland
143 K 18 Nowy Targ, Poland
152 M 9 Noyabr'sk, Russian Federation
129 R 3 Noyon, France
128 K 6 Nozay, France
216 I 8 Nsambi, Democratic Republic of Congo
219 R 6 Nsanje, Malawi
215 T 15 Nsoc, Equatorial Guinea
219 P 3 Nsombo, Zambia
215 Q 13 Nsukka, Nigeria
216 I 9 Ntandembele, Democratic Republic of Congo
219 R 5 Ntcheu, Malawi
216 D 7 Ntoum, Gabon
217 R 8 Ntungamo, Uganda
218 M 8 Ntwetwe Pan, Botswana ꞥ
188 J 9 Nu Shan, China ▲
213 E 18 Nuba Mountains, Sudan ▲
213 G 14 Nubian Desert, Sudan ◇
235 Y 10 Nubu, Fiji
89 U 13 Nudo de Zempoaltépetl, Mexico ▲
84 J 4 Nueltin Lake, Nunavut, Canada ꞥ
90 K 5 Nueva Arcadia, Honduras
104 L 3 Nueva Bolivia, Venezuela
89 X 12 Nueva Coahuila, Mexico
105 P 2 Nueva Esparta, Venezuela ⊡
110 I 13 Nueva Galia, Argentina
92 G 5 Nueva Gerona, Cuba
91 Q 10 Nueva Guinea, Nicaragua
106 C 8 Nueva Loja, Ecuador
111 G 19 Nueva Lubecka, Argentina
110 L 6 Nueva Pompeya, Argentina
89 P 5 Nueva Rosita, Mexico

90 I 7 Nueva San Salvador, El Salvador
89 R 8 Nueva Villa de Padilla, Mexico
113 C 16 Nueve de Julio, Argentina
92 L 5 Nuevitas, Cuba
89 Q 6 Nuevo Laredo, Mexico
89 R 7 Nuevo León, Mexico ⊡
213 O 20 Nugaal, Somalia
234 J 3 Nuguria Islands, Papua New Guinea ⇄
182 I 9 Nuh, India
232 O 12 Nuhaka, New Zealand
236 F 5 Nui, Tuvalu ⇄
79 Q 3 Nuiqsut, Alaska, U.S.A.
234 J 5 Nukiki, Solomon Islands
234 B 3 Nuku, Papua New Guinea
236 I 11 Nuku'alofa, Tonga ●
236 F 6 Nukufetau, Tuvalu ⇄
236 G 6 Nukulaelae, Tuvalu ⇄
234 L 4 Nukumanu Islands, Papua New Guinea ⇄
236 K 6 Nukunonu, Tokelau Islands ⇄
236 J 6 Nukunonu, Tokelau Islands
237 P 15 Nukuoro, Federated States of Micronesia ⇄
178 M 10 Nukus, Uzbekistan
230 H 6 Nullagine, Western Australia, Australia
230 M 10 Nullarbor, South Australia, Australia
230 L 10 Nullarbor Plain, Western Australia, Australia ◇
187 F 15 Nulu'erhu Shan, China ▲
183 R 9 Num, Nepal
193 V 11 Num, Indonesia ⇄
215 U 11 Numan, Nigeria
133 G 14 Numansdorp, Netherlands
199 J 15 Numata, Japan
199 K 17 Numazu, Japan
231 O 2 Numbulwar, Northern Territory, Australia
84 J 2 Nunavut, Canada ⊡
127 S 7 Nuneaton, United Kingdom
183 X 12 Nungba, India
186 F 11 Nungnain Sum, China
78 L 9 Nunivak Island, Alaska, U.S.A. ⇄
153 Z 6 Nunligran, Russian Federation
132 K 11 Nunspeet, Netherlands
141 C 17 Nuoro, Italy
235 P 7 Nupani, Solomon Islands ⇄
175 N 5 Nuqrah, Saudi Arabia
104 G 6 Nuquí, Colombia
179 N 6 Nura, Kazakhstan
176 I 10 Nūrābād, Iran
179 P 12 Nurata, Uzbekistan
137 I 21 Nuremberg, Germany
88 J 5 Nuri, Mexico
157 S 2 Nurlat, Russian Federation
135 N 14 Nurmes, Finland
177 W 9 Nurpur, Pakistan
182 I 5 Nurpur, India
192 M 14 Nusa Tenggara Barat, Indonesia ⊡
193 O 15 Nusa Tenggara Timur, Indonesia ⊡
171 Q 13 Nusaybin, Turkey
177 S 11 Nushki, Pakistan
45 O 11 Nuugaatsiaq, Greenland
44 M 12 Nuuk, Greenland ▣
45 N 11 Nuussuaq, Greenland ▶
45 O 10 Nuussuaq, Greenland
152 K 9 Nyagan', Russian Federation
217 U 7 Nyahururu, Kenya
184 K 10 Nyainqêntanglha, China ▲
184 L 10 Nyainqêntanglha Shan, China ▲
217 S 9 Nyakaliro, Tanzania
213 A 18 Nyala, Sudan
219 O 8 Nyamandhiovu, Zimbabwe
213 C 20 Nyamlell, Sudan
154 K 9 Nyandoma, Russian Federation
216 E 10 Nyanga, Gabon ⊡
216 F 9 Nyanga, Congo

217 T 8 Nyanza, Kenya ⊡
149 I 19 Nyasvizh, Belarus
219 O 7 Nyathi, Zimbabwe
191 E 15 Nyaunglebin, Myanmar
135 E 18 Nybergsund, Norway
135 C 25 Nyborg, Denmark
135 G 24 Nybro, Sweden
217 V 8 Nyeri, Kenya
213 E 20 Nyerol, Sudan
184 M 11 Nyingchi, China
143 N 22 Nyírbátor, Hungary
143 M 22 Nyíregyháza, Hungary
135 D 26 Nykøbing, Denmark
135 H 21 Nyköping, Sweden
135 H 21 Nynäshamn, Sweden
231 T 10 Nyngan, New South Wales, Australia
149 G 18 Nyoman, Belarus ꞥ
138 A 9 Nyon, Switzerland
129 U 12 Nyons, France
155 S 10 Nyrob, Russian Federation
143 G 16 Nysa, Poland
198 J 10 Nyūdō-zaki, Japan ▶
217 P 11 Nyunzu, Democratic Republic of Congo
192 M 9 Nyurang, Indonesia
153 S 10 Nyurba, Russian Federation
153 S 11 Nyuya, Russian Federation
151 U 9 Nyzhni Sirohozy, Ukraine
151 U 9 Nyzhni Torhayi, Ukraine
151 U 11 Nyzhn'ohirs'kyy, Ukraine
216 E 10 Nzambi, Congo
217 S 10 Nzega, Tanzania
214 H 12 Nzérékoré, Guinea
218 F 2 N'zeto, Angola
217 P 10 Nzingu, Democratic Republic of Congo

O

198 H 8 Ō-shima, Japan ⇄
199 K 17 Ō-shima, Japan ⇄
78 C 7 Oahu, Hawaii, U.S.A. ⇄
59 O 11 Oak Bluffs, Massachusetts, U.S.A.
74 J 4 Oak City, Utah, U.S.A.
65 H 14 Oak Creek, Wisconsin, U.S.A.
75 P 3 Oak Creek, Colorado, U.S.A.
76 G 6 Oak Harbor, Washington, U.S.A.
65 H 16 Oak Lawn, Illinois, U.S.A.
60 J 8 Oak Ridge, Tennessee, U.S.A.
62 I 7 Oakdale, Louisiana, U.S.A.
127 U 6 Oakham, United Kingdom
77 I 20 Oakhurst, California, U.S.A.
61 Q 2 Oakland, Maryland, U.S.A.
67 P 13 Oakland, Nebraska, U.S.A.
76 F 12 Oakland, Oregon, U.S.A.
77 G 19 Oakland, California, U.S.A.
68 I 3 Oakley, Kansas, U.S.A.
73 N 13 Oakley, Idaho, U.S.A.
230 H 5 Oakover, Western Australia, Australia ꞥ
76 G 12 Oakridge, Oregon, U.S.A.
232 J 12 Oakura, New Zealand
232 J 6 Oakura, New Zealand
233 F 23 Oamaru, New Zealand
199 D 19 Ōasa, Japan
77 N 15 Oasis, Nevada, U.S.A.
241 R 14 Oates Land, Antarctica ◇
89 T 14 Oaxaca, Mexico
89 S 14 Oaxaca, Mexico ⊡
152 L 10 Ob', Russian Federation ꞥ
86 B 5 Oba, Ontario, Canada
215 T 14 Obala, Cameroon
124 F 12 Oban, United Kingdom
233 D 23 Obelisk, New Zealand ▲
112 F 10 Oberá, Argentina
139 Q 8 Oberdrauburg, Austria
139 I 2 Oberlin, Kansas, U.S.A.
139 Q 5 Oberndorf, Austria
139 Q 4 Oberösterreich, Austria
137 K 20 Oberpfälzer Wald, Germany ▲
139 Y 6 Oberpullendorf, Austria
137 H 26 Oberstdorf, Germany

⬚ Country ⬚ Internal administrative region: State/Province/Territory/Dependent territory ⬘ Capital city ▲ Mountain range/Undersea ridge ▲ Mountain peak/Volcano/Seamount ◇ Geographic feature ▶ Headland/Point/Cape/Peninsula ⚏ Desert ⚏ Island/Island group ⬚ Antarctic base ⊚ Ocean ≈ Sea ≈ Bay/Gulf/Channel/Strait ᔑ Lake ⬚ Salt pan/Dry/Intermittent lake ᔓ River

Legend: ◻ Country · ◻ Internal administrative region: State/Province/Territory/Dependent territory · ♣ Capital city · ▲ Mountain range/ Undersea ridge · ▲ Mountain peak/ Volcano/Seamount · ◇ Geographic feature · ▶ Headland/Point/ Cape/Peninsula · ▦ Desert · ◻ Island/Island group · ▦ Antarctic base · ⊗ Ocean · ⇌ Sea · ⇌ Bay/Gulf/Channel/Strait · ⤸ Lake · ⤸ Salt pan/Dry/ Intermittent lake · River

Patton Seamount – Phou Set

41 R 2 **Patton Seamount**, Pacific Ocean ▲
183 U 14 **Patuakhali**, Bangladesh
91 P 5 **Patuca**, Honduras
89 P 12 **Pátzcuaro**, Mexico
128 M 14 **Pau**, France
108 C 13 **Pauini**, Brazil
190 C 12 **Pauk**, Myanmar
82 E 8 **Paulatuk**, Northwest Territories, Canada
108 O 13 **Paulista**, Brazil
108 N 13 **Paulo Afonso**, Brazil
69 N 11 **Pauls Valley**, Oklahoma, U.S.A.
190 C 9 **Paungbyin**, Myanmar
191 D 14 **Paungde**, Myanmar
182 K 7 **Pauri**, India
181 E 20 **Pavagada**, India
156 L 3 **Pavelets**, Russian Federation
140 C 7 **Pavia**, Italy
148 C 11 **Pāvilosta**, Latvia
146 J 8 **Pavlikeni**, Bulgaria
150 J 3 **Pavlivka**, Ukraine
179 U 4 **Pavlodar**, Kazakhstan ▣
179 U 3 **Pavlodar**, Kazakhstan
151 V 6 **Pavlohrad**, Ukraine
157 O 1 **Pavlovo**, Russian Federation
156 M 6 **Pavlovsk**, Russian Federation
156 L 11 **Pavlovskaya**, Russian Federation
140 F 9 **Pavullo nel Frignano**, Italy
194 A 15 **Pawai**, Singapore
69 P 8 **Pawhuska**, Oklahoma, U.S.A.
69 O 8 **Pawnee**, Oklahoma, U.S.A.
147 H 26 **Paximadia**, Greece
147 A 17 **Paxoi**, Greece
79 S 8 **Paxson**, Alaska, U.S.A.
191 E 15 **Payagyi**, Myanmar
192 D 11 **Payakumbuh**, Indonesia
138 C 8 **Payerne**, Switzerland
72 J 10 **Payette**, Idaho, U.S.A.
230 G 10 **Paynes Find**, Western Australia, Australia
67 Q 7 **Paynesville**, Minnesota, U.S.A.
128 L 6 **Pays de la Loire**, France ▣
112 E 13 **Paysandu**, Uruguay ▣
113 D 14 **Paysandú**, Uruguay
74 K 11 **Payson**, Arizona, U.S.A.
74 K 3 **Payson**, Utah, U.S.A.
192 G 12 **Payung**, Indonesia
104 K 6 **Paz de Ariporo**, Colombia
171 Q 7 **Pazar**, Turkey
170 F 7 **Pazarbaşi Burnu**, Turkey ▶
170 M 12 **Pazarcik**, Turkey
146 H 10 **Pazardzhik**, Bulgaria ▣
146 H 10 **Pazardzhik**, Bulgaria
83 H 16 **Peace**, Alberta, Canada
83 H 17 **Peace River**, Alberta, Canada
74 H 9 **Peach Springs**, Arizona, U.S.A.
77 F 16 **Peanut**, California, U.S.A.
74 M 14 **Pearce**, Arizona, U.S.A.
189 R 12 **Pearl**, China
62 L 5 **Pearl**, Mississippi, U.S.A.
78 B 7 **Pearl City**, Hawaii, U.S.A.
78 B 7 **Pearl Harbor**, Hawaii, U.S.A.
63 U 6 **Pearson**, Georgia, U.S.A.
81 N 2 **Peary Channel**, Nunavut, Canada
45 R 10 **Peary Land**, Greenland ◇
85 N 8 **Peawanuck**, Ontario, Canada
219 T 6 **Pebane**, Mozambique
106 G 10 **Pebas**, Peru
111 L 23 **Pebble Island**, Falkland Islands
145 K 15 **Peć**, Serbia and Montenegro
62 I 8 **Pecan Island**, Louisiana, U.S.A.
155 P 3 **Pechora**, Russian Federation
155 S 5 **Pechora**, Russian Federation
155 Q 2 **Pechorskaya Guba**, Russian Federation
152 K 6 **Pechorskoye More**, Russian Federation
70 H 8 **Pecos**, Texas, U.S.A.
75 S 12 **Pecos**, New Mexico/Texas, U.S.A.
133 C 20 **Pecq**, Belgium
143 H 26 **Pécs**, Hungary
91 W 15 **Pedasí**, Panama
93 P 8 **Pedernales**, Dominican Republic
218 F 6 **Pediva**, Angola
109 M 16 **Pedra Azul**, Brazil
43 B 17 **Pedra Badejo**, Cape Verde
109 E 14 **Pedras Negras**, Brazil
91 S 14 **Pedregal**, Panama
112 K 4 **Pedregulho**, Brazil
89 N 7 **Pedriceña**, Mexico
108 K 13 **Pedro Afonso**, Brazil
92 K 9 **Pedro Bank**, Jamaica
110 G 5 **Pedro de Valdivia**, Chile
109 G 18 **Pedro Juan Caballero**, Paraguay
112 G 13 **Pedro Osório**, Brazil
65 M 20 **Peebles**, Ohio, U.S.A.
58 K 11 **Peekskill**, New York, U.S.A.
125 G 16 **Peel**, United Kingdom
82 B 10 **Peel**, Yukon Territory/Northwest Territories, Canada
136 M 9 **Peene**, Germany
136 M 8 **Peenemünde**, Germany
233 I 20 **Pegasus Bay**, New Zealand
137 J 20 **Pegnitz**, Germany
191 D 15 **Pegu**, Myanmar ▣
191 E 16 **Pegu**, Myanmar
191 D 14 **Pegu Yoma**, Myanmar
192 B 8 **Pegunungan Barisan**, Indonesia
195 P 10 **Pegunungan Boven Kapuas**, Malaysia
195 R 8 **Pegunungan Dulit**, Malaysia
195 R 9 **Pegunungan Hose**, Malaysia
195 T 10 **Pegunungan Iran**, Indonesia/Malaysia
193 X 12 **Pegunungan Maoke**, Indonesia
192 K 11 **Pegunungan Muller**, Indonesia
192 J 11 **Pegunungan Schwaner**, Indonesia
127 Z 11 **Pegwell Bay**, United Kingdom
113 B 17 **Pehuajó**, Argentina
0 G 20 **Peiraias**, Greece
194 B 14 **Peirce Reservoir**, Singapore
109 J 14 **Peixe**, Brazil
192 H 10 **Pejantan**, Indonesia
194 E 8 **Pekan**, Malaysia
192 E 10 **Pekanbaru**, Indonesia
194 B 8 **Pelabuhan Kelang**, Malaysia
195 X 5 **Pelabuhan Sandakan**, Malaysia
192 M 10 **Pelawanbesar**, Indonesia
86 B 15 **Pelee Island**, Ontario, Canada
86 B 15 **Pelee Point**, Ontario, Canada ▶
193 P 11 **Peleng**, Indonesia
143 D 18 **Pelhřimov**, Czech Republic
92 K 1 **Pelican Point**, The Bahamas
146 C 13 **Pelister**, Macedonia (F.Y.R.O.M.) ▲
63 Q 3 **Pell City**, Alabama, U.S.A.
134 K 11 **Pello**, Finland
136 F 8 **Pellworm**, Germany
82 B 13 **Pelly**, Yukon Territory, Canada
84 M 1 **Pelly Bay**, Nunavut, Canada
82 B 12 **Pelly Crossing**, Yukon Territory, Canada
75 O 12 **Pelona Mountain**, New Mexico, U.S.A. ▲
147 D 21 **Peloponnese**, Greece
147 E 22 **Peloponnisos**, Greece ▣
159 Q 9 **Peloponnisos–Cretan Ridge**, Mediterranean Sea ◇
112 H 13 **Pelotas**, Brazil
112 H 10 **Pelotas**, Brazil
194 F 9 **Pemanggil**, Malaysia
192 I 10 **Pemangkat**, Indonesia
192 C 9 **Pematangsiantar**, Indonesia
219 N 6 **Pemba**, Zambia
219 U 4 **Pemba**, Mozambique
217 W 11 **Pemba Channel**, Tanzania
217 X 11 **Pemba Island**, Tanzania
230 G 12 **Pemberton**, Western Australia, Australia
83 G 21 **Pemberton**, British Columbia, Canada
67 N 2 **Pembina**, North Dakota, U.S.A.
64 G 10 **Pembine**, Wisconsin, U.S.A.
193 X 14 **Pembre**, Indonesia
126 K 10 **Pembroke**, United Kingdom
86 H 10 **Pembroke**, Ontario, Canada
127 O 9 **Pen y Fan**, United Kingdom ▲
127 R 1 **Pen-y-ghent**, United Kingdom ▲
131 N 1 **Pena Prieta**, Spain ▲
130 I 5 **Penafiel**, Portugal
131 N 4 **Peñafiel**, Spain
131 O 5 **Peñalara**, Spain ▲
108 L 11 **Penalva**, Brazil
112 I 5 **Penápolis**, Brazil
130 M 6 **Peñaranda de Bracamonte**, Spain
130 L 10 **Peñarroya-Pueblonuevo**, Spain
127 O 11 **Penarth**, United Kingdom
72 K 3 **Pend Oreille Lake**, Idaho, U.S.A.
76 J 9 **Pendleton**, Oregon, U.S.A.
217 N 11 **Penge**, Democratic Republic of Congo
189 Y 12 **P'enghu Tao**, Taiwan
187 G 19 **Penglai**, China
189 P 7 **Pengshui**, China
190 B 12 **Pengwa**, Myanmar
189 O 6 **Pengxi**, China
192 L 15 **Penida**, Indonesia
111 G 25 **Península Brecknock**, Chile ▶
91 V 15 **Península de Azuero**, Panama ▶
111 G 25 **Península de Brunswick**, Chile ▶
91 O 12 **Península de Nicoya**, Costa Rica ▶
91 R 14 **Península de Osa**, Costa Rica ▶
111 E 20 **Península de Taitao**, Chile ▶
111 H 26 **Península Hardy**, Chile ▶
111 I 25 **Península Mitre**, Argentina ▶
107 D 18 **Peninsula Paracas**, Peru ▶
104 L 1 **Peninsula Paraguaná**, Venezuela ▶
111 E 21 **Península Tres Montes**, Chile ▶
111 J 17 **Peninsula Valdés**, Argentina ▶
113 B 19 **Península Verde**, Argentina ▶
111 E 22 **Península Wharton**, Chile ▶
87 S 6 **Péninsule de Gaspé**, Québec, Canada ▶
85 P 5 **Pèninsule d'Ungava**, Québec, Canada ▶
131 U 7 **Peñíscola**, Spain
173 V 3 **Penjwin**, Iraq
127 R 6 **Penkridge**, United Kingdom
128 H 6 **Penmarch**, France
140 J 13 **Penne**, Italy
241 Q 14 **Pennell Coast**, Antarctica ◇
125 I 14 **Pennines**, United Kingdom
127 R 1 **Pennines Dales**, United Kingdom ◇
60 L 7 **Pennington Gap**, Virginia, U.S.A.
58 H 14 **Pennsville**, New Jersey, U.S.A.
58 E 12 **Pennsylvania**, U.S.A. ▣
231 N 10 **Penong**, South Australia, Australia
91 V 14 **Penonomé**, Panama
41 R 8 **Penrhyn Basin**, Pacific Ocean ◇
125 I 15 **Penrith**, United Kingdom
126 J 15 **Penryn**, United Kingdom
63 P 7 **Pensacola**, Florida, U.S.A.
241 N 6 **Pensacola Mountains**, Antarctica
107 M 18 **Pensamiento**, Bolivia
195 U 7 **Pensiangan**, Malaysia
235 R 10 **Pentecost**, Vanuatu
83 H 21 **Penticton**, British Columbia, Canada
126 K 14 **Pentire Point**, United Kingdom ▶
231 T 5 **Pentland**, Queensland, Australia
124 H 7 **Pentland Firth**, United Kingdom
181 E 20 **Penukonda**, India
127 O 8 **Penybont**, United Kingdom
127 N 10 **Penywaun**, United Kingdom
157 P 4 **Penza**, Russian Federation
126 I 15 **Penzance**, United Kingdom
137 J 25 **Penzberg**, Germany
157 P 4 **Penzenskaya Oblast'**, Russian Federation ▣
153 Y 9 **Penzhinskaya Guba**, Russian Federation
65 F 17 **Peoria**, Illinois, U.S.A.
232 K 9 **Pepepe**, New Zealand
194 B 7 **Perak**, Malaysia ▣
194 B 7 **Perak**, Malaysia
131 S 6 **Perales del Alfambra**, Spain
147 I 26 **Perama**, Greece
181 F 22 **Perambalur**, India
134 N 12 **Peranka**, Finland
87 U 6 **Percé**, Québec, Canada
139 X 4 **Perchtoldsdorf**, Austria
230 J 5 **Percival Lakes**, Western Australia, Australia
150 H 6 **Perechyn**, Ukraine
104 H 6 **Pereira**, Colombia
112 H 5 **Pereira Barreto**, Brazil
157 N 8 **Perelazovskiy**, Russian Federation
157 S 5 **Perelyub**, Russian Federation
150 J 4 **Peremyshlyany**, Ukraine
151 V 5 **Pereshchepyne**, Ukraine
154 J 14 **Pereslavl'-Zalesskiy**, Russian Federation
157 V 5 **Perevolotskiy**, Russian Federation
151 Q 4 **Pereyaslav-Khmel'nyts'kyy**, Ukraine
77 H 14 **Perez**, California, U.S.A.
139 T 4 **Perg**, Austria
113 C 15 **Pergamino**, Argentina
194 D 5 **Perhentian Besar**, Malaysia
135 K 15 **Perhonjoki**, Finland
85 S 10 **Péribonca**, Québec, Canada
110 I 6 **Perico**, Argentina
88 L 7 **Pericos**, Mexico
129 O 11 **Périgueux**, France
147 H 17 **Peristera**, Greece
111 G 20 **Perito Moreno**, Argentina
136 K 11 **Perleberg**, Germany
194 A 4 **Perlis**, Malaysia ▣
155 T 12 **Perm'**, Russian Federation
145 L 21 **Përmet**, Albania
155 T 12 **Permskaya Oblast'**, Russian Federation ▣
108 O 13 **Pernambuco**, Brazil ▣
43 J 14 **Pernambuco Abyssal Plain**, Atlantic Ocean ◇
43 I 14 **Pernambuco Seamounts**, Atlantic Ocean
146 F 9 **Pernik**, Bulgaria ▣
146 F 9 **Pernik**, Bulgaria
139 W 5 **Pernitz**, Austria
89 S 12 **Perote**, Mexico
129 R 15 **Perpignan**, France
126 J 14 **Perranporth**, United Kingdom
71 O 5 **Perrin**, Texas, U.S.A.
63 T 4 **Perry**, Georgia, U.S.A.
63 T 8 **Perry**, Florida, U.S.A.
69 N 9 **Perry**, Oklahoma, U.S.A.
69 Q 3 **Perry Lake**, Kansas, U.S.A.
70 L 1 **Perryton**, Texas, U.S.A.
107 L 18 **Perseverancia**, Bolivia
175 T 3 **Persian Gulf**, Asia
230 G 11 **Perth**, Western Australia, Australia
124 I 12 **Perth**, United Kingdom
86 I 11 **Perth**, Ontario, Canada
39 T 8 **Perth Basin**, Indian Ocean ◇
128 L 9 **Pertuis Breton**, France
128 L 9 **Pertuis d'Antioche**, France
107 E 15 **Peru**, South America ■
65 J 18 **Peru**, Indiana, U.S.A.
107 J 16 **Perú**, Bolivia
41 Y 9 **Peru Basin**, Pacific Ocean ◇
140 G 11 **Perugia**, Italy
112 D 12 **Perugorría**, Argentina
112 K 8 **Peruibe**, Brazil
41 Z 7 **Peru–Chile Trench**, Pacific Ocean ◇
133 D 21 **Peruwelz**, Belgium
151 Q 7 **Pervomays'k**, Ukraine
151 T 11 **Pervomays'ke**, Ukraine
156 M 3 **Pervomayskiy**, Russian Federation
157 W 5 **Pervomayskiy**, Russian Federation
151 V 5 **Pervomays'kyy**, Ukraine
153 Y 8 **Pervorechenskiy**, Russian Federation
152 I 10 **Pervoural'sk**, Russian Federation
140 H 10 **Pesaro**, Italy
140 J 13 **Pescara**, Italy
177 W 7 **Peshawar**, Pakistan
145 L 17 **Peshkopi**, Albania
146 H 10 **Peshtera**, Bulgaria
179 R 9 **Peski Muyunkum**, Kazakhstan ◇
179 V 8 **Peski Saryyesik-Atyrau**, Kazakhstan ◇
179 U 9 **Peski Taukum**, Kazakhstan ◇
90 L 7 **Pespire**, Honduras
154 H 12 **Pestovo**, Russian Federation
172 F 9 **Petah Tiqwa**, Israel
147 D 22 **Petalidi**, Greece
77 F 19 **Petaluma**, California, U.S.A.
133 K 26 **Pètange**, Luxembourg
89 P 13 **Petatlán**, Mexico
219 P 5 **Petauke**, Zambia
64 E 12 **Petenwell Lake**, Wisconsin, U.S.A.
240 H 8 **Peter I Island**, Norway
83 K 16 **Peter Pond Lake**, Saskatchewan, Canada
86 B 6 **Peterbell**, Ontario, Canada
231 P 11 **Peterborough**, South Australia, Australia
127 V 7 **Peterborough**, United Kingdom
86 F 12 **Peterborough**, Ontario, Canada
124 J 10 **Peterhead**, United Kingdom
45 P 12 **Petermann Bjerg**, Greenland ▲
61 T 6 **Petersburg**, Virginia, U.S.A.
79 X 11 **Petersburg**, Alaska, U.S.A.
127 T 12 **Petersfield**, United Kingdom
87 T 9 **Petitodiac**, New Brunswick, Canada
83 F 15 **Petitot**, British Columbia, Canada
89 Z 11 **Peto**, Mexico
64 K 10 **Petoskey**, Michigan, U.S.A.
172 G 12 **Petra**, Jordan
146 F 12 **Petrich**, Bulgaria
151 P 9 **Petrivka**, Ukraine
151 U 9 **Petrivka**, Ukraine
104 J 4 **Petrólea**, Colombia
108 N 13 **Petrolina**, Brazil
179 R 1 **Petropavlovsk**, Kazakhstan
153 Z 11 **Petropavlovsk-Kamchatskiy**, Russian Federation
112 N 6 **Petrópolis**, Brazil
150 H 11 **Petroșani**, Romania
157 P 4 **Petrovsk**, Russian Federation
153 Q 14 **Petrovsk-Zabaykal'skiy**, Russian Federation
154 G 9 **Petrozavodsk**, Russian Federation
150 M 7 **Petrușeni**, Moldova
151 U 6 **Petrykivka**, Ukraine
132 G 9 **Petten**, Netherlands
71 P 12 **Pettus**, Texas, U.S.A.
152 J 11 **Petukhovo**, Russian Federation
156 L 1 **Petushki**, Russian Federation
127 U 12 **Petworth**, United Kingdom
139 S 3 **Peuerbach**, Austria
192 C 8 **Peureula**, Indonesia
153 X 6 **Pevek**, Russian Federation
143 G 21 **Pezinok**, Slovakia
177 V 9 **Pezu**, Pakistan
137 J 23 **Pfaffenhofen an der Ilm**, Germany
137 F 22 **Pforzheim**, Germany
137 G 25 **Pfullendorf**, Germany
138 K 8 **Pfunds**, Austria
219 P 10 **Phalaborwa**, Republic of South Africa
177 X 8 **Phalia**, Pakistan
180 C 12 **Phalodi**, India
191 O 21 **Phan Rang**, Vietnam
191 O 21 **Phan Ri**, Vietnam
191 O 22 **Phan Thiêt**, Vietnam
191 K 15 **Phang Khon**, Thailand
191 F 24 **Phangnga**, Thailand
183 R 9 **Phaplu**, Nepal
191 H 25 **Phatthalung**, Thailand
191 H 14 **Phayao**, Thailand
63 R 4 **Phenix City**, Alabama, U.S.A.
191 H 20 **Phet Buri**, Thailand
191 I 16 **Phetchabun**, Thailand
191 H 17 **Phichit**, Thailand
58 I 14 **Philadelphia**, Pennsylvania, U.S.A.
79 R 4 **Philip Smith Mountains**, Alaska, U.S.A.
133 G 22 **Philippeville**, Belgium
61 P 3 **Philippi**, West Virginia, U.S.A.
40 K 6 **Philippine Basin**, Pacific Ocean ◇
196 L 11 **Philippine Sea**, Asia
40 J 5 **Philippine Trench**, Pacific Ocean ◇
197 F 20 **Philippines**, Asia ■
73 O 6 **Philipsburg**, Montana, U.S.A.
68 L 2 **Phillipsburg**, Kansas, U.S.A.
191 J 18 **Phimai**, Thailand
191 H 16 **Phitsanulok**, Thailand
191 L 21 **Phnom Penh**, Cambodia
191 K 21 **Phnum Aôral**, Cambodia ▲
191 J 20 **Phnum Tumpôr**, Cambodia ▲
236 K 4 **Phoenix**, Kiribati
74 I 12 **Phoenix**, Arizona, U.S.A.
236 H 4 **Phoenix Islands**, Kiribati
191 J 17 **Phon**, Thailand
190 K 11 **Phong Thô**, Vietnam
190 I 11 **Phôngsali**, Laos
191 J 14 **Phou Bia**, Laos ▲
191 L 15 **Phou Cô Pi**, Laos ▲
190 I 13 **Phou Houie Moc**, Laos ▲
190 J 13 **Phou San**, Laos ▲
191 M 17 **Phou Set**, Laos ▲

■ Country ▣ Internal administrative region: State/Province/Territory/Dependent territory · Capital city · Mountain range/Undersea ridge · ▲ Mountain peak/Volcano/Seamount · ◇ Geographic feature · ▶ Headland/Point/Cape/Peninsula · Desert · Island/Island group · Antarctic base · Ocean · Sea · Bay/Gulf/Channel/Strait · Lake · Salt pan/Dry/Intermittent lake · River

323

▣ Country   ▣ Internal administrative region: State/Province/Territory/Dependent territory   ▲ Capital city   ▲ Mountain range/Undersea ridge   ▲ Mountain peak/Volcano/Seamount   ◇ Geographic feature   ▶ Headland/Point/Cape/Peninsula   ⇄ Desert   ⇄ Island/Island group   Antarctic base   Ocean   Sea   ≈ Bay/Gulf/Channel/Strait   ↘ Lake   Salt pan/Dry/Intermittent lake   ↘ River

324

Pokaran – Presa Miguel Alemán

180 B 12 **Pokaran**, India
232 K 9 **Pokeno**, New Zealand
183 O 9 **Pokhara**, Nepal
157 T 3 **Pokhvistnevo**, Russian Federation
134 L 9 **Pokka**, Finland
217 O 6 **Poko**, Democratic Republic of Congo
153 T 11 **Pokrovsk**, Russian Federation
156 K 9 **Pokrovskoye**, Russian Federation
176 J 10 **Pol-e Fāsā**, Iran
177 U 6 **Pol-e Khomrī**, Afghanistan
143 J 20 **Polana**, Slovakia
142 F 11 **Poland**, Europe
142 G 9 **Polanów**, Poland
170 G 9 **Polatli**, Turkey
149 K 14 **Polatsk**, Belarus
45 R 9 **Pole Plain**, Arctic Ocean
193 N 12 **Polewali**, Indonesia
215 U 12 **Poli**, Cameroon
189 X 2 **Poli**, China
142 D 10 **Police**, Poland
147 K 17 **Polichnitos**, Greece
129 U 8 **Poligny**, France
196 H 11 **Polillo**, Philippines
196 H 10 **Polillo Islands**, Philippines
196 H 10 **Polillo Strait**, Philippines
170 G 15 **Polis**, Cyprus
151 O 2 **Polis'ke**, Ukraine
181 E 22 **Pollachi**, India
131 Y 7 **Pollença**, Spain
232 J 9 **Pollok**, New Zealand
151 W 8 **Polohy**, Ukraine
197 L 23 **Polomoloc**, Philippines
181 G 24 **Polonnaruwa**, Sri Lanka
150 M 4 **Polonne**, Ukraine
150 H 12 **Polovragi**, Romania
126 L 15 **Polperro**, United Kingdom
146 J 7 **Polski Trŭmbesh**, Bulgaria
72 M 4 **Polson**, Montana, U.S.A.
151 U 5 **Poltava**, Ukraine
148 H 7 **Põltsamaa**, Estonia
154 M 4 **Poluostrov Kanin**, Russian Federation
154 I 1 **Poluostrov Rybachiy**, Russian Federation
153 O 7 **Poluostrov Taymyr**, Russian Federation
152 M 7 **Poluostrov Yamal**, Russian Federation
148 I 8 **Põlva**, Estonia
147 I 23 **Polyaigos**, Greece
154 I 1 **Polyarnyy**, Russian Federation
155 T 5 **Polyarnyy Ural**, Russian Federation
147 G 14 **Polygyros**, Greece
146 E 13 **Polykastro**, Greece
236 F 3 **Polynesia**, Oceania
130 H 7 **Pombal**, Portugal
219 R 9 **Pomene**, Mozambique
142 F 9 **Pomerania**, Poland
65 N 20 **Pomeroy**, Ohio, U.S.A.
234 G 4 **Pomio**, Papua New Guinea
136 N 9 **Pommersche Bucht**, Germany
77 K 24 **Pomona**, California, U.S.A.
90 K 3 **Pomona**, Belize
146 N 9 **Pomorie**, Bulgaria
154 I 6 **Pomorskiy Bereg**, Russian Federation
155 O 3 **Pomorskiy Proliv**, Russian Federation
63 Y 13 **Pompano Beach**, Florida, U.S.A.
141 J 16 **Pompei**, Italy
69 N 8 **Ponca City**, Oklahoma, U.S.A.
93 U 8 **Ponce**, Puerto Rico
68 M 8 **Pond Creek**, Oklahoma, U.S.A.
181 H 19 **Pondicherry**, India
90 M 9 **Poneloya**, Nicaragua
130 K 2 **Ponferrada**, Spain
143 M 15 **Poniatowa**, Poland
157 V 3 **Ponomarevka**, Russian Federation
154 L 4 **Ponoy**, Russian Federation
197 L 17 **Ponson**, Philippines
133 F 21 **Pont-à-Celles**, Belgium
129 U 4 **Pont-à-Mousson**, France
140 A 7 **Pont-Canavese**, Italy
109 N 17 **Ponta da Baleia**, Brazil
219 R 10 **Ponta da Barra**, Mozambique
219 R 9 **Ponta da Barra Falsa**, Mozambique
218 F 2 **Ponta das Palmeirinhas**, Angola
218 F 4 **Ponta das Salinas**, Angola
42 O 2 **Ponta Delgada**, Azores
218 F 6 **Ponta do Enfião**, Angola
43 A 15 **Ponta do Sol**, Cape Verde
42 N 5 **Ponta do Sol**, Madeira
112 I 8 **Ponta Grossa**, Brazil
112 J 11 **Ponta Imbituba**, Brazil
109 H 18 **Ponta Porã**, Brazil
219 S 7 **Ponta Timbué**, Mozambique
129 V 8 **Pontarlier**, France
128 K 7 **Pontchâteau**, France
109 K 14 **Ponte Alta do Tocantins**, Brazil
130 H 4 **Ponte da Barca**, Portugal
130 H 4 **Ponte de Lima**, Portugal
130 H 8 **Ponte de Sor**, Portugal
130 H 3 **Ponteareas**, Spain
140 I 5 **Pontebba**, Italy
127 T 3 **Pontefract**, United Kingdom
109 F 15 **Pontes e Lacerda**, Brazil
130 H 2 **Pontevedra**, Spain
65 G 17 **Pontiac**, Illinois, U.S.A.
65 M 14 **Pontiac**, Michigan, U.S.A.
194 E 10 **Pontian Kechil**, Malaysia
192 I 11 **Pontianak**, Indonesia
128 J 5 **Pontivy**, France
129 P 4 **Pontoise**, France
84 I 8 **Ponton**, Manitoba, Canada
63 N 2 **Pontotoc**, Mississippi, U.S.A.
140 D 9 **Pontremoli**, Italy
131 V 4 **Ponts**, Spain
127 O 10 **Pontypool**, United Kingdom
127 O 10 **Pontypridd**, United Kingdom
91 V 15 **Ponuga**, Panama
149 J 15 **Ponya**, Belarus
231 O 11 **Poochera**, South Australia, Australia
216 H 9 **Pool**, Congo
127 R 13 **Poole**, United Kingdom
127 R 14 **Poole Bay**, United Kingdom
231 R 11 **Pooncarie**, New South Wales, Australia
232 K 6 **Poor Knights Islands**, New Zealand
151 V 6 **Popasne**, Ukraine
104 G 8 **Popayán**, Colombia
148 C 10 **Pope**, Latvia
133 A 19 **Poperinge**, Belgium
73 X 3 **Poplar**, Montana, U.S.A.
69 Y 7 **Poplar Bluff**, Missouri, U.S.A.
62 M 7 **Poplarville**, Mississippi, U.S.A.
89 R 12 **Popocatépetl**, Mexico
216 I 11 **Popokabaka**, Democratic Republic of Congo
140 I 13 **Popoli**, Italy
234 E 6 **Popondetta**, Papua New Guinea
146 L 7 **Popovo**, Bulgaria
143 K 19 **Poprad**, Slovakia
90 I 3 **Poptún**, Guatemala
233 M 14 **Porangahau**, New Zealand
109 J 15 **Porangatu**, Brazil
181 A 15 **Porbandar**, India
42 J 6 **Porcupine Abyssal Plain**, Atlantic Ocean
140 H 6 **Pordenone**, Italy
157 Q 2 **Poretskoye**, Russian Federation
234 B 4 **Porgera**, Papua New Guinea
135 J 18 **Pori**, Finland
233 K 16 **Porirua**, New Zealand
134 I 11 **Porjus**, Sweden
154 E 12 **Porkhov**, Russian Federation
127 N 12 **Porlock**, United Kingdom
231 R 2 **Pormpuraaw**, Queensland, Australia
128 K 7 **Pornic**, France
197 L 17 **Poro**, Philippines
153 X 13 **Poronaysk**, Russian Federation
147 G 21 **Poros**, Greece
149 F 19 **Porozava**, Belarus
241 W 13 **Porpoise Bay**, Antarctica
43 L 25 **Porpoise Point**, Ascension
138 C 6 **Porrentruy**, Switzerland
140 E 9 **Porreta Terme**, Italy
134 K 6 **Porsangen**, Norway
135 C 20 **Porsgrunn**, Norway
93 N 8 **Port-à-Piment**, Haiti
83 F 22 **Port Alberni**, British Columbia, Canada
219 N 15 **Port Alfred**, Republic of South Africa
76 G 6 **Port Angeles**, Washington, U.S.A.
92 L 8 **Port Antonio**, Jamaica
231 T 15 **Port Arthur**, Tasmania, Australia
71 U 10 **Port Arthur**, Texas, U.S.A.
93 O 7 **Port-au-Prince**, Haiti
231 P 10 **Port Augusta**, South Australia, Australia
218 K 15 **Port Beaufort**, Republic of South Africa
217 S 7 **Port Bell**, Uganda
181 N 22 **Port Blair**, India
71 T 10 **Port Bolivar**, Texas, U.S.A.
86 D 14 **Port Burwell**, Ontario, Canada
183 T 14 **Port Canning**, India
87 R 4 **Port-Cartier**, Québec, Canada
233 F 24 **Port Chalmers**, New Zealand
63 W 12 **Port Charlotte**, Florida, U.S.A.
65 M 16 **Port Clinton**, Ohio, U.S.A.
86 F 14 **Port Colborne**, Ontario, Canada
93 O 6 **Port-de-Paix**, Haiti
194 C 9 **Port Dickson**, Malaysia
231 T 3 **Port Douglas**, Queensland, Australia
219 P 13 **Port Edward**, Republic of South Africa
86 C 11 **Port Elgin**, Ontario, Canada
87 U 9 **Port Elgin**, New Brunswick, Canada
219 N 15 **Port Elizabeth**, Republic of South Africa
126 M 10 **Port Eynon**, United Kingdom
232 L 7 **Port Fitzroy**, New Zealand
216 D 8 **Port-Gentil**, Gabon
62 L 5 **Port Gibson**, Mississippi, U.S.A.
124 G 13 **Port Glasgow**, United Kingdom
79 P 10 **Port Graham**, Alaska, U.S.A.
215 R 14 **Port Harcourt**, Nigeria
83 E 21 **Port Hardy**, British Columbia, Canada
87 X 9 **Port Hawkesbury**, Nova Scotia, Canada
230 G 5 **Port Hedland**, Western Australia, Australia
79 N 12 **Port Heiden**, Alaska, U.S.A.
90 K 4 **Port Honduras**, Belize
64 M 12 **Port Hope**, Michigan, U.S.A.
85 X 8 **Port Hope Simpson**, Newfoundland and Labrador, Canada
92 M 3 **Port Howe**, The Bahamas
65 M 14 **Port Huron**, Michigan, U.S.A.
126 K 14 **Port Isaac Bay**, United Kingdom
71 Q 15 **Port Isabel**, Texas, U.S.A.
156 K 10 **Port Katon**, Russian Federation
71 R 12 **Port Lavaca**, Texas, U.S.A.
231 O 12 **Port Lincoln**, South Australia, Australia
214 F 11 **Port Loko**, Sierra Leone
38 B 12 **Port Louis**, Mauritius
231 V 10 **Port Macquarie**, New South Wales, Australia
38 E 7 **Port Mathurin**, Rodrigues Island
87 T 4 **Port-Menier**, Québec, Canada
234 E 6 **Port Moresby**, Papua New Guinea
93 N 3 **Port Nelson**, The Bahamas
218 I 13 **Port Nolloth**, Republic of South Africa
124 F 8 **Port of Ness**, United Kingdom
93 Y 14 **Port of Spain**, Trinidad and Tobago
76 E 13 **Port Orford**, Oregon, U.S.A.
233 B 26 **Port Pegasus**, New Zealand
231 P 11 **Port Pirie**, South Australia, Australia
61 P 15 **Port Royal**, South Carolina, U.S.A.
61 U 4 **Port Royal**, Virginia, U.S.A.
61 P 15 **Port Royal Sound**, South Carolina, U.S.A.
212 F 7 **Port Said**, Egypt
64 M 13 **Port Sanilac**, Michigan, U.S.A.
219 P 13 **Port Shepstone**, Republic of South Africa
63 R 8 **Port St Joe**, Florida, U.S.A.
219 O 14 **Port St Johns**, Republic of South Africa
111 K 24 **Port Stephens**, Falkland Islands
213 H 14 **Port Sudan**, Sudan
62 M 9 **Port Sulphur**, Louisiana, U.S.A.
127 N 10 **Port Talbot**, United Kingdom
129 R 15 **Port-Vendres**, France
235 Q 11 **Port Vila**, Vanuatu
232 K 9 **Port Waikato**, New Zealand
231 P 11 **Port Wakefield**, South Australia, Australia
194 A 6 **Port Weld**, Malaysia
231 S 14 **Port Welshpool**, Victoria, Australia
125 E 16 **Portadown**, United Kingdom
64 F 13 **Portage**, Wisconsin, U.S.A.
84 I 10 **Portage la Prairie**, Manitoba, Canada
130 I 9 **Portalegre**, Portugal
130 I 8 **Portalegre**, Portugal
75 U 11 **Portales**, New Mexico, U.S.A.
131 Y 3 **Portbou**, Spain
127 T 13 **Portchester**, United Kingdom
109 L 16 **Porteirinha**, Brazil
108 I 10 **Portel**, Brazil
130 I 10 **Portel**, Portugal
77 J 22 **Porterville**, California, U.S.A.
127 O 10 **Porth**, United Kingdom
127 N 11 **Porthcawl**, United Kingdom
126 M 5 **Porthmadog**, United Kingdom
147 B 20 **Porthmos Zakynthou**, Greece
131 W 9 **Portinatx**, Spain
127 P 10 **Portishead**, United Kingdom
231 Q 13 **Portland**, Victoria, Australia
59 P 7 **Portland**, Maine, U.S.A.
65 K 18 **Portland**, Indiana, U.S.A.
71 Q 13 **Portland**, Texas, U.S.A.
76 G 9 **Portland**, Oregon, U.S.A.
232 O 13 **Portland Island**, New Zealand
43 K 26 **Portland Point**, Ascension
125 D 18 **Portlaoise**, Republic of Ireland
130 H 5 **Porto**, Portugal
130 H 5 **Porto**, Portugal
108 I 11 **Porto Alegre**, Brazil
112 H 12 **Porto Alegre**, Brazil
218 G 3 **Porto Amboim**, Angola
109 H 15 **Porto Artur**, Brazil
112 J 10 **Porto Belo**, Brazil
108 I 10 **Pôrto de Moz**, Brazil
109 G 14 **Porto dos Gaúchos**, Brazil
141 I 23 **Porto Empedocle**, Italy
109 F 16 **Porto Esperidião**, Brazil
108 K 12 **Porto Franco**, Brazil
108 I 9 **Porto Grande**, Brazil
43 B 17 **Porto Inglês**, Cape Verde
109 G 16 **Porto Jofre**, Brazil
42 N 4 **Porto Moniz**, Madeira
109 G 18 **Porto Murtinho**, Brazil
43 A 15 **Porto Novo**, Cape Verde
215 O 13 **Porto-Novo**, Benin
140 I 11 **Porto Recanati**, Italy
43 B 17 **Porto Rincão**, Cape Verde
140 I 11 **Porto San Giorgio**, Italy
42 O 4 **Porto Santo**, Madeira
112 G 6 **Porto São José**, Brazil
109 N 16 **Porto Seguro**, Brazil
141 B 16 **Porto Torres**, Italy
129 Y 15 **Porto-Vecchio**, France
108 D 13 **Porto Velho**, Brazil
91 W 13 **Portobelo**, Panama
140 E 12 **Portoferraio**, Italy
77 H 17 **Portola**, California, U.S.A.
106 B 9 **Portoviejo**, Ecuador
124 F 10 **Portree**, United Kingdom
127 T 13 **Portsmouth**, United Kingdom
59 O 8 **Portsmouth**, New Hampshire, U.S.A.
61 V 7 **Portsmouth**, Virginia, U.S.A.
65 M 20 **Portsmouth**, Ohio, U.S.A.
93 Y 10 **Portsmouth**, Dominica
134 L 9 **Porttipahdan tekojärvi**, Finland
130 G 12 **Portugal**, Europe
104 M 3 **Portuguesa**, Venezuela
111 H 25 **Porvenir**, Chile
135 M 19 **Porvoo**, Finland
187 K 20 **Poryŏng**, South Korea
112 E 10 **Posadas**, Argentina
138 J 10 **Poschiavo**, Switzerland
154 J 12 **Poshekhon'ye**, Russian Federation
176 L 8 **Posht-e Badam**, Iran
134 M 11 **Posio**, Finland
193 O 11 **Poso**, Indonesia
171 R 7 **Posof**, Turkey
187 L 22 **Posŏng**, South Korea
106 A 10 **Posorja**, Ecuador
109 K 15 **Posse**, Brazil
71 O 5 **Possum Kingdom Lake**, Texas, U.S.A.
70 K 5 **Post**, Texas, U.S.A.
210 L 13 **Post Weygand**, Algeria
144 B 8 **Postojna**, Slovenia
67 U 10 **Postville**, Iowa, U.S.A.
144 G 13 **Posušje**, Bosnia and Herzegovina
197 I 17 **Potatan**, Philippines
69 R 11 **Poteau**, Oklahoma, U.S.A.
71 O 11 **Poteet**, Texas, U.S.A.
141 L 16 **Potenza**, Italy
131 N 1 **Potes**, Spain
171 Q 6 **P'ot'i**, Georgia
215 T 10 **Potiskum**, Nigeria
72 J 5 **Potlatch**, Idaho, U.S.A.
61 U 4 **Potomac**, Maryland, U.S.A.
69 X 5 **Potosi**, Missouri, U.S.A.
107 J 21 **Potosí**, Bolivia
107 J 23 **Potosí**, Bolivia
136 M 13 **Potsdam**, Germany
58 I 5 **Potsdam**, New York, U.S.A.
58 H 13 **Pottstown**, Pennsylvania, U.S.A.
58 G 12 **Pottsville**, Pennsylvania, U.S.A.
181 H 25 **Pottuvil**, Sri Lanka
177 W 8 **Potwar Plateau**, Pakistan
58 J 10 **Poughkeepsie**, New York, U.S.A.
232 M 13 **Poukawa**, New Zealand
127 P 2 **Poulton-le-Fylde**, United Kingdom
235 O 13 **Poum**, New Caledonia
64 G 11 **Pound**, Wisconsin, U.S.A.
112 L 6 **Pouso Alegre**, Brazil
191 K 20 **Poŭthĭsăt**, Cambodia
232 O 12 **Poverty Bay**, New Zealand
130 H 4 **Póvoa de Varzim**, Portugal
157 N 6 **Povorino**, Russian Federation
73 Y 6 **Powder**, Montana, U.S.A.
73 W 11 **Powder River**, Wyoming, U.S.A.
73 X 8 **Powder River Basin**, Wyoming, U.S.A.
73 T 9 **Powell**, Wyoming, U.S.A.
43 G 22 **Powell Basin**, Atlantic Ocean
83 F 21 **Powell River**, British Columbia, Canada
64 H 10 **Powers**, Michigan, U.S.A.
61 S 6 **Powhatan**, Virginia, U.S.A.
65 O 18 **Powhatan Point**, Ohio, U.S.A.
188 K 4 **Powo**, China
194 A 14 **Poyan Reservoir**, Singapore
189 V 7 **Poyang Hu**, China
185 U 11 **PoyangHu**, China
139 Y 2 **Poysdorf**, Austria
89 S 11 **Poza Rica**, Mexico
170 J 12 **Pozanti**, Turkey
144 M 10 **Požarevac**, Serbia and Montenegro
144 K 12 **Požega**, Serbia and Montenegro
142 G 12 **Poznań**, Poland
131 P 11 **Pozo Alcón**, Spain
109 G 19 **Pozo Colorado**, Paraguay
107 M 20 **Pozo del Tigre**, Bolivia
110 J 8 **Pozo Hondo**, Argentina
130 M 10 **Pozoblanco**, Spain
141 K 24 **Pozzallo**, Italy
192 F 12 **Prabumulih**, Indonesia
191 G 21 **Prachuap Khiri Khan**, Thailand
143 G 17 **Praděd**, Czech Republic
129 Q 15 **Prades**, France
109 N 16 **Prado**, Brazil
139 O 7 **Prägraten**, Austria
143 C 17 **Prague**, Czech Republic
43 B 17 **Praia**, Cape Verde
108 H 10 **Prainha**, Brazil
76 J 11 **Prairie City**, Oregon, U.S.A.
191 J 18 **Prakhon Chai**, Thailand
148 G 5 **Prangli**, Estonia
192 D 9 **Prapat**, Indonesia
191 J 18 **Prasat**, Thailand
38 B 9 **Praslin**, Seychelles
112 J 4 **Prata**, Brazil
140 F 10 **Prato**, Italy
68 L 6 **Pratt**, Kansas, U.S.A.
41 S 2 **Pratt Seamount**, Pacific Ocean
63 Q 4 **Prattville**, Alabama, U.S.A.
127 N 15 **Prawle Point**, United Kingdom
192 L 15 **Praya**, Indonesia
149 J 14 **Prazaroki**, Belarus
139 S 7 **Predlitz**, Austria
139 T 3 **Pregarten**, Austria
148 I 12 **Preiļi**, Latvia
71 P 14 **Premont**, Texas, U.S.A.
64 E 10 **Prentice**, Wisconsin, U.S.A.
136 M 11 **Prenzlau**, Germany
191 B 18 **Preparis Island**, Myanmar
191 B 17 **Preparis North Channel**, Myanmar
191 B 18 **Preparis South Channel**, Myanmar
143 G 18 **Přerov**, Czech Republic
89 W 14 **Presa de la Angostura**, Mexico
89 P 12 **Presa del Infiernillo**, Mexico
89 T 13 **Presa Miguel Alemán**, Mexico

Country · Internal administrative region: State/Province/Territory/Dependent territory · Capital city · Mountain range/Undersea ridge · Mountain peak/Volcano/Seamount · Geographic feature · Headland/Point/Cape/Peninsula · Desert · Island/Island group · Antarctic base · Ocean · Sea · Bay/Gulf/Channel/Strait · Lake · Salt pan/Dry/Intermittent lake · River

Presa Nezahualcóyotl – Punto Fijo

89 V 13 **Presa Nezahualcóyotl**, Mexico
74 I 11 **Prescott**, Arizona, U.S.A.
86 J 11 **Prescott**, Ontario, Canada
233 A 25 **Preservation Inlet**, New Zealand
145 N 16 **Preševo**, Serbia and Montenegro
112 B 10 **Presidencia Roque Sáenz Peña**, Argentina
41 S 10 **President Thiers Seamount**, Pacific Ocean
112 C 10 **Presidente de la Plaza**, Argentina
108 L 11 **Presidente Dutra**, Brazil
112 H 6 **Presidente Epitácio**, Brazil
112 I 6 **Presidente Prudente**, Brazil
112 H 6 **Presidente Venceslau**, Brazil
70 H 10 **Presidio**, Texas, U.S.A.
179 Q 2 **Presnovka**, Kazakhstan
143 L 19 **Prešov**, Slovakia
59 R 1 **Presque Isle**, Maine, U.S.A.
127 O 4 **Prestatyn**, United Kingdom
127 P 2 **Preston**, United Kingdom
67 U 9 **Preston**, Minnesota, U.S.A.
69 T 6 **Preston**, Missouri, U.S.A.
73 P 13 **Preston**, Idaho, U.S.A.
60 K 6 **Prestonburg**, Kentucky, U.S.A.
219 O 10 **Pretoria**, Republic of South Africa
147 B 17 **Preveza**, Greece
78 J 11 **Pribilof Islands**, Alaska, U.S.A.
144 J 13 **Priboj**, Serbia and Montenegro
143 C 18 **Příbram**, Czech Republic
74 L 4 **Price**, Utah, U.S.A.
149 E 16 **Prienai**, Lithuania
218 L 13 **Prieska**, Republic of South Africa
72 K 2 **Priest Lake**, Idaho, U.S.A.
72 J 3 **Priest River**, Idaho, U.S.A.
143 I 20 **Prievidza**, Slovakia
144 F 10 **Prijedor**, Bosnia and Herzegovina
144 J 13 **Prijepolje**, Serbia and Montenegro
146 D 12 **Prilep**, Macedonia (F.Y.R.O.M.)
149 A 15 **Primorsk**, Russian Federation
154 E 10 **Primorsk**, Russian Federation
146 N 10 **Primorsko**, Bulgaria
156 J 11 **Primorsko-Akhtarsk**, Russian Federation
83 K 17 **Primrose Lake**, Saskatchewan, Canada
218 L 15 **Prince Albert**, Republic of South Africa
83 M 17 **Prince Albert**, Saskatchewan, Canada
82 G 6 **Prince Albert Peninsula**, Northwest Territories, Canada
82 F 7 **Prince Albert Sound**, Northwest Territories, Canada
85 P 1 **Prince Charles Island**, Nunavut, Canada
241 V 5 **Prince Charles Mountains**, Antarctica
38 H 12 **Prince Edward Fracture Zone**, Indian Ocean
87 V 8 **Prince Edward Island**, Prince Edward Island, Canada
87 V 8 **Prince Edward Island**, Canada
38 I 11 **Prince Edward Islands**, Republic of South Africa
61 V 4 **Prince Frederick**, Maryland, U.S.A.
61 U 6 **Prince George**, Virginia, U.S.A.
83 F 18 **Prince George**, British Columbia, Canada
241 U 2 **Prince Harald Coast**, Antarctica
231 R 1 **Prince of Wales Island**, Queensland, Australia
79 X 12 **Prince of Wales Island**, Alaska, U.S.A.
82 J 5 **Prince of Wales Island**, Nunavut, Canada
82 F 6 **Prince of Wales Strait**, Northwest Territories, Canada
80 M 3 **Prince Patrick Island**, Northwest Territories, Canada
81 P 5 **Prince Regent Inlet**, Nunavut, Canada
83 C 18 **Prince Rupert**, British Columbia, Canada
79 S 9 **Prince William Sound**, Alaska, U.S.A.
61 W 4 **Princess Anne**, Maryland, U.S.A.
241 P 2 **Princess Astrid Coast**, Antarctica
231 S 2 **Princess Charlotte Bay**, Queensland, Australia
241 V 7 **Princess Elizabeth Land**, Antarctica
241 R 2 **Princess Ragnhild Coast**, Antarctica
83 D 19 **Princess Royal Island**, British Columbia, Canada
58 I 13 **Princeton**, New Jersey, U.S.A.
60 D 6 **Princeton**, Kentucky, U.S.A.
61 O 6 **Princeton**, West Virginia, U.S.A.
65 F 16 **Princeton**, Illinois, U.S.A.
65 H 21 **Princeton**, Indiana, U.S.A.
69 T 1 **Princeton**, Missouri, U.S.A.
76 J 12 **Princeton**, Oregon, U.S.A.
216 C 7 **Príncipe**, São Tomé and Príncipe
76 H 11 **Prineville**, Oregon, U.S.A.
133 G 15 **Prinsenbeek**, Netherlands
91 R 7 **Prinzapolca**, Nicaragua
91 P 7 **Prinzapolka**, Nicaragua
154 F 9 **Priozersk**, Russian Federation
149 L 22 **Pripet**, Belarus
149 H 21 **Pripet Marshes**, Belarus
145 M 15 **Priština**, Serbia and Montenegro
136 K 11 **Pritzwalk**, Germany
129 T 12 **Privas**, France
157 P 7 **Privolzhskaya Vozvyshennost'**, Russian Federation
157 R 4 **Privolzh'ye**, Russian Federation
157 O 11 **Priyutnoye**, Russian Federation
145 L 16 **Prizren**, Serbia and Montenegro
141 I 22 **Prizzi**, Italy
144 G 10 **Prnjavor**, Bosnia and Herzegovina
192 K 14 **Probolinggo**, Indonesia
71 O 7 **Proctor**, Texas, U.S.A.
71 O 7 **Proctor Lake**, Texas, U.S.A.
105 W 6 **Professor van Blommestein Meer**, Suriname
133 G 21 **Profondeville**, Belgium
89 Y 10 **Progreso**, Mexico
90 L 5 **Progreso**, Honduras
77 G 15 **Project City**, California, U.S.A.
157 O 13 **Prokhladnyy**, Russian Federation
145 J 16 **Prokletije**, Albania
145 N 14 **Prokuplje**, Serbia and Montenegro
153 T 7 **Proliv Dmitriya Lapteva**, Russian Federation
152 K 6 **Proliv Karskiye Vorota**, Russian Federation
153 X 5 **Proliv Longa**, Russian Federation
45 V 7 **Proliv Vil'kitskogo**, Arctic Ocean
153 P 5 **Proliv Vil'kitskogo**, Russian Federation
141 L 14 **Promontorio del Gargano**, Italy
149 N 18 **Pronya**, Belarus
231 T 5 **Proserpine**, Queensland, Australia
142 H 13 **Prosna**, Poland
76 G 13 **Prospect**, Oregon, U.S.A.
197 M 20 **Prosperidad**, Philippines
43 N 25 **Prosperous Bay**, St Helena
143 G 18 **Prostějov**, Czech Republic
43 N 18 **Protea Seamount**, Atlantic Ocean/Indian Ocean
146 M 8 **Provadiya**, Bulgaria
129 U 14 **Provence**, France
129 V 13 **Provence-Alpes-Côte-d'Azur**, France
59 N 10 **Providence**, Rhode Island, U.S.A.
60 E 6 **Providence**, Kentucky, U.S.A.
153 Z 6 **Provideniya**, Russian Federation
59 P 10 **Provincetown**, Massachusetts, U.S.A.
129 R 5 **Provins**, France
74 K 3 **Provo**, Utah, U.S.A.
112 H 8 **Prudentópolis**, Brazil
79 R 3 **Prudhoe Bay**, Alaska, U.S.A.
143 H 17 **Prudnik**, Poland
137 B 19 **Prüm**, Germany
150 I 12 **Prundeni**, Romania
142 K 13 **Pruszków**, Poland
150 L 7 **Prut**, Moldova
138 L 7 **Prutz**, Austria
149 F 20 **Pruzhany**, Belarus
151 V 9 **Pryazovs'ke**, Ukraine
241 X 6 **Prydz Bay**, Antarctica
151 R 3 **Pryluky**, Ukraine
151 W 9 **Prymors'k**, Ukraine
151 O 11 **Prymors'ke**, Ukraine
151 V 11 **Prymors'kyy**, Ukraine
151 P 2 **Pryp"yat**, Ukraine
142 L 11 **Przasnysz**, Poland
143 J 15 **Przedbórz**, Poland
143 N 17 **Przemyśl**, Poland
143 N 17 **Przeworsk**, Poland
147 G 19 **Psachna**, Greece
147 J 18 **Psara**, Greece
156 L 13 **Psebay**, Russian Federation
154 D 12 **Pskov**, Russian Federation
154 D 13 **Pskovskaya Oblast'**, Russian Federation
179 N 4 **Pskovskiy**, Kazakhstan
151 T 3 **Ps'ol**, Ukraine
147 D 14 **Ptolemaïda**, Greece
159 P 9 **Ptolemy Trench**, Mediterranean Sea
149 K 21 **Ptsich**, Belarus
149 K 21 **Ptsich**, Belarus
144 D 6 **Ptuj**, Slovenia
191 H 14 **Pua**, Thailand
189 N 10 **Pu'an**, China
106 G 10 **Puca Urco**, Peru
107 E 14 **Pucallpa**, Peru
189 Q 3 **Pucheng**, China
189 X 8 **Pucheng**, China
154 L 14 **Puchezh**, Russian Federation
187 L 19 **Puch'ŏn**, South Korea
197 H 15 **Pucio Point**, Philippines
150 J 12 **Pucioasa**, Romania
111 F 15 **Pucón**, Chile
134 M 12 **Pudasjärvi**, Finland
127 Q 13 **Puddletown**, United Kingdom
154 I 9 **Pudozh**, Russian Federation
89 R 12 **Puebla**, Mexico
89 S 13 **Puebla**, Mexico
130 K 3 **Puebla de Sanabria**, Spain
75 S 6 **Pueblo**, Colorado, U.S.A.
131 Q 11 **Pueblo de Don Fadrique**, Spain
77 K 14 **Pueblo Mountain**, Oregon, U.S.A.
91 N 7 **Pueblo Nuevo**, Nicaragua
91 N 5 **Pueblo Viejo**, Honduras
111 I 15 **Puelches**, Argentina
111 H 14 **Puelén**, Argentina
188 K 12 **Pu'er**, China
88 G 3 **Puertecitos**, Mexico
111 F 20 **Puerto Aisen**, Chile
104 L 11 **Puerto Alfonso**, Colombia
89 T 15 **Puerto Ángel**, Mexico
91 S 14 **Puerto Armuelles**, Panama
104 H 9 **Puerto Asís**, Colombia
105 N 6 **Puerto Ayacucho**, Venezuela
107 B 19 **Puerto Ayora**, Ecuador
107 C 19 **Puerto Baquerizo Moreno**, Ecuador
90 K 4 **Puerto Barrios**, Guatemala
112 C 10 **Puerto Bermejo**, Argentina
104 I 5 **Puerto Berrío**, Colombia
105 N 2 **Puerto Cabello**, Venezuela
91 R 7 **Puerto Cabezas**, Nicaragua
91 S 5 **Puerto Cabo Gracias á Dios**, Nicaragua
105 N 6 **Puerto Carreño**, Colombia
107 J 16 **Puerto Cavinas**, Bolivia
111 F 19 **Puerto Cisnes**, Chile
111 H 23 **Puerto Coig**, Argentina
90 K 4 **Puerto Cortés**, Honduras
91 R 13 **Puerto Cortés**, Costa Rica
88 H 3 **Puerto de Lobos**, Mexico
42 O 11 **Puerto del Rosario**, Canary Islands
89 S 14 **Puerto Escondido**, Mexico
106 D 9 **Puerto Francisco de Orellana**, Ecuador
107 K 16 **Puerto Génova**, Bolivia
107 K 20 **Puerto Grether**, Bolivia
111 I 26 **Puerto Harberton**, Argentina
107 I 17 **Puerto Heath**, Bolivia
105 N 7 **Puerto Inírida**, Colombia
110 K 5 **Puerto Irigoyen**, Argentina
91 O 12 **Puerto Jesus**, Costa Rica
104 I 10 **Puerto Leguizamo**, Colombia
91 Q 5 **Puerto Lempira**, Honduras
88 H 4 **Puerto Libertad**, Mexico
111 I 17 **Puerto Lobos**, Argentina
104 K 1 **Puerto Lopez**, Colombia
106 A 9 **Puerto López**, Ecuador
89 W 15 **Puerto Madero**, Mexico
111 I 18 **Puerto Madryn**, Argentina
107 H 16 **Puerto Maldonado**, Peru
106 A 11 **Puerto Máncora**, Peru
111 F 17 **Puerto Montt**, Chile
90 L 8 **Puerto Morazáno**, Nicaragua
107 B 14 **Puerto Morin**, Peru
111 F 24 **Puerto Natáles**, Chile
104 L 6 **Puerto Nuevo**, Colombia
91 Z 14 **Puerto Obaldía**, Panama
92 L 5 **Puerto Padre**, Cuba
105 N 5 **Puerto Páez**, Venezuela
106 D 11 **Puerto Pardo**, Peru
88 G 2 **Puerto Peñasco**, Mexico
104 J 10 **Puerto Pizarro**, Colombia
93 Q 6 **Puerto Plata**, Dominican Republic
107 F 15 **Puerto Portillo**, Peru
197 D 18 **Puerto Princesa**, Philippines
91 Q 13 **Puerto Quepos**, Costa Rica
112 F 10 **Puerto Rico**, Argentina
93 T 8 **Puerto Rico**, U.S.A.
42 D 11 **Puerto Rico Trench**, Atlantic Ocean
111 H 22 **Puerto San Julián**, Argentina
90 M 9 **Puerto Sandino**, Nicaragua
111 H 22 **Puerto Santa Cruz**, Argentina
109 G 18 **Puerto Sastre**, Paraguay
107 K 17 **Puerto Siles**, Bolivia
106 H 10 **Puerto Socorro**, Peru
107 O 21 **Puerto Suárez**, Bolivia
88 M 11 **Puerto Vallarta**, Mexico
107 E 15 **Puerto Victoria**, Peru
91 S 12 **Puerto Viejo**, Costa Rica
107 A 19 **Puerto Villamil**, Ecuador
111 I 19 **Puerto Visser**, Argentina
111 H 25 **Puerto Yartou**, Chile
131 N 10 **Puertollano**, Spain
157 R 5 **Pugachev**, Russian Federation
188 L 9 **Puge**, China
76 G 6 **Puget Sound**, Washington, U.S.A.
141 M 15 **Puglia**, Italy
87 V 9 **Pugwash**, Nova Scotia, Canada
135 O 16 **Puhos**, Finland
131 W 3 **Puigcerdà**, Spain
129 P 15 **Puigmal**, France
131 X 3 **Puigmal d'Err**, Spain
214 G 12 **Pujehun**, Sierra Leone
236 M 7 **Pukapuka**, Cook Islands
84 H 7 **Pukatawagan**, Manitoba, Canada
187 M 16 **Pukch'ŏng**, North Korea
145 K 16 **Pukë**, Albania
232 K 9 **Pukekohe**, New Zealand
233 E 19 **Pukekura**, New Zealand
187 L 16 **Puksubaek-san**, North Korea
141 C 19 **Pula**, Italy
107 J 22 **Pulacayo**, Bolivia
193 N 10 **Pulai**, Indonesia
197 J 15 **Pulanduta Point**, Philippines
192 L 12 **Pulangpisau**, Indonesia
237 N 15 **Pulap**, Federated States of Micronesia
58 G 7 **Pulaski**, New York, U.S.A.
60 E 10 **Pulaski**, Tennessee, U.S.A.
61 O 7 **Pulaski**, Virginia, U.S.A.
193 X 14 **Pulau Dolak**, Indonesia
195 Y 7 **Pulau Gaya**, Malaysia
193 N 9 **Pulau Maratua**, Indonesia
237 N 15 **Pulawat**, Federated States of Micronesia
143 M 14 **Puławy**, Poland
127 V 13 **Pulborough**, United Kingdom
135 M 14 **Pulkkila**, Finland
76 L 8 **Pullman**, Washington, U.S.A.
236 I 15 **Pulo Anna**, Palau
142 L 12 **Pułtusk**, Poland
184 I 7 **Pulu**, China
39 Z 2 **Pulu Capelok**, Cocos Islands
39 Z 2 **Pulu Pandang**, Cocos Islands
171 P 10 **Pülümür**, Turkey
237 N 15 **Pulusuk**, Federated States of Micronesia
110 H 6 **Puna de Atacama**, Argentina
233 F 18 **Punakaiki**, New Zealand
183 U 9 **Punakha**, Bhutan
107 J 20 **Punata**, Bolivia
193 W 12 **Puncak Jaya**, Indonesia
193 Y 13 **Puncak Mandala**, Indonesia
193 X 13 **Puncak Trikora**, Indonesia
182 I 7 **Pundri**, India
181 C 17 **Pune**, India
194 B 13 **Punggol**, Singapore
187 M 15 **P'ungsan**, North Korea
217 O 8 **Punia**, Democratic Republic of Congo
177 X 10 **Punjab**, Pakistan
182 H 6 **Punjab**, India
107 H 19 **Puno**, Peru
107 G 18 **Puno**, Peru
88 G 6 **Punta Abreojos**, Mexico
141 N 19 **Punta Alice**, Italy
89 Z 11 **Punta Allen**, Mexico
130 L 15 **Punta Almina**, Spain
113 B 19 **Punta Alta**, Argentina
88 J 9 **Punta Arena**, Mexico
111 G 25 **Punta Arenas**, Chile
107 E 19 **Punta Atico**, Peru
41 Y 5 **Punta Baja**, Easter Island
88 F 3 **Punta Baja**, Mexico
113 B 21 **Punta Bermeja**, Argentina
91 S 15 **Punta Burica**, Costa Rica
91 S 12 **Punta Cahuita**, Costa Rica
104 H 2 **Punta Canoas**, Colombia
141 B 15 **Punta Caprara**, Italy
91 N 4 **Punta Caxinas**, Honduras
104 F 7 **Punta Chirambirá**, Colombia
90 L 8 **Punta Cosigüina**, Nicaragua
41 Z 5 **Punta Cuidado**, Easter Island
110 F 12 **Punta Curaumilla**, Chile
111 H 24 **Punta de Arenas**, Argentina
131 P 13 **Punta de las Entinas**, Spain
88 M 11 **Punta de Mita**, Mexico
91 R 9 **Punta de Perlas**, Nicaragua
93 N 6 **Punta de Quemado**, Cuba
91 R 10 **Punta del Mono**, Nicaragua
113 G 15 **Punta del Palmar**, Uruguay
111 J 18 **Punta Delgada**, Argentina
111 H 22 **Punta Desengaño**, Argentina
88 F 5 **Punta Eugenia**, Mexico
106 A 8 **Punta Galera**, Ecuador
111 E 16 **Punta Galera**, Chile
104 K 1 **Punta Gallinas**, Colombia
91 Y 15 **Punta Garachiné**, Panama
110 F 2 **Punta Gorda**, Chile
90 J 4 **Punta Gorda**, Belize
91 R 10 **Punta Gorda**, Nicaragua
91 R 6 **Punta Gorda**, Nicaragua
91 O 12 **Punta Guiones**, Costa Rica
89 Z 11 **Punta Herrero**, Mexico
110 F 5 **Punta Jorjino**, Chile
111 E 14 **Punta Lavapié**, Chile
110 F 10 **Punta Lengua de Vaca**, Chile
111 H 23 **Punta León**, Argentina
91 W 15 **Punta Mala**, Panama
104 E 9 **Punta Manglares**, Colombia
91 X 12 **Punta Manzanillo**, Panama
91 V 15 **Punta Mariato**, Panama
130 L 14 **Punta Marroquí**, Spain
111 I 21 **Punta Medanosa**, Argentina
106 A 12 **Punta Negro**, Peru
111 J 18 **Punta Ninfas**, Argentina
111 J 17 **Punta Norte**, Argentina
111 J 17 **Punta Norte**, Argentina
106 A 11 **Punta Pariñas**, Peru
91 Q 4 **Punta Patuca**, Honduras
88 G 4 **Punta Prieta**, Mexico
113 B 21 **Punta Rasa**, Argentina
104 F 8 **Punta Reyes**, Colombia
89 U 12 **Punta Roca Partida**, Mexico
88 J 6 **Punta Rosa**, Mexico
41 Z 4 **Punta Rosalia**, Easter Island
90 L 4 **Punta Sal**, Honduras
107 C 16 **Punta Salinasó Lachay**, Peru
88 G 6 **Punta San Hipólito**, Mexico
41 Y 4 **Punta San Juan**, Easter Island
90 J 8 **Punta San Juan**, El Salvador
91 Q 14 **Punta San Pedro**, Costa Rica
106 A 10 **Punta Santa Elena**, Ecuador
107 D 18 **Punta Santa Maria**, Peru
113 E 17 **Punta Sur**, Argentina
89 N 13 **Punta Tejupan**, Mexico
110 F 12 **Punta Topocalma**, Chile
91 O 12 **Puntarenas**, Costa Rica
104 L 2 **Punto Fijo**, Venezuela

Country · Internal administrative region: State/Province/Territory/Dependent territory · Capital city · Mountain range/Undersea ridge · Mountain peak/Volcano/Seamount · Geographic feature · Headland/Point/Cape/Peninsula · Desert · Island/Island group · Antarctic base · Ocean · Sea · Bay/Gulf/Channel/Strait · Lake · Salt pan/Dry/Intermittent lake · River

Country ▣ Internal administrative region: State/Province/Territory/Dependent territory ▪ Capital city ▲▲ Mountain range/ Undersea ridge ▲ Mountain peak/ Volcano/Seamount ◇ Geographic feature ▶ Headland/Point/ Cape/Peninsula ☱ Desert ☱ Island/Island group ☱ Antarctic base ☱ Ocean ☱ Sea ≈ Bay/Gulf/Channel/Strait ↘ Lake ☱ Salt pan/Dry/ Intermittent lake ↘ River

327

126 J 9 **Ramsey Island**, United Kingdom 🏝
86 C 8 **Ramsey Lake**, Ontario, Canada 💧
127 Z 11 **Ramsgate**, United Kingdom
176 G 9 **Rāmshīr**, Iran
135 G 17 **Ramsjö**, Sweden
234 C 4 **Ramu**, Papua New Guinea 〰
183 W 15 **Ramu**, Bangladesh
180 D 13 **Rana Pratap Sagar**, India 💧
110 G 12 **Rancagua**, Chile
133 F 23 **Rance**, Belgium
181 I 14 **Ranchi**, India
89 O 9 **Rancho Grande**, Mexico
141 K 22 **Randazzo**, Italy
135 C 24 **Randers**, Denmark
134 H 11 **Randijaure**, Sweden 💧
214 F 8 **Ranérou**, Senegal
233 E 23 **Ranfurly**, New Zealand
191 I 26 **Rangae**, Thailand
183 V 14 **Rangamati**, Bangladesh
183 W 10 **Rangapara North**, India
232 I 5 **Rangaunu Bay**, New Zealand ≋
59 O 5 **Rangeley**, Maine, U.S.A.
75 N 3 **Rangely**, Colorado, U.S.A.
71 O 6 **Ranger**, Texas, U.S.A.
86 B 8 **Ranger**, Ontario, Canada
183 V 10 **Rangia**, India
232 L 12 **Rangipo**, New Zealand
232 K 9 **Rangiriri**, New Zealand
232 M 12 **Rangitaiki**, New Zealand
233 F 21 **Rangitata**, New Zealand
232 L 13 **Rangitikei**, New Zealand 〰
191 E 16 **Rangoon**, Myanmar 🏛
183 T 11 **Rangpur**, Bangladesh
90 K 3 **Ranguana Cay**, Belize 🏝
181 D 20 **Ranibennur**, India
183 R 13 **Raniganj**, India
70 K 8 **Rankin**, Texas, U.S.A.
84 L 4 **Rankin Inlet**, Nunavut, Canada ≋
181 A 14 **Rann of Kachchh**, India ◇
157 U 5 **Ranneye**, Russian Federation
219 W 9 **Ranohira**, Madgascar
191 F 23 **Ranong**, Thailand
234 J 6 **Ranongga**, Solomon Islands 🏝
191 H 25 **Ranot**, Thailand
193 V 11 **Ransiki**, Indonesia
192 L 12 **Rantau**, Indonesia
65 G 18 **Rantoul**, Illinois, U.S.A.
134 M 12 **Ranua**, Finland
173 U 2 **Rānya**, Iraq
186 O 9 **Raohe**, China
140 C 9 **Rapallo**, Italy
181 A 14 **Rapar**, India
66 G 9 **Rapid City**, South Dakota, U.S.A.
64 H 9 **Rapid River**, Michigan, U.S.A.
148 I 8 **Räpina**, Estonia
148 G 6 **Rapla**, Estonia
138 H 7 **Rapperswil**, Switzerland
196 K 13 **Rapurapu**, Philippines 🏝
58 I 7 **Raquette Lake**, New York, U.S.A. 💧
237 O 11 **Rarotonga**, Cook Islands 🏝
212 F 9 **Râs**, Egypt
174 K 6 **Rās Abū Madd**, Saudi Arabia ▶
212 H 13 **Rās Abu Shagara**, Sudan ▶
175 Z 9 **Rās ad Daqm**, Oman
173 N 1 **Ra's al 'Ayn**, Syria
172 H 3 **Rās al Basīṭ**, Syria ▶
175 Z 7 **Rās al Ḩadd**, Oman
175 Z 7 **Rās al Ḩadd**, Oman ▶
159 Q 12 **Rās al Hilāl**, Mediterranean Sea ▶
175 S 13 **Rās al Kalb**, Yemen ▶
175 X 5 **Ras al Khaimah**, United Arab Emirates
175 Z 10 **Rās al Madrakah**, Oman ▶
175 S 3 **Rās al Mish'āb**, Saudi Arabia
211 Y 7 **Rās al Muraysah**, Libya ▶
212 B 7 **Rās al Muraysah**, Egypt ▶
159 R 12 **Rās al Tīn**, Mediterranean Sea ▶
159 U 12 **Rās 'Alam el Rûm**, Mediterranean Sea ▶
172 G 12 **Rās an Naqb**, Jordan
174 I 3 **Rās ash Shaykh Ḩumayd**, Saudi Arabia
211 X 7 **Rās at Tīn**, Libya ▶
175 S 4 **Rās az Zawr**, Saudi Arabia ▶
175 O 15 **Rās Bāb al Mandab**, Yemen ▶
212 G 12 **Râs Banâs**, Egypt ▶
174 K 6 **Rās Barīdī**, Saudi Arabia ▶
213 O 22 **Rās Cabaad**, Somalia ▶
213 O 18 **Rās Caluula**, Somalia ▶
213 O 18 **Rās Caseyr**, Somalia ▶
213 I 18 **Rās Dashen**, Ethiopia ▲
213 O 20 **Rās Durdura**, Somalia ▶
176 G 10 **Rās-e Barkan**, Iran ▶
176 H 11 **Rās-e Halīleh**, Iran ▶
177 N 14 **Rās-e Meydanī**, Iran ▶
212 D 7 **Râs el Kanâyis**, Egypt ▶
159 U 12 **Rās el Kenâyis**, Mediterranean Sea ▶
175 V 12 **Rās Fartak**, Yemen ▶
213 O 20 **Rās Gabbac**, Somalia ▶
212 H 13 **Rās Hardârba**, Sudan ▶
174 L 8 **Rās Ḩāṭibah**, Saudi Arabia ▶
213 O 21 **Rās Ilig**, Somalia ▶
175 O 13 **Rās 'Īsá**, Yemen ▶
177 Q 14 **Ras Jaddi**, Pakistan ▶
176 M 14 **Rās Jagīn**, Iran ▶
158 K 10 **Rās Kaboudia**, Mediterranean Sea ▶
174 K 5 **Rās Karkūmā**, Saudi Arabia ▶
213 I 15 **Rās Kasar**, Sudan/Eritrea ▶
213 M 19 **Rās Khansiir**, Somalia ▶
213 O 20 **Rās Macbar**, Somalia ▶
175 X 11 **Rās Mirbāţ**, Oman ▶
175 X 14 **Rās Momi**, Yemen ▶
177 T 15 **Ras Muari**, Pakistan ▶
212 G 10 **Râs Muhammad**, Egypt ▶
175 X 11 **Rās Naws**, Oman ▶
210 A 14 **Râs Nouâdhibou**, Western Sahara ▶
214 E 5 **Râs Nouâdhibou**, Mauritania ▶
177 P 14 **Ras Nuh**, Pakistan ▶
177 R 14 **Ras Ormara**, Pakistan ▶
176 H 11 **Rās osh Shaţţ**, Iran ▶
175 W 11 **Rās Sājir**, Oman ▶
175 Y 10 **Rās Şawqirah**, Oman ▶
217 X 9 **Ras Shaka**, Kenya ▶
175 Y 10 **Rās Sharbithāt**, Oman ▶
175 V 14 **Rās Shu'ab**, Yemen ▶
175 Z 9 **Rās Şirāb**, Oman
213 N 19 **Rās Surud**, Somalia ▶
175 S 3 **Rās Tanāqīb**, Saudi Arabia ▶
175 T 4 **Rās Tannūrah**, Saudi Arabia
214 E 6 **Râs Timirist**, Mauritania ▶
213 O 19 **Rās Xaafuun**, Somalia ▶
197 C 19 **Rasa**, Philippines 🏝
149 D 14 **Raseiniai**, Lithuania
213 E 19 **Rashad**, Sudan
151 T 4 **Rashivka**, Ukraine
176 K 6 **Rashm**, Iran
176 H 4 **Rasht**, Iran
191 K 17 **Rasi Salai**, Thailand
145 L 14 **Raška**, Serbia and Montenegro
177 Q 11 **Raskoh**, Pakistan ⛰
84 L 1 **Rasmussen Basin**, Nunavut, Canada ≋
82 L 7 **Rasmussen Bay**, Nunavut, Canada ≋
149 L 16 **Rasna**, Belarus
150 J 11 **Râşnov**, Romania
43 A 16 **Raso**, Cape Verde 🏝
157 N 4 **Rasskazovo**, Russian Federation
137 E 22 **Rastatt**, Germany
134 L 6 **Rásttigáisa**, Norway ▲
191 G 19 **Rat Buri**, Thailand
78 C 13 **Rat Island**, Alaska, U.S.A. 🏝
78 C 12 **Rat Islands**, Alaska, U.S.A. 🏝
233 L 14 **Rata**, New Zealand
237 X 2 **Ratak Chain**, Marshall Islands 🏝
182 H 9 **Ratangarh**, India
135 F 16 **Rätansbyn**, Sweden
182 L 11 **Rath**, India
190 A 12 **Rathedaung**, Myanmar
136 K 13 **Rathenow**, Germany
181 D 14 **Ratlam**, India
181 C 18 **Ratnagiri**, India
181 G 25 **Ratnapura**, Sri Lanka
150 J 1 **Ratne**, Ukraine
177 U 12 **Rato Dero**, Pakistan
75 S 8 **Raton**, New Mexico, U.S.A.
139 N 6 **Rattenberg**, Austria
194 C 8 **Raub**, Malaysia
113 D 17 **Rauch**, Argentina
175 R 3 **Raudhatain**, Kuwait
232 O 11 **Raukumara Range**, New Zealand ⛰
135 J 18 **Rauma**, Finland
181 I 15 **Raurkela**, India
198 M 3 **Rausu**, Japan
232 O 10 **Rautoria**, New Zealand
150 I 3 **Rava-Rus'ka**, Ukraine
72 M 4 **Ravalli**, Montana, U.S.A.
176 M 9 **Rāvar**, Iran
133 H 16 **Ravels**, Belgium
77 I 16 **Ravendale**, California, U.S.A.
140 G 9 **Ravenna**, Italy
137 G 25 **Ravensburg**, Germany
231 T 4 **Ravenshoe**, Queensland, Australia
230 H 11 **Ravensthorpe**, Western Australia, Australia
177 X 10 **Ravi**, Pakistan 〰
179 N 14 **Ravnina**, Turkmenistan
173 Q 5 **Rāwah**, Iraq
177 W 8 **Rawalpindi**, Pakistan
173 T 1 **Rawāndiz**, Iraq
193 U 11 **Rawas**, Indonesia
182 G 8 **Rawatsar**, India
143 G 14 **Rawicz**, Poland
230 K 10 **Rawlinna**, Western Australia, Australia
73 V 13 **Rawlins**, Wyoming, U.S.A.
111 I 18 **Rawson**, Argentina
185 N 11 **Rawu**, China
66 H 3 **Ray**, North Dakota, U.S.A.
172 H 6 **Rayak**, Lebanon
153 U 14 **Raychikhinsk**, Russian Federation
175 P 12 **Raydah**, Yemen
157 V 2 **Rayevskiy**, Russian Federation
127 Y 10 **Rayleigh**, United Kingdom
76 F 8 **Raymond**, Washington, U.S.A.
71 P 15 **Raymondville**, Texas, U.S.A.
191 I 20 **Rayong**, Thailand
62 J 4 **Rayville**, Louisiana, U.S.A.
177 V 8 **Razani**, Pakistan
146 L 7 **Razgrad**, Bulgaria ▣
146 L 7 **Razgrad**, Bulgaria
146 G 11 **Razlog**, Bulgaria
127 U 11 **Reading**, United Kingdom
58 H 13 **Reading**, Pennsylvania, U.S.A.
65 K 20 **Reading**, Ohio, U.S.A.
64 E 13 **Readstown**, Wisconsin, U.S.A.
110 J 13 **Realicó**, Argentina
191 J 20 **Reăng Kesei**, Cambodia
211 Q 8 **Rebaa**, Algeria
134 I 7 **Rebbenesøy**, Norway 🏝
211 W 12 **Rebiana Sand Sea**, Libya ◇
154 G 7 **Reboly**, Russian Federation
198 I 3 **Rebun-tō**, Japan 🏝
149 M 20 **Rechytsa**, Belarus
108 O 13 **Recife**, Brazil
111 F 14 **Recinto**, Chile
112 C 12 **Reconquista**, Argentina
110 I 9 **Recreo**, Argentina
190 K 11 **Red**, Asia 〰
57 P 12 **Red**, Texas, U.S.A. 〰
60 H 10 **Red Bank**, Tennessee, U.S.A.
63 O 2 **Red Bay**, Alabama, U.S.A.
85 X 8 **Red Bay**, Newfoundland and Labrador, Canada
77 G 16 **Red Bluff**, California, U.S.A.
66 M 15 **Red Cloud**, Nebraska, U.S.A.
83 J 19 **Red Deer**, Alberta, Canada
68 J 7 **Red Hills**, Kansas, U.S.A. ◇
74 H 9 **Red Lake**, Arizona, U.S.A. 💧
84 J 10 **Red Lake**, Ontario, Canada
73 S 8 **Red Lodge**, Montana, U.S.A.
212 H 11 **Red Sea**, Africa/Asia ⛵
213 G 14 **Red Sea**, Sudan ▣
67 T 8 **Red Wing**, Minnesota, U.S.A.
194 D 5 **Redang**, Malaysia 🏝
125 K 15 **Redcar**, United Kingdom
77 G 16 **Redding**, California, U.S.A.
127 R 8 **Redditch**, United Kingdom
108 J 12 **Redenção**, Brazil
108 L 13 **Redenção do Gurguéia**, Brazil
66 M 8 **Redfield**, South Dakota, U.S.A.
154 H 14 **Redkino**, Russian Federation
77 K 24 **Redlands**, California, U.S.A.
76 H 11 **Redmond**, Oregon, U.S.A.
65 L 20 **Redoak**, Ohio, U.S.A.
126 J 15 **Redruth**, United Kingdom
67 Q 8 **Redwood Falls**, Minnesota, U.S.A.
77 F 17 **Redwood Valley**, California, U.S.A.
64 J 13 **Reed City**, Michigan, U.S.A.
66 H 6 **Reeder**, North Dakota, U.S.A.
76 E 11 **Reedsport**, Oregon, U.S.A.
61 V 5 **Reedville**, Virginia, U.S.A.
233 G 17 **Reefton**, New Zealand
137 B 15 **Rees**, Germany
171 N 9 **Refahiye**, Turkey
63 O 3 **Reform**, Alabama, U.S.A.
71 Q 12 **Refugio**, Texas, U.S.A.
142 E 9 **Rega**, Poland 〰
137 M 22 **Regen**, Germany
137 K 22 **Regensburg**, Germany
210 L 11 **Reggane**, Algeria
140 E 8 **Reggio**, Italy
141 L 21 **Reggio di Calabria**, Italy
150 J 9 **Reghin**, Romania
83 N 19 **Regina**, Saskatchewan, Canada
177 R 10 **Registan**, Afghanistan ◇
112 K 8 **Registro**, Brazil
183 X 8 **Regong**, India
130 I 10 **Reguengos de Monsaraz**, Portugal
218 I 10 **Rehoboth**, Namibia
61 X 3 **Rehoboth Beach**, Delaware, U.S.A.
61 Q 8 **Reidsville**, North Carolina, U.S.A.
127 V 11 **Reigate**, United Kingdom
129 S 3 **Reims**, France
138 F 7 **Reinach**, Switzerland
83 M 16 **Reindeer**, Saskatchewan, Canada 〰
83 M 14 **Reindeer Lake**, Saskatchewan, Canada 💧
131 N 2 **Reinosa**, Spain
139 Y 2 **Reinthal**, Austria
82 J 12 **Reliance**, Northwest Territories, Canada
210 L 6 **Relizane**, Algeria
211 Q 8 **Remada**, Tunisia
137 C 18 **Remagen**, Germany
192 J 14 **Rembang**, Indonesia
211 Q 8 **Remel el Abiod**, Tunisia ⛰
133 M 26 **Remich**, Luxembourg
65 H 17 **Remington**, Indiana, U.S.A.
129 V 6 **Remiremont**, France
157 O 10 **Remontnoye**, Russian Federation
137 C 16 **Remscheid**, Germany
190 F 6 **Renam**, Myanmar
65 F 21 **Rend Lake**, Illinois, U.S.A. 💧
234 K 6 **Rendova**, Solomon Islands 🏝
136 G 8 **Rendsburg**, Germany
86 H 10 **Renfrew**, Ontario, Canada
192 E 11 **Rengat**, Indonesia
110 G 12 **Rengo**, Chile
189 T 10 **Renhua**, China
151 N 11 **Reni**, Ukraine
231 Q 11 **Renmark**, South Australia, Australia
234 L 8 **Rennell**, Solomon Islands 🏝
128 L 5 **Rennes**, France
84 J 10 **Rennie**, Manitoba, Canada
77 I 17 **Reno**, Nevada, U.S.A.
58 E 11 **Renovo**, Pennsylvania, U.S.A.
187 D 18 **Renqiu**, China
189 N 7 **Renshou**, China
193 O 15 **Reo**, Indonesia
179 N 13 **Repetek**, Turkmenistan
108 F 10 **Represa de Balbina**, Brazil 💧
112 H 9 **Represa de Foz de Areia**, Brazil 💧
112 L 5 **Represa de Furnas**, Brazil 💧
112 F 8 **Represa de Itaipu**, Brazil/Paraguay 💧
112 G 8 **Represa de Salto Santiago**, Brazil 💧
112 G 7 **Represa Ilha Grande**, Brazil 💧
112 H 4 **Represa Porto Primavera**, Brazil 💧
112 I 3 **Represa São Simão**, Brazil 💧
109 J 15 **Represa Serra da Mesa**, Brazil 💧
109 L 17 **Represa Três Marias**, Brazil 💧
108 J 11 **Represa Tucuruí**, Brazil 💧
90 L 5 **Repressa el Cajón**, Honduras 💧
64 G 9 **Republic**, Michigan, U.S.A.
76 J 6 **Republic**, Washington, U.S.A.
218 M 12 **Republic of South Africa**, Africa ■
144 F 10 **Republica Srpska**, Bosnia and Herzegovina ▣
85 N 2 **Repulse Bay**, Nunavut, Canada
106 E 12 **Requena**, Peru
131 S 8 **Requena**, Spain
129 Q 13 **Réquista**, France
170 M 9 **Reşadiye**, Turkey
171 S 11 **Reşadiye**, Turkey
146 C 12 **Resen**, Macedonia (F.Y.R.O.M.)
112 H 8 **Reserva**, Brazil
75 N 12 **Reserve**, New Mexico, U.S.A.
86 I 8 **Réservoir Baskatong**, Québec, Canada 💧
86 I 8 **Réservoir Cabonga**, Québec, Canada 💧
86 H 8 **Réservoir Dozois**, Québec, Canada 💧
86 K 6 **Réservoir Gouin**, Québec, Canada 💧
85 P 9 **Réservoir la Grande Deux**, Québec, Canada 💧
85 Q 9 **Réservoir la Grande Trois**, Québec, Canada 💧
87 P 4 **Réservoir Manic Trois**, Québec, Canada 💧
87 P 2 **Réservoir Manicouagan**, Québec, Canada 💧
85 Q 9 **Réservoir Opinaca**, Québec, Canada 💧
87 O 4 **Réservoir Outardes Quatre**, Québec, Canada 💧
87 N 4 **Réservoir Pipmuacan**, Québec, Canada 💧
151 T 5 **Reshetylivka**, Ukraine
112 C 10 **Resistencia**, Argentina
150 F 11 **Reşiţa**, Romania
142 E 9 **Resko**, Poland
81 P 4 **Resolute Bay**, Nunavut, Canada
233 A 24 **Resolution Island**, New Zealand 🏝
85 T 4 **Resolution Island**, Nunavut, Canada 🏝
156 L 12 **Respublika Adygeya**, Russian Federation ▣
152 M 13 **Respublika Altay**, Russian Federation ▣
157 W 2 **Respublika Bashkortostan**, Russian Federation ▣
153 R 13 **Respublika Buryatiya**, Russian Federation ▣
157 R 15 **Respublika Dagestan**, Russian Federation ▣
157 Q 10 **Respublika Kalmykiya**, Russian Federation ▣
154 H 6 **Respublika Kareliya**, Russian Federation ▣
153 N 13 **Respublika Khakasiya**, Russian Federation ▣
155 R 7 **Respublika Komi**, Russian Federation ▣
155 O 14 **Respublika Mariy El**, Russian Federation ▣
157 O 3 **Respublika Mordoviya**, Russian Federation ▣
153 R 10 **Respublika Sakha**, Russian Federation ▣
157 O 14 **Respublika Severnaya Osetiya-Alaniya**, Russian Federation ▣
157 S 1 **Respublika Tatarstan**, Russian Federation ▣
153 O 13 **Respublika Tyva**, Russian Federation ▣
90 F 6 **Retalhuleu**, Guatemala
110 F 13 **Retén Llico**, Chile
127 T 4 **Retford**, United Kingdom
129 S 3 **Rethel**, France
147 H 26 **Rethymno**, Greece
139 W 2 **Retz**, Austria
38 B 14 **Réunion**, France ▣
137 G 23 **Reutlingen**, Germany
138 L 6 **Reutte**, Austria
66 H 7 **Reva**, South Dakota, U.S.A.
129 P 14 **Revel**, France
83 H 20 **Revelstoke**, British Columbia, Canada
106 A 12 **Reventazón**, Peru
41 V 5 **Revillagigedo Islands**, Mexico 🏝
172 E 11 **Revivim**, Israel
182 M 12 **Rewa**, India
182 I 9 **Rewari**, India
73 P 10 **Rexburg**, Idaho, U.S.A.
107 I 18 **Reyes**, Bolivia
134 A 11 **Reykanestá**, Iceland ▶
45 N 14 **Reykjanes Basin**, Arctic Ocean ◇
45 N 15 **Reykjanes Ridge**, Arctic Ocean ⛰
134 B 11 **Reykjavík**, Iceland 🏛
89 R 7 **Reynosa**, Mexico
148 I 12 **Rēzekne**, Latvia
151 N 8 **Rezina**, Moldova
144 N 12 **Rgotina**, Serbia and Montenegro
127 N 8 **Rhayader**, United Kingdom
136 D 13 **Rheine**, Germany
138 E 6 **Rheinfelden**, Switzerland
137 D 20 **Rheinland-Pfalz**, Germany ▣
138 H 9 **Rheinwaldhorn**, Switzerland ▲
129 W 5 **Rhine**, Europe 〰
64 F 10 **Rhinelander**, Wisconsin, U.S.A.
217 R 6 **Rhino Camp**, Uganda
136 K 12 **Rhinow**, Germany
133 H 21 **Rhisnes**, Belgium
59 N 11 **Rhode Island**, U.S.A. ▣
59 O 11 **Rhode Island Sound**, Rhode Island, U.S.A. ≋
147 O 24 **Rhodes**, Greece 🏝
159 U 9 **Rhodes Basin**, Mediterranean Sea ◇
146 G 11 **Rhodope Mountains**, Bulgaria ⛰

■ Country ▣ Internal administrative region: State/Province/Territory/Dependent territory 🏛 Capital city ⛰ Mountain range/Undersea ridge ▲ Mountain peak/Volcano/Seamount ◇ Geographic feature ▶ Headland/Point/Cape/Peninsula 🏜 Desert 🏝 Island/Island group ⛺ Antarctic base 🌊 Ocean ⛵ Sea ≋ Bay/Gulf/Channel/Strait 💧 Lake ⬚ Salt pan/Dry/Intermittent lake 〰 River

137 G 19 **Rhön**, Germany ⛰
127 N 10 **Rhondda**, United Kingdom ◇
129 T 12 **Rhône**, France/Switzerland ∫
129 U 11 **Rhône-Alpes**, France ◘
158 G 5 **Rhône Fan**, Mediterranean Sea ◇
127 O 5 **Rhosllanerchrugog**, United Kingdom
126 L 10 **Rhossili**, United Kingdom
125 I 18 **Rhyl**, United Kingdom
127 O 4 **Rhyl**, United Kingdom
215 S 15 **Riaba**, Equatorial Guinea
108 K 12 **Riachão**, Brazil
109 L 14 **Riachão das Neves**, Brazil
109 J 15 **Rialma**, Brazil
130 G 2 **Rías Bajas**, Spain ◇
192 E 10 **Riau**, Indonesia ◘
131 O 5 **Riaza**, Spain
109 H 18 **Ribas do Rio Pardo**, Brazil
219 T 5 **Ribáuè**, Mozambique
127 Q 2 **Ribble**, United Kingdom ∫
135 B 25 **Ribe**, Denmark
112 J 8 **Ribeira**, Brazil ∫
130 G 2 **Ribeira**, Spain
42 O 2 **Ribeira Grande**, Azores
112 K 5 **Ribeirão Preto**, Brazil
107 J 16 **Riberalta**, Bolivia
131 X 3 **Ribes de Freser**, Spain
144 C 8 **Ribnica**, Slovenia
151 O 8 **Rîbniţa**, Moldova
136 K 8 **Ribnitz-Damgarten**, Germany
88 L 4 **Ricardo Flores Magón**, Mexico
140 H 10 **Riccione**, Italy
64 D 10 **Rice Lake**, Wisconsin, U.S.A.
69 S 11 **Rich Mountain**, Arkansas, U.S.A. ▲
63 U 2 **Richard B. Russell Lake**, Georgia, U.S.A. 🏞
214 E 7 **Richard Toll**, Senegal
219 Q 12 **Richards Bay**, Republic of South Africa
61 O 11 **Richburn**, South Carolina, U.S.A.
72 M 11 **Richfield**, Idaho, U.S.A.
58 I 8 **Richfield Springs**, New York, U.S.A.
87 T 8 **Richibucto**, New Brunswick, Canada
71 R 7 **Richland**, Texas, U.S.A.
64 E 13 **Richland Center**, Wisconsin, U.S.A.
60 M 7 **Richlands**, Virginia, U.S.A.
218 L 13 **Richmond**, Republic of South Africa
231 S 5 **Richmond**, Queensland, Australia
233 I 16 **Richmond**, New Zealand
60 J 5 **Richmond**, Kentucky, U.S.A.
61 T 6 **Richmond**, Virginia, U.S.A.
86 M 10 **Richmond**, Québec, Canada
63 W 5 **Richmond Hill**, Georgia, U.S.A.
233 H 17 **Richmond Range**, New Zealand ⛰
127 V 10 **Richmond upon Thames**, United Kingdom
72 K 13 **Riddle**, Idaho, U.S.A.
77 K 22 **Ridgecrest**, California, U.S.A.
51 N 15 **Ridgeland**, South Carolina, U.S.A.
58 D 11 **Ridgway**, Pennsylvania, U.S.A.
139 R 4 **Ried im Innkreis**, Austria
137 G 24 **Riedlingen**, Germany
137 M 16 **Riesa**, Germany
148 C 13 **Rietavas**, Lithuania
140 H 13 **Rieti**, Italy
75 O 4 **Rifle**, Colorado, U.S.A.
134 C 9 **Rifstangi**, Iceland ▶
217 U 6 **Rift Valley**, Kenya ◘
215 V 9 **Rig-Rig**, Chad
148 F 11 **Rīga**, Latvia ⌂
2 K 7 **Riggins**, Idaho, U.S.A.
48 E 6 **Riguldi**, Estonia
241 N 3 **Riiser-Larsen Ice Shelf**, Antarctica ◇
241 U 2 **Riiser-Larsen Peninsula**, Antarctica ▶
43 N 23 **Riiser–Larsen Sea**, Atlantic Ocean ∿
148 F 6 **Riisipere**, Estonia
215 Q 10 **Rijau**, Nigeria
132 M 11 **Rijssen**, Netherlands
198 L 4 **Rikubetsu**, Japan
146 G 10 **Rila**, Bulgaria ⛰
69 O 3 **Riley**, Kansas, U.S.A.
76 J 12 **Riley**, Oregon, U.S.A.
133 F 16 **Rilland**, Netherlands
143 K 21 **Rimavská Sobota**, Slovakia
140 H 10 **Rimini**, Italy
87 Q 6 **Rimouski**, Québec, Canada
193 N 15 **Rinca**, Indonesia 🏝
188 K 6 **Rinda**, China
147 J 21 **Rineia**, Greece 🏝
180 D 12 **Ringas**, India
62 H 4 **Ringgold**, Louisiana, U.S.A.
71 P 4 **Ringgold**, Texas, U.S.A.
215 S 10 **Ringim**, Nigeria
135 B 24 **Ringkøbing**, Denmark
68 M 12 **Ringling**, Oklahoma, U.S.A.
73 R 6 **Ringling**, Montana, U.S.A.
135 D 25 **Ringsted**, Denmark
134 I 7 **Ringvassøy**, Norway 🏝
127 S 13 **Ringwood**, United Kingdom
108 C 13 **Rio Branco**, Brazil
112 J 8 **Rio Branco do Sul**, Brazil
109 H 18 **Rio Brilhante**, Brazil
111 F 16 **Río Bueno**, Chile
112 K 6 **Rio Claro**, Brazil
93 Z 14 **Rio Claro**, Trinidad and Tobago
113 A 19 **Río Colorado**, Argentina
110 J 11 **Río Cuarto**, Argentina
112 N 7 **Rio de Janeiro**, Brazil
112 N 6 **Rio de Janeiro**, Brazil ◘
91 U 15 **Río de Jesús**, Panama
112 I 10 **Rio do Sul**, Brazil
111 H 23 **Río Gallegos**, Argentina
113 H 14 **Rio Grande**, Brazil
56 L 12 **Rio Grande**, U.S.A., U.S.A. ∫
111 I 25 **Río Grande**, Argentina
89 O 8 **Río Grande**, Mexico
71 O 15 **Rio Grande City**, Texas, U.S.A.
89 N 10 **Rio Grande de Santiago**, Mexico ∫
108 O 12 **Rio Grande do Norte**, Brazil ◘
112 F 11 **Rio Grande do Sul**, Brazil ◘
43 J 17 **Rio Grande Fracture Zone**, Atlantic Ocean ◇
43 H 17 **Rio Grande Gap**, Atlantic Ocean ⛰
43 H 17 **Rio Grande Rise**, Atlantic Ocean ⛰
91 W 14 **Río Hato**, Panama
112 G 12 **Río Jacuí**, Brazil ∫
89 Z 10 **Río Lagartos**, Mexico
130 G 8 **Rio Maior**, Portugal
107 J 21 **Río Mulatos**, Bolivia
112 I 9 **Rio Negro**, Brazil
111 I 16 **Río Negro**, Argentina ◘
113 D 14 **Río Negro**, Uruguay ◘
112 H 12 **Rio Pardo**, Brazil
75 P 10 **Rio Rancho**, New Mexico, U.S.A.
106 D 10 **Río Tigre**, Peru
197 B 20 **Rio Tuba**, Philippines
109 I 17 **Rio Verde**, Brazil
111 G 24 **Río Verde**, Chile
89 Q 10 **Río Verde**, Mexico
106 B 9 **Riobamba**, Ecuador
104 J 2 **Ríohacha**, Colombia
106 C 12 **Rioja**, Peru
129 R 10 **Riom**, France
131 Q 10 **Riópar**, Spain
151 Q 1 **Ripky**, Ukraine
127 S 1 **Ripley**, United Kingdom
127 S 5 **Ripley**, United Kingdom
60 A 9 **Ripley**, Tennessee, U.S.A.
61 N 4 **Ripley**, West Virginia, U.S.A.
65 L 20 **Ripley**, Ohio, U.S.A.
131 X 3 **Ripoll**, Spain
127 S 1 **Ripon**, United Kingdom
133 K 15 **Rips**, Netherlands
150 M 7 **Rîşcani**, Moldova
91 S 13 **Risco**, Panama ∫
198 I 3 **Rishiri-tō**, Japan 🏝
198 I 3 **Rishiri-yama**, Japan ▲
172 F 9 **Rishon Le Ẕiyyon**, Israel
135 D 15 **Rissa**, Norway
135 N 17 **Ristiina**, Finland
134 N 13 **Ristijärvi**, Finland
148 C 6 **Ristna**, Estonia
181 N 21 **Ritchie's Archipelago**, India 🏝
76 K 7 **Ritzville**, Washington, U.S.A.
140 F 6 **Riva del Garda**, Italy
110 K 6 **Rivadavia**, Argentina
110 G 9 **Rivadavia**, Chile
113 A 16 **Rivadavia**, Argentina
91 N 10 **Rivas**, Nicaragua
214 H 13 **River Cess**, Liberia
64 C 11 **River Falls**, Wisconsin, U.S.A.
113 E 16 **River Plate**, Argentina/Uruguay ∫
112 F 13 **Rivera**, Brazil
112 F 13 **Rivera**, Uruguay
113 A 18 **Rivera**, Argentina
112 E 13 **Rivera**, Uruguay ◘
58 L 12 **Riverhead**, New York, U.S.A.
215 Q 14 **Rivers**, Nigeria ◘
64 H 12 **Rivers**, Wisconsin, U.S.A.
233 D 24 **Riversdale**, New Zealand
233 L 16 **Riversdale Beach**, New Zealand
71 S 8 **Riverside**, Texas, U.S.A.
77 K 25 **Riverside**, California, U.S.A.
73 U 11 **Riverton**, Wyoming, U.S.A.
87 U 9 **Riverview**, New Brunswick, Canada
71 P 14 **Riviera**, Texas, U.S.A.
87 T 5 **Rivière-au-Renard**, Québec, Canada
85 Q 7 **Rivière aux Feuilles**, Québec, Canada ∫
85 R 7 **Rivière aux Mélèzes**, Québec, Canada ∫
87 V 4 **Rivière-aux-Saumons**, Québec, Canada
87 P 7 **Rivière-du-Loup**, Québec, Canada
38 B 11 **Rivière du Rempart**, Mauritius
87 R 4 **Rivière-Pentecôte**, Québec, Canada
93 Z 11 **Rivière-Pilote**, Martinique
150 L 3 **Rivne**, Ukraine
140 A 7 **Rivoli**, Italy
218 K 6 **Rivungo**, Angola
175 R 6 **Riyadh**, Saudi Arabia ⌂
171 P 8 **Rize**, Turkey
189 X 2 **Rizhao**, China
170 J 15 **Rizokarpason**, Cyprus
93 V 7 **Road Town**, Virgin Islands, United Kingdom ⌂
74 M 5 **Roan Plateau**, Utah, U.S.A. ◇
129 S 9 **Roanne**, France
57 W 9 **Roanoke**, Virginia, U.S.A.
61 Q 6 **Roanoke**, Virginia, U.S.A.
63 R 4 **Roanoke**, Alabama, U.S.A.
61 W 9 **Roanoke Island**, North Carolina, U.S.A. 🏝
61 T 8 **Roanoke Rapids**, North Carolina, U.S.A.
91 N 3 **Roatán**, Honduras
127 O 10 **Roath**, United Kingdom
231 S 14 **Robbins Island**, Tasmania, Australia 🏝
69 R 10 **Robert S. Kerr Reservoir**, Oklahoma, U.S.A. 🏞
241 R 14 **Roberts Butte**, Antarctica ▲
183 O 12 **Robertsganj**, India
240 I 3 **Robertson Island**, Antarctica 🏝
214 G 13 **Robertsport**, Liberia
86 M 6 **Roberval**, Québec, Canada
231 R 12 **Robinvale**, Victoria, Australia
131 Q 9 **Robledo**, Spain
84 H 9 **Roblin**, Manitoba, Canada
107 N 21 **Robore**, Bolivia
71 P 13 **Robstown**, Texas, U.S.A.
141 J 14 **Roccaraso**, Italy
113 F 15 **Rocha**, Uruguay
113 G 15 **Rocha**, Uruguay ◘
127 R 3 **Rochdale**, United Kingdom
129 O 10 **Rochechouart**, France
109 H 17 **Rochedo**, Brazil
128 L 9 **Rochefort**, France
133 I 23 **Rochefort**, Belgium
154 M 8 **Rochegda**, Russian Federation
127 X 11 **Rochester**, United Kingdom
58 E 8 **Rochester**, New York, U.S.A.
59 O 8 **Rochester**, New Hampshire, U.S.A.
65 I 17 **Rochester**, Indiana, U.S.A.
67 T 9 **Rochester**, Minnesota, U.S.A.
233 D 24 **Rock and Pillar Range**, New Zealand ⛰
65 E 16 **Rock Falls**, Illinois, U.S.A.
61 O 11 **Rock Hill**, South Carolina, U.S.A.
73 T 14 **Rock Springs**, Wyoming, U.S.A.
73 W 5 **Rock Springs**, Montana, U.S.A.
42 J 6 **Rockall Bank**, Atlantic Ocean ◇
42 J 6 **Rockall Trough**, Atlantic Ocean ◇
71 Q 9 **Rockdale**, Texas, U.S.A.
65 F 15 **Rockford**, Illinois, U.S.A.
231 V 7 **Rockhampton**, Queensland, Australia
61 Q 11 **Rockingham**, North Carolina, U.S.A.
66 L 2 **Rocklake**, North Dakota, U.S.A.
59 Q 6 **Rockland**, Maine, U.S.A.
65 H 22 **Rockport**, Indiana, U.S.A.
76 H 6 **Rockport**, Washington, U.S.A.
70 M 10 **Rocksprings**, Texas, U.S.A.
65 H 19 **Rockville**, Indiana, U.S.A.
67 R 12 **Rockwell City**, Iowa, U.S.A.
60 I 9 **Rockwood**, Tennessee, U.S.A.
86 B 8 **Rocky Island Lake**, Ontario, Canada 🏞
61 T 8 **Rocky Mount**, North Carolina, U.S.A.
73 O 3 **Rocky Mountain**, Montana, U.S.A. ▲
83 I 19 **Rocky Mountain House**, Alberta, Canada
56 J 4 **Rocky Mountains**, Montana, U.S.A. ⛰
218 G 8 **Rocky Point**, Namibia ▶
110 G 10 **Rodeo**, Argentina
75 N 15 **Rodeo**, New Mexico, U.S.A.
129 Q 12 **Rodez**, France
137 L 21 **Roding**, Germany
150 J 8 **Rodna**, Romania
146 H 13 **Rodolivos**, Greece
147 O 23 **Rodos**, Greece
38 E 7 **Rodrigues Island**, Mauritius ◘
230 F 6 **Roebourne**, Western Australia, Australia
230 I 4 **Roebuck Bay**, Western Australia, Australia ≈
230 I 4 **Roebuck Plains Roadhouse**, Western Australia, Australia
133 K 17 **Roermond**, Netherlands
85 N 3 **Roes Welcome Sound**, Nunavut, Canada ≈
133 A 18 **Roesbrugge-Haringe**, Belgium
133 B 18 **Roeselare**, Belgium
141 L 17 **Rofrano**, Italy
144 I 13 **Rogatica**, Bosnia and Herzegovina
69 S 8 **Rogers**, Arkansas, U.S.A.
64 L 10 **Rogers City**, Michigan, U.S.A.
77 K 23 **Rogers Lake**, California, U.S.A. 🏞
72 M 13 **Rogerson**, Idaho, U.S.A.
41 X 11 **Roggeveen Basin**, Pacific Ocean ◇
129 Y 14 **Rogliano**, France
141 M 19 **Rogliano**, Italy
150 J 5 **Rohatyn**, Ukraine
139 S 3 **Rohrbach**, Austria
177 U 12 **Rohri**, Pakistan
182 I 8 **Rohtak**, India
148 E 6 **Rohuküla**, Estonia
191 K 17 **Roi Et**, Thailand
183 Z 8 **Roing**, India
148 D 10 **Roja**, Latvia
113 B 15 **Rojas**, Argentina
148 G 13 **Rokiškis**, Lithuania
198 K 8 **Rokkasho**, Japan
199 H 14 **Rokkō-zaki**, Japan ▶
150 M 2 **Rokytne**, Ukraine
135 A 19 **Røldal**, Norway
69 W 5 **Rolla**, Missouri, U.S.A.
138 B 9 **Rolle**, Switzerland
231 U 7 **Rolleston**, Queensland, Australia
86 F 7 **Rollet**, Québec, Canada
134 K 5 **Rolvsøya**, Norway 🏝
231 U 8 **Roma**, Queensland, Australia
193 R 14 **Roma**, Indonesia 🏝
57 O 15 **Roma**, Texas, U.S.A.
43 J 14 **Romanche Gap**, Atlantic Ocean ◇
150 G 10 **Romania**, Europe □
153 R 13 **Romanovka**, Russian Federation
197 I 14 **Romblon**, Philippines
197 I 14 **Romblon**, Philippines 🏝
197 H 14 **Romblon Passage**, Philippines ≈
141 H 14 **Rome**, Italy ⌂
58 H 8 **Rome**, New York, U.S.A.
63 R 2 **Rome**, Georgia, U.S.A.
65 M 14 **Romeo**, Michigan, U.S.A.
127 W 10 **Romford**, United Kingdom
129 R 5 **Romilly-sur-Seine**, France
61 R 2 **Romney**, West Virginia, U.S.A.
151 S 3 **Romny**, Ukraine
135 B 25 **Rømø**, Denmark 🏝
157 P 2 **Romodanovo**, Russian Federation
129 P 7 **Romorantin-Lanthenay**, France
194 D 9 **Rompin**, Malaysia ∫
127 S 12 **Romsey**, United Kingdom
191 M 15 **Ron**, Vietnam
130 M 13 **Ronda**, Spain
104 K 5 **Rondón**, Colombia
109 E 14 **Rondônia**, Brazil ◘
109 H 16 **Rondonópolis**, Brazil
189 Q 11 **Rong'an**, China
188 J 5 **Rongbaca**, China
187 I 19 **Rongcheng**, China
237 W 1 **Rongelap Atoll**, Marshall Islands 🏝
189 Q 10 **Rongjiang**, China
237 X 1 **Rongrik**, Marshall Islands 🏝
189 R 12 **Rongxian**, China
135 F 26 **Rønne**, Denmark
240 I 7 **Ronne Entrance**, Antarctica ≈
240 L 7 **Ronne Ice Shelf**, Antarctica ◇
135 G 24 **Ronneby**, Sweden
135 F 15 **Rönnöfors**, Sweden
133 D 19 **Ronse**, Belgium
43 O 15 **Rookery Point**, Tristan da Cunha ▶
182 J 7 **Roorkee**, India
133 G 15 **Roosendaal**, Netherlands
74 K 12 **Roosevelt**, Arizona, U.S.A.
241 O 11 **Roosevelt Island**, Antarctica 🏝
143 M 17 **Ropczyce**, Poland
231 N 2 **Roper Bar**, Northern Territory, Australia
128 M 13 **Roquefort**, France
108 E 8 **Roraima**, Brazil ◘
135 E 16 **Røros**, Norway
151 Q 5 **Ros'**, Ukraine ∫
106 B 8 **Rosa Zárate**, Ecuador
92 I 9 **Rosalind Bank**, Jamaica ≈
112 G 6 **Rosana**, Brazil
104 K 3 **Rosario**, Venezuela
113 C 14 **Rosario**, Argentina
196 F 9 **Rosario**, Philippines
196 G 12 **Rosario**, Philippines
88 M 9 **Rosario**, Mexico
92 E 8 **Rosario Bank**, Cayman Islands ≈
110 J 7 **Rosario de la Frontera**, Argentina
112 F 12 **Rosário do Sul**, Brazil
88 E 2 **Rosarito**, Mexico
88 G 5 **Rosarito**, Mexico
88 I 6 **Rosarito**, Mexico
141 L 20 **Rosarno**, Italy
66 L 7 **Roscoe**, South Dakota, U.S.A.
70 L 6 **Roscoe**, Texas, U.S.A.
125 C 17 **Roscommon**, Republic of Ireland
64 K 11 **Roscommon**, Michigan, U.S.A.
125 D 19 **Roscrea**, Republic of Ireland
236 L 8 **Rose**, American Samoa 🏝
38 B 12 **Rose Belle**, Mauritius
38 B 12 **Rose Hill**, Mauritius
74 M 12 **Rose Peak**, Arizona, U.S.A. ▲
93 Y 10 **Roseau**, Dominica ⌂
76 F 12 **Roseburg**, Oregon, U.S.A.
133 H 22 **Rosée**, Belgium
213 G 19 **Roseires Reservoir**, Sudan 🏞
71 S 10 **Rosenburg**, Texas, U.S.A.
137 K 25 **Rosenheim**, Germany
131 Y 3 **Roses**, Spain
140 J 12 **Roseto degli Abruzzi**, Italy
83 L 19 **Rosetown**, Saskatchewan, Canada
65 D 17 **Roseville**, Illinois, U.S.A.
218 I 12 **Rosh Pinah**, Namibia
140 E 11 **Rosignano Marittimo**, Italy
150 J 13 **Roșiori de Vede**, Romania
156 H 2 **Roslavl'**, Russian Federation
154 M 11 **Roslvatino**, Russian Federation
231 T 15 **Ross**, Tasmania, Australia
233 F 19 **Ross**, New Zealand
241 O 11 **Ross Ice Shelf**, Antarctica ◇
241 Q 12 **Ross Island**, Antarctica 🏝
127 Q 9 **Ross-on-Wye**, United Kingdom
82 C 13 **Ross River**, Yukon Territory, Canada
241 N 12 **Ross Sea**, Antarctica ∿
125 C 15 **Rossan Point**, Republic of Ireland ▶
234 I 7 **Rossel Island**, Papua New Guinea 🏝
125 E 20 **Rosslare**, Republic of Ireland
214 E 7 **Rosso**, Mauritania
156 L 7 **Rossosh'**, Russian Federation
134 F 12 **Røssvatnet**, Norway 🏞
176 J 13 **Rostāq**, Iran
136 J 9 **Rostock**, Germany
154 J 14 **Rostov**, Russian Federation
156 L 10 **Rostov-na-Donu**, Russian Federation
156 M 9 **Rostovskaya Oblast'**, Russian Federation ◘
63 S 2 **Roswell**, Georgia, U.S.A.
75 S 12 **Roswell**, New Mexico, U.S.A.
236 A 9 **Rota**, Northern Mariana Islands 🏝
193 P 15 **Rote**, Indonesia 🏝
136 G 11 **Rotenburg**, Germany
137 E 17 **Rothaargebirge**, Germany ⛰
137 H 21 **Rothenburg ob der Tauber**, Germany
240 H 5 **Rothera**, Antarctica ⁙
127 S 4 **Rotherham**, United Kingdom

Rothschild Island – St Helena Sound

240 I 6 Rothschild Island, Antarctica
127 U 7 Rothwell, United Kingdom
193 P 15 Roti, Indonesia
233 G 19 Rotomanu, New Zealand
141 N 17 Rotondella, Italy
232 M 11 Rotorua, New Zealand
139 T 6 Rottenmann, Austria
132 G 13 Rotterdam, Netherlands
132 M 5 Rottumeroog, Netherlands
132 L 4 Rottumerplaat, Netherlands
137 F 24 Rottweil, Germany
235 W 8 Rotuma, Fiji
129 Q 1 Roubaix, France
129 O 3 Rouen, France
60 F 6 Rough River Lake, Kentucky, U.S.A.
38 C 11 Round Island, Mauritius
71 P 9 Round Rock, Texas, U.S.A.
74 M 8 Round Rock, Arizona, U.S.A.
73 T 6 Roundup, Montana, U.S.A.
124 I 6 Rousay, United Kingdom
86 F 7 Rouyn, Québec, Canada
134 L 11 Rovaniemi, Finland
154 L 9 Rovdino, Russian Federation
151 Z 7 Roven'ky, Ukraine
138 H 10 Roveredo, Switzerland
140 F 6 Rovereto, Italy
191 L 19 Rôvieng Tbong, Cambodia
140 G 8 Rovigo, Italy
150 H 12 Rovinari, Romania
157 Q 6 Rovnoye, Russian Federation
61 R 11 Rowland, North Carolina, U.S.A.
85 O 1 Rowley Island, Nunavut, Canada
39 U 7 Rowley Shoals, Indian Ocean
197 I 16 Roxas, Philippines
197 E 17 Roxas, Philippines
197 H 14 Roxas, Philippines
61 R 8 Roxboro, North Carolina, U.S.A.
231 P 10 Roxby Downs, South Australia, Australia
73 T 4 Roy, Montana, U.S.A.
75 S 9 Roy, New Mexico, U.S.A.
127 S 8 Royal Leamington Spa, United Kingdom
127 X 12 Royal Tunbridge Wells, United Kingdom
58 M 7 Royalton, Vermont, U.S.A.
128 L 10 Royan, France
129 Q 3 Roye, France
127 W 9 Royston, United Kingdom
63 U 2 Royston, Georgia, U.S.A.
145 L 15 Rožaje, Serbia and Montenegro
142 L 11 Różan, Poland
151 T 11 Rozdol'ne, Ukraine
143 K 20 Rožňava, Slovakia
132 F 13 Rozenburg, Netherlands
132 K 13 Rozendaal, Netherlands
150 K 3 Rozhyshche, Ukraine
145 K 17 Rrëshen, Albania
157 O 5 Rtishchevo, Russian Federation
127 P 5 Ruabon, United Kingdom
218 G 7 Ruacana, Namibia
233 L 14 Ruahine Range, New Zealand
232 J 6 Ruakaka, New Zealand
233 C 26 Ruapuke Island, New Zealand
232 M 11 Ruatahuna, New Zealand
232 J 7 Ruawai, New Zealand
175 Q 10 Rub' al Khālī, Saudi Arabia
151 Y 5 Rubizhne, Ukraine
152 L 13 Rubtsovsk, Russian Federation
79 P 7 Ruby, Alaska, U.S.A.
77 M 17 Ruby Mountains, Nevada, U.S.A.
150 J 11 Rucăr, Romania
148 B 12 Rucava, Latvia
189 U 10 Rucheng, China
61 S 4 Ruckersville, Virginia, U.S.A.
177 Q 11 Rudbar, Afghanistan
156 G 1 Rudnya, Russian Federation
157 P 6 Rudnya, Russian Federation
179 O 3 Rudnyy, Kazakhstan
137 J 17 Rudolstadt, Germany
189 Z 5 Rudong, China
129 P 2 Rue, France
213 F 17 Rufa'a, Sudan
129 N 9 Ruffec, France
113 A 16 Rufino, Argentina
219 O 5 Rufunsa, Zambia
189 Y 5 Rugao, China
125 K 20 Rugby, United Kingdom
127 T 7 Rugby, United Kingdom
66 K 3 Rugby, North Dakota, U.S.A.
127 R 6 Rugeley, United Kingdom
136 L 8 Rügen, Germany
217 Q 8 Ruhengeri, Rwanda
148 E 9 Ruhnu, Estonia
189 Z 8 Rui'an, China
189 V 7 Ruichang, China
75 R 13 Ruidoso, New Mexico, U.S.A.
189 V 10 Ruijin, China
188 H 11 Ruili, China
217 U 12 Ruipa, Tanzania
88 M 10 Ruiz, Mexico
148 G 9 Rūjiena, Latvia
134 N 11 Ruka, Finland
217 R 12 Rukwa, Tanzania
124 E 11 Rum, United Kingdom
93 N 3 Rum Cay, The Bahamas
144 K 10 Ruma, Serbia and Montenegro
175 R 5 Rumāh, Saudi Arabia
173 Y 12 Rumaila, Iraq
213 D 21 Rumbek, Sudan
234 A 4 Rumginae, Papua New Guinea
198 J 4 Rumoi, Japan
219 R 3 Rumphi, Malawi
189 U 4 Runan, China
127 P 4 Runcorn, United Kingdom
218 J 7 Rundu, Namibia
217 P 6 Rungu, Democratic Republic of Congo
217 T 12 Rungwa, Tanzania
188 L 4 Ru'nying, China
135 O 17 Ruokolahti, Finland
184 K 6 Ruoqiang, China
134 M 6 Ruostefjelbma, Norway
192 E 10 Rupat, Indonesia
150 J 10 Rupea, Romania
61 O 5 Rupert, West Virginia, U.S.A.
240 M 12 Ruppert Coast, Antarctica
107 I 18 Rurrenabaque, Bolivia
219 Q 7 Rusape, Zimbabwe
150 I 7 Ruscova, Romania
146 K 6 Ruse, Bulgaria
146 K 6 Ruse, Bulgaria
187 H 20 Rushan, China
127 U 8 Rushden, United Kingdom
65 D 18 Rushville, Illinois, U.S.A.
149 C 14 Rusnė, Lithuania
148 I 12 Rušonu ezers, Latvia
60 L 4 Russell, Kentucky, U.S.A.
68 L 4 Russell, Kansas, U.S.A.
234 L 6 Russell Islands, Solomon Islands
60 H 7 Russell Springs, Kentucky, U.S.A.
60 F 7 Russellville, Kentucky, U.S.A.
63 O 2 Russellville, Alabama, U.S.A.
69 U 10 Russellville, Arkansas, U.S.A.
152 J 9 Russian Federation, Europe
240 M 12 Russkaya, Antarctica
153 V 7 Russkoye Ust'ye, Russian Federation
171 U 7 Rust'avi, Georgia
219 N 11 Rustenburg, Republic of South Africa
62 I 4 Ruston, Louisiana, U.S.A.
135 C 17 Ruten, Norway
193 O 15 Ruteng, Indonesia
77 M 18 Ruth, Nevada, U.S.A.
60 M 10 Rutherfordton, North Carolina, U.S.A.
58 L 7 Rutland, Vermont, U.S.A.
181 N 22 Rutland Island, India
184 H 8 Rutog, China
86 D 9 Rutter, Ontario, Canada
157 R 15 Rutul, Russian Federation
132 M 12 Ruurlo, Netherlands
217 U 14 Ruvuma, Tanzania
219 S 3 Ruvuma, Mozambique/Tanzania
175 V 6 Ruweis, United Arab Emirates
157 P 3 Ruzayevka, Russian Federation
149 F 19 Ruzhany, Belarus
143 J 19 Ružomberok, Slovakia
217 Q 9 Rwanda, Africa
156 M 2 Ryazan', Russian Federation
156 M 2 Ryazanskaya Oblast', Russian Federation
156 M 3 Ryazhsk, Russian Federation
240 J 7 Ryberg Peninsula, Antarctica
154 J 13 Rybinsk, Russian Federation
154 I 12 Rybinsk Reservoir, Russian Federation
143 I 17 Rybnik, Poland
127 T 13 Ryde, United Kingdom
231 S 13 Rye, Victoria, Australia
127 Y 12 Rye, United Kingdom
127 Y 13 Rye Bay, United Kingdom
73 T 6 Ryegate, Montana, U.S.A.
143 M 14 Ryki, Poland
156 I 5 Ryl'sk, Russian Federation
198 I 13 Ryōtsu, Japan
142 J 11 Rypin, Poland
199 N 24 Ryukyu Islands, Japan
40 K 5 Ryukyu Trench, Pacific Ocean
142 D 12 Rzepin, Poland
143 M 17 Rzeszów, Poland
154 G 14 Rzhev, Russian Federation

S

132 L 13 's-Heerenberg, Netherlands
133 I 14 's-Hertogenbosch, Netherlands
90 I 5 Sa de las Minas, Guatemala
191 M 22 Sa Đec, Vietnam
113 D 18 Sa del Tandil, Argentina
191 I 19 Sa Kaeo, Thailand
213 K 24 Saacow, Somalia
137 J 15 Saale, Germany
137 J 18 Saalfeld, Germany
139 Q 6 Saalfelden, Austria
137 C 21 Saarbrücken, Germany
137 B 20 Saarburg, Germany
148 D 9 Sääre, Estonia
148 D 8 Saaremaa, Estonia
135 L 16 Saarijärvi, Finland
137 C 21 Saarland, Germany
138 E 10 Saas Fee, Switzerland
172 J 6 Sab' Ābār, Syria
93 W 8 Saba, Netherlands Antilles
144 J 10 Šabac, Serbia and Montenegro
131 W 4 Sabadell, Spain
199 G 16 Sabae, Japan
195 W 6 Sabah, Malaysia
180 E 12 Sabalgarh, India
90 M 7 Sabamagrande, Honduras
104 L 3 Sabana Grande, Venezuela
104 I 2 Sabanalarga, Colombia
104 L 3 Sabaneta, Venezuela
192 B 8 Sabang, Indonesia
196 G 7 Sabangan, Philippines
150 L 9 Săbăoani, Romania
181 G 25 Sabaragamuwa, Sri Lanka
141 H 15 Sabaudia, Italy
107 I 21 Sabaya, Bolivia
172 H 9 Şabḩā, Jordan
211 T 11 Sabhā, Libya
71 N 11 Sabinal, Texas, U.S.A.
131 T 3 Sabiñánigo, Spain
89 Q 6 Sabinas Hidalgo, Mexico
62 H 6 Sabine, Louisiana, U.S.A.
62 H 8 Sabine Lake, Louisiana, U.S.A.
211 T 8 Sabkhat al Hayshah, Libya
211 X 9 Sabkhat al Qunayyin, Libya
211 W 9 Sabkhat Ghuzayyil, Libya
197 F 14 Sablayan, Philippines
215 S 9 Sabon Kafi, Niger
128 M 13 Sabres, France
241 X 12 Sabrina Coast, Antarctica
196 H 2 Sabtang, Philippines
130 J 6 Sabugal, Portugal
193 N 15 Sabulu, Indonesia
175 O 11 Şabyā, Saudi Arabia
176 M 6 Sabzevār, Iran
76 K 10 Sacajawea Peak, Oregon, U.S.A.
131 Q 6 Sacedón, Spain
187 M 21 Sach'ŏn, South Korea
137 M 16 Sachsen, Germany
136 J 12 Sachsen-Anhalt, Germany
58 G 6 Sackets Harbor, New York, U.S.A.
73 V 2 Saco, Montana, U.S.A.
197 I 22 Sacol, Philippines
77 G 19 Sacramento, California, U.S.A.
77 G 17 Sacramento, California, U.S.A.
75 R 13 Sacramento Mountains, New Mexico, U.S.A.
77 G 16 Sacramento Valley, California, U.S.A.
172 I 5 Şadad, Syria
175 O 11 Şa'dah, Yemen
191 H 26 Sadao, Thailand
181 E 18 Sadaseopet, India
173 V 4 Sadd Darband-i Khān, Iraq
173 T 8 Saddat al Hindīyah, Iraq
175 X 11 Şadḩ, Oman
213 G 20 Sadi, Ethiopia
177 V 12 Sadiqabad, Pakistan
183 Y 9 Sadiya, India
198 I 13 Sadoga-shima, Japan
151 U 11 Sadove, Ukraine
157 P 9 Sadovoye, Russian Federation
177 V 4 Safed Khirs, Afghanistan
177 P 7 Safed Koh, Afghanistan
135 E 21 Säffle, Sweden
74 L 13 Safford, Arizona, U.S.A.
127 X 8 Saffron Walden, United Kingdom
210 G 8 Safi, Morocco
177 O 10 Safidabeh, Iran
172 H 4 Şāfītā, Syria
156 I 1 Safonovo, Russian Federation
173 Z 12 Safwān, Iraq
234 E 4 Sag Sag, Papua New Guinea
184 I 10 Saga, China
199 B 21 Saga, Japan
199 E 21 Saga, Japan
198 K 12 Sagae, Japan
190 C 10 Sagaing, Myanmar
190 D 11 Sagaing, Myanmar
199 K 17 Sagami-nada, Japan
199 K 16 Sagami-wan, Japan
67 U 2 Saganaga Lake, Minnesota, U.S.A.
191 F 21 Saganthif Kyun, Myanmar
181 F 14 Sagar, India
153 S 7 Sagastyr, Russian Federation
183 P 10 Sagauli, India
176 L 8 Saghand, Iran
64 L 13 Saginaw, Michigan, U.S.A.
64 L 13 Saginaw Bay, Michigan, U.S.A.
178 J 6 Sagiz, Kazakhstan
64 G 9 Sagola, Michigan, U.S.A.
131 P 11 Sagra, Spain
130 G 12 Sagres, Portugal
190 C 13 Sagu, Myanmar
92 M 6 Sagua de Tánamo, Cuba
92 J 4 Sagua la Grande, Cuba
75 Q 6 Saguache, Colorado, U.S.A.
87 N 6 Saguenay, Québec, Canada
87 N 6 Saguenay, Québec, Canada
131 T 8 Sagunto, Spain
79 R 3 Sagwon, Alaska, U.S.A.
172 H 9 Saḩāb, Jordan
210 I 13 Sahara, Algeria
42 J 10 Saharan Seamounts, Atlantic Ocean
182 J 7 Saharanpur, India
183 R 11 Saharsa, India
171 V 10 Şahbuz, Azerbaijan
183 S 12 Sahibganj, India
177 X 10 Sahiwal, Pakistan
177 W 9 Sahiwal, Pakistan
177 O 9 Sahlābād, Iran
173 T 12 Şaḩrā' al Ḩijāra, Iraq
88 J 4 Sahuaripa, Mexico
89 O 11 Sahuayo, Mexico
39 V 6 Sahul Shelf, Indian Ocean
213 B 20 Sa'id Bundas, Sudan
210 L 6 Saïda, Algeria
172 G 6 Saïda, Lebanon
234 D 4 Saidor, Papua New Guinea
183 T 11 Saidpur, Bangladesh
199 E 17 Saigō, Japan
183 X 14 Saiha, India
187 B 14 Saihan Tal, China
199 E 20 Saijō, Japan
199 D 21 Saiki, Japan
135 N 17 Saimaa, Finland
177 P 11 Saindak, Pakistan
124 J 13 St Abb's Head, United Kingdom
139 W 5 St Aegyd am Neuwalde, Austria
126 J 15 St Agnes, United Kingdom
129 O 7 St-Aignan, France
85 Y 10 St Alban's, Newfoundland and Labrador, Canada
127 V 10 St Albans, United Kingdom
60 M 4 St Albans, West Virginia, U.S.A.
127 R 14 St Alban's Head, United Kingdom
129 Q 8 St-Amand-Montrond, France
129 U 9 St-Amour, France
139 U 8 St Andrä, Austria
38 B 14 St-André, Réunion
63 X 6 St Andrew Sound, Georgia, U.S.A.
124 I 12 St Andrews, United Kingdom
38 B 9 Ste Anne, Seychelles
87 R 5 Ste-Anne-des-Monts, Québec, Canada
85 X 9 St Anthony, Newfoundland and Labrador, Canada
138 K 7 St Anton am Arlberg, Austria
231 R 13 St Arnaud, Victoria, Australia
233 H 17 St Arnaud, New Zealand
127 O 4 St Asaph, United Kingdom
85 W 9 St-Augustin, Québec, Canada
63 W 8 St Augustine, Florida, U.S.A.
126 K 15 St Austell, United Kingdom
126 K 15 St Austell Bay, United Kingdom
93 X 8 St Barthélémy, France, France
129 N 15 St-Béat, France
38 B 14 St-Benoit, Réunion
126 J 9 St Bride's Bay, United Kingdom
128 J 5 St-Brieuc, France
129 O 6 St-Calais, France
86 F 13 St Catharines, Ontario, Canada
42 B 6 St Catherine Point, Bermuda
127 T 14 St Catherine's Point, United Kingdom
129 P 12 St-Céré, France
73 Q 13 Saint Charles, Idaho, U.S.A.
69 X 4 St Charles, Missouri, U.S.A.
126 L 9 St Clears, United Kingdom
67 R 7 St Cloud, Minnesota, U.S.A.
93 V 8 St Croix, Virgin Islands, U.S.A.
64 C 10 St Croix Falls, Wisconsin, U.S.A.
87 O 9 St-Damien-de-Buckland, Québec, Canada
126 J 9 St David's, United Kingdom
126 J 9 St David's Head, United Kingdom
42 B 7 St David's Island, Bermuda
38 A 14 St-Denis, Réunion
129 W 5 St-Dié, France
129 T 5 St Dizier, France
129 T 10 St-Étienne, France
93 X 8 St Eusatius, Netherlands Antilles
87 P 6 St-Fabien, Québec, Canada
86 M 6 St-Félicien, Québec, Canada
129 S 6 St-Florentin, France
129 R 11 St-Flour, France
68 G 2 St Francis, Kansas, U.S.A.
138 I 6 St Gallen, Switzerland
129 N 15 St-Gaudens, France
231 U 9 St George, Queensland, Australia
42 C 7 St George, Bermuda
61 P 14 St George, South Carolina, U.S.A.
74 H 7 St George, Utah, U.S.A.
87 S 10 St George, New Brunswick, Canada
63 S 8 St George Island, Florida, U.S.A.
78 J 11 St George Island, Alaska, U.S.A.
139 U 3 St Georgen, Austria
93 Y 13 St George's, Grenada
105 Y 7 St Georges, French Guiana
87 O 9 St-Georges, Québec, Canada
87 X 9 St George's Bay, Nova Scotia, Canada
85 W 11 St Georges Bay, Newfoundland and Labrador, Canada
125 E 21 St George's Channel, Republic of Ireland/United Kingdom
234 H 3 St George's Channel, Papua New Guinea
42 B 7 St George's Island, Bermuda
139 R 5 St Gilgen, Austria
133 F 17 St-Gillis-Waas, Belgium
129 O 15 St-Girons, France
126 K 10 St Govan's Head, United Kingdom
64 K 12 Saint Helen, Michigan, U.S.A.
43 M 25 St Helena, U.K.
218 J 14 Saint Helena Bay, Republic of South Africa
43 J 16 Saint Helena Fracture Zone, Atlantic Ocean
61 P 15 St Helena Sound, South Carolina, U.S.A.

Country · Internal administrative region: State/Province/Territory/Dependent territory · Capital city · Mountain range/Undersea ridge · Mountain peak/Volcano/Seamount · Geographic feature · Headland/Point/Cape/Peninsula · Desert · Island/Island group · Antarctic base · Ocean · Sea · Bay/Gulf/Channel/Strait · Lake · Salt pan/Dry/Intermittent lake · Riv

231 T 15 **St Helens**, Tasmania, Australia
127 P 3 **St Helens**, United Kingdom
76 F 9 **St Helens**, Oregon, U.S.A.
125 J 26 **St Helier**, United Kingdom
133 J 23 **St-Hubert**, Belgium
86 L 10 **St-Hyacinthe**, Québec, Canada
64 K 10 **St Ignace**, Michigan, U.S.A.
126 I 15 **St Ives**, United Kingdom
127 W 7 **St Ives**, United Kingdom
126 J 15 **St Ives Bay**, United Kingdom ≈
132 J 6 **St Jacobiparochie**, Netherlands
139 O 8 **St Jakob**, Austria
128 K 14 **St-Jean-de-Luz**, France
129 V 11 **St-Jean-de-Maurienne**, France
128 K 8 **St-Jean-de-Monts**, France
87 O 8 **St-Jean-de-Port-Joli**, Québec, Canada
86 L 11 **St-Jean-sur-Richelieu**, Québec, Canada
86 K 10 **St-Jérôme**, Québec, Canada
139 P 6 **St Johann in Tirol**, Austria
87 S 10 **Saint John**, New Brunswick, Canada
68 L 5 **St John**, Kansas, U.S.A.
85 U 13 **St John**, New Brunswick, Canada
93 V 8 **St John**, Virgin Islands, U.S.A. 🏝
65 K 14 **Saint Johns**, Michigan, U.S.A.
85 Z 10 **St John's**, Newfoundland and Labrador, Canada
93 Y 9 **St John's**, Antigua and Barbuda 🏛
74 M 11 **St Johns**, Arizona, U.S.A.
60 E 10 **St Joseph**, Tennessee, U.S.A.
62 K 5 **St Joseph**, Louisiana, U.S.A.
69 R 2 **St Joseph**, Missouri, U.S.A.
38 B 15 **St-Joseph**, Réunion
63 R 8 **St Joseph Bay**, Florida, U.S.A. ≈
71 Q 13 **St Joseph Island**, Texas, U.S.A. 🏝
86 A 9 **St Joseph Island**, Ontario, Canada 🏝
86 J 10 **St-Jovité**, Québec, Canada
129 O 10 **St-Junien**, France
126 J 15 **St Keverne**, United Kingdom
93 X 8 **St Kitts**, St Kitts and Nevis 🏝
93 X 9 **St Kitts and Nevis**, North America □
105 X 6 **St-Laurent-du-Maroni**, French Guiana
81 W 11 **St Lawrence**, Québec, Canada ∿
78 K 7 **St Lawrence Island**, Alaska, U.S.A. 🏝
133 K 25 **St-Léger**, Belgium
86 M 9 **St-Léonard**, Québec, Canada
87 Q 8 **St-Léonard**, New Brunswick, Canada
38 A 15 **St Leu**, Réunion
128 L 4 **St-Lô**, France
69 X 4 **St Louis**, Missouri, U.S.A.
214 D 7 **St-Louis**, Senegal
38 A 15 **St-Louis**, Réunion
93 Z 11 **St Lucia**, North America □
93 Y 11 **St Lucia Channel**, St Lucia ≈
93 W 8 **St Maarten**, Netherlands Antilles 🏝
128 K 4 **St-Malo**, France
93 O 7 **St Marc**, Haiti
129 P 8 **St-Marcel**, France
133 E 19 **St-Maria-Lierde**, Belgium
38 B 14 **Ste-Marie**, Réunion
87 N 9 **Ste-Marie**, Québec, Canada
63 T 7 **St Marks**, Florida, U.S.A.
93 X 8 **St Martin**, France, France 🏝
231 P 10 **St Mary Peak**, South Australia, Australia ▲
69 P 3 **Saint Marys**, Kansas, U.S.A.
85 Z 11 **St Mary's Bay**, Newfoundland and Labrador, Canada ≈
78 J 9 **St Matthew Island**, Alaska, U.S.A. 🏝
234 F 2 **St Matthias Group**, Papua New Guinea 🏝
126 K 15 **St Mawes**, United Kingdom
128 M 9 **St-Maxient-l'École**, France
129 W 14 **Ste-Maxime**, France
139 R 7 **St Michael**, Austria
139 U 6 **St Michael**, Austria
86 K 9 **St-Michel-des-Saints**, Québec, Canada
138 J 9 **St Moritz**, Switzerland
128 K 7 **St-Nazaire**, France
127 V 8 **St Neots**, United Kingdom
133 F 17 **St-Niklaas**, Belgium
138 E 10 **St Niklaus**, Switzerland
139 S 6 **St Nikolai**, Austria
129 Q 1 **St-Omer**, France
87 O 8 **St-Pacôme**, Québec, Canada
128 L 14 **St-Palais**, France
87 O 7 **St-Pascal**, Québec, Canada
38 A 14 **St Paul**, Réunion
66 M 14 **St Paul**, Nebraska, U.S.A.
67 S 8 **St Paul**, Minnesota, U.S.A.
42 H 13 **Saint Paul Fracture Zone**, Atlantic Ocean ◇
39 O 10 **St Paul Island**, France 🏝
78 J 11 **St Paul Island**, Alaska, U.S.A. 🏝
87 Y 7 **St Paul Island**, Nova Scotia, Canada 🏝
41 Y 15 **St Paul's Point**, Pitcairn Island ▶
136 F 8 **St Peter-Ording**, Germany
125 J 25 **St Peter Port**, United Kingdom
87 Y 9 **St Peter's**, Nova Scotia, Canada
87 W 8 **St Peters**, Prince Edward Island, Canada
154 F 10 **St Petersburg**, Russian Federation
63 V 11 **St Petersburg**, Florida, U.S.A.
38 A 15 **St-Pierre**, Réunion
81 Z 10 **St-Pierre**, St Pierre and Miquelon 🏛
85 Y 11 **St-Pierre**, France, Canada
85 X 11 **St Pierre and Miquelon**, France ▣
128 L 9 **St-Pierre-d'Oléron**, France
128 I 4 **St-Pol-de-Léon**, France
139 W 4 **St Pölten**, Austria
129 Q 14 **St-Pons-de-Thomiéres**, France
129 R 9 **St-Pourçain-sur-Sioule**, France
87 Q 7 **St Quentin**, New Brunswick, Canada
129 R 2 **St-Quentin**, France
129 W 14 **St-Raphaël**, France
72 L 4 **Saint Regis**, Montana, U.S.A.
38 B 15 **Ste-Rose**, Réunion
87 O 7 **St Siméon**, Québec, Canada
61 Q 13 **St Stephen**, South Carolina, U.S.A.
79 W 10 **St Terese**, Alaska, U.S.A.
86 L 10 **Ste-Thérese**, Québec, Canada
86 C 14 **St Thomas**, Ontario, Canada
93 V 8 **St Thomas**, Virgin Islands, U.S.A. 🏝
87 N 8 **St-Tite-des-Caps**, Québec, Canada
129 W 14 **St-Tropez**, France
133 I 19 **St-Truiden**, Belgium
129 O 2 **St-Valery-en-Caux**, France
139 T 8 **St Veit an der Glan**, Austria
93 Y 12 **St Vincent**, St Vincent and the Grenadines 🏝
93 X 12 **St Vincent and the Grenadines**, North America □
63 R 8 **St Vincent Island**, Florida, U.S.A. 🏝
93 Y 11 **St Vincent Passage**, St Lucia ≈
83 L 17 **St Walburg**, Saskatchewan, Canada
93 Z 10 **Sainte-Marie**, Martinique
93 Y 9 **Sainte-Rose**, Guadeloupe, France
128 M 10 **Saintes**, France
236 A 8 **Saipan**, Northern Mariana Islands 🏛
236 A 8 **Saipan**, Northern Mariana Islands 🏝
190 B 11 **Saitlai**, Myanmar
199 C 23 **Saito**, Japan
107 H 20 **Sajama**, Bolivia
210 J 6 **Saka**, Morocco
199 G 18 **Sakai**, Japan
199 F 19 **Sakaide**, Japan
199 E 18 **Sakaiminato**, Japan
174 M 2 **Sakākah**, Saudi Arabia
219 W 9 **Sakaraha**, Madgascar
214 K 12 **Sakassou**, Côte d'Ivoire
198 J 12 **Sakata**, Japan
153 X 13 **Sakhalin**, Russian Federation 🏝
171 W 7 **Şäki**, Azerbaijan
215 O 12 **Saki**, Nigeria
149 D 15 **Šakiai**, Lithuania
199 M 26 **Sakishima-shotō**, Japan 🏝
191 K 16 **Sakon Nakhon**, Thailand
177 U 14 **Sakrand**, Pakistan
218 K 13 **Sakrivier**, Republic of South Africa
199 J 15 **Saku**, Japan
199 L 16 **Sakura**, Japan
151 T 12 **Saky**, Ukraine
43 B 16 **Sal**, Cape Verde 🏝
135 H 20 **Sala**, Sweden
41 W 10 **Sala y Gómez**, Chile 🏝
86 K 11 **Salaberry-de-Valleyfield**, Québec, Canada
148 F 9 **Salacgrīva**, Latvia
112 D 11 **Saladas**, Argentina
113 C 16 **Saladillo**, Argentina
112 B 12 **Salado**, Argentina ∿
89 P 5 **Salado**, Mexico ∿
214 I 11 **Saladou**, Guinea
173 T 2 **Salahuddin**, Iraq
215 W 8 **Salal**, Chad
212 H 13 **Salâla**, Sudan
175 W 11 **Şalālah**, Oman
90 H 5 **Salamá**, Guatemala
110 F 11 **Salamanca**, Chile
130 L 5 **Salamanca**, Spain
58 D 10 **Salamanca**, New York, U.S.A.
215 Y 10 **Salamat**, Chad ▣
172 I 4 **Salamīyah**, Syria
148 C 12 **Salantai**, Lithuania
110 H 6 **Salar de Arizaro**, Argentina 💧
110 H 4 **Salar de Ascotán**, Chile 💧
110 G 5 **Salar de Atacama**, Chile 💧
107 I 21 **Salar de Coipasa**, Bolivia 💧
107 I 22 **Salar de Uyuni**, Bolivia 💧
131 O 3 **Salas de los Infantes**, Spain
192 J 14 **Salatiga**, Indonesia
157 W 3 **Salavat**, Russian Federation
193 T 11 **Salawati**, Indonesia 🏝
181 A 15 **Salaya**, India
193 O 13 **Salayar**, Indonesia 🏝
127 N 15 **Salcombe**, United Kingdom
218 J 15 **Saldanha**, Republic of South Africa
148 D 11 **Saldus**, Latvia
231 T 13 **Sale**, Victoria, Australia
152 L 8 **Salekhard**, Russian Federation
181 E 22 **Salem**, India
59 O 9 **Salem**, Massachusetts, U.S.A.
65 F 21 **Salem**, Illinois, U.S.A.
69 W 6 **Salem**, Missouri, U.S.A.
74 K 3 **Salem**, Utah, U.S.A.
76 G 10 **Salem**, Oregon, U.S.A.
141 H 22 **Salemi**, Italy
141 O 16 **Salentina Peninsula**, Italy ▶
141 K 16 **Salerno**, Italy
127 Q 3 **Salford**, United Kingdom
143 J 21 **Salgótarján**, Hungary
108 N 13 **Salgueiro**, Brazil
210 L 11 **Sali**, Algeria
193 R 9 **Salibabu**, Indonesia 🏝
75 Q 5 **Salida**, Colorado, U.S.A.
149 J 20 **Salihorsk**, Belarus
219 R 4 **Salima**, Malawi
69 N 4 **Salina**, Kansas, U.S.A.
74 J 5 **Salina**, Utah, U.S.A.
89 U 14 **Salina Cruz**, Mexico
111 I 16 **Salina Gualicho**, Argentina 💧
106 A 10 **Salinas**, Ecuador
77 G 21 **Salinas**, California, U.S.A.
89 P 9 **Salinas**, Mexico
110 I 5 **Salinas Grandes**, Argentina 💧
108 K 9 **Salinópolis**, Brazil
127 S 12 **Salisbury**, United Kingdom
61 W 4 **Salisbury**, Maryland, U.S.A.
61 P 9 **Salisbury**, North Carolina, U.S.A.
85 P 3 **Salisbury Island**, Nunavut, Canada 🏝
127 R 12 **Salisbury Plain**, United Kingdom ◇
150 I 11 **Săliște**, Romania
172 I 8 **Şalkhad**, Syria
131 W 4 **Sallent**, Spain
113 A 17 **Salliqueló**, Argentina
69 R 10 **Sallisaw**, Oklahoma, U.S.A.
85 Q 4 **Salluit**, Québec, Canada
183 N 9 **Sallyana**, Nepal
173 U 7 **Salmān Pāk**, Iraq
176 E 3 **Salmās**, Iran
148 D 8 **Salme**, Estonia
72 L 7 **Salmon**, Idaho, U.S.A. ∿
73 N 8 **Salmon**, Idaho, U.S.A.
83 H 21 **Salmon Arm**, British Columbia, Canada
41 P 5 **Salmon Bank**, Pacific Ocean ▲
72 M 8 **Salmon River Mountains**, Idaho, U.S.A. ⛰
135 L 19 **Salo**, Finland
140 E 6 **Salò**, Italy
129 U 14 **Salon-de-Provence**, France
150 F 9 **Salonta**, Romania
110 I 10 **Salsacate**, Argentina
156 M 11 **Sal'sk**, Russian Federation
74 K 12 **Salt**, Arizona, U.S.A. ∿
70 F 7 **Salt Basin**, Texas, U.S.A. 💧
70 F 7 **Salt Flat**, Texas, U.S.A.
74 J 2 **Salt Lake City**, Utah, U.S.A.
177 W 8 **Salt Range**, Pakistan ◇
110 I 6 **Salta**, Argentina
110 I 6 **Salta**, Argentina ▣
126 M 14 **Saltash**, United Kingdom
89 P 7 **Saltillo**, Mexico
112 D 13 **Salto**, Uruguay
113 C 15 **Salto**, Argentina
112 E 13 **Salto**, Uruguay ▣
109 H 19 **Salto del Guairá**, Paraguay
77 M 25 **Salton Sea**, California, U.S.A. 💧
135 J 19 **Saltvik**, Finland
61 N 12 **Saluda**, South Carolina, U.S.A.
172 M 2 **Salūq**, Syria
197 N 20 **Salvacion**, Philippines
109 N 15 **Salvador**, Brazil
110 J 4 **Salvador Mazza**, Argentina
175 T 6 **Salwah**, Saudi Arabia
190 F 13 **Salween**, Myanmar ∿
60 L 5 **Salyersville**, Kentucky, U.S.A.
139 Q 7 **Salzburg**, Austria ▣
139 Q 5 **Salzburg**, Austria
137 H 14 **Salzgitter**, Germany
139 Q 5 **Salzkammergut**, Austria ⛰
136 I 12 **Salzwedel**, Germany
191 G 16 **Sam Ngao**, Thailand
71 U 7 **Sam Rayburn Reservoir**, Texas, U.S.A. 💧
190 M 13 **Sâm Son**, Vietnam
107 K 21 **Samaipata**, Bolivia
197 M 22 **Samal**, Philippines 🏝
197 H 23 **Samales Group**, Philippines 🏝
212 E 9 **Samâlût**, Egypt
93 R 7 **Samaná**, Dominican Republic
177 T 6 **Samangān**, Afghanistan ▣
197 L 15 **Samar**, Philippines 🏝
157 T 3 **Samara**, Russian Federation ∿
157 S 3 **Samara**, Russian Federation
234 G 7 **Samarai**, Papua New Guinea
192 M 11 **Samarinda**, Indonesia
179 Q 13 **Samarkand**, Uzbekistan
179 P 12 **Samarqand Wiloyati**, Uzbekistan ▣
173 S 6 **Sāmarrā'**, Iraq
157 T 4 **Samarskaya Oblast'**, Russian Federation ▣
179 Y 5 **Samarskoye**, Kazakhstan
183 Q 11 **Samastipur**, India
171 Y 8 **Şamaxi**, Azerbaijan
217 O 10 **Samba**, Democratic Republic of Congo
218 H 2 **Samba Cajú**, Angola
181 I 16 **Sambalpur**, India
192 I 10 **Sambas**, Indonesia
219 Z 5 **Sambava**, Madgascar
150 H 5 **Sambir**, Ukraine
133 E 22 **Sambre**, Belgium ∿
187 N 19 **Samch'ŏk**, South Korea
219 O 3 **Samfya**, Zambia
187 M 15 **Samjiyŏn**, North Korea
171 V 8 **Şämkir**, Azerbaijan
211 T 11 **Samnū**, Libya
236 J 7 **Samoa**, Oceania □
41 Q 9 **Samoa Basin**, Pacific Ocean ◇
236 J 8 **Samoan Islands**, Samoa/American Samoa 🏝
146 G 10 **Samokov**, Bulgaria
143 G 21 **Šamorín**, Slovakia
147 M 20 **Samos**, Greece
147 L 20 **Samos**, Greece 🏝
147 I 14 **Samotharaki**, Greece 🏝
159 S 6 **Samothraki**, Mediterranean Sea 🏝
159 S 6 **Samothraki Plateau**, Mediterranean Sea ◇
192 K 12 **Sampit**, Indonesia
234 H 4 **Sampun**, Papua New Guinea
217 P 13 **Sampwe**, Democratic Republic of Congo
135 D 25 **Samsø**, Denmark 🏝
191 H 19 **Samut Prakan**, Thailand
191 H 19 **Samut Sakhon**, Thailand
191 H 19 **Samut Songkhram**, Thailand
143 N 19 **San**, Poland ∿
113 D 18 **San Agustín**, Argentina
110 H 10 **San Agustín de Valle Fértil**, Argentina
77 H 19 **San Andreas**, California, U.S.A.
90 I 2 **San Andrēs**, Guatemala
196 I 13 **San Andres**, Philippines
196 K 13 **San Andres**, Philippines
107 K 18 **San Andrés**, Bolivia
75 Q 12 **San Andres Mountains**, New Mexico, U.S.A. ⛰
89 U 12 **San Andrés Tuxtla**, Mexico
70 M 8 **San Angelo**, Texas, U.S.A.
105 N 8 **San Antonio**, Venezuela
105 Q 3 **San Antonio**, Venezuela
110 H 11 **San Antonio**, Argentina
110 I 9 **San Antonio**, Argentina
110 F 12 **San Antonio**, Chile
196 F 11 **San Antonio**, Philippines
71 O 11 **San Antonio**, Texas, U.S.A.
71 P 11 **San Antonio**, Texas, U.S.A. ∿
75 P 12 **San Antonio**, New Mexico, U.S.A.
90 J 3 **San Antonio**, Belize
90 J 5 **San Antonio**, Honduras
90 L 6 **San Antonio**, Honduras
131 W 9 **San Antonio Abad**, Spain
197 B 20 **San Antonio Bay**, Philippines ≈
110 I 6 **San Antonio de los Cobres**, Argentina
90 M 6 **San Antonio de Oriente**, Honduras
111 J 16 **San Antonio Oeste**, Argentina
140 J 12 **San Benedetto del Tronto**, Italy
138 H 9 **San Bernadino**, Switzerland
77 K 24 **San Bernardino**, California, U.S.A.
77 K 24 **San Bernardino Mountains**, California, U.S.A. ⛰
197 K 14 **San Bernardino Strait**, Philippines ≈
110 G 12 **San Bernardo**, Chile
88 K 7 **San Blas**, Mexico
107 J 18 **San Borja**, Bolivia
110 K 6 **San Camilo**, Argentina
105 O 9 **San Carlos**, Venezuela
107 L 20 **San Carlos**, Bolivia
111 F 14 **San Carlos**, Chile
113 F 16 **San Carlos**, Uruguay
196 G 9 **San Carlos**, Philippines
197 J 17 **San Carlos**, Philippines
88 H 7 **San Carlos**, Mexico
91 Q 12 **San Carlos**, Costa Rica
91 P 10 **San Carlos**, Nicaragua
91 W 14 **San Carlos**, Panama
111 G 17 **San Carlos de Bariloche**, Argentina
113 B 17 **San Carlos de Bolívar**, Argentina
141 O 16 **San Cataldo**, Italy
110 F 13 **San Clemente**, Chile
77 K 25 **San Clemente**, California, U.S.A.
77 J 26 **San Clemente Island**, California, U.S.A. 🏝
90 H 5 **San Crisóbal Verapez**, Guatemala
235 N 7 **San Cristobal**, Solomon Islands 🏝
112 B 12 **San Cristobal**, Argentina
104 J 11 **San Cristóbal**, Colombia
104 K 4 **San Cristóbal**, Venezuela
110 K 9 **San Cristóbal**, Argentina
42 M 11 **San Cristóbal de la Laguna**, Canary Islands
89 W 13 **San Cristóbal de las Casas**, Mexico
90 I 6 **San Cristobal Frontera**, Guatemala
71 P 13 **San Diego**, Texas, U.S.A.
77 K 26 **San Diego**, California, U.S.A.
140 H 7 **San Donà di Piave**, Italy
104 M 2 **San Felipe**, Venezuela
110 G 11 **San Felipe**, Chile
88 G 3 **San Felipe**, Mexico
89 P 10 **San Felipe**, Mexico
110 G 12 **San Fernando**, Chile
113 D 15 **San Fernando**, Argentina
130 K 13 **San Fernando**, Spain
196 F 10 **San Fernando**, Philippines
196 F 8 **San Fernando**, Philippines
77 J 24 **San Fernando**, California, U.S.A.
88 G 4 **San Fernando**, Mexico
89 S 8 **San Fernando**, Mexico
93 Y 14 **San Fernando**, Trinidad and Tobago
105 N 4 **San Fernando de Apure**, Venezuela
105 N 7 **San Fernando de Atabapo**, Venezuela
112 B 13 **San Francisco**, Argentina
77 F 19 **San Francisco**, California, U.S.A.
77 G 19 **San Francisco Bay**, California, U.S.A. ≈
110 J 9 **San Francisco del Chañar**, Argentina
90 L 7 **San Francisco Gotera**, El Salvador
131 W 10 **San Francisco Javier**, Spain

□ Country ▣ Internal administrative region: State/Province/Territory/Dependent territory 🏛 Capital city ⛰ Mountain range/Undersea ridge ▲ Mountain peak/Volcano/Seamount ◇ Geographic feature ▶ Headland/Point/Cape/Peninsula 🏜 Desert 🏝 Island/Island group ⁂ Antarctic base 🌊 Ocean 🌀 Sea ≈ Bay/Gulf/Channel/Strait 💧 Lake ⊟ Salt pan/Dry/Intermittent lake ∿ River

106 C 8 San Gabriel, Ecuador
93 T 8 San Germán, Puerto Rico
140 E 11 San Gimignano, Italy
141 N 19 San Giovanni in Fiore, Italy
107 J 18 San Ignacio, Bolivia
107 M 19 San Ignacio, Bolivia
106 B 12 San Ignacio, Peru
88 H 6 San Ignacio, Mexico
90 J 2 San Ignacio, Belize
196 H 9 San Ildefonso Peninsula, Philippines ▶
91 Q 13 San Isidro, Costa Rica
197 K 14 San Jacinto, Philippines
107 K 18 San Javier, Bolivia
112 B 13 San Javier, Argentina
77 G 19 San Joaquin, California, U.S.A. ⤳
77 H 20 San Joaquin Valley, California, U.S.A. ◇
113 B 14 San Jorge, Argentina
236 A 8 San Jose, Northern Mariana Islands
196 G 9 San Jose, Philippines
197 G 14 San Jose, Philippines
65 F 18 San Jose, Illinois, U.S.A.
75 R 10 San Jose, New Mexico, U.S.A.
77 G 20 San Jose, California, U.S.A.
113 E 15 San José, Uruguay ▣
90 H 7 San José, Guatemala
90 M 5 San José, Honduras
91 Q 12 San José, Costa Rica ♣
197 H 17 San Jose de Buenavista, Philippines
107 N 20 San José de Chiquitos, Bolivia
112 D 12 San José de Feliciano, Argentina
88 J 4 San José de Gracia, Mexico
110 H 10 San José de Jáchal, Argentina
110 J 10 San José de la Dormida, Argentina
113 E 15 San José de Mayo, Uruguay
107 D 16 San José de Quero, Peru
89 Q 8 San José de Raíces, Mexico
88 J 9 San José del Cabo, Mexico
104 J 8 San José del Guaviare, Colombia
110 H 10 San Juan, Argentina
110 G 10 San Juan, Argentina ▣
89 T 13 San Juan, Mexico
91 Q 11 San Juan, Nicaragua ⤳
93 U 7 San Juan, Puerto Rico ♣
93 Q 7 San Juan, Dominican Republic
41 Z 1 San Juan Bautista, Juan Fernández Islands
109 G 20 San Juan Bautista, Paraguay
105 N 3 San Juan de los Morros, Venezuela
111 J 25 San Juan de Salvamento, Argentina
91 Q 11 San Juan del Norte, Nicaragua
89 Q 11 San Juan del Río, Mexico
91 N 10 San Juan del Sur, Nicaragua
90 G 4 San Juan Ixcoy, Guatemala
75 P 7 San Juan Mountains, Colorado, U.S.A. ▲▲
88 H 6 San Juanico, Mexico
110 L 10 San Justo, Argentina
107 J 18 San Lorenzo, Bolivia
106 B 7 San Lorenzo, Ecuador
107 H 16 San Lorenzo, Peru
113 B 14 San Lorenzo, Argentina
90 L 7 San Lorenzo, Honduras
107 K 22 San Lucas, Bolivia
88 H 6 San Lucas, Mexico
88 J 9 San Lucas, Mexico
110 I 11 San Luis, Argentina
110 I 12 San Luis, Argentina
89 Q 10 San Luis de la Paz, Mexico
112 D 10 San Luis del Palmar, Argentina
77 H 23 San Luis Obispo, California, U.S.A.

75 P 6 San Luis Peak, Colorado, U.S.A. ▲
89 P 10 San Luis Potosí, Mexico
89 P 9 San Luis Potosí, Mexico
88 G 1 San Luis Río Colorado, Mexico
88 H 3 San Luisito, Mexico
71 P 10 San Marcos, Texas, U.S.A.
89 R 14 San Marcos, Mexico
90 F 5 San Marcos, Guatemala
90 M 7 San Marcos de Colón, Honduras
140 H 10 San Marino, Europe ▣
240 I 5 San Martin, Antarctica ▦
106 C 13 San Martín, Peru
107 L 18 San Martín, Bolivia ⤳
110 H 11 San Martín, Argentina
110 I 9 San Martín, Argentina
111 G 16 San Martín de Los Andes, Argentina
131 N 6 San Martín de Valdeiglesias, Spain
77 F 20 San Mateo, California, U.S.A.
90 F 4 San Mateo Ixtatán, Guatemala
107 O 19 San Matías, Bolivia
107 M 20 San Miguel, Bolivia
107 L 18 San Miguel, Bolivia ⤳
90 K 7 San Miguel, El Salvador
91 X 14 San Miguel, Panama
196 J 12 San Miguel Bay, Philippines ≈
107 J 19 San Miguel de Huachi, Bolivia
110 J 7 San Miguel de Tucumán, Argentina
113 C 16 San Miguel del Monte, Argentina
77 H 24 San Miguel Island, California, U.S.A. ⤱
197 C 21 San Miguel Islands, Philippines ⤱
91 P 10 San Miguelito, Nicaragua
91 X 13 San Miguelito, Panama
113 B 15 San Nicolás de los Arroyos, Argentina
77 I 25 San Nicolas Island, California, U.S.A. ⤱
141 C 18 San Nicoló Gerrei, Italy
107 L 19 San Pablo, Bolivia
196 G 12 San Pablo, Philippines
110 I 6 San Pedro, Argentina
112 F 9 San Pedro, Argentina
113 C 15 San Pedro, Argentina
197 G 14 San Pedro, Philippines
88 J 8 San Pedro, Mexico
90 L 1 San Pedro, Belize
214 J 14 San-Pédro, Côte d'Ivoire
90 H 4 San Pedro Carchá, Guatemala
89 O 7 San Pedro de las Colonias, Mexico
93 R 7 San Pedro de Macoris, Dominican Republic
131 S 11 San Pedro del Pinatar, Spain
90 K 4 San Pedro Sula, Honduras
88 F 3 San Quintín, Mexico
110 H 12 San Rafael, Argentina
91 P 11 San Rafael, Costa Rica
91 N 7 San Rafael del Norte, Nicaragua
107 K 17 San Ramón, Bolivia
107 M 20 San Ramón, Bolivia
140 A 10 San Remo, Italy
71 O 8 San Saba, Texas, U.S.A.
112 D 13 San Salvador, Argentina
90 J 7 San Salvador, El Salvador ♣
93 N 3 San Salvador, The Bahamas
110 I 5 San Salvador de Jujuy, Argentina
111 H 25 San Sebastián, Argentina
42 L 12 San Sebastián de la Gomera, Canary Islands
141 L 14 San Severo, Italy
77 G 22 San Simeon, California, U.S.A.
196 H 5 San Vicente, Philippines
88 F 2 San Vicente, Mexico
90 J 7 San Vicente, El Salvador

107 D 17 San Vicente de Cañete, Peru
104 I 8 San Vicente del Caguán, Colombia
175 P 13 Şan'ā', Yemen ♣
213 N 19 Sanaag, Somalia ▣
241 P 1 Sanae, Antarctica ▦
78 L 14 Sanak Islands, Alaska, U.S.A. ⤱
176 F 5 Sanandaj, Iran
175 U 11 Sanaw, Yemen
184 H 5 Sanchakou, China
180 B 13 Sanchor, India
155 O 14 Sanchursk, Russian Federation
197 N 20 Sanco Point, Philippines ▶
129 Q 8 Sancoins, France
92 J 5 Sancti Spíritus, Cuba
181 B 22 Sand Cay, India ⤱
66 H 12 Sand Hills, Nebraska, U.S.A. ▲▲
69 P 9 Sand Springs, Oklahoma, U.S.A.
199 G 18 Sanda, Japan
192 I 11 Sandai, Indonesia
195 X 5 Sandakan, Malaysia
191 M 20 Sândăn, Cambodia
146 G 12 Sandanski, Bulgaria
234 A 4 Sandaun, Papua New Guinea ▣
124 I 6 Sanday, United Kingdom ⤱
127 Q 5 Sandbach, United Kingdom
70 J 10 Sanderson, Texas, U.S.A.
230 H 5 Sandfire Roadhouse, Western Australia, Australia
127 T 11 Sandhurst, United Kingdom
182 L 10 Sandila, India
139 U 3 Sandl, Austria
135 A 20 Sandnes, Norway
216 M 13 Sandoa, Democratic Republic of Congo
143 M 16 Sandomierz, Poland
134 K 12 Sandön, Sweden
65 F 21 Sandoval, Illinois, U.S.A.
191 C 14 Sandoway, Myanmar
127 T 14 Sandown, United Kingdom
72 K 2 Sandpoint, Idaho, U.S.A.
230 H 9 Sandstone, Western Australia, Australia
67 S 6 Sandstone, Minnesota, U.S.A.
189 T 10 Sandu, China
64 M 13 Sandusky, Michigan, U.S.A.
65 M 16 Sandusky, Ohio, U.S.A.
135 E 15 Sandvika, Norway
127 Z 11 Sandwich, United Kingdom
218 H 10 Sandwich Bay, Namibia ≈
183 V 14 Sandwip, Bangladesh
183 V 14 Sandwip, Bangladesh ⤱
127 V 8 Sandy, United Kingdom
74 K 3 Sandy, Utah, U.S.A.
43 N 26 Sandy Bay, St Helena ≈
231 W 7 Sandy Cape, Queensland, Australia ▶
84 K 9 Sandy Lake, Ontario, Canada ⤳
84 K 9 Sandy Lake, Ontario, Canada
179 N 15 Sandykachi, Turkmenistan
59 O 7 Sanford, Maine, U.S.A.
61 R 10 Sanford, North Carolina, U.S.A.
63 X 9 Sanford, Florida, U.S.A.
181 C 17 Sangamner, India
177 O 7 Sangan, Iran
153 T 10 Sangar, Russian Federation
129 P 1 Sangatte, France
197 H 22 Sangboy Islands, Philippines ⤱
193 N 15 Sangeang, Indonesia ⤱
77 I 21 Sanger, California, U.S.A.
58 H 8 Sangerfield, New York, U.S.A.
137 J 16 Sangerhausen, Germany
188 M 5 Sanggarmai, China

192 J 10 Sanggau, Indonesia
216 H 7 Sangha, Congo ▣
216 H 5 Sangha-Mbaéré, Central African Republic
177 U 14 Sanghar, Pakistan
147 E 23 Sangiás, Greece ▲
193 Q 9 Sangir, Indonesia ⤱
187 M 20 Sangju, South Korea
181 C 18 Sangli, India
215 U 15 Sangmélima, Cameroon
219 P 9 Sango, Zimbabwe
75 Q 6 Sangre de Cristo Range, Colorado, U.S.A. ▲
93 Z 14 Sangre Grande, Trinidad and Tobago
188 J 4 Sangruma, China
182 I 7 Sangrur, India
109 G 14 Sangue, Brazil ⤳
131 S 3 Sangüesa, Spain
128 L 12 Sanguinet, France
63 W 13 Sanibel Island, Florida, U.S.A. ⤱
81 T 10 Sanikiluaq, Nunavut, Canada
173 R 6 Saniyah, Iraq
176 G 4 Sanjbod, Iran
188 K 11 Sanjiachang, China
198 J 13 Sanjō, Japan
130 K 13 Sanlúcar de Barrameda, Spain
141 C 18 Sanluri, Italy
86 K 7 Sanmaur, Québec, Canada
189 S 3 Sanmenxia, China
189 W 10 Sanming, China
142 J 12 Sanniki, Poland
143 N 18 Sanok, Poland
140 I 10 Sansepolcro, Italy
144 F 10 Sanski Most, Bosnia and Herzegovina
189 Q 9 Sansui, China
131 U 6 Sant Carles de la Ràpita, Spain
131 Y 4 Sant Feliu de Guíxols, Spain
107 B 14 Santa, Peru
72 K 4 Santa, Idaho, U.S.A.
90 I 3 Santa Amelia, Guatemala
77 K 25 Santa Ana, California, U.S.A.
88 I 3 Santa Ana, Mexico
90 I 6 Santa Ana, El Salvador
107 K 17 Santa Ana de Yacuma, Bolivia
71 N 7 Santa Anna, Texas, U.S.A.
104 L 4 Santa Barbara, Venezuela
77 I 24 Santa Barbara, California, U.S.A.
90 K 5 Santa Bárbara, Honduras
77 H 24 Santa Barbara Channel, California, U.S.A. ≈
112 K 6 Santa Bárbara d'Oeste, Brazil
77 J 25 Santa Barbara Island, California, U.S.A. ⤱
110 G 6 Santa Catalina, Chile
91 U 14 Santa Catalina, Panama
77 J 25 Santa Catalina Island, California, U.S.A. ⤱
112 H 10 Santa Catarina, Brazil ▣
88 F 4 Santa Catarina, Mexico
104 L 12 Santa Clara, Colombia
77 G 20 Santa Clara, California, U.S.A.
92 I 4 Santa Clara, Cuba
77 J 24 Santa Clarita, California, U.S.A.
106 E 10 Santa Clotilde, Peru
107 L 20 Santa Cruz, Bolivia
107 L 21 Santa Cruz, Bolivia ▣
111 H 22 Santa Cruz, Argentina ▣
111 G 23 Santa Cruz, Argentina ⤳
196 E 9 Santa Cruz, Philippines
196 G 12 Santa Cruz, Philippines
77 G 20 Santa Cruz, California, U.S.A.
91 O 12 Santa Cruz, Costa Rica
90 G 4 Santa Cruz Barillas, Guatemala
42 L 11 Santa Cruz de la Palma, Canary Islands
131 O 10 Santa Cruz de Mudela, Spain
42 M 11 Santa Cruz de Tenerife, Canary Islands

90 L 5 Santa Cruz de Yojoa, Honduras
131 O 7 Santa Cruz del al Zarza, Spain
90 G 5 Santa Cruz del Quiché, Guatemala
131 N 7 Santa Cruz del Retamar, Spain
92 K 6 Santa Cruz del Sur, Cuba
112 G 12 Santa Cruz do Sul, Brazil
77 I 24 Santa Cruz Island, California, U.S.A. ⤱
235 P 7 Santa Cruz Islands, Solomon Islands ⤱
112 C 13 Santa Elena, Argentina
71 O 15 Santa Elena, Texas, U.S.A.
105 S 6 Santa Elena de Uairén, Venezuela
75 Q 9 Santa Fe, New Mexico, U.S.A.
112 B 13 Santa Fé, Argentina
112 C 12 Santa Fé, Argentina ▣
91 U 14 Santa Fé, Panama
92 G 5 Santa Fé, Cuba
88 I 9 Santa Genoveva, Mexico ▲
108 L 11 Santa Inês, Brazil
109 F 15 Santa Isabel, Brazil
110 H 13 Santa Isabel, Argentina
90 I 4 Santa Isabel, Guatemala ⤳
91 X 13 Santa Isabel, Panama
108 D 9 Santa Isabel do Rio Negro, Brazil
112 C 11 Santa Lucia, Argentina
90 G 6 Santa Lucia, Guatemala
77 G 21 Santa Lucia Range, California, U.S.A. ▲▲
43 A 15 Santa Luzia, Cape Verde ⤱
108 K 11 Santa Luzia, Brazil
42 O 2 Santa Maria, Azores ⤱
43 B 16 Santa Maria, Cape Verde
112 G 12 Santa Maria, Brazil
77 I 23 Santa Maria, California, U.S.A.
91 U 14 Santa Maria, Panama ⤳
110 I 7 Santa María, Argentina
89 X 12 Santa María, Mexico
91 N 6 Santa María, Honduras
108 J 13 Santa Maria das Barreiras, Brazil
108 E 9 Santa Maria do Boiaçu, Brazil
104 I 2 Santa Marta, Colombia
77 J 24 Santa Monica, California, U.S.A.
130 K 11 Santa Ollala del Cala, Spain
90 L 5 Santa Rita, Honduras
107 J 18 Santa Rosa, Bolivia
107 G 18 Santa Rosa, Peru
110 H 12 Santa Rosa, Argentina
111 I 16 Santa Rosa, Argentina
112 F 10 Santa Rosa, Brazil
113 A 17 Santa Rosa, Argentina
75 S 10 Santa Rosa, New Mexico, U.S.A.
77 F 18 Santa Rosa, California, U.S.A.
89 Y 11 Santa Rosa, Mexico
90 J 5 Santa Rosa de Copán, Honduras
107 M 19 Santa Rosa de la Roca, Bolivia
108 B 13 Santa Rosa do Purus, Brazil
77 H 25 Santa Rosa Island, California, U.S.A. ⤱
88 H 6 Santa Rosalia, Mexico
112 A 11 Santa Sylvina, Argentina
113 G 15 Santa Vitória, Brazil
109 H 23 Santa Vitória do Palmar, Brazil
189 N 6 Santai, China
109 L 15 Santana, Brazil
112 G 13 Santana da Boa Vista, Brazil
108 I 13 Santana do Araguaia, Brazil
112 F 12 Santana do Livramento, Brazil
104 J 5 Santander, Colombia ▣

131 O 1 Santander, Spain
197 J 19 Santander, Philippines
141 B 19 Sant'Antioco, Italy
131 Y 8 Santanyí, Spain
108 H 19 Santarém, Brazil
130 H 8 Santarém, Portugal ▣
130 G 8 Santarém, Portugal
92 J 2 Santaren Channel, The Bahamas
61 Q 13 Santee, South Carolina, U.S.A. ⤳
110 F 12 Santiago, Chile ♣
110 F 12 Santiago, Chile ▣
112 F 11 Santiago, Brazil
196 H 8 Santiago, Philippines
88 J 9 Santiago, Mexico
91 U 15 Santiago, Panama
93 Q 7 Santiago, Dominican Republic
89 U 14 Santiago Astata, Mexico
130 H 1 Santiago del Compostela, Spain
110 J 8 Santiago del Estero, Argentina
110 J 7 Santiago del Estero, Argentina ▣
130 G 11 Santiago do Cacém, Portugal
70 H 10 Santiago Mountains, Texas, U.S.A. ▲
70 I 10 Santiago Peak, Texas, U.S.A. ▲
193 O 10 Santigi, Indonesia
138 I 7 Säntis, Switzerland ▲
131 P 10 Santisteban del Puerto, Spain
112 F 11 Santo, Brazil
71 P 6 Santo, Texas, U.S.A.
109 M 18 Santo Amaro de Campos, Brazil
112 L 7 Santo André, Brazil
43 A 15 Santo Antão, Cape Verde ⤱
107 N 20 Santo Corazón, Bolivia
107 H 17 Santo Domingo, Peru
88 H 7 Santo Domingo, Mexico
91 P 9 Santo Domingo, Nicaragua
93 R 8 Santo Domingo, Dominican Republic ♣
130 H 4 Santo Tirso, Portugal
107 G 18 Santo Tomás, Peru
88 F 2 Santo Tomás, Mexico
90 L 8 Santo Tomás, Nicaragua
112 E 11 Santo Tomé, Argentina
112 L 7 Santos, Brazil
43 H 17 Santos Plateau, Atlantic Ocean ◇
189 Q 15 Sanya, China
189 O 2 Sanying, China
189 Q 3 Sanyuan, China
218 H 1 Sanza Pombo, Angola
186 J 7 Sanzhan, China
112 K 7 São Bernardo do Campo, Brazil
112 E 11 São Borja, Brazil
112 J 6 São Carlos, Brazil
109 I 14 São Félix do Araguaia, Brazil
108 I 12 São Félix do Xingu, Brazil
43 A 17 São Filipe, Cape Verde
108 M 13 São Francisco, Brazil ⤳
112 F 12 São Francisco de Assis, Brazil
112 I 12 São Francisco de Paula, Brazil
112 J 9 São Francisco do Sul, Brazil
112 F 12 São Gabriel, Brazil
108 C 9 São Gabriel da Cachoeira, Brazil
112 N 7 São Gonçalo, Brazil
108 C 9 São João, Brazil
112 O 6 São João da Barra, Brazil
109 J 15 São João d'Aliança, Brazil
108 J 12 São João do Araguaia, Brazil
108 M 13 São João do Piauí, Brazil
112 I 11 São Joaquim, Brazil
42 N 1 São Jorge, Azores ⤱
112 J 10 São José, Brazil
112 H 13 São José do Norte, Brazil
112 I 5 São José do Rio Preto, Brazil

▣ Country ▣ Internal administrative region: State/Province/Territory/Dependent territory ♣ Capital city ▲▲ Mountain range/Undersea ridge ▲ Mountain peak/Volcano/Seamount ◇ Geographic feature ▶ Headland/Point/Cape/Peninsula ▦ Desert ⤱ Island/Island group ▦ Antarctic base ◎ Ocean ⤳ Sea ≈ Bay/Gulf/Channel/Strait ⤳ Lake ⤳ Salt pan/Dry/Intermittent lake ⤳ River

332

São José dos Campos – Selat Sape

112 L 7 São José dos Campos, Brazil
112 J 9 São José dos Pinhais, Brazil
112 H 13 São Lourenço do Sul, Brazil
108 L 10 São Luís, Brazil
109 H 21 São Luís Gonzaga, Brazil
112 F 11 São Luiz Gonzaga, Brazil
109 G 15 São Manuel, Brazil
109 M 17 São Mateus, Brazil
42 O 2 São Miguel, Azores
109 I 15 São Miguel do Araguaia, Brazil
112 G 9 São Miguel d'Oeste, Brazil
43 A 16 São Nicolau, Cape Verde
112 I 5 São Paulo, Brazil
109 K 19 São Paulo, Brazil
42 I 13 São Pedro e São Paulo, Atlantic Ocean
109 K 16 São Romão, Brazil
112 L 5 São Sebastião do Paraíso, Brazil
112 G 12 São Sepé, Brazil
112 I 4 São Simão, Brazil
43 B 17 São Tiago, Cape Verde
216 B 7 São Tomé, São Tomé and Príncipe
216 B 8 São Tomé, São Tomé and Príncipe
216 B 7 São Tomé and Príncipe, Africa
43 A 15 São Vicente, Cape Verde
42 N 5 São Vicente, Madeira
112 K 7 São Vicente, Brazil
129 U 7 Saône, France
170 F 8 Sapanca, Turkey
215 Q 13 Sapele, Nigeria
147 J 13 Sapes, Greece
90 K 3 Sapodilla Cays, Belize
198 J 6 Sapporo, Japan
141 L 17 Sapri, Italy
112 L 6 Sapucai, Brazil
192 K 14 Sapudi, Indonesia
69 P 9 Sapulpa, Oklahoma, U.S.A.
195 V 7 Sapulut, Malaysia
176 F 5 Saqqez, Iran
176 F 5 Sar Dasht, Iran
177 S 6 Sar-e Pol, Afghanistan
177 S 6 Sar-e Pol, Afghanistan
173 T 1 Sar i Kōrāwa, Iraq
177 S 6 Sar-i-Pul, Afghanistan
145 L 17 Šar Planina, Serbia and Montenegro
146 B 11 Šar Planina, Macedonia (F.Y.R.O.M.)
197 J 16 Sara, Philippines
191 H 18 Sara Buri, Thailand
176 G 4 Sarāb, Iran
173 U 7 Sarābādī, Iraq
70 H 8 Saragosa, Texas, U.S.A.
106 B 11 Saraguro, Ecuador
181 H 16 Saraipali, India
144 H 12 Sarajevo, Bosnia and Herzegovina
177 P 6 Sarakhs, Iran
178 M 15 Sarakhs, Turkmenistan
157 W 4 Saraktash, Russian Federation
190 D 8 Saramati, Myanmar
106 C 11 Sarameriza, Peru
179 T 5 Saran', Kazakhstan
58 J 6 Saranac Lake, New York, U.S.A.
145 K 22 Sarandë, Albania
112 G 10 Sarandi, Brazil
113 F 14 Sarandí del Yí, Uruguay
113 E 15 Sarandí Grande, Uruguay
197 M 25 Sarangani, Philippines
197 L 24 Sarangani Bay, Philippines
197 M 24 Sarangani Islands, Philippines
197 L 25 Sarangani Strait, Philippines
181 H 16 Sarangarh, India
181 E 14 Sarangpur, India
157 P 3 Saransk, Russian Federation
155 S 14 Sarapul, Russian Federation
172 I 3 Sarāqib, Syria
63 V 11 Sarasota, Florida, U.S.A.
151 O 10 Sarata, Ukraine
195 O 10 Saratok, Malaysia
157 Q 5 Saratov, Russian Federation
157 P 5 Saratovskaya Oblast', Russian Federation
157 Q 4 Saratovskoye Vodokhranilishche, Russian Federation
177 P 13 Saravan, Iran
191 M 17 Saravan, Laos
195 R 9 Sarawak, Malaysia
170 C 7 Saray, Turkey
172 H 3 Şarāyā, Syria
214 G 9 Saraya, Senegal
170 D 11 Sarayköy, Turkey
170 H 11 Sarayönü, Turkey
177 P 13 Sarbāz, Iran
177 O 9 Sarbīsheh, Iran
143 I 24 Sárbogárd, Hungary
110 F 9 Sarco, Chile
182 G 8 Sardarshahr, India
141 C 17 Sardegna, Italy
141 C 17 Sardinia, Italy
91 O 11 Sardinia, Costa Rica
158 J 7 Sardinia–Corsica Trough, Mediterranean Sea
158 H 8 Sardino–Balearic Abyssal Plain, Mediterranean Sea
62 M 2 Sardis Lake, Mississippi, U.S.A.
69 Q 11 Sardis Lake, Oklahoma, U.S.A.
138 I 7 Sargans, Switzerland
42 E 10 Sargasso Sea, Atlantic Ocean
177 X 9 Sargodha, Pakistan
215 X 11 Sarh, Chad
176 K 5 Sārī, Iran
147 M 25 Saria, Greece
236 A 7 Sarigan, Northern Mariana Islands
171 R 9 Sarikamiş, Turkey
195 O 10 Sarikei, Malaysia
231 U 6 Sarina, Queensland, Australia
131 T 4 Sariñena, Spain
211 V 13 Sarīr Tibesti, Libya
187 K 18 Sariwŏn, North Korea
170 D 7 Sariyer, Turkey
170 L 11 Sariz, Turkey
125 J 25 Sark, United Kingdom
179 X 8 Sarkand, Kazakhstan
170 F 11 Şarkikaraagaç, Turkey
135 O 17 Särkisalmi, Finland
170 L 10 Şarkişla, Turkey
147 M 14 Şarköy, Turkey
193 X 11 Sarmi, Indonesia
135 E 17 Särna, Sweden
138 F 8 Sarnen, Switzerland
86 B 13 Sarnia, Ontario, Canada
150 L 2 Sarny, Ukraine
198 L 3 Saroma-ko, Japan
147 G 20 Saronic Gulf, Greece
170 A 8 Saros Körfezi, Turkey
143 M 21 Sárospatak, Hungary
157 O 2 Sarova, Russian Federation
177 V 7 Sarowbī, Afghanistan
157 P 10 Sarpa, Russian Federation
129 W 4 Sarrebourg, France
129 W 4 Sarreguemines, France
90 J 4 Sarstoon, Belize
177 V 13 Sartanahu, Pakistan
129 Y 15 Sartène, France
147 H 15 Sarti, Greece
198 K 6 Saru, Japan
171 U 9 Särur, Azerbaijan
143 G 23 Sárvár, Hungary
176 I 11 Sarvestān, Iran
179 U 12 Sary-Tash, Kyrgyzstan
178 I 8 Sarykamys, Kazakhstan
178 L 11 Sarykamyshkoye Ozero, Turkmenistan
179 W 9 Saryozek, Kazakhstan
179 T 8 Saryshagan, Kazakhstan
179 Q 8 Sarysu, Kazakhstan
179 W 5 Sarzhal, Kazakhstan
192 D 10 Sasak, Indonesia
234 K 5 Sasamungga, Solomon Islands
183 O 12 Sasaram, India
199 A 22 Sasebo, Japan
182 J 3 Saser Kangri, India
83 L 15 Saskatchewan, Canada
83 M 18 Saskatoon, Saskatchewan, Canada
153 R 8 Saskylakh, Russian Federation
219 O 11 Sasolburg, Republic of South Africa
157 N 2 Sasovo, Russian Federation
214 I 14 Sass Town, Liberia
214 J 14 Sassandra, Côte d'Ivoire
141 C 16 Sassari, Italy
132 G 12 Sassenheim, Netherlands
136 M 8 Sassnitz, Germany
140 F 9 Sassuolo, Italy
199 C 24 Sata-misaki, Japan
68 H 6 Satanta, Kansas, U.S.A.
181 C 18 Satara, India
107 E 16 Satipo, Peru
157 X 1 Satka, Russian Federation
183 T 14 Satkhira, Bangladesh
182 M 12 Satna, India
143 M 21 Sátoraljaújhely, Hungary
179 Q 7 Satpayev, Kazakhstan
181 D 15 Satpura Range, India
199 C 24 Satsuma-hantō, Japan
191 H 20 Sattahip, Thailand
182 J 3 Satti, India
150 H 7 Satu Mare, Romania
191 H 26 Satun, Thailand
192 L 14 Saubi, Indonesia
112 D 12 Sauce, Argentina
179 R 9 Saudakent, Kazakhstan
175 S 8 Saudi Arabia, Asia
67 Q 6 Sauk Centre, Minnesota, U.S.A.
137 G 24 Saulgau, Germany
129 S 7 Saulieu, France
148 F 10 Saulkrasti, Latvia
64 K 9 Sault Sainte Marie, Michigan, U.S.A.
86 A 8 Sault Sainte Marie, Ontario, Canada
57 T 5 Sault Ste Marie, Michigan, U.S.A.
193 U 14 Saumlakki, Indonesia
129 N 7 Saumur, France
241 N 11 Saunders Coast, Antarctica
218 J 2 Saurimo, Angola
105 T 8 Sauriwaunawa, Guyana
144 H 10 Sava, Bosnia and Herzegovina/Serbia and Montenegro
91 N 5 Savá, Honduras
236 J 8 Savai'i, Samoa
215 O 12 Savalou, Benin
65 E 15 Savanna, Illinois, U.S.A.
92 K 8 Savanna-la-Mar, Jamaica
60 C 10 Savannah, Tennessee, U.S.A.
61 N 14 Savannah, South Carolina, U.S.A.
63 W 5 Savannah, Georgia, U.S.A.
191 L 16 Savannakhét, Laos
84 K 11 Savant Lake, Ontario, Canada
170 C 9 Savaştepe, Turkey
176 I 6 Sāveh, Iran
129 W 4 Saverne, France
149 M 22 Savichy, Belarus
140 A 8 Savigliano, Italy
145 I 14 Šavnik, Serbia and Montenegro
140 B 9 Savona, Italy
135 O 17 Savonlinna, Finland
78 K 7 Savoonga, Alaska, U.S.A.
171 R 7 Şavşat, Turkey
193 P 15 Savu, Indonesia
134 M 10 Savukoski, Finland
235 X 11 Savusavu, Fiji
190 F 7 Sawan, Myanmar
191 G 16 Sawankhalok, Thailand
199 L 15 Sawara, Japan
198 I 13 Sawasaki-bana, Japan
127 W 8 Sawston, United Kingdom
231 W 10 Sawtell, New South Wales, Australia
193 O 15 Sawu Sea, Indonesia
127 U 4 Saxilby, United Kingdom
127 Z 8 Saxmundham, United Kingdom
215 O 9 Say, Niger
178 I 9 Say-Utes, Kazakhstan
172 H 4 Sāyā, Syria
179 V 7 Sayak, Kazakhstan
107 C 16 Sayán, Peru
193 T 10 Sayang, Indonesia
179 O 13 Sayat, Turkmenistan
90 H 3 Sayaxché, Guatemala
175 U 13 Sayḥūt, Yemen
178 F 5 Saykhin, Kazakhstan
213 K 19 Sāylac, Somalia
185 N 3 Sayn-Ust, Mongolia
185 S 4 Saynshand, Mongolia
184 I 4 Sayram Hu, China
68 J 10 Sayre, Oklahoma, U.S.A.
89 N 11 Sayula, Mexico
89 U 13 Sayula, Mexico
175 S 12 Say'ūn, Yemen
145 J 20 Sazan, Albania
177 X 6 Sazin, Pakistan
182 G 2 Sazin, India
154 H 11 Sazonovo, Russian Federation
210 L 10 Sbaa, Algeria
78 K 8 Scammon Bay, Alaska, U.S.A.
140 F 12 Scansano, Italy
150 M 12 Scânteia, Romania
124 I 7 Scapa Flow, United Kingdom
127 V 1 Scarborough, United Kingdom
86 F 13 Scarborough, Ontario, Canada
93 Z 13 Scarborough, Trinidad and Tobago
233 H 19 Scargill, New Zealand
124 E 9 Scarp, United Kingdom
133 F 19 Schaerbeek, Belgium
137 F 25 Schaffhausen, Germany
138 G 5 Schaffhausen, Switzerland
132 H 9 Schagen, Netherlands
139 R 3 Schärding, Austria
133 E 14 Scharendijke, Netherlands
136 E 9 Scharhörn, Germany
138 M 6 Scharnitz, Austria
132 N 6 Scheemda, Netherlands
81 V 9 Schefferville, Newfoundland and Labrador, Canada
139 V 4 Scheibbs, Austria
139 T 7 Scheifling, Austria
77 N 19 Schell Creek Range, Nevada, U.S.A.
58 J 9 Schenectady, New York, U.S.A.
71 O 11 Schertz, Texas, U.S.A.
132 F 12 Scheveningen, Netherlands
132 G 13 Schiedam, Netherlands
132 L 5 Schiermonnikoog, Netherlands
138 I 8 Schiers, Switzerland
133 G 17 Schilde, Belgium
140 F 6 Schio, Italy
150 M 9 Schitu Duca, Romania
137 K 16 Schkeuditz, Germany
139 S 6 Schladming, Austria
137 B 18 Schleiden, Germany
137 K 18 Schleiz, Germany
136 G 8 Schleswig, Germany
136 G 9 Schleswig-Holstein, Germany
139 S 4 Schlierbach, Austria
43 N 18 Schmidt-Ott Seamount, Atlantic Ocean
137 I 25 Schongau, Germany
133 D 16 Schoondijke, Netherlands
137 D 25 Schopfheim, Germany
133 G 17 Schoten, Belgium
234 C 3 Schouten Islands, Papua New Guinea
218 J 12 Schroffenstein, Namibia
138 J 7 Schruns, Austria
71 Q 10 Schulenburg, Texas, U.S.A.
125 B 21 Schull, Republic of Ireland
77 J 18 Schurz, Nevada, U.S.A.
137 I 21 Schwabach, Germany
137 G 22 Schwäbisch, Germany
137 G 23 Schwäbisch Gmünd, Germany
137 G 17 Schwalmstadt, Germany
137 K 21 Schwandorf, Germany
139 N 7 Schwaz, Austria
136 N 11 Schwedt, Germany
137 H 19 Schweinfurt, Germany
136 J 10 Schwerin, Germany
136 J 10 Schweriner See, Germany
138 G 8 Schwyz, Switzerland
141 H 22 Sciacca, Italy
73 X 2 Scobey, Montana, U.S.A.
127 Z 7 Scole, United Kingdom
43 E 21 Scotia Ridge, Atlantic Ocean
43 G 21 Scotia Sea, Atlantic Ocean
124 G 12 Scotland, United Kingdom
71 O 5 Scotland, Texas, U.S.A.
61 U 8 Scotland Neck, North Carolina, U.S.A.
87 N 10 Scotstown, Québec, Canada
241 Q 12 Scott Base, Antarctica
68 H 4 Scott City, Kansas, U.S.A.
241 Q 12 Scott Coast, Antarctica
82 K 13 Scott Lake, Saskatchewan, Canada
219 P 13 Scottburgh, Republic of South Africa
66 G 13 Scottsbluff, Nebraska, U.S.A.
63 Q 1 Scottsboro, Alabama, U.S.A.
65 J 21 Scottsburg, Indiana, U.S.A.
231 T 15 Scottsdale, Tasmania, Australia
74 J 12 Scottsdale, Arizona, U.S.A.
60 G 7 Scottsville, Kentucky, U.S.A.
77 L 20 Scotty's Junction, Nevada, U.S.A.
58 H 11 Scranton, Pennsylvania, U.S.A.
127 U 3 Scunthorpe, United Kingdom
138 K 8 Scuol, Switzerland
156 I 11 Sea of Azov, Russian Federation/Ukraine
147 H 24 Sea of Crete, Greece
199 G 16 Sea of Japan, Asia
170 C 8 Sea of Marmara, Turkey
153 X 11 Sea of Okhotsk, Russian Federation
124 E 10 Sea of the Hebrides, United Kingdom
61 W 3 Seaford, Delaware, U.S.A.
43 O 16 Seal Bay, Tristan da Cunha
71 R 10 Sealy, Texas, U.S.A.
77 N 23 Searchlight, Nevada, U.S.A.
69 W 10 Searcy, Arkansas, U.S.A.
59 R 5 Searsport, Maine, U.S.A.
76 F 9 Seaside, Oregon, U.S.A.
127 O 13 Seaton, United Kingdom
76 G 7 Seattle, Washington, U.S.A.
233 I 18 Seaward Kaikoura Range, New Zealand
91 N 8 Sebaco, Nicaragua
59 O 7 Sebago Lake, Maine, U.S.A.
194 A 15 Sebarok, Singapore
63 Y 10 Sebastian, Florida, U.S.A.
210 K 6 Sebdou, Algeria
192 E 11 Seberida, Indonesia
150 H 10 Sebeş, Romania
171 N 9 Sebinkarahisar, Turkey
150 G 9 Sebiş, Romania
210 L 12 Sebkha Azzel Matti, Algeria
210 L 12 Sebkha Mekerrhane, Algeria
214 E 6 Sebkha Narhamcha, Mauritania
214 H 3 Sebkha Oumm ed Droûs Telli, Mauritania
214 G 5 Sebkhet Chemchâm, Mauritania
214 H 3 Sebkhet Oumm ed Droûs Guebli, Mauritania
214 J 4 Sebkhet Ti-n-Bessaïs, Mauritania
90 I 4 Sebol, Guatemala
63 W 11 Sebring, Florida, U.S.A.
192 M 12 Sebuku, Indonesia
106 A 12 Sechura, Peru
233 A 23 Secretary Island, New Zealand
181 F 18 Secunderabad, India
148 C 12 Seda, Lithuania
69 T 4 Sedalia, Missouri, U.S.A.
181 E 18 Sedam, India
129 T 3 Sedan, France
69 P 7 Sedan, Kansas, U.S.A.
131 O 2 Sedano, Spain
127 Q 1 Sedbergh, United Kingdom
233 J 17 Seddon, New Zealand
172 F 11 Sede Boqer, Israel
177 N 8 Sedeh, Iran
172 E 10 Sederot, Israel
172 F 10 Sedom, Israel
74 J 10 Sedona, Arizona, U.S.A.
138 M 7 Seefeld in Tirol, Austria
218 J 11 Seeheim, Namibia
136 N 13 Seelow, Germany
129 N 5 Sées, France
137 H 15 Seesen, Germany
139 V 6 Seewiesen, Austria
214 G 12 Sefadu, Sierra Leone
194 D 9 Segamat, Malaysia
215 P 11 Ségbana, Benin
154 I 7 Segezha, Russian Federation
141 H 14 Segni, Italy
104 I 5 Segovia, Colombia
131 N 5 Segovia, Spain
128 M 6 Segré, France
78 H 14 Seguam Island, Alaska, U.S.A.
78 G 13 Seguam Pass, Alaska, U.S.A.
215 U 5 Séguédine, Niger
214 J 12 Séguéla, Côte d'Ivoire
71 P 11 Seguin, Texas, U.S.A.
78 D 13 Segula Island, Alaska, U.S.A.
218 L 8 Sehithwa, Botswana
181 E 14 Sehore, India
234 G 7 Sehulea, Papua New Guinea
177 T 13 Sehwan, Pakistan
138 C 7 Seignelégier, Switzerland
134 J 6 Seiland, Norway
68 K 9 Seiling, Oklahoma, U.S.A.
135 K 16 Seinäjoki, Finland
129 O 3 Seine, France
142 N 8 Sejny, Poland
192 F 12 Sekayu, Indonesia
199 I 17 Seki, Japan
194 B 8 Selangor, Malaysia
191 K 17 Selaphum, Thailand
191 K 17 Selaphum, Laos
193 T 15 Selaru, Indonesia
192 L 15 Selat Alas, Indonesia
192 L 15 Selat Bali, Indonesia
192 F 11 Selat Berhala, Indonesia
192 C 11 Selat Bungalaut, Indonesia
193 T 11 Selat Dampir, Indonesia
193 S 11 Selat Jailolo, Indonesia
194 A 14 Selat Jurong, Singapore
192 H 11 Selat Karimata, Indonesia
192 L 13 Selat Laut, Indonesia
192 L 15 Selat Lombok, Indonesia
192 K 14 Selat Madura, Indonesia
193 R 12 Selat Manipa, Indonesia
192 D 11 Selat Mentawai, Indonesia
193 R 11 Selat Obi, Indonesia
193 Q 15 Selat Ombai, Indonesia
193 P 11 Selat Peleng, Indonesia
193 P 15 Selat Rote, Indonesia
192 M 15 Selat Sape, Indonesia

Country · Internal administrative region: State/Province/Territory/Dependent territory · Capital city · Mountain range/Undersea ridge · Mountain peak/Volcano/Seamount · Geographic feature · Headland/Point/Cape/Peninsula · Desert · Island/Island group · Antarctic base · Ocean · Sea · Bay/Gulf/Channel/Strait · Lake · Salt pan/Dry/Intermittent lake · River

◻ Country ⬜ Internal administrative region: State/Province/Territory/Dependent territory ◼ Capital city ▲ Mountain range/Undersea ridge ▲ Mountain peak/Volcano/Seamount ◇ Geographic feature ▶ Headland/Point/Cape/Peninsula ◻ Desert ≖ Island/Island group ▲ Antarctic base ◇ Ocean ◿ Sea ≈ Bay/Gulf/Channel/Strait ↳ Lake ↳ Salt pan/Dry/Intermittent lake ↳ River

179	R 12	**Sirdaryo Wiloyati**, Uzbekistan ◘
150	L 7	**Siret**, Romania
183	Q 10	**Sirha**, Nepal
176	L 13	**Sīrīk**, Iran
191	H 15	**Sirikit Reservoir**, Thailand ∽
176	L 11	**Sīrjān**, Iran
171	R 12	**Şirnak**, Turkey
176	J 13	**Sīrrī**, Iran 🏝
182	H 7	**Sirsa**, India
181	D 20	**Sirsi**, India
181	F 17	**Sirsilla**, India
211	U 8	**Sirte**, Libya
159	O 12	**Sirte Rise**, Mediterranean Sea ◇
149	G 15	**Širvintos**, Lithuania
173	V 4	**Sirwan**, Iraq ∫
191	K 18	**Sisaket**, Thailand
189	P 3	**Sishilipu**, China
171	V 9	**Sisian**, Armenia
191	J 19	**Sisŏphŏn**, Cambodia
234	B 3	**Sissano**, Papua New Guinea
67	O 7	**Sisseton**, South Dakota, U.S.A.
177	P 13	**Sīstān Va Balūchestān**, Iran ◘
130	L 7	**Sistema Central**, Spain ⛰
131	O 4	**Sistema Ibérico**, Spain ⛰
131	N 12	**Sistemas Béticos**, Spain ⛰
129	V 13	**Sisteron**, France
181	N 22	**Sisters**, India 🏝
76	H 11	**Sisters**, Oregon, U.S.A.
183	V 14	**Sitakunda**, Bangladesh
182	L 9	**Sitapur**, India
147	K 26	**Siteia**, Greece
131	W 5	**Sitges**, Spain
79	W 11	**Sitka**, Alaska, U.S.A.
191	D 14	**Sittang**, Myanmar ∫
133	K 18	**Sittard**, Netherlands
127	Y 11	**Sittingbourne**, United Kingdom
190	B 13	**Sittwe**, Myanmar
91	P 7	**Siuna**, Nicaragua
183	R 13	**Siuri**, India
181	F 23	**Sivaganga**, India
176	J 10	**Sīvand**, Iran
170	M 9	**Sivas**, Turkey
171	O 12	**Siverek**, Turkey
151	Y 5	**Sivers'k**, Ukraine
154	E 11	**Siverskiy**, Russian Federation
170	G 10	**Sivrihisar**, Turkey
212	B 9	**Siwa**, Egypt
193	O 12	**Siwa**, Indonesia
212	B 8	**Siwa Oasis**, Egypt ◇
182	J 6	**Siwalik Range**, India ⛰
183	P 11	**Siwan**, India
64	J 13	**Six Lakes**, Michigan, U.S.A.
91	S 13	**Sixaola**, Costa Rica
189	W 4	**Sixian**, China
189	W 4	**Siyang**, China
171	Y 7	**Siyäzän**, Azerbaijan
135	D 25	**Sjaelland**, Denmark 🏝
145	K 14	**Sjenica**, Serbia and Montenegro
151	S 10	**Skadovs'k**, Ukraine
135	C 22	**Skagen**, Denmark
135	B 23	**Skagerrak**, Denmark ≈
79	W 9	**Skagway**, Alaska, U.S.A.
147	E 22	**Skala**, Greece
150	L 6	**Skala-Podil's'ka**, Ukraine
135	E 24	**Skälderviken**, Sweden ≈
147	H 17	**Skantzoura**, Greece 🏝
177	Y 6	**Skardu**, Pakistan
182	I 2	**Skardu**, India
135	A 19	**Skare**, Norway
143	L 15	**Skarżysko-Kamienna**, Poland
210	C 12	**Skaymat**, Western Sahara
127	X 4	**Skegness**, United Kingdom
134	J 13	**Skellefteå**, Sweden
135	D 20	**Ski**, Norway
147	F 17	**Skiathos**, Greece 🏝
147	G 17	**Skiathos**, Greece
134	I 7	**Skibotn**, Norway
149	F 18	**Skidal'**, Belarus
135	C 20	**Skien**, Norway
142	K 13	**Skierniewice**, Poland
211	O 5	**Skikda**, Algeria
127	V 2	**Skipsea**, United Kingdom
127	R 2	**Skipton**, United Kingdom
135	B 24	**Skive**, Denmark
147	F 16	**Sklithro**, Greece
126	J 10	**Skokholm Island**, United Kingdom 🏝
150	I 5	**Skole**, Ukraine
126	J 9	**Skomer Island**, United Kingdom 🏝
147	G 17	**Skopelos**, Greece 🏝
147	G 17	**Skopelos**, Greece
146	D 10	**Skopje**, Macedonia (F.Y.R.O.M.) ⌂
135	F 22	**Skövde**, Sweden
153	T 13	**Skovorodino**, Russian Federation
59	P 5	**Skowhegan**, Maine, U.S.A.
135	D 20	**Skrimfjell**, Norway ▲
148	C 11	**Skrunda**, Latvia
135	A 20	**Skudeneshavn**, Norway
219	P 10	**Skukuza**, Republic of South Africa
148	C 12	**Skuodas**, Lithuania
151	O 5	**Skvyra**, Ukraine
142	E 12	**Skwierzyna**, Poland
124	F 10	**Skye**, United Kingdom 🏝
147	H 18	**Skyropoula**, Greece 🏝
147	I 18	**Skyros**, Greece
147	H 18	**Skyros**, Greece 🏝
135	D 25	**Slagelse**, Denmark
79	S 8	**Slana**, Alaska, U.S.A.
125	E 19	**Slaney**, Republic of Ireland ∫
154	D 11	**Slantsy**, Russian Federation
150	I 13	**Slatina**, Romania
70	K 5	**Slaton**, Texas, U.S.A.
153	Y 8	**Slautnoye**, Russian Federation
80	M 9	**Slave**, Northwest Territories, Canada ∫
215	O 13	**Slave Coast**, Nigeria ◇
83	I 17	**Slave Lake**, Alberta, Canada
156	K 12	**Slavyansk-na-Kubani**, Russian Federation
149	N 18	**Slawharad**, Belarus
142	G 8	**Sławno**, Poland
127	V 5	**Sleaford**, United Kingdom
85	O 7	**Sleeper Island**, Ontario, Canada 🏝
81	S 9	**Sleeper Islands**, Nunavut, Canada 🏝
142	H 12	**Ślesin**, Poland
58	J 10	**Slide Mountain**, New York, U.S.A. ▲
62	M 8	**Slidell**, Louisiana, U.S.A.
125	C 16	**Sligo**, Republic of Ireland
125	C 16	**Sligo Bay**, Republic of Ireland ≈
146	L 9	**Sliven**, Bulgaria ◘
146	K 9	**Sliven**, Bulgaria
146	K 6	**Slivo Pole**, Bulgaria
151	O 7	**Slobidka**, Ukraine
155	P 12	**Slobodskoy**, Russian Federation
150	M 13	**Slobozia**, Romania
132	N 6	**Slochteren**, Netherlands
135	B 16	**Slogen**, Norway ▲
143	K 17	**Słomniki**, Poland
149	G 19	**Slonim**, Belarus
132	J 8	**Slotermeer**, Netherlands ∽
127	U 10	**Slough**, United Kingdom
143	I 21	**Slovak Ore Mountains**, Slovakia ⛰
143	I 20	**Slovakia**, Europe □
151	N 2	**Slovechne**, Ukraine
144	C 7	**Slovenia**, Europe □
144	D 6	**Slovenska Bistrica**, Slovenia
151	X 5	**Slov"yans'k**, Ukraine
149	L 22	**Slovyechna**, Belarus ∫
142	D 12	**Słubice**, Poland
150	L 2	**Sluch**, Ukraine ∫
133	C 16	**Sluis**, Netherlands
142	H 13	**Słupca**, Poland
142	G 8	**Słupsk**, Poland
134	H 13	**Slussfors**, Sweden
149	J 19	**Slutsk**, Belarus
125	A 17	**Slyne Head**, Republic of Ireland ▶
153	P 14	**Slyudyanka**, Russian Federation
59	P 7	**Small Point**, Maine, U.S.A. ▶
85	U 8	**Smallwood Reservoir**, Newfoundland and Labrador, Canada ∽
149	J 17	**Smalyavichy**, Belarus
149	H 16	**Smarhon'**, Belarus
144	L 10	**Smederevo**, Serbia and Montenegro
144	M 11	**Smederevska Palanka**, Serbia and Montenegro
151	R 5	**Smila**, Ukraine
149	J 17	**Smilavichy**, Belarus
148	H 10	**Smiltene**, Latvia
68	L 2	**Smith Center**, Kansas, U.S.A.
85	P 5	**Smith Island**, Nunavut, Canada 🏝
77	E 14	**Smith River**, California, U.S.A.
81	Q 2	**Smith Sound**, Nunavut, Canada ≈
86	I 11	**Smiths Falls**, Ontario, Canada
69	R 12	**Smithville**, Oklahoma, U.S.A.
68	L 4	**Smoky Hill**, Kansas, U.S.A. ∫
68	K 3	**Smoky Hills**, Kansas, U.S.A. ◇
135	C 15	**Smøla**, Norway 🏝
156	H 1	**Smolensk**, Russian Federation
156	I 1	**Smolenskaya Oblast'**, Russian Federation ◘
156	H 1	**Smolensko-Moskovskaya Vozvyshennost'**, Russian Federation ◇
147	C 15	**Smolikas**, Greece ▲
146	I 11	**Smolyan**, Bulgaria ◘
146	I 12	**Smolyan**, Bulgaria
73	Q 12	**Smoot**, Wyoming, U.S.A.
86	D 5	**Smooth Rock Falls**, Ontario, Canada
146	L 8	**Smyadovo**, Bulgaria
240	J 7	**Smyley Island**, Antarctica 🏝
61	W 2	**Smyrna**, Delaware, U.S.A.
134	D 10	**Snaefell**, Iceland ▲
134	C 11	**Snaekollur**, Iceland ▲
127	T 3	**Snaith**, United Kingdom
73	P 10	**Snake**, Idaho/Washington, U.S.A. ∫
72	M 12	**Snake River Plain**, Idaho, U.S.A. ◇
135	E 14	**Snåsvatn**, Norway ∽
132	J 7	**Sneek**, Netherlands
132	K 7	**Sneekermeer**, Netherlands ∽
134	A 11	**Snňfellsjökull**, Iceland ▲
127	X 5	**Snettisham**, United Kingdom
153	O 8	**Snezhnogorsk**, Russian Federation
143	E 16	**Sněžka**, Czech Republic ▲
151	S 9	**Snihurivka**, Ukraine
143	M 19	**Snina**, Slovakia
135	C 16	**Snöhetta**, Norway ▲
135	B 20	**Snønuten**, Norway ▲
135	C 16	**Snota**, Norway ▲
61	W 4	**Snow Hill**, Maryland, U.S.A.
82	L 12	**Snowbird Lake**, Northwest Territories, Canada ∽
126	M 5	**Snowdon**, United Kingdom ▲
74	L 11	**Snowflake**, Arizona, U.S.A.
240	I 3	**Snowhill Island**, Antarctica 🏝
72	L 3	**Snowshoe Peak**, Montana, U.S.A. ▲
74	J 1	**Snowville**, Utah, U.S.A.
93	O 4	**Snug Corner**, The Bahamas
85	X 8	**Snug Harbour**, Newfoundland and Labrador, Canada
191	M 20	**Snuŏl**, Cambodia
150	K 6	**Snyatyn**, Ukraine
68	K 12	**Snyder**, Oklahoma, U.S.A.
70	L 6	**Snyder**, Texas, U.S.A.
219	X 6	**Soalala**, Madgascar
187	L 22	**Soan-kundo**, South Korea 🏝
219	Z 6	**Soanierana-Ivongo**, Madgascar
187	M 21	**Sobaek-sanmaek**, South Korea ⛰
213	E 20	**Sobat**, Sudan ∫
143	C 19	**Soběslav**, Czech Republic
108	M 11	**Sobral**, Brazil
191	M 23	**Soc Trăng**, Vietnam
142	K 13	**Sochaczew**, Poland
156	L 13	**Sochi**, Russian Federation
146	G 13	**Sochos**, Greece
41	R 9	**Society Archipelago**, French Polynesia 🏝
110	H 6	**Socompa**, Argentina
104	I 5	**Socorro**, Colombia
75	P 12	**Socorro**, New Mexico, U.S.A.
175	W 14	**Socotra**, Yemen 🏝
77	M 23	**Soda Lake**, California, U.S.A. ∽
73	Q 12	**Soda Springs**, Idaho, U.S.A.
134	L 10	**Sodankylä**, Finland
135	H 18	**Söderhamn**, Sweden
213	D 17	**Sodiri**, Sudan
213	H 21	**Sodo**, Ethiopia
193	Q 15	**Soë**, Indonesia
219	P 9	**Soekmekaar**, Republic of South Africa
148	D 7	**Soela Väin**, Estonia ≈
132	I 12	**Soest**, Netherlands
147	D 17	**Sofades**, Greece
219	R 7	**Sofala**, Mozambique ◘
146	G 9	**Sofia**, Bulgaria ⌂
147	F 20	**Sofiko**, Greece
146	H 9	**Sofiya**, Bulgaria ◘
151	T 7	**Sofiyivka**, Ukraine
184	M 10	**Sog**, China
104	J 6	**Sogamoso**, Colombia
135	A 17	**Sognefjorden**, Norway ∫
197	L 17	**Sogod**, Philippines
187	L 23	**Sŏgwip'o**, South Korea
212	E 10	**Sohâg**, Egypt
127	W 7	**Soham**, United Kingdom
181	I 16	**Sohapur**, India
177	X 8	**Sohawa**, Pakistan
133	J 21	**Soheit-Tinlot**, Belgium
42	F 9	**Sohm Abyssal Plain**, Atlantic Ocean ◇
133	F 20	**Soignies**, Belgium
129	R 3	**Soissons**, France
199	E 19	**Sōja**, Japan
197	I 18	**Sojoton Point**, Philippines ▶
187	M 18	**Sokch'o**, South Korea
170	B 11	**Söke**, Turkey
179	S 12	**Sokh**, Uzbekistan
171	Q 5	**Sokhumi**, Georgia
144	N 13	**Sokobanja**, Serbia and Montenegro
215	N 12	**Sokodé**, Togo
154	K 11	**Sokol**, Russian Federation
144	I 12	**Sokolac**, Bosnia and Herzegovina
151	P 6	**Sokolivka**, Ukraine
142	O 10	**Sokółka**, Poland
151	U 9	**Sokolohirne**, Ukraine
142	M 12	**Sokołów Podlaski**, Poland
215	P 9	**Sokoto**, Nigeria
215	P 9	**Sokoto**, Nigeria ◘
157	V 5	**Sol'-Iletsk**, Russian Federation
182	J 6	**Solan**, India
233	A 25	**Solander Island**, New Zealand 🏝
181	D 13	**Solapur**, India
151	N 7	**Soldănești**, Moldova
138	L 8	**Sölden**, Austria
104	I 2	**Soledad**, Colombia
77	G 21	**Soledad**, California, U.S.A.
112	H 11	**Soledade**, Brazil
129	Y 15	**Solenzara**, France
171	Q 10	**Solhan**, Turkey
154	L 12	**Soligalich**, Russian Federation
127	S 7	**Solihull**, United Kingdom
155	T 10	**Solikamsk**, Russian Federation
108	D 11	**Solimões**, Brazil ∫
137	C 16	**Solingen**, Germany
171	Y 6	**Şollar**, Azerbaijan
135	H 15	**Sollefteå**, Sweden
131	Y 7	**Soller**, Spain
150	L 5	**Soloblovtsi**, Ukraine
192	D 11	**Solok**, Indonesia
90	G 5	**Sololá**, Guatemala
235	O 6	**Solomon Islands**, Oceania □
234	G 6	**Solomon Sea**, Solomon Islands/Papua New Guinea ◒
186	H 10	**Solon**, China
59	P 5	**Solon**, Maine, U.S.A.
64	D 9	**Solon Springs**, Wisconsin, U.S.A.
193	P 15	**Solor**, Indonesia 🏝
156	M 2	**Solotcha**, Russian Federation
138	E 7	**Solothurn**, Switzerland
154	I 6	**Solovetskiy**, Russian Federation
154	I 5	**Solovetskiye Ostrova**, Russian Federation 🏝
143	I 24	**Solt**, Hungary
176	I 6	**Soltānābād**, Iran
177	N 5	**Soltānābād**, Iran
136	G 12	**Soltau**, Germany
154	E 12	**Sol'tsy**, Russian Federation
125	H 15	**Solway Firth**, United Kingdom ≈
219	N 4	**Solwezi**, Zambia
198	L 13	**Sōma**, Japan
170	C 9	**Soma**, Turkey
213	M 22	**Somali**, Ethiopia ◘
38	J 5	**Somali Basin**, Indian Ocean ◇
213	K 24	**Somalia**, Africa □
218	K 2	**Sombo**, Angola
144	I 8	**Sombor**, Serbia and Montenegro
133	G 21	**Sombreffe**, Belgium
89	N 9	**Sombrerete**, Mexico
111	H 24	**Sombrero**, Chile
150	H 8	**Şomcuta Mare**, Romania
180	C 12	**Somdari**, India
133	K 16	**Someren**, Netherlands
72	M 3	**Somers**, Montana, U.S.A.
42	A 7	**Somerset**, Bermuda
60	I 7	**Somerset**, Kentucky, U.S.A.
65	N 19	**Somerset**, Ohio, U.S.A.
75	O 5	**Somerset**, Colorado, U.S.A.
42	A 7	**Somerset Island**, Bermuda 🏝
81	P 4	**Somerset Island**, Nunavut, Canada 🏝
58	H 11	**Somersville**, Pennsylvania, U.S.A.
58	J 13	**Somerville**, New Jersey, U.S.A.
71	R 9	**Somerville**, Texas, U.S.A.
71	Q 9	**Somerville Lake**, Texas, U.S.A. ∽
173	Y 9	**Someydeh**, Iraq
137	I 16	**Sömmerda**, Germany
134	E 12	**Sømna**, Norway 🏝
235	Y 11	**Somosomo**, Fiji
90	M 8	**Somotillo**, Nicaragua
181	I 17	**Sompeta**, India
133	J 15	**Son**, Netherlands
183	N 12	**Son**, India ∫
190	K 12	**Son La**, Vietnam
91	U 15	**Soná**, Panama
187	J 17	**Sŏnch'ŏn**, North Korea
135	C 26	**Sønderborg**, Denmark
137	I 16	**Sonderhausen**, Germany
140	D 5	**Sondrio**, Italy
195	Q 10	**Song**, Malaysia
191	O 19	**Sông Cau**, Vietnam
191	L 24	**Sông Đôc**, Vietnam
187	G 16	**Song Range**, China ⛰
189	T 9	**Songbai**, China
217	U 14	**Songea**, Tanzania
186	K 13	**Songhua Hu**, China ∽
191	H 25	**Songkhla**, Thailand
186	G 9	**Songling**, China
188	L 10	**Songming**, China
187	K 18	**Songnim**, North Korea
218	G 1	**Songo**, Angola
219	Q 5	**Songo**, Mozambique
188	M 5	**Songpan**, China
183	U 11	**Songsak**, India
189	Y 9	**Songxi**, China
189	S 4	**Songxian**, China
186	J 11	**Songyuan**, China
189	S 7	**Songzi**, China
186	C 13	**Sonid Zuoqi**, China
182	J 8	**Sonipat**, India
177	T 14	**Sonmiani**, Pakistan
177	S 14	**Sonmiani Bay**, Pakistan ≈
88	H 2	**Sonoita**, Mexico
70	L 9	**Sonora**, Texas, U.S.A.
77	H 19	**Sonora**, California, U.S.A.
88	I 4	**Sonora**, Mexico ◘
88	I 4	**Sonora**, Mexico ∫
74	G 13	**Sonoran Desert**, Arizona, U.S.A. ◇
90	I 7	**Sonsonate**, El Salvador
236	I 15	**Sonsorol Islands**, Palau 🏝
153	Z 10	**Sopka Klyuchevskaya**, Russian Federation ▲
153	Z 11	**Sopka Koryakskaya**, Russian Federation ▲
153	Z 10	**Sopka Shiveluch**, Russian Federation ▲
142	I 8	**Sopot**, Poland
143	F 22	**Sopron**, Hungary
151	T 1	**Sopych**, Ukraine
241	S 2	**Sor Rondane Mountains**, Antarctica ⛰
141	I 14	**Sora**, Italy
187	M 18	**Sŏrak-san**, South Korea ▲
131	Q 13	**Sorbas**, Spain
86	L 10	**Sorel**, Québec, Canada
170	K 9	**Sorgun**, Turkey
131	Q 4	**Soria**, Spain
113	D 15	**Soriano**, Uruguay ◘
181	J 16	**Soro**, India
112	K 7	**Sorocaba**, Brazil
157	U 4	**Sorochinsk**, Russian Federation
236	K 15	**Sorol**, Federated States of Micronesia 🏝
193	T 11	**Sorong**, Indonesia
217	T 7	**Soroti**, Uganda
134	J 6	**Sørøya**, Norway 🏝
134	J 6	**Sørøysundet**, Norway ≈
141	J 16	**Sorrento**, Italy
134	N 9	**Sorsatunturi**, Finland ▲
134	H 12	**Sorsele**, Sweden
196	K 13	**Sorsogon**, Philippines
154	F 8	**Sortavala**, Russian Federation
134	G 8	**Sortland**, Norway
134	F 9	**Sørvågen**, Norway
219	O 10	**Soshanguve**, Republic of South Africa
155	Q 7	**Sosnogorsk**, Russian Federation
154	H 6	**Sosnovets**, Russian Federation
154	K 4	**Sosnovka**, Russian Federation
154	F 10	**Sosnovo**, Russian Federation
154	E 10	**Sosnovyy Bor**, Russian Federation
143	J 17	**Sosnowiec**, Poland
151	R 2	**Sosnytsya**, Ukraine
152	J 10	**Sos'va**, Russian Federation
135	N 14	**Sotkamo**, Finland
110	I 10	**Soto**, Argentina
89	R 9	**Soto la Marina**, Mexico
135	A 18	**Sotra**, Norway 🏝
89	Y 10	**Sotuta**, Mexico
216	G 6	**Souanké**, Congo
214	J 13	**Soubré**, Côte d'Ivoire
147	H 26	**Souda**, Greece
146	K 12	**Soufli**, Greece
214	G 11	**Souguéta**, Guinea
38	B 13	**Souillac**, Mauritius
129	P 11	**Souillac**, France
211	P 5	**Souk Ahras**, Algeria
210	I 6	**Souk el Arbaâ du Rharb**, Morocco
128	L 10	**Soulac-sur-Mer**, France
172	F 7	**Soûr**, Lebanon
107	G 18	**Source of the Amazon**, Peru ◇
108	J 10	**Soure**, Brazil
87	W 8	**Souris**, Prince Edward Island, Canada

□ Country ◘ Internal administrative region: State/Province/Territory/Dependent territory ⌂ Capital city ⛰ Mountain range/Undersea ridge ▲ Mountain peak/Volcano/Seamount ◇ Geographic feature ▶ Headland/Point/Cape/Peninsula ◓ Desert 🏝 Island/Island group ⁙ Antarctic base ◎ Ocean ◒ Sea ≈ Bay/Gulf/Channel/Strait ∽ Lake ▚ Salt pan/Dry/Intermittent lake ∫ River

108 N 12 **Sousa**, Brazil
211 Q 6 **Sousse**, Tunisia
159 O 6 **South Adriatic Basin**, Mediterranean Sea ◇
181 N 22 **South Andaman**, India 🏝
231 O 9 **South Australia**, Australia ▣
39 U 10 **South Australian Basin**, Indian Ocean ◇
39 W 11 **South Australian Plain**, Indian Ocean ◇
75 P 12 **South Baldy**, New Mexico, U.S.A. ▲
65 M 16 **South Bass Island**, Ohio, U.S.A. 🏝
86 C 10 **South Baymouth**, Ontario, Canada
65 J 16 **South Bend**, Indiana, U.S.A.
61 R 7 **South Boston**, Virginia, U.S.A.
61 O 12 **South Carolina**, U.S.A. ▣
185 T 15 **South China Sea**, Asia 🌊
66 H 8 **South Dakota**, U.S.A. ▣
127 U 12 **South Downs**, United Kingdom ◇
218 M 10 **South East**, Botswana ▣
43 L 26 **South East Bay**, Ascension ≈
231 S 15 **South East Cape**, Tasmania, Australia ▶
41 O 10 **South Fiji Basin**, Pacific Ocean ◇
75 P 6 **South Fork**, Colorado, U.S.A.
77 E 16 **South Fork**, California, U.S.A.
241 T 9 **South Geomagnetic Pole**, Antarctica ◇
43 H 21 **South Georgia**, U.K. 🏝
183 V 14 **South Hatia Island**, Bangladesh 🏝
65 I 15 **South Haven**, Michigan, U.S.A.
84 K 4 **South Henik Lake**, Nunavut, Canada 💧
61 S 7 **South Hill**, Virginia, U.S.A.
217 V 6 **South Horr**, Kenya
181 L 20 **South Huvadhu Atoll**, Maldives 🏝
159 S 9 **South Ikaria Basin**, Mediterranean Sea ◇
39 V 13 **South Indian Basin**, Indian Ocean ◇
81 P 10 **South Indian Lake**, Manitoba, Canada
233 G 19 **South Island**, New Zealand 🏝
39 Z 3 **South Island**, Cocos Islands 🏝
181 B 23 **South Island**, India 🏝
197 E 20 **South Islet**, Philippines 🏝
84 I 11 **South Junction**, Manitoba, Canada
187 K 20 **South Korea**, Asia □
77 I 18 **South Lake Tahoe**, California, U.S.A.
181 M 17 **South Maalhosmadulu Atoll**, Maldives 🏝
241 V 14 **South Magnetic Pole**, Antarctica ◇
181 L 18 **South Male Atoll**, Maldives 🏝
181 L 17 **South Miladunmadulu Atoll**, Maldives 🏝
127 N 12 **South Molton**, United Kingdom
92 K 8 **South Negril Point**, Jamaica ▶
240 H 1 **South Orkney Islands**, U.K. 🏝
43 G 22 **South Orkney Rise**, Atlantic Ocean ⛰
59 O 6 **South Paris**, Maine, U.S.A.
75 T 3 **South Platte**, Colorado, U.S.A. 〰
43 K 26 **South Point**, Ascension ▶
64 L 11 **South Point**, Michigan, U.S.A. ▶
241 P 8 **South Pole**, Antarctica ◇
86 F 10 **South River**, Ontario, Canada
124 I 7 **South Ronaldsay**, United Kingdom 🏝
43 I 22 **South Sandwich Islands**, U.K. 🏝
43 I 21 **South Sandwich Trench**, Atlantic Ocean ◇
83 L 19 **South Saskatchewan**, Saskatchewan, Canada 〰
240 G 3 **South Shetland Islands**, U.K. 🏝
43 E 22 **South Shetland Trough**, Atlantic Ocean ◇
125 K 15 **South Shields**, United Kingdom
60 L 4 **South Shore**, Kentucky, U.S.A.
41 N 9 **South Solomon Trench**, Pacific Ocean ◇
85 P 1 **South Spicer Island**, Nunavut, Canada 🏝
232 J 13 **South Taranaki Bight**, New Zealand ≈
39 Y 11 **South Tasman Rise**, Indian Ocean ⛰
85 P 9 **South Twin Island**, Québec, Canada 🏝
124 D 10 **South Uist**, United Kingdom 🏝
43 K 26 **South West Bay**, Ascension ≈
233 B 26 **South West Cape**, New Zealand ▶
43 M 26 **South West Point**, St Helena ▶
127 T 13 **Southampton**, United Kingdom
58 M 12 **Southampton**, New York, U.S.A.
85 N 3 **Southampton Island**, Nunavut, Canada 🏝
58 M 10 **Southbridge**, Massachusetts, U.S.A.
39 O 10 **Southeast Indian Ridge**, Indian Ocean ⛰
41 U 14 **Southeast Pacific Basin**, Pacific Ocean ◇
83 M 15 **Southend**, Saskatchewan, Canada
127 Y 10 **Southend-on-Sea**, United Kingdom
213 G 22 **Southern**, Ethiopia ▣
214 G 12 **Southern**, Sierra Leone ▣
218 L 10 **Southern**, Botswana ▣
219 N 6 **Southern**, Zambia ▣
219 R 5 **Southern**, Malawi ▣
181 G 26 **Southern**, Sri Lanka ▣
233 C 22 **Southern Alps**, New Zealand ⛰
237 O 10 **Southern Cook Islands**, Cook Islands 🏝
230 H 10 **Southern Cross**, Western Australia, Australia
213 A 19 **Southern Darfur**, Sudan ▣
234 B 5 **Southern Highlands**, Papua New Guinea ▣
84 J 6 **Southern Indian Lake**, Manitoba, Canada 💧
84 J 6 **Southern Indian Lake**, Manitoba, Canada
213 E 19 **Southern Kordofan**, Sudan ▣
90 K 2 **Southern Lagoon**, Belize 💧
235 Y 12 **Southern Lau Group**, Fiji 🏝
237 R 6 **Southern Line Islands**, Kiribati 🏝
90 L 2 **Southern Long Cays**, Belize 🏝
39 U 14 **Southern Ocean**, Indian Ocean 🌀
125 H 14 **Southern Uplands**, United Kingdom ⛰
83 N 19 **Southey**, Saskatchewan, Canada
82 O 7 **Southhampton Island**, Nunavut, Canada 🏝
233 C 24 **Southland**, New Zealand ▣
231 S 15 **Southport**, Tasmania, Australia
127 O 3 **Southport**, United Kingdom
61 T 12 **Southport**, North Carolina, U.S.A.
38 I 10 **Southwest Indian Ridge**, Indian Ocean ⛰
41 P 12 **Southwest Pacific Basin**, Pacific Ocean ◇
234 D 2 **Southwest Point**, Papua New Guinea ▶
127 Z 7 **Southwold**, United Kingdom
141 M 20 **Soverato**, Italy
141 M 19 **Soveria Mannelli**, Italy
149 C 15 **Sovetsk**, Russian Federation
155 P 13 **Sovetsk**, Russian Federation
152 J 9 **Sovetskiy**, Russian Federation
219 N 8 **Sowa Pan**, Botswana 💧
219 N 11 **Soweto**, Republic of South Africa
198 J 2 **Sōya-misaki**, Japan ▶
198 J 2 **Sōya-wan**, Japan ≈
89 W 13 **Soyaló**, Mexico
218 F 1 **Soyo**, Angola
149 N 18 **Sozh**, Belarus 〰
146 N 9 **Sozopol**, Bulgaria
133 K 21 **Spa**, Belgium
240 J 6 **Spaatz Island**, Antarctica 🏝
179 O 8 **Space Launching Center**, Kazakhstan
131 Q 8 **Spain**, Europe □
127 W 6 **Spalding**, United Kingdom
86 C 9 **Spanish**, Ontario, Canada
77 I 17 **Sparks**, Nevada, U.S.A.
60 H 9 **Sparta**, Tennessee, U.S.A.
61 O 8 **Sparta**, North Carolina, U.S.A.
60 M 11 **Spartanburg**, South Carolina, U.S.A.
147 E 22 **Sparti**, Greece
83 J 21 **Sparwood**, British Columbia, Canada
156 I 2 **Spas-Demensk**, Russian Federation
156 M 2 **Spas-Klepiki**, Russian Federation
153 V 15 **Spassk-Dal'niy**, Russian Federation
66 G 9 **Spearfish**, South Dakota, U.S.A.
70 K 1 **Spearman**, Texas, U.S.A.
43 N 26 **Speery Island**, St Helena 🏝
93 Z 12 **Speightstown**, Barbados
67 Q 11 **Spencer**, Iowa, U.S.A.
231 O 11 **Spencer Gulf**, South Australia, Australia ≈
233 C 24 **Spencer Peak**, New Zealand ▲
147 F 22 **Spetses**, Greece 🏝
147 F 22 **Spetses**, Greece
124 H 10 **Spey**, United Kingdom 〰
137 E 21 **Speyer**, Germany
136 D 9 **Spiekeroog**, Germany 🏝
139 W 8 **Spielfeld**, Austria
43 L 21 **Spiess Seamount**, Atlantic Ocean ▲
138 E 9 **Spiez**, Switzerland
147 I 26 **Spili**, Greece
177 S 10 **Spin**, Afghanistan
141 M 16 **Spinazzola**, Italy
232 H 4 **Spirits Bay**, New Zealand ≈
83 L 18 **Spiritwood**, Saskatchewan, Canada
69 R 11 **Spiro**, Oklahoma, U.S.A.
171 T 8 **Spitak**, Armenia
45 U 11 **Spitsbergen**, Svalbard 🏝
139 R 8 **Spittal**, Austria
139 V 3 **Spitz**, Austria
71 T 9 **Splendora**, Texas, U.S.A.
138 I 9 **Splügen**, Switzerland
127 S 2 **Spofforth**, United Kingdom
148 I 13 **Špoģi**, Latvia
76 K 7 **Spokane**, Washington, U.S.A.
140 H 12 **Spoleto**, Italy
64 C 9 **Spooner**, Wisconsin, U.S.A.
73 X 8 **Spotted Horse**, Wyoming, U.S.A.
76 K 7 **Sprague**, Washington, U.S.A.
76 J 10 **Spray**, Oregon, U.S.A.
144 H 10 **Spreča**, Bosnia and Herzegovina 〰
133 J 21 **Sprimont**, Belgium
63 V 10 **Spring Hill**, Florida, U.S.A.
65 I 14 **Spring Lake**, Michigan, U.S.A.
218 J 13 **Springbok**, Republic of South Africa
69 S 9 **Springdale**, Arkansas, U.S.A.
85 X 10 **Springdale**, Newfoundland and Labrador, Canada
75 S 8 **Springer**, New Mexico, U.S.A.
58 L 10 **Springfield**, Massachusetts, U.S.A.
58 M 8 **Springfield**, Vermont, U.S.A.
60 F 8 **Springfield**, Tennessee, U.S.A.
65 F 19 **Springfield**, Illinois, U.S.A.
65 L 19 **Springfield**, Ohio, U.S.A.
67 Q 9 **Springfield**, Minnesota, U.S.A.
69 T 7 **Springfield**, Missouri, U.S.A.
75 U 7 **Springfield**, Colorado, U.S.A.
76 G 11 **Springfield**, Oregon, U.S.A.
87 V 9 **Springhill**, Nova Scotia, Canada
233 G 18 **Springs Junction**, New Zealand
231 U 7 **Springsure**, Queensland, Australia
58 D 9 **Springville**, New York, U.S.A.
61 Q 3 **Spruce Knob**, West Virginia, U.S.A. ▲
77 N 16 **Spruce Mountain**, Nevada, U.S.A. ▲
133 G 15 **Sprundel**, Netherlands
127 W 3 **Spurn Head**, United Kingdom ▶
233 I 18 **Spy Glass Point**, New Zealand ▶
83 G 21 **Squamish**, British Columbia, Canada
144 J 8 **Srbobran**, Serbia and Montenegro
191 K 22 **Srê Âmbel**, Cambodia
153 Y 9 **Sredinnyy Khrebet**, Russian Federation ⛰
146 M 6 **Sredishte**, Bulgaria
153 W 8 **Srednekolymsk**, Russian Federation
156 J 3 **Sredne–Russkaya Vozvyshennost'**, Russian Federation ◇
155 T 10 **Sredniy Ural**, Russian Federation ⛰
146 H 9 **Srednogorie**, Bulgaria
142 G 13 **Śrem**, Poland
153 S 13 **Sretensk**, Russian Federation
195 O 11 **Sri Aman**, Malaysia
181 F 25 **Sri Jayewardenepura Kotte**, Sri Lanka 🏛
181 H 23 **Sri Lanka**, Asia □
181 I 18 **Srikakulam**, India
183 V 12 **Srimangal**, Bangladesh
182 H 3 **Srinagar**, India
182 K 7 **Srinagar**, India
142 G 13 **Środa Wielkopolska**, Poland
136 G 10 **Stade**, Germany
135 A 16 **Stadlandet**, Norway 🏝
132 N 7 **Stadskanaal**, Netherlands
127 R 6 **Stafford**, United Kingdom
58 M 10 **Stafford Springs**, Connecticut, U.S.A.
139 S 6 **Stainach**, Austria
127 V 11 **Staines**, United Kingdom
139 V 8 **Stainz**, Austria
151 Y 6 **Stakhanov**, Ukraine
139 Q 8 **Stall**, Austria
143 M 16 **Stalowa Wola**, Poland
127 V 6 **Stamford**, United Kingdom
58 K 12 **Stamford**, Connecticut, U.S.A.
58 J 9 **Stamford**, New York, U.S.A.
70 M 5 **Stamford**, Texas, U.S.A.
127 U 1 **Stamford Bridge**, United Kingdom
218 J 10 **Stampriet**, Namibia
138 L 7 **Stams**, Austria
69 R 1 **Stanberry**, Missouri, U.S.A.
219 O 11 **Standerton**, Republic of South Africa
64 L 13 **Standish**, Michigan, U.S.A.
73 R 5 **Stanford**, Montana, U.S.A.
219 P 12 **Stanger**, Republic of South Africa
151 R 9 **Stanislav**, Ukraine
111 L 24 **Stanley**, Falkland Islands 🏛
66 H 3 **Stanley**, North Dakota, U.S.A.
72 L 9 **Stanley**, Idaho, U.S.A.
153 S 12 **Stanovoy Khrebet**, Russian Federation ⛰
153 R 12 **Stanovoye Nagor'ye**, Russian Federation ◇
231 V 9 **Stanthorpe**, Queensland, Australia
127 Y 7 **Stanton**, United Kingdom
60 J 5 **Stanton**, Kentucky, U.S.A.
132 L 9 **Staphorst**, Netherlands
127 T 5 **Stapleford**, United Kingdom
66 K 13 **Stapleton**, Nebraska, U.S.A.
143 L 19 **Stará-Lubovna**, Slovakia
146 J 9 **Stara Zagora**, Bulgaria ▣
146 J 9 **Stara-Zagora**, Bulgaria
143 L 15 **Starachowice**, Poland
154 F 12 **Staraya Russa**, Russian Federation
237 Q 5 **Starbuck Island**, Kiribati 🏝
142 E 10 **Stargard-Szczeciński**, Poland
154 G 14 **Staritsa**, Russian Federation
63 V 8 **Starke**, Florida, U.S.A.
63 N 3 **Starkville**, Mississippi, U.S.A.
137 I 25 **Starnberger See**, Germany 💧
146 N 8 **Staro Oryakhovo**, Bulgaria
151 Y 5 **Starobil's'k**, Ukraine
142 I 9 **Starogard Gdański**, Poland
150 M 4 **Starokostyantyniv**, Ukraine
156 K 10 **Starominskaya**, Russian Federation
156 J 12 **Starotitarovskaya**, Russian Federation
151 V 5 **Starovirivka**, Ukraine
127 N 15 **Start Bay**, United Kingdom ≈
127 N 15 **Start Point**, United Kingdom ▶
151 V 12 **Staryy Krym**, Ukraine
152 L 9 **Staryy Nadym**, Russian Federation
156 K 5 **Staryy Oskol**, Russian Federation
151 W 4 **Staryy Saltiv**, Ukraine
149 K 19 **Staryya Darohi**, Belarus
143 L 16 **Staszów**, Poland
58 E 12 **State College**, Pennsylvania, U.S.A.
58 J 13 **Staten Island**, New York, U.S.A. 🏝
61 O 9 **Statesville**, North Carolina, U.S.A.
45 R 10 **Station Nord**, Greenland
135 A 20 **Stavanger**, Norway
233 F 20 **Staveley**, New Zealand
127 S 4 **Staveley**, United Kingdom
133 E 15 **Stavenisse**, Netherlands
157 N 12 **Stavropol'**, Russian Federation
157 N 11 **Stavropol'skiy Kray**, Russian Federation ▣
147 G 14 **Stavros**, Greece
142 M 10 **Stawiski**, Poland
142 H 13 **Stawiszyn**, Poland
75 P 3 **Steamboat Springs**, Colorado, U.S.A.
60 I 7 **Stearns**, Kentucky, U.S.A.
78 M 7 **Stebbins**, Alaska, U.S.A.
240 J 5 **Steele Island**, Antarctica 🏝
83 H 14 **Steen River**, Alberta, Canada
133 F 15 **Steenbergen**, Netherlands
77 J 14 **Steens Mountain**, Oregon, U.S.A. ▲
132 K 9 **Steenwijk**, Netherlands
230 E 8 **Steep Point**, Western Australia, Australia ▶
82 H 4 **Stefansson Island**, Nunavut, Canada 🏝
139 X 7 **Stegersbach**, Austria
150 G 9 **Ştei**, Romania
139 V 7 **Steiermark**, Austria ▣
84 I 10 **Steinbach**, Manitoba, Canada
133 K 25 **Steinfort**, Luxembourg
137 D 14 **Steinfurt**, Germany
218 J 13 **Steinkopf**, Republic of South Africa
133 E 14 **Stellendam**, Netherlands
129 T 3 **Stenay**, France
136 K 13 **Stendal**, Germany
148 D 10 **Stende**, Latvia
147 F 25 **Steno Antikythiro**, Greece ≈
147 F 23 **Steno Elafonisou**, Greece ≈
147 M 24 **Steno Karpathou**, Greece ≈
150 L 2 **Stepan'**, Ukraine
71 O 7 **Stephenville**, Texas, U.S.A.
85 X 10 **Stephenville**, Newfoundland and Labrador, Canada
179 S 3 **Stepnogorsk**, Kazakhstan
157 P 13 **Stepnoye**, Russian Federation
144 K 11 **Stepojevac**, Serbia and Montenegro
147 F 19 **Sterea Ellas**, Greece ▣
66 K 5 **Sterling**, North Dakota, U.S.A.
75 T 2 **Sterling**, Colorado, U.S.A.
70 L 7 **Sterling City**, Texas, U.S.A.
65 M 14 **Sterling Heights**, Michigan, U.S.A.
61 T 3 **Sterling Park**, Virginia, U.S.A.
157 W 2 **Sterlitamak**, Russian Federation
83 J 19 **Stettler**, Alberta, Canada
65 O 18 **Steubenville**, Ohio, U.S.A.
127 V 9 **Stevenage**, United Kingdom
64 F 11 **Stevens Point**, Wisconsin, U.S.A.
79 R 6 **Stevens Village**, Alaska, U.S.A.
63 Q 1 **Stevenson**, Alabama, U.S.A.
79 Q 11 **Stevenson Entrance**, Alaska, U.S.A. ≈
83 D 17 **Stewart**, British Columbia, Canada
233 C 26 **Stewart Island**, New Zealand 🏝
67 T 9 **Stewartville**, Minnesota, U.S.A.
87 V 10 **Stewiacke**, Nova Scotia, Canada
139 T 4 **Steyr**, Austria
132 K 6 **Stiens**, Netherlands
64 H 11 **Stiles Junction**, Wisconsin, U.S.A.
127 T 1 **Stillington**, United Kingdom
69 N 9 **Stillwater**, Oklahoma, U.S.A.
77 J 18 **Stillwater Range**, Nevada, U.S.A. ⛰
144 G 12 **Štilt**, Bosnia and Herzegovina
127 V 7 **Stilton**, United Kingdom
70 K 1 **Stinnett**, Texas, U.S.A.
146 E 11 **Štip**, Macedonia (F.Y.R.O.M.)
124 H 12 **Stirling**, United Kingdom
134 J 6 **Stjernøya**, Norway 🏝
137 F 25 **Stockach**, Germany
139 X 3 **Stockerau**, Austria
135 H 21 **Stockholm**, Sweden 🏛
127 R 4 **Stockport**, United Kingdom
43 I 15 **Stocks Seamount**, Atlantic Ocean ▲
127 S 3 **Stocksbridge**, United Kingdom
68 K 3 **Stockton**, Kansas, U.S.A.
69 T 6 **Stockton**, Missouri, U.S.A.

□ Country ▣ Internal administrative region: State/Province/Territory/Dependent territory 🏛 Capital city ⛰ Mountain range/Undersea ridge ▲ Mountain peak/Volcano/Seamount ◇ Geographic feature ▶ Headland/Point/Cape/Peninsula ◭ Desert 🏝 Island/Island group ⁙ Antarctic base 🌀 Ocean 🌊 Sea ≈ Bay/Gulf/Channel/Strait 💧 Lake ⚑ Salt pan/Dry/Intermittent lake 〰 River

77 H 19 **Stockton**, California, U.S.A.
64 E 8 **Stockton Island**, Wisconsin, U.S.A. 🌴
69 S 6 **Stockton Lake**, Missouri, U.S.A. 💧
70 J 9 **Stockton Plateau**, Texas, U.S.A. ◇
142 M 13 **Stoczek**, Poland
143 B 18 **Stod**, Czech Republic
191 M 19 **Stœng Trêng**, Cambodia
127 R 5 **Stoke-on-Trent**, United Kingdom
144 N 11 **Stol**, Serbia and Montenegro ▲
152 L 5 **Stolbovoy**, Russian Federation
149 I 21 **Stolin**, Belarus
43 O 16 **Stoltenhoff Island**, Tristan da Cunha 🌴
127 R 5 **Stone**, United Kingdom
86 G 9 **Stonecliffe**, Ontario, Canada
124 J 11 **Stonehaven**, United Kingdom
61 T 7 **Stony Creek**, Virginia, U.S.A.
81 N 10 **Stony Rapids**, Saskatchewan, Canada
79 O 9 **Stony River**, Alaska, U.S.A.
43 O 16 **Stonyhill Point**, Tristan da Cunha ▶
134 I 12 **Storavan**, Sweden 💧
135 A 19 **Stord**, Norway 🌴
135 C 25 **Store Baelt**, Denmark ≈
135 D 15 **Støren**, Norway
134 G 11 **Storjord**, Norway
82 H 5 **Storkerson Peninsula**, Nunavut, Canada ▶
135 E 15 **Storlien**, Norway
67 Q 11 **Storm Lake**, Iowa, U.S.A.
124 F 8 **Stornoway**, United Kingdom
155 P 9 **Storozhevsk**, Russian Federation
150 K 7 **Storozhynets'**, Ukraine
135 F 15 **Storsjön**, Sweden 💧
132 H 6 **Stortemelk**, Netherlands ≈
134 H 13 **Storuman**, Sweden
134 H 13 **Storuman**, Sweden 💧
127 X 9 **Stour**, United Kingdom 〜
127 R 7 **Stourbridge**, United Kingdom
127 Q 7 **Stourport-on-Severn**, United Kingdom
84 J 9 **Stout Lake**, Ontario, Canada 💧
127 S 9 **Stow-on-the-Wold**, United Kingdom
149 I 18 **Stowbtsy**, Belarus
127 Y 8 **Stowmarket**, United Kingdom
125 D 15 **Strabane**, United Kingdom
159 T 11 **Strabo Trench**, Mediterranean Sea ◇
231 S 15 **Strahan**, Tasmania, Australia
133 J 25 **Straimont**, Belgium
85 X 9 **Strait of Belle Isle**, Newfoundland and Labrador, Canada ≈
141 C 15 **Strait of Bonifacio**, Italy ≈
87 X 9 **Strait of Canso**, Nova Scotia, Canada ≈
127 Z 13 **Strait of Dover**, France/United Kingdom ≈
83 F 21 **Strait of Georgia**, British Columbia, Canada ≈
130 K 15 **Strait of Gibraltar**, Africa/Spain ≈
176 K 14 **Strait of Hormuz**, Iran ≈
56 F 3 **Strait of Juan de Fuco**, Oregon, U.S.A. ≈
111 G 25 **Strait of Magellan**, Chile ≈
39 R 4 **Strait of Malacca**, Indian Ocean ≈
194 B 9 **Strait of Malacca**, Indonesia/Malaysia ≈
159 O 7 **Strait of Otranto**, Mediterranean Sea ≈
63 Y 15 **Straits of Florida**, Cuba/U.S.A ≈
143 C 19 **Strakonice**, Czech Republic
136 L 8 **Stralsund**, Germany
125 F 16 **Strangford Lough**, United Kingdom ≈
135 H 20 **Strängnäs**, Sweden
125 G 15 **Stranraer**, United Kingdom
129 X 4 **Strasbourg**, France
61 R 3 **Strasburg**, Virginia, U.S.A.
139 R 5 **Strasswalchen**, Austria
232 J 13 **Stratford**, New Zealand
69 N 11 **Stratford**, Oklahoma, U.S.A.
70 J 1 **Stratford**, Texas, U.S.A.
86 D 13 **Stratford**, Ontario, Canada
127 S 8 **Stratford-upon-Avon**, United Kingdom
231 S 15 **Strathgordon**, Tasmania, Australia
86 C 14 **Strathroy**, Ontario, Canada
59 O 4 **Stratton**, Maine, U.S.A.
58 L 8 **Stratton Mountain**, Vermont, U.S.A. ▲
137 L 22 **Straubing**, Germany
134 A 9 **Straumnes**, Iceland ▶
76 K 11 **Strawberry Mountain**, Oregon, U.S.A. ▲
74 L 3 **Strawberry Reservoir**, Utah, U.S.A. 💧
231 N 11 **Streaky Bay**, South Australia, Australia
150 G 12 **Strehaia**, Romania
148 G 9 **Strenči**, Latvia
140 C 6 **Stresa**, Italy
141 L 22 **Stretta di Messina**, Italy ≈
73 N 13 **Strevell**, Idaho, U.S.A.
143 B 18 **Stříbro**, Czech Republic
234 A 5 **Strickland**, Papua New Guinea 〜
113 B 20 **Stroeder**, Argentina
141 L 20 **Stromboli**, Italy ▲
124 I 7 **Stromness**, United Kingdom
67 N 14 **Stromsburg**, Nebraska, U.S.A.
135 D 21 **Strömstad**, Sweden
135 G 15 **Strömsund**, Sweden
124 I 7 **Stronsay**, United Kingdom 🌴
127 R 10 **Stroud**, United Kingdom
69 O 9 **Stroud**, Oklahoma, U.S.A.
58 I 12 **Stroudsburg**, New Jersey, U.S.A.
135 B 24 **Struer**, Denmark
146 B 12 **Struga**, Macedonia (F.Y.R.O.M.)
146 F 11 **Struma**, Bulgaria 〜
126 K 8 **Strumble Head**, United Kingdom ▶
146 E 12 **Strumica**, Macedonia (F.Y.R.O.M.)
150 I 5 **Stryy**, Ukraine
143 H 16 **Strzelce Opolskie**, Poland
143 G 16 **Strzelin**, Poland
142 H 12 **Strzelno**, Poland
63 Y 11 **Stuart**, Florida, U.S.A.
138 L 7 **Stubaier Alpen**, Austria ⛰
127 R 8 **Studley**, United Kingdom
156 L 2 **Stupino**, Russian Federation
241 S 15 **Sturge Island**, Antarctica 🌴
64 H 11 **Sturgeon Bay**, Wisconsin, U.S.A.
86 E 9 **Sturgeon Falls**, Ontario, Canada
66 G 9 **Sturgis**, South Dakota, U.S.A.
127 Q 12 **Sturminster Newton**, United Kingdom
143 I 22 **Štúrovo**, Slovakia
231 Q 8 **Sturt Stony Desert**, South Australia, Australia ◇
219 N 14 **Stutterheim**, Republic of South Africa
137 F 23 **Stuttgart**, Germany
69 W 12 **Stuttgart**, Arkansas, U.S.A.
134 A 10 **Stykkishólmur**, Iceland
147 E 18 **Stylida**, Greece
149 H 21 **Styr**, Belarus/Ukraine 〜
195 R 8 **Suai**, Malaysia
213 H 14 **Suakin**, Sudan
216 K 12 **Suana**, Democratic Republic of Congo
189 Z 11 **Suao**, Taiwan
192 H 9 **Subi Besar**, Indonesia 🌴
141 H 14 **Subiaco**, Italy
68 I 6 **Sublette**, Kansas, U.S.A.
144 J 7 **Subotica**, Serbia and Montenegro
186 F 13 **Subrag**, China
150 L 8 **Suceava**, Romania
150 K 7 **Suceviţa**, Romania
142 N 10 **Suchowola**, Poland
104 I 4 **Sucre**, Colombia ▣
105 Q 3 **Sucre**, Venezuela ▣
107 K 21 **Sucre**, Bolivia 🏛
106 C 8 **Sucumbíos**, Ecuador ▣
108 F 11 **Sucunduri**, Brazil 〜
112 H 4 **Sucuriú**, Brazil 〜
215 T 15 **Sud**, Cameroon ▣
217 P 9 **Sud-Kivu**, Democratic Republic of Congo ▣
215 S 14 **Sud-Ouest**, Cameroon ▣
151 V 12 **Sudak**, Ukraine
213 B 19 **Sudan**, Africa ◘
127 X 8 **Sudbury**, United Kingdom
86 D 9 **Sudbury**, Ontario, Canada
213 D 21 **Sudd**, Sudan ◇
136 E 8 **Süderoogsand**, Germany 🌴
143 E 16 **Sudeten**, Czech Republic ⛰
156 M 1 **Sudogda**, Russian Federation
156 I 5 **Sudzha**, Russian Federation
131 T 8 **Sueca**, Spain
212 F 8 **Suez**, Egypt
212 F 8 **Suez Canal**, Egypt ◇
61 V 7 **Suffolk**, Virginia, U.S.A.
71 S 10 **Sugar Land**, Texas, U.S.A.
43 N 25 **Sugar Loaf Point**, St Helena ▶
197 N 18 **Sugbuhan Point**, Philippines ▶
186 H 9 **Sugehe**, China
184 H 5 **Sugun**, China
185 Q 7 **Suhait**, China
175 Y 6 **Şuḩār**, Oman
185 S 4 **Sühbaatar**, Mongolia ▣
185 Q 2 **Sühbaatar**, Mongolia
137 I 18 **Suhl**, Germany
144 F 12 **Šuica**, Bosnia and Herzegovina
189 X 8 **Suichang**, China
189 U 10 **Suichuan**, China
189 R 1 **Suide**, China
181 B 14 **Suigam**, India
186 K 10 **Suihua**, China
188 M 8 **Suijiang**, China
186 K 9 **Suileng**, China
189 O 6 **Suining**, China
189 R 10 **Suining**, China
129 T 4 **Suippes**, France
125 D 20 **Suir**, Republic of Ireland 〜
189 R 14 **Suixi**, China
189 V 4 **Suixi**, China
189 U 3 **Suixian**, China
189 P 8 **Suiyang**, China
187 G 16 **Suizhong**, China
189 T 5 **Suizhou**, China
177 U 15 **Sujawal**, Pakistan
192 H 14 **Sukabumi**, Indonesia
192 I 11 **Sukadana**, Indonesia
199 K 14 **Sukagawa**, Japan
192 J 12 **Sukaramai**, Indonesia
195 X 5 **Sukau**, Malaysia
135 M 14 **Sukeva**, Finland
156 J 2 **Sukhinichi**, Russian Federation
154 M 10 **Sukhona**, Russian Federation 〜
191 G 16 **Sukhothai**, Thailand
177 U 12 **Sukkur**, Pakistan
211 U 10 **Sūknah**, Libya
218 I 8 **Sukses**, Namibia
155 T 13 **Suksun**, Russian Federation
199 E 21 **Sukumo**, Japan
135 A 17 **Sula**, Norway 🌴
151 S 4 **Sula**, Ukraine 〜
193 R 12 **Sulabesi**, Indonesia 🌴
177 U 12 **Sulaiman Ranges**, Pakistan ⛰
157 R 14 **Sulak**, Russian Federation
197 M 15 **Sulat**, Philippines
193 O 12 **Sulawesi**, Indonesia 🌴
193 N 13 **Sulawesi Selatan**, Indonesia ▣
193 P 12 **Sulawesi Tengah**, Indonesia ▣
193 P 14 **Sulawesi Tenggara**, Indonesia ▣
193 P 10 **Sulawesi Utara**, Indonesia ▣
173 U 4 **Sulaymān Beg**, Iraq
142 E 13 **Sulechów**, Poland
215 R 12 **Suleja**, Nigeria
143 J 15 **Sulejów**, Poland
136 F 12 **Sulingen**, Germany
106 A 12 **Sullana**, Peru
63 O 3 **Sulligent**, Alabama, U.S.A.
65 H 20 **Sullivan**, Indiana, U.S.A.
69 W 5 **Sullivan**, Missouri, U.S.A.
146 L 11 **Süloğlu**, Turkey
62 H 7 **Sulphur**, Louisiana, U.S.A.
69 O 12 **Sulphur**, Oklahoma, U.S.A.
211 W 8 **Sultan**, Libya
86 B 7 **Sultan**, Ontario, Canada
170 I 11 **Sultanhani**, Turkey
183 N 10 **Sultanpur**, India
197 E 26 **Sulu Archipelago**, Philippines 🌴
193 O 7 **Sulu Sea**, Malaysia/Philippines 🌊
197 N 17 **Suluan**, Philippines 🌴
170 G 10 **Sülüklü**, Turkey
179 R 12 **Sülüktü**, Kyrgyzstan
211 W 7 **Sulunḩah**, Libya
211 W 7 **Sulūq**, Libya
137 K 20 **Sulzbach-Rosenberg**, Germany
241 N 12 **Sulzberger Bay**, Antarctica ≈
192 D 11 **Sumatera Barat**, Indonesia ▣
192 F 12 **Sumatera Selatan**, Indonesia ▣
192 D 9 **Sumatera Utara**, Indonesia ▣
192 F 10 **Sumatra**, Indonesia 🌴
193 N 15 **Sumba**, Indonesia 🌴
193 N 14 **Sumbawa**, Indonesia 🌴
192 M 15 **Sumbawabesar**, Indonesia
217 R 12 **Sumbawanga**, Tanzania
218 G 4 **Sumbe**, Angola
219 O 2 **Sumbu**, Zambia
124 J 5 **Sumburgh Head**, United Kingdom ▶
188 K 7 **Sumdo**, China
176 H 4 **Sume'eh Sarā**, Iran
213 C 20 **Sumeih**, Sudan
192 K 14 **Sumenep**, Indonesia
199 O 22 **Sumiyō**, Japan
173 R 1 **Summēl**, Iraq
76 I 13 **Summer Lake**, Oregon, U.S.A. 💧
61 P 14 **Summerville**, South Carolina, U.S.A.
63 R 2 **Summerville**, Georgia, U.S.A.
83 E 15 **Summit Lake**, British Columbia, Canada
199 G 19 **Sumoto**, Japan
143 G 17 **Šumperk**, Czech Republic
190 F 7 **Sumprabum**, Myanmar
171 Z 8 **Sumqayit**, Azerbaijan
61 P 12 **Sumter**, South Carolina, U.S.A.
151 U 3 **Sumy**, Ukraine
77 K 25 **Sun City**, California, U.S.A.
183 Q 9 **Sun Kosi**, Nepal 〜
155 P 13 **Suna**, Russian Federation
198 J 5 **Sunagawa**, Japan
187 K 17 **Sunan**, North Korea
175 X 6 **Şunaynah**, Oman
73 P 2 **Sunburst**, Montana, U.S.A.
65 M 18 **Sunbury**, Ohio, U.S.A.
112 B 13 **Sunchales**, Argentina
187 L 21 **Sunch'ŏn**, South Korea
39 S 3 **Sunda Shelf**, Indian Ocean ◇
192 G 13 **Sunda Strait**, Indonesia ≈
73 Z 9 **Sundance**, Wyoming, U.S.A.
183 S 14 **Sundarbans**, India ◇
125 K 15 **Sunderland**, United Kingdom
170 F 9 **Sündiken Dağlari**, Turkey
135 H 17 **Sundsvall**, Sweden
217 W 10 **Sunga**, Tanzania
194 B 8 **Sungai Besar**, Malaysia
192 D 8 **Sungai Petani**, Malaysia
192 E 11 **Sungaidareh**, Indonesia
192 E 11 **Sungaipenuh**, Indonesia
194 A 5 **Sungei Petani**, Malaysia
194 B 13 **Sungei Seletar Reservoir**, Singapore 💧
216 I 8 **Sungu**, Democratic Republic of Congo
170 J 9 **Sungurlu**, Turkey
104 H 6 **Sunia**, Colombia
135 E 20 **Sunne**, Sweden
76 I 8 **Sunnyside**, Washington, U.S.A.
77 G 20 **Sunnyvale**, California, U.S.A.
231 W 8 **Sunshine Coast**, Queensland, Australia ◇
153 S 11 **Suntar**, Russian Federation
177 P 14 **Suntsar**, Pakistan
186 K 7 **Sunwu**, China
199 C 20 **Suō-nada**, Japan ≈
134 N 13 **Suomussalmi**, Finland
191 L 21 **Suŏng**, Cambodia
154 G 8 **Suoyarvi**, Russian Federation
64 C 8 **Superior**, Wisconsin, U.S.A.
74 K 13 **Superior**, Arizona, U.S.A.
171 R 10 **Süphan Daği**, Turkey ▲
193 W 11 **Supiori**, Indonesia 🌴
61 S 12 **Suppli**, North Carolina, U.S.A.
173 X 11 **Sūq ash Shuyūkh**, Iraq
189 W 4 **Suqian**, China
175 Z 7 **Şūr**, Oman
91 R 14 **Sur**, Costa Rica
157 Q 2 **Sura**, Russian Federation 〜
171 Z 7 **Şuraabad**, Azerbaijan
177 S 12 **Surab**, Pakistan
192 K 14 **Surabaya**, Indonesia
192 J 14 **Surakarta**, Indonesia
197 L 23 **Surallah**, Philippines
231 U 8 **Surat**, Queensland, Australia
181 C 15 **Surat**, India
191 G 23 **Surat Thani**, Thailand
182 G 7 **Suratgarh**, India
149 M 14 **Surazh**, Belarus
156 H 3 **Surazh**, Russian Federation
173 U 3 **Sūrdāsh**, Iraq
150 M 12 **Surdila-Greci**, Romania
145 N 15 **Surdulica**, Serbia and Montenegro
181 B 15 **Surendranagar**, India
58 J 14 **Surf City**, New Jersey, U.S.A.
231 W 9 **Surfers Paradise**, Queensland, Australia
92 H 4 **Surgidero de Batabanó**, Cuba
152 L 10 **Surgut**, Russian Federation
181 F 18 **Suriapet**, India
197 M 18 **Surigao**, Philippines
197 M 18 **Surigao Strait**, Philippines ≈
191 K 18 **Surin**, Thailand
105 V 7 **Suriname**, Suriname ◘
182 M 8 **Surkhet**, Nepal
179 Q 14 **Surkhondaryo Wiloyati**, Uzbekistan ▣
171 O 8 **Sürmene**, Turkey
157 N 8 **Surovikino**, Russian Federation
138 F 7 **Sursee**, Switzerland
157 Q 2 **Surskoye**, Russian Federation
134 B 12 **Surtsey**, Iceland 🌴
171 N 13 **Sürüş**, Turkey
199 J 17 **Suruga-wan**, Japan ≈
192 E 12 **Surulangun**, Indonesia
171 W 9 **Şuşa**, Azerbaijan
140 A 7 **Susa**, Italy
199 C 19 **Susa**, Japan
199 E 21 **Susaki**, Japan
199 G 20 **Susami**, Japan
176 G 8 **Süsangerd**, Iran
77 H 16 **Susanville**, California, U.S.A.
138 J 8 **Susch**, Switzerland
171 N 9 **Suşehri**, Turkey
191 G 25 **Suso**, Thailand
58 F 13 **Susquehanna**, Pennsylvania, U.S.A. 〜
110 I 5 **Susques**, Argentina
87 T 10 **Sussex**, New Brunswick, Canada
83 E 17 **Sustut Peak**, British Columbia, Canada ▲
153 W 9 **Susuman**, Russian Federation
184 M 3 **Sutay Uul**, Mongolia ▲
218 K 14 **Sutherland**, Republic of South Africa
76 F 12 **Sutherlin**, Oregon, U.S.A.
177 W 11 **Sutlej**, Pakistan 〜
61 O 4 **Sutton**, West Virginia, U.S.A.
127 S 7 **Sutton Coldfield**, United Kingdom
127 T 5 **Sutton in Ashfield**, United Kingdom
85 N 8 **Sutton Ridges**, Ontario, Canada ⛰
198 I 6 **Suttsu**, Japan
185 Q 3 **Süüj**, Mongolia
148 H 9 **Suur Munamägi**, Estonia ▲
179 U 11 **Suusamyr**, Kyrgyzstan
235 X 12 **Suva**, Fiji 🏛
151 O 11 **Suvorove**, Ukraine
142 N 8 **Suwałki**, Poland
191 K 17 **Suwannaphum**, Thailand
199 B 26 **Suwanose-jima**, Japan 🌴
237 N 8 **Suwarrow**, Cook Islands 🌴
172 G 9 **Suwayliḩ**, Jordan
187 L 19 **Suwon**, South Korea
179 R 9 **Suzak**, Kazakhstan
199 I 15 **Suzaka**, Japan
154 K 14 **Suzdal'**, Russian Federation
189 Y 6 **Suzhou**, China
189 V 4 **Suzhou**, China
199 H 14 **Suzu**, Japan
199 H 14 **Suzu-misaki**, Japan ▶
199 H 18 **Suzuka**, Japan
45 S 10 **Svalbard**, Norway ▣
135 F 26 **Svaneke**, Denmark
134 J 10 **Svappavaara**, Sweden
134 J 12 **Svartlå**, Sweden
151 Y 5 **Svatove**, Ukraine
191 M 21 **Svay Rieng**, Cambodia
148 G 13 **Svėdasai**, Lithuania
135 F 17 **Sveg**, Sweden
149 C 14 **Švėkšna**, Lithuania
135 C 26 **Svendborg**, Denmark
135 F 16 **Svenstavik**, Sweden
151 Z 6 **Sverdlovs'k**, Ukraine
81 N 2 **Sverdrup Channel**, Nunavut, Canada ≈
146 E 11 **Sveti Nikole**, Macedonia (F.Y.R.O.M.)
153 W 14 **Svetlaya**, Russian Federation
157 N 12 **Svetlograd**, Russian Federation
149 A 15 **Svetlyy**, Russian Federation
154 E 9 **Svetogorsk**, Russian Federation
134 C 11 **Svíahnúkar**, Iceland ▲
143 M 19 **Svidník**, Slovakia
146 K 11 **Svilengrad**, Bulgaria
149 H 15 **Svir**, Belarus
146 J 7 **Svishtov**, Bulgaria
149 F 19 **Svislach**, Belarus
143 F 18 **Svitavy**, Czech Republic
153 U 13 **Svobodnyy**, Russian Federation
146 G 8 **Svoge**, Bulgaria

◘ Country ▣ Internal administrative region: State/Province/Territory/Dependent territory 🏛 Capital city ⛰ Mountain range/Undersea ridge ▲ Mountain peak/Volcano/Seamount ◇ Geographic feature ▶ Headland/Point/Cape/Peninsula ◓ Desert 🌴 Island/Island group ⁂ Antarctic base 🌀 Ocean 🌊 Sea ≈ Bay/Gulf/Channel/Strait 💧 Lake ⚑ Salt pan/Dry/Intermittent lake 〜 River

- 144 N 13 **Svrljig**, Serbia and Montenegro
- 149 L 20 **Svyetlahorsk**, Belarus
- 137 F 24 **Swabian Alp**, Germany ⛰
- 127 X 6 **Swaffham**, United Kingdom
- 236 K 7 **Swains**, American Samoa 🏝
- 63 V 4 **Swainsboro**, Georgia, U.S.A.
- 218 H 9 **Swakopmund**, Namibia
- 127 S 1 **Swale**, United Kingdom ∫
- 235 Q 7 **Swallow Islands**, Solomon Islands 🏝
- 231 R 12 **Swan Hill**, Victoria, Australia
- 84 H 9 **Swan River**, Manitoba, Canada
- 127 R 14 **Swanage**, United Kingdom
- 61 V 9 **Swanquarter**, North Carolina, U.S.A.
- 59 R 6 **Swans Island**, Maine, U.S.A. 🏝
- 231 T 15 **Swansea**, Tasmania, Australia
- 231 V 11 **Swansea**, New South Wales, Australia
- 126 M 10 **Swansea**, United Kingdom
- 142 G 12 **Swarzędz**, Poland
- 219 P 11 **Swaziland**, Africa □
- 135 F 22 **Sweden**, Europe □
- 76 G 11 **Sweet Home**, Oregon, U.S.A.
- 60 J 9 **Sweetwater**, Tennessee, U.S.A.
- 70 L 6 **Sweetwater**, Texas, U.S.A.
- 218 K 15 **Swellendam**, Republic of South Africa
- 143 N 15 **Świdnik**, Poland
- 142 E 9 **Świdwin**, Poland
- 142 E 13 **Świebodzin**, Poland
- 142 I 10 **Świecie**, Poland
- 83 M 20 **Swift Current**, Saskatchewan, Canada
- 127 S 10 **Swindon**, United Kingdom
- 127 V 5 **Swineshead**, United Kingdom
- 142 D 9 **Świnoujście**, Poland
- 138 B 8 **Switzerland**, Europe □
- 154 K 11 **Syamzha**, Russian Federation
- 149 L 15 **Syanno**, Belarus
- 154 G 10 **Syas'troy**, Russian Federation
- 156 I 1 **Sychevka**, Russian Federation
- 143 H 15 **Syców**, Poland
- 231 V 11 **Sydney**, New South Wales, Australia
- 87 Y 8 **Sydney**, Nova Scotia, Canada
- 151 Y 5 **Syeverodonets'k**, Ukraine
- 136 F 12 **Syke**, Germany
- 155 P 9 **Syktyvkar**, Russian Federation
- 63 R 3 **Sylacauga**, Alabama, U.S.A.
- 183 W 12 **Sylhet**, Bangladesh
- 183 V 12 **Sylhet**, Bangladesh ▣
- 136 E 7 **Sylt**, Germany 🏝
- 60 K 10 **Sylva**, North Carolina, U.S.A.
- 63 W 4 **Sylvania**, Georgia, U.S.A.
- 63 T 6 **Sylvester**, Georgia, U.S.A.
- 147 N 23 **Symi**, Greece 🏝
- 151 V 6 **Synel'nykove**, Ukraine
- 135 C 18 **Synnfjell**, Norway ▲
- 155 S 5 **Synya**, Russian Federation
- 241 U 2 **Syowa**, Antarctica ⁂
- 141 L 23 **Syracuse**, Italy
- 58 G 8 **Syracuse**, New York, U.S.A.
- 68 G 5 **Syracuse**, Kansas, U.S.A.
- 179 Q 10 **Syrdar'ya**, Kazakhstan ∫
- 172 K 4 **Syria**, Asia □
- 191 D 16 **Syriam**, Myanmar
- 172 K 8 **Syrian Desert**, Jordan ◇
- 147 L 24 **Syrna**, Greece 🏝
- 147 I 21 **Syros**, Greece 🏝
- 135 N 15 **Syväri**, Finland ≃
- 157 R 3 **Syzran'**, Russian Federation
- 142 F 12 **Szamotuły**, Poland
- 142 D 10 **Szczecin**, Poland
- 142 F 9 **Szczecinek**, Poland
- 143 J 16 **Szczekociny**, Poland
- 142 M 10 **Szczuczyn**, Poland
- 142 L 10 **Szczytno**, Poland
- 143 K 25 **Szeged**, Hungary
- 143 L 24 **Szeghalom**, Hungary
- 143 I 23 **Székesfehérvár**, Hungary
- 143 I 25 **Szekszárd**, Hungary
- 143 K 24 **Szentes**, Hungary
- 143 H 26 **Szentőrinc**, Hungary
- 143 L 21 **Szerencs**, Hungary
- 143 K 23 **Szolnok**, Hungary
- 143 F 23 **Szombathely**, Hungary
- 143 E 14 **Szprotawa**, Poland
- 142 H 11 **Szubin**, Poland

T

- 190 F 12 **Ta-Kaw**, Myanmar
- 190 I 11 **Ta Loung San**, Laos ▲
- 196 K 13 **Tabaco**, Philippines
- 234 H 3 **Tabar Islands**, Papua New Guinea 🏝
- 176 M 8 **Ṭabas**, Iran
- 89 V 12 **Tabasco**, Mexico ▣
- 176 M 10 **Tabāsīn**, Iran
- 108 B 11 **Tabatinga**, Brazil
- 210 J 10 **Tabelbala**, Algeria
- 83 K 20 **Taber**, Alberta, Canada
- 217 P 7 **Tabili**, Democratic Republic of Congo
- 236 E 3 **Tabiteuea**, Kiribati 🏝
- 197 H 14 **Tablas**, Philippines 🏝
- 197 H 15 **Tablas Strait**, Philippines ≈
- 197 D 18 **Table Point**, Philippines ▶
- 69 S 8 **Table Rock Reservoir**, Missouri, U.S.A. ≃
- 143 D 19 **Tábor**, Czech Republic
- 217 S 11 **Tabora**, Tanzania ▣
- 217 S 11 **Tabora**, Tanzania
- 179 R 12 **Taboshar**, Tajikistan
- 214 I 14 **Tabou**, Côte d'Ivoire
- 176 F 3 **Tabrīz**, Iran
- 237 P 1 **Tabuaeran**, Kiribati 🏝
- 234 A 4 **Tabubil**, Papua New Guinea
- 174 K 3 **Tabūk**, Saudi Arabia
- 196 G 7 **Tabuk**, Philippines
- 184 J 3 **Tacheng**, China
- 104 K 5 **Tachira**, Venezuela ▣
- 197 L 16 **Tacloban**, Philippines
- 104 L 11 **Tacna**, Colombia
- 107 H 20 **Tacna**, Peru
- 107 H 20 **Tacna**, Peru ▣
- 110 J 6 **Taco Pozo**, Argentina
- 76 G 7 **Tacoma**, Washington, U.S.A.
- 58 K 10 **Taconic Range**, New York, U.S.A. ⛰
- 90 H 5 **Tactic**, Guatemala
- 113 E 14 **Tacuarembo**, Uruguay ▣
- 112 E 13 **Tacuarembó**, Uruguay
- 197 L 23 **Tacurong**, Philippines
- 127 T 2 **Tadcaster**, United Kingdom
- 235 Q 14 **Tadine**, New Caledonia
- 211 N 12 **Tadjmout**, Algeria
- 213 K 19 **Tadjoura**, Djibouti
- 210 M 7 **Tadjrouna**, Algeria
- 87 O 7 **Tadoussac**, Québec, Canada
- 181 E 20 **Tadpatri**, India
- 187 M 18 **T'aebaek-sanmaek**, North Korea/South Korea ⛰
- 187 J 19 **Taech'ŏng-do**, South Korea 🏝
- 187 M 20 **Taegu**, South Korea
- 187 K 22 **Taehŭksan-kundo**, South Korea 🏝
- 187 L 20 **Taejŏn**, South Korea
- 187 L 23 **Taejŏng**, South Korea
- 131 R 3 **Tafalla**, Spain
- 110 I 7 **Tafi Viejo**, Argentina
- 210 F 9 **Tafraoute**, Morocco
- 176 K 9 **Taft**, Iran
- 181 O 24 **Tafwap**, India
- 213 E 14 **Tagab**, Sudan
- 156 L 10 **Taganrog**, Russian Federation
- 214 H 6 **Tagant**, Mauritania ▣
- 199 C 21 **Tagawa**, Japan
- 197 K 18 **Tagbilaran**, Philippines
- 210 K 9 **Taghit**, Algeria
- 83 B 15 **Tagish Lake**, British Columbia, Canada ≃
- 179 O 15 **Tagtabazar**, Turkmenistan
- 109 K 14 **Taguatinga**, Brazil
- 234 H 8 **Tagula**, Papua New Guinea
- 234 H 8 **Tagula Island**, Papua New Guinea 🏝
- 197 M 22 **Tagum**, Philippines
- 42 K 9 **Tagus Abyssal Plain**, Atlantic Ocean ◇
- 186 J 5 **Tahe**, China
- 77 I 18 **Tahoe City**, California, U.S.A.
- 70 K 5 **Tahoka**, Texas, U.S.A.
- 76 F 7 **Taholah**, Washington, U.S.A.
- 232 K 12 **Tahora**, New Zealand
- 215 Q 8 **Tahoua**, Niger
- 215 Q 8 **Tahoua**, Niger ▣
- 173 V 9 **Taḥrīr**, Iraq
- 176 M 11 **Tahrūd**, Iran
- 212 E 10 **Tahta**, Egypt
- 170 K 13 **Tahtali Dağlari**, Turkey ⛰
- 107 I 16 **Tahuamanu**, Bolivia ∫
- 193 Q 9 **Tahulandang**, Indonesia 🏝
- 232 L 9 **Tahuna**, New Zealand
- 193 Q 9 **Tahuna**, Indonesia
- 214 I 13 **Taï**, Côte d'Ivoire
- 189 Y 6 **Tai Hu**, China ≃
- 189 V 2 **Tai'an**, China
- 189 P 4 **Taibai**, China
- 189 Q 2 **Taibai**, China
- 189 P 4 **Taibai Shan**, China ▲
- 189 Y 11 **T'aichung**, Taiwan
- 233 E 24 **Taieri**, New Zealand ∫
- 147 E 22 **Taigetos**, Greece ⛰
- 189 S 1 **Taigu**, China
- 189 T 2 **Taihang Shan**, China ⛰
- 232 L 13 **Taihape**, New Zealand
- 189 U 9 **Taihe**, China
- 189 V 4 **Taihe**, China
- 189 V 6 **Taihu**, China
- 189 U 4 **Taikang**, China
- 191 D 16 **Taikkyi**, Myanmar
- 186 I 10 **Tailai**, China
- 231 Q 12 **Tailem Bend**, South Australia, Australia
- 124 H 9 **Tain**, United Kingdom
- 189 Z 12 **T'ainan**, Taiwan
- 189 Z 10 **Taipei**, Taiwan ♜
- 189 O 13 **Taiping**, China
- 189 U 12 **Taiping**, China
- 194 B 6 **Taiping**, Malaysia
- 186 G 9 **Taiping Ling**, China ▲
- 199 B 26 **Taira-jima**, Japan 🏝
- 232 L 9 **Tairua**, New Zealand
- 176 E 6 **Tairuq**, Iran
- 192 E 13 **Tais**, Indonesia
- 189 T 13 **Taishan**, China
- 189 Z 12 **T'aitung**, Taiwan
- 134 M 12 **Taivalkoski**, Finland
- 189 Y 11 **Taiwan**, Asia □
- 189 Y 12 **Taiwan Strait**, Taiwan/China ≈
- 186 I 6 **Taiyanggou**, China
- 189 S 1 **Taiyuan**, China
- 189 Y 5 **Taizhou**, China
- 189 Z 7 **Taizhou**, China
- 175 P 14 **Ta'izz**, Yemen
- 211 T 12 **Tajarḥī**, Libya
- 179 S 13 **Tajikistan**, Asia □
- 199 K 14 **Tajima**, Japan
- 88 I 3 **Tajitos**, Mexico
- 130 L 7 **Tajo**, Spain ∫
- 191 G 16 **Tak**, Thailand
- 176 G 5 **Takāb**, Iran
- 217 X 6 **Takabba**, Kenya
- 233 I 15 **Takaka**, New Zealand
- 199 F 19 **Takamatsu**, Japan
- 199 D 23 **Takanabe**, Japan
- 199 H 15 **Takaoka**, Japan
- 232 J 8 **Takapuna**, New Zealand
- 199 B 26 **Takara-jima**, Japan 🏝
- 199 J 15 **Takasaki**, Japan
- 218 M 10 **Takatokwane**, Botswana
- 199 G 18 **Takatsuki**, Japan
- 199 E 21 **Takatsuki-yama**, Japan ▲
- 199 H 16 **Takayama**, Japan
- 199 C 25 **Take-shima**, Japan 🏝
- 199 G 17 **Takefu**, Japan
- 192 B 8 **Takengon**, Indonesia
- 199 B 21 **Takeo**, Japan
- 176 H 5 **Tākestān**, Iran
- 199 C 22 **Taketa**, Japan
- 191 L 22 **Takêv**, Cambodia
- 177 V 6 **Takhār**, Afghanistan ▣
- 177 S 10 **Takhta Pul Post**, Afghanistan
- 198 J 5 **Takikawa**, Japan
- 198 K 4 **Takinoue**, Japan
- 234 G 3 **Takis**, Papua New Guinea
- 83 E 18 **Takla Lake**, British Columbia, Canada ≃
- 184 H 6 **Taklimakan Desert**, China ◇
- 153 R 12 **Taksimo**, Russian Federation
- 191 F 24 **Takua Pa**, Thailand
- 215 S 12 **Takum**, Nigeria
- 237 P 10 **Takutea**, Cook Islands 🏝
- 234 K 4 **Takuu Islands**, Papua New Guinea 🏝
- 113 F 15 **Tala**, Uruguay
- 110 H 10 **Talacasto**, Argentina
- 149 L 16 **Talachyn**, Belarus
- 177 W 8 **Talagang**, Pakistan
- 181 F 23 **Talaimannar**, Sri Lanka
- 192 G 12 **Talangbatu**, Indonesia
- 106 A 11 **Talara**, Peru
- 179 T 10 **Talas**, Kyrgyzstan
- 234 F 4 **Talasea**, Papua New Guinea
- 179 T 11 **Talasskaya Oblast'**, Kyrgyzstan ▣
- 130 M 7 **Talavera de la Reina**, Spain
- 110 F 13 **Talca**, Chile
- 111 E 14 **Talcahuano**, Chile
- 181 J 16 **Talcher**, India
- 179 W 8 **Taldykorgan**, Kazakhstan
- 179 V 10 **Talgar**, Kazakhstan
- 127 O 9 **Talgarth**, United Kingdom
- 213 E 22 **Tali Post**, Sudan
- 193 Q 11 **Taliabu**, Indonesia 🏝
- 197 K 18 **Talibon**, Philippines
- 181 D 19 **Talikota**, India
- 179 P 13 **Talimardzhan**, Uzbekistan
- 171 W 10 **Talish Mountains**, Azerbaijan ⛰
- 192 L 15 **Taliwang**, Indonesia
- 173 Q 2 **Tall 'Afar**, Iraq
- 172 K 1 **Tall al Aḥmar**, Syria
- 173 W 11 **Tall al Laḥm**, Iraq
- 173 O 1 **Tall Baydar**, Syria
- 172 J 7 **Tall Ghāb**, Syria ▲
- 173 Q 2 **Tall Ḥuqnah**, Iraq
- 173 R 2 **Tall Kayf**, Iraq
- 173 Q 1 **Tall Kūjik**, Syria
- 172 L 7 **Tall Salāh**, Jordan ▲
- 173 N 1 **Tall Tamir**, Syria
- 173 Q 1 **Tall 'Uwaynāt**, Iraq
- 63 S 7 **Tallahassee**, Florida, U.S.A.
- 148 F 5 **Tallinn**, Estonia ♜
- 62 K 5 **Tallulah**, Louisiana, U.S.A.
- 150 I 11 **Tălmaciu**, Romania
- 210 G 8 **Talmest**, Morocco
- 151 P 6 **Tal'ne**, Ukraine
- 213 E 19 **Talodi**, Sudan
- 177 V 5 **Tāloqān**, Afghanistan
- 185 O 4 **Talshand**, Mongolia
- 148 D 10 **Talsi**, Latvia
- 110 F 7 **Taltal**, Chile
- 193 P 10 **Taludaa**, Indonesia
- 192 E 11 **Taluk**, Indonesia
- 191 O 17 **Tam Ky**, Vietnam
- 236 E 3 **Tamana**, Kiribati 🏝
- 210 F 8 **Tamanar**, Morocco
- 211 T 11 **Tamanhint**, Libya
- 211 O 14 **Tamanrasset**, Algeria
- 190 D 8 **Tamanthi**, Myanmar
- 126 L 14 **Tamar**, United Kingdom ∫
- 143 H 25 **Tamási**, Hungary
- 89 R 9 **Tamaulipas**, Mexico ▣
- 89 R 10 **Tamazunchale**, Mexico
- 214 F 9 **Tambacounda**, Senegal
- 192 H 10 **Tambelan Besar**, Indonesia 🏝
- 152 M 7 **Tambey**, Russian Federation
- 195 Z 6 **Tambisan**, Malaysia
- 231 T 7 **Tambo**, Queensland, Australia
- 107 G 20 **Tambo**, Peru ∫
- 106 A 12 **Tambo Grande**, Peru
- 219 W 7 **Tambohorano**, Madgascar
- 217 N 4 **Tamboura**, Central African Republic
- 157 N 4 **Tambov**, Russian Federation
- 157 N 4 **Tambovskaya Oblast'**, Russian Federation ▣
- 195 V 5 **Tambunan**, Malaysia
- 213 C 22 **Tambura**, Sudan
- 214 H 7 **Tâmchekket**, Mauritania
- 181 F 22 **Tamil Nadu**, India ▣
- 138 I 8 **Tamins**, Switzerland
- 144 L 10 **Tamiš**, Serbia and Montenegro ∫
- 135 L 20 **Tammisaari**, Finland
- 63 V 10 **Tampa**, Florida, U.S.A.
- 63 U 11 **Tampa Bay**, Florida, U.S.A. ≈
- 135 L 17 **Tampere**, Finland
- 89 S 10 **Tampico**, Mexico
- 194 C 9 **Tampin**, Malaysia
- 194 B 14 **Tampines**, Singapore
- 175 Q 9 **Tamrah**, Saudi Arabia
- 106 F 11 **Tamshiyacu**, Peru
- 139 S 7 **Tamsweg**, Austria
- 231 U 10 **Tamworth**, New South Wales, Australia
- 127 S 6 **Tamworth**, United Kingdom
- 191 M 22 **Tân An**, Vietnam
- 210 E 10 **Tan-Tan**, Morocco
- 134 M 6 **Tana Bru**, Norway
- 199 G 20 **Tanabe**, Japan
- 78 E 13 **Tanaga Island**, Alaska, U.S.A. 🏝
- 194 C 5 **Tanah Merah**, Malaysia
- 192 C 11 **Tanahbala**, Indonesia 🏝
- 192 M 11 **Tanahgrogot**, Indonesia
- 193 O 14 **Tanahjampea**, Indonesia 🏝
- 192 C 11 **Tanahmasa**, Indonesia 🏝
- 182 L 8 **Tanakpur**, India
- 230 M 5 **Tanami Desert**, Northern Territory, Australia ◇
- 79 Q 6 **Tanana**, Alaska, U.S.A.
- 187 M 16 **Tanch'ŏn**, North Korea
- 214 L 12 **Tanda**, Côte d'Ivoire
- 183 N 10 **Tanda**, India
- 197 N 19 **Tandag**, Philippines
- 150 M 12 **Tăndărei**, Romania
- 195 V 4 **Tandek**, Malaysia
- 113 D 18 **Tandil**, Argentina
- 215 W 11 **Tandjilé**, Chad ▣
- 177 U 14 **Tando Adam**, Pakistan
- 199 C 25 **Tanega-shima**, Japan 🏝
- 143 N 16 **Tanew**, Poland ∫
- 210 K 15 **Tanezrouft**, Algeria ⛰
- 217 W 11 **Tanga**, Tanzania ▣
- 217 W 11 **Tanga**, Tanzania
- 234 H 3 **Tanga Islands**, Papua New Guinea 🏝
- 188 L 9 **Tangdan**, China
- 188 L 4 **Tanggor**, China
- 184 K 9 **Tanggula Shan**, China ⛰
- 189 S 5 **Tanghe**, China
- 210 I 6 **Tangier**, Morocco
- 61 W 5 **Tangier Island**, Virginia, U.S.A. 🏝
- 189 U 10 **Tangjiang**, China
- 194 B 14 **Tanglin**, Singapore
- 199 F 17 **Tango**, Japan
- 232 N 13 **Tangoio**, New Zealand
- 184 J 9 **Tangra Yumco**, China ≃
- 192 B 8 **Tangse**, Indonesia
- 187 F 17 **Tangshan**, China
- 189 U 2 **Tangyin**, China
- 186 M 10 **Tangyuan**, China
- 219 V 9 **Tanjona Ankaboa**, Madgascar ▶
- 219 Z 4 **Tanjona Bobaomby**, Madgascar ▶
- 219 Z 6 **Tanjona Masoala**, Madgascar ▶
- 219 W 6 **Tanjona Vilanandro**, Madgascar ▶
- 219 W 11 **Tanjona Vohimena**, Madgascar ▶
- 192 L 11 **Tanjung**, Indonesia
- 193 O 10 **Tanjung Arus**, Indonesia ▶
- 194 A 7 **Tanjung Beras Basah**, Malaysia ▶
- 195 X 5 **Tanjung Bidadari**, Malaysia ▶
- 192 J 14 **Tanjung Bugel**, Indonesia ▶
- 192 F 13 **Tanjung Cina**, Indonesia ▶
- 194 M 10 **Tanjung Datu**, Malaysia ▶
- 193 X 11 **Tanjung d'Urville**, Indonesia ▶
- 194 E 7 **Tanjung Gelang**, Malaysia ▶
- 192 G 14 **Tanjung Guhakolak**, Indonesia ▶
- 195 O 9 **Tanjung Jerijih**, Malaysia ▶
- 193 O 10 **Tanjung Kandi**, Indonesia ▶
- 195 Q 8 **Tanjung Kidurong**, Malaysia ▶
- 193 O 13 **Tanjung Koku**, Indonesia ▶
- 192 L 13 **Tanjung Layar**, Indonesia ▶
- 193 S 11 **Tanjung Libobo**, Indonesia ▶
- 192 G 12 **Tanjung Lumut**, Indonesia ▶
- 193 N 10 **Tanjung Mangkalihat**, Indonesia ▶
- 192 L 15 **Tanjung Mebulu**, Indonesia ▶
- 192 I 10 **Tanjung Munggeresak**, Indonesia ▶
- 193 R 12 **Tanjung Palpetu**, Indonesia ▶
- 195 R 8 **Tanjung Payung**, Malaysia ▶
- 195 N 10 **Tanjung Po**, Malaysia ▶
- 192 J 12 **Tanjung Puting**, Indonesia ▶
- 194 E 9 **Tanjung Resang**, Malaysia ▶
- 192 I 12 **Tanjung Sambar**, Indonesia ▶
- 192 L 13 **Tanjung Selatan**, Indonesia ▶
- 195 V 4 **Tanjung Simpang Mangayau**, Malaysia ▶
- 195 N 10 **Tanjung Sipang**, Malaysia ▶
- 195 O 9 **Tanjung Sirik**, Malaysia ▶
- 193 S 9 **Tanjung Sopi**, Indonesia ▶
- 195 W 4 **Tanjung Sugut**, Malaysia ▶
- 195 W 4 **Tanjung Sumangat**, Malaysia ▶
- 194 C 9 **Tanjung Tuan**, Malaysia ▶
- 193 X 15 **Tanjung Vals**, Indonesia ▶
- 193 R 12 **Tanjung Waka**, Indonesia ▶
- 192 H 12 **Tanjungpandan**, Indonesia
- 192 F 10 **Tanjungpinang**, Indonesia
- 192 L 9 **Tanjungredeb**, Indonesia
- 192 M 9 **Tanjungselor**, Indonesia
- 177 V 9 **Tank**, Pakistan
- 182 K 3 **Tankse**, India
- 235 R 12 **Tanna**, Vanuatu 🏝
- 197 J 18 **Tañon Strait**, Philippines ≈
- 215 S 8 **Tanout**, Niger
- 183 O 9 **Tansen**, Nepal
- 212 E 8 **Tanta**, Egypt
- 172 F 8 **Tantura**, Israel
- 78 L 9 **Tanunak**, Alaska, U.S.A.
- 217 S 11 **Tanzania**, Africa □
- 189 S 8 **Taojiang**, China
- 186 I 11 **Taonan**, China
- 141 L 21 **Taormina**, Italy
- 75 R 8 **Taos**, New Mexico, U.S.A.
- 210 I 6 **Taounate**, Morocco
- 210 J 6 **Taourirt**, Morocco
- 210 J 9 **Taouz**, Morocco

□ Country ▣ Internal administrative region: State/Province/Territory/Dependent territory ♜ Capital city ⛰ Mountain range/Undersea ridge ▲ Mountain peak/Volcano/Seamount ◇ Geographic feature ▶ Headland/Point/Cape/Peninsula ◓ Desert 🏝 Island/Island group ⁂ Antarctic base Ⓞ Ocean ≋ Sea ≈ Bay/Gulf/Channel/Strait ≃ Lake ⊡ Salt pan/Dry/Intermittent lake ∫ River

Key:
⊡ Country ⊡ Internal administrative region: State/Province/Territory/Dependent territory ⌐ Capital city ▲ Mountain range/ Undersea ridge ▲ Mountain peak/ Volcano/Seamount ◇ Geographic feature ▶ Headland/Point/ Cape/Peninsula ▲ Desert ⌐ Island/Island group ⌖ Antarctic base ⌐ Ocean ◢ Sea ≈ Bay/Gulf/Channel/Strait ⌐ Lake ⌐ Salt pan/Dry/ Intermittent lake ⌐ River

233 F 23	Tokarahi, New Zealand
199 N 25	Tokasiki-jima, Japan ⇄
170 L 9	Tokat, Turkey
187 K 19	Tŏkchŏk-to, South Korea ⇄
236 J 5	Tokelau Islands, New Zealand ▣
232 K 12	Tokirima, New Zealand
198 L 5	Tokkachi, Japan ↳
151 V 8	Tokmak, Ukraine
232 O 11	Tokomaru Bay, New Zealand
198 L 4	Tokoro, Japan ↳
232 L 11	Tokoroa, New Zealand
214 H 11	Tokounuo, Guinea
179 T 11	Toktogul, Kyrgyzstan
236 I 10	Toku, Tonga ⇄
199 N 22	Toku-no-shima, Japan ⇄
199 N 22	Tokunoshima, Japan
199 F 19	Tokushima, Japan
199 D 20	Tokuyama, Japan
199 K 16	Tokyo, Japan ▪
199 K 16	Tōkyō-wan, Japan ≈
177 S 6	Tokzār, Afghanistan
232 O 11	Tolaga Bay, New Zealand
219 X 11	Tôlanaro, Madagascar
157 W 2	Tolbazy, Russian Federation
184 M 3	Tolbo, Mongolia
91 U 14	Tolé, Panama
179 T 9	Tole Bi, Kazakhstan
112 G 8	Toledo, Brazil
131 O 7	Toledo, Spain
197 J 17	Toledo, Philippines
65 L 16	Toledo, Ohio, U.S.A.
76 F 10	Toledo, Oregon, U.S.A.
62 H 6	Toledo Bend Reservoir, Louisiana, U.S.A. ↳
184 J 3	Toli, China
219 V 10	Toliara, Madagascar
219 W 9	Toliara, Madagascar
104 H 7	Tolima, Colombia ▣
193 O 10	Tolitoli, Indonesia
179 U 10	Tolmak, Kyrgyzstan
140 H 5	Tolmezzo, Italy
144 A 7	Tolmin, Slovenia
143 I 25	Tolna, Hungary
216 J 9	Tolo, Democratic Republic of Congo
197 I 19	Tolong Bay, Philippines ≈
131 R 1	Tolosa, Spain
89 Q 12	Toluca, Mexico
141 M 16	Tolve, Italy
157 R 3	Tol'yatti, Russian Federation
219 O 9	Tom Burke, Republic of South Africa
230 G 6	Tom Price, Western Australia, Australia
64 E 12	Tomah, Wisconsin, U.S.A.
198 K 6	Tomakomai, Japan
198 J 4	Tomamae, Japan
195 Y 6	Tomanggong, Malaysia
195 U 6	Tomani, Malaysia
179 U 7	Tomar, Kazakhstan
156 J 6	Tomarovka, Russian Federation
170 K 11	Tomarza, Turkey
143 O 16	Tomaszów Lubelski, Poland
143 K 14	Tomaszów Mazowiecki, Poland
88 M 11	Tomatlán, Mexico
63 O 5	Tombigbee, Alabama, U.S.A. ↳
218 F 1	Tomboco, Angola
74 L 15	Tombstone, Arizona, U.S.A.
218 F 6	Tombua, Angola
111 F 14	Tomé, Chile
193 Q 13	Tomea, Indonesia ⇄
131 P 9	Tomelloso, Spain
179 Q 9	Tomenaryk, Kazakhstan
198 L 13	Tomioka, Japan
104 M 6	Tomo, Colombia ↳
216 H 6	Tomori, Central African Republic
58 J 14	Toms River, New Jersey, U.S.A.
152 M 12	Tomsk, Russian Federation
153 V 9	Tomtor, Russian Federation
193 U 12	Tomu, Indonesia

199 N 25	Tonaki-jima, Japan ⇄
89 V 14	Tonalá, Mexico
108 C 11	Tonantins, Brazil
76 J 5	Tonasket, Washington, U.S.A.
58 D 8	Tonawanda, New York, U.S.A.
127 W 11	Tonbridge, United Kingdom
193 Q 10	Tondano, Indonesia
135 B 26	Tønder, Denmark
240 K 10	Toney Mountain, Antarctica ▲
236 I 9	Tonga, Oceania ▣
41 P 10	Tonga Trench, Pacific Ocean ◇
189 X 11	Tong'an, China
237 P 6	Tongareva, Cook Islands ⇄
236 I 11	Tongatapu, Tonga ⇄
236 H 12	Tongatapu Group, Tonga ⇄
189 T 5	Tongbai, China
186 K 9	Tongbei, China
189 W 6	Tongcheng, China
187 M 17	T'ongch'ŏn, North Korea
189 Q 3	Tongchuan, China
189 R 10	Tongdao, China
133 J 19	Tongeren, Belgium
189 U 8	Tonggu, China
189 R 3	Tongguan, China
189 T 8	Tongguan, China
187 N 19	Tonghae, South Korea
188 L 11	Tonghai, China
186 L 10	Tonghe, China
187 K 15	Tonghua, China
186 O 9	Tongjiang, China
186 H 13	Tongliao, China
189 W 6	Tongling, China
235 R 11	Tongoa, Vanuatu ⇄
197 H 24	Tongquil, Philippines ⇄
189 Q 9	Tongren, China
189 Q 15	Tongshi, China
124 H 8	Tongue, United Kingdom
189 N 3	Tongwei, China
187 E 17	Tongxian, China
185 Q 8	Tongxin, China
186 E 13	Tongxing, China
186 I 12	Tongyu, China
189 O 8	Tongzi, China
88 J 5	Tónichi, Mexico
213 D 21	Tonj, Sudan
180 D 12	Tonk, India
176 I 5	Tonkābon, Iran
190 L 11	Tonkin, Vietnam ◇
191 K 20	Tônlé Sab, Cambodia ↳
129 S 6	Tonnerre, France
136 F 8	Tönning, Germany
77 K 19	Tonopah, Nevada, U.S.A.
91 V 15	Tonosí, Panama
135 D 20	Tønsberg, Norway
74 J 3	Tooele, Utah, U.S.A.
231 V 9	Toowoomba, Queensland, Australia
213 O 18	Tooxin, Somalia
230 M 3	Top Springs, Northern Territory, Australia
69 Q 4	Topeka, Kansas, U.S.A.
150 J 9	Topliţa, Romania
42 N 1	Topo, Azores
77 N 24	Topock, California, U.S.A.
146 C 12	Topolčani, Macedonia (F.Y.R.O.M.)
88 K 7	Topolobampo, Mexico
146 K 10	Topolovgrad, Bulgaria
151 N 3	Toporyshche, Ukraine
127 N 13	Topsham, United Kingdom
232 J 7	Topuni, New Zealand
127 N 14	Tor Bay, United Kingdom ≈
170 B 11	Torbalı, Turkey
177 O 7	Torbat-e Heydariyeh, Iran
177 O 6	Torbat-e Jām, Iran
130 M 4	Tordesillas, Spain
134 K 12	Töre, Sweden
151 Y 7	Torez, Ukraine
137 L 15	Torgau, Germany
136 N 10	Torgelow, Germany
179 O 5	Torghay, Kazakhstan
133 B 18	Torhout, Belgium
213 E 23	Torit, Sudan

154 E 11	Torkovichi, Russian Federation
134 I 9	Torneälven, Sweden ↳
134 I 9	Torneträsk, Sweden
134 I 9	Torneträsk, Sweden
85 T 5	Torngat Mountains, Québec, Canada ▲
70 E 8	Tornillo, Texas, U.S.A.
134 K 12	Tornio, Finland
113 B 18	Tornquist, Argentina
215 S 11	Toro, Nigeria
130 M 4	Toro, Spain
77 L 25	Toro Peak, California, U.S.A. ▲
215 O 9	Torodi, Niger
234 J 5	Torokina, Papua New Guinea
143 K 23	Törökszentmiklós, Hungary
86 F 13	Toronto, Ontario, Canada
154 F 14	Toropets, Russian Federation
217 T 7	Tororo, Uganda
126 L 15	Torpoint, United Kingdom
127 N 14	Torquay, United Kingdom
131 N 3	Torquemada, Spain
77 J 25	Torrance, California, U.S.A.
130 H 10	Torrão, Portugal
131 V 3	Torre de Cadí, Spain
130 J 5	Torre de Moncorvo, Portugal
130 M 13	Torrecilla, Spain ▲
131 O 1	Torrelavega, Spain
89 O 7	Torreón, Mexico
112 I 11	Torres, Brazil
235 P 9	Torres Islands, Vanuatu ⇄
130 H 8	Torres Novas, Portugal
193 Y 15	Torres Strait, Asia/Oceania ≈
130 G 8	Torres Vedras, Portugal
131 T 11	Torrevieja, Spain
234 A 3	Torricelli Mountains, Papua New Guinea ▲
140 C 9	Torriglia, Italy
58 L 10	Torrington, Connecticut, U.S.A.
73 Z 13	Torrington, Wyoming, U.S.A.
135 F 14	Torrön, Sweden ↳
135 F 19	Torsby, Sweden
111 F 21	Tortel, Chile
179 T 4	Tortkuduk, Kazakhstan
93 V 8	Tortola, Virgin Islands, United Kingdom ◇
171 Q 9	Tortum, Turkey
176 L 6	Ţorūd, Iran
171 O 8	Torul, Turkey
142 H 11	Toruń, Poland
148 H 9	Tõrva, Estonia
154 H 14	Torzhok, Russian Federation
199 E 20	Tosa, Japan
199 F 21	Tosa-wan, Japan ≈
199 E 21	Tosashimizu, Japan
134 F 13	Tosbotn, Norway
218 M 11	Tosca, Republic of South Africa
140 F 11	Toscana, Italy ▣
179 R 11	Toshkent Wiloyati, Uzbekistan ▣
112 B 12	Tostado, Argentina
148 F 8	Tõstamaa, Estonia
136 G 11	Tostedt, Germany
170 J 8	Tosya, Turkey
131 R 11	Totana, Spain
154 L 11	Tot'ma, Russian Federation
127 N 14	Totnes, United Kingdom
105 V 6	Totness, Suriname
110 F 8	Totoral, Chile
235 Y 12	Totoya, Fiji ⇄
157 U 4	Totskoye, Russian Federation
199 F 17	Tottori, Japan
214 I 12	Touba, Côte d'Ivoire
214 E 8	Touba, Senegal
214 I 8	Touboro, Cameroon
207 O 7	Touggourt, Algeria
214 G 10	Tougué, Guinea
235 P 13	Touho, New Caledonia
214 H 8	Touil, Mauritania
129 U 4	Toul, France

129 V 15	Toulon, France
129 P 14	Toulouse, France
214 J 13	Toumodi, Côte d'Ivoire
215 U 12	Toungo, Nigeria
191 E 14	Toungoo, Myanmar
215 V 9	Tourba, Chad
133 C 20	Tournai, Belgium
107 E 14	Tournavista, Peru
129 T 11	Tournon-sur-Rhône, France
129 T 8	Tournus, France
108 O 12	Touros, Brazil
129 N 7	Tours, France
185 Q 3	Töv, Mongolia ▣
156 J 2	Tovarkovo, Russian Federation
171 U 7	Tovuz, Azerbaijan
198 K 9	Towada, Japan
198 K 9	Towada-ko, Japan ↳
58 G 10	Towanda, Pennsylvania, U.S.A.
127 T 8	Towcester, United Kingdom
66 J 3	Towner, North Dakota, U.S.A.
73 Q 6	Townsend, Montana, U.S.A.
231 T 4	Townsville, Queensland, Australia
213 G 22	Towot, Sudan
59 U 2	Towson, Maryland, U.S.A.
198 J 6	Tōya-ko, Japan ↳
70 H 8	Toyah, Texas, U.S.A.
199 H 15	Toyama, Japan
199 H 14	Toyama-wan, Japan ≈
90 L 4	Toyós, Honduras
199 I 17	Toyota, Japan
199 I 18	Toyohashi, Japan
199 F 17	Toyooka, Japan
211 P 7	Tozeur, Tunisia
171 S 6	Tqibuli, Georgia
171 Q 5	Tqvarch'eli, Georgia
191 M 23	Tra Vinh, Vietnam
130 K 4	Trabazos, Spain
171 C 8	Trabzon, Turkey
139 W 4	Traisen, Austria
125 B 20	Tralee, Republic of Ireland
135 F 22	Tranås, Sweden
110 I 7	Trancas, Argentina
191 G 25	Trang, Thailand
193 V 14	Trangan, Indonesia ⇄
112 E 13	Tranqueras, Uruguay
241 N 7	Transantarctic Mountains, Antarctica ▲
38 H 9	Transkei Basin, Indian Ocean ◇
150 G 10	Transylvania, Romania ◇
150 G 11	Transylvanian Alps, Romania ▲▲
150 H 8	Transylvanian Basin, Romania ◇
141 H 21	Trapani, Italy
214 F 6	Trarza, Mauritania ▣
183 V 9	Trashigang, Bhutan
191 J 20	Trat, Thailand
139 T 4	Traun, Austria
139 S 5	Traunsee, Austria ↳
136 I 9	Travemünde, Germany
64 J 11	Traverse City, Michigan, U.S.A.
140 D 8	Travo, Italy
127 N 5	Trawsfynydd, United Kingdom
143 E 19	Třebíč, Czech Republic
145 H 15	Trebinje, Bosnia and Herzegovina
143 M 20	Trebišov, Slovakia
233 C 22	Treble Cone, New Zealand ▲
144 C 8	Trebnje, Slovenia
181 B 22	Tree Island, India ⇄
126 K 15	Tregony, United Kingdom
113 G 14	Treinta y Tres, Uruguay
113 F 14	Treinta y Tres, Uruguay ▣
111 I 18	Trelew, Argentina
135 E 26	Trelleborg, Sweden
126 M 6	Tremadog Bay, United Kingdom ≈
38 B 15	Tremblet, Réunion

74 J 1	Tremonton, Utah, U.S.A.
64 I 9	Trenary, Michigan, U.S.A.
143 H 20	Trenčín, Slovakia
113 A 17	Trenque Lauquen, Argentina
127 U 5	Trent, United Kingdom ↳
140 F 5	Trentino-Alto Adige, Italy ▣
140 F 6	Trento, Italy
58 I 13	Trenton, New Jersey, U.S.A.
69 T 2	Trenton, Missouri, U.S.A.
86 H 12	Trenton, Ontario, Canada
85 Z 11	Trepassey, Newfoundland and Labrador, Canada
113 C 18	Tres Arroyos, Argentina
108 E 12	Três Casas, Brazil
111 H 21	Tres Cerros, Argentina
112 L 6	Três Corações, Brazil
104 H 9	Tres Esquinas, Colombia
112 B 9	Tres Isletas, Argentina
112 H 5	Três Lagoas, Brazil
111 G 22	Tres Lagos, Argentina
89 V 14	Tres Picos, Mexico
75 Q 8	Tres Piedras, New Mexico, U.S.A.
90 K 4	Tres Puntas, Guatemala ▶
112 N 6	Três Rios, Brazil
135 D 18	Tretten, Norway
140 D 7	Treviglio, Italy
140 G 6	Treviso, Italy
126 K 14	Trevose Head, United Kingdom ▶
145 N 16	Trgovište, Serbia and Montenegro
147 M 24	Tria Nisia, Greece ⇄
68 G 4	Tribune, Kansas, U.S.A.
181 D 22	Trichur, India
139 T 6	Trieben, Austria
137 B 20	Trier, Germany
140 I 7	Trieste, Italy
144 A 6	Triglav, Slovenia ▲
147 D 16	Trikala, Greece
181 G 24	Trincomalee, Sri Lanka
107 K 18	Trinidad, Bolivia
113 E 15	Trinidad, Uruguay
75 S 7	Trinidad, Colorado, U.S.A.
92 I 5	Trinidad, Cuba
93 Z 14	Trinidad, Trinidad and Tobago ◇
93 Y 13	Trinidad and Tobago, North America ▣
71 T 9	Trinity, Texas, U.S.A. ↳
85 Z 10	Trinity Bay, Newfoundland and Labrador, Canada ≈
79 P 12	Trinity Islands, Alaska, U.S.A. ⇄
38 B 11	Triolet, Mauritius
211 S 7	Tripoli, Libya ▪
147 E 21	Tripoli, Greece
172 G 5	Tripoli, Lebanon
158 K 11	Tripolitanian Valley, Mediterranean Sea ◇
183 V 13	Tripura, India ▣
136 F 9	Trischen, Germany ⇄
43 O 15	Tristan da Cunha, Tristan da Cunha ⇄
43 N 15	Tristan da Cunha, U.K. ▣
43 I 18	Tristan da Cunha Fracture Zone, Atlantic Ocean ◇
90 M 8	Triunfo, Honduras
181 D 24	Trivandrum, India
141 K 14	Trivento, Italy
143 G 21	Trnava, Slovakia
234 G 6	Trobriand Islands, Papua New Guinea ⇄
179 P 2	Troebratskåy, Kazakhstan
134 F 12	Trofors, Norway
144 E 12	Troglav, Bosnia and Herzegovina ▲
141 L 15	Troia, Italy
87 P 7	Trois-Pistoles, Québec, Canada
133 K 21	Trois-Ponts, Belgium
86 L 9	Trois-Rivières, Québec, Canada
152 I 11	Troitsk, Russian Federation
155 S 8	Troitsko-Pechorsk, Russian Federation
135 E 22	Trollhättan, Sweden
108 G 9	Trombetas, Brazil ↳

219 N 13	Trompsburg, Republic of South Africa
134 I 7	Tromsø, Norway
135 D 15	Trondheim, Norway
135 D 15	Trondheimsfjorden, Norway ≈
183 U 9	Trongsa, Bhutan
125 G 14	Troon, United Kingdom
147 D 20	Tropaia, Greece
141 L 20	Tropea, Italy
42 J 11	Tropic Seamount, Atlantic Ocean ◇
151 U 3	Trostyanets', Ukraine
64 K 9	Trout Lake, Michigan, U.S.A.
83 F 14	Trout Lake, Northwest Territories, Canada ↳
84 K 10	Trout Lake, Ontario, Canada ↳
73 S 9	Trout Peak, Wyoming, U.S.A. ▲
127 R 11	Trowbridge, United Kingdom
58 K 9	Troy, New York, U.S.A.
63 Q 5	Troy, Alabama, U.S.A.
69 X 3	Troy, Missouri, U.S.A.
72 K 2	Troy, Montana, U.S.A.
77 M 19	Troy Peak, Nevada, U.S.A. ▲
146 I 8	Troyan, Bulgaria
129 S 5	Troyes, France
151 Y 4	Troyits'ke, Ukraine
75 R 9	Truchas Peak, New Mexico, U.S.A. ▲
77 I 17	Truckee, California, U.S.A.
104 L 3	Trujillo, Venezuela ▣
107 B 14	Trujillo, Peru
130 L 8	Trujillo, Spain
91 N 4	Trujillo, Honduras
146 E 9	Trŭn, Bulgaria
126 J 15	Truro, United Kingdom
87 V 10	Truro, Nova Scotia, Canada
83 F 16	Trutch, British Columbia, Canada
75 P 13	Truth Or Consequences, New Mexico, U.S.A.
146 J 9	Tryavna, Bulgaria
66 J 13	Tryon, Nebraska, U.S.A.
144 D 10	Tržac, Bosnia and Herzegovina
142 F 11	Trzcianka, Poland
142 E 12	Trzciel, Poland
143 G 15	Trzebnica, Poland
144 B 6	Tržič, Slovenia
185 U 3	Tsagaannuur, Mongolia
157 Q 9	Tsagan Aman, Russian Federation
134 I 9	Tsåktso, Sweden ▲
171 T 7	Ts'alka, Georgia
146 N 10	Tsarevo, Bulgaria
151 U 6	Tsarychanka, Ukraine
185 N 4	Tseel, Mongolia
156 M 10	Tselina, Russian Federation
218 J 11	Tses, Namibia
218 L 9	Tsetseng, Botswana
215 N 13	Tsévié, Togo
218 L 11	Tshabong, Botswana
218 L 10	Tshane, Botswana
216 F 11	Tshela, Democratic Republic of Congo
216 L 12	Tshibala, Democratic Republic of Congo
216 L 13	Tshibwika, Democratic Republic of Congo
216 K 11	Tshikapa, Democratic Republic of Congo
217 P 12	Tshimbo, Democratic Republic of Congo
219 Q 10	Tshokwane, Republic of South Africa
218 K 9	Tshootsha, Botswana
82 C 9	Tsiigehtchic, Northwest Territories, Canada
157 N 9	Tsimlyanskoye Reservoir, Russian Federation ↳
218 L 11	Tsineng, Republic of South Africa
219 W 11	Tsiombe, Madagascar
219 W 7	Tsiroanomandidy, Madagascar
157 Q 1	Tsivil'sk, Russian Federation
171 T 6	Ts'khinvali, Georgia

▣ Country ▣ Internal administrative region: State/Province/Territory/Dependent territory ▪ Capital city ▲ Mountain range/Undersea ridge ▲ Mountain peak/Volcano/Seamount ◇ Geographic feature ▶ Headland/Point/Cape/Peninsula Desert ⇄ Island/Island group Antarctic base Ocean Sea ≈ Bay/Gulf/Channel/Strait Lake Salt pan/Dry/Intermittent lake River

171 V 7 **Tsnori**, Georgia
182 K 4 **Tso Morari Lake**, India ◣
219 O 13 **Tsolo**, Republic of South Africa
171 R 6 **Tsqaltubo**, Georgia
199 H 18 **Tsu**, Japan
199 L 15 **Tsuchiura**, Japan
198 J 8 **Tsugarū-kaikyō**, Japan ≈
199 D 21 **Tsukumi**, Japan
218 I 7 **Tsumeb**, Namibia
218 I 10 **Tsumis Park**, Namibia
218 J 8 **Tsumkwe**, Namibia
199 G 17 **Tsuruga**, Japan
199 F 20 **Tsurugi-san**, Japan ▲
198 J 12 **Tsuruoka**, Japan
199 A 20 **Tsushima**, Japan 🏝
199 F 18 **Tsuyama**, Japan
219 N 11 **Tswelelang**, Republic of South Africa
149 N 20 **Tsyerakhowka**, Belarus
151 S 9 **Tsyurupyns'k**, Ukraine
83 F 14 **Tthenaagoo**, Northwest Territories, Canada
232 N 12 **Tuai**, New Zealand
232 K 9 **Tuakau**, New Zealand
125 C 17 **Tuam**, Republic of Ireland
237 T 8 **Tuamotu Archipelago**, French Polynesia 🏝
41 T 9 **Tuamotu Fracture Zone**, Pacific Ocean ◇
190 J 11 **Tuân Giao**, Vietnam
196 G 6 **Tuao**, Philippines
156 L 13 **Tuapse**, Russian Federation
195 U 5 **Tuaran**, Malaysia
194 A 14 **Tuas**, Singapore
236 J 8 **Tuasivi**, Samoa
74 K 9 **Tuba City**, Arizona, U.S.A.
193 S 11 **Tubalai**, Indonesia 🏝
192 J 14 **Tuban**, Indonesia
112 J 11 **Tubarão**, Brazil
172 G 8 **Tūbās**, Israel
197 E 20 **Tubbataha Reefs**, Philippines 🏝
137 F 23 **Tübingen**, Germany
133 F 20 **Tubize**, Belgium
214 G 13 **Tubmanburg**, Liberia
237 T 12 **Tubuai**, French Polynesia 🏝
41 T 10 **Tubuai Island**, French Polynesia 🏝
107 O 21 **Tucavaca**, Bolivia
142 H 10 **Tuchola**, Poland
63 T 2 **Tucker**, Georgia, U.S.A.
42 B 7 **Tucker's Town**, Bermuda
74 K 14 **Tucson**, Arizona, U.S.A.
110 I 8 **Tucumán**, Argentina ◘
75 T 10 **Tucumcari**, New Mexico, U.S.A.
110 H 10 **Tucunuco**, Argentina
108 J 11 **Tucuruí**, Brazil
131 R 3 **Tudela**, Spain
148 I 6 **Tudu**, Estonia
183 Y 10 **Tuensang**, India
175 S 4 **Ţufayḩ**, Saudi Arabia
234 F 6 **Tufi**, Papua New Guinea
41 S 2 **Tufts Abyssal Plain**, Pacific Ocean ◇
197 M 16 **Tugnug Point**, Philippines ▶
196 G 7 **Tuguegarao**, Philippines
153 V 13 **Tugur**, Russian Federation
232 K 12 **Tuhua**, New Zealand
130 H 3 **Tui**, Spain
42 N 12 **Tuineje**, Canary Islands
213 M 21 **Tukayel**, Ethiopia
150 H 6 **Tukhol'ka**, Ukraine
179 U 14 **Tŭkhtamish**, Tajikistan
211 W 7 **Tūkrah**, Libya
82 C 8 **Tuktoyaktuk**, Northwest Territories, Canada
148 E 11 **Tukums**, Latvia
217 T 13 **Tukuyu**, Tanzania
156 K 2 **Tula**, Russian Federation
89 Q 9 **Tula**, Mexico
234 M 6 **Tulaghi**, Solomon Islands
177 Q 8 **Tulak**, Afghanistan
89 R 11 **Tulancingo**, Mexico
77 I 22 **Tulare**, California, U.S.A.
77 H 22 **Tulare Lake Bed**, California, U.S.A. ◣
106 B 8 **Tulcán**, Ecuador
151 N 12 **Tulcea**, Romania
70 K 3 **Tulia**, Texas, U.S.A.
186 H 6 **Tulihe**, China
82 E 11 **Tulít'a**, Northwest Territories, Canada
60 G 10 **Tullahoma**, Tennessee, U.S.A.
125 D 18 **Tullamore**, Republic of Ireland
129 P 11 **Tulle**, France
139 X 3 **Tulln**, Austria
62 J 5 **Tullos**, Louisiana, U.S.A.
231 T 4 **Tully**, Queensland, Australia
150 L 10 **Tulnici**, Romania
134 M 9 **Tulppio**, Finland
69 P 9 **Tulsa**, Oklahoma, U.S.A.
156 K 3 **Tul'skaya Oblast'**, Russian Federation ◘
153 P 13 **Tulun**, Russian Federation
234 J 4 **Tulun Islands**, Papua New Guinea 🏝
156 M 2 **Tuma**, Russian Federation
91 O 8 **Tuma**, Nicaragua ∫
104 F 8 **Tumaco**, Colombia
216 M 9 **Tumba**, Democratic Republic of Congo
192 K 11 **Tumbangsamba**, Indonesia
106 A 11 **Tumbes**, Peru
83 G 18 **Tumbler Ridge**, British Columbia, Canada
231 O 11 **Tumby Bay**, South Australia, Australia
187 M 14 **Tumen**, China ∫
105 S 5 **Tumeremo**, Venezuela
197 E 26 **Tumindao**, Philippines 🏝
181 E 21 **Tumkur**, India
194 C 5 **Tumpat**, Malaysia
105 V 8 **Tumuc-Humac Mountains**, Brazil/Suriname ⛰
171 O 10 **Tunceli**, Turkey
189 R 15 **Tunchang**, China
215 R 10 **Tundun-Wada**, Nigeria
217 V 14 **Tunduru**, Tanzania
146 J 9 **Tundzha**, Bulgaria ∫
215 S 12 **Tunga**, Nigeria
181 D 20 **Tungabhadra Reservoir**, India ◣
213 E 19 **Tungaru**, Sudan
197 I 22 **Tungawan**, Philippines
195 Z 6 **Tungku**, Malaysia
91 P 7 **Tungla**, Nicaragua
106 C 9 **Tungurahua**, Ecuador ◘
181 H 18 **Tuni**, India
62 L 1 **Tunica**, Mississippi, U.S.A.
211 Q 5 **Tunis**, Tunisia ▙
211 P 6 **Tunisia**, Africa □
158 L 11 **Tunisian Plateau**, Mediterranean Sea ◇
104 J 6 **Tunja**, Colombia
91 P 7 **Tunki**, Nicaragua
134 F 13 **Tunnsjøen**, Norway ◣
127 W 2 **Tunstall**, United Kingdom
110 G 12 **Tunuyán**, Argentina
179 W 10 **Tüp**, Kyrgyzstan
112 I 6 **Tupã**, Brazil
237 R 9 **Tupai**, French Polynesia 🏝
112 G 11 **Tupanciretã**, Brazil
63 N 2 **Tupelo**, Mississippi, U.S.A.
108 J 13 **Tupiratins**, Brazil
107 J 23 **Tupiza**, Bolivia
58 I 6 **Tupper Lake**, New York, U.S.A. ◣
186 H 11 **Tuquan**, China
153 P 10 **Tura**, Russian Federation
183 U 11 **Tura**, India
179 S 10 **Tura-Ryskulova**, Kazakhstan
175 N 8 **Turabah**, Saudi Arabia
233 K 14 **Turakina**, New Zealand
233 K 16 **Turakirae Head**, New Zealand ▶
234 B 5 **Turama**, Papua New Guinea ∫
178 K 13 **Turan Lowland**, Turkmenistan ◇
232 L 12 **Turangi**, New Zealand
149 J 21 **Turaw**, Belarus
174 L 1 **Turayf**, Saudi Arabia
177 Q 14 **Turbat**, Pakistan
61 P 13 **Turbeville**, South Carolina, U.S.A.
104 G 4 **Turbo**, Colombia
150 I 9 **Turda**, Romania
237 X 11 **Tureia**, French Polynesia 🏝
142 I 13 **Turek**, Poland
179 T 4 **Turgay**, Kazakhstan
146 L 8 **Tŭrgovishte**, Bulgaria
146 L 8 **Turgovishte**, Bulgaria ◘
170 B 11 **Turgutlu**, Turkey
170 L 9 **Turhal**, Turkey
110 G 4 **Turi**, Chile
148 G 7 **Türi**, Estonia
131 S 8 **Turia**, Spain ∫
108 L 10 **Turiaçu**, Brazil
140 A 7 **Turin**, Italy
150 J 2 **Turiys'k**, Ukraine
150 H 5 **Turka**, Ukraine
170 B 8 **Türkeli**, Turkey 🏝
179 Q 10 **Turkestan**, Kazakhstan
179 Q 12 **Turkestan Range**, Uzbekistan ⛰
170 M 10 **Turkey**, Asia/Europe □
70 L 3 **Turkey**, Texas, U.S.A.
157 O 5 **Turki**, Russian Federation
178 H 12 **Turkmenbashi**, Turkmenistan
178 M 12 **Turkmenistan**, Asia □
178 I 13 **Turkmenskiy Zaliv**, Turkmenistan ≈
170 L 12 **Türkoğlu**, Turkey
93 Q 4 **Turks and Caicos Islands**, United Kingdom, United Kingdom ◘
93 Q 5 **Turks Islands**, Turks and Caicos Islands 🏝
135 K 19 **Turku**, Finland
77 H 20 **Turlock**, California, U.S.A.
90 L 2 **Turneffe Islands**, Belize 🏝
133 H 16 **Turnhout**, Belgium
139 W 4 **Türnitz**, Austria
83 K 15 **Turnor Lake**, Saskatchewan, Canada ◣
150 J 14 **Turnu Măgurele**, Romania
184 L 5 **Turpan**, China
184 L 5 **Turpan Depression**, China ◇
139 S 8 **Turrach**, Austria
69 Y 10 **Turrell**, Arkansas, U.S.A.
91 R 12 **Turrialba**, Costa Rica
173 V 7 **Tursāq**, Iraq
178 M 11 **Turtkul'**, Uzbekistan
197 C 23 **Turtle Islands**, Philippines 🏝
64 C 10 **Turtle Lake**, Wisconsin, U.S.A.
153 N 9 **Turukhansk**, Russian Federation
74 J 9 **Tusayan**, Arizona, U.S.A.
63 O 3 **Tuscaloosa**, Alabama, U.S.A.
140 D 9 **Tuscan Archipelago**, Italy 🏝
58 E 14 **Tuscarora Mountains**, Pennsylvania, U.S.A. ⛰
65 G 19 **Tuscola**, Illinois, U.S.A.
70 M 7 **Tuscola**, Texas, U.S.A.
171 S 10 **Tutak**, Turkey
181 E 24 **Tuticorin**, India
195 S 6 **Tutong**, Brunei
146 L 6 **Tutrakan**, Bulgaria
66 K 5 **Tuttle**, North Dakota, U.S.A.
69 O 3 **Tuttle Creek Reservoir**, Kansas, U.S.A. ◣
137 F 24 **Tuttlingen**, Germany
193 R 15 **Tutuala**, East Timor
236 K 8 **Tutuila**, American Samoa 🏝
219 N 8 **Tutume**, Botswana
233 L 16 **Tuturumuri**, New Zealand
135 N 15 **Tuusniemi**, Finland
236 G 5 **Tuvalu**, Oceania □
174 L 7 **Tuwwal**, Saudi Arabia
89 O 12 **Tuxpan**, Mexico
89 S 11 **Tuxpan**, Mexico
89 V 14 **Tuxtla Gutiérrez**, Mexico
191 N 20 **Tuy Duc**, Vietnam
191 O 19 **Tuy Hoa**, Vietnam
190 L 11 **Tuyên Quang**, Vietnam
170 I 11 **Tuz Gölü**, Turkey ◣
173 U 4 **Tūz Khurmātū**, Iraq
144 I 11 **Tuzla**, Bosnia and Herzegovina
151 N 13 **Tuzla**, Romania
170 J 13 **Tuzla**, Turkey
154 H 14 **Tver'**, Russian Federation
154 H 13 **Tverskaya Oblast'**, Russian Federation ◘
143 J 19 **Tvrdošín**, Slovakia
146 K 9 **Tvŭrdista**, Bulgaria
124 J 13 **Tweed**, United Kingdom ∫
77 M 24 **Twentynine Palms**, California, U.S.A.
73 P 7 **Twin Bridges**, Montana, U.S.A.
63 V 4 **Twin City**, Georgia, U.S.A.
72 M 12 **Twin Falls**, Idaho, U.S.A.
72 M 9 **Twin Peaks**, Idaho, U.S.A. ▲
76 I 6 **Twisp**, Washington, U.S.A.
233 E 21 **Twizel**, New Zealand
64 H 12 **Two**, Wisconsin, U.S.A.
43 L 26 **Two Boats Village**, Ascension
143 I 17 **Tychy**, Poland
71 S 6 **Tyler**, Texas, U.S.A.
62 L 6 **Tylertown**, Mississippi, U.S.A.
147 I 26 **Tympaki**, Greece
153 T 13 **Tynda**, Russian Federation
125 I 15 **Tyne**, United Kingdom ∫
60 J 6 **Tyner**, Kentucky, U.S.A.
135 D 16 **Tynset**, Norway
135 D 19 **Tyrifjorden**, Norway ◣
147 E 16 **Tyrnavos**, Greece
58 D 12 **Tyrone**, Pennsylvania, U.S.A.
158 L 7 **Tyrrhenian Basin**, Mediterranean Sea ◇
141 E 15 **Tyrrhenian Sea**, Europe 🌊
152 K 11 **Tyukalinsk**, Russian Federation
157 W 4 **Tyul'gan**, Russian Federation
152 J 10 **Tyumen'**, Russian Federation
126 M 9 **Tywi**, United Kingdom ∫

U

237 X 6 **Ua Huka**, French Polynesia 🏝
237 W 6 **Ua Pou**, French Polynesia 🏝
108 D 11 **Uarini**, Brazil
108 F 10 **Uatumã**, Brazil ∫
108 N 13 **Uauá**, Brazil
90 I 2 **Uaxactún**, Guatemala
109 L 18 **Ubá**, Brazil
112 N 5 **Ubá**, Brazil
109 N 15 **Ubaitaba**, Brazil
216 J 5 **Ubangi**, Central African Republic ∫
173 N 7 **Ubaylah**, Iraq
199 C 20 **Ube**, Japan
131 O 11 **Úbeda**, Spain
112 K 4 **Uberaba**, Brazil
112 J 3 **Uberlândia**, Brazil
137 F 25 **Überlingen**, Germany
194 B 13 **Ubin**, Singapore 🏝
191 I 16 **Ubolratna Reservoir**, Thailand ◣
219 Q 12 **Ubombo**, Republic of South Africa
191 L 17 **Ubon Ratchathani**, Thailand
217 N 8 **Ubundu**, Democratic Republic of Congo
107 E 14 **Ucayali**, Peru ◘
107 E 14 **Ucayali**, Peru ∫
133 F 19 **Uccle**, Belgium
153 P 10 **Uchami**, Russian Federation
179 X 7 **Ucharal**, Kazakhstan
199 C 24 **Uchinoura**, Japan
198 I 7 **Uchiura-wan**, Japan ≈
179 O 11 **Uchkuduk**, Uzbekistan
127 W 12 **Uckfield**, United Kingdom
73 W 9 **Ucross**, Wyoming, U.S.A.
153 U 13 **Uda**, Russian Federation ∫
153 R 9 **Udachnyy**, Russian Federation
182 H 9 **Udaipur**, India
151 S 3 **Uday**, Ukraine ∫
135 D 22 **Uddevalla**, Sweden
134 H 12 **Uddjaure**, Sweden ◣
133 J 15 **Uden**, Netherlands
140 I 6 **Udine**, Italy
41 S 13 **Udintsev Fracture Zone**, Pacific Ocean ◇
181 C 21 **Udipi**, India
155 R 13 **Udmurtskaya Respublika**, Russian Federation ◘
191 J 15 **Udon Thani**, Thailand
136 M 10 **Uecker**, Germany ∫
199 I 15 **Ueda**, Japan
216 L 5 **Uele**, Democratic Republic of Congo ∫
153 Z 5 **Uelen**, Russian Federation
153 Z 6 **Uel'kal'**, Russian Federation
136 I 12 **Uelzen**, Germany
199 H 18 **Ueno**, Japan
157 W 1 **Ufa**, Russian Federation ∫
157 W 1 **Ufa**, Russian Federation
148 D 10 **Ugāle**, Latvia
217 R 6 **Uganda**, Africa □
141 O 18 **Ugento**, Italy
153 W 13 **Uglegorsk**, Russian Federation
154 J 13 **Uglich**, Russian Federation
153 Z 6 **Ugol'nyye**, Russian Federation
156 I 2 **Ugra**, Russian Federation
143 G 19 **Uherské Hradiště**, Czech Republic
65 O 18 **Uhrichsville**, Ohio, U.S.A.
124 F 10 **Uig**, United Kingdom
218 G 2 **Uíge**, Angola
218 G 1 **Uíge**, Angola ◘
187 L 18 **Uijongbu**, South Korea
178 J 5 **Uil**, Kazakhstan
155 T 13 **Uinskoye**, Russian Federation
74 L 3 **Uinta Mountains**, Utah, U.S.A. ⛰
218 H 9 **Uis**, Namibia
132 H 11 **Uithoorn**, Netherlands
237 W 2 **Ujae**, Marshall Islands 🏝
143 M 22 **Újfehértó**, Hungary
199 G 18 **Uji**, Japan
199 B 24 **Uji-guntō**, Japan 🏝
199 K 14 **Ujiie**, Japan
181 D 14 **Ujjain**, India
193 N 13 **Ujung Pandang**, Indonesia
192 C 8 **Ujung Tamiang**, Indonesia ▶
215 Q 11 **Ukata**, Nigeria
199 O 22 **Uke-jima**, Japan 🏝
217 S 9 **Ukerewe Island**, Tanzania 🏝
155 Q 7 **Ukhta**, Russian Federation
235 N 7 **Uki**, Solomon Islands 🏝
76 J 10 **Ukiah**, Oregon, U.S.A.
77 F 17 **Ukiah**, California, U.S.A.
149 F 14 **Ukmergė**, Lithuania
151 O 6 **Ukraine**, Europe □
218 G 4 **Uku**, Angola
199 A 21 **Uku-jima**, Japan 🏝
185 R 3 **Ulaanbaatar**, Mongolia ▙
184 M 2 **Ulaangom**, Mongolia
187 A 15 **Ulan Hua**, China
157 R 11 **Ulan Khol**, Russian Federation
153 Q 14 **Ulan-Ude**, Russian Federation
184 L 8 **Ulan Ul Hu**, China ◣
179 S 9 **Ulanbel'**, Kazakhstan
186 H 11 **Ulanhot**, China
170 C 7 **Ulaş**, Turkey
146 N 12 **Ulaş**, Turkey
170 M 10 **Ulaş**, Turkey
235 N 7 **Ulawa**, Solomon Islands 🏝
187 N 19 **Ulchin**, South Korea
145 J 17 **Ulcinj**, Serbia and Montenegro
185 T 2 **Uldz**, Mongolia ∫
185 S 3 **Uldz**, Mongolia
181 C 17 **Ulhasnagar**, India
186 E 11 **Uliastai**, China
185 O 3 **Uliastay**, Mongolia
236 K 14 **Ulithi**, Federated States of Micronesia 🏝
179 N 5 **Ul'kayak**, Kazakhstan ∫
231 U 12 **Ulladulla**, New South Wales, Australia
124 G 9 **Ullapool**, United Kingdom
187 O 19 **Ullŭng-do**, South Korea 🏝
137 H 24 **Ulm**, Germany
150 H 8 **Ulmeni**, Romania
144 H 13 **Ulog**, Bosnia and Herzegovina
219 R 5 **Ulongue**, Mozambique
187 N 20 **Ulsan**, South Korea
135 D 16 **Ulsberg**, Norway
125 D 15 **ULSTER**, United Kingdom ◘
90 K 5 **Ulúa**, Honduras ∫
170 D 8 **Ulubat Gölü**, Turkey ◣
170 D 9 **Uludağ**, Turkey ▲
184 G 5 **Ulugqat**, China
170 J 12 **Ulukişla**, Turkey
237 N 14 **Ulul**, Federated States of Micronesia 🏝
219 P 12 **Ulundi**, Republic of South Africa
184 L 3 **Ulungur Hu**, China ◣
82 G 7 **Uluqsaqtuuq**, Northwest Territories, Canada
230 M 7 **Uluru**, Northern Territory, Australia ▲
127 P 1 **Ulverston**, United Kingdom
151 P 7 **Ul'yanovka**, Ukraine
157 S 2 **Ul'yanovsk**, Russian Federation
157 S 3 **Ul'yanovskaya Oblast'**, Russian Federation ◘
179 T 5 **Ul'yanovskiy**, Kazakhstan
68 H 6 **Ulysses**, Kansas, U.S.A.
179 Q 6 **Ulytau**, Kazakhstan
151 P 6 **Uman'**, Ukraine
177 V 14 **Umarkot**, Pakistan
76 J 9 **Umatilla**, Washington, U.S.A.
154 I 4 **Umba**, Russian Federation
140 G 11 **Umbertide**, Italy
234 E 4 **Umboi Island**, Papua New Guinea 🏝
140 H 12 **Umbria**, Italy ◘
234 F 2 **Umbukul**, Papua New Guinea
135 J 15 **Umeå**, Sweden
135 I 14 **Umeälven**, Sweden ∫
157 N 4 **Umet**, Russian Federation
175 R 3 **Umgharah**, Kuwait
79 Q 4 **Umiat**, Alaska, U.S.A.
82 I 8 **Umingmaktok**, Nunavut, Canada
219 P 13 **Umlazi**, Republic of South Africa
175 X 5 **Umm al Qaiwain**, United Arab Emirates
173 R 5 **Umm al Tūz**, Iraq
213 C 17 **Umm Bel**, Sudan
174 K 5 **Umm Lajj**, Saudi Arabia
173 Z 12 **Umm Qaşr**, Iraq
213 E 18 **Umm Ruwaba**, Sudan
211 Y 7 **Umm Sa'ad**, Libya
175 U 6 **Umm Sa'id**, Qatar
213 E 17 **Umm Saiyala**, Sudan
174 J 5 **Umm Urūmah**, Saudi Arabia 🏝
45 O 9 **Ummannaq**, Greenland
78 J 14 **Umnak Island**, Alaska, U.S.A. 🏝
218 I 4 **Umpulo**, Angola
219 O 14 **Umtata**, Republic of South Africa
215 R 13 **Umuahia**, Nigeria
112 F 7 **Umuarama**, Brazil
109 N 16 **Una**, Brazil
144 E 10 **Una**, Bosnia and Herzegovina ∫
78 K 14 **Unalaska Island**, Alaska, U.S.A. 🏝
134 L 10 **Unari**, Finland ◣
134 L 10 **Unari**, Finland
193 O 11 **Unauna**, Indonesia 🏝
172 G 12 **'Unayzah**, Jordan
175 P 5 **'Unayzah**, Saudi Arabia
66 J 4 **Underwood**, North Dakota, U.S.A.
234 F 4 **Unea Island**, Papua New Guinea 🏝
156 H 3 **Unecha**, Russian Federation
85 S 5 **Ungava Bay**, Québec, Canada ≈
217 X 9 **Ungwana Bay**, Kenya ≈

□ Country ◘ Internal administrative region: State/Province/Territory/Dependent territory ▙ Capital city ⛰ Mountain range/Undersea ridge ▲ Mountain peak/Volcano/Seamount ◇ Geographic feature ▶ Headland/Point/Cape/Peninsula ◢ Desert 🏝 Island/Island group ⁙ Antarctic base ◎ Ocean 🌊 Sea ≈ Bay/Gulf/Channel/Strait ◣ Lake ◩ Salt pan/Dry/Intermittent lake ∫ River

União da Vitória – Velká Bíteš

112 H 9 **União da Vitória**, Brazil
43 L 26 **Unicorn Point**, Ascension
78 L 13 **Unimak Island**, Alaska, U.S.A.
78 J 13 **Unimak Pass**, Alaska, U.S.A.
108 D 10 **Unini**, Brazil
69 X 4 **Union**, Missouri, U.S.A.
58 B 10 **Union City**, Pennsylvania, U.S.A.
60 B 8 **Union City**, Tennessee, U.S.A.
63 R 5 **Union Springs**, Alabama, U.S.A.
58 B 14 **Uniontown**, Pennsylvania, U.S.A.
69 T 1 **Unionville**, Missouri, U.S.A.
175 W 6 **United Arab Emirates**, Asia
125 J 16 **United Kingdom**, Europe
56 H 8 **United States of America**, North America
76 K 11 **Unity**, Oregon, U.S.A.
139 P 6 **Unken**, Austria
182 L 10 **Unnao**, India
124 K 3 **Unst**, United Kingdom
91 O 11 **Upala**, Costa Rica
105 R 4 **Upata**, Venezuela
127 S 11 **Upavon**, United Kingdom
218 K 12 **Upington**, Republic of South Africa
181 A 15 **Upleta**, India
236 J 8 **Upolu**, Samoa
78 E 8 **Upolu Point**, Hawaii, U.S.A.
58 H 14 **Upper Darby**, Pennsylvania, U.S.A.
233 K 16 **Upper Hutt**, New Zealand
76 G 13 **Upper Klamath Lake**, Oregon, U.S.A.
77 I 14 **Upper Lake**, California, U.S.A.
213 F 20 **Upper Nile**, Sudan
67 Q 3 **Upper Red Lake**, Minnesota, U.S.A.
65 L 17 **Upper Sandusky**, Ohio, U.S.A.
135 H 20 **Uppsala**, Sweden
84 K 11 **Upsala**, Ontario, Canada
182 J 4 **Upshi**, India
73 Z 9 **Upton**, Wyoming, U.S.A.
175 N 5 **'Uqlat aş Şuqūr**, Saudi Arabia
173 N 6 **Uqlat Şawāb**, Iraq
185 R 6 **Urad Houqi**, China
198 L 5 **Urahoro**, Japan
198 L 6 **Urakawa**, Japan
157 V 5 **Ural**, Kazakhstan/Russian Federation
152 I 11 **Ural Mountains**, Russian Federation
152 G 10 **Ural'sk**, Russian Federation
178 I 4 **Ural'sk**, Kazakhstan
172 I 2 **Urām aş Şughrá**, Syria
217 S 11 **Urambo**, Tanzania
231 P 5 **Urandangi**, Queensland, Australia
109 L 15 **Urandi**, Brazil
75 N 6 **Uravan**, Colorado, U.S.A.
199 K 16 **Urawa**, Japan
152 J 9 **Uray**, Russian Federation
175 S 5 **Uray'irah**, Saudi Arabia
65 G 19 **Urbana**, Illinois, U.S.A.
140 G 10 **Urbania**, Italy
140 G 10 **Urbino**, Italy
107 G 17 **Urcos**, Peru
184 M 3 **Urdgol**, Mongolia
179 X 7 **Urdzhar**, Kazakhstan
127 S'1 **Ure**, United Kingdom
155 N 13 **Uren'**, Russian Federation
152 M 9 **Urengoy**, Russian Federation
235 Q 9 **Uréparapara**, Vanuatu
178 M 11 **Urgench**, Uzbekistan
184 K 3 **Urho**, China
182 G 3 **Uri**, India
179 P 3 **Uritskiy**, Kazakhstan
132 J 9 **Urk**, Netherlands
170 A 10 **Urla**, Turkey
215 Q 13 **Uromi**, Nigeria
145 M 16 **Uroševac**, Serbia and Montenegro
179 R 12 **Üroteppa**, Tajikistan
185 P 5 **Urt**, Mongolia
88 K 5 **Uruáchic**, Mexico
109 J 15 **Uruaçu**, Brazil
89 P 12 **Uruapan**, Mexico
108 G 10 **Urucará**, Brazil
108 L 12 **Uruçuí**, Brazil
112 E 12 **Uruguaiana**, Brazil
110 O 8 **Uruguay**, South America
113 F 14 **Uruguay**, South America
184 K 5 **Ürümqi**, China
177 T 8 **Urūzgān**, Afghanistan
157 N 6 **Uryupinsk**, Russian Federation
155 P 14 **Urzhum**, Russian Federation
150 L 12 **Urziceni**, Romania
151 X 9 **Urzuf**, Ukraine
155 S 4 **Usa**, Russian Federation
199 C 21 **Usa**, Japan
197 F 24 **Usada**, Philippines
170 D 10 **Uşak**, Turkey
144 L 13 **Ušće**, Serbia and Montenegro
174 L 8 **'Usfān**, Saudi Arabia
174 M 8 **'Ushayrah**, Saudi Arabia
199 B 23 **Ushibuka**, Japan
179 W 8 **Ushtobe**, Kazakhstan
111 H 25 **Ushuaia**, Argentina
234 D 4 **Usino**, Papua New Guinea
155 S 4 **Usinsk**, Russian Federation
127 O 10 **Usk**, United Kingdom
170 D 7 **Usküdar**, Turkey
137 G 15 **Uslar**, Germany
156 M 5 **Usman'**, Russian Federation
148 C 10 **Usmas ezers**, Latvia
155 O 7 **Usogorsk**, Russian Federation
153 Q 13 **Usol'ye-Sibirskoye**, Russian Federation
197 K 15 **Uson**, Philippines
151 W 7 **Uspenivka**, Ukraine
179 V 3 **Uspenka**, Kazakhstan
129 Q 10 **Ussel**, France
153 V 15 **Ussuriysk**, Russian Federation
153 Q 13 **Ust'-Barguzin**, Russian Federation
153 P 12 **Ust'-Ilimsk**, Russian Federation
153 Z 10 **Ust'-Kamchatsk**, Russian Federation
179 X 4 **Ust'-Kamenogorsk**, Kazakhstan
155 R 9 **Ust'-Kulom**, Russian Federation
153 P 12 **Ust'-Kut**, Russian Federation
153 T 8 **Ust'-Kuyga**, Russian Federation
153 U 11 **Ust'-Maya**, Russian Federation
155 R 9 **Ust'-Nem**, Russian Federation
153 V 9 **Ust'-Nera**, Russian Federation
153 R 7 **Ust'-Olenek**, Russian Federation
153 W 10 **Ust'-Omchug**, Russian Federation
154 L 7 **Ust'-Pinega**, Russian Federation
153 O 8 **Ust'-Port**, Russian Federation
155 P 5 **Ust'-Tsil'ma**, Russian Federation
179 O 2 **Ust'-Uyskoye**, Kazakhstan
154 L 8 **Ust'-Vayen'ga**, Russian Federation
143 C 16 **Ústí nad Labem**, Czech Republic
142 G 8 **Ustka**, Poland
156 L 12 **Ust'Labinsk**, Russian Federation
146 L 10 **Ustrem**, Bulgaria
142 F 8 **Ustronie Morskie**, Poland
143 N 18 **Ustrzyki Dolne**, Poland
178 J 9 **Ustyurt Plateau**, Kazakhstan
154 I 12 **Ustyuzhna**, Russian Federation
90 K 8 **Usulután**, El Salvador
89 X 13 **Usumacinta**, Mexico
193 W 13 **Uta**, Indonesia
74 J 4 **Utah**, U.S.A.
74 J 3 **Utah Lake**, Utah, U.S.A.
75 T 9 **Ute Reservoir**, New Mexico, U.S.A.
149 G 14 **Utena**, Lithuania
217 W 12 **Utete**, Tanzania
191 H 17 **Uthai Thani**, Thailand
177 T 14 **Uthal**, Pakistan
58 I 8 **Utica**, New York, U.S.A.
90 M 4 **Utila**, Honduras
199 B 22 **Uto**, Japan
183 N 10 **Utraula**, India
132 H 12 **Utrecht**, Netherlands
132 I 12 **Utrecht**, Netherlands
237 Y 1 **Utrik**, Marshall Islands
134 L 7 **Utsjoki**, Finland
199 K 15 **Utsunomiya**, Japan
157 Q 11 **Utta**, Russian Federation
182 L 10 **Uttar Pradesh**, India
191 H 15 **Uttaradit**, Thailand
182 K 6 **Uttaranchal**, India
182 K 6 **Uttarkashi**, India
184 K 3 **Utubulak**, China
235 Q 8 **Utupua**, Solomon Islands
237 S 9 **Uturoa**, French Polynesia
135 L 16 **Uurainen**, Finland
135 J 19 **Uusikaupunki**, Finland
181 G 25 **Uva**, Sri Lanka
144 J 13 **Uvac**, Serbia and Montenegro
70 M 11 **Uvalde**, Texas, U.S.A.
149 M 20 **Uvaravichy**, Belarus
157 N 5 **Uvarovo**, Russian Federation
217 R 11 **Uvinza**, Tanzania
234 G 5 **Uvol**, Papua New Guinea
185 N 2 **Uvs**, Mongolia
185 N 2 **Uvs Nuur**, Mongolia
199 D 21 **Uwajima**, Japan
175 Y 7 **'Uwayfī**, Oman
211 S 10 **'Uwaynāt Wannīn**, Libya
153 O 12 **Uyar**, Russian Federation
185 R 5 **Üydzin**, Mongolia
215 R 14 **Uyo**, Nigeria
179 S 10 **Uyuk**, Kazakhstan
179 O 11 **Uzbekistan**, Asia
149 I 18 **Uzda**, Belarus
129 P 10 **Uzerche**, France
129 T 13 **Uzès**, France
151 N 3 **Uzh**, Ukraine
150 G 6 **Uzhhorod**, Ukraine
144 K 12 **Užice**, Serbia and Montenegro
179 V 10 **Uzunaghach**, Kazakhstan
170 B 7 **Uzunköprü**, Turkey
148 D 13 **Užventis**, Lithuania

V

218 M 12 **Vaal**, Republic of South Africa
134 M 13 **Vaala**, Finland
133 L 19 **Vaals**, Netherlands
135 J 16 **Vaasa**, Finland
132 K 11 **Vaassen**, Netherlands
148 F 13 **Vabalninkas**, Lithuania
143 J 22 **Vác**, Hungary
112 I 11 **Vacaria**, Brazil
77 G 19 **Vacaville**, California, U.S.A.
38 B 12 **Vacoas**, Mauritius
181 C 15 **Vadodara**, India
134 M 6 **Vadsø**, Norway
138 I 7 **Vaduz**, Liechtenstein
234 K 5 **Vaghena**, Solomon Islands
134 H 8 **Vågsfjorden**, Norway
143 H 19 **Váh**, Slovakia
237 X 10 **Vahitahi**, French Polynesia
236 G 6 **Vaiaku**, Tuvalu
75 Q 4 **Vail**, Colorado, U.S.A.
237 X 10 **Vairaatea**, French Polynesia
148 E 6 **Väiri**, Estonia
236 F 5 **Vaitupu**, Tuvalu
216 M 2 **Vakaga**, Central African Republic
129 W 10 **Val d'Isere**, France
86 G 7 **Val-d'Or**, Québec, Canada
83 M 20 **Val Marie**, Saskatchewan, Canada
138 D 10 **Valais**, Switzerland
146 E 12 **Valandovo**, Macedonia (F.Y.R.O.M.)
147 H 18 **Valaxa**, Greece
111 I 16 **Valcheta**, Argentina
154 G 12 **Valday**, Russian Federation
131 P 9 **Valdepeñas**, Spain
130 M 3 **Valderas**, Spain
79 S 9 **Valdez**, Alaska, U.S.A.
111 F 16 **Valdivia**, Chile
43 M 17 **Valdivia Seamount**, Atlantic Ocean
63 U 7 **Valdosta**, Georgia, U.S.A.
135 C 18 **Valdres**, Norway
171 S 7 **Vale**, Georgia
76 L 12 **Vale**, Oregon, U.S.A.
150 G 8 **Valea lui Mihai**, Romania
109 N 15 **Valença**, Brazil
108 M 12 **Valença do Piauí**, Brazil
129 T 11 **Valence**, France
105 N 3 **Valencia**, Venezuela
131 S 3 **Valencia**, Spain
131 T 3 **Valencia**, Spain
197 L 21 **Valencia**, Philippines
158 E 7 **Valencia Basin**, Mediterranean Sea
130 J 8 **Valencia de Alcántara**, Spain
130 L 3 **Valencia de Don Juan**, Spain
158 E 7 **Valencia Trough Shel**, Mediterranean Sea
129 R 1 **Valenciennes**, France
66 K 11 **Valentine**, Nebraska, U.S.A.
70 G 9 **Valentine**, Texas, U.S.A.
140 C 8 **Valenza**, Italy
196 G 11 **Valenzuela**, Philippines
41 Q 12 **Valerie Guyot**, Pacific Ocean
148 H 9 **Valga**, Estonia
144 K 1' **Valjevo**, Serbia and Montenegro
148 H 9 **Valka**, Latvia
133 J 16 **Valkenswaard**, Netherlands
151 V 4 **Valky**, Ukraine
131 N 4 **Valladolid**, Spain
89 Z 10 **Valladolid**, Mexico
141 L 15 **Vallata**, Italy
140 A 6 **Valle D'Aosta**, Italy
105 N 3 **Valle de La Pascua**, Venezuela
104 G 7 **Valle Del Cauca**, Colombia
89 T 13 **Valle Nacional**, Mexico
104 J 2 **Valledupar**, Colombia
87 O 9 **Vallée-Jonction**, Québec, Canada
77 G 19 **Vallejo**, California, U.S.A.
110 F 9 **Vallenar**, Chile
141 K 26 **Valletta**, Malta
66 M 5 **Valley City**, North Dakota, U.S.A.
76 I 13 **Valley Falls**, Oregon, U.S.A.
196 H 6 **Valley Head**, Philippines
61 P 4 **Valley Head**, West Virginia, U.S.A.
60 G 5 **Valley Station**, Kentucky, U.S.A.
83 H 17 **Valleyview**, Alberta, Canada
140 G 9 **Valli di Comacchio**, Italy
141 K 17 **Vallo della Lucania**, Italy
138 B 8 **Vallorbe**, Switzerland
131 V 5 **Valls**, Spain
148 G 9 **Valmiera**, Latvia
128 L 3 **Valognes**, France
149 H 17 **Valozhyn**, Belarus
181 E 23 **Valparai**, India
65 H 16 **Valparaiso**, Indiana, U.S.A.
110 F 11 **Valparaíso**, Chile
110 F 11 **Valparaíso**, Chile
112 I 5 **Valparáiso**, Brazil
138 H 9 **Vals**, Switzerland
181 C 16 **Valsad**, India
135 F 14 **Valsjöbyn**, Sweden
156 K 7 **Valuyki**, Russian Federation
42 K 12 **Valverde**, Canary Islands
130 J 11 **Valverde del Camino**, Spain
135 K 18 **Vammala**, Finland
171 S 11 **Van**, Turkey
59 R 1 **Van Buren**, Maine, U.S.A.
69 X 7 **Van Buren**, Missouri, U.S.A.
191 O 19 **Vân Canh**, Vietnam
230 M 1 **Van Diemen Gulf**, Northern Territory, Australia
171 S 11 **Van Gölü**, Turkey
70 F 8 **Van Horn**, Texas, U.S.A.
65 K 17 **Van Wert**, Ohio, U.S.A.
171 T 8 **Vanadzor**, Armenia
237 X 11 **Vanavana**, French Polynesia
153 P 11 **Vanavara**, Russian Federation
59 S 3 **Vanceboro**, Maine, U.S.A.
76 G 9 **Vancouver**, Washington, U.S.A.
83 G 22 **Vancouver**, British Columbia, Canada
83 E 22 **Vancouver Island**, British Columbia, Canada
65 F 20 **Vandalia**, Illinois, U.S.A.
231 P 3 **Vanderlin Island**, Northern Territory, Australia
181 F 21 **Vandivasi**, India
148 G 7 **Vändra**, Estonia
135 E 21 **Vänern**, Sweden
135 E 22 **Vänersborg**, Sweden
219 Y 10 **Vangaindrano**, Madgascar
234 K 6 **Vangunu**, Solomon Islands
235 Q 8 **Vanikoro Islands**, Solomon Islands
234 A 3 **Vanimo**, Papua New Guinea
153 W 14 **Vanino**, Russian Federation
150 G 12 **Vânju Mare**, Romania
153 Z 5 **Vankarem**, Russian Federation
134 I 6 **Vanna**, Norway
128 J 6 **Vannes**, France
218 J 14 **Vanrhynsdorp**, Republic of South Africa
85 O 2 **Vansittart Island**, Nunavut, Canada
135 L 19 **Vantaa**, Finland
235 Z 11 **Vanua Balavu**, Fiji
235 Q 9 **Vanua Lava**, Vanuatu
235 X 10 **Vanua Levu**, Fiji
235 S 11 **Vanuatu**, Oceania
214 L 11 **Varalé**, Côte d'Ivoire
140 B 6 **Varallo**, Italy
176 I 6 **Varāmīn**, Iran
183 O 11 **Varanasi**, India
155 R 2 **Varandey**, Russian Federation
134 M 6 **Varangerfjorden**, Norway
134 M 6 **Varangerhalvøya**, Norway
149 I 14 **Varapayeva**, Belarus
135 D 23 **Varberg**, Sweden
147 C 20 **Varda**, Greece
146 D 11 **Vardar**, Macedonia (F.Y.R.O.M.)
135 B 25 **Varde**, Denmark
171 V 9 **Vardenis**, Armenia
134 N 6 **Vardø**, Norway
136 E 10 **Varel**, Germany
149 F 16 **Varėna**, Lithuania
140 C 6 **Varese**, Italy
150 J 8 **Vârful Ineu**, Romania
150 J 11 **Vârful Moldoveanu**, Romania
150 J 11 **Vârful Omu**, Romania
150 G 11 **Vârful Peleaga**, Romania
150 I 8 **Vârful Pietrosu**, Romania
150 G 12 **Vârful Svinecea Mare**, Romania
150 K 9 **Vârful Toaca**, Romania
112 L 6 **Varginha**, Brazil
110 F 6 **Varillas**, Chile
135 N 16 **Varkaus**, Finland
147 G 20 **Varkiza**, Greece
135 E 20 **Värmeln**, Sweden
146 N 8 **Varna**, Bulgaria
146 N 8 **Varna**, Bulgaria
135 F 23 **Värnamo**, Sweden
148 D 13 **Varniai**, Lithuania
149 H 15 **Varnyany**, Belarus
171 Q 10 **Varto**, Turkey
140 C 8 **Varzi**, Italy
143 N 21 **Vásárosnamény**, Hungary
155 N 7 **Vashka**, Russian Federation
149 L 21 **Vasilyevichy**, Belarus
150 M 9 **Vaslui**, Romania
64 L 13 **Vassar**, Michigan, U.S.A.
134 G 12 **Västansjö**, Sweden
135 G 17 **Västbäcka**, Sweden
135 G 20 **Västerås**, Sweden
135 E 18 **Västerdalälven**, Sweden
135 G 23 **Västervik**, Sweden
140 K 13 **Vasto**, Italy
135 E 20 **Västra Silen**, Sweden
143 F 24 **Vasvár**, Hungary
151 V 8 **Vasylivka**, Ukraine
151 P 4 **Vasyl'kiv**, Ukraine
151 V 7 **Vasyl'kivka**, Ukraine
129 P 7 **Vatan**, France
124 D 11 **Vatersay**, United Kingdom
141 H 14 **Vatican City**, Europe
134 C 11 **Vatnajökull**, Iceland
219 Y 8 **Vatomandry**, Madgascar
150 J 8 **Vatra Dornei**, Romania
135 F 22 **Vättern**, Sweden
235 W 12 **Vatulele**, Fiji
138 B 9 **Vaud**, Switzerland
75 R 11 **Vaughn**, New Mexico, U.S.A.
104 L 9 **Vaupés**, Colombia
129 S 14 **Vauvert**, France
236 J 10 **Vava'u Group**, Tonga
181 G 24 **Vavuniya**, Sri Lanka
149 M 17 **Vawkavichy**, Belarus
149 F 19 **Vawkavysk**, Belarus
135 F 24 **Växjö**, Sweden
171 U 9 **Vayk**, Armenia
136 E 12 **Vechta**, Germany
181 F 23 **Vedaranniyam**, India
150 K 14 **Vedea**, Romania
113 B 16 **Vedia**, Argentina
149 M 21 **Vedrych**, Belarus
132 N 7 **Veendam**, Netherlands
132 J 13 **Veenendaal**, Netherlands
134 E 12 **Vega**, Norway
70 J 2 **Vega**, Texas, U.S.A.
133 J 15 **Veghel**, Netherlands
181 L 19 **Veimandu Channel**, Maldives
135 B 25 **Vejle**, Denmark
42 N 1 **Velas**, Azores
137 C 16 **Velbert**, Germany
139 S 9 **Velden**, Austria
144 C 6 **Velenje**, Slovenia
146 D 11 **Veles**, Macedonia (F.Y.R.O.M.)
131 Q 11 **Vélez Rubio**, Spain
144 M 10 **Velika**, Serbia and Montenegro
144 D 9 **Velika Kladuša**, Bosnia and Herzegovina
154 E 12 **Velikiy Novgorod**, Russian Federation
155 N 10 **Velikiy Ustyug**, Russian Federation
154 E 14 **Velikiye Luki**, Russian Federation
146 J 8 **Veliko Tŭrnovo**, Bulgaria
146 J 8 **Veliko Tŭrnovo**, Bulgaria
214 F 9 **Vélingara**, Senegal
146 H 10 **Velingrad**, Bulgaria
156 G 1 **Velizh**, Russian Federation
143 F 19 **Velká Bíteš**, Czech Republic

Country · Internal administrative region: State/Province/Territory/Dependent territory · Capital city · Mountain range/Undersea ridge · Mountain peak/Volcano/Seamount · Geographic feature · Headland/Point/Cape/Peninsula · Desert · Island/Island group · Antarctic base · Ocean · Sea · Bay/Gulf/Channel/Strait · Lake · Salt pan/Dry/Intermittent lake · River

234 J 5 **Vella Lavella**, Solomon Islands 🏝
181 F 21 **Vellore**, India
147 G 22 **Velopoula**, Greece 🏝
154 L 10 **Vel'sk**, Russian Federation
66 J 3 **Velva**, North Dakota, U.S.A.
151 R 9 **Velyka Korenykha**, Ukraine
151 T 8 **Velyka Lepetykha**, Ukraine
151 X 4 **Velykyy Burluk**, Ukraine
42 G 12 **Vema Fracture Zone**, Atlantic Ocean ◇
43 M 17 **Vema Seamount**, Atlantic Ocean ▲
113 B 15 **Venado Tuerto**, Argentina
130 H 9 **Vendas Novas**, Portugal
155 O 7 **Vendinga**, Russian Federation
129 O 6 **Vendôme**, France
140 G 7 **Veneto**, Italy ▣
156 L 2 **Venev**, Russian Federation
105 N 5 **Venezuela**, Venezuela □
42 E 12 **Venezuelan Basin**, Atlantic Ocean ◇
140 G 7 **Venice**, Italy
62 M 9 **Venice**, Louisiana, U.S.A.
63 V 12 **Venice**, Florida, U.S.A.
133 L 16 **Venlo**, Netherlands
133 K 15 **Venray**, Netherlands
148 C 11 **Venta**, Latvia/Lithuania ∿
219 N 13 **Venterstad**, Republic of South Africa
140 A 10 **Ventimiglia**, Italy
111 F 17 **Ventisquero**, Argentina ▲
127 T 14 **Ventnor**, United Kingdom
148 C 10 **Ventspils**, Latvia
77 I 24 **Ventura**, California, U.S.A.
112 B 12 **Vera**, Argentina
131 R 12 **Vera**, Spain
89 T 12 **Veracruz**, Mexico
89 R 10 **Veracruz**, Mexico ▣
181 A 16 **Veraval**, India
140 C 6 **Verbania**, Italy
140 B 7 **Vercelli**, Italy
135 E 14 **Verdalsøra**, Norway
74 J 11 **Verde**, Arizona, U.S.A. ∿
196 F 12 **Verde Island Passage**, Philippines ≈
129 T 4 **Verdun**, France
113 G 14 **Vergara**, Uruguay
58 L 6 **Vergennes**, Vermont, U.S.A.
151 U 8 **Verkhiniy Rohachyk**, Ukraine
155 N 12 **Verkhnespasskoye**, Russian Federation
154 G 2 **Verkhnetulomskoye Vodokhranilishche**, Russian Federation 💧
156 K 4 **Verkhov'ye**, Russian Federation
153 T 7 **Verkhoyanskiy Khrebet**, Russian Federation ⛰
83 K 18 **Vermilion**, Alberta, Canada
62 J 8 **Vermilion Bay**, Louisiana, U.S.A. ≈
67 T 3 **Vermilion Lake**, Minnesota, U.S.A. 💧
67 O 11 **Vermillion**, South Dakota, U.S.A.
58 K 7 **Vermont**, U.S.A. ▣
240 H 4 **Vernadsky**, Antarctica ⁘
74 M 3 **Vernal**, Utah, U.S.A.
86 E 9 **Verner**, Ontario, Canada
129 O 4 **Verneuil-sur-Avre**, France
63 O 3 **Vernon**, Alabama, U.S.A.
71 N 4 **Vernon**, Texas, U.S.A.
74 J 3 **Vernon**, Utah, U.S.A.
83 H 21 **Vernon**, British Columbia, Canada
63 Y 11 **Vero Beach**, Florida, U.S.A.
147 E 14 **Veroia**, Greece
140 F 7 **Verona**, Italy
113 E 16 **Verónica**, Argentina
129 P 4 **Versailles**, France
65 J 20 **Versailles**, Indiana, U.S.A.
69 U 5 **Versailles**, Missouri, U.S.A.
138 A 10 **Versoix**, Switzerland
92 K 5 **Vertientes**, Cuba
151 R 2 **Vertiyivka**, Ukraine
133 K 20 **Verviers**, Belgium
129 S 2 **Vervins**, France
83 M 20 **Verwood**, Saskatchewan, Canada
129 Z 14 **Vescovato**, France
151 U 9 **Vesele**, Ukraine
156 M 10 **Veselovskoye Vodokhranilishche**, Russian Federation 💧
157 N 7 **Veshenskaya**, Russian Federation
129 V 6 **Vesoul**, France
63 Q 3 **Vestavia Hills**, Alabama, U.S.A.
135 A 21 **Vestbygd**, Norway
134 G 8 **Vesterålen**, Norway 🏝
134 G 9 **Vestfjorden**, Norway ≈
134 G 9 **Vestvågøy**, Norway 🏝
141 J 16 **Vesuvius**, Italy ▲
154 J 12 **Ves'yegonsk**, Russian Federation
143 H 24 **Veszprém**, Hungary
135 G 23 **Vetlanda**, Sweden
155 N 13 **Vetluga**, Russian Federation
154 M 14 **Vetluzhskiy**, Russian Federation
146 K 6 **Vetovo**, Bulgaria
140 G 13 **Vetralla**, Italy
146 M 9 **Vetren**, Bulgaria
133 A 17 **Veurne**, Belgium
138 C 9 **Vevey**, Switzerland
129 U 12 **Veynes**, France
170 K 8 **Vezirköprü**, Turkey
112 H 12 **Viamão**, Brazil
130 H 3 **Viana do Castelo**, Portugal ▣
130 H 4 **Viana do Castelo**, Portugal
133 L 24 **Vianden**, Luxembourg
132 I 13 **Vianen**, Netherlands
190 H 12 **Viangphoukha**, Laos
140 E 10 **Viareggio**, Italy
141 M 20 **Vibo Valentia**, Italy
135 C 24 **Viborg**, Denmark
131 X 4 **Vic**, Spain
128 M 14 **Vic-en-Bigorre**, France
140 F 7 **Vicenza**, Italy
104 M 6 **Vichada**, Colombia ▣
104 L 7 **Vichada**, Colombia ∿
129 R 9 **Vichy**, France
68 K 9 **Vici**, Oklahoma, U.S.A.
62 K 5 **Vicksburg**, Mississippi, U.S.A.
112 N 5 **Viçosa**, Brazil
67 U 12 **Victor**, Iowa, U.S.A.
73 Q 11 **Victor**, Idaho, U.S.A.
231 P 12 **Victor Harbor**, South Australia, Australia
230 M 3 **Victoria**, Northern Territory, Australia ∿
231 T 13 **Victoria**, Australia ▣
38 A 9 **Victoria**, Seychelles 🏛
113 B 14 **Victoria**, Argentina
196 F 10 **Victoria**, Philippines
71 Q 11 **Victoria**, Texas, U.S.A.
83 F 22 **Victoria**, British Columbia, Canada
90 L 5 **Victoria**, Honduras
218 M 7 **Victoria Falls**, Zimbabwe
82 H 6 **Victoria Island**, Nunavut, Canada 🏝
241 R 12 **Victoria Land**, Antarctica ◇
197 C 19 **Victoria Peak**, Philippines ▲
90 J 3 **Victoria Peak**, Belize ▲
230 M 3 **Victoria River**, Northern Territory, Australia
218 L 14 **Victoria West**, Republic of South Africa
86 M 10 **Victoriaville**, Québec, Canada
110 I 13 **Victorica**, Argentina
77 K 24 **Victorville**, California, U.S.A.
110 J 12 **Vicuña Mackenna**, Argentina
73 X 3 **Vida**, Montana, U.S.A.
77 N 24 **Vidal**, California, U.S.A.
150 J 13 **Videle**, Romania
130 I 10 **Vidigueira**, Portugal
146 E 6 **Vidin**, Bulgaria ▣
146 F 6 **Vidin**, Bulgaria
145 H 14 **Viduša**, Bosnia and Herzegovina ⛰
149 H 14 **Vidzy**, Belarus
113 B 21 **Viedma**, Argentina
148 D 12 **Viekšniai**, Lithuania
131 V 2 **Vielha**, Spain
133 K 22 **Vielsalm**, Belgium
139 X 3 **Vienna**, Austria 🏛
61 N 3 **Vienna**, West Virginia, U.S.A.
65 F 23 **Vienna**, Illinois, U.S.A.
69 V 5 **Vienna**, Missouri, U.S.A.
129 T 10 **Vienne**, France
191 J 15 **Vientiane**, Laos 🏛
137 B 16 **Viersen**, Germany
138 F 8 **Vierwaldstätter See**, Switzerland 💧
129 P 7 **Vierzon**, France
148 G 12 **Viesīte**, Latvia
141 M 14 **Vieste**, Italy
190 L 12 **Viêt Tri**, Vietnam
134 I 10 **Vietas**, Sweden
190 L 13 **Vietnam**, Asia □
93 Z 11 **Vieux Fort**, St Lucia
196 K 12 **Viga**, Philippines
196 F 7 **Vigan**, Philippines
140 C 7 **Vigevano**, Italy
89 Z 11 **Vigía Chico**, Mexico
128 M 15 **Vignemale**, France/Spain ▲
130 H 3 **Vigo**, Spain
177 X 10 **Vihari**, Pakistan
135 L 19 **Vihti**, Finland
148 I 10 **Viļaka**, Latvia
148 I 11 **Viļāni**, Latvia
135 M 15 **Viitasaari**, Finland
148 H 5
181 G 19 **Vijayawada**, India
134 E 13 **Vik**, Norway
134 C 12 **Vík**, Iceland
146 G 11 **Vikhren**, Bulgaria ▲
83 K 18 **Viking**, Alberta, Canada
134 E 13 **Vikna**, Norway 🏝
109 F 15 **Vila Bela da Santíssima Trindade**, Brazil
108 B 10 **Vila Bittencourt**, Brazil
43 A 16 **Vila da Ribeira Brava**, Cape Verde
43 B 16 **Vila da Sal Rei**, Cape Verde
219 R 6 **Vila de Sena**, Mozambique
130 G 12 **Vila do Bispo**, Portugal
43 B 17 **Vila do Tarrafal**, Cape Verde
67 T 4 **Virginia**, Minnesota, U.S.A.
130 G 9 **Vila Franca de Xira**, Portugal
130 J 5 **Vila Nova de Foz Coa**, Portugal
130 H 5 **Vila Nova de Gaia**, Portugal
43 A 17 **Vila Nova Sintra**, Cape Verde
108 F 9 **Vila Novo Paraíso**, Brazil
130 I 5 **Vila Real**, Portugal ▣
130 I 5 **Vila Real**, Portugal
112 O 5 **Vila Velha**, Brazil
107 K 22 **Vilacaya**, Bolivia
130 J 1 **Vilalba**, Spain
219 R 9 **Vilanculos**, Mozambique
181 E 23 **Vilatikkulam**, India
135 H 14 **Vilhelmina**, Sweden
109 F 14 **Vilhena**, Brazil
151 T 12 **Viline**, Ukraine
148 G 8 **Viljandi**, Estonia
149 D 15 **Vilkaviškis**, Lithuania
149 E 15 **Vilkija**, Lithuania
110 L 8 **Villa**, Argentina
107 K 22 **Villa Abecia**, Bolivia
88 M 3 **Villa Ahumada**, Mexico
112 B 10 **Villa Angela**, Argentina
112 B 10 **Villa Berthet**, Argentina
113 C 15 **Villa Constitución**, Argentina
110 J 10 **Villa del Rosario**, Argentina
110 I 11 **Villa Dolores**, Argentina
89 W 14 **Villa Flores**, Mexico
113 E 17 **Villa Gesell**, Argentina
88 I 7 **Villa Insurgentes**, Mexico
113 A 19 **Villa Iris**, Argentina
141 J 16 **Villa Literno**, Italy
113 A 14 **Villa María**, Argentina
107 I 22 **Villa Martín**, Bolivia
107 L 23 **Villa Montes**, Bolivia
112 C 11 **Villa Ocampo**, Argentina
88 M 6 **Villa Ocampo**, Mexico
110 J 9 **Villa Ojo de Agua**, Argentina
110 H 9 **Villa Unión**, Argentina
88 M 9 **Villa Unión**, Mexico
89 N 8 **Villa Unión**, Mexico
110 I 12 **Villa Valeria**, Argentina
130 K 2 **Villablino**, Spain
131 P 11 **Villacarrillo**, Spain
131 N 6 **Villacastín**, Spain
139 S 9 **Villach**, Austria
130 M 3 **Villada**, Spain
130 J 2 **Villafranca del Bierzo**, Spain
141 I 22 **Villafrati**, Italy
89 Q 8 **Villagrán**, Mexico
112 C 13 **Villaguay**, Argentina
89 W 13 **Villahermosa**, Mexico
131 T 10 **Villajoyosa**, Spain
113 B 20 **Villalonga**, Argentina
111 J 16 **Villálonga**, Argentina
130 M 4 **Villalpando**, Spain
141 B 16 **Villanova Monteleone**, Italy
131 P 10 **Villanueva de los Infantes**, Spain
143 I 26 **Villány**, Hungary
130 M 4 **Villardefrades**, Spain
111 F 15 **Villarrica**, Chile
131 Q 8 **Villarrobledo**, Spain
141 C 19 **Villasimius**, Italy
104 J 7 **Villavicencio**, Colombia
130 M 1 **Villaviciosa de Asturias**, Spain
107 K 23 **Villazon**, Bolivia
86 F 8 **Ville-Marie**, Québec, Canada
129 P 12 **Villefranche-de-Rouergue**, France
129 T 9 **Villefranche-sur-Saône**, France
131 S 10 **Villena**, Spain
67 R 14 **Villisca**, Iowa, U.S.A.
149 G 16 **Vilnius**, Lithuania 🏛
137 L 23 **Vilsbiburg**, Germany
137 M 23 **Vilshofen**, Germany
133 G 18 **Vilvoorde**, Belgium
149 I 16 **Vilyeyka**, Belarus
153 S 10 **Vilyuy**, Russian Federation ∿
153 Q 10 **Vilyuyskoye Vodokhranilishche**, Russian Federation 💧
130 G 1 **Vimianzo**, Spain
129 N 4 **Vimoutiers**, France
110 E 11 **Viña del Mar**, Chile
59 R 6 **Vinalhaven Island**, Maine, U.S.A. 🏝
219 Z 6 **Vinanivao**, Madgascar
131 U 6 **Vinarós**, Spain
65 H 21 **Vincennes**, Indiana, U.S.A.
241 Y 11 **Vincennes Bay**, Antarctica ≈
181 C 15 **Vindhya Ranges**, India ⛰
150 F 10 **Vinga**, Romania
191 L 14 **Vinh**, Vietnam
191 N 16 **Vinh Linh**, Vietnam
191 M 22 **Vinh Long**, Vietnam
191 L 23 **Vinh Rach Gia**, Vietnam ≈
130 J 4 **Vinhais**, Portugal
146 E 11 **Vinica**, Macedonia (F.Y.R.O.M.)
69 Q 8 **Vinita**, Oklahoma, U.S.A.
151 N 5 **Vinnytsya**, Ukraine
240 L 7 **Vinson Massif**, Antarctica ▲
216 G 10 **Vinza**, Congo
140 F 4 **Vipiteno**, Italy
196 K 13 **Virac**, Philippines
181 B 14 **Viramgam**, India
171 P 13 **Viranşehir**, Turkey
177 W 15 **Virawah**, Pakistan
84 H 10 **Virden**, Manitoba, Canada
128 M 4 **Vire**, France
218 G 6 **Virei**, Angola
93 V 7 **Virgin Corda**, Virgin Islands, United Kingdom 🏝
93 V 7 **Virgin Islands**, United Kingdom, United Kingdom ▣
93 V 8 **Virgin Islands**, U.S.A., U.S.A. ▣
219 N 12 **Virginia**, Republic of South Africa
57 R 5 **Virginia**, Minnesota, U.S.A.
61 Q 5 **Virginia**, U.S.A. ▣
65 E 19 **Virginia**, Illinois, U.S.A.
61 W 7 **Virginia Beach**, Virginia, U.S.A.
73 P 8 **Virginia City**, Montana, U.S.A.
77 I 18 **Virginia City**, Nevada, U.S.A.
86 F 7 **Virginiatown**, Ontario, Canada
135 N 18 **Virojoki**, Finland
133 J 26 **Virton**, Belgium
148 E 7 **Virtsu**, Estonia
107 B 14 **Virú**, Peru
77 I 21 **Visalia**, California, U.S.A.
197 J 15 **Visayan Sea**, Philippines 🌊
135 H 23 **Visby**, Sweden
108 B 11 **Visconde do Rio Branco**, Brazil
45 O 7 **Viscount Melville Sound**, Arctic Ocean ≈
81 N 4 **Viscount Melville Sound**, Nunavut, Canada ≈
133 K 19 **Visé**, Belgium
144 J 12 **Višegrad**, Bosnia and Herzegovina
130 I 6 **Viseu**, Portugal ▣
130 I 6 **Viseu**, Portugal
181 H 18 **Vishakhapatnam**, India
146 L 11 **Vishegrad**, Bulgaria ▲
179 S 4 **Vishnevka**, Kazakhstan
138 E 10 **Visp**, Switzerland
142 J 12 **Vistula**, Poland ∿
149 A 16 **Vistula Lagoon**, Russian Federation ≈
151 S 8 **Visun'**, Ukraine ∿
146 I 7 **Vit**, Bulgaria ∿
140 G 13 **Viterbo**, Italy
235 W 11 **Viti Levu**, Fiji 🏝
130 K 5 **Vitigudino**, Spain
112 O 5 **Vitória**, Brazil
109 M 16 **Vitória da Conquista**, Brazil
108 I 10 **Vitória do Xingu**, Brazil
131 Q 2 **Vitoria-Gasteiz**, Spain
43 H 16 **Vitória Seamount**, Atlantic Ocean ▲
146 F 9 **Vitosha**, Bulgaria ⛰
128 L 5 **Vitré**, France
129 T 4 **Vitry-le-François**, France
149 M 14 **Vitsyebsk**, Belarus
149 L 15 **Vitsyebskaya Voblasts'**, Belarus ▣
134 J 10 **Vittangi**, Sweden
129 U 5 **Vittel**, France
141 J 23 **Vittoria**, Italy
41 P 6 **Vityaz Seamount**, Pacific Ocean ▲
130 J 1 **Viveiro**, Spain
131 T 7 **Viver**, Spain
219 O 9 **Vivo**, Republic of South Africa
129 N 9 **Vivonne**, France
146 N 11 **Vize**, Turkey
181 H 18 **Vizianagaram**, India
155 P 10 **Vizinga**, Russian Federation
150 M 12 **Viziru**, Romania
145 K 20 **Vjosë**, Albania ∿
133 I 19 **Vlaams Brabant**, Belgium ▣
132 F 13 **Vlaardingen**, Netherlands
145 N 15 **Vladičin Han**, Serbia and Montenegro
157 P 14 **Vladikavkaz**, Russian Federation
156 M 1 **Vladimir**, Russian Federation
146 G 7 **Vladimirovo**, Bulgaria
153 V 15 **Vladivostok**, Russian Federation
132 O 7 **Vlagtwedde**, Netherlands
144 I 12 **Vlasenica**, Bosnia and Herzegovina
144 G 11 **Vlašić**, Bosnia and Herzegovina ▲
143 D 18 **Vlašim**, Czech Republic
145 N 14 **Vlasotince**, Serbia and Montenegro
132 H 6 **Vlieland**, Netherlands 🏝
133 D 16 **Vlissingen**, Netherlands
145 J 20 **Vlorë**, Albania
143 C 18 **Vltava**, Czech Republic ∿
139 R 4 **Vöcklabruck**, Austria
155 Q 7 **Vodnyy**, Russian Federation
215 T 12 **Vogel Peak**, Nigeria ▲
137 F 18 **Vogelsberg**, Germany ⛰
219 Y 9 **Vohilava**, Madgascar
148 D 7 **Võhma**, Estonia
148 G 7 **Võhma**, Estonia
217 W 10 **Voi**, Kenya
150 I 11 **Voineasa**, Romania
214 H 12 **Voinjama**, Liberia
129 U 10 **Voiron**, France
139 V 7 **Voitsberg**, Austria
144 J 9 **Vojvodina**, Serbia and Montenegro ▣
215 U 12 **Voko**, Cameroon
73 X 7 **Volborg**, Montana, U.S.A.
90 H 6 **Volcán Agua**, Guatemala ▲
110 G 6 **Volcán Antofalla**, Argentina ▲
110 H 4 **Volcán Apagado**, Chile ▲
91 S 14 **Volcán Barú**, Panama ▲
110 G 8 **Volcán Copiapó**, Chile ▲
111 F 18 **Volcán Corcovado**, Chile ▲
106 B 9 **Volcán Cotopaxi**, Ecuador ▲
107 A 18 **Volcán Darwin**, Ecuador ▲
90 I 7 **Volcán de Santa Ana**, El Salvador ▲
89 W 15 **Volcán de Tacaná**, Mexico ▲
111 G 14 **Volcán Domuyo**, Argentina ▲
110 G 2 **Volcán Guallatiri**, Chile ▲
91 R 12 **Volcán Irazu**, Costa Rica ▲
107 A 18 **Volcán La Cumbre**, Ecuador ▲
111 F 16 **Volcán Lanin**, Argentina ▲
88 H 5 **Volcán Las Tres Vírgenes**, Mexico ▲
110 H 5 **Volcán Licancábur**, Chile ▲
110 G 6 **Volcán Llullaillaco**, Chile ▲
91 P 11 **Volcán Miravalles**, Costa Rica ▲
107 G 19 **Volcán Misti**, Peru ▲
107 I 23 **Volcán Ollagüe**, Bolivia ▲
91 Q 12 **Volcán Poás**, Costa Rica ▲
110 G 12 **Volcán San José**, Chile ▲
106 B 10 **Volcán Sangay**, Ecuador ▲
104 G 8 **Volcán Sotará**, Colombia ▲
107 H 20 **Volcán Tacora**, Chile/Peru ▲
90 F 5 **Volcán Tajumulco**, Guatemala ▲
111 G 14 **Volcán Tromen**, Argentina ▲
111 F 16 **Volcán Villarrica**, Chile ▲
107 A 18 **Volcán Wolf**, Ecuador ▲
78 E 9 **Volcano**, Hawaii, U.S.A.
155 R 8 **Vol'dino**, Russian Federation
132 I 10 **Volendam**, Netherlands
152 F 10 **Volga**, Russian Federation ∿
157 O 8 **Volga–Don Canal**, Russian Federation ∿
157 N 9 **Volgodonsk**, Russian Federation
157 P 8 **Volgograd**, Russian Federation
157 O 7 **Volgogradskaya Oblast'**, Russian Federation ▣
157 Q 7 **Volgogradskoye Vodokhranilishche**, Russian Federation 💧

□ Country ▣ Internal administrative region: State/Province/Territory/Dependent territory 🏛 Capital city ⛰ Mountain range/Undersea ridge ▲ Mountain peak/Volcano/Seamount ◇ Geographic feature ▶ Headland/Point/Cape/Peninsula 🏜 Desert 🏝 Island/Island group ⁘ Antarctic base 🌐 Ocean 🌊 Sea ≈ Bay/Gulf/Channel/Strait 💧 Lake ⚑ Salt pan/Dry/Intermittent lake ∿ River

Völkermarkt – Watertown

139 T 9 **Völkermarkt**, Austria
154 G 11 **Volkhov**, Russian Federation
151 X 7 **Volnovakha**, Ukraine
153 P 8 **Volochanka**, Russian Federation
150 L 5 **Volochys'k**, Ukraine
151 P 5 **Volodarka**, Ukraine
151 X 8 **Volodars'ke**, Ukraine
150 J 3 **Volodymyr-Volyns'kyy**, Ukraine
150 L 2 **Volodymyrets'**, Ukraine
154 K 12 **Vologda**, Russian Federation
154 K 10 **Vologodskaya Oblast'**, Russian Federation
151 W 5 **Volokhiv Yar**, Ukraine
156 J 1 **Volokolamsk**, Russian Federation
156 K 6 **Volokonovka**, Russian Federation
147 F 17 **Volos**, Greece
151 Z 5 **Voloshino**, Ukraine
156 L 8 **Voloshino**, Russian Federation
156 K 3 **Volovo**, Russian Federation
157 Q 5 **Vol'sk**, Russian Federation
112 M 6 **Volta Redonda**, Brazil
140 E 11 **Volterra**, Italy
157 R 1 **Volzhsk**, Russian Federation
157 P 8 **Volzhskiy**, Russian Federation
219 X 10 **Vondrozo**, Madgascar
147 B 18 **Vonitsa**, Greece
148 I 8 **Võnnu**, Estonia
132 J 12 **Voorhuizen**, Netherlands
132 G 12 **Voorschoten**, Netherlands
134 D 10 **Vopnafjörður**, Iceland
149 G 17 **Voranava**, Belarus
139 S 5 **Vorchdorf**, Austria
132 L 12 **Vorden**, Netherlands
135 D 26 **Vordingborg**, Denmark
147 K 18 **Voreio Aigaio**, Greece
147 G 18 **Voreioi Sporades**, Greece
147 F 18 **Voreios Evvoïkos Kolpos**, Greece
45 T 15 **Voring Plateau**, Arctic Ocean
155 U 2 **Vorkuta**, Russian Federation
148 E 6 **Vormsi**, Estonia
156 L 5 **Voronezh**, Russian Federation
156 L 5 **Voronezhskaya Oblast'**, Russian Federation
151 U 4 **Vorskla**, Ukraine
148 G 8 **Võrtsjärv**, Estonia
148 I 9 **Võru**, Estonia
179 S 12 **Vorukh**, Tajikistan
218 L 13 **Vosburg**, Republic of South Africa
179 R 14 **Vose**, Tajikistan
129 W 6 **Vosges**, France
156 L 1 **Voskresensk**, Russian Federation
155 N 14 **Voskresenskoye**, Russian Federation
135 A 18 **Voss**, Norway
179 X 5 **Vostochnyy Kazakhstan**, Kazakhstan
153 N 13 **Vostochnyy Sayan**, Russian Federation
237 R 6 **Vostok**, Kiribati
241 T 9 **Vostok**, Antarctica
155 R 13 **Votkinsk**, Russian Federation
155 S 13 **Votkinskoye Vodokhranilishche**, Russian Federation
112 I 5 **Votuporanga**, Brazil
129 T 3 **Vouziers**, France
151 W 7 **Vovcha**, Ukraine
151 W 3 **Vovchans'k**, Ukraine
154 G 5 **Voynitsa**, Russian Federation
155 R 8 **Voyvozh**, Russian Federation
155 O 6 **Vozhgora**, Russian Federation
151 Q 8 **Voznesens'k**, Ukraine
151 R 8 **Vozsiyats'ke**, Ukraine
149 J 20 **Vozyera Chyrvonaye**, Belarus
151 P 8 **Vradiyivka**, Ukraine
145 N 15 **Vranjska Banja**, Serbia and Montenegro
143 M 20 **Vranov nad Toplou**, Slovakia
146 G 8 **Vratsa**, Bulgaria
146 G 8 **Vratsa**, Bulgaria
144 B 7 **Vrhnika**, Slovenia
133 D 15 **Vrouwenpolder**, Netherlands
144 M 9 **Vršac**, Serbia and Montenegro
144 E 10 **Vrtoče**, Bosnia and Herzegovina
218 M 11 **Vryburg**, Republic of South Africa
219 P 12 **Vryheid**, Republic of South Africa
143 H 19 **Vsetín**, Czech Republic
145 M 15 **Vučitrn**, Serbia and Montenegro
133 I 15 **Vught**, Netherlands
151 X 7 **Vuhledar**, Ukraine
155 S 6 **Vuktyl'**, Russian Federation
219 P 11 **Vukuzakhe**, Republic of South Africa
153 Y 10 **Vulkan Ichinskiy**, Russian Federation
191 N 22 **Vung Tau**, Vietnam
235 X 12 **Vunisea**, Fiji
135 M 18 **Vuohijarvi**, Finland
134 J 11 **Vuollerim**, Sweden
134 H 11 **Vuolvojaure**, Sweden
134 L 9 **Vuotso**, Finland
157 T 1 **Vyatka**, Russian Federation
157 S 1 **Vyatskiye Polyany**, Russian Federation
156 I 1 **Vyaz'ma**, Russian Federation
157 N 1 **Vyazniki**, Russian Federation
154 E 9 **Vyborg**, Russian Federation
155 N 9 **Vychegda**, Russian Federation
148 J 13 **Vyerkhnyadzvinsk**, Belarus
149 N 20 **Vyetka**, Belarus
149 K 14 **Vyetryna**, Belarus
149 H 20 **Vyhanashchy**, Belarus
157 N 2 **Vyksa**, Russian Federation
151 O 11 **Vylkove**, Ukraine
150 H 7 **Vylok**, Ukraine
154 E 11 **Vyrista**, Russian Federation
150 K 4 **Vyshnivets'**, Ukraine
154 G 13 **Vyshniy-Volochek**, Russian Federation
143 G 19 **Vyškov**, Czech Republic
149 E 20 **Vysokaye**, Belarus
151 O 2 **Vystupovychi**, Ukraine
154 I 10 **Vytegra**, Russian Federation

W

133 I 14 **Waal**, Netherlands
133 I 14 **Waalwijk**, Netherlands
213 E 21 **Waat**, Sudan
234 C 4 **Wabag**, Papua New Guinea
83 I 16 **Wabasca**, Alberta, Canada
83 I 16 **Wabasca-Desmarais**, Alberta, Canada
65 J 17 **Wabash**, Indiana, U.S.A.
65 H 18 **Wabash**, Indiana/Illinois, U.S.A.
67 U 8 **Wabasha**, Minnesota, U.S.A.
63 U 9 **Waccasassa Bay**, Florida, U.S.A.
71 Q 7 **Waco**, Texas, U.S.A.
68 L 2 **Waconda Lake**, Kansas, U.S.A.
177 S 13 **Wad**, Pakistan
213 C 18 **Wad Banda**, Sudan
213 F 16 **Wad Hamid**, Sudan
213 F 17 **Wad Medani**, Sudan
211 U 9 **Waddān**, Libya
132 H 6 **Waddeneilanden**, Netherlands
132 H 8 **Waddenzee**, Netherlands
126 K 14 **Wadebridge**, United Kingdom
67 Q 6 **Wadena**, Minnesota, U.S.A.
138 G 7 **Wädenswil**, Switzerland
61 Q 10 **Wadesboro**, North Carolina, U.S.A.
173 X 14 **Wādī al Bāṭin**, Iraq
175 T 12 **Wādī al Masīlah**, Yemen
172 G 9 **Wādī as Sīr**, Jordan
173 R 3 **Wādī ath Tharthār**, Iraq
212 E 13 **Wadi Halfa**, Sudan
173 O 7 **Wādī Ḥawrān**, Iraq
172 G 12 **Wādī Mūsá**, Jordan
63 V 4 **Wadley**, Georgia, U.S.A.
199 N 23 **Wadomari**, Japan
187 H 17 **Wafangdian**, China
132 K 13 **Wageningen**, Netherlands
84 M 2 **Wager Bay**, Nunavut, Canada
231 T 12 **Wagga Wagga**, New South Wales, Australia
230 G 11 **Wagin**, Western Australia, Australia
138 G 7 **Wägiteler See**, Switzerland
75 S 9 **Wagon Mound**, New Mexico, U.S.A.
142 G 11 **Wągrowiec**, Poland
177 X 8 **Wah**, Pakistan
74 H 5 **Wah Wah Mountains**, Utah, U.S.A.
193 S 12 **Wahai**, Indonesia
232 L 10 **Waharoa**, New Zealand
213 D 20 **Wahda**, Sudan
78 C 7 **Wahiawa**, Hawaii, U.S.A.
67 O 6 **Wahpeton**, North Dakota, U.S.A.
233 H 19 **Waiau**, New Zealand
233 H 18 **Waiau**, New Zealand
139 U 4 **Waidhofen an der Ybbs**, Austria
193 T 11 **Waigeo**, Indonesia
232 I 5 **Waiharara**, New Zealand
232 O 11 **Waihau Bay**, New Zealand
232 K 8 **Waiheke Island**, New Zealand
232 L 9 **Waihi**, New Zealand
232 O 11 **Waihirere**, New Zealand
233 E 25 **Waihola**, New Zealand
193 N 15 **Waikabubak**, Indonesia
233 K 15 **Waikanae**, New Zealand
233 H 19 **Waikari**, New Zealand
232 K 11 **Waikato**, New Zealand
233 F 24 **Waikouaiti**, New Zealand
78 D 7 **Wailuku**, Hawaii, U.S.A.
233 G 16 **Waimarie**, New Zealand
233 G 22 **Waimate**, New Zealand
78 A 6 **Waimea**, Hawaii, U.S.A.
78 B 7 **Waimea**, Hawaii, U.S.A.
78 E 8 **Waimea**, Hawaii, U.S.A.
127 X 5 **Wainfleet All Saints**, United Kingdom
193 O 15 **Waingapu**, Indonesia
233 L 16 **Wainuioru**, New Zealand
79 O 3 **Wainwright**, Alaska, U.S.A.
83 K 18 **Wainwright**, Alberta, Canada
232 M 11 **Waiotapu**, New Zealand
232 L 13 **Waiouru**, New Zealand
233 D 25 **Waipahi**, New Zealand
233 H 19 **Waipara**, New Zealand
233 M 14 **Waipawa**, New Zealand
232 J 7 **Waipu**, New Zealand
233 M 14 **Waipukurau**, New Zealand
233 I 17 **Wairau**, New Zealand
233 I 17 **Wairau Valley**, New Zealand
232 N 12 **Wairoa**, New Zealand
232 M 12 **Waitahanui**, New Zealand
232 L 9 **Waitakaruru**, New Zealand
232 J 8 **Waitakere**, New Zealand
233 E 22 **Waitaki**, New Zealand
233 F 24 **Waitati**, New Zealand
232 K 13 **Waitotara**, New Zealand
232 J 9 **Waiuku**, New Zealand
199 H 14 **Wajima**, Japan
216 K 7 **Waka**, Democratic Republic of Congo
199 G 17 **Wakasa-wan**, Japan
199 G 19 **Wakayama**, Japan
68 J 3 **WaKeeney**, Kansas, U.S.A.
127 S 3 **Wakefield**, United Kingdom
199 F 19 **Waki**, Japan
198 J 8 **Wakinosawa**, Japan
198 J 3 **Wakkanai**, Japan
218 H 4 **Waku-Kungo**, Angola
234 J 4 **Wakunai**, Papua New Guinea
186 J 4 **Walagan**, China
143 F 16 **Wałbrzych**, Poland
231 V 10 **Walcha**, New South Wales, Australia
73 W 13 **Walcott**, Wyoming, U.S.A.
142 F 10 **Wałcz**, Poland
75 Q 2 **Walden**, Colorado, U.S.A.
137 D 24 **Waldkirch**, Germany
61 U 4 **Waldorf**, Maryland, U.S.A.
76 F 11 **Waldport**, Oregon, U.S.A.
69 S 11 **Waldron**, Arkansas, U.S.A.
137 E 25 **Waldshut**, Germany
193 P 11 **Waleabahi**, Indonesia
127 N 8 **Wales**, United Kingdom
133 L 25 **Walferdange**, Luxembourg
231 T 9 **Walgett**, New South Wales, Australia
240 K 9 **Walgreen Coast**, Antarctica
217 P 8 **Walikale**, Democratic Republic of Congo
67 Q 4 **Walker**, Minnesota, U.S.A.
77 J 18 **Walker Lake**, Nevada, U.S.A.
66 H 9 **Wall**, South Dakota, U.S.A.
76 K 9 **Walla Walla**, Washington, U.S.A.
39 S 7 **Wallaby Plateau**, Indian Ocean
61 T 11 **Wallace**, North Carolina, U.S.A.
72 K 4 **Wallace**, Idaho, U.S.A.
83 H 18 **Wallace Mountain**, Alberta, Canada
86 B 14 **Wallaceburg**, Ontario, Canada
231 P 11 **Wallaroo**, South Australia, Australia
137 G 20 **Walldürn**, Germany
138 H 7 **Wallensee**, Switzerland
236 I 8 **Wallis**, Wallis and Futuna Islands
236 H 7 **Wallis and Futuna Islands**, France
138 D 10 **Walliser Alpen**, Switzerland
64 K 10 **Walloon Lake**, Michigan, U.S.A.
69 X 9 **Walnut Ridge**, Arkansas, U.S.A.
230 G 12 **Walpole**, Western Australia, Australia
127 R 6 **Walsall**, United Kingdom
75 S 7 **Walsenburg**, Colorado, U.S.A.
181 H 18 **Waltair**, India
63 S 5 **Walter F. George Reservoir**, Georgia, U.S.A.
61 O 14 **Walterboro**, South Carolina, U.S.A.
38 J 9 **Walters Shoal**, Indian Ocean
127 W 10 **Waltham Abbey**, United Kingdom
127 U 6 **Waltham on the Wolds**, United Kingdom
87 U 10 **Walton**, Nova Scotia, Canada
127 Z 9 **Walton-on-the-Naze**, United Kingdom
218 H 9 **Walvis Bay**, Namibia
218 H 10 **Walvis Bay**, Namibia
43 L 17 **Walvis Ridge**, Atlantic Ocean
193 Y 14 **Wamal**, Indonesia
216 L 8 **Wamba**, Democratic Republic of Congo
217 P 6 **Wamba**, Democratic Republic of Congo
91 P 5 **Wampusirpi**, Honduras
177 V 9 **Wana**, Pakistan
231 R 9 **Wanaaring**, New South Wales, Australia
233 D 22 **Wanaka**, New Zealand
189 U 9 **Wan'an**, China
193 W 13 **Wanapiri**, Indonesia
86 E 8 **Wanapitie Lake**, Ontario, Canada
193 W 12 **Wandai**, Indonesia
45 S 10 **Wandel Sea**, Arctic Ocean
188 I 11 **Wanding**, China
191 G 14 **Wang Nua**, Thailand
191 I 16 **Wang Saphung**, Thailand
233 K 14 **Wanganui**, New Zealand
232 K 13 **Wanganui**, New Zealand
231 S 12 **Wangaratta**, Victoria, Australia
183 T 9 **Wangdue-Phodrang**, Bhutan
137 G 25 **Wangen**, Germany
136 E 9 **Wangerooge**, Germany
189 S 11 **Wanggao**, China
193 P 13 **Wangiwangi**, Indonesia
189 O 11 **Wangmo**, China
186 M 13 **Wangqing**, China
83 H 17 **Wanham**, Alberta, Canada
217 N 7 **Wanie-Rukula**, Democratic Republic of Congo
213 L 24 **Wanlaweyn**, Somalia
189 R 15 **Wanning**, China
91 P 5 **Wanquibila**, Honduras
127 S 10 **Wantage**, United Kingdom
189 Q 6 **Wanxian**, China
189 P 5 **Wanyuan**, China
189 U 8 **Wanzai**, China
65 L 18 **Wapakoneta**, Ohio, U.S.A.
76 I 8 **Wapato**, Washington, U.S.A.
132 L 11 **Wapenveld**, Netherlands
69 Y 7 **Wappapello Lake**, Missouri, U.S.A.
213 D 21 **Warab**, Sudan
213 D 21 **Warab**, Sudan
230 K 7 **Warakurna Roadhouse**, Western Australia, Australia
213 L 21 **Warandab**, Ethiopia
181 F 18 **Warangal**, India
127 W 7 **Warboys**, United Kingdom
137 F 15 **Warburg**, Germany
231 P 8 **Warburton**, South Australia, Australia
230 K 8 **Warburton**, Western Australia, Australia
177 U 7 **Wardag**, Afghanistan
181 F 16 **Wardha**, India
173 P 2 **Wardīyah**, Iraq
133 C 19 **Waregem**, Belgium
127 Q 13 **Wareham**, United Kingdom
133 I 20 **Waremme**, Belgium
136 L 10 **Waren**, Germany
137 E 14 **Warendorf**, Germany
231 V 6 **Warginburra Peninsula**, Queensland, Australia
231 V 9 **Warialda**, New South Wales, Australia
142 L 13 **Warka**, Poland
232 K 7 **Warkworth**, New Zealand
76 H 10 **Warm Springs**, Oregon, U.S.A.
77 L 19 **Warm Springs**, Nevada, U.S.A.
193 U 11 **Warmandi**, Indonesia
218 J 12 **Warmbad**, Namibia
127 R 11 **Warminster**, United Kingdom
230 K 3 **Warmun**, Western Australia, Australia
136 K 8 **Warnemünde**, Germany
63 U 4 **Warner Robins**, Georgia, U.S.A.
133 B 19 **Warneton**, Belgium
181 F 16 **Warora**, India
231 Q 12 **Warracknabeal**, Victoria, Australia
231 S 9 **Warrego**, Queensland, Australia
58 C 10 **Warren**, Pennsylvania, U.S.A.
65 M 15 **Warren**, Michigan, U.S.A.
65 O 17 **Warren**, Ohio, U.S.A.
67 O 3 **Warren**, Minnesota, U.S.A.
71 T 9 **Warren**, Texas, U.S.A.
69 T 4 **Warrensburg**, Missouri, U.S.A.
218 M 12 **Warrenton**, Republic of South Africa
61 T 4 **Warrenton**, Virginia, U.S.A.
215 Q 14 **Warri**, Nigeria
127 Q 4 **Warrington**, United Kingdom
63 P 7 **Warrington**, Florida, U.S.A.
63 P 2 **Warrior**, Alabama, U.S.A.
231 R 13 **Warrnambool**, Victoria, Australia
67 P 2 **Warroad**, Minnesota, U.S.A.
142 L 12 **Warsaw**, Poland
58 E 9 **Warsaw**, New York, U.S.A.
61 T 10 **Warsaw**, North Carolina, U.S.A.
65 J 17 **Warsaw**, Indiana, U.S.A.
69 T 5 **Warsaw**, Missouri, U.S.A.
213 M 24 **Warshiikh**, Somalia
143 I 14 **Warta**, Poland
181 F 16 **Warud**, India
231 V 9 **Warwick**, Queensland, Australia
127 S 8 **Warwick**, United Kingdom
59 N 11 **Warwick**, Rhode Island, U.S.A.
188 K 8 **Warzhong**, China
74 J 5 **Wasatch Range**, Utah, U.S.A.
76 I 9 **Wasco**, Oregon, U.S.A.
177 Q 13 **Washap**, Pakistan
64 E 8 **Washburn**, Wisconsin, U.S.A.
181 E 16 **Washim**, India
58 A 13 **Washington**, Pennsylvania, U.S.A.
61 U 9 **Washington**, North Carolina, U.S.A.
61 S 4 **Washington**, Virginia, U.S.A.
65 F 18 **Washington**, Illinois, U.S.A.
65 M 19 **Washington**, Ohio, U.S.A.
67 V 13 **Washington**, Iowa, U.S.A.
76 H 7 **Washington**, U.S.A., U.S.A.
61 U 3 **Washington, D.C.**, District of Columbia, U.S.A.
64 I 10 **Washington Island**, Wisconsin, U.S.A.
85 P 10 **Waskaganish**, Québec, Canada
83 L 17 **Waskesiu Lake**, Saskatchewan, Canada
91 Q 6 **Waspán**, Nicaragua
133 H 14 **Waspik**, Netherlands
214 F 9 **Wassadou**, Senegal
137 K 24 **Wasserburg**, Germany
137 G 18 **Wasserkuppe**, Germany
234 E 4 **Wasu**, Papua New Guinea
234 B 6 **Wasua**, Papua New Guinea
193 O 13 **Watampone**, Indonesia
181 L 18 **Wataru Channel**, Maldives
62 M 2 **Water Valley**, Mississippi, U.S.A.
58 L 11 **Waterbury**, Connecticut, U.S.A.
61 O 11 **Wateree Lake**, South Carolina, U.S.A.
125 D 20 **Waterford**, Republic of Ireland
126 J 14 **Watergate Bay**, United Kingdom
133 G 20 **Waterloo**, Belgium
67 U 11 **Waterloo**, Iowa, U.S.A.
86 D 13 **Waterloo**, Ontario, Canada
127 U 13 **Waterlooville**, United Kingdom
64 F 9 **Watersmeet**, Michigan, U.S.A.
58 H 6 **Watertown**, New York, U.S.A.

Country · Internal administrative region: State/Province/Territory/Dependent territory · Capital city · Mountain range/Undersea ridge · Mountain peak/Volcano/Seamount · Geographic feature · Headland/Point/Cape/Peninsula · Desert · Island/Island group · Antarctic base · Ocean · Sea · Bay/Gulf/Channel/Strait · Lake · Salt pan/Dry/Intermittent lake · River

- 67 N 8 **Watertown**, South Dakota, U.S.A.
- 125 A 21 **Waterville**, Republic of Ireland
- 57 Z 5 **Waterville**, Maine, U.S.A.
- 69 N 2 **Waterville**, Kansas, U.S.A.
- 76 I 7 **Waterville**, Washington, U.S.A.
- 127 V 10 **Watford**, United Kingdom
- 66 G 3 **Watford City**, North Dakota, U.S.A.
- 58 G 9 **Watkins Glen**, New York, U.S.A.
- 68 L 9 **Watonga**, Oklahoma, U.S.A.
- 217 Q 6 **Watsa**, Democratic Republic of Congo
- 216 K 8 **Watsi Kengo**, Democratic Republic of Congo
- 83 M 18 **Watson**, Saskatchewan, Canada
- 83 D 14 **Watson Lake**, Yukon Territory, Canada
- 77 G 20 **Watsonville**, California, U.S.A.
- 60 I 9 **Watts Bar Lake**, Tennessee, U.S.A. 💧
- 138 H 7 **Wattwil**, Switzerland
- 213 C 21 **Wau**, Sudan
- 234 E 5 **Wau**, Papua New Guinea
- 231 N 5 **Wauchope**, Northern Territory, Australia
- 63 W 11 **Wauchula**, Florida, U.S.A.
- 65 H 15 **Waukegan**, Illinois, U.S.A.
- 65 G 14 **Waukesha**, Wisconsin, U.S.A.
- 64 F 12 **Waupaca**, Wisconsin, U.S.A.
- 68 M 12 **Waurika**, Oklahoma, U.S.A.
- 64 F 11 **Wausau**, Wisconsin, U.S.A.
- 64 F 12 **Wautoma**, Wisconsin, U.S.A.
- 230 M 3 **Wave Hill**, Northern Territory, Australia
- 127 Z 7 **Waveney**, United Kingdom ∿
- 58 G 10 **Waverly**, Pennsylvania, U.S.A.
- 60 D 8 **Waverly**, Tennessee, U.S.A.
- 67 P 14 **Waverly**, Nebraska, U.S.A.
- 133 G 20 **Wavre**, Belgium
- 211 U 11 **Wāw al Kabīr**, Libya
- 215 P 11 **Wawa**, Nigeria
- 86 A 6 **Wawa**, Ontario, Canada
- 91 Q 6 **Wawa**, Nicaragua ∿
- 234 B 5 **Wawoi**, Papua New Guinea ∿
- 71 Q 6 **Waxahachie**, Texas, U.S.A.
- 193 S 9 **Wayabula**, Indonesia
- 193 T 10 **Wayag**, Indonesia 🏝
- 63 V 6 **Waycross**, Georgia, U.S.A.
- 60 D 10 **Waynesboro**, Tennessee, U.S.A.
- 61 R 5 **Waynesboro**, Virginia, U.S.A.
- 63 N 6 **Waynesboro**, Mississippi, U.S.A.
- 63 V 3 **Waynesboro**, Georgia, U.S.A.
- 60 L 10 **Waynesville**, North Carolina, U.S.A.
- 68 L 8 **Waynoka**, Oklahoma, U.S.A.
- 215 V 10 **Waza**, Cameroon
- 177 T 9 **Wazi Khwa**, Afghanistan
- 177 Y 8 **Wazirabad**, Pakistan
- 142 H 10 **Wda**, Poland ∿
- 235 Q 13 **Wé**, New Caledonia
- 68 K 10 **Weatherford**, Oklahoma, U.S.A.
- 77 F 15 **Weaverville**, California, U.S.A.
- 84 M 9 **Webequie**, Ontario, Canada
- 40 K 8 **Weber Basin**, Pacific Ocean ◇
- 58 F 8 **Webster**, New York, U.S.A.
- 234 G 7 **Wedau**, Papua New Guinea
- 43 H 23 **Weddel Abyssal Plain**, Atlantic Ocean ◇
- 111 K 24 **Weddell Island**, Falkland Islands 🏝
- 240 K 5 **Weddell Sea**, Antarctica 🌊
- 231 U 10 **Wee Waa**, New South Wales, Australia
- 77 G 15 **Weed**, California, U.S.A.
- 58 D 11 **Weedville**, Pennsylvania, U.S.A.
- 133 I 16 **Weelde**, Belgium
- 133 K 17 **Weert**, Netherlands
- 132 H 11 **Weesp**, Netherlands
- 142 L 8 **Węgorzewo**, Poland
- 142 M 12 **Węgrów**, Poland
- 192 B 8 **Weh**, Indonesia 🏝
- 189 N 3 **Wei**, China ∿
- 187 E 15 **Weichang**, China
- 137 K 20 **Weiden**, Germany
- 187 G 20 **Weifang**, China
- 187 I 19 **Weihai**, China
- 137 J 17 **Weimar**, Germany
- 189 Q 3 **Weinan**, China
- 189 N 9 **Weining**, China
- 231 R 1 **Weipa**, Queensland, Australia
- 61 O 1 **Weirton**, West Virginia, U.S.A.
- 72 J 9 **Weiser**, Idaho, U.S.A.
- 188 K 10 **Weishan**, China
- 189 V 3 **Weishan Hu**, China 💧
- 189 U 3 **Weishi**, China
- 63 R 2 **Weiss Lake**, Alabama, U.S.A. 💧
- 137 I 22 **Weissenburg in Bayern**, Germany
- 137 N 15 **Weisswasser**, Germany
- 133 L 23 **Weiswampach**, Luxembourg
- 139 U 2 **Weitra**, Austria
- 188 J 9 **Weixi**, China
- 189 N 8 **Weixin**, China
- 139 W 7 **Weiz**, Austria
- 142 H 8 **Wejherowo**, Poland
- 233 G 15 **Wekakura Point**, New Zealand ▶
- 61 N 6 **Welch**, West Virginia, U.S.A.
- 213 I 19 **Weldiya**, Ethiopia
- 77 J 22 **Weldon**, California, U.S.A.
- 41 T 2 **Welker Seamount**, Pacific Ocean ▲
- 213 H 21 **Welk'īt'ē**, Ethiopia
- 219 N 12 **Welkom**, Republic of South Africa
- 86 F 14 **Welland Canal**, Ontario, Canada ∿
- 181 G 25 **Wellawaya**, Sri Lanka
- 231 Q 3 **Wellesley Islands**, Queensland, Australia 🏝
- 133 I 23 **Wellin**, Belgium
- 127 V 8 **Wellingborough**, United Kingdom
- 231 U 11 **Wellington**, New South Wales, Australia
- 233 L 16 **Wellington**, New Zealand 🏛
- 233 L 16 **Wellington**, New Zealand ◘
- 127 Q 6 **Wellington**, United Kingdom
- 127 P 12 **Wells**, United Kingdom
- 77 M 15 **Wells**, Nevada, U.S.A.
- 127 Y 5 **Wells-next-the-Sea**, United Kingdom
- 232 K 7 **Wellsford**, New Zealand
- 64 J 12 **Wellston**, Michigan, U.S.A.
- 139 S 4 **Wels**, Austria
- 127 O 6 **Welshpool**, United Kingdom
- 85 P 9 **Wemindji**, Québec, Canada
- 76 J 7 **Wenatchee**, Washington, U.S.A.
- 189 R 15 **Wenchang**, China
- 189 Y 8 **Wencheng**, China
- 188 M 6 **Wenchuan**, China
- 137 E 17 **Wenden**, Germany
- 74 H 12 **Wenden**, Arizona, U.S.A.
- 187 H 19 **Wendeng**, China
- 127 U 10 **Wendover**, United Kingdom
- 77 N 16 **Wendover**, Nevada, U.S.A.
- 138 E 9 **Wengen**, Switzerland
- 189 Z 8 **Wenling**, China
- 237 O 15 **Weno**, Federated States of Micronesia
- 65 F 17 **Wenona**, Illinois, U.S.A.
- 184 J 4 **Wenquan**, China
- 184 L 9 **Wenquan**, China
- 188 M 12 **Wenshan**, China
- 231 R 11 **Wentworth**, New South Wales, Australia
- 69 X 4 **Wentzville**, Missouri, U.S.A.
- 189 S 3 **Wenxi**, China
- 189 N 4 **Wenxian**, China
- 189 Y 8 **Wenzhou**, China
- 133 K 21 **Werbomont**, Belgium
- 218 L 10 **Werda**, Botswana
- 213 L 21 **Werdēr**, Ethiopia
- 139 R 6 **Werfen**, Austria
- 137 E 15 **Werl**, Germany
- 137 K 21 **Wernberg-Köblitz**, Germany
- 137 I 15 **Wernigerode**, Germany
- 213 H 19 **Werota**, Ethiopia
- 137 H 16 **Werra**, Germany ∿
- 137 G 20 **Wertheim**, Germany
- 132 I 9 **Wervershoof**, Netherlands
- 137 B 15 **Wesel**, Germany
- 137 G 15 **Weser**, Germany ∿
- 59 S 4 **Wesley**, Maine, U.S.A.
- 231 O 1 **Wessel Islands**, Northern Territory, Australia 🏝
- 71 Q 7 **West**, Texas, U.S.A.
- 158 B 9 **West Alboran Basin**, Mediterranean Sea ◇
- 240 L 7 **West Antarctica**, Antarctica ◇
- 172 G 9 **West Bank**, Israel ◇
- 62 M 9 **West Bay**, Louisiana, U.S.A. ≈
- 63 Q 7 **West Bay**, Florida, U.S.A.
- 64 G 13 **West Bend**, Wisconsin, U.S.A.
- 183 R 14 **West Bengal**, India ◘
- 127 T 5 **West Bridgford**, United Kingdom
- 127 R 7 **West Bromwich**, United Kingdom
- 73 Q 2 **West Butte**, Montana, U.S.A. ▲
- 233 A 25 **West Cape**, New Zealand ▶
- 40 K 7 **West Caroline Basin**, Pacific Ocean ◇
- 233 E 19 **West Coast**, New Zealand ◘
- 71 S 11 **West Columbia**, Texas, U.S.A.
- 111 J 23 **West Falkland**, Falkland Islands 🏝
- 236 M 15 **West Fayu**, Federated States of Micronesia 🏝
- 73 N 2 **West Glacier**, Montana, U.S.A.
- 59 S 4 **West Grand Lake**, Maine, U.S.A. 💧
- 241 X 6 **West Ice Shelf**, Antarctica ◇
- 39 Y 2 **West Island**, Cocos Islands 🏝
- 39 Y 3 **West Island Settlement**, Cocos Islands
- 65 I 18 **West Lafayette**, Indiana, U.S.A.
- 126 L 14 **West Looe**, United Kingdom
- 86 C 14 **West Lorne**, Ontario, Canada
- 40 K 6 **West Mariana Basin**, Pacific Ocean ◇
- 69 Y 10 **West Memphis**, Arkansas, U.S.A.
- 234 F 5 **West New Britain**, Papua New Guinea ◘
- 219 P 8 **West Nicholson**, Zimbabwe
- 63 Z 12 **West Palm Beach**, Florida, U.S.A.
- 69 V 8 **West Plains**, Missouri, U.S.A.
- 61 U 6 **West Point**, Virginia, U.S.A.
- 63 R 3 **West Point Lake**, Alabama, U.S.A. 💧
- 43 E 22 **West Scotia Ridge**, Atlantic Ocean ⛰
- 38 J 2 **West Sheba Ridge**, Indian Ocean ⛰
- 152 L 9 **West Siberian Plain**, Russian Federation ◇
- 132 I 6 **West-Terschelling**, Netherlands
- 67 U 10 **West Union**, Iowa, U.S.A.
- 61 O 3 **West Virginia**, U.S.A. ◘
- 133 A 18 **West-Vlaanderen**, Belgium ◘
- 231 T 11 **West Wyalong**, New South Wales, Australia
- 73 Q 9 **West Yellowstone**, Montana, U.S.A.
- 64 D 13 **Westby**, Wisconsin, U.S.A.
- 75 R 6 **Westcliffe**, Colorado, U.S.A.
- 132 M 8 **Westerbork**, Netherlands
- 217 T 7 **Western**, Kenya ◘
- 218 L 6 **Western**, Zambia ◘
- 234 B 5 **Western**, Papua New Guinea ◘
- 234 J 6 **Western**, Solomon Islands ◘
- 181 F 25 **Western**, Sri Lanka ◘
- 183 O 9 **Western**, Nepal ◘
- 214 F 12 **Western Area**, Sierra Leone ◘
- 230 J 7 **Western Australia**, Australia ◘
- 213 C 21 **Western Bahr el Ghazal**, Sudan ◘
- 218 L 14 **Western Cape**, Republic of South Africa ◘
- 213 A 17 **Western Darfur**, Sudan ◘
- 212 C 9 **Western Desert**, Egypt ◇
- 148 F 11 **Western Dvina**, Belarus/Latvia ∿
- 213 D 22 **Western Equatoria**, Sudan ◘
- 181 C 17 **Western Ghats**, India ⛰
- 41 X 14 **Western Harbour**, Pitcairn Island ≈
- 234 C 4 **Western Highlands**, Papua New Guinea ◘
- 213 D 19 **Western Kordofan**, Sudan ◘
- 210 C 12 **Western Sahara**, Africa □
- 133 D 16 **Westerschelde**, Netherlands ≈
- 58 B 9 **Westfield**, New York, U.S.A.
- 132 K 5 **Westgat**, Netherlands ≈
- 66 J 2 **Westhope**, North Dakota, U.S.A.
- 133 G 16 **Westmalle**, Belgium
- 61 T 2 **Westminster**, Maryland, U.S.A.
- 61 O 3 **Weston**, West Virginia, U.S.A.
- 127 O 11 **Weston-super-Mare**, United Kingdom
- 233 G 17 **Westport**, New Zealand
- 125 B 17 **Westport**, Republic of Ireland
- 76 E 7 **Westport**, Washington, U.S.A.
- 124 I 6 **Westray**, United Kingdom 🏝
- 84 H 8 **Westray**, Manitoba, Canada
- 86 D 7 **Westree**, Ontario, Canada
- 65 I 16 **Westville**, Indiana, U.S.A.
- 126 L 12 **Westward Ho!**, United Kingdom
- 193 R 14 **Wetar**, Indonesia 🏝
- 83 J 19 **Wetaskiwin**, Alberta, Canada
- 217 X 11 **Wete**, Tanzania
- 127 S 2 **Wetherby**, United Kingdom
- 137 E 18 **Wetzlar**, Germany
- 133 C 19 **Wevelgem**, Belgium
- 78 M 3 **Wevok**, Alaska, U.S.A.
- 63 S 8 **Wewahitchka**, Florida, U.S.A.
- 234 C 3 **Wewak**, Papua New Guinea
- 69 O 11 **Wewoka**, Oklahoma, U.S.A.
- 125 E 20 **Wexford**, Republic of Ireland
- 83 N 19 **Weyburn**, Saskatchewan, Canada
- 139 U 5 **Weyer Markt**, Austria
- 137 D 17 **Weyerbusch**, Germany
- 127 Q 14 **Weymouth**, United Kingdom
- 59 O 10 **Weymouth**, Massachusetts, U.S.A.
- 87 T 11 **Weymouth**, Nova Scotia, Canada
- 127 Q 14 **Weymouth Bay**, United Kingdom ≈
- 82 G 12 **Wha Ti**, Northwest Territories, Canada
- 232 M 11 **Whakamaru**, New Zealand
- 232 J 6 **Whakapara**, New Zealand
- 233 M 15 **Whakataki**, New Zealand
- 232 N 10 **Whakatane**, New Zealand
- 232 N 13 **Whakatu**, New Zealand
- 84 L 4 **Whale Cove**, Nunavut, Canada
- 124 K 4 **Whalsay**, United Kingdom 🏝
- 232 M 9 **Whangamata**, New Zealand
- 232 K 12 **Whangamomona**, New Zealand
- 233 H 15 **Whanganui Inlet**, New Zealand ≈
- 232 O 10 **Whangaparaoa**, New Zealand
- 232 O 11 **Whangara**, New Zealand
- 232 J 6 **Whangarei**, New Zealand
- 127 U 1 **Wharram le Street**, United Kingdom
- 39 R 7 **Wharton Basin**, Indian Ocean ◇
- 70 M 2 **Wheeler**, Texas, U.S.A.
- 63 P 1 **Wheeler Lake**, Alabama, U.S.A. 💧
- 75 R 8 **Wheeler Peak**, New Mexico, U.S.A. ▲
- 77 N 18 **Wheeler Peak**, Nevada, U.S.A. ▲
- 61 O 1 **Wheeling**, West Virginia, U.S.A.
- 65 G 15 **Wheeling**, Illinois, U.S.A.
- 232 L 8 **Whenuakite**, New Zealand
- 127 Q 1 **Whernside**, United Kingdom ▲
- 127 N 13 **Whiddon Down**, United Kingdom
- 232 I 6 **Whirinaki**, New Zealand
- 83 G 21 **Whistler**, British Columbia, Canada
- 125 L 16 **Whitby**, United Kingdom
- 127 P 5 **Whitchurch**, United Kingdom
- 127 T 12 **Whitchurch**, United Kingdom
- 66 H 10 **White**, South Dakota, U.S.A. ∿
- 85 X 10 **White Bay**, Newfoundland and Labrador, Canada ≈
- 66 H 6 **White Butte**, North Dakota, U.S.A. ▲
- 59 Q 3 **White Cap Mountain**, Maine, U.S.A. ▲
- 76 G 13 **White City**, Oregon, U.S.A.
- 231 R 10 **White Cliffs**, New South Wales, Australia
- 87 X 8 **White Hill**, Nova Scotia, Canada ▲
- 232 N 9 **White Island**, New Zealand 🏝
- 62 I 8 **White Lake**, Louisiana, U.S.A. 💧
- 77 K 20 **White Mountain**, California, U.S.A. ▲
- 59 N 6 **White Mountains**, New Hampshire, U.S.A. ⛰
- 213 F 18 **White Nile**, Sudan ◘
- 213 D 21 **White Nile**, Sudan ∿
- 76 I 9 **White Salmon**, Oregon, U.S.A.
- 45 W 13 **White Sea**, Arctic Ocean 🌊
- 154 I 5 **White Sea**, Russian Federation 🌊
- 61 P 5 **White Sulphur Springs**, West Virginia, U.S.A.
- 73 R 6 **White Sulphur Springs**, Montana, U.S.A.
- 83 J 18 **Whitecourt**, Alberta, Canada
- 58 K 6 **Whiteface Mountain**, New York, U.S.A. ▲
- 72 M 2 **Whitefish**, Montana, U.S.A.
- 64 K 8 **Whitefish Bay**, Michigan, U.S.A. ≈
- 64 J 8 **Whitefish Point**, Michigan, U.S.A.
- 58 K 7 **Whitehall**, New York, U.S.A.
- 64 D 12 **Whitehall**, Wisconsin, U.S.A.
- 125 H 15 **Whitehaven**, United Kingdom
- 83 B 14 **Whitehorse**, Yukon Territory, Canada
- 74 L 12 **Whiteriver**, Arizona, U.S.A.
- 60 A 10 **Whiteville**, Tennessee, U.S.A.
- 61 S 11 **Whiteville**, North Carolina, U.S.A.
- 75 N 13 **Whitewater Baldy**, New Mexico, U.S.A. ▲
- 125 H 15 **Whithorn**, United Kingdom
- 61 N 11 **Whitmire**, South Carolina, U.S.A.
- 86 G 10 **Whitney**, Ontario, Canada
- 126 L 15 **Whitsand Bay**, United Kingdom ≈
- 231 U 5 **Whitsunday Group**, Queensland, Australia 🏝
- 64 L 12 **Whittemore**, Michigan, U.S.A.
- 79 R 9 **Whittier**, Alaska, U.S.A.
- 127 V 7 **Whittlesey**, United Kingdom
- 82 K 12 **Wholdaia Lake**, Northwest Territories, Canada 💧
- 231 P 11 **Whyalla**, South Australia, Australia
- 191 G 14 **Wiang Pa Pao**, Thailand
- 190 G 13 **Wiang Phran**, Thailand
- 86 D 11 **Wiarton**, Ontario, Canada
- 73 Z 5 **Wibaux**, Montana, U.S.A.
- 69 N 6 **Wichita**, Kansas, U.S.A.
- 71 N 4 **Wichita**, Texas, U.S.A. ∿
- 71 O 4 **Wichita Falls**, Texas, U.S.A.
- 68 L 11 **Wichita Mountains**, Oklahoma, U.S.A. ⛰
- 124 I 8 **Wick**, United Kingdom
- 74 I 12 **Wickenburg**, Arizona, U.S.A.
- 127 Z 8 **Wickham Market**, United Kingdom
- 60 B 7 **Wickliffe**, Kentucky, U.S.A.
- 125 F 19 **Wicklow Head**, Republic of Ireland ▶
- 127 P 4 **Widnes**, United Kingdom
- 137 E 15 **Wiedenbrück**, Germany
- 137 D 17 **Wiehl**, Germany
- 136 L 7 **Wiek**, Germany
- 142 L 10 **Wielbark**, Poland
- 143 I 15 **Wieluń**, Poland
- 139 X 5 **Wiener Neustadt**, Austria
- 143 M 14 **Wieprz**, Poland ∿
- 137 E 19 **Wiesbaden**, Germany
- 137 C 18 **Wiesemscheid**, Germany
- 137 F 21 **Wiesloch**, Germany
- 127 P 3 **Wigan**, United Kingdom
- 75 S 3 **Wiggins**, Colorado, U.S.A.
- 127 T 7 **Wigston**, United Kingdom
- 133 K 14 **Wijchen**, Netherlands
- 132 J 13 **Wijk bij Duurstede**, Netherlands
- 213 I 17 **Wik'ro**, Ethiopia
- 138 H 6 **Wil**, Switzerland
- 76 J 7 **Wilbur**, Washington, U.S.A.
- 231 R 10 **Wilcannia**, New South Wales, Australia
- 136 E 12 **Wildeshausen**, Germany
- 138 D 9 **Wildhorn**, Switzerland ▲
- 139 W 8 **Wildon**, Austria
- 138 L 8 **Wildspitze**, Austria ▲
- 83 I 18 **Wildwood**, Alberta, Canada
- 105 V 7 **Wilhelmina Gebergte**, Suriname ⛰
- 136 E 10 **Wilhelmshaven**, Germany
- 58 H 11 **Wilkes Barre**, Pennsylvania, U.S.A.
- 241 W 13 **Wilkes Coast**, Antarctica ◇
- 241 V 12 **Wilkes Land**, Antarctica ◇
- 61 O 8 **Wilkesboro**, North Carolina, U.S.A.
- 76 F 11 **Willamette**, Oregon, U.S.A. ∿

□ Country ◘ Internal administrative region: State/Province/Territory/Dependent territory 🏛 Capital city ⛰ Mountain range/Undersea ridge ▲ Mountain peak/Volcano/Seamount ◇ Geographic feature ▶ Headland/Point/Cape/Peninsula ∴ Desert 🏝 Island/Island group ⁂ Antarctic base Ⓞ Ocean 🌊 Sea ≈ Bay/Gulf/Channel/Strait 💧 Lake ⚐ Salt pan/Dry/Intermittent lake ∿ River

76 E 8 **Willapa Bay**, Washington, U.S.A. ≈
65 M 17 **Willard**, Ohio, U.S.A.
75 Q 11 **Willard**, New Mexico, U.S.A.
74 M 14 **Willcox**, Arizona, U.S.A.
133 F 18 **Willebroek**, Belgium
93 S 13 **Willemstad**, Netherlands Antilles 🏛
127 P 8 **Willersley**, United Kingdom
231 O 9 **William Creek**, South Australia, Australia
230 G 11 **Williams**, Western Australia, Australia
74 J 10 **Williams**, Arizona, U.S.A.
77 G 18 **Williams**, California, U.S.A.
83 F 20 **Williams Lake**, British Columbia, Canada
60 K 7 **Williamsburg**, Kentucky, U.S.A.
61 U 6 **Williamsburg**, Virginia, U.S.A.
60 L 6 **Williamson**, Kentucky, U.S.A.
58 F 11 **Williamsport**, Pennsylvania, U.S.A.
61 U 9 **Williamston**, North Carolina, U.S.A.
218 K 14 **Williston**, Republic of South Africa
63 V 8 **Williston**, Florida, U.S.A.
66 G 3 **Williston**, North Dakota, U.S.A.
83 F 17 **Williston Lake**, British Columbia, Canada ∿
127 O 12 **Williton**, United Kingdom
77 F 17 **Willits**, California, U.S.A.
67 Q 8 **Willmar**, Minnesota, U.S.A.
77 F 15 **Willow Creek**, California, U.S.A.
58 E 13 **Willow Hill**, Pennsylvania, U.S.A.
69 V 7 **Willow Springs**, Missouri, U.S.A.
218 M 15 **Willowmore**, Republic of South Africa
77 G 17 **Willows**, California, U.S.A.
61 W 1 **Wilmington**, Delaware, U.S.A.
61 T 12 **Wilmington**, North Carolina, U.S.A.
65 G 17 **Wilmington**, Illinois, U.S.A.
65 L 19 **Wilmington**, Ohio, U.S.A.
65 O 17 **Wilmott**, Ohio, U.S.A.
127 R 4 **Wilmslow**, United Kingdom
61 T 9 **Wilson**, North Carolina, U.S.A.
231 S 14 **Wilsons Promontory**, Victoria, Australia ▶
127 R 12 **Wilton**, United Kingdom
59 P 5 **Wilton**, Maine, U.S.A.
66 J 5 **Wilton**, North Dakota, U.S.A.
133 K 24 **Wiltz**, Luxembourg
230 H 8 **Wiluna**, Western Australia, Australia
233 M 15 **Wimbledon**, New Zealand
127 R 13 **Wimborne Minster**, United Kingdom
65 I 17 **Winamac**, Indiana, U.S.A.
219 N 12 **Winburg**, Republic of South Africa
127 Q 12 **Wincanton**, United Kingdom
127 Y 12 **Winchelsea**, United Kingdom
127 S 12 **Winchester**, United Kingdom
60 J 5 **Winchester**, Kentucky, U.S.A.
60 G 10 **Winchester**, Tennessee, U.S.A.
61 S 3 **Winchester**, Virginia, U.S.A.
72 K 6 **Winchester**, Idaho, U.S.A.
73 R 11 **Wind River Range**, Wyoming, U.S.A. ⛰
63 T 2 **Winder**, Georgia, U.S.A.
127 P 1 **Windermere**, United Kingdom
218 I 9 **Windhoek**, Namibia 🏛
84 K 9 **Windigo Lake**, Ontario, Canada ∿
139 T 5 **Windischgarsten**, Austria
67 Q 10 **Windom**, Minnesota, U.S.A.
231 R 7 **Windorah**, Queensland, Australia
127 U 11 **Windsor**, United Kingdom
58 L 10 **Windsor**, Connecticut, U.S.A.
61 U 8 **Windsor**, North Carolina, U.S.A.
86 B 14 **Windsor**, Ontario, Canada
87 U 10 **Windsor**, Nova Scotia, Canada
93 Z 9 **Windward Islands**, Caribbean 🏝
93 N 7 **Windward Passage**, Cuba ≈
69 O 7 **Winfield**, Kansas, U.S.A.
86 C 12 **Wingham**, Ontario, Canada
73 S 4 **Winifred**, Montana, U.S.A.
84 M 9 **Winisk**, Ontario, Canada ∫
85 N 8 **Winisk**, Ontario, Canada
191 F 17 **Winkana**, Myanmar
139 Q 8 **Winklern**, Austria
77 K 15 **Winnemucca**, Nevada, U.S.A.
77 J 16 **Winnemucca Lake**, Nevada, U.S.A. ∿
66 K 10 **Winner**, South Dakota, U.S.A.
73 T 5 **Winnett**, Montana, U.S.A.
86 G 8 **Winneway**, Québec, Canada
62 I 5 **Winnfield**, Louisiana, U.S.A.
71 U 10 **Winnie**, Texas, U.S.A.
84 J 10 **Winnipeg**, Manitoba, Canada
62 J 5 **Winnsboro**, Louisiana, U.S.A.
57 S 12 **Winona**, Mississippi, U.S.A.
67 U 9 **Winona**, Minnesota, U.S.A.
132 O 7 **Winschoten**, Netherlands
136 H 11 **Winsen**, Germany
59 Q 5 **Winslow**, Maine, U.S.A.
74 K 10 **Winslow**, Arizona, U.S.A.
58 K 10 **Winsted**, Connecticut, U.S.A.
61 P 8 **Winston-Salem**, North Carolina, U.S.A.
63 W 9 **Winter Park**, Florida, U.S.A.
67 S 13 **Winterset**, Iowa, U.S.A.
132 N 13 **Winterswijk**, Netherlands
138 G 6 **Winterthur**, Switzerland
231 R 6 **Winton**, Queensland, Australia
233 C 25 **Winton**, New Zealand
61 U 8 **Winton**, North Carolina, U.S.A.
127 W 6 **Wisbech**, United Kingdom
59 Q 6 **Wiscasset**, Maine, U.S.A.
64 D 12 **Wisconsin**, U.S.A. ▣
64 E 12 **Wisconsin Rapids**, Wisconsin, U.S.A.
73 N 7 **Wisdom**, Montana, U.S.A.
60 L 7 **Wise**, Virginia, U.S.A.
79 Q 5 **Wiseman**, Alaska, U.S.A.
66 L 6 **Wishek**, North Dakota, U.S.A.
143 I 18 **Wisła**, Poland
136 J 9 **Wismar**, Germany
62 K 5 **Wisner**, Louisiana, U.S.A.
129 X 4 **Wissembourg**, France
142 O 13 **Wisznice**, Poland
127 V 5 **Witham**, United Kingdom ∫
127 N 13 **Witheridge**, United Kingdom
127 W 2 **Withernsea**, United Kingdom
127 S 9 **Witney**, United Kingdom
64 F 11 **Wittenberg**, Wisconsin, U.S.A.
136 J 12 **Wittenberge**, Germany
136 I 10 **Wittenburg**, Germany
230 G 6 **Wittenoom**, Western Australia, Australia
137 C 19 **Wittlich**, Germany
136 K 11 **Wittstock**, Germany
234 F 4 **Witu Islands**, Papua New Guinea 🏝
218 J 9 **Witvlei**, Namibia
137 G 16 **Witzenhausen**, Germany
142 J 11 **Wkra**, Poland ∫
142 H 7 **Władysławowo**, Poland
142 I 12 **Włocławek**, Poland
143 O 14 **Włodawa**, Poland
143 J 15 **Włoszczowa**, Poland
231 T 12 **Wodonga**, Victoria, Australia
143 K 16 **Wodzisław**, Poland
143 I 17 **Wodzisław Śląski**, Poland
132 H 12 **Woerden**, Netherlands
138 F 6 **Wohlen**, Switzerland
241 R 2 **Wohlthat Mountains**, Antarctica ⛰
193 V 13 **Wokam**, Indonesia 🏝
186 N 10 **Woken**, China
127 V 11 **Woking**, United Kingdom
127 U 11 **Wokingham**, United Kingdom
136 M 10 **Woldegk**, Germany
236 L 15 **Woleai**, Federated States of Micronesia 🏝
216 F 6 **Woleu-Ntem**, Gabon ▣
73 P 5 **Wolf Creek**, Montana, U.S.A.
79 P 6 **Wolf Mountain**, Alaska, U.S.A. ▲
73 X 3 **Wolf Point**, Montana, U.S.A.
139 U 8 **Wolfsberg**, Austria
136 I 13 **Wolfsburg**, Germany
87 U 10 **Wolfville**, Nova Scotia, Canada
136 M 9 **Wolgast**, Germany
138 F 7 **Wolhusen**, Switzerland
142 D 9 **Wolin**, Poland
83 L 14 **Wollaston Lake**, Saskatchewan, Canada ∿
82 H 7 **Wollaston Peninsula**, Nunavut, Canada ▶
231 P 3 **Wollogorang Roadhouse**, Northern Territory, Australia
231 U 12 **Wollongong**, New South Wales, Australia
143 F 14 **Wołów**, Poland
66 M 9 **Wolsey**, South Dakota, U.S.A.
142 F 13 **Wolsztyn**, Poland
132 K 8 **Wolvega**, Netherlands
127 R 7 **Wolverhampton**, United Kingdom
230 G 10 **Wongan Hills**, Western Australia, Australia
187 M 19 **Wonju**, South Korea
83 G 16 **Wonowon**, British Columbia, Canada
187 L 17 **Wŏnsan**, North Korea
231 S 14 **Wonthaggi**, Victoria, Australia
63 N 1 **Woodall Mountain**, Mississippi, U.S.A. ▲
58 I 15 **Woodbine**, New Jersey, U.S.A.
63 V 6 **Woodbine**, Georgia, U.S.A.
127 Z 8 **Woodbridge**, United Kingdom
61 T 4 **Woodbridge**, Virginia, U.S.A.
76 G 10 **Woodburn**, Oregon, U.S.A.
233 H 20 **Woodend**, New Zealand
59 S 4 **Woodland**, Maine, U.S.A.
76 G 9 **Woodland**, Washington, U.S.A.
77 G 18 **Woodland**, California, U.S.A.
234 H 6 **Woodlark Island**, Papua New Guinea 🏝
64 E 9 **Woodruff**, Wisconsin, U.S.A.
65 O 19 **Woodsfield**, Ohio, U.S.A.
233 H 16 **Woodstock**, New Zealand
127 S 9 **Woodstock**, United Kingdom
61 S 3 **Woodstock**, Virginia, U.S.A.
65 F 15 **Woodstock**, Illinois, U.S.A.
86 D 13 **Woodstock**, Ontario, Canada
87 R 9 **Woodstock**, New Brunswick, Canada
233 L 14 **Woodville**, New Zealand
62 K 6 **Woodville**, Mississippi, U.S.A.
71 U 8 **Woodville**, Texas, U.S.A.
68 K 8 **Woodward**, Oklahoma, U.S.A.
193 W 11 **Woöi**, Indonesia
231 F 10 **Woomera**, South Australia, Australia
59 N 10 **Woonsocket**, Rhode Island, U.S.A.
230 F 8 **Wooramel Roadhouse**, Western Australia, Australia
65 N 17 **Wooster**, Ohio, U.S.A.
213 L 19 **Woqooyi Galbeed**, Somalia ▣
218 K 15 **Worcester**, Republic of South Africa
127 R 8 **Worcester**, United Kingdom
59 N 10 **Worcester**, Massachusetts, U.S.A.
139 O 6 **Wörgl**, Austria
193 V 14 **Workai**, Indonesia 🏝
125 H 15 **Workington**, United Kingdom
127 T 4 **Worksop**, United Kingdom
132 J 8 **Workum**, Netherlands
73 U 10 **Worland**, Wyoming, U.S.A.
137 E 20 **Worms**, Germany
126 L 10 **Worms Head**, United Kingdom ▶
127 V 13 **Worthing**, United Kingdom
67 Q 10 **Worthington**, Minnesota, U.S.A.
237 W 2 **Wotho**, Marshall Islands 🏝
237 Y 2 **Wotje**, Marshall Islands 🏝
193 O 12 **Wotu**, Indonesia
193 P 13 **Wowoni**, Indonesia 🏝
127 V 4 **Wragby**, United Kingdom
153 Y 5 **Wrangel Island**, Russian Federation 🏝
45 T 5 **Wrangel Sea**, Arctic Ocean ≋
79 Y 11 **Wrangell**, Alaska, U.S.A.
79 S 8 **Wrangell Mountains**, Alaska, U.S.A. ⛰
127 W 5 **Wrangle**, United Kingdom
75 U 3 **Wray**, Colorado, U.S.A.
218 I 13 **Wreck Point**, Republic of South Africa ▶
63 V 3 **Wrens**, Georgia, U.S.A.
127 P 5 **Wrexham**, United Kingdom
197 L 15 **Wright**, Philippines
73 X 10 **Wright**, Wyoming, U.S.A.
240 K 10 **Wright Island**, Antarctica 🏝
71 T 5 **Wright Patman Lake**, Texas, U.S.A. ∿
181 N 21 **Wrightmyo**, India
82 E 12 **Wrigley**, Northwest Territories, Canada
143 G 15 **Wrocław**, Poland
142 F 12 **Wronki**, Poland
142 H 12 **Września**, Poland
142 F 13 **Wschowa**, Poland
189 P 7 **Wu**, China ∫
189 T 2 **Wu'an**, China
230 G 10 **Wubin**, Western Australia, Australia
186 G 10 **Wuchagou**, China
186 L 12 **Wuchang**, China
187 A 15 **Wuchuan**, China
189 R 14 **Wuchuan**, China
187 F 14 **Wudan**, China
175 R 11 **Wuday'ah**, Saudi Arabia
187 E 19 **Wudi**, China
215 S 10 **Wudil**, Nigeria
188 L 10 **Wuding**, China
189 N 4 **Wudu**, China
189 R 7 **Wufeng**, China
189 R 9 **Wugang**, China
185 R 7 **Wuhai**, China
189 U 6 **Wuhan**, China
189 W 4 **Wuhe**, China
189 X 6 **Wuhu**, China
189 V 11 **Wuhua**, China
215 S 12 **Wukari**, Nigeria
187 H 20 **Wuleidao Wan**, China ≈
188 K 11 **Wuliang Shan**, China ⛰
193 T 14 **Wuliaru**, Indonesia 🏝
139 T 2 **Wullowitz**, Austria
215 S 13 **Wum**, Cameroon
188 M 10 **Wumeng Shan**, China ⛰
189 P 12 **Wuming**, China
213 C 20 **Wun Rog**, Sudan
189 V 10 **Wuping**, China
137 C 16 **Wuppertal**, Germany
137 H 20 **Würzburg**, Germany
137 L 16 **Wurzen**, Germany
189 R 6 **Wushan**, China
189 T 11 **Wushi**, China
43 L 18 **Wüst Seamount**, Atlantic Ocean ▲
187 B 17 **Wutai Shan**, China ▲
133 G 16 **Wuustwezel**, Belgium
234 B 2 **Wuvulu Island**, Papua New Guinea 🏝
189 W 6 **Wuwei**, China
189 Y 5 **Wuxi**, China
189 Q 6 **Wuxi**, China
189 P 13 **Wuxu**, China
189 R 12 **Wuxuan**, China
189 V 10 **Wuyi Shan**, China ⛰
186 M 8 **Wuyiling**, China
189 X 8 **Wuyishan**, China
189 W 7 **Wuyuan**, China
187 A 17 **Wuzhai**, China
185 Q 7 **Wuzhong**, China
189 S 12 **Wuzhou**, China
231 T 8 **Wyandra**, Queensland, Australia
127 P 8 **Wye**, United Kingdom ∫
127 Y 12 **Wye**, United Kingdom
230 K 3 **Wyndham**, Western Australia, Australia
69 X 10 **Wynne**, Arkansas, U.S.A.
73 V 8 **Wyola**, Montana, U.S.A.
65 J 14 **Wyoming**, Michigan, U.S.A.
73 U 11 **Wyoming**, U.S.A. ▣
73 Q 11 **Wyoming Range**, Wyoming, U.S.A. ⛰
142 L 12 **Wyszków**, Poland
142 K 12 **Wyszogród**, Poland
61 O 7 **Wytheville**, Virginia, U.S.A.
143 M 15 **Wyżyna Lubelska**, Poland ⛰
143 J 17 **Wyżyna Małopolska**, Poland ⛰

X

89 Z 10 **X-Can**, Mexico
218 I 3 **Xá-Muteba**, Angola
213 O 19 **Xaafuun**, Somalia
90 G 4 **Xaclbal**, Guatemala ∫
171 Y 7 **Xaşşmaz**, Azerbaijan
219 Q 10 **Xai-Xai**, Mozambique
184 K 10 **Xainza**, China
190 K 13 **Xam Hua**, Laos
108 K 12 **Xambioá**, Brazil
218 G 6 **Xangongo**, Angola
171 W 9 **Xankändi**, Azerbaijan
137 B 15 **Xanten**, Germany
146 I 13 **Xanthi**, Greece
112 H 9 **Xanxeré**, Brazil
213 N 23 **Xarardheere**, Somalia
188 K 4 **Xar'oi**, China
131 T 9 **Xàtiva**, Spain
184 J 11 **Xêgar**, China
65 L 19 **Xenia**, Ohio, U.S.A.
218 M 8 **Xhumo**, Botswana
186 E 12 **Xi Ujimqin Qi**, China
189 X 11 **Xiamen**, China
189 Q 4 **Xi'an**, China
189 Q 7 **Xianfeng**, China
189 T 10 **Xiang**, China ∫
188 J 7 **Xiangcheng**, China
189 S 5 **Xiangfan**, China
191 J 14 **Xiangkhoang**, Laos
191 J 14 **Xiangkhoang Plateau**, Laos ◇
189 Z 7 **Xiangshan**, China
189 X 3 **Xiangshui**, China
189 T 8 **Xiangtan**, China
189 V 8 **Xiangtang**, China
189 Y 7 **Xianju**, China
189 T 7 **Xianning**, China
189 T 7 **Xiantao**, China
189 W 8 **Xianxia Ling**, China ⛰
189 Q 3 **Xianyang**, China
189 X 10 **Xianyou**, China
185 W 1 **Xiao Higgan Ling**, China ⛰
186 K 6 **Xiao Hinggan Range**, China ⛰
186 I 8 **Xiao'ergou**, China
189 U 6 **Xiaogan**, China
188 L 6 **Xiaojin**, China
189 V 3 **Xiaoxian**, China
189 S 1 **Xiaoyi**, China
189 Y 9 **Xiapu**, China
188 L 8 **Xichang**, China
189 N 12 **Xichou**, China
187 J 14 **Xifeng**, China
189 O 9 **Xifeng**, China
189 P 2 **Xifeng**, China
184 K 10 **Xigazê**, China
186 K 10 **Xiji**, China
186 B 13 **Xil**, China
189 N 11 **Xilin**, China
186 D 13 **Xilinhot**, China
185 O 6 **Ximiao**, China
186 F 9 **Xin Barag Zuoqi**, China
186 C 13 **Xin Hot**, China
187 J 15 **Xinbin**, China
187 E 14 **Xinbo**, China
189 S 11 **Xindu**, China
189 R 10 **Xing'an**, China
189 V 8 **Xingan**, China
187 G 16 **Xingcheng**, China
189 V 10 **Xingguo**, China
187 C 16 **Xinghe**, China
189 X 4 **Xinghua**, China
187 E 16 **Xinglong**, China
186 K 10 **Xinglongzhen**, China
189 V 11 **Xingning**, China
189 R 6 **Xingshan**, China
189 U 1 **Xingtai**, China
187 C 18 **Xingtang**, China
108 I 13 **Xingu**, Brazil ∫
108 J 12 **Xinguara**, Brazil
189 N 10 **Xingyi**, China
189 Q 9 **Xinhuang**, China
185 P 8 **Xining**, China
189 S 2 **Xinjiang**, China
184 I 6 **Xinjiang Uygur**, China ▣
188 M 6 **Xinjin**, China
186 O 8 **Xinlincun**, China
187 H 15 **Xinlitun**, China
188 K 6 **Xinlong**, China
187 I 15 **Xinmin**, China
186 M 8 **Xinqing**, China
189 S 9 **Xinshao**, China
189 W 2 **Xintai**, China
189 T 3 **Xinxiang**, China
189 S 12 **Xinxing**, China
189 U 5 **Xinyang**, China
189 W 3 **Xinyi**, China
189 Q 15 **Xinying**, China
189 U 9 **Xinyu**, China
184 J 4 **Xinyuan**, China
186 L 13 **Xinzhan**, China
186 H 7 **Xinzhangfang**, China
189 T 3 **Xinzheng**, China
185 R 6 **Xinzhoa**, China ▲
187 A 18 **Xinzhou**, China
187 T 4 **Xiping**, China
188 K 2 **Xiqing Shan**, China ⛰
109 M 14 **Xique-Xique**, Brazil
189 O 8 **Xishui**, China
189 V 6 **Xishui**, China
214 E 10 **Xitole**, Guinea-Bissau
189 X 7 **Xiuning**, China
189 Q 8 **Xiushan**, China
189 U 7 **Xiushui**, China
189 T 3 **Xiuwu**, China
187 I 16 **Xiuyan**, China
189 S 4 **Xixia**, China
189 U 5 **Xixian**, China
189 P 5 **Xixiang**, China
187 H 17 **Xizhong Dao**, China 🏝
213 M 19 **Xjis**, Somalia
171 U 10 **Xok**, Azerbaijan
191 N 21 **Xom Duc Hanh**, Vietnam
184 L 7 **Xorkol**, China
189 Q 7 **Xuan'en**, China
187 C 16 **Xuanhua**, China

□ Country ▣ Internal administrative region: State/Province/Territory/Dependent territory 🏛 Capital city ⛰ Mountain range/Undersea ridge ▲ Mountain peak/Volcano/Seamount ◇ Geographic feature ▶ Headland/Point/Cape/Peninsula ∴ Desert 🏝 Island/Island group ⁂ Antarctic base 🌊 Ocean ≋ Sea ≈ Bay/Gulf/Channel/Strait ∿ Lake ⚑ Salt pan/Dry/Intermittent lake ∫ River

188	M 10	**Xuanwei**, China
189	X 6	**Xuanzhou**, China
189	T 4	**Xuchang**, China
213	L 23	**Xuddur**, Somalia
213	N 20	**Xudun**, Somalia
189	W 3	**Xuecheng**, China
189	X 3	**Xugou**, China
186	L 7	**Xunhe**, China
186	L 7	**Xunke**, China
189	V 11	**Xunwu**, China
189	Q 5	**Xunyang**, China
189	Q 3	**Xunyi**, China
189	R 8	**Xupu**, China
189	R 14	**Xuwen**, China
189	N 8	**Xuyong**, China
189	W 3	**Xuzhou**, China
147	F 20	**Xylokastro**, Greece

Y

188	L 7	**Ya'an**, China
213	I 23	**Yabēlo**, Ethiopia
146	H 8	**Yablanitsa**, Bulgaria
215	P 10	**Yabo**, Nigeria
172	I 6	**Yabrūd**, Syria
186	L 12	**Yabuli**, China
76	F 11	**Yachats**, Oregon, U.S.A.
189	Q 15	**Yacheng**, China
107	L 23	**Yacuiba**, Bolivia
107	J 18	**Yacuma**, Bolivia ∿
186	I 8	**Yadong**, China
157	P 1	**Yadrin**, Russian Federation
199	M 26	**Yaeyama-rettō**, Japan 🏝
211	S 8	**Yafran**, Libya
43	E 21	**Yaghan Basin**, Atlantic Ocean ◇
198	J 4	**Yagishiri-tō**, Japan 🏝
153	W 9	**Yagodnoye**, Russian Federation
83	I 21	**Yahk**, British Columbia, Canada
151	R 4	**Yahotyn**, Ukraine
216	M 7	**Yahuma**, Democratic Republic of Congo
199	J 17	**Yaizu**, Japan
188	K 6	**Yajiang**, China
216	J 5	**Yaka**, Central African Republic
186	G 8	**Yakeshi**, China
76	I 8	**Yakima**, Washington, U.S.A.
177	Q 12	**Yakmach**, Pakistan
146	G 11	**Yakoruda**, Bulgaria
199	D 25	**Yaku-shima**, Japan 🏝
198	I 7	**Yakumo**, Japan
79	U 10	**Yakutat**, Alaska, U.S.A.
153	T 10	**Yakutsk**, Russian Federation
151	V 9	**Yakymivka**, Ukraine
191	I 26	**Yala**, Thailand
217	N 8	**Yaleko**, Democratic Republic of Congo
216	M 4	**Yalinga**, Central African Republic
216	I 4	**Yaloké**, Central African Republic
170	E 8	**Yalova**, Turkey
151	U 13	**Yalta**, Ukraine
187	J 16	**Yalu**, China ∿
152	J 11	**Yalutorovsk**, Russian Federation
170	F 11	**Yalvaş**, Turkey
198	L 10	**Yamada**, Japan
199	C 22	**Yamaga**, Japan
198	K 12	**Yamagata**, Japan
199	C 20	**Yamaguchi**, Japan
157	X 2	**Yamantau**, Russian Federation ▲
199	N 22	**Yamato**, Japan
213	C 23	**Yambio**, Sudan
146	L 10	**Yambol**, Bulgaria ▣
146	L 9	**Yambol**, Bulgaria
152	M 8	**Yamburg**, Russian Federation
193	T 14	**Yamdena**, Indonesia 🏝
196	H 1	**Y'ami**, Philippines 🏝
214	K 13	**Yamoussoukro**, Côte d'Ivoire ♜
75	N 3	**Yampa**, Colorado, U.S.A. ∿
151	N 7	**Yampil'**, Ukraine
151	T 1	**Yampil'**, Ukraine
182	L 11	**Yamuna**, India ∿
184	L 11	**Yamzho Yumco**, China 💧
187	E 16	**Yan Shan**, China ⛰
153	T 8	**Yana**, Russian Federation ∿
234	H 7	**Yanaba Island**, Papua New Guinea 🏝
199	E 20	**Yanadani**, Japan
199	D 20	**Yanai**, Japan
181	H 19	**Yanam**, India
189	Q 2	**Yan'an**, China
155	S 14	**Yanaul**, Russian Federation
174	K 6	**Yanbu' al Baḩr**, Saudi Arabia
189	Y 4	**Yancheng**, China
185	N 7	**Yanchiwan**, China
189	R 1	**Yanchuan**, China
216	I 9	**Yandja**, Democratic Republic of Congo
216	K 3	**Yangalia**, Central African Republic
217	N 7	**Yangambi**, Democratic Republic of Congo
184	L 10	**Yangbajain**, China
188	J 10	**Yangbi**, China
189	S 3	**Yangcheng**, China
189	S 13	**Yangchun**, China
186	O 11	**Yanggang**, China
187	C 16	**Yanggao**, China
189	V 2	**Yanggu**, China
189	S 13	**Yangjiang**, China
189	T 1	**Yangquan**, China
189	T 11	**Yangshan**, China
189	R 11	**Yangshuo**, China
189	V 7	**Yangtze**, China ∿
188	L 11	**Yangwu**, China
189	P 4	**Yangxian**, China
189	U 7	**Yangxin**, China
187	M 18	**Yangyang**, South Korea
187	C 16	**Yangyuan**, China
189	X 5	**Yangzhou**, China
189	Q 8	**Yanhe**, China
186	M 13	**Yanji**, China
188	M 8	**Yanjin**, China
188	J 7	**Yanjing**, China
67	N 11	**Yankton**, South Dakota, U.S.A.
188	J 8	**Yanmen**, China
187	D 16	**Yanqing**, China
187	E 19	**Yanshan**, China
188	M 12	**Yanshan**, China
189	R 11	**Yanshan**, China
189	W 8	**Yanshan**, China
153	T 7	**Yanskiy Zaliv**, Russian Federation ≈
187	H 19	**Yantai**, China
149	A 15	**Yantarnyy**, Russian Federation
186	K 13	**Yantongshan**, China
189	Y 8	**Yantou**, China
146	J 6	**Yantra**, Bulgaria ∿
189	X 3	**Yanweigang**, China
188	K 8	**Yanyuan**, China
189	V 2	**Yanzhou**, China
188	K 10	**Yao'an**, China
215	T 14	**Yaoundé**, Cameroon ♜
189	Q 3	**Yaoxian**, China
236	K 14	**Yap**, Federated States of Micronesia 🏝
236	L 15	**Yap**, Federated States of Micronesia ▣
40	K 7	**Yap Trench**, Pacific Ocean ◇
193	W 11	**Yapen**, Indonesia 🏝
88	J 5	**Yaqui**, Mexico ∿
104	M 3	**Yaracuy**, Venezuela ▣
155	O 13	**Yaransk**, Russian Federation
170	E 14	**Yardimci Burnu**, Turkey ►
171	Y 10	**Yardimli**, Azerbaijan
127	Z 6	**Yare**, United Kingdom ∿
237	U 1	**Yaren**, Nauru ♜
155	P 9	**Yarensk**, Russian Federation
104	J 10	**Yari**, Colombia ∿
175	P 13	**Yarīm**, Yemen
108	H 9	**Yaripo**, Brazil
184	H 6	**Yarkant He**, China ∿
170	H 12	**Yarma**, Turkey
87	S 12	**Yarmouth**, Nova Scotia, Canada
154	J 13	**Yaroslavl'**, Russian Federation
154	J 12	**Yaroslavskaya Oblast'**, Russian Federation ▣
156	H 1	**Yartsevo**, Russian Federation
104	H 5	**Yarumal**, Colombia
235	W 11	**Yasawa Group**, Fiji 🏝
157	N 11	**Yashalta**, Russian Federation
215	R 10	**Yashi**, Nigeria
215	P 11	**Yashikera**, Nigeria
157	P 11	**Yashkul'**, Russian Federation
150	I 7	**Yasinya**, Ukraine
149	C 14	**Yasnoye**, Russian Federation
191	K 17	**Yasothon**, Thailand
231	U 12	**Yass**, New South Wales, Australia
176	I 9	**Yāsūj**, Iran
170	M 7	**Yasun Burnu**, Turkey ►
170	C 12	**Yatağan**, Turkey
235	Q 14	**Yaté**, New Caledonia
69	P 6	**Yates Center**, Kansas, U.S.A.
84	K 3	**Yathkyed Lake**, Nunavut, Canada 💧
217	N 7	**Yatolema**, Democratic Republic of Congo
199	C 22	**Yatsushiro**, Japan
172	F 10	**Yatta**, Israel
107	E 19	**Yauca**, Peru
107	G 18	**Yauri**, Peru
106	F 11	**Yavari**, Brazil/Peru ∿
88	J 6	**Yávaros**, Mexico
181	F 16	**Yavatmal**, India
91	Z 14	**Yaviza**, Panama
179	Q 2	**Yavlenka**, Kazakhstan
150	I 4	**Yavoriv**, Ukraine
199	D 21	**Yawatahama**, Japan
176	K 9	**Yazd**, Iran
176	L 9	**Yazd**, Iran ▣
176	I 9	**Yazd-e Khast**, Iran
177	O 8	**Yazdan**, Iran
171	N 11	**Yazihan**, Turkey
62	L 4	**Yazoo City**, Mississippi, U.S.A.
139	U 4	**Ybbs an der Donau**, Austria
147	G 22	**Ydra**, Greece 🏝
147	G 21	**Ydra**, Greece
191	F 18	**Ye**, Myanmar
215	X 5	**Yebbi-Bou**, Chad
184	H 6	**Yecheng**, China
131	S 10	**Yecla**, Spain
88	K 5	**Yécora**, Mexico
191	D 14	**Yedashe**, Myanmar
149	I 14	**Yedy**, Belarus
213	K 23	**Yeed**, Somalia
63	X 11	**Yeehaw Junction**, Florida, U.S.A.
154	H 11	**Yefimovskiy**, Russian Federation
156	K 4	**Yefremo**, Russian Federation
171	U 9	**Yeghegnadzor**, Armenia
179	V 5	**Yegindybulak**, Kazakhstan
215	N 12	**Yégué**, Togo
191	C 15	**Yegyi**, Myanmar
213	E 23	**Yei**, Sudan
213	D 22	**Yei**, Sudan ∿
152	J 10	**Yekaterinburg**, Russian Federation
157	T 1	**Yelabuga**, Russian Federation
157	O 6	**Yelan'**, Russian Federation
151	R 8	**Yelanets'**, Ukraine
156	L 4	**Yelets**, Russian Federation
155	U 3	**Yeletskiy**, Russian Federation
157	T 3	**Yelkhovka**, Russian Federation
124	J 4	**Yell**, United Kingdom 🏝
189	R 2	**Yellow**, China ∿
72	L 8	**Yellow Pine**, Idaho, U.S.A.
185	X 8	**Yellow Sea**, China ◓
82	H 12	**Yellowknife**, Northwest Territories, Canada
73	U 7	**Yellowstone**, Montana, U.S.A. ∿
73	S 9	**Yellowstone Lake**, Wyoming, U.S.A. 💧
157	O 2	**Yel'niki**, Russian Federation
179	N 14	**Yeloten**, Turkmenistan
149	L 21	**Yel'sk**, Belarus
215	P 11	**Yelwa**, Nigeria
61	O 15	**Yemassee**, South Carolina, U.S.A.
175	T 12	**Yemen**, Asia □
150	M 3	**Yemil'chyne**, Ukraine
154	K 8	**Yemtsa**, Russian Federation
155	P 8	**Yemva**, Russian Federation
190	L 11	**Yên Bai**, Vietnam
190	C 13	**Yenangyaung**, Myanmar
216	F 10	**Yénéganou**, Congo
184	G 6	**Yengisar**, China
216	H 7	**Yengo**, Congo
170	E 8	**Yenişehir**, Turkey
153	N 10	**Yenisey**, Russian Federation ∿
45	X 9	**Yeniseykiy Zaliv**, Arctic Ocean ≈
153	N 11	**Yeniseyskiy Kryazh**, Russian Federation ◇
127	P 13	**Yeovil**, United Kingdom
88	K 5	**Yepachi**, Mexico
231	V 6	**Yeppoon**, Queensland, Australia
178	L 13	**Yerbent**, Turkmenistan
153	Q 11	**Yerbogachen**, Russian Federation
171	T 9	**Yerevan**, Armenia ♜
179	T 4	**Yereymentau**, Kazakhstan
77	J 18	**Yerington**, Nevada, U.S.A.
170	J 9	**Yerköy**, Turkey
181	D 17	**Yermala**, India
153	T 13	**Yerofey**, Russian Federation
172	F 11	**Yeroham**, Israel
157	R 5	**Yershov**, Russian Federation
190	C 11	**Yesagyo**, Myanmar
179	P 4	**Yesil'**, Kazakhstan
170	J 11	**Yeşilhisar**, Turkey
170	E 12	**Yeşilova**, Turkey
157	N 13	**Yessentuki**, Russian Federation
171	W 8	**Yevlax**, Azerbaijan
151	T 12	**Yevpatoriya**, Ukraine
189	T 4	**Yexian**, China
156	K 10	**Yeysk**, Russian Federation
148	L 13	**Yezyaryshcha**, Belarus
186	J 9	**Yi'an**, China
189	N 8	**Yibin**, China
189	R 6	**Yichang**, China
189	S 6	**Yicheng**, China
189	R 2	**Yichuan**, China
186	L 9	**Yichun**, China
189	U 8	**Yichun**, China
188	J 6	**Yidun**, China
189	U 8	**Yifeng**, China
189	Q 3	**Yijun**, China
186	J 8	**Yilaha**, China
186	M 10	**Yilan**, China
170	L 9	**Yildizeli**, Turkey
186	I 6	**Yilehuli Shan**, China ⛰
188	M 11	**Yiliang**, China
188	M 9	**Yiliang**, China
188	L 9	**Yimen**, China
186	L 11	**Yimianpo**, China
186	G 4	**Yimuhe**, China
189	W 2	**Yinan**, China
185	Q 7	**Yinchuan**, China
189	T 6	**Yingcheng**, China
189	T 11	**Yingde**, China
188	I 11	**Yingjiang**, China
188	M 7	**Yingjing**, China
187	H 16	**Yingkou**, China
189	O 6	**Yingshan**, China
189	T 6	**Yingshan**, China
189	V 5	**Yingshang**, China
189	W 8	**Yingtan**, China
187	B 17	**Yingxian**, China
184	J 4	**Yining**, China
189	P 8	**Yinjiang**, China
188	L 10	**Yipinglang**, China
189	P 9	**Yiquan**, China
213	E 22	**Yirol**, Sudan
186	G 10	**Yirxie**, China
189	Q 11	**Yishan**, China
189	X 2	**Yishui**, China
194	B 13	**Yishun**, Singapore
186	H 6	**Yitulihe**, China
189	Y 7	**Yiwu**, China
187	H 15	**Yixian**, China
186	J 4	**Yixiken**, China
189	Y 6	**Yixing**, China
189	S 8	**Yiyang**, China
189	W 8	**Yiyang**, China
189	W 2	**Yiyuan**, China
189	T 10	**Yizhang**, China
148	C 12	**Ylakiai**, Lithuania
134	L 12	**Yli-Kärppä**, Finland
134	K 11	**Ylitornio**, Finland
45	Q 11	**Ymer Nunatak**, Greenland ▲
153	V 11	**Ynykchanskiy**, Russian Federation
215	T 10	**Yobe**, Nigeria ▣
198	I 6	**Yobetsu-dake**, Japan ▲
213	K 19	**Yoboki**, Djibouti
196	K 12	**Yog Point**, Philippines ►
192	I 14	**Yogyakarta**, Indonesia
192	I 15	**Yogyakarta**, Indonesia ▣
199	F 17	**Yōka**, Japan
215	V 14	**Yokadouma**, Cameroon
199	N 21	**Yokate-jima**, Japan 🏝
199	H 18	**Yokkaichi**, Japan
215	U 13	**Yoko**, Cameroon
199	K 16	**Yokohama**, Japan
199	K 16	**Yokosuka**, Japan
198	K 11	**Yokote**, Japan
215	U 12	**Yola**, Nigeria
216	M 9	**Yolombo**, Democratic Republic of Congo
199	E 18	**Yonago**, Japan
199	L 26	**Yonaguni-jima**, Japan 🏝
198	K 13	**Yonezawa**, Japan
194	E 10	**Yong Peng**, Malaysia
189	W 10	**Yong'an**, China
189	V 4	**Yongcheng**, China
187	N 20	**Yŏngch'ŏn**, South Korea
189	O 7	**Yongchuan**, China
189	V 9	**Yongfeng**, China
189	R 11	**Yongfu**, China
187	M 19	**Yŏngju**, South Korea
189	Y 7	**Yongkang**, China
188	J 10	**Yongping**, China
188	L 10	**Yongren**, China
188	M 8	**Yongshan**, China
188	K 9	**Yongsheng**, China
189	R 8	**Yongshun**, China
189	T 10	**Yongxing**, China
189	U 9	**Yongxing**, China
189	V 7	**Yongxiu**, China
189	S 10	**Yongzhou**, China
58	K 12	**Yonkers**, New York, U.S.A.
230	G 11	**York**, Western Australia, Australia
127	T 2	**York**, United Kingdom
58	F 14	**York**, Pennsylvania, U.S.A.
63	O 4	**York**, Alabama, U.S.A.
67	N 14	**York**, Nebraska, U.S.A.
86	E 13	**York**, Ontario, Canada
59	O 8	**York Harbor**, Maine, U.S.A.
231	P 11	**Yorke Peninsula**, South Australia, Australia ►
231	O 12	**Yorketown**, South Australia, Australia
127	R 1	**Yorkshire Dales**, United Kingdom ◇
127	U 1	**Yorkshire Wolds**, United Kingdom ◇
83	N 18	**Yorkton**, Saskatchewan, Canada
61	V 6	**Yorktown**, Virginia, U.S.A.
65	G 16	**Yorkville**, Illinois, U.S.A.
90	M 5	**Yoro**, Honduras
199	N 22	**Yoro-jima**, Japan 🏝
199	O 23	**Yoron-tō**, Japan 🏝
77	I 20	**Yosemite Village**, California, U.S.A.
155	O 14	**Yoshkar-Ola**, Russian Federation
187	M 21	**Yŏsu**, South Korea
172	F 12	**Yotvata**, Israel
125	C 20	**Youghal**, Republic of Ireland
125	D 21	**Youghal Bay**, Republic of Ireland ≈
231	T 12	**Young**, New South Wales, Australia
110	M 11	**Young**, Uruguay
241	S 15	**Young Island**, Antarctica 🏝
41	X 14	**Young's Rock**, Pitcairn Island ►
65	O 17	**Youngstown**, Ohio, U.S.A.
210	G 7	**Youssoufia**, Morocco
189	Q 8	**Youyang**, China
152	M 14	**Youyi Feng**, Russian Federation ▲
127	Z 8	**Yoxford**, United Kingdom
170	J 9	**Yozgat**, Turkey
77	G 14	**Yreka**, California, U.S.A.
234	F 2	**Ysabel Channel**, Papua New Guinea ≈
135	E 26	**Ystad**, Sweden
127	N 9	**Ystalyfera**, United Kingdom
179	V 10	**Ysyk-Köl**, Kyrgyzstan 💧
193	T 11	**Yu**, Indonesia 🏝
189	Z 11	**Yü Shan**, Taiwan ▲
185	X 13	**Yü-Shan**, Taiwan ▲
189	R 8	**Yuan**, China ∿
189	Q 10	**Yuanbao Shan**, China ▲
188	L 12	**Yuanjiang**, China
189	R 8	**Yuanling**, China
188	L 10	**Yuanmou**, China
187	B 18	**Yuanping**, China
189	S 3	**Yuanqu**, China
77	G 17	**Yuba City**, California, U.S.A.
198	K 5	**Yūbari-sanchi**, Japan ⛰
89	Y 10	**Yucatán**, Mexico ▣
89	Y 9	**Yucatan Channel**, Mexico ≈
89	Y 11	**Yucatan Peninsula**, Mexico ►
189	T 1	**Yuci**, China
187	E 14	**Yudaokou**, China
186	H 4	**Yudi Shan**, China ▲
230	M 6	**Yuendumu**, Northern Territory, Australia
189	Z 8	**Yueqing**, China
188	L 8	**Yuexi**, China
189	V 6	**Yuexi**, China
189	T 7	**Yueyang**, China
189	W 8	**Yugan**, China
155	S 1	**Yugorskiy Poluostrov**, Russian Federation ►
189	R 1	**Yuhebu**, China
189	V 8	**Yujiang**, China
153	X 7	**Yukagirskoye Ploskogor'ye**, Russian Federation ◇
148	K 13	**Yukhavichy**, Belarus
156	J 2	**Yukhnov**, Russian Federation
216	K 10	**Yuki**, Democratic Republic of Congo
80	I 6	**Yukon**, Yukon Territory, Canada ∿
79	R 5	**Yukon Flats**, Alaska, U.S.A. ◇
82	B 13	**Yukon Territory**, Canada ▣
171	T 12	**Yüksekova**, Turkey
199	C 20	**Yukuhashi**, Japan
230	M 7	**Yulara**, Northern Territory, Australia
157	X 4	**Yuldybayevo**, Russian Federation
63	W 7	**Yulee**, Florida, U.S.A.
189	Z 12	**Yüli**, Taiwan
185	S 7	**Yulin**, China
189	R 13	**Yulin**, China
188	K 9	**Yulongxue Shan**, China ▲
74	G 13	**Yuma**, Arizona, U.S.A.
216	I 9	**Yumbi**, Democratic Republic of Congo
217	O 8	**Yumbi**, Democratic Republic of Congo
185	O 7	**Yumen**, China
188	L 10	**Yun Gui Gaoyuan**, China ⛰
170	G 10	**Yunak**, Turkey
189	S 12	**Yunan**, China
78	I 14	**Yunaska Island**, Alaska, U.S.A. 🏝
189	R 3	**Yuncheng**, China
189	V 2	**Yuncheng**, China
189	S 12	**Yunfu**, China
107	J 20	**Yungas**, Bolivia ⛰
189	T 6	**Yunmeng**, China
188	K 11	**Yunnan**, China ▣
231	Q 11	**Yunta**, South Australia, Australia

□ Country ▣ Internal administrative region: State/Province/Territory/Dependent territory ♜ Capital city ⛰ Mountain range/Undersea ridge ▲ Mountain peak/Volcano/Seamount ◇ Geographic feature ► Headland/Point/Cape/Peninsula ☗ Desert 🏝 Island/Island group ⁙ Antarctic base 🌊 Ocean ◓ Sea ≈ Bay/Gulf/Channel/Strait 💧 Lake ⚑ Salt pan/Dry/Intermittent lake ∿ River

□ Country ☐ Internal administrative region: State/Province/Territory/Dependent territory ▲ Capital city ▲ Mountain range/Undersea ridge ▲ Mountain peak/Volcano/Seamount ◇ Geographic feature ▶ Headland/Point/Cape/Peninsula ◆ Desert ☲ Island/Island group ☷ Antarctic base ⊘ Ocean ↘ Sea ≈ Bay/Gulf/Channel/Strait ↘ Lake ◆ Salt pan/Dry/Intermittent lake ↘ River

CREDITS

PHOTO CREDITS

Key t=top; l=left; r=right; tl=top left; tc=top center; tr=top right; cl=center left; c=center; cr=center right; b=bottom; bl=bottom left; bc=bottom center; br=bottom right

AAP = Australian Associated Press; APL/Corbis = Australian Picture Library/Corbis; COR = Corel Corp.; DS = Digital Stock; GI = Getty Images; IOT = Images on Tap; N_E = NASA/Earth Observatory; N_ES = NASA/Earth from Space; N_J = NASA/Jet Propulsion Laboratory; N_T = NASA/TOMS; N_V = NASA/Visible Earth; NASA = National Aeronautics and Space Administration; PD = Photodisc; PE = PhotoEssentials; PL = photolibrary.com

2t Craig Mahew & Robert Simmon/NASA/GSFC **5**bl Serg Andrefouet & Frank Muller-Karger/Institute for Marine Remote Sensing/University of South Florida; br DS **6**tc, tc AV HRR/NDVI/Seawifs/MODIS/NCEP/DMSP/Sky2000 star catalog/AVHRR & Seawifs/Reto Stockli/Marit Jentoft-Nilsen; tl PL; tr GI; Globes N_V **7**tc, tc, tl AVHRR/NDVI/Seawifs/ODIS/NCEP/DMSP/ Sky2000 star catalog/AVHRR & Seawifs/Reto Stockli/Marit Jentoft-Nilsen; tr Jerry Stebbins; Globes N_V **12**t PL **14**tc NASA/GSFC; c NASA/GSFC/METI/ERSDAC/JAROS/US/ Japan ASTER Science Team; bc PL **17**b APL/Corbis; br, cr, tr GI **18**c NASA; cl APL/Corbis; tr DS **19**cr AAP/AFP; tr APL/Corbis **20**cr, tr APL/Corbis; tr PL **21**cr, br APL/Corbis **22**cr, br APL/ Corbis **23**tr REU **24**c, tr APL/Corbis **25**br, cr APL/Corbis **26**tr APL/Corbis **27**br, tc, tr APL/Corbis **28**t PL **32**bl APL/Corbis **33**br, tc, tl APL/Corbis **34**c METI/ERSDAC/JAROS/US/Japan ASTER Science Team/NASA/GSFC **36**bl Liam Gumley/MODIS Atmosphere Team/University of Wisconsin-Madison; cr COR **37**c APL/Corbis **38**cl APL/Corbis/AFP **39**tr APL/Corbis **40**bc, br, tc, tr APL/Corbis; c AAP **42**br, cl, tr APL/Corbis **43**c APL/Corbis **44**bc, br, c, cr, tr APL/Corbis **46**c Craig Mahew & Robert Simmon/NASA/GSFC **48**c NASA/GSFC/MITI/ERSDAC/JAROS/US/Japan ASTER Science Team; b APL/ Corbis; t Professor Stanley Herwitz/Clark University/NASA **49**c SRTM Team/NASA/JPL/NIMA **50**bl DS; br NASA/GSFC/LaRC/JPL/MISR Team; c Jacques Descloitres/ MODIS Land Rapid Response Team/NASA/GSFC **51**bl N_J; c Jeff Schmaltz/MODIS Rapid Response Team/NASA/GSFC **52**cl GI **55**br NASA; bc, c, cl, tc APL/Corbis **56**tc, tr APL/Corbis **57**br GI; tl APL/Corbis **58**tc PD; tr APL/Corbis **59**c, cl GI; cl APL/Corbis **61**bc, cr APL/Corbis **62**c GI; cl DS **63**cr GI; tr DS **64**cl APL/Corbis **65**br, cr, tr APL/Corbis **67**br, tr APL/Corbis; cr PD **68**cl APL/Corbis **69**bl, tr APL/Corbis **70**br APL/Corbis **71**bc, tc, tc, tr APL/Corbis; tl PD **72**bc, br APL/Corbis; tc GI **75**tc, tr APL/Corbis **76**br GI; br COR **77**bc, bl PD; cr APL/ Corbis **78**bl, c, tc, tr GI; c PD **80**tc, tr APL/Corbis **81**br, cr APL/Corbis **82**cl GI; tl PD **83**bc, tc APL/Corbis **84**c GI; cl COR **85**br APL/Corbis; cr COR **86**br GI; tr APL/Corbis **87**tr GI **88**bc, br, cr APL/Corbis **89**tc, tl GI **90**br, cr APL/Corbis **91**c, tc, tl APL/Corbis **92**bl GI; cl APL/Corbis **94**c Craig Mahew & Robert Simmon/NASA/GSFC **96**bl, br, tr GI; **97**c Sea WiFS Project/NASA/Goddard Space Flight Centre/ORBIMAGE **98**br APL/Corbis; c NASA/GSFC/MITI/ERSDAC/JAROS/US/Japan Aster Science Team; cl GI **99**bl APL/ Corbis; c Sea WiFS Project/NASA/Goddard Space Flight Centre/ORBIMAGE; tr NASA/EFS **100**tl PD **103**br, c, cl, tr APL/Corbis; tl GI **104**bc APL/Corbis; br PD **105**bc, bl APL/ Corbis; c GI **106**c GI; cl APL/Corbis **107**tl, cr PD; tr PE **109**bc, cr, tc APL/Corbis; bc, bl PD **110**cr APL/Corbis; br GI **111**tl, tr GI **112**cl, cr, tl, tr APL/Corbis **113**c APL/Corbis **114**c Craig Mayhew & Robert Simmon/NASA/GSFC **116**bl NASA/GSFC/ MITI/ERSDAC/ JAROS/US/Japan ASTER Science Team; br, t NASA/GSFC/METI/ERSDAC/JAROS/US/Japan ASTER Science Team **117**c NASA/Our Earth as Art/USGC **118**bc APL/ Corbis; cl Jacques Descloitres/MODIS Rapid Response Team/NASA/GSFC tl PL **119**bl NASA/GSFC/LaRC/JPL/MISR Team; c Earth Sciences and Image Analysis, NASA-Johnson Space Center **120**cr PL **123**c, cr APL/Corbis; tr AAP/Associated Press **124**bc APL/Corbis; br GI **125**tl GI **126**c, tc, tr APL/Corbis **127**br, tr APL/Corbis **129**br, cr GI; cr APL/Corbis; tr PD **130**c COR; cl IOT **132**bl APL/Corbis; cl COR; tl GI **133**tc APL/Corbis; tl IOT **135**c PE; cr GI **136**br GI **137**br APL/Corbis; tr GI **138**tc, tr GI **139**tl GI **141**tc, tr APL/Corbis **142**bc Georg Gerster; br GI **143**tr PE **145**c, cl, tc, tr APL/Corbis; tl GI **147**tc APL/Corbis; tl Guido Alberto Rossi **149**bc, cr, APL/Corbis; tr GI **150**br APL/Corbis **151**tc, tr APL/ Corbis **152**tc GI; cl, tr APL/Corbis **154**bl, cl APL/Corbis **155**br, tc, tr APL/Corbis **156**c APL/Corbis **157**bc APL/Corbis; c GI **158**bc, br APL/Corbis; c PD **159**bl Guido Alberto Rossi; br APL/Corbis **160**c Craig Mahew & Robert Simmon/NASA/GSFC **162**b, c N_J cr NASA/GSFC/METI/ERSDAC/JAROS/US/Japan Aster Science Team **163**br N_J **164**bc Jacques Descloitres /MODIS Land Rapid Response Team; bl APL/Corbis; cr Jeff Schmaltz/MODIS Rapid Response Team/NASA/GSFC **165**bl Jacques Descloitres/MODIS Land Rapid Response Team/ NASA/GSFC; cl Jacues Descloitres/MODIS Land Rapid Response Team/ NASA/GSFC **168**bl APL/Corbis **169**tc AAP/AFP; cl, tr APL/Corbis **170**bl APL/Corbis **171**bc, bl APL/Corbis **172**br, cr GI **173**br, tr APL/Corbis; cr GI **174**br APL/Corbis **175**br, tr APL/Corbis; tc GI **176**cl, c, tc, tr APL/Corbis **177**br APL/Corbis **178**tc, tr APL/ Corbis **179**tr APL/Corbis **180**bc AAP/EPA AFPI; c APL/Corbis **181**c APL/Corbis **182**c, cl, cr APL/Corbis **183**bl APL/Corbis **184**bc AAP/Associated Press/XINHUA NEWS AGENCY; br, cl APL/ Corbis; c PD **185**br PD **186**br, tl PD; cl, tc APL/Corbis **188**br AAP Image/EPA/Michael Reynolds; c, cl APL/Corbis **189**br GI **190**c, cl, cr APL/Corbis **191**tr APL/Corbis; cr PD **192**bc GI bl AAP/Associated Press AP cr APL/Corbis **194**cr, tr APL/Corbis **195**bl, tr APL/Corbis **196**br, cr APL/Corbis **197**bl, cr APL/Corbis **198**tc GI; tr APL/Corbis **199**bl, tl GI; cr, tc APL/Corbis **200**c Craig Mahew & Robert Simmon/NASA/GSFC **202**bl, br, tr N_J **203**c Jacques Descloitres/MODIS Rapid Response Team/NASA/GSFC **204**br, cr APL/ Corbis; cl Jacques Descloitres/MODIS Land Science Team/NASA/GSFC; cl Jacques Descloitres/MODIS Land Rapid Response Team/NASA/GSFC **205**br, cl APL/Corbis; c Jacques Descloitres/ MODIS Land Rapid Response Team/ NASA/GSFC **206**cr GI **209**cr, tc, tr APL/Corbis **210**c, cl APL/Corbis **211**bc AAP/Associated Press; c APL/Corbis **212**cr APL/Corbis **213**cl, tl, tr APL/Corbis **214**cl APL/Corbis **215**br APL/ Corbis **216**cl PL **217**br, cr APL/Corbis **219**bc, bl, c, tr APL/Corbis **220**c Craig Mahew & Robert Simmon/NASA/GSFC **222**t Jacques Descloitres/MODIS Rapid Response Team/NASA/GSFC; tl NASA/GSFC/MITI/ERSDAC/JAROS/US/Japan Aster Science Team **223**cr Jacques Descloitres/MODIS Land Science Team; tr GSFC/Landsat Team/Australian Ground Receiving Station Teams/NASA **224**bl APL/Corbis; br, c N_ES **225**, cr N_ES **228**bl, br APL/Corbis **229**br PL; c Paul Hoehenberger/pacific-picture Bildagentur; cl, cr APL/Corbis **230**br APL/Corbis **231**bl, cr, tr APL/Corbis **232**c, cr APL/Corbis **233**bl, bc, c, cl APL/Corbis **234**bc, br, cr, tr APL/Corbis **236**br, cl, tr APL/Corbis **237**bl, tc APL/Corbis **238**c PL **240**c, tr APL/Corbis **241**br, cr, tr APL/Corbis **242**c APL/Corbis; cr PL **243**c, br, tc APL/Corbis; cr N_T **244**t Jerry Stebbins

ILLUSTRATION CREDITS

Richard Bonson/Tom Connell/Wildlife Art: 18 **John Bull**: 1 **Andrew Davies/Creative Communication**: 16, 18, 20, 22, 23, 24, 26, 27, 36, 37, 44, 52, 54, 56, 59, 60, 62, 65, 66, 68, 71, 72, 75, 76, 79, 80, 83, 84, 87, 88, 90, 93, 99, 100, 102, 104, 106, 108, 110, 113, 120, 124, 126, 128, 130, 132, 134, 136, 138, 140, 142, 144, 146, 148, 150, 155, 157, 159, 166, 167, 168, 169, 170, 172, 174, 177, 178, 180, 182, 184, 187, 188, 190, 193, 194, 195, 196, 198, 206, 210, 211, 212, 215, 217, 218, 230, 231, 233, 235, 240, 242, 243, 248
Chris Forsey: 164 **Mark A. Garlick/space-art.co.uk**: 14, 15 **Rob Mancini** 21 **Map Illustrations**: 18, 30, 32, 33, 36, 37, 38, 39, 40, 41, 42, 43, 44, 50, 51, 52, 54, 55, 59, 74, 77, 79, 80, 81, 82, 84, 86, 88, 90, 92, 98, 99, 100, 102, 103, 104, 106, 108, 110, 112, 118, 119, 120, 121, 122, 123, 124, 126, 128, 130, 131, 132, 134, 135, 136, 138, 140, 142, 144, 146, 148, 150, 154, 156, 158, 164, 165, 167, 168, 169, 170, 172, 174, 176, 178, 180, 181, 182, 183, 184, 186, 188, 190, 192, 194, 196, 198, 204, 205, 206, 207, 208, 209, 210, 211, 212, 214, 216, 218, 224, 225, 226, 227, 228, 230, 232, 234, 236, 237, 240, 246, 247 **Map Illustrations/Creative Communication**: 56, 58, 60, 62, 64, 66, 68, 70, 72, 74, 76, 78
Edwina Riddell: 20, 21 **Suzanne Tawansi**: 10, 11, 31, 208, 209, 226, 229 **Richard Bonson/Wildlife Art**: 16 **Rod Westblade**: 50 **Murray Zanoni**: 39, 41, 44, 57, 63, 67, 68, 70, 74, 80, 84, 89, 91, 105, 109, 110, 113, 126, 127, 128, 132, 137, 138, 140, 142, 144, 146, 148, 151, 156, 159, 170, 172, 174, 179, 183, 191, 193, 195, 196, 210, 213, 214, 216, 219, 231, 232

ACKNOWLEDGMENTS

Conceived and produced by Weldon Owen Pty Ltd
59 Victoria Street, McMahons Point
Sydney, NSW 2060, Australia

Chief Executive Officer John Owen
President Terry Newell
Publisher Sheena Coupe
Creative Director Sue Burk
Vice President International Sales Stuart Laurence
Administrator International Sales Kristine Ravn

Project Manager Sarah Anderson
Art Director Suzanne Tawansi

Project Editors/Text Jenni Bruce, Scott Forbes
Editorial Assistant Karen Penzes

Designers Clare Forte, Liz Murphy
Design Assistant Nika Markovtzev
Initial Design Concept John Bull

Production Manager Caroline Webber
Production Coordinator James Blackman

Systems Administrator Margaret Hilliard
Editorial Coordinator Jennifer Losco

Picture Researcher Jo Collard

Maps Map Illustrations
Chief Cartographer Laurie Whiddon
Cartographic Team Bil Andersen, Andrew Davies,
Kerrie deGruchy, Sydney Gubbay, Ian Faulkner,
Brian Johnston, Brad McLean, Karen Reithmuller

Cityscape Illustrations Murray Zanoni
Information Graphics Andrew Davies, Suzanne Tawansi
Illustrators Richard Bonson/Wildlife Art Ltd,
Tom Connell/Wildlife Art Ltd, Mark A. Garlick, Rob Mancini,
Edwina Riddell, Peter Scott/Wildlife Art Ltd
Flags Flag Society of Australia

Color reproduction by Colourscan Overseas Co Pte Ltd
Printed in Singapore by Tien Wah Press (Pte) Limited

A WELDON OWEN PRODUCTION

Weldon Owen would like to thank the following people for their assistance in the production of this
book: Tony Burton (Flag Society of Australia), Melanie Calabretta, Brendan Cotter, Janine Flew, Helen
Flint, Angela Handley, Emma Hutchinson, Tessy Grabo, Global Forest Watch, Matthew Hall, Ralph Kelly
(Flag Society of Australia), Professor Kim Lowell (Département des sciences du bois et de la forêt,
Université Laval, Canada), Rory Moore, Michael Nahas, Grace Newell, Sarah Plant (Puddingburn
Publishing Services), Deborah Smith, Kiren Thandi, Shannon Tufui.
Text: Jenni Bruce (thematic map pages), Scott Forbes (regional map pages), Dr Stephen Gale (Geographic
Terms), Margaret McPhee (satellite image pages).

Notes
1. All population statistics quoted in this atlas are projected 2005 figures. National population statistics
have been sourced from the U.S. Census Bureau. City Population statistics have been sourced from the
United Nations Population Division, World Urbanization Prospects: The 2001 Revision.
2. All city population statistics quoted in this atlas are of urban agglomerations. The combined
population of a city and its suburbs is known as an urban agglomeration.
3. Billion is defined as 1,000 million (1,000,000,000) in this atlas.

FLAGS OF THE WORLD

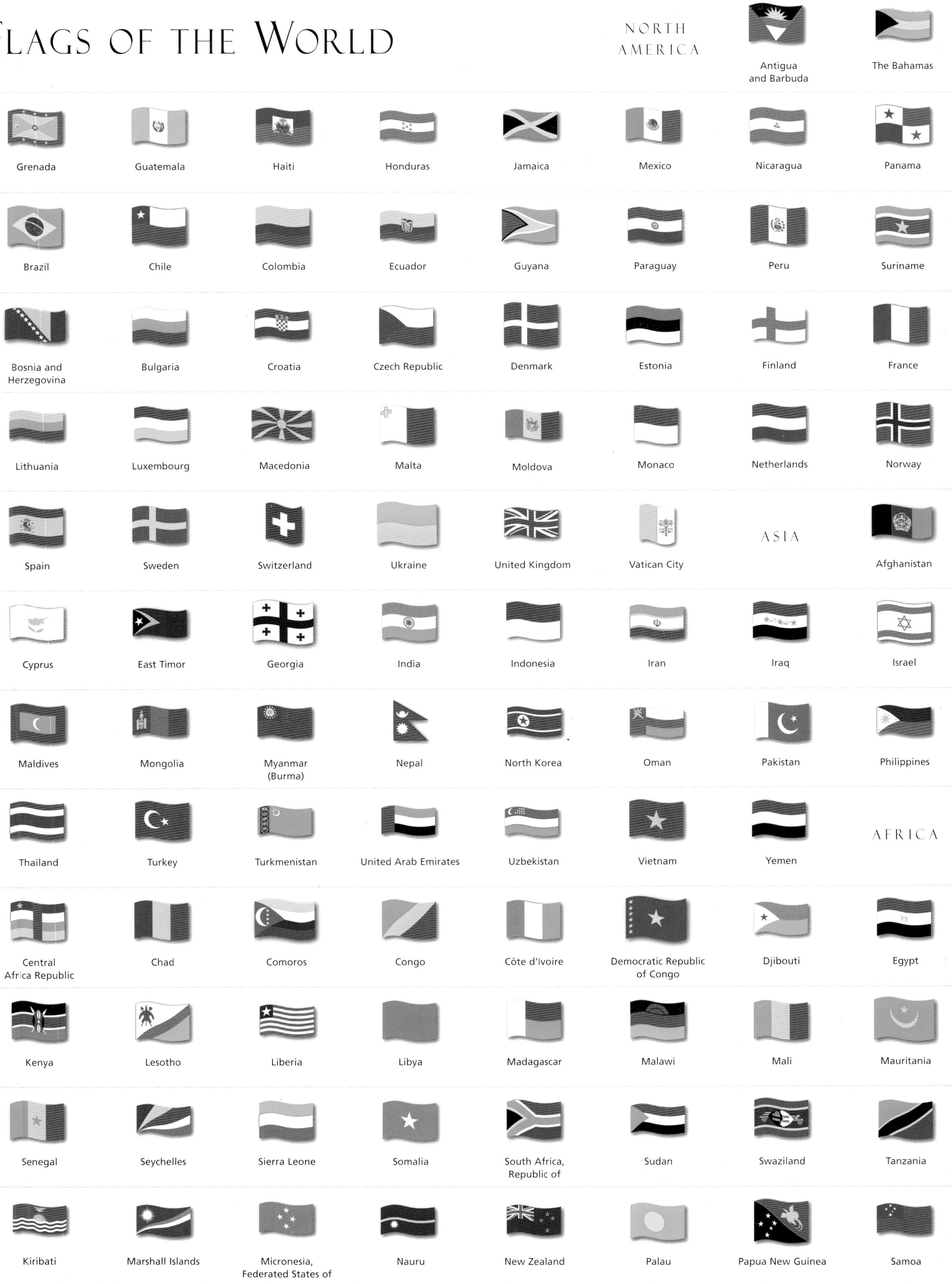

NORTH AMERICA

Antigua and Barbuda

The Bahamas

Grenada

Guatemala

Haiti

Honduras

Jamaica

Mexico

Nicaragua

Panama

Brazil

Chile

Colombia

Ecuador

Guyana

Paraguay

Peru

Suriname

Bosnia and Herzegovina

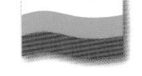
Bulgaria

Croatia

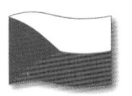
Czech Republic

Denmark

Estonia

Finland

France

Lithuania

Luxembourg

Macedonia

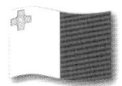
Malta

Moldova

Monaco

Netherlands

Norway

Spain

Sweden

Switzerland

Ukraine

United Kingdom

Vatican City

ASIA

Afghanistan

Cyprus

East Timor

Georgia

India

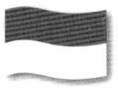
Indonesia

Iran

Iraq

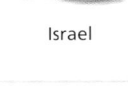
Israel

Maldives

Mongolia

Myanmar (Burma)

Nepal

North Korea

Oman

Pakistan

Philippines

Thailand

Turkey

Turkmenistan

United Arab Emirates

Uzbekistan

Vietnam

Yemen

AFRICA

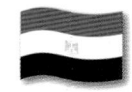

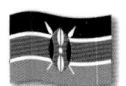
Central Africa Republic

Chad

Comoros

Congo

Côte d'Ivoire

Democratic Republic of Congo

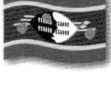
Djibouti

Egypt

Kenya

Lesotho

Liberia

Libya

Madagascar

Malawi

Mali

Mauritania

Senegal

Seychelles

Sierra Leone

Somalia

South Africa, Republic of

Sudan

Swaziland

Tanzania

Kiribati

Marshall Islands

Micronesia, Federated States of

Nauru

New Zealand

Palau

Papua New Guinea

Samoa